EMPLOYMENT LAW

WITHDRAWN

EMPLOYMENT LAW

Gillian Phillips MA (Cantab), LLM, Solicitor, Part-time Employment Judge, Employment Tribunals

Karen Scott LLB, LLM, Solicitor, Part-time Employment Judge, Employment Tribunals

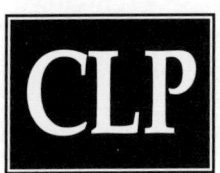

Published by

College of Law Publishing,
Braboeuf Manor, Portsmouth Road, St Catherines, Guildford GU3 1HA

British Library Cataloguing-in-Publication Data

A catalogue record for this book is available from the British Library.

ISBN 978 1 912363 71 1

Typeset by Style Photosetting Ltd, Mayfield, East Sussex

Tables and index by Moira Greenhalgh, Carnforth, Lancashire

Preface

This book has been written primarily for students of the Employment Law and Practice elective on the Legal Practice Course. It covers a number of important areas of individual employment law, although it does not deal with trade union law or collective agreements.

For the sake of brevity, the masculine pronoun is used to include the feminine.

The law is stated as at 1 October 2018, although some later developments have been referred to where possible.

We express our thanks to the many previous authors and contributors to this book. In particular, we would like to thank Peter Rumbelow, for all his sterling efforts over the years. We would also like to express our thanks to Elizabeth Ajagbe, Jo Bingham, Sarah Brown, David Capron, Penny Hayhurst, Stuart Roberts, Christine Taylor, Christine Pashley and the rest of the Employment Law team at the University of Law for their comments on the previous editions of this book. Though we benefitted enormously from their advice, all errors are strictly of our own making. Thanks too to John Moore, formerly of Bevan Brittan LLP.

Thanks as always to David Stott for his help and guidance.

GILLIAN PHILLIPS
KAREN SCOTT

Contents

Table of Cases

C

D

F

G

H

L

O

S

T

X

Table of Statutes

Table of Secondary Legislation and Codes of Practice

EU secondary legislation

Codes of Practice and Guidance

Introductory Note

Responsible government departments

Responsibility for employment law is currently spread across a number of different government departments, including the Department for Work and Pensions, the Department for Business, Energy and Industrial Strategy (BEIS), the Ministry of Justice and the Home Office.

In June 2009, the Department for Business, Enterprise and Regulatory Reform (DBERR) (the former Department of Trade and Industry (DTI)) became the Department for Business, Innovation and Skills (BIS). A number of the websites referred to in this book were originally DTI/DBERR/BIS websites. In July 2016, BIS and the Department of Energy and Climate Change (DECC) merged to form BEIS. The authors have endeavoured to change web addresses where necessary; in most instances, however, pre-existing DTI/DBERR/BIS website addresses remain operative and will automatically redirect the user to the correct web page. References to DTI/DBERR/BIS are retained where relevant for historical purposes.

Brexit

The UK voted on 23 June 2016 to leave the EU (the 'Brexit' vote). Article 50 of the Treaty on European Union (TEU) allows a Member State to notify the EU of its withdrawal and obliges the EU to try to negotiate a withdrawal agreement with that State. A number of individuals challenged in the courts the Government's decision to trigger Article 50 without the approval of Parliament. The High Court ruled in a judgment handed down on 3 November 2016 that the Prime Minister could not invoke the royal prerogative as legal authority for a notification to be sent under Article 50 of the TEU, to begin the withdrawal process. The Government appealed that decision to the Supreme Court, which heard it in December 2016 (*R (Miller) v Secretary of State for Exiting the European Union* [2017] UKSC 5). The Lord Justices ruled, by a majority of eight to three, that the Prime Minister could not lawfully bypass MPs and peers by using the royal prerogative to trigger Article 50 and start the two-year process of negotiating the UK's divorce from its EU partners. The Government therefore put forward to Parliament the EU (Notification of Withdrawal) Bill. On 16 March 2017, the Queen gave Royal Assent to that Bill, giving the Government the formal power to trigger Article 50. Article 50 was officially triggered by the Prime Minister on 28 March 2017, when she signed a letter informing the European Commission of Britain's intention to leave the European Union, which will occur before 29 March 2019. Until then, the UK continues to be bound by its EU obligations.

Parliament issued a briefing paper on 20 October 2016 (before the High Court judgment) entitled 'Brexit: employment law', which sets out what is anticipated would happen in the normal course of events to legislation guaranteed by EU law in the event of Brexit. Areas that derive from EU legislation and could be impacted include TUPE (see **Chapter 7**), redundancy consultation (see **Chapter 4**), working time, holiday pay and agency workers' rights (see **Chapter 1**), as well as discrimination (see **Chapter 8**) and family-friendly rights (see **Chapter 14**).

On 12 July 2018, the Government published a White Paper on the future relationship between the United Kingdom and the European Union. At para 123, it proposes that there be no regression in employment laws. That means that no EU-based laws will be repealed, so, for example, TUPE 2006, the Working Time Regulations 1998 and much discrimination legislation will not be amended when the UK leaves the EU. However, the UK will no longer, after Brexit, retain the European Charter of Fundamental Rights. The European Union

(Withdrawal) Act 2018 (see below) specifically excludes the Charter (s 5(4)) from continuing to be part of UK domestic law. Although many of the areas covered by the Charter are also included in the European Convention on Human Rights (which is part of UK law through the Human Rights Act 1998), for example the right to a private life, freedom of association and non-discrimination, the Charter also covers a broader set of economic and social rights. The Government says that protections enshrined in the Charter either already exist in UK law or else will be individually implemented.

One important question is what would happen to precedents already set by the Court of Justice of the European Union (CJEU) and European Court of Justice (ECJ). Claire Darwin of Matrix Chambers has said that '[a] key issue for lawyers will be the status of judgments of the [CJEU] ...'. In the view of Lewis Silkin:

> On leaving the EU, the ECJ would no longer have jurisdiction and its future decisions would not be binding on UK courts. It seems likely, however, that if we retain any laws originating from the EU (which is probable) our courts would still take account of future ECJ judgments as persuasive, albeit not binding, when ruling on those laws. In that case, the ECJ would continue to exert an appreciable influence.

And, according to Gavin Williams of Herbert Smith Freehills LLP, 'The one certainty is that we can expect a period of uncertainty.'

On 26 June 2018, the European Union (Withdrawal) Act 2018 was passed. A number of other separate but related Bills, that will together provide the legislative underpinning for Brexit, are still going through Parliament. The content of these Bills indicate that the Government is still preparing to leave both the Single Market and the Customs Union and to end the free movement of people – what some have called a 'hard Brexit'. However, the Bills also suggest that the Government is prioritising the economy and trade in its Brexit preparations.

The European Union (Withdrawal) Act 2018 is the main vehicle for implementing Brexit. It repeals the European Communities Act 1972 (which legislated for the incorporation of EU law into the domestic law of the United Kingdom) and ends the authority of EU law and the CJEU within the UK, and it transfers into UK law the existing provisions of EU law applicable at this point in time. The 2018 Act states that when interpreting retained EU law after Brexit, UK courts and tribunals will not be bound by any decisions made on or after exit day but 'may have regard to' such decisions 'so far as it is relevant to any matter before the Court or tribunal'. The 2018 Act also (controversially) gives (s 8) Ministers delegated powers to make secondary legislation (through the use of what is known as a 'Henry VIII' clause – so named from the Statute of Proclamations 1539, which gave King Henry VIII power to legislate by proclamation) to amend any law that does not operate appropriately once the UK has left the EU (eg references to EU institutions which no longer have jurisdiction). This allows changes to be made to legislation by Ministers without any parliamentary scrutiny.

The seven remaining pieces of Brexit legislation are set out below. These are at various different legislative stages. Some have been pushed back following the agreement between the EU and the Government of a standstill transition period after the official exit date of 29 March 2019. In some cases, no draft legislation has yet been published.

- The Taxation (Cross-border) Trade Act 2018 (which received royal assent on 13 September 2018) will enable the UK to establish and operate a standalone customs and indirect taxation regime after Brexit.
- The Trade Bill (the second reading took place on 11 September 2018) is focused on converting trade deals between the EU and third countries into bilateral deals with Britain. It will equip the Government with the powers to operate an independent trade policy.
- The Immigration Bill, which will create a new immigration system, will end the free movement of EU citizens and their families and bring them under the UK immigration

rules. Employers are expected to see this as an opportunity to advocate what skills they require to support their growth and say whether there is sufficient supply within the UK domestic labour market or whether certain visas or categories of work permit may be required.

- The Fisheries Bill (the first formal reading took place on 25 October 2018) will establish national management of UK waters and national fishing quotas and govern foreign access to UK waters.

- The Agriculture Bill (now committed to a Public Bill Committee) will replace the Common Agricultural Policy and introduce a new domestic scheme to support farmers and protect the natural environment.

- The Nuclear Safeguards Act 2018 (which received royal assent on 26 June 2018) will give the Office for Nuclear Regulation the powers to fulfil the UK's safeguard and non-proliferation obligations and ensure continued civil nuclear trade outside the Euratom regime.

- The Sanctions and Anti-Money Laundering Act 2018 (which received royal assent on 23 May 2018) will provide a domestic legislative framework for the Government to impose restrictive sanctions measures on individuals and organisations, as well as to license certain sanctioned activities

Depending on the outcome of the Article 50 negotiations and the model ultimately chosen, the UK is likely to remain bound by much of the existing European employment law and regulation. For now, therefore, it is still business as usual, and we have updated this edition on that basis.

Key European developments

Working time

(See **Chapter 1**.) Working time has long been a vexed issue, at both European and national level. Talks on a revised Working Time Directive to replace the 1993 Directive (implemented in the UK through the Working Time Regulations 1998) have been ongoing since the European Commission issued a proposal for its amendment in September 2004.

During the period 2004–09, there were extensive discussions in the Council of Europe and the European Parliament on a common legislative proposal that would have made a number of changes to the Directive. The EU's talks focused particularly on two key issues: an individual's right to opt out of the 48-hour working week, and whether time spent on call is counted as working time. In mid-September 2008, the Council of the European Union reached an agreement on amendments to the Directive. To amend the Directive there must be agreement between the Member States (represented by 'The Council' of ministers from each Member State) and the European Parliament. The European Parliament did not support the proposed amendments and in December 2008 voted for considerable amendments of its own, including the phasing out of the opt-out provisions over three years and for the entire period of on-call time, including any inactive part, to count as working time. A period of intense negotiation (known as conciliation) followed, but on 27 April 2009 the negotiations failed. It was agreed that as the European Parliament and Member States were unable to resolve their long-standing differences over whether to retain the opt-out or not, there was no point in continuing the negotiations.

Following the failure of the previous efforts to revise the Directive, the Commission moved to a two-stage consultation with EU-level social partners. The first stage involved the launch, in March 2010, of a consultation paper, following which the Commission concluded that 'changes to the current working time rules are urgently needed'. The second-stage consultation process began in December 2010 and asked for the social partners' (workers and employers' representatives) views on two options for revision of the Directive:

- a focused review, dealing only with the issues of on-call time and compensatory rest;
- a comprehensive review, dealing with a wider range of matters highlighted by the social partners in their responses to the first consultation, including the individual opt-out from the Directive's 48-hour maximum working week.

In November 2011, the EU-level social partners indicated that they would enter into talks to revise the Directive. Under the process provided for by Article 155 of the Treaty on the Functioning of the European Union (TFEU), they had nine months in which to negotiate an agreement. In August 2012 the deadline was extended to December 2012. These negotiations failed to reach agreement by 31 December 2012 and, after further exploratory meetings, it was announced that negotiations were at an end. This once again put the initiative for reform back onto the Commission.

In December 2014, the Commission published a further public consultation on the Directive, with the aim 'to gather insights and contributions from the public in the context of the on-going review and impact assessment process concerning the Directive and possible changes to it'. The consultation included looking at the general impact of the Directive, as well as at some of its specific provisions, including the 48-hour opt-out, how to treat on-call time, the application of the Directive to the emergency services and healthcare sectors, and whether specific rules should be introduced to cover teleworking, zero hours contracts and flexitime.

On 24 May 2017, the European Commission published an Interpretative Communication on the Directive 'concerning certain aspects of the organisation of working time' ([2017] OJ C165/1). This includes an examination of the current state of play of the implementation of the Directive, taking into consideration national reports (including the views of national and European social partners), previous Commission reports on implementation, information collected from EU pilot and infringement procedures, contributions from independent experts and research done by the Commission itself.

The most important findings, many of which apply equally to the UK, included the following:

- *Exclusions from the Directive's scope of application:* The Directive has for the most part been transposed in both the public and private sectors. However, in some Member States, some categories of workers are excluded from the scope of the legislation. In the public sector this is most commonly the case for the armed forces, police and other security forces, and also for civil protection services such as prison staff and public service firefighters. As for the private sector, several Member States exclude domestic workers. Such exclusions are not consistent with the requirements of the Working Time Directive.
- *Workers with more than one employment contract:* The Working Time Directive does not explicitly state whether its provisions set absolute limits in case of employees who have concurrent contracts with one or more employer(s) or if they apply to each employment relationship separately. The CJEU has not yet had to rule on this point. The Commission considers that, in the light of the Directive, its provisions should apply as far as possible per worker. Taking into account the need to ensure that the health and safety objective of the Working Time Directive is given full effect, Member States' legislation should provide for appropriate mechanisms for monitoring and enforcement. While it is noted that Member State practices vary on this point, the UK does apply the Directive per worker.
- *Definition of 'working time' and 'on-call time':* In general, the formal definition of 'working time' set out in the Directive (ie that the worker 'is working, at the employer's disposal and carrying out his activity or duties') does not appear to give rise to problems of application. Most Member States do not have specific legal provisions defining the status of what is referred to as on-call work. 'On-call time' refers to periods where a worker is required to remain at the workplace or another place determined by the employer, ready to carry out his or her duties if requested to do so. According to the Court's rulings, all on-call time must be fully counted as working time for the purposes

of the Directive. This principle applies both to periods where the worker is working in response to a call ('active' on-call time) and to periods where he or she is allowed to rest while waiting for a call ('inactive' on-call time), provided that he or she remains at the workplace. Where a specific mention of on-call work is made in national rules, this is generally consistent with the Court's interpretation. Furthermore, national courts have generally in practice introduced EU case law. Compliance among the Member States with the requirement to treat on-call time as working time is improving, but there are still some issues.

- *Breaks and rest periods:* Article 4 provides for a rest break where the working day is longer than 6 hours, without specifying its duration or defining it in more detailed terms. The Directive requires that these details shall be 'laid down in collective agreements or agreements between the two sides of industry or, failing that, by national legislation'. The Directive allows collective agreements to establish the duration and terms of the break. Nevertheless, the duty to transpose the Directive lies with the Member States. It is therefore their responsibility to ensure that all workers, including those who may not be covered by collective agreements, are entitled to a break. This provision appears in general to have been satisfactorily transposed. Most Member States set out minimum provisions for the length and timing of a rest break during the working day. However, some Member States do not set a minimum duration or timing for the rest break by law, and it is not clear whether collective agreements in all cases cover these aspects. As regards rest (Articles 3 and 5 of the Directive), the Directive sets out out minimum provisions for the length of rest of 11 consecutive hours per 24-hour period and a minimum uninterrupted rest period of 24 hours per seven-day period, plus the 11 hours of daily rest. The Directive provides a possibility for the weekly rest to be reduced to 24 hours for objective reasons. These core requirements appear satisfactorily transposed into national law by Member States for most sectors. A few Member States appear to have transposed the requirement for weekly rest incorrectly in some respects, eg because the requirement is not transposed for a certain sector or by providing for the use of a 24-hour rest period without the presence of concrete objective reasons.

- *Limits to working time:* Under Article 6 of the Directive, average weekly working time (including overtime) must not exceed 48 hours per week. In general, this limit has been satisfactorily transposed, and many Member States actually lay down more protective standards. Several countries have amended their legislation for certain groups of workers in order to comply with the Directive. In general, there are still a few cases where the Directive's limit is exceeded, including in Ireland (social care workers) and Greece (doctors).

- *Annual leave:* The core right to paid annual leave (Article 7 of the Directive) is generally transposed satisfactorily. All Member States explicitly provide for a right to at least 4 weeks' paid annual leave, and all provide for the worker to receive his or her 'average pay', his or her 'normal weekly rate', 'average monthly remuneration' or similar while he or she is on leave. Two main problems have been identified. First, some Member States impose conditions on acquiring or taking paid annual leave in the first year of employment that go further than provided for by the Directive as interpreted by the Court of Justice. For example, they lay down qualification periods which are too long (6– 8 months) before leave can be taken. A few Member States have systems in which the right to annual leave with pay is acquired based on the worker's earnings in a qualifying year which precedes the year in which the paid annual leave can be taken ('the holiday year'). The worker is entitled to time off in the holiday year, but without pay. These rules may result in a delay of more than a year before accrued paid annual leave can be taken. The second main problem is the lapsing of the right to paid annual leave which the worker has not been able to take. The CJEU has held that a worker who is unable to work due to illness continues to build up paid annual leave entitlement during the period of sick leave. Member States may place a limit on the possibility to carry over annual leave that cannot be taken due to justified incapacity. However, the Court has also framed that possibility and held that 'any carry-over period must be substantially longer than the reference period in respect of which it is granted'. Many Member States have provisions that entitle the worker to carry over or postpone acquired periods of annual leave when taking such leave would coincide with a period of sick leave. But in several countries, the period before the worker loses his or her right to leave with pay appears too short, as it is not longer than the one-year reference period.

- *Night work (Article 16):* Member States generally limit the average working time of night workers to 8 hours. However, a number of Member States, including the UK, have chosen to let the working time of night workers be averaged over a period of 4 months. The reference period applicable for night work should be substantially shorter than the period used for the maximum working week. Thus, the Commission is of the opinion that a reference period of 4 months is too long.

- *Derogations (Articles 17 and 18 of the Directive):* Member States have generally transposed these derogations and make use of them. As to the sectors and activities concerned, Member States have generally taken up the activities listed in the Directive itself.

- *Opt-out (Article 22):* Member States have the option not to apply the maximum limit to weekly working time as long as the general principles of the protection of health and safety of workers are respected and certain protective measures are put in place. The worker may not be obliged to work more than an average of 48 hours a week unless he or she has first given his or her explicit, free and informed advance consent to perform such work. The Member State must ensure that the employer does not subject the worker to any detriment if the worker is not willing to give his or her agreement to perform such work. The Member State must also ensure that the employer keeps up-to-date records of all workers who carry out such work and places these records at the disposal of the competent authorities, who may, for reasons connected with the safety and/or health of workers, prohibit or restrict the possibility of exceeding the maximum weekly working hours. Some 18 Member States now provide for the use of the opt-out. Of these, six (including the UK) allow the use of the opt-out irrespective of sector, whereas the other 12 limit its use to jobs that make extensive use of on-call time, such as health services or emergency services. The remaining 10 Member States do not use the opt-out.

In general terms, the review concluded that a large majority of workers in the EU are subject to working time rules that respect EU legislation. In many cases national rules afford greater protection than what is required under the Directive, and the compliance of Member State legislation with the Directive is improving. Given that many of these issues remain unresolved and will not be resolved before the UK leaves the EU, it is unlikely that any further changes made will impact the UK, although some commentators believe that the Working Time Regulations 1998 are ripe for change post-Brexit.

Data protection (see **15.5**)

The EU General Data Protection Regulation (GDPR) was passed in April 2016. It now applies in all Member States (since 25 May 2018) and replaces the Data Protection Directive (95/46/EC). Although the GDPR is an EU Regulation, and so was applicable in the UK without the need for domestic UK legislation as the UK was still in the EU when it became effective, as a Regulation, the GDPR would have automatically fallen away when the UK leaves the EU, and so the UK Government has implemented domestic legislation to retain the GDPR via the Data Protection Act 2018. The 2018 Act is intended to ensure that the country's data protection framework is 'suitable for our new digital age, allowing citizens to better control their data'.

Whistleblowers

On 23 April 2018, in response to a request from the European Parliament, the European Commission published a proposal for a Directive on whistleblower protections for those reporting violations of EU law. There is already a degree of protection for whistleblowers in the UK via the Public Interest Disclosure Act 1998 and, more recently, in the Trade Secrets (Enforcement etc) Regulations 2018 (implementing the EU Trade Secrets Directive 2016/943, which became effective on 5 July 2016 but gave Member States until 9 June 2018 to implement), which precludes whistleblowers from liability for reporting misconduct or illegal activity, even if it relates to trade secrets.

Key UK employment law and procedure developments

Employment law reforms

The Government has confirmed, on a number of occasions, its intention to repeal the Human Rights Act 1998 and reform the UK human rights framework so as to deliver on the Government's 2015 election manifesto pledge to introduce a British Bill of Rights and reform human rights law. No timeframe was set out in the Queen's Speech.

In February 2017, Her Majesty's Courts and Tribunals Service (HMCTS) launched its online register of employment tribunal judgments. This was the first time that there had been an online central register of tribunal judgments. The service currently covers cases from 2016 and 2017, but all new judgments will be made available going forward. EAT judgments are available as before via <www.judiciary.gov.uk/judgments/>.

Employment tribunal reforms

The Briggs Review of the Civil Courts Structure was published in July 2016 (<www.judiciary.gov.uk/civil-courts-structure-review/civil-courts-structure-review-ccsr-final-report-published/>). It was commissioned by the Lord Chief Justice and the Master of the Rolls in July 2015 to coincide with a programme for reform of the courts by HMCTS as well as to look at civil court structures and judicial processes more generally. The final report followed the publication of an interim report in January 2016. The review makes a number of recommendations intended to inform the current programme of wider court modernisation being undertaken by HMCTS. It also makes a number of recommendations on different aspects of the civil justice system, many of which are not within the scope of this work. Those that are are summarised briefly below:

- *Online Court* – a new standalone court, designed to be used by people with minimum assistance from lawyers, with its own set of user-friendly rules. This may include employment cases at some time in the future.
- *Enforcement of judgments and orders* – there should be a single court as the default court for the enforcement of the judgments and orders of all the civil courts (including the new Online Court). This should normally be the County Court.
- *Boundaries between jurisdictions* – Lord Justice Briggs acknowledged that there continued to be a case for convergence between the Employment Tribunal (and Employment Appeal Tribunal) and the civil courts. He found that there was broad support for 'the creation of an Employment and Equalities Court, as a civil court with specialist judiciary, forming part of the civil court structure, but with exclusive jurisdiction in relation to employment and equality disputes, its own rules, procedure and culture, and a route of first appeal to the EAT as a specialist appeal court' and that 'there was no significant support for leaving the ET and the EAT in their state of current isolation' (para 11.15). Acknowledging that practical and possible political difficulties with creating a new court may prevent change in the short to medium term, he said: 'It will nonetheless be necessary to address the unsatisfactory jurisdictional limits which currently prevent many employment cases being dealt with, in full, in the civil courts or in the ET' (para 11.18). He concluded that while 'there continues to be a case for convergence between the Employment Tribunal (and Employment Appeal Tribunal) and the civil courts, the detail is a matter beyond the scope of this review' (para 12.15(60)).

In October 2016, the Ministry of Justice announced plans for streamlined and largely digital courts. These were part of an ambitious £1 billion six-year package of civil and criminal justice reforms intended to conclude in April 2022.

In December 2016, the Government published a specific consultation on reforming the employment tribunal system. BEIS and the Ministry of Justice said that tribunals 'have not kept pace with changes in society, in particular, with the way that users want and need to interact with our systems'. However, the Government noted that while most reforms to tribunals can be dealt with by secondary legislation within existing powers in the Tribunals, Courts and Enforcement Act 2007, changes to employment tribunals can only happen through amendments to primary legislation, namely the Employment Tribunals Act 1996. 'This means that the employment tribunals and the employment appeal tribunal are likely to be the last major tribunals to be fully reformed. They will, therefore, benefit from improvements identified during the implementation of reforms in other tribunals.'

The consultation paper noted that, uniquely among tribunals managed by HMCTS, BEIS is responsible for policy and legislation on procedural matters in employment tribunals. The paper proposes transferring responsibility for procedural rules to the independent tribunal procedure committee, whose membership would be expanded to include 'appropriate' employment sector representatives such as employment judges and 'suitably experienced' practitioners. The paper proposed that case management functions would be delegated to relevant (administrative) staff, albeit dependent on the judiciary's agreement. BEIS would retain responsibility for employment law policy. The paper seeks views on the factors that might make particular cases 'suitable to deal with through a digital medium'. The paper did not specifically address the issue of tribunal fees, stating that the Government would publish the conclusions of its review on tribunal fees 'in due course and any adjustments to the current fee structure will be brought for consultation'. The consultation closed on 20 January 2017.

On 31 January 2017, the Government published its post implementation review of employment tribunal fees (see below).

In February 2017, the Government published its response to the employment tribunal system consultation and the results of the consultation process. These indicated that the majority of respondents broadly agreed that some digitisation of the system would be beneficial but the extent of support for the proposal varied. The main theme to emerge was concern that the move to a digital system would not be well managed or properly resourced and that measures should be in place to ensure staff and judiciary have proper access and training to use the new tools so as not to hinder their take-up. The Government's response was, broadly, that as any reform of the employment tribunal system would come at the end rather than the beginning of the digital transformation plans, they would 'be able to benefit from practical lessons learnt from similar types of reform taking place in other courts and tribunals'. As far as delegation of case management was concerned, as stated in para 26 of the consultation document, the intention is that tribunal caseworkers would be either legally trained or qualified. The Government believed such delegation would be useful but expected that any delegation would 'only be implemented following further engagement between the Senior President of Tribunals, employment tribunal judiciary and tribunal users'. The Government said it therefore intends to proceed with its proposal to amend the Employment Tribunals Act 1996 to provide for the Tribunal Procedure Committee to be able to make rules concerning the delegation of judicial functions to HMCTS staff. 'This power will specifically provide for the rules to delegate to the Senior President of Tribunals the authority to designate both the functions to be delegated and the categories of staff who may exercise those delegated functions.' These changes will be brought forward as soon as parliamentary time allows.

The Government also acknowledged the importance of non-legal members in cases where their workplace experience is needed to help determine the case and stated that 'they will continue to be involved in proceedings where they are needed'. However, the Government proposed that the appointment of non-legal members should no longer be with Ministers but with the Senior President and said that it intends to proceed with this proposal through an amendment to the Employment Tribunals Act 1996.

The Government also proposed that the responsibility for Employment Tribunal and Employment Appeal Tribunal rules should be transferred to the Tribunal Procedure Committee, which 'will allow those rules and procedures to be more responsive to the challenges of resolving complex workplace disputes and the wider reforms being introduced generally across the justice system than the current legislative framework allows'. They proposed the appointment of two additional members to the Tribunal Procedure Committee in the form of an employment judge and a legal practitioner with specific experience of the employment tribunal system.

In April 2017, the Prime Minister, Theresa May, called a General Election. One result of this was that the Prisons and Courts Bill (which was to be used to implement the new online dispute resolution system for civil cases proposed by Briggs, as well as numerous other criminal and civil justice measures) was not included in the 'wash up' before the dissolution of Parliament on 3 May. However, a new Prison and Courts Reform Bill was included in the post-Election Queen's Speech, which included an intention to take advantage of new technology 'to make our court system fit for purpose in the 21st century, speeding up cases for litigants and reducing costs'.

In September 2018, the Law Commission published a Consultation Paper on Employment Law Hearing Structures. The terms of reference are to review the jurisdictions of the employment tribunal, the Employment Appeal Tribunal and the civil courts in employment and discrimination matters and make recommendations for reform. Issues raised include extending tribunal limitation deadlines from three to six months as well as removing the £25,000 limit on contract claims in tribunals. The consultation closed on 11 January 2019.

Employment tribunal fees – see also Chapter 6

The Government introduced employment tribunal fees in July 2013. The introduction of fees for claimants in employment tribunals led to a significant drop in the number of cases brought, approaching 70%. According to a House of Commons Report published in June 2016 (see below), the number of single cases brought declined by about 67% to around 4,500 per quarter from October 2013 to June 2015; and the number of multiple cases declined by 72%, from 1,500 per quarter in the year leading to June 2013 to around 400 per quarter since October 2013.

The Government launched a post-implementation review of the fees on 11 June 2015.

The House of Commons Justice Committee published a Report into the effect of employment tribunal fees in June 2016. The Committee concluded that 'the regime of employment tribunal fees has had a significant adverse impact on access to justice for meritorious claims'. It cited statistics, comparing cases brought in the first three months of 2013 and of 2015, that showed reductions in the number of cases for the most common types of claims: Working Time Directive, down 78%; unauthorised deductions from wages, down 56%; unfair dismissal, down 72%; equal pay, down 58%; breach of contract, down 75%; and sex discrimination, down 68%.

On 31 January 2017, the Government published its post-implementation review of employment tribunal fees. The review concluded that the current system of fees and remissions had been 'generally successfully in meeting the scheme's original objective' and was 'generally working effectively and is operating lawfully'. It stated that 'there is no conclusive evidence that ET fees have prevented people from bringing claims'.

In the July 2017 review of employment practices by Matthew Taylor (see section on the 'gig economy' below), concern was expressed about the impact fees were having, and the Government was urged to change the system.

A judicial review brought by Unison against the fees was heard by the Supreme Court in March 2017. Unison's challenge was successful (R *(on the application of UNISON) v Lord Chancellor* [2017] UKSC 51). A seven-judge Supreme Court unanimously held that the Fees Order was unlawful *ab initio* and must therefore be quashed. The Supreme Court's conclusion was based on the fact that fees were 'inconsistent with access to justice' and had resulted in a substantial fall in claims being brought. It said that the fees were contrary to the Equality Act 2010 as they disproportionately affected women. The statistics indicated that there had been a significant reduction in claims in areas such as pregnancy discrimination. On this basis the Supreme Court was unanimous in finding that the fee regime was unlawful. Lord Reed (with whom all six Justices agreed) noted that:

> [§8] ETs are intended to provide a forum for the enforcement of employment rights by employees and workers, including the low paid, those who have recently lost their jobs, and those who are vulnerable to long term unemployment. They are designed to deal with issues which are often of modest financial value, or of no financial value at all, but are nonetheless of social importance.

His judgment went on:

> [§ 28] [I]t is necessary to bear in mind that the use which people make of ETs is governed more by circumstances than by choice. Every individual who is in employment may require to have resort to an ET, usually unexpectedly: for example, if they find themselves unfairly dismissed or the victim of discrimination. Persons whose employment rights have been breached, or who believe them to have been breached, are often under a practical compulsion to apply to an ET for redress.

Lady Hale endorsed Lord Reed's speech but added her own judgment on the underlying discrimination complaint that had formed the basis for the claim in the first place. She observed that the charging of fees for all complaints had clearly 'deterred meritorious claims at least as much as, if not more than, unmeritorious claims'. As a result of this applying across the board, and thus to those with protected characteristics who were to bring a discrimination complaint, she easily concluded that this must mean that there was discrimination in itself by deterring those discrimination complaints.

In the light of the Supreme Court ruling in the *Unison* case, a number of practical matters needed to be resolved:

(1)   As a result of the ruling, the Government immediately stated that it would refund the more than £27 million to the thousands of people charged for taking claims to tribunal since July 2013, when fees were first introduced; this is likely to be a complicated process. While there is likely to be a central record of all fees paid by employment tribunal claimants, where a claimant won his or her case, in most situations the losing employer would be ordered to pay the value of the employment tribunal fees to the claimant as part of a costs award. Problems of double recovery may arise. There is also a question about what should happen if the fee was taken into account in arriving at a settlement figure. The Employment Tribunals Rules of Procedure 2013 also contain rules related to fees and will need to be amended by legislation. In the meantime, they will need to be read in line with the Supreme Court's judgment. From November 2017, a process has been put in place for anyone who paid a fee to apply to be reimbursed.

(2)   There was an issue about those who had effectively been denied access to an employment tribunal between 2013 and the handing down of the judgment. On 9 August 2017, the President of the Employment Tribunals in England and Wales issued a Case Management Order to the effect that all employment claims or applications brought to tribunal which relied on the Supreme Court decision were stayed. On 18 August 2017, the stay was lifted with immediate effect. It was announced that:

(a)   applications for reimbursement of fees, however paid or by whom, shall be made in accordance with administrative arrangements set out by the Ministry of Justice and HMCTS (see above);

(b)   applications for the reinstatement of claims (of whatever kind) rejected or dismissed for non-payment of fees shall be made in accordance with administrative arrangements to be announced by the Ministry of Justice and HMCTS shortly;

(c)   all other claims or applications brought to the Employment Tribunal in England and Wales in reliance upon the decision of the Supreme Court in *Unison* shall proceed to be considered judicially in accordance with the appropriate legal and procedural principles in the usual way.

(3)   The Government announced the repeal of the Fees Order and, since the judgment, fees have not been sought for those issuing claims.

(4)   As of 3 August 2017, the form that can be used to submit claims online was amended to remove any reference to fees.

(5)   What will be the impact on the role of Acas and the pre-claim conciliation process, and on the tribunal system, and do they have the resources to cope?

According to figures released by the Ministry of Justice in September 2018, following the abolition of fees in July 2017, tribunal claims increased by 165% in the second quarter of 2018 compared to the same period in 2017. The increase has led to a significant backlog in hearing tribunal claims (between January and March 2018 there was a 24% increase in outstanding caseload over the same period the previous year). From the launch of the fee refund scheme in October 2017 to 31 March 2018, 9,500 applications for refunds were received and 7,700 payments made, with a total value of £6,555,600. As at September 2018, £10,650,000 had been refunded.

In June 2018, the Government confirmed that it had launched a review on 'how' it would charge fees in the future. In November, the Ministry of Justice said it was confident that it could find a balance that helps fund the court system while being 'proportionate and progressive'. It therefore appears that it is only a question of time before a new fee scheme is introduced. However, at the time of writing, nothing had been announced.

Employment tribunal awards

Employment tribunal compensation awards are increased each year in line with inflation, based on the September retail price index (RPI). Last year this increased by 2%. The Employment Rights (Increase of Limits) Order 2017 (SI 2017/175) increased tribunal compensation limits in line with this for awards on and after 6 April 2017. The maximum basic award increased from £14,370 to £14,670. The maximum compensatory award for unfair dismissal was raised from £78,962 to £80,541. The maximum amount of a week's pay, used to calculate statutory redundancy payments and various awards including the basic and additional awards for unfair dismissal, was raised from £479 to £489. The minimum basic award for certain categories of unfair dismissal increased from £5,835 to £5,970 (see **Chapter 5** in particular).

Other matters

Cyber bullying

A new type of workplace bullying – cyber bullying – has emerged in recent years. Acas defines cyber bullying as 'any form of bullying, harassment or victimisation online'. Cyber bullying can include leaking sensitive personal information about individuals, threatening or abusive comments online, inappropriate comments and the posting of pictures. Although it is not possible to bring an employment tribunal claim in respect of bullying/cyber bullying in isolation, it can generally be tagged on to discrimination, harassment or victimisation claims or constructive or unfair dismissal claims. Acas has recently released guidance on cyber bullying and how it can be dealt with in the workplace. Employers should make sure they have an up-to-date policy in place that deals with cyber bullying, not least because this can happen outside the workplace and can occur through the work email system in and out of working hours.

The gender pay gap

The Equality Act 2010 (Gender Pay Gap Information) Regulations 2017 (SI 2017/172), which require larger public and private sector employers with over 250 employees to publish their gender pay gap figures, came into force in April 2017. The Regulations require private and public sector employers to publish annually six pieces of mandatory information about the pay and bonuses of men and women in their organisations. The Regulations clarify who is covered by the obligation (most workers but not genuinely self-employed workers or, for example, partners in firms). The information must be signed off as accurate by a director and published on the organisation's website, so that it is accessible to staff and the public. The same information must be provided to the Government, which will also publish the details on its gender pay gap website. Acas and the Government Equalities Office have published joint guidance on the new law. The first statistics had to be published by 4 April 2018, and over 10,000 employers submitted data. Those employers have to follow through on any initiatives identified to close gender pay gaps. Many reported big gaps between men and women's pay (Ryanair reported a 71.8% median hourly gap and a 97% male top quartile).

The 'gig economy' (see 1.3)

The 'gig economy' has been defined as 'a labour market characterised by the prevalence of short-term contracts or freelance work, as opposed to permanent jobs'. In the gig economy, instead of a regular wage, workers get paid for the 'gigs' they do, such as a food delivery or a car journey. It has been estimated that five million people in the UK are employed in this type of capacity. Jobs include courier and delivery services, plumbing and minicab driving. Proponents of the gig economy claim that people can benefit from flexible hours, with control over how much time they can work as they juggle other priorities in their lives. Most of those working in the gig economy are classed as self-employed independent contractors, which has meant that they are not viewed as workers or employees, so have no protection against unfair dismissal, no right to redundancy payments and no right to receive the national minimum wage, paid holiday or sickness pay. In October 2016, Matthew Taylor, chief executive of the Royal Society of the Arts, was tasked with looking at how working practices in the modern economy needed to change in order to keep pace with modern business models.

On 11 July 2017, the Taylor Review was published. In its opening paragraph detailing its rationale, the report advocates change in the 'British way' – building on existing strengths and existing regulation. 'Seven steps towards fair and decent work with realistic scope for development and fulfilment' are proposed:

- *Good work for all'*: There is a need for a national strategy to provide good work (defined to include wages, employment quality, education and training, working conditions, work life balance and consultative participation and collective representation) for all 'for which government needs to be held accountable'. The report does not suggest the banning of zero hours contracts. It recognises that some workers may want to work in this way. It does, however, acknowledge the importance of 'good work'.

- *Dependent contractors*: The distinction between employees, workers and the genuinely self-employed should be retained, but people who work for platform-based companies, such as Deliveroo and Uber, who are under their control and supervision, should be classed as 'dependent contractors'. Such 'dependent contractors' should be entitled to certain minimum wage, holiday and sickness rights, and employers in these industries should pay national insurance. Individuals who prefer flexible working should be allowed to continue but they should be granted fairness at work. There should be a clear statutory legal distinction made between dependent contractors and those who are legitimately self-employed. The need for an element of personal service in employment contracts should be retained, but a requirement to perform work personally would no longer be crucial to being a 'worker' – the focus would be on control. The rationale for this is that it is unfair that individuals who, in theory at least, have the right to provide a substitute should not be able to gain 'worker' (or 'dependent contractor') status.

- *National Living Wage:* This is 'a powerful tool' to raise the financial base line of low paid workers. Strategies must be put in place, particularly for low paid sectors, to make sure workers do not get stuck on this rate of pay.

- *Cost of employment:* The Government should avoid further increasing the non-wage costs of employing a person. The review highlighted the apprenticeship levy as an expense companies have raised concerns about. The Government must provide additional protections for dependent contractors.

- *Good corporate governance:* National regulation is not needed to provide good work. Companies must practise responsible corporate governance, good management and strong employment relations within their organisations.

- *Developing skills:* Everyone should feel they have realistically attainable ways to strengthen their future prospects at work. Individuals should be able to develop their skills through 'formal and informal learning' as well as 'on the job and off the job activities'.

- *A healthy workplace:* The UK needs to develop a more proactive approach to workplace health which will benefit companies, workers and the wider public interest.

The Review also contains recommendations for:

- individuals to be able to have their employment status determined by a tribunal, without having to pay a fee. The Review also suggests that the burden of proof should be on an employer where employment status is in dispute;

- a right to return for individuals who have been absent due to a long-term sickness absence;

- extending the right to a written statement of terms (ERA 1996, s 1) to workers as well as employees, to include a description of statutory rights and with a standalone right to compensation if a statement is not provided;

- requiring written statements to be given on day one of employment;

- preserving continuity of employment where any gap in employment is less than one month, rather than one week;

- HMRC to have responsibility for enforcing the right to holiday pay and sick pay for low paid workers.

The recommendations have been critiqued by unions as being 'weak and business-friendly'. The review consists of a set of recommendations for the Government to consider. In February 2018, the Government published 'Good Work', its response to the Taylor Review. It has said that it will take forward all but one of the Review's 53 recommendations (it has rejected a proposal to change National Insurance contributions). However, it is only proposed initially to consult on a number of issues raised by the Review. The consultations included employment status, and whether to rename workers who are neither self-employed nor employees as 'dependent contractors', as well as how to align employment status and tax status frameworks. The Government also consulted on a number of other recommendations from the Review, including the strengthening of rights of those with flexible working patterns, and the provision of a 'list of rights' to which individuals are entitled. The Government has also consulted on proposals to make the enforcement of employment tribunal awards against employers simpler. All consultations have now closed, and further developments are awaited.

Modern slavery

The Modern Slavery Act 2015 requires certain organisations to produce and publish an annual statement setting out the steps taken to ensure that no form of modern slavery exists anywhere in its business or its supply chain. The aim is to encourage organisations to take responsibility not only for their own labour force, but also for the use of labour in the organisations that supply goods and services to them. The Act applies to all commercial organisations producing goods or services that do business in the UK and have an annual global turnover of over £36 million. Those organisations covered by the Act have to produce their first statement within six months of the end of the first financial year. Those companies whose financial year end was on 31 December 2016 had until 30 June 2017 to produce their first statement. In August 2018, the first CPS Modern Slavery Report was published. This showed that, while charges for modern slavery offences had risen by 27% since 2017, the number of convictions remained almost the same as the previous year, and down from 2015/16. Referrals from police and other agencies to the CPS rose by 31% to 355.

National minimum wage

In April 2018, in response in part to a recommendation in the Taylor Review (see 'Gig economy' above), the Low Pay Commission opened a consultation seeking views on existing national living wage rates and the rates that should apply from April 2019. The consultation closed on 1 June 2018. The Low Pay Commission will recommend new rates to the Government in October 2018. The Government usually increases rates in line with the Commission's recommendations.

Reviews and reports

The Work and Pensions Committee in its May 2017 report on self-employment and the 'gig economy' (see more above) found that 'established definitions of employment and self-employment [see **1.3**] are straining at the leash'.

Sexual harassment

In January and March 2016, the Trades Union Congress (TUC) sought information about women's experience of sexual harassment in the workplace (see **Chapter 11**). A Report, 'Still just a bit of banter?', was published in August 2016. An online version is available at <www.tuc.org.uk/sites/default/files/SexualHarassmentreport2016.pdf>. Key findings included:

- More than half (52%) of all women polled have experienced some form of sexual harassment.
- Thirty-five per cent of women have heard comments of a sexual nature being made about other women in the workplace.
- Thirty-two per cent of women have been subject to unwelcome jokes of a sexual nature.
- Twenty-eight per cent of women have been subject to comments of a sexual nature about their body or clothes.
- Nearly one-quarter of women have experienced unwanted touching (such as a hand on the knee or lower back).
- One-fifth of women have experienced unwanted sexual advances.
- More than one in 10 women reported experiencing unwanted sexual touching or attempts to kiss them.
- In the vast majority of cases, the perpetrator was a male colleague, with nearly one in five reporting that their direct manager or someone else with direct authority over them was the perpetrator.
- Four out of five women did not report the sexual harassment to their employer.

The Report made the following recommendations for government:

- abolition of employment tribunal fees;
- reinstatement of third party harassment legislation;
- reinstatement of employment tribunal powers to make wider recommendations;
- reinstatement of Statutory Equality Questionnaire;
- recognition and facility time for union equality representatives;
- extending the full range of statutory employment rights to all workers, regardless of employment status or type of contract.

In March 2018, the Equalities and Human Rights Commission (EHRC) published a report, 'Turning the tables: ending sexual harassment at work', which raises serious concerns about sexual harassment in the workplace. It identified widespread failures by employers and set out a number of recommendations in a call to the Government to take action, including:

- a statutory code of practice, with tribunal discretion to increase compensation by 25% for non-compliance;
- safeguards against employers using confidentiality agreements to prevent the disclosure of past acts of harassment;
- extension of the limitation period for bringing a sexual harassment claim;
- reinstatement of protection from third party harassment (without the requirement to show two previous incidents).

Trade union reforms

Although collective rights are beyond the scope of this work, in May 2016, one of the most significant pieces of trade union legislation for many years was passed. The Trade Union Act 2016 includes changes to the way in which lawful industrial action can be voted for. Although the Act received the Royal Assent on 4 May 2016, it did not become law until March 2017. In January 2017, the Government published draft regulations giving more details on what constitutes 'important public services' and a revised code of practice on industrial action ballots and notice to employers. Those regulations have now become law, with effect from 1 March 2017.

The new rules require unions to include more detailed information on the ballot paper sent to members. This must now summarise the dispute in enough detail that members can understand what issues are unresolved, the action planned, and the period during which it is expected to take place. Any ballot sent to union members from 1 March 2017 must meet the requirements. Unions must now provide all eligible voters and the employer with certain prescribed information relating to the result of the ballot. In addition to a majority voting in favour, a minimum turnout of 50% of those entitled to vote in now required. In certain essential services (including health, education, fire, border security and transport), at least 40% of those entitled to vote in a ballot must vote in favour of action. Unions will be required to give employers 14 rather than the current 7 days' notice of industrial action. A ballot for strike action will cease to provide a mandate after 6 months (extendable to 9 months if the employer agrees). Ultimately, after a transitional period of 12 months, new trade union members will only have to pay the political levy if they actively opt in to do so. As a measure to tackle intimidation during strike action, it is now a requirement for a union to appoint a supervisor to oversee any picketing for picketing to qualify for protection.

General

For some years now, there have been common commencement dates for the introduction of employment policy. The two dates for commencement of domestic employment law for which BEIS has responsibility are 6 April and 1 October of each year. BEIS publishes an annual statement of forthcoming employment legislation every January. An e-mail alert system is also available on the BIS website.

In June 2018, the Ministry of Justice published Quarterly Tribunal Statistics and Tables for January to March 2018.

In the year leading up to March 2018, the employment tribunal received 122,400 claims. This represents an increase of 118% compared to the same period in the previous year and reflects the general upward trend since fees were removed in July 2017 (fees were introduced in July 2013) (191,541 in 2012–13, 105,803 in 2013–14 61,308 in 2014–15, 83,031 in 2015–16, 88,476 in 2016–17). The number of claims in the most recent quarter (April–June 2018) is up 165% on the same period last year.

In March 2018, Acas released statistics on early conciliation for the period April 2017– December 2018. These show that while between the start of April 2017 and the end of July 2017, Acas received about 1,700 early conciliation notices a week, since the Supreme Court ruling on fees, this has risen to about 2,200 notifications a week. Since the end of August, there has been a 57% increase in ET1 receipts and a 25% increase in early conciliation notifications. Over this same period, 26% of notifications proceeded to a claim in the employment tribunal and 26% were settled via a COT3 or withdrawn. (See **Chapter 6**.)

In 2017–18, according to Ministry of Justice annual employment tribunal statistics, the median unfair dismissal award was £8,015 and the average (mean) award was £15,007. The median race discrimination award was £11,299 and the average (mean) award was £24,322. For sex discrimination claims, the figures were £10,638 and £13,212, for disability claims £16,523 and £30,698, for religious or belief discrimination £5,696 and £5,074, for sexual orientation £12,550 and £12,550, and for age discrimination £6,184 and £6,796 respectively. The highest discrimination award was £242,130 in a disability discrimination claim. Costs were awarded to the claimant in 169 cases and to the respondent in 310 cases. The maximum costs award was £20,000 and the median was £2,409. Since the launch of the employment tribunal refund scheme in October 2017 to 31 March 2018, 9,500 applications for a refund were received and 7,700 refund payments made, totalling £6,555,600.

For the most up-to-date and detailed analysis of the trends in employment tribunal claims, readers are directed to the quarterly and annual reports (and supporting data files) provided online by the Justice Statistics Analytical Services Division of the Ministry of Justice.

Reference resources

Useful information for employees may be found at <http://www.direct.gov.uk>. The site contains guidance on a number of employment matters, such as starting a new job, pay, employment contracts, work and families, discrimination and redundancy. The site also contains links to guidance on flexible working and maternity rights.

The EHRC has sections on its website <http://www.equalityhumanrights.com> containing guidance on all aspects of discrimination. The website also contains past publications and reports governing disability, gender and race.

The Acas website <http://www.acas.org.uk> provides a series of online publications which are free to download (for example on topics such as discipline and grievances at work, redundancy, stress, flexible working and holiday pay). It also offers a range of e-learning courses.

A number of law firms with employment law practices also provide a range of useful publications and guidance on their websites.

Table of Abbreviations

Legislation

ASCLA 2009	Apprenticeships, Skills, Children and Learning Act 2009
CPR 1998	Civil Procedure Rules 1998
DDA 1995	Disability Discrimination Act 1995
DPA 2018	Data Protection Act 2018
EA 2002	Employment Act 2002
EPA 1970	Equal Pay Act 1970
EP(C)A 1978	Employment Protection (Consolidation) Act 1978
ERA 1996	Employment Rights Act 1996
ERA 1999	Employment Relations Act 1999
ERRA 2013	Enterprise and Regulatory Reform Act 2013
ETA 1996	Employment Tribunals Act 1996
GDPR	General Data Protection Regulation
HRA 1998	Human Rights Act 1998
HSWA 1974	Health and Safety at Work etc Act 1974
ICE Regulations	Information and Consultation of Employees Regulations 2004
ITEPA 2003	Income Tax (Earnings and Pensions) Act 2003
MPLPAL(A)R 2006	Maternity and Parental Leave etc and Paternity and Adoption Leave (Amendment) Regulations 2006
MPLR 1999	Maternity and Parental Leave etc Regulations 1999
NMWA 1998	National Minimum Wage Act 1998
PALR 2002	Paternity and Adoption Leave Regulations 2002
PIDA 1998	Public Interest Disclosure Act 1998
RRA 1976	Race Relations Act 1976
SDA 1975	Sex Discrimination Act 1975
TULR(C)A 1992	Trade Union and Labour Relations (Consolidation) Act 1992

Employment case reports

ICR	Industrial Cases Reports
IRLR	Industrial Relations Law Reports

Other abbreviations

AAL	additional adoption leave
Acas	Advisory, Conciliation and Arbitration Service
AML	additional maternity leave
APL	additional paternity leave
BIS	Department for Business, Innovation and Skills
CJEU	Court of Justice of the European Union
CRE	Commission for Racial Equality
DfWP	Department for Work and Pensions
DRC	Disability Rights Commission
DTI	Department of Trade and Industry
EAT	Employment Appeal Tribunal
ECHR	European Convention on Human Rights
ECtHR	European Court of Human Rights
ECJ	European Court of Justice
EDT	effective date of termination (of employment)

EHRC	Equality and Human Rights Commission
EOC	Equal Opportunities Commission
ETO	economic, technical or organisational (reason for dismissal on transfer of an undertaking)
EWC	expected week of childbirth
HMRC	HM Revenue and Customs
HSE	Health and Safety Executive
ICO	Information Commissioner's Office
MA	maternity allowance
NICs	National Insurance Contributions
NJC	National Joint Council for Local Authorities' Administrative, Professional, Technical and Clerical Services
NMW	national minimum wage
OAL	ordinary adoption leave
OML	ordinary maternity leave
OPL	ordinary paternity leave
OTS	Office of Tax Simplification
PAYE	Pay As You Earn (in relation to Schedule E Income Tax)
PCP	provision, criterion or practice
PILON	payment in lieu of notice
ROET	Regional Office of the Employment Tribunals
RRO	restricted reporting order
S2P	Second State Pension Scheme
SAP	statutory adoption pay
SMP	statutory maternity pay
SOSR	some other substantial reason
SPP	statutory paternity pay
TEU	Treaty on European Union
TFEU	Treaty on the Functioning of the European Union

THE CONTRACT OF EMPLOYMENT

LEARNING OUTCOMES

After reading this chapter you will be able to:

- understand and explain the differences between an employee and a worker, and identify which statutory rights apply to which
- understand and explain the difference between a written statement of terms and an employment contract
- identify statutory restrictions on the freedom to contract
- understand how implied terms operate in an employment contract
- list the key terms that *must* be included in a written statement of terms/contract of employment
- list the key additional terms that *may* be included in a written contract of employment, and understand the importance of and the enforceability of restrictive covenants
- understand how the protection of wages legislation works
- understand the Working Time Regulations
- advise as to the enforceability of post-termination duties.

1.1 INTRODUCTION

Employment law in the UK derives from various sources – not only common law and statute, but also codes of practice and European Union (EU) law. In recent years, EU legislation has had a particularly significant influence, in terms both of legislation and judgments of the Court of Justice of the European Union (CJEU).

On 23 June 2016, the UK voted to leave the EU. Article 50 of the Treaty on European Union (TEU) has been triggered by the UK Government, and the UK will leave the EU on 29 March 2019.

Further, quite separately, decisions of the European Court of Human Rights (ECtHR) in Strasbourg (which originates separately from the EU through the Council of Europe) have influenced its development. This book will attempt to explain the impact and effect of all these areas on UK employment law. The main emphasis of this book is on individual employment rights – that is to say, the law that relates to employers and their employees and workers. There is very little commentary on collective areas of labour law such as trade unions, but these areas are touched upon where relevant.

1.2   BACKGROUND

Set out below is a summary of the main sources of employment law and their relevance.

1.2.1   Common law

Prior to the enactment of legislation affecting the relationship of employer and employee, the obligations each owed to the other were largely governed by the law of contract. Case law developed as the courts were called upon to interpret express contractual provisions, and to determine the nature and extent of implied contractual rights and duties. Case law has also developed on the interpretation of statutory provisions, many of which depend on the concept of 'reasonableness'.

This book considers reports of decisions reached by the UK courts and by the employment tribunals, as both forums can be used to determine issues of employment law. Judgments of the ECJ and ECtHR are also referred to, where relevant.

1.2.1.1   Employment tribunals

Employment tribunals have jurisdiction (through statute) to hear claims arising out of breaches of most aspects of the employment relationship, for example unfair dismissal, wrongful dismissal, redundancy payments, discrimination claims, equal pay claims and protection of wages claims (see **6.2.1** for further details). Tribunals also have jurisdiction to hear some claims by workers (eg, claims under the protection of wages legislation – see **1.10** below – and discrimination claims). For the distinction between a worker and an employee, see s 230 of the Employment Rights Act 1996 (ERA 1996) and **1.3** below.

1.2.1.2   The Employment Appeal Tribunal

The Employment Appeal Tribunal (EAT) hears appeals on questions of law from an employment tribunal. Its decisions are binding on employment tribunals. An appeal from the EAT lies to the Court of Appeal and from there to the Supreme Court.

1.2.1.3   The civil courts

In addition to the appellate function of the civil courts, the High Court and county court can hear breach of contract claims (eg wrongful dismissal) (see **Chapter 2**). Further, the civil courts can grant injunctive relief (eg where a restraint of trade clause has been breached, see **1.8.7.1**).

Note that the last House of Lords hearings took place in July 2009. The House of Lords has been replaced by the Supreme Court.

1.2.2   Legislation

The Industrial Relations Act 1971 attempted for the first time to introduce a comprehensive regulatory framework for all aspects of employment law, from collective bargaining to individual rights. Prior to this, employment issues had had to be dealt with in the common law courts under the common law. There were no special provisions or protections. There were no concepts of fairness – an employer was free to dismiss an employee as long as it did so in a contractually correct manner. The 1971 Act introduced the right to complain of 'unfair' dismissal. The majority of individual rights were consolidated, first in the Employment Protection (Consolidation) Act 1978 (EP(C)A 1978) and most recently in the ERA 1996. The 1996 Act was amended by the Employment Relations Acts 1999 and 2004 (ERA 1999 and 2004), the Employment Act 2002 (EA 2002) and the Work and Families Act 2006.

The Trade Union and Labour Relations (Consolidation) Act 1992 (TULR(C)A 1992), as amended by the Trade Union Reform and Employment Rights Act 1993 and the ERA 1999, consolidated all statute law containing trade union and group provisions. In the field of equal pay and discrimination, the Equal Pay Act 1970 (EPA 1970), the Sex Discrimination Act 1975 (SDA 1975), the Race Relations Act 1976 (RRA 1976) and the Disability Discrimination Act 1995 (DDA 1995) have all been repealed and replaced by the provisions of the Equality Act 2010 (see **Chapter 8**).

In addition to statutes there is a plethora of delegated legislation regulating employment law (much of it driven by EU law – see **1.2.4**), which will be referred to where relevant.

1.2.3 Codes of practice

A code of practice is not legally binding and is intended to give guidance to employers on good employment practices. It may, however, be used in evidence. For example, the Advisory, Conciliation and Arbitration Service (Acas) Code of Practice on Discipline and Grievance is often referred to by tribunals (see **Chapter 5**).

1.2.4 European Union law – applicability to Member States

1.2.4.1 Treaty provisions and Regulations

Provisions of EU treaties and EU Regulations which give clear, precise and unconditional rights to individuals are generally directly enforced in national courts because they have direct applicability (see *Van Gend en Loos v Nederlandse Administratie der Belastingen* (Case 26/62) [1963] ECR 1). One important example is Article 157 TFEU (ex Article 119 EEC/141 EC), which provides that 'Each Member State shall ensure that the principle of equal pay for male and female workers for equal work or work of equal value is applied'.

In the case of *Barber v Guardian Royal Exchange Assurance Group* (Case C-262/88) [1990] 2 All ER 660, Article 157 TFEU was applied directly in favour of a man in order to entitle him to the same benefits as a woman under an occupational pension scheme. The scheme was discriminatory as it permitted women to receive a pension from age 50, but men only from age 55. Article 157 TFEU was applied despite the fact that different retiring ages in pension schemes were apparently permitted under the SDA 1975 and the EPA 1970. In equal work cases, Article 157 TFEU is directly effective and overrides inconsistent national law.

1.2.4.2 Directives

A Directive is secondary EU legislation. It is not directly applicable in a Member State but must be implemented by national legislation. However, if a Directive gives clear, precise and unconditional rights to an individual, and the State fails to implement it at all or to implement it properly within the stipulated time frame, the individual has a right to rely on the Directive directly against the State or an emanation of the State.

This means that Directives that have not been properly implemented in a Member State can be directly enforced, but only by employees of the State or of an emanation of the State. In *Marshall v Southampton and South West Hampshire AHA* [1986] QB 401, a female former employee of the Area Health Authority was able to rely on the Equal Treatment Directive 76/207 in order to challenge contractual retirement ages which discriminated on the grounds of sex. A challenge was possible in this case because the Area Health Authority was found to be an emanation of the State; Ms Marshall would not have been able to rely directly on the Directive if she had been employed in the private sector. (However, see *Kucukdeveci v Swedex GmbH & Co KG* (Case C-555/07) where the general principle of non-discrimination on grounds of age was given effect between individuals by the ECJ.)

The ECJ, in *Impact v Ministry for Agriculture and Food (Ireland)* (Case C-268/06) [2008] IRLR 552, confirmed that public sector employees can bring such claims in employment tribunals as well as in the national courts.

1.2.4.3   Interpretation of national legislation

Employees who cannot rely on direct effect, for example if they work in the private sector, may seek to enforce rights conferred by EU Directives which have not been properly implemented by asking their national courts to interpret their national legislation in the light of the EU Directive (indirect effect).

Section 2(4) of the European Communities Act 1972 provides that 'any enactment passed or to be passed ... shall be construed and have effect subject to [EU law]'. Where UK legislation had been passed to implement an EU Directive, the English courts interpreted the UK legislation so as to comply with EU law. For example, in *Litster v Forth Dry Dock & Engineering Co Ltd* [1989] IRLR 161 (see **7.2.2.3**), the House of Lords (now Supreme Court) put a very strained interpretation on the Transfer of Undertakings (Protection of Employment) Regulations 1981 (SI 1981/1794) in order to make the Regulations comply with the Acquired Rights Directive 77/187, which they were intended to implement. The ECJ held in *Marleasing SA v La Comercial Internacional de Alimentacion SA* [1990] ECR I-4135 that national courts must 'as far as possible' interpret national law in light of EU law, irrespective of whether the national law was adopted before or after the Directive in question. In *Webb v EMO Air Cargo (UK) Ltd* [1993] IRLR 27, the House of Lords followed *Marleasing* and stated that

> it is for a UK court to construe domestic legislation ... so as to accord with the interpretation of [a] Directive as laid down by the European Court, if that can be done without distorting the meaning of the domestic legislation.

1.2.4.4   Action against the State

If a State fails to implement a Directive at all (or incorrectly), an employee who is affected can bring a claim against the State for damages under the principle in *Francovich (Andrea) and Bonifaci (Danila) v Italy* (Cases C-6 and 9/90) [1992] IRLR 84.

1.2.4.5   Brexit

The UK voted on 23 June 2016 to leave the EU (the Brexit vote). Following the vote, Article 50 of the Treaty on European Union was triggered by the UK Government on 29 March 2017. The UK is due to leave the UK on or before 29 March 2019. The European Union (Withdrawal) Act 2018 will repeal the European Communities Act 1972 (which became effective on 1 January 1973 when the UK joined the European Community (EC) and ceded sovereignty on areas covered by EC law, such as some employment and discrimination laws, to the EC). The 2018 Act signifies the end of the position of EU law and the CJEU within the UK, but transfers into UK law the provisions of EU law applicable at the time the UK leaves the EU. The 2018 Act states that when interpreting retained EU law after Brexit, UK courts and tribunals will not be bound by any decisions made on or after exit day but 'may have regard to' such decisions 'so far as it is relevant'. The 2018 Act also expressly states that the EU Charter of Fundamental Rights will not apply to the UK after Brexit (see Introductory Note for more details). Depending on the outcome of Article 50 negotiations and the terms on which the UK leaves the EU, the influence of EU employment law and regulation will remain strong.

1.2.5   Human Rights Act 1998

The Human Rights Act 1998 (HRA 1998) came into force on 2 October 2000. Courts and tribunals in the UK now have to interpret national law in the light of the rights contained in the European Convention for the Protection of Human Rights and Fundamental Freedoms ('the Convention' or ECHR), and where this is not possible, the High Court is empowered to declare such law incompatible with Convention rights. Employees of public authorities have a direct cause of action against their employer under the Act for contravention of the Act (see **Chapter 15**).

1.2.6 Recruitment and induction

Employers should take care not to discriminate when they advertise jobs. A job applicant can bring a claim against a potential employer for discrimination (Equality Act 2010, s 39) in terms of the arrangements made for recruitment, the terms offered or as a result of a refusal or deliberate failure to offer employment.

1.2.6.1 Immigration, Asylum and Nationality Act 2006 and Immigration Act 2014

For all employees employed on or after 16 May 2014, an employer must undertake required checks before an individual commences working. (For employees employed before 16 May 2014, the position was dealt with by the 2006 Act and a 2008 Code of Practice; and for employees employed before 29 February 2008 by the Asylum and Immigration Act 1996.) An employer is *not* exempt from carrying out checks on employees acquired as a result of a transfer under the Transfer of Undertakings (Protection of Employment) Regulations 2006 (SI 2006/246) (see **Chapter 7**).

Section 15 of the Immigration, Asylum and Nationality Act 2006 provides that an employer who negligently employs a person subject to immigration control who does not have the right to take employment, shall be guilty of a civil offence. The Act allows employers to avoid a civil penalty if they have carried out specific document checks before they employ the employee. The Act also makes it a criminal offence to employ someone whom the employer knows or has reasonable cause to believe has no permission to work in the UK (s 21).

The Government published a consultation document on 9 July 2013, 'Prevention of illegal working: strengthening and simplifying the civil penalty system'. Following the consultation, two new codes of practice for employers came into effect on 16 May 2014, the first relating to the prevention of illegal working, and the second avoiding unlawful discrimination while preventing illegal working. The detail of these is beyond the scope of this book.

An employer who is found to have employed someone illegally may be fined up to £20,000 per individual illegal worker if it has not carried out the necessary checks before employing the person. For knowingly employing an illegal worker, or having 'reasonable cause to believe' a person has no permission to work in the UK, the sanctions are up to five years' imprisonment and unlimited fines.

All UK citizens have the right to work in the UK. Citizens of the European Economic Area (EEA) also have the right to work in the UK subject to proving that they have such citizenship. Otherwise, no one has the right to work in the UK unless he is granted the right to work by the Home Office – generally by a visa. Asylum seekers can apply for permission to work if they have waited more than 12 months for a decision from the Home Office. All asylum seekers who apply for permission to work and are not considered responsible for the delay are restricted to national shortage occupations. Students, if studying at foundation degree level or above, can work part time during terms, for no more than 20 hours a week. Students, if studying below foundation degree level, can work part time during terms, for no more than 10 hours a week.

Dismissal of an employee on the basis that he does not have the right to work in the UK may involve a consideration of issues relating to whether he has contravened a statutory enactment (ERA 1996, s 98(2)(d)), some other substantial reason and illegality (see **1.2.7** and **Chapter 5** below), as well as discrimination (see **Chapter 8** onwards).

Readers should log on to the Home Office UK Visa and Immigration website <http://ukba.homeoffice.gov.uk> for further detailed guidance (see also **8.4.1**).

Note that the 'Brexit' vote in June 2016 is likely to impact on the ability of employers to employ EU citizens, but for the time being there are no immediate changes. Down the line, some immigration requirements may change.

1.2.6.2   Illegality

An employee whose contract is illegal may be prevented from asserting his contractual and statutory rights. There has long been a common law doctrine of illegality, which can defeat claims in contract or tort. The doctrine is rooted in public policy. The underlying principle was identified by Lord Mansfield in *Holman v Johnson* (1775) 1 Cowp 341:

> The objection, that a contract is immoral or illegal as between plaintiff and defendant ... is founded in general principles of policy ... The principle of public policy is this; ex dolo malo non oritur actio. No court will lend its aid to a man who founds his cause of action upon an immoral or an illegal act. If, from the plaintiff's own stating or otherwise, the cause of action appears to arise ex turpi causa, or the transgression of a positive law of this country, there the court says he has no right to be assisted. It is upon that ground the court goes; not for the sake of the defendant, but because they will not lend their aid to such a plaintiff. So if the plaintiff and defendant were to change sides, and the defendant was to bring his action against the plaintiff, the latter would then have the advantage of it; for where both are equally in fault, potior est conditio defendentis.

There are three categories of case where a contract may be tainted with illegality. These were identified by Peter Gibson LJ in *Hall v Woolston Leisure Services Ltd* [2000] IRLR 578 (paras 30–31). The judgment also contains a useful run-through of the previous case law in an employment context. The first category is where the contract is entered into with the intention of committing an illegal act. The second is where the contract is expressly or impliedly prohibited by statute. The third category is where the contract was lawful when made but has been performed illegally, and the party seeking the assistance of the court knowingly participated in the illegal performance. In the first two types of cases, case law has established that illegality in these situations generally renders a contract void and unenforceable from the outset. In the first type, the contract may not be unenforceable if the activities do not form part of the contract. In the third, the contract is legal on its face but the illegality may prevent a party from enforcing it. The most common example of the third type in an employment situation often involves some sort of tax fraud. In order to fall within the third category, it is traditionally said that there are two requirements:

(a)   knowledge of the illegal performance; and

(b)   participation in the illegal performance.

See, for example, *Ashmore, Benson Ltd v Dawson* [1973] 1 WLR 828, *Tomlinson v Dick Evans 'U' Drive Ltd* [1978] IRLR 77 and *Davidson v Pillay* [1979] IRLR 275.

Knowledge requires that the employee must have knowledge of the facts which render the performance illegal. However, it is irrelevant whether the party appreciates that what he is doing is illegal: ignorance of the law is no excuse. In *San Ling Chinese Medicine Centre v Miss Lian Wei Ji* (UKEAT/0370/09) the EAT applied *Hall* and upheld the tribunal's decision that the claimant's contract was not tainted by illegality in circumstances where the claimant's work permit *might* be revoked. There was no illegality unless and until the permit *was* revoked.

Participation requires active participation. There are cases in which the courts have held that mere knowledge of the illegality coupled with a failure to do anything about it can constitute participation. In *Hall* it came to the employee's attention that her employers were deceiving the Revenue and not paying the appropriate tax. The Court of Appeal held that this was not sufficient to render the contract an illegal one because there was no illegality by Mrs Hall:

> Her acquiescence in the employer's conduct, which is the highest her involvement in the illegality can be put, no doubt reflects the reality that she could not compel her employer to change its conduct.

In the context of discriminations claims, the Supreme Court considered the issue in *Hounga v Allen* [2014] UKSC 47. The Supreme Court had to consider in what circumstances the defence of illegality should defeat a complaint by an employee that an employer has discriminated against him. The claimant was working illegally in the UK when she was dismissed by her employer. The Court of Appeal had decided that the illegality of the contract of employment formed a material part of the claimant's complaint and that to uphold it would be to condone the illegality. The Supreme Court allowed the appeal and held that entry into the illegal contract and its continued operation provided no more than the context in which the employer perpetrated the discriminatory act. There was not a sufficiently close connection between the illegality and the discrimination claim for the claim to be defeated by illegality. Furthermore, the decision of the Court of Appeal to uphold Mrs Allen's defence of illegality to her complaint ran counter, on the facts, to the public policy against trafficking and in favour of the protection of its victims, according to a majority of the Supreme Court.

In the context of unfair dismissal claims, it was settled law that if the underlying contract of employment was illegal then it was against public policy to allow the claim to be pursued: *Tomlinson v Dick Evans*, applied in *Davidson v Pillay*, cited with approval in *Hall*. Moreover, the employee could not count any period during which he was employed under an illegal contract as part of his period of continuous employment for the purpose of obtaining the requisite continuity to pursue a claim. In *Hyland v JH Barker (North West) Ltd* [1985] ICR 861, continuity was broken by a four-week period during which the employee received a tax-free benefit which both parties knew to be illegal. (See also *Salvesen v Simons* [1994] IRLR 52 and *Enfield Technical Services v Payne*; *Grace v BF Components Ltd* [2008] IRLR 500.)

However, readers should note the relatively recent decision in *Patel v Mirza* [2016] UKSC 42. The Supreme Court encourages a more flexible assessment of whether the public interest would be harmed by enforcement of an illegal contract:

> The essential rationale of the illegality doctrine is that it would be contrary to the public interest to enforce a claim if to do so would be harmful to the integrity of the legal system .... In assessing whether the public interest would be harmed in that way, it is necessary a) to consider the underlying purpose of the prohibition which has been transgressed and whether that purpose will be enhanced by denial of the claim, b) to consider any other relevant public policy on which the denial of the claim may have an impact and c) to consider whether denial of the claim would be a proportionate response to the illegality, bearing in mind that punishment is a matter for the criminal courts.

It seems clear therefore that the more flexible policy-based approach will apply to unfair dismissal cases too. Readers should have regard to the case if they are advising where there is illegality in employment contracts.

In *Okedina v Chikale* (UKEAT/0152/17) (a domestic worker case), the EAT considered the impact of an illegal contract of employment upon an employee's right to bring claims of unfair dismissal, race discrimination and for arrears of pay. It noted that there were two types of illegality which rendered a contract unenforceable from the outset: (i) where the contract is entered into with the intention of committing an illegal act; and (ii) where the contract is expressly prohibited by statute. Neither of these applied here. The EAT noted a third category where a party might be prevented from enforcing a contract lawfully made but later illegally performed. In this case, the employee was not involved in the illegal performance, and as such she was entitled to bring her claims to the tribunal.

1.2.6.3 Criminal record and other background checks

Any data that employers acquire as a result of job applications, must be processed fairly in accordance with an employer's obligations (as a data controller) under the Data Protection Act (DPA) 2018 (see **15.5**). There are six data protection principles that apply when processing personal data. These include keeping the data secure, but also that the data should be kept no longer than is necessary, and that any that are retained are accurate, relevant and not excessive. This also applies to data retained/stored after termination of employment.

Some employers may also be tempted to conduct their own background 'research' on applicants via social media. Such searches should be for specific and good reason. Under the Equality Act 2010, it is unlawful to ask candidates about protected characteristics, whether they are married or plan to have children. Questions should only be asked about health or disability if there are necessary requirements of the job that cannot be met with reasonable adjustments. Age should only be sought on an application form if there are age requirements for the job. These matters can be asked about on separate equality monitoring forms. Drug screening can only be undertaken with an individual's explicit consent, but the use of drug and alcohol tests should be justified as necessary and proportionate (eg safety-critical jobs).

The same data protection principles referred to above will also apply when 'processing' these sorts of data. Part One of the Employment Practices Code on recruitment and selection (see **15.5**) sets out a number of recommendations, a key one of which is that any checks need to be justified by reference to the vacant position, so that the checks conducted on a van driver will be different from those for a senior management position. The Code warns employers against placing reliance on 'information collected from possibly unreliable sources'. The Information Commission has warned employers about using deception, such as claiming to be a friend, in order to access an applicant's social media information. Applicants should be given the opportunity to make representations on the accuracy of the information and any adverse findings.

The Employment Practices Code draws a distinction between obtaining information in order to 'verify' something and obtaining information in order to 'vet' someone. The latter will generally be regarded as a more intrusive act than the former, so it should only be used where there are 'particular and significant risks involved to the employer, clients, customers or others and where there is no less intrusive and reasonably practicable alternative'. In some limited circumstances, such as for those in the financial sector or as regards employees coming into contact with vulnerable individuals, vetting is a legal requirement. The Financial Services and Market Act 2000, for example, requires individuals working in controlled functions, such as senior customer-facing roles, to be 'fit and proper', meeting honesty, competence and financial soundness criteria. The Conduct of Employment Agencies and Employment Business (Amendment) Regulations 2014 (SI 2014/3351) (which came into force in April 2014) require agencies to screen candidates adequately, giving employers information on why they might be unsuitable. Agencies should also pass on any information they later obtain showing that the person might after all be unsuitable, for up to three months.

After *Smith v Carillion (JM) Ltd* [2015] EWCA Civ 209, the Employment Relations Act 1999 (Blacklists) Regulations 2010 (SI 2010/493) now make it unlawful for employers, employment agencies and others to compile, supply or use a blacklist of trade union members or activists for discriminatory purposes such as employment vetting. They also make it unlawful to refuse to employ someone for a set of specified 'prohibited' reasons.

Pre-employment screening can be a legal minefield, not least because data protection and privacy requirements differ from country to country, and in some instances pre-employment screening without consent may be unlawful. Employers need to consider not only the laws of the country where the applicant is to be employed, but also the laws of the country from which the applicant is being considered. Further, job applicants are increasing aware of their data protection and privacy rights. In Europe, Article 8 of the ECHR gives individuals the right to respect for their private and family life, their home and correspondence. In UK law, this right is enshrined in the Human Rights Act 1988 (see **15.4.2**).

Employers should make sure they comply with relevant data protection laws affecting the storage of personal data. Employees and applicants (as well as clients and customers) are entitled to make subject access requests to obtain any personal data that an organisation, including their employer, holds on them. Companies should have policies in place to deal with subject access requests, which have strict time limits (see **15.5**).

If employers want to know whether job applicants have a criminal record, they should have a proper reason for doing so, in terms of the job role. Employers can specifically ask the applicant to declare any criminal record on any application form (but see, regarding spent convictions, **1.2.7**) and/or they can use the Disclosure and Barring Service (formerly the Criminal Records Bureau), which does not disclose spent convictions. A practice had developed of employers circumventing the protection against revealing spent convictions by insisting that job applicants make a data protection subject access request (see **15.5.2**) to get hold of their full criminal record and provide it to the prospective employer. It is a specific criminal offence (DPA 2018, s 184) to require a job applicant (or indeed existing employees) to produce a copy of his criminal record through a subject access request.

1.2.6.4 Rehabilitation of Offenders Act 1974

Job applicants do not generally have to disclose spent convictions. Some excepted professions (eg teachers, healthcare practitioners and lawyers) may have to disclose information about spent convictions, if required. Amendments to the Rehabilitation of Offenders Act 1974, included in the Legal Aid and Sentencing and Punishment of Offenders Act 2012, which came into effect in March 2014, mean that the length of time that it takes for criminal convictions to become 'spent' has been reduced. Where an offender receives a custodial sentence of six months or less, the conviction becomes spent at the end of 24 months from the date the sentence is completed. Custodial sentences of more than four years or a public protection sentence never become spent.

A spent conviction or a failure to declare one is not a proper ground for dismissing an employee. The Ministry of Justice has issued guidance on this topic.

1.2.6.5 Guidance on recruitment and induction

Acas has published a number of guides which are helpful in this area. They include 'Recruiting staff', 'Employment references', 'Starting staff: induction', 'Social media' and 'Recruitment and unconscious bias'. (See too **8.4** and **12.12**.)

1.3 THE RELATIONSHIP OF EMPLOYER AND EMPLOYEE

1.3.1 Introduction

Not all persons who perform work for others are employees, ie employed under a contract of service (a name derived from the old-fashioned terminology of master and servant). Some are workers (see **1.3.3**) and some are truly independent contractors who work under a contract *for services*. In marginal cases, it may be difficult to distinguish a contract of service from a contract for services.

The difference is important in practice because, for example, only employees are entitled to redundancy payments or to present a claim of unfair dismissal. Further, there are different income tax regimes. Employees pay income tax, which is deducted at source under the PAYE scheme, whereas independent contractors pay income tax under a different regime. There are also differences in National Insurance contributions (NICs) and entitlement to benefits.

Certain employment-related rights, such as discrimination, are not limited to employees and, increasingly, protections are being applied to 'workers' rather than the more narrow 'employee'. The term 'worker' includes employees but is wider (see ERA 1996, s 230(3)). It can be difficult to distinguish between a worker and an employee, and between a worker and those who are to be regarded as carrying on a business (see *Byrne Brothers (Formwork) Ltd v Baird* [2002] IRLR 96 for a discussion) (see below at **1.3.3**).

The Taylor Review (see Introductory Note) suggested that there should be a new categorisation of 'dependent contractor', who should be given certain basic rights around minimum wage, holiday pay and sickness pay. It is possible that someone who has registered as self-employed for tax purposes may still be a 'worker' for paid holiday entitlement and national minimum wage purposes and also an employee under the Equality Act 2010 where there is an extended definition of 'employee'. No single factor is determinative of status, and a number of factors must be considered (see further below), such as 'personal service', 'control', 'mutuality of obligations', 'integration into the business' and 'who bears the financial risk'. In *Hall (Inspector or Taxes) v Lorimer* [1994] IRLR 171, the Court of Appeal stated that, when determining employment status, the process includes 'paint[ing] a picture from the accumulation of detail', and that approach was confirmed most recently by the Supreme Court in *Pimlico Plumbers Ltd v Smith* [2018] UKSC 29, which held that employment status must be considered on the individual facts of each case and that what actually happens on the ground is more important than the wording of the contract.

1.3.2 Employee

Section 230(1) of the ERA 1996 defines an employee as 'an individual who ... works under ... a contract of employment'. Section 230(2) defines contract of employment as 'a contract of service ... whether express or implied, and (if it is express) whether oral or in writing'. Section 230(3) defines a worker (see **1.3.3**). The definitions of employee and worker both require there to be a contract in existence: see the Court of Appeal in *Secretary of State for Justice v Windle* [2016] EWCA Civ 459. This appears to be an absolute requirement and needs to be determined before any discussion can take place on whether a person is an employee or a worker. For a contract to exist, there must be, expressly or impliedly, an offer, acceptance, consideration and an intention to create legal relations. See too *Sharpe v Bishop of Worcester* [2015] IRLR 663 and *O'Brien v Ministry of Justice* [2013] ICR 499.

Over the years, the courts have formulated a variety of tests to identify the existence of a contract of service. These tests have included the 'control' test (see, eg, *Yewens v Noakes* (1880) 6 QBD 530); the 'integration' test (see, eg, *Stevenson Jordan & Harrson Ltd v McDonald and Evans* [1952] 1 TLR 101); and the 'economic reality' test (see, eg, *Market Investigations Ltd v Minister of Social Security* [1969] 2 QB 173). The 'multiple factor' test advocated by McKenna J in *Ready Mixed Concrete (South East) Ltd v Minister of Pensions and National Insurance* [1968] 1 All ER 433) was approved by the Supreme Court in *Autoclenz v Belcher* [2011] UKSC 41.

McKenna J stated that a contract of service existed if three conditions were fulfilled:

(a)   the servant agrees that, in consideration of a wage or other remuneration, he will provide his own work and skill in the performance of some service for his master ('mutuality of obligation', ie on the employer to pay for the work and on the employee to personally do the work ('personal service'));

(b)   the servant agrees, expressly or impliedly, that in the performance of that service he will be subject to the other's control in a sufficient degree to make that other master (control);

(c)   the other provisions of the contract are consistent with its being a contract of service.

Freedom to do a job by one's own hands or by another's is inconsistent with a contract of service, though a limited or occasional power of delegation may not be. (These principles were recently confirmed by the Supreme Court in *Autoclenz Ltd v Belcher*.)

When, if at all, might an express agreement be challenged? This was considered by the Supreme Court in *Autoclenz Ltd v Belcher* (above). The Court of Appeal, in its judgment ([2010] IRLR 70), set out the circumstances in which courts can look behind the express terms of the parties' agreement. The EAT had held that the 20 car valets who worked for Autoclenz at its premises in Derbyshire were not employees but were workers within the meaning of s 230(3) of the ERA 1996. The Court of Appeal disagreed. The terms of the agreement between Autoclenz and the valets provided that:

(a) there was no obligation on the valets to perform any work or for Autoclenz to provide it;

(b) the valets' services would be engaged from time to time;

(c) the valets could arrange for a substitute to carry out their valeting duties; and

(d) the valets paid their own tax and had to purchase their own insurance, uniforms and materials.

However, according to the Court of Appeal, the above terms did not accurately reflect the relationship between the parties:

(a) the valets were required to notify Autoclenz whether or not they would be turning up for work; and

(b) whilst there existed a substitution clause, the valets would not, in practice, be permitted to send a substitute in their place and were expected to turn up and provide services in person.

The Court of Appeal, upholding the Employment Judge's decision at first instance, held that the valets were employees. The Court said that tribunals should focus on the actual legal obligations of the parties rather than merely relying on the written terms of an agreement when determining what kind of employment relationship existed. The fact that Autoclenz described the valets as workers and not employees was not conclusive. The tribunal has to consider whether or not the words represent the actual legal obligations of the parties. The Court of Appeal said it was not necessary to find any deliberate intention to deceive. The written terms are always the starting point, but where an issue is raised the tribunal must ask if the parties ever realistically intended or envisaged that its terms would be carried out as written.

The Supreme Court agreed with the Court of Appeal that the individual valets were not self-employed subcontractors and, although it was not necessary for the claims for minimum wage and holiday which only necessitated a finding that the valets were workers, it also upheld the finding that they were 'employees'. The Supreme Court held the real situation trumped what was written in the contract. It was not necessary for the valets to prove a 'sham', in the sense that the parties intended to mislead HM Revenue and Customs (HMRC). The fact that the employer had written a 'substitution clause' into the contracts did not reflect the reality, as everyone expected the valets to carry out their duties personally. The essential question was: What was the true nature of the agreement between the parties? That *might* be what is written down, but was not necessarily so.

See also *Protectacoat Firthglow Ltd v Szilagyi* [2009] EWCA Civ 98 and *Windle* (above). There is a helpful review of the legal distinctions between a contract of service and a contract for services in *Drake v Ipsos Mori UK Ltd* (UKEAT/0604/11).

1.3.2.1 Case law

Mutual obligations

The courts draw a distinction between mutuality on the one hand (which is necessary for there to be a contract at all) and, where there is a contract, the nature of that contract. That will be determined by the *nature* of the mutual obligations: mutual obligations on the employee to work personally for another, and on the employer to pay for the work. It is useful to repeat part of Elias J's judgment in *Stephenson v Delphi Diesel Systems Ltd* [2003] ICR 471:

11   The significance of mutuality is that it determines whether there is a contact in existence at all. The significance of control is that it determines whether, if there a contract in place, it can properly be classified as a contract of service, rather than some other kind of contract.

12   The issue of whether there is a contract at all arises most frequently in situations where a person works for an employer, but only on a casual basis from time to time. It is often necessary then to show that the contract continues to exist in the gaps between the periods of employment. Cases frequently have had to decide whether there is an over-arching contract or what is sometimes called an 'umbrella contract' which remains in existence even when the individual concerned is not working. It is in that context in particular that courts have emphasised the need to demonstrate some mutuality of obligation between the parties but, as I have indicated, all that is being done is to say that there must be something from which a contract can properly be inferred. Without some mutuality, amounting to what is sometimes called the 'irreducible minimum of obligation', no contract exists.

13   The question of mutuality of obligation, however, poses no difficulties during the period when the individual is actually working. For the period of such employment a contract must, in our view, clearly exist. For that duration the individual clearly undertakes to work and the employer in turn undertakes to pay for the work done. This is so, even if the contract is terminable on either side at will. Unless and until the power to terminate is exercised, these mutual obligations (to work on the one hand and to be paid on the other) will continue to exist and will provide the fundamental mutual obligations.

Carmichael v National Power [2000] IRLR 43 illustrates this point. Mrs Leese and Mrs Carmichael applied, were interviewed and were told:

I am pleased to note that you are agreeable to be employed by the CEGB at Blyth 'A' and 'B' Power Stations on a casual as required basis as a station guide.

When your services are required you will be paid at the rate of 376.56 pence per hour being the minimum of Band I of the NJIC Agreement. Your salary will be paid by credit transfer.

Please find enclosed a pre-typed reply letter which should be returned to me confirming your acceptance of this offer together with the completed method of payment form.

The employment tribunal held that their case 'founder[ed] on the rock of absence of mutuality', that is that, when *not* working as guides, they were in no contractual relationship of any kind with the company. The House of Lords held that the employment tribunal's decision that the 'documents did no more than provide a framework for a series of successive ad hoc contracts of service or for services which the parties might subsequently make; and that when they were not working as guides they were not in any contractual relationship with [the company]' was correct. When they were not working as guides, they were not in employment because the company did not promise to offer work, and the claimants were not agreeing to do work. The contracts did not create mutuality of obligation and therefore could not be contracts of employment. The company was not obliged to provide guide work as might become available in future and they were not obliged to undertake such work when made available.

In *Cornwall County Council v Prater* [2006] EWCA Civ 102, the Court of Appeal upheld the EAT's decision that, whilst there was no umbrella contract, there was sufficient mutuality of obligation during each assignment carried out by a teacher while the individual contracts were in force. During each assignment there was an obligation on the teacher to teach the pupil and an obligation on the council to pay her, and the gaps between the individual contracts when she was not carrying out work for the County Council were 'temporary cessations of work' which were bridged by s 212 of the ERA 1996 (the Council did not appeal that finding).

In *St Ives Plymouth Ltd v Haggerty* (UKEAT/0107/08), the EAT upheld the tribunal's decision that a casual worker was an employee and that there was a sufficient mutuality of obligation in the gaps when no work was performed to infer the existence of a contract of employment. Although there was no obligation upon the casual worker to accept offers of work, the tribunal was persuaded that, had she persistently declined offers of work, her name would have been removed from the list of casuals. Equally, although there was no guaranteed minimum amount of work, the claimant had an expectation that she would be offered a reasonable amount of work. On that basis, the EAT held that the tribunal had been entitled to find that there was an 'overarching' contract because there was sufficient mutuality of obligation.

The EAT in *Little v BMI Chiltern Hospital* (UK/EAT/0021/09) held that the fact that the employer could and did send hospital porters home during a shift, without pay for the rest of the shift, when their services were not needed, negated the existence of mutuality of obligation and meant there was only a contract for freelance services, and not, as the porter contended, a succession of specific engagement contracts of employment. The contract itself stated that the porter was an independent contractor who would work on an 'as and when required' basis for an hourly rate. The EAT held that the contract reflected the 'true intentions' of the parties. However, the EAT in *Drake v Ipsos Mori UK Ltd* (UKEAT/0604/11) held that *Little* should not be treated as authority for the proposition that a right to terminate work at will is inconsistent with a contract of employment. In that case, the claimant worked for the respondent as a market researcher under a succession of individual assignments. The EAT held:

(1)   'Applying the reasoning in *Stephenson* to the case in hand, I have no doubt that there was a contract in place – and the requisite mutuality – when the Claimant was actually undertaking an assignment for the Respondent. The fact that the assignment could be brought to an end does not mean that there was no contract in existence while the assignment was continuing. Plainly there was a contract while the assignment was continuing: there was an agreement to undertake work in return for payment. When the Respondent in its Handbook described the acceptance of an assignment as a 'contract' it was correct. The fact that either side might terminate the contract at will does not mean that there was no contract.'

(2)   The case should be remitted for the tribunal to decide 'whether ... the assignments [were] carried out under a series of contracts of employment, as the Claimant contends, or merely under a series of contracts for services, as the Respondent contends' by considering whether under each contract the claimant was obliged to work personally for the respondent unless and until he returned or completed the assignment or the respondent withdrew it; the extent to which the terms of each contract placed obligations on the claimant to work under the control of the respondent; and, finally, whether other terms were consistent with the contracts being contracts *of* service/ employment as opposed to contracts *for* services.

The authors respectfully suggest that *Little* could and should have been otherwise decided.

In *Knight v BCCP* (UKEAT/0413/10), the EAT again emphasised the importance of mutuality – without mutual obligations to offer and to accept work, there can be no employment relationship under s 230 of the ERA 1996. Mr Knight was a licensed private hire driver, who was engaged by the respondent company for just over six weeks between 1 September and 14 October 2008. There was no contractual documentation. He was told that he would receive mileage rates for the work that he did, and that he had to provide his car upon the basis that he paid the insurance as well as the running costs including petrol, maintenance bills and other expenses. He was paid by submitting an invoice based on the company's records. He had to pay his own tax and National Insurance contributions and did not have any set working hours. He worked under the company's control to a degree in that it dictated the dress to be worn, how the car was to be presented, how the claimant was to deal with opening doors and procedure at airports and stations. He received wages only for the occasions when he actually worked. The relationship between the claimant and the company terminated when he was asked to complete a detailed security questionnaire in connection with cars provided for government purposes, and he decided he did not want to disclose the detailed information which it required. The issue before the employment tribunal was whether he was entitled to one week's statutory notice pay under s 86 of the ERA 1996, which necessitated his being an employee. The employment tribunal found that Mr Knight was under no obligation to accept work and the company was under no obligation to offer work to him, and as such, he was not an employee. The EAT upheld the tribunal's decision.

See also on mutuality, *Stringfellows Restaurants Ltd v Quashie* [2013] IRLR 99, at **1.3.2.2** below.

Personal service

In *Express and Echo Publications v Tanton* [1999] IRLR 367, the Court of Appeal emphasised that, to be a contract of service, a contract had to contain an obligation on the part of the employee to provide his services personally. Generally, therefore, if a worker is entitled to substitute personal service (ie to ask a replacement to do his work) then that will usually demonstrate that the contract is not a contract of service because the worker lacks the obligation required. However, in *McFarlane v Glasgow City Council* [2001] IRLR 7, the EAT said that a lack of personal service is not necessarily conclusive:

> [P]roperly regarded, [the decision in] *Tanton* does not oblige the tribunal to conclude that under a contract of service the individual has, always and in every event ... to personally provide his services.

Whether a power to delegate work to a substitute is determinative may depend on whether the right to delegate is fettered and/or the nature of the duties that may be delegated. In *McFarlane*, the claimant could not unilaterally refuse to work; it was only in circumstances where he was unable to attend that a substitute could be provided, and any substitute had to be approved by the employer. In the circumstances he was an employee.

By contrast, in *Real Time Civil Engineering Ltd v Callaghan* (UKEAT/0516/05), the EAT held that the tribunal in this case was wrong to ignore a contractual provision giving an individual an unfettered right to delegate his duties to a substitute simply because the individual had not, in reality, ever done so. The difference in this case was that the individual's right to delegate was unfettered: the agreement contained a term allowing for substitute to be sent without restriction. That term was, held the EAT, inconsistent with a contract of service.

In *Autoclenz v Belcher* (above) the Supreme Court confirmed that in determining whether an individual is free to choose whether he will do the work himself or send someone else to do it (in which case he is neither an employee nor a worker), the relative bargaining power of the parties must be taken into account in deciding whether the terms of any written agreement in truth represent what was agreed, and the true agreement will often have to be gleaned from all the circumstances of the case, of which the written agreement is only a part.

The Court of Appeal reviewed the existing authorities in relation to personal service in *Pimlico Plumbers Ltd v Smith* [2017] EWCA Civ 51, a case about whether plumbers were workers or independent contractors (see **1.3.3** below) and summarised the principles (at [84]):

> Firstly, an unfettered right to substitute another person to do the work or perform the services is inconsistent with an undertaking to do so personally. Secondly, a conditional right to substitute another person may or may not be inconsistent with personal performance depending upon the conditionality. It will depend on the precise contractual arrangements and, in particular, the nature and degree of any fetter on a right of substitution or, using different language, the extent to which the right of substitution is limited or occasional. Thirdly, by way of example, a right of substitution only when the contractor is unable to carry out the work will, subject to any exceptional facts, be consistent with personal performance. Fourthly, again by way of example, a right of substitution limited only by the need to show that the substitute is as qualified as the contractor to do the work, whether or not that entails a particular procedure, will, subject to any exceptional facts, be inconsistent with personal performance. Fifthly, again by way of example, a right to substitute only with the consent of another person who has an absolute and unqualified discretion to withhold consent will be consistent with personal performance.

Control

In the *Ready Mixed Concrete* case (**1.3.2** above), McKenna J described control as including 'the power of deciding the thing to be done, the way ..., the means ..., the time ... and the place'.

The Court of Appeal, in *Montgomery v Johnson Underwood Ltd* [2001] IRLR 269, confirmed that for a contract of service to exist there had to be control, that control is a separate factor, and no less important than mutuality of obligation when considering whether there is a contract of service. Control requires a general ultimate direct authority over an employee in the performance of his work. Control in itself, however, is not conclusive: an independent contractor can agree to submit himself to the same control as an employee without actually becoming an employee (see, for example, *Ready Mixed Concrete*); and many employees will, by virtue of seniority for example, be subject to very little control.

The EAT confirmed in *White and Another v Troutbeck SA* (UKEAT/0177/12) that the issue of control concerns whether there is, to a sufficient degree, a contractual right of control over the worker, and not whether in practice the worker has day-to-day control of his own work. The EAT's decision was upheld by the Court of Appeal ([2013] EWCA Civ 1171), which emphasised the need to address the cumulative effect of the totality of provisions in any written agreement and all the circumstances of the relationship created by it.

1.3.2.2   Other matters

An employment tribunal must consider the overall picture. The tribunal should not adopt a 'checklist' approach but consider all aspects, with no single factor being in itself conclusive, and each of which may vary in weight and direction (see eg *Hall v Lorimer* [1994] IRLR 171).

Among matters that may be relevant to consider as to whether the person is an employee are:

(a)   How is the individual paid?

(b)   Who pays tax and National Insurance?

(c)   Who provides the tools and equipment?

(d)   How integral to the business is the individual's role?

(e)   Is the individual paid for sickness and holiday?

(f)   Is the individual subject to the disciplinary and grievance policy?

(g)   Is the individual a member of a company pension scheme?

(h)   Where does the economic risk lie?

(i)   How did the parties view the relationship at the outset

(j)   How was the arrangement terminable?

The Court of Appeal, in *Enfield Technical Services Limited v Payne; Grace v BF Components Limited* [2008] IRLR 500, decided that individuals who characterise themselves as self-employed but who are in fact employees, can still bring unfair dismissal claims, unless they have misrepresented the real nature of the working relationship. In these cases, both claimants had described themselves as self-employed and had not paid tax via PAYE. When the working relationship ended, unfair dismissal claims were brought. The tribunal found, on the facts, that the claimants were employees. The employer argued that it would be contrary to public policy to allow the claim to continue and that the contract had been performed illegally. The Court of Appeal said that a failure to categorise employment status correctly, which deprives the Revenue of tax, does not of itself make a contract illegal, particularly where there is some legal uncertainty about the nature of the relationship. For a contract to be illegal, there must be some false representation about it.

In *Stringfellows Restaurants Ltd v Quashie* [2013] IRLR 99, the Court of Appeal reinstated an employment tribunal's finding that it had no jurisdiction to hear a claim for unfair dismissal brought by a lap dancer at 'Stringfellows' night club as she was not an employee. The claimant was a lap dancer who was paid entirely from customers' vouchers, which were changed into cash at the end of the night. She had to comply with house rules, including that she was required to work set nights as rostered. There was a dress code and she had to do a certain number of free dances each shift. The employment tribunal had decided that she was not an employee, as there was no obligation on the employer to pay her anything.

The employment tribunal found that, in a number of respects, conditions for there to be an employment relationship were met: the supply of her services was personal to the claimant; she could not send a substitute; the employer exercised sufficient control over the claimant for there to be an employment contract. However, while there was also plainly a contract in existence between the parties, as there were some mutual obligations in play (eg to work when rostered and for her to be allowed to dance when at work), the crucial question was not whether there was a contract but whether the contract was a contract of employment. In coming to the conclusion that it was not, the employment tribunal found there was no obligation on the employer to pay the claimant anything, so the claimant took the financial risk, she negotiated her own fees with customers; in the circumstances, she paid the club to give her an opportunity to earn money by dancing. This finding was reinforced by the fact that the terms of the contract involved the claimant being responsible for her own tax and National Insurance, and not being entitled to sick pay or holiday pay.

The EAT had reversed the tribunal decision and held that the claimant was an employee and could bring a claim for unfair dismissal. It had also held that there was an umbrella contract which covered gaps in the evenings when the claimant did not dance.

The Court of Appeal, in overturning the EAT, looked at the nature of the mutual obligations required for the purposes of a contract of employment. The leading judgment was given by Elias LJ. He revisited his earlier assessment of mutuality in *Stephenson v Delphi* (**1.3.2.1** above) and said that in so far as he had suggested that once some mutuality was shown, the only question was whether there was sufficient control, that was too sweeping: even where the work-wage relationship exists and there is substantial control, there may be other features of the relationship which entitle a tribunal to conclude there was no employment contract, even during individual engagements. In this case, the fact that the employer was under no obligation to pay the dancer and she took the economic risk supported the tribunal's finding that she was not an employee. Given its findings that there was no employment contract during individual engagements, the Court of Appeal did not feel it necessary to look at whether there was an umbrella contract in existence.

See too the Court of Appeal decision in *Secretary of State for Justice v Windle* [2016] EWCA Civ 459 that the absence of an overriding or umbrella contract for a series of assignments or engagements could be crucial: 'the fact that a person supplying services is only doing so on an assignment-to-assignment basis may tend to indicate a degree of independence, or lack or subordination, in the relationship while at work which is incompatible with employee status ...'.

1.3.3 Workers

A number of statutory employment protections apply not solely to employees but to a wider class of 'worker' (which includes employees). See, for example, s 13 of the ERA 1996 (relating to deductions from wages – see **1.11** below), the National Minimum Wage Regulations 1999 (SI 1999/584) (see **1.8.3.1** below), the Working Time Regulations 1988 (SI 1988/1833) (see **1.12** below) and the Part-time Workers (Prevention of Less Favourable Treatment) Regulations 2000 (SI 2000/1551) (see **8.10** below).

A worker is defined under s 230(3) of the ERA 1996 to mean

> an individual who has entered into or works under (or where employment has ceased worked under)
>
> (a)   a contract of employment; or

(b) any other contract, whether express or implied and (if it is express) whether oral or in writing, whereby the individual undertakes to do or perform personally any work or services for another party to the contract whose status is not by virtue of the contract that of a client or customer of any profession or business undertaking carried on by the individual.

The reference to a contract of employment in para (a) above means that an employee is also a worker. The same definition appears in the National Minimum Wage Regulations 1999, the Working Time Regulations 1998 and the Part-time Workers Regulations 2000.

There are thus four requirements that need to be satisfied in limb (b):

(a) the worker has to be an individual who has entered into or works under a contract;

(b) with another party for work or services;

(c) the individual undertakes to do or perform personally the work or services for the other party;

(d) that other party must not, by virtue of the contract, have the status of a client or customer of any profession or business undertaking carried on by the individual who is to perform the work or services.

As far as the requirement for a contract is concerned, readers are reminded that there must be an offer, acceptance, consideration and an intention to create legal relations. See *Windle v Secretary of State for Justice* [2015] ICR 156, *O'Brien v Ministry of Justice* [2013] ICR 499 (where the Supreme Court dispensed with the requirement for a contract, applying the Framework Directive 97/81/EC, which referenced a broader concept of 'employment relationship') and *Gilham v Ministry of Justice* (UKEAT/0087/16).

As far as the third and fourth requirements are concerned, there are a number of authorities, dealt with below.

Readers should note again the Supreme Court decision in *Autoclenz* (above) where the Court held that

> the ET was entitled to hold that the documents did not reflect the true agreement between the parties and that, on the basis of the ET's findings, four essential contractual terms were agreed: (1) that the valeters would perform the services defined in the contract for Autoclenz within a reasonable time and in a good and workmanlike manner; (2) that the valeters would be paid for that work; (3) that the valeters were obliged to carry out the work offered to them and Autoclenz undertook to offer work; and (4) that the valeters must personally do the work and could not provide a substitute to do so. See in particular, per Aikens LJ at para 97. It follows that, applying the principles identified above, the Court of Appeal was correct to hold that those were the true terms of the contract and that the ET was entitled to disregard the terms of the written documents, in so far as they were inconsistent with them.

In *Byrne Brothers (Formwork) Ltd v Baird* [2002] IRLR 96, the EAT held that a tribunal had not erred in holding that various labour-only subcontractors who worked as carpenters in the construction industry were workers within the meaning of the Working Time Regulations, and had therefore correctly concluded that they were entitled to holiday pay: as the applicants undertook to perform work or services for the company personally, they fell within the definition of 'worker' in limb (b) above, notwithstanding that the contract provided that, in certain circumstances, the services could be provided by someone other than the subcontractor with the prior express agreement of the contractor.

The EAT said, usefully:

> Thus the essence of the intended distinction must be between, on the one hand, workers whose degree of dependence is essentially the same as that of employees and, on the other, contractors who have a sufficiently arms-length and independent position to be treated as being able to look after themselves in the relevant respects.
>
> ...

> Drawing [the] distinction [between workers and independent contractors] will involve all or most of the same considerations as arise in drawing the distinction between a contract of service and a contract for services – but with the boundary pushed further in the putative worker's favour. It may, for example, be relevant to assess the degree of control exercised by the putative employer, the exclusivity of the engagement and its typical duration, the method of payment, what equipment the putative worker supplies, the level of risk undertaken etc. The basic effect of limb (b) is ... to lower the pass mark, so that cases which failed to reach the mark necessary to qualify for protection as employees might do so as workers (at 101).

The EAT, following *McFarlane* (**1.3.2.1** above), held that a limited power to appoint a substitute was not inconsistent with an obligation to provide services personally and that the purpose of limb (b) is 'to create an intermediate class of protected worker who is on the one hand not an employee, but on the other hand cannot in some narrower sense be regarded as carrying on a business'. In looking at the policy behind limb (b), the EAT said that it was to extend protection to workers who were 'substantively and economically' in the same position as employees.

The EAT emphasised that what was important were the rights and obligations of the parties *under the contract* and not what happened *in practice*, although that 'may shed light' on the contractual position. The EAT thought that the carpenters in *Byrne* were a good example of the kind of workers for whom the intermediate category in limb (b) was designed. The carpenters were clearly not carrying on a business, and Byrne Brothers were not their clients. There was sufficient mutuality of obligation between the parties for it to be said that there was a contract for services within the meaning of limb (b).

In *Premier Groundworks Ltd v Jozsa* (UKEAT/0494/08), the EAT held that an individual who worked under a contract which gave him complete freedom to delegate could not be a worker for the purpose of the Working Time Regulations. The position would be different, according to the EAT, if the right not to perform the obligations depended on some other event, such as whether the party was ill. Here, the freedom was unfettered and therefore the individual could not be a 'worker'. See too *MPG Contracts Ltd v England* (UK/EAT/0488/08), where an option allowing a father-and-son team to appoint a subcontractor (albeit with a provision that the contractor could refuse to accept unsuitable substitutes) meant that the contract was not one to provide services personally, and therefore the claimants were not workers for the purposes of bringing a holiday pay claim.

In *Redrow Homes (Yorkshire) Ltd v Buckborough and Another* (UKEAT/0528/07), the issue was (as it also was in *Redrow Homes (Yorkshire) Ltd v Wright* [2004] IRLR 720) whether workmen (bricklayers) engaged by Redrow to work on its building sites were workers for the purposes of reg 2(1) of the Working Time Regulations, or were self-employed contractors. The standard contract between Redrow and the workmen provided that the men agreed to provide such labour as was necessary to maintain the required rate of progress but were not obliged to perform the labour themselves. The EAT upheld the employment tribunal's finding that the men were workers, and said that its finding that the obligations provision in the contract was a sham did not contain any error of law. The EAT said that an express contractual arrangement could also be a sham where neither party intends the relevant provision(s) in the contract to have effect.

In *Clarkson v Pensher Security Doors Ltd* (UKEAT/0107/07) the EAT held that the purported worker was not a worker but rather that he carried on a business undertaking for a customer. The EAT agreed with the tribunal that the case came very close to the dividing line between the two, and readers should read the decision for further guidance.

In *Yorkshire Window Company Ltd v Parkes* (UKEAT/0484/09) the EAT helpfully drew the following from the authorities:

> We would draw the following principles from the authorities to which we have referred, (a), the question whether or not a contract provides for the performance of personal services is essentially a

matter of construction, (b), the court is concerned with construing the contract, rather than with general policy considerations, (c), the fact that the individual chooses personally to supply the services is irrelevant; the issue is whether he is contractually obliged to do so, (d), the right or obligation to employ a substitute will not necessarily mean that there is no obligation on the part of the 'contractor' to perform personal services unless that right to employ a substitute is unfettered, (e), in cases where the 'contractor' is unable as opposed to unwilling, to carry out specified services, and has accepted an obligation to perform those services, but is unable to do so, and where he himself does not bear the costs of employing a substitute, a limited or occasional power of delegation may not be inconsistent with a contract to provide personal services, (f), a worker holds an intermediate position between an employee and someone who carries on his own business undertaking.

The fourth requirement is there, as Mr Recorder Underhill QC (as he then was) noted in *Byrne Brothers (Formwork) Ltd v Baird and Others* [2002] IRLR 96, to

> create an intermediate class of protected worker, who is on the one hand not an employee but on the other hand cannot in some narrower sense be regarded as carrying on a business. ... it is sometimes said that the effect of the exception is that the regulations do not extend to the 'genuinely self-employed'; but that is not a particularly helpful formulation since it is unclear how 'genuinely' self-employment is to be defined.

It is clear that not all those who might properly be described as self-employed are engaged in a business undertaking. The question whether the 'worker' carries on a business undertaking of which the 'employer' is a client or customer is, of course, closely linked to the issue of whether the 'worker' provides services personally. It must be determined whether the essence of the relationship is that of a worker or somebody who is employed, albeit in a small way, in a business undertaking. In many cases, it might assist, as Langstaff J suggested in *Cotswold Developments Construction Ltd v Williams* [2006] IRLR 281, para 53, to focus upon 'whether the purported worker actively markets his services as an independent person to the world in general ... or whether he is recruited by the principal to work for that principal as an integral part of the principal's operations'. As Elias J said in *James v Redcats (Brands) Ltd* [2007] ICR 1006, the question is whether the obligation for personal service is the dominant feature of the contractual arrangement or not. If it is, then the contract lies in the employment field; if it is not – if, for example, the dominant feature of the contract is a particular outcome or objective and the obligation to provide personal service is an incidental or secondary consideration – it will lie in the business field and the person concerned will not be a worker.

In *Yorkshire Window Company Ltd v Parkes* (above), the Employment Judge held that the claimant was not an employee because, in particular, he had treated himself as self-employed in relation to VAT and income tax, and prepared accounts on that basis, was entitled to refuse referrals and could elect which leads he wished to pursue. The Judge went on to find, however, that the claimant was a worker because, on the facts, the claimant had to carry out the work personally (there was no unfettered right to provide a substitute) and he was not pursuing a business; the claimant was not conducting a business enterprise of a general character to the benefit of a larger class of beneficiaries. The claimant was required to confine his services to the respondent and did so as the terms of the contract made clear. The EAT upheld the decision.

In *Community Dental Centres Ltd v Sultan-Darmon* (UKEAT/0532/09), the EAT held that a dentist was not a worker (nor an employee) as he did not 'undertake to do or perform personally any work or services' as required by s 230(3) of the ERA 1996 because of the existence of an unfettered right of substitution in his contract. The EAT said that it was not sufficient that the individual might be obliged personally to find a substitute; that analysis was inconsistent with the established authorities.

The Court of Appeal, in *The Hospital Medical Group Ltd v Westwood* [2012] EWCA Civ 1005, had to consider whether a GP who, aside from his job, carried out hair restoration surgery for the respondent's clients on a Saturday morning, was a worker. The claimant brought claims of unlawful deductions, accrued holiday pay and age discrimination. The employment tribunal ruled, applying *Autoclenz v Belcher* (**1.3.2** above), that the claimant was not an employee but that he was a worker within s 230(3)(b) of the ERA 1996. The claimant was 'clearly in business on his own account, and was engaged under a contract for services as a self-employed independent contractor' (para 30). Nevertheless, he was engaged personally to carry out the work himself (as the respondent conceded); he had no right to delegate the work to others; he was engaged by the respondent because of his skills (para 31).

The EAT upheld the decision of the employment tribunal. The EAT said the claimant was not performing work or services for the respondent as a client or customer of any profession or business carried on by him. The Court of Appeal agreed, Maurice Kay LJ commenting that:

> The striking thing about the judgments in *Cotswold* and *Redcats* is that neither propounds a test of universal application. Langstaff J's 'integration' test was considered by him to be demonstrative 'in most cases' and Elias J said that the 'dominant purpose' test 'may help' tribunals 'in some cases' (paragraph 68). In my judgment, both were wise to eschew a more prescriptive approach which would gloss the words of the statute. ... (at [18])

> ... HMG was not just another purchaser of Dr Westwood's various medical skills. Separately from his general practice and his work at the Albany Clinic, he contracted specifically and exclusively to carry out hair restoration surgery on behalf HMG. In its marketing material, HMG referred to him as 'one of our surgeons'. Although he was not working for HMG pursuant to a contract of employment, he was clearly an integral part of its undertaking when providing services in respect of hair restoration, even though he was in business on his own account. ... (at [19])

In *Macalinden T/A Charm Offensive v Lazarov* (UKEAT/0453/13), the EAT allowed an appeal by a theatre producer that five stage actors were workers, such as to entitle them to the national minimum wage. The EAT said that the evidence before the employment tribunal raised a real issue as to whether the claimants were carrying on a 'business or undertaking' and remitted the case back to the employment tribunal for further consideration.

Readers are also referred to *O'Brien v Ministry of Justice* [2013] UKSC 6, where the Supreme Court explained its decision (delivered in July 2012) that a part-time Crown Court recorder was a part-time worker for the purposes of the provisions preventing less favourable treatment regarding part-time workers (see **8.10**). However, the EAT held in *Gilham v Ministry of Justice* (UKEAT/0087/16) that a District Judge was not a worker. The distinction between the *O'Brien* judge and the *Gilham* judge is that the judge in the former case was relying on the Part-time Workers Regulations 2000 (which derive from European legislation), whereas Ms Gilham was relying on the ERA 1996 (s 47B/whistleblowing), which does not derive from European legislation.

The ECJ recently defined a worker (for the purpose of the Working Time Directive) as someone who pursues real, genuine activities, to the exclusion of activities on such a small scale as to be regarded as purely marginal and ancillary (*Fenoll v Centre d'aide par le travail 'La Jouvene'* (Case C-316/13) [2016] IRLR 67). As Caspar Glyn QC blogged, 'the case potentially opens the door for individuals who fall outside the domestic s 230(3) ERA 1996 definition of worker to bring claims for working time rights derived from EU law'. (See also *Balkaya* below.)

In *Suhail v Herts Urgent Care* (UKEAT/0416/11), the EAT held that out-of-hours GPs were self-employed individuals carrying on a business or profession. See also *Suhail v Barking, Havering and Redbridge University Hospitals NHS Trust* (UKEAT/0536/13), where the EAT upheld a tribunal finding that an out-of-hours GP was neither an employee nor a worker for the purposes of bringing a whistleblowing detriment claim pursuant to s 47B of the ERA 1996. The EAT held that the GP was not a worker because the health service provider was a client or customer of his own business.

The leading domestic authority on worker status is *Clyde & Co LLP and Another v Bates van Winkelhof* [2014] IRLR 641, where the Supreme Court held that an equity partner who spent most of her time on secondment in Tanzania was a worker. As an equity partner, Ms Bates was unable to market her services to anyone other than the LLP, and she played an integral part within the business. The fact that she was not in a subordinate position as regards the LLP was irrelevant. See too *Plastering Contractors Stanmore Ltd v Holden* (UKEAT/0074/14).

Note

BIS has published a 'worker' checklist in connection with national minimum wage claims (search 'national minimum wage worker checklist'). In March 2017, Acas published new guidance for employers on employment status.

Finally, note that the ECJ held in *Balkaya v Kiesel Abbruch- und Recycling Technik GmbH* (Case C-229/14) that a director and an unpaid trainee may fall within the concept of 'worker' under the Collective Redundancies Directive (98/59/EC) (see **4.8**). But note that the EU definition of 'worker' is, and has been since 1986, different from that in the UK.

The 'gig economy'

The 'gig economy' has been defined as 'a labour market characterised by the prevalence of short-term contracts or freelance work, as opposed to permanent jobs'. In the gig economy, instead of a regular wage, workers get paid for the 'gigs' they do, such as a food delivery or a car journey. Jobs include courier and delivery services, plumbing and minicab driving. Proponents of the gig economy claim that people can benefit from independence, flexible hours, with control over how much time they can work as they juggle other priorities in their lives. Most of those working in the gig economy are classed as self-employed independent contractors, which has meant that they are not viewed as workers or employees, so have no protection against unfair dismissal, no right to redundancy payments and no right to receive the national minimum wage, paid holiday or sickness pay. The Taylor Review recommended a new category of 'dependent contractor' to cover these sorts of workers and said that they should be entitled to certain minimum basic rights.

There have been a number of 'gig economy' cases recently heard by the employment tribunals, which were seeking to determine whether individuals were workers (s 230(3)) or self-employed. The claimant in *Dewhurst v CitySprint UK Ltd* (ET/220512/2016) was a cycle courier who worked typically over a four-day week. Jobs were assigned based on a tracking system which a courier had to sign into and remain in contact with during the assignment. The employer argued that the courier was self-employed. An employment tribunal felt that there was a discrepancy between the contractual terms and conditions and the reality of how she worked. It decided that the claimant was a worker while she was logged into the tracking system. In reality she was fully integrated into and working for the business. As was the case in *CitySprint*, employment tribunals are not bound by the labels the parties attach to their relationships, although the way in which they describe their relationship will carry some weight (see *Quashie* and *Autoclenz* above).

In *Boxer v Excel Group Services* (ET/3200365/2016), an employment tribunal again found that the written contract did not reflect the reality of the working arrangements and held that another cycle courier was also a worker. Mr Boxer worked 9 hours per day, 5 days per week as a cycle courier for Excel Group Services (Excel). Mr Boxer's contract with Excel described him as a 'subcontractor' and he was registered as self-employed with HMRC. Excel did not pay Mr Boxer when he took a week's holiday between 8 and 15 March 2016 and so he brought a claim for his holiday pay. Excel offered to pay him for his holiday but would not make any concessions about his status. He sought a declaration about his status and succeeded in persuading the tribunal that he was a worker, with rights to holiday pay. As with the *Dewhurst* case, the tribunal was willing to look beyond the employment contract that existed and examine the reality of the relationship. In this case, the claimant was clearly under the direction of another and was not working as an independent contractor running his own business. This, accompanied by the requirement for a high degree of commitment to Excel, meant that the essential features of a working relationship were found to be present.

In *Pimlico Plumbers Ltd v Smith* [2018] UKSC 29, the Supreme Court got to consider the issues for the first time. It held that a plumber, carrying out plumbing and maintenance work on behalf of the company, was a 'worker'. Mr Smith wore a branded uniform, drove a branded van, carried an identity card and was bound by a number of restrictive covenants regarding his working activities post-termination. The Court of Appeal ([2017] EWCA Civ 51) had previously set out the applicable principles as to the requirement for personal performance:

> Firstly, an unfettered right to substitute another person to do the work or perform the services is inconsistent with an undertaking to do so personally. Secondly, a conditional right to substitute another person may or may not be inconsistent with personal performance depending upon the conditionality. It will depend on the precise contractual arrangements and, in particular, the nature and degree of any fetter on a right of substitution or, using different language, the extent to which the right of substitution is limited or occasional. Thirdly, by way of example, a right of substitution only when the contractor is unable to carry out the work will, subject to any exceptional facts, be consistent with personal performance. Fourthly, again by way of example, a right of substitution limited only by the need to show that the substitute is as qualified as the contractor to do the work, whether or not that entails a particular procedure, will, subject to any exceptional facts, be inconsistent with personal performance. Fifthly, again by way of example, a right to substitute only with the consent of another person who has an absolute and unqualified discretion to withhold consent will be consistent with personal performance. (para 84)

The Court of Appeal held that the employment tribunal was correct to find that, on the proper interpretation of the 2009 agreement, Mr Smith undertook to provide his services personally. The express wording of the agreement between the company and Mr Smith required personal performance by Mr Smith. It provided, for example, in para 2.1 that 'You shall provide such building trade services as are within *your* skills'; in para 2.2 that 'You shall provide the services for such periods as may be agreed with the company ... The actual days on which *you* will provide the services will be agreed between you and the company ...'; in para 2.4 that '*you* will be competent to perform the work which *you* agree to carry out', and 'you will promptly correct ... any errors in your work ...'; in para 2.5 that 'If *you* are unable to work due to illness or injury ... you shall notify the company'; and in para 3.9 that 'You will have *personal* liability for the consequences of your services to the company' (in all cases emphasis added) and that there was no express right of substitution or delegation. The Court of Appeal also found that the tribunal had legitimately found that there was an umbrella contract that placed a continuing obligation on Mr Smith to make himself available for work. In the view of the Supreme Court, the employment tribunal was entitled on the evidence to conclude that Pimlico Plumbers was not (looking at the extended definition of worker in s 230(3)(b) of the ERA 1996) a 'client or customer' of Mr Smith.

In *Aslam, Farrar & Others v Uber* (ET/2202550/2015 & Others), another employment tribunal held that 'any driver who (a) has the App switched on, (b) is within the territory in which he is authorised to work, and (c) is able and willing to accept assignments, is, for so long as those conditions are satisfied, working for Uber under a "worker" contract ...' and as such is entitled to the National Minimum Wage and to receive holiday pay.

Uber sought to argue that the company merely connects taxi drivers with passengers, rather than being a provider of taxi services itself, and that a contract exists between the driver and passenger and that therefore drivers were self-employed contractors. The tribunal found that Uber runs a transportation business and that drivers provided their work personally and satisfied the definition of s 230(3)(b) of the ERA 1996 because of the following factors:

(1)   The contradiction in the Rider Terms between the fact that [Uber] purports to be the drivers' agent and its assertion of 'sole and absolute discretion' to accept or decline bookings.

(2)   The fact that Uber interviews and recruits drivers.

(3)   The fact that Uber controls the key information (in particular the passenger's surname, contact details and intended destination) and excludes the driver from it.

(4)   The fact that Uber requires drivers to accept trips and/or not to cancel trips, and enforces the requirement by logging off drivers who breach those requirements.

(5)   The fact that Uber sets the (default) route and the driver departs from it at his peril.

(6)   The fact that [Uber] fixes the fare and the driver cannot agree a higher sum with the passenger. (The supposed freedom to agree a lower fare is obviously nugatory.)

(7)   The fact that Uber imposes numerous conditions on drivers (such as the limited choice of acceptable vehicles), instructs drivers as to how to do their work and, in numerous ways, controls them in the performance of their duties.

(8)   The fact that Uber subjects drivers through the rating system to what amounts to a performance management/disciplinary procedure.

(9)   The fact that Uber determines issues about rebates, sometimes without even involving the driver whose remuneration is liable to be affected.

(10)   The guaranteed earnings schemes (albeit now discontinued).

(11)   The fact that Uber accepts the risk of loss which, if the drivers were genuinely in business on their own account, would fall upon them.

(12)   The fact that Uber handles complaints by passengers, including complaints about the driver.

(13)   The fact that Uber reserves the power to amend the drivers' terms unilaterally.

The tribunal noted that the 'notion that Uber in London is a mosaic of 30,000 small businesses linked by a common "platform" is to our minds faintly ridiculous', although it accepted that Uber *could* devise a business model not involving them employing drivers as workers. Uber appealed the decision. The appeal was heard in late September 2017, with Uber arguing that it operates as an agency for self-employed drivers. The judgment was handed down on 10 November 2017. In brief, the EAT held that the employment tribunal had been entitled to reject Uber's characterisation of the relationship between Uber and Uber drivers in the written contractual documentation. The EAT dismissed Uber's appeal against the tribunal's judgment. The EAT agreed that the tribunal was able to look behind the contractual documentation and rejected the argument that Uber was simply a technology platform acting as an agent for the drivers. Uber appealed the EAT's decision and the appeal was heard by the Court of Appeal on 30–31 October 2018. At the time of writing, no judgment had been handed down.

In *Lange v Addison Lee Ltd* (ET/2208029/2016), an employment tribunal ruled that a group of Addison Lee drivers were not self-employed but were workers who were entitled to the national minimum wage and holiday pay. In *Addison Lee Ltd v Gascoigne* (UKEAT/0289/17), the EAT upheld a tribunal's finding that a cycle courier was a worker within the meaning of reg 2 of the Working Time Regulations 1998 and s 230(3)(b) of the ERA 1996 when he was logged on to the Addison Lee app, and so was entitled to holiday pay. There was mutuality when he was logged on to the app. Finally, the CAC decided on 14 November 2017 that Deliveroo riders were not workers for the purposes of trade union recognition (TURI/985/2016) because, in brief, the right to provide a substitute was real and operable on the facts.

While cases in this area will always be fact specific, there is an increasing line of authority emerging that those working in the gig economies, even where technologically novel working practices are used, will more often than not be found to be, at a minimum, workers (with some employment rights) rather than self-employed independent contractors (with none).

Zero hours contracts

There is no legal definition of what constitutes a zero hours contract. If they are freely entered into, they are not illegal under UK domestic law. In a Private Member's Bill introduced by MP Andy Sawford in 2013, the following definition of a zero hours contract was included:

(1)   A zero hours contract is a contract or arrangement for the provision of labour, which— (a) fails to specify guaranteed working hours, ...

A typical contractual wording might read: 'We are under no obligation to provide work to you at any time and you are under no obligation to accept any work offered by us at any time.'

Zero hours contracts are essentially any contract where an individual works with no stipulation as to minimum hours of work or pay, and often no stipulation about the manner of the work. The individual will only be paid for the hours they actually work. The zero hours label serves, however, as shorthand for a large body of people who work at the unregulated margins of the UK's workforce under a variety of contractual and non-contractual arrangements. Historically, these arrangements were prevalent in areas of female workers and industries such as construction, fishing and docking, but more recently in food service and care, as well as the gig economy cases discussed above. Terms such as 'on call', 'reserve', 'bank', 'casuals', 'regular causals' and 'key-time' intermingle with the more traditional binary and tripartite delineations of employees, workers and the self-employed (or freelance).

In the UK Labour Force Survey (LFS) for the period December 2017 to February 2018, just over 900,000 people or about 2.8% of the workforce said that they were on a zero hours contract. The Business Survey indicated that, as at November 2017, employers said they had issued 1.8 million 'non-guaranteed hours contracts' (NGHCs). The number of contracts actually issued is likely to be larger than this, because, for example, some people will hold more than one such contract. The LFS statistics show that the number of people reporting zero hours did not change much between 2000 and 2012, but from 2012 onwards, the numbers increased rapidly – rising two and half times between 2012 and 2016, from 0.8% of the workforce to 2.8%. The Business Survey figures suggest a 22% increase in contracts issued between 2014 and 2017.

There are often negative concerns around zero hours contracts, including lower earnings, difficulties for planning finances due to the variability of earnings, lack of employment rights and security, and that the choice to turn down work is often in reality 'illusory'. On the other hand, others emphasise the positives that come from the flexibility and lack of ties for both employers and those working under such arrangements.

Trying to analyse and apply legal protections to those on zero hours contracts using the traditional binary or tripartite scheme of employees, workers and the self employed creates difficulties. The absence of any stipulation as to minimum hours and the absence of any future commitment will generally be regarded as indicative of an absence of mutuality of obligations (see eg *Nethermere (St Neots) Ltd v Gardiner and Another* [1984] ICR 612, *Carmichael* (above) and *O'Kelly v Trust House Forte plc* [1983] IRLR 369) and so presents a serious impediment for anyone seeking to argue that there is an employment or even a worker relationship between the parties. Even if each single individual arrangement could be said to fulfill the s 230 ERA 1996 definition, the difficulty in establishing any sort of global or umbrella contract may mean that there is insufficient continuity to fall within many of the statutory protections. In some instances where the traditional analysis creates obvious difficulties, the courts have started to look at the 'reality' of the arrangement (see for example Lord Hoffman in *Carmichael* ([1999] 1 WLR 2042 at 2050G); Langstaff J in *Cotswold Developments Construction Ltd v Williams* (UKEAT/0457/05), where he expressed concern that courts may have misunderstood that mutuality does not deprive the existence of an underlying contract where an employee has the right to refuse work or an employer to withhold it; the Supreme Court in *Autoclenz* (above), giving effect to the parties' 'actual legal obligations'; and *Pulse Healthcare Ltd v Carewatch Care Services Ltd* (UKEAT 0123/12) where the contractual agreement was found not to reflect the true agreement between the parties). In *Haggerty* (above), the EAT found that while there was a zero hours contract, there were 'mutual obligations subsisting between the employer and the employee during the periods when the employee, as a casual worker, was not actually engaged on any particular shift'. This was based on a finding of a long and well-established regular work pattern. It is therefore possible that a zero hours contract could be classified as one of employment, although there may be complications around continuity of service in terms of access to certain rights (see eg *Stephenson and Prater* (above) and *McMeechan v Secretary of State for Employment* [1997] IRLR 353). Even where a zero hours worker is not an employee, they may still be (as indeed the recent gig economy cases indicate) a worker and therefore still have access to some statutory rights in terms of holiday pay, minimum wage legislation etc.

The Taylor Review (see Introductory Note)

In October 2016, Matthew Taylor, chief executive of the Royal Society of the Arts, was tasked by the Government with looking at how working practices in the modern economy needed to change in order to keep pace with modern business models. The 'Taylor review of modern working practices' was published in July 2017. In brief, the report recommends the following:

- The distinction between employee, worker and self-employment should be retained, but there should be greater clarity between 'worker' status and self-employment and workers should be renamed as 'dependent contractors'.

- Such 'dependent contractors' should be entitled to certain minimum wage, holiday and sickness rights, and employers in these industries should pay national insurance.

- Individuals who prefer flexible working should be allowed to continue, but they should be granted fairness at work.

- There should be a clear statutory legal distinction made between dependent contractors and those who are legitimately self-employed. The need for an element of personal service in employment contracts should be retained, but a requirement to perform work personally would no longer be crucial to being a 'worker' – the focus would be on control, which should be of greater importance in determining the new 'dependent contractor' status than not performing work personally.

The Government published its response to the Taylor Review in February 2018 and has said that it will consult on the vast majority of its recommendations, including around employment status.

1.3.4 Other relevant qualifying definitions

Although the definitions of 'employee' and 'worker' contained in s 230(1) and (3) of the ERA 1996 are the most common definitions of those terms (see **1.3.2** and **1.3.3**), it is important nonetheless to check what definition is relevant to any particular legislation. Set out below are two areas where wider definitions appear.

1.3.4.1 Public Interest Disclosure Act 1998

So far as a claim under the Public Interest Disclosure Act 1998 (PIDA 1998) is concerned (see **5.5.5**), workers have a right not to be subjected to a detriment on the grounds that they have made a protected disclosure (ERA 1996, s 47B). Employees will be regarded as unfairly dismissed if the principal reason for their dismissal is that they made a protected disclosure (ERA 1996, s 103A). Workers who are dismissed for making a protected disclosure must complain, however, that dismissal is a detriment (ERA 1996, s 47B(2)). Different compensation regimes apply: under s 49(6) of the ERA 1996, workers cannot get more than if they had brought a successful unfair dismissal claim. 'Worker' is given an extended definition beyond the standard definition in s 230(3) of the ERA (see s 43K of the ERA 1996). In particular, the definition is extended to cover agency workers (s 43K(1)(a)), and covers those who would be defined as a worker within s 230(3) if the words 'personally or otherwise' were substituted for 'personally' in s 230(3)(b) (see above) (s 43K(1)(b)). Section 43K(2) contains an extended definition of 'employer'. It provides that with regard to agency and similar workers, 'employer' includes the person who substantially determines the terms on which those workers were engaged. The *Clyde & Co* case referred to at **1.3.3** above was a public interest disclosure case.

Section 43K was considered by the EAT in *Croke v Hydro Aluminium Worcester Ltd* [2007] ICR 1303. The EAT concluded that in construing the definition of 'worker' in s 43K, it was appropriate to adopt a purposive approach. Accordingly, where an individual supplied his services to an employment agency through his own company, and the employment agency, in turn, provided the services of that company to an end-user, it may be that in appropriate circumstances the individual is a 'worker' of the end-user for the purposes of s 43K. (See also on this area *Keppel Seghers UK Ltd v Hinds* (UKEAT/0019/14).)

Following *Clyde & Co v Bates* (see **1.3.3**), partners in LLPs can be workers, and accordingly, while they do not have unfair dismissal rights, they do have protection against being subjected to a detriment. In *McTigue v University Hospital Bristol NHS Foundation Trust* (EAT/0354/15) the EAT confirmed that some agency workers come within s 43K(1)(a).

The Court of Appeal considered s 43K in *Day v Lewisham & Greenwich NHS Trust* [2017] EWCA Civ 329. The Court held that words should be read into s 43K to exclude a claim by an employee or worker falling within s 230(3) but allow a claim by the same person under s 43K against a different respondent. In this case a doctor has brought a claim against the Trust and Health Education England (HEE) (a training body). The EAT had upheld the employment tribunal's decision that he was precluded from bringing a claim against the HEE because the Trust was his employer under s 230(3). The Court of Appeal decided that the doctor fell within s 43K notwithstanding his worker relationship with the Trust.

1.3.4.2 Discrimination legislation

By s 83(2) of the Equality Act 2010:

> 'Employment' means ... employment under a contract of employment, a contract of apprenticeship or a contract personally to do work ...

This definition applies to discrimination which is 'because of' any of the protected characteristics (see **Chapter 8**). It is similar, but not identical to the wording that appeared in the old legislation (for example SDA 1975, s 82(1); RRA 1976, s 78; DDA 1995, s 68).

The definition clearly covers employees and workers, and it also extends to individuals who are self-employed, provided that their 'employment' contract obliges them to perform the work personally: in other words, if they are not permitted to sub-contract any part of the work.

The ECJ held in *Allonby v Accrington and Rossendale College* (Case C-256/01) [2004] ICR 1328 that 'the term worker ... cannot be defined by reference to the legislation of the Member States but has a Community meaning. Moreover, it cannot be interpreted restrictively.' It went on to hold that under European law a worker is a person who, for a certain period of time performs services for and under the direction of another person in return for which he receives remuneration, but that the authors of the EC Treaty did not intend the term 'worker', within the meaning of Article 141(1) EC (now Article 157(1) TFEU), to include independent providers of services who are not in a relationship of subordination with the person who receives the services. The question whether such a relationship exists must be answered, said the ECJ, in each particular case having regard to all the factors and circumstances by which the relationship between the parties is characterised.

The UK courts have emphasised that the important question is to ascertain what the dominant objective of the contract was. The Court of Appeal in *Mirror Group Newspapers Ltd v Gunning* [1986] IRLR 27 said the key question was whether the dominant purpose of the contract in that case was the personal execution of any work or labour. It held that the words 'a contract personally to execute any work or labour' (in the extended definition of 'employment' in the SDA 1975, s 82(1)) contemplated a contract the dominant purpose of which is that the party contracting to provide services under it performs personally the work or labour which forms the subject matter of the contract. In *Gunning*, a contract for the distribution of newspapers was not to be considered an 'employment' contract under the discrimination legislation. The dominant purpose of the contract was to secure effective distribution of the paper.

However, according to the Supreme Court in *Jivraj v Hashwani* [2011] UKSC 40, the dominant purpose test is not the key test. The focus must be on the contract and the relationship between the parties. Lord Clarke emphasised the words in the statute 'employment under', and held that

> [an arbitrator's] role is not one of employment under a contract personally to do work. Although an arbitrator may be providing services for the purposes of VAT and he of course receives fees for his work, and although he renders personal services which he cannot delegate, he does not perform those services or earn his fees for and under the direction of the parties as contemplated in ... *Allonby*. He is rather in the category of an independent provider of services who is not in a relationship of subordination with the parties who receive his services ...

An arbitrator appointed by the parties to a dispute was not therefore a worker within the meaning of the discrimination legislation.

In *X v Mid Sussex CAB* [2013] IRLR 146, the Supreme Court confirmed that a volunteer worker at a Citizens Advice Bureau was not entitled to claim disability discrimination because the legislation does not extend protection to voluntary workers without a contract. The lack of remuneration was held to be the key. A similar interpretation would apply to discrimination on the grounds of race, sex, sexual orientation, religion or belief, and age.

In *Halawi v WDFG UK Ltd t/a World Duty Free and Another* [2015] IRLR 50, H, a beauty consultant working in a duty-free cosmetics outlet at Heathrow Airport was found not to be in 'employment' for the purposes of bringing a discrimination claim. She provided her services via a limited company to an agency, which contracted with a cosmetics company, which in turn had an arrangement with WDF. As such, there was no contract, either of employment or 'personally to do work', between H and either WDF or the agency. Further, she did not satisfy the test of control, as all WDF could do was restrict her access to the workplace. Moreover, H was not required to carry out the work personally, as she could use a substitute. The Court of Appeal expressed some concern that it was unable to provide her with a remedy for the alleged discrimination, but said it had no option, given the employment tribunal's findings of fact as to her complicated working arrangements.

In *Secretary of State for Justice v Windle* [2016] EWCA Civ 459, the Court of Appeal held that the claimants did not satisfy the extended definition of employee in s 83(2) of the Equality Act 2010. The claimants were interpreters engaged on an 'as and when' basis to provide interpretation services in courts. They were not obliged to accept work and there was no requirement that they be offered work. It was argued that they were under 'a contract personally to do work'. Underhill LJ said that the test for 'a contract personally to do work' is the same as the test for 'workers' (see **1.3.2**) and agreed with the reasoning in *Quashie v Stringfellows Restaurant* [2012] EWCA Civ 1735 (which found that there was insufficient mutuality of obligation for a lap dancer to be an employee of the club where she worked). The Court decided that although mutuality of obligation between assignments is not a strict requirement for the purposes of meeting the extended definition of 'employee', it is something that can be taken into account. Underhill LJ said:

> [I]t does not follow that the absence of mutuality of obligation outside that period [of the assignment] may not influence, or shed light on, the character of the relationship within it. It seems to me a matter of common sense and common experience that the fact that a person supplying services is only doing so on an assignment-by-assignment basis may tend to indicate a degree of independence, or lack of subordination, in the relationship while at work which is incompatible with the employee status even in the extended sense [under the Equality Act 2010].

Windle was applied in *Capita Translation v Siauciunas* (UKEAT/0181/16). Mr Siauciunas was an interpreter registered with Capita working within the HM Courts Service via a framework agreement to provide his services on an assignment by assignment basis. In considering his status for a discrimination claim, the employment tribunal found that he was an 'employee', applying s 83(2), because he personally provided services and because it held, applying the EAT decision in *Windle*, that a lack of obligation between assignments for Capita to provide work to him and for him to accept work was not relevant. After the employment tribunal's judgment, the Court of Appeal overturned the EAT's decision in *Windle*. Capita's appeal succeeded, with the EAT following the Court of Appeal in *Windle* that a lack of mutuality of obligation between assignments was relevant when determining employment status. Offers for work could be, and on the facts were, declined, and Mr Siauciunas had never committed himself or been obliged to commit himself to work exclusively for Capita. The case was remitted to a new employment tribunal for further factual investigation.

It seems to the authors that requiring mutuality of obligation between assignments seriously undermines the reach of the extended definition of employee in s 83(2) and does not sit well with, for example, the *Uber* and *Pimlico Plumbers* cases (see **1.3.3** above). (Note though that permission to appeal in the *Windle* case was declined, so the case remains as a binding precedent.) For the time being, therefore, the hurdle for proving 'employee' status in the wider s 83(2) is higher than proving worker status under s 230(3) of the ERA 1996.

Note that s 41 of the Equality Act also protects contract workers from being discriminated against by their principals, ie the client who engages them. Such workers may also be separately protected from discrimination by the agency they work for (if it is their employer) (see s 39 and **8.12**). Sections 44 and 45 protect partners.

For a pre-Equality Act 2010 decision on the meaning of 'contract worker' in discrimination legislation, see *Leeds City Council v Woodhouse* [2010] IRLR 625. There, the Court of Appeal held that an employee of an 'arm's-length' management organisation (which carried out property management for Leeds Council) was a contract worker of the Council.

1.3.5 Apprenticeship

In *Thorpe v Dul, Brooksby Melton College and Learning Skills Council* [2003] ICR 1556, the EAT held that a 'modern' apprenticeship, ie one established under a government-funded scheme, is not a contract of employment, and therefore modern apprentices are not automatically protected by unfair dismissal and other statutory rights. However, the EAT also said that there could also be, on the facts in any case, in addition to the apprenticeship, a contract of employment.

The current statutory scheme for apprenticeships in England and Wales is set out in the Apprenticeships, Skills, Children and Learning Act (ASCLA) 2009. At common law, a contract of apprenticeship was a common law creation distinct from a contract of employment. These 'traditional' apprenticeships have been almost completely replaced by apprenticeships governed by the ASCLA regime. Apprenticeship agreements under the ASCLA 2009 are expressly given (s 35) the status of contracts of service, not the (traditional) status of contracts of apprenticeship. This means that ASCLA apprentices are entitled to all of the same employment rights and protections as an employee. There is a special apprenticeship rate of the national minimum wage (£3.30 per hour as at October 2015).

For a recent case examining contracts of apprenticeship, see *Commissioners for HMRC v Jones and Others T/A Holmescales Riding Centre* (UKEAT/0458/13).

(For readers interested in more information about apprenticeships, there was a very useful article looking at both traditional common law apprenticeships and modern arrangements established under statutory schemes in the IDS Employment Law Brief 1002 (August 2014).)

1.3.6 Agency workers

Much of the detail in relation to the status of agency workers is beyond the scope of this book, but this is a developing area of law (see eg *Franks v Reuters and Another* [2003] IRLR 423, CA; *Dacas v Brook Street Bureau (UK) Ltd* [2004] IRLR 358, CA; *Astbury v Gist Ltd* [2007] All ER (D) 480, *Bunce v Skyblue* [2005] IRLR 557, CA and *RNLI v Bushaway* [2005] IRLR 674; *Cable & Wireless plc v Muscat* [2006] IRLR 354, CA). Agency workers may be employees of the agency, or of the end-user or of neither.

In *National Grid Electricity Transmission plc v Wood* [2007] All ER (D) 358 (Oct), the EAT was prepared to uphold a tribunal decision that Mr Wood, who had been supplied to the respondent company by an agency, was employed by the end-user under an implied contract of employment. Case law suggests, however, that tribunals will rarely find implied contracts of service between agency workers and the end-user (the client to whom they are supplied).

In *Dacas* (above), endorsed in *Muscat* (above), the Court of Appeal directed tribunals always to consider the possibility of an implied employment contract between an agency worker and client (or end-user) where there is a triangular relationship between the agency worker, agency and end-user.

The Court of Appeal offered the following guidance to tribunals on when a contract of employment should be implied between the worker and the end-user:

(a)   Where the arrangements between agency, agency worker and end-user are genuine and reflect the actual working relationship – such as where there was no pre-existing employment relationship between the agency, worker and end-user – then it will be a rare case in which the evidence justifies the tribunal implying a contract. Such evidence would need to show that the agency worker is working pursuant to mutual obligations with the end-user, and that these obligations are incompatible with the agency arrangement.

(b)   The mere passage of time does not in itself justify the implication of a contract on the ground of necessity. Something more is required to show that it is necessary to imply a contract.

(c)   It would be more readily open to a tribunal to infer a contract where, as in *Muscat*, the agency arrangement had been superimposed on a pre-existing employment relationship between worker and end-user, although, strictly speaking, the tribunal would be finding that the agency arrangements did not bring the original contract to an end.

The Court of Appeal's view is that whether a contract of employment should be implied between an agency worker and an end-user is a question of fact for the tribunal.

In *Cairns v Visteon Ltd* [2007] IRLR 175, the EAT, while not ruling out the possibility that two employment contracts could exist in parallel between an individual and two employers in respect of the same work, said the concept was problematic, and that there was no good policy reason for extending unfair dismissal protection where an individual already had an express contract of employment with the agency. The EAT went on to say that, for a contract to be implied between the agency worker and the end-user, it is necessary to show that the conduct of the parties is consistent with there being a contract of employment between them. The EAT also held in two other cases (*Heatherwood & Wexham Park Hospitals NHS Trust v Kulubowila* [2007] All ER (CD) 496 and *Astbury v Gist Ltd* [2007] All ER (D) 480) that agency workers were not employees of the end-user.

In *Consistent Group Limited v Kalwak and Others* [2008] IRLR 505, the issue was whether Polish migrant agency workers could be employees of an agency, despite a lack of detailed control over their day-to-day work. In this case, there was a contractual statement that provided that the workers were not employees of the agency and that there was no mutuality of obligation between the agency and the workers. The EAT held that the express terms did not reflect the reality and that the arrangements were therefore a sham. The Court of Appeal overruled the EAT, emphasising that it is not possible to imply into a contract a term that conflicts with an express term. If there was nothing to indicate that the relevant terms were included by the parties in order to be deliberately misleading, the finding of 'sham' must be overturned. The case was remitted to the employment tribunal to be reheard.

See also *Protectacoat Firthglow Ltd v Szilagyi* [2009] IRLR 365 and the Court of Appeal decision in *Autoclenz Ltd v Belcher* [2010] IRLR 70 (confirmed by the Supreme Court) at **1.3.2** above.

It was hoped that the Court of Appeal would take the opportunity to consider some of the various and conflicting agency decisions when *James v Greenwich Borough Council* [2008] IRLR 302 came before it on appeal. However, Mummery LJ asserted that 'there is no significant difference between the law stated and applied in the decisions of this court and in those of the EAT. It is apparently thought in some quarters that they are in conflict. I do not think so.'

Ms James had a 'Temporary Worker Agreement' with an employment agency, which found her a position as a housing support worker with Greenwich Council. After several years the Council replaced her with another worker supplied by the agency. In response to her claim for unfair dismissal, the Council disputed her legal status as an employee. She was paid by the agency following receipt by the agency from her of completed weekly timesheets. The tribunal found that the Council's Disciplinary Procedure and Grievance Policy did not apply to Ms James and that she was not entitled to benefit from the Council's sick pay or holiday pay provisions applicable to employees. The decisions of both the tribunal and the EAT were that she was not employed by the Council under a contract of service. The Court of Appeal held that the 'real issue' in agency worker cases is whether a contract should be implied between the worker and the end-user in a tripartite situation of worker, agency and end-user, rather than whether the irreducible minimum of mutual obligation exists. Mutuality is important in deciding whether a contract that has been concluded is a contract of employment or some other kind of contract. The correct approach is for an employment tribunal to decide – as a question of fact – whether, applying common law principles, it is necessary to imply a contractual relationship between the agency worker and the end-user client. In many cases, agency workers will fall outside the scope of protection because neither the workers nor the end-users are in any kind of express contractual relationship with each other and it is not necessary to imply one in order to explain the work undertaken by the worker for the end-user. The Court of Appeal held that the EAT in *James* had not erred in holding that the circumstances did not exist which could justify the inference of an implied contract. The provision of work by the local authority, its payments to the agency, and the performance of the work by Ms James were all explained by their respective express contracts with the agency, so it was not necessary to imply the existence of another contract in order to give business reality to the relationship between the parties. The Court of Appeal expressly approved the guidance given in paras 53–61 of the EAT's decision, and readers advising on this topic should therefore also read the EAT's judgment.

Muschett v HM Prison Service [2010] EWCA Civ 25 is yet another example of the difficulties of establishing a contractual relationship between an agency worker and the end-user. The Court of Appeal emphasised that in tripartite arrangements a contract could only be implied between the agency worker and the end-user where it was necessary to do so to reflect the business reality of the situation. To find necessity, it required evidence from which a tribunal could conclude that the agency relationship no longer adequately reflected how the work was actively being performed. The Court of Appeal in this case said the 'meagre collection of facts' relied upon by the claimant could not justify making a finding that the claimant was an employee.

In *Tilson v Alstom Transport* [2010] EWCA Civ 1038, the Court of Appeal was again reluctant to imply a contractual relationship between the agency worker and the end-user. In this case, the ongoing relationship was conducted on the basis that no contract of employment existed (on two occasions, Alstom asked Mr Tilson to become an employee but on each occasion he declined because he preferred to be an independent contractor); and even though there was evidence of a significant degree of integration of an agency worker into an organisation (Mr Tilson was supervised by Alstom's managers and had to apply to his line manager to take holiday; he also supervised Alstom staff), the court held that that was not inconsistent with an agency relationship in which there is no contract between worker and end-user. The Court of Appeal also held that the need to apply to a line manager before taking annual leave was not sufficient to justify the implication of a contract. This case reinforces the position that while it is not impossible to find an employment contract between an agency worker and the end-user (see, for an example, *McMeechan v Secretary of State for Employment* [1997] ICR 549), a contract of employment will not be implied where it is not necessary to do so to explain a working relationship. In many such cases, the 'irreducible minimum' requirement for an employment contract – mutuality of obligation and control exercised by the employer – will not be met. It is also likely that deduction of National Insurance and PAYE in such situations will be regarded as a neutral factor (since ss 44–47 of the Income Tax (Earnings and Pensions) Act 2003 necessitate it). The only exception may be where there is evidence that both parties have deliberately entered into a sham arrangement to prevent a relationship of employer and employee from arising (see too *BIS v Studders* (UKEAT/0571/10)).

It should be remembered, of course, that even if the agency worker is not an employee, he may still benefit from some protections, eg the anti-discrimination legislation (see **1.3.4.2**), national minimum wage legislation and working time legislation (see, for example, *Electronic Data Systems Ltd v Hanbury and Brook Street Bureau* (UKEAT/128/00)), as a worker.

1.3.6.1 Agency Workers Regulations 2010

Following the coming into force of the EC Directive on conditions for temporary (agency) work (Directive 2008/104/EC) in December 2008, the Agency Workers Regulations 2010 (SI 2010/93), as amended by SI 2011/1941, came into force on 1 October 2011. The Regulations create a right for agency workers to receive the same basic terms and conditions as if they had been directly recruited by the end-user. The detail is beyond the scope of this book. However, a short summary appears below.

The Regulations provide that agency workers (defined as individuals having a contract of employment with the agency or a contract with the agency to perform work and services temporarily) will have equal access to facilities (such as canteen, childcare facilities, vacancy lists etc) and information on job vacancies as direct employees of the end-user from day 1. Otherwise, for the more detailed requirements, such as equal treatment in terms of pay and other basic working conditions (annual leave, rest breaks, rest periods, duration of working time, length of night work – and pregnant agency workers must be allowed to take paid time off for ante-natal appointments), there is a 12-week qualifying period, so short-term agency temps will not qualify for these rights. The 12 weeks do not have to be continuous; there can be breaks between assignments and absences on grounds of, say, sickness or jury service.

The number of hours that the worker has worked during the reference period is calculated differently depending on the type of work done by the worker.

There are four types of work:

(a)   time work;

(b)   salaried hours work;

(c)   output work;

(d)   unmeasured work.

The rules vary according to the type of work done, and readers should consult the Regulations for the detail. For example, lunch breaks will not count as hours worked for time workers but will count for salaried hours workers if they form part of the workers' basic minimum hours under the contract.

In May 2011, the BIS published Guidance on the Agency Workers Regulations 2010. The Guidance seeks to assist in interpreting the Regulations and gives illustrations in relation to issues such as:

•   Who is an agency worker?

•   What terms and conditions are covered by the requirement of equal treatment?

•   Is a comparator needed?

•   How to calculate the 12-week qualifying period

- Who will be responsible if the Regulations are breached?

There have been relatively few reported cases on the Regulations.

In *Bray v Monarch Personnel Refuelling (UK) Ltd* (ET/1801581/12), the tribunal considered the application of what is known as the 'Swedish derogation' (contained in reg 10 of the Agency Workers Regulations 2010, which effectively prevents agency workers getting parity on pay and holiday pay with permanent workers in certain defined situations). The tribunal decision offers some useful guidance on the interpretation of reg 10. It held that the claimants fell within the derogation and so were not entitled to equal pay to permanent workers.

In *Moran v Ideal Cleaning Services Ltd* [2014] IRLR 172, the EAT held that 'agency' workers did not come within the scope of the Regulations because they apply (reg 3) to those working 'temporarily', where their agency relationship was on an indefinite and not a temporary basis. In *Brooknight Guarding Ltd v Matei* (UKEAT/0309/17) the EAT considered *Moran* and the definition of 'agency worker'. It held that an employee on a zero hours contract could be an agency worker if he was temporary rather than permanent.

Stevens v Northolt High School (ET/3300621/2014) was a case where an agency was able to avoid any liability because it had taken reasonable steps to determine the pay and conditions of a comparable worker at a school. The school, however, had to pay the locum music teacher over £10,000 because she had been underpaid by £98 for 111 days. The claim for underpayment was brought under regs 5 and 6 (which require that after 12 weeks, temporary workers are paid the same amount as permanent staff in the same position).

In *Coles v Ministry of Defence* (UKEAT/0403/14), the EAT considered whether, under the Regulations, in a redeployment situation, agency workers only have to be informed of vacancies or whether they have to be given preference ahead of permanent staff. The EAT held that Article 6 of the Directive only provides a right to information about vacancies. Beyond that, it was up to an employer to decide how to conduct any recruitment process and whether preference would be given to people in a redeployment pool. The aim was to make sure that temporary agency workers had the same chance as others in the relevant undertaking to find permanent employment. Article 6 did not mean that an employer was prevented, in a redeployment situation, from giving priority to permanent staff over temporary agency staff.

In *Kocur v Angard Staffing Solutions Ltd and Another* (UKEAT/0181/17) the EAT upheld an agency worker's claim for the same annual leave and rest break entitlement as a direct recruit, even though he was paid more, in total, for each shift; the Regulations require a term by term comparison, not a package-based approach.

The EAT gives some useful guidance on apportioning liability for a breach of the Regulations between agency and hirer in *Amissah v Trainpeople Co UK Ltd* (UKEAT/0187/16).

In *Brooknight Guarding Ltd v Matei* (UKEAT/0309/17), the EAT held that a security guard employed on a zero hours contract was not a permanent employee but was an agency worker under the Regulations. As a result, he was entitled to the same terms and conditions as a comparable employee.

Given that this is a complex and developing area, readers should always ensure that they look at the most up-to-date case law on this topic.

1.3.7   Other categories

In *The New Testament Church of God v Stewart* [2007] IRLR 178, the presumption that all ministers were office holders and not employees was successfully challenged. The Court of Appeal upheld the EAT's decision that a Christian minister was an employee of his church. In *The President of the Methodist Conference v Preston* [2013] UKSC 29, the Supreme Court said that a Methodist minister was not an employee for the purposes of an unfair dismissal claim. Baroness Hale dissented, saying that 'it quacks like a duck and swims like a duck'. The majority, after consideration of the internal arrangements of the Methodist Church, concluded that there was no intention to create legal relations in such cases. The Court of Appeal upheld an employment tribunal decision that there was no contract between a Church of England rector and the Bishop because the relationship was governed by ecclesiastical law and was not a contractual arrangement (*Sharpe v Bishop of Worcester* [2015] EWCA Civ 399). It is clear that each case will depend on its facts.

In X *v Mid Sussex Citizens Advice Bureau* [2013] IRLR 146, the Supreme Court held that the Equal Treatment Framework Directive (2000/78) did not cover a volunteer at a Citizens Advice Bureau, at least when the volunteer's activity was not undertaken pursuant to a contract (and so did not fall within the expanded definition of 'employment' in discrimination legislation; s 83 of the Equality Act 2010, see **1.3.4.2**). The Supreme Court identified nine reasons for rejecting the argument that voluntary activity was covered by the Directive, based around a careful textual analysis of the language used in the Framework Directive, including its French version.

In *Gladwell v Secretary of State for Trade and Industry* [2007] ICR 264, EAT, the EAT held that the fact that a claimant was a company director with a shareholding of 50% did not preclude him from being an employee. Mr Justice Elias commented, 'a majority shareholder will in practice act as the employer, making decisions on behalf of the company, but that does not prevent him being an employee'.

In *Secretary of State for BERR v Neufeld* [2009] EWCA Civ 280, the Court of Appeal had to determine whether a controlling shareholder of a company could also be an employee. Mr Neufeld claimed to have been an employee (under ERA 1996, s 230) of the company for which he worked. The company was insolvent and he claimed that he was entitled as an employee to a payment from the Secretary of State under s 182 of the ERA 1996 (which provides that employees of insolvent employers can recover certain debts from the National Insurance Fund, including up to eight weeks' arrears of pay, notice pay and a basic award in an unfair dismissal claim). He was a controlling shareholder and a director of the company. The tribunal held that Mr Neufeld was not an employee, but the EAT reversed that finding. The Court of Appeal, after reviewing the authorities, confirmed that the leading case on employees, shareholders and directors was *Secretary of State for Trade and Industry v Bottrill* [1999] ICR 592, and that being a controlling shareholder was one factor that had to be taken into account when deciding, in all the circumstances, whether a person was an employee or not, but that there is no reason in principle why a person who was a shareholder and director of a company could not also be an employee of the company under a contract of employment, even if that person had a controlling interest in, or even total control of, the company.

The Court of Appeal in *Neufeld* approved, in essence, the approach taken by the EAT in *Clark v (1) Clark Construction Initiatives Ltd (2) Utility Consultancy Services Ltd* (UKEAT/0225/07). In that case the EAT concluded that 'what we have to do is to look at the whole picture, which we have done. We should balance out all the factors and make a reasoned conclusion'. The EAT listed three circumstances (although not exhaustive ones) in which it said it might be possible for a tribunal to see through what was on its face a legitimate employment contract:

(a)   where the company is itself a sham (ie it is the *alter ego* of the individual) – this would be an 'exceptional' case;

(b)   where the contract was entered into for an ulterior purpose, eg to secure a redundancy payment from the Secretary of State;

(c)   where the parties do not conduct their relationship in accordance with the contract, either because:

   (i)   they never intended to, or

   (ii)   the relationship in practice has ceased to reflect the contractual terms.

The EAT then listed a number of other factors which it said would need to be considered when deciding whether to give effect to the contract.

The Court of Appeal held, on the facts, that Mr Neufeld was an employee. The Court summed up the position as follows:

> In a case in which no allegation of sham is raised, or in which the claimant proves that no question of sham arises, the question ... for the court or tribunal will be whether the claimed contract amounts to a true contract of employment. ... [G]iven that the critical question in cases such as those under appeal is as to whether the putative employee was an employee at the time of the company's insolvency, it will or may be necessary to inquire into what has been done under the claimed contract: there will or may therefore need to be the like inquiry as in cases in which an allegation of sham is made. In order for the employee to make good his case, it may well be insufficient merely to place reliance on a written contract made, say, five years earlier. The tribunal will want to know that the claimed contract, perhaps as subsequently varied, was still in place at the time of the insolvency. In a case in which the alleged contract is not in writing, or is only in brief form, it is obvious that it will usually be necessary to inquire into how the parties have conducted themselves under it.

See also *Stack v Ajar-Tec Ltd* [2015] EWCA Civ 46, where the Court upheld an employment tribunal decision that a director and shareholder who performed part-time work for the respondent company without pay for three years was an employee and a worker. See *Department for Employment and Learning v Morgan* [2016] IRLR 350 and *Dugdale v DDE Law Ltd* (UKEAT/0169/16) for two decisions applying *Neufield*.

1.4   THE CONTRACT OF EMPLOYMENT

The general common law provisions that apply to any assessment of whether a binding and legally enforceable contract exists (ie offer, acceptance, certainty, intention to create legal relations, consideration) apply equally to employment contracts (see *MacInnes v Gross* [2017] EWHC 46 (QB)). Generally, courts adopt an objective approach to interpreting contracts, including employment contracts, but in doing so they rely on a number of 'tools' in order to assess the objective meaning – including the language and commercial implications. Where contracts have been drafted or negotiated by professionals, there may be more willingness to rely on textual analysis, but where contracts are informal or brief or lack skilled professional input, or there is inequality of bargaining position, courts may place greater emphasis on the factual matrix (see eg *Wood v Capita Insurance Services Ltd* [2017] UKSC 24).

Parties to an employment relationship will often, but not always, put the terms and conditions that govern that relationship into writing. However, there is no legal requirement for the contract of employment to be in writing. It may be written, oral or a mixture of both. In some circumstances the court will imply a contract of employment (see, eg, *Dacas v Brook Street Bureau (UK) Ltd* (**1.3.6**)). Where there is no written contract of employment, the law requires employers to provide what is known as a written statement of terms to their employees. In the absence of any written contract, the written statement should set out some minimum details about the terms governing the employment relationship.

Even where there is a written contract that sets out the express terms which govern the relationship, the courts will in certain situations imply additional terms into that contract (see **1.5**). This section and those following consider the written statement of terms, some of the terms which may be implied into a contract of employment, including the regulation of working time and minimum wage legislation, and the principal terms which should be considered for express inclusion in a written contract, including restrictive covenants. The protection of wages is addressed in **1.11**.

Readers should note the Contracts (Rights of Third Parties) Act 1999. The full operation of the Act is beyond the scope of this book, but in outline, the Act reforms the doctrine of privity of contract but expressly provides that no rights are conferred on a third party to enforce any term of an employment contract against an employee. However, the Act does not prevent third parties from enforcing relevant contractual terms against the employer where, for example, the terms of the contract purport to confer a benefit on a third party, eg a company car. The

Act must be considered when drafting employment contracts or compromise agreements (see **6.5**).

Where the employer and the employee have agreed the terms of their contract, those terms cannot be changed without both parties agreeing to the changes. In other words, employers cannot unilaterally change the terms and conditions of the contract (see **1.9** below).

1.4.1 Types of contract

The two most common types of employment contract are:

(a)   the indefinite contract – this is a 'continuing' contract which is terminable by either the employer or the employee on giving the requisite period of notice; and

(b)   the 'fixed-term' (or 'limited-term') contract – which provides for employment for a fixed (limited), definite period of time (see **1.8.1.2**).

These contracts may be used whether the contract is for full-time or part-time work.

Increasingly, employers are utilising a variety of non-standard contracts, such as zero hours contracts, in order to achieve flexible working arrangements. Zero hours contracts are casual contracts where the hours to be worked are left (deliberately) undefined and unguaranteed, but employees may be required to be available for work at any time or at specified times. The employer is not obliged to offer any minimum amount of work (or pay), effectively putting the employee on call. In June 2014, the Government announced plans to ban exclusivity clauses in zero hours contracts (whereby employees are prohibited from working under any other contract) and to improve the transparency of zero hours contracts by increasing the availability of information for employees. This change was introduced through the Small Business, Enterprise and Employment Act 2015, which came into force on 26 May 2015. Section 27A renders unenforceable any term prohibiting the worker working under another contract or from doing so without consent. The Exclusivity Terms in Zero Hours Contracts (Redress) Regulations 2015 (SI 2015/2012) came into force on 1 January 2016. These provide, inter alia, that dismissal for breach of an exclusivity clause is automatically unfair (see **5.5**), and it is unlawful to subject an employee or worker to a detriment if they work for another employer in breach of such a clause. The Government has announced that it will encourage businesses and unions to develop codes of practice, and has also published 'Zero hours contracts: guidance for employers'.

Note: With effect from 1 September 2013, a new category of employee status has been introduced, whereby employees may give up employment rights in return for shares. The detail is beyond the scope of the book, but, in brief, individuals can opt to receive at least €2,000 of shares in return for giving up rights to claim unfair dismissal, the right to a statutory redundancy payment, and the right to request flexible working and time off to study or for training. The employee will have to receive independent advice, paid for by the employer.

The Taylor review

The Review (see **1.3.3**) recommends that the Government should ask the Low Pay Commission (LPC), in its next remit, to advise on the impact of bringing in a higher National Minimum Wage for hours which are not guaranteed in a contract (zero hours contracts) hoping that might incentivise employers to schedule guaranteed hours.

1.4.2 Written statement of terms

By s 1 of the ERA 1996 (as amended by the EA 2002), the employer must, within no later than two months of employment commencing, give the employee a written statement of terms and conditions relating to the following particulars:

(a)   identity of the parties;

(b)   date employment began;

(c)   date continuous employment began (taking into account any relevant employment with a previous employer);

(d)   scale or rate of remuneration and intervals of pay;

(e)   hours of work;

(f)   any terms relating to:

    (i)   holidays and holiday pay;

    (ii)   sickness and sick pay;

    (iii)   pensions and pension schemes;

(g)   length of notice required to determine the contract;

(h)   in the case of non-permanent employment, the period for which it is expected to continue or, if it is for a fixed term, the date it is to end;

(i)   job title or a brief description of work;

(j)   place or places of work;

(k)   particulars of any collective agreements which directly affect the terms and conditions of employment;

(l)   where employees are required to work outside the UK for a period of more than one month, the period of such work, currency in which payment is made, benefits provided and terms relating to the return to the UK;

(m)   details of the disciplinary and dismissal rules and grievance procedures (ERA 1996, s 3) (to avoid the procedures becoming contractual in nature, the s 1 statement should make it clear they are not); these can be set out in the body of the particulars, or reference may be made to another reasonably accessible document;

(n)   whether a contracting out certificate is in force (under the Pension Schemes Act 1993).

If there are no particulars to be entered under any of the heads above, that fact must be stated (ERA 1996, s 2(1)).

Although the statement must be given to the employee, it may refer him to a document that is reasonably accessible and which contains full details of the terms relating to pension schemes and dismissal and disciplinary procedures and grievance procedures (ERA 1996, ss 2(2) and 3(1)(aa)).

Any changes in the terms of employment must be notified by the employer in writing within one month of the change (ERA 1996, s 4).

An example of a statement of terms under s 1 may be found in **Appendix 1**.

The Employment Rights Act 1996 (Itemised Pay Statement) (Amendment) Orders 2018, which come into force on 6 April 2019, will extend the right to receive an itemised pay statement (or payslip) to all workers and not just employees. They require payslips to state the number of hours being paid where wages vary according to time worked, either as an aggregate number of hours or as separate figures for different types of work or rate of pay. While employees have been entitled to an itemised payslip (ERA 1996, s 58), workers have not. The Government estimated that some 290,000 workers (1% of the workforce) did not receive a payslip. It hopes that by providing workers with itemised payslips, the greater transparency over how much they are paid and why, will ensure that they are paid correctly. This implements one of the recommendations of the Taylor Review (see Introductory Note).

1.4.2.1   Exceptions

Excluded classes

No written statement needs to be given to any employee if his employment continues for less than one month.

Written contract

If the contract of employment is in writing and contains all the particulars that need to be referred to under s 1 of the ERA 1996, no separate written statement of terms need be given to the employee (ERA 1996, s 7A). (See **1.8** for written contracts.) Employers may decide not to set out the disciplinary and dismissal rules and grievance procedures in the contract to avoid giving the procedures contractual status (see **Chapter 3**).

1.4.2.2   Disputes about the statement

The written statement of terms given by the employer under s 1 of the ERA 1996 merely states what the contract terms are, it is not the contract itself. The employee may dispute the accuracy of the statement, or, alternatively, the employer may fail to give the employee a written statement. In *Lovett v Wigan Metropolitan Borough Council* [2001] EWCA Civ 12, the Court of Appeal confirmed that a s 1 statement did not form part of the contract of employment. An employee did not agree to any variation of existing terms by signing to 'confirm receipt' of the particulars. If it is intended that the s 1 statement is to have contractual force, it must expressly state so and signing must be stated to confirm agreement to the contractual terms. A mere acknowledgement of receipt will be insufficient to bind an employee.

By s 11 of the ERA 1996, where the employer fails to give the employee a written statement as required, or where a dispute arises as to its accuracy, either party may refer the matter to an employment tribunal. The tribunal's duty is to determine what particulars should have been contained in the written statement. The tribunal does not have power to invent terms or impose terms on the parties which had not been agreed between them (*Eagland v British Telecommunications plc* [1992] IRLR 323, CA). See too *Southern Cross Healthcare v Perkins and Others* [2010] EWCA Civ 1442 where the Court of Appeal said that ss 11 and 12 of the ERA 1996 do not give a tribunal rights to construe the terms of the contract or amend the agreement. Such a power can arise only in the context of a breach of contract claim in the civil courts. The only power the tribunal has is to amend the statutory statement so that it corresponds with any written agreement.

The EA 2002 states that the tribunals must award compensation of two to four (gross) weeks' pay (up to the statutory maximum – £489 as at 6 April 2017) to the employee, where the absence of particulars becomes evident upon a successful tribunal claim being brought under any of the tribunal jurisdictions listed in Sch 5 to EA 2002 (which covers most common tribunal complaints) (EA 2002, s 38). There is no free-standing right to claim compensation. The tribunal must award the minimum of two weeks' pay and may, if it considers it just and equitable in the circumstances, award four weeks' pay (ie a maximum of £1,956 as at 6 April 2017) in respect of the failure. The tribunal does not have to make an award if there are exceptional circumstances that make it unjust to make an award.

1.5   IMPLIED TERMS

In certain situations, even where there is a written statement or a written contract, terms will be implied into the contract. Terms may be implied into a contract of employment either at common law, where there is no express term (see **1.7**), or under statute (see **1.6**). The terms of a collective agreement (an agreement between an employer and a trade union) may be incorporated into a contract of employment by implication. Collective agreements are beyond the scope of this book.

In *Newcastle upon Tyne Hospitals NHS Foundation Trust v Haywood* [2018] UKSC 22, the Supreme Court held that a term will be implied into all employment contracts that notice of termination will only start to run from the date the employee receives written notice of their dismissal and has had a reasonable opportunity to read it, if different. This will therefore be the default position unless there is an express contractual clause making clear that, for example, notice is effective from the date of delivery. Contracts will need to set out clearly how notice can be served and when it will be considered to have been received.

1.6 TERMS IMPLIED BY STATUTE

The Working Time Regulations 1998 (see **1.12**) provide an example of terms implied by statute, as does the National Minimum Wage Act 1998 (NMWA – see **1.8.3.1**). The 'equality clause' arising under the Equality Act 2010 (see **8.9.1.1**) is also a term implied by statute.

1.7 TERMS IMPLIED BY COMMON LAW

In addition to terms which are implied by statute, terms may also be implied into a contract by the common law. The principal implied duties are set out below. These may conveniently be divided into employers' duties and employees' duties.

1.7.1 Employers' duties

1.7.1.1 Duty to pay wages and provide work

At common law, the general rule is that an employee has no right to work. Provided that the employer pays the employee, there is no breach of an implied term if the employee is kept idle (*Turner v Sawdon* [1901] 2 KB 653).

There are, however, increasing exceptions to this rule. It has long been established, for example, that workers whose livelihood depends on publicity, for example actors and singers, have the right to work. Similarly, if the employee is paid by commission or is a piece worker, there is an implied duty to provide the employee with work. Furthermore, in *William Hill Organisation Ltd v Tucker* [1998] IRLR 313, the Court of Appeal held that the employee in question had the right to be provided with work during his notice period. The Court of Appeal stated that whether an employee has the right to be provided with work is a 'question of construction of the ... contract in light of its surrounding circumstances'. The Court of Appeal pointed to three factors which, on the facts, supported the right to work:

(a)   The employee was in a specific and unique post, both in substance as well as form. The employee was the only senior dealer – he was the person appointed to conduct a new and specialised business.

(b)   The skills necessary to the proper discharge of such duties as a senior dealer in spread betting required their frequent exercise.

(c)   The terms of the contract itself. The contract provided for the days and hours of work, and specifically imposed on the employee an obligation to work those hours necessary to do the job in a full and professional manner. The court said that if the work was available it was inconsistent with that provision if the employee was bound to draw his pay without doing the work. In addition the contract provided for only a limited power of suspension in narrow circumstances.

Many senior employees will fall within the criteria referred to above, with the result that they will enjoy the right to work (see also **1.8.7.3**). An implied right to work is less likely to be implied into more junior employees' contracts.

In *SG&R Valuation Service v Boudrais* [2008] EWHC 1340 (QB), the High Court held that the implied right to work is subject to the qualification that employees have not, as a result of some other breach of contract or duty, made it 'impossible or reasonably impracticable' for the employer to provide work (in this case because the employees concerned had collected confidential information to use with a new employer and had sought to poach staff).

In *Standard Life Healthcare Ltd v Gorman and Others* [2009] EWCA Civ 1292, where employees were paid on a commission only basis, the Court of Appeal, whilst holding that they had a right to work, held that where an employee was in breach of his duty of good faith (see **1.7.2.4**), the employer was released from its obligation to provide work.

1.7.1.2 Duty to indemnify employee

The employer is under a duty to indemnify the employee for expenses and liabilities incurred by the employee in the course of his employment (*In re Famatina Development Corporation Ltd* [1914] 2 Ch 271).

1.7.1.3 Duty to take reasonable care of the employee's safety and working conditions

There are implied contractual duties on the employer to provide adequate plant and premises, competent fellow workers and a safe system of work (*Wilsons & Clyde Coal Co Ltd v English* [1938] AC 57). This duty to take reasonable care of an employee's safety and working conditions extends only to the employee's personal safety, not to safeguarding his property.

The employer also has statutory duties in respect of health and safety imposed by the Health and Safety at Work etc Act 1974 (HSWA 1974). Further, the Employers' Liability (Compulsory Insurance) Act 1969 requires the employer to take out employers' liability insurance for the benefit of his employees.

In *Waltons and Morse v Dorrington* [1997] IRLR 488, a term was implied in favour of a non-smoker in a smoking environment, that the employer should provide and monitor, so far as is reasonably practicable, a working environment which is reasonably suitable for the performance of contractual obligations.

In *Moores v Bude-Stratton Town Council* [2000] IRLR 676, the EAT held that the employer was under a duty to take reasonable steps to protect employees from unacceptable treatment.

1.7.1.4 Duty of mutual trust and confidence

There is a duty of mutual trust and confidence owed by the employer and the employee to each other. As far as the employer is concerned, it was stated in *Woods v WM Car Services (Peterborough) Ltd* [1983] IRLR 413, CA (approved by the House of Lords in *Malik and Another v BCCI SA (in compulsory liquidation)* [1998] AC 20), that employers will not 'without reasonable and proper cause, conduct themselves in a manner calculated or likely to destroy or seriously damage the relationship of mutual confidence and trust between employer and employee'. This is particularly important in the area of constructive dismissal. (See **3.4.3** for further details.)

1.7.1.5 Duty to take reasonable care in giving references

There is an implied term to take reasonable care in compiling or giving a reference and in verifying the information on which it is based. An employer may be liable to the employee or former employee for any economic loss suffered as a result of a negligent misstatement (see *Caparo Industries v Dickman* [1990] 2 AC 605 (re the test to be applied when establishing whether or not a duty of care is owed) and *Spring v Guardian Assurance plc* [1994] IRLR 460 (re references)).

In *Bartholomew v London Borough of Hackney* [1999] IRLR 246, the Court of Appeal held that where an employer decides to give a reference, there is a duty of care to provide a reference that is 'true, accurate and fair' (ie not misleading). By 'fair', the Court of Appeal meant in terms of the overall impression given of the employee, as well as being factually correct in its component parts. In *Kidd v Axa Equity and Law Life Assurance Society plc and Another* [2000] IRLR 301, the High Court rejected an employee's claim that he had a right to a 'full and comprehensive' reference. The court said that the duty owed by a referee is

> not to give misleading information ... whether as a result of the unfairly selective provision of information, or by the inclusion of facts or opinions in such a manner as to give rise to a false or mistaken inference in the mind of a reasonable recipient.

The EAT held in *TSB Bank plc v Harris* [2000] IRLR 157 that an employee was entitled to resign and claim constructive dismissal on the basis that a reference provided to a prospective employer was in breach of the implied duty of mutual trust and confidence. Ms Harris's employer provided a reference limited to the factual history of Ms Harris's employment. It recorded that there had been 17 complaints against her, 15 more than she knew of, and that four of them had been upheld and eight remained outstanding. The reference said nothing about Ms Harris's character, nor her ability to undertake her job.

The EAT upheld the tribunal's decision that Ms Harris had been unfairly constructively dismissed. The employer should have made Ms Harris aware of the complaints before the reference had been given in order to allow her the opportunity to address the damaging information which was on her file. The reference supplied was unfair and misleading, and not prepared with due skill and care. The approach of the EAT was reinforced by the Court of Appeal in *Cox v Sun Alliance Life Ltd* [2001] IRLR 448. The Court emphasised that the duty of care owed by an employer with regard to the provision of a reference is not only to take reasonable care to provide an accurate reference, but also to take reasonable care to provide a fair one. A reference does not generally 'have to provide a full and comprehensive report on all the material facts concerning the subject'.

In *McKie v Swindon College* [2011] EWHC 469 (QB), the High Court held that an employer owed a duty to its former employee to take reasonable care when referring to that former employee in communications with a third party (an email sent by a former employer to a current employer which resulted in the employee's dismissal). This extends the scope of *Spring* to include circumstances beyond that of simply providing a reference. The case is a useful reference for the process that a court will follow in order to determine whether a duty of care is owed.

Employers, especially public authority employers, need to take care that nothing they write when acting as a referee could be taken to amount to an interference with employees' private or family lives, unless one of the exceptions set out in Article 8(2) of the ECHR applies (see **15.4.2**).

The DPA 1998 (see **Chapter 15**) regulates when and how information concerning an employee may be held, obtained and disclosed. An employer who provides a reference will be processing data for the purposes of the DPA 1998. However, the Act excludes the disclosure to employees of references provided for future employment, although employees may be able to obtain the same from the recipient of the reference. It is clear that while there is no common law duty to provide a reference, an employee may be able to see one if it is provided.

1.7.1.6   Duty to notify on termination without notice

In *Société Générale v Geys* [2013] IRLR 122, the Supreme Court held that an employer must notify an employee in clear terms that the contract is ended.

1.7.1.7   Duty to give reasonable notice

Readers are referred to **2.3.3**.

1.7.2   Employees' duties

1.7.2.1   Duty to give personal service

The relationship of employer and employee is a personal one, and the employee may not delegate performance of his duties. This can be crucial in determining whether someone is an employee or not (see **1.3** above).

1.7.2.2   Duty to obey reasonable orders

The employee is under a contractual duty not wilfully to disobey a lawful order (*Laws v London Chronicle Ltd* [1959] 2 All ER 285). Neither must the employee act in a manner designed to frustrate the commercial aspect of the contract. A 'work to rule' may amount to a breach of contract if designed to disrupt work (*Secretary of State for Employment v Associated Society of Locomotive Engineers and Firemen (ASLEF) (No 2)* [1972] 2 QB 455).

1.7.2.3 Duty of reasonable care and indemnity

The employee is under a duty to exercise reasonable care and skill in the performance of his duties. An employee will be in breach of this duty if he performs his duties negligently or incompetently. If an employee is in breach of this duty, he is also liable to indemnify the employer for any loss suffered by the employer by reason of the employee's breach (*Lister v Romford Ice and Cold Storage Co Ltd* [1957] AC 555).

1.7.2.4 Duty of fidelity or good faith

The duty of fidelity or good faith is sometimes referred to as the employee's part of the mutual duty of trust and confidence. The duty consists principally of a number of aspects of confidentiality and non-competition, some of which also apply after employment has ceased (see **1.7.2.6–1.7.2.8** and **1.8.6**).

In *Crowson Fabrics Ltd v Rider and Others* [2007] EWHC 2942 (Ch), the High Court held that employees who had copied customer contact details and sales figures during employment, had not acted in breach of their implied duty of confidentiality because the information was not confidential (it was in the public domain). However, they were held to have breached their duty of fidelity and, in the case of the senior employee, the fiduciary duty (see **2.5.3**).

In *Kynixa Ltd v Hynes and Others* [2008] EWHC 1495 (Comm), the court held that three senior employees had breached their duty of fidelity by deliberately misleading their employer about their intention to work for a competitor, with which they had been in discussions for at least two months prior to departure.

The High Court held that a senior employee breached his contract and fiduciary duties when he helped set up a business that would compete with his employer's business during 'garden leave' (see **1.8.7.3**) (*Imam-Sadeque v Blue Bay Asset Management (Services) Ltd* [2012] EWHC 3511 (QB)).

1.7.2.5 Secret profits

An employee must not make a secret profit. If he does so, he can be compelled to account to his employer for the profit made (*Boston Deep Sea Fishing and Ice Co v Ansell* (1888) 39 Ch D 339) (see **2.5.3**).

1.7.2.6 Competition

In the absence of an express prohibition in the contract, taking a job outside working hours is not necessarily a breach of the employee's duty of fidelity, even where that job involves working for a competitor. Much will depend on how damaging that other employment is to the employer's business.

In *Hivac Ltd v Park Royal Scientific Instruments Ltd* [1946] Ch 169, five skilled manual workers who assembled hearing aids worked for their employer's sole competitor on Sundays. The Court of Appeal held that they were in breach of the implied duty of fidelity because it could not be consistent with their contract of employment for them to do in their spare time something which could potentially inflict such harm on their employers. Clearly, the fact that they worked for the only other competitor in the market was of great significance.

For the employee's duty of fidelity to be breached in this situation, the employee must normally occupy a position where he has access to confidential information or trade secrets such that the employer is at risk of such information being passed to a competitor. Therefore, in *Nova Plastics Ltd v Frogatt* [1982] IRLR 146, an odd-job man who worked for a competitor in his spare time was not in breach of contract.

After employment, the ex-employee may compete with his former employer without restriction. Any restrictive covenant which attempts to restrict such competition is subject to the doctrine of restraint of trade (see **1.8.7**).

1.7.2.7 Conflict of interest and duty

During employment, the employee must not allow his duty of fidelity to his employer to conflict with his personal interest. In particular, an employee who is intending to leave his employment and set up in competition may wish to obtain information from his employer or entice away his employer's customers and staff. It is a breach of the duty of fidelity to make lists of existing customers with the intention of using it after the termination of the employment relationship (*Roger Bullivant Ltd v Ellis* [1987] ICR 464) or even deliberately to memorise such a list for such a purpose (*Robb v Green* [1895] 2 QB 315). It is also a breach of the duty to entice away or agree to work personally for existing customers of the employer, or to induce other employees to break their contracts of employment (*Sanders v Parry* [1967] 2 All ER 803). (See also *Kynixa* at **1.7.2.4** above.)

1.7.2.8 Trade secrets and confidential information

During employment, an employee is in breach of his duty of fidelity if he uses or reveals trade secrets or other information which by its nature is confidential, or which has been impressed upon the employee as being confidential (*Faccenda Chicken Ltd v Fowler* [1986] 1 All ER 617). Such other information which by its nature is confidential would include lists of customers (see **1.7.2.7** above). A particular method of doing work, though not a trade secret, could be confidential information if the employee had been told of its confidentiality. However, information of a trivial or mundane character, or information that is available from public sources, cannot be turned into confidential information, even by an express term of the contract.

See too the statutory definition of trade secrets and the position after employment has ended at **1.8.6** and **1.8.7**.

1.7.3 Other implied terms

As well as the above general terms, which are seen as a necessary part of contracts of employment, terms may also be implied into contracts where the court is satisfied that the term is necessary to give business efficacy to the contract or that the term is so obvious that the parties must have intended it. It is only appropriate to imply a term where, on a consideration of the express terms of the agreement and the facts and circumstances surrounding it, an implication arises that the parties actually intended the term in question to be part of their original contract.

Terms may also be implied (increasingly rarely) where it is the normal custom and practice to include such a term in contracts of that kind. The custom must be 'reasonable, notorious and certain'. Implication from custom or usage should only normally be on the basis that it does not conflict with an express term. In *Park Cakes Ltd v Shumba* [2013] EWCA Civ 974, the Court of Appeal reviewed the authorities relating to when a contractual term may be implied from past custom or practice and provided a useful summary of the applicable principles relating to the provision of past benefits.

Lastly, a term may be implied by the courts (albeit rarely) where an intention to include the term (at the time of entering into the contract) is shown by the way the contract has been performed.

1.8 WRITTEN CONTRACTS

Although a contract of employment may be oral, written, or partly oral and partly written, it is advisable in the interests of certainty and to avoid disputes for the contract to be in writing and expressly to set out all the essential terms of the employment. There is no prescribed form for a written contract. An example is set out in **Appendix 1**.

Issues of interpretation or construction of express terms are determined objectively: what would, at the time, objectively have been understood? The subjective views of the parties are technically not relevant (see *The Basildon Academies v Amadi and Fox* (EAT/0342/14)).

One of the practical difficulties that may occur is deciding what documents form part of the contract and give rise to binding terms. For example, is the disciplinary procedure contractual? This may cause problems if an employer wishes to change a policy. Generally speaking, if it is a term of the contract, it cannot be changed unilaterally, ie without the employee's consent (see **1.9**).

In *Harlow v Artemis International Corporation Ltd* [2008] EWHC 1126 (QB), the High Court said that a redundancy policy, referred to in Mr Harlow's contract but contained in a staff handbook, was an express term of the employee's contract, and he was therefore contractually entitled to an enhanced payment under the policy. The policy spoke of 'entitlement', which set it aside from true policies, said the Court. Just because a document is referred to in a contract, though, does not mean it automatically becomes a contractual term. It will depend on the facts. The EAT held in *Worrall v Wilmott Dixon Partnership* (UKEAT/0521/09) that to incorporate a term of a collective agreement into a contract, the term must be brought to the employees' notice or agreed. It said it was not sufficient for the term simply to be in a readily available document, such as a handbook. The EAT held:

> [I]t cannot be right that a party is bound by a contractual document which he has not received merely because it was a document available to him. The fact that a document was available to the claimant does not show that he had notice of its terms or that he had agreed to them.

On the facts, a term in a collective agreement providing for enhanced redundancy pay was held not to have been incorporated into the claimants' contracts, as there was no evidence of it being brought to the claimants' notice or agreed.

Nevertheless, care needs to be taken if an employer wishes to refer the employee to a policy or procedure but wants to remain free to change that policy or procedure at its discretion. (See, eg, clause 17 of the sample Service Contract in **Appendix 1**.) A non-exhaustive list of considerations to take into account when determining whether the provisions of a policy were incorporated into a contract of employment was set out in *Albion Automotive Ltd v Walker* [2002] EWCA Civ 946. That case concerned whether employees who had been made redundant were entitled to enhanced redundancy payments because the employers had made such payments on previous occasions. The employees did not have written contracts of employment. Peter Gibson LJ, with whom the other members of the Court of Appeal agreed, endorsed the submission of the employees' counsel (set out at [15]) that when assessing whether a policy originally produced unilaterally by management had acquired contractual status, a number of considerations are relevant, including the following:

(a)   whether the policy was drawn to the attention of employees;

(b)   whether it was followed without exception for a substantial period;

(c)   the number of occasions on which it was followed;

(d)   whether payments were made automatically;

(e)   whether the nature of communication of the policy supported the inference that the employers intended to be contractually bound;

(f)   whether the policy was adopted by agreement;

(g)   whether employees had a reasonable expectation that the enhanced payment would be made;

(h)   whether terms were incorporated in a written agreement;

(i)   whether the terms were consistently applied.

If a policy is not meant to be contractual, the policy or contract should clearly state this. See also *Bateman v Asda Stores* at **1.4** above.

Note: In *Rock Advertising Ltd v MWB Business Exchange Centres Ltd* [2018] UKSC 24 (a rent arrears case), the Supreme Court upheld the validity of a contractual clause that required any variations to the contract to be in writing and signed. This meant that a subsequent oral agreement to vary the contract was not valid. Employers sometimes try to rely on the assertion that, after a change to a working term or practice is unilaterally introduced, ie without express agreement, it is impliedly accepted if employees continue to work. In *Abrahall v Nottingham City Council* [2018] EWCA Civ 796, the Court of Appeal held that a group of employees, who had continued to work following their employer's imposition of a pay freeze, did not implicitly agree to a variation. The question of what, if any, inferences are to be drawn from continuing to work will depend on the particular circumstances of each case. (See **1.9** below.)

Some of the other *principal* clauses which should be considered for inclusion in a contract and some points to consider when drafting them are outlined below. The desirability of the clauses and their content will vary depending upon whether the employer or employee is being advised.

1.8.1 Duration clause

1.8.1.1 Indefinite contracts

In a contract for an indefinite term, the duration clause should specify the notice period to be given by the employer and the employee to terminate the contract.

In the case of managerial, professional and other senior employees, it may be appropriate to make the notice period fairly long, for example six months to be given by either party. This is mutually beneficial for employer and employee. It means that the employer should not be deprived of the services of a key employee on short notice and it gives the employee a degree of security. It may be worth considering reducing the notice period in the early stages of employment, to allow earlier termination if either the employer finds the employee unsuitable or the employee dislikes the job. For example, only one month's notice might be required to terminate within one year of commencing employment.

For less skilled employees, it may be appropriate to make the notice period shorter, but it must comply with the statutory minimum required by s 86 of the ERA 1996 (see **2.3.3**). In many cases, the contractual notice period would be the statutory minimum.

If there is no express term in the employment contract as to notice, then a term will be implied that the notice be of 'reasonable length'. In *Clark v Fahrenheit 451 (Communications) Ltd* (UKEAT/591/99), the EAT said that determining what is a reasonable length is a mixed question of law and fact and depends on all the circumstances of the case.

Consideration should also be given to whether to include a pay in lieu of notice (PILON) clause in the contract. This may protect an employer from an unlawful damages claim where a contract is terminated without notice (see **2.3.3**). It gives the employer the option of terminating a contract immediately by making a payment in lieu rather than waiting for the employee to work his notice. This can mean that restrictive covenants remain enforceable, because there has been no breach by the employer (see *General Billposting Co Ltd v Atkinson* [1909] AC 118, below at **1.8.7.2**). However, it is important, where a PILON clause is relied on, that an employer makes this clear and unambiguous (see *Société Général, London Branch v Geys*, at **2.3.3**).

1.8.1.2 Fixed (limited)-term contracts

In the case of key, senior employees, the employer may wish to secure the employee's services for a longer period by entering into a fixed-term contract, for example for a period of five years from a specified date. This will bind both the employer and the employee for the fixed period.

If advising the employer on a fixed-term contract, the following matters should also be considered:

(a)   A clause that permits a fixed-term contract to be lawfully ended before expiry is known as a 'break' clause. The 'break' clause may permit the employer, or the employee, or both to have the right to end the contract by giving notice to the other. If a break clause is inserted, it should comply with the statutory minimum notice periods. For example, if the employer is in a strong enough bargaining position, he may wish to insert a clause under which he can terminate the contract at any time by giving the employee three months' notice. This effectively binds the employee for the full fixed term, but allows the employer to bring the contract to an end by giving notice. If there is no express 'break' clause, then the contract cannot be brought to an end by notice. The statutory minimum notice periods are not relevant in that situation.

(c)   Whether or not there is a break clause dealing with notice, it is advisable to insert a 'termination' clause into a fixed-term contract, under which the employer may terminate the contract without notice on the happening of specified events, such as bankruptcy of the employee. This is a more limited form of 'break' clause. In an indefinite contract, such a clause would not be necessary unless the notice period was very long.

(d)   If the employee is a director of the employer company, fixed-term contracts in excess of two years require the approval of the members of the company, otherwise the contract becomes terminable by reasonable notice (Companies Act 2006, ss 188 and 189).

(e)   It is unlawful to treat employees on fixed-term contracts less favourably than permanent employees without objective justification (Fixed-term Employees (Prevention of Less Favourable Treatment) Regulations 2002 (SI 2002/2034)) (see **8.11**).

1.8.1.3   Continuous employment

Section 1 of the ERA 1996 requires the employee to be informed whether any previous employment is continuous with the current employment and the date of commencement of the period of continuous employment (see **1.4.2**). This would normally be dealt with in the duration clause.

1.8.2   Duties and mobility

The duties and mobility clauses are concerned with defining the job which the employee is engaged to perform and the place or places where he can be required to perform it.

1.8.2.1   Job title

The job title or brief description should be stated to comply with s 1 of the ERA 1996. Although s 1 of the Act requires only the job title, the ECJ held in *Helmut Kampelmann and Others v Landschaftsverband Westfalen-Lippe* (Cases C-253/96 to 256/96) [1997] ECR I-6907 that the Proof of Employment Directive requires the employee to be told the nature of his employment, or be given a brief description of his work. The employer may wish to address matters such as job flexibility, or mobility, within a job description.

1.8.2.2   Duties

Defining duties

From the employer's point of view, the employee's duties should be defined widely. The clause should cover all duties that the employer envisages that the employee may be asked to do, and any possible changes in duties. In the case of a senior manager, for example, the contract could require him to carry out 'such duties as the employer may from time to time direct'. However, even if the duties are widely defined, they will be limited to some extent by the job title. For example, in *Hayden v Cowan* [1982] IRLR 314, the applicant's job title was 'divisional contracts surveyor'. The Court of Appeal held that the employer could not therefore transfer him to any job as a quantity surveyor, despite a term in his contract which stated that he was 'required to undertake, at the direction of the company, any and all duties which reasonably fell within [his] capabilities'.

The duties of junior employees would usually be more narrowly defined. However, the employer must still bear in mind any changes he may wish to make to the employee's duties in the future, so that the changes can be made without the employer being in breach of contract.

How widely duties are defined may be relevant in determining if an employee is redundant (see **4.2.3.2**).

Time devoted to duties

From the employer's point of view, senior employees should be required to devote their whole time and attention to their duties. This does not mean that they have to work 24 hours a day, seven days a week, but it does mean that they are not restricted to specific hours. With junior employees, it is usual to specify the hours to be worked but, if appropriate, the contract should specify that the employee can be compelled to work overtime. Note that the Working Time Regulations 1998 regulate the hours that employees can be required to work (see **1.11**).

Consideration should be given as to whether there should be a term prohibiting the employee from taking part in any other business during employment. In the absence of any express term, an employee is only prohibited from working for a competitor during employment, and only then if he possesses information of a confidential nature (see **1.7.2**). The term prohibiting working for any other business will allow the employer, if appropriate, to obtain an injunction against the employee in the event of breach.

Qualifications

If the employee is required to hold a particular qualification (eg to possess a driving licence), or to pass a test or medical examination, this should be made an express term of the contract. The courts will not imply such a term unless it is necessary to make the contract work (*Stubbes v Trower, Still and Keeling* [1987] IRLR 321).

1.8.2.3   Place of work and mobility

Section 1 of the ERA 1996 requires the place or places of work to be stated (see **1.4.2**). A mobility clause defines the area within which the employee can be required to work. From an employer's perspective, such a clause, particularly for a senior employee, should be drawn widely so that the employer is entitled to change the employee's place of work if necessary. It might, for example, require an employee to work anywhere within the UK. This can be very important when considering the question of redundancy (see **4.2.2**). If the employee will, or may, be required to work elsewhere, a mobility clause should be included. Even where the contract does contain a mobility clause, the court has held that the employer must not exercise that clause in such a manner as to breach the implied duty of trust and confidence (*United Bank Ltd v Akhtar* [1989] IRLR 507). In *Kellogg Brown & Root (UK) Ltd v Fitton & Another* (UKEAT/0205/16), the claimants were dismissed following a workplace closure. The closure was announced in April 2015 and the employees were told they would move in July 2015. The claimants had refused to relocate and they were dismissed. The mobility clause provided:

> The location of your employment is _____ but the company may require you to work at a different location including any new office location of the company either in the UK or overseas either on a temporary or permanent basis. You agree to comply with this requirement unless exceptional circumstances prevail.

The employment tribunal concluded that the mobility clause was too wide and uncertain and had been unreasonably invoked by the respondent.

Furthermore, it may be argued that a mobility clause is indirectly discriminatory on the grounds of sex, on the basis that it is likely to be more difficult for women than men to comply with the requirement to move, as a greater proportion of women are secondary earners (see **Chapter 10**).

Where there is no express mobility clause, the court is very unlikely to imply one where the written particulars state the place of work as required under ERA 1996, s 1. Even if there is no place of work clause, the court may still refuse to imply a mobility clause where there is no need to do so to give the contract business efficacy (*Aparau v Iceland Frozen Foods plc* [1996] IRLR 119).

The implication of a term is a matter for the court or tribunal, and whether or not a term is implied depends upon the intention of the parties, as collected from the words of the agreement and the surrounding circumstances. An implied term will usually be made in two situations: first, where it is necessary to give business efficacy to the contract, and, secondly, where the term implied represents the obvious, but unexpressed intention of the parties (see **1.7.3**).

Whether the court or tribunal will imply a mobility clause into the contract of employment will therefore depend upon the particular contractual relationship of the parties. If the tribunal is prepared to imply a mobility clause into the contract, as a rule of thumb, it may be possible to expect an employee to be mobile within a reasonable daily travelling distance from his home (see *Jones v Associated Tunnelling Co Ltd* [1981] IRLR 477, where the Court of Appeal held that since the employer was in business as a contractor working at different sites, the parties must have envisaged a degree of mobility). In *O'Brien v Associated Fire Alarms Ltd* [1968] 3 ITR 183, the Court of Appeal would not imply a term requiring an employee to move 120 miles. The Court of Appeal held that the only term that could be implied into the employee's contract was that he should be employed within a reasonable distance of his home. In *Managers (Holborn) Ltd v Hohne* [1977] IRLR 230, the EAT implied a term requiring the employee to work anywhere in Central London, since the employee was a commuter and the whole of central London was accessible to her by public transport.

1.8.2.4 Employee's viewpoint

The above guidelines are expressed from the point of view of the employer. From the employee's viewpoint, it is desirable to have a narrower definition of duties and mobility.

1.8.3 Remuneration, illness and holidays

In order to comply with s 1 of the ERA 1996, terms relating to pay, sickness and sick pay, holidays and holiday pay must be notified to the employee in the contract or s 1 statement.

In *Judge v Crown Leisure Ltd* [2005] IRLR 823, the Court of Appeal held that in order for there to be a legally binding contractual commitment, there must be certainty as to the contractual commitment entered into. Otherwise, a promise amounts to nothing more than a statement of intention. Therefore, on the facts, an employee was not entitled to rely on a promise made at a Christmas party that he would be paid the same as his colleagues 'eventually'.

1.8.3.1 Pay, benefits and commission

The remuneration clause should specify how the employee's remuneration is calculated (eg hourly wage or annual salary) and when payment is due (eg weekly or monthly). The contract should also specify any fringe benefits to which the employee is entitled (eg a company car or medical insurance).

Legislation on payslips means that all employees (ERA 1996, s 8) should receive itemised payslips showing gross and net amounts, and where different amounts are paid in different ways, this must be shown. These rights will be extended to workers from April 2019.

The NMWA 1998 established the legislative framework for the national minimum wage (NMW).

The National Minimum Wage Regulations 1999, outlining the detail of the NMW, came into force on 1 April 1999 (now the 2015 Regulations (SI 2015/621), which remade the 1999 Regulations and consolidated amendments). The National Minimum Wage (Amendment) Regulations 2016 (SI 2016/68) came into force on 1 April 2016. These set a 'national living wage' for workers aged 25 and over. They raised the previous national minimum wage for those aged 25 and over from £6.70 to £7.20 per hour, which was a 10.8% increase and the largest uplift since 2001. The National Minimum Wage (Amendment) Regulations 2018 (SI 2018/455) increased the minimum wage rates in April 2018.

The 2016 Regulations:

(a)   set a rate for the national living wage for those aged 25 and over (£7.83 from 1 April 2018);

(b)   set a rate for the NMW for those aged 21 and over (£7.38 from 1 April 2018);

(c)   set modified rates for 18–20-year-olds (£5.90 from 1 April 2018);

(d)   provided that workers aged below 18 who have ceased to be of compulsory school age qualify for the NMW (£4.20 for such workers from 1 April 2018);

(e)   exempt non-employed apprentices under 26 in the first year of their apprenticeship. Persons who are workers on specified government schemes at pre-apprenticeship level will not be entitled to the NMW, whether they are employed by the employer or not;

(f)   set rates for employed apprentices under the age of 19, or 19 or above in their first year of apprenticeship (£3.70 from 1 April 2018);

(g)   set the pay reference period for averaging NMW pay at a maximum of one month;

(h)   determined how to calculate hours worked for which the NMW is payable;

(i)   required employers to issue a statement of the NMW to workers; and

(j)   required employers to keep records.

The Government updated its guidance on the NMW in April 2017 (<www.gov.uk/government/uploads/system/uploads/attachment_data/file/605397/nmw-nlw-calculating-minimum-wage-guidance.pdf>).

It is a useful document but readers should always ensure that they consider up-to-date case law. The detail is beyond the scope of this book but the following issues are examples of things to consider:

(a)   The process for determining whether the NMW has been paid is set out in reg 7. Part 4 sets out how to determine which payments qualify as remuneration, and Part 5 sets out how to calculate the hours worked for the purposes of the calculation.

(b)   The number of hours that the worker has worked during the reference period is calculated differently depending on the type of work done by the worker.

(c)   On-call or standby time outside normal working hours may be working time.

(d)   The Government Guidance document states that:

The hours of work that count for minimum wage purposes for time and salaried work includes any time when a worker is:

-    at the workplace working:
    -    For time work this will exclude the length of the rest breaks they take and any payment for these
    -    For salaried work, rest breaks may count for minimum wage purposes if provided for by the worker's contract [so, for example, if someone is employed for 40 hours per week and that includes his lunch break, the employee is entitled to count lunch into the number of hours worked per week]
    -    For both time and salaried work, time spent working may include time when the worker is asleep (see [regs 27 and 32])

- required to be available for work either on standby or on-call at or near their workplace – however there is an exception if the worker is permitted to sleep during this time and is provided with suitable sleeping facilities
- time spent travelling on business

(e) Regulation 10 sets out what payments are and are not permitted to count towards the NMW (eg tips, commission).

Sleeping time

Much of the case law around the NWM has concentrated on on-call hours and time when a worker is permitted to sleep. Under the NMW legislation, salaried hours workers and time work workers who are 'on call' are regarded as working when they are available at or near a place of work for the purpose of doing work and are required to be available for such work, unless they are at home. However, when they are provided with suitable facilities for sleeping, only time when they are awake for the purposes of working is treated as time work or salaried work.

In the conjoined cases of *Focus Care Agency Ltd v Roberts, Frudd v The Partington Group Ltd and Royal Mencap Society v Tomlinson-Blake* (UKEAT/0143/16), the President of the EAT considered all of the recent appellate case law on the question whether employees who sleep in, in order to carry out duties if required, engage in 'time work' for the full duration of the night shift or whether they are only entitled to the NMW when they are awake and carrying out relevant duties. She considered and rejected a challenge to the approach taken in a number of the earlier decisions on this issue, including *British Nursing Association (BNA) v Inland Revenue* [2002] IRLR 480 and *Scottbridge Construction Ltd v Wright* [2003] IRLR 21. She held that 'a multifactorial evaluation is required. No single factor is determinative and the relevance and weight of particular factors will vary with and depend on the context and circumstances of the particular case.'

In the BNA case, the Court of Appeal held that nurses providing an overnight telephone service from home were 'working' throughout their shifts so that all their work amounted to time work within reg 30 (as amended), even though they could do what they wished between calls. Regulation 32 (as amended), which deems certain 'on-call' work to be time work, therefore had no application on the facts of the case. The Court observed that:

> No one would say that an employee sitting at the employer's premises during the day waiting for phone calls was only working, in the sense of only being entitled to be remunerated, during the periods when he or she was actually on the phone. Exactly the same consideration seems to me to apply if the employer chooses to operate the very same service during the night-time, not by bringing the employees into his office (which would no doubt impose substantial overhead costs on the employer and lead to significant difficulties of recruitment), but by diverting calls from the central switchboard to employees sitting waiting at home. It was indeed as a continuation of the day-time service that the employer presented the night-time service to his employees and recruited them for that purpose.

The decision was applied by the EAT in *Burrow Down Support Services Ltd v Rossiter* [2008] ICR 1172 (decided under the amended Regulations).

In *South Manchester Abbeyfield Society v Hopkins and Woodworth* [2011] IRLR 300, the EAT concluded that case law showed a 'clear dichotomy' between:

- cases where an employee is working merely by being present at the employer's premises (eg a night watchman) whether or not provided with sleeping accommodation (in which case sleeping time will count towards the NMW under the definition of time work in reg 26/30); and
- cases where the employee is provided with sleeping accommodation and is simply on call (in which case, because of the terms of reg 27/32, only those hours spent awake for the purpose of working will count in the calculation of the NMW).

The sheltered accommodation workers who were required to be on call at night were held to fall within reg 27, so that only hours spent awake for the purpose of working were held to count for the purpose of the NMW.

In *Wray v JW Lees & Co (Brewers)* [2012] ICR 43, a pub manager was required to reside and sleep at the pub premises simply to deal with any emergencies during the night, such as break-ins. It was held that because sleeping facilities were provided, the case fell within reg 27, so that only time spent awake dealing with such an emergency counted.

In the *Royal Mencap Society* case, the EAT had upheld the tribunal's finding that a care worker who provided care for two vulnerable adults with local authority assessed care plans, specifying 24-hour support, was working for the entirety of her sleep-in shifts. As a result of the EAT's decision, the Government changed its guidance to require all employers to pay the NMW for sleep-in shifts. This has had an enormous impact on social care providers and local authorities. The Government also put in place a social care compliance scheme (SCCS) to assist employers with back pay liabilities.

The EAT's decision was overturned by the Court of Appeal in *Royal Mencap Society v Tomlinson-Blake* [2018] EWCA Civ 1641, which held that such carers were not on call and were only entitled to have sleep-in hours counted for minimum wage purposes when they are, and are required to be, awake for the purpose of performing some specific activity. Underhill LJ reviewed all the previous authorities and held that at least one of them (*Burrow Down*) was wrongly decided. He rejected the multifactorial approach suggested by the EAT and held (at [43]) that since the sleep-in exception (1999 Regulations, regs 15, 16; 2015 Regulations, regs 32, 37) only applies when a worker is 'available for work' and not in cases where the worker is actually working, while it is first necessary to ascertain into which of these two categories a worker who is 'sleeping in' falls, that is an 'unnecessarily elaborate approach' as 'the self-evident intention of the relevant provisions' is to deal comprehensively with the position of sleep-in workers: the draftsperson clearly regarded them as being 'available for work rather than actually working'.

In reaching this conclusion, Underhill LJ distinguished a number of previous cases (*BNA*, *Scottbridge*). He found that if a worker is expected to sleep, the time must fall into the 'available for work' provisions. For Underhill LJ, a night watchman falls comfortably on the 'actual work' side of the line. The decision has been welcomed in some quarters and criticised in others: care providers concerned about potentially vast back pay liabilities have welcomed it; those sleep-in carers who provide already relatively low paid work will be less pleased. Unison, which supported Tomlinson-Blake's case, has lodged an application for permission to appeal to the Supreme Court. If accepted, this is likely to be heard in late 2019. Despite the Court of Appeal's ruling, the Government is continuing with the SCCS.

Regulations 27 and 32 only become relevant if the tribunal decides that the worker is not working by being present during the period in question.

Note: Regulation 57(3) contains an exemption for family workers. This exemption is being challenged on the basis that it amounts to indirect sex discrimination: see *Puthenveetil v Alexander and Another* (UKEAT/0407/17).

Penalties

With effect from 6 April 2009, with the introduction of the Employment Act 2008, employers have to pay all arrears at the current rate where these are higher than the rate that applied when the underpayment was made. In addition, if an HMRC investigation finds that an employer has underpaid workers, notices of underpayment will require the employer to pay a financial penalty to the Secretary of State within 28 days of service. The penalty is set at 100% of the total underpayment of the NMW. The minimum penalty payable is £100 and the maximum penalty is £20,000 per worker. If the employer complies with the notice within 14 days of its service, the financial penalty will be reduced by 50%. The 2008 Act also gives some new powers to help HMRC inspectors carry out their investigations.

For employers who refuse to cooperate with the above civil regime, criminal proceedings are possible. The fine on conviction for each offence is up to £5,000 (level 5) in the magistrates' court, or an unlimited fine in the Crown Court. The Employment Act 2008 also gives HMRC the power to use the search and seize powers in the Police and Criminal Evidence Act 1984 when investigating criminal offences under the NMWA 1998. The Government has started publishing a list 'naming and shaming' employers who fail to pay workers the NMW. In the first list, published in February 2017, 360 employers who had underpaid a total of 15,520 workers by a total of £995,233 were named. The sectors with the most offenders were retail, hospitality and hairdressing. HMRC has issued penalties in the region of £800,000 as well.

Note: The Small Business, Enterprise and Employment Act 2015 increased the maximum fine to £20,000, and for this to be on a 'per worker' (rather than per employer) basis. The Act came into force on 26 May 2015).

1.8.3.2 Deductions

If deductions are to be made from salary or wages, for example, to repay loans from the employer or, in the case of employees who handle money, to recoup any shortages, the contract should give the employer the right to make such deductions. This is to comply with the requirements of the ERA 1996 and is dealt with in more detail at **1.11**.

1.8.3.3 Sick pay

The contract should state whether the employer pays sick pay (other than statutory sick pay (SSP)). If sick pay is paid, the contract should state the period for which it is payable, how much is payable and whether SSP is deducted in calculating it. An employee who is off sick for a period of more than three consecutive days is entitled to receive SSP from his employer.

This clause should also specify that the employer is entitled to require the employee to provide a medical certificate if absent for more than, say, seven days.

With effect from 6 April 2018, the rate of SSP is £92.05, which is payable for a maximum period of 28 weeks in any three years.

The relationship between holidays and sickness is considered at **1.12.5**.

The Government abolished employers' ability to recover payments of SSP made to their employees on 6 April 2014. This means that now employers pay SSP. The money the Government saves is to be used to set up Health Advisory Centres, aimed at getting employees who are on long-term sick leave back to work. The Fitness for Work Service will provide an occupational health assessment, and will give advice to employees, employers and GPs. Where an employee has been absent from work for four weeks, or is expected to be so absent, due to sickness, he should normally be referred by his GP for an assessment. Following assessment, a Return to Work Plan will be issued. See <fitforwork.org>.

1.8.3.4 Holidays and holiday pay

The clause should specify how many days paid holiday the employee is entitled to each year and when it can be taken. Paid holiday can originate from two different sources: statute and contract. In general, statute lays down minimums, which can be topped up by contract. Note that minimum paid annual leave in the UK is now regulated by the Working Time Regulations 1998 (see **1.12**). The Working Time Directive (93/104) lays down a minimum of four weeks' paid leave. The 1998 Regulations provide an additional minimum for UK workers of 1.6 weeks. The ECJ held in *Lock v British Gas Trading Ltd* (Case C-539/12) that an employee should receive 'normal pay' during his UK statutory annual leave – that is, not limited to bare pay but including compensation for allowances and commission which the employee would have received had he been working during leave (see **1.12.5.3**).

1.8.4 Pension

The contract should specify whether or not the employer has an occupational pension scheme which the employee is entitled to join. An employee cannot be compelled to join an occupational pension scheme and is entitled to enter into a personal pension scheme instead.

If the employer has an occupational pension scheme, there will usually be a contracting out certificate in force under the Pension Schemes Act 1993. If there is no contracting out certificate in force, the employee will be entitled to a second State pension under the Second State Pension Scheme (S2P). An employee who is contracted out of S2P pays lower National Insurance contributions.

Employers must, unless exempt (eg employing fewer than five employees, or offering an occupational pension that all staff can join within a year of starting work), give their employees access to a stakeholder pension scheme.

Since 1 October 2012, there has been a requirement to enrol employees automatically in a pension scheme, and the employer will be obliged to contribute. The new employer duties are being introduced over six years. Employers employing 50 or more employees are now obliged to auto-enrol their employees, and employers with fewer than 50 employees have been given staging dates between 1 June 2015 and 1 April 2017. Further details may be found at <www.pensionsadvisoryservice.org.uk>.

1.8.5 Inventions and discoveries

In the case of employees who are likely to make discoveries or inventions, for example senior scientific and technical employees, the employer should ensure that the contract provides that any invention or discovery made in the course of employment belongs to the employer.

Such a clause is subject to the provisions of the Patents Act 1977 and the Copyright, Designs and Patents Act 1988. Details of these Acts are beyond the scope of this book but the basic rule is that inventions made in the course of employment belong to the employer. Other inventions belong to the employee and this cannot be varied by agreement. Even if the invention is made in the course of employment, the employee may be entitled to an award of compensation if the invention is of outstanding benefit to the employer.

1.8.6 Confidentiality

1.8.6.1 During employment

During employment, it is an implied term that an employee shall not reveal any confidential information (*Faccenda Chicken Ltd v Fowler* [1986] 1 All ER 617 – see **1.7.2.8**). Although there is an implied term that the employee shall not reveal any confidential information, it is advisable, in the case of employees who have access to confidential information, to insert an express term making it clear that they may not reveal such information during employment. The clause may also state what information the employer regards as confidential, though mundane information or information already in the public domain cannot be made confidential even by an express clause. The purpose of this clause is to draw the employee's attention to the duty of confidentiality and so to prevent the disclosure of such information.

1.8.6.2 After employment

After employment, only trade secrets and equivalent highly confidential information are protected by the implied term (see *Faccenda Chicken Ltd v Fowler*, **1.8.6.1** above). In *Faccenda Chicken*, the Court of Appeal set out a number of factors to be taken into account to determine whether particular information falls within the category that ought not to be disclosed after the employment has ended (applied recently in *Vestergaard Frandsen Als and Others v Bestnet Europe Ltd and Others* [2009] EWHC 657 (Ch)):

(a) What was the nature of the employment?

(b) What was the nature of the information?

(c) Did the employer tell the employee that he regarded the information as confidential?

(d) Could the information be easily isolated from the other information which the employee was free to use?

(See too the new Trade Secrets Directive adopted on 27 May 2016 and **1.8.7.1** below.)

On the facts of *Faccenda Chicken Ltd*, although Mr Fowler's knowledge of customers, sales and prices information was confidential and therefore could not be used or even memorised deliberately during employment, it was not confidential information equivalent to a trade secret, and thus his employer was not entitled to an injunction restraining the former employee from using information which he had generally acquired in his employment. If, however, Mr Fowler had made a copy of the list of customers or deliberately memorised it during his employment, that would amount to a breach of the duty of fidelity and the employer would have been able to restrain him from using that information in a competing business after the employment had ended (see, eg, *Bullivant v Ellis* [1987] ICR 464 and *Robb v Green* above – see **1.7.2.7**)

In *Stephenson Ltd v Mandy* [2000] IRLR 233, the High Court considered whether a distinction could be made between information which had been 'deliberately learned' and that which was 'innocently carried in the head'. The court said such a distinction could not be definitive of what information could be legitimately protected by means of a restrictive covenant. In that case, a list of clients was held to be part of information the employer was entitled to protect, even though some of it was in the employee's head 'innocently'. See too *Force India Formula One Team Ltd v Aerolab Srl and Another* [2013] EWCA Civ 780.

In order to prevent an employee taking up a position where he may use such information, a restraint of trade clause (see **1.8.7.1**) should also be included.

The High Court held in *Eurasion Natural Resources Corporation Ltd v Judge* [2014] EWHC 3556 (QB) that the implied duty of confidentiality did not require the ex-employee to 'deliver up' the highly confidential to the former employer. However, in *Arthur J Gallagher Services (UK) Ltd and Others v Skriptchenko and Others* [2016] EWHC 603 (QB), the High Court granted an application for permission to inspect the defendant's electronic devices and computer and for the deletion of any confidential information found on them.

The advent of social media has meant that what is confidential information is not as clear-cut as it once was. For example, if an employee, with his employer's implied or express knowledge, uses Facebook, or Twitter or LinkedIn to communicate with customers or clients, these can be commercially valuable tools. Do those contacts belong to the employer or to the employee? Often, employees use their work e-mail addresses for personal and work purposes – who 'owns' their contacts lists? Employers need to have clear policies regarding these issues. In a recent case, *Whitmar Publications Ltd v Gamage* [2013] EWHC 1881 (Ch), the court issued an interim injunction to Whitmar, requiring its three employees to give Whitmar 'exclusive access, management and control' of four LinkedIn groups, which one of the employees (Wright) had had responsibility for operating in her role at Whitmar. The High Court held that Wright had been 'responsible for dealing with the LinkedIn groups as part of her employment duties at Whitmar', and that they had been 'operated for Whitmar's benefit and promoted its business' using the company's computers. The information in these accounts had been used when the new company set up by the employees had issued a press release, in breach of the duty of good faith.

Data protection law (see **Chapter 14**) may now provide additional protection for employers against employees leaving and taking confidential information with them. The UK's Information Commissioner's Office (ICO) announced in June 2016 that it had brought an enforcement action under s 55 of the Data Protection Act 1998 (now s 149 of the 2018 Act) against an individual who had left to join a competitor and taken a list of over 900 clients with him, including their purchase history and other commercial data. Section 55 makes it an offence for a person to knowingly or recklessly obtain or disclose personal data without the consent of the data controller. The individual concerned pleaded guilty to an offence under s 55 and was fined £300 and ordered to pay just over £400 in costs. While in most cases it will not be possible for an employer to bring a private prosecution itself against a former employee, it can report it to the ICO which has power to investigate and prosecute. A criminal record may serve as a more effective deterrent to an employee than the risk of civil injunction proceedings.

While it is well established that an employer cannot enforce restrictive covenants contained in the contract of employment if he is in repudiatory breach (see *General Billposting Company Ltd v Atkinson* [1909] AC 118 and **1.8.7.5**), it seems likely that any express term relating to confidentiality will continue notwithstanding any repudiation of the contract by the employer and that, in the absence of an express provision, the implied duty will, in any event, continue. Nevertheless, the issue is not beyond doubt (*Campbell v Frisbee* [2003] ICR 141).

1.8.7   Restrictive covenants

In order to prevent unfair competition after employment ends, it is advisable for an employer, where it is possible, to insert a restrictive covenant into the employee's contract.

In the absence of an effective restrictive covenant, an ex-employee may compete with the ex-employer, solicit the former customers of the ex-employer and poach its staff.

1.8.7.1   Restraint of trade

A restrictive covenant restraining an ex-employee from working in a competing business or soliciting ex-customers is prima facie void as being in restraint of trade. An employer is not entitled to protect himself against competition as such; he must have an interest to protect.

In order for a restrictive covenant to be enforceable:

(a)   the employer must have a legitimate business interest to protect. Legitimate business interests are:

    (i)   trade secrets or other highly confidential information which 'if disclosed to a competitor, would be liable to cause real or significant damage to the owner of the secret which the owner had tried to limit dissemination of' (*Lansing Linde Ltd v Kerr* [1991] 1 All ER 418, CA). Readers should note that the Trade Secrets (Enforcement, etc) Regulations 2018 (SI 2018/597) came into force on 9 June 2018 and define trade secrets as information which '(a) is secret in the sense that it is not generally known among, or readily accessible to, persons within the circles that normally deal with the kind of information in question, (b) has commercial value ..., and (c) has been subject to reasonable steps ... to keep it secret';

    (ii)   trade connections, eg employers' relationships with their customers and clients (goodwill). The employer will have to demonstrate that a breach would result in actual or potential harm to the employer's business (see eg *Jack Allen (Sales and Service) Ltd v Smith* [1999] IRLR 19);

    (iii)   the employer's interest in maintaining a stable and trained workforce (see eg *Dawnay, Day & Co Ltd v Braconier d'Alphen & Others* [1997] IRLR 442).

A restrictive covenant can be valid only if imposed on a person who has such information, for example a senior technical employee with knowledge of trade secrets, or a manager or salesperson who has knowledge of trade connections.

In *Thomas v Far plc* [2007] EWCA Civ 118, the Court of Appeal held that an employer was entitled to seek to protect its pricing and financial information by way of a non-compete clause in the contract (see **1.8.7.2**).

(b) the restraint must also be reasonable in time and area, and it must be no wider than necessary to protect the employer's business interest (ie, the activity prohibited must be no wider than necessary; see **1.8.7.2**).

A restrictive covenant will not be enforced unless its terms are sufficiently clear.

In *Kynixa* (see above at **1.7.2.4**) the High Court upheld terms preventing two employees from competing with their employer ('*in any business competing with the Business*'); from soliciting customers of the employer ('*any person who is, or has been at any time, in the previous 6 months, a customer of the Business*'); and from poaching employees for a period of 12 months ('*solicit or entice away or endeavour to solicit or entice away any consultant, director or employee of the Group engaged in the Business*').

The Court held that the employer

> had a legitimate interest in seeking to prevent the solicitation of its customers. Equally it had a legitimate interest in seeking to prevent solicitation of [employees]. Given the nature of its business, the competitive nature of the market in which it operated, the fact that the … [Defendants] were well known to the customers of the Claimant and the fact that with some customers, at least, arrangements for the provision of services by the Claimant between … it and the customer would remain in place for a fixed period time (measured often in two year periods) but then be reviewed … a restraint lasting twelve months was entirely reasonable. [The Court] also had regard to the fact that the … Defendants had a choice about whether or not to enter the shareholder agreement [where the terms were contained] and in each case they chose to do so for (potentially) substantial gain …

The Court also held that the *anti-competition clause was justified*. The defendants were very senior employees and were privy to confidential information which the claimant was justified in seeking to protect.

1.8.7.2 Contents of the clause

Restrictive covenants can cover competition by the ex-employee after the employment ends, the soliciting of (or dealing with) former customers and clients, and also the poaching of former employees. The basic rules set out above apply to all these areas.

Non-competition

The typical non-competition clause prohibits the employee, for a specified number of months or years after the end of the employment, from carrying on or being associated with the business in which the employer is engaged, within a specified number of miles of the employer's premises at which the employee was employed.

The clause must be no wider than is necessary to protect the employer's business:

(a) The business activity from which the employee is barred must be no wider than the business in which he was employed. In *Scully UK Ltd v Lee* [1998] IRLR 259, the Court of Appeal refused to grant an injunction enforcing a covenant prohibiting an ex-employee from dealing with companies which were not in direct competition with the former employer. Mr Lee worked as a technical sales engineer for Scully, who were involved in the design and manufacture of systems for use in the oil and gas industry. In January 1997, he resigned from Scully and went to work as a sales manager for a company concerned with the supply of fuel distribution products and gauges. The Court of Appeal struck down a clause which prohibited the ex-employee from having any involvement in any business dealing with the type of equipment provided by Scully, on grounds that it extended to non-competing businesses (ie, businesses not involved in the oil and gas industry) and was therefore wider than necessary to protect their legitimate interests in customer connections and confidential information.

(b)   A time restraint in excess of one year can usually be justified only in exceptional circumstances. One year may be too long in some cases, especially if the employer's trade connections are subject to rapid change.

(c)   The area within which the ex-employee is barred from competing must be reasonable. It must not be wider than the area within which the employer did business.

In *Hollis & Co v Stocks* [2000] IRLR 712, a covenant restraining a solicitor from working (as a solicitor) within a 10-mile radius of a small firm of solicitors in Nottinghamshire for a period of one year was held to be enforceable; and in *Corporate Express Ltd v Day* [2004] EWHC 2943 (QB), the court upheld a six-month ban on working for competitors because there was a real risk that the employee would use her knowledge to benefit her new employer.

The Court of Appeal held in *Thomas v Far plc* (see **1.8.7.1**) that a clause in the contract of a managing director of a firm of insurance brokers, which prevented him from competing with the company for 12 months, was enforceable. The employee had argued on appeal that the non-solicitation and confidentiality clauses in the managing director's contract adequately protected the employer and that the non-compete clause was unnecessary. The Court of Appeal held that because of the problems of differentiating between confidential and non-confidential information, and the fact that the solicitation of clients was unlikely to be done by the managing director himself, the non-compete clause was necessary to protect the legitimate business interest. It was accepted, on the facts, that the 12-month non-compete clause did not prevent Mr Thomas from acting as an insurance broker in sectors other than social housing, and since most insurance policies in the social housing sector were for longer than 12 months, the 12-month period was reasonable.

In *Christie Owen & Davies v Walton* [2008] CSOH 37, the Court of Session upheld a non-compete clause that prevented the employee from working for a competitor in the care sector in any capacity, because the employee had been 'materially involved' in the business of the former employer (ie had knowledge of the former employer's client base and potential client base).

It is important to remember to review contracts when employees are promoted. In *PAT Systems v Neilly* [2012] EWHC 2609 (QB), the High Court refused to enforce a 12-month non-compete clause which had been entered into when the employee started employment in a junior role. The court said that the clause had to be assessed at the time it was entered into – because of the employee's very junior role, it was not reasonable to have a 12-month non-complete covenant, so it was unenforceable from the outset, and the promotion could not, absent express agreement to the clause from the employee, make it enforceable.

The High Court also expressed the provisional view that a 12-month non-compete clause was too long on the facts, having regard to the nature of the market in which the claimant operated and the transparent market in which the employer operated.

For a recent case on a non-compete clause, see *Tillman v Egon Zehnder Ltd* [2017] EWCA Civ 1054, which yet again emphasises the need for careful drafting of restrictive covenants.

Non-solicitation

The non-solicitation clause will prohibit the employee from seeking business from persons who were customers of the employer within a specified period prior to the employee leaving employment. Such a clause is more likely to be upheld if it is restricted to those customers with whom the employee has had personal contact during a specified period before termination (see, eg, *WRN Ltd v Ayris* [2008] EWHC 1080 (QB) where the term was held to be too wide because it was not restricted to customers with whom the employee had actually dealt). The clause should be no wider than necessary to protect the employer's business. Again, the clause is more likely to be upheld if it is restricted to those persons who were the employer's customers within a comparatively short time prior to the employee leaving. What is reasonable will depend on the nature of the business, eg how often customers come and go.

In *Associated Foreign Exchange Ltd v International Foreign Exchange (UK) Ltd* [2010] EWHC 1178 (Ch) the High Court held that there was insufficient evidence that a non-solicitation restriction of 12 months went no further than was reasonably necessary to protect an employer's legitimate business interests. The contract also contained a six-month non-dealing clause. The High Court refused to grant an injunction to prevent an ex-employee soliciting customers. It said that the non-dealing clause gave the employer adequate protection because the employee in question was not particularly senior and had not played a key part in building up new business for AFEX. Such protection as was sought by the non-solicitation clause would only be appropriate where a business could show that building up a relationship with its potential customers was a long and difficult process involving significant investment in time and money.

In *Coppage & Another v Safetynet Security Ltd* [2013] EWCA Civ 1176, the Court of Appeal upheld a six-month non-solicitation clause which prevented a director approaching anyone who had been a customer of the employer during the director's four-year term of employment. Although not restricted to customers with whom the employee had had personal contact, it was, in the court's opinion, reasonable because the term was 'only' six months and it was a non-solicitation clause and not a non-competition clause. However, in *Bartholomews Agri Food Ltd v Thornton* [2016] EWHC 648 (QB), the High Court refused to award an injunction in a case where the clause was not restricted to customers with whom the employee had been in contact.

Non-poaching

A non-poaching clause will prevent the employee from persuading other employees to go with him to a new employer. Such clauses are probably best restricted to senior employees known to the employee, where the employer has a legitimate interest to protect in the stability of its workforce (see, eg, *TSC Europe (UK) Ltd v Massey* [1999] IRLR 22 and, more recently, *UBS Wealth Management (UK) Ltd v Vesta Wealth LLP and Others* [2008] EWHC 1974 (QB)). Any clause will need to consider how long it will take for an employee's influence to end.

In deciding whether to grant an injunction to prevent an employee from poaching other employees, courts apply a 'balance of convenience test' (see **2.5.2**). For a recent decision on how the balance of convenience test is applied on an interim injunction application invoking the impact of the movements of senior employees on more junior employees left behind, see *Willis v Jardine Lloyd Thompson Group plc* [2015] AC 9301548.

Non-dealing

A non-dealing clause will prevent the employee from dealing with clients even if the clients approach the employee.

In *Allan Janes LLP v Johal* [2006] EWHC 286 (Ch), the High Court upheld a non-dealing covenant prohibiting a senior solicitor from dealing with the firm's clients (in the 12 months before termination) for a period of one year post termination.

In *Beckett Investment Management Group Limited v Hall* [2007] EWCA Civ 613, the Court of Appeal upheld a 12-month non-dealing clause imposed by a holding company, even though on a literal interpretation of the clause the employees were not in breach. Beckett Investment Management Group Ltd (BIMG) was the holding company within a group of companies that provided financial advice. BIMG did not itself provide direct financial advice. This was done by a subsidiary, Beckett Financial Services Ltd (BFS). Hall and Yadev, who were both senior employees employed by BIMG but based at BFS's offices, left to start up their own competing business. Their contracts contained post-termination restrictions preventing them from providing financial advice of a type provided by the Company (defined as BIMG) to certain clients. Hall and Yadev continued to deal with BFS's clients and argued that the non-dealing restriction was unenforceable. The Court of Appeal said that the phrase the business of 'the Company' should be construed as the business undertaken by the subsidiaries. In terms of the length of the restriction, the Court said that 12 months was reasonable having regard to the nature of the financial services business, the seniority of Hall and Yadev, and evidence of an industry standard of 12 months. However, the Court said that a period longer than 12 months would have been unreasonable and unenforceable.

In this case, the clause was trying to protect the business for which the employees were actually working. It is important when drafting such restrictions to ensure that these clauses not only reflect the employee's actual circumstances, but also properly protect the actual business in which they are working.

Enforcement

If the clause is in restraint of trade, either because the employer has no interest to protect or because it is drafted too widely and therefore is unreasonable in time or area, it is void and hence unenforceable.

The 'blue pencil' test

If a clause is drafted too widely and is found to be in restraint of trade, the court may be able to apply the 'blue pencil' test to sever that part of the clause that is too wide and leave the remainder as an enforceable clause. Therefore, if drafting a restrictive covenant, draft for severance so that if one part of a clause is found to be void it can be severed, leaving the remainder valid. The court must be able to sever the offending part by striking a 'blue pencil' through it. The court cannot rewrite the clause (eg by substituting a shorter time-limit). The Court of Appeal in *Scully UK Ltd v Lee* (see above) stated that severance of part of a covenant was permissible only in cases where the obligation to be severed was truly a separate obligation to that to be enforced. If the obligations were in any way interdependent, then severance would not be permitted.

The Court of Appeal confirmed a three-stage approach in *Beckett Investment Management Ltd v Hall* [2007] EWCA Civ 613:

(a)   Can the provision be removed without needing to modify the wording of the other terms?

(b)   Are the remaining terms supported by adequate consideration?

(c)   Does the removal change the character of the contract so that it becomes 'not the sort of contract that the parties entered into at all'?

In *Corporate Express Ltd v Day* [2004] EWHC 2943 (QB), the High Court upheld a restrictive covenant for a senior manager imposing a six-month ban in the post-employment soliciting of clients and the working for 10 named competitors. In *TFS Derivatives Ltd v Morgan* [2005] IRLR 246, the EAT considered a restrictive covenant involving a City equity broker. It concerned the enforceability of a fairly wide-ranging covenant which did not allow the broker for a period of six months following termination of employment to 'undertake, carry on or be employed, engaged or interested in any capacity in either any business which is competitive with *or similar to* a relevant business within the territory, or any business an objective or anticipated result of which is to compete with a relevant business within the territory' (emphasis added). Mrs Justice Cox stated that, if there is ambiguity and two possible constructions, rather than holding that the covenant is an unreasonable restraint of trade, the court should construe it on the basis that the parties are to be deemed to have intended their bargain to be lawful. In this case, rather than holding that the covenant was too wide to be reasonable, she severed the words 'or similar to'.

Drafting a series of cumulative restrictions leaving the court to decide where the line should be drawn (eg restraint for three years, followed by restraint for two years, followed by restraint for one year) is very likely to be void for uncertainty and is not recommended. Particular care needs to be taken where there is a transfer of an undertaking (see **7.4.1.1**).

In *Prophet Plc v Huggett* [2014] EWCA Civ 1013, the Court of Appeal, while holding that the wording of a non-compete clause was 'absurd', reiterated that while a court is able to 'blue pencil' (delete) bits of covenants to make them enforceable, it cannot add new words to make effective a provision that is not. While it might be possible to construe an ambiguous covenant in a way that made it enforceable, where the clause was not ambiguous but plain wrong and ineffective, as here, it could not be rescued.

For a recent case where a restrictive covenant was held to be unenforceable on the basis that it was too wide, see *Bartholomews Agri Food Ltd v Thornton* [2016] EWHC 648 (QB). For a case where a covenant was held to be properly drafted and enforceable, see *Pickwell and Nicholls v Pro Cam CP Ltd* [2016] EWHC 1304 (QB).

Mode of enforcement

The employer's remedy when an employee is in breach of an effective restrictive covenant will be an injunction where damages are not an adequate remedy, that is, an injunction to prevent the ex-employee from carrying on a competing business, soliciting customers or poaching staff, whichever is appropriate. The employer may also claim damages if he has suffered pecuniary loss. The employee can be compelled to hand over, for example, copies of lists of customers and details of trade secrets in his possession. See *Roger Bullivant Ltd v Ellis* (at **1.8.6.2** above) and, more recently, *UBS Wealth Management (UK) Ltd v Vestra Wealth LLP* (above), where a business was granted a 'springboard' injunction to prevent a rival business, its founder and four defecting employees from doing business with and attempting to poach clients and other staff. See, most recently, *CEF Holdings Ltd and Another v Mundey and Others* [2012] EWHC 1524 (QB), where the High Court determined a number of issues arising out of an employer's attempts to stop its former employees setting up a rival company. The case set out some important principles in relation to without notice injunctions and the obligation of full and frank disclosure. The court also held that a number of restrictive covenants were too wide and invalid or, in some cases, unnecessary.

Damages awards can be a vexed issue. In *Marathon Asset Management LLP v Seddon & Bridgeman* [2017] EWHC 300 (Comm), the High Court considered the approach to assessing damages in a claim against two former employees who had unlawfully removed approximately 40,000 documents when they resigned to set up a competing business. The court found that the defendants had breached their duties of confidence but had only made very limited use of the documents. Marathon's case was that it did not matter what use was actually made of any of the files or that no loss had been shown: the defendants unlawfully took its confidential information and must pay for the value of what they took. It claimed that £15 million was the appropriate value to be placed on an award of damages. In a 74-page judgment following a nine-day High Court trial, involving factual and expert evidence and 'citation of case law and legal scholarship filling no fewer than 11 volumes', Marathon's arguments were rejected and nominal damages of only £1 were awarded against each of the two defendants. The misuse of confidential information had neither caused Marathon to suffer any financial loss nor resulted in the defendants making any financial gain, so it was hard to see how Marathon could be entitled to any remedy other than an award of nominal damages. It was only if and to the extent that any use was actually made of any of the files that it might be possible to show that any significant benefit was obtained by the defendants from wrongful use of the confidential information.

Effect of wrongful dismissal

If the contract terminates in circumstances where neither party is in breach of contract, or where the employee is rightfully dismissed for his own breach, the restrictive covenant can be enforced by the employer provided it is not void as being in restraint of trade.

However, the House of Lords held in *General Billposting Company Ltd v Atkinson* [1909] AC 118, that an otherwise valid restrictive covenant cannot be enforced if the employee has been wrongfully dismissed by the employer.

Thus, according to *Billposting*, where there is a repudiatory breach of contract by the employer, the employee is released from the obligations under the covenant.

Whilst *Billposting* remains good law, some judges have expressed reservations as to the correctness of the principle (see eg *Rock Refrigeration Ltd v Jones* [1996] IRLR 675). Support for the view that confidentiality covenants can survive wrongful dismissal can be found in *Campbell v Frisbee* [2003] ICR 141.

Note that where the contract expressly provides that payment may be made in lieu of notice, the employer may dismiss the employee without proper notice and still be able to enforce any restrictive covenants (provided they are otherwise reasonable). This is because the employer is not then in breach of contract. This is the principal reason for the inclusion of a pay in lieu of notice provision (see **2.3.3**).

Employee's viewpoint

Ideally, an employee would want to avoid restrictive covenants, or limit them so as not to prejudice his ability to change employment. However, it may be in the employee's interest to agree to a restrictive covenant which is patently too wide and hence unenforceable.

1.8.7.3 'Garden leave' clauses

The term 'garden leave' is used to mean the period of time during which the employee is paid but is required to stay at home rather than attend work. The employer can thus hold the employee to the terms of his contract and prevent him from working for a competitor during the period. The clause will be invoked where either party gives notice of termination but the employer does not want the employee to attend at work during the notice period or to work for a competitor during that period.

A garden leave clause is more likely to be enforceable than a simple restriction precluding the employee joining a competitor for a period post-termination because it ensures that the employee does not suffer financially during the period of garden leave (*Eurobrokers Ltd v Rabey* [1995] IRLR 206). Nevertheless, the clause will not be enforced unless it is a reasonable restraint and the employer can show a legitimate business interest that he is seeking to protect (*Provident Financial Group plc v Hayward* [1989] ICR 160; *Symbian Ltd v Christensen* [2001] IRLR 77; *JH Finn & Co v Holliday* [2013] EWHC 3450 (QB)).

A long period of garden leave may be unduly onerous for an employee, and it is a matter for the court's discretion as to whether and to what extent the provision should be enforced. The court may, if the restraint during garden leave is drafted too widely, 'whittle it down' to something reasonable.

An employer who wishes to be sure that an employee can be sent home on garden leave should ensure that there is an express clause in the employee's contract sanctioning this course of action. This is because, in some cases (see **1.7.1**), the contract may give the employee the right to be provided with work during the notice period, or such a right may be implied and failure by the employer to observe that right may prevent him from relying on the garden leave clause; indeed, it could amount to a breach of contract by the employer (*William Hill Organisation Ltd v Tucker* [1998] IRLR 313).

In *SG&R Valuation Service v Boudrais* (see **1.7.1.1**), the High Court held that an employer can, however, send an employee on garden leave, in the absence of an express contractual right to do so, where there is evidence of actual wrongdoing by the employee (here helping himself to confidential information as part of a planned move to a competitor).

In *Credit Suisse Asset Management Ltd v Armstrong* [1996] IRLR 450, the court held that there was no relationship between the restrictive covenant and garden leave clause such as to allow the court, in any but an exceptional case, to order a set-off for the period of garden leave against the period covered by the restrictive covenant. Provided that the restrictive covenant was valid, it should be enforced by the court, once the garden leave has come to an end.

Table 1.1 Solicitation, poaching, competition and confidentiality: summary chart

	Solicitation (clients/ customers) or Poaching (fellow employees)	Competition	Confidentiality
During contract			
(a) *Implied terms*	Not to solicit customers and/or employees of the employer Not to copy list of customers	Must not compete with employer Cannot 'moonlight' for a competitor if causes harm	Respect any confidential information
(b) *Express terms*	To increase employee's duty and/or clarify implied position	To increase employee's duty – eg devote 'full time' clause – to prevent all moonlighting	To clarify implied position – eg to define what counts as confidential information
After contract			
(a) *Implied terms*	No implied term	No implied term	Only 'highly confidential' information/trade secrets are protected
(b) *Express terms*	Covenant protecting legitimate interest (eg, customer connections/ stable workforce). Covenant must be reasonable in terms of (a) the activity prohibited (eg customers with whom employee had personal contact/senior employees known to the employee); and (b) time (eg customers from the last 6 months and for the next 6 months).	Covenant protecting legitimate interest (eg trade secrets) (see *Lansing Linde*). Covenant must be reasonable in terms of (a) the activity prohibited (eg no wider than the business in which employee employed, such as not to work for a competitor); (b) time; and (c) area covered (eg no wider than the area where the employer carries on business).	Covenant protecting legitimate interest (eg trade secrets or other highly confidential information which if disclosed would cause real harm to the employer (*Lansing Linde*)). To clarify the implied position, ie what the employer considers highly confidential information (cannot increase the duty).

1.8.7.4 Reviews

Employers should regularly review their restrictive covenants, to make sure they remain relevant and that the business interests to be protected are properly described. Where new restrictive covenants are imposed, for example where a business is acquired and new employees are merged into existing teams, it will be necessary not only to ensure that the employees agree to any changes but also, in certain situations, for consideration to be paid, in order to ensure that there is an enforceable covenant. In *Re-use Collections Ltd v Sendall and May Glass Recycling Ltd* [2014] EWHC 3852 (QB), Re-use sought to rely on express restrictive covenants to prevent former employees from setting up a competing business. The High

Court emphasised that for a binding contract to exist, there needed to be 'consideration', ie some benefit provided in return for the obligation accepted by the employee. In this case, although there had been a pay rise, that had not been awarded in connection with the acceptance of new terms and conditions. Continued employment will be sufficient consideration only if it is dependent on acceptance of the covenants.

1.8.7.5   Government review of 'non-compete clauses'

In May 2016, the Government issued a consultation on whether post-termination restrictions unfairly hinder the free movement of employees or stifle entrepreneurship. The closing date for responses was 19 July 2016. The outcome of the consultation is awaited.

1.8.8   Disciplinary and grievance procedures

Details of disciplinary and grievance procedures may be included to comply with s 1 of the ERA 1996 (see **1.4.2**). If employers wish to have the power, on appeal by an employee, to increase any disciplinary sanction, they will need to reserve that power expressly (see *McMillan v Airedale NHS Foundation Trust* [2014] EWCA Civ 1031 and **5.4.2.2** below).

Note: where a disciplinary procedure forms part of an employee's contract of employment, civil remedies for breach of contract may be used during the course of disciplinary proceedings. In *West London Mental Health NHS Trust v Chhabra* [2013] UKSC 60, the Supreme Court granted an injunction preventing an NHS Trust from holding a disciplinary hearing against the claimant as a result of a number of irregularities in the proceedings against the claimant, which cumulatively rendered the convening of the disciplinary panel unlawful as a material breach of her contract

1.8.9   Surrender of papers

It is common for the employment contract to require the employee, on the termination of the contract, to surrender all notes and documents that he has in his possession which relate to the employer's business.

1.8.10   Other issues

Consideration should be given to inclusion of other clauses in the contract and policy statements, for example:

(a)   a PILON clause (see **Chapter 2**);

(b)   a whistle-blowing policy (see **5.6.5**);

(c)   computer/telephone usage policies (see **15.5.2**);

(d)   an equal opportunities policy (see **Chapter 8**);

(e)   a health and safety policy;

(f)   a maternity, paternity and parental leave policy (see **Chapter 14**);

(g)   a flexible working policy (see **Chapter 14**).

1.9   VARIATION OF CONTRACTUAL TERMS

Where the employer and employee have agreed the terms of their contract, those terms cannot be changed without both parties agreeing to the changes. In other words, employers cannot unilaterally change the terms and conditions of the contract. The test as to when express variation clauses will be permitted was set out by the Court of Appeal in *Wandsworth London Borough Council v D'Silva* [1998] IRLR 193. The Court said that employers need to use clear and unambiguous language in a contract to be able to rely upon a clause allowing unilateral variation. Even if such a clause exists, terms must be used in a manner that is not oppressive or capricious. Problems can arise with staff handbooks, which may or may not form part of the contractual terms. If they are contractual, changing them may become problematic.

Where an employer does try to impose a unilateral variation on an employee, an employee has four choices (see *Robinson v Tescom Corporation* [2008] IRLR 408):

(a)   to agree to the variation (either expressly, or by continuing to work without protest);

(b)   to resign and complain of unfair constructive dismissal (see **3.4.3**) and wrongful dismissal (see **Chapter 2**);

(c)   to refuse to work under the new terms and force the employer to take such steps as it thinks are appropriate;

(d)   to stand and sue, ie continue to work under protest and seek damages (either for breach of contract – see for example *Rigby v Ferodo* [1987] IRLR 516 – or, if the breach is so serious as to bring the original contract to an end, unfair dismissal).

In *Robinson v Tescom*, the employee agreed to changes 'under protest', but then refused to work under the new terms and was dismissed. The EAT said the decision to dismiss him was fair because, having agreed (albeit under protest) to the changes, he could not then renege on what he had agreed – he was refusing to obey a lawful and reasonable instruction.

Careful regard should be had to the contract to see whether the terms are wide enough to allow for the proposed change. Often a contract will permit variations to certain terms, eg hours of work and place of work. However, employers must also have regard to the implied duty of mutual trust and confidence, even where the contractual terms permit a variation. An employer should, for example, consult with employees before introducing changes.

It is quite common for employers to include so-called 'flexibility clauses' in contracts, which purport to allow the employer to vary some terms unilaterally, ie without agreement. The courts are generally wary of such clauses, and terms that purport to give employers the right to change any terms of the contract, eg 'the right to vary this contract from time to time', have usually been construed narrowly. If the change might produce an unreasonable result, the tribunals must 'seek to avoid such a result' (*Wandsworth London Borough Council v D'Silva* [1998] IRLR 193).

In *Bateman v Asda Stores* (UKEAT/0221/09) the EAT held that conditions in the Asda staff handbook were incorporated in the claimants' contracts of employment, and the wording in the staff handbook was wide enough to permit Asda to change the pay and work structure, with the result that Asda was entitled to impose changes in the claimants' pay and work provisions without the need to obtain their express consent. The contract provided, 'The company reserves the right to review, revise, amend or replace the contents of this handbook.' Note that the employer had consulted and sought agreement, and most employees had agreed to the changes; only one employee (out of 700) alleged financial detriment from the changes.

In *Slade & Others v TNT UK Ltd* (UKEAT/0113/11), the employer sought to change terms of employment by making an offer to 'buy out' certain existing terms, but warned that refusal would result in dismissal with an offer of re-engagement on the proposed new terms. The offer was rejected and the employer dismissed with notice and re-employed on new terms and conditions. The employment tribunal held that the employer did not unfairly dismiss where the terms of offered re-employment did not include the terms of the 'buy out' as part of the new terms (see **Chapter 5**).

Sometimes, when an employer wants to try to change a term of a policy, it will maintain that the term is not contractual and so consent is not needed (see **1.8**). In *Norman v National Audit Office* (UKEAT/0276/14), an employer imposed changes to sick pay and privilege leave days after unsuccessful negotiations. The terms of the contract contained a clause that said that the conditions of service were 'subject to amendment', and that any significant changes would be notified by management, policy circulars or general orders, changes to employees' particular terms being notified separately. The employment tribunal accepted that the 'subject to amendment' provision permitted the variation. The EAT disagreed: it said that the wording was not sufficiently clear and unambiguous to permit the changes the employer was trying to make; 'subject to amendment' came 'nowhere near' the standard of being clear and unambiguous. The references to amendment and notification raised the possibility of change occurring, and how that would be communicated, but did not establish a clear power to change terms. The EAT also held that the relevant provision was not incorporated into the actual contracts as it was contained in a staff handbook, which largely addressed collective bargaining issues and was not the 'stuff of terms and conditions'.

In *Hart v St Mary's School* (UKEAT/0305/14), a teacher's contract stated that her part-time hours were 'subject to variation'. The school tried to change her three-day week by spreading it over five days. The teacher resigned and claimed constructive unfair dismissal. The EAT held that the reference to variation was not sufficiently clear to give rise to a power to the employer to vary contractual terms unilaterally, and decided that the provision meant that a variation could be at either party's request.

In *Sparks v Department for Transport* [2015] EWHC 181 (QB); [2016] EWCA Civ 360, seven employees who worked for different agencies within the Department of Transport (such as the DVLA and the Highways Agency) applied to the High Court for a declaration that their employer had breached their contracts of employment by unilaterally imposing a change to the attendance management provisions of what they argued was a contractual staff handbook. In July 2012, following unsuccessful negotiations with the trade unions, the Department of Transport sought to introduce standardised attendance management terms across all its agencies. As some agencies had pre-existing different terms, this had the effect of unilaterally changing some employees' terms of service. The Departmental Staff Handbook for each agency provided as follows:

1.1   Contract of employment

    1.1.1 ... Your terms and conditions of employment include those set out in

        (1)   ...

        (2)   the DfT Departmental Staff Handbook which contains terms and conditions and procedures and guidance applying specifically to you as a Crown employee ...

1.2   The Departmental Staff Handbook

    1.2.1 The Departmental Staff Handbook, as applying to you, sets out many of your terms and conditions. It is the intention of the recognised trade unions ... and of the Crown that all of the provisions of the Departmental Staff Handbook which apply to you and are apt for incorporation should be incorporated into your contract of employment.

    1.2.2 The Departmental Staff Handbook is in two parts:

    Part A contains terms and conditions. Without prejudice to the generality of paragraph 1.2.1 above, all of Part A and all annexes of Part A which apply to you and which are apt for incorporation, will be incorporated into your contract of employment; and

    Part B contains procedures and guidance relevant to your employment relationship with the Crown. Those procedures and guidance can be relevant to the operation of your contractual terms and conditions set out in Part A, but in the event of inconsistency between Part A and Part B it is Part A which prevails.

The High Court held that the terms relating to attendance management were incorporated into the individual employees' contracts and that the Department of Transport's attempts to impose variations on them unilaterally should not be permitted, as the relevant terms provided that any proposals to change the relevant terms and conditions should have been the subject of consultation, 'with a view to reaching agreement'. If no agreement could be reached, the High Court said that 'unilateral changes could then have been made but only if they were not detrimental to the employee'. On the facts, the court found the changes were detrimental. The court also held that certain clauses were not apt for contractual incorporation, for example clauses relating to reporting obligations when sick. The High Court's analysis was upheld by the Court of Appeal: the attendance management provisions were contractual and could only be amended in accordance with the contract.

Where an employer wishes to vary the terms of a contract, it is first necessary to identify whether the terms are contractual or not. Where terms are contained in staff handbooks, this can give rise to uncertainty as to the contractual effect of clauses and how to change them. Where terms are not contractual, and subject to a power being provided to allow change, as long as there is a consultation, then, generally speaking, such terms can ultimately be varied without agreement. Where terms are contractual, employers will either need to obtain the express agreement of the employees to any variation, or, in an extreme case, they could terminate the employment and offer to re-employ on the new terms. This might give rise to an unfair dismissal claim (see **Chapter 5**). If employers wish to rely on a clause purporting to give them a power to make unilateral variations to a contact, such a clause will need to be very clear and unambiguous. Even if there is a power to impose changes unilaterally, the employer still needs to consider how changes will be communicated, and needs to consult about the proposed change. Failure to do so may give rise to a breach of the implied duty of trust and confidence (see **1.7.1.4** and **3.4.3**).

See also *Rock Advertising Ltd v MWB Business Exchange Centres Ltd* and *Abrahall v Nottingham City Council* at **1.8** above.

1.10 HUMAN RIGHTS ACT 1998

From a contractual perspective, the individual rights recognised by the HRA 1998 (see **Chapter 15**) may be given greater weight, especially when they have to be balanced against managerial interests. This could be achieved by two routes. First, the courts may be persuaded to accept that those rights are implicitly incorporated into individual contracts of employment. Secondly, if that is a step too far, it may be argued that they are part and parcel of the development of the implied duty of mutual trust and confidence. Thus, even though the HRA 1998 is not directly enforceable between private individuals, if there is a breach of a Convention right, that may give rise to a claim for breach of contract.

Additionally, as courts and tribunals are obliged to act compatibly with the HRA 1998 (s 6), it has also been argued that the HRA 1998 will impact on the construction of terms of the contract of employment, in particular terms relating to confidentiality and restraint of trade, and the HRA 1998 may well limit the 'scope' of 'managerial prerogative' in the context of giving orders and the obligation of an employee to obey (lawful and reasonable) orders.

Note that the current Government gave a manifesto commitment to repeal the HRA 1998 and replace it with a British Bill of Rights. At the time of writing, no Bill has been produced.

Although there is nothing specifically stated in the HRA 1998, it has long been accepted that rights under the ECHR can be waived by contract. The ECtHR's jurisprudence makes it clear, however, that:

(a) any waiver must be clear and unequivocal;

(b) simply signing a contract may not amount to a waiver – an employee's attention must be drawn to any specific provision;

(c) even where there is a waiver in a contract, it is not deemed to be conclusive of the matter; courts will still scrutinise and assess any such waiver.

In *Rommelfanger v Germany* (1989) 62 DR 151, Mr Rommelfanger was a German doctor working in a Catholic hospital. He expressed views on abortion in the press which ran counter to those of the Catholic Church, and was dismissed as a result. In his contract, he had accepted a duty of loyalty to the Catholic Church. It was held that he had accepted a limitation on his freedom of expression but had not thereby deprived himself of the protection of Article 10 of the ECHR. Notwithstanding the contractual limitation, the Court maintains a supervisory jurisdiction to look at the substantive issue and weigh up the competing interests of the employer and employee. The Court will give weight to contractual waivers, but there may be situations where the restriction on the right is too extreme, in which case the Court will interfere. As the Catholic Church was an organisation based on certain fundamental convictions and beliefs which it considered essential, it was entitled to its freedom of expression.

In *Ahmad v UK* (1982) 4 EHRR 126, a local authority teacher complained of constructive dismissal after he was refused permission to attend a mosque during working hours. It was accepted by the Court that his right to exercise his freedom of religion (Article 9) could be limited by contractual obligations such as requirements relating to the hours of work, timetabling etc, provided that his employers did not arbitrarily disregard his freedom of religion.

In *Stedman v UK* (1997) 23 EHRR CD 168, the Commission rejected the employee's claim that her employer had breached Article 9 by requiring her to work on Sundays; the employee was not dismissed because of her religious beliefs but because she refused to work her contractual hours (see now, however, s 10 of the Equality Act 2010 – at **8.2.3**).

1.11   PROTECTION OF WAGES

If an employer fails to pay remuneration due under the employment contract, the employee (or worker – see **1.3** above) will often be able to rely on what is commonly referred to as the 'protection of wages' legislation – set out in Pt II of the ERA 1996. This part of the ERA 1996 expressly includes workers as well as employees within its protections (as defined in s 230). The term 'worker' is wider and expressly encompasses an individual who works under a contract of employment (s 230(3)), and will be used below when describing the protection provided. Notice pay is not covered by Pt II and s 14 expressly excludes deductions made in respect of an overpayment of wages or expenses (see **1.11.4** below). The normal remedies for breach of contract are also available in all these situations. Most workers utilise the protection of wages legislation where it is available in addition to or in preference to the normal breach of contract remedies.

Readers should also bear in mind that such claims may also arise as a shortfall in holiday pay or a failure to pay the NMW and that workers may have a variety of overlapping legal grounds on which to bring such claims, each of which may have different limits and restrictions applying to them. It may sometimes be necessary to rely on all possible heads of claim. This may be particularly significant where there are relatively short limitation periods for bringing claims. For example, under the ERA 1996 and the Working Time Regulations 1998, claims must generally be brought within three months, whereas for breach of contract claims, there is a six-year limitation period.

Two aspects of the statutory protection for unpaid wages that exist in Pt II of the ERA 1996 are considered below: first, the need for authority before the employer is entitled to make deductions from wages; and, secondly, the method of enforcement by employment tribunals.

1.11.1   Deductions from wages

The basic right given to workers by Pt II of the ERA 1996 is stated in s 13, whereby an employer must not make any deduction from wages unless:

(a)   it is authorised by statute (eg Pay As You Earn (PAYE) and National Insurance); or

(b)   it is authorised by the worker's contract; or

(c)   the worker has previously signified in writing his consent to the making of it.

A deduction is defined in s 13(3) as follows:

> Where the total amount of wages paid on any occasion by an employer to a worker employed by him is less than the total amount of wages properly payable by him to the worker on that occasion ... the amount of the deficiency shall be treated ... as a deduction ...

Therefore, if the total amount paid to the worker is less than the total amount properly payable (which will not include pure errors of computation), it will be a deduction.

Non-payment of a sum due may amount to a deduction, provided that the sum relates to a period of employment. Non-payment of wages in lieu of notice after termination of the contract does not therefore fall under the ERA 1996 (*Delaney v Staples* [1991] IRLR 112).

A unilateral reduction in wages may amount to a deduction, as may a non-payment of commission.

An employer may also make deductions where those deductions are covered by one of the exemptions in s 14 (see **1.11.4**).

If the employer wishes to make any deductions from a worker's wages, for example penalties for substandard work or to recoup 'till shortages' from workers handling money, authority to make the deduction should be specified in the contract.

For workers in retail employment, deductions for cash shortages or stock deficiencies must not, except for the final payment of wages, exceed one-tenth of the employee's gross wages (ERA 1996, s 17).

If the employer wishes to make deductions of a type not provided for in the contract, for example, if the employer makes a loan to be repaid by deductions from wages, the worker must give his written consent to the deduction. (In the example given, this would usually be done in the loan agreement.)

1.11.2   What are 'wages'?

The ERA 1996 prohibits deductions from 'wages', and s 27 of the ERA 1996 defines wages as 'any sums payable to the worker [by his employer] in connection with his employment … including any fee, bonus, commission, holiday pay or other emolument referable to his employment, whether payable under his contract or otherwise'. There is a list of excluded payments in s 27(2).

In *Kent Management Services Ltd v Butterfield* [1992] IRLR 394, the EAT held that although the contract described the commissions and bonuses as discretionary and non-contractual, nevertheless both the employer and worker would expect them to be paid unless there were exceptional circumstances. Such payments, which were identifiable sums, were therefore 'wages', whether contractual or not, and the employer could not withhold them even though he was of the opinion that the contract had not been properly performed. If the employer had wanted the right to withhold the payments in certain circumstances then he should have included the necessary authority in the worker's contract.

The EAT held in *Hellewell v AXA Services* (UK/EAT/0084/11) that the contract relieved the employers of any obligation to pay bonuses where, as was the case here, employees had committed gross misconduct. The bonus was not therefore 'properly payable', and thus there was no unlawful deduction (see **1.10.3** below).

In *Coors Brewers v Adcock* [2007] EWCA Civ 19, the Court of Appeal held that claims by employees (who were still employed, so could not bring a tribunal claim for breach of contract) for bonuses under a share scheme, were in reality claims for unliquidated (unspecified) damages and therefore fell outside the scope of an unlawful deduction claim. Wall LJ stated that the unlawful deduction regime applied only to 'a specific sum of money' or an 'identifiable sum'. Where a detailed investigation was required as to the level of the alleged underpayment, the proper route was to bring a breach of contract claim (which in this case would have to be brought in the civil court, as the employees were still employed).

In *Tradition Securities & Futures SA v Alexandre Mouradian* [2009] EWCA Civ 60, the Court of Appeal held that an employee was entitled to bring a claim relating to the amount of his bonus in the employment tribunal under the unlawful deduction from wages provisions because the amount of the bonus was quantifiable according to a precise formula for calculating the bonus.

As stated above, payments in lieu of notice are not wages under ERA 1996, s 27.

Following the EAT's decision in *Bear Scotland* (see **1.12.5.3** below), the Government passed the Deduction from Wages (Limitation) Regulations 2014 (SI 2014/3322), which took effect from 8 January 2015. The Regulations apply to claims presented to the employment tribunal on or after 1 July 2015. Although designed to limit back claims for holiday pay to two years, they also amend the ERA 1996 so that all complaints presented on or after 17 July 2015 of unauthorised deductions from wages can only be brought in respect of deductions occurring within two years of presentation of the claim (but excluding some very specific statutory payments, such as SSP (see **1.8.3.3**) and statutory maternity pay (SMP, see **14.2**), as set out in s 27(1)(b)–(j) of the ERA 1996). The Regulations also amended the Working Time Regulations 1998 by stating that the right to payment in respect of annual leave is not contractual but purely statutory, thus preventing the bringing of contractual claims under the protection of wages legislation for statutory holiday pay claims. This also now overrules one of the findings of the House of Lords in *HMRC v Stringer* [2009] UKHL 31.

One area that can be particularly complex is how you actually calculate what a day's wages are. Where someone is paid an annual salary, should you divide it by 365, or by some lesser fraction to allow for non-working days such as weekends? The Supreme Court had to look at this in *Hartley v King Edward VI College* [2017] UKSC 39. A county court ruled that teachers who had been on strike should have 1/260 of their annual pay deducted for each strike day. Contractually most full-time teachers are directed to work 195 days per year. They also have to undertake work during undirected time. The claimants argued that the proportion to be deducted should be 1/365 for each strike day. The county court followed the decision in *Amey v Peter Symonds College* [2014] IRLR 206 and ruled that the proper deduction should be 1/260. The Court of Appeal held, applying s 2 of the Apportionment Act 1870, that monies are apportioned on the basis that payment accrues daily, but that does not necessarily mean that it accrues at an even rate on each day. In this case, the respondent employer's interpretation of the contract, that pay accrued at a rate of 1/260 on working days and days of paid holiday, rather than 1/365 as contended by the claimant teachers, was correct. That fraction was based on the premise that the teachers' working days were Monday to Friday, and that all work days should be included, even those that did not have to be worked because of holidays. So the formula applied was:

5 working days a week x 52 weeks a year = 260 working days a year

The Supreme Court allowed the appeal and directed that 1/365th should be deducted.

1.11.3 'Properly payable'

The Court of Appeal held in *New Century Cleaning Co Ltd v Church* [2000] IRLR 27 that wages will be 'properly payable' only if the worker has a legal (although not necessarily contractual) entitlement to the wages. In *Hellewell v AXA Services* (**1.11 2** above) the EAT confirmed that the claimants were not entitled to a bonus because the contract was clear – no bonus was payable where the employees had committed gross misconduct. The EAT held, in *Agarwal v Cardiff University* (UKEAT/0210/16), that the employment tribunal has no jurisdiction to construe a contract in order to determine a claim under s 13 of the ERA 1996 not to suffer an unauthorised deduction from wages. The decision of the Court of Appeal in *Southern Cross Healthcare Co Ltd v Perkins* (see **1.4.2.2** above) applies to s 13 claims too. However, the EAT decided in *Weatherilt v Cathay Pacific Airways Ltd* (UKEAT/0333/16), relying on Court of Appeal authorities not considered in *Agarwal*, that *Agarwal* was wrongly decided (such that Southern Cross does not apply to s 13 claims) and that the tribunal was entitled to construe the employee's contract to decide whether allowances were payable during periods of sickness absence. In *East v Valentine* (UKEAT/0325/16) (see **1.12.1.1** below), the EAT said that it preferred the approach in *Weatherilt* to that in *Agarwal*. The matter has finally been put to rest by the Court of Appeal in *Agarwal* ([2018] EWCA Civ 2084). The Court held that tribunals do have jurisdiction to interpret contracts in s 13 claims.

1.11.4 Exceptions

1.11.4.1 Overpayment of wages or expenses

An employer may make deductions to recover overpayments of wages or expenses previously paid by mistake to the worker (ERA 1996, s 14(1)). Any dispute as to the lawfulness of such a deduction must be resolved in the civil courts. Such overpayments are recoverable unless the employer has led the worker to believe the money was his and the worker changes his position (eg spends the money) and the overpayment was not the worker's fault (*Kleinwort Benson Ltd v Lincoln City Council and Other Appeals* [1999] 2 AC 349).

1.11.4.2 Deductions in respect of industrial action

If the worker is not performing any of his duties, the employer may deduct an amount which represents a fair proportion of his salary.

1.11.5 Enforcement

If an employer makes an unauthorised deduction from wages, the worker may present a complaint to an employment tribunal within three months of the payment from which the deduction was made (or within three months of the last in a series of deductions, so allowing a claim to go back more than three months if the underpayments form part of a series). Note that the Deduction from Wages (Limitation) Regulations 2014, which took effect from 8 January 2015 (see **1.11.2**), apply to claims that are presented to the employment tribunal on or after 1 July 2015. Although designed to limit back claims for holiday pay to two years, these Regulations also amend the ERA 1996 so that all claims of unauthorised deductions from wages can only be brought in respect of deductions occurring within two years of presentation of the claim (but excluding some very specific statutory payments such as SSP and SMP, as set out in s 27(1)(b)–(j) of the ERA 1996). Where a claim for unpaid holiday pay is made and further deductions are made by the employer, the ET Presidential Direction of 27 March 2015 permits the claimant to apply to amend the claim to add further complaints of alleged non-payment of holiday pay.

Where the complaint is upheld, the tribunal will order the employer to pay to the worker the amount of the unauthorised deduction (ERA 1996, s 27). Alternatively, an employee could pursue a claim for breach of contract in the civil courts. See also the chart at **5.6.2.5**.

1.12 WORKING TIME REGULATIONS 1998

The Working Time Regulations 1998 (the Regulations) implement the Working Time Directive (93/104).

The Government has issued guidance on the limits of working time and some of the entitlements provided for in the 1998 Regulations (see <http://www.direct.gov.uk>). The guidance explains how the Regulations work and how employers may seek to comply with them – what questions they need to consider and what action they should take. The guidance is intended to be just that, and should not be regarded as a complete or authoritative statement of the law.

Note that the Regulations apply to workers as well as employees (see **1.3**). As the definition of worker encompasses that of employee, that term will be used below. What follows is an introduction to the Regulations.

1.12.1 The nature and scope of the Regulations

1.12.1.1 Working time

The Regulations provide (reg 2) that, in relation to a worker, 'working time' means:

(a)   any period during which he is working, at his employer's disposal and carrying out his activity or duties;

(b)   any period during which he is receiving 'relevant training'; and

(c)   any additional period which is to be treated as working time under a relevant agreement.

The Government's guidance gives some examples:

(i)   On-call time will be working time when a worker is required to be at his place of work – when a worker is away from the workplace when on-call, and accordingly free to pursue his leisure activities, on-call time is not working time (see *Sindicato de Medicos de Asistencia Publica (SiMAP) v Conselleria de Sanidad y Consumo de la Generalidad Valenciana* [2000] IRLR 845, ECJ). The ECJ confirmed in *Landeshauptstadt Kiel v Jaeger* [2003] IRLR 804 that the three criteria mentioned in (a) above are cumulative. In the *Jaeger* case the ECJ held that on-call time spent at a hospital was working time, even though the doctor was allowed to sleep when not required, because all three criteria in (a) were met.

In *Hughes v G and L Jones t/a Graylyns Residential Home* (UKEAT/0159/08), the EAT held that working time included the period the care worker was on call between 9pm and 8am, seven days a week, during which time she occupied a flat on site at a reduced rent.

In *Ville de Nivelles v Matzak* (Case C-518/15), the ECJ held that stand-by time spent at home by a volunteer fireman, which was within eight minutes' travelling distance of a workplace, was working time.

(ii)   A lunch break spent at leisure will not be working time, although a working lunch would be.

(iii) Time spent working abroad will be working time.

(iv) Time spent travelling to and from a place of work is unlikely to be working time as a worker will probably neither be working nor carrying out his duties, but a worker may well be doing both if he is engaged by travel that is required by the job. In *Federación de Servicios Privados del sindicato Comisiones obreras v Tyco Integrated Security SL* (Case C-266/14), the ECJ held that Article 2 of the Directive should be interpreted as meaning that the time spent travelling at the beginning and end of the day by a peripatetic worker who was not assigned to a fixed place of work but was required to travel every day from home to the premises of a different customer of the employer and to return home from the premises of another, different customer (following a route or list that was determined for the worker by the employer the previous day) constituted 'working time' and was not a 'rest period'. So for technicians who do repair or maintenance work, time spent travelling between home and the first and last visits of the day is working time.

Working time includes any period during which the employee is in work, at the employer's disposal (ie legally obliged to obey its instructions) and carrying out his activity or duties for that employer. In *East v Valentine* (UKEAT/0325/16), the claimant was a support worker assisting disabled persons in the community. He had to travel from place to place using his car. At the beginning of a period of work, he would drive directly from his home to the first assignment, and when he finished his last assignment he would drive directly home. The claimant's contract set out working hours and pay and specifically stated that his working hours did not include time taken to travel to and from work. There was also a clause stating that additional hours would generally be taken as time off in lieu. The question arose as to whether this time should be counted as working time. The EAT overruled the employment tribunal's finding based on *Tyco* that there was an unlawful deduction from wages. They said that the

Regulations were not concerned with questions of payment. A finding that a journey is working time does not give rise to any statutory right to payment, and moreover the contractual position here was very clear.

(v)   In *Edwards v Encirc Ltd* (UKEAT/0367/14), the EAT overturned an employment tribunal's finding that a trade union shop steward and a health and safety representative were not working when they attended meetings at their workplace between night shifts. In the EAT's view, the tribunal had adopted an unduly restrictive approach to the questions of whether the employees were at their employer's disposal and carrying out their duties when attending the meetings. In September 2013, E, who worked night shifts, attended a health and safety meeting during the day. This meant he had only six hours between the end of the meeting and the start of his next night shift. Likewise, M attended a trade union meeting during the day. He also had a break of six hours between the end of the meeting and the start of his next night shift. Both E and M brought employment tribunal claims arguing that they had been denied their right (see **1.12.4.1**) to 11 hours' consecutive rest in any period of 24 hours (reg 10(1)). The EAT pointed out that in order for workers to be at their employer's disposal, it is not necessary that they be under the employer's specific control and direction. The Directive allows for a broader approach, and can cover the situation where an employer has required an employee to be in a specific place and to hold himself out as ready to work for the employer's benefit. Similarly, there was no requirement that the activity or duties referred to in reg 2(1)(a) must be solely the specified contractual duties. If a worker is engaged in activities that arise from the employment relationship, are for the benefit of the employer and done with the employer's knowledge, at and in an approved time and manner, then this could amount to working time.

1.12.1.2   Worker

Subject to the exclusions outlined below, the Regulations will apply to individuals over the minimum school leaving age who can be categorised as 'employees' (ie those working under contracts of service or apprenticeship) plus a wider group who undertake to perform personally any work or services (eg freelancers) (see, eg, *Willoughby v County Home Care Ltd* (ET/1100310/99)). Those whose work amounts to carrying out business activity on their own account (with whom there is a relationship of client/customer rather than employer) are excluded; such individuals are likely to be paid on the basis of an invoice rather than receiving wages (see discussion at **1.3**).

The Regulations specifically exclude domestic servants in private households from the provisions of working time and night work. However, they are covered by the provisions on rest periods and annual leave.

The Regulations distinguish between 'adult workers' (workers who have attained the age of 18) and 'young workers' (who are over compulsory school age but below the age of 18). Only adult workers are dealt with below.

1.12.1.3   Excluded activities and sectors of activity

Prior to 1 August 2003, most of the entitlements under the Regulations did not apply to workers in air, road, sea, inland waterway and lake transport; sea fishing and other work at sea; and doctors in training. However, since 1 August 2003, the Regulations now generally apply in full to non-mobile workers within these industries.

Regulation 2 defines a mobile worker as 'any worker employed as a member of travelling or flying personnel by an undertaking which operates transport services for passengers or goods by road or air'. The position with regard to mobile workers in these industries is more complicated, and often mobile workers are protected under sector-specific legislation or are only covered by certain parts of the Regulations.

The armed forces and the police and emergency services are partially exempt from the Regulations.

Young workers in the armed forces, the police and emergency services, the aviation sector and the road transport sector, are covered by the young workers provisions in the Working Time Regulations.

The UK Regulations do now apply to junior doctors.

Detailed consideration of the above provisions is beyond the scope of this book.

1.12.2 Summary of the limits, rights and duties

Almost all of the rights and limits introduced by the Regulations are subject to exceptions and qualifications. The basic provisions with regard to day workers and adults are summarised below. There are also specific provisions relating to night work and young workers which are outside the scope of this book.

1.12.2.1 Limits on working time

Weekly working time (reg 4)

In a 17-week period (which may be extended), no worker is permitted to work more than an average of 48 hours per week.

1.12.2.2 Adult workers' rights

Daily rest period (reg 10)

Eleven consecutive hours' rest in every 24-hour period. See **1.12.4**.

Weekly rest period (reg 11)

An uninterrupted rest period of not less than 24 hours in each seven-day period (in addition to the daily rest period).

Daily rest period (reg 12)

Twenty minutes' rest break, provided that the working day is longer than six hours.

Annual leave (reg 13)

An entitlement to 5.6 weeks' (ie 28 days for a 5-day per week employee) paid annual leave (see **1.12.5**).

1.12.3 Maximum weekly working time (reg 4)

The Regulations set a limit on the amount of working time which may be undertaken by a worker each week. The general rule is that a worker's working time (including overtime) in any reference period shall not exceed an average of 48 hours for each seven days. An employer is under a positive duty to take all reasonable steps, in keeping with the need to protect the health and safety of workers, to ensure that this limit is not exceeded.

1.12.3.1 'Reference period'

For the purposes of the maximum weekly working time-limits, the reference period which applies in the case of a worker is any period of 17 weeks in the course of his employment (unless a relevant agreement (see below) between an employer and a trade union/workforce representative or an individual stipulates which successive periods of 17 weeks amount to such a reference period). This means that, so long as the employee has not worked more than the average in the 17 weeks preceding and including today, then the rules are not breached. In view of this, employers are well advised to put in place early warning systems to check whether an employee is nearing the limit on each rolling period.

The reference period may also be extended to a period not exceeding 52 weeks, by means of a collective or workforce agreement, for objective or technical reasons or reasons concerning the organisation of work. The 17-week reference period is extended to a 26-week period where a worker is engaged in 'special case' activities (eg security or surveillance, hospitals, prisons, broadcasting, tourism, rail transport) where the worker's activities are intermittent.

1.12.3.2 'Average working time'

A worker's 'average working time' is normally calculated by identifying the number of weeks in the reference period (C) and the aggregate number of hours of working time worked by the worker in that period (A) and dividing A by C to produce an average figure. However, where a worker will not have worked certain days during the reference period because of, for example, annual leave, sick leave or maternity leave, A will be increased by the number of hours worked immediately after the reference period during the number of working days on which the worker was absent in the reference period (B).

The Regulations contain the following formula for calculating average working time for each seven days during a reference period:

$$\frac{A + B}{C}$$

In *Barber and Others v RJB Mining (UK) Ltd* [1999] IRLR 308, five pit deputies sought and obtained declarations that they need not work beyond the 48-hour average, irrespective of what their contract required. The High Court ruled that the Regulations imposed a contractual obligation on the employer which was enforceable in the High Court.

1.12.3.3 'Unmeasured' working time

The limit on weekly working time does not apply in relation to a worker where, on account of the specific characteristics of the activity in which he is engaged, the duration of his working time is not measured or predetermined, or can be determined by the worker himself.

Essentially, this applies to workers who have complete control over the hours they work and whose time is not monitored or determined by their employer. The Guidance states that an indicator may be if the worker is able to decide when to do his work and for how long.

The Regulations provide the following examples of situations in which this exception may apply (see reg 20(1)):

(a)   managing executives or other persons with autonomous decision-taking powers;

(b)   family workers (eg family members who work in a shop and live in a flat above it); or

(c)   workers officiating at religious ceremonies in churches and religious communities.

Note, however, that where a 'normal' worker voluntarily works in excess of his contractual hours, those extra hours count towards the 48-hour limit.

1.12.3.4 'Opt out' agreements (reg 5)

A worker may agree in writing with his employer that the 48-hour limit on average working time does not apply to him. Such an agreement may either relate to a specified period or apply indefinitely, but the agreement shall always be terminable by the worker giving not less than seven days' notice to his employer in writing (or such other period of notice not exceeding three months specified in the agreement).

An 'opt out' agreement will be binding only if the employer keeps up-to-date records of workers who have agreed to opt out.

The employer cannot make an employee sign an 'opt out' agreement. A worker will be protected against detrimental treatment if he refuses to sign an 'opt out' agreement. If such a refusal leads to an employee's dismissal, that dismissal will be treated as automatically unfair, irrespective of the length of service of the employee concerned (see, for example, *Brown v Controlled Packaging Services Ltd* (ET/1402252/98)).

1.12.3.5 Sanctions

A failure to observe the weekly working time-limit in respect of a worker will render an employer liable to the sanctions and penalties presently available to the Health & Safety Executive (HSE) and local authorities under health and safety legislation. Under this legislation, the HSE/local authorities can issue improvement and prohibition notices. In extreme cases, criminal proceedings may be commenced, and this may lead to unlimited fines.

As employers have a general duty to protect the health and safety at work of their workers, employers could be in breach of this common law duty of care if the weekly working time-limit is exceeded. This common law duty of care is bolstered by the Regulations which contain a statutory duty on an employer to observe the limits on weekly working time. If the employer fails to observe this statutory duty, a worker may enforce it as a civil claim in the courts.

The Regulations also give workers two further rights if they refuse to work in excess of the maximum weekly working time-limit. First, a worker has the right not to be subjected to any detriment by any act, or any deliberate failure to act, by his employer for (inter alia) refusing to work in excess of an average 48 hours per week. Secondly, an employee shall be regarded as unfairly dismissed (irrespective of length of service) if the principal reason for his dismissal is that he has (inter alia) refused to exceed the weekly limit on his working hours (see **Chapter 5**).

Additionally, as the weekly working units underpin contractual rights, an employee will be entitled to enforce these rights through a contract claim in the civil courts. In the *Barber* case (see **1.12.3.2** above), the High Court indicated that a declaration, rather than an injunction, would normally be the appropriate remedy.

Prosecutions for breach have been few. In 2002, Fourboys newsagent was fined £5,000 because the managers worked, on average, 71.3 hours per week. In 2007, a construction company (CFR Group plc) was fined £750 for breaching reg 4(1) on weekly working time limits.

1.12.4 Rest (regs 10, 11, 12)

The rest entitlements provided by the Regulations differ depending upon whether a person is a worker or a young worker. The rest entitlements provided for young workers are more generous than those provided for workers. See reg 10.

1.12.4.1 Daily rest period (reg 10)

An adult worker is entitled to a rest period of at least 11 consecutive hours in each 24-hour period during which he works for the employer. This entitlement is subject to the following exceptions:

(a) where working time is unmeasured (see **1.12.3.3**);

(b) where the worker is engaged in one of the 'special case' activities;

(c) where a shift worker changes shift and cannot take the daily rest period between the end of one shift and the start of the next one;

(d) where the worker is engaged in activities involving periods of work split up over the day (eg cleaning staff);

(e) where the right is modified or excluded by a collective or workforce agreement (see **1.12.6**).

Where any of these exceptions applies (other than the unmeasured working time exception), the employer must allow the worker to take an equivalent period of compensatory rest and, in exceptional cases where this is not possible for objective reasons, the employer must afford the worker such protection as may be appropriate in order to safeguard the worker's health and safety.

1.12.4.2   Weekly rest period (reg 11)

Adult workers are entitled to an uninterrupted rest period of not less than 24 hours in each seven-day period. This right is additional to the daily rest entitlement except where objective, technical or work organisation conditions justify incorporating all or part of the daily entitlement into the weekly rest period. Daily rest and weekly rest should be taken consecutively, ie giving an uninterrupted period of 35 hours.

If the employer so determines, the seven-day reference period can be averaged over a reference period of 14 days. In these circumstances, the employer can choose between:

(a)   two uninterrupted rest periods each of not less than 24 hours in each 14-day period; and

(b)   one uninterrupted rest period of not less than 48 hours in each such 14-day period.

The ECJ held in *Maio Marques da Rosa v Varzim* (Case C-306/16) that there is no requirement for a rest day to be at the end of a 7-day period.

The relevant reference period shall be taken to begin at midnight between Sunday and Monday of each week or (as the case may be) every other week unless a relevant agreement provides to the contrary.

The weekly rest entitlement of adult workers is subject to the same exceptions as are outlined in relation to daily rest (**1.12.4.1** above).

1.12.4.3   Daily rest breaks (reg 12)

Adult workers are entitled to a daily rest break where their daily working time is more than six hours. The details of this rest break (including its duration and the terms on which it is granted) may be set by a collective or workforce agreement. In the absence of such an agreement, the break must be an uninterrupted period of not less than 20 minutes. The worker shall be entitled to spend this break away from his workstation if he has one.

In *Grange v Abellio London Ltd* (UKEAT/0130/16), the EAT held that even if the worker does not expressly request breaks, employers must provide them, and a claim can be brought if provision is not made. Employers must take active steps to ensure that their working arrangements enable workers to take the requisite rest breaks. Workers cannot be forced to take rest breaks, but they are to be positively enabled to.

This entitlement is subject to the following exceptions:

(a)   where working time is unmeasured;

(b)   where the worker is engaged in one of the 'special case' activities;

(c)   where the right is modified or excluded by a collective or workforce agreement (see **1.12.6**).

Where (b) or (c) applies, the employer must allow the worker to take an equivalent period of compensatory rest and, in exceptional cases where this is not possible for objective reasons, must afford the worker such protection as may be appropriate in order to safeguard the worker's health and safety. In *Hughes v Corps of Commissioners Management Ltd* [2011] EWCA Civ 1061, the Court of Appeal held that there should be a proper uninterrupted break from work during a rest period, of at least 20 minutes, and then considered the approach to be taken in assessing the special case exception. Readers should have regard to the case when considering these exceptions.

In *McCartney v Oversley House Management* [2006] IRLR 514, the EAT held that the on-call time of a live-in employee was working time, and could not therefore count as a 'rest period', even if the employee was entitled to 'rest' while on call.

In *Gallacher v Alpha Catering Services* [2005] IRLR 102, the EAT said a 'break' was a period when employees were not at their employer's disposal.

In *Crawford v Network Rail Infrastructure Ltd* (UKEAT/0316/16), the EAT said that an employer was not entitled to meet the 20-minute rest period requirement by aggregating breaks of a shorter duration.

1.12.4.4   Sanctions

A worker may present a complaint to a tribunal that his employer has not allowed him to exercise his right to a daily/weekly rest period or rest break, or has failed to provide an equivalent period of compensatory rest. Such complaints must be brought within three months of the act or omission complained of, unless the tribunal considers that it was not reasonably practicable to bring the complaint within this period. The EAT confirmed in *Miles v Linkage Community Trust Ltd* (UKEAT/0618/07) that time will run from the date of the refusal by the employer.

In *Grange v Abellio London Ltd* (see **1.12.4.3**) the claimant was told that he would have to work an eight-hour shift without a break, finishing half an hour earlier (previously he received a half-hour break, finishing later). The issue was whether he had been *refused* a break. The EAT held that:

> Adopting an approach that both allows for a common sense construction of Regulation 30(1), read together with Regulation 12(1), and still meets the purpose of the WTD, I consider the answer is thus to be found in the EAT's Judgment in *Truslove*: the employer has an obligation ('duty') to afford the worker the entitlement to take a rest break (paragraph 32 *Truslove*). That entitlement will be '*refused*' by the employer if it puts into place working arrangements that fail to allow the taking of 20 minute rest breaks (*MacCartney*). If, however, the employer has taken active steps to ensure working arrangements that enable the worker to take the requisite rest break, it will have met the obligation upon it: workers cannot be forced to take the rest breaks but they are to be positively enabled to do so.

If the tribunal upholds such a complaint, it must make a declaration to that effect and may also award compensation. The amount of compensation is such as the tribunal considers just and equitable in all the circumstances having regard to the employer's default in refusing to permit the exercise of the worker's entitlement and any loss sustained by the worker as a consequence of that default. Compensation for injury to feelings is not available (*Santos Gomes v Higher Level Care Ltd* (EAT/0017/16)).

The Regulations also provide that a worker has the right not to be subjected to any detriment by any act, or any deliberate failure to act, by his employer on the ground that the worker has refused (or proposed to refuse) to forgo a rest entitlement, has brought proceedings against the employer to enforce such an entitlement or has alleged that the employer has infringed such a right. If this is the principal reason for an employee's dismissal, the dismissal will be treated as unfair (irrespective of the employee's length of service).

1.12.5   Annual leave and holiday pay

The Working Time Directive (93/104) provides for a basic period of four weeks' annual leave per year. The Regulations, however, go further than this for UK workers and provide that a worker is entitled to a minimum of 5.6 weeks' annual leave in each leave year (ie 28 days for full-time employees, ie those who work five days a week). This is effectively to compensate for the eight bank holidays. Thus a UK worker's paid holiday entitlement is made up of:

- four weeks' basic annual leave (20 days for full-time employees) each year (Article 7 and reg 13(1));

- an additional 1.6 weeks' annual leave (eight days for full-time employees) each year (reg 13A).

These basic minimums can also be topped up, enhanced or extended by express contractual terms. Different rules can apply as to how holiday leave is paid and impacted on by termination or sick pay, depending on whether the paid holiday entitlement is basic, additional or contractual. So, for example, while basic paid holiday must be used or lost and cannot be paid for in lieu or accrued over from year to year (unless on termination), additional leave can be carried over but cannot be paid in lieu, and any contractual paid holiday above and beyond these minimums can be treated as having been agreed in the contract, so may be able to be carried over or paid in lieu. The general view when looking at paid holiday entitlement is that the basic holiday accrues first, followed by the additional, followed by any contractual entitlement. This can be important because of the different rules that apply (see below for more details).

A worker's leave year will normally be specified in the contract of employment. If not, a 'leave year' starts on 1 October 1998 or, if later, the date on which the worker starts work, and each subsequent anniversary of that date.

Regulation 13(9) provides that:

(a)   the leave may only be taken in the leave year in respect of which it is due;

(b)   a worker's leave may not be replaced by a payment in lieu (except at termination of employment) (see **1.12.5.6** below).

Contractual and statutory annual leave will continue to accrue during maternity/adoption, etc leave (see **Chapter 14**).

1.12.5.1   Joiners and leavers

There are special rules relating to joiners and leavers. For joiners, their rights to annual leave are proportionate to the amount of the 'leave year' for which they work. For leavers, workers have a right to be paid in lieu for any untaken leave to which they are entitled. (See *Kreuziger v Land Berlin* and *Max-Planck-Gesellschaft zur Förderung der Wissenschaften eV v Shimizu* (Cases C-619/16 and C-684/16) for the position upon termination in respect of a worker who has not applied to take leave during the year.)

In *Leisure Leagues UK Ltd v Maconnachie* [2002] IRLR 600, the EAT held that holiday pay should be calculated on the basis of the number of working days in the year and not the number of calendar days. See also *Yarrow v Edwards Chartered Accountants* (UKEAT/0116/07).

The Court of Appeal decided in *Bamsey and Others v Albion Engineering and Manufacturing plc* [2004] IRLR 457 that, when calculating holiday pay, compulsory but non-guaranteed overtime does not need to be taken into account in computing a week's pay.

Regulation 14(4) provides that an employer can recover payment for excess holiday taken by a leaver only if there is express agreement between the employer and employee. That means that if an employer wants to be able to recover compensation from an employee who is leaving and has taken more holiday than that to which he was entitled at the date of termination, this should be provided for in the contract of employment. The EAT confirmed in in *Hill v Chappell* [2003] IRLR 19, that an employer cannot use the ERA 1996 to claw back the money.

1.12.5.2   Notice

A worker does not have the right to take leave at any time he chooses. Subject to variation or exclusion by a relevant agreement, a worker is required under reg 15 to give written notice to his employer specifying the dates on which leave is to be taken twice as many days in advance of the earliest day specified in the notice as the number of days to which the notice relates. A similar notice requiring a worker to take leave on particular days may be issued by the employer.

An employer also has the power to issue a notice to a worker requiring him *not* to take leave on particular days. Such a notice must be given to the worker as many days in advance of the earliest day specified in the notice as the number of days to which the notice relates. Again, this right is subject to modification or exclusion by a relevant agreement. (See the decision of the Supreme Court in *Russell v Transocean International* [2011] UKSC 57 on when leave can be taken.)

The ECJ has recently held, in *Shimizu* (above) that the mere fact that a worker did not apply for leave during a given year does not automatically mean that leave is lost and cannot be carried over. An employer must 'diligently' bring it to a worker's attention that leave will be lost; the burden of proof will be on the employer.

1.12.5.3 Calculating holiday pay

A worker is entitled to a 'week's pay' for each week of annual leave (reg 16). Article 7 of the Working Time Directive requires workers to be paid 'normal remuneration' during the holiday to which they are entitled under EU law (ie the basic four weeks). For the purposes of reg 16 of the 1998 Regulations, a 'week's pay' is defined in accordance with the Employment Rights Act 1996 (ss 221–224). If the pattern of work is settled and normal, regular working hours are involved, it should be straightforward to calculate normal pay (ERA 1996, ss 221–223). If there are not 'normal' working hours, a 12-week average period is used (ERA 1996, s 224; *Brazel v The Harpur Trust* (UKEAT/0102/17)). Employers commonly use, as a shorthand way of calculating holiday leave entitlement, a calculation of 12.07% of hours worked. The calculation is based on a standard working year of 52 weeks, less 5.6 weeks' annual leave, leaving 46.4 weeks: 5.6 divided by 46.4 = 12.07%. However, where someone such as Mrs Brazel, a part-time music teacher, only worked in term time (32 weeks), her holiday pay needed to be calculated on the average of her last 12 working weeks at 5.6 divided by 32 weeks, giving 17.5% of pay. The EAT said there was no requirement to ensure that full-time workers were not treated less favourably than part-time workers (as opposed to the other way round). Care therefore needs to be taken when calculating the holiday pay of casual or zero hours staff.

In 2012, the ECJ, in *Williams v British Airways plc* (Case C-155/10) (see **1.12.5** above), confirmed that a worker must be no worse off financially during annual leave than if he had continued working, and that workers are entitled to their 'normal remuneration' when on holiday. Different considerations may apply where additional or contractual holiday is concerned. In *Williams*, the ECJ had been asked by the UK Supreme Court to consider whether or not 'normal remuneration' during a period of annual leave should include allowances on top of basic pay, in the context of a dispute over how the holiday pay of British Airways pilots, who were paid flying allowances as well as basic pay, should be calculated. The ECJ gave a wider definition to 'normal pay' under the Directive than had previously been assumed. Accordingly, holiday pay was not confined to basic pay but included the supplementary payments for time spent flying, as well as allowances linked to the pilots' professional and personal status. Since *Williams*, tribunals have considered a number of claims concerning whether overtime arrangements, commission and various other financial supplements paid to workers formed part of 'normal remuneration' for the purposes of calculating holiday pay.

Commission payments

By s 221(4), commission or similar payments which vary with the amount of work done are included, but not if they depend on results rather than the amount of work done (*Evans v Malley Organisation Ltd* [2003] ICR 432, CA).

The reasoning in *Williams* (above) was also adopted by the ECJ in *Lock v British Gas Trading Ltd* [2014] ICR 813, a case concerning the right to paid annual leave under Article 7 of the Working Time Directive. In *Lock*, the ECJ held that commission payments that were directly and intrinsically linked to an individual's work must be reflected in the worker's holiday pay. Mr Lock was employed as a sales consultant. He was remunerated by a basic salary plus a sales-based commission payment, which accounted for approximately 60% of his total pay.

While he was on holiday, he did not get any commission. When the case returned to the employment tribunal, the tribunal held that it could read the 1998 Regulations compatibly with the EU Directive by adding words to the Regulations. The new words inserted into reg 16(3) are as follows:

> (e)   as if, in the case of the entitlement under regulation 13, a worker with normal working hours whose remuneration includes commission or similar payment shall be deemed to have remuneration which varies with the amount of work done for the purpose of section 221 [of the ERA 1996].

Both the EAT (UKEAT/0189/15) and the Court of Appeal ([2016] EWCA Civ 983) upheld the tribunal's decision and dismissed British Gas's appeal, ruling that the 1998 Regulations can be interpreted to provide that calculating 'normal pay' for the four weeks' paid holiday derived from the Working Time Directive must include regular commission payments.

Overtime

Overtime payments should be ignored when they relate to work done outside normal working hours (s 222(3); *Tarmac Roadshow Holdings Ltd v Peacock* [1973] ICR 273, CA (see below)).

In the joined cases of *Bear Scotland Ltd & Others v Fulton & Others*, *Hertel (UK) Ltd v Woods & Others* and *Amec Group Ltd v Law & Others* (UKEATS/0047/13, UKEAT/0160/14 and UKEAT/0161/14), the EAT (Langstaff J, President of the EAT, sitting alone), applying the *Marleasing* principle (see **1.2.4.3** above), considered what constitutes 'normal remuneration' for holiday pay purposes and, if a worker has been underpaid, how far back he can claim. The appeal concerned the decisions of two employment tribunals that supplementary payments normally received by workers, including overtime payments, should count towards holiday pay. The EAT held:

- Holiday pay must correspond to 'normal' remuneration, which is pay that is normally received, including 'non-guaranteed' overtime, commission and other allowances forming a worker's normal pay (but only in relation to the first four weeks of statutory leave, which are covered by the Working Time Directive).

- There is, however, limited scope for workers to recover underpayments of holiday pay by way of an unlawful deduction from wages claim.

The EAT concluded therefore that overtime, including non-guaranteed overtime and other allowances 'intrinsically linked to the performance of the tasks' (in this case 'radius allowances' and 'travelling time payments'), must be included when calculating holiday pay.

The decision only applies in relation to basic holiday pay payable in respect of the first four weeks of holiday entitlement (1998 Regulations, reg 13), which derives from the Working Time Directive. While under UK law, workers are entitled to 5.6 weeks' annual leave, only the first four weeks of leave derive from the Directive. The additional 1.6 weeks come under reg 13A and are a matter of UK law only. As reg 13A leave is not derived from the Directive, the wider interpretation of 'normal pay' does not apply here.

While the EAT has ruled (*Bear Scotland*) that compulsory overtime pay should be included when calculating holiday pay, it had not dealt with the issue of payment for voluntary overtime payments until recently. There had been a couple of employment tribunal judgments that had looked at the issue. In *Brettle, White & Others v Dudley Metropolitan Borough Council* (ET/1300537/15) the tribunal helpfully analysed the current position regarding the calculation of holiday pay, what it should include and what counts as a 'regular' payment where voluntary overtime is concerned. The tribunal heard from five lead claimants (there were 56 claimants in total) employed by Dudley Council in the repair and improvement department for social housing. They were all tradesmen with a variety of skills – including plumbers, roofers, electricians and carpenters – each of whom worked different types of voluntary overtime and/or were on stand-by/on-call rotas on a 'regular' basis, receiving payments for these additional hours when worked (but not whilst they were on annual leave). The tradesmen were invited to work on a Saturday on a purely voluntary basis while working on the council's stock of social housing. They also elected to go on standby every four weeks, to deal with emergency call-outs and repairs – again, not at the employer's discretion. The voluntary overtime and on-call rota had been in place for such a period, and with such regularity, that it was argued it had become part of their 'normal work' and accordingly part of their 'normal pay'. The council argued that it did not form part of 'contractual pay'. But the judge ruled that the payment for that work had to be included in the calculation of holiday pay for the first 20 days of annual leave, under reg 13 of the 1998 Regulations. The employment judge emphasised that the question of whether a payment is 'intrinsically linked to normal work, paid in such a manner and with such sufficient regularity to be considered part of normal remuneration' is fact specific (see too *Whitehead v EMH Housing* (ET/2600493/4/6)). The EAT held in *Dudley Metropolitan Borough Council v Willetts* (UKEAT/0334/16) that voluntary overtime, normally worked, is pay for the purposes of calculating holiday pay. This was followed by the EAT in *Flowers v East of England Ambulance Trust* (UKEAT/0235/17), which said that voluntary overtime was part of normal remuneration if it was paid over a sufficient period. (See too the 2018 Acas Guidance on Overtime.)

How far back can a claim be made?

Under the 1998 Regulations, workers can only claim underpayments under reg 13 arising in the three months prior to the presentation of their claim. However, in *HMRC v Stringer* (see **1.12.5** above), the House of Lords established that a failure to pay holiday pay under the 1998 Regulations can also be framed as an unlawful deduction from wages claim, contrary to s 13 of the ERA 1996 (see **1.11** above). A worker can bring a s 13 claim in respect of a 'series of deductions'; in such a case, the claim must be brought within three months of the last deduction in the series (ERA 1996, s 23). It was assumed that using this route allowed claimants to link together a series of underpayments in order to bring a backdated claim, regardless of the length of time that had elapsed between each deduction. This decision meant that if workers brought a claim under the protection of wages provisions of the ERA 1996 for a series of deductions of wages, there would be more flexibility on time restrictions than there would be if a claim were brought under the 1998 Regulations. In the employment tribunal case of *Neal v Freightliner Ltd* (ET/1315342/2012) (which was settled before an appeal to the EAT was heard), the tribunal allowed a worker to claim for underpayments going back to 2007 when his employment began.

However, the EAT in *Bear Scotland* (above) (and confirmed in UKEATS/0010/16) concluded that the workers could not claim any consequent holiday underpayment as forming part of a series of deductions of wages where more than three months had elapsed between the 'deductions'. The EAT stated that 'any series punctuated from the next succeeding series by a gap of more than three months is one in respect of which the passage of time has extinguished the jurisdiction to consider a complaint that it was unpaid'. This analysis thus severely restricts the amount of time that a worker may potentially look back at as the chances of a worker having a long (if any) series of untaken reg 13 leave over a number of years is likely to be minimal. However, going forward, employers will need to take into account overtime when calculating the first four weeks of any worker's holiday pay. At the end of November 2014, Unite announced that it was not pursuing an appeal in the *Bear Scotland* case, so the position remains that other than cases where there has not been a three-month break period between leave periods, most claims will have been restricted. As *Bear Scotland* conflicts with other, higher authority on the meaning of 'series', it is, however, likely to be an area that is revisited by the courts sooner rather than later.

Following the EAT's decision in *Bear Scotland* and the joined cases, the Government introduced legislation to 'reduce potential costs to employers and give certainty to workers on their rights following the recent court decisions on holiday pay' (Government Press Release, 18 December 2014). The Deduction from Wages (Limitation) Regulations 2014 took effect from 8 January 2015, and apply to claims presented to the employment tribunal on or after 1 July 2015. Designed to limit back claims for holiday pay to two years, these Regulations also amended the 1998 Regulations by stating that the right to payment in respect of annual leave is not contractual but purely statutory, thus preventing the bringing of contractual claims for statutory holiday pay.

However, the ECJ in *King v The Sash Window Workshop Ltd* (Case C-214/16) (a case referred to the ECJ by the Court if Appeal following an employment tribunal decision to award £25,000 in respect of untaken holiday stretching back 13 years, Mr King's claim having been brought as a series of unlawful deductions under s 13 of the ERA 1996, and pre-dating the 2014 Regulations) held that workers' denied paid holiday can carry over their four weeks' statutory entitlement indefinitely and be paid in lieu of the entire accrued untaken entitlement on termination.

In this case, the employer wrongly classed Mr King as self-employed and therefore maintained that he had no right to paid holidays. As a result, he did not take most of his holiday entitlement from 1999 to 2012 (over 24 weeks'). The ECJ said it did not matter that the worker had not put in holiday requests. It also said that Article 7 of the Directive had to be interpreted as precluding national provisions which prevent a worker from carrying over and/or accumulating until termination paid annual leave rights.

This decision (although it only applies to the basic four weeks under reg 13 and not to the additional eight days in the UK under reg 13A) runs directly counter to the decision of the EAT in *Bear Scotland* (above) and appears to obviate the two-year backstop implemented by the 2014 Regulations. The case has now been referred back to the Court of Appeal and is listed for hearing in late November 2018. Until then, the situation remains uncertain. Under *Bear Scotland*, the 'no more than three months gap' between deductions may prove problematic, but it is open to the Court of Appeal to find that it is incompatible with EU law.

1.12.5.4 'Rolled-up' holiday pay

The ECJ held in *Robinson-Steele v RD Retail Services and other cases* (Case C-131/04) that it is contrary to the Working Time Directive for a payment for annual leave to be made in the form of payments staggered over the year and paid together with remuneration for work done, rather than in the form of a payment in respect of a specific period during which the worker actually takes leave.

Notwithstanding that ruling in 2006, rolled-up holiday pay continues for many workers. Current UK Government guidance states: 'Holiday pay should be paid for the time when annual leave is taken. An employer cannot include an amount for holiday pay in the hourly rate. ... If a current contract still includes rolled-up pay, it needs to be re-negotiated.' However, where it continues it would appear that, so long as payments are clearly identified as holiday pay, an employer is entitled to offset rolled-up holiday pay against a claim by a worker for his holiday entitlement (see *Lyddon v Englefield Brickwork Ltd* (EAT/0301/07)).

1.12.5.5 Annual leave and sickness

The analysis below is relevant to the four weeks' annual leave entitlement under the Working Time Directive (different considerations may apply in respect of additional leave beyond four weeks, which is not derived from the Directive). Article 7, as implemented by reg 13 of the 1998 Regulations, provides that an employee is entitled to paid annual leave of at least four weeks. Regulation 13(9) of the Regulations provides that annual leave may only be taken in the leave year in respect of which it is due. However, the following principles can be distilled from domestic and European case law:

(1)   A sick employee must be permitted to take annual leave whilst sick (*HMRC v Stringer*).

(2)   An employee who is permitted to take paid annual leave during a period of sick leave cannot be required to do so (*Pereda v Madrid Mouilidad* (Case C-277/08); *Plumb v Duncan Print Group Ltd* (EAT/0071/15)).

(3)   The Working Time Directive does not preclude national legislation or practices which prevent an employee from taking paid annual leave during a period of sickness absence provided, however, that the worker has the opportunity to take annual leave at a later date or be paid for it if the employment relationship ends before the employee can take the leave (*Schultz-Hoff v Deutsche Rentenversicherung Bund* [2009] IRLR 214; see too *NHS Leeds v Larner* [2012] EWCA Civ 1034).

(4)   EU law does not confer an unlimited right to carry over periods of annual leave to subsequent years. The Working Time Directive, at most, only requires that employees on sick leave are able to take annual leave within a period of 18 months of the end of the leave year in respect of which the annual leave arises. Consequently, reg 13(9) of the Regulations is to be read as permitting a worker to take annual leave within 18 months of the end of the leave year in which it accrued (or be entitled to payment on termination for the paid annual leave), where the worker was unable or unwilling to take annual leave because he was on sick leave and, as a consequence, did not exercise his right to annual leave (*Plumb v Duncan Print Group Ltd*). A year is too short a period. National law restricting the period to 15 months is acceptable (*KHS AG v Schulte* [2012] IRLR 156).

(5)   A worker who becomes unfit during annual leave must be allowed to take the part of the annual leave that coincides with sickness at a later date and to carry it forward to the next holiday year if unable to use it (*Pereda v Madrid Mouilidad* and *Sobczyszyn v Szkola Podstawowa w Rzeplinie* (Case C-178/15)).

(6)   In *NHS Leeds v Larner* [2012] EWCA Civ 1034, the Court of Appeal commented, on an obiter basis, that reg 14(2) (which allows for payment, on termination, in respect of untaken but accrued holiday during the last year of employment) could be read and interpreted (so as to comply with Article 7 of the Directive) to include a provision requiring an employer to make a payment on termination in respect of any untaken holiday pay from a previous holiday year which was rolled over due to sickness. Under reg 30(1), a worker can bring a claim for any amount which is unpaid but due under reg 14(2).

Where the employer in question is the state or an emanation of the state (see **1.2.4.2**), the employee will be able to rely on the direct effect of Article 7 of the Working Time Directive. In other cases the court will be asked to interpret domestic law in line with EU law. The Court of Appeal suggested in *Larner* (above) that reg 13 could be construed in line with Article 7.

1.12.5.6   Annual leave and maternity/paternity leave

As employment rights are protected in the UK while on maternity/paternity leave (see **Chapter 14**), paid holiday will continue to accrue. Generally, this will be taken before or after the maternity/paternity leave period. This applies to both statutory and contractual annual leave entitlements. (See the ECJ case of *Tribunalul Botosani v Dicu* on the ability of EU States' laws to disapply the accrual of annual leave during parental leave, distinguishing it from maternity leave and sickness, for which the Working Time Directive does not presuppose that the worker is actually at work.)

1.12.5.7   Summary of current state of affairs on annual leave in the UK

Generally statutory annual leave must be taken in the year in which it falls due and cannot be carried forward. Case law has established that where someone is on sick leave, maternity leave or has not been permitted to take annual leave, their holiday continues to be due and accrue. Case law now suggests that untaken holiday cannot be carried forward indefinitely and should be limited to 18 months after the end of the holiday year in question. This only applies to the four weeks' annual leave mandated by the Directive, and different considerations will apply to the additional 1.6 weeks allowed under UK law and any separate express contractual holiday pay provisions, which will be governed by the terms of the contract.

When calculating how much an employee should be paid in respect of annual leave, it is necessary to work out what a 'week's pay' means. Where a worker has 'normal working hours' and is on a fixed salary, this is a fairly straightforward exercise. Where the worker receives variable pay depending on the amount of work he does or when he does it, a week's pay is averaged out over the previous 12 weeks. Both guaranteed and non-guaranteed contractual overtime payments, as well as commission payments, should be included. There is nothing in principle that appears likely to prevent voluntary overtime, at least where this is worked regularly (so as to constitute work 'normally carried out' and amount to an 'appropriately permanent feature' so as to form part of a worker's 'normal hours'), from also having to be taken into account (see *Patterson v Castlereagh Borough Council* (NIIT/1793/13). Likewise, any payments that are linked to productivity, and travel time payments that exceed expenses incurred and so amount to additional taxable remuneration. These sums only apply when calculating the four weeks to which employees are entitled under the Working Time Directive.

Workers can only bring claims for holiday pay in the employment tribunal. Claims can be brought either under the Regulations, or as a series of unlawful deductions from wages under the ERA 1996. However, both claims have to be brought within three months of the date of the last payment. A gap of more than three months will restrict a 'series' claim under the unlawful deductions for wages provisions in the ERA 1996. Any claims for statutory annual holiday pay issued after 1 July 2015 can in any event only go back a maximum of two years.

Holiday pay – summary of relevant case law

	ECJ	SC	CA	EAT	ET
On call	SiMAP (C-303/98) [2000] IRLR 845, paras 48–49; Grigore (C-258/10), para 53; Jaeger (C-151/02) [2003] IRLR 804, para 63; Matzak (C-518/15)			Hughes (UKEAT/0159/08)	
Travelling to work	Tyco Integrated Security (C-266/14)			Valentine (UKEAT/0325/16)	
Normal remuneration/ week's pay	Williams (C-155/10)			Bear Scotland (UKEATS/ 0047/13)	
Commission payments	Williams (C-155/10); Lock [2014] ICR 813		Evans [2003] ICR 432; Lock [2016] EWCA Civ 983		
Overtime			Peacock [1973] ICR 273; Patterson [2015] IRLR 721	Bear Scotland (UKEATS/ 0047/13); Willetts (UKEAT/0334/16); Flowers (UKEAT/0235/17)	Brettle (ET/1300537/15); Whitehead (ET/2600493/4/ 6)
Sickness	Pereda (C-277/08); Schultz-Hoff [2009] IRLR 214; Sobczyszyn (C-178/15)	Stringer [2009] UKHL 31	Larner [2010] EWCA Civ 1034	Plumb (UKEAT/0071/15)	
Calculation		Stringer [2009] UKHL 31		Brazel (UKEAT/ 0102/17)	
Limitations on back pay: Deduction from Wages (Limitation) Regulations 2016	King (C-214/16)			Bear Scotland (UKEATS/ 0047/13)	Neal (ET/1315342/2012)
Rolling up	Robinson-Steele (C-131/04)				

1.12.5.8 Zero hours contracts

In *Heimann v Kaiser GmbH* [2013] IRLR 48, the ECJ ruled that national legislation could provide for workers on zero hours contracts to be entitled to be paid annual leave on a pro rata basis, since their situation was analogous to that of part-time workers. Accordingly, claimants do not accrue untaken annual leave during the period of their zero hours arrangement.

1.12.5.9 Bank holidays

This is another potentially vexed area. Some employers only give the benefit of bank or public holidays if the holiday in question falls on a day when the worker would normally be at work. However, this may be in breach of the Part-Time Workers Regulations 2000 (see **8.10**) because some part-time workers (generally those who do not work on Mondays or whose working days are variable) could be treated less favourably than comparable full-time workers. In general it is simplest to give part-time workers a pro rata entitlement to public holidays, regardless of which days they normally work.

1.12.5.10 Holidays and discrimination

While most Christian festivals such as Christmas and Easter are provided for as public holidays, there is no such provision for non-Christian festivals. This may lead to requests in some businesses for a large volume of days off at the same time, outside the designated public holidays. Employers need to be wary of avoiding putting employees of particular religions or beliefs at a disadvantage if they refuse such requests. They will need to ensure they are acting reasonably in how they deal with such requests. Similar issues can arise in regard to request for leave during school holidays in respect of possible indirect sex discrimination claims. See by way of illustration the approach of the EAT in *Garreddu v London Underground Ltd* (see **8.2.3.1** below).

1.12.5.11 Sanctions

The sanctions for failing to provide a worker with paid annual leave are very similar to the sanctions that are imposed in respect of a breach of a worker's rest entitlements outlined at **1.12.4.4** above. However, where the complaint is of failure to provide due pay for a period of annual leave or pay in lieu of untaken leave on termination of employment, the tribunal must order payment of the amount due by the employer. (See the chart at **5.6.2.5**.)

1.12.5.12 Law Society practice note

The Law Society has a useful practice note on its website about holiday entitlement, advising on calculating entitlement to paid annual leave, how entitlement is affected by working part time, for a fixed term or on a temporary contract, and the difference between contractual and statutory entitlement.

1.12.6 Relevant agreements

The Regulations enable workers and employers to enter into agreements to establish the way in which some of the working time rules apply to their own workplaces. Provision is made for the following agreements which, collectively, are referred to as 'relevant agreements':

(a)   workforce agreements, ie agreements with workforce representatives;

(b)   collective agreements with independent recognised trade unions;

(c)   written agreements, ie any other agreement in writing which is legally enforceable between the worker and his employer.

1.12.6.1 Which rights/limits can be modified or excluded?

The main situation in which a written agreement between a worker and his employer can be utilised is to modify or exclude the limits on weekly working time.

Collective or workforce agreements can be used (inter alia) to modify or exclude the following rights:

(a)   length of night work;

(b)   daily and weekly rest periods; and

(c)   rest breaks.

In each case where a collective or workforce agreement is utilised to modify or exclude these rights, the employer must allow the worker wherever possible to take an equivalent period of compensationary rest and, if this is not possible for objective reasons, must afford the worker such protection as may be appropriate in order to safeguard the worker's health and safety.

In *Industry and Commerce Maintenance v Briffa* (UKEAT/021508/07), the EAT held that the basic requirements in reg 15 could be varied or excluded by a contractual term which covered the position and was legally enforceable as a relevant agreement under reg 2.

1.12.6.2   Workforce agreements: the legal requirements

The Regulations lay down detailed provisions with regard to a valid workforce agreement. For example, the agreement has to be in writing, and it cannot last longer than five years.

1.13   CHECKLISTS

1.13.1   Terms and conditions

(1)   Is the individual an employee or a worker? For the definition of 'employee' see s 230(1) of the ERA 1996; for the definition of 'worker' see s 230(3) of the 1996 Act.

(2)   Within two months of starting employment, employers must give their employees a written statement of the main terms of their contract.

(3)   There are certain key terms that *must* be included in a written statement of terms and conditions (see ERA 1996, s 1(3)–(4)).

(4)   Consider whether to include other express terms as well (see **1.4** and **Appendix 1**).

(5)   Check that any restrictive covenants are reasonable in terms of time and area, and are necessary to protect the employer's business interests.

(6)   Check that the National Minimum Wage Regulations and Working Time Regulations are not being broken.

(7)   Check that the employee signs and returns the statement/contract, and that both the employer and the employee have copies.

1.13.2   Summary of basic working time rights, enforcement and exceptions

SUMMARY OF BASIC WORKING TIME RIGHTS

Maximum working week	48 hours/week
Daily break	20 minutes/6 hours
Daily rest	11 hours/24 hours
Weekly rest	24 hours/7 days
Paid annual leave	5.6 weeks/52 weeks

ENFORCEMENT

	Health & Safety etc	Declaration and Compensation	No Detriment	Unfair Dismissal
WORKING WEEK	✓		✓	✓
NIGHT WORK	✓		✓	✓
REST PERIODS		✓	✓	✓
REST BREAKS		✓	✓	✓
ANNUAL LEAVE		✓	✓	✓

EXCEPTIONS

	Written Agreement	Unmeasured Working Time	Special Case Activities	Shift/Split Period Workers	Collective/ Workforce Agreements
WORKING WEEK	✓	✓			
NIGHT WORK		✓	✓		✓
REST PERIODS		✓	✓	✓	✓
REST BREAKS		✓	✓		✓
ANNUAL LEAVE					

1.14 FURTHER READING

Harvey, *Industrial Relations and Employment Law* (Butterworths), Divs A, B and C.

Lewis, *Employment Law – an adviser's handbook*, 12th revised edn (LAG, 2017).

Selwyn's Law of Employment, 20th edn (OUP, 2018).

Blackstone's Employment Law Practice, 10th edn (OUP, 2019).

Bowers, *A Practical Approach to Employment Law*, 9th edn (OUP, 2017), chs 1–6.

Howard, *Drafting Employment Contracts*, 3rd edn (Law Society).

SUMMARY

This chapter has looked at the various sources of UK employment law (common law, statute, codes of practice and EU law (**1.2** and **1.4**)). It has identified that there are some important differences between employees, workers and those who work for themselves as far as statutory protections are concerned. Certain rights, such as unfair dismissal and the right to a redundancy payment, apply only to employees; others (eg the National Minimum Wage Regulations and the Working Time Regulations) apply to a wider category of worker (**1.3**).

Section 1 of the ERA 1996 provides that employers must give their employees a written statement of the main terms of their contract (**1.4** and **Appendix 1**). A statement of terms and conditions is not a contract, but it does confirm the main express terms of the employment contract. It is not definitive of the entire contract, but it does provide an evidential basis of the most important terms.

Contracts of employment, where both sides agree the terms, may be written or oral, but it is sensible to put them in writing. Even where there is a written contract with express terms, statute and the courts will sometimes imply terms into a contract (**1.4**). The most important implied term is that of mutual trust and confidence. Where this term is broken, it may entitle either side to bring the relationship to an end. If an employer breaches it, it may entitle an employee with the requisite period of continuous employment to resign and claim constructive unfair dismissal (**3.4.3**).

The contract should, as a minimum, deal with all the matters set out in s 1(3) and (4) of the ERA 1996. This includes pay, job description, hours of work, place of work and whether the employee can be made to move, holiday, pension and sickness provisions, the length of notice that needs to be given by either side to terminate the arrangement (s 86 of the ERA 1996 sets out certain minimum notice periods), disciplinary and grievance procedures, and the obligations of confidentiality that an employee owes his employer (**1.4–1.8, Appendix 1**). It is also possible to include terms which protect an employer's business after the employee has left. These terms are known as restrictive covenants. They may be expressly included in a contract, so long as they are reasonable in terms of time and area and are necessary to protect the employer's business interests (**1.8.7**).

The protection of wages legislation set out in Pt II of the ERA 1996 protects an employee if an employer fails to pay the proper wages due under the contract, and prevents an employer from making deductions from an employee's wages unless they are authorised (**1.11**). For claims presented after 1 July 2015, there is a maximum of two years' deductions that can be claimed (**1.11.2**).

The Working Time Regulations 1998 set out maximum weekly working hours and provide for certain minimum rights to have breaks and paid annual leave (**1.12**). For claims presented after 1 July 2015, there is a maximum of two years' back pay that can be claimed.

CHAPTER 2

TERMINATION OF THE CONTRACT OF EMPLOYMENT – WRONGFUL DISMISSAL

LEARNING OUTCOMES

After reading this chapter you will be able to:

- describe and understand the differences between a claim of wrongful dismissal based on a breach of contract and the statutory claim of unfair dismissal, and the remedies that are available for wrongful dismissal

- explain when a wrongful dismissal claim arises

- understand the main ways in which a contract of employment may come to an end and the relevance of notice periods

- understand the significance of constructive dismissal

- understand the relevant principles to apply when calculating an employee's damages following a wrongful dismissal

- understand what remedies are available to an employer if an employee is in repudiatory breach of contract.

2.1 INTRODUCTION

Before considering in detail three of the main potential claims an employee might have on termination of a contract of employment (wrongful dismissal (see **2.2**), unfair dismissal (see **Chapter 5**) and the right to a redundancy payment (see **Chapter 4**)), it is useful to have a preliminary overview of these claims.

2.1.1 Wrongful dismissal (breach of contract)

This is a common law contractual claim for breach of contract, which may be brought by workers or employees, based *solely* on the fact that the dismissal by the employer was in breach of contract. The remedy is therefore damages for breach of contract.

For example:

(a)   termination of the contract with no notice or short notice (see **2.3.3**); or

(b)   where the employee/worker establishes he has been constructively dismissed (see **2.3.5**); or

(c)   termination of the contract before the expiry of a limited term where there is no break clause (see **2.3.8**).

A breach of contract claim can be brought in the civil courts or in the employment tribunal. However, an employment tribunal's contract jurisdiction is limited (Employment Tribunals Act (ETA) 1996, ss 3 and 8; Employment Tribunal's Extension of Jurisdiction Order 1994). In *London Borough of Enfield v Sivanandan* [2005] EWCA Civ 10, the Court of Appeal held that where a breach of contract claim is struck out (as opposed to being withdrawn – see *Sajid v Chowdhury* [2002] IRLR 113) by an employment tribunal, it is an abuse of process to re-issue it in the civil courts. Even if a claim is withdrawn, it may be an abuse of process to re-issue it if the claim in the employment tribunal covered the same facts and was worth less than £25,000. If a claim is withdrawn but it is intended to pursue the claim in the civil courts, the claimant should tell the employment tribunal that that is the reason the claim is being withdrawn.

There is no limit to the amount of damages recoverable in a court action, although there is a restriction on tribunal awards. This is currently £25,000. Breach of contract claims can be brought in a tribunal where the claim follows termination of the employment together with a claim for unfair dismissal. Claimants need to be aware, though, that if they bring a high-value breach of contract claim in the tribunal, they will not be permitted to seek to recover any excess over £25,000 in the civil courts. The Court of Appeal, in *Fraser v HLMAD* [2006] EWCA Civ 738, said that once the claimant had lodged an ET1 claim form, which included a claim for breach of contract for wrongful dismissal, the claims had 'merged' and there was no independent claim left which he could pursue. The Court of Appeal said that claimants wishing to bring high-value breach of contract claims should do so in the civil courts, unless they are willing to limit damages to £25,000.

Limitation periods for bringing claims in the tribunal and courts are also different (see **2.2**).

When considering a breach of contract claim, no account is taken of the reasonableness of an employer's action in terminating the contract. This allows employers to write in contractual provisions entitling them to terminate the contract and dismiss the employee without facing any common law claim for breach of contract (the contractual notice period must not be shorter than the statutory minimum period required by s 86 of the ERA 1996 – see **2.3.3**). So, for example, if an employer dismisses an employee with the correct notice, generally no claim for breach of contract will arise. To redress the balance, in the 1960s, statute began to intervene in the hitherto unfettered rights of the employer. In particular, concepts of fairness and reasonableness were introduced. Two statutory rights given to the employee are the right to claim unfair dismissal and/or the right to claim a redundancy payment on termination.

Note that workers and employees with less than a year's service will also be entitled to bring a claim for unpaid notice if their contract is terminated with insufficient notice (but note that ERA 1996, s 86 – relating to minimum notice periods – applies only to employees).

2.1.2   Unfair dismissal

This is a statutory claim that can be brought only by certain employees who satisfy eligibility criteria. It can be brought only before an employment tribunal.

The success of the claim does not rest on the issue of breach of contract. The tribunal looks instead into whether or not there was a fair reason for dismissal and at the reasonableness of the employer's actions.

A successful applicant may receive a basic award of compensation calculated in accordance with a set formula. In addition, he may receive a compensatory award to compensate for actual financial loss suffered (in a similar way to an award of damages for breach of contract). This compensatory award is subject to a maximum limit, which was £78,962 as at 6 April 2016 (note the limit is subject to revision in February each year – the Secretary of State can, each year, increase or decrease that sum in accordance with the Retail Price Index).

2.1.3 Redundancy payment

This is another statutory claim, which is in the nature of a reward for past services; it is compensation for the loss of a secure job rather than for future financial losses.

The claimant must, again, be eligible and the claim is pursued (where necessary) in the employment tribunal.

The payment is calculated in accordance with a set formula, which is the same as the basic award formula for unfair dismissal.

2.1.4 Conclusion

There is overlap, in terms of the remedy afforded to an employee, between the three claims, which is considered after looking in detail at each of them (see **6.8**).

The remainder of this chapter deals with the common law claim of wrongful dismissal in breach of contract.

The statutory claims of unfair dismissal and redundancy payments are dealt with in **Chapters 3–5**.

2.2 WRONGFUL DISMISSAL (DISMISSAL IN BREACH OF CONTRACT)

At common law, an employee (or worker) will have a claim for damages against his employer if the employer has dismissed him in breach of contract. This breach of contract claim is known as the claim for 'wrongful dismissal'. See **2.3** for when termination of the contract amounts to a breach of contract (ie gives rise to a wrongful dismissal claim). If there is no dismissal, there cannot be a claim for wrongful dismissal. Instead, there would be a general breach of contract claim.

This claim may be pursued in the civil courts or in the employment tribunal.

In the courts, the limitation period is six years and there is no upper limit on the level of damages which may be awarded. If the claim is worth less than £5,000 and is pursued in the county court, it will automatically be referred to the small claims track.

If a wrongful dismissal claim is pursued in the employment tribunal, there are certain preconditions (ETA 1996, ss 3 and 8; Employment Tribunal's Extension of Jurisdiction Order 1994):

(a)   the claim must be for breach of a contract of employment or other contract connected with employment and must arise or be outstanding on the *termination* of employment. In *Capek v Lincolnshire County Council* [2000] IRLR 590, the Court of Appeal held that tribunals have no jurisdiction to hear claims for breach of contract which are lodged prior to the termination of the employee's contract (ETA 1996, s 3(2));

(b)   the only remedy available is compensation;

(c)   the employment tribunal will not be able to award more than £25,000 in respect of a contract claim (1994 Order, art 10);

(d)   the tribunal cannot hear all claims arising out of an alleged breach – for example claims relating to contractual terms of confidentiality and restrictive covenants are excluded (1994 Order, arts 3, 5);

(e)   the employer will be able to raise a counterclaim (alleging that the employee has also breached the contract of employment);

(f)   the claim will have to be brought within three months of termination (see **6.3.6**).

2.3 TERMINATION OF CONTRACT

2.3.1 Introduction

At common law, the contract of employment may come to an end in a number of ways. Only if the termination amounts to a breach of contract by the employer will the employee be entitled to claim damages for wrongful dismissal. The main ways in which an employment contract can come to an end are set out below.

2.3.2 Termination by agreement

The parties may at any time agree to bring the contract to an end. Neither party will be in breach of contract and no claim for wrongful dismissal will arise.

2.3.3 Termination by notice

A contract of employment for an indefinite term may be terminated by either party giving the other proper notice. Provided proper notice is given, the contract will terminate with no liability for breach of contract, whatever the reason for the termination. If the contract is ended by the employer with proper notice, there can be no wrongful dismissal claim by the employee because the employer has acted within the terms of the contract.

In *Newcastle upon Tyne Hospitals NHS Foundation Trust v Haywood* [2018] UKSC 22, the Supreme Court held that a term will be applied into all employment contracts that notice of termination will only start to run from the date the employee received written notice of their dismissal and has had a reasonable opportunity to read it, if different. This will be the default position unless there is an express contractual clause making clear that, for example, notice is effective from the date of delivery.

This rule applies only to contracts for an indefinite term. In the absence of a 'break' clause, limited-term contracts cannot be terminated by notice.

If the contract contains an express term stating the period of notice to be given by either party, then a party giving shorter notice to terminate will be in breach of contract, subject to **2.3.4**. If an expressly agreed period of notice is shorter than the statutory minimum period required by ERA 1996, s 86 (see below), the longer statutory minimum period must be given. The parties should agree the period of notice when the contract is entered into.

In the absence of an express term, it is an implied term of every indefinite contract of employment that it can be terminated by reasonable notice given by either party. What period is reasonable will depend on the facts of each case. The more senior the employee, the longer the period of notice required. The courts have held, for example, that three months was a reasonable period of notice for a salesman and an airline pilot, but only one week was required in the case of a milk carrier. In *Clark v Fahrenheit 451 (Communications) Ltd* (UKEAT/591/99), the EAT held that an employee's seniority and status and the employer's financial position are to be taken into account in determining what is a reasonable period of notice. Clearly, a reasonable amount must not be less than the statutory minimum.

When advising employers on reasonable periods of notice, it must be remembered that for senior, highly-skilled employees, reasonable notice can be quite long. For professional employees such as solicitors, accountants, highly-skilled technical employees, scientists or middle-managers, reasonable notice is likely to be in the region of three to six months. For a very senior employee, such as a managing director, it could be 12 months. For the unskilled and semi-skilled employee, reasonable notice is unlikely to exceed the statutory minimum period required by ERA 1996, s 86. The problem should be avoided by incorporating expressly agreed periods of notice into the employees' contracts.

Where a contract of employment is terminable by notice, s 86 of the ERA 1996 lays down the statutory minimum period of notice which must be given to employees. The statutory minimum period prevails over any shorter contractual period. However, as the parties may agree longer periods, any contractual provisions should be checked as, if these are more beneficial to the employee, they will override the statutory minimum. In *Newcastle upon Tyne NHS Foundation Trust v Haywood* [2017] EWCA Civ 153, the Court of Appeal held that notice of termination of employment is given when the employee actually receives the notice, because the contents of the letter had to be communicated to the employee. So the day a letter was written or the day it was posted or the day the letter arrived at the claimant's house were not relevant (see also **3.5.2.1**).

The statutory minimum period of notice required to be given by an employer under s 86(1) is:

Period of continuous employment	Notice
1 month to 2 years	1 week
2 years to 12 years	1 week for each year
12 years plus	12 weeks

The only statutory minimum notice required to be given by an employee is one week's notice after one month's continuous employment (s 86(2)).

See **3.5** for the meaning of continuous employment. Either party may waive notice (s 86(3)).

Sometimes the employer will terminate a contract without notice or with short notice but give the employee a payment in lieu of the notice period due ('PILON'). What is the effect of such a payment? There are two possibilities (the second of which is the norm):

(a) The employee accepts the PILON, although there is no provision in the contract permitting such a payment, and agrees, expressly or impliedly, to waive the requirement for notice. In this case there will either be no breach by the employer, or the breach has been waived by the employee for consideration. In either case, there will be no liability for wrongful dismissal.

(b) The employer pays the employee in lieu of notice, but there is no provision in the contract permitting such a payment to be made and the employee, while taking the money, does not accept the payment as waiving his right to notice. In this case the employer is in breach of contract and technically the employee could claim wrongful dismissal. However, unless the payment in lieu of notice is significantly less than the damages likely to be awarded (see **2.4.1**), the claim would not be worth pursuing in financial terms.

In *Société Générale, London Branch v Geys* [2013] IRLR 122, the Supreme Court settled a long-running question as to whether a party's repudiation of a contract of employment itself automatically terminates the contract, or whether the contract comes to an end only when the other party accepts the repudiation (the elective theory). The elective theory is in accordance with the general common-law rule that a repudiated contract is not terminated unless and until the repudiation is accepted by the innocent party. This is primarily because it would be manifestly unjust to allow the wrongdoer to determine a contract by a repudiatory breach where the innocent party wished to affirm the contract for good reason. The effect of the automatic theory of termination is to reward the wrong-doer.

The Supreme Court favoured the elective theory, by a 4:1 majority. The claimant was the managing director at a bank. His contract had a clause saying it could be terminated after three months' notice. The staff handbook provided that the bank reserved the right to terminate the employment at any time with immediate effect by making a payment in lieu of notice. The contract gave the claimant an entitlement to a termination payment, under which, if his contract terminated after 31 December 2007, he would receive a figure calculated by reference to his salary in 2006 and 2007. If his employment terminated before that date, his termination payment was to be calculated by reference to two earlier years, when his salary was much lower. So it was a key issue as to whether the contact terminated in 2007 or 2008.

At a meeting on 29 November 2007, the claimant was given a letter informing him that his employment was being terminated 'with immediate effect'. No reference was made to the PILON clause, so this appeared on its face to be a repudiatory breach of contract. On 18 December, the bank paid a sum into the claimant's bank account that would have satisfied the PILON clause, but again there was no reference to the PILON clause. The claimant became aware of the payment at some point before the end of December, and on 2 January 2008 the claimant told the bank that he was affirming his contract. On 4 January, the bank wrote to the claimant for the first time making express reference to an intention to make the payment pursuant to the PILON clause and terminate his contract with effect from 29 November 2007. Under the contract, notices were deemed to be received on the second day after posting, ie on 6 January. The claimant therefore argued that his contract was not actually terminated until that date. The bank argued that the contract was terminated on 29 November or, in the alternative, on 18 December. The High Court accepted the claimant's argument, but the Court of Appeal decided that the correct date was 18 December. The Supreme Court decided that the elective theory of termination was correct, so that the bank's breach of contract did not actually terminate the claimant's contract unless or until it was accepted by the claimant (which it was not), thus preferring the line of authority in cases such as *Gunton v Richmond-upon-Thames Borough Council* [1980] IRLR 321. That meant that the contract terminated on 6 January, when the bank lawfully terminated the claimant's contract by validly exercising the PILON clause. However, the Supreme Court rejected the suggestion (of Buckley LJ in *Gunton*) that a court could easily infer acceptance: real acceptance was required in the sense of a conscious intention to bring the contract to an end or doing an act inconsistent with its continuation.

The Supreme Court rejected the suggestion that the payment into the claimant's account amounted to the exercise of the PILON clause. The Court emphasised the need for notices to be given in clear and unambiguous terms; thus it was not sufficient to make the payment in lieu, the employee also had to receive a clear and unambiguous notice that the payment had been made in exercise of the right to terminate under the PILON clause. Even if writing is not required by the contract, a sensible employer will give notice in writing; otherwise notice can be given by a clear verbal statement to the effect that the contract is at an end.

It therefore follows that:

(a)   the elective theory applies equally to repudiatory breaches by an employee;

(b)   there is no difference in principle between a resignation and a dismissal – the elective theory applies in all instances;

(c)   a justified summary dismissal (as opposed to a repudiatory breach) will still be effective to bring a contract an end;

(d)   for the purpose of the effective date of termination (EDT), which is a statutory concept, s 97(3)(b) of the ERA 1996 provides that the EDT is 'the date when the contract of employment was terminated by the employer' (plus any statutory notice required by s 86 of the ERA 1996) (see **3.5.2.1**). Although this was not discussed by the Supreme Court, the Court of Appeal did consider this and held that the EDT would not necessarily be the same date as the repudiatory acceptance, so could precede that date.

Note: Where a contract expressly allows the employer to terminate the contract either by notice or by making a payment in lieu of notice, the dismissal does not become wrongful even if the employer fails to make the payment. The employee's claim in this situation is for a sum due under the contract (a debt owed), *not* for damages for breach of contract (*Abrahams v Performing Rights Society Ltd* [1995] IRLR 486, CA). Because the sum is for the recovery of a debt, the employee is not under a duty to mitigate losses. By contrast an employee who brings a claim for wrongful dismissal is under a duty to mitigate losses (see **2.4**).

In *Cerberus Software Ltd v Rowley* [2001] IRLR 160, the employee's contract provided for termination by either party giving six months' notice. It went on to provide that the employer 'may make a payment in lieu of notice to the employee'. The Court of Appeal held that in this situation, where the employer gave neither, the case was one of wrongful dismissal and the measure of damages was what the employee would have earned under the contract, subject to the ordinary duty of mitigation. The Court of Appeal distinguished the case from *Abrahams* (above), on the basis that the contract gave the employer the choice whether to pay or not to pay. In *Abrahams* the contractual clause provided that the employee *was* entitled to notice or payment in lieu. Thus, provided a PILON clause is carefully drafted, an employer will still receive the benefit of any mitigation by former employees as the employee's claim will be for wrongful dismissal where the employer gives neither notice nor payment in lieu of notice. However, as the employer has acted in breach of contract, that will render any restrictive covenants in the contract unenforceable (see **1.8.7**).

A PILON paid under the terms of the contract is always regarded as an 'emolument' from that employment and will be chargeable to income tax (*EMI Group Electronics Ltd v Coldicott (Inspector of Taxes)* [1999] IRLR 630, CA). Thus, such payments are not treated as falling within the Income Tax (Earnings and Pensions) Act 2003 exemption relating to termination payments up to £30,000 (see **2.4.1.8**).

Readers should consult the latest information on the HMRC website when giving advice on the tax implications of termination payments (www.hmrc.gov.uk).

2.3.4 Dismissal for employee's breach – 'summary dismissal'

If the employee commits a repudiatory breach of contract, the employer is entitled to treat the contract as discharged, ie to dismiss the employee without notice.

Any repudiatory breach of an express or implied term by the employee will justify the employer dismissing without notice. Non-exhaustive examples would include revealing trade secrets, wilful disobedience of lawful orders, theft from the employer or other gross misconduct and negligence if sufficiently serious. The crucial factor is the seriousness of the breach. It must be repudiatory (or fundamental), ie sufficiently serious to entitle the employer to treat the contract as discharged. In cases of gross negligence, the test is whether the negligent dereliction of duty was 'so grave and weighty' (*Neary v Dean of Westminster* [1999] IRLR 288). For two examples, see (misconduct) *Pepper v Webb* [1969] All ER 216 and (performance) *Alidair v Taylor* [1978] IRLR 82. In *Dunn & Another v AAH Ltd* [2010] EWCA Civ 183, the Court of Appeal held that an employee who had failed to follow instructions to report risk of fraud to HQ over a five-month period had so undermined the duty of trust and confidence by virtue of his wilful neglect of duty that the employer could accept the breach of contract and dismiss without notice. See too *Adesokan v Sainsbury's Supermarkets Ltd* [2017] EWCA Civ 22.

In *Kearns v Glencore UK Ltd* [2013] EWHC 3976 (QB), the High Court held that the conduct of the claimant over a period of time – being late or absent from work (due to binge drinking) – was such that he had repudiated his contract, and the employer accepted that repudiation by dismissing him. Alternatively, the claimant's conduct on the day of his dismissal – failing to turn up for a business meeting due to his binge drinking – was such as to amount to gross misconduct, which meant that the employer was entitled to dismiss him summarily, without notice. This case confirms that in effect, the so-called 'last straw' doctrine (see **3.4.3** below – where the 'last straw' can be fairly minor if there is a sufficient series of events, such that while the final act must not be completely trivial, it need not by itself be a fundamental breach of contract) also applies to employees.

When dealing with a suspected repudiatory breach, the employer must reserve its position so as not to waive the breach if it does not intend to take immediate disciplinary action (see *Cook v MSHK Ltd and Ministry of Sound Recordings Ltd* [2009] EWCA Civ 624). Otherwise it will be deemed to have affirmed the contract (and waived the breach).

Dismissal without notice can be justified by discovery of sufficient grounds *after* dismissal has taken place. In *Boston Deep Sea Fishing and Ice Co v Ansell* (1888) 39 Ch D 339, the misconduct of a managing director in taking bribes was discovered only after his dismissal. The tribunal held that the employer could rely on the latter acquired knowledge to justify the decision summarily to dismiss the employee. For a recent example, see *Williams v Leeds Football Club* [2015] EWHC 376 (QB). However, the Court of Appeal held in *Cavenagh v Williams Evans Ltd* [2012] EWCA Civ 697 that the employer could not rely on after-discovered gross misconduct in circumstances where it had already agreed to make a contractual payment in lieu of notice.

If the employer is mistaken about the seriousness of the breach and dismisses without notice in circumstances where he is not entitled to, the employer will have dismissed in breach of contract and be liable for wrongful dismissal (see **2.3.3**). It will be for the tribunal (or court) to decide whether the conduct amounted to a repudiatory breach of contract. In theory the employee has a choice whether to accept the breach or waive it, but in practice an employee has little choice but to accept the breach because he cannot perform his duties (*Boyo v Lambeth London Borough Council* [1995] IRLR 50).

2.3.5 Resignation and constructive dismissal

Normally, an employee who resigns will have no claim for wrongful dismissal. This is because it is the employee, not the employer, who has terminated the contract. For an example of how difficult it will be for an employee to claim that his unambiguous words of resignation amount to a dismissal, see *Ali v Birmingham City Council* (UKEAT/0313/08). Indeed, if the employee does not give proper notice or terminates a fixed-term contract before its expiry date, it is the employee who will be in breach of contract.

However, if the employer commits a repudiatory breach of an express or implied term of the contract of employment, the employee is entitled to accept the breach, resign and treat the contract as discharged. This is known as a constructive dismissal. The employee must leave within a reasonable time of the breach, otherwise he may be taken to have affirmed the contract and waived the breach. If the employee can establish that he has been constructively dismissed, he will have a claim for wrongful dismissal (dismissal in breach of contract).

Note that the employer's breach must be repudiatory; a minor breach will not entitle the employee to leave and claim that he has been constructively dismissed. Note too that the date of the resignation may be relevant as to when time starts to run to bring an employment tribunal claim. If an employee resigns without notice, the employment will end there and then, and time will start to run; the employer does not need to 'accept' the resignation, nor is he obliged to give the employee a 'cooling-off period', though some employers do so (see, eg, *Secretary of State for Justice v Hibbert* (UKEAT/0289/13)).

See **3.4.3** for details of constructive dismissal.

In *East Kent Hospitals University NHS Foundation Trust v Levy* (UKEAT/0232/17) the EAT held that giving notice does not automatically amount to an unambiguous act of resignation. The claimant was made a conditional offer of a new role within the same NHS trust. She sent a letter giving one month's notice for the old job. The conditional offer was later withdrawn and the claimant sought to withdraw her notice. The NHS trust refused, her employment ended and she brought an unfair dismissal claim. The tribunal found the wording of the notice to be ambiguous and concluded that the letter was merely signifying an intention to move jobs. The EAT agreed.

2.3.6 Frustration

If the contract of employment is frustrated, it terminates automatically by operation of law. Neither party will be in breach and neither party will have a claim against the other, other than for wages due to the date of frustration. Frustration occurs where, without the fault of either party, some event occurs which prevents performance of the contract. The event must not have been provided for by the contract. The principal events which may frustrate a contract of employment are as follows.

2.3.6.1 The death of either party

The death of the employee clearly frustrates the contract. The death of a sole trader employer will also frustrate the contract. However, if the employees are re-employed by the personal representatives of the deceased, or the business is transferred to another employer who re-employs the employees, continuity of employment will usually be preserved (see **3.5.5**).

2.3.6.2 Illness or injury of the employee

Long-term or permanent illness or injury which prevents the employee from performing his duties *may* frustrate the contract. Factors which will be taken into account in deciding whether or not a contract is frustrated include:

(a)   the nature of the work;

(b)   the length of employment;

(c)   the nature, length and effect of the illness or injury;

(d)   the need for the work to be done and the need for a replacement to do it; and

(e)   whether in all the circumstances a reasonable employer could be expected to wait any longer (*Egg Stores (Stamford Hill) Ltd v Leibovici* [1976] IRLR 376);

(f)   how likely it is that the employee will return to work.

The terms of the contract must also be considered. If the contract makes provision for a period of absence due to ill-health, then the contract would not be frustrated if the employee was likely to return to work within that period.

In practice, especially with contracts terminable by notice, the courts and employment tribunals are extremely reluctant to find that a contract has been frustrated. The effect of holding that a contract is frustrated deprives the employee of any remedy that he might have had if he had been dismissed. Nevertheless, in rare cases the court may find that the contract has been frustrated. In *Collins v Secretary of State for Trade and Industry* (UKEAT/1460/99), the EAT held that a contract had been frustrated by an employee's long-term illness. Of particular relevance, on the facts, was the length of time the employee was off work (three years) and the unlikeliness of any return to work.

In *Warner v Armfield Retail & Leisure Ltd* (UKEAT/0376/12), the EAT held that, in the case of a disabled person, before the doctrine of frustration can apply there is an additional factor which must be considered over and above the factors set out above – namely whether the employer is in breach of its duty to make reasonable adjustments (see **Chapter 13**). While there is something which it is reasonable to expect the employer to do, the doctrine of frustration cannot apply. On the facts, the tribunal having found no breach of the duty to make reasonable adjustments, the tribunal's decision that the contract had been frustrated was upheld.

2.3.6.3 Imprisonment of the employee

A problem arises when a contract is terminated on the imprisonment of an employee. The employer will allege frustration and termination by operation of law. The employee will argue that he has been dismissed, frustration not being applicable as imprisonment constitutes 'self-induced frustration'. This would give the employee a potential claim for wrongful dismissal, even though in the majority of cases the dismissal would be justified.

The Court of Appeal in *FC Shepherd & Co Ltd v Jerrom* [1987] 1 QB 301 decided the imprisoned employee had no claim. Balcombe LJ found that the frustrating event was the actual imposition of the sentence, not the misconduct by the employee, but Lawton and Mustill LJJ held that the rule against reliance on self-induced frustration only meant that neither party could rely on his own misconduct to establish a defence of frustration. But since the employer was relying on the employee's fault, that requirement was satisfied and thus frustration could succeed.

In *Chakki v United Yeast Co Ltd* [1982] 2 All ER 446, the EAT held that certain elements need to be considered when deciding whether or not a prison sentence has frustrated the contract of employment. It distinguished between a situation where a sentence of imprisonment was a cause of 'instantaneous' frustration of a contract of employment and one where it was merely a 'potentially frustrating event' depending on the time at which frustration occurred, being the time at which the parties became aware of the cause and the likely outcome of the interruption and had to decide on a future course of action. The EAT said:

> [I]t seems to us that in some cases a sentence of imprisonment will be similar to an accident or an illness and thus a potentially frustrating event rather than a cause of instantaneous frustration. It has to be recognised, however, that a sentence of imprisonment differs from an accident to an illness in that, unless and until it is varied on appeal, the length of the employee's absence and the affect on the contract of employment is immediately predictable. One has therefore to try to find that moment at which the question of frustration or not has to be determined.

In *Four Seasons Healthcare Ltd v Maughan* [2005] IRLR 324, the EAT held that frustration requires that there should be some outside event or extraneous change of situation, not foreseen or provided for by the parties within the contract. The EAT commented, in a situation where there was a detailed disciplinary procedure in the employment contract which made specific reference to the misconduct which the claimant had been dismissed over (namely physical abuse directed towards residents), 'it seems to us that the presence of such a detailed disciplinary procedure should indeed ... inhibit us from being too ready to find in favour of frustration'. In this case, therefore, the contract was not frustrated until the custodial sentence made its performance impossible. Thus, a very short custodial sentence might not have the effect of frustrating a contract.

2.3.7 Partnerships and companies

The dissolution of a partnership or the winding up of a company may terminate the employees' contracts.

2.3.7.1 Partnerships

Usually, a change of partners where the employer is a partnership will have no effect on the employees' contracts of employment.

However, if the contract is of a personal nature, ie the identity of the partners is material to the contract, then if the relevant partner leaves, the employee's contract will automatically be terminated (*Phillips v Alhambra Palace Co* [1901] 1 KB 59). If the partner leaves voluntarily (eg by retirement), there will be a wrongful dismissal of the employee unless proper notice was given. If the partner dies, the employee's contract will be frustrated. In practice, it is rare for the contract to be of a personal nature, the usual rule being that a change of partners does not affect the employee's contract.

Even if an employee's contract is terminated in such circumstances, there will be no break in the continuity of his employment if he is re-employed by the new partners (see **3.5.5**).

2.3.7.2 Companies

An order for the compulsory winding up of a company and a resolution to wind up an insolvent company will usually terminate the employees' contracts automatically. Dismissal will be wrongful unless proper notice is given. The making of an administration order or the appointment of a receiver by debenture holders would not normally terminate employees' contracts.

2.3.8 Limited-term contracts

At common law, a limited-term contract expires by effluxion of time at the end of the term. For example, a contract for a limited term of three years commencing on 1 February 2013 will come to an end on 31 January 2016 with no liability on either party if it is not renewed.

There is no implied term allowing a party to terminate a limited-term contract before its expiry date. If the employer or employee terminates a limited-term contract, with or without notice, before its expiry date, there will be a breach of contract unless:

(a)   the other party is in repudiatory breach of the contract; or

(b)   there is express power in the contract allowing early termination (a 'break' clause) (see below); or

(c)   the termination is by mutual agreement.

One or both parties (often only the employer) may be able to terminate the contract before the end of the limited term if the contract contains a 'break' clause. A 'break' clause allows a party to bring the contract to an end within the limited term, usually by giving notice. The 'break' clause may, for example, allow the employer to terminate in any circumstances by giving the employee, say, six months' notice, or it may allow termination in specific circumstances only (eg on the employee's bankruptcy or long-term illness) (see **1.8.1.2**).

2.4 EMPLOYEE'S REMEDIES FOR WRONGFUL DISMISSAL

In practice, the employee/worker who is wrongfully dismissed will usually have little choice but to accept the dismissal. It is virtually unheard of for a court to grant an injunction to prevent a dismissal, but it may depend on the precise terms of the contract. In *West London Mental Health NHS Trust v Chhabra* [2013] UKSC 60, the Supreme Court granted an injunction, preventing the Trust from holding a disciplinary hearing into matters said by the Trust to constitute 'gross misconduct' (see **1.8.8**), because this was not in accordance with the contractual disciplinary procedure. The employee/worker may then claim damages for wrongful dismissal against the employer.

2.4.1 Damages for wrongful dismissal

2.4.1.1 Introduction

Damages for wrongful dismissal are damages for breach of contract. They are governed by the normal rules of the law of contract:

(a)   the loss claimed must not be too remote, ie it must either arise naturally from the breach or be such as may reasonably be supposed to have been in the contemplation of both parties at the time of contract, as the probable result of the breach (*Hadley v Baxendale* (1854) 9 Exch 341);

(b)   the measure of damages, for loss which is not too remote, is the sum required to put the claimant, so far as money can, in the same position as if the contract had been performed (*Robinson v Harman* (1848) 1 Exch 850).

In *Boyo v Lambeth London Borough Council* [1994] ICR 727, CA, it was held that the correct measure of damages following the employer's repudiatory breach of contract was the amount the employee would be entitled to receive if dismissed in accordance with the terms of the contract. See also *Société Général, London Branch v Geys* at **2.3.3** above.

In the case of wrongful dismissal, damages are usually assessed as follows.

2.4.1.2   Loss of net wages

The starting point in calculating damages in the case of a contract for an indefinite term is the salary or wages that the employee/worker would have earned during the proper notice period. In the case of a fixed-term contract it would be the salary for the remainder of the fixed term. There is an exception in the case of a fixed term where the employer was entitled to terminate under a 'break' clause, in which case it is the salary which would have been earned during the period of notice due under the 'break' clause.

Note that there is a danger in using the term 'ex gratia'. In *Publicis Consultants v O'Farrell* (UKEAT/ 0430/10) Mrs O'Farrell's contract entitled her to three months' notice of termination. The letter of dismissal said she would be paid statutory redundancy pay, holiday pay and a sum which, although equivalent to three months' gross salary, was said to be an ex gratia payment. An issue arose (in her successful unfair dismissal claim) as to whether she was entitled to receive three months' notice pay as damages for her dismissal without notice. The EAT said she was. The starting point in any exercise of the construction of documents must be with the words the parties have used. An 'ex gratia' payment is, on its ordinary construction, a payment made freely and not under obligation. Further, the *contra proferentem* rule meant that, as this was the company's own unilateral document, if it was ambiguous it had to be read with 'the construction least favourable to the author'.

Where an employer fails to follow a contractual disciplinary procedure, the employee is generally only entitled to receive compensation for the wages he would have received during the course of the disciplinary procedure (see *Gunton v London Borough of Richmond* [2000] IRLR 703) plus any contractual notice. This remains the case even if the employee is able to show that the disciplinary process, if followed, would have meant that the employee was not dismissed. This is because, at common law, employers are entitled to dismiss on notice without proper cause. The only recourse for an employee in this situation is to bring an unfair dismissal claim (see **Chapter 5**).

The Court of Appeal held in *Edwards v Chesterfield Royal Hospital NHS Foundation Trust* [2010] IRLR 702 that compensation for reputational damage caused by a flawed disciplinary procedure might be recovered 'at large' as it was not caused by the dismissal but rather by failure to follow an express contractual disciplinary procedure, if that failure led to the misconduct finding and the resultant inability to secure permanent NHS employment. The Court therefore permitted a claim for £4 million loss of earnings to proceed. The Court of Appeal rejected a submission that the principles laid down by the House of Lords in *Johnson v Unisys Ltd* [2001] IRLR 279 (see **2.4.1.5** and **5.6.2.2**) precluded recovery of the lossed claimed. *Unisys* does not apply where there is a breach of an express contractual term – it restricts compensation to the unfair dismissal regime where what is said to cause the loss is the manner of dismissal.

Edwards was appealed to the Supreme Court. A majority of the Supreme Court overruled the Court of Appeal's decision. The majority held that breach of contract claims for an alleged failure to follow an express disciplinary process could not proceed: as the claims for financial loss caused by damage to reputation were inextricably linked to the dismissal process, they fell within the exclusion indentified by the House of Lords in *Johnson v Unisys* and unfair dismissal was the appropriate claim. (There is an excellent and detailed analysis of the case and its significance in IDS Employment Law Brief No 943, February 2012, at p 3 onwards.)

2.4.1.3   Accrued holiday pay

Under the employee's contract and/or the Working Time Regulations 1998, reg 14, the employee/worker will be entitled to payment in lieu of any holiday to which he was entitled but had not yet taken, subject to a maximum of two years' back pay (see **1.12.5**).

In *Leisure Leagues UK Ltd v Maconnachie* [2002] IRLR 600, the EAT gave guidance on calculating holiday pay. The EAT held that the correct method of calculating holiday pay for a worker with regular hours and an annual salary is to divide the worker's annual salary by the number of working (not calendar) days in a year, multiplied by the number of days' leave the worker has outstanding (see **1.12.5**).

2.4.1.4   Additional loss

In addition to such lost salary or wages, the employee/worker may claim damages for loss of other benefits to which he was entitled under the contract. This would cover lost commission in the case of employees/workers remunerated wholly or partly by commission. It would also cover loss of fringe benefits such as a company car and also loss of pension rights if the employee/worker was entitled to a pension. In *Silvey v Pendragon plc* [2001] IRLR 685, the Court of Appeal held that an employee who was wrongfully dismissed 12 days short of his 55th birthday was entitled to claim damages for loss of significant pension rights that would have accrued when he attained the age of 55.

Loss of pension entitlement may in some cases involve a large sum, and it can be difficult to calculate this loss. There are two forms of pension loss which may be suffered: the loss of the pension position earned to the date of dismissal, and loss of future pension opportunity. Usually the sum lost will be based on the amount of employee's and employer's contributions made to a future pension. Where an employee/worker is close to retirement, the court may look at the cost of purchasing an annuity to produce the pension lost by the employee/worker.

The Government Actuary's Department (GAD) had produced guidelines to assist in calculating pension loss, the latest (third) edition being produced in 2003. The Court of Appeal, in *Griffin v Plymouth Hospital NHS Trust* [2014] EWCA Civ 1240, called for there to be an updated version of the guidelines, but in 2015 they were withdrawn on the basis that they were out-of-date. The guidelines had drawn a helpful distinction between money purchase schemes and final salary schemes, and set out two approaches to calculating future pension losses – a simplified approach and a substantial loss approach. The former was for use where there was either a money purchase scheme or a final salary scheme where there was a relatively short period of continuing pension loss. The substantial loss approach was for use only in cases concerning final salary schemes where there was long-term or whole career loss. A working group of Employment Judges produced a consultation paper in March 2016 to review the 2003 guidelines. The consultation closed on 20 May 2016.

The EAT's decision in *Chief Constable of West Midlands Police v Gardner* (UKEAT/0174/11) provides a useful discussion of the various approaches to pension loss calculation.

The Court of Appeal held in *Bentwood Brothers (Manchester) Ltd v Shepherd* [2003] IRLR 364 that an employee should be compensated for 10 years' future loss of pension following an unfair dismissal, even though the award for loss of earnings was for only two and a half years. The Court agreed that whilst Ms Shepherd might well be able to find alternative employment on similar pay, she would not be able to do so with a final salary scheme which she had at Bentwood Brothers.

The employee/worker is only awarded damages for loss of benefits to which he was entitled under the contract. Thus, the established orthodoxy has always been that an employee/worker will not generally be awarded damages for loss of a discretionary contractual payment which he might have expected to receive, such as a Christmas bonus or an annual salary increase (*Lavarack v Woods of Colchester Ltd* [1967] 1 QB 278). However, in *Clark v BET plc and Another*

[1997] IRLR 348, the employee successfully argued that, although his contract only entitled him to an annual salary increase 'by such amount as the board shall in its absolute discretion decide', this term amounted to a contractual obligation to increase his salary each year. The court said that contractual provisions relating to salary increases must be interpreted realistically and not on the basis that any discretion would have been exercised to give the employee the least possible benefit. Similar reasoning was applied in respect of a 'discretionary' bonus scheme entitlement under his contract of employment. Similarly in *Clark v Nomura International plc* [2000] IRLR 766, Burton J held that it was a breach of contract for an employer to exercise discretionary powers in a manner that was irrational or perverse. The Court of Appeal's decision in *Mallone v BPB Industries plc* [2002] IRLR 452 confirms that an employer must not exercise its discretion in an irrational manner (see also *Horkulak v Cantor Fitzgerald International* [2004] IRLR 942, *Commerzbank AG v Keen* [2006] EWCA Civ 1536 and *Paturel v DB Services (UK) Ltd* [2015] EWHC 3659 (QB)). Readers should also note the Supreme Court's decision in *Braganza v BP Shipping Ltd and Another* [2015] UKSC 17, where the Court applied *Wednesbury* unreasonableness to death benefits in an employment case. In that case the Supreme Court held that, although the decision not to pay a widow death in service benefit was not 'arbitrary, capricious or perverse', it was unreasonable in the *Wednesbury* sense, having been formed without taking relevant matters into account. Whether the same approach might be taken to bonus cases remains to be seen, but the Court indicated that might not be the case at para 57 of its judgment:

> In cases such as *Clark v Nomura International Plc*, *Keen v Commerzbank AG* and *Horkulak v Cantor Fitzgerald International* [2005] ICR 402 the courts have reviewed contractual decisions on the grant of performance-related bonuses where there were no specific criteria of performance or established formulae for calculating a bonus. In such cases the employee is entitled to a bona fide and rational exercise by the employer of its discretion. The courts are charged with enforcing that entitlement but there is little scope for intensive scrutiny of the decision-making process. The courts are in a much better position to review the good faith and rationality of the decision-making process where the issue is whether or not a state of fact existed, such as whether an employee's wilful act caused his death.

In *Hills v Niksun Inc* [2016] EWCA Civ 115, the issue was whether the judge was right to interfere with Niksun's exercise of what it described as the broad discretion provided to it in the contractual documents. The first instance judge concluded that the decision-making power as to commission-split rested with Niksun, but that Niksun was not given 'a general discretion such as is found in the banker's bonus cases'. The Court of Appeal concluded that the judge was justified in saying that the absence of evidence from Niksun as to the decision-making process meant that he could not assume that the decision was a rational one.

The difference between *Hills* (and *Braganza*) to other banker's bonus cases is that in those other cases the employer had a complete discretion, meaning that the decision whether to award a bonus or not is subject to the 'irrationality' test. In *Hills*, by contrast, there were rules in place, so what was being challenged was the reasonable application of the company's rules.

The Court of Appeal held in *Levett v Biotrace International plc* [1999] IRLR 375 that an option to purchase shares did not lapse in circumstances where employment was terminated in breach of contract unless the scheme rules so provided.

Damages may also be claimed for the loss of opportunity to earn tips in occupations where tips are usual (eg in the case of waiters and waitresses).

An employee cannot claim damages for breach of contract in respect of a loss of opportunity to bring an unfair dismissal claim (see **Chapter 5**). (See, eg, *The Wise Group v Mitchell* [2005] ICR 896.) The Court of Appeal held in *Harper v Virgin Net Ltd* [2004] IRLR 390 that an employee dismissed in breach of contract with less than one year's service, cannot claim damages for wrongful dismissal on the basis that she lost the chance of recovering unfair dismissal compensation that she would have received if she had been given her *contractual* notice of termination. Brooke LJ stated:

> I do not consider it is open to the courts, through the machinery of an award of damages for wrongful dismissal, to rewrite Parliament's scheme and to place a financial burden on employers which Parliament decided not to impose on them.

Chadwick LJ added that Parliament

> did not – as it easily could have done – postpone the effective date of termination to whichever should be the later of the expiry of the periods of contractual or statutory notice. That must be seen as a deliberate policy choice.

The other reason given for the decision is the need to be consistent with the House of Lords decision in *Johnson v Unisys Ltd* [2001] IRLR 279 (as explained in *Eastwood and Another v Magnox Electric plc* [2004] IRLR 733) (see below and **5.6.2.2**). These cases are authority for the rule that damages for breach of contract cannot include losses arising out of the fact and manner of dismissal.

2.4.1.5 Pecuniary loss only

Damages can usually be claimed for pecuniary loss only, so damages cannot generally be claimed for loss of future prospects or injured feelings (*Bliss v South East Thames Regional Health Authority* [1985] IRLR 308).

In *Malik v BCCI; Mahmud v BCCI* [1997] IRLR 462, HL, it was held that an employee might be entitled to 'stigma' damages, for example where the employer's business was conducted in a wholly dishonest manner which affected the employees' future prospects because of the stigma attaching to their reputations. The Court of Appeal's decision in *Bank of Credit and Commerce International SA (in compulsory liquidation) v Ali and Others (No 3)* [2002] IRLR 460 confirms that loss of employment prospects is almost impossible to prove without strong evidence, preferably from prospective employers.

The House of Lords held in *Johnson v Unisys Ltd* [2001] IRLR 279 that a claimant cannot recover contractual damages for psychiatric illness arising from the dismissal. Their Lordships distinguished the *Malik* case on the basis that that claim arose from a breach of the implied term of trust and confidence *during* the employment relationship; it did not arise on dismissal. Similarly, in *Gogay v Hertfordshire County Council* [2000] IRLR 703, the Court of Appeal held that the employer was in breach of the implied term of trust and confidence when it suspended an employee pending further investigation of a disciplinary charge, because it had no reasonable grounds for suspending her. Mrs Gogay was able to recover damages at common law for psychiatric injury on the facts, because the loss arose from breach of the implied duty of trust and confidence *during* the subsistence of the employment relationship.

The House of Lords in *Eastwood v Magnox; McCabe v Cornwall County Council and Another* [2004] IRLR 733, two cases concerning the overlap between common law claims for damages for breach of trust and confidence, and the statutory unfair dismissal regime, held that a distinction must be drawn between those cases where the employer has breached the term of trust and confidence *prior* to the dismissal – for which an (unlimited) common law claim can be brought – and cases where the *decision* to dismiss amounts to a breach of trust and confidence. These latter cases fall within the statutory unfair dismissal regime, and are therefore subject to the cap on compensation which cannot be circumvented by bringing a breach of contract claim in the civil courts. Lord Nicholls recognised the artificiality of the distinction but said it was nevertheless a distinction that had to be observed. At para 28 of his judgment he said:

> In the ordinary course ... an employer's failure to act fairly in the steps leading to dismissal does not of itself cause the employee financial loss. The loss arises when the employee is dismissed and it arises by reason of his dismissal. Then the resultant claim for loss falls squarely within the *Johnson* exclusion area. ... Exceptionally financial loss may flow directly from the employer's failure to act fairly when taking steps leading to dismissal. Financial loss flowing from suspension is an instance ... [and] cases

... when an employee suffers financial loss from psychiatric or other illness caused by his pre-dismissal unfair treatment.

The existence of such an exclusion area may mean that in some cases a continuing course of conduct, such as a disciplinary process followed by dismissal, may need to be chopped up artificially. Where financial losses flow directly from a pre-dismissal action, that can give rise to a cause of action which arises independently from the dismissal. Lord Nicholls noted two instances where problems will arise: financial losses flowing from suspension without pay and financial losses (as occurred in these two cases) flowing from psychiatric illness caused by pre-dismissal unfair treatment. He said that in such cases 'the employee has a common law cause of action which precedes, and is independent of, his subsequent dismissal'. He went on to note that in some circumstances an employer would be better off dismissing an employee than suspending him.

2.4.1.6   Duty to mitigate

The employee is under a duty to mitigate his loss. Once the employment is terminated, he must take steps to obtain suitable alternative employment. He will be in breach of this duty if he refuses a reasonable offer of re-employment. The employee is not entitled to damages in respect of any loss that has been mitigated or would have been mitigated but for the employee's breach of duty (*Brace v Calder and Others* [1895] 2 QB 253).

The employee is only under a duty to accept reasonable offers of re-employment, not any other job offered. For example, there would be no need to accept an offer involving serious demotion. If the old employer offers to re-engage the employee, the employee would be in breach of his duty to mitigate if he failed to accept, provided that the job offered was reasonable and there was still a relationship of mutual trust and confidence between employer and employee.

2.4.1.7   Benefits reducing loss

If the employer has paid money in lieu of notice to the employee, this will be taken into account in assessing the damages awarded. Certain other benefits received by the employee which reduce his loss will also be set against the damages awarded, for example, jobseeker's allowance and income support. If a pension becomes payable during the period for which damages are claimed, this does not reduce the damages awarded (*Hopkins v Norcross plc* [1994] IRLR 18, CA). The rule on pensions is based on public policy.

Overlap with redundancy payments and awards of compensation for unfair dismissal are dealt with at **6.7**.

2.4.1.8   Tax and National Insurance contributions

The basic rule is that income tax and NICs that would have been paid on the wages or salary, if earned, are deducted in assessing damages (*British Transport Commission v Gourley* [1956] AC 185; *Shove v Downs Surgical plc* [1984] IRLR 17). Damages are therefore generally awarded in respect of loss of *net* earnings. This puts the employee in the position as though the contract had been performed.

However, the effect of the Income Tax (Earnings and Pensions) Act 2003 (ITEPA 2003) has to be considered. Guidance on the Act may be found in the HMRC guide CWG2 (2009), *Employer's Further Guide to PAYE and NICs*. It is available on HMRC's website <http://www.hmrc.gov.uk/guidance/cwg2.pdf>. An employer is exempt from paying tax on termination payments, including damages for wrongful dismissal, which do not exceed £30,000 (ITEPA 2003, s 401). The exemption applies only if the payment is not otherwise subject to tax under any other head; only then can it be taxed as a termination payment. This means considering whether the payment is a contractual payment made in return for services (see, eg, *Delaney v Staples* [1992] 1 All ER 944 and *SCA Packaging v Revenue and Customs* [2007] EWHC 270 (Ch)). If the payment or benefit is earnings from the employment, tax is due under s 62 of the ITEPA 2003 (and there is no £30,000 exemption). As the employee receives only his net loss of earnings, it is therefore the employer who benefits from the rule. Termination payments exceeding £30,000 are subject to income tax on the excess over £30,000. Therefore, if the damages for wrongful dismissal exceed £30,000, the award of damages will have to be grossed up to compensate the employee for the double tax that the employee will have to pay. Note, however, that pure damages for breach of contract in a tribunal are subject to a £25,000 jurisdictional limit. In reality, damages for breach of contract in a tribunal claim will need to be grossed up only where other awards, such as compensation for unfair dismissal, take the award over £30,000 (see **5.7.2.2**).

For example, in the case of *Shove v Downs Surgical plc* (above), the court assessed the ex-employee's total loss as being £70,300. The court deducted an element for failure to mitigate and accelerated receipt (see **2.4.1.9** below), giving a net loss of £60,729. Damages of £88,447 were therefore payable by the employer to ensure that, after paying tax, the ex-employee was left with £60,729 in his hands, the remainder going to the Revenue.

Note that where the contract of employment contains an express PILON provision, the £30,000 tax and the unlimited NICs exemption will not be available in respect of the sum paid by way of compensation or for wrongful dismissal (see *EMI Group Electronics Ltd v Coldicott (Inspector of Taxes)* [1999] IRLR 630 and *Cerberus Software Ltd v Rowley* [2001] IRLR 160). This is because HMRC takes the view that, in such cases, the pay in lieu is due under the contract and is not, therefore, a true severance payment (see **2.3.3**). In practice, this means that awards for unpaid notice pursuant to a PILON clause should always be paid grossed up, because they are taxable as earnings and are not covered by the £30,000 exemption.

Where there is no PILON clause, even if a payment is made, termination without notice is strictly speaking still a breach of contract and the payment does not therefore flow from the contract. Note that the tax position where a contract is terminated without notice and there is a discretion to give a PILON is complex and beyond the scope of the book (see *Richardson v Delaney* [2001] IRLR 663, the Revenue's Tax Bulletin 63, February 2003 and the Revenue's Employment Income Manual 12800 (updated 2010)). (See though **5.6.2.5** and see also **Table 5.1**.)

2.4.1.9 Accelerated receipt

In the majority of cases, any award of damages for wrongful dismissal will be made after the employee's contract could have been properly terminated by the employer. In this situation, no question of accelerated receipt arises.

However, in the case of a long fixed-term contract, the employee may receive his damages before he would have earned some of the salary that they represent. In this case, a deduction will be made from the damages as the accelerated receipt will allow the employee to invest the money (eg in an annuity) and obtain a return on it (*Bold v Brough, Nicholson & Hall Ltd* [1964] 1 WLR 201). In *Brentwood Brothers (Manchester) Ltd v Shepherd* [2003] IRLR 364, the Court of Appeal questioned whether the 5% discount rate normally applied by tribunals remained appropriate in 2004, given that the discount in personal injury cases was by then 2.5%. The court also held that any deductions should be done on the basis of an appropriate percentage deduction year on year and not one single deduction. A Government consultation on the personal injury discount rate closed on 7 May 2013. In August 2014, the Ministry of Justice said that it would appoint a panel of experts to review the rate, with a report due in April 2015. No report has yet been published.

2.4.1.10 Adjustment to an award for unreasonable failure to follow Acas Code of Practice

Note that the Employment Tribunal cannot award an Acas uplift to wrongful dismissal damages (see **Chapter 5**).

2.4.2 Other remedies

The employee will usually have little choice but to accept dismissal and claim monetary compensation. The courts will not award specific performance of contracts of employment, nor will they usually issue an injunction restraining the employer from terminating the employment in breach of contract. In exceptional circumstances the courts have granted an injunction, the effect of which is to keep the contract alive until proper notice would have expired, but the employer was not required to allow the employee to do work during the period covered by the injunction (*Hill v C A Parsons & Co Ltd* [1972] 1 Ch 305). Occasionally, the courts will grant an interim injunction restraining an employer from dismissing an employee (eg pending an appeal hearing). Such an injunction can be granted only if there is sufficient mutual trust and confidence between employer and employee (*Powell v London Borough of Brent* [1987] IRLR 466). These remedies are exceptional and details are beyond the scope of this book.

2.5   EMPLOYER'S REMEDIES

If the employee is in repudiatory breach of contract, the employer may dismiss him without notice ('summarily') (see **2.3.4**). Other remedies available to the employer include damages, injunction and account of profit.

2.5.1   Damages

Any breach of contract by the employee theoretically entitles the employer to claim damages. In practice, it is a remedy which employers rarely pursue.

(a)   An employee may be in breach of contract by resigning without giving proper notice or leaving before a fixed-term contract has expired. The usual measure of damages in such cases would be the additional cost of providing a substitute to do the work (*National Coal Board v Galley* [1958] 1 WLR 16). The remedy is not usually worth pursuing because the amount involved would usually be too small.

(b)   If an employer suffers loss by reason of the employee's negligence, the employer may be entitled to an indemnity from the employee (see *Lister v Romford Ice and Cold Storage Co Ltd* [1957] AC 555, at **1.7.2.3**). The remedy is rarely pursued, partly because it can lead to bad industrial relations and also because the employer is often insured against the loss. The employee may, anyway, have insufficient funds to meet a substantial award of damages.

(c)   Damages might be an appropriate remedy where the employer has suffered loss by reason of the employee's breach of the duty of good faith, for example where the employee has revealed trade secrets or competed with the employer's business. In *Gamatronic (UK) Ltd v Hamilton* [2016] EWHC 2225 (QB), two employees set up a rival firm during their employment. The employer sought to recover the employees' salaries for the period of breach (they were still employed). The judge rejected the claim to recover salaries. There was no causal connection between the wrongful acts and the loss claimed (the salaries paid) and no failure of consideration. The evidence failed to establish that the employees failed to dedicate proper time and attention to their work for Gamatronic.

2.5.2   Injunction

An injunction may be awarded to an employer to restrain certain actions of an employee where damages would be an inadequate remedy:

(a)   It may be used to restrain or prevent breaches of the duty of fidelity, for example by restraining an employee from using or revealing trade secrets. In *Robb v Green* [1895] 2 QB 315, an employee who had made a list of customers was ordered to deliver up the list and was restrained by injunction from copying it.

(b)   It is the appropriate remedy to enforce a valid restrictive covenant after employment, by restraining the employee from working in contravention of it (see **1.8**).

(c)   Where an employee is required by contract to give a period of notice, the employer might obtain an injunction to prevent him from breaching that term by taking up a new position before expiry of his contractual notice period.

In deciding whether and to what extent to grant an injunction the court will apply the 'balance of convenience' test (*American Cyanamid v Ethicon Ltd* [1975] AC 398). The court will take into account the following factors:

(a)   actual or potential damage to the employer's business (eg loss of important clients who may follow the employee);

(b)   inconvenience (financial and other) to the employee;

(c)   whether the employee has given an adequate undertaking to abide by the contract;

(d)   no more relief should be granted than is absolutely necessary – any injunction need not necessarily be for the full contractual period (*GFI Group Inc v Eaglestone* [1994] IRLR 119).

For a decision which provides a useful analysis of the general principles on injunctions, see *Vestergaard Frandsen Als and Others v Bestnet Europe Ltd and Others* [2009] EWHC 1456 (Ch) and *QBE Management Services (UK) Ltd v Dymoke and Others* [2012] IRLR 458.

In *Sunrise Brokers LLP Rodgers* [2014] EWHC 2633 (QB), the High Court granted Sunrise an injunction that meant that Mr Rodgers had to abide by his contract until the expiry of his notice period. There was no obligation on Sunrise to put him on garden leave (see **1.8.7.3**), and as Mr Rodgers refused to come into work, Sunrise was not obliged to pay him. The High Court also issued an injunction holding Mr Rodgers to the terms of his restrictive covenants.

Where the employer is not at fault and an employee has walked out, refusing to pay the recalcitrant employee will not allow him to argue that the employer is in breach.

2.5.3   Action for account of profits

Usually in breach of contract claims the measure of damages is the loss suffered by the claimant, and not the profit made by the respondent. Account of profits is, however, assessed on the profits made by the respondent. Until recently, an action for account of profits was available as a remedy only in the special case where there is a breach of the implied duty of good faith, by using the employer's confidential information to make a secret profit (see **1.7.2.5**), or breach of a fiduciary duty (see *Nottingham University v Fishel and Another* [2000] IRLR 471, where the High Court confirmed that the employment relationship is not a fiduciary one but that fiduciary duties may arise from the relationship, *Kynixa Ltd v Hynes and Others* [2008] EWHC 1495 (Comm), where the High Court held that the company director owed a fiduciary duty and that a second employee was also subject to a fiduciary duty by virtue of her senior status as a clinical services manager, and *Samsung Semiconductor Europe Ltd v Docherty and Another* [2011] CSOH 32, where the Court of Session held that a QA manager who worked with the employer's most important customer was subject to a fiduciary duty). In *Attorney-General v Blake and Jonathan Cape Ltd* [2001] IRLR 36, it was held that exceptionally a respondent may be required, as a remedy for breach of contract, to pay over to the claimant the profits received from the breach, even where the claimant has suffered no financial loss as a result of the breach and the wrongdoer is not in breach of a fiduciary duty. The House of Lords said a useful guide, although not exhaustive, is whether the employer had a legitimate interest in preventing the employee's profit-making activity and, hence, in depriving him of a profit.

2.6   CHECKLIST

(1)   How did contract end – has there been a breach of contract by employer?

(2)   Can employer raise employee's conduct as defence to a wrongful dismissal claim? (Remember after-acquired knowledge can be used.)

(3)   Is contract for a fixed term or terminable on notice?

(4)   What was employee's net pay?

(5)   Are there any factors which will increase/decrease starting point?

(6)   Are damages in excess of £30,000? If so, consider the tax position.

2.7   FURTHER READING

Textbooks dealing with termination at common law include:

Harvey, *Industrial Relations and Employment Law* (Butterworths), Div A.

Duggan, *Wrongful Dismissal and Breach of Contract*, 2nd edn (Duggan Press, 2019).

Duggan, *Contracts of Employment: Law and Guidance*, 3rd edn (Duggan Press, 2019).

Lewis, *Employment Law – an adviser's handbook*, 12th revised edn (LAG, 2017).

Selwyn, *Law of Employment*, 20th edn (OUP, 2018).

Blackstone's Employment Law Practice, 10th edn (OUP, 2019).

SUMMARY

This chapter has looked at the differences between the breach of contract claim known as wrongful dismissal and the statutory claim of unfair dismissal, and at the extent to which they may overlap (**2.1, 2.2**). Provided that a contract is terminated in accordance with any express or implied terms (eg s 86 of the ERA 1996 sets out minimum periods of notice), neither party will be in breach of contract. The chapter has looked at the main ways in which a contract of employment may come to an end and the relevance of notice periods (**2.3**). It has also considered when a summary dismissal claim may be justified (**2.3.4**). It explains the principles to be applied when calculating an employee's damages following a wrongful dismissal (**2.4**) and the remedies available to an employer if an employee is in repudiatory breach of contract (**2.5**). A flowchart summarising wrongful dismissal and breach of contract claims is set out in **Figure 2.1** below.

Figure 2.1 Flowchart: Wrongful Dismissal/Breach of Contract Claims

1. Has there been a dismissal?

- actual dismissal
- constructive dismissal
  - Employer commits a repudiatory/fundamental (not minor) breach of express/implied term so that employee is entitled to resign in response (with or without notice) and treat the contract as discharged
  - Employee must resign within a reasonable time of the breach in response to the breach

NB Expiry of a limited-term contract is not a dismissal for the purposes of wrongful dismissal

Time limit

Claim in employment tribunal within 3 months of dismissal

Claim in civil court within 6 years of dismissal

NO → **No claim**

YES

2. Is the dismissal wrongful?

- actual dismissal with no notice or insufficient notice unless justified by the employee's repudiatory breach (gross misconduct)

NB 1. Look at contractual notice period – must not be less than statutory minimum

2. Consider impact of a PILON clause

OR

- dismissal *before* the expiry of a limited term unless
  - in accordance with terms of a break clause
  - justified by the employee's repudiatory breach (gross misconduct)*

*NB** Employee's after-discovered but pre-dismissal misconduct may justify dismissal without notice – *Boston Deep Sea Fishing v Ansell*

OR

- constructive dismissal – the employer's repudiatory breach renders the dismissal wrongful

NO

YES

3. Compensation: damages for breach of contract

Normal contractual damages rules (*Hadley v Baxendale*; loss of *net* wages) for proper notice period or until end of limited term (unless break clause)

PLUS any additional *contractual* losses (eg commission, pension, health insurance, car, bonuses, holiday pay, etc)

Reducing factors

payments made (eg payment in lieu)

certain benefits

duty to mitigate

accelerated receipt

Employment tribunal – maximum award £25,000

Civil court – no maximum

NB Overlapping claims – damages for wrongful dismissal will be set off against any overlapping unfair dismissal compensatory award (usually the 'immediate loss of earning' element) arising from the same dismissal

NB Compensation may be:

- Increased by up to 25% for an unreasonable failure to follow the Acas Code of Practice
- Decreased by up to 25% for an unreasonable failure to follow the Acas Code of Practice

(Consider too bringing a claim under the Working Time Regulations for unused statutory leave on termination in the absence of a contractual right to payment for unused holiday on termination.)

CHAPTER 3

DISMISSAL – ELIGIBILITY TO PRESENT A STATUTORY CLAIM

LEARNING OUTCOMES

After reading this chapter you will be able to:

- list the eligibility factors that must be satisfied before a person may bring a claim for unfair dismissal and/or a redundancy payment
- explain the difference between an actual and a constructive dismissal
- understand the significance of the non-renewal of a fixed-term contract
- understand the importance of continuity of employment
- calculate continuous employment
- explain when an employment tribunal will not have jurisdiction to hear a claim of unfair dismissal and/or for a redundancy payment.

3.1 INTRODUCTION

In addition to the common law claim for wrongful dismissal (see **Chapter 2**), there are two further claims that may be available to an employee on termination of his employment. These claims arise as a result of statutory rights given to an employee, namely, the right to a redundancy payment and the right not to be unfairly dismissed.

These claims differ from wrongful dismissal in many respects, most notably because not every employee is eligible to present a claim for redundancy or unfair dismissal. In this chapter, we consider the eligibility requirements for both statutory claims.

3.2 ELIGIBILITY FACTORS

In order to claim a redundancy payment or to pursue a complaint of unfair dismissal, a person must:

(a)   be an employee;

(b)   have been dismissed;

(c)   have been continuously employed for the requisite period;

(d)   not be within an excluded class.

In certain situations, a person may be unable to bring a claim for jurisdictional reasons.

Each of these issues will be considered in more detail below.

3.3   EMPLOYEES ONLY

The claimant must be an employee (ERA 1996, ss 94, 135). An employee is defined as 'an individual who ... works under ... a contract of employment' (ERA 1996, s 230(1)). The self-employed, workers and independent contractors are excluded from entitlement (see **1.3**).

3.4   DISMISSAL

The fact that the contract has terminated does not in itself give rise to a statutory claim.

In order to be entitled to a redundancy payment or to claim unfair dismissal, an employee must show (ie has the burden of proving) that he has been 'dismissed' within the meaning of the legislation. An employee who resigns, leaves by mutual agreement, or whose contract is frustrated has not been dismissed and is not eligible to pursue a statutory claim.

The word 'dismissal' for the purpose of unfair dismissal and redundancy payments is defined by ss 95 and 136 of the ERA 1996, respectively, and differs in one important respect from the common law definition (see (b) below).

Under ERA 1996, dismissal may arise in one of three ways:

(a)   the contract is terminated by the employer; or

(b)   a limited term expires without being renewed; or

(c)   the employee is constructively dismissed.

The following paragraphs consider each of these situations in detail.

3.4.1   The contract is terminated by the employer – actual dismissal

An employee is treated as dismissed if 'the contract under which he is employed ... is terminated by the employer (whether with or without notice)' (ERA 1996, ss 95(1)(a) and 136(1)(a)).

(a)   This includes the most common of the three dismissal situations – where the employer simply gives the employee notice in accordance with the terms of the contract.

(b)   It also covers the situation where the employer terminates the contract without notice, ie he dismisses summarily. In this case, even though the dismissal may have been provoked by the employee's conduct, it is the employer's action in treating the contract as discharged which terminates the contract and thus constitutes dismissal.

> **EXAMPLE**
>
> If an employee is absent without leave and the employer refuses to allow him to return to work, this will operate as a dismissal (*London Transport Executive v Clark* [1981] IRLR 166, CA).

(c)   Occasionally, there is some doubt as to whether there has been a dismissal or a resignation where the words used by the employer are ambiguous.

> **EXAMPLE**
>
> The employer may use the words 'get lost' (or something even less polite) in an argument with the employee. If the employee takes him at his word, can he claim to have been dismissed?

> If the words used by the employer are ambiguous, then the test is to consider how the words would have been understood by the reasonable listener. The test is an objective one and the question of whether or not there has been a dismissal must be considered in light of all the surrounding circumstances (*Southern v Franks Charlesly & Co* [1981] IRLR 278). There is one authority (*Tanner v DT Kean* [1978] IRLR 110) for the proposition that the intention of the speaker is the relevant test, but none of the other cases supports this view.
>
> In *Futty v Brekkes (D & D) Ltd* [1974] IRLR 130, a foreman had a conversation with an employee which ended with the foreman saying 'if you don't like the job, you can f*** off'. The employee left and claimed that he had been dismissed. The tribunal decided that there was no dismissal, but only a 'general exhortation'.
>
> However, note that in appropriate circumstances, speaking to an employee in a disrespectful manner may, through the employer's breach of the implied term of mutual trust and confidence, constitute a constructive dismissal (see **3.4.3**).

(d) There are cases where the employer will offer the employee a 'choice' – resign or be dismissed. If the employee chooses to resign, as this has been forced upon him by his employer, it will be treated as a dismissal by his employer (see, eg, *Martin v MBS Fastenings (Glynwed) Distribution Ltd* [1983] IRLR 198, CA).

In *Sandhu v Jan de Rijk Transport Ltd* [2007] EWCA Civ 430, an employee was summoned to a meeting and informed that his contract would be ended. He agreed severance terms in the meeting. Both the employment tribunal and the EAT held that he had resigned. The Court of Appeal overturned that finding. The Court said that resignation involves some degree of negotiation, discussion and genuine choice on the part of the employee. In this case, the employee had had no advance knowledge of what was to be discussed in the meeting, no time to take advice and no opportunity for reflection. The Court said he was not negotiating freely and had therefore been dismissed.

3.4.2 A limited term expires without being renewed or is ended early

Unlike the position at common law, the non-renewal of a limited-term contract is treated as a dismissal for the purpose of pursuing the statutory claims.

(a) An employee is treated as dismissed if 'he is employed under a limited-term contract and that contract terminates by virtue of the limiting term without being renewed under the same contract' (ERA 1996, ss 95(1)(b) and 136(1)(b)).

(b) A limited-term contract may contain a 'break' clause under which one party, usually the employer, is entitled to terminate by giving notice before the term expires. If such a contract expires by effluxion of the limited term and the contract is not renewed, the employee is treated as being dismissed under this subsection. If the employer terminates the contract by giving notice under the 'break' clause, the employee is dismissed under s 95(1)(a) or s 136(1)(a) (see **3.4.1**).

3.4.3 The employee is constructively dismissed

Generally, an employee will not be regarded as having been dismissed if he resigns (but see *Southern v Franks Charlesly & Co* [1981] IRLR 278, *Sovereign House Security v Savage* [1989] IRLR 115 and *Greater Glasgow Health Board v Mackay* 1989 SLT 729). However, an employee is to be treated as dismissed if 'the employee terminates the contract under which he is employed (with or without notice) in circumstances in which he is entitled to terminate it without notice by reason of the employer's conduct' (ERA 1996, ss 95(1)(c) and 136(1)(c)).

(a) An employee who leaves in such circumstances is said to be constructively dismissed. In order for an employee to treat himself as constructively dismissed within this provision, the employer's conduct must either amount to a significant breach going to the heart of the contract, or show that the employer no longer intends to be bound by one or more of the essential terms of the contract. The employee is then entitled to treat the contract as discharged at common law (*Western Excavating Ltd v Sharp* [1978] QB 761, CA). The test is an objective one; whether the employer intended to breach the contract or not is irrelevant.

(b)   A breach of an express term of the contract by the employer can amount to such a constructive dismissal. Examples would include:

(i)   *Reduction of pay*

A unilateral reduction in pay will amount to repudiation of the contract. This would include, for example, reduction in fringe benefits or refusal to pay overtime at overtime rates. In *Cantor Fitzgerald International v Callaghan and Others* [1999] IRLR 234, the Court of Appeal emphasised the importance of pay in any contract of employment; it said there was a crucial distinction between an employer's failure to pay or delay in paying agreed remuneration, perhaps due to a mistake or oversight, which would 'not necessarily' go to the root of the contract, and a deliberate refusal to do so, which the Court said would undermine the whole basis of the contract. See, more recently, *Mostyn v S and P Casuals Ltd* (UKEAT/0158/17).

(ii)   *Pay below the national minimum wage*

Where an employee is paid well below the national minimum wage, that may amount to such an obvious and egregious breach as to amount to a clear repudiatory breach (see *Mruke v Khan* [2018] EWCA Civ 280).

(ii)   *Job description*

A fundamental change in the nature of the job will amount to repudiation if there is no term allowing the employer to make such a change. In *Land Securities Trillium Ltd v Thornley* [2005] IRLR 765, EAT, it was held that there was a repudiatory breach when the employer moved the employee from a 'hands on' role to a managerial position, because the contract of employment did not include that flexibility for the employer. In so deciding, the EAT stated that the tribunal should look not only at the claimant's job description, but also at the work she actually did. Although her contract said that the claimant 'would perform to the best of [her] abilities ... any other duties which may reasonably be required of [her]', this, said the EAT, imposed a requirement of reasonableness on any request by the employer.

(c)   A significant breach of an implied term by the employer will entitle the employee to treat himself as constructively dismissed. There is implied into contracts of employment a term that employers will not 'without reasonable and proper cause, conduct themselves in a manner calculated or likely to destroy or seriously damage the relationship of confidence and trust between the employer and employee' (*Woods v WM Car Services (Peterborough) Ltd* [1983] IRLR 413, CA; see also *Malik v BCCI*; *Mahmud v BCCI* [1997] ICR 606, HL and *Baldwin v Brighton and Hove City Council* [2007] ICR 680). This is known as the duty of trust and confidence.

This duty is very wide in its application. Employers have been held to be in breach of this duty by, for example, making unjustified accusations of theft on scant evidence, making unjustified allegations that an employee was incapable of doing his job and falsely telling an employee who wanted a transfer that no vacancies were available. In *Stanley Cole (Wainfleet) Ltd v Sheridan* [2003] IRLR 52, the EAT upheld the tribunal's decision that the unjustified imposition of a final written warning amounted to a repudiatory breach entitling the employee to resign and claim she had been unfairly constructively dismissed; and in *Greenhof v Barnsley Metropolitan BC* [2006] IRLR 98, the EAT held that a serious breach of the employer's duty to make reasonable adjustments (see **Chapter 13**) amounted to a breach of the implied duty of trust and confidence (see also *Shaw v CCL Ltd* (UKEAT/0512/06), where the employer's actions, which amounted to sex discrimination, were held to breach the implied duty (discrimination against an employee will usually amount to a repudiatory breach)). In *Private Medicine Intermediaries Ltd v Hodkinson and Others* (EAT/0134/15), the EAT upheld a tribunal decision that an employer committed a repudiatory breach by raising performance concerns during a period of sick leave, and that the claimant has been constructively unfairly dismissed. (The case demonstrates the need for a sensitive approach when contacting absent employees.) Performance issues and grievances should, as far as possible, be dealt with separately.

If an employer acts in an unreasonable way there may be a breach of this duty, but the test remains that in *Western Excavating Ltd v Sharp* (see (a) above). The employer's conduct has to amount to a repudiatory breach of contract. In *Brown v Merchant Ferries* [1998] IRLR 682, the Court of Appeal accepted that if the employer's conduct is seriously unreasonable, this may provide evidence that there has been a repudiatory breach of contract but, on the facts, held that the conduct in question fell far short of a repudiatory breach by the employer. Mere unreasonable behaviour is not enough. The Court of Appeal has confirmed that the 'range of reasonable responses' test (see **Chapter 5**) has no relevance to the issue of whether an employee has been constructively dismissed, in *Bournemouth University Higher Education Corporation v Buckland* [2010] EWCA Civ 121 (see below).

In *Morrow v Safeway Stores plc* [2002] IRLR 9, the EAT held that the employment tribunal had erred in holding that although a manager's conduct in giving the applicant a public reprimand amounted to a breach of the implied contractual term of trust and confidence, it was not sufficiently serious to amount to a repudiation entitling the applicant to resign and claim constructive dismissal. The EAT held that where an employer breaches the implied term of trust and confidence, that breach is 'inevitably' fundamental, and thus such a breach goes to the root of the contract and amounts to a repudiatory breach, entitling the employee to resign and claim constructive dismissal. If the employer's conduct is insufficiently serious, there is no breach of the implied term. The EAT remitted the case for re-hearing: was the breach sufficiently serious or not?

Marshall Specialist Vehicles Ltd v Osborne (UKEAT/101/02) is a case concerning when employees can claim constructive dismissal arising out of stress at work. A tribunal had implied a term that employers should take reasonable care to avoid imposing a workload, or acquiescing in an employee's assumption of a workload, that would forseeably cause mental or physical injury. It found that the term had been breached and awarded maximum unfair dismissal damages. The EAT overturned this decision and criticised the tribunal for 'manufacturing' a term which was designed to provide the means to achieve a predetermined result. The EAT stated that there is already a general implied term that employers should take reasonable care for the safety of their employees. To show a breach giving rise to constructive dismissal an employee had to:

(i)   establish that the risk of injury was foreseeable;

(ii)   show that the employer was in breach of its duty;

(iii)   show that the breach was a foreseeable breach.

In *Horkulak v Cantor Fitzgerald International* [2003] IRLR 756, a senior director successfully claimed that the managing director's use of foul and abusive language was in breach of the implied duty of trust and confidence. The High Court held that the frequent use of such language did not 'sanitise its effect' so as to remove its power to offend, and held that the fact that an employee is very highly paid does not entitle an employer to apply a different standard of behaviour in its treatment of the employee.

For some years there was a debate about the relevance of the 'range of reasonable responses' test (see **Chapter 5**) when determining whether an employee has been constructively dismissed. For example, the EAT, in *Claridge v Daler Rowney Ltd* [2008] IRLR 672, held that for an employer's mishandling of a grievance to amount to a breach of trust and confidence, it was necessary for the employee to show that the conduct complained of was calculated or likely to destroy or seriously damage the employment relationship, and that the employee will not be able to satisfy that test unless the behaviour is outside the band of reasonable responses. On the facts it was held that a delay of some four and a half months in notifying the employee of the outcome of the grievance was not a fundamental breach; the employer's conduct did not fall outside the band of reasonable responses (see too *Abbey National v Fairbrother* [2007] IRLR 320). In *Savola v Chiltern Herb Farms* [1982] IRLR 166, the Court of Appeal decided that a constructive dismissal (the resignation was in response to a breach of an express term) could be a fair dismissal, ie that in some circumstances an employer who is in breach may still act reasonably. In *Bournemouth University Higher Education Corporation v Buckland* (UKEAT/0492/08) the EAT held that the band of reasonable responses test is not relevant when considering whether an employee has been constructively dismissed. At this stage, held the EAT, the only question for the tribunal is whether the employer had conducted himself in a manner calculated or likely to destroy or seriously damage the employment relationship (although as the EAT stated in *Nationwide Building Society v Niblett* (UKEAT/0524/08), it is perhaps 'difficult to envisage circumstances in which an employer will be in breach of the implied term of trust and confidence unless the employer's conduct has been unreasonable').

The Court of Appeal upheld the *Buckland* decision ([2010] EWCA Civ 121) and held that the only question for the tribunal is whether the employer had without reasonable or proper cause conducted himself in a manner calculated or likely to destroy or seriously damage the employment relationship; the range of reasonable responses test should be relevant only when considering whether or not the dismissal (be it actual or constructive) is fair or unfair (see **Chapter 5**). The Court of Appeal also said it was clear as a matter of general contract law that an anticipatory breach of contract could be withdrawn at any time up to the moment of acceptance, but once a repudiatory breach had been committed the defaulting party had 'crossed the Rubicon' and was unable to retreat, ie the breach cannot be cured; the other party could then elect whether or not to accept the breach.

In *RDF Media Group v Clements* [2008] IRLR 207, the High Court gave a very clear explanation of the implied term of trust and confidence (see paras 100–106). Importantly, the High Court held that an employee was not constructively dismissed because he himself was in repudiatory breach of the mutual obligation of trust and confidence. He could not therefore rely on the employer's later breach of the obligation. This applies even where the employer only subsequently finds out about the employee's breach.

In *Chakrabarty v Ipswich Hospital NHS Trust* [2014] EWHC 2735 (QB), the High Court held, in the context of a hospital doctor, that there was no freestanding and discrete implied contractual term of fairness. The court said that 'where the authorities contemplate questions of fairness, they do so in the context of the implied term of trust and confidence, or on a narrower basis by reference to an implied term that disciplinary processes will be conducted fairly, without unjustified delay'. Fairness is part of the fulfilment of the implied term of trust and confidence and, in the context of the disciplinary proceedings, these should be conducted fairly. In *Coventry University v Mian* [2014] EWCA Civ 1275, the Court of Appeal considered whether an employer had breached its duty of care to an employee by pursuing disciplinary proceedings without a proper basis for doing so. This was a personal injury claim, which had succeeded in the High Court. The Court of Appeal held that the employer did not breach its duty of care to the employee by bringing disciplinary proceedings against her. In the *Mian* case, Coventry University commenced disciplinary proceedings against Dr Mian to investigate and consider an allegation that she had been complicit in preparing false references. The disciplinary hearing was due to take place in April 2007, but was delayed for various reasons until November. Dr Mian was signed off sick from April 2007 and did not attend the disciplinary hearing – although she submitted written responses to the allegations and was represented at the hearing by her union representative. Dr Mian was acquitted at the disciplinary hearing and subsequently brought proceedings against Coventry alleging that it had been in breach of contract and/or negligent in commencing disciplinary proceedings without undertaking further enquiries and that this caused her psychiatric injury. The judge in the High Court found that a proper investigation had not been carried out. The judge found that the charges brought against Dr Mian were unjustified and that the University was in breach of contract. The University appealed. The Court of Appeal allowed the appeal and dismissed the claim.

The Court of Appeal confirmed that the correct test in such situations is whether the decision was 'unreasonable' in the sense that it had been outside the range of reasonable decisions open to an employer in all of the circumstances. The Court of Appeal held that this requires an objective assessment and 'in the circumstances' includes consideration of both the evidence which was available to the employer at the time and such other evidence as would or should have been available as the result of a (non-negligently) conducted investigation. It was not appropriate to assess the overall merits; in this case a reasonable employer could have concluded that there was a case for Dr Mian to answer on the basis of the evidence available at the time proceedings were instigated. The University, accordingly, was not in breach of its duty of care.

The duty not to act in a manner likely to undermine trust and confidence was looked at again by the EAT in *McBride v Falkirk Football Club* (UKEATS/0058/10). The claimant was the Club's under-19s team manager. He resigned after his right to pick his team was arbitrarily removed after an Academy Director was appointed. The tribunal implied into his contract a term that he would relinquish his right to pick his team once an Academy Director was appointed, and on that basis found no breach of contract by the Club, and rejected his claim for constructive dismissal. The EAT, in overturning the employment tribunal's decision and substituting a finding of constructive dismissal, said that the test to be applied in trust and confidence cases was to be judged from an objective standpoint, so that an employer could not rely upon factors in a particular industry – such as 'an autocratic style of management' being 'the norm in football' – as a defence to a breach of the implied term of trust and confidence. The EAT also held that a term ought not to be implied into a contract of employment which contradicted an express term or which was imprecise, unnecessary or not obvious. Useful guidance on when to imply terms in a contact is set out at paras 54 and 55.

In *Assamoi v Spirit Pub Company* (UKEAT/0050/11), the employer upheld an employee's grievance about treatment by his immediate manager and took steps to rectify the situation. The EAT held that this prevented the employee relying on the treatment to show a breach of the implied term of trust and confidence. The actions of the more senior manager had prevented the matter escalating into a state of affairs that would have justified the employee leaving and claiming that he had been constructively dismissed.

For a case where the employer was held to have reasonable and proper cause for its conduct, see *Sharfugeen v T J Morris Ltd* (UKEAT/0272/16).

In *Agoreyo v London Borough of Lambeth* [2017] EWHC 2019 (QB) the High Court held that suspension of a teacher for alleged excessive force against two children was a breach of trust and confidence.

(d)   In some instances, while an act may not of itself be sufficiently serious, it is possible to look at the cumulative effect of a number of minor breaches, through what is known as the 'last straw' doctrine. In *London Borough of Waltham Forest v Omilaju* [2005] IRLR 35, the Court of Appeal (referring to *Malik v BCCI* [1998] AC 20 and *Lewis v Motorworld Garages Ltd* [1986] ICR 157) restated that 'the last action of the employer which leads to the employee leaving need not itself be a breach of contract'. In *Omilaju*, the 'straw that broke the camel's back' was, looked at objectively, perfectly reasonable, justifiable and permissible conduct. What is clear is that a last straw must not be 'utterly trivial' or innocuous and must contribute something to the breach, and an entirely innocuous act cannot be a final straw.

Most recently, in *Kaur v Leeds Teaching Hospitals NHS Trust* [2018] EWCA Civ 978, the Court of Appeal again restated the general principles to be applied in last straw cases and what questions a tribunal should ask itself, namely:

(1)   What was the most recent act (or omission) on the part of the employer which the employee says caused, or triggered, his or her resignation?

(2)   Has he or she affirmed the contract since that act?

(3)   If not, was that act (or omission) by itself a repudiatory breach of contract [ie entitling the employee to treat the contract as at an end]?

(4)   If not, was it nevertheless a part ... of a course of conduct comprising several acts and omissions which, viewed cumulatively, amounted to a (repudiatory) breach of [the implied term of trust and confidence]? (If it was, there is no need for any separate consideration of a possible previous affirmation ...)

(5)   Did the employee resign in response (or partly in response) to that breach?

In *Kaur*, given that the employer's disciplinary procedure had been perfectly properly applied, there could be no 'last straw' and hence no constructive dismissal. The Court of Appeal also confirmed in *Kaur* that, in relying on previous acts, an employee claiming constructive dismissal could rely on a previously affirmed repudiatory breach where there were then subsequent breaches, based on the cumulative effect of all the breaches. A final straw will revive the opportunity to resign; otherwise an employee who soldiers on and does not object at the first opportunity would lose their right to rely on all conduct up to that point, which would not be right.

See also (g) below.

(e)   A threat to change terms and conditions, and to dismiss an employee if he does not accept the changes, may amount to a constructive dismissal even if the employee resigns before implementation of the changes. The employer's threats could amount to anticipatory breach of contract (*Greenaway Harrison Ltd v Wiles* [1994] IRLR 380). See also *Buckland* (above).

(f)   It is *not* possible to argue that the *manner* of a dismissal is a breach of the implied term of trust and confidence. The House of Lords, in *Johnson v Unisys Ltd* [2001] IRLR 279, was unwilling to develop the common law to imply a contractual term that an employer must carry out a dismissal in good faith, given the existence of the statutory unfair dismissal regimes which specifically cover the process of dismissal. (This decision also had implications for what damages may be recovered in a wrongful dismissal claim – see **2.4.1.5** and **5.6.2.2**.) The EAT held in *Bethnal Green and Shoreditch Education Trust v Dippenaar* (UKEAT/0064/15) that subjecting an employee to capability proceedings with no reasonable and proper cause amounted to a repudiatory breach.

(g)   It is important to determine, once a repudiation has been established, whether 'the repudiatory breach played a part in the dismissal' (see *Abbey Cars (West Horndon) Ltd v Ford* (UKEAT/0472/07). However, it is an error of law to look for 'the' effective cause, ie the principal or main cause (see *Wright v North Ayrshire Council* [2014] ICR 77). The EAT referred to *Nottingham CC v Meckle* [2005] ICR 1 in *Wright*, where the Court of Appeal stated:

The proper approach, therefore, once a repudiation of the contract by the employer has been established, is to ask whether the employee has accepted that repudiation by treating the contract of employment as at an end.

So even if an employee leaves for a whole host of reasons, he can still claim constructive dismissal if the repudiatory breach is one of the factors relied on. (See *Ishaq v Royal Mail Group* (UKEAT/0156/16) for a case where the tribunal's decision that the real reason for resignation was to avoid disciplinary proceedings and not in response to the employer's breach was upheld by the EAT.)

It is possible to look to the cumulative effects of the employer's actions. The final act may not in itself amount to a repudiatory breach of contract but could be the 'last straw' entitling the employee to claim constructive dismissal. Where there is a series of incidents, none of which individually amounts to a serious breach but which together amount to a breach of the implied duty of trust and confidence, if the employee continues to work, any implied waiver of the breach will be conditional upon there being no repetition of the breach (*JV Strong & Co Ltd v Hamill* (UKEAT/1179/99)). Where there is a series of incidents, the employee's response has to be measured from the last incident. In *Abbey National plc v Robinson* [2000] All ER (D) 1884, the EAT found that an employee was entitled to claim constructive dismissal when she resigned almost a year after a breach of contract by her employers. There was a series of incidents culminating with the 'last straw' (the withdrawal of a job offer) and her resignation was tendered shortly after that last incident.

Note that, according to the Court of Appeal in *London Borough of Waltham Forest v Omilaju* (above), the final straw must contribute something to that breach, although what it adds may be relatively 'insignificant'. If the alleged final straw is an entirely innocuous act (here, a justified refusal to pay) on the part of the employer, this cannot be the last straw.

(h)   Founded as it is on the contractual concept of repudiatory breach, the employee must leave within a reasonable period following the breach to avoid being taken as having affirmed the contract and waived the breach. In *Bunning v GT Bunning & Sons Ltd* [2005] EWCA Civ 293, the employer had breached the claimant's contract when it failed to carry out adequate risk assessments when the claimant said she was pregnant. However, the Court of Appeal held that she waived the breach when she accepted an alternative job with the employer.

How long is too long is a question of fact. In *Munchkins Restaurant Ltd and Another v Karmazyn and Others* (UKEAT/0359/09), the waitresses in question put up with the employer's conduct for several years. The tribunal made the point that in its view the waitresses were migrant workers with no certainty of continued employment, save at Munchkins; that there were considerations of convenience for one; that they were constrained by financial and in some cases parental pressure; that they had the fear that they might not obtain other work; that they had the comfort of one manager acting as a cushion until she left; and that they managed, therefore, to find a balance between conduct which was unwelcome and unlawful and the advantages which their job gave them. It was not therefore, according to the EAT, completely beyond the scope of reason to think that women in this particular situation should behave as they did.

Mere delay by itself (unaccompanied by any express or implied affirmation of contract) does not constitute affirmation of the contract, but if it is prolonged it may be evidence of an implied affirmation. In *Mrs A Fereday v South Staffordshire NHS Primary Care Trust* (UKEAT/0513/10), the claimant invoked the grievance procedure, which resulted in a decision adverse to her on 13 February 2009, but she only resigned by a letter dated 24 March 2009. The EAT upheld the employment tribunal's decision that the respondent had repudiated the contract of employment but that the claimant had affirmed the contract by her delay. The EAT held that the employment tribunal was entitled to take the prolonged delay of nearly six weeks between the grievance decision and the claimant's resignation as an implied affirmation, bearing in mind that the claimant was expecting or requiring the respondent (the employer) to perform its part of the contract of employment by paying her sick pay. See also *Mari v Reuters Ltd* (UKEAT/0539/13) (where the EAT set out the case law and relevant principles of law on the question of affirmation and the significance of accepting sick pay), *Wess v Science Museum Group* (UKEAT/0120/14) (where the EAT said that delay alone might be neutral, but where terms had an immediate impact, affirmation was more likely to be found) and, most recently, the Court of Appeal's decision in *Abrahall v Nottingham City Council* [2018] EWCA Civ 796, where employees who had continued working two years after a pay freeze was imposed were held not to have accepted the variation.

The High Court in *Brown v Neon Management Services Ltd* [2018] EWHC 2137 (QB) held that resignation on long notice (six months or more) constituted affirmation of the contract of employment, although further breaches during the notice period entitled the employees to resign and allege constructive dismissal, and on that basis the claims succeeded.

Delay is one of many factors to which the tribunal may have regard to when deciding whether the contract has been affirmed. Other relevant factors might be illness (see,eg, *Chindove v Morrisons Supermarkets plc* (UKEAT/0201/13 and UKEAT/0043/14)), whether a grievance has been raised, whether there are ongoing discussions as to whether or not some accommodation might be reached, etc. The important question is, in the end, whether, in all the circumstances, the employee's conduct had demonstrated an intention to continue the contract. See too *Adjei-Frempong v Howard Frank Ltd* (EAT/0044/15).

(i) The employee's acceptance of the breach must be unambiguous and unequivocal (see *Atlantic Air Ltd v Holt* (UKEAT/0602/07), but it need not be communicated to the employer. The Court of Appeal, in *Weathersfield v Sargeant* [1999] IRLR 94, stated that the fact that an employee left her employment without giving a reason at the time did not preclude her from claiming that she had been constructively dismissed, although such conduct would usually make it more difficult to obtain such a finding. The Court rejected the notion that there could be no acceptance of a repudiation unless the employee told the employer at the time that he was leaving because of the employer's repudiatory conduct. The EAT held in *Wright v North Ayrshire Council* (UKEAT/0017/13) that the issue is whether the breach 'played a part in the [resignation]'. The repudiatory breach need not be the only cause but must be 'an' (cf 'the') effective cause of the resignation. The fact that an employee had other non-repudiatory reasons would not vitiate the acceptance of the repudiation.

(j) The date of the resignation and whether it is with or without notice may be important when establishing the effective date of termination for the purpose of bringing an unfair dismissal claim (see **3.5.1** and **6.3.1**). In *Secretary of State for Justice v Hibbert* (UKEAT/0289/13), the EAT held that a claimant's letter of resignation was immediate and unambiguous, and did not include a four-week period of notice. This meant that her unfair dismissal claim was out of time. Where the resignation is clear, the employer does not need to accept the resignation, nor is it obliged to offer a 'cooling-off period' where a resignation is made in the heat of the moment (though many employers do as good practice).

(k) A prior repudiatory breach by an employee will not prevent that employee from claiming constructive dismissal – even if he might have been dismissed for gross misconduct if the employer had known of it. Under employment law principles, an unaccepted repudiation has no effect. However, the misconduct will be relevant to remedy (see *Aberdeen City Council v McNeill* [2014] IRLR 114 and *Atkinson v Community Gateway Association* (UKEAT/0457/12).

3.5 CONTINUOUS EMPLOYMENT

In order to be eligible to present a statutory claim, the claimant must have the requisite period of 'continuous employment' prior to the dismissal.

In calculating periods of continuous employment, a month means a calendar month and a year means 12 calendar months. If, for example, an employee commenced employment on 20 April 2014 and worked continuously for his employer from that date, his period of two years' continuous employment is complete on 19 April 2016. (See, eg, *Pacitti Jones v O'Brien* [2005] IRLR 889.)

Continuous employment usually means working for the same employer without a break. Sometimes, employment can be regarded as continuous in spite of short breaks (ERA 1996, s 212(3)(c) (see **3.5.3**)). Sometimes, time spent with a previous employer may be added on (eg where there are 'associated employers', such as teachers within one local education authority who work for different schools).

3.5.1 Periods of employment required

3.5.1.1 Unfair dismissal

From 6 April 2012, for employees who start work on or after that date, to be entitled to present a complaint of unfair dismissal, the dismissed employee must have been continuously employed for a period of not less than two years, starting on the date that employment commenced and ending on the 'effective date of termination' (EDT) (ERA 1996, s 108(1)). For employees who started work before 6 April 2012, only one year is required.

It is advisable for employers to review the employment of new employees well before they have been continuously employed for two years. This will enable an employer to dismiss an unsatisfactory employee with proper notice, before he becomes entitled to present a complaint of unfair dismissal. However, note that even if an employee does not have the necessary length of service, he is eligible to present a claim for discrimination if relevant on the facts (see **Chapters 8** and **13**).

Exceptionally, an employee does not need a qualifying period of continuous employment to present an unfair dismissal claim, for example an employee who is dismissed for trade union reasons (**5.5.1**), for having stopped work on health and safety grounds (**5.5.4**), for having asserted a statutory right (**5.5.3**) or because she is pregnant (**Chapter 14**).

3.5.1.2 Redundancy payment

To be entitled to claim a redundancy payment, the dismissed employee must have been employed for a period of not less than two years, starting on the date that employment commenced and ending on the 'relevant date' (ERA 1996, s 155). See further **Chapter 4**.

3.5.2 Calculating continuous employment

3.5.2.1 Unfair dismissal and the effective date of termination

The EDT is defined by ss 97 and 145 of the ERA 1996 to mean:

(a) for an employee whose contract is terminated by notice, whether given by the employer or employee, the date on which that notice expires. In *Palfrey v Transco plc* [2004] IRLR 916, the EAT said that the employee's EDT was his leaving date as agreed with the employer, and not the termination date given in the notice of dismissal (see also *Wedgewood v Ministergate Hull Ltd* (UKEAT/0137/10);

(b) for an employee whose contract is terminated without notice, the date on which termination takes effect (see *Heaven v Whitbread Group plc* (UKEAT/0084/10), the Court of Appeal's decision in *Société Général, London Branch v Geys* at **2.3.3** above and more recently *Cosmeceuticals Ltd v Parkin* (UKEAT/0049/17)); and

(c) for an employee with a limited-term contract which expires without renewal, the date on which the term expires.

Dismissals, resignations and EDT can often be complex matters to ascertain in practice (see, eg, *Secretary of State for Justice v Hibbert* at **3.4.3(i)** above). As a rule of thumb, the EDT is the last day on which the employee worked for the employer.

Note that:

(a)   if an employee is dismissed without notice but given wages in lieu, the EDT is still the date the employee was told to go (see, eg, *Robert Cort & Son Ltd v Charman* [1981] ICR 816);

(b)   with a constructive dismissal, where the employee resigns the EDT is the date of departure, ie the employee's acceptance of the repudiation. Where an employee resigns and gives notice, the EDT will be the date the notice expires.

The Court of Appeal held that the EDT is a statutory construct and cannot be fixed by agreement between the parties (*Fitzgerald v University of Kent at Canterbury* [2004] IRLR 300).

The EDT may be important in determining whether an employee has presented a case to a tribunal within the requisite time-limits (see **6.3**). In *Gisda Cyf v Barratt* [2010] UKSC 41, the Supreme Court held that the EDT of an employee dismissed for gross misconduct was the date she opened and read the letter from her employer, informing her of her dismissal. See also *Robinson v Bowskill* (UKEAT/0313/12) and *Cosmeceuticals Ltd v Parkin* (above). The position is the same under the common law (see **2.3.3** above).

In *Hawes v Curtis Ltd v Arfan* [2012] ICR 1244, it was accepted that an altered decision on an appeal against dismissal might change the EDT, for example where the appeal expressly varied the date on which termination took effect.

Extension of EDT in special circumstances

The main purpose of this rule is to ensure that employers do not deprive employees of their statutory rights by wrongfully dismissing them without notice just before they reach the qualifying period to present a claim of unfair dismissal.

In circumstances where the employee is entitled to a statutory minimum period of notice under s 86 of the ERA 1996 (see **2.3.3**), if he is dismissed without notice or with less notice than the statutory minimum, for certain purposes his EDT will be extended by the statutory minimum period of notice to which he was entitled but did not receive (ERA 1996, s 97(2)):

(a)   The EDT is extended only by the statutory minimum period of notice, not by any longer contractual period to which he may have been entitled.

(b)   The EDT is extended only if the employee was entitled to notice. It is not extended if a limited-term contract terminates (except under a 'break' clause), or if an employer is entitled to dismiss the employee without notice (ERA 1996, s 86(6)). In *Lancaster and Duke Ltd v Wileman* (UKEAT/0256/17), the EAT emphasised that where there is a genuine entitlement to summarily dismiss, an employee cannot rely on the deeming provisions in s 86 of the ERA 1996 to get to two years' qualifying service. In this case, Ms Wileman was dismissed for gross misconduct with no notice, two days before her two-year anniversary. No process was carried out before her dismissal and there was no right of appeal. The tribunal extended her period by adding in the statutory minimum one week's notice and found that she was unfairly dismissed. The EAT overturned this because the tribunal had not made any finding as to whether Ms Wileman has been guilty of gross misconduct, such that the s 86(6) provision would apply. There needed to be a wrongful dismissal claim for the additional week to be added.

(c)   A constructively dismissed employee is also entitled to extend the EDT by the statutory minimum period for the purposes of bringing an unfair dismissal claim (see (d) below). The statutory minimum period of notice that would have been due from the employer had the employer terminated, will start to run from the date that the employee gave notice (ERA 1996, s 97(4)).

(d)   The EDT is extended only for some purposes, such as the qualification period to present an unfair dismissal claim, the calculation of awards for such a claim and entitlement to be given a written statement of reasons for dismissal (see **5.2.3**). It does *not* extend the EDT for the purposes of extending the time-limits to present claims.

> **EXAMPLE**
>
> Natalie commenced employment on 3 April 2015. There is no break in her continuity of employment. Her employer wrongfully dismissed her without notice on 30 March 2017. On this date she had been continuously employed for more than one month but less than two years. Under s 86 of the ERA 1996 she was entitled to one week's statutory minimum notice (see **2.3.3**). Her EDT is extended by one week to 6 April 2017 (the seven days' notice starts on 31 March and expires on 6 April), which gives her the necessary two years' continuous employment to present an unfair dismissal claim.

3.5.2.2 Redundancy payments and the relevant date

The relevant date is defined by ERA 1996, s 145 in exactly the same way as the EDT is for unfair dismissal (see **3.5.2.1** above).

Extension of the relevant date in special circumstances

Again, the rules are designed to prevent an employer wrongfully dismissing an employee just before he reaches the qualifying period for presenting a redundancy payment claim. Points (a), (b) and (d) at **3.5.2.1** above apply to extension of the relevant date also (s 145(5)).

Point (c) above does not apply. The relevant date will be extended by the statutory minimum period to which the employee is entitled but did not receive, but only where there is an actual dismissal by the employer. The relevant date is *not* extended by the statutory minimum period for the purposes of making a redundancy payment claim where the employee has been constructively dismissed.

> **EXAMPLE**
>
> George commenced employment on 3 April 2015. There is no break in his continuity of employment. He resigns on 30 March 2017, alleging that he has been constructively dismissed. On this date he has been employed for just less than two years. Although, under ERA 1996, s 86, he is entitled to one week's statutory minimum notice, the relevant date will *not* be extended by the statutory minimum period. He is not eligible to claim a redundancy payment.

3.5.3 Continuity of employment

Periods of employment must be continuous. If a period of employment is broken so that it is not continuous with a later period, the employee will commence a new period of employment after the break, starting again at week one. He will not be able to add the old period of employment to the new.

There is a presumption in favour of the employee that employment is continuous (ERA 1996, s 210(5)). This may, however, be rebutted by the employer.

A week counts towards the period of continuous employment if in that week the employee actually works or the employee's relationship with the employer is governed by a contract.

Weeks during which the employee is *not employed* under a contract of employment do not count. However, such weeks *will* count in the following circumstances (ERA 1996, s 212):

(a)   if the employee is absent due to sickness, injury, pregnancy or confinement up to a maximum of 26 weeks;

(b)   if there is a temporary cessation of work (see *Cornwall County Council v Prater* (UKEAT/ 0055/05)) (the case was appealed to the Court of Appeal on different grounds; there was no appeal on this point ([2006] IRLR 362) and *Ford v Warwickshire CC* [1983] ICR 273, HL (applied in *Hussain v Acorn Independent College Ltd* (UKEAT/0199/10)));

(c)   if the employee is absent in circumstances where, by arrangement or custom, the employee is regarded as continuously in employment (see *Curr v Marks & Spencer plc* [2003] IRLR 74 for a decision of the Court of Appeal on this issue).

It is necessary to rely on these provisions to preserve continuity only where there is no continuing contract of employment. If there is a subsisting contractual relationship, continuity of employment will be preserved, even though the employee does not work due to, for example, sickness or holiday or maternity leave. If an employee is reinstated following an unfair dismissal finding, continuity will be assumed as if there had been no dismissal.

For a recent decision considering the statutory construction of s 212 of the ERA 1996, see the EAT's decision in *Welton v Deluxe Retail Ltd (t/a Madhouse)* [2013] IRLR 166, which looked at the situation where there was a gap of just over a week between the claimant ending work at one of the employer's stores and starting work at another.

Note that continuity is a statutory concept. In *London Probation Board v Kirkpatrick* [2005] IRLR 443, the EAT held that it was open to an employer and an employee to arrange (under ERA 1996, s 212(3)(c)) that absence from work could count towards continuity of employment and that reinstatement could qualify as such an arrangement. The EAT in *Welton* disagreed with this analysis, preferring the line of authority in *Murphy v Birrell & Sons Ltd* [1978] IRLR 458 and *Morris v Walsh Western UK Ltd* [1997] IRLR 562, that an 'arrangement' had to exist beforehand, or arise contemporaneously with the relevant absence from work; it could not be made retrospectively to cure gaps in employment. This is because the wording of the section is in the present tense, 'he is regarded as *continuing in* the employment of his employer' (emphasis added).

3.5.4   Industrial action

Industrial action does not break continuity of employment, but days during which the employee is on strike or locked out by the employer do not count in computing the length of employment (ERA 1996, s 216).

This is achieved by postponing the beginning of the period of continuous employment by the number of days between the last working day before the strike or lockout and the day on which work was resumed.

EXAMPLE

An employee, whose continuous employment commenced on 7 September 2016, goes on strike at lunchtime on Friday 11 November 2017. She resumes work on Tuesday 15 November 2017. Her period of continuous employment will now be treated as beginning on 11 September 2016. It is postponed by the four days (ie 11, 12, 13, 14 November) between the last working day before the strike (10 November 2017) and the day work resumed (15 November 2017). The days 12 and 13 November are 'lost' by the employee, even though they are a Saturday and Sunday and not working days.

3.5.5   Change of employer

The basic rule is that for employment to be continuous, it must be with the same employer. A change of employer will break continuity (ERA 1996, s 218).

Although a change of employer breaks continuity, a change of job with the same employer will not break it.

In the following circumstances, continuity of employment is preserved despite a change of employer:

(a) there is a transfer of an undertaking within TUPE 2006 (see **Chapter 7**);

(b) on the death of an employer, the employee is employed by the personal representatives of the deceased;

(c) there is a change of partners who are the employers;

(d) the new employer is an associated employer of the old employer (ERA 1996, s 218(6)). Employers are associated if one is a company of which the other has control, or if both are companies of which a third person has control (ERA 1996, s 231). Therefore, if an employee is moved between companies within a 'group', his continuity will be preserved (see the EAT's decision in *Schwarzenbach and Anor v Jones* (UKEAT/0100/15)).

3.6 EXCLUDED CLASSES

The ERA 1996 excludes certain classes of employee from entitlement to the statutory claims. For example, members of the armed forces, the police service and 'share' mariners are excluded from the right to present a claim of unfair dismissal. Crown employees, 'share' mariners and certain domestic servants employed by close relations are not entitled to redundancy payments. Diplomatic and state immunity may also protect certain classes of employees (see eg *Reyes v Al-Malki* [2015] EWCA Civ 32, *Benkharbouche and Anor v Embassy of the Republic of Sudan* [2015] IRLR 301 and *USA v Nolan* [2015] UKSC 63). Further details of these exclusions may be found in Harvey, *Industrial Relations and Employment Law* (Butterworths), Division C. The Supreme Court held in *Reyes v Al-Malki & Another* [2017] UKSC 61 that embassy employees do not have immunity from claims brought by their domestic staff.

3.7 JURISDICTION

Many employers have mobile or globally based workforces. Generally speaking, employees who ordinarily work in Great Britain will be protected under UK employment laws. For peripatetic employees, their bases will normally be regarded as their place of work. The contract may be relevant here, although courts tend to focus on the actual position in practice rather than on what the contract says, if there is a conflict.

In cases where there is a foreign element, for example expatriate employees working abroad for a UK company, or employees who spend some, but not all, of their time working abroad, the question arises whether a tribunal has jurisdiction to hear the case at all or whether it should be heard in a foreign court.

The right of an employee not to be unfairly dismissed by his employer is embodied in s 94(1) of the ERA 1996. When the right not to be unfairly dismissed first made its appearance (as s 22 of the Industrial Relations Act 1971), it was accompanied by a provision (s 27(2)) which said that s 22 did not apply 'to any employment where under his contract of employment the employee ordinarily works outside Great Britain'. When the legislation was consolidated, ultimately in ERA 1996, the geographical limitation for unfair dismissal claims appeared in s 196(3) under the heading 'Employment outside Great Britain'.

Section 196 of the ERA 1996 provided, inter alia, that the unfair dismissal provisions of the Act did not apply in relation to employment during any period when the employee was working outside Great Britain, unless the employee ordinarily worked in Great Britain for the same employer, or his contract was governed by the law of England and Wales (or Scotland). However, the whole of s 196 was repealed by s 32(3) of the ERA 1999, with effect from 25 October 1999. This repeal left uncertain the extent to which tribunals had jurisdiction to hear unfair dismissal claims under s 94(1) (which simply states that an employee has the right not to be unfairly dismissed by his employer).

It has therefore been left to the courts to imply whatever geographical limitations seem appropriate to the substantive right. Read literally, s 94(1) of the ERA 1996 applies to any individual who works under a contract of employment anywhere in the world. Nonetheless, as pointed out by the House of Lords in the leading case, *Serco Ltd v Lawson and Others* [2006] UKHL 3, it is inconceivable that Parliament was intending to confer rights upon employees working in foreign countries and having no connection with Great Britain. The argument has been over what those limitations should be. In the absence of statutory guidance, guidance on the developing domestic law principles of territoriality and jurisdiction in the enforcement of employment law rights has been provided by the appellate courts. There are now a number of important authorities on this issue of the legislative reach of s 94(1).

Some issues were resolved by the House of Lords in *Serco Ltd v Lawson and Others* [2006] UKHL 3. Hoffmann LJ, giving the judgment, identified three categories of case:

(a)   where the employee was working in Great Britain at the time of the dismissal (so long as that was not a casual visit) – he said that this was the 'normal' case and s 94(1) would generally apply;

(b)   the peripatetic employee – where the 'commonsense [approach] of treating the base' as the place of employment would apply (see *Todd v British Midland Airways Ltd* [1978] ICR 959); and

(c)   expatriate employees – where there would have to be 'unusual' or 'exceptional' circumstances for an employee to be protected under British employment law.

Two examples were given:

(i)   an employee posted abroad by a British employer for the purposes of a business carried on in Britain,

(ii)   an employee of a British employer operating in a British enclave in a foreign country.

Lord Hoffmann said that there might be other examples of employees who 'have equally strong connections with Great Britain and British employment law' but that he could not think of any.

In *Duncombe and Others v Secretary of State for Children, Schools and Families* [2011] UKSC 36, the Supreme Court held that teachers working abroad in schools in Europe and employed by a UK government department were protected under the expatriate employee category identified in *Serco* above because they were another example of employees who have equally strong connections with Britain – the employees' employment had an overwhelmingly closer connection to Britain than anywhere else. The factors that were important were that the Government employed the employees; their contracts were governed by English law; they were employed in international enclaves and it would be anomalous if a teacher employed by the British Government working in a European school in England were protected but these employees working in a school in another country were not.

Lady Hale, delivering the judgment of the Supreme Court remarked (para 8) that it was a mistake to try to torture the circumstances of one employment to make them fit one of the examples given, for 'they are merely examples of the application of the general principle'. She went on to say:

> In our view, these cases do form another example of an exceptional case where the employment has such an overwhelmingly closer connection with Britain and with British employment law than with any other system of law that it is right to conclude that Parliament must have intended that the employees should enjoy protection from unfair dismissal.

In *Ravat v Halliburton Manufacturing and Services Ltd* [2012] UKSC 1 and *Ministry of Defence v Wallis* [2011] EWCA Civ 231, the courts considered the extent to which, if at all, an employment tribunal can go beyond the three categories of case identified by Lord Hoffmann in *Serco*. In *Wallis*, the Court of Appeal upheld the tribunal's decision that the claimants fell within the expatriate category of employee, making it clear that each case must be decided on its own facts. The fact that the claimants were recruited by the MoD, were eligible for the posts as dependants of serving members of the army posted abroad and were employed on terms governed by English law were all factors which meant that the claimants had 'clear, firm, sound connections with Britain'. In *Ravat*, the Supreme Court, on an appeal from the Scottish Court of Session (which was divided as to the extent to which it was possible to depart from Lord Hoffman's categories), held that a British citizen who lived in England but worked in Libya on what was known as a commuter or rotational basis (he worked 28 days in Libya, then was in England for 28 days), could bring an unfair dismissal claim. He was employed by Halliburton Manufacturing and Services Ltd, a UK subsidiary of Halliburton Inc, a US company. The work he carried out was for the benefit of a German subsidiary of Halliburton Inc. He was paid in sterling and paid UK tax. At the time of his dismissal he was working in Libya. The Supreme Court held that he had sufficiently strong connections with Great Britain to be able to bring a claim of unfair dismissal in England.

In a unanimous judgment, Lord Hope pointed out that Mr Ravat did not fit into any of the three categories identified by Lord Hoffmann in *Serco*. He was not working in Great Britain at the time of his dismissal. He was not a peripatetic employee. He was not working abroad as an expatriate in a political or social British enclave. Nor had he been posted abroad to work for a business conducted in Great Britain, as he was commuting from his home in Preston and the company for whose benefit he was working in Libya was a German company.

Lord Hope referred to the warning given by Lady Hale in *Duncombe* against adopting too restrictive an approach to the problem, and concluded:

> The question in each case is whether section 94(1) applies to the particular case, notwithstanding its foreign elements. Parliament cannot be taken to have intended to confer rights on employees having no connection with Great Britain at all. The paradigm case for the application of the subsection is, of course, the employee who was working in Great Britain. But there is some scope for a wider interpretation, as the language of section 94(1) does not confine its application to employment in Great Britain ... the starting point needs to be more precisely identified. It is that the employment relationship must have a stronger connection with Great Britain than with the foreign country where the employee works. The general rule is that the place of employment is decisive. But it is not an absolute rule. The open-ended language of section 94(1) leaves room for some exceptions where the connection with Great Britain is sufficiently strong to show that this can be justified. The case of the peripatetic employee who was based in Great Britain is one example. The expatriate employee, all of whose services were performed abroad but who had nevertheless very close connections with Great Britain because of the nature and circumstances of employment, is another. But it does not follow that the connection that must be shown in the case of those who are not truly expatriate, because they were not both working and living overseas, must achieve the high standard that would enable one to say that their case was exceptional. The question whether, on given facts, a case falls within the scope of section 94(1) is a question of law, but it is also a question of degree. The fact that the commuter has his home in Great Britain, with all the consequences that flow from this for the terms and conditions of his employment, makes the burden in his case of showing that there was a sufficient connection less onerous. Mr Cavanagh said that a rigorous standard should be applied, but I would not express the test in those terms. The question of law is whether section 94(1) applies to this particular employment. The question of fact is whether the connection between the circumstances of the employment and Great Britain and with British employment law was sufficiently strong to enable it to be said that it would be appropriate for the employee to have a claim for unfair dismissal in Great Britain.

On the facts, the factors that pointed to a sufficiently close connection with Britain were:

(a)   Mr Ravat's home was in Britain;

(b)   he was paid in sterling;

(c)   he was treated as a commuter under his employer's assignment policy; and

(d)   his contract was stated to be subject to UK law.

A number of other appellate decisions have examined this vexed area. These include:

- *Jackson v Ghost Inc* [2003] IRLR 824, EAT – store manager of a New York store, who lived and worked in New York, and who was recruited in America; the only connection with the UK was the ownership of the ultimate corporate entity; held, not subject to the employment tribunal's jurisdiction.

- *Financial Times Ltd v Bishop* (UKEAT/0147/03) – sales executive employed by Financial Times Limited at its London office; subsequently he moved to a similar role in New York; later he took up the post of advertising and circulation manager in Singapore, where he remained for two years before transferring back to New York and ultimately to San Francisco, where his role was to take in-house the selling of the *Financial Times'* advertising; the employment tribunal determined that it had jurisdiction to consider his unfair dismissal complaint; the EAT held that the tribunal had applied the wrong test and the case was remitted to a differently constituted tribunal.

- *Ministry of Defence v Wallis* [2011] ICR 617, CA – spouses of UK military personnel, based in Germany, working at an international school; held, they were subject to the employment tribunal's jurisdiction.

- *Clyde & Co LLP and Another v Bates van Winkelhof* [2012] IRLR 992, CA – an LLP partner in a London-based law firm, who was based in and worked mainly in Tanzania but who retained property in the UK and visited regularly – 100 days a year (78 work/22 personal) – held, was subject to the employment tribunal's jurisdiction.

- *Dhunna v Credit Sights Ltd* [2014] EWCA Civ 1238 – an employee of the London office of a US-based company was permanently relocated to Dubai, where he worked for the benefit of the US-based business in Dubai; the employment tribunal held that there was insufficient connection with the UK; the EAT allowed his appeal but the Court of Appeal restored the tribunal's finding.

- *Powell v OMV Exploration & Production Ltd* [2014] IRLR 80, EAT – the claimant worked for an Isle of Man company, which was ultimately owned by a German company; there was no place of business in the UK and the administration of the company was based in Austria; the claimant worked for three weeks abroad and then 'rested' for one week in the UK; in total, over the period for which he was employed, from November 2010 until February 2012 when his contract was terminated, he worked a total of 20 full working days in the UK; the employment tribunal held he fell outside its territorial jurisdiction scope; the EAT dismissed the claimant's appeal.

- *Lodge v Dignity & Choice in Dying* (UKEAT/0252/14) – the EAT found that an Australian citizen, who was not an expatriate and had not been posted abroad, who was employed as head of finance for a UK company and who worked remotely in Australia for family reasons, was entitled to pursue unfair dismissal and whistleblowing claims in the UK. The fact that she was a 'virtual employee' in Australia rather than a 'physical employee' in London did not mean she fell outside the protection of the UK courts.

- *Jeffery v The British Council* (UKEAT/0036/16) – the EAT found that an expatriate (UK citizen) employee who had worked abroad for the British Council for over 20 years, latterly as a teaching centre manager in Bangladesh, who did not have a home in the UK and returned to the UK only to visit his parents, was entitled to bring claims of constructive unfair dismissal and whistleblowing to an employment tribunal. His contract was governed by English law, and he was entitled to a civil service pension.

Although each case ultimately is determined on its own facts, the following principles may be derived from the decisions:

(a)   The essential question for the tribunal to ask itself is: 'Does s 94(1) of the ERA 1996 apply to the employee in question?' This is a question of law and degree on the facts (*Ravat* (paras 28, 29)).

(b)   The starting point and general rule is that the place of employment is decisive (*Serco* (para 11); *Ravat* (para 27); *Dhunna* (para 50); *Bates, CA* (para 92)), but the open-ended language of s 94(1) leaves room for some exceptions (*Serco*).

(c)   It is not necessary to try to fit each case within one of the examples given by Lord Hoffmann in *Serco* (*Duncombe* (para 8)).

(d)   For an exception to apply, as a minimum, the connection of an employee with Great Britain/the UK and with British/UK employment law must be 'sufficiently strong' as 'to enable it to be said that Parliament would have regarded it as appropriate for the Tribunal to deal with the claim' (*Ravat* (para 35)).

(e)   Where the employee concerned is peripatetic or an 'international commuter' who commutes from a UK base, a 'sufficiently strong' connection test applies (*Ravat* (paras 28, 29, 33, 35); *Dhunna* (para 50); *Powell* (paras 47, 48). See also *Olsen v Gearbulk Services Ltd* (UKEAT/0345/14), where a Danish citizen carrying on an international role in Switzerland with a Bermudan company subject to Bermudan law and jurisdiction, who spent just under half his working time in the UK, was not permitted to bring an unfair dismissal claim in the UK.

(f)   The two further examples given by Lord Hoffmann in *Serco* as exceptional cases are:

   (i)   an employee who is posted abroad by a British employer for the purposes of a business carried on in Great Britain; and

   (ii)   an expatriate employee of a British employer, who is operating within what amounts to an extra-territorial British enclave in a foreign country.

(g)   Although Lord Hoffmann described the two examples given at (f) above as 'expatriate' examples, a distinction is now drawn between 'expatriate' cases, where the employee in fact maintains some work or personal link to the UK/Great Britain, and 'true expatriate' cases, where the employee works and lives wholly abroad;

(h)   There is a more onerous test for a 'true' expatriate employee who works and lives outside Great Britain/the UK, where there must be an 'especially strong' connection (see, eg, *Duncombe* (para 8); *Ravat* (paras 28, 29, 33).

(i)   There is no need, in the 'sufficiently strong' connection cases, for any comparative exercise to be applied between the UK/Great Britain and the other jurisdiction.

The EAT, in *Bleuse v MBT Transport* [2008] IRLR 264, had caused confusion by holding that different rules on jurisdiction apply depending on the statutory basis for the claim. The EAT said that *Serco* applies only where the legislation is primarily a UK concept, but it does not apply where the legislation derives from EU legislation with direct effect (such as the Working Time Regulations). This means that, in these cases, a weaker link with the UK *might* suffice. *Bleuse* was endorsed by the Court of Appeal in *Duncombe* (above), which said that the *Serco* test should be modified in its application to UK law where necessary to give effect to directly effective rights derived from EU law – this is likely to have most impact when determining territorial jurisdiction in discrimination cases. However, in *Clyde & Co LLP and Another v Bates van Winkelhof* the Court of Appeal upheld an employment tribunal's decision with regard to jurisdiction and agreed that it was right to apply the *Serco* test of a *sufficiently* strong connection to Great Britain to discrimination claims. Elias LJ did say that, in cases where the employee works *wholly* abroad (on the facts the employee lived and/or worked for part of the time in Great Britain), a comparative approach would be appropriate to decide where the stronger connection is.

The law on territorial jurisdiction continues to be a live issue. Other recent cases have included *Fuller v United Healthcare Services Inc* (UKEAT/0464/13) (US employee on assignment in London), *Swania v Standard Chartered Bank* (EAT/0181/14) (Italian banker living and working in Singapore), *Creditsights Ltd v Dhunna* [2014] EWCA Civ 1238, *Olsen v Gearbulk Services Ltd* (UKEAT/0345/14), *Green v SIG Trading Ltd* (UKEAT/0282/16) and the joined cases of *Nogueira v Crewlink and Oscar v Ryanair* (Cases C-168/16 and C-169/16) decided by the CJEU in September

2017. The CJEU said that jurisdiction could not be displaced by clauses in a contract so as to prevent proceedings being brought in the State where the employee habitually works.

Note: The Equality Act 2010, which deals with discrimination claims, is silent as to its territorial scope (see para 15 of the Explanatory Notes). Paragraph 10.70 of the EHRC's Statutory Code of Practice on Employment (see **Chapter 8**) states that discrimination protection in employment is required 'when there is a sufficiently close link between the employment relationship and Great Britain'. This therefore requires a similar approach to that for unfair dismissal when determining if an employment tribunal has jurisdiction to hear a claim. In R (*on the application of Hottak and Anor*) *v Secretary of State for Foreign and Commonwealth Affairs and Anor* [2015] EWHC 1953 (Admin), the High Court held that there was no jurisdiction to hear claims brought by Afghan interpreters working with the British military in Afghanistan, who were employed by the British Government. The Court of Appeal upheld the decision and confirmed that the same test (in *Lawson*) applies to discrimination claims ([2016] EWCA Civ 438).

In *Smania v Standard Chartered Bank* (UKEAT/0181/14), the EAT said that the test for territorial jurisdiction in a claim alleging dismissal or detriment based on a protected disclosure is the same test as for ordinary unfair dismissal. It upheld an employment tribunal decision that it had no jurisdiction to hear a whistleblowing claim by an Italian banker who lived and worked in Singapore, and whose head office was based in Great Britain. (See also *Fuller v United Healthcare Services Inc* (UKEAT/0464/13).)

3.8 CONTRACTING OUT

Any provision purporting to contract out of the employee's rights under the ERA 1996 is void except in so far as it is permitted by the Act (see eg **6.5**).

3.9 FURTHER READING

Textbooks dealing with eligibility include:

Selwyn's Law of Employment, 20th edn (OUP, 2018).

Harvey, *Industrial Relations and Employment Law* (Butterworths), Div DI.

Lewis, *Employment Law – an adviser's handbook*, 12th revised edn (LAG, 2017).

Duggan, *Unfair Dismissal: Law, Practice and Precedents*, 2nd edn (Duggan Press, 2019).

SUMMARY

This chapter has looked at two statutory claims which might be available to an employee on the termination of his employment in addition to the common law claim for wrongful dismissal covered in **Chapter 2** – unfair dismissal and/or for a redundancy payment. It has covered eligibility to present these claims to an employment tribunal. In order to claim a redundancy payment or pursue a complaint of unfair dismissal a person must be an employee (**1.3**), must have been dismissed (actually, constructively or on the expiry of a fixed-term contract) (**3.4**), must have the requisite two years' continuous employment (**3.5**) and must not fall within any of the excluded classes (**3.6**). Additionally, the tribunal must have the necessary jurisdiction to hear the claim (**3.7** and **6.2.1**).

It is therefore sensible always to check the following matters in order to determine if someone is eligible to bring a claim:

(1)   commencement date;

(2)   EDT;

(3)   no break;

(4)   starting date in the event of industrial action;

(5)   two years' service (for employees who started work with their employer before 6 April 2012, one year for unfair dismissal).

REDUNDANCY

LEARNING OUTCOMES

After reading this chapter you will be able to:

- describe the three different definitions of redundancy
- explain how an employee may make a redundancy payment claim
- explain when an employee may lose his entitlement to a redundancy payment
- calculate a redundancy payment.

4.1 INTRODUCTION

An eligible employee, dismissed by reason of redundancy, will be entitled, at a minimum, to a statutory redundancy payment from his employer (ERA 1996, s 163). The contract of employment may provide for more generous payments. *Note:* where an employee is dismissed by reason of redundancy, this may *also* give rise to potential wrongful dismissal and/or unfair dismissal claims (see **Chapters 2** and **5**). The right to claim a redundancy payment is a separate right, which will arise irrespective of whether the dismissal is unfair or wrongful.

A redundancy payment is in the nature of a reward for past services, and so an eligible employee is entitled to receive the full payment even when he manages to find another job immediately.

Often the employer accepts that the employee is redundant and will simply calculate the amount of the redundancy payment and make payment without the need for any formal application to an employment tribunal. However, where there is a dispute over the right to receive the payment or over the correct amount, an application will need to be made and the tribunal will determine these matters.

4.1.1 Eligibility

Before advising on the right to a redundancy payment, eligibility must be checked. Employees must have two years' continuous service before they are eligible to claim a redundancy payment (ERA 1996, s 155). There must also, of course, be a dismissal (see **3.4** for the definition of dismissal).

4.1.2 Redundancy

The next point to consider is whether the situation which led to the dismissal fits the statutory definition of redundancy. In other words, is the reason for the dismissal redundancy? If it is not, there will be no right to a redundancy payment. The scope of the definition is considered below at **4.2**.

4.2 DEFINITION OF REDUNDANCY

The definition of redundancy is contained in s 139(1) of the ERA 1996:

> For the purposes of this Act an employee who is dismissed shall be taken to be dismissed by reason of redundancy if the dismissal is wholly or mainly attributable to—
>
> (a)   the fact that his employer has ceased or intends to cease—
>
>   (i)   to carry on the business for the purposes of which the employee was employed by him, or
>
>   (ii)   to carry on that business in the place where the employee was so employed, or
>
> (b)   the fact that the requirements of that business—
>
>   (i)   for employees to carry out work of a particular kind, or
>
>   (ii)   for employees to carry out work of a particular kind in the place where the employee was employed by the employer,
>
> have ceased or diminished or are expected to cease or diminish.

Looking at this definition, it may be seen that redundancy occurs in three main situations: job redundancy, place of work redundancy and employee redundancy (our labels). Each of these is now considered in turn.

4.2.1 Cessation of business – 'job redundancy'

Within s 139(1)(a)(i) of the ERA 1996, an employee who is dismissed by reason of the closure of the employer's business will be dismissed by reason of redundancy. This will be the case whether the cessation of business is permanent or temporary.

4.2.2 Cessation or reduction in work at place of employment – 'place of work redundancy'

Here, *the place* where the employee is employed is being relocated (ERA 1996, s 139(1)(a)(ii)). This sounds a simple proposition, but there were, in the past, difficulties in determining whether 'place of work' is where the employee *could be required to work according to the contract of employment* (the 'contractual' test), or alternatively where the employee *actually* works (the 'factual' test). In *Bass Leisure Ltd v Thomas* [1994] IRLR 104, the EAT held that an employee's place of work, for the purposes of redundancy, is a question of 'fact', taking into account where the employee 'actually' worked.

The decision was approved by the Court of Appeal in *High Table Ltd v Horst* [1997] IRLR 513. The applicants were all employed as waitresses by High Table, who provided in-house catering services for city companies. The three applicants had always worked at Hill Samuel, but their contracts did contain a mobility clause. Hill Samuel reduced their requirements and the three applicants were dismissed. The Court held that for the purposes of redundancy, an employee's place of work was not to be decided solely by reference to the contract of employment regardless of where the employee actually worked. The place where the employee was employed for the purposes of s 139(1)(a)(ii) was to be established by a factual inquiry, taking into account the employee's fixed place or changing places of work and any contractual terms which might assist.

The Court said that if an employee had worked in only one location under his contract of employment for the purposes of the employer's business (as was the case, on the facts, in *High Table*), it defied common sense to widen the extent of the place where he was so employed merely because of the existence of the mobility clause. However, if the work of the employee for the employer had involved a change of location, then the contract of employment might be helpful to determine the extent of the place where the employee was employed.

Thus the position is as follows:

(a) if an employee has worked in only one location, that is his place of work, regardless of any mobility clause in his contract;

(b) if an employee has worked from several locations, the place of work is still to be established by a factual enquiry, taking into account any contractual terms that might assist in evidencing his place of work, for example a mobility clause.

4.2.2.1 Mobility clauses in the context of a 'place of work' redundancy situation

As noted above, when considering an employee's 'place' of work, the existence of a contractual mobility clause is irrelevant to that particular analysis where the employee worked in one location only.

However, mobility clauses are nevertheless still relevant when considering whether an employee is entitled to a redundancy payment on the facts, even if you have established that there is a redundancy situation within the meaning of s 139. This is because the cause of the dismissal must still be established. To be entitled to a redundancy payment, the employee's dismissal must have been caused by the redundancy situation. Whilst a mobility clause is not always relevant to identifying the place of work (see above), it is still a valid term of the contract. If an employee has a mobility clause in his contract, but refuses to obey a lawful request from his employer to move in accordance with the contractual term, then the dismissal may be due to the employee's misconduct rather than the underlying redundancy situation which has given rise to the need to implement the mobility clause (see *Home Office v Evans* [2008] IRLR 59 and *Kellogg Brown & Root (UK) Ltd v Fitton* (UKEAT/0205/16) (see also **1.8.2.3**)).

4.2.3 Reduction in requirement for employees to do work of a particular kind – 'employee redundancy'

An employee is dismissed by reason of redundancy within s 139(1)(b) of the ERA 1996 if the reason for his dismissal is that the requirement for employees to do work of a particular kind has ceased or diminished. This will clearly cover the situation where the dismissed employee's own job has disappeared through lack of work, but the section also covers other situations, some of which may not be so obvious.

4.2.3.1 Surplus employees

If the requirement for employees to do the work is reduced, even though the same amount of work is still being done, this will come within the ambit of the section.

EXAMPLES

(a) Initial overstaffing may mean fellow employees can absorb the work done by the dismissed employee.

(b) New technology means that some employees are dismissed and replaced by machines.

(c) A reorganisation of work methods may produce a more efficient system requiring less manpower so some employees are dismissed.

(d) The work carried out by an employee may be done in fewer hours, so the employer seeks to reduce the employee's hours (not the overall employee headcount). The employee does not agree and is dismissed (see *Packman v Fauchon* (UKEAT/0017/12)).

> (e)   An independent contractor may be taken on to do the same work, for example instead of employing an office cleaner the employer may engage the services of a cleaning company, and the cleaner therefore will be dismissed. Note in this example the effect of the Transfer of Undertakings (Protection of Employment) Regulations 2006 (see **Chapter 7**).

4.2.3.2   Work of a particular kind

What if a change in the nature of a job leads to the dismissal of an employee? Will the dismissal be by reason of redundancy? If the nature of the work has changed fundamentally so that work of a particular kind has ceased or diminished, even though it has been replaced by different work, this will amount to redundancy. For example, in *Murphy v Epsom College* [1984] IRLR 271, as a result of the installation of a new heating system, a plumber was replaced by a heating technician and was held to have been made redundant. The dismissal was for redundancy because the employer no longer needed to carry out work of the particular kind done by him. However, a mere reallocation of duties or introduction of new methods will not amount to redundancy. See, for example, *North Riding Garages Ltd v Butterwick* [1967] 2 QB 56, where no redundancy situation arose when a garage manager was asked to sell cars in addition to his other duties.

The contract test or the function test?

Historically, there have been two conflicting tests used for determining whether work of a particular kind has ceased or diminished: the contract test and the function test. The contract test focused on how the duties of the employee were *defined* in the contract of employment. The function test focused on the duties *actually performed* by the employee. Historically, the contract test prevailed.

According to the contract test, if duties are narrowly defined as the actual job being carried out by the employee, and that job has gone, the employee is redundant. However, if the duties are widely defined in the contract, whilst the job performed by that employee may have gone, there may be other available jobs he could still be required to perform under his contract. In this case his dismissal will not be by reason of redundancy if the alternative job is offered (*Haden Ltd v Cowan* [1982] IRLR 314). According to the function test, if the actual job carried out by the employee has gone, the employee is redundant regardless of whether, under his contract, he could be required to do other work.

However, the EAT held in *Safeway Stores v Burrell* [1997] IRLR 200 that neither the contract nor the function test should be applied. Judge Peter Clark held that the test to establish whether or not a redundancy situation existed under s 139(1)(b) should be a three-stage process:

(1)   Was the employee dismissed? If so,

(2)   Had the requirements of the employer's business for employees to carry out work of a particular kind ceased or diminished, or were they expected to cease or diminish? If so,

(3)   Was the dismissal of the employee caused wholly or mainly by that state of affairs?

In determining at stage (2) whether there was a true redundancy situation, the only question to be asked is whether there was a diminution/cessation in the employer's requirements for *employees* (not the applicant) to carry out work of a particular kind, or an expectation of such a diminution/cessation in the future. The terms of the applicant's contract are irrelevant to that question.

The House of Lords confirmed in *Murray and Another v Foyle Meats Ltd* [1999] IRLR 562 that neither the contract nor the function test is determinative of the matter.

Their Lordships approved the reasoning and conclusion of Judge Peter Clark in the *Safeway* case above (see stages (2) and (3) in *Safeway* above). Lord Irvine held that the definition of redundancy in s 139(1)(b)

> is ... simplicity itself [and] asks two questions of fact. The first is ... whether the requirements of the business for employees to carry out work of a particular kind have diminished. The second ... is whether the dismissal is *attributable*, wholly or mainly to that state of affairs. This is a question of causation. (emphasis added)

Thus, the dismissal of an employee may be attributable to a diminution in the employer's need for employees, irrespective of the terms of the contract or the function which the employee performed. The causal connection between the need for fewer employees to carry out work of a particular kind and the dismissal of the employee is a matter of fact, not law. Clearly at stage (3), contractual terms which allow the employer to move the employee from one job to another (flexibility clauses) may be a relevant fact to take into account. If an employee is asked, for example, to move to another job (under his contractual terms) and refuses, then the dismissal may be due to the employee's misconduct rather than the underlying redundancy situation.

As commentators have pointed out (see Rubenstein [1997] IRLR 197, [1999] IRLR 505), the weakness of the approach in *Safeway* and *Murray* is that no weight is given to the words 'work of a particular kind'. However, the commentator considers that this is also the strength of the House of Lords decision. By directing the focus on causation, a dismissal will now be by reason of redundancy if it is attributable to the business's diminished need for employees to do work of a particular kind. In *Martland and Others v Cooperative Insurance Society and Others* (UKEAT/0220/07 and 0221/07), the EAT held that the words 'work of a particular kind' referred to the generic type of job, not the specific terms and conditions, so where financial advisers were dismissed and immediately offered re-engagement on new terms and conditions, the dismissals were not for redundancy but for some other substantial reason. The job was essentially the same, albeit that time spent selling was to increase by 50% and commission paid was to be reduced.

In *Shawkat v Nottingham City Council NHS Trust (No 2)* [2001] IRLR 555, the Court of Appeal held that the tribunal was entitled to find that dismissal of a thoracic surgeon, following a re-organisation as a result of which he was asked to carry out cardiac surgery in addition to thoracic surgery, was not by reason of redundancy. The requirements for employees to carry out thoracic surgery had not diminished even though a re-organisation changed the work which the employees in the thoracic department, including the applicant, were required to carry out.

It is clear, then, that not all re-organisations will amount to redundancies. The restructuring must, to fall within the statutory definition, entail a reduction in the number of employees required to work of a particular kind. If, for example, the employer dismisses employees and replaces them with less well-paid employees, that will not amount to a redundancy situation.

The EAT also considered the three-stage test in *Hachette Filipacchi UK Ltd v Johnson* (UKEAT/0452/05). The employee had moved to a new position within the company as a project director, 'revitalising' a magazine published by the company. Her old job was filled. Subsequently, the company decided to end production of the magazine in question and the employee was dismissed. The EAT agreed with the employment tribunal that she had been dismissed by reason of redundancy applying the three-stage test: she had been dismissed; the employer's requirements for a project director had ceased; and her dismissal had been caused wholly or mainly by that state of affairs.

4.2.3.3 'Bumping'

'Bumping' occurs where employee A's job disappears. However, employee A is moved to do employee B's job and it is B who is dismissed. In *W Gimber & Sons Ltd v Spurrett* (1967) 2 ITR

308, it was held that the dismissal of B was by reason of redundancy within what is now s 139(1)(b) of the ERA 1996. Work of 'a particular kind', ie A's work, has ceased.

In *Church v West Lancashire NHS Trust* [1998] IRLR 4, the EAT decided it was not bound by *Gimber v Spurrett* and held that dismissal of a 'bumped' employee was not by reason of redundancy. The EAT held that 'work of a particular kind' within ERA 1996, s 139(1)(b) meant work of a particular kind that the *dismissed* employee was employed to do. However, the EAT stated in *Safeway Stores v Burrell* [1997] IRLR 200 that bumping dismissals may be dismissals by reason of redundancy, and the House of Lords confirmed in *Murray and Another v Foyle Meats Ltd* [1999] IRLR 562 that the wording of s 139(1)(b) can include 'bumping' redundancies. Thus, although the House of Lords did not expressly overrule *Church*, it should not be followed in future 'bumping' cases.

'Bumping' may also be relevant to the issue of whether a dismissal by reason of redundancy is fair or unfair (see **5.3**).

4.3   PRESUMPTION OF REDUNDANCY

In many cases there will be no dispute as to whether or not the employee is redundant. However, if the employer will not accept the claim and the employee refers the matter to an employment tribunal, there is a presumption that the dismissal was by reason of redundancy (ERA 1996, s 163(2)). The presumption applies only in the case of a claim for a redundancy payment and may be rebutted by the employer showing that the reason for the dismissal was not redundancy but was for another reason, such as misconduct.

4.4   OFFERS OF RE-EMPLOYMENT

A redundancy payment is intended to compensate the employee for loss of his job with that employer. Therefore, if the employee is re-employed by his employer, or by an associated employer, he does not need compensation and may not be entitled to a redundancy payment.

Section 141 of the ERA 1996 therefore provides that if the employee is offered a job, he may lose his entitlement to a redundancy payment.

4.4.1   Offers to renew or re-engage

An offer to renew is the offer of the employee's old job back where, for example, the employer secures a new customer and finds that work is beginning to increase again.

An offer of re-engagement involves an offer of a different job with the same or an associated employer.

Even if dismissed by reason of redundancy, an employee will lose his entitlement to a redundancy payment if he unreasonably refuses an offer of suitable alternative employment made in accordance with the provisions of s 141 of the ERA 1996.

4.4.1.1   The offer

By s 141(2)–(4) of the ERA 1996, an employee is not entitled to a redundancy payment if he unreasonably refuses an offer, whether oral or written:

(a)   made by his employer or an associated employer; and

(b)   made before the contract of employment comes to an end;

(c)   to re-employ him in the same or some other suitable employment;

(d)   provided that the renewal or re-engagement is to take effect within four weeks of the end of the original contract.

The employer's offer must comply with all the above requirements, otherwise the employee will be entitled to a redundancy payment, even if he unreasonably refuses it.

4.4.1.2   Acceptance of the offer

If the employee accepts an offer made in accordance with the provisions set out above, the employee is treated as though he had not been dismissed. Thus his continuity of employment is not broken but, as there is deemed to have been no dismissal, there is no entitlement to a redundancy payment. This will be the case whether or not the alternative employment was 'suitable'.

4.4.1.3   Rejection of the offer

If the employee rejects the offer then the question of whether or not he is entitled to a redundancy payment turns on two issues:

(a)   suitability of the alternative offered; and

(b)   the reasonableness of the employee's refusal.

If the alternative offered was unsuitable, the employee will be entitled to a redundancy payment without more analysis. However, if the alternative is suitable, then the second issue must be considered. If the employee has unreasonably refused suitable alternative employment, the right to the redundancy payment is lost.

(a)   The alternative employment has to be suitable for the particular employee and is ultimately a question for the employment tribunal to decide using an objective test. The key factors are pay, nature of duties, status, hours and place. The question is whether the new job is substantially equivalent to the old job. In *Commission for Healthcare Audit and Inspection v Ward* (UKEAT/0579/07), the EAT held that a tribunal is entitled to have regard to the degree of suitability of a job when deciding if a refusal is reasonable. So, if a new job offer is overwhelmingly suitable, it may be easier for the employer to show that a refusal was unreasonable than if suitability is less obvious.

(b)   When looking at the reasonableness of a refusal, a subjective test is used, taking into account personal circumstances, for example domestic circumstances.

Even if a job is deemed suitable, a particular employee may still be reasonable to refuse it. In *Redman v Devon PCT* [2013] EWCA Civ 1110, the Court of Appeal confirmed that the reasonableness or otherwise of an employee's refusal depends on factors personal to the employee and the test is therefore subjective. The case was remitted to the tribunal for reconsideration of whether the employee's refusal to work in a hospital, having worked in the community for 30 years, was reasonable. The EAT held in *Dunne v Colin & Avril Ltd* (UKEAT/0293/16) that an employee can rely at tribunal stage on a reason for refusal that he or she has not raised expressly with the employer when refusing the offer.

4.4.1.4   Trial period

It may be difficult for the employee to decide whether or not the alternative employment offered is suitable. The employer may also have doubts as to the employee's suitability for the new job. To assist both parties to decide whether the new employment is suitable, s 138 of the ERA 1996 provides that there may be a 'trial period' of four weeks (calendar weeks), beginning with the date on which the employee starts work under the new contract.

In *Optical Express Ltd v Williams* [2007] IRLR 936, the claimant was a manager in charge of a dental clinic. The dental clinic closed and a redundancy situation arose. The claimant was offered an alternative position as manager of an optical store. Whilst she did not consider the post suitable, she accepted a four-week trial period, in accordance with the provisions of s 138 of the ERA 1996. The claimant gave notice to terminate the contract two weeks after the four-week trial period had expired. An employment tribunal upheld her claim for a redundancy payment and stated she had a 'common law' reasonable period in addition to the statutory trial period because this was a constructive dismissal case (her employers were in breach of the implied term of trust and confidence by imposing on her a new contract which was clearly unsuitable). The EAT allowed the appeal and held that where there is an offer and acceptance of a new contract of employment by reference to the four-week trial period in s 138, the claimant could not claim a redundancy payment unless within the trial period she exercised the rights given by s 138 to terminate the contract. It is now clear that where an acceptance of alternative employment is made under the statutory trial period scheme, the employee must give notice of termination within the 4-week statutory trial period in order to receive a redundancy payment.

If either the employer or the employee terminates the contract during the statutory trial period for a reason connected with the change, the original dismissal by reason of redundancy will revive. Whether or not the employee is then entitled to a redundancy payment still turns on whether the alternative employment offered was suitable. However, there will now be evidence available from the trial period.

(a)   There is no 'trial period' if there is no change in the terms of employment, ie if the only change is in the identity of the employer.

(b)   If the new employment involves retraining, the parties may agree, before the employee starts work under the new contract, to extend the trial period. The agreement must specify the date on which the extended period ends.

4.5   CHANGE OF EMPLOYER

4.5.1   Death, etc, of employer

Exceptionally, by s 136(5) of the ERA 1996, where any act by or affecting an employer terminates the contract of employment by operation of law, such termination takes effect as termination by the employer. The effect of this is that if a business closes down by virtue of the death of the employer or dissolution of a partnership then, although at common law the contract may be frustrated, it will be treated as a dismissal for the purposes of redundancy payments. Thus, an eligible employee will, if the business ceases or his job comes to an end, be entitled to a redundancy payment.

This provision may not apply if the employee continues in his job. If he is employed by the personal representatives on the death of an employer, or if there is effectively only a change in partners despite a dissolution of the partnership, the employee will not be dismissed and there will be continuity of employment (see **3.5.5**).

4.5.2   Associated employer

If an employee is re-employed by an associated employer, this will be a re-engagement within **4.4.1**. See **3.5.5** for the definition of associated employer.

4.5.3   Transfer of undertakings

A business closure should be distinguished from a transfer of the business to a new employer. In the latter situation the employees will usually be transferred to the new employer without being dismissed, so the employee will not be entitled to a redundancy payment. This is by virtue of the Transfer of Undertakings (Protection of Employment) Regulations 2006 (see **Chapter** 7).

4.6   COMPUTATION OF THE STATUTORY REDUNDANCY PAYMENT

A redundancy payment is computed by applying a formula based on an age factor, length of service and a 'week's pay' (ERA 1996, s 162). It is not based on loss suffered.

(a)   Working *back* from the date of termination of employment, the employee is entitled to:

(i)   one-and-a-half weeks' *gross* pay for each complete year of continuous employment in which the employee was 41 or over;

(ii) one week's *gross* pay for each earlier year in which the employee was 22 or over (but under 41);

(iii) half a week's *gross* pay for each earlier year.

(b) The total number of years to be taken into account is subject to a maximum of 20.

(c) A 'week's pay' is calculated in accordance with ERA 1996, s 221. In the majority of cases where there is a normal weekly wage, a week's pay would be the *gross* basic pay to which the employee was entitled in the week ending with the dismissal, subject to a statutory maximum of £508 (at 6 April 2018).

EXAMPLE 1

Doris is aged 63 when dismissed in November 2018 by reason of redundancy. Her normal retiring age is 65. She has been continuously employed for 35 years and her gross basic week's pay in her last week was £520.

Her redundancy payment will be:

1½ × 20 (years) × £508 = £15,240.

This is the maximum possible redundancy payment.

The number of years is 20, not 35, as this is the maximum.

The age factor is 1½ as all years that count are aged 41 or over – taking the most 'valuable' year first, ie working back from the date of dismissal.

The 'week's pay' is the maximum of £508, not the £520 actually earned.

EXAMPLE 2

Ron is aged 43 when dismissed by reason of redundancy in November 2018. He has been continuously employed for just over 6 years and his gross basic week's pay in his last week was £580.

His redundancy payment will be:

1½ × 2 years × £508 (= £1,524) (ie for ages 42 and 41)

plus 1 × 4 years × £508 (= £2,032) (ie for ages 40, 39, 38, 37) giving a total of £3,556.

The age factor is 1½ for the 2 complete years worked after the 41st birthday and 1 for the other 4 years.

EXAMPLE 3

Jack is aged 24 when dismissed by reason of redundancy in November 2018. He has been continually employed for 8 years and his gross basic week's pay in his last week was £350.

His redundancy payment will be:

1 × 2 × £350 (= £700) (ie for ages 23 and 22)

½ × 6 × £350 (= £1,050) (ie for ages 21, 20, 19, 18, 17, 16)

giving a total of £1,750.

The age factor is 1 for 2 complete years worked after the 22nd birthday and ½ for the 6 years between 18 and 21.

Note: The Business Link website <http://www.businesslink.gov.uk> features an interactive redundancy payment calculator. Select Employment and Skills; Redundancy and Dismissal; Calculate the statutory redundancy pay due to your employee.

4.7 ENFORCEMENT

4.7.1 Employer's liability

The person primarily liable to pay a redundancy payment is the employer. In the majority of cases the employer will simply make the payment without dispute. When the employer makes a statutory redundancy payment, he must give the employee a written statement of how the amount has been calculated (ERA 1996, s 165). The employee can then check its accuracy.

4.7.2 Reference to employment tribunal

If the employer fails to make a payment or there is a dispute about the amount, the employee may refer the matter to an employment tribunal. There is a time limit which must be observed.

By s 164 of the ERA 1996, an employee is not entitled to a redundancy payment unless, within six months of the dismissal:

(a)   a payment is agreed and made; or

(b)   he has given the employer written notice of the claim; or

(c)   a question as to the right to, or amount of, the payment has been referred to an employment tribunal; or

(d)   a complaint of unfair dismissal has been presented to the employment tribunal.

An employment tribunal may, if it considers it just and equitable that the employee should receive a redundancy payment, extend the time-limit to 12 months from dismissal, but employees should regard the six months' time-limit as strict.

It is not necessary to refer the matter to an employment tribunal within six months of dismissal, provided written notice of the claim has been given to the employer within that time.

4.7.3 Employer's insolvency

Where an employee is entitled to a statutory redundancy payment from his employer, but the employer is declared legally insolvent and the redundancy payment remains unpaid, the employee may apply for payment out of the National Insurance Fund to the Redundancy Payment Office (RPO) using Form RP1 (available at <http://www.insolvency.gov.uk>). The RPO, if satisfied that the employee is entitled to the payment, will make the payment out of the Fund (ERA 1996, s 166). The RPO then has a statutory right to recover the amount of the payment from the employer. The employee must have claimed the payment from his employer within the relevant time-limit, and the payment must have been owed when the employer became insolvent (see *Secretary of State for Business, Innovation & Skills v Pengelly & Another* (UKEAT/0287/12 & 0312/12) (see **4.7.2**).

4.8 CONSULTATION

4.8.1 Duty to consult representatives

4.8.1.1 The duty to consult under TULR(C)A 1992, s 188

What follows is a very brief introduction to the collective provisions, which are set out in the Trade Union and Labour Relations (Consolidation) Act 1992 (TULR(C)A 1992). On 6 April 2013, Acas published Guidance entitled *How to manage collective redundancies*. The Guidance is intended to make it easier for employers to understand the law on collective redundancies. It includes a useful flow chart and case studies, as well as a checklist and sample selection matrix.

Where an employer is proposing to dismiss as redundant 20 or more employees at one establishment (but see below as to what is meant by 'establishment' and whether that limitation is lawful) within a period of 90 days or less, he should consult the 'appropriate representatives' (representative of any independent trade union which is recognised, or elected employee representatives) of any employees who may be affected by the proposed dismissals or measures taken in connection with the dismissals, unless there are special circumstances that mean it is not reasonably practicable to consult (see *GMB and Amicus v Beloit Walmsley Ltd (in administration)* [2004] IRLR 18) (TULR(C)A 1992, s 188, as amended). In *Hardy v Tourism South East* [2005] IRLR 242, the EAT confirmed that the s 188 duty to consult applies even when the employer intends to offer alternative employment to the majority of employees, thereby bringing the number actively dismissed below 20. The employer must also inform the Secretary of State (Form HR1). Failure to do so is a criminal offence.

Regulation 3 of the Collective Redundancies and Transfer of Undertakings (Protection of Employment) (Amendment) Regulations 2014 (SI 2014/16), inserted new ss 198A and 198B into TULR(C)A 1992. These provide that the statutory obligation to consult over collective redundancies may be discharged by a prospective employer where the redundancy dismissals are consequent on a TUPE transfer (see **Chapter 7**). The Government considered that it made practical sense to allow a transferee to consult affected employees before a transfer, about redundancies that might occur after the transfer, even though at that stage they were still employees of the transferor.

Redundancy has a different meaning, for the purposes of this consultation exercise, from the s 139 definition set out in **4.2** above. Here, redundancy is defined as a 'dismissal for a reason not related to the individual concerned or for a number of reasons all of which are not so related'. This definition will also, therefore, include a reorganisation where an employer gives notice to end existing terms and offer new terms of employment, and is therefore wider than the s 139 definition.

Fixed-term employees are excluded from the scope of collective redundancy consulation where their fixed-term contract will expire on an agreed date within the redundancy period.

Under UK law, officers in the police service are also excluded from the collective consultation rights. However, in *Vining v Wandsworth LBC* [2017] EWCA Civ 1092, the Court of Appeal ruled that this exclusion infringed their right to association under Article 11 of the ECHR.

Consultation must begin in good time. In particular, if 100 or more employees are to be dismissed at one establishment within a 90-day period, the employer must consult at least 45 days before the first dismissal is to take effect; otherwise, for at least 20 but fewer than 100 employees, he must consult at least 30 days before the first dismissal takes effect. Employers should ensure that the consultation period has ended before giving notice of dismissal to those employees who are to be dismissed by reason of redundancy (see *Junk v Kuhnel* [2005] IRLR 310 and *Leicestershire County Council v Unison* [2005] IRLR 920). Even if there are good reasons for shortening the 30-day consultation period, the obligation to consult remains (see *Shanahan Engineering v Unite* (UKEAT/0411/09)).

The obligation to consult includes consulting about ways of avoiding dismissals, reducing the numbers of employees to be dismissed and mitigating the consequences of those dismissals. In *UK Coal Mining Ltd v National Union of Mineworkers (Northumberland Area)* (UKEAT/0397/06), the EAT held that the duty to consult includes consultation over the business reason(s) for a closure. The decision overturned 15 years of established authority. The Court of Appeal referred the matter to the ECJ in *USA v Nolan* [2010] EWCA Civ 1223. The issue arose as to whether collective consultation should have started when the US Government was proposing to close a UK army base in Hampshire, so that redundancies might be said to be foreseeable or inevitable, or did it only have to consult after the decision to close had been taken? The ECJ held (*USA v Nolan* (Case C-583/10)) that it had no jurisdiction to respond to the reference because the Collective Redundancies Directive (98/59/EC) excludes employees of public administrative bodies. In October 2015, the Supreme Court handed down its judgment in *USA v Nolan*. However, it did not deal with the consultation issue, which awaits prior determination by the Court of Appeal. The Supreme Court determined that the relevant UK legislation did apply to the base in the UK and so the US Government was under a duty to consult; even if the decision to dismiss was made in Washington, the dismissals related to the base in the UK. Further, as the US had not invoked state immunity early in the proceedings, it was now prevented from relying on it. In the meantime, employers would be advised to follow *UK Coal Mining*.

Employers who recognise a trade union *must* consult with representatives of that trade union; they cannot choose to consult with elected employee representatives. If there is no recognised trade union, the employer must arrange for employee representatives to be elected and *must* consult with them.

The employer must disclose the reasons for the redundancies, numbers and descriptions of the employees to be made redundant and the method of selection. The consultation must consider the possibility of avoiding or reducing the redundancies and mitigating their effects.

In *GMB and AEEU v Campbells UK Ltd* (ET/26787/96), the tribunal held that it was not enough for an employer who was proposing to close a factory simply to consult on how the ensuing redundancies should be handled. The tribunal stated that consultation must include consultation about ways of avoiding dismissals, and this is so even where what is being proposed is a total shutdown (see also *Middlesborough Borough Council v TGWU and Another* [2002] IRLR 332, EAT). The Court of Appeal stated in *Susie Radin Ltd v GMB and Others* [2004] IRLR 400 that the obligation set out in s 188 placed an 'absolute obligation on the employer to consult, and to consult meaningfully'. This means that the employer must disclose the reasons for the redundancies, the number and description of employees to be made redundant, and the method of selection. See also *Kelly and Another v The Helsey Group* [2013] IRLR 515.

What amounts to an 'establishment' is a fact-sensitive issue. The Acas Guidance notes that the Court of Justice of the European Union (CJEU) indicated that 'establishment' means 'depending on the circumstances, the unit to which the workers made redundant are assigned to carry out their duties'. The Guidance sets out some useful questions that might be asked in order to clarify what amounts to an 'establishment' for these purposes:

*   Is it a distinct entity?
*   Does it have a degree of permanence and stability?
*   Does it have the ability to carry out the tasks it has been assigned?
*   Does it have a workplace, technical means and organisational structure to carry out work assigned?

The Guidance suggests that an establishment can be made up of more than one place, but distinct entities do not need to have geographical separation, legal, economic, financial, administrative, technological or managerial autonomy or independence.

In *USDAW v WW Realisation 1 Ltd* (UKEAT/0548/12), the EAT struck out the words 'at any one establishment' from the definition in s 188 of TULR(C)A 1992, on the basis that it was an incorrect transposition of the Collective Redundancies Directive (98/59/EC). The case was based around the closure of a number of Woolworths and Ethel Austin stores. In both instances, administrators argued that each store was a separate establishment, and so sought to limit the impact of the obligation to consult on a collective basis: a large number of employees were employed at stores with fewer than 20 employees (3,233 Woolworths employees out of a total of 4,400, and 720 Ethel Austin employees out of a total workforce of 1,210). No consultation was undertaken (not uncommon in insolvencies), but only those employees at larger establishments would be entitled to a protective award (see **4.8.1.2** below). The employment tribunal found that 'establishment' meant each individual shop, so while staff at shops with 20 or more staff were entitled to a protective award, staff at the smaller stores were not. The EAT reviewed the wording of the Collective Redundancies Directive and held that the UK wording did not uphold the Directive's core objective of protecting workers' rights. This meant that where it was proposed to dismiss 20 or more employees, it did not matter if they were located at different stores. The Secretary of State appealed the EAT judgment. The Court of Appeal decided to refer the case to the ECJ, to clarify whether the 20 or more redundancies have to be at the same establishment, and also whether the relevant provisions of the Directive have direct effect.

In April 2015, the ECJ, following the Advocate General's Opinion in February, ruled that the definition of 'establishment' in s 188 of the TULR(C)A 1992 does comply with the EU Collective Redundancies Directive, and employers are not therefore required to aggregate dismissals across all establishments. The ECJ confirmed that the Directive does allow establishments to be treated separately for the purposes of the 20-employee threshold for collective consultation. This effectively overrules the finding of the EAT, and means that employers with multiple sites can rely on the position as it was before the EAT's ruling and approach any future consultation exercises over collective redundancies and dismissals on a more local basis. The ECJ was concerned to apply a consistent approach, ruling that 'establishment' must be given the same meaning throughout the EU (in contrast to the earlier Opinion of the Advocate General, who thought that it was up to the national courts to reach a national definition). According to the ECJ, 'establishment' means 'the entity to which the workers are assigned to carry out their duties'. The Advocate General talked in terms of 'local employment unit'. It is not essential that the unit in question is endowed with a management that can independently effect collective redundancies. An establishment may consist of a distinct entity having a certain degree of permanence and stability, which is assigned to perform given tasks and has a workforce, technical means and organisational structure allowing for that. The entity may be a part of an undertaking and does not need to have autonomy – whether legal, economic, administrative or technological – in order to be an 'establishment'. In light of these factors, the ECJ concluded that where an undertaking comprises several entities meeting the criteria for 'establishment', it is the entity to which the workers made redundant are assigned to carry out their duties that constitutes the 'establishment' for collective consultation purposes. The ECJ said that it is up to the UK courts to decide if each Woolworth store was an 'establishment'. Determining the unit will be normally be a question of fact for a tribunal. The ECJ has formally referred the 'Woolworths' case back to the Court of Appeal for it to decide whether, in light of the clarification now given, the employment tribunal was correct in finding that the stores to which the employees made redundant were assigned were separate 'establishments'. The ECJ has confirmed the approach it took in the 'Woolworths' case in two further decisions: *Lyttle v Bluebird UK Bidco2* (Case C-182/13) and *Rabal Canas v Nexea Gestation Documental* (Case C-392/13).

Note that the Collective Redundancies Directive talks about 'workers' being 'employed'. In *Balkaya v Kiesel Abbruch- und Recycling Technik GmbH* (Case C-229/14), the ECJ held that 'worker' could include a director and an unpaid trainee when deciding whether an obligation to consult arose. The Court stated that the concept of worker in Article 1(1)(a) of the Directive could not be defined by reference to the legislation of the Member States but had to be given an autonomous and independent meaning. Otherwise, the methods for calculation of the thresholds would be within the discretion of the Member States, which would allow the latter to alter the scope of the Directive and thus to deprive it of its full effect.

4.8.1.2 Protective award

If the employer fails to consult in accordance with the TULR(C)A 1992 provisions, the trade union, elected employee representatives or affected employees may present a complaint to an employment tribunal. If the complaint is well founded, the tribunal must make a declaration to that effect and may make a 'protective award' of wages per employee for such 'protected period' as the tribunal considers just and equitable. A protective award is an award of pay to the employees affected by the failure to consult properly.

The maximum 'protected period' is 90 days. In *TGWU v Morgan Platts Ltd* (UKEAT/0646/02) the EAT ruled that the starting point for tribunals in calculating protective awards should be the maximum period. From there the tribunal should then consider whether there are reasons for reducing the amount. On the facts of the case there were not, as the company had failed to consult at all. Once a protective award is made, relevant employees are entitled to one week's gross pay for each week of the 'protected period'. The award is not capped.

For many years the courts treated protective awards as compensatory in nature (see, for example, *Spillers-French (Holdings) Ltd v USDAW* [1980] ICR 31), but in *Susie Radin Ltd v GMB* [2004] IRLR 400 the Court of Appeal held that the purpose of the protective award was to punish the employer and should act as an effective sanction and deterrent. The Court held that the starting point is the maximum 90 days, which should be reduced only where there are mitigating circumstances.

In *Amicus v GBS Tooling Ltd* [2005] IRLR 683, the EAT agreed that the tribunal was entitled to take into account the fact that the employer had kept employees informed up to the point that the redundancy proposals were formulated. The EAT therefore upheld the tribunal's decision to award 70 days' pay, rather than 90. (See too *Evans v Permacell Finesse* (UKEAT/0350/07).)

In *Lancaster University v UCU* (UKEAT/0278/10), the EAT upheld an award of 60 days' pay where the tribunal had accepted as mitigation the fact that the union had, for a number of years, condoned the employer's practice so far as consultation was concerned.

In *Independent Insurance Co Ltd v Aspinall and Others* (UKEAT/0051/11) there was no recognised union and no employee representative. The employment tribunal upheld a complaint by the individuals who complained, but also extended this to a further 350 employees who had not brought a claim or who had their claims settled or dismissed. The employment tribunal rejected a submission that it only had jurisdiction to make an award in respect of a person who complained. The EAT overturned that decision – which it said would produce an 'absurd result'.

In *AEI Cables Ltd v GMB & Others* (UKEAT/0375/12), the fact that the employer was insolvent and therefore unable to trade resulted in a protective award of 90 days being reduced by the EAT to 60 days.

It is a defence to a claim for a protective award for the employer to show that '... there [were] special circumstances which render[ed] it not reasonably practicable for the employer to comply with [the duty to consult]' (TULR(C)A 1992, s 188(7)). In *Clarks of Hove Ltd v The Bakers' Union* [1978] IRLR 366, the Court of Appeal held that 'special circumstances' had to be something out of the ordinary and uncommon, such as a sudden disaster.

4.8.2 Information and Consultation Regulations 2004

Directive 2002/14 gives employees in the covered undertakings a right to be informed about the undertaking's economic situation, informed and consulted about employment prospects, and informed and consulted with a view to reaching agreement about decisions likely to lead to substantial changes in work organisation or contractual relations, including, but not limited to, collective redundancies and transfers (see **Chapter 7**).

The Information and Consultation of Employees Regulations 2004 (SI 2004/3426) (ICE Regulations) apply to undertakings employing 50 or more employees. They require employers to set up information and consultation arrangements to ensure that employees are consulted on a wide range of matters. However, the obligations are triggered only on a valid request from at least 10% of employees.

The detail of the ICE Regulations is beyond the scope of this book, but note that where there is an overlap between the duty under the ICE Regulations and the duty to consult under s 188 (**4.8.1.1** above), the ICE obligations cease to apply once the employer informs the representatives in writing that he will comply with his s 188 duty. BIS has produced a guide for explaining the requirements to inform and consult employees, which is available on its website.

The EAT is empowered to award penalties of up to £75,000 for breaches of the ICE Regulations. In *Amicus v Macmillan Publishers Ltd* (UKEAT/0185/07), Macmillan were fined £55,000 for failing to comply with the Regulations. This was the first penalty so awarded. The EAT took into account the following factors in imposing the penalty:

(a) the fact that the legislation had clearly been ignored;

(b) Macmillan had committed other breaches of the legislation, including a failure to provide information;

(c) Macmillan had unacceptably 'dragged its feet' in dealing with the employee request;

(d) Macmillan had not adequately explained its failure to comply.

The EAT concluded that a penalty of £55,000 was appropriate as it would deter other employers from adopting a similarly 'cavalier' attitude to their obligations, but the breach in this case was not sufficiently grave to warrant the maximum penalty. The EAT in its decision commented that employers must recognise the importance of the rights under the ICE Regulations and that the provisions must be complied with.

See also **Chapter 7**, at **7.7**, which deals with the (similar but not identical) collective consultation requirements under the 2006 TUPE Regulations.

4.8.3 Duty to notify Secretary of State

Where 20 or more redundancies are proposed there is a duty to notify the Secretary of State of the proposals. Notification is made on form HR1 (available at <http://www.insolvency.gov.uk>).

4.8.4 Unfair dismissal

Failure to consult with individual employees about proposed redundancies can render the dismissals unfair (see **5.4.2.3**). Redundant employees in such circumstances may be able to bring claims for a redundancy payment and unfair dismissal.

4.9 CASE STUDY: REDUNDANCY PAYMENT, UNPAID NOTICE AND HOLIDAY PAY

Facts

(1) R was an independent working men's club. It was not for profit and was registered under the Industrial and Provident Societies Act (IPSA) 1965 with the Financial Services Authority. Its members and employees were governed by the rules of the Club. The premises from which the Club operated were leased to the Club under a full maintenance and repairing lease.

(2) C was employed by R as a bar steward/cleaner. She started work with R in September 2002. She continued to work for R until her dismissal on 28 April 2016. Over that period, she worked approximately 40 hours a week every week, apart from when she took holidays. She was paid £8.00 an hour and took home a net weekly wage of £256 (gross £320).

(3) On or around 28 April 2016, C was informed by a member of R's committee that the Club was in severe financial difficulties and was being wound up. The committee member gave C 48 hours' notice. She was paid one week's notice. She was informed that there was no money to pay her any redundancy payment or any other outstanding monies due to her, such as in respect of untaken but accrued holiday. A subsequent letter received by C indicated that there had been mismanagement at R for several years,

and that because of the parlous financial state of R, it had been shut down. Rent had not been paid for several months and various suppliers were owed money. The premises were being advertised for sale. It did not appear that any steps had been taken with regard to liquidating R. All the committee members had resigned.

(4)   Under the provisions of the IPSA 1965, Ch 12, s 57, no individual officer, member or servant is personally liable for any of the debts of the Club. The situation therefore remains somewhat in limbo as far as the legal status of R is concerned. On the face of it, it appears to be insolvent.

(5)   At the time of the termination of her employment, C, who was aged 57 as at the date of her dismissal, had achieved some 13 years' continuous employment. She was disappointed that none of the committee members had expressed any concerns about her situation and appeared to feel no moral responsibility towards her predicament, notwithstanding that they appeared to have been aware of the Club's difficulties for some time.

Claims

(6)   In her ET1, C brings claims of unpaid notice, breach of contact, unpaid wages and unpaid holiday pay. She also seeks a redundancy payment. She did not complain about unfair dismissal.

Evidence

(7)   C appeared before the Employment Judge (sitting alone) and gave evidence. She produced various items of paperwork, including letters from the Insolvency Service relating to her claim. She also had with her the originals of her pay slips. Although a committee member had submitted a brief ET3/Response Form, which said that R had been wound up, no one appeared for R at the hearing.

Issues

(8)   Although C had a long service record with R, she had not included a claim for unfair dismissal in her ET1. This omission was discussed at a Case Management Discussion (CMD). The notes of this recorded that C said she had not realised she could bring such a claim. By the time the CMD took place, it was over four and half months since the termination of C's contract. The Employment Judge found as a preliminary issue that any claim for unfair dismissal would amount to a new claim, that it was not implicit from the matters set out in the ET1, that it was out of time and that there was nothing to suggest that it was not reasonably practicable for the claim to have been made within the time limit, ignorance of the law per se being no defence (see **Chapter 8**).

(9)   On that basis, the Tribunal had to determine the following matters:
   (a)   Was C an employee of R?
   (b)   Was C entitled to a redundancy payment; and if so, to how much?
   (c)   Had C been paid her proper notice?
   (d)   Had C been paid the holiday pay due on the termination of her employment?

Findings

(10)   On the basis of the evidence before it, the Employment Judge found as follows:
   (a)   C was an employee of R. Although she had no written contract, this was not a difficult issue on the facts. C had worked regularly for R for nearly 14 years. There was no issue that she expected to work each week and expected to be paid for her work. She gave evidence about the hours she worked, from whom she took instructions, that the materials she used, for example, to clean were all provided by R, that she had had her PAYE and National Insurance deducted from her wages,

and that she had been paid for her holidays. She produced her wage slips to support this.

(b)   C was entitled to a redundancy payment, as the reason for her dismissal was clearly a reason that fell within the definition in s 139 of the ERA 1996, namely, the closure of the business. C had 13 years' completed service at the date of her dismissal; as she was aged 41 and over for the duration of her employment with R, she was entitled to one and a half week's gross pay for each completed year of continuous service (ERA 1996, ss 162 and 221): 13 x 1.5 x £320 = £6,240. R was ordered to pay to C the sum of £6,240 in respect of a redundancy payment.

(c)   R was in breach of C's contract of employment by failing to give her proper notice or to pay her due notice entitlement. Although R paid C one week's notice, under s 86 of the ERA 1996, the statutory minimum period of notice required to be given to an employee with 12 years' plus service is 12 weeks' notice. C is therefore entitled to be paid for 11 weeks' notice at her net weekly wage (£256) per week: 11 x £256 = £2,816. R is ordered to pay damages to C in the sum of £2,816 (net).

(d)   C's complaint that R had failed to pay holiday pay due on the termination of the employment was well founded. Regulation 14 of the Working Time Regulations allows an employee to be paid in lieu of any accrued but untaken holiday as at the date of dismissal. As at the date of her dismissal, C had 15 days' holiday accrued and due. C is therefore due payment in respect of 15 days' holiday, calculated on the basis of an eight-hour working day and a net weekly wage of £256 (8 hours x £6.40 (net)) = £51.20 per day rate x 15 = £768 (net). R is ordered to pay to C the sum of £768 (net).

Note: Given that R has been wound up/appears to be insolvent, and that there are no apparent assets, C is unlikely to be able to get any money back from R. In this sort of case, C would be able to make a claim from the National Insurance Fund, by completing Form RP1, in respect of any redundancy pay, unpaid wages (up to a maximum of eight weeks), holiday pay (up to a maximum of six weeks), notice pay (one week after one calendar month's service, rising to one week per year of service up to a maximum of 12 weeks, but new earnings will be taken into account), and any basic award for unfair dismissal. To qualify for a redundancy payment, C will need to show that she has been made redundant, has worked continuously for her employer for two years or more, and that she either made a written claim to her employer for her redundancy payment, or made a complaint to an employment tribunal, within six months of her dismissal. She will be able to attach the Tribunal's decision as evidence of these matters. There is a current limit of £508 (at April 2018) a week on the amount C can claim for her weekly pay.

4.10   FURTHER READING

Textbooks covering redundancy include:

Selwyn's Law of Employment, 20th edn (OUP, 2018).

See also:

Harvey, *Industrial Relations and Employment Law* (Butterworths), Div E.

Lewis, *Employment Law – an adviser's handbook*, 12th revised edn (LAG, 2017).

Blackstone's Employment Law Practice, 10th edn (OUP, 2019).

SUMMARY

This chapter has set out the mechanisms for making a claim for a redundancy payment. A redundancy payment is in the nature of a reward for past services. Where there is a dispute over the right to receive a redundancy payment or over the amount due, an employment tribunal has jurisdiction to determine the matter (**4.3**). Employees must be eligible to bring a claim. They must have at least two years' continuous service and there must also be a dismissal by reason of redundancy (**3.4**).

The definition of 'redundancy' is contained in s 139(1) of the ERA 1996. Redundancy occurs in three main situations: job redundancy (ie where the business closes down – ERA 1996, s 139(1)(a)(i)); place of work redundancy (ie where there is a cessation or reduction in work *at the place* where the employee works – ERA 1996, s 139(1)(a)(ii)); and employee redundancy (ie there is a reduction in the requirement for employees to do work of a particular kind – ERA 1996, s 139(1)(b)) (**4.2**).

An eligible employee, dismissed by reason of redundancy, will be entitled, at a minimum, to a statutory redundancy payment from his employer (ERA 1996, s 163). The contract of employment may provide for more generous payments.

If the employee is offered a suitable alternative job by his employer, which he unreasonably refuses, he may lose his entitlement to a redundancy payment (ERA 1996, s 141). It is possible to have a trial period of four weeks in order to determine whether the job is suitable (ERA 1996, s 138) (**4.4**). If a business is sold as a going concern, so that employees are not dismissed, they may not be entitled to a redundancy payment (see **Chapter 7** on the transfer of undertakings).

A redundancy payment is calculated by applying a formula based on age, length of service and 'a week's pay' (ERA 1996, s 162) (**4.6**).

Where an employee is dismissed by reason of redundancy, this may also give rise to wrongful (**Chapter 3**) and/or unfair dismissal (**Chapter 5**) claims. The right to claim a redundancy payment is a separate right that will arise irrespective of whether the dismissal is unfair.

Under s 188 of the Trade Unions and Labour Relations (Consolidation) Act 1992, obligations are imposed on employers to consult appropriate employee representatives (**4.8**).

In summary, in each case, consider the following.

- Is the employee eligible (**3.4**)?
- Has there been a dismissal (**3.4**)?
- Do the circumstances fit the statutory definition of redundancy (**4.2**)?
- Was the dismissal caused by the redundancy situation?
- Has there been a suitable offer of alternative employment (**4.4**)?
- Is the employee reasonable in refusing this (**4.4**)?

A flowchart showing the redundancy payment system is set out at **Figure 4.1** below.

Figure 4.1 Flowchart: Redundancy payments

UNFAIR DISMISSAL

LEARNING OUTCOMES

After reading this chapter you will be able to:

- describe the statutory claim of unfair dismissal and how it differs from wrongful dismissal

- list the potentially fair reasons for dismissal set out in ERA 1996, s 98 and understand their ambit

- understand the different procedural steps that should normally be followed before dismissal, depending on the reason for dismissal

- understand the relevance of the Acas Code of Practice on Disciplinary and Grievance Procedures

- understand the significance of *BHS v Burchell* in a misconduct case

- explain and apply the range of reasonable responses test

- be aware of the relevant maximum for unfair dismissal awards, and understand and be able to apply the relevant principles for calculating damages for unfair dismissal.

5.1 INTRODUCTION

In the UK, every eligible employee has the right not to be unfairly dismissed by his employer (ERA 1996, s 94). Note that, although much employment law in Europe is underpinned by common principles, very significant differences exist when it comes to dismissals. Do not assume that following UK principles will necessarily be sufficient when dismissing employees based abroad. International law firm CMS (now CMS Cameron McKenna Nabarro Olswang) issued in February 2018 two helpful guides to dismissal – one relating to Europe (covering 24 countries, plus Russia) and one relating to China, Singapore and UAE.

At common law, an employer can dismiss any employee whenever he chooses, whether he has any good reason or not. Provided he gives full notice and otherwise complies with the contract, the employee has no remedy. Even where the contract is breached, the award of damages is often relatively small (see **Chapter 2**).

In order to give a measure of protection against dismissal at the whim of the employer, the statutory claim of unfair dismissal introduced the concept of fairness into termination of contracts of employment. The employer must be able to show not only that he had a good reason to dismiss, but also that he acted fairly in, for example, the way in which he handled the dismissal.

5.1.1 Eligible employee

See **Chapter 3** for details of eligibility, but check in particular that the individual is an employee (not a worker) and has the necessary two years' continuous employment (ERA 1996, s 108), as relevant. (There are exceptions where the dismissal is for a reason relating to, for example, trade union membership, health and safety, or on the grounds of pregnancy. These exceptions are dealt with at **5.5**).

5.1.2 Dismissal

The employee must have been dismissed. See **3.4** for the definition of dismissal.

Where an employee intends to rely on s 95(1)(c) of the ERA 1996 – constructive dismissal – rather than on actual dismissal, he should consider using the grievance procedure set out in the Acas Code of Practice on Disciplinary and Grievance Procedures (see **5.4.1** below) before he resigns, or before he submits the ET1. A failure to follow the Code, where it applies, gives tribunals a discretionary power to increase or decrease awards by up to 25%, if they consider that the employer's/employee's failure to comply with the Code was unreasonable.

The Code sets out the process for dealing with grievances, which is as follows:

*   Let the employer know the nature of the grievance.
*   Hold a meeting with the employee to discuss the grievance.
*   Allow the employee to be accompanied at the meeting.
*   Decide on appropriate action.
*   Allow the employee to take the grievance further if not resolved.
*   Overlapping grievance and disciplinary cases: where an employee raises a grievance during a disciplinary process, the disciplinary process may be suspended temporarily in order to deal with the grievance. Where the grievance and disciplinary cases are related, it may be appropriate to deal with both issues concurrently.

To complement the Code, Acas has published guidance. Tribunals cannot adjust awards on account of any failure to follow the guidance, neither are they required to have regard to the guidance.

Where there is an actual dismissal, an employer should also consider the Code (see **5.4.1**). A failure to follow the Code gives tribunals a discretionary power to increase or decrease awards by up to 25% if they consider that the employer's/employee's failure to comply with the Code was unreasonable.

5.1.3 Potentially fair reason for dismissal

The onus is on the employer to show that the dismissal is for one of the five permitted reasons (see **5.2**). If the employer cannot show that the dismissal was for one of these permitted reasons, the dismissal will be unfair.

5.1.4 Fairness

Where the reason for the dismissal falls within one of the five permitted reasons, the tribunal must then go on to decide whether the employer acted reasonably in all the circumstances under ERA 1996, s 98(4) (see **5.3**) in dismissing this employee for this reason.

5.1.5 Remedies

Remedies are dealt with at **5.6**.

5.2 REASONS FOR DISMISSAL

The employer must be able to establish that the only or principal reason for the dismissal was a potentially fair reason. The burden of proof is on the employer, but it is not a heavy burden to discharge (see *Kuzel v Roche Products Ltd* [2008] IRLR 530). If he is unable to show that the dismissal was for one of the five permitted reasons, the dismissal will be held to be unfair. This is the case whether there is an actual or a constructive dismissal. Where the employee is basing his claim on a constructive dismissal, the reason for the dismissal given by the employer will be the reason for which the employer allegedly breached the contract.

The employer should try to ensure that he states the correct reason for dismissal on the ET1 to avoid being at risk of the dismissal being held to be unfair. However, the employment tribunal will seek to discover the real reason for dismissal, and if the employer has made a genuine mistake in how it has labelled the reason but the factual basis for the dismissal is clear to the employee, the tribunal can ignore an incorrect label. In *Abernethy v Mott, Hay and Anderson* [1974] ICR 323, CA, the employee refused to relocate and was dismissed for redundancy. The tribunal held that the employee was actually fairly dismissed for incapability. The Court of Appeal upheld the fairness of the dismissal, since the facts were clear to the employee at the time of the dismissal and the employer should not be penalised for attaching the wrong legal label.

In *Wilson v Post Office* [2000] IRLR 834, the Court of Appeal confirmed that the characterisation of the reason for a dismissal is a matter of legal analysis, and that since this was not a case in which the employer had tried to change the nature of the case, it was open to the EAT to say that the dismissal was to be characterised as for SOSR when it was originally formulated by the employer in terms of capability. So, where an employer wrongly labels the reason for dismissal, but still seeks to justify the dismissal on factual grounds made clear at the time of dismissal, he will not be bound by the wrong label. (See also *Screene v Seatwave Ltd* (UKEAT/0020/11).)

However, different considerations apply where the employer seeks to change the factual basis of the dismissal. In *Hotson v Wisbech Conservative Club* [1984] ICR 859, the EAT allowed an appeal by Ms Hotson, a club barmaid dismissed for gross inefficiency, because the real reason was suspected dishonesty, which went beyond a mere change of label. The allegation of dishonesty should have been put to the employee at the outset, to allow her to answer it. See too *Screene v Seatwave* (above) (where the EAT said a tribunal was entitled to make its decision on the basis of what it considered to be the real reason for dismissal) and *Perkin v St George's Healthcare NHS Trust* [2005] IRLR 934 (at **5.4.2.5** below).

Thus, provided the factual basis of the employer's argument is adhered to, it should not matter that the wrong reasons are pleaded. However, it would be good practice for an employer to state the reason for dismissal expressly, and, where there is a genuine uncertainty as to which of the reasons apply, state in the alternative. But reasons should not be stated in the alternative unless there is genuine uncertainty, because s 98(1)(a) requires the employer to show the reason or, if more than one, the principal reason.

5.2.1 The five permitted reasons

By s 98(1) and (2) of the ERA 1996, in determining whether a dismissal is fair or unfair, it is for the employer to establish the only or principal reason for the dismissal, and that it is a reason falling within the following:

(a)   relating to the capability or qualifications of the employee to do work of the kind which he was employed to do (s 98(2)(a)); or

(b)   relating to the conduct of the employee (s 98(2)(b)); or

(c)   that the employee was redundant (s 98(2)(c)); or

(d)   that the employee could not continue to work in the position held without contravening some statutory provision (s 98(2)(d)); or

(e)   there was some other substantial reason (SOSR) that could justify the dismissal of an employee holding the position that employee held (s 98(1)(b)).

In *Kuzel v Roche Products Ltd* [2008] IRLR 530, the Court of Appeal confirmed that the burden is on the employer to show the reason for dismissal; but that where the employee asserts there was a different reason, the employee must produce some evidence of that. Where there is such evidence, it will be for the employer to show that the potentially fair reason was, in fact, the principal reason (see also *East Lancs Coachbuilders Ltd v Hilton* (UKEAT/0054/06)). It will then be for the tribunal to consider the evidence and make a finding of fact.

5.2.2   The ambit of the five reasons

This section deals with the ambit or scope of each of the five reasons. If the employer shows the dismissal is for one of these reasons, it has overcome the first hurdle. However, showing the reason does not of itself make the dismissal fair. The employment tribunal still has to decide whether the employer acted reasonably in dismissing the employee for that reason. We shall look at how fairness relates to these reasons in more detail below (see **5.4**).

5.2.2.1   Capability and qualifications

Section 98(2)(a) provides that an employer may fairly dismiss an employee for a reason that 'relates to the capability or qualifications of the employee for performing work of the kind which he was employed by the employer to do'. Capability is defined in s 98(3)(a) as 'capability assessed by reference to skill, aptitude, health or any other physical or mental quality'. There is always the potential for a degree of overlap between conduct and capability.

The incapability or lack of qualification for which the employee is dismissed must relate to the work which the employee was employed to do. Incapability within the provision may be incapability to do the job by virtue of incompetence, or an inherent inability to perform the job. It also extends to the inability of the employee to do his job by reason of illness or injury. Therefore sickness of an employee is a reason which may justify dismissal, even where that illness has been caused by the employer (see **5.4.2.1**).

Note: The Acas Code of Practice on Disciplinary and Grievance Procedures 2015 covers culpable (ie incompetent) poor performance dismissals but not ill health dismissals.

5.2.2.2   Conduct

The 'conduct' reason (s 98(2)(b)) may cover conduct of virtually any sort, but it would usually be misconduct within the employment. The EAT confirmed in *JP Morgan Securities plc v Ktorza* (UKEAT/0311/16) that there is no requirement for the conduct to be culpable. Of course, culpability or otherwise may be relevant to reasonableness (see **5.3**). It would include, for example, a range of conduct, from minor incidents (such as bad time-keeping) through to more serious matters such as disobedience of orders, breach of the duty of fidelity, dishonesty, fighting, sexual harassment or absence without permission. Conduct does not need to be gross, as opposed to serious, to be a fair dismissal. In *Mbubaegbu v Homerton University Hospital NHS Foundation Trust* (UKEAT/0218/17), the EAT upheld an employment tribunal's decision that multiple alleged breaches, even absent a single act of gross misconduct, could amount to a fair dismissal. A 'series of acts, demonstrating a pattern of conduct' could be of 'sufficient seriousness to undermine the relationship of trust and confidence'. See also *Quintiles Commercial UK Ltd v Barongo* (UKEAT/0255/17).

To minimise his potential liability for unfair dismissal, the employer should have a comprehensive set of disciplinary rules (see **Chapter 1** and the Acas Code of Practice on

Disciplinary and Grievance Procedures at **5.4.2.2** below) that differentiate between the sorts of conduct regarded as minor or serious, and which set out how such incidents will be treated and what the possible consequence may be. The distinction between misconduct and gross misconduct can be important: generally speaking, only gross misconduct will justify summary dismissal, ie dismissal without notice, and one incident of a minor nature would not usually justify dismissal as a sanction, whereas a series of minor incidents or repeatedly bad behaviour could be expected to do so. What is important is that it is made clear to the employee what sort of response can be expected following particular sorts of misconduct. The exact nature of the employer's disciplinary rules and procedures will depend on the size of the organisation. Larger firms should have a comprehensive set of detailed rules and procedures which should be carefully followed (although a minor deviation will not necessarily lead to a finding of unfair dismissal). A smaller firm may have a much less formal procedure, although it should still ensure that there is a fair investigation and a reasonable sanction. Note that a dismissal for gross misconduct can be unfair (see, for example, *Arnold Clark Automobiles Ltd v Spoor* [2017] IRLR 500).

Dismissal for misconduct outside employment, such as criminal offences committed elsewhere, will also come within this reason, but for such a dismissal to be fair the outside misconduct must usually have an effect on the employment relationship (see **5.4.2.2** below). For example, if a cashier is charged with a motoring offence, this would have no employment implications. However, a charge of theft clearly could have.

In order for the employer to rely on misconduct to justify a dismissal, the misconduct must have been known to the employer at the time of dismissal. He cannot rely on subsequently discovered misconduct to justify the dismissal (*W Devis & Sons Ltd v Atkins* [1977] AC 931, HL). For example, an employee is dismissed because his employer does not like him. After he leaves, his employer discovers that he has been submitting bogus expense claims. The employer cannot rely on this conduct when giving his reason for the dismissal.

However, note that it is at the point of actual dismissal beyond which after-acquired knowledge cannot be taken into account. The employer is entitled to take into account factors that occur until dismissal, even after notice of termination has been given (*Alboni v Ind Coope Retail Ltd* [1998] IRLR 131, CA), both in determining the reason for the dismissal and whether the employer acted reasonably in the circumstances in treating it as a sufficient reason for dismissal. Note also that after-acquired knowledge may affect the amount of compensation an employee may receive (see **5.6.2**).

5.2.2.3 Redundancy

As we have seen, a dismissal by reason of redundancy may give rise to a claim for a redundancy payment (see **Chapter 4**). However, redundancy is also a potentially fair reason for dismissing an employee. If an employer does not handle a redundancy situation fairly, that can give rise, separately, to an unfair dismissal claim (see **5.4.2.3**). The definition of redundancy has already been dealt with, and the same definition in ERA 1996, s 139 applies here (see **4.2**).

Redundancy dismissals are not covered by the Acas Disciplinary and Grievance Code.

5.2.2.4 Contravention of a statutory provision ('illegality')

If an employee seeks to enforce employment rights that are found to arise from an illegal contract, he may be unable to do so. Contravention of a statutory provision (s 98(2)(d)) covers the situation where it becomes illegal by statute either for the employee to work in the position held, or for the employer to employ him in it. The burden of proving illegality is on an employer.

One of the more common types of dismissal for this reason is the dismissal of the driver of a motor vehicle who is disqualified by a court from driving because of a motoring offence (see, eg, *Appleyard v FM Smith (Hull) Ltd* [1972] IRLR 19). Another common situation that arises is where employers fail to pay an employee's tax and/or National Insurance (see for example *Newland v Simons & Willer (Hairdressers) Ltd* [1981] IRLR 359, *Hewcastle Catering Ltd v Ahmed* [1991] IRLR 473 and *Salvesen v Simons* [1994] IRLR 52).

Another area is the employment of someone who is in the UK illegally, or who does not have permission to work. See **1.2.6** for more analysis and the recent case of *Okedina v Chikale* (UKEAT/0152/17), which re-emphasised that an employer will not be able to avoid liability on a contract which is performed illegally by it (eg because appropriate tax deductions were not made) if the employee is not complicit in those acts.

5.2.2.5   Some other substantial reason

Some other substantial reason is not limited by the four reasons above. The employer may show any substantial reason outside the four above as the reason for the dismissal of an employee holding the position held, but the onus of proof is on the employer to show that it is a substantial reason that could justify the dismissal. Provided the reason is not 'whimsical, unworthy or trivial', it will suffice. In *Scott and Co v Richardson* (UKEAT/0074/04), Mr Scott carried out debt recovery services and decided to introduce shift work. Mr Richardson refused to accept the proposed change to his contract of employment on the basis that he should continue to be paid overtime for working in the evening. He was dismissed. The EAT held that what the employer had to demonstrate to the tribunal was that it reasonably believed/ concluded that the reorganisation of working hours had advantages – it was not necessary to go beyond that to see whether it did have those advantages. In this case there was a commercial reason for carrying out the reorganisation, and the EAT said the tribunal was bound to find that the employer had shown that the reason for dismissal was for some other substantial reason.

It is not possible to give a comprehensive list of other reasons which may justify dismissal, but reasons which have been held to be a potentially fair reason for dismissal include refusal to accept a reorganisation affecting working hours (*Muggeridge and Slade v East Anglia Plastics Ltd* [1973] IRLR 163 and *Scott and Co v Richardson* (UKEAT/0074/04)), replacement by a better qualified employee (*Priddle v Dibble* [1978] 1 All ER 1058), end of genuine temporary employment (*Terry v East Sussex County Council* [1977] 1 All ER 567), dismissal because of a clash of personalities between employees (*Gorfin v Distressed Gentlefolk's Aid Association* [1973] IRLR 290; see also *Perkin v St George's Healthcare NHS Trust* [2005] EWCA Civ 1174), marriage of an employee to a competitor, where there was a real risk of a leak of trade secrets (*Foot v Eastern Counties Timber Co Ltd* [1972] IRLR 83), refusal of employees to accept a new restraint of trade clause in their contracts (even if the clause was unreasonable) (*Willow Oak Developments Ltd t/a Windsor Recruitment v Silverwood & Others* [2006] IRLR 607), loss of trust and confidence in the employee, in exceptional cases (*Ezsias v North Glamorgan NHS Trust* [2011] IRLR 550 and *Governing Body of Tubbenden Primary School v Sylvester* (UKEAT/0527/11)), risk of damage to the employer's reputation (*Leach v Office of Communications* [2012] EWCA Civ 959), third-party pressure (*Mr S Bancroft v Interserve (Facilities Management) Ltd* (UKEAT/0329/12)) and a series of repeated short absences where health is not the issue as far as the employer is concerned (see *Ridge v HM Land Registry* (EAT/0485/12)).

Note: Not all 'some other substantial reason' dismissals are covered by the Acas Code of Practice on Disciplinary and Grievance Procedures (see *Phoenix House Ltd v Stockman* (UKEAT/ 0264/15)).

5.2.3   Statement of reasons for dismissal

An employee who has been continuously employed for at least two years (or one year if employed by the employer before 6 April 2012) is entitled to request that he be provided by his employer, within 14 days of the request, with a written statement of the reason for his dismissal (ERA 1996, s 92). The statement is admissible in evidence in any proceedings. If a woman is dismissed while pregnant or during her maternity leave period, she is entitled, without prior request, to a written statement (see **14.9.2**).

If the employer unreasonably fails to comply with the request or the particulars given are inadequate or untrue, the employee may present a complaint to an employment tribunal. The time-limit to present the complaint is the same as that for a complaint of unfair dismissal (see **6.3.1**), generally three months from the EDT (see **3.5**). If the complaint is well founded, the tribunal must order the employer to pay the employee two weeks' pay (gross) (ERA 1996, s 93). There is no upper limit on a week's pay for this purpose (ERA 1996, s 227).

5.3 FAIRNESS OF DISMISSAL

Once the employer has shown that the reason for the dismissal falls within one of the permitted reasons, the tribunal must then decide whether the employer has acted reasonably within s 98(4) of the ERA 1996 in dismissing the employee for that reason.

In practice, it is usually relatively easy for the employer to show the reason for the dismissal. Persuading the tribunal that he has acted reasonably on the evidence presented may be more difficult.

By s 98(4) of the ERA 1996, the tribunal must decide whether the dismissal was fair or unfair, having regard to the reason shown by the employer, *and* whether, in the circumstances (including the size and administrative resources of the employer's undertaking), the employer acted reasonably or unreasonably in treating that reason as a sufficient reason for dismissing the employee; *and* that question shall be determined in accordance with equity and the substantial merits of the case. It is not for the tribunal to decide if the employee did do what was alleged, nor is it for the tribunal to decide what it would have done: the test is an objective one.

5.3.1 ERA 1996, s 98(4): general

Each case will turn on its own facts, but there are a number of principles the tribunal must follow in determining reasonableness.

5.3.1.1 Has the employer acted reasonably?

In *Iceland Frozen Foods Ltd v Jones* [1982] IRLR 439, the EAT summarised the correct approach for the tribunal to adopt in answering the question posed by s 98(4) of the ERA 1996:

(a)   the starting point should always be the words of s 98(4) themselves;

(b)   in applying the section an employment tribunal must consider the reasonableness of the employer's conduct, not simply whether they (the members of the employment tribunal) consider the dismissal to be fair;

(c)   in judging the reasonableness of the employer's conduct an employment tribunal must not substitute its decision as to what is the right course to adopt for that of the employer;

(d)   in many (though not all) cases there is a band of reasonable responses to the employee's conduct within which one employer might reasonably take one view, another quite reasonably take another;

(e)   the function of the employment tribunal, as an industrial jury, is to determine whether in the particular circumstances of each case the decision to dismiss the employee fell within the band of reasonable responses that a reasonable employer might have adopted. If the dismissal falls within the band, the dismissal is fair: if the dismissal falls outside the band, it is unfair.

The question for the tribunal to determine, therefore, is whether the respondent's decision to dismiss the employee fell within the band (or range) of reasonable responses of a reasonable employer. It is sufficient that a reasonable employer would regard the circumstances as a sufficient reason for dismissing – it is not necessary that all reasonable employers would dismiss in those circumstances. However, the tribunal should be careful to not substitute its own view for what the employer should have done, for this would be an error in law which is appealable. Provided that the tribunal does not fall into this error, almost any decision may be justified, because it is for the tribunal to determine what a reasonable employer could or should have done. In *London Ambulance Service NHS Trust v Small* [2009] IRLR 563 the Court of Appeal held that the tribunal substituted its view of the facts for that of the employer. It is useful to quote from the judgment:

> 41. The ET ought to have confined its consideration to facts relating to the Trust's handling of Mr Small's dismissal: the genuineness of the Trust's belief and the reasonableness of the grounds of its belief about the conduct of Mr Small at the time of the dismissal. Instead, the ET introduced its own findings of fact about the conduct of Mr Small, including aspects of it that had been disputed at the disciplinary hearing. For example, the ET found that the daughter, who did not give evidence to the ET, had not told Mr Small that her mother was hypertensive and diabetic. Further, on the point whether Mr Small had done a risk assessment before asking the patient to walk, the ET held that there was no evidence that he had failed to carry out a risk assessment, but Mr Suter gave evidence to the ET that the crucial issue before the disciplinary panel was that Mr Small had not carried out a proper patient assessment, before the decision was made.

> 42. The ET used its findings of fact to support its conclusion that, at the time of dismissal, the Trust had no reasonable grounds for its belief about Mr Small's conduct and therefore no genuine belief about it. By this process of reasoning the ET found that the dismissal was unfair. In my judgment, this amounted to the ET substituting itself and its findings for the Trust's decision-maker in relation to Mr Small's dismissal.

> 43. It is all too easy, even for an experienced ET, to slip into the substitution mindset. In conduct cases the claimant often comes to the ET with more evidence and with an understandable determination to clear his name and to prove to the ET that he is innocent of the charges made against him by his employer. He has lost his job in circumstances that may make it difficult for him to get another job. He may well gain the sympathy of the ET so that it is carried along the acquittal route and away from the real question – whether the employer acted fairly and reasonably in all the circumstances at the time of the dismissal.

See *Fuller v London Borough of Brent* [2011] EWCA Civ 267, *Crawford and Another v Suffolk Mental Health Partnership NHS Trust* [2012] IRLR 402 and *Newbound v Thames Water Utilities Ltd* [2015] EWCA Civ 677 for decisions of the Court of Appeal finding that there was no error of law and that a reasonable employment tribunal could find that dismissal was outside the range of reasonable responses.

The approach set out in *Iceland* was re-stated by the Court of Appeal in the joined cases *HSBC (formerly Midland Bank) v Madden; Post Office v Foley* [2000] IRLR 827, CA, and in *London Ambulance Service NHS Trust v Small* [2009] EWCA Civ 220. In *Sarkar v West London Mental Health NHS Trust* [2010] IRLR 508 and *Salford Royal NHS Foundation Trust v Roldan* [2010] IRLR 721, the Court of Appeal appeared to endorse a more interventionist approach by employment tribunals when applying the range of reasonable responses test. In *Roldan*, the Court of Appeal said that the tribunal had been entitled to find that the dismissal was unfair, given the conflict in evidence which meant that the Trust should have investigated the issues in more depth. In *North West London Hospitals NHS Trust v Bowater* [2011] EWCA Civ 63, the Court of Appeal upheld an employment tribunal's decision that the decision to dismiss could not possibly be within the band of reasonable responses. The employee had made a lewd comment, but one that 'a large proportion of the population would consider ... to be merely humorous'. The Court said (at [26]):

> It is important that, in cases of this kind, the EAT pays proper respect to the decision of the ET. It is the ET to whom Parliament has entrusted the responsibility of making what are, no doubt sometimes, difficult and borderline decisions in relation to the fairness of dismissal. An appeal to the EAT only lies on a point of law and it goes without saying that the EAT must not, under the guise of a charge of perversity, substitute its own judgment for that of the ET.

In *Graham v The Secretary of State for Work & Pensions (Jobcentre Plus)* [2012] EWCA Civ 903 (a conduct case), the Court said (at [36]) that

> the ET must then decide on the reasonableness of the response by the employer. In performing the latter exercise, the ET must consider, by the objective standards of the hypothetical reasonable employer, rather than by reference to the ET's own subjective views, whether the employer has acted within a '*band or range of reasonable responses*' to the particular misconduct found of the particular employee. If the employer has so acted, then the employer's decision to dismiss will be reasonable. However, this is not the same thing as saying that a decision of an employer to dismiss will only be regarded as unreasonable if it is shown to be perverse. The ET must not simply consider whether they think that the dismissal was fair and thereby substitute their decision as to what was the right course to adopt for that of the employer. The ET must determine whether the decision of the employer to dismiss the employee fell within the band of reasonable responses which '*a reasonable employer might have adopted*'. An ET must focus its attention on the fairness of the conduct of the employer at the time of the investigation and dismissal (or any internal appeal process) and not on whether in fact the employee has suffered an injustice.

The Court of Appeal confirmed in *Davies v Sandwell Metropolitan BC* [2012] EWCA Civ 135, that the fairness of a decision to dismiss for misconduct, which relies on a previous final warning, should be assessed under s 98(4) principles; but that in assessing reasonableness, while a tribunal may assess whether the final warning was issued in good faith or was 'manifestly inappropriate', it is not the tribunal's function to re-hear earlier internal disciplinary proceedings.

Note that the 'range of reasonable responses' test applies not just to the substantive reason for the dismissal, but also to the procedural aspects of the employer's actions. In *Sainsbury's Supermarkets Ltd v Hitt* [2003] IRLR 23, the Court of Appeal held that the range of reasonable responses test applied as much to whether a reasonable investigation had been carried out as it does to the reasonableness of the decision to dismiss for the conduct reason. The Court of Appeal confirmed this in *Bournemouth University Higher Education Corporation v Buckland* [2010] EWCA Civ 121.

For a useful discussion of some of the authorities, see *EAGA plc v Tideswell* (UKEAT/0007/11) and, more recently, *Newbound v Thames Water Utilities Ltd* [2015] EWCA Civ 677.

In *Reilly v Sandwell MBC* [2018] UKSC 18, the Supreme Court held that it was fair to dismiss a school head teacher for failing to disclose a close relationship with a man convicted of making indecent images of children. The employment tribunal held that the dismissal was procedurally unfair (due to technical failures in the appeal process) but that the reason for dismissal was a fair and sufficient reason (conduct) for dismissal. It directed (i) a 90% reduction in any compensation in accordance with the approach endorsed in *Polkey v AE Dayton Services Ltd* [1988] 1 AC 344 (see below), and (ii) a 100% reduction due to blameworthy conduct. The Supreme Court raised some doubt about the relevance of the test in *BHS Ltd v Burchell* [1980] ICR 303 (see below) to s 98(4) (as opposed to s 98(1)–(3) – reason and belief) but ultimately concluded:

> [N]o harm has been done by the extravagant view taken of the reach of [that] judgment ... In effect it has been considered only to require the tribunal to inquire whether the dismissal was within a range of reasonable responses ... and had been preceded by a reasonable amount of investigation.

5.3.1.2 Matters known to the employer

The employer must generally justify the decision to dismiss on the basis of the information known to him at the time of dismissal (*W Devis & Sons Ltd v Atkins* [1977] AC 931, HL). See also *Alboni v Ind Coope Retail Ltd* [1998] IRLR 131, CA (see **5.2.2.2**). The Court of Appeal held in *Orr v Milton Keynes Council* [2011] EWCA Civ 62 that 'known to the employer' means facts known to the decision maker or facts that he could reasonably acquire through the appropriate disciplinary procedure.

The Court of Appeal in *Royal Mail Ltd v Jhuti* [2017] EWCA Civ 1632 (a whistleblowing case) gives some useful examples at paras 60–63. Interestingly, Underhill LJ opined that where the 'manipulation' is carried out by somebody very senior, there might be a case for attributing the motivation to the employer.

5.3.1.3 Size of the undertaking

The tribunal must take into account the size and administrative resources of the undertaking. An employer with a small workforce might, for example, find it more difficult than a larger firm to find other employees to do the work of an employee who is absent sick for a long period. This might justify a dismissal and replacement of a sick employee in circumstances where a large firm would not be acting reasonably. A small firm is also less likely to have suitable alternative employment for employees who lose their own jobs through redundancy. A small firm may also have less formal disciplinary and consultation procedures than a large one.

5.3.1.4 Does the reason justify dismissal?

The tribunal must decide whether dismissal was within a range of reasonable responses. Would a reasonable employer have demoted or suspended instead?

5.3.1.5 Pressure on the employer

In deciding whether the employer acted reasonably, the tribunal must not take into account any pressure put on the employer, by way of industrial action or the threat of industrial action, to dismiss the employee (ERA 1996, s 107).

5.3.1.6 Breach of contract

The fact that a dismissal is in breach of contract will not of itself render it unfair. The test is whether the employer acted reasonably.

5.3.1.7 Equitable considerations

A long-serving employee deserves more consideration before dismissal. For example, an employee with 20 years' service who is convicted of an offence of dishonesty unrelated to his employment, might be demoted to a position which would not give him an opportunity for breach of trust rather than be dismissed.

5.3.1.8 Consistency

The employer should consider how previous similar situations have been dealt with in the past. Nevertheless, it will be rare that the circumstances of one employee are truly comparable with those of another. In *Hadjioannou v Coral Casinos Ltd* [1981] IRLR 352, the EAT said that inconsistency of treatment would be relevant only in limited circumstances. In *Paul v East Surrey District HA* [1995] IRLR 305, the Court of Appeal held that the employee's dismissal was fair on the ground that there was a clear and rational basis for distinguishing between the cases of the two employees. For a recent decision on consistency of treatment, see *MBNA Ltd v Jones* (UKEAT/0120/15).

5.3.1.9 Human rights

Although the Human Rights Act 1998 (HRA 1998) is only directly effective between victims and public authorities (see **Chapter 15**), for employees pursuing their private sector employers for unfair dismissal, the HRA 1998 may be used to 'shape and determine' the outcome of the claim. In *Pay v Lancashire Probation Service* [2004] IRLR 129, the EAT agreed that the ERA 1996, s 98(4) must be read in a way which is compatible with human rights. However, on the facts, the EAT decided that the activities in which the applicant was involved (performing in fetish clubs and merchandising of products connected with bondage, domination and sado-masochism; photographs were available on the Internet of him involved in these activities) were not private, and that the interference with freedom of expression was justified and accordingly there was no infringement of the applicant's rights under Articles 8 or 10 (freedom of expression) of the ECHR. Mr Pay was a probation officer who worked with sex offenders. The EAT said that the interference with Article 10 was justified on the facts because of the competing interests of the employer to protect its reputation and maintain public confidence. Dismissal was a proportionate response.

In X *v* Y [2004] IRLR 625, the Court of Appeal dealt with the question of whether tribunals must take account of the HRA 1998 (in this case Article 8 of the Convention) when deciding unfair dismissal claims brought against private sector employers. The majority of the Court of Appeal held that Article 8 was not engaged. Mummery LJ went on to state that there should be no difference in approach, whether the employer is private or public sector. He said the Convention had an 'oblique' effect rather than a horizontal one, and that the right to respect for private life 'blended' with the law on unfair dismissal, but without creating new private law causes of action against private employers. See **15.4.2**.

It has also been suggested that Article 6 (the right to a fair hearing) might apply to internal disciplinary hearings. In R (*G*) *v* The Governors of X School [2011] UKSC 30, the Supreme Court held that Article 6 *may* be engaged in internal disciplinary hearings where the consequences of an internal disciplinary proceeding were sufficiently linked to the determination of an individual's civil rights to practise his chosen profession (in the sense of having a 'substantial influence or effect' on the outcome of a subsequent process which is determinative of civil rights (in this case the outcome of the Independent Safeguarding Authority's process, which could have meant that the claimant's name was added to the register)).

Statutory provisions obliged the school, when it made a serious finding of misconduct, to make a reference to what became the Independent Safeguarding Authority (ISA) (originally the Secretary of State) to consider whether the claimant should be should be placed on the 'children's barred list' and prevented from working with children in the future. Under this statutory framework, the claimant would have a right to legal representation before the ISA; and if dissatisfied with its decision, there was a right of appeal. Applying that test to the facts, the fact that ISA was required by statutory provisions and published guidance to 'exercise its own independent judgment both in relation to finding facts and making an assessment of their gravity and significance', before forming a view as to whether G should be placed on the barred list, was significant in the Supreme Court's view. The Supreme Court considered that the governors' determination that G had been guilty of gross misconduct would *not* have a 'substantial influence or effect' on the ISA's decision-making process. It followed that G's Article 6 rights were not engaged at the internal disciplinary stage, but only at the subsequent ISA hearing (see further **15.4.1**).

Other rights may be of relevance, for example an excessively long period of suspension could amount to inhuman or degrading treatment or punishment under Article 3; or unjustified surveillance of an employee before or as part of an investigation process in a disciplinary matter may be a breach of the right to respect for private life under Article 8 (see **15.4.2**).

5.4 PROCEDURAL UNFAIRNESS

An employer may be justified in dismissing an employee for the substantive reason, but the dismissal may still be unfair if the employer does not follow a fair procedure in reaching the decision to dismiss. There can be different procedural requirements, depending on the reason for the dismissal. These matters are dealt with in more detail in **5.4.2** in relation to each of the different reasons for dismissal.

5.4.1 Codes of practice

Any relevant Code (for example, the Acas Code of Practice on Disciplinary and Grievance Procedures, available at <http://www.acas.org.uk>) should be considered by the tribunal. If the employer fails to comply with the Code, that will be taken into account by the tribunal when deciding fairness. It may also have an effect on the amount of compensation awarded.

The Acas Code of Practice on Disciplinary and Grievance Procedures (latest version March 2015) is intended to provide basic practical guidance on the key procedural principles that underpin the handling of disciplinary and grievance situations at work. It sets down minimum standards only.

The key points to note are:

- A failure to follow the Code will not in itself make a dismissal automatically unfair, but tribunals can adjust awards by up to 25% for any unreasonable failure to comply with any of its provisions (EA 2008, s 3).
- The Code applies to disciplinary and grievance matters, but the text also refers to performance issues, suggesting that the disciplinary procedure guidance should also be applied to handling capability dismissals. Note that while misconduct involves culpable conduct, poor performance is capable of involving both culpable and non-culpable conduct. Where poor performance is the result of genuine ill health or injury, the Code will not apply. The position will be different where ill health leads to a failure to comply with a sickness absence procedure or is not believed to be genuine. In these sort of cases there is culpable conduct which it will be appropriate to investigate under the Code.
- If the employer purports to dismiss for a culpability-related reason, the Code applies even if a tribunal does not accept that reason as genuine (see *Bethnal Green and Shoreditch Education Trust v Dippenaar* (UKEAT/0064/15)).
- The Code does not apply to other dismissals, such as redundancy, 'some other substantial reason' (SOSR) dismissals for breakdown in working relationships (*Phoenix House Ltd v Stockman* (UKEAT/0264/15)), the termination of a fixed-term contract and cases of medical incapability (*Holmes v Qinetic Ltd* (UKEAT/0206/15), although it would apply to allegations of misuse of a sickness system. There is some doubt about the decision in *Stockman*, because in that case there was a disciplinary element to the case, and the authors respectfully consider that it may have been wrongly decided. Employers will be required to satisfy a tribunal that the termination procedure is fair according to the general fairness principles set out in the ERA 1996 and case law (see **5.4.2.3**).
- The Code does not require employees to submit a grievance before bringing a tribunal claim, but employees who unreasonably fail to do this may suffer a reduction in any tribunal award of up to 25%. Note that grievances must be in writing, so the Code does not apply to oral grievances (*Cadogan Hotel Partners Ltd v Ozog* (UKEAT/0001/14)).

The Acas Code is not legally binding, but its provisions will be taken into account by employment tribunals where appropriate when deciding whether a dismissal is fair or unfair. In *Lock v Cardiff Railway Co Ltd* [1998] IRLR 358, the EAT emphasised (it was dealing with the old Acas Code) the importance of tribunals examining and taking into account the Acas Code. Not to do so would amount to a misdirection of law.

The Acas Code applies to disciplinary situations, and para 1 states that 'disciplinary situations include misconduct and poor performance', so it is also applicable in a capability dismissal.

The Code sets out the process for disciplinary matters, which is as follows:

- Establish the facts of each case.
- Inform the employee of the problem.
- Hold a meeting with the employee.
- At that meeting, allow the employee to be accompanied.
- Decide on the appropriate action.
- Provide the employee with an opportunity to appeal.

(See **5.4.2.1** and **5.4.2.2** below for further detail.) While an employer may lay down its own procedures, it will need to ensure that these meet the minimum standards of the Acas Code.

Under s 10 of the ERA 1999, workers have a statutory right to be accompanied at a disciplinary hearing. This right applies only where the worker 'reasonably requests' the presence of a companion. Where the worker's request is reasonable, the employer must permit the companion to attend (see eg *Roberts v The Regard Partnership* (ET/2104545/09)). Note that while the worker may choose whom he wishes to accompany him, his choice of companion is limited under s 10 to trade union officials or fellow workers. Some organisation will, however, permit a wider choice of companion in their disciplinary procedures. There may be limited circumstances where the employee asks to be accompanied by a person other than a colleague or trade union representative and where a denial of such a request could amount to a breach of trust and confidence (see *Stevens v University of Birmingham* [2015] EWHC 2300 (QB)).

Note that by virtue of ss 37 and 38 of the ERA 2004 (amending s 10 of the ERA 1999), employers must now allow a companion who accompanies an employee to a disciplinary hearing to address the hearing to put an employee's case, to sum up that case and to respond on the employee's behalf. However, the companion is not entitled to answer questions on the worker's behalf. If the employer fails to tell the employee of his right to be accompanied to a disciplinary hearing, or does not allow a companion to attend, this can be taken into account when considering fairness (see Acas Code of Practice at **5.4.1** below). (Note that these provisions also apply to workers – see **1.3.3**.)

Two cases have considered the right to be accompanied. In *Toal v GB Oils Ltd* (UKEAT/0569/12), the claimant requested that he be accompanied at a grievance hearing by a member of his trade union. The manager refused to allow the union member to attend, because he considered that he might prejudice the hearing. The claimant asked another union member to represent him. The grievance was not upheld and the claimant complained to an employment tribunal under s 10. The EAT, overturning the decision of the tribunal, held that the claimant had an absolute right to choose his companion: the use of the word 'reasonably' in s 10(1)(b) applied to the right to request to be accompanied but not to the choice of companion. Although the Acas Code (see below) suggests that 'it would not normally be reasonable for workers to insist on being accompanied by a companion whose presence would prejudice the hearing', the Code was not an available aid to the interpretation of a statute. The Acas Code has twice been amended in the light of this decision. In *Gnahoua v Abellio London Ltd* (ET/2303661/2015), however, a tribunal confirmed that in such a case, where a nominated companion was within the statutory categories but was otherwise unsuitable, only nominal damages may be appropriate.

In *Leeds Dental Team Ltd v Mrs D Rose* (UK EAT/0016/13), the claimant wanted to be accompanied to a disciplinary hearing by the former owner of the dental practice. The respondent refused: the claimant went off sick and then resigned, bringing a constructive unfair dismissal claim, including the refusal to allow her to be accompanied by the former owner. The tribunal held that the respondent's refusal was unreasonable and contributed to a breach of trust and confidence. There was no breach of s 10 on the facts, but the refusal contributed to a breach of trust and confidence. (See too *Stevens v University of Birmingham* [2015] EWHC 2300 (QB), where the High Court held it was unfair for the University to refuse the claimant a companion of his choosing, and that amounted to a breach of the implied term of trust and confidence, such that the claimant was entitled to a declaration that he had permission to be accompanied by his choice of person.)

As noted above, a failure to follow the Code, where it applies, gives tribunals a discretionary power to increase or decrease the unfair dismissal award (and presumably other awards that also arise out of the disciplinary process or dismissal on grounds of misconduct or capability, eg claims of unlawful discrimination, wrongful dismissal, unlawful deduction of wages) by up to 25%, if they consider that the employer's/employee's failure to comply with the Code was unreasonable. It is for the tribunal to decide what uplift (or reduction) would be just and equitable. The full list of claims to which this regime applies is set out in Sch A2 to TULRCA 1992.

To complement the Code, Acas has published guidance. Tribunals cannot adjust awards on account of any failure to follow the guidance, neither are they required to have regard to the guidance. However, it is anticipated that in many cases tribunals will refer to the guidance to assist them in determining whether the employer's handling of misconduct and poor performance matters has complied with general principles of fairness. For that reason, when dealing with disciplinary matters, employers and their advisers should read the relevant section of the guidance and ensure that they comply with it.

5.4.2 Procedural unfairness: particular reasons

The general principles dealt with in **5.3.1** apply to dismissals for any reason. However, where procedural unfairness is concerned, particular reasons may require a particular procedural approach (see below).

The application of an unfair procedure will render a dismissal unfair even though compliance with a fair procedure would have produced the same result of dismissal (*Polkey v AE Dayton Services Ltd* [1987] ICR 301). However, the fact that compliance would have still led to dismissal may be taken into account when considering compensation (a 'Polkey' deduction) (see **5.6.2.2**).

5.4.2.1 Capability and qualifications

The approach to capability and qualifications should vary depending on whether the incapability is due to incompetence or sickness. The Acas Code covers poor performance/incompetence.

Incompetence

Before dismissing any employee for incompetence, an employer should normally have met with the employee, warned the employee about his standard of work and given him the opportunity to improve. Where appropriate, adequate training should have been given and review periods set down. In some cases, for example where an employee has been moved to a job beyond his capabilities, the employer should consider whether it is possible to move the employee to a job within his capabilities. Acas gives the following example in the guidance:

> A member of staff in accounts makes a number of mistakes on invoices to customers. You bring the mistakes to his attention, make sure he has had the right training and impress on him the need for accuracy but the mistakes continue. You invite the employee to a disciplinary meeting and inform him of his right to be accompanied by a colleague or employee representative. At the meeting the employee does not give a satisfactory explanation for the mistakes so you decide to issue an improvement note setting out: the problem, the improvement required, the timescale for improvement, the support available and a review date. You inform the employee that a failure to improve may lead to a final written warning.

In *Williams v Meddygfa Rhydbach Surgery* (ET/1600487/2016), an employment tribunal decision, the tribunal found that Mrs Williams had been constructively unfairly dismissed when she was bullied during a mishandled performance management process. Following various personnel changes, Mrs Williams, who had been employed for 30 years, was considered to have been over-promoted and was no longer well regarded by some of the practice. During a performance meeting, one of the doctors raised his voice and banged his fist on the table. Mrs Williams brought a grievance and, when it was not upheld, resigned. The employment tribunal found that the performance management had not been properly carried out and she had been bullied. This is a first instance decision and could be appealed, but it serves as a reminder of the importance of dealing with performance management issues in a structured and measured way.

Readers should always have regard to the guidance produced by Acas (see the overview chart reproduced at **5.4.2.2**).

Sickness

The Acas Code does not explicitly cover dismissals by reason of ill-health, but the guidance produced by Acas includes a section dealing with ill-health absences, which employers would be well advised to read.

Absence may be due to sickness or may be a misconduct issue, which means that different procedural considerations may arise and may be appropriate.

An employee may be fairly dismissed for long-term sickness. The nature and likely duration of the illness and the length of service of the employee are relevant, as are the needs of the employer. A key employee or an employee in a small firm may need to be replaced by an employer more quickly than a less vital employee or one in a larger firm. Ultimately, the test is whether the employer could reasonably be expected to wait any longer for the employee (*Spencer v Paragon Wallpapers Ltd* [1976] IRLR 373).

The employer should consult with the employee concerning the nature and likely length of the illness, seek medical advice relating to the condition of the employee and consider whether suitable alternative employment can be offered. Under the Access to Medical Reports Act 1988, the written consent of an employee is required before the employer can obtain a medical report from the employee's specialist or doctor. The medical practitioner must be responsible for the clinical care of the individual. For this reason, reports prepared by occupational doctors are normally exempt. Warnings would not normally be appropriate, but an employee who takes a large number of short breaks for illness could be warned about his attendance record.

The EAT held in *DB Schenker Rail (UK) Ltd v Doolan* (UKEATS/0053/09) that where there is a conflict in medical evidence, the employer need only show that it acted within the range of reasonable responses when preferring the evidence of one expert over another. The decision to dismiss in capability cases is a managerial one for the employer and not a medical one for doctors.

According to the EAT in *Edwards v Governors of Hanson School* [2001] IRLR 733, if an employer has

> acted maliciously, or wilfully caused an employee incapacitating ill-health, we see no reason why dismissal, however fair the ultimate procedures in themselves, should not lead to a finding of unfair dismissal.

This may mean that a dismissal of an employee on long-term sick absence caused by bullying and mismanagement at work may be unfair.

In *Frewin v Consignia plc* [2003] All ER (D) 314 (Jul), the EAT stated that, when considering the fairness of a dismissal, a tribunal is entitled to take into account whether the incapacity was caused by the employer. The EAT said that

> the weight to be attached to that factor would depend on all the circumstances of the case. In some instances, the existence of causation could render the decision to dismiss unfair; in other cases it might not. Thus the existence of a causative link would not require the conclusion that the decision to dismiss had been unfair or raise any presumption of unfairness. It was merely a factor to be considered and weighed in the balance.

In *McAdie v RBS* [2007] IRLR 895, Mrs McAdie's ill-health was stress-related. The tribunal concluded it had been caused by the way her grievances about various matters had been handled, and by other treatment by her line managers. She was subsequently dismissed on ill-health grounds and brought a claim for unfair dismissal. The employment tribunal held that the dismissal was unfair on the basis that the employer had caused Mrs McAdie's health problems. On appeal, the EAT held that the tribunal had asked itself the wrong question. The question it should have asked was whether it was reasonable for the employer to dismiss Mrs

McAdie in the circumstances as they then were, including the fact that its mishandling of the situation had led to her illness. The Court of Appeal upheld the EAT's decision; it stated that the EAT had applied the correct test and had been right to find that Mrs McAdie had not been unfairly dismissed. The fact an employer has caused the incapacity in question cannot preclude him dismissing fairly. However, where the employer is responsible for the incapacity, it may be expected, as the EAT said in this case (approved by the Court of Appeal), to 'go the extra mile in finding alternative employment for such an employee or to put up with a longer period of sickness than would otherwise be reasonable'. This approach was confirmed in the recent case of L v M (UKEAT/0382/13). If an employer is responsible for an employee's ill-health, this will be a relevant consideration as to whether and when it is reasonable to dismiss for that incapacity.

In *First Leeds v Haigh* (UKEAT/0246/07), the EAT held that a capability dismissal will normally be unfair if an employer fails to take reasonable steps to ascertain whether an employee is entitled to an ill-health retirement (see also *Apsden v Webb Poultry & Meat Group (Holdings) Ltd* [1996] IRLR 521).

In *O'Brien v Bolton St Catherine's Academy* [2017] IRLR 547, the claimant had been off work for over a year, and there was no evidence that she would be fit to return in the foreseeable future, if at all, when the decision to dismiss was taken. However, the position had changed by the time of the appeal hearing. There was now evidence, albeit not unproblematic, that she was fit to return to work at once. The Court of Appeal held that it was open to the tribunal to hold that it was unreasonable for the school to disregard that new evidence without at least a further assessment by its own occupational health advisers. The dismissal was therefore unfair.

The impact of the disability discrimination provisions of the Equality Act 2010 should always be considered in relation to an ill-health dismissal. This area is considered further in **Chapter 13**.

5.4.2.2   Conduct

As mentioned previously, the type of misconduct may vary greatly, from incidents of a minor nature (eg bad time-keeping) to gross misconduct (eg theft or divulging trade secrets).

It is important, however, to determine what the real reason for the dismissal is – for example, if the reason for the dismissal is a breakdown in trust and confidence caused by the employee's behaviour, an employer does not need to follow its contractual conduct dismissal procedure (see *Ezsias v North Glamorgan NHS Trust* (UKEAT/0399/09)). In *Ezsias*, the EAT upheld the tribunal's decision that Mr Ezsias had been fairly dismissed for 'some other substantial reason' where Mr Ezsias' behaviour had led to relationships in the department breaking down (see **5.4.2.5**).

The important feature here, when considering the reasonableness of the employer's actions, is how he handled the situation.

The Acas guidance gives an overview on 'Handling discipline', as shown in **Figure 5.1**.

Figure 5.1   Handling discipline – an overview

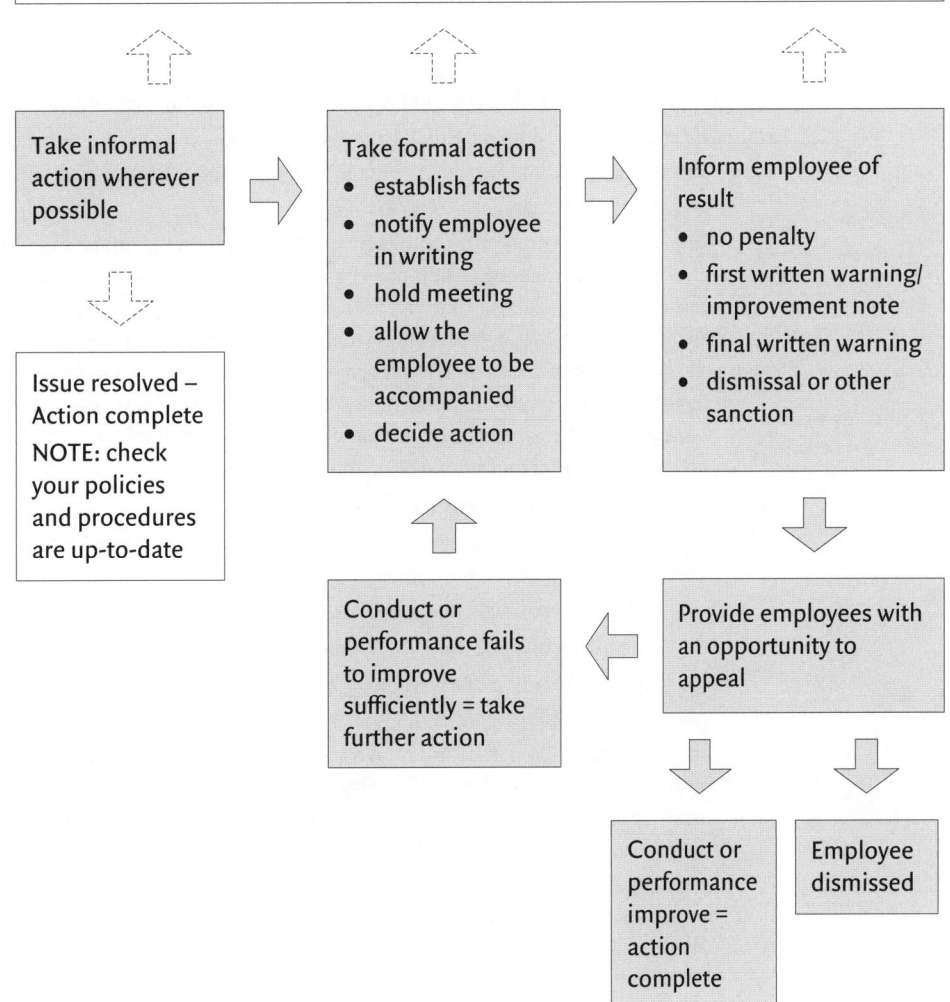

Source: Acas, *Discipline and grievances at work*

An extract from the Code follows:

Keys to handling disciplinary issues in the workplace

Establish the facts of each case

5.   It is important to carry out necessary investigations of potential disciplinary matters without unreasonable delay to establish the facts of the case. In some cases this will require the holding of an investigatory meeting with the employee before proceeding to any disciplinary hearing. In others, the investigatory stage will be the collation of evidence by the employer for use at any disciplinary hearing.

6.   In misconduct cases, where practicable, different people should carry out the investigation and disciplinary hearing.

7.   If there is an investigatory meeting this should not by itself result in any disciplinary action. Although there is no statutory right for an employee to be accompanied at a formal investigatory meeting, such a right may be allowed under an employer's own procedure.

8.   In cases where a period of suspension with pay is considered necessary, this period should be as brief as possible, should be kept under review and it should be made clear that this suspension is not considered a disciplinary action.

Inform the employee of the problem

9.   If it is decided that there is a disciplinary case to answer, the employee should be notified of this in writing. This notification should contain sufficient information about the alleged misconduct or poor performance and its possible consequences to enable the employee to prepare to answer the case at a disciplinary meeting. It would normally be appropriate to provide copies of any written evidence, which may include any witness statements, with the notification.

10.   The notification should also give details of the time and venue for the disciplinary meeting and advise the employee of their right to be accompanied at the meeting.

Hold a meeting with the employee to discuss the problem

11.   The meeting should be held without unreasonable delay whilst allowing the employee reasonable time to prepare their case.

12.   Employers and employees (and their companions) should make every effort to attend the meeting. At the meeting the employer should explain the complaint against the employee and go through the evidence that has been gathered. The employee should be allowed to set out their case and answer any allegations that have been made. The employee should also be given a reasonable opportunity to ask questions, present evidence and call relevant witnesses. They should also be given an opportunity to raise points about any information provided by witnesses. Where an employer or employee intends to call relevant witnesses they should give advance notice that they intend to do this.

Allow the employee to be accompanied at the meeting

13.   Workers have a statutory right to be accompanied by a companion where the disciplinary meeting could result in:

-    a formal warning being issued; or

-    the taking of some other disciplinary action; or

-    the confirmation of a warning or some other disciplinary action (appeal hearings).

14.   The statutory right is to be accompanied by a fellow worker, a trade union representative, or an official employed by a trade union. A trade union representative who is not an employed official must have been certified by their union as being competent to accompany a worker. Employers must agree to a worker's request to be accompanied by any companion from one of these categories. Workers may also alter their choice of companion if they wish. As a matter of good practice, in making their choice workers should bear in mind the practicalities of the arrangements. For instance, a worker may choose to be accompanied by a companion who is suitable, willing and available on site rather than someone from a geographically remote location.

15.   To exercise the statutory right to be accompanied workers must make a reasonable request. What is reasonable will depend on the circumstances of each individual case. A request to be accompanied does not have to be in writing or within a certain timeframe. However, a worker should provide enough time for the employer to deal with the companion's attendance at the meeting. Workers should also consider how they make their request so that it is clearly understood, for instance by letting the employer know in advance the name of the companion where possible and whether they are a fellow worker or trade union official or representative.

16.   If a worker's chosen companion will not be available at the time proposed for the hearing by the employer, the employer must postpone the hearing to a time proposed by the worker provided that the alternative time is both reasonable and not more than five working days after the date originally proposed.

17.   The companion should be allowed to address the hearing to put and sum up the worker's case, respond on behalf of the worker to any views expressed at the meeting and confer with the worker during the hearing. The companion does not, however, have the right to answer questions on the worker's behalf, address the hearing if the worker does not wish it or prevent the employer from explaining their case.

Decide on appropriate action

18.   After the meeting decide whether or not disciplinary or any other action is justified and inform the employee accordingly in writing.

19. Where misconduct is confirmed or the employee is found to be performing unsatisfactorily it is usual to give the employee a written warning. A further act of misconduct or failure to improve performance within a set period would normally result in a final written warning.

20. If an employee's first misconduct or unsatisfactory performance is sufficiently serious, it may be appropriate to move directly to a final written warning. This might occur where the employee's actions have had, or are liable to have, a serious or harmful impact on the organisation.

21. A first or final written warning should set out the nature of the misconduct or poor performance and the change in behaviour or improvement in performance required (with timescale). The employee should be told how long the warning will remain current. The employee should be informed of the consequences of further misconduct, or failure to improve performance, within the set period following a final warning. For instance that it may result in dismissal or some other contractual penalty such as demotion or loss of seniority.

22. A decision to dismiss should only be taken by a manager who has the authority to do so. The employee should be informed as soon as possible of the reasons for the dismissal, the date on which the employment contract will end, the appropriate period of notice and their right of appeal.

23. Some acts, termed gross misconduct, are so serious in themselves or have such serious consequences that they may call for dismissal without notice for a first offence. But a fair disciplinary process should always be followed, before dismissing for gross misconduct.

24. Disciplinary rules should give examples of acts which the employer regards as acts of gross misconduct. These may vary according to the nature of the organisation and what it does, but might include things such as theft or fraud, physical violence, gross negligence or serious insubordination.

25. Where an employee is persistently unable or unwilling to attend a disciplinary meeting without good cause the employer should make a decision on the evidence available.

Provide employees with an opportunity to appeal

26. Where an employee feels that disciplinary action taken against them is wrong or unjust they should appeal against the decision. Appeals should be heard without unreasonable delay and ideally at an agreed time and place. Employees should let employers know the grounds for their appeal in writing.

27. The appeal should be dealt with impartially and wherever possible, by a manager who has not previously been involved in the case.

28. Workers have a statutory right to be accompanied at appeal hearings.

29. Employees should be informed in writing of the results of the appeal hearing as soon as possible.

The Acas Guidance gives the following examples:

---

1. An employee in a small firm makes a series of mistakes in letters to one of your key customers promising impossible delivery dates. The customer is upset at your firm's failure to meet delivery dates and threatens to take his business elsewhere.

   You are the owner of the business and carry out an investigation and invite the employee to a disciplinary meeting. You inform her of her right to be accompanied by a colleague or an employee representative.

   Example outcome of meeting

   At the meeting the employee does not give a satisfactory explanation for the mistakes and admits that her training covered the importance of agreeing realistic delivery dates with her manager. During your investigation, her team leader and section manager told you they had stressed to the employee the importance of agreeing delivery dates with them before informing the customer. In view of the seriousness of the mistakes and the possible impact on the business, you issue the employee with a final written warning. You inform the employee that failure to improve will lead to dismissal and of her right to appeal.

Example outcome of meeting in different circumstances

At the meeting, the employee reveals that her team leader would not let her attend training as the section was too busy. Subsequently the team leader was absent sick and the employee asked the section manager for help with setting delivery dates. The manager said he was too busy and told the employee to 'use her initiative'. Your other investigations support the employee's explanation. You inform the employee that you will not be taking disciplinary action and will make arrangements for her to be properly trained. You decide to carry out a review of general management standards on supervision and training.

2.   A member of your telephone sales team has been to lunch to celebrate success in an exam. He returns from lunch in a very merry mood, is slurring his speech and is evidently not fit to carry out his duties. You decide to send him home and invite him in writing to a disciplinary meeting setting out his alleged behaviour of gross misconduct for which he could be dismissed. Your letter includes information about his right to be accompanied by a colleague or an employee representative. At the meeting he admits he had too much to drink, is very apologetic and promises that such a thing will not happen again. He is one of your most valued members of staff and has an exemplary record over his 10 years service with you. You know that being unfit for work because of excessive alcohol is listed in your company rules as gross misconduct. In view of the circumstances and the employee's record, however, you decide not to dismiss him but give him a final written warning. You inform the employee of his right to appeal.

Note: The Guidance is not the same as the Code and is not statutorily binding; although it can still be referred to in terms of fairness, breaches of it do not count for s 207A purposes (see **5.6.2**).

Some principles derived from case law

Characterisation of the misconduct

As mentioned above (**5.2.2.2**), it is important that employers correctly characterise misconduct, in particular if it is said to be gross misconduct, as this may trigger different procedural routes in any disciplinary policy, but will also be relevant as to whether a decision to dismiss is reasonable. It will also have implications for wrongful dismissal (see **Chapter 2**). Ultimately, to dismiss for gross misconduct, an employee's conduct has to be so serious that it warrants dismissal without prior warnings and without notice.

This was considered by the EAT in the case of *Eastlands Homes Partnership Ltd v Cunningham* (UKEAT/0272/13), where Mr Cunningham had been a caretaker in a care home for the elderly, run by the respondent housing association, for 32 years. He had an exemplary record. One of the tenants left his entire estate to Mr Cunningham and his wife. Mr Cunningham's wife was appointed sole executor of his will. The respondent's code of conduct prevented employees accepting gifts worth more than £50, but also stated that any gifts must be approved by the management. Mr Cunningham failed to notify the respondent of his inheritance until after a disciplinary investigation had begun. He was dismissed for gross misconduct on the basis of a serious breach of trust occasioned by his non-disclosure. The employment tribunal said that the dismissal was unfair and wrongful. The EAT allowed the respondent's appeal. The EAT said that the tribunal had failed to analyse the misconduct or the respondent's approach to that misconduct, in terms of whether it was capable of amounting to gross misconduct or whether it was reasonable for the respondent to believe it was gross misconduct.

In most cases of misconduct, notice (or, if the contract so provides, payment in lieu) should still be given in accordance with the contract. However, in the case of gross misconduct, this amounts to a repudiation of the contract by the employee, entitling the employer to terminate without notice or give payment in lieu (see **Chapter 2**).

Note that where a tribunal finds that the conduct justifying a dismissal was not gross misconduct, so as not to justify summary dismissal (ie without notice), this will not (necessarily) mean that the dismissal is unfair, although it may mean that the dismissal is wrongful if no notice was given.

Warnings

The Acas Code of Practice provides for a graduated system of warnings. Warnings are a critical part of the disciplinary and dismissal process. Depending on the seriousness of the misconduct, they may be oral, written or final. Warnings should usually have some sort of fixed time-limit. For serious misconduct, however, it may be appropriate to skip the imposition of a first written warning and, for gross misconduct, to dismiss without warning (see paras 18–22 of the Code, above). In *Sandwell & West Birmingham Hospitals NHS Trust v Westwood* (UKEAT/0032/09), the EAT held that the question of what amounts to gross misconduct is a mixed question of law and fact: as a matter of law it connotes deliberate wrongdoing or gross negligence. Thus tribunals must consider the character of the conduct and whether it was so serious as to amount to gross misconduct (see above).

In *Davies v Sandwell MBC* [2013] IRLR 374, the Court of Appeal held that it is not open to the Employment Tribunal (ET) to re-open a warning. Rather, 'the function of the ET is to apply the objective statutory test of reasonableness to determine whether the ... warning was a circumstance, which a reasonable employer could reasonably take into account ...' The Court of Appeal agreed that it is relevant for the ET to consider 'whether the final warning was issued in good faith, whether there were prima facie grounds for following the warning procedure and whether it was manifestly inappropriate to issue the warning'.

In *General Dynamics Information Technology Ltd v Carranza* (UKEAT/0107/14), the EAT allowed an appeal against an employment tribunal decision holding that a dismissal was unfair because the employer had not revised a final written warning. See too *John-Charles v NHS Business Services Authority* (EAT/0105/15) where the EAT held that it was not unreasonable for the employer to take a warning into account, notwithstanding that the employee had appealed it. However, whilst relevant to the decision, it was unfair that the employee was not told that the decision maker became minded to dismiss only once she learned of the warning – he should have been entitled to make representations on that factor. In *Way v Spectrum Property Care Ltd* [2015] EWCA Civ 381, the Court of Appeal remitted a case where bad faith in issuing a warning was alleged, but not decided upon by the ET.

It is clear that where a previous warning has expired, it may not be taken into account in a case in which, but for the previous warning, the employer would not have shown a reason for dismissing the employee (*Diosynth Ltd v Thomson* [2006] IRLR 284). However, the Court of Appeal confirmed in *Airbus UK Ltd v Webb* [2008] IRLR 309 that an expired warning may be taken into account where the expired final warning was not the reason, or the principal reason, shown for dismissal, but rather its relevance was to whether the range of reasonable responses to the later misconduct included dismissal for that misconduct. It might also be relevant where an allegation of inconsistent treatment is raised by the employee. The absence of previous misconduct and of a final warning may provide a reason for imposing a lesser penalty on another employee. (See too *Stratford v Auto Trail VR Ltd* (UKEAT/0116/16).)

If an employee is at risk of dismissal, he must be told of this in advance of the hearing, otherwise the dismissal may be unfair. See, for example, *Boyd v Renfrewshire Council* [2008] CSIH 36. Mr Boyd was summarily dismissed for gross misconduct in 'deliberately and wilfully' taking an unauthorised break and failing to complete his work. The tribunal found that the dismissal was unfair because it had not been alleged until after the disciplinary hearing that Mr Boyd's actions were 'wilful', nor had there previously been any mention of gross misconduct or the possibility of dismissal. The tribunal's decision was upheld by the Court of Session.

In *Way v Spectrum Property Care Ltd* [2015] EWCA Civ 381, the Court of Appeal looked at whether, where an employee alleges that a previous warning was in bad faith, there is any obligation on the employer or the employment tribunal to reconsider that. The claimant was dismissed for misconduct in December 2013. Previously, in December 2010, he had been given a final 12-month written warning and informed of his right of appeal against the imposition of the warning. He said he was told not to appeal, as there was a risk it could end up with dismissal. The warning letter stated that the claimant needed to be familiar with the policies and procedures in the Staff Handbook. Both before and after the December 2010 warning (which was not connected to sending e-mails), the claimant had sent 'inappropriate' e-mails, which were not in accordance with the staff policies and procedures. Management carried out a general crackdown on inappropriate e-mail usage, and judged this employee's e-mails to fall into a 'red' category, which meant that they were regarded as warranting a final warning (as opposed to a gold warning, which would have meant that they were sufficiently serious to initiate the gross misconduct disciplinary process, or an amber warning, which would have resulted only in a letter of concern). However, because the claimant was already on a final written warning, it was decided there should be a disciplinary hearing, as a result of which the claimant was dismissed. At his appeal, he raised what he said was the bad faith of the previous warning. That contention was rejected. The employment tribunal and the EAT both found the dismissal to be fair, relying principally on the live final written warning. The claimant appealed. The Court of Appeal referred to *Davies v Sandwell* (above), which held that the essential principle is that it is legitimate for an employer to rely on a final warning when deciding to dismiss for a further offence, provided that it was issued in good faith, there were at least prima facie grounds for imposing it and it must not have been manifestly inappropriate to issue it. The Court also referred to *Wincanton Group plc v Stone* [2013] IRLR 178, where the EAT gave specific guidance to tribunals (para 37) to the effect:

> If a tribunal is not satisfied that the first warning was issued for an oblique motive or was manifestly inappropriate or, put another way, was not issued in good faith nor with prima facie grounds for making it, then the earlier warning will be valid. If it is so satisfied, the earlier warning will not be valid and cannot and should not be relied upon subsequently.

The Court of Appeal said that the fact that the claimant had been given a final warning was highly relevant to the reasonableness or otherwise of any subsequent decision to dismiss him, as it meant that he had been found guilty of misconduct and had been warned that a further act of misconduct meant he was likely to be dismissed. The warning had therefore taken him a step further down the disciplinary road to dismissal. The Court of Appeal went on to say, however, that where a warning is given in bad faith, it should not be taken into account in deciding whether there is, or was, sufficient reason for dismissing an employee. It was not reasonable for an employer to take into account such a warning; and it would not be in accordance with equity or the substantial merits of the case to do so. Whether a warning was given in bad faith was a matter of fact, which a tribunal would, in an appropriate case, have to determine for itself on the evidence. The tribunal could not therefore rely on the employer's own assessment of the position.

Bandara v BBC (UKEAT/0335/15) is a case where a tribunal held that even though a final written warning was manifestly inappropriate, the dismissal was fair. The EAT overturned that decision. While noting that the general rule is that earlier disciplinary decisions should not be reopened as a matter of course, according to the EAT, a tribunal must:

> examine whether the employer relied on the final written warning.... Much will depend, therefore, on whether the employer attached significant weight to the manifestly inappropriate final warning. If the employer did not, for example if it treated the warning as no more than background or as indicative of the standard to be expected of an employee, and if in reality it dismissed for the misconduct alleged in the new disciplinary proceedings, the Employment Tribunal may be entitled to find that the dismissal

was fair, though it must take care to apply the s 98(4) test. But if the employer attached significant weight to the warning, for example starting from the proposition that the employee was to be dismissed for any significant misconduct because he was already subject to a final written warning, then it is difficult to see how the employer's decision can have been reasonable.

Suspension

In July 2018, Acas published updated guidance on when and how to suspend employees and the process that should be adopted. Readers should refer to this where appropriate, bearing in mind that it is not binding.

Depending on all the facts, an employer may wish to suspend the employee pending the outcome of an investigation. So long as the employer is not under an obligation to provide the employee with work (see **1.7.1.1**), he will not normally be acting in breach of contract to suspend the employee with pay. Clearly, if there is a contractual clause allowing for suspension with pay, there can then be no argument about breach of the right to be provided with work.

Note, however, that in *Gogay v Hertfordshire County Council* [2000] IRLR 703 (see **2.4.1.5**), the Court of Appeal upheld the High Court's finding that suspension of an employee was in breach of the implied duty of trust and confidence. The woman employee had been suspended (on full pay under a contractual clause) pending the outcome of an investigation. The letter sent to the employee said that 'the issue to be investigated is an allegation of sexual abuse by a young person in our care'. In the event, the investigation concluded that there was no case to answer and that the child had never said anything which might be construed as an allegation of abuse. The Court of Appeal says that it does not inevitably follow that an employee should be suspended merely because there are reasonable grounds for an investigation. There are other options open to an employer, such as transfer. There must be reasonable and proper cause for a suspension. In the recent case of *Agoreyo v London Borough of Lambeth* [2017] EWHC 2019 (QB), the High Court was critical of a 'knee-jerk' suspension. The High Court stressed that suspension is not a neutral act but 'inevitably casts a shadow over the employee's competence'. Explanations given at the time should be considered, along with alternatives to suspension. The High Court did not accept in this case that suspension of a teacher was necessary for child protection reasons.

Factors to consider before suspending include:

- How serious is the alleged offence?
- Are fuller preliminary investigations appropriate before suspending?
- Are there risks if an employee remains (theft, damage, repeat, danger to others)?
- Might the employee influence the investigation (influence witnesses, remove evidence)?
- What is the employee's role, length of service, disciplinary record?
- How have others been treated?
- Are there alternatives available?

The Acas guidance makes it clear that suspension with pay may be considered for certain cases such as gross misconduct or where relationships have broken down, or where it is considered that there is a risk to an employer's property or responsibilities to others. However, the guidance emphasises that such suspension should be imposed only after careful consideration and should be reviewed to ensure that it is not unnecessarily protracted.

The High Court held in *Agoreyo v London Borough of Lambeth* [2017] EWHC 2019 (QB) that suspension of a teacher who was accused of using excess force to restrain schoolchildren was a kneejerk reaction and a breach of trust and confidence (see **3.4.3** above).

Investigations

The Acas Code sets out that an employer should establish the facts of each case. This means that, generally speaking, before there is a disciplinary hearing, an employer will need to carry out an investigation into the alleged misconduct. Depending on the size of the organisation, it is preferable for different people to carry out the investigation and the hearing. The employer should carry out the investigation as quickly as possible.

An investigation may require the employer to interview the employee and get his account of the incident, and also to interview any witnesses or others involved in the incident. The employer should try to take notes of any such interviews. It may be appropriate for an employer to examine any physical evidence that may exist, for example where something is recorded on CCTV.

The employer should consider the results of the investigation and decide whether it is appropriate to proceed to a disciplinary hearing. Where the matter is to proceed to a hearing, the employer should normally make any notes of interview and other evidence relied upon available to the employee before the hearing.

The Court of Appeal considered the scope of a reasonable investigation in a conduct dismissal in *Shrestha v Genesis Housing Association Ltd* [2015] EWCA Civ 94. The claimant contended, when challenged over allegations of inflating his expenses, that there was an obligation on his employer to investigate in full all the defences he advanced. The Court of Appeal said such an approach would add an 'unwarranted gloss' to the range of reasonable responses test. Any investigation should be looked at as a whole. Employers must consider those defences that are advanced, but whether and to what extent it is necessary to carry out a specific inquiry into each of them will depend on the circumstances. On the facts in this case, the assessment, that the claimant's explanations were not plausible, was a reasonable assessment in the circumstances, with the result that it was unnecessary for the employer to pursue any further inquiries into the claimant's explanations.

The Court of Appeal held, in *Sainsbury's Supermarkets Ltd v Hitt* [2003] IRLR 23, that the range of reasonable responses test 'applies as much to the question of whether the investigation into the suspected misconduct was reasonable in all the circumstances as it does to ... the decision to dismiss'. In *Gratton v Hutton* (2003) unreported, 1 July, the EAT emphasised that the test is not whether further investigation might reasonably have been carried out but whether the investigation which *had* been carried out could be regarded by a reasonable employer as adequate. Furthermore, the Court of Appeal held in *Panama v London Borough of Hackney* [2003] IRLR 278 that the employer's failure to obtain evidence to support an allegation of misconduct meant that it neither had reasonable grounds for its belief, nor had it carried out as much investigation into the matter as was reasonable in all the circumstances.

In *Salford Royal NHS Foundation Trust v Roldan* [2010] IRLR 721, the Court of Appeal confirmed that when carrying out an investigation into allegations of gross misconduct, employers should take into account the gravity of the potential consequences for an employee. This may mean a more thorough investigation is required in cases where there are potentially significant consequences for the employee if he loses his job. In *Roldan*, the employee, who was a nurse, lost her work permit and consequently her right to stay in the UK, and also became the subject of a criminal investigation by the police.

An investigation need not necessarily be recorded in writing, although a written record of witnesses' evidence is generally required (*Now Motor Retailing Ltd v Mulvihill* (UKEAT/0052/15)).

In *NHS 24 v Pillar* (UKEATS/0005/16), the EAT decided that an employment tribunal was wrong to find a dismissal unfair because an investigation report included details of previous incidents that had not resulted in disciplinary proceedings. Applying *Sandwell & West Birmingham Hospitals NHS Trust v Westwood* (UKEAT/0032/09), the tribunal concluded that it was reasonable for the employer to regard the claimant's conduct as gross misconduct when taking into account the previous incidents. However, it said that the investigation was not reasonable. The EAT allowed the appeal: while there may be cases where an unfair dismissal investigation might fall foul of *BHS v Burchell* (below), the starting point was the 'sufficiency' of the investigation, not the gathering of too much information. This case is also useful in highlighting the differences between an investigator and the person hearing the disciplinary proceedings.

Conduct of the hearing

In *Ramsey v Walkers Snack Foods Ltd* [2004] IRLR 754 the EAT confirmed that it is possible to have a fair procedure where witnesses for the employer insist on anonymity because, on the facts, there was a very real fear of reprisals against the witnesses. In *Linfood Cash & Carry Ltd v Thompson* [1989] IRLR 235 the EAT set out guidelines to assist in balancing the need for a fair hearing with protecting witnesses. In outline, the employer should ensure that the information given by the informant is reduced into writing, noting key facts such as date, time and place, clarity of observation, circumstantial evidence, such as the reason for the presence of the informer and why certain small details are memorable, whether the informant has suffered at the hands of the accused or has any other reason to fabricate, whether from personal grudge or any other reason.

Further investigation can then take place, including inquiries into the character and background of the informant, or any other information which may tend to add or detract from the value of the information. If the employer is satisfied that the fear is genuine then a decision will need to be made whether or not to continue with the disciplinary process. If it is to continue, it is best if, at each stage of the process, the member of management responsible for the hearing should himself interview the informant and satisfy himself that weight is to be given to the information. The written statement of the informant, if necessary with omissions to avoid identification, should be made available to the employee and his representatives. Full and careful notes should be taken during all stage of the disciplinary process, and if evidence from an investigating officer is to be taken at a hearing, it should, where possible, be prepared in a written form.

The tribunal will want to make clear findings as to the extent of the respondent's investigation into the reasons why the informant is insisting on anonymity, and then carry out a balancing act between the respondent's perceived need to protect the identity of the informant and natural justice that the claimant should know sufficiently the nature of the case against him, applying the band of reasonable responses test.

The EAT confirmed that there is 'no rule of law which renders it incumbent on an employer, when dismissing an employee for misconduct ... [to give] the employee who is liable to be dismissed the opportunity to cross-examine the person making the complaint' (*Santamera v Express Cargo Forwarding t/a IEC Ltd* [2003] IRLR 273).

In *Corus UK Ltd v Mainwaring* (UKEAT/0053/07) the EAT held that there is no obligation to take a witness statement from an employee who 'tips off' an employer about a malingering employee, where the employer subsequently relies on his own evidence (eg, video/medical) before dismissing.

In *Hargreaves v Governing Body of Manchester Grammar School* (UKEAT/0048/18) the EAT held that it was within the band of reasonable responses for an employer not to disclose to a disciplinary panel evidence from potential witnesses, who said that they had seen nothing. The tribunal was entitled to conclude that the employer had conducted a fair investigation and that the dismissal was not unfair.

Care needs to be taken as to who the decision maker is – ie who takes the actual decision to dismiss. This would usually be a manager. Managers may need, on occasions, to take advice from human resources (HR) about the process and any issues that arise during the hearing. If the manager's decision is improperly influenced by HR, it is likely that this will render any dismissal unfair (see *Chabra v West London Mental Health NHS Trust* [2014] ICR 194 and *Ramphal v Department for Transport* (UKEAT/0352/14)). An investigating or disciplinary officer is entitled to call on advice from HR, but HR must limit advice to questions of law, procedure and/or process; HR should avoid straying into areas of culpability and appropriateness of sanctions.

Failure to attend a hearing

An employer may be faced with an employee who is unable or refuses to attend a disciplinary hearing by reason of ill-health. This can cause a dilemma for the employer, who may be keen to get the hearing dealt with quickly. It may be sensible in this situation to ask the employee to produce a note from his GP to the effect that he is not fit to attend the hearing (a 'fit note' stating that the employee cannot work may not be sufficient). Alternatively, an employer might ask its occupational health department to assess the employee. Other options, such as a telephone hearing or a hearing at a neutral venue near the employee's home, or allowing the employee to make written submissions, should be considered where appropriate. If none of these options is possible, the employer should consider adjourning the hearing for a short period. Ultimately, it may be necessary to go ahead in the employee's absence. Tribunals will expect the employer to explain why it went ahead and what efforts were made to get the employee to attend, and to have a full note of the hearing. The employer should also take great care to make sure that the decision, especially if it is one of dismissal, is communicated properly to the employee.

In *Talon Engineering Ltd v Smith* (UKEAT/0236/17), the EAT held that the employment tribunal was entitled to conclude that a refusal to postpone a hearing for two weeks to allow Mrs Smith's union representative to accompany her was, in the circumstances, outside the range of reasonable responses. Although the employer had complied with the rules governing the right to be accompanied, this did not automatically mean that the dismissal was procedurally fair.

Right of appeal

The employee should have the right to appeal against any disciplinary action taken. In *Afzal v East London Pizza Ltd* (UKEAT/0265/17), the EAT emphasised that the whole dismissal process, including an appeal, was relevant to the question of fairness. There has been some discussion over the years as to whether an appeal can remedy procedural defects at the initial hearing. Most appeals are not a full rehearing of all the facts and evidence but tend to be reviews of what has gone before. The conventional wisdom was that procedural defects at the initial hearing could only be cured by an appeal which took the form of a full rehearing (which was a matter of substance not label – see, for example, *Whitbread & Co v Mills* [1988] IRLR 501). However, the Court of Appeal in *Taylor v OCS Group Ltd* [2006] EWCA Civ 702 disapproved of that approach, and said that the essential question, when deciding whether a dismissal is fair under ERA 1996, s 98(4), is whether the employer acted reasonably. The Court held that where a first hearing is defective, the appeal can cure the defect if the appeal is comprehensive, and that the distinction drawn in previous case law between reviews and rehearings is not helpful. According to Smith LJ, 'what matters is not whether the internal appeal was technically a rehearing or a review but whether the disciplinary process as a whole was fair'. In *Adeshina v St George's University Hospitals NHS Foundation Trust and Others* (UKEAT/0293/14), the EAT held that procedural defects were cured at an appeal hearing and thus rendered a dismissal fair.

In *Patel v Folkestone Nursing Home Ltd* [2018] EWCA Civ 1689, the Court of Appeal, applying *Salmon v Castlebeck Care (Teesdale) Ltd* (UKEAT/0304/14), found that an appeal, which had overturned an earlier dismissal finding, revoked the dismissal and reinstated the employee who was therefore prevented from bringing unfair and wrongful dismissal claims.

In *McMillan v Airedale NHS Foundation Trust* [2014] EWCA Civ 1031, the Court of Appeal held that as a right to appeal against a disciplinary sanction is for the employee's benefit, an increase in sanction would be permitted only if there was an express term in the employment contract allowing this. In McMillan the claimant, a hospital consultant, was disciplined and given a final written warning, following a finding of misconduct. She appealed against the sanction. The appeal panel upheld the finding (after a rehearing) and took steps to reconvene to consider the appropriate sanction. The claimant withdrew her appeal and sought an injunction to prevent the appeal panel considering sanctions. The High Court held:

(a)   that the appeal panel could not, in the absence of express contractual power, impose a more severe sanction;

(b)   because the appeal was withdrawn, the appeal panel could not reconvene to consider sanctions.

An injunction was granted. The Court of Appeal rejected the hospital's appeal and upheld the High Court's decision. Underhill LJ did accept that there was nothing wrong in principle with an employer's reserving an express power to increase sanctions on appeal.

The EAT held in *Adeshina v St George's University Hospitals NHS Foundation Trust and Others* (UKEAT/ 0293/14) that it endorsed the Acas advice that the person hearing the appeal be more senior to the original decision taker but that, on the facts, a less senior member of a panel of three (where the other two were more senior) did not render the decision unfair.

Dealing with grievances during a disciplinary process

It can often be a vexed issue for an employer whether a disciplinary process should be put on hold where an employee issues or has an on-going grievance. Employers can be wary of what might be seen as a delaying tactic. The Acas Code provides that the disciplinary process 'may' be temporarily suspended in order to deal with a grievance. The Acas Guidance suggests that where a grievance is raised during a meeting, 'it may sometimes be appropriate' to stop the meeting. An important consideration may be the extent to which the grievance and the disciplinary process are related or arise out of the same facts, or where the grievance is directed against an individual who is involved in the disciplinary process. It is in any event sensible for an employer in this situation, who does not suspend the disciplinary process, to keep a note of why it was not considered appropriate to do so.

The issue of whether the disciplinary process should be suspended was considered by the EAT in *Jinadu v Dockland Buses Ltd* (UKEAT/0434/14). Ms Jinadu was a bus driver for the respondent. Her driving was considered to be below standard and she was instructed to arrange a driving assessment. She did not do so and was eventually dismissed for gross misconduct. She appealed against the decision to dismiss her. The appeal was adjourned to allow her to take her assessment, as a result of which she was required to undertake some corrective training. She failed the training and the appeal was reconvened. At the appeal hearing, Ms Jinadu made various complaints, including of discrimination, against a number of members of the respondent's management. Her appeal against dismissal failed, on the basis of her failure to display an adequate standard of driving and the interests of public safety. An employment tribunal rejected her claim for unfair dismissal. She appealed to the EAT. One of the grounds of appeal was that the respondent should have considered suspending the disciplinary process while Ms Jinadu's grievances were considered. This ground was rejected by the EAT, although it gave no reasons for this. (Ms Jinadu succeeded in her appeal on other grounds.)

Social media

Social media have increasingly become relevant in unfair dismissal cases (see Acas research paper, *Workplaces and Social Networking – the Implications for Employment Relations* at <http:// www.acas.org.uk>). Employers often use information posted on Facebook and other social media sites as evidence of employees' wrongdoing. This can give rise to a question whether employers should be entitled to rely on such evidence (have they, for example, breached their employee's privacy in accessing the information, or are they interfering with an employee's right to free speech – see **Chapter 15**), but there may also be issues about the employee's use of social media sites during working hours and about what the employer regards as other inappropriate use of social media by staff.

In *Taylor v Somerfield Stores Ltd* (ETS/107487/2007), a supermarket warehouse employee was dismissed for posting video footage on YouTube which captured a colleague hitting another colleague with a plastic bag full of plastic bags in one of the employer's warehouses. The footage did not show who the employees were but did reveal the uniforms they were wearing. The footage was taken down after three days and had only eight hits while it was up, three of which were by the supermarket's managers after they discovered the footage was online. The supermarket held a disciplinary process and dismissed the employee for bringing the supermarket into disrepute and breaching health and safety rules. The employment tribunal found there was no evidence to indicate that the supermarket had been brought into disrepute and found the dismissal unfair. (See also *Teggert v TeleTech UK Ltd* (NIET/00704/11) and *Preece v JD Wetherspoons plc* (ET/2104806/10).)

The EAT held in *British Waterways Board v Smith* (UKEAT/0004/15) that it was fair to dismiss on the facts for derogatory comments made about the employer on Facebook. (In August 2016, a policeman (PC Graham Wise), who tweeted abuse about celebrities, was summarily dismissed by Cleveland Police after being found guilty of gross misconduct.) What is important is that employers have a policy on social networking, treat 'electronic behaviour' consistently with 'non-electronic behaviour' and react reasonably to issues around social networking.

In *Plant v API Microelectronics Ltd* (ET/3401454/2016), an employment tribunal held that the dismissal of a long-serving employee with a clean disciplinary record who had made derogatory remarks over social media about her employer was fair. There was a social media policy, the claimant was aware of it and what it entailed.

See '"I Lost My Job Over a Facebook Post – Was That Fair?" Discipline and Dismissal for Social Media Activity', 2019 *International Journal of Comparative Labour Law and Industrial Relations* (31 October 2018) for a good account of this area (available to download on SSRN at https://papers.ssrn.com/sol3/papers.cfm?abstract_id=3276055).

Suspected misconduct: the approach in *British Home Stores v Burchell* [1978] IRLR 379

What if the employer *suspects* misconduct by an employee? Does he have to be able to prove the employee did the act? An employer can still be fair in dismissing, provided the tribunal is satisfied that:

(a)   the employer had a genuine belief in guilt (this is really relevant to the reason for the dismissal);

(b)   the employer had reasonable grounds upon which to base the belief; and

(c)   the employer carried out a reasonable investigation.

Note: The burden of proof in relation to (b) and (c) is a neutral one, but (as a result of s 6 of the Employment Act 1980) the onus of proof (with regard to the reason for dismissal) lies on the employer. The first of the three elements of *Burchell* is relevant to reason, *not* reasonableness.

In *Boys and Girls Welfare Society* [1996] IRLR 129, the EAT said *BHS v Burchell* was inappropriate if there was no conflict on the facts, for example the employee admitted or did not dispute his guilt. Nevertheless, in *Whitbread plc (t/a Whitbread Medway Inns) v Hall* [2001] IRLR 275, the Court of Appeal made it clear that even where misconduct is admitted (so that an employer does not need to prove that it had reasonable grounds for its belief), an employer is still under a duty to follow a fair procedure, such as hearing explanations and considering other penalties besides dismissal (unless the offence is so heinous that a reasonable employer following good industrial practice could conclude that no explanation or mitigation would make any difference to the decision to dismiss). In *John Lewis plc v Coyne* [2001] IRLR 139, an employment tribunal held that a dismissal for making personal telephone calls (which was not denied), in breach of company rules, was unfair because the employer had failed to investigate the seriousness of the offence, including the purpose of the calls, whether there was any element of personal crisis and whether or not the conduct was persistent.

Criminal offences

What if an employee is charged with a criminal offence but denies guilt? This should be grounds for dismissal only where it has employment implications. For example:

(a)   Was the offence committed in the course of employment?

(b)   Was it an offence of dishonesty?

(c)   Was the employee in a position of trust?

(d)   Is the employee to be detained in custody?

The outcome of any subsequent criminal proceedings does not necessarily have any bearing on the issue of reasonableness. For example, in *Da Costa v Optalis* [1976] IRLR 178, the employee in question was dismissed from his job as a bookkeeper for not keeping proper accounts. He was later prosecuted but was acquitted. The employment tribunal held his dismissal to have been fair. The issues involved were different, as was the standard of proof to be applied.

An employer does not have to delay his decision pending the outcome of any criminal proceedings. He may, however, decide to suspend the employee pending the decision of the criminal court. In *A v B* [2003] IRLR 405, the EAT emphasised that 'the investigator ... should focus no less on any potential evidence that may exculpate or at least point to the innocence of the employee as he should on the evidence directed toward proving the charges against him'.

The EAT held in *Gondalia v* Tesco Stores (UKEAT/0320/14) that an Employment Judge had not erred when, in considering the fairness of a dismissal for allegedly dishonest conduct, he did not apply the criminal law test for dishonesty (known as the '*Ghosh* test': *R v Ghosh* [1982] 3 WLR 110). The appropriate question is whether the employer acted reasonably in treating the alleged dishonesty as a sufficient reason for dismissal.

Absence

Dealing with an employee's absence can be a complicated issue. In the first instance it can be important that an employer makes the right decision as to whether to treat absence as a conduct issue or as a capability issue. If the latter is appropriate, then a different procedure will need to be adopted from that which would be applied if the absence was a misconduct issue (see **5.4.2.1** above). Persistent lateness or absence may be a conduct issue, as would unauthorised absences and late returns from holiday. These may be properly dealt with under disciplinary processes.

In *Brighton & Sussex University Hospitals HNS Trust v Akinwunmi* (UKEAT/0345/16), the claimant, who was a consultant neurosurgeon, was dismissed after he took 20 months of unauthorised absence following complaints made about him by colleagues. There was a long and complicated history of tit-for-tat complaints. The hospital undertook a number of investigations and reports during the absence. The tribunal accepted that the hospital genuinely believed that the claimant's 20-month unauthorised absence was misconduct and that it had reasonable grounds for that belief. The key issue, however, was whether it was within the band of reasonable responses for them to dismiss the claimant for that reason. The tribunal found that the claimant had been unfairly dismissed. In its view, the situation here was similar to that of an employee who is disciplined for failing to obey a reasonable management instruction. What the hospital did not do during the absence was have any meaningful contact with the claimant. The tribunal found it had made no real efforts to address the claimant's concerns about his colleagues, and as such it had been reasonable for the claimant to refuse to return. In effect the tribunal viewed this as a reasonable failure by the claimant to follow an unreasonable management instruction. The EAT upheld the tribunal's decision. The case is a cautionary tale about dismissals for absence. While unauthorised absence can often be a straightforward misconduct issue – on the face of it an unauthorised absence of over a year would be thought to be a straightforward case for a fair dismissal finding – employers still need to look at the reason for the absence and, where it is or appears to be work-related, they will need to adopt appropriate processes to try to resolve it.

Summary

In coming to a decision whether a conduct dismissal is unfair, a tribunal has to consider not just the reason given by the employer for the dismissal, but whether it was a genuinely held reason, as well as whether dismissal was within the range of reasonable responses of a reasonable employer and whether a fair procedure was followed. This can involve the tribunal making findings of fact on the evidence as it is presented to it.

The Court of Appeal, in the recent case of *Newbound v Thames Water Utilities Ltd* [2015] EWCA Civ 677, looked in detail at when an employment tribunal was justified in finding that a decision to dismiss on the grounds of conduct was unfair (and also at when such a finding can be challenged on appeal). Mr Newbound was dismissed by Thames Water for misconduct after 34 years of service. He was employed to maintain Thames Water's water assets, including valves known as 'penstocks', which open and close sewers. During a complex, though routine, maintenance operation, which was supervised by others more senior, the claimant and a contractor carried out an inspection without wearing breathing apparatus, which was required for health and safety reasons. This was reported and an investigation was carried out. The claimant was not interviewed as part of the investigation. Possible charges of gross misconduct were identified against the claimant and another less experienced but more senior employee. In the event, gross misconduct charges were laid against the claimant and misconduct charges against the other employee. The claimant was told the nature of the charge and was suspended on full pay. Further investigations were carried out, including into the claimant's record and history. The claimant was not interviewed as part of this investigation. A disciplinary hearing found that he had committed a serious infringement of health and safety rules that amounted to gross misconduct. He was summarily dismissed for this, and it was later added that there was also some other substantial reason as there was a 'loss of trust and confidence'. (The Court of Appeal felt that although this was added as an 'afterthought', and was not an allegation that the claimant had had to meet before, nothing turned on this in that it was 'simply another label attached to the same set of facts'). The claimant appealed against the decision to dismiss him, acknowledging that there had been an error of judgement on his part, but stated that he was sorry and was willing to undergo refresher training. He also referred to his 34 years of service. The decision to dismiss him was upheld. The other employee received a 12-month written warning and had to undergo some additional training.

The claimant decided to issue a claim for unfair dismissal. He sought assistance from his trade union. The union refused to support him and, in a letter to him expressed in 'trenchant' terms, said that because he had been dismissed for 'a very significant and potentially very dangerous breach of health and safety, to both you and others … the failure to abide by the requirements as set out by the on site briefing is totally damning'. At some point this letter came into the possession of the employers, who made use of it in the tribunal proceedings when cross-examining the claimant. The employment tribunal judge did not mention this in his judgment, but said during the hearing that the views expressed in it could not be binding on him. (The Court of Appeal said that the judge was right to ignore the views expressed in the letter.)

The employment tribunal found that the claimant had been unfairly dismissed but held that he had made a 40% contribution to his dismissal (which impacted on the compensation he was awarded – see **5.6.2.2**). It was accepted that the reason for the dismissal was conduct. The employment tribunal judge expressed some concerns about the investigation but held that, overall, it was reasonable. (That finding was not challenged before the Court of Appeal.) The crucial question for the judge was 'whether the respondent acted reasonably or unreasonably in treating the claimant's conduct as a sufficient reason for dismissal, a question to be decided having regard to equity and the substantial merits of the case'. On the facts, the judge concluded that 'no reasonable employer would have dismissed the employee in the circumstances and that the decision to terminate his employment was perverse'. He also relied on the disparate treatment between the two employees.

The employers appealed to the EAT, which allowed their appeal and dismissed the claimant's claim. The EAT held, inter alia, that the judge had 'failed to consider the reasonableness of the gravity with which' the employer viewed the claimant's conduct. It criticised the judge for relying on the evidence that was given at the hearing before him, rather than on the evidence that was before the employer when taking the decision to dismiss. The EAT found he had 'impermissibly substituted his view of the importance' of a number of factors. On the disparate treatment point, the EAT held that this was 'erroneously based on the EJ's own view of the relative culpability' of the two employees.

The claimant appealed to the Court of Appeal. One of the issues for the Court was the extent to which appellate courts could interfere with the findings of an employment tribunal, the only legal basis for an appeal from an employment tribunal being on a question of law (ETA 1996, s 21(1)). One consequence of this is that a finding of primary fact by an employment tribunal cannot be overturned on appeal unless there is no evidence to support it (*Fuller v London Borough of Brent* [2011] IRLR 414). The Court found that the employment tribunal judge was entitled to reach the conclusions that he had, that he made no error of law and that the EAT should not have interfered with his decision. With regard to the judge's reliance on the claimant's length of service, the Court held that 'the fact that Mr Newbound was an employee of 34 years' service with a clean disciplinary record was a factor the judge was fully entitled to take into account: it would have been extraordinary if he had not done so'. On the disparity of treatment issue, the Court held that there had rarely been 'such an obvious case of unjustified disparity'.

This case is a very useful and recent point of reference as to how an employment tribunal approaches an unfair dismissal case. It is well worth a read.

5.4.2.3 Redundancy

(The Acas Code of Practice on Disciplinary and Grievance Procedures does not apply to redundancy dismissals, but there is an Acas advisory booklet on handling redundancy.)

Where a dismissal is for redundancy, the tribunal must be satisfied that it was reasonable to dismiss *that* employee by reason of redundancy. It is not enough to show that it was reasonable to dismiss *an* employee (*Williams v Compair Maxam Ltd* [1982] IRLR 83).

In *Kellogg Brown & Root (UK) Ltd v Fitton & Another* (UKEAT/0205/16), the claimants were dismissed following a workplace closure. The closure was announced in April 2015 and the employees were told they would move in July 2015. The claimants had refused to relocate and they were dismissed.

The mobility clause provided:

> The location of your employment is _____ but the company may require you to work at a different location including any new office location of the company either in the UK or overseas either on a temporary or permanent basis. You agree to comply with this requirement unless exceptional circumstances prevail.

The tribunal asked whether the instruction had been legitimate – in the sense that it was a valid contractual requirement – and concluded that it was not; whether the instruction was reasonable, again concluding that it was not; finally, whether the refusal was reasonable, concluding that it was (the claimants faced an additional 100 mile commute each day, one had brought a property near to his former workplace and did not have a car (although a car share might be possible), and the other had worked near to his home town for the respondent for 25 years, would soon be 64 and was due to retire a year later). The judgment cites and applies *United Bank Ltd v Akhtar* (see above at **1.8.2.3**). The tribunal concluded that the dismissals were unfair.

The essence of a fair redundancy dismissal is (1) fair selection (fair criteria applied fairly), (2) warning and consultation, and (3) alternative employment (*Williams*). In *Polkey v AE Dayton Services Ltd* [1988] ICR 142, HL, it was stated that in the case of redundancy, the employer will not normally act reasonably unless he:

(a)   warns and consults any employees affected or their representatives;

(b)   adopts a fair basis on which to select for redundancy, ie identifies an appropriate pool from which to select, and uses objective criteria and applies those criteria fairly (see *British Aerospace plc v Green* [1995] IRLR 433, CA); and

(c)   takes such steps as may be reasonable to avoid or minimise redundancy by redeployment within his own organisation.

See also *Buchanan v Tilcon Ltd* [1983] IRLR 417, *FDR Ltd v Holloway* [1995] IRLR 400, *John Brown Engineering Ltd v Brown and Others* [1997] IRLR 90 and *King v Eaton Ltd* [1996] IRLR 199. Where a trade union is involved, readers should refer to *Williams and Others v Compair Maxam Ltd* (above).

Issues of fairness and reasonableness still need to be judged by reference to the 'range of reasonable responses' test (see *Beddell v West Ferry Printers* [2000] ICR 1263). In *Drake International Systems Ltd v O'Hare* (UKEAT/0384/03), the EAT emphasised that tribunals should not impose their own views as to the reasonableness of the selection criteria or the implementation of the criteria: the correct question was whether the selection was one that a reasonable employer acting reasonably could have made. One of the tricky areas in redundancy is how an employer determines the 'pool' of employees that is being considered for redundancy, even if it might be thought that only one role is being lost and that there should therefore be a pool of just one. Employers need to consult about the pool and to consider whether there are other employees occupying similar roles who should be included in it. In *Hendy Banks v Fairbrother* (UKEAT/0691/04) the EAT confirmed that the 'range of reasonable responses' test applied when deciding whether an employer had acted reasonably in selecting a pool for redundancy, ie the group of employees from which those to be made redundant will be selected. The tribunal must first decide whether the pool selected by the employer fell within a 'range of reasonable responses'. In *Wrexham Golf Club Ltd v Ingham* (UKEAT/0190/12) the EAT held that it can be reasonable to focus upon a single employee without developing a pool or even considering developing a pool. In *Leventhal Ltd v North* (UKEAT/0265/04) the EAT upheld a decision that a redundancy dismissal was unfair (on the facts) because the employer had not considered 'bumping' (see also *Fulcrum Pharma (Europe) Ltd v Bonassera and Another* (UKEAT/0198/10) (see **4.2.3.3**). However, in *Halpin v Sandpiper Books Ltd* (UKEAT/0171/11) the EAT held that it was not unreasonable not to 'bump' another employee and that a pool of one was reasonable. (See also *Capita Hartshead Ltd v Byard* (UKEAT/0445/11), where the EAT held that a redundancy dismissal was unfair where the employer used a selection pool of one.) In *Fulcrum Pharma (Europe) Ltd v Bonassera*, the EAT said that the following factors should be considered when assessing whether others should be included in a pool, where one post is being made redundant:

•   whether there is a vacancy

•   how different the jobs are

•   how different the salaries are

•   the relative lengths of service of those holding the jobs

- the qualifications of the employee in danger of redundancy.

Ultimately, the test is whether the employer has 'genuinely applied its mind' to the composition of the pool and whether the dismissal fell within the range of reasonable responses. The *Capita* case contains a useful summary of the law on redundancy selection.

Having decided upon the pool for selection, the employer must then fairly select for redundancy. There is no one fair method of selection. Last in, first out ('LIFO') is sometimes used as a basis for selection, but following the introduction of the Employment Equality (Age) Regulations 2006 there was concern that LIFO was potentially age discriminatory against younger employees who were presumed to have less service. Both the Acas guide on 'Age in the Workplace' and the Government guide 'Age Positive' counsel against the use of LIFO, although the High Court in *Rolls Royce plc v Unite the Union* [2008] EWHC 2420 (QB) held that including length of service as part of a matrix of selection criteria was not unlawful. LIFO may also be potentially sex discriminatory. However, there are advantages to it, not least that it is completely objective. Where there is a contractual procedure, an employer should follow it.

Some of the selection criteria commonly used include:

(a) skills or experience;

(b) standard of work performance or aptitude for work;

(c) attendance or disciplinary record.

In *De Belin v Eversheds Legal Services Ltd* (ET/1804069/09) the employment tribunal held that a decision to inflate the billing score of a woman on maternity leave was discriminatory on the ground of sex. The decision was upheld by the EAT (UKEAT/0352/10).

Having drawn up fair objective selection criteria, as the Acas booklet on handling redundancies makes clear, 'the selection will still be unfair if those criteria are carelessly or mistakenly applied'.

One of the most difficult questions for tribunals is the extent to which they should examine the marking that has been applied in a selection exercise. It is clear that one of the requirements for fair consultation in a redundancy exercise involves giving an employee sufficient information about and explanation for his scoring so that he understands them and has a meaningful chance to comment on and challenge the scores.

In *Pinewood Repro Limited t/a County Print (County Print) v Page* (UKEAT/0028/10), the employer agreed the selection criteria (attendance, quality, productivity, abilities, skills, experience, disciplinary record and flexibility) with the trade union, ensured that the scoring was carried out by two senior managers and gave the employee a right to appeal his selection for redundancy, but did not explain to Mr Page why he had received lower scores than the two other people in the selection pool. Mr Page was provided with a copy of his scores; he queried why he had been marked down for 'abilities, skills and experience' given his level of qualifications and 27 years' experience. He also queried why he had been marked down for flexibility as he was 'as flexible as the next man'. He was given no explanation as to how the scores had been arrived at, being told only that 'we believe that the scores given by the assessors are responsible and appropriate'. On appeal he was told that the employers were 'satisfied that the scoring was factual and correct'.

A tribunal found that Mr Page had been unfairly dismissed. The EAT upheld its decision and took the opportunity to review the relevant authorities and, whilst cautioning against an impermissible 'microscopic analysis' of scoring by tribunals, indicated that, particularly with subjective criteria, employees should have sufficient information to understand their scores and an opportunity to challenge them.

It is also important that employers make (and keep) written notes of why a particular score was awarded and what it was based on: the EAT in *Page* was critical of the 'complete absence of comments on the scoring sheet'. In *Dabson v David Cover & Sons* (UKEAT/0374/2011), the EAT emphasised, however, that when assessing the fairness of selection for redundancy, the marks awarded in the selection exercise should be investigated only in exceptional circumstances such as bias or obvious mistake.

The employer should always consider whether there are any alternative vacancies before implementing redundancies. It may be necessary for an employer, when considering whether a dismissal for redundancy is within the 'range of reasonable responses' test, to consider 'bumping' (see **4.2.3.3** above): *Mirab v Mentor Graphics* (UKEAT/0172/17), and it may not be necessary for the employee to have specifically raised this. An employer should provide information about the financial prospects of alternative positions (*Fisher v Hoopoe Finance Ltd* (UKEAT/0043/05). The EAT held in *Morgan v The Welsh Rugby Union* (UKEAT/0314/10) that it was fair to apply subjective criteria when deciding whom to appoint to a suitable alternative vacancy where there were multiple applicants. The 'classic' redundancy guidance set out in *Williams v Compair Maxam Ltd* [1982] ICR 156 does not apply where redundant employees are applying for a new and different role. The principles in *Williams* apply to selection for redundancy not selection for a new role, even where redundancies arise in consequence of such a process. The EAT accepted that in new role cases after a reorganisation, the employer's decision must of necessity be forward looking and may involve something more like an interview process than the application of selection criteria. In that case, *Morgan* directs tribunals back to an 'unvarnished' s 98(4) reasonableness test. Note, however, the EAT's decision in *Green v London Borough of Barking and Dagenham* (UKEAT/0157/16), a case in which the tribunal had taken the view that it was inappropriate to apply the redundancy fairness rules in *Williams* (above) because this was, they thought, a '*Morgan v Welsh RFU* case'. The EAT held that the case was not on all fours with *Morgan* because the nature of the work had not changed significantly; and even if it had been, it was not clear that the tribunal had considered the s 98(4) reasonableness test. See also *Akzo Coatings plc v Thompson* (UKEAT/117/94) and *Darlington Memorial Hospital NHS Trust v Edwards and Vincent* (UKEAT/678/95).

In *Mental Health Care (UK) Ltd v Bilvan and Another* (UKEAT/0248/12), the EAT upheld a tribunal's decision that the use of recruitment criteria to select for redundancy, without any regard to past appraisals or the views of managers who worked with the employees, was unfair.

In *Dunne v Colin & Avril Ltd* (see **4.4.1.3** above), even if a claimant is disentitled to a redundancy payment on the basis that she has unreasonably refused an offer of suitable alternative employment, that does not necessarily mean that the dismissal was fair.

Note that there are some special cases:

(a)   It is automatically unfair to select an employee for redundancy for a 'trade union' reason (see **5.5.1** for details).

(b)   It is automatically unfair to select an employee for redundancy because she is pregnant. There are also special rules concerning offers of alternative employment to pregnant employees (see **14.9**).

The tribunal will also take into account whether or not the employer has complied with his statutory duties to consult (see **4.8**).

A tribunal's findings of fact may also be relevant as regards compensation. If an employer dismissed an employee without consultation, a tribunal must take account of the possibility of alternative employment arising during the period of consultation (see *King v Royal Bank of Canada Europe* (UKEAT/0333/10)).

5.4.2.4   Contravention of a statutory provision

If it becomes illegal for an employee to continue in his employment because to do so would contravene a statutory provision, dismissal will often be fair. However, the employer should consider whether it is possible to redeploy the employee to another job. For example, if a driver has been disqualified from driving, is there any suitable alternative job, such as vehicle maintenance, that he could do without a driving licence? For two cases in this area, see *Kelly v University of Southampton* (UKEAT/0295/07) and *Klusova v London Borough of Hounslow* [2007] EWCA Civ 1127. (See **1.2.6**.)

5.4.2.5 Some other substantial reason

The natures of 'some other substantial reason' dismissals are so varied that no specific rules can be laid down. The general principles must be followed and, in particular, the dismissal must be within the reasonable range of responses. For example, in a business reorganisation which involves making changes to certain terms and conditions, the employer must weigh the commercial needs of the business against the detriment suffered by individual employees.

In *Genower v Ealing AHA* [1980] IRLR 297, the applicant was a general administrative assistant in the supplies department of a hospital. In order to solve a problem of corruption, the respondent decided to move certain grades of employees to different posts at different hospitals. The applicant was ordered to become a purchasing officer at another hospital quite outside the terms of his contract. The EAT held that the applicant's resignation amounted to a constructive dismissal but that the dismissal was fair: the respondent had initiated an internal reorganisation with the intention of preventing corruption.

It is clear from the authorities that where it is sought to justify a dismissal as being for some other substantial reason, there must be some kind of pressure on the employer; it is not enough for an employer simply to say that it is convenient or helpful to carry out a business reorganisation or that to do so would reduce employment costs. It is often appropriate to consider the procedural aspects in a similar way to that suggested in *Polkey* (see **5.4.2.3**).

In *Perkin v St George's Healthcare NHS Trust* [2005] EWCA Civ 1174 the Court of Appeal said employers were entitled to dismiss employees for having a difficult personality even if they were technically good at their jobs.

The Court of Appeal held that the three-stage test set out in *BHS Ltd v Burchell* [1978] IRLR 379 (see **5.4.2.2** above) applies when dismissing an employee for some other substantial reason (a breakdown in trust and confidence). The tribunal will have to determine whether the employer had reasonable grounds following a reasonable investigation for deciding that trust and confidence has been damaged.

In *Ezsias v North Glamorgan NHS Trust* (UKEAT/0399/09) the EAT upheld the tribunal's decision that Mr Ezsias had been dismissed for 'some other substantial reason' (ie the fact of a breakdown in relationships) rather than for misconduct, and that the dismissal was fair. The tribunal relied upon *Perkin* (see above). The distinction was important because if the tribunal had found that the reason for dismissal was misconduct, the Trust would have had to follow Whitley Council procedures. Those did not apply, however, because Mr Ezsias was found to have been dismissed for 'some other substantial reason' – he was dismissed because of the *fact* that relationships had broken down, not because his behaviour had caused the breakdown.

The EAT did make it clear that, even if the behaviour which had caused the breakdown of working relationships with his colleagues in the department had been the reason for his dismissal, it is possible that the action which the Trust took against Mr Ezsias should have been classified as action taken against him because of his conduct. But it would not *necessarily* follow that it should have been classified in that way. In *Perkin*, the Court of Appeal classified the reason for Mr Perkin's dismissal as coming within the category of 'some other substantial reason', even though it was his manner and management style which had led to the breakdown of relationships. Employers must be clear as to the reason for dismissal because procedure follows the reason.

The EAT also counselled employment tribunals to be on the lookout, in cases of this kind, to see whether an employer is using the rubric of 'some other substantial reason' as a pretext to conceal the real reason for the employee's dismissal.

In *Governing Body of Tubbenden Primary School v Sylvester* (UKEAT/0527/11), a deputy head teacher maintained a friendship, discreetly, with a fellow teacher, who was arrested and suspended for having indecent images of children. Some nine months after it was indicated to her by the School and local education authority that there was nothing wrong in her continuing with this friendship, and with three days' prior warning, she was suspended and disciplinary proceedings were initiated, and ultimately she was dismissed for 'some other substantial reason'. The employment tribunal accepted this but found the dismissal unfair in the circumstances, especially since the employer had not only failed to warn the deputy of the risk to her employment, but also had appeared to condone her conduct in maintaining the friendship.

It was contended that in a case of dismissal for some other substantial reason for loss of confidence, a tribunal was not entitled to have regard to the causes of that loss but should be restricted merely to the fact of it. This was rejected: s 98(4) entitled the tribunal to take a broader view, and the context was analogous to a dismissal for conduct, in which case a warning or its absence was highly relevant to any consideration of fairness.

In *Leach v Office of Communications* [2012] EWCA Civ 959, the Court of Appeal upheld a tribunal's decision that an employee had been fairly dismissed, for 'some other substantial reason' on the basis of a breakdown of trust and confidence, after the police had disclosed to the employer credible but untested allegations that the employee had committed child sex offences. The employer had adopted a sufficiently critical approach to the allegations and had not accepted them at face value. Even though the claimant had denied all of the allegations at a disciplinary hearing, the risk of damage to the employer's reputation was sufficient to justify dismissal. Arguments based on Articles 6 and 8 of the ECHR (which was directly applicable to Ofcom as a public authority employer) were also rejected. The EAT had upheld the tribunal's findings, but Mr Justice Underhill had stated that the EAT did not find the terminology of 'trust and confidence' particularly helpful. He observed 'a growing trend among parties to employment litigation to regard the invocation of "loss of trust and confidence" as an automatic solvent of obligations', which it is not. The Court of Appeal also noted that the duty of trust and confidence was an obligation at the heart of the employment relationship, and was not a convenient label to stick on any situation in which the employer feels let down by an employee or which the employer can use as a valid reason for dismissal whenever a conduct reason is unavailable or inappropriate. Courts are particularly aware that reliance by employers on 'trust and confidence' carries a danger of omitting the procedural safeguards that would apply to a conduct dismissal (see, eg, *Ezsias v North Glamorgan NHS Trust* [2011] IRLR 550, where the EAT pointed out that tribunals must be alert to employers using 'some other substantial reason' as a pretext for dismissal when conduct is the real concern).

In *Windsor Recruitment v Silverwood* (UKEAT/0339/05) the EAT looked at dismissals for refusing to accept a restrictive covenant in terms of some other substantial reason. It said the reasonableness of the covenant was relevant to general fairness, not to the reason.

In *Garside & Laycock v Booth* (UKEAT/0003/11) the EAT held that where a dismissal is for failure to accept a wage cut, the question whether the dismissal is fair for some other substantial reason has to be determined by reference to whether it was reasonable for the employer to dismiss, and not whether it was reasonable for the employee to accept the lesser term offered to him. All employees were asked to take a 5% pay cut. Mr Booth was the only one still refusing. The EAT overturned the tribunal's decision that the dismissal was unfair. The employee's reasonableness in refusing is only one factor to weigh in the balance – the correct focus of the tribunal should be on whether the employer acted reasonably in all the circumstances, not on whether it was reasonable for the employee to resist the attempt to reduce his pay.

In *Slade & Others v TNT UK Ltd* (UKEAT/0113/11), the employer sought to change terms of employment by making an offer to 'buy out' certain existing terms, but warned that refusal would result in dismissal with an offer of re-engagement on the proposed new terms. The offer was rejected and the employer dismissed with notice. Each of those who had been thus dismissed accepted re-engagement on the new terms, but under protest, and reserved their right to claim that their dismissal had been unfair.

The employment tribunal held that the employer did not act unfairly where the terms of offered re-employment did not include the terms of the 'buy out' as part of the new terms. That decision was upheld by the EAT. The tribunal had correctly considered whether the reason for the dismissal was a substantial reason – the burden of proof being on the respondent. If the reason for the dismissals was for a sound business reason, or one which the respondent reasonably believed was a sound business reason, then it would be a substantial reason. It was not necessary for the action to be the only available action to avert a business disaster, but on the other hand a reason must not be trivial. On the facts the tribunal was entitled to find that the reason was a business restructuring, namely a change of remuneration structure with a view to reduction of costs and an increase in efficiency to combat falling revenues and an alarming fall in operating profits. The tribunal found that the respondent had not been successful in all it set out to do in terms of cost reduction, but was satisfied it had an honest and reasonable belief that taking the proposed steps would achieve those aims. Those aims were legitimate and necessary, and constituted a substantial reason satisfying the provisions of s 98(1). That conclusion was not challenged.

The EAT held that the tribunal had correctly considered whether the dismissal was fair having regard to s 98(4) and had legitimately concluded that the employer had acted reasonably. The EAT held that the tribunal applied itself to the correct test and came to a conclusion which was open to it, namely that what the respondent did was within the bands of reasonable responses to the situation in which it found itself: the tribunal rejected the contention that the *only* reasonable response for the respondent would be to offer re-engagement on terms which included the buy-out sum.

The approach adopted by the EAT in *Booth* and *Slade* was reiterated by the EAT most recently in *General Vending Services v Schofield* (UKEAT/0137/13). In this case, the employer wanted, for business reasons, to make changes to the terms and conditions of its engineers, which would lead, amongst other things, to a reduction in salary. Twenty to 30 employees accepted the new terms. Mr Schofield did not, and he was dismissed, being offered re-engagement on the new terms. His claim succeeded before the employment tribunal, on the basis that he was reasonable in rejecting the changes. The EAT overturned the decision, stating that just because the employee is reasonable, that does not mean that the employer was unreasonable in dismissing. The EAT held that 'while the reaction of employees was a relevant matter which an employer would take into account, it could not be decisive'. It added that the number of employees who agree to a change could be persuasive (see, eg, *Catamaran Cruises Ltd v Williams* [1994] IRLR 386 and *St John of God (Care Services) Ltd v Brooks* [1992] IRLR 546).

In *Bancroft v Interserve* (**5.2.2.5** above), the EAT confirmed that where an employee is dismissed as a result of third-party pressure, the dismissal will be fair if the employer has done everything he reasonably can to avoid or mitigate the injustice brought about by the stance of the client, by trying to get the client to change his mind or, if that is not possible, by trying to find alternative work for the employee.

In *Bancroft*, Interserve had a contract with the Home Office to provide catering at a bail hostel. Mr Bancroft was a chef at the hostel but fell out with the hostel manager. Following a disciplinary hearing, Mr Bancroft was given a warning. However, relying on a term on the contract, the Home Office asked for Mr Bancroft to be replaced. No inquiry was made as to whether the request was justified and no efforts were made to persuade the Home Office to change its mind. Mr Bancroft was offered an alternative, but with more traveling, fewer hours and less pay, which he refused. He was dismissed for 'some other substantial reason'. The employment tribunal found the dismissal fair.

The EAT said that the tribunal had not asked the right question: was there any injustice to Mr Bancroft, and whether Interserve had done 'everything they could to mitigate the injustice'? As the tribunal had not explored why Interserve had not looked into the relationship between Mr Bancroft and the hostel manager, the EAT send the case back to the tribunal to consider again in light of the EAT's conclusions.

5.5   OTHER SPECIAL CASES

There is a number of other special cases where the normal rules relating to unfair dismissal are varied. In summary, these are:

(a)   pregnancy or maternity-related dismissals (see **Chapter 14**);

(b)   dismissal for trade union reasons (see **5.5.1**);

(c)   selection for redundancy based on either of the above (see **5.4.2.3** and **5.5.1**);

(d)   dismissal following industrial action (see **5.5.2**);

(e)   dismissal for asserting a statutory right (see **5.5.3**);

(f)   health and safety dismissals (see **5.5.4**);

(g)   some dismissals on transfer of a business (see **Chapter 7**);

(h)   dismissal by reason of political opinions or affiliation (see **5.5.5**);

(i)   dismissals where the worker has made a protected disclosure (see **5.5.6**);

(j)   if the reason for the dismissal relates to a prohibited list (ERA 1996, s 104F(1)) (there is a statutory prohibition on compiling trade union blacklists – see Employment Relations Act 1999 (Blacklists) Regulations 2010);

(k)   dismissals where an employee is dismissed because of a breach of an exclusivity clause rendered unenforceable by s 27A(3) of the ERA 1996 (see **1.4.1**).

In the case of pregnancy or maternity-related dismissals, dismissals for trade union reasons (or selection for redundancy on either of these grounds), dismissals for asserting a statutory right, health and safety dismissals, some dismissals for a reason connected with a transfer of a business and dismissals for making a protected disclosure, the dismissal will be 'automatically' unfair. This means that once the tribunal has established that the reason for the dismissal falls under one of these heads, it will not have to go on to consider the reasonableness of the decision under s 98(4).

5.5.1   Dismissals for trade union reasons

The general principle is that an employee is free to join a trade union or not to join as he chooses. Consequently, it is unfair to dismiss any employee either because he is or because he is not a member of a trade union or because of involvement in union activities (see *Jet2.com v Denby* (UKEAT/0070/17).

By s 152(1) of TULR(C)A 1992:

... the dismissal of an employee [is] unfair if the reason for it ... was that the employee—

(a)   was, or proposed to become, a member of an independent trade union, or

(b)   had taken part, or proposed to take part, in the activities of an independent trade union at an appropriate time, or

(c)   was not a member of any trade union, or of a particular trade union ... or [refused] to become or remain a member.

An 'appropriate time' within s 152(1)(b) above is either outside working hours or within them at a time to which the employer has agreed (s 152(2)). 'Activities of an independent trade union' would cover such matters as union meetings. It does not extend to industrial action. The Court of Appeal held in *Morris v Metrolink RATP DEV Ltd* [2018] EWCA Civ 1350 that misconduct did not, on the facts, take the conduct outside the scope of 'trade union activities' for the purpose of s 152.

No qualifying period of continuous employment is necessary to bring a claim within this section because employees would be at risk of dismissal for these reasons shortly after commencing employment.

It is automatically unfair to select an employee for redundancy for one of the reasons within s 152 of TULR(C)A 1992 listed above (TULR(C)A 1992, s 153).

Where a complaint is made that the dismissal was on trade union membership grounds, the applicant may also seek interim relief (TULR(C)A 1992, s 161) (ie an injunction to preserve the status quo until a full hearing: in effect reinstatement until final judgment).

As to burden of proof, see *Kuzel* at **5.5.6.4** (confirmed in *Dahou v Serco Ltd* [2016] EWCA Civ 832).

5.5.2 Industrial action

Industrial action includes strikes and other industrial action (eg a 'work to rule') by employees and lock-outs by the employer. The right of the employee to present a complaint of unfair dismissal depends whether the industrial action is 'unofficial' or 'other' ('official') industrial action. Basically, industrial action is 'official' if either:

(a)   authorised or endorsed by a trade union; or

(b)   none of those taking part is a member of a trade union.

5.5.2.1 Unofficial industrial action

By s 237 of the TULR(C)A 1992, if at the time of his dismissal the employee was taking part in unofficial industrial action, the employment tribunal has no jurisdiction to hear a complaint of unfair dismissal. This is not to say that the dismissal is fair, but merely that the employee is not eligible to present a claim. This means that in the event of unofficial strikes and other unofficial industrial action, the employer can select employees, such as the ringleaders of the strike, for dismissal without fear of a claim for unfair dismissal.

5.5.2.2 Other industrial action

All employees taking part in official strike action are protected from dismissal during the first 12 weeks of the strike action. There is no qualifying period of employment. Section 238A of the TULR(C)A 1992 provides that a dismissal will be automatically unfair if the reason (or, if more than one, the principal reason for the dismissal) is that the employee took 'protected' industrial action, provided the dismissal occurred within the 12-week period, or if after that period the employee was dismissed when they had ceased to take part in the action, or if the dismissal occurs after the 12-week period, but the employer had not taken proper steps for the purposes of resolving the dispute.

5.5.3 Dismissal for asserting a statutory right

5.5.3.1 ERA 1996, s 104

It is unfair to dismiss an employee (or to select for redundancy) because:

(a)   he has brought proceedings against an employer to enforce a relevant statutory right; or

(b)   he has alleged that the employer has infringed a right of his which is a relevant statutory right.

'Relevant statutory rights' include, for example, claims under s 13 of the ERA 1996 (protection of wages), or a claim to a written statement of terms under ERA 1996, s 1.

No qualifying period of continuous employment is necessary.

Note: there is some scope for an overlap with a public interest disclosure claim (see **5.5.5** below). Section 104 does not cover breaches of contractual obligations (unless it is a wages claim) but the PIDA 1998 might cover this. Section 104 does not cover detriments.

5.5.4 Health and safety dismissals

5.5.4.1 ERA 1996, s 100

It is unfair to dismiss an employee who 'stops the job' on health and safety grounds. No period of continuous employment is required.

5.5.5 Political dismissals

Following the case of *Redfearn v UK* in the ECtHR (see **Chapter 8**), where the Court ruled that the UK had not sufficiently implemented Article 11 of the ECHR (the right of assembly), the requirement for a qualification period where someone claims he has been dismissed due to political opinion or affiliation was removed. This does not make dismissals on this ground automatically unfair; it simply means that no qualifying period is required. This change affects dismissals after 25 June 2013. The Government could have dealt with the effect of *Redfearn* by allowing a free-standing claim for unlawful discrimination on political grounds, but chose instead to create a further exception to the qualifying period.

5.5.6 Public Interest Disclosure Act 1998

5.5.6.1 Introduction

The PIDA 1998, often referred to as the 'whistleblower's charter', introduced special rights and protections for workers who disclose wrongdoing by their employers to a third party in specific circumstances. It was introduced after a series of disasters (such as the Zeebrugge ferry, Piper Alpha oil platform and the Clapham rail crash) which highlighted the need for a law to protect workers who 'blew the whistle' in the public interest.

The PIDA 1998 aims to promote better relations between employers and their workforce over wrongdoing in the workplace, and to end the so-called 'cover-up culture', so that workers are not scared to tell their bosses or others about problems relating to matters such as health and safety or criminal activities for fear of being dismissed or victimised. The Act assumes that whistleblowing is in the public interest. This approach offers some protection to whistleblowers but does little to encourage them. Some commentators have argued that the UK should adopt a similar approach to that in the USA (see the Dodd-Frank legisation), which permits a percentage of any fine imposed to be paid to the whistleblower and has encouraged the flow of information to US regulators.

The provisions of the PIDA 1998 apply not just to employees and workers but also to third-party contractors whose work is controlled by an employer. (See **1.3.4.1** for the definition of a 'worker' in a PIDA claim. Members of an LLP are workers for these purposes – see *Clyde & Co LLP and Another v Bates van Winkelhof* [2014] UKSC 32 – and some agency workers may be covered (ERA 1996, s 43K(1)(a) – see *McTigue v University Hospital Bristol NHS Foundation Trust* (EAT/0354/15).) The Act does not create a general right for all whistleblowing. Only certain categories of information will be protected in certain situations. Claims under the PIDA 1998 may be brought in respect of treatment which subjects the claimant to a detriment (ERA 1996, s 47B) and, in respect of employees only, for unfair dismissal (ERA 1996, s 103A). A claim may therefore relate both to treatment during the employment relationship and to the termination of it. This section of the book deals with dismissal claims, whether by an employee or a worker, and is meant only as an introduction to what is a complex topic.

In March 2015, BIS published *Whistleblowing Guidance for Employers and Code of Practice*, and in June 2015 it published *Blowing the whistle to a prescribed person – List of prescribed persons and bodies*.

The *Guidance* is intended to help employers understand the law on whistleblowing and put in place whistleblowing policies. The prescribed persons guidance sets out information on the role of prescribed people and how they should handle disclosures. The International Bar Association published, in April 2018, a useful guide on whistleblower protections.

In order to assess whether a dismissal/detriment falls within the PIDA 1998, the following matters will need to be considered:

(1) Is there a qualifying disclosure (ERA 1996, s 43B (as amended by the Enterprise and Regulatory Reform Act 2013, s 17))?
   - has there been a disclosure of information,
   - which, in the reasonable belief of the worker,
   - is made in the public interest, and
   - tends to show one or more of a number of failures?

(2) Was that disclosure made to an appropriate person?

(3) Was that disclosure the reason or principal reason for the dismissal (or detriment)?

See below for more details on each of these areas. In *Blackbay Ventures Ltd v Gahir* [2014] IRLR 416, the EAT gave some guidance to tribunals when considering how to approach a protected disclosure case.

5.5.6.2 Qualifying disclosure

Disclosure of information

The word 'disclosure' is not defined in the ERA 1996; the phrase is intended, however, to have a wide reach. The question is to be determined in the light of the statute itself – whether there is a disclosure of information. It has to show or tend to show something that comes within the section (s 43B(1)). An employee simply has to communicate the information by some effective means in order for the communication to constitute a disclosure of the information. There is no requirement in the legislation that the disclosure needs to be in writing. However, there is room for disagreement where broad communications, especially verbal conversations, are relied upon, not least because of the evidential issues that can arise where a conversation is disputed. There is also no need for the disclosure to be of information that is formerly unknown or secret (s 43L(3)): telling someone something they already know can be a disclosure. It is clear that a disclosure of information must convey some sort of factual information that goes beyond a mere allegation or opinion (*Cavendish Munro Professional Risks Management Ltd v Geduld* [2010] IRLR 38). In *Geduld*, the court said that a disclosure was the 'giving of information' and the 'conveying of facts'. *Geduld* was followed in *Goode v Marks and Spencer plc* (UKEAT/0442/09) where a distinction was sought to be drawn between information and an allegation. In *Blitz v Vectone Group Holdings Ltd* (UKEAT/0253/10), the EAT held that there was no disclosure of information in an email that was interpreted as seeking advice and requesting information rather than supplying it. In *Norbrook Laboratories (GB) Ltd v Shaw* (UKEAT/0150/13), the EAT accepted that concerns raised in separate documents over a number of days with different individuals may be taken together to form a disclosure of information. More recently, in *Eiger Securities LLP v Korshunova* [2017] ICR 561, the EAT found that there had been a disclosure of information.

Whether something is an allegation or a fact continues to cause difficulties, not least because the margins between the two can be fine and they can be intertwined. In *Kilraine v London Borough of Wandsworth* [2018] EWCA Civ 1436, the Court of Appeal, while declining to give comprehensive guidance on what constituted a disclosure, said that an allegation could constitute 'information', but words that were too general and devoid of factual content would not do so (eg saying the words 'have not been cleaned for two weeks' discloses information, whereas saying 'you are in breach of health and safety law', without more, is not sufficient).

Words that would otherwise fall short can, however, be boosted by context or surrounding circumstances.

Reasonable belief

The Court of Appeal gave general guidance in *Babula v Waltham Forest College* [2007] EWCA Civ 1154 as to what is meant by 'reasonable belief'. It held that there may be a qualifying disclosure even if the employee is wrong, so long as the belief was reasonable in the circumstances at the time of the disclosure. Further guidance was provided on this in *Goode v Marks and Spencer plc* (UKEAT/0442/09). In *Soh v Imperial College* (UKEAT/0350/14) the EAT held that what matters is whether there is a reasonable belief that the *information being disclosed* shows one of the wrongdoings in paras (a)–(f) of s 43B(1) of the ERA 1996 (not whether there is a reasonable belief that the colleague had (in this case) failed to comply with a legal obligation). The Court of Appeal held in *Beatt v Croydon Health Services NHS Trust* [2017] EWCA Civ 401 that the belief of the decision maker as to whether the disclosure is protected is irrelevant when deciding whether the disclosure is protected.

Public interest

All disclosures must be in the 'public interest' to qualify. This was added by the Enterprise and Regulatory Reform Act 2013, s 17, to ensure that all disclosures are in the public interest, so as to avoid workers using this section to raise concerns about private employment rights such as a breach of their own contracts (see *Parkins v Sodexho*, above). However, public interest is not defined, and employees may still try to argue that complaints about breaches of their contracts do pass the test. In *Chesterton Global Ltd v Nurmohamed* [2017] EWCA Civ 979, the Court of Appeal had the opportunity to consider the application of the 'public interest' test. An employment tribunal had found that a complaint by an employee about the misstatement of costs and liabilities in his employer's accounts, which could have had an impact on his and other colleagues' bonuses, was a disclosure of information. The employment tribunal concluded that while the claimant was motivated by self-interest, he was also concerned about financial probity and the wider interests of his colleagues. In the tribunal's view, this was a sufficiently large section of the public for the claimant reasonably to believe that his disclosure was in the public interest. The tribunal said it was not necessary for the disclosure to be of interest to the entirety of the public. The EAT, upholding the tribunal's decision, said that s 43B(1) of the 1996 Act imposes a subjective test, since it asks whether the claimant had a reasonable belief (at the time of making the disclosure) in two matters:

(a)   that his disclosure was in the public interest; and

(b)   that the disclosure tended to show that one of the five relevant failures had occurred or was likely to occur (see below).

The Court of Appeal upheld that reasoning. It held:

> The statutory criterion of what is 'in the public interest' does not lend itself to absolute rules, still less when the decisive question is not what is in fact in the public interest but what could reasonably be believed to be. I am not prepared to rule out the possibility that the disclosure of a breach of a worker's contract of the *Parkins v Sodexho* kind may nevertheless be in the public interest, or reasonably be so regarded, if a sufficiently large number of other employees share the same interest. I would certainly expect employment tribunals to be cautious about reaching such a conclusion, because the broad intent behind the amendment of section 43B(1) is that workers making disclosures in the context of private workplace disputes should not attract the enhanced statutory protection accorded to whistleblowers – even, as I have held, where more than one worker is involved. But I am not prepared to say never. In practice, however, the question may not often arise in that stark form. The larger the number of persons whose interests are engaged by a breach of the contract of employment, the more likely it is that there will be other features of the situation which will engage the public interest.
>
> Against that background, in my view the correct approach is as follows. In a whistleblower case where the disclosure relates to a breach of the worker's own contract of employment (or some other matter

under section 43B(1) where the interest in question is personal in character), there may nevertheless be features of the case that make it reasonable to regard disclosure as being in the public interest as well as in the personal interest of the worker .... The question is one to be answered by the Tribunal on a consideration of all the circumstances of the particular case, but [counsel for the employee's] fourfold classification of relevant factors which I have reproduced ... above may be a useful tool. As he says, the number of employees whose interests the matter disclosed affects may be relevant, but that is subject to the strong note of caution which I have sounded in the previous paragraph.

The four factors the Court referred to are:

(1)   the numbers in the group whose interests the disclosure served;

(2)   the nature of the interests affected and the extent to which they are affected by the wrongdoing disclosed – a disclosure of wrongdoing directly affecting a very important interest is more likely to be in the public interest than a disclosure of trivial wrongdoing affecting the same number of people, and all the more so if the effect is marginal or indirect;

(3)   the nature of the wrongdoing disclosed – disclosure of deliberate wrongdoing is more likely to be in the public interest than the disclosure of inadvertent wrongdoing affecting the same number of people;

(4)   the identity of the alleged wrongdoer: 'the larger or more prominent the wrongdoer (in terms of the size of its relevant community, ie staff, suppliers and clients), the more obviously should a disclosure about its activities engage the public interest' – though this should not be taken too far.

On the facts, given that numbers affected were high; the misstatements in the accounts were to the tune of £2 million–£3 million; the wrongdoing concerned deliberate falsification of accounts; and the employer was a national estate agent and a major player in the London property market, the disclosures were in the public interest.

The guidance in *Chesterton* was followed in *Underwood v Wincanton plc* (UKEAT/0163/15) when the EAT held that the test can be satisfied by a group of employees raising a matter specific to their conditions of employment. It appears that the test of public interest is a relatively easy hurdle to jump.

In a whistleblowing claim, a disclosure can still qualify for protection if the belief in its public interest was mistaken but reasonable. The approach of the Court of Appeal suggests that the introduction of the element of 'public interest' imposes a relatively low threshold for a claimant.

Morgan v Royal Mencap Society (EAT/0272/15) is another recent decision on public interest which again suggests that the threshold is relatively low. In that case the claimant had complained about working in cramped conditions which were affecting her knee. She subsequently resigned and brought a number of claims, including that she had been automatically unfairly dismissed and subject to detriments on the basis that her complaints about health and safety were protected disclosures. The employment tribunal dismissed her claim at a preliminary hearing on the basis that it had no reasonable prospect of success, because while these matters were very important to the claimant, such disclosures were not in the public interest. The EAT allowed the claimant's appeal. It was reasonably arguable that an employee may, even if they were the principal person affected, consider such health and safety complaints to be made in the wider interests of employees generally. 'The question is not whether the disclosure is actually in the public interest, but whether the worker making it has the belief, and whether the belief is reasonable.' In *Parsons v Airplus International Ltd* (UKEAT/ 0111/17) the EAT said that a disclosure made purely out of self-interest could not constitute sufficient grounds for a reasonable belief that the disclosures were made in the public interest.

Relevant failures

There are limits on the matters about which an employee may complain. The PIDA 1998 inserts a provision into the ERA 1996 (s 43B(1)), which provides that a 'qualifying disclosure' means any disclosure of information which in the reasonable (ie there is an objective element to the test) belief of the worker (ie this is overall a subjective test at the time of disclosure) tends to show wrongdoing of one or more of the following kinds (past, present or future) of 'relevant failures':

(a)   a criminal offence (see *Babula v Waltham Forest College* [2007] EWCA Civ 1154);

(b)   a failure to comply with a legal obligation (see *Parkins v Sodexho Ltd* [2002] IRLR 109, *Douglas v Birmingham City Council* (UKEAT/0518/02) and *Eiger Securities LLP v Korshunova* (UKEAT/0149/16));

(c)   a miscarriage of justice;

(d)   the health and safety of any individual is endangered;

(e)   the environment is being damaged;

(f)   information relating to any of the above areas is being deliberately concealed.

A similar approach to that adopted with regard to public interest will be applied to the assessment of the 'reasonable belief'.

5.5.6.3   Relevant person and procedure

In order to qualify for protection, there is a tiered disclosure regime:

(a)   a disclosure to an employer or (where the failure related to a person other than an employer) to that other person (s 43C);

(b)   a disclosure to a legal adviser in the course of obtaining legal advice (s 43D);

(c)   where the employer is appointed under any statute by a Minister of the Crown, a disclosure to a Minister of the Crown (s 43E);

(d)   a disclosure to a prescribed person under s 43F. (Details of prescribed bodies and the matters in respect of which they are prescribed are set out in the Public Interest Disclosure (Prescribed Persons) Order 2014 (SI 2014/2418) (as amended). The list includes bodies such as HMRC and the HSE.)

These four methods of disclosure are very specific. In addition, there are two much more general provisions which impose more complex tests:

(a)   A disclosure, reasonably believing that the information disclosed is substantially true, which is not made for personal gain, where the employee reasonably believes that if he discloses the information to his employer or a prescribed person he will suffer a detriment, or he has previously made a disclosure of substantially the same information to the employer or the prescribed person. In deciding whether it is reasonable for the employee to make the disclosure, the Act lays down a number of circumstances that should be borne in mind, including the identity of the person to whom the disclosure is made, the seriousness of the relevant failure and how the employer responded to the earlier disclosure (s 43G).

(b)   A disclosure of 'exceptionally serious' material such as merits bypassing one of the other procedures.

In *Goode v Marks and Spencer plc* (**5.5.5.2** above), one of the reasons Goode's claim failed was because the tribunal found that his disclosure to the media was different from his internal expressions of concern and did not therefore satisfy the test for the wider disclosure under s 43G(2)(c)(i), which requires a worker to have 'previously made a disclosure of substantially the same information to his employer'.

In *Collins v National Trust* (ET/2507255/05), C was able to avail himself of the 'exceptionally serious circumstances' provisions, such that his disclosure to a local newspaper of a confidential report about dangers on a public beach was protected. (Compare this to the circumstances in *Holbrook v Queen Mary's Sidcup NHS Trust* (ET/1101904/06).)

In *Barton v Royal Borough of Greenwich* (UKEAT/0041/14), the EAT upheld an employment tribunal's decisions that:

(a)   a disclosure to the Information Commissioner's Office (ICO) by an employee, although a qualifying disclosure, was not protected because it was made to an external body, so needed to satisfy the higher standard of 'reasonable belief' that the information was substantially true. As the employee had taken no steps to verify the information before contacting the ICO, he was not able to satisfy that requirement;

(b)   the call the employee made to the ICO did not convey 'information' (it was seeking advice) and so was not a protected disclosure.

Employers should have an appropriate disclosure policy in their staff handbooks so as to avoid whistleblowing cases reaching the tribunal. This should ensure they receive early notification of any problems. Since April 2010, claimants bringing a whistleblowing claim against their employer can tick a box on the claim form, requesting that the tribunal forward details of their whistleblowing allegations to the appropriate regulator for investigation.

Until 2013, there was a good faith requirement for disclosures. In *Street v Derbyshire Unemployed Workers Centre* [2004] IRLR 687, the Court of Appeal held that an employee's disclosure was not 'protected' because she had been motivated by a grudge and therefore had not acted in good faith. The Court of Appeal emphasised that a person could 'reasonably believe' in the substantial truth of an allegation, but still not make a disclosure in 'good faith'. It said the phrase did not mean 'honesty'. It said a disclosure would not be made in good faith where the 'dominant or pre-dominant purpose' of making the disclosure was for an ulterior motive and was not for the public interest in the disclosure of wrongdoing. The motive should be 'public spirited' (which is the underlying principle of the whistleblowing legislation). (See also *Smith v Ministry of Defence* (IDS Brief 788/12).) In the Harold Shipman inquiry, the chair, Dame Janet Smith, expressed concerns that the 'good faith' test should be removed from the PIDA 1998. The ERRA 2013 removed the good faith requirement for a disclosure. However, tribunals now have a power to reduce compensation by 25% if a disclosure was not in good faith.

In *Onyango v Berkeley* (EAT/0407/12), the EAT held that a claimant could rely on a post-termination protected disclosure in a claim brought under s 47B of the ERA 1996 (the right not to be subjected to a detriment on the ground that he had made a protected disclosure), as long as the disclosure preceded the related detriment.

5.5.6.4   Causation

The disclosure must be the reason or principal reason for the dismissal (or detriment). Section 103A of the ERA 1996 requires that the protected disclosure be 'the reason (or, if more than one reason, the principal reason) for the dismissal'. In *Royal Mail Group Ltd v Jhuti* [2018] IRLR 251, the Court of Appeal considered when a dismissal decision will be treated as connected with whistleblowing. The claimant made a protected disclosure to her line manager, who then misled the person who made the decision to dismiss. The tribunal dismissed the claim, finding that the disclosures were not the reason for the dismissal. The EAT found that the dismissal was automatically unfair within s 103A of the ERA 1996, holding that a decision made in ignorance of true facts due to 'manipulation by someone in a management position' can be attributed to the employer of both of them. The Court of Appeal held that the dismissal was fair because the dismissing officer was not aware of the protected disclosures (the Court suggested that the claimant might recover damages for losses sustained by the dismissal as part of her detriment claim (her manager's actions amounted to detriments)).

In a case where the claimant has made multiple disclosures, the question is whether the cumulative impact was the principal reason for the dismissal (*El-Megrisi v Azad University (IR) in Oxford* (UKEAT/0448/08)). In detriment cases, the test is whether the protected disclosure *materially influences* the employer's treatment of the whistleblower. That, as the Court of Appeal noted in *NHS Manchester v Fecitt and Others* [2012] IRLR 641, means that there are different tests. See too *Eiger Securities LLP v Korshunova* (UKEAT/0149/16).

In *Panayiotou v (1) Chief Constable Paul Kernaghan and (2) Police and Crime Commissioner for Hampshire* (UKEAT/0436/13), the EAT held that an employer was able to dismiss an employee after the latter made a series of disclosures, where the decision to dismiss was motivated by the manner in which the employee pursued the case, rather than by the fact that he made a disclosure. In *Beatt v Croydon Health Services NHS Trust* [2017] IRLR 748, the issue in dispute before the Court of Appeal, it having been accepted that Mr Beatt had made protected disclosures, was whether he could succeed in his claim when the employer did not believe he had made a protected disclosure. The Court distinguished between two questions: (1) Was the making of the disclosure the reason/principal reason for the dismissal? and (2) Was the disclosure in question a protected one? The first question requires a finding as to what was in the decision maker's mind; the second does not. Therefore if the disclosure was the reason for the dismissal, and it was found by the tribunal to be protected, then the claim would succeed.

5.5.6.5   Burden of proof

Employees will be treated as having been automatically unfairly dismissed where the reason or principal reason for the dismissal was that they made a protected disclosure. There is no continuous employment requirement. However, the employee's continuity of employment will still matter.

If the employee has the requisite continuity of employment to bring an 'ordinary' unfair dismissal claim, the burden of proving the reason for the dismissal is on the employer to show that he had a potentially fair reason for the dismissal. There is no burden on the employee to disprove the reason put forward by the employer, but he will have to produce some evidence supporting the positive case that he was dismissed by reason of making a protected disclosure. It will then be for the tribunal to consider the evidence as a whole and make findings of fact on the basis of the direct evidence and/or by reasonable inferences from primary facts established by the evidence (*Kuzel v Roche Products Ltd* [2008] IRLR 530). In *Royal Mail Group Ltd v Jhuti* [2017] EWCA Civ 1632, the Court of Appeal confirmed that it is only the mental processes of the dismissing officer that are relevant; if that person was not aware of proceedings, the dismissal could not be by reason of those disclosures.

Where an employee does not have the requisite continuous employment required for an 'ordinary' unfair dismissal claim, the burden of proof is on the employee to prove that the protected disclosure was the employer's reason or principal reason for the dismissal (see the EAT's reasoning on this in *Kuzel* (UKEAT/0516/06). In a detriment case, the worker must prove that he made the relevant disclosure and prove the detrimental treatment. The employer then has to prove another reason for the treatment. If it does not prove another reason, the tribunal must conclude that it was by reason of the protected disclosure.

In dismissal cases, the standard of proof is different from that in detriment cases (s 48(2)/s 47B – see *Fecitt v NHS Manchester* [2012] IRLR 64; where a worker alleges that he was dismissed by reason of making a protected disclosure, he will need to rely on the detriment provisions because only employees are able to allege unfair dismissal). See also *International Petroleum Ltd v Osipov* (UKEAT/0058/17) which looks at a number of issues, including when an individual decision maker can be sued by the whistleblower, the approach to burden of proof and inference drawing as well as various issues on remedies in a whistleblowing context.

5.5.6.6 Vicarious liability

The ERRA 2013 includes a provision making employers vicariously liable when their employees victimise a whistleblowing colleague. This came into effect on 25 June 2013. There is a defence for an employer of having taken all reasonable steps to prevent such treatment.

5.5.6.7 Enforcement and remedies

The usual three-month time limit applies for bringing a claim (see **6.3.1**). Where the employee is dismissed, time runs from the date of dismissal. Where the complaint is one of detrimental treatment, this can sometimes be problematic where the act complained of and the detriment occur on different dates – see *Vivian v Bournemouth Borough Council* (UKEAT/0254/10). Where this happens, time runs from the date of the act which has been done on the ground that the worker has made a protected disclosure, not the later date of the detriment suffered as a result. In this case, the act was placing the employee in the redeployment pool, and time ran from that act, not from the consequences of that act. However, it may be found not to have been reasonably practicable to bring the complaint until the detriment occurred, so the claim may be admissible if it is brought within a further reasonable period (see **6.3.1**).

Since April 2010 claimants have been invited to tick a box on the ET1 (see **Chapter 6**) indicating whether their claim includes protected disclosure allegations and, if so, whether the claimant wishes the tribunal to refer the allegation on to the relevant authority.

In whistleblowing cases, there is the possibility of 'interim relief' (ERA 1996, s 128). An employee who has been dismissed can ask the tribunal to order the employer to continue to pay his wages through to trial (and any subsequent appeal). An order may be made where the employment judge considers the employee is 'likely to succeed'. 'Likely' means having a 'pretty good chance' of success (see *Taplin v Shippam Ltd* [1978] ICR 1068, *Raja v Secretary of State for Justice* [2010] All ER (D) 134 and *His Highness Sheikh Khalid bin Saqr Al Qasimi v Robinson* (UKEAT/0283/17)).

Where an individual makes the decision to dismiss, in a whistleblowing case, then they may be personally liable (as well as the employer) for all losses arising (*International Petroleum Ltd and Others v Osipor and Others* (UKEAT/0058/17)).

Where an employee has made a protected disclosure and is dismissed for that reason, that is an automatically unfair dismissal (ERA 1996, s 103A). No qualifying period of service will be necessary to bring a claim. There are no limits on the amounts which may be awarded by way of compensatory award, and the tribunal may award reinstatement/re-engagement. It is also unlawful to subject an employee who has made a protected disclosure to any other detriment (ERA 1996, s 47B). That will include dismissal for workers. There is an express provision making it unlawful to contract out of the PIDA 1998. Note that damages will be awarded on different bases, depending on whether the claim is for a detriment (akin to a discrimination claim) or unfair dismissal (unfair dismissal principles will apply). Thus, in detriment cases, compensation can include compensation for injury to feelings. The ERRA 2013 gives tribunals a power to reduce compensation by 25% if a disclosure was not given in good faith.

See *Small v Shrewsbury and Telford Hospitals NHS Trust* [2017] EWCA Civ 882 for a recent case on damages awards in whistleblowing cases. The Court of Appeal recognised in this case that bringing a whistleblowing claim may be 'career-ending' and said that a tribunal should consider whether to award long-term loss of earnings in such cases, even if not specifically raised by the claimant.

5.5.6.8 Human Rights Act 1998

Article 10 of the ECHR, as incorporated by the HRA 1998, contains a right to freedom of expression. That includes the right to hold opinions, and to give and receive information and opinions. That right is subject to balancing restrictions such as are necessary in a democratic society. There is considerable overlap between this and the protection offered by the PIDA 1998. However, Article 10 may provide assistance in areas which are not deemed to be 'protected disclosures' under the 1998 Act.

5.6 AWARDS FOR UNFAIR DISMISSAL

The remedies available for an unfairly dismissed employee are either:

(a)   reinstatement or re-engagement; or

(b)   compensation.

Section 112(2) of the ERA 1996 requires an employment tribunal to explain to a successful complainant what awards are available by way of reinstatement and re-engagement, and when they may be made, and to ask the complainant if he wants such an order to be made. The wording is mandatory. A failure to comply with s 112(2) does not render the decision void, but it does make it voidable, depending on whether the failure caused injustice and unfairness (see *Cowley v Manson Timber Ltd* [1995] ICR 367).

5.6.1 Reinstatement and re-engagement

If the employee wants his job back, he may ask for reinstatement (ERA 1996, s 114) or re-engagement (ERA 1996, s 115). Reinstatement is to his old job as though he had not been dismissed. Re-engagement is in a different job with the same employer, his successor or an associated employer. The EAT held in *Dafiaghor-Olomu v Community Integrated Care* (UKEAT/ 0001/17) that a 'successor employer' does not include a relevant TUPE transfer where there is no change in ownership, because the definition of successor in s 235 of the ERA 1996 requires a change in legal ownership of the undertaking itself. Reinstatement or re-engagement orders are very rare, occurring in less than 1% of unfair dismissal cases that were successful at tribunal.

5.6.1.1 Availability of the order

In deciding whether to make an order for reinstatement or re-engagement, the tribunal must take into account:

(a)   whether the complainant wishes to be reinstated or re-engaged;

(b)   whether it is practicable for the employer to comply with the order;

(c)   whether it would be just to make the order where the complainant has caused or contributed to his dismissal (ERA 1996, s 116(1)).

Where a tribunal orders re-engagement, the terms must be specified with a degree of detail and precision (*Lincolnshire CC v Lupton* (EAT/0328/15)).

The order will not be made unless the employee asks for it. When considering whether to make such an order, the relevant time to assess practicability is the time of the hearing or when the order is to take effect, not the position at the time of dismissal (see *Great Ormond Street Hospital for Children NHS Trust v Patel* (UKEAT/0085/07), *Rembiszewski v Atkins Ltd* (UKEAT/ 0402/11) and *Dafiaghor-Olomu v Community Integrated Care* (above)). It is unlikely to be made if the employee substantially contributed to his own dismissal. In practice, few reinstatement or re-engagement orders are made. Those which are made are often found where the employer is a large organisation such that it is practical to order the employee to return. Where, as is often the case, the employment relationship is permanently damaged, an order will not be made. (See, for example, *Central and NW London NHS Trust v Ambimbola* (UKEAT/0542/08), where the EAT held that the existence of mutual trust and confidence was a relevant factor when addressing the issue of practicability of compliance.)

In *McBride v Scottish Police Authority* [2016] UKSC 27, the Supreme Court emphasised that the only obligation under s 114 was that a claimant be restored to their contractual employment. Reinstatement terms cannot alter contractual terms of employment, but reinstatement does not require the recreation of the precise factual conditions at the point of dismissal. The judgment contains a useful analysis of the principles applicable to reinstatement, as does *United Lincolnshire Trust v Farren* (UKEAT/0198/16).

5.6.1.2 Contents of the order

Where the tribunal orders reinstatement in the old job, it will make consequential orders that the employee be paid arrears of pay, maintains seniority and maintains pension rights (ERA 1996, s 114).

Where the tribunal orders re-engagement in a different job, it will make consequential orders relating to the nature of employment, remuneration, arrears of pay, seniority and pension rights (ERA 1996, s 115).

5.6.1.3 Non-compliance with order

If an order for reinstatement or re-engagement is made but not complied with by the employer, the employer cannot be compelled to reinstate or re-engage the employee. The tribunal must then make an award of compensation in favour of the employee instead (ERA 1996, s 117). Section 117 provides for an award of compensation, and also the making of an additional award of compensation, unless the employer satisfies the tribunal that it was not practicable to comply with the order. Practicability of compliance is thus assessed at two separate stages: a provisional determination at the first stage (see **5.6.1**), and a second conclusive determination, with the burden on the employer at the second stage (under s 117).

This award of compensation will consist of a basic, compensatory and additional award.

The basic award is calculated in the usual way (see **5.6.2.1**).

The compensatory award will be assessed in the same way as usual, but instead of being limited to £83,682 or 52 weeks' gross pay (whichever is the lower) (see **5.6.2.2**), the limit will be the higher of £83,682 (as at 6 April 2018) or the value of the employee's arrears of pay and benefits which should have been paid to him under the original order for reinstatement or re-engagement. The amount of any award already made under s 112(5) shall be deducted from any compensation awarded under s 117.

For example, if the reinstatement order required the employer to pay the employee the sum of £85,000 by way of arrears of pay and the employer fails to comply, the compensatory award will be £85,000 not £83,682.

Lastly, the tribunal must make an additional award unless the employer can satisfy the tribunal that it was not practicable to comply with the reinstatement or re-engagement order. The employer could put forward new evidence to show this. If the tribunal makes an additional award, this will be an amount equivalent to between 26 and 52 weeks' gross pay. A week's pay is subject to a maximum of £508 as at 6 April 2018.

5.6.2 Compensation

If the tribunal considers that the complaint is well founded, but no order for reinstatement or re-engagement is made, it must make an award of compensation. The award will consist of two elements:

(a)   the basic award; and

(b)   the compensatory award (ERA 1996, s 118).

5.6.2.1 Basic award

The basic award is generally calculated in the same way as a redundancy payment, by applying the formula based on age factor, length of service and one week's pay. The same maximum of 20 years' service and £508 (as at 6 April 2018) for one week's pay applies (ERA 1996, s 119).

(See **4.6** for details.) A gross weekly figure is used (subject to the maximum cap). The maximum basic award is currently £15,240 (since 6 April 2018).

There are, however, a number of differences between the calculations of the basic award and a redundancy payment:

(a)   In certain circumstances, such as where an employee is unfairly dismissed for being a member of a trade union or refusing to be a member of one, or where a health and safety official is dismissed, the basic award is subject to a minimum, which is £6,203 as at 6 April 2018.

(b)   The basic award may be subject to reduction. Section 122(1) and (2) provide that the basic award may be reduced by such sum as is just and equitable having regard to the claimant's unreasonable refusal to accept an offer of reinstatement and/or the claimant's pre-dismissal conduct (even if the conduct did not contribute to the dismissal).

Redundancy payments should also be deducted from the basic award. Note that in *Bowyer v Siemens Communications* (UKEAT/0021/05) the EAT held that a payment made by an employer which purported to be a redundancy payment, but which was not in fact because there was no redundancy situation, could not be set off against the basic award in an unfair dismissal claim. Such a payment could be offset (under ERA 1996, s 122(4)) only where the true reason for the dismissal was redundancy. (In practice, this will have an impact only where the compensatory award exceeds the statutory cap, as usually such sum will be set off against the compensatory award.)

Note, when calculating the basic award, that age, length of continuous service and pay are all artificially defined by statute. This contrasts with the approach to the compensatory award which is almost entirely discretionary. Thus the approach to the calculation of the two awards is necessarily different. The formula for a week's pay is set out in s 229 of the ERA 1996. For continuity of the period of employment, regard needs to be had to s 218 of the ERA 1996.

Determining what amounts to a week's pay can sometimes be a complicated process. In the context of the calculation of the basic award, it is subject to a statutory cap. But it may still require some complex working out – especially where employees work on flexible hours, or where their pay includes a rate for overtime or holiday pay. Note also that the ERA 1996, s 207A increase for breach of a Code of Practice (see below) only applies to the compensatory award, not the basic award.

5.6.2.2   Compensatory award

Unlike the basic award, which is based on a formula, the compensatory award is designed to compensate the employee for the loss that he has suffered.

By s 123(1) of the ERA 1996, the compensatory award consists of 'such amount as the tribunal considers just and equitable in all the circumstances having regard to the loss sustained by the complainant in consequence of the dismissal in so far as that loss is attributable to action taken by the employer'.

Maximum award

The compensatory award is subject to a maximum, which is £83,682 (from 6 April 2018) or 52 weeks' gross pay (whichever is the lower) (Unfair Dismissal (Variation of the Limit of Compensatory Award) Order 2013 (SI 2013/1949)). So, for example, if an employee was earning £36,000 per annum, the cap will be £36,000. This maximum is applied *after* any reductions have been made (see 'Reducing factors' below).

In the context of calculating the compensatory element of an award, a week's pay is not subject to any limit (as it is for calculating the basic award). Where an employee receives non-variable pay for their working hours, the amount of a week's pay is 'the amount that is payable by the employer' under the contract. In *University of Sunderland v Drossou* (UKEAT/0341/16), the

EAT upheld a tribunal decision that a week's pay could include the employer's pension contributions – even though this was paid into a pension fund and the employee did not receive it as income in hand. For example, an employee earns £1,000 per week gross and his employer contributes £150 into a pension scheme each week. If pension contributions are not included, the maximum award would be £52,000 (£1,000 x 52 weeks). If the pension is included then the maximum award would be £59,800 (£1,150 x 52 weeks). The EAT noted that the wording of s 221(2) of the ERA 1996 is different from the wording in s 27 (unlawful deductions from wages claims). Whereas the wording of s 27 ('sums payable to the worker') would rule out including a pension contribution, s 221(2) refers to wages as 'sums payable to the worker'. This can make a significant difference to an award, and would appear to cover other financial rewards.

Note that the maximum does not apply to whistleblowing cases or to dismissals for asserting statutory rights.

Note: The £83,682 maximum applies only to the compensatory element of the award. A claimant could therefore receive £83,682 (or, if less, 12 months' pay) plus a basic award of up to £15,240 (as at 6 April 2018).

In *Tao Herbs and Acupuncture Ltd v Jin* (UKEAT/1477/09), the EAT confirmed that it was not appropriate when assessing compensation under s 123 of the ERA 1996 to take account of the employer's ability to pay (even if it would mean the business went into liquidation): the prime consideration is the loss suffered by the claimant.

In *W Devis & Sons Ltd v Atkins* [1977] AC 931 the dismissal of an abattoir manager was held to be unfair, but because the employer subsequently discovered information suggesting that the employee had been dishonest during his employment, the court held that it was just and equitable to order no compensatory award.

Whether an employee can recover non-economic loss was the subject of discussion in *Johnson v Unisys Ltd* [2001] IRLR 279. The employee received the maximum compensatory award from a tribunal. He then made a claim for breach of contract in the county court, claiming that his dismissal without a fair hearing was in breach of the duty of trust and confidence, and that this breach resulted in his having a mental breakdown. He sought damages for this. His claim was dismissed on two grounds. First, because the implied duty of trust and confidence was said to be inappropriate to the termination of the employment relationship (see **2.4.1.5**) and, secondly, because the employee had already exercised his statutory right to claim unfair dismissal. In the course of his judgment, Lord Hoffmann commented that while 'in the early days' the compensatory award was only there to compensate financial loss, that was

> too narrow a construction. The emphasis is upon the tribunal awarding such compensation as it thinks just and equitable. So I see no reason why in an appropriate case it should not include compensation for distress, humiliation, damage to reputation in the community or to family life.

However, in *Dunnachie v Kingston Upon Hull* [2004] IRLR 727, the House of Lords unanimously held that damages for non-economic loss are not recoverable for unfair dismissal, and that s 123 of the ERA 1996 only allows a tribunal to award financial losses. Thus it is not possible to recover damages for injury to feelings as part of unfair dismissal compensation. This overrides the Court of Appeal's decision (see [2004] IRLR 287).

Dunnachie was heard by the House of Lords at the same time as *Eastwood v Magnox; McCabe v Cornwall County Council and Another* [2004] IRLR 733, two cases concerning the overlap between common law claims for damages for breach of trust and confidence, and the statutory unfair dismissal regime. In these cases the House of Lords confirmed that a common law claim for breach of the implied term of trust and confidence will be allowed for events leading up to the dismissal, but not for the dismissal itself (because that would amount to a circumvention of the statutory cap placed on compensation for unfair dismissal) (see further **2.4.1.5**). So the employee who suffers psychiatric harm arising out of the events leading up to dismissal cannot recover damages for the loss suffered as part of his unfair dismissal claim because such a loss does not flow from the dismissal, but he might be able to bring a personal injury claim and/or a claim for breach of contract in the civil courts for such pre-dismissal loss. Damages for losses arising out of breach of an implied term flowing from the dismissal are only recoverable in an employment tribunal (where the cap on damages applies).

The Supreme Court confirmed that the so-called *Johnson* exclusion area also applies to cases in which the breach relied upon is of an express contractual term (*Edwards v Chesterfield Royal Hospital NHS Foundation Trust* [2013] UKSC 58). Therefore, an employee who is dismissed cannot bring proceedings for breach of contract based on a failure to follow contractual disciplinary procedures because that would, according to the Supreme Court, undermine the statutory unfair dismissal regime (see **Chapter 2**).

In *GAB Robins v Triggs* [2008] IRLR 317 (an unfair constructive dismissal claim), the Court of Appeal held, applying *Johnson* and *Eastwood*, that in assessing the claimant's loss of earnings for unfair dismissal purposes, no regard could be had to losses which flowed from the bullying that led to her taking time off ill and subsequently resigning, and which resulted in reduced earning capacity thereafter. Regard must be had, for the purposes of s 123 of the ERA 1996, only to losses flowing from the dismissal (by which time the claimant was already ill). The claimant's reduced earning capacity by reason of her illness was not a loss suffered 'in consequence of the dismissal'. Rather, it was caused by the bullying, and therefore the claimant could recover damages in respect of it only by bringing a separate claim at common law, such as for psychiatric injury.

A tribunal must, in deciding whether to make a compensatory award (see *Saunders v OCS Group* (UKEAT/0051/09)):

(a)   identify what loss the employee has suffered at the date of dismissal; and then

(b)   decide whether the employer's action (in dismissing the employee) caused the loss.

Heads of loss

Compensation will usually be assessed under the following main heads:

(a)   Immediate loss of net earnings to which the employee was entitled, from the date of dismissal to the date of the hearing or until the employee finds a new job, if earlier (provided that job is higher-paid). In *Whelan and Another (t/a Cheers Off Licence) v Richardson* [1998] IRLR 14, the EAT said, when calculating unfair dismissal compensation, that the applicant should be compensated for all losses arising from the date of dismissal until the date on which higher-paid alternative employment is found.

In *Burlo v Langley & Carter* [2006] EWCA Civ 1778, the Court of Appeal dealt with the principles for calculating compensation during an employee's notice period. Ms Burlo worked as a nanny for Mr Langley and Ms Carter. Her employment was subject to a written contract which provided for eight weeks' notice of termination on either side. The contract also provided that, during periods of sickness, the employers would pay 'sickness benefit in accordance with government statutory sick pay legislation'. Following an argument about money, Ms Burlo threatened to resign. Mr Langley said that she would be required to work her notice. Ms Burlo continued at work, but some days later she had a car accident and was provided with a sick note to say that she would be off work for several weeks. In the meantime, her employers engaged another nanny and wrote saying that they would not now require Ms Burlo to work out her notice. Ms Burlo brought a number of claims in the employment tribunal, including claims for wrongful and unfair dismissal. Both these claims succeeded. The tribunal assessed damages for the notice period at £3,440 (eight weeks at her normal weekly wage). They did not explain why they held that the damages should be based on the normal weekly wage rather than on the statutory sick pay to which the employee would have been entitled whilst off sick under her contract of employment. The Court of Appeal held that if Ms Burlo had not been dismissed, she would have received statutory sick pay during her period of absence. Consequently, statutory sick pay was the correct measure of her weekly loss during the notice period. Note, however, that where an employee is entitled only to statutory minimum notice, the employer must pay full pay during the notice period, even where the employee is off work sick (ERA 1996, ss 87 and 88).

In *Paggetti v Cobb* (UKEAT/136/01), the EAT held that when assessing the compensatory (and basic) awards, the tribunal must have regard to the minimum wage.

(b) Future loss of net earnings to which the employee was entitled from the date of hearing until the employee obtains new employment. No award will be made under this head if the employee is permanently re-employed in an equally well remunerated job at the date of hearing. If he loses that new job, the tribunal will have to assess whether the chain of causation has been broken (*Cowen v Rentokil Ltd* (UKEAT/0473/07)). If the employee takes a less well-paid job, he will be compensated for the difference in pay for such period as the tribunal thinks appropriate in the circumstances. If the employee remains unemployed at this date, the tribunal will have to estimate if and when the employee is likely to be re-employed. Compensation for future loss of earnings is not limited to the employee's contractual notice period. The tribunal will take into account local employment conditions, the skills of the employee, his age and general employability. If an employee could and would have worked beyond the age of 65, compensation may be awarded for potential loss of earnings after 65. If evidence shows that the employee would shortly have lost his job anyway, due, for example, to redundancy, compensation will be limited.

(c) Loss of pension rights and net fringe benefits from the date of dismissal to the date at (b) above. The value of lost pension rights is very difficult to calculate, and depends on a number of factors, such as the duration of the loss, the type of scheme, the benefits paid and the benefits receivable on retirement. There are two main approaches – a simplified approach and a substantial approach. Where there is a defined contribution scheme, calculation should be relatively straightforward, since the loss will be the value of the contributions that have not been paid. Where there is a defined benefit scheme, the position will be more complicated to assess, and may depend on whether an individual is able to transfer the value of his pension to a new fund. The detail of these approaches is beyond the scope of this work. In *Department for Work and Pensions v Coulson* (UKEAT/0572/12), the EAT upheld a pension award reflecting compensation for the pension the claimant would have received if she had remained in employment until her retirement (the claimant was 42 at the date of dismissal). See the Court of Appeal's decision in *Griffin v Plymouth Hospital NHS Trust* [2014] EWCA Civ 1240 for a more recent consideration of the calculation of pension loss.

In March 2016 a working group of Employment Judges produced a 4th edition of the *Compensation for Loss of Pension Rights* booklet on the approach to be adopted in calculating pension losses. The booklet sets out that there should be a default assumption that as far as state pension rights were concerned, there were no losses. As far as occupational pensions are concerned, there should be two possible approaches, depending on whether a case is simple or complex. In simple cases (usually defined contribution or money purchase schemes), the value should be calculated using the amount of lost employer future service contributions from the date of dismissal, taking account where appropriate of any mitigation. In complex cases, such as loss of defined benefit rights for a substantial period of time (in the absence of any agreement between the parties on pension loss), pension loss should be determined using factors set out in what are known as the Ogden tables (actuarial table commonly used to assess compensation in personal injury cases), valued by expert actuaries. Following publication, the Presidents of Employment Tribunals in England and Wales and Scotland have issued Presidential Guidance on the principles to be applied when compensating for pension loss, applying from 10 August 2017. The principles adopt the approach set out in the booklet referred to above. Readers are advised to refer to this Guidance and the booklet when advising on calculating pension losses.

(d)   Loss of statutory rights. The loss of accrued redundancy rights is compensated for by the basic award, but the tribunal will order a sum for the loss of the right to bring an unfair dismissal claim for one year. Conventionally, this sum is about £350.

The employee may exceptionally also be awarded up to half-a-week's net pay for each week of the statutory minimum period of notice to which he had been entitled at the end of employment. For example, an employee with 20 years' service would have been entitled to the maximum 12-week notice period. He may be awarded ½ × 12 × net weekly pay (ie six weeks) to compensate for the loss of this. This payment will be made only in exceptional circumstances, because it depends on the double contingency that the employee will get a new job and be dismissed from it before building up the same period of notice. More often than not, a tribunal will simply award the £350 above for loss of statutory rights.

(e)   Expenses in looking for work; removal expenses incurred in taking up a new job.

(f)   A premium for delayed payment may be awarded (the reverse of accelerated receipt – see 'Reducing factors' below) (*Melia v Magna Kansei* (UKEAT/0339/04)).

Compulsory increase of the compensatory award

Section 38 of the EA 2002 states that a tribunal must award compensation to an employee where, upon a successful claim being made under any of the jurisdictions listed in Sch 5 to the EA 2002 (which include unfair dismissal), it becomes apparent that the employer was in breach of his duty to provide full and accurate written particulars (under ERA 1996, s 1). This is not a free-standing claim, it is dependent upon a claim under one of the listed jurisdictions being successful. The tribunal must award the minimum amount of two weeks' pay and may, if it considers it just and equitable, in the circumstances, award a higher amount of four weeks' pay (subject to the maximum of £508 (as at 6 April 2018)). This is on top of any award the tribunal might already have made in respect of the main claim. The tribunal does not have to make any award if there are exceptional circumstances that would make it unjust or inequitable to make an award or increase an award.

Discretionary increase of compensation

Where there has been an unreasonable failure by the employer to comply with the Acas Code, the tribunal has power to increase compensation by up to 25% (TULR(C)A 1992, s 207A). It should be noted that this adjustment option does not apply to the basic award.

It remains to be seen what will constitute an unreasonable failure to comply with the Code, and what factors will be relevant to the question of whether it is 'just and equitable' to make an adjustment to an award. In *Lawless v Print Plus* (UKEAT/0333/09), a case decided under the old statutory minimum procedures, the EAT said the factors to be taken into account when considering the size of the uplift include:

(a)   whether the procedures were ignored altogether or applied to some extent;

(b)   whether the failure to apply the procedures was deliberate or inadvertent;

(c)   whether there are circumstances which might mitigate the blameworthiness of the failure;

(d)   the size and resources of the employer which may aggravate or mitigate the culpability and/or seriousness of the failure.

In *Shifferaw v Hudson Music Co Ltd* (UKEAT/0294/15) the employment tribunal dealt with the uplift issue as follows:

> 65. ... Whilst we rejected ... some other complaints of failure to comply with the ACAS code, we found unreasonable failure to comply in relation to James De Wolfe having not been an independent person to deal with the Claimant's grievance. We considered that this was a serious failure because he was the

person considering her whole grievance and she was not given a right of appeal. The just and equitable uplift was more than the 10% proposed by [the respondent]. However, there were *some* measures taken to address her concerns internally, and other complaints had not succeeded before us [tribunal's emphasis]. Overall, within the statutory range of 0% to 25%, we considered a 20% uplift would be fair in this case.

There was no challenge to that decision. The EAT held that where there are concurrent unfair dismissal and wrongful dismissal claims, it is a matter for the judge's discretion whether the uplift should be applied from the date of dismissal or from the end of the notice period (wrongful dismissal is not included in Sch A2). The case was remitted for the judge to determine that question. In the authors' opinion, the uplift ought to apply to the unfair dismissal compensatory award from the date of dismissal. In such cases wrongful dismissal damages would become a notional award (see **6.7.1**).

Note that because s 207A only 'bites' on claims where the relevant Code of Practice applies, and because, as we saw earlier, the only Code of Practice published to date does not apply to dismissals by reason of redundancy or where the dismissal was as a result of the expiry of a fixed-term contract, no adjustment will be made to redundancy payment awards or unfair dismissal awards where the reason for the dismissal was redundancy or expiry of a fixed-term contract. The EAT held in *Lund v St Edmund's School, Canterbury* (UKEAT/0514/12) that the Code applies to 'some other substantial reason' dismissals where the reason related to the employee's behaviour. The claimant was dismissed because the school had lost confidence in him as a result of the claimant's actions at work. The EAT held that 'his claim concerned the conduct on his part which led the school to consider whether he should be dismissed, even if it was not his conduct but the effect of his conduct ... which was the ultimate reason for his dismissal'.

In *Phoenix House Ltd v Stockman* (UKEAT/0264/15), it was held that the 25% uplift does not apply to dismissals for some other substantial reason due to a breakdown in working relations. (This conflicts with the 'provisional view' given in *Hussain v Jurys Inns Group Ltd* (UKEAT/0283/15).) In *Holmes v Qinetiq Ltd* [2016] IRLR 664, the EAT held that the Acas Code did not apply to ill-health dismissals where no disciplinary procedure was invoked.

Note also that uplifts can only be applied to employees and not workers (see *Local Government Yorkshire v Shah* (UKEAT/0587/11)).

Reducing factors

Note that early pension payments should *not* be deducted from the compensatory award (*Smoker v London Fire and Civil Defence Authority* [1991] ICR 449, followed in *Knapton & Others v ECC Card Clothing Ltd* [2006] IRLR 756).

(a) *Mitigation*

The employee is under a duty to mitigate his loss by taking reasonable steps to obtain alternative employment. Compensation will not be awarded for any loss that should have been mitigated but was not (*Kyndall Spirits v Burns* (EAT/29/02)). The burden of raising and proving an unreasonable failure to mitigate is on the employer. In practice, an employee should keep records of his job applications to show the tribunal that he has tried to mitigate his loss. Where an employee turns down an offer of employment, the ultimate question for the tribunal is whether he acted unreasonably in turning it down. The tribunal must consider all the surrounding circumstances (*Wilding v British Telecommunications plc* [2002] IRLR 524). Failure to mitigate can reduce the compensatory award but not the basic award. Similarly, if the employee has secured an alternative job by the time of the hearing, wages from that new job will be taken into account. The EAT held in *Window Machinery Sales Ltd t/a Promac Group v Luckey* (UKEAT/0301/14) that the tribunal should ask first what steps were reasonable for the claimant to have taken; secondly, whether the claimant did take reasonable steps; and thirdly, to what extent, if any, the claimant would have actually mitigated the loss if he had taken those steps; and that the burden of proof is on the employer at all stages.

In *Cooper Contracting Ltd v Lindsey* (EAT/0184/15), the EAT summarised the following principles as being relevant when assessing mitigation of loss:

(1)   It is not for the employee to prove that they mitigated their loss: the burden of proof is on the employer.

(2)   If the employer does not address the issue of mitigation, the Tribunal need not consider it.

(3)   If the employer does raise the issue, it must prove that the employee acted unreasonably; the employee does not have to show that what they did was reasonable. While it might be reasonable for an employee to accept the most lucratively paid job, it is not necessarily unreasonable for them to accept a lesser paid job due to a preference for the nature of that particular role: 'there may come a time in a person's working life when some types of work are no longer appropriate ... Mr Lindsey's evidence was that he preferred to be his own boss having had the experience of employment with the Respondent. It is very much his own choice.'

(4)   The employee does not have to take all reasonable steps to mitigate their loss. If such a position were adopted, an employer would be able to argue that an employee's compensation should be reduced on the basis of a single reasonable step not taken.

(5)   Ultimately, it is the Tribunal's view of what is unreasonable in all the circumstances that matters, which can include the views and wishes of the employee.

(6)   It is not for the claimant to be put on trial when looking at mitigation of loss; they are not the party at fault in the proceedings.

The Court of Appeal in *Burlo* (see 'Heads of loss' above) looked closely at the decision of the National Industrial Relations Court (Sir John Donaldson presiding) in *Norton Tool Co Ltd v Tewson* [1973] 1 WLR 45. It said that *Norton Tool* settled two basic points of law on the calculation of compensation for unfair dismissal in an actual dismissal. First, compensation could not be awarded for injury to feelings. (*Norton Tool* was expressly approved on this point by the House of Lords in *Dunnachie v Kingston upon Hull City Council* (see above).) Secondly, where an employer summarily dismissed an employee in a situation where notice should have been given but was not, an employee was entitled to be awarded compensation for wages in lieu of notice without any deduction for wages which were actually earned, or could have been earned, with an alternative employer during the notice period. In *Babcock FATA Ltd v Addison* [1987] ICR 805, the employer had challenged (unsuccessfully) *Norton Tool* on the wages in lieu of notice point. Although the employer won its appeal on the particular facts in *Babcock*, the Court of Appeal in that case were unanimous in not accepting the contention that *Norton Tool* was wrong in holding that the employee should not have to give credit for the wages that he had received from alternative employment during the period of notice. It was argued in *Burlo* that the House of Lords in *Dunnachie* had impliedly overruled the *Norton Tool* principle that credit need not be given by an employee for other earnings during the notice period. The Court of Appeal said that issue had to be left for another case to determine, but in the meantime a claimant should not have to give credit for monies earned during the notice period. The Court of Appeal in *Stuart Peters v Bell* [2009] EWCA Civ 938 held that this principle does not apply to a constructive dismissal. In a constructive dismissal case, credit has to be given for wages earned during the notice period.

(b)   *Accelerated receipt for future loss of earnings*

See **2.4.1.9** for a discussion of this reducing factor.

(c)   *Ex gratia payments made by the employer to the employee*

(d)   *'Polkey' deductions*

One of the factors that a tribunal has to consider when assessing compensation where there have been procedural failings in the dismissal process, is whether the employee would still have been dismissed if a proper procedure had been followed. If the tribunal concludes that even if a fair procedure had been followed, dismissal would still have occurred, then that can sound in the compensation that is awarded. Such a conclusion can have two main effects:

(i)   on the period of time over which compensation is awarded; and

(ii)   on the actual amount,

in that a percentage reduction (up to 100%) may be made by the tribunal to take account of the tribunal's assessment of the likelihood that dismissal would still have occurred. An employment tribunal's task, when deciding what compensation is just and equitable for future loss of earnings in these circumstances, will almost inevitably involve a consideration of uncertainties. What the tribunal has to do is to 'construct, from evidence not speculation, a framework which is a working hypothesis about what would have happened had the [employer] behaved differently and fairly' (*Gover and Others v Property Care Ltd* [2006] EWCA Civ 286).

In *Polkey v AE Dayton Services Ltd* [1988] ICR 142, the House of Lords ended what was known as the 'no difference' rule, which had allowed procedurally irregular dismissals to be ruled as fair where it could be shown that carrying out a proper procedure would have made no difference to the outcome. Their Lordships said this was not relevant to fairness, but it would sound in the assessment of damages because s 123 of the ERA 1996 refers to 'such amount as the tribunal considers just and equitable in all the circumstances'. Lord Mackay of Clashfern approved the remarks of Browne-Wilkinson J in *Sillifant v Powell Duffryn Timber Ltd* [1983] IRLR 91, at 92:

> Where in the circumstances known at the time of the dismissal, it was not reasonable for the employer to dismiss without giving an opportunity to explain, but facts subsequently discovered or proved ... show that the dismissal was in fact merited, compensation would be reduced to nil. Such an approach ensures that an employee who could have been fairly dismissed does not get compensation.

Lord Bridge also approved the remarks of Browne-Wilkinson J at 96:

> There is no need for an 'all or nothing' decision; if the industrial tribunal thinks there is a doubt whether or not the employee would have been dismissed, this element can be reflected by reducing the normal amount of compensation by a percentage representing the chance that the employee would still have lost his employment.

In *Lambe v 186K* [2005] ICR 307, the Court of Appeal considered how tribunals should approach the question of compensation in cases where a dismissal might have occurred in any event. Giving the judgment of the Court, Wall LJ (at 323) cited with approval the judgment of Lord Prosser in the Court of Session in *King v Eaton Ltd (No 2)* [1998] IRLR 686. The procedure by which an applicant was made redundant in *King* was found to be unfair, and the issue was whether the applicant would have been made redundant had a fair procedure been followed. Lord Prosser stated (at para 19):

> It seems to us that the matter will be one of impression and judgment, so that a tribunal will have to decide whether the unfair departure from what should have happened was of a kind which makes it possible to say, with more or less confidence, that the failure made no difference, or whether the failure was such that one cannot sensibly reconstruct the world as it might have been.

Wall LJ stated that the formulation 'provides tribunals with a straightforward and sensible yardstick with which to approach such cases'. At para 60, Wall LJ adopted that approach and stated:

> [That] approach to the facts of the instant case leads us to the conclusion that on the evidence available to it, the Tribunal was entitled to conclude that in the Appellant's case, whilst both the process of selection for redundancy and the absence of consultation was unfair, it was unlikely

that the Appellant would have found alternative employment with the Respondent or any of its associated companies at the conclusion of an extended period of consultation. The Tribunal was entitled to find that what the Appellant wanted was his job back, and that he was not willing to consider the alternative offered by the Respondent, which the Tribunal found was both a promotion and commanded a higher income. In short, this was not a case in which it was impossible for the Tribunal sensibly to reconstruct the world as it never was: the Tribunal was entitled to come to the conclusion that an extended period of consultation should have taken place, but that at the end of it, the Appellant would still have left the Respondent's employment.

Where a fair procedure would have delayed an otherwise inevitable dismissal, compensation will be awarded for the time the procedure would have taken to conduct properly (see, for example, *Slaughter v Breuer* [1990] ICR 730).

In *O'Donoghue v Redcar and Cleveland BC* [2001] IRLR 615, the Court of Appeal upheld the tribunal's finding that the claimant would have been dismissed fairly within a further period of six months because of her antagonistic attitude. Compensation was therefore limited to six months (see also *Gover and Others v Property Care Ltd* [2006] EWCA Civ 286).

In *Software 2000 Ltd v Andrews and Others* [2007] ICR 825, Elias J reviewed and summarised the principles to be extracted from all the authorities on *Polkey*.

The EAT confirmed in *Zebrowski v Concentric Birmingham Ltd* (UKEAT/0245/16) that, in summary, tribunals have three *alternative* options when assessing how long a period to make an award for:

*   to find that it is certain that the employee would have been dismissed by the end of a particular period and so limit compensation to that period (see *O'Donoghue* above);

*   to find that the employment relationship would have continued unaffected for a certain period but thereafter there was a percentage chance that the employee would have ceased to be employed (see, for example, *Frith Accountants Ltd v Law* (EAT/0460/13));

*   to assess the percentage likelihood of the employment terminating in any event.

Polkey deductions may be made whether the dismissal is substantively unfair or procedurally unfair, although it will be easier to assess if the failure is procedural (*King v Eaton Ltd (No 2)* [1998] IRLR 686). For decisions considering a *Polkey* reduction (i) in a redundancy situation, where there was a procedurally unfair dismissal, see *Contract Bottling Ltd v Cave* (UKEAT/0525/12), and (ii) in an unfair dismissal case, see *Anderson v Chesterfield High School* (UKEAT/0206/14).

(e) *Discretionary reduction in compensation*

Where there has been an unreasonable failure by the employee to comply with the Acas Code, a reduction of up to 25% is possible. (See the discussion above of the discretionary increase of compensation.)

(f) *Contributory fault*

If the tribunal finds that the complainant caused or contributed to his dismissal (this must be pre-dismissal conduct), the compensatory award *must* be reduced by such proportion as it considers just and equitable (ERA 1996, s 123(6)). If the employee substantially contributed to his own dismissal, this will mean a substantial percentage reduction in the awards, even of 100%, leaving the employee with a finding of unfair dismissal but no compensation. This is usually relevant only in misconduct dismissals. It is unusual in capability dismissals, for example on health grounds, where the employee is not culpable or blameworthy (but see *Jinadu v Dockland Buses Ltd* (UKEAT/0166/16) where the claimant's compensatory (and basic) award was reduced by 75% in a capability case). The tribunal does not necessarily need to reduce basic and compensatory awards by the same percentage, but it often does so in practice. The question for the tribunal is whether, in a misconduct case, the claimant was in fact guilty of the blameworthy or culpable conduct which to any extent caused or contributed to the dismissal. The employer's conduct is irrelevant (*Sandwell & West Birmingham Hospitals NHS Trust v Westwood* (UKEAT/0032/09), but tribunals must consider mitigating factors before making a reduction.

(g)   *Pre-dismissal misconduct discovered after dismissal*

The tribunal, in deciding what amount is just and equitable, may take into account any misconduct of the employee discovered after dismissal and reduce both the basic and compensatory awards accordingly (ss 122(2) and 123(1)). Post-dismissal conduct is not relevant.

(h)   *Contractual redundancy payments in excess of the basic award.*

(i)   *Payments in lieu – compensatory award only*

If the employee receives a payment in lieu of notice or an ex gratia payment from his employer, this will be taken into account in assessing his compensation (*Babcock FATA Ltd v Addison* [1987] IRLR 173, CA).

(j)   *Conduct of the employee post dismissal*, in so far as it might breach the chain of causation when considering future loss (see *Cumbria County Council & Governing Body of Dowdales School v Bates* (UKEAT/0398/11 & 0039/13).

Order of compensatory award adjustments

The correct order of adjustments once the net loss is calculated is (see *Ministry of Defence v Wheeler* [1998] IRLR 23, CA, and *Digital Equipment Co Ltd v Clements (No 2)* [1998] IRLR 134, CA):

(a)   deduct payments in lieu/ex gratia payments made by the employer;

(b)   deduct sums earned by the employee from new employment, or make deductions (notional earnings) by reason of a failure to mitigate;

(c)   deduct benefits other than jobseeker's allowance and income support (see also **5.6.2.4** below);

(d)   make any *Polkey* deduction;

(e)   reduce the award or increase by up to 25% for a failure to comply with the Acas Code;

(f)   make any contributory fault deduction/deduction for misconduct discovered after dismissal (ERA 1996, s 123(6));

(g)   deduct contractual redundancy payment made by the employer which is in excess of basic award;

(h)   add in any award for sums awarded for failure to provide written particulars of employment (EA 2002, ss 31 and 38) (s 31(5));

(i)   apply statutory cap of £83,682 (as at 6 April 2018) (if appropriate);

(j)   gross up (if appropriate).

5.6.2.3   Interest

Interest may be awarded on compensation for unfair dismissal. It begins to run from the day after the decision is sent to the parties. However, if the amount is paid in full within 14 days, no interest is payable.

The current rate of interest is set out in s 17 of the Judgments Act 1833 and Article 4 of the Employment Tribunals (Interest) Order 1990 (SI 1990/479). Since 1 April 1993, this rate has been 8% per annum.

5.6.2.4   Recoupment of social security benefits

The Employment Protection (Recoupment of Jobseeker's Allowance and Income Support) Regulations 1996 (SI 1996/2349) (as amended and updated by the Welfare Reform Act 2007 and the Social Security (Miscellaneous Amendments) (No 5) Regulations 2010 (SI 2010/2429)) allow the Government to recoup jobseeker's allowance, income support and (from 1

November 2010) income-related employment and support allowance (IRESA) paid to an employee who gets an unfair dismissal award of compensation. These benefits received by the employee are not deducted by the tribunal in computing the compensatory award. (*Note:* Contributory employment and support allowance is not covered by the recoupment regulations.)

The Employment Tribunals Act 1996 (ETA 1996), ss 16 and 17 operate as follows:

(a) where the employee has received jobseeker's allowance, income support or IRESA between the EDT and the hearing, the tribunal designates the 'immediate loss of earnings' part of the award as the 'prescribed element' and notifies the Department for Work and Pensions (DfWP);

(b) the employer withholds the 'prescribed element' from the employee until notified by the DfWP of the amount of jobseeker's allowance, income support and IRESA to be recouped (up to the maximum of the 'prescribed element');

(c) the amount to be recouped is then paid by the employer to the DfWP and any balance of the 'prescribed element' paid to the employee.

EXAMPLE

Whilst awaiting a hearing, the employee receives income support *totalling* £1,500. The tribunal awards compensation of £10,000.

£2,000 of this represents immediate loss of wages (the 'prescribed element').

The employer pays £8,000 to the employee immediately and tells DfWP that he has retained £2,000.

DfWP tells the employer to account for £1,500.

The employer pays £1,500 to DfWP and £500 to the employee.

Note: the recoupment regulations do not apply to settlements.

5.6.2.5 Taxation

If an award is made for termination of employment that exceeds £30,000, it is subject to taxation (see Income Tax (Earnings and Pensions) Act 2003, Ch 3, Pt 6, s 401(1)). This covers payments for 'being' an employee, including emoluments from the employer and rewards for services past, present and future. Any awards over £30,000 should therefore be grossed up to ensure that the net loss is actually paid to the claimant (see **2.4.1.8**). The EAT explains how to calculate the grossed up figure in *Hall v Durham CC and Ors* (UKEAT/0256/14) and confirms in *Chief Constable of Northumbria Police v Erichsen* (UKEAT/0027/15) that since pension loss is assessed on a gross basis, that loss should not be grossed up.

A detailed explanation of how taxation impacts in practice on tribunal awards is beyond the scope of this work, but a summary chart is set out in **Table 5.1** below. Tribunals generally make awards that reflect a claimant's losses, but should take into account when doing so any prospective tax liability. From 6 April 2011, employers must deduct PAYE from post-termination payments at the appropriate marginal rate.

Readers should note that, from 6 April 2018, significant changes were introduced to the tax treatment of termination payments to ensure that payments in respect of the contractual notice period will be taxable, even if the employee does not work the notice period, ensuring that NICs due on sums above £30,000 will be payable and clarifying that the exception does not apply to termination payments relating to injury to feelings awards. In essence, the new rules treat all employment contracts as if they contain a payment in lieu of notice (PILON) clause, so that the basic pay the employee would have received during the notice period will be taxed as earnings (and subject to income tax and national insurance contributions). The £30,000 exemption will remain potentially available for any balance which is genuinely compensation for loss of office. Payments for injury to feelings (except where the injury amounts to a psychiatric injury or other recognised medical condition) will fall outside the injury payments exemption.

In August 2013, the Office of Tax Simplification (OTS) produced an interim report which looked at s 401 of the Income Tax (Earnings and Pensions) Act 2003. The report noted that there was an unfair distinction made with regard to PILON, where properly advised employees might be better able to avoid paying tax, and the Government should consider increasing the £30,000 threshold.

In its final report in July 2014, the OTS concluded that the existing system was fraught with confusion and uncertainty. The Office found that employers want to pay the correct amount of tax but that the complexities of the system often prevent this from being achieved. The OTS concluded that, above all, employers want a system that is clear and easy to administer, and employees want certainty about the amounts they will receive. The OTS found cases where employees and employers had been asked to pay additional tax following the employee's departure from the employer, and cases where employers had deducted too much tax because they were unable to determine the correct tax treatment due to the complexity of the rules. The OTS also concluded that the current system was unfair, because those who are better paid and better advised were often able to structure their affairs so that they benefitted from the tax exemptions.

In July 2015, HMRC published a consultation on 'Simplification of the tax and National Insurance treatment of termination payments'. The consultation contained proposals:

(a)   to remove distinctions between contractual and non-contractual payments; and

(b)   to review the existing exemptions, with consideration given to removing some, or all, of them.

The OTS also considered that the current £30,000 threshold would probably be unaffordable if the distinction between contractual and non-contractual termination payments were to be removed. The OTS suggested two potential options for reform of the taxation of termination payments. One suggestion was a blanket exemption, the other was to link the availability of any tax exemption to the payment of statutory redundancy. However, the OTS acknowledged that there would be difficulties with this system, as there are a number of people who are not able to benefit from statutory redundancy.

HMRC had evidence that some employees and employers attempt to change the nature of their termination payments. This is so that the employee can benefit from the £30,000 exemption and the employer avoids liability for employer national insurance contributions (NICs). For example, there have been cases where employees and employers argue that a PILON (subject to tax and NICs) is actually a payment for breach of contract, so there is no NIC liability and the payment is only taxable on amounts over £30,000. With such a complex tax treatment of termination payments, it is often difficult for HMRC to disprove such claims.

The Government has acknowledged that there are difficulties with the taxation of termination payments. It has indicated that it wants to review the treatment, with the aim of creating a regime that is fair, easy for employers to administer and for employees to understand, and which avoids uncertainty.

The consultation closed on 16 October 2015. In December 2016, in response to the July 2015 consultation, HMRC published draft legislation intended to change the way termination payments are taxed. This became effective in April 2018.

The stated aims of the proposals are to make the taxation of termination payments simpler for both employees and employers to understand and operate, clearer and more certain, fairer and not unduly expensive to implement and operate.

The existing distinction between contractual/customary termination payments from the employer, such as holiday pay (which are taxable), and non-contractual ones, such as statutory redundancy pay (which currently are not subject to tax), is to be retained. In the responses to the proposals, it was pointed out by a significant number of responses that to change this state of affairs would involved a considerable amount of legislative changes, which would increase complexity. However, it will be made clearer that only payments directly relating to termination will be exempt, and reference will need to be made to the contractual terms and conditions of employment in order to ascertain which payments are contractual. The excess of any non-contractual payments over £30,000 will be taxable, and the existing £30,000 threshold is to be retained.

> **EXAMPLE**
>
> Suppose a tribunal awards £50,000 as the compensatory element of an award for unfair dismissal. HM Revenue and Customs regards this as taxable as a termination payment. The first £30,000 is tax free (if statutory redundancy has also been paid this would count towards the £30,000). The remaining £20,000 is taxed as income. What tax rate is applicable will depend on what the employee has already earned in the tax year. If his total gross earnings in the year do not exceed £42,385, the appropriate tax rate will be 20%. The award will need to be grossed up (which will provide a figure of £25,000 (20,000 ÷ 0.8)). Then add back in the £30,000. The tribunal will need to award £55,000 to the employee to ensure that the employee is left, after the employer pays the tax due on £25,000 (being £5,000), with the true net loss of £50,000.

Table 5.1 Taxation of tribunal awards

Type of Award	Gross/Net	Explanation
Unlawful deduction from wages [ERA 1996, s 24] (see **1.11.1**)	Gross (but see wording in ERA 1996, s 13(3)) NI is also payable	Wages. This is deferred remuneration; it is a contractual payment which is taxable in the hands of the employee. It is not a payment on termination and does not come within the £30K exemption.
Unpaid holiday pay (whether under contract or under WTR) (see **1.12.5**)	Gross NI is also payable	Wages. This is deferred remuneration; it is a contractual payment which is taxable in the hands of the employee. It is not a payment on termination and does not come within the £30K exemption.
Unpaid notice: (a) PILON clause (see **2.4.1.8**)	(a) Gross NI is also payable	(a) This is a contractual payment which is taxable in the hands of the employee. It is not a payment on termination and does not come within the £30K exemption.

Type of Award	Gross/Net	Explanation
(b) No PILON clause	(b) Net (after notional deduction of tax and NICs)	(b) (This will be rare due to changes introduced from April 2018 – see above.) Where there is no PILON clause, this will not be a contractual payment but rather is damages for breach of contract. Damages are generally awarded in respect of net loss of earnings as this puts the employee in the same position as if the contract had been performed. An employee is exempt from paying tax on termination payments, including damages for wrongful dismissal, which do not exceed £30K. This sum should be included as part of the £30K exemption as it is a payment on termination under IT(EP)A 2003, Pt 6. Sums in excess of £30K will need to be grossed up.
Damages for wrongful dismissal (such as genuine compensation for loss of office (over and above any notice pay)) – generally calculated on basis of a sum equal to the wages payable during the contractual notice period (see **2.4**) (See *British Transport Commission v Gourley* [1955] 3 All ER 796)	Net (after notional deduction of tax and NICs)	This is not a contractual payment but rather is damages for breach of contract. An employee is exempt from paying tax on termination payments, including damages for wrongful dismissal, which do not exceed £30K. This sum should therefore be included as part of the £30K exemption as it is a payment on termination. NB: there is a £25K jurisdictional limit on tribunal awards for breach of contract, so in reality this will require grossing up only where other awards, such as compensation for unfair dismissal, take the award over £30K.
Employment Act 2002, s 38 payment (see **5.6.2.2**)	Gross (subject to the weekly pay cap)	This is not wages and therefore is not normally taxable. Not included within the £30K exemption.
UD reinstatement or re-engagement (where arrears of wages etc will have to be paid)	Net	The Court of Appeal in *Wilson v Clayton* [2005] IRLR 108 said this was not earnings but a payment in consequence of dismissal. An employee is exempt from paying tax on termination payments which do not exceed £30,000. This sum should be included as part of the £30,000 exemption.
UD basic award and compensation award (ERA 1996, s 118) (see **5.6.2.1** and **5.6.2.2**)	Net (after notional deduction of tax and NI)	Not taxable *unless* in excess of £30K exemption, when will have to gross up the amount which exceeds £30K. (See *British Transport Commission v Gourley* [1955] 3 All ER 796.)

Type of Award	Gross/Net	Explanation
Compensation award for unlawful discrimination – treated as statutory tort (see **8.13.2.1**)	Net (after notional deduction of tax and NI)	Not taxable unless in excess of £30K exemption, when will have to gross up the amount which exceeds £30K. (See *Walker v Adams* [2001] STC 101.)
Discrimination – injury to feelings and personal injury award (ITEPA 2003, s 406) (see *Moorthy v HMRC* [2018] EWCA Civ 847 and *Timothy James Consulting Ltd v Wilton UK* (EAT/0082/14)) (see **8.8.2.2**)	Simple figure awarded	If the injury to feelings award relates to conduct before termination then it is not earnings, is not taxable and does not need to be grossed up. Prior to April 2018, if an injury to feelings award arose out of the termination of employment then it was not taxable. From April 2018, payments arising out of termination of employment will be exempt only if they relate to a psychiatric injury or other recognised medical condition.

5.7 PENALTIES FOR EMPLOYERS

Section 16 of the ERRA 2013 introduced, from 6 April 2014, financial penalties for employers who lose a claim (see ETA 1996, s 12A). Any penalty goes to the Government, not to the claimant. A penalty may be imposed where the employer's breach has 'one or more aggravating features'. The level of penalty is subject to a minimum of £100 and a maximum of £5,000.

If a financial award has been made to a claimant, the penalty will be half the total award made by the tribunal (subject to the maximum level). A 50% reduction will be applied if the penalty is paid within 21 days.

The penalty is designed to encourage employers to take their legal responsibilities seriously. There is no definition of what amounts to an aggravating feature. The Government's Explanatory Note to s 16 of the ERRA 2013 states that a tribunal may be more likely to find aggravating features where the employer's actions were deliberate or committed with malice, the employer was an organisation with a dedicated human resources department, or the employer repeatedly breaches the employment rights. It therefore appears that the penalty is not intended to be applied where there is 'inadvertent error'.

Even if a tribunal finds an aggravating feature, it will still have a discretion whether to impose a penalty, taking into account factors such as size, duration of the breach, the behaviour of the parties and ability to pay. (See too **6.4.10.5**)

5.8 CASE STUDY 1: UNFAIR DISMISSAL, REDUNDANCY PAYMENT AND UNPAID WAGES

Facts

(1)   R ran a graphic design agency employing a number of designers. C was employed by R as a senior designer. On 1 October 2017, C was given her wage cheque for September. That cheque bounced. By 13 October 2017, the entire workforce, including C, had been sent home on full pay. The workshop was closed. R indicated to its workforce that the company expected a payment and that wages would be honoured. There was considerable uncertainty amongst the members of the workforce as to what was happening, and other than as indicated below, there appears to have been no formal notification to C either of the fact that she was being made redundant, or of when she

was being made redundant. C was born on 2 February 1991. She worked for R between June 2014 and October 2017. Her ET1 was dated 28 October 2017. In her ET1, C says that on 28 October 2017 she phoned R to ask what was happening and was told that she was being made redundant. Her basic wage was £30,000 per annum. Her normal working week was 40 hours.

Claims

(2)   C complained in her ET1 of unfair dismissal, and that R had not paid her wages and/or had not paid the notice pay and/or outstanding holiday pay to which she was entitled by her contract.

Evidence

(3)   Oral evidence was heard on oath from C, who produced a bundle of papers relating to her claim, including payslips and her contract of employment. C confirmed that she had not been paid for September or October, and that she had not been given any notice. Her contract confirmed that she was entitled to one month's notice of termination.

Findings

(4)   The decision of the tribunal was that C was unfairly dismissed by R, and that she was entitled to a redundancy payment and wages in breach of contract.

Reasons

(5)   There was some confusion over the effective date of termination for C. One of her colleagues had received a letter confirming that his last date of employment was 20 October 2017, although C had not received such a letter. As C had submitted her ET1 on 30 October 2017, two days after she had been told she was being made redundant, the tribunal concluded that 28 October was the appropriate date from which to assume that the employment relationship with R had ended.

(6)   The tribunal (which heard the claim in May 2018) concluded that:
   (a)   this was a genuine redundancy situation in accordance with s 139 of the ERA 1996, and that redundancy was the reason for C's dismissal;
   (b)   as C had two years' service, she was entitled to complain of unfair dismissal and was entitled to a redundancy payment;
   (c)   on the basis of the evidence, her dismissal was unfair. Notwithstanding that there had been some communication with her on 13 October, when she had been sent home on full pay, after that date she was not given any further information about the company's situation and had to find things out for herself. On that basis, there had not been proper, adequate or reasonable warning or consultation. There was clearly no attempt to consider any help or assistance with regard to alternative employment. However, as it was clear that even had there been proper warning, consultation, etc, it was highly likely that C would still have been dismissed, the tribunal made a 100% *Polkey* reduction in respect of the compensatory element of the unfair dismissal award;
   (d)   unauthorised deductions had been made from C's wages, in that she had not been paid money properly due and payable in respect of wages, as set out below; further, the tribunal found as fact that R had failed to pay notice pay and holiday pay to which C was entitled.
   (e)   in addition, C was owed overtime in respect of hours worked in September.

Remedy

(7)   R was order to pay C:

Unpaid wages awards:

Four weeks' (gross) salary for September	£2,500.00
Four weeks' (gross) salary for October	£2,500.00
September overtime (gross) (45 hours at time and a half) (best estimate)	£3,750.00

Wrongful dismissal award:

Four weeks' salary in lieu of notice (net)	£2,000.00

Holiday pay:

Ten days' unpaid leave (gross)	£1,153.84
TOTAL	£11,903.84

In addition, C was entitled to a redundancy payment/unfair dismissal basic award of 1 x 2 x £508 (max gross week's pay as at date of calculation) = £1,016. There was no compensatory element to this award in the light of the *Polkey* finding.

GRAND TOTAL	£12,919.84

All the amounts detailed above have been calculated gross unless otherwise stated. Where a sum is stated to be gross, the respondent will account to HMRC directly in respect of tax and National Insurance due thereon as is appropriate.

5.9   CASE STUDY 2: UNFAIR DISMISSAL

Facts

(1)   C commenced employment with R (Isle of Sodor Train Company (ISTC)) on 3 December 2008, as a Revenue Protection Assistant based at Sodor Town station. He was summarily dismissed with effect from 3 October 2017, as result of an incident on Sodor Town station on 10 September 2017, when he was accused by a customer of having taken money for two single tickets valued at £5.80, and failing to issue either a receipt or tickets. V (Group Revenue Protection Manager, Isle of Sodor) conducted an investigation into the incident. C was interviewed on 11, 16, 19 and 23 September. He was suspended on basic pay pending the investigation. In addition, W (Senior Revenue Protection Inspector), X (Senior Revenue Protection Inspector), Y (Acting Senior Revenue Protection Inspector) and Z (RO2, Sodor Town) were interviewed.

(2)   At the conclusion of the investigatory process, C was invited, by letter dated 23 September, to attend a disciplinary hearing. C was told that he was being charged under para 9 of the ISTC Disciplinary Procedure 'with the following irregularity of gross misconduct', namely, of misappropriating £5.80 of Isle of Sodor Trains' monies. That letter informed C of his right to be accompanied at the disciplinary hearing. C's representative was sent all the relevant paperwork.

(3)   A disciplinary hearing was held on 2 and 3 October. H, Group Station Manager, Sodor Town, conducted it. C was accompanied by a trade union representative. Z was called by C to give evidence on his behalf. The hearing was adjourned to enable H and C's trade union representative to view some CCTV footage. At the conclusion of the disciplinary process, H found that:

(a)   money was taken from the customers;

(b)   the ticket issuing machine was switched off;

(c)   no tickets were issued;

(d)   the money that was taken was not accounted for and that 'no credible reason has been given for not issuing the tickets', and that 'Therefore I believe that C took the money and did not intend to issue the tickets thereby misappropriating ISTC monies'.

H found that the charge was proved, and he decided that C should be dismissed with immediate effect. H confirmed his decision in writing in a letter dated 3 October. That letter also set out details of the right to appeal against the decision.

(4)   C appealed against:

(a)   the severity of the punishment; and

(b)   the interpretation of the facts by H.

N, Retail Manager, Isle of Sodor, heard the appeal on 10 October. C was again accompanied by his trade union representative. N upheld the decision to dismiss C. N believed that 'it has been proven beyond doubt that C intentionally pocketed the £5.80 by making a conscious decision not to issue the tickets'. His decision was confirmed in writing by letter dated 10 October.

(5)   C's contract refers at para 17 to 'Disciplinary and other rules'. At para 2.1, disciplinary procedures are stated to apply to '(f) misconduct or negligence' and '(l) irregularities involving cash'. Procedure Agreement 4 is headed 'Discipline' and an Annex contains the relevant agreed procedure. This allows, inter alia, for witnesses to be called and for the employee to be accompanied. Paragraph 9 states that in cases of 'exceptionally grave misconduct which may warrant summary dismissal' the usual procedure shall not apply. Paragraph 17 of C's contract stated that ISTC may

> at any time ... dismiss without notice, or suspend from duty, and after inquiry, dismiss without notice, or suspend from duty as a disciplinary measure an employee for certain offences including but not limited to ... (c) misconduct or negligence ... (e) cash procedure irregularities (f) a serious or repeated breach of the rules.

Claims

(6)   C complained of unfair dismissal. He said in his ET1 Claim Form (box 11) that he believed his dismissal was unfair because 'the company did not properly and thoroughly investigate the matter because they clearly did not take into account all the information I gave them regarding the incident'. C seeks reinstatement. R, in its ET3 Claim Form, maintained that C's dismissal was fair and, in the alternative, that if it were to be found that the dismissal was unfair, that C's own conduct caused or contributed to his dismissal.

Evidence

(7)   Disclosure took place in the usual way and paginated bundles were prepared which included extracts from C's personal file, extracts from the ISTC Disciplinary Procedure, other rules and regulations, Procedure Agreement 4, plus papers relating to C's dismissal and a Schedule of Loss from C setting out his claim for compensation.

(8)   Although standard directions were made for the exchange of witness statements prior to the hearing, and witness statements were provided by R to C prior to the hearing, C did not provide one. Although R complained about this failure, in the circumstances the tribunal felt that in the light of the pre-litigation correspondence R was well aware of C's case and the grounds of his complaint. As such the tribunal did not believe R had been prejudiced by this failure. On the basis that there was little information in the ET1 about C's case, it was agreed that the tribunal would first of all read the relevant documents and that C would present his evidence first. C, who was not legally represented at the hearing but was assisted by his brother, read out as his evidence-in-chief a letter that he had written to the RMT Regional Organiser dated 21 November, which set out his complaints in some detail. In addition, the tribunal had written statements, on R's side, from P (Group Revenue Protection Manager, Isle of Sodor), who conducted the final part of the investigation, H (Group Station Manager, Sodor Town, who conducted the disciplinary hearing) and N (Retail Manager, Isle of Sodor, who heard C's appeal). Oral evidence was given on oath by all witnesses, except P who affirmed.

(9)   At the hearing, all witnesses who gave oral evidence were cross-examined and the tribunal had the opportunity to ask questions of them. C also submitted a written statement from Ms A, whose evidence he wanted the tribunal to take into account, but who was unable to give oral evidence. Although R pointed out that it had not had advance notice of this, having had the opportunity over a short adjournment to consider the contents of the statement, R did not object to the tribunal reading Ms A's statement; nevertheless, R reminded the tribunal that it had not had the opportunity to cross-examine Ms A.

(10)   There was some discussion during the case about whether the tribunal should see CCTV footage, stills of which had been available at the time of the investigation and the footage of which was viewed as part of the disciplinary hearing. Although both sides agreed that it might be of assistance for the tribunal to see the CCTV in the presence of the parties, unfortunately there was a problem getting the equipment to work and it was not possible to view it during the hearing. After discussion it was agreed that the tribunal would watch the CCTV footage in chambers.

(11)   At the conclusion of the evidence, both sides made oral submissions on liability and remedy. All these matters were taken into consideration by the tribunal before reaching its decision.

The issues to be decided

(12)   The principal issue for the tribunal to determine was whether the dismissal was fair within s 98(4) of the ERA 1996:

(a)   What was the reason for C's dismissal?

(b)   Was this a potentially fair reason for dismissal?

(c)   Was the dismissal substantively fair?

(d)   Was the dismissal procedurally fair?

(e)   Depending on the outcome, a remedy might need to be considered.

Submissions

(13)   On behalf of C it was submitted that, on the facts, even if the dismissal was for the potentially fair reason of conduct under s 98(2) of the ERA 1996, R did not act reasonably in treating that as a sufficient reason for dismissal under s 98(4) of the 1996 Act. Procedurally, C said that R did not acknowledge C's denial and did not accept the counter-evidence that was produced. In particular, it was submitted that R's investigation was flawed, and that it did not properly and thoroughly investigate the matter in that:

(a)   it was neither full nor impartial;

(b)   evidence was not examined, or was improperly concluded;

(c)   it was at best based on assumptions and speculation; and

(d)   it did not take into account all the information C gave to R.

It was submitted that it was unfair to dismiss on suspicion of misconduct without a full examination of the evidence. C said that there was no evidence that he deliberately set out to steal money from the company; there was no evidence that, as per the charge, funds had been misappropriated – no search was made of C and what money was found was in the float bag, which in the event contained more than it should have done because of money added by C. C says that it is not possible to conclude that 'no stone was left unturned in getting to the bottom of the facts'.

(14)   R's representative submitted that the reason for the dismissal was a potentially fair reason, namely, misconduct, and that procedurally R had done all that it should have done. R submitted that it honestly believed that C was guilty of misappropriating £5.80; that there were reasonable grounds for that belief following a reasonable investigation;

and that dismissal was within the range of reasonable responses, as C was in a position of trust. In the alternative, it was submitted that if the tribunal found that the dismissal was unfair, then C's conduct caused or contributed to his dismissal and any award should be reduced by 100% to zero.

The law

(15) Where there is a potentially fair reason for dismissal, the tribunal must decide whether the employer acted reasonably or unreasonably in treating that as a sufficient reason for dismissal. The material statutory provisions are set out in s 98(4) of the ERA 1996, which, so far as relevant, read as follows:

>   (4) Where the employer has fulfilled the requirements of subsection (1), the determination of the question whether the dismissal is fair or unfair (having regard to the reason shown by the employer—
>
>   (a) depends on whether in the circumstances (including the size and administrative resources of the employer's undertaking) the employer acted reasonably or unreasonably in treating it as a sufficient reason for dismissing the employee, and
>
>   (b) shall be determined in accordance with equity and the substantial merits of the case.

(16) Tribunals should not, when considering these matters, look at what they would have done but should judge, on the basis of the range of reasonable responses test, what the employers actually did. The appropriate test is whether the dismissal of the applicant lay within the range of conduct that a reasonable employer could have adopted.

(17) The Court of Appeal in the joined cases of *HSBC (formerly Midland Bank) v Madden; Post Office v Foley* [2000] IRLR 827, reiterated that the correct approach for a tribunal to adopt was that set out by the EAT in *Iceland Frozen Foods Ltd v Jones* [1982] IRLR 439, namely, that it was not for a tribunal to substitute its own view as to an employer's conduct and that tribunals should determine in each case whether the decision to dismiss fell within the 'band of reasonable responses' which a reasonable employer might have adopted towards the employee's conduct. That approach was re-emphasised by the Court of Appeal in *Post Office v Burkett* [2003] EWCA Civ 748 and most recently in *London Ambulance Service NHS Trust v Small* [2009] EWCA Civ 220.

(18) Section 98 does not require the dismissing employer to be satisfied, on the balance of probabilities, that the employee whose conduct is in question has actually done what he or she is alleged to have done. The EAT, in *British Home Stores v Burchell* [1978] IRLR 379, held that where an employer *suspects* misconduct, a dismissal can still be fair provided that the employer (i) had a genuine belief in guilt; (ii) had reasonable grounds upon which to base that belief; and (iii) carried out a proper investigation.

(19) The Court of Appeal in *Sainsbury's Supermarkets Ltd v Hitt* [2003] IRLR 23, held that the range of reasonable responses test

>   applies as much to the question of whether the investigation into suspected misconduct was reasonable in all the circumstances as it does to other procedural and substantive aspects of the decision to dismiss a person from his employment for a conduct reason. ... The objective standards of the reasonable employer must be applied to all aspects of the question whether an employee was fairly and reasonably dismissed. ... The objective standard ... did not require [the employer] to carry out further investigations of the kind which the tribunal majority considered ought to have been carried out. ... The purpose of the investigation was not to establish whether or not the applicant was guilty of the alleged theft but whether there were reasonable grounds for the employer's belief that there had been misconduct on his part to which a reasonable response was to dismiss him.

(20) The test to be applied in a case of suspected misconduct is not whether further investigation should have been carried out, or whether more could have been done, but whether the investigation that had been carried out could be regarded by a reasonable employer as adequate. Even in the most serious of cases, it is unrealistic and

inappropriate to require the standards and safeguards of a criminal trial, but a careful and conscientious investigation of the facts is necessary, and the person carrying out the investigation should focus carefully on the potential evidence, particularly if it points towards innocence, as opposed to concentrating on evidence which goes to prove the charges being made. In these sorts of cases, the more grave the charges and the potential impact of dismissal, the more rigorous the process that is required.

The tribunal's findings

(21) The unanimous decision of the tribunal was that C was fairly dismissed by reason of conduct. C was a Revenue Inspection Assistant. Trust and integrity are at the heart of such a role. The tribunal believed that in that circumstances, the dismissal of C for the offence charged was within the range of reasonable responses, and that this accordingly was a fair dismissal.

(22) The tribunal found that C's dismissal was for the potentially fair reason of conduct. The dismissal was a result of the employer's belief that C had appropriated money.

(23) The tribunal then considered s 98(4) of the ERA 1996. Since no burden of proof exists on either party to establish the reasonableness or unreasonableness of a dismissal under s 98(4), this is a question for the tribunal to determine 'neutrally'. The tribunal is not able to re-hear the evidence or to re-examine C's case. In particular, it is not for the tribunal to determine whether C is guilty or innocent. This was emphasised most recently by the Court of Appeal in *London Ambulance Service v Small*, where the Court reiterated that a tribunal must review the fairness of the employer's decision to dismiss, not substitute its own view on the facts. The Court of Appeal said the tribunal should have concentrated on the employer's handling of the dismissal rather than making its own findings about Small's conduct.

(24) The tribunal considered the following questions:

(a) *Did R have a genuine belief that C had behaved in the manner alleged?* In the tribunal's judgment, having heard the evidence of H, who conducted the disciplinary interview, and N, who conducted the appeal, and having read and considered the investigatory interviews, R did have a genuine belief that C had behaved in the manner charged. In particular, R believed he had misappropriated the ticket money.

(b) *Did R have reasonable grounds for that belief?* In the tribunal's judgment, R did have reasonable grounds for that belief. The tribunal noted that:

   (i) the initial allegation came from a customer;

   (ii) there was no dispute that C had taken money from the customer;

   (iii) there was no conclusive evidence that C had issued or attempted to issue any tickets: the customer said he had not; the ticket issuing machine 'bleed and print' did not show that any tickets had been issued; the CCTV was inconclusive on this point;

   (iv) C had altered his account of what had happened: initially he said that he had issued tickets and had then disposed of them in a plastic rubbish bag – a subsequent search did not produce the tickets; subsequently he said that he must have been confused and had not issued the tickets; later still he said he had not taken any money, or that he must have returned it all to the customer;

   (v) C said initially that his ticket issuing machine was switched off because he had 'just' returned from a toilet break – the CCTV showed him at the barrier for an unbroken period of 30 minutes before the incident;

   (vi) C failed to do a full cashing-up when asked to do 'an end of shift' and to cash up – he did only a partial cash-up: in particular, he did not remove his float before cashing up; his shift sheet should have shown a surplus of £5.80 but did not.

The tribunal considered that each explanation C gave was examined in full by R. An employer is not obliged to accept a denial, neither is it obliged to accept counter-evidence; what it must do is give it due consideration. The tribunal believes R did this.

C questioned whether there was sufficient evidence of 'intent'. He said that the CCTV appeared to show him trying to issue a ticket. In fact, the tribunal felt that the CCTV was inconclusive on this. H found that 'the money that was taken was not accounted for', that 'no credible reason has been given for not issuing the tickets' and that 'Therefore I believe that C took the money and did not intend to issue the tickets thereby misappropriating ISTC monies'. In answer to a question from C in cross-examination about this, H said he concluded 'intent' because 'no attempt was made to issue a ticket'. In *Post Office v Burkett*, the Court of Appeal said that the crucial question was whether the Post Office's response to the facts before it was reasonable. The question whether there were reasonable grounds for an honest belief had to be answered not by reference to the tribunal's own objective views formed subsequently, but by reference to its assessment of what it was open to a reasonable employer to conclude on the material before it. In the tribunal's judgment, there were sufficient grounds for H to reach the conclusion that he did. C was 'charged' with misappropriating £5.80. Disciplinary hearings are not criminal hearings. The issue for R was, put simply, whether it felt C had made an innocent mistake or not in taking money and not issuing a ticket. It concluded that he had not. In the tribunal's judgment, R was entitled to reach that conclusion on the evidence before it.

(c) *Did R conduct an investigation which was fair and proportionate having regard to the employer's capacity and resources?* This was at the heart of the way C framed his initial complaint – namely, that ISTC did not 'properly and thoroughly investigate the matter because they clearly did not take into account all the information I gave them regarding the incident'. Although there was no attempt made to contact the initial complainant or to elicit a statement from him, in the tribunal's judgment the investigation conducted was fair, full and thorough. There is no obligation as matter of law to turn over every stone. The tribunal concluded that R operated a fair, adequate and reasonable procedure. C was interviewed on a number of occasions. Any matters raised by him in his interviews were followed up and checked. Z was interviewed, all the Revenue Inspection Officers who were involved in the initial process were questioned, and the CCTV was considered. The disciplinary appeal was adjourned to allow C's representative to look at the CCTV footage (as opposed to the stills) and Z gave evidence. In a situation where an employee's livelihood is at stake and the allegation is a serious one, there is a heightened obligation on an employer as to the thoroughness of its investigation. The tribunal had no doubt that this investigation met that standard. In the tribunal's judgment there was a reasonable investigation.

(d) *Other procedural shortcomings.* In addition to the areas identified above, the tribunal looked at whether there were any procedural or other lapses by ISTC. One matter the tribunal considered was the so-called 'Paragraph 9 Summary Procedure'. The Tribunal looked at this against the Acas Code of Practice, which emphasised that workers should be aware of the likely consequences of breaking rules. The tribunal noted that there was no specific list of offences or examples of matters which would amount to serious (or 'exceptionally gross') misconduct, and thus no indication as to precisely when the para 9 procedure would be invoked. Paragraph 9 (which deals with the procedure in cases of 'exceptionally grave misconduct which may warrant summary action') stated that the 'usual' procedure shall not apply. Paragraph 12 contained a list of 'recordable punishments', of which the last was dismissal. Paragraph 17 of C's contract stated that R might

> at any time ... dismiss without notice, or suspend from duty, and after inquiry, dismiss without notice, or suspend from duty as a disciplinary measure an employee for certain offences including but not limited to ... (c) misconduct or negligence ... (e) cash procedure irregularities (f) a serious or repeated breach of the rules.

Overall, while the tribunal felt that the position could have been spelled out more clearly, in its judgment R's procedure did make clear to C that a possible consequence of misconduct was summary dismissal – the letter summoning C to interview contained a heading that alerted him to this. While the tribunal felt it might be preferable to identify some examples of serious misconduct – as opposed to less serious misconduct – so that the procedure and the possible consequences would be very clearly set out, it did not feel that this was sufficient *per se* to render the dismissal unfair.

The tribunal examined the initial letter informing C that he was to attend a disciplinary hearing, which did not contain any specific mention of the possible consequences of the disciplinary action that was to be taken. It contained a heading, 'Clause 9 Summary Procedure', and it then specified that the charge was considered to amount to gross misconduct. The Clause 9 Summary Procedure states that the usual procedure shall not apply in cases of 'exceptionally grave misconduct, which may warrant summary action'. Again while the tribunal felt it would have been preferable if this letter had set out the possible consequences of the proposed action, bearing in mind that it was not for the tribunal to substitute its own views, it did not feel, either in isolation or taken with the other matters set out here, that this rendered the dismissal procedurally unfair. Both C and his representative appeared to understand the Clause 9 Procedure and its significance.

In general, subject to the above, the tribunal had no criticisms about the way in which the investigatory process or the actual disciplinary hearing were conducted. There was a long, detailed and thorough investigation. The tribunal felt that C was aware of the accusations made against him in advance, and that he was given a proper opportunity to know the case against him and to state his case. It noted that he was entitled to and did call Z at the disciplinary hearing. It also noted that a representative accompanied C to both the disciplinary and the appeal hearings. The tribunal heard no evidence that made it doubt that those conducting the disciplinary hearing and the appeal were anything other than independent, or that they acted in anything but good faith.

(e) *The substantive decision to dismiss – was it within the range of responses of a reasonable employer in the circumstances?* The Court of Appeal, in *Post Office v Burkett* [2003] EWCA Civ 748, said that the crucial question for a tribunal was whether an employer's response to the facts before it was reasonable. The real question in these cases is whether R acted fairly and reasonably in all the circumstances at the time of the dismissal. If satisfied of R's fair conduct of the dismissal in those respects, the tribunal then has to decide whether the dismissal of C was a reasonable response to the misconduct. In all the circumstances, the tribunal held that decision of H to dismiss C, albeit over a very small sum of money, could not be said to fall outside the range of reasonable responses. The tribunal felt that given that C was in a position of trust in handling money as a Revenue Inspection Assistant, the misconduct that R believed him to have committed amounted to serious dishonesty. Contributory fault arises for decision only if it is established that the dismissal was unfair. As the tribunal had concluded the dismissal was fair, there was no need for it to consider contribution or remedy.

5.10 FURTHER READING

Textbooks include:

Lewis, *Employment Law – an adviser's handbook*, 12th revised edn (LAG, 2017).

Harvey, *Industrial Relations and Employment Law* (Butterworths), Div D1.

Selwyn's Law of Employment, 20th edn (OUP, 2018).

Blackstone's Employment Law Practice, 10th edn (OUP, 2019).

Gray, *Employment Tribunal Remedies Handbook 2018–19* (Bath Publishing).

Duggan, *Unfair Dismissal: Law, Practice and Precedents*, 2nd edn (Duggan Press, 2019).

SUMMARY

At common law, provided the employer gives the correct notice and otherwise complies with the terms of the contract, he may dismiss any employee he chooses, whether he has a good reason or not (see **Chapter 2**). The statutory claim of unfair dismissal introduced the concept of reasonableness into the termination of contracts of employment. Now every eligible employee (see **Chapter 3**) has a statutory right not to be unfairly dismissed by his employer under s 94 of the ERA 1996.

An employer must be able to establish that the only or principal reason for the dismissal was one of five potentially fair reasons as listed in s 98 of the ERA 1996 (conduct, capability, redundancy, illegality and some other substantial reason) (**5.2**).

Once an employer has shown the existence of one of the five permitted reasons, the tribunal must then decide if the employer acted reasonably, as defined by s 98(4) of the ERA 1996, having regard to the reason shown by the employer, in dismissing the employee (**5.3**).

When deciding whether the dismissal was fair or unfair, in addition to having regard to the reason, the tribunal should also have regard to all the circumstances, including the Acas Code of Practice on Disciplinary and Grievance Procedures (**5.4.1**) and the size and administrative resources of the employer, as well as to equity and the substantial merits of the case. Each case will ultimately turn on its own facts, but tribunals will generally look at both the substantive reason for the dismissal and any appropriate procedure (**5.4**). The test is ultimately one of reasonableness, and tribunals will ask themselves whether the dismissal was within the range of responses of a reasonable employer (see *Iceland Frozen Foods Ltd v Jones* [1982] IRLR 439 (**5.3.1.1**)).

There are a number of special cases where the normal rules relating to unfair dismissal either do not apply or are varied (**5.5**).

The remedies available for unfair dismissal are either reinstatement or re-engagement (together with any consequential awards relating to arrears of pay, etc), or compensation. Awards which exceed £30,000 are subject to income tax and may need to be grossed up to ensure that the net loss is actually paid to the claimant (**5.6**).

In summary, the following questions should be asked:

- Do any of the special rules apply (**5.5**)?
- Is the employee eligible (**Chapter 3**)?
- Has there been a dismissal (**3.4**)?
- Is there a potentially fair reason (**5.2**)?
- Has the employer acted reasonably (**5.3** and **5.4**)?
- Has the employee asked for reinstatement or re-engagement (**5.6.1**)?
- How much will the basic award be (**5.6.2.1**)?
- What are the relevant heads of compensatory award (**5.6.2.2**)?
- Are there any relevant increasing factors?
- Are there any relevant reducing factors?

Figure 5.2 Flowchart: Unfair Dismissal

---

1. **Eligibility** (burden of proof on employee)
- time limits (3 months (less 1 day) from EDT)
- employee
- 2 years' service (for employees employed by current employer on or after 6 April 2012; 1 year for all others)
- not excluded class

↓

2. **Dismissal** (burden of proof on employee)
- expiry and non-renewal of limited-term contract or
- actual dismissal or
- constructive dismissal

NB Definition in *Western Excavating v Sharp*

↓

3. **Reason for dismissal (ERA 1996, s 98(2))** (burden of proof on employer)
- what is the main reason for the dismissal?
- does that reason fall within one of the five potentially fair reasons?

NB If reason is redundancy, consider claim for both unfair dismissal and a redundancy payment

↓

4. **Consider fairness of dismissal (ERA 1996, s 98(4))**
Test – range of reasonable responses (Iceland Frozen Foods)
Question of fact for tribunal
- size and administrative resources of employer
- equity
- sufficiency of the reason given by the employer
- substantial merits
- procedure (depends on reason)
- Acas Code if conduct/capability

↓

5. **Remedies**
- reinstatement (old job back)
- re-engagement (job elsewhere in business)
- compensation
  — basic award: age factor (½/1/1½) x gross weekly pay (max £508 from 6 April 2018) x number of complete years service (max 20 years) (EA 2002, s 38)
  — compensatory award (consider heads of loss/deductions) (max £83,682 or 52 weeks' gross pay from 6 April 2018)
    immediate loss of net earnings etc
    future losses including pension
    mitigation; other deductions (*Polkey*/contribution)

NB Award (basic and compensatory) can be increased or decreased by up to 25% for unreasonable failure to follow Acas Code

↓

6. **Consider other claims**
- redundancy payment/wrongful dismissal/discrimination

NB Employee cannot be compensated twice for same loss

CHAPTER 6

PRACTICE AND PROCEDURE, SETTLEMENTS AND OVERLAPPING CLAIMS

LEARNING OUTCOMES

After reading this chapter you will be able to:

- describe the relevant employment tribunal procedures for bringing a claim, from submitting a claim form to the giving of a judgment
- understand the different time-limits that apply to tribunal claims
- explain the options that are available other than bringing a tribunal claim
- describe the different ways in which claims may be settled
- understand the significance of overlapping claims.

6.1 INTRODUCTION

This chapter deals with the procedure for making a claim to the employment tribunal and, in outline, the hearing of a complaint by the tribunal. It also covers settlement and overlapping claims.

The Department for Business, Energy and Industrial Strategy and the Ministry of Justice launched a joint consultation 'Reforming the Employment Tribunal System' in late 2016. The Government set out how it intends to proceed in a response to the consultation in April 2017. The Government has said that it aims to:

- digitise the claims process (including offering 'innovative resolution methods');
- delegate some case management decisions to 'case workers';
- provide for the Senior President of Tribunals to be able to have responsibility for determining panel composition in employment tribunals.

6.2 APPLICATIONS TO THE EMPLOYMENT TRIBUNAL

6.2.1 Jurisdiction

The following claims may all be brought by presenting a complaint to the employment tribunal:

(a) unfair dismissal;

(b) claims of discrimination on the grounds of sex, race, religion or belief, disability, sexual orientation and age from employees and job applicants (Equality Act 2010);

(c) equal pay;

(d) complaints that unlawful deductions from wages have been made under Pt II of the ERA 1996 (these claims may also be brought in the county court);

(e) redundancy payments;

(f) complaints in relation to maternity rights, paternity rights, adoption leave rights, parental rights, dependant rights and flexible working rights;

(g) complaints in relation to failure to provide written reasons;

(h) complaints of victimisation because an employee has exerted any of his statutory rights;

(i) certain claims for damages for breach of contract, including (subject to a maximum award of £25,000) wrongful dismissal (contractual claims may also be brought in the county court);

(j) complaints under the Part-time Workers (Prevention of Less Favourable Treatment) Regulations 2000;

(k) complaints under some provisions of the Working Time Regulations 1998;

(l) complaints under the Agency Workers Regulations 2010.

The above list is not exhaustive. In most instances, these claims must be brought by employees, although there are some exceptions (eg, claims under the protection of wages legislation (see **1.10**) and discrimination claims) where claims by workers can be dealt with. For the distinction between a worker and an employee, see s 230 of the ERA 1996 and **1.1.1** and **1.3**.

6.2.2 Mandatory pre-claim Early Conciliation

6.2.2.1 Introduction

Anyone considering bringing an employment tribunal claim must make an Early Conciliation notification to Acas, to see whether the dispute can be resolved through conciliation. The legislative framework for the Early Conciliation scheme is contained in the ERRA 2013. The details of the scheme itself are set out in the Schedule to the Employment Tribunals (Early Conciliation: Exemptions and Rules of Procedure) Regulations 2014 (SI 2014/254) (the Early Conciliation Regulations). The scheme came into effect on 6 April 2014, but only became mandatory for claims presented on or after 6 May 2014. The 2013 Employment Tribunals Rules of Procedure (see **6.4**) were amended to provide for the rejection of claims in accordance with the Early Conciliation scheme. Rule 10 now provides (added by the Employment Tribunal (Constitution and Rules of Procedure) (Amendment) Regulations 2014 (SI 2014/271)) that a tribunal shall reject a claim if it does not contain either an Early Conciliation number, or confirmation that the Early Conciliation proceedings do not apply to the claim or that an exemption applies. The new scheme does not affect Acas's pre-existing duty to conciliate claims that were already in the system (see **6.4.7.6**).

The details of the scheme are set out in ss 18A and 18B of the ETA 1996. These are the key stages of the compulsory Early Conciliation scheme:

(a) the prospective claimant must send information to Acas in the 'prescribed manner', ie via the prescribed form or via the telephone using a prescribed number;

(b)   a Conciliator will make contact with the claimant;

(c)   the Conciliator must try to promote settlement within the 'prescribed period' of one month (subject to a maximum extension of two weeks);

(d)   if at any time the Conciliator concludes it is not possible to reach settlement, or time expires, a certificate is issued;

(e)   the claimant cannot start most claims without the certificate.

Acas has published a guidance note on how Early Conciliation will work, available at <http://www.acas.org.uk/media/pdf/h/o/Early-Conciliation-explained.pdf>.

Employers will also be able to use Early Conciliation if they believe there is a workplace dispute that is likely to lead to 'relevant' tribunal proceedings. Relevant proceedings are listed in s 18(1A) of the ETA 1996. There are two areas that are not expressly included in the list:

(a)   the right to be accompanied under ss 10–13 of the ERA 1999 (but this appears to be indirectly incorporated, as Part V of the ERA 1996 is included in the s 18 list); and

(b)   claims under regs 12 and 16 of the Transfer of Undertakings (Protection of Employment) Regulations 2006, but the view is that these claims are indirectly covered via the Regulations (see regs 12(7) and 16(1)).

There are some exceptions to the requirement to make an Early Conciliation notification: for example, if many people are making a claim against the same employer and one person has already made a request to Acas about the same issue, other potential claimants may not have to. The full list of exemptions is set out in reg 3(1) of the Early Conciliation Regulations.

6.2.2.2   Procedure

Tribunal claims will not be accepted unless the complaint has been referred to Acas and a conciliation certificate issued. There is a prescribed notification form. The easiest way to access this is through the Acas website at <http://www.acas.org.uk/earlyconciliation>. The notification form asks for basic contact details for the claimant and the employer. Claimants need to take care to include the correct name of their employer, as the name of the employer on any subsequent ET1 will need to correspond to the name on the form. If the names are different, this could lead to the claim being rejected by the tribunal. Rule 4 of the Tribunal Rules says that if there is more than one prospective respondent, a separate form must be presented for each.

When Acas receives an Early Conciliation notification form, it will contact the sender and check whether the claimant wants to proceed with Early Conciliation. If he does, Acas will then approach the employer. According to the Acas guidance, a Conciliator will aim to make contact with both parties by the end of the following working day, to explore with them how the potential claim might be resolved. If a Conciliator cannot contact either of the parties, or the prospective claimant does not wish to proceed with conciliation, the case will be closed and an Early Conciliation certificate will be issued to the prospective claimant. This will allow the prospective claimant to progress his claim. Likewise, if the prospective respondent is not willing to participate, the prospective claimant will be informed and a certificate issued.

The initial period of Early Conciliation is intended to last for up to one calendar month. However, if both parties agree, the period may be extended by a further 14 days. If after this period the matter has not been resolved, the Conciliation will end and the claimant will be free to make a tribunal claim. The formal certificate that Early Conciliation has finished will include a unique reference number. Claimants will need to include this when issuing their claim form/ET1 to prove that they have complied with the Early Conciliation notification requirement. Failure to include the unique reference number will result in the claim being rejected (see **6.2.2.3** below). If settlement is reached, this will be recorded using an Acas settlement document (known as a COT3 – see **6.5.1** below).

6.2.2.3 Time-limits

In order to allow time for Early Conciliation to take place, changes have been made (ERA 1996, s 207B) to the usual time-limits within which an employee must bring an employment tribunal claim. These time-limits are dealt with in detail at **6.3** below, but the usual three or six calendar months (depending on the type of claim) are suspended (ie the clock is stopped) during the conciliation period. Even if a the time-limit would normally expire less than a month after the end of the conciliation period, a claimant will have a full month (not one month less one day, as originally suggested by HM Courts & Tribunals Service Booklet T420) from when he receives the certificate to lodge his claim with the employment tribunal office. This will mean that where a claimant approaches Acas towards the end of the normal maximum limitation period, he will be able to have up to two and a half months longer to bring a claim (the one-month initial period, the two-week extension, plus a further month after it ends). See **6.3.7** for a detailed analysis of how Early Conciliation will affect time-limits.

6.2.2.4 Cases

In the years since Early Conciliation was introduced, there have been a number of cases, many of them at first instance, that have considered the interpretation of some of the key provisions. (For cases on Early Conciliation time-limits see **6.3.7** below.) While first instance decisions are not binding on other tribunals, they are still a useful reference point.

In *Masih-Rogers v Hammersmith Hairdressing and others* (ET/2201248/14) (heard on 2 October 2014), the claimant's Early Conciliation certificate only referred to the second respondent, not the first. The Employment Judge concluded that Rule 10(1)(b)(3) of the Tribunal Rules had not been complied with and that there was no jurisdiction to consider the claimant's complaint.

In *Hudson v Plymouth Hospitals NHS Trust* (ET/1401148/2014) (heard on 9 October 2014), an employment tribunal considered what was meant by reg 3(1)(c) (which provides that a claimant can claim an exemption where his 'employer has already been in touch with Acas'). There had been preceding discussions at Acas between the claimant's representative and the employer about two other, similar cases. The claimant's case was not actually discussed. No Early Conciliation certificate had been obtained. The employment tribunal held that the respondent had not contacted Acas in connection with this dispute and struck out the claimant's claim for want of jurisdiction.

In *Ngomoto v Carltech Community Services* (ET/1304618/2014) (heard on 16 October 2014) an employment tribunal considered what was meant by reg 3(1)(d) (which provides that a claimant can claim an exemption where his 'claim contains an application for interim relief'). The claimant had issued a claim of automatically unfair dismissal on the grounds of public interest disclosure, and had included an application for interim relief under s 128 of the ERA 1996. No Early Conciliation certificate had been obtained. The employment tribunal held (somewhat controversially) that there was no basis in law for the interim relief application but as it was genuinely made, there was jurisdiction to hear the claim.

Section 18A(1) of the ETA 1996 provides that before a claim is presented 'relating to any matter', information must be provided to Acas 'about that matter'. Does 'matter' require a full detailed particularisation of the specific dispute and the legal basis for the claim, or might this be a more broad-brush reference? In *Ellis v Brighton & Hove Golf Club* (ET/2301658/2014) (heard on 30 January 2015), the date of the Early Conciliation certificate was 22 June 2014. This was obtained two days before the claimant's employment was terminated, ostensibly by reason of redundancy. The employer argued that the unfair dismissal claim that the claimant sought to bring could not be covered by the Early Conciliation certificate as it pre-dated the dismissal. The Employment Judge looked at matters in the round and said that the Early Conciliation certificate could only be said to have been obtained in connection with the likely termination of employment, and it did not matter that the prospect of redundancy as the reason had not previously been raised. The claimant had complied with the requirements of Rule 10 and the tribunal had jurisdiction to hear the claim. See too *Mortimer v The Golden Holiday Company Ltd and Another* (ET/2300983/15); *Science Warehouse Ltd v Mills* (EAT/0224/15); *Drake International Systems Ltd and Others v Blue Arrow Ltd* (EAT/0282/15); and *Mist v Derby Community Health Services NHS Trust* (EAT/0170/15).

In *Joseph v Royal College of Surgeons of England* (ET/2202074/14) (heard on 27 February 2015), the claimant brought claims of unfair dismissal and discrimination on the grounds of race and age. The employer sought to argue that because the Early Conciliation process had not considered a number of the specific allegations relied upon, the claimant should not be able to bring those claims. The Employment Judge noted that the conciliation process itself was confidential, and it was not appropriate for the tribunal to know all the details of that process. The Employment Judge concluded that 'matter' must be interpreted broadly, without any detailed particularisation of the facts.

In *Cranwell v Cullen* UKEATS/0046/14 (heard by the EAT on 20 March 2015), the claimant's claims of sexual harassment and other demeaning treatment were rejected because she had not obtained an Early Conciliation certificate from Acas before making the claim. She found the very thought of conciliation on the facts of her claim problematic, as it would involve her talking to someone who had treated her in the manner she described. Further, she said that her former employer had been subject to a court order which prohibited him from contacting her. So, she said, she simply could not conciliate with him. She had ticked the box indicating that she was exempt from Early Conciliation. However, none of the exemptions applied to her and the tribunal rejected her claim on that basis. She appealed. The EAT dismissed her appeal. Although it was sympathetic, it ruled that s 18A of the ETA 1996 imposed a mandatory obligation. This was reinforced by Rule 10 of the Tribunal Rules, which makes it clear that a tribunal must reject a claim if the Early Conciliation details are not included in the claim. Rule 6 (which deals with irregularities and failures to comply with the Rules) could not be construed as 'entitling the Tribunal to avoid having to satisfy an obligation which is placed upon the Tribunal itself in absolute and strict terms'.

Several cases have confirmed that a claim will be rejected if the Early Conciliation number is omitted or incorrect (eg *Sterling v United Learning Trust* (UKEAT/0439/14); *Adams v BT plc* (EAT/0342/15)) (see **6.3.1** below). In *Giny v SNA Transport Ltd* (UKEAT/0317/16), an error was made in the name of the respondent during the Early Conciliation process. The error was corrected when the claim was issued. The EAT applied the two-stage test and rejected the claimant's application for reconsideration:

(1)   Is it a minor error? No – the claim will be rejected.

(2)   If it is a minor error, is it in the interests of justice to allow the claim to go ahead?

In this case, the EAT felt that the error was not minor.

In *Compass Group UK and Ireland Ltd v Morgan* (UKEAT/0060/16), the EAT held that an Early Conciliation certificate could still be valid for events that occurred after the certificate had been issued, in this case a constructive dismissal after a disability discrimination claim. This is likely to be the case unless the matters in dispute at the time of the certificate were wholly different to those arising thereafter.

In *De Mota v (1) ADR Network and (2) The Co-operative Group Ltd* (UKEAT/0305/16) the claimant named two respondents on one form, and Acas issued a certificate naming both. Rule 4, however, requires a separate form for each prospective respondent. An employment tribunal held that it lacked jurisdiction to hear the claim because the certificate was improperly issued. The EAT allowed the claimant's appeal and said that the Acas certificate was sufficient to give jurisdiction, notwithstanding the error.

In *HMRC v Garau* (UKEAT/0348/16), the EAT said that issuing a second Early Conciliation certificate in the same matter does not extend time to make a claim.

6.2.2.5 Summary

Below is a summary of some of the main principles that have emerged from these cases:

- Claimants only have to commence the Early Conciliation process once; provided there is a certificate, tribunals will not usually look behind it.
- The 'stop the clock' provisions (ERA 1996, s 207B) only apply to the first period of conciliation.
- Claimants (probably) can take the benefit of the 'stop the clock' provisions that provide them with the longest time to issue their claim.
- If a claimant fails to commence Early Conciliation until after the normal limitation period for bringing a claim, they will need to get an extension of time from the tribunal (under ERA 1996, s 123).
- If the claimant does not commence Early Conciliation before issuing their claim, they will not be able to proceed with it.
- Getting the name of an employer wrong will not necessarily invalidate an Early Conciliation certificate.
- A separate Early Conciliation certificate is needed for each respondent.

6.2.3 Insolvency

Where a winding-up order has been made, no action or proceedings can be started or continued without the leave of the insolvency court. The liquidator, when appointed, will become the appropriate party, and any proceedings which will be against the company in liquidation will be stayed. If there is a creditors' voluntary winding up, any proceedings will continue. If there is an administration order, no legal proceedings can be started or continued without the consent of the administrator or the court's permission.

6.3 TIME-LIMITS IN EMPLOYMENT TRIBUNALS

Time-limits differ depending upon the complaint. The main limits are set out below. A claimant who fails to present a claim in time will generally lose the right to bring the claim, although there are escape clauses. Time-limits go to a tribunal's jurisdiction, so they are not simply matters of procedure that the parties can waive. There are two types of escape clause – that it is 'not reasonably practicable' to present the claim in time, or that it is 'just and equitable' to grant an extension. These are discussed in more detail below.

6.3.1 Unfair dismissal

The time-limits for an unfair dismissal claim are set out in s 111 of the ERA 1996. The complaint must normally be presented to the tribunal within three months starting with the 'effective date of termination' (EDT), or within such further period as the tribunal considers reasonable where it was not reasonably practicable for the complaint to be presented within three months (ERA 1996, s 111). The EDT for this purpose is the basic EDT as defined by s 97 of the ERA 1996 (see **3.5.2**). It is not extended where the employee did not receive the statutory minimum period of notice (see **3.5.2**). The three months start with (ie includes) the EDT (see *Trow v Ind Coope (West Midlands) Ltd* [1967] 2 QB 899 and *Hammond v Haigh Castle & Co Ltd* [1973] ICR 148). This effectively means three months less a day (see *Pacitti Jones v O'Brien* [2005] IRLR 889 (Court of Session)).

In *Gisda Cyf v Barratt* [2010] UKSC 41, the Supreme Court held that in a summary dismissal, the EDT would be the date the employee actually learned of the decision to dismiss. In the case, Barratt dismissed Mrs Syf in a letter, delivered by recorded delivery and signed for by her son, on 30 November 2006. She was expecting the decision letter to arrive, but was away at the time it arrived as her sister was giving birth, and as a result she did not actually open the letter until 4 December. She subsequently presented an unfair dismissal claim on 2 March. If the EDT was the date the letter was sent and received, namely 30 November, then her unfair dismissal claim was out of time. If it was the date she read it, 4 December, then her unfair dismissal claim would have been presented in time. The Supreme Court held that the EDT was 4 December, ie when she actually read the letter. It held that she should not be criticised for wanting the letter to remain at home unopened, instead of asking her son to read to her, as its contents were private. There was nothing to indicate that she had deliberately not opened the letter or gone away to avoid reading it. The Supreme Court stated that, on policy grounds, it was desirable to interpret the time-limit legislation in a way favourable to the employee, and that strict contractual laws concerning termination of contracts should not displace the statutory framework. In *Robinson v Bowskill* (UKEAT/0313/12) the EAT held that this also applies where the dismissal is communicated through a third party.

In *Wang v University of Keele* (UKEAT/0223/10), the EAT held that, unless a contract specifically provides otherwise, contractual notice, whether oral or written, runs from the day after the notice is given. Dr Wang was given three months' notice of dismissal by a letter e-mailed on the afternoon of 3 November. He read it that afternoon. He presented a claim for unfair dismissal on 2 May. The employment tribunal rejected his claim on the basis that it was a day out of time, saying the notice period ran from 3 November to 2 February. The EAT, having reviewed all the relevant authorities, said that unless there was an express term in the contract, the law does not take account of fractions of a day so notice may not always run from the time of actual knowledge. In cases of oral notice of dismissal given during the working day, notice cannot take effect until the following day.

The complaint should actually be received by the appropriate Regional Office of the Employment Tribunals (ROET) within the appropriate time-limit. For example, s 111 of the ERA 1996 provides that an unfair dismissal claim must be presented (although a tribunal does have the power to extend the period where it was not 'reasonably practicable' to present the complaint within three months – see below) 'before the end of the period of three months beginning with the effective date of termination'. So, if an employee is dismissed on 15 January, his claim form must arrive at ROET before midnight on 14 April. If an employee is dismissed on 30 November, his claim must be presented by 28 February.

Where the normal three-month time-limit expires on a non-working day (such as a Saturday, Sunday or bank holiday), care will need to be taken to ensure that the claim reaches the tribunal beforehand. Rule 4(2) of the Rules of Procedure *cannot* be relied upon to extend the date to the next working day (see *Miah v Axis Security Services Ltd* (UKEAT/0290/17)).

The time-limit for presenting a complaint of unfair dismissal should be regarded as strict. Claim forms may be delivered not only by post but also by hand, by fax and by e-mail. Generally speaking, it is up to the party (or his solicitor) to make sure that the claim form is received within the relevant time-limit.

The tribunal's discretionary power to extend the time-limit is subject to a two-part test. First, the tribunal must be satisfied that it was not reasonably practicable for the claim to be presented in time. Secondly, the tribunal must be satisfied that the claim was presented within such further period as the tribunal considers reasonable. In *Palmer v Southend on Sea BC* [1984] ICR 372, the Court of Appeal said that 'reasonably practicable' does not mean reasonably or physically possible but rather something like 'reasonably feasible'. The determination of what is reasonably practicable is a question of fact for the tribunal (see *Miller v Community Links Trust Ltd* (UK EAT/0486/07). The burden of proof is on the claimant.

In *Sealy v Consignia plc* [2002] IRLR 624, the Court of Appeal held that in determining whether it is reasonably practicable for a claim to have been presented in time, a complainant is entitled to rely on the 'ordinary course of post', such that a letter sent by first class post may be assumed to be delivered on the second day after it was posted (excluding weekends and bank holidays), and if it does not so arrive, it may be regarded (for the purposes of an application to extend) as not reasonably practicable for the complaint to be presented in time. The current line of authority stands for three propositions: first, that 'where a claimant does an act within the period prescribed, which in the ordinary event would result in the complaint being made within the specified period, and that is prevented from having its normal and expected result by some unforeseen circumstance', the 'escape clause' is available; secondly, that if the condition is satisfied, it does not matter why the complainant has waited until the last moment; and, thirdly, that the question whether the condition has been satisfied is a question of fact, to be determined by the tribunal on the evidence before it. (See also *Coldridge v HM Prison Service* (UKEAT/0728/04) and *John Lewis Partnership v Charman* (UKEAT/0079/11), where the EAT held it was not reasonably practicable for a claimant to present his unfair dismissal claim in time because he was awaiting the outcome of an internal appeal.)

Where a claim form is sent by e-mail, a claimant is entitled to assume that it will be delivered at the tribunal within an hour (unless there is an indication that it has not been received, such as a bounce-back message). In *Initial Electronic Security Systems Ltd v Avdic* (UKEAT/0281/05), the EAT held the *Consignia* 'escape route' is also available where a claim form is served by e-mail (so long as the claimant sends it at least an hour before midnight on the day time expires). If an e-mail is not received then a tribunal should assume that it was not reasonably practicable for the complaint to be presented in time, and consider whether the claimant acted reasonably promptly in re-submitting the claim form, once he realised it had not been received.

General guidance on e-mail transmission was set out by the EAT in *Initial Electronic Security Systems Ltd v Audic* [2005] ICR 1598. *Beasley v National Grid* (UKEAT/0626/06) is an illustration of how strictly the time-limits are enforced. In that case, the EAT upheld a tribunal decision not to accept an unfair dismissal claim which was presented by e-mail 88 seconds late. The employment tribunal held that it was 'reasonably practicable' to present the claim in time. The claimant knew on 5 May 2006 that the three-month period expired on 6 May 2006, but he misread the e-mail address of place to which the claim form had to be sent and sent it at 23.44 on 6 May 2006 to 'qsi' and not to the correct address, which was 'gsi'. The claim form was returned to the claimant at 23.45 and he sent a test message (rather than the claim form) to the correct address at 23.57 on 6 May 2006. The claimant then sent the claim form to the correct address so that it arrived at 00.01 and 28 seconds on 7 May 2006, ie late. The EAT held that the tribunal had considered the reasonable practicability issue properly, taking into account all relevant matters: it had considered whether the claimant knew of the three-month period; the steps taken by him to ensure that the claim was brought in time; and the impediments preventing him from bringing the claim within the prescribed three-month period. The Court of Appeal refused leave to appeal.

For a contrasting case to *Beasley* (above), see *Powell v Newcastle College Group* (ET/2514148/09).

The remedy of unfair dismissal is considered to be sufficiently well known that ignorance of the remedy will not be accepted as an excuse (see *Reed in Partnership Ltd v Fraine* (UKEAT/0520/10). Generally, the question in all cases is whether the claimant ought to have known of his rights. In *John Lewis Partnership v Charman* (UKEAT/0079/11), the EAT upheld a decision of the employment tribunal that because the claimant was 'young and inexperienced', and prior to his dismissal he knew nothing about employment tribunals or any right to claim for unfair dismissal, it was not reasonably practicable for him to have presented his claim in time. The starting-point, said the EAT, is that if an employee is reasonably ignorant of the relevant time-limits it cannot be said to be reasonably practicable for him to comply with them. The EAT held in *Adams v BT plc* (EAT/0342/15) that, while the employment tribunal was correct to reject a claim for unfair dismissal where the Early Conciliation number was wrong, the tribunal should have accepted the claim when re-presented (out of time), because it was not reasonably practicable to re-present the claim in time as the claimant was not aware of the need to re-present the claim until she was advised of the error in the first claim. (See too *Walls Meat Co Ltd v Khan* [1979] ICR 52.)

What of carelessness by the employee or his adviser? Generally, this will not be sufficient. If the employee's solicitor misses the time-limit, the tribunal will not extend it, unless there are wholly exceptional circumstances, such as the claimant and the solicitor being misled by the employer as to a material factual matter. Where a professional adviser is careless, this could lead to a negligence claim by the employee against his solicitor if the tribunal does not exercise its discretion to extend time.

In *Marks and Spencer plc v William-Ryan* [2005] IRLR 562, the Court of Appeal held that the employment tribunal had been entitled to find that it had not been reasonably practicable for a claimant to present her unfair dismissal claim within three months because she had received misleading information from her employer, who had advised her that she could not present a claim until she had been through the employer's appeal procedure. Whilst the employee had sought advice from a CAB, the nature of the advice was to seek to resolve the matter with her employer, and the CAB had not advised about making a claim in the Employment Tribunal.

In *Northamptonshire County Council v Entwhistle* (UKEAT/0540/09), however, the EAT held that an employment tribunal had erred in finding that it was not reasonably practicable for a claimant to present his unfair dismissal claim in time in circumstances where his solicitor had been negligent; notwithstanding erroneous advice from the employer, the solicitor should have known the limitation period and filed the claim in time. The EAT said that:

> ... the Judge was right not to read Lord Phillips' endorsement of the *Dedman* principle in *Williams-Ryan* as meaning that in no case where a claimant has consulted a skilled adviser and received wrong advice about the time limit can he claim that it was not reasonably practicable for him to present his claim in time. It is perfectly possible to conceive of circumstances where the adviser's failure to give the correct advice is itself reasonable. Waller LJ made this very point in *Riley*: see at page 336 B. The paradigm case, though not the only example, of such circumstances would be where both the claimant and the adviser had been misled by the employer as to some material factual matter (for example something bearing on the date of dismissal, which is not always straightforward). ...

> ... in a case where a claimant has consulted skilled advisers the question of reasonable practicability is to be judged by what he could have done if he had been given 'such [advice] as they should reasonably in all the circumstances have given him': see the judgment of Brandon LJ in the *Walls* case quoted at para. 5 (3) above. It necessarily follows from the finding of negligence that Mr Lee did not give the Claimant the advice which he should reasonably, in all the circumstances, have given him.

In *Paczkowski v Sieradzka* (UKEAT 0111/16), the claimant was told, by three separate advisers (the CAB, Acas and her local trade union adviser), that she could not bring an unfair dismissal claim without two years' service. The tribunal had concluded that it was not reasonably practicable for the claimant to lodge her claim in time. The EAT remitted the case to the tribunal to determine whether the advice given to the claimant was reasonable in the particular circumstances of this case and – at the same time – was the information provided by the claimant and specific questions raised by her also reasonable? The tribunal could, held the EAT, only arrive at a final conclusion on that question once it had made findings as to the actual instructions given and questions asked as to the status of the advisers and advice received. In *DHL Supply Chain Ltd v Fazackerley* (UKEAT/0019/18), the EAT said that it was not reasonably practicable for an employee to present a claim for unfair dismissal in time, where the delay was due to erroneous advice from Acas. The position is different for erroneous advice from a solicitor or adviser. Acas is a government agency which should not be offering advice.

The discovery of new relevant facts can give grounds for an extension of time (see *Machine Tool Industry Research Association v Simpson* [1988] ICR 558 and *Cambridge and Peterborough Foundation*

NHS Trust v Crouchman [2009] ICR 1306). Illness of the claimant may also be a relevant factor (see *Chouafi v London United Busways Ltd* [2006] EWCA Civ 689).

Even if a claimant satisfies a tribunal that it was not reasonably practicable to present a claim within the three-month time-limit, the tribunal must still go on to consider whether the claim was presented within such further period as it considers reasonable. The length of any further period will be determined by the facts in any given case. In *Nolan v Balfour Beatty Engineering Services* (UKEAT/0109/11), the EAT said that tribunals must bear in mind the surrounding context, including the primary time-limit and the general principle that litigation should be progressed efficiently and without delay. Tribunals should then go on to consider all the circumstances of a particular case, including what the claimant did; what he or she knew, or reasonably ought to have known, about time-limits; and why it was that the further delay had occurred. The basic rule is that tribunals expect claimants who present a claim late to act to rectify the delay as soon as they become aware of it. In *Marks and Spencer plc v William-Ryan* (above), the Court of Appeal emphasised the importance of considering what a claimant knew and what knowledge she should have had, had she acted reasonably. For two cases where a delay of several months beyond the initial three months was still held to be reasonable, see *Remploy v Brain* (UKEAT/0465/10) and *Locke v Tabfine Ltd t/a Hands Music Centre* (UKEAT/0517/10).

6.3.2 Redundancy payments

An employee will lose his entitlement to a redundancy payment unless, before the end of a period of six months beginning with the 'relevant date', the employee has, where no payment has been made, made a claim in writing to the employer for the payment or presented a claim to the tribunal. The 'relevant date' is defined by s 145 of the ERA 1996 (see **3.5.2**).

6.3.3 Discrimination

Any complaints of discrimination must be brought within three months starting with the date the act or actions to which the complaint relates took place, or such other period as the tribunal considers just and equitable (Equality Act 2010, s 123(1)). (This is considered further at **8.8**.) See, most recently, the decision in *Abertawe Bro Morgannwg University Local Health Board v Morgan* [2018] EWCA Civ 640, where the Court of Appeal explored the principles behind extending time-limits.

This represents a slight change from the pre-Equality Act 2010 position, which provided that a claim was out of time after three months and for a discretion to bring a claim out of time.

6.3.4 Equal pay

There is, in practice, no time-limit for a claim in respect of the ongoing operation of an equality clause whilst still in employment. A claim should be brought within six months of the employee leaving that employment.

6.3.5 Deductions from wages

The time-limit for presenting a claim for unlawful deduction of wages (ERA 1996, s 13) is three months starting with the date of the deduction, or later if it was not reasonably practicable for the claim to be presented in time (see **6.3.1**).

6.3.6 Wrongful dismissal

The time-limit for presenting a claim for wrongful dismissal is three months starting with the EDT, or later if it was not reasonably practicable for the claim to be presented within the time-limit (see **6.3.1**).

6.3.7 Acas Early Conciliation – effect on time-limits

One of the consequences of the requirements around Early Conciliation is that if there are problems which cause delay, they can impact on time-limits and may mean that claims are submitted out of time. There have been a number of cases looking at these issues, which are summarised below.

The new system of mandatory Acas Early Conciliation applies to claims presented on or after 6 May 2014. The list of relevant proceedings is set out in s 18(1) of the ETA 1996. The claims to which Early Conciliation does not apply are set out in reg 3 of the Early Conciliation Regulations 2014, but it will apply to all of the most common claims.

6.3.7.1 Early Conciliation

When a claimant contacts Acas, this will 'pause' the time-limit for presenting his claim to a tribunal from the date Acas is notified. This pause can be for up to one calendar month, plus a further 14 days if more time is needed. The time-limit will start to run again when the claimant receives his formal acknowledgement (the Certificate) that Early Conciliation has finished. Once Early Conciliation has ended, the claimant will have at least one calendar month in which to present his claim. If a claimant was already out of time for making a tribunal claim when requesting Early Conciliation, he will still be late afterwards. Provisions to extend time have been inserted into primary and secondary legislation by:

- Sch 2 to the ERRA 2013;
- art 3 of and the Schedule to the Employment Tribunals Act 1996 (Application of Conciliation Provisions) Order 2014 (SI 2014/431);
- art 2 of and the Schedule to the ERRA 2013 (Consequential Amendments) (Employment) Order 2014 (SI 2014/386);
- the ERRA 2013 (Consequential Amendments) (Employment) (No 2) Order 2014 (SI 2014/853), which amended TUPE 2006 with effect from 20 April 2014.

The guide below is provided by the Citizens' Advice Bureau at:

<www.adviceguide.org.uk/england/work_e/work_problems_at_work_e/early_conciliation_how_it_affects_the_time_limit_for_making_a_claim.htm>.

> Early conciliation has an important implication for the time limit for making a claim. It stops the clock so that time is suspended while you are in the early conciliation process.
>
> It is essential that you read this page to find out how early conciliation affects the time limit for making your claim.
>
> **Time limits in employment cases**
>
> The normal time limit for making a claim in most employment cases is three months minus one day.
>
> In redundancy pay and equal pay cases, the time limit is six months minus one day.
>
> If early conciliation applies to your case, this will affect the time limit for presenting your case to an employment tribunal.
>
> **How long does early conciliation last?**
>
> Early conciliation (EC) can last up to one calendar month starting on the date on which you notify Acas of your potential claim.
>
> This one-month period can be extended by up to 14 days if, towards the end of the month, Acas thinks that there is a reasonable prospect of settling the case within those extra 14 days.
>
> If you do not wish to take part in early conciliation, or you can't settle all parts of your dispute, Acas must issue an early conciliation certificate.
>
> This can be:
>
> - at any point during the early conciliation period, or
> - at the end of the one-month conciliation period, or
> - at the end of the extended one-month-and-14-day period.
>
> **When will the certificate be treated as having been received?**
>
> When you will be treated as having received the early conciliation certificate depends on how it is sent to you.

If the EC certificate is sent by email

You will be treated as having received it on the same day it was sent.

If the EC certificate is sent by post

If the certificate is sent by post, you will be treated as having received it on the second working day after it was sent.

A working day does not include Sundays and public holidays.

The early conciliation period

This is also called the **pause period** or the **stop the clock** period. The early conciliation period:

* starts on the day after you contact Acas, either by telephone or by completing the online EC form (Day A), and

* ends on the day you receive your early conciliation certificate (Day B).

The early conciliation period could be as long as one calendar month plus 14 days from the day after the day on which you contact Acas, or as short as one day.

Example of a short conciliation period

You present your form online or telephone Acas on 1 May. Acas establishes on 2 May that you or your employer do not wish to conciliate, and emails you the early conciliation certificate on 2 May. The early conciliation period lasted one day.

Example of a long conciliation period

You present your form online or telephone Acas on 1 May. This is Day A. The conciliation period starts on 2 May. Conciliation may continue for up to one calendar month starting that day. In this case, the early conciliation period is from 2 May to 1 June.

On 1 June, Acas thinks that there's a reasonable prospect of settlement, and so the period is extended by 14 days, from 2 to 15 June.

Unfortunately, negotiations break down and no settlement is reached. You receive the Acas early conciliation certificate by email on 15 June. The end of the conciliation period is 15 June, known as Day B.

How the early conciliation period affects the time limit for making your claim

Early conciliation extends the time you have to make your claim. This is because while you are taking part in early conciliation, the clock stops. If negotiations fail, the clock starts running again from the date you are deemed to have received your early conciliation certificate (Day B). Time is added to the original time limit for making a claim to make up for the pause during the early conciliation period.

However, you will not know the exact new time limit until conciliation has ended and you have received your early conciliation certificate.

If your original time limit falls between Day A and one month after Day B

If your original time limit falls between Day A and one month after Day B (the date on which you receive your early conciliation certificate), the new time limit will be one month after Day B.

Example 1

You were dismissed on 31 May. The original time limit would expire on 30 August. You enter into conciliation on 15 August, Day A, but this fails on 5 September, Day B.

The original time limit falls within the period which began with Day A and ended a month after Day B, that is, from 15 August to 5 October. Therefore time will expire on 5 October.

If your original time limit falls more than one month after Day B

If the original time limit falls more than one month after Day B, then time will be extended by a period equivalent to the early conciliation period. The length of the early conciliation period is calculated from the day after Day A up to and including Day B.

Example 2

You were dismissed on 31 May. The original time limit for making your claim would be 30 August. You enter into conciliation on 15 June, Day A, but this fails after 20 days on 5 July, Day B.

The original time limit does not fall within a period which began with Day A and ended a month after Day B, that is, from 15 June to 5 August. The early conciliation period took 20 days. Therefore, 20 days will be added to the original time limit of 30 August. The new time limit is therefore 19 September.

So, in every case, as shown in the two examples above, you will sometimes have more, but will never have less, than one month from the date you receive your early conciliation certificate (Day B) to present your claim to the employment tribunal, provided that you contact Acas before the original time limit expires.

If your original time limit falls before you contact Acas

If the original time limit for your claim expired before you contact Acas to start the early conciliation process, you should contact Acas immediately to start early conciliation and contact a specialist adviser for help and advice.

Even if you are making a claim out of time, you will need your early conciliation certificate to complete the ET1.

As mentioned above (**6.2.2.3**), changes have been made to time-limits to allow time for Early Conciliation to take place. The unfair dismissal and other time-limits (see **6.3.1**) are now subject to the provisions of s 207B of the ERA 1996. There has, however, been considerable uncertainty as to the interpretation and effect of these time-limits. There are, as illustrated below, many traps for the unwary. Many of the cases discussed below are first instance cases, and first instance decisions are not binding on other tribunals, though they are still, nonetheless, a useful reference point.

In *Booth v Pasta King UK Ltd* (ET/1401231/2014) (heard in October 2014), the tribunal looked at the effect of s 207B of the ERA 1996. The claimant was dismissed on 2 April 2014. He sought to bring an unfair dismissal claim, and his ET1 was therefore due on or before 1 July 2014. He made contact with Acas on 21 May 2014 (day A). He received the Early Conciliation certificate on 21 June 2014 (day B). He submitted his ET1 on 24 July 2014. Under s 207B(3) (as relied upon by the claimant), 'the period beginning with the day after day A (22 May) and ending with Day B (21 June) is not be counted'. On this basis, 31 days could be discounted, leaving a date of 1 August. However, under s 207B(4) (as relied upon by the employer), 'if a time limit set by a relevant provision would (if not extended by this subsection) expire during the period beginning with day A (21 May) and ending one month after day B (21 July), the time limit expires instead at the end of that period'. On this basis, the last date for filing the ET1 was 21 July. The question for the tribunal was which, if either, subsection prevailed. The Employment Judge determined that Parliament could not have intended that a claimant should fail to have the benefit of s 207B(3) just because s 207B(4) was also available. She determined that the two provisions should not be read or applied in isolation, and held that the claim was in time. (See too *Wass v Delta Global Source (UK) Ltd* (ET/2600605/15).)

In *Chandler v Thanet District Council* (ET/2301782/14), the claimant was dismissed on 14 May 2014. He sought to bring an unfair dismissal claim, and his ET1 was due on or before 13 August 2014. He made contact with Acas on 8 May 2014. He received the Early Conciliation certificate on 7 June 2014 (day B). He submitted his ET1 on 10 September 2014. Argument focused on whether the time spent in Early Conciliation prior to the termination date (some five days) should be counted. The employer argued that they should not. On this basis, only 25 days could be counted, leaving a final date of 8 September. The claimant argued that all 30 days should be counted. The Employment Judge determined in favour of the claimant, finding that the period for submitting the claim was extended to 13 September, and therefore that the claim had been presented in time. Section 207B of the ERA 1996 should be interpreted so that time spent in Early Conciliation should always in effect be added on to the normal time-limit, even where the Early Conciliation period starts before time begins to run. Some commentators have said that s 207B does not easily support the employment judge's interpretation. Until the issue is resolved by appellate authority, claimants would be advised to be cautious about relying on it, but the same approach was also adopted by another tribunal in *Myers v Nottingham City Council* (2015).

In *Thomas v Nationwide Building Society* (ET/1601342/14) (heard in October 2014), no Early Conciliation certificate had been obtained, and the claim was rejected at the first stage sift under Rules 10 and 12. The claimant applied for a reconsideration under Rule 13. At a preliminary hearing to consider this, a later Early Conciliation certificate was presented. The employment tribunal held (somewhat controversially) that this remedied the defect and that there was therefore jurisdiction to hear the claim. Rule 13(4) provides that in a case where the original rejection was correct but the defect has been rectified, the claim shall be treated as presented on the date that the defect was rectified. In this case, the Employment Judge held that the claim should be treated as if presented at the date the defect was rectified (7 October, which was the date when Early Conciliation was completed) and listed a further hearing to consider whether the claim was out of time.

The EAT considered the meaning of 'one month *after*' (s 207B(4)) in *Tanveer v East London Bus and Coach Co Ltd* (UKEAT/0022/16). The claimant contacted Acas on 18 June 2015 and received the Early Conciliation certificate on 30 June 2015. The claim was issued on 31 July 2015. The issue was: 'what was "one month after"'? The employment tribunal concluded that one month was a calendar month, which meant that time expired on 30 July 2015. On appeal, the claimant argued that a calendar month meant that time expired on the last day of the calendar month, ie 31 July 2015, because the language of 'one month *after*' differs from the usual language (within the relevant period beginning with a date). The EAT disagreed and held that time expired on the corresponding date, ie 30 July 2015.

In *Hardy v Balfour Beatty Group Employment Ltd* (ET/13066954/14), the relationship between s 207B(3) and (4) was again considered. The claimant was dismissed on 15 July 2014. He sought to bring claims of unfair dismissal, non-payment of holiday pay and breach of contract, and his ET1 was therefore due on or before 14 October 2014. He made contact with Acas on 2 October 2014 (day A). He received the Early Conciliation certificate on 16 November 2014 (day B). Under s 207B(3), this stopped the clock for 45 days, which extended the period to 28 November. He submitted his ET1 on 22 December. However, under s 207B(4) (as relied upon by the claimant), the revised limitation period (28 November) would fall during the period beginning with day A (2 October) and ending one month after day B (16 December). On this basis, the last date for filing the ET1 was 16 December. So on either basis, the claim appeared to have been filed out of time. The claimant sought to argue that the two sections were cumulative, and he could therefore add the 45 days to day B, thus extending the period until 31 December. The Employment Judge disagreed with this analysis. If the extended date under s 207B(3) falls *within* day A and day B, s 207B(4) is engaged. The 45 days in s 207B(3) must be added to day B and not to the original limitation period. Section 207B(4) can be relied upon where the circumstances in s 207B(3) might be disadvantageous.

In *Luton Borough Council v Haque* (UKEAT/0260/17), a case which again concerned the relationship between s 207B(3) and (4), the effective date of termination was 20 June 2016. The claimant went to Acas on 22 July 2016 (Day A). The Early Conciliation certificate was issued on 22 August 2016 (Day B). The three months statutory time-limit therefore expired on 19 September 2016. The period of conciliation was 31 days. The claim form was presented on 18 October 2016. A dispute arose as to whether the 31 days period of conciliation extended the time limit from 19 September to 20 October (ie 31 days after 19 September) or whether the effect of s 207B(4) meant that time expired one month after Day B, ie 22 September (in which case the claim would be out of time). The employment tribunal ruled that the claimant's claims had been presented in time and should proceed to a full hearing. The respondent appealed. The EAT referred the case to a full hearing in an effort to resolve the ambiguity of the approach to the relationship between s 207B(3) and (4). In its judgment on allowing the appeal to go to a full hearing, the EAT referred to *Booth v Pasta King UK Ltd* (above) and *Savory and 58 Others v South Western Ambulance Service NHS Foundation Trust and Another* (ET/1400119/2016). In its substantive judgment (UKEAT/0180/17), the EAT said that the statutory provisions are to be applied sequentially and not as alternatives. First, the time-limit is extended by the period of conciliation. Next (and only if the time-limit would then expire prior to a month after Day B), the time-limit expires at the end of that month. Subsection (3) applies in every case. By contrast, subsection (4) expressly applies only in the circumstances to which it refers: the EAT therefore found that the claimant's claims has been presented in time.

In *Ullah v London Borough of Hounslow* (EAT/0084/16) the EAT confirmed that the statutory provisions did not require the period between date A and B to be added to the usual limitation period: they did not deal with 'adding time at all'; they only provided that time was 'not to be counted'. Therefore, 'whatever part of the usual time limit would run between A and B is ignored when reckoning the expiry of 3 months'.

In *Compass Group UK and Ireland Ltd v Morgan* (UKEAT/0060/16), the EAT held that a claimant's constructive dismissal claim was covered by an Early Conciliation certificate issued before she resigned.

In *Revenue and Customs Commissioners v Garau* (UKEAT/0348/16), the EAT held that there is no provision for a second certificate to be issued, and therefore such second certificate that was issued could have no effect on the time-limit.

6.4 TRIBUNAL RULES

The practice and procedure of employment tribunals is governed by the Employment Tribunals (Constitution and Rules of Procedure) Regulations 2013, which came into force on 29 July 2013. Schedule 1 sets out the Tribunal Rules of Procedure.

Rule 2 states that the 'overriding objective' of the Rules is to enable tribunals to deal with cases fairly and justly. This includes, so far as practicable:

(a) ensuring the parties are on an equal footing;

(b) dealing with the case in ways that are proportionate to the complexity and importance of the issues;

(c) avoiding unnecessary formality and seeking flexibility in the proceedings;

(d) avoiding delay, so far as compatible with a proper consideration of the issues; and

(e) saving expense.

The parties have a duty to assist the tribunal in furthering the overriding objective. Tribunals are obliged to apply the overriding objective when interpreting every rule or exercising any power.

In *Harris v Academies Enterprise Trust* [2015] IRLR 208, the EAT compared the wording of the overriding objective as it appeared in the Employment Tribunal Rules and as it was worded in rule 3.9 of the Civil Procedure Rules (CPR) 1998. The claimant brought a number of claims against the Trust, including for whistleblowing, disability discrimination, victimisation and harassment. Witness statements were due to be exchanged on 19 February 2014, and a full hearing had been listed to start on 3 March 2014. The employer applied for an extension of time to exchange witness statements, but this was refused. On 26 February, the claimant applied for an unless order (see **6.4.8.3**). The Employment Judge did not make the order but stated that she was considering striking out the ET3/response under Rule 37(1) because of non-compliance with the original order to exchange witness statements (see **6.4.8.2**). At the beginning of the hearing on 3 March, the claimant applied to strike out the response. The Employment Judge accepted that there had been a failure to comply with a tribunal order and that the employer had acted unreasonably in not providing the witness statements, but noted that the overriding objective in the Tribunal Rules required tribunals to deal with cases fairly and justly, and went on to assess the relative prejudice to each of the parties. Having done so, the Employment Judge did not consider it appropriate to strike out the ET3/response, on the basis that it would not be proportionate, and the case was adjourned to the following Monday. The claimant's appeal was dismissed by the EAT. The EAT noted that the correct approach was to focus on the consequences of default before determining the proportionate response. The EAT noted that there were differences between the wording of the overriding objective in the CPR 1998 and in the Employment Tribunal Rules, and concluded, 'Though, it seems to me, there is much of principle that applies to both, it would be a mistake to suggest that the CPR applied in the tribunals in the same way as they apply in the civil courts.'

Rule 3 states that the tribunal shall, whenever practicable and appropriate, encourage the use of alternative means to settle the dispute.

Rule 4 sets out the rules on 'calculating time limits' for any act required under the Rules in Sch 1. (See eg **6.4.3** below.) The tribunal has a wide discretion to extend or shorten time-limits.

6.4.1 Litigants in person

A key area where the overriding objective comes into play is when dealing with unrepresented parties or litigants in person. Employment tribunals are accustomed to dealing with litigants in person. In 1995, the Woolf Report noted, 'All too often the litigant in person is regarded as a problem for judges and for the court system rather than a person for whom the system of civil justice exists.'

In March 2013, the Master of the Rolls issued practice guidance on dealing with litigants in person applicable to courts, and a judicial working group was established, chaired by Mr Justice Hickinbottom, which reported in July 2013 (*The Judicial Working Group on Litigants in Person: Report*). The Hickinbottom Report reiterated what the Woolf Report had noted, namely, that it is the court's or tribunal's duty to ensure that litigants have every reasonable opportunity to present their case, without assisting them with it.

The starting point for any consideration of this area is Rule 2 of the Employment Tribunal Rules and the overriding objective. The Court of Appeal in *Drysdale v Department of Transport (The Maritime and Coastguard Agency)* [2014] EWCA Civ 1083 provided some guidance on how employment tribunals should apply the overriding objective in the context of litigants in person. Mr Drysdale was represented by his wife during his employment tribunal proceedings. During the hearing, Mrs Drysdale, with her husband's apparent consent, asked that the claim be withdrawn. The tribunal asked her if her husband agreed and she confirmed that he did. The tribunal then dismissed the claim. The respondent employer then made a costs application, and Mr and Mrs Drysdale walked out after an acrimonious exchange. They subsequently appealed against the dismissal, challenging whether the tribunal had taken adequate steps to ensure that Mr Drysdale had taken a properly considered decision to withdraw the claim.

The Court of Appeal set out (at para 49) a number of general principles:

(a)   It is desirable for courts generally, and employment tribunals in particular, to provide appropriate assistance to litigants in the formulation and presentation of their case.

(b)   What level of assistance or intervention is 'appropriate' depends upon the circumstances of each particular case, including whether the litigant is represented or not, whether any representative is legally qualified and, in any case, the apparent level of competence and understanding of the litigant and/or his representative.

(c)   The appropriate level of assistance or intervention is constrained by the overriding requirement that the tribunal must at all times be, and be seen to be, impartial as between the parties, and that injustice to either side must be avoided.

(d)   How much assistance or intervention is appropriate is for the judgment of the tribunal hearing the case, and for the tribunal's assessment and 'feel' for what is fair in all the circumstances of the specific case. Rigid obligations or rules of law should be avoided.

(e)   There is a wide margin of appreciation available to a tribunal in assessing such matters, and an appeal court will not normally interfere with the tribunal's exercise of its judgment in the absence of an act or omission on the part of the tribunal which no reasonable tribunal, properly directing itself on the basis of the overriding objective, would have done/omitted to do, and which amounts to unfair treatment of a litigant.

In *U v Butler and Wilson* (UKEAT/0354/13), the EAT considered a tribunal's approach to adjournment, where the claimant wanted time to collect his papers from a nearby printing shop and to challenge the dismissal of his case in his absence because he arrived late. The right to a fair hearing may require a judge to adjourn a hearing even without an application from a party. The EAT held that the Employment Judge had failed to properly exercise her case management powers to adjourn in order to permit the claimant an opportunity to reflect on what course he wished to pursue. Furthermore, the tribunal had been in error in not explaining to the claimant that he had an option to make a written application for a review rather than proceeding immediately with an oral application. It was an important factor that the tribunal knew that the claimant was disabled with post-traumatic stress disorder and episodic psychosis, which should have been taken into account when making case management decisions. The EAT held:

> Anyone conducting a judicial or quasi-judicial hearing confronted with a person who is plainly unwell would necessarily and obviously adjourn the hearing for a brief time to enable them to recover sufficiently to present their case, or their evidence, if possible during the course of the hearing.

A distinction between *Drysdale* and *Butler and Wilson* is that, in the latter case, it could not be said the claimant was 'participating effectively' in his hearing.

6.4.2   The claim (Rule 8)

The complaint must be made in writing on the prescribed claim form ET1. (Only the official ETS versions of the forms are acceptable – they can be downloaded from <http://www.employmenttribunals.gov.uk>.) The ET1 *must* contain the following information:

(a)   each claimant's name;

(b)   each claimant's address;

(c)   each respondent's name;

(d)   each respondent's address;

(e)   details relating to Early Conciliation, including the Early Conciliation number.

Rule 10(1) states that if a claim is not presented on the prescribed form, or where the claim does not include the minimum information referred to above or does not contain an early conciliation number or confirmation that one is not required, it will be rejected. (Rule 10(1) was amended by the Employment Tribunals (Constitution and Rules of Procedure) (Amendment) Regulations 2014 (SI 2014/271) to bring it up to date with regard to the early conciliation procedure.)

Rule 12 states that a claim form may be referred to an Employment Judge, and the Judge can strike out a claim, if it appears that (a) a tribunal has no jurisdiction to consider the claim or part of it, or (b) if it cannot sensibly be responded to or is an abuse of process. This then effectively allows the Employment Judge to conduct a preliminary 'sift' of the claim. In *Higgins v Home Office* (UKEAT/0296/14), the claimant sought to bring an unfair constructive dismissal claim six years after the employment relationship ended. The employment tribunal rejected the claim as an abuse of process under the sifting procedure in Rule 12. The EAT said that striking out a valid claim as an abuse of process should be the last resort (see *Wallis v Valentine* [2002] EWCA Civ 1034). Claims should only be rejected in the sift in the most plain and obvious cases; borderline cases should be dealt with under Rule 27 (no reasonable prospect of success). As the tribunal had failed to appreciate that the claimant may have had significant mental health issues, the case was remitted back to a fresh tribunal to reconsider it under Rule 12 and under Rule 27. In *Secretary of State for Business, Energy and Industrial Strategy v Parry* [2018] EWCA Civ 672, the Court of Appeal considered the scope and ambit of Rule 12(1)(b), which allows for rejection of a claim without a hearing. It held that the rejection of a claim under Rule 12(1)(b) is not a 'determination of proceedings' within s 7 of the Employment Tribunals Act 1996. Rule 12 has to be read with Rule 8, which states that proceedings only commence when a completed claim form is presented. Further, a rejection is not a determination – it is a judicial act of a different quality which does not go to the substance of the claim or the quality of the issues.

Rule 12 also make provision for the rejection of a defective claim including:

> (f)   one which institutes relevant proceedings and the name of the respondent on the claim form is not the same as the name of the prospective respondent on the early conciliation certificate to which the early conciliation number relates.

Rule 12(2A) states that the claim (or part of it):

> shall be rejected if the Judge considers that the claim, or part of it, is of a kind described in sub-paragraph (e) or (f) of paragraph (1) unless the Judge considers that the claimant made a minor error in relation to a name or address and it would not be in the interests of justice to reject the claim.

In *Giny v SNA Transport Ltd* (UKEAT/0317/16), the claimant's Early Conciliation Certificate named the respondent as a 'Mr A' (the correct name was 'SNA Ltd', of whom Mr A was the director). The claimant gave the correct address. He subsequently took legal advice and the ET1 was issued in the correct name. The tribunal struck the claim out under Rule 12(1)(f), considering that this was not a minor error and declining to exercise its discretionary power that it would not be in the interests of justice to reject the claim. The EAT held that this was a decision that the tribunal could properly come to, having applied the two-stage test.

A claimant may apply under Rule 13 for reconsideration of a decision to reject a claim form under Rules 10 or 12, if he considers the rejection erroneous or if the notified defect can be rectified.

The form should be sent to the appropriate ROET. The complaint must be received at the ROET within the relevant time-limit (see **6.3** above). Generally, as a matter of practice, claims will be held in the 'relevant' tribunal region for the claimant's postcode – work or home. However, there is no 'right' for a claimant to have a case heard in a particular region (see *Faleye and Another v UK Mission Enterprise Ltd* (UKEAT/0359/10)). Requests for transfers between regions are purely a matter, subject to any injustice, of discretion for an Employment Judge to determine.

A complaint may be posted, delivered by hand or sent electronically (see Rule 85). (See also **6.3.1**.)

A copy of the complaint will be sent by the ROET to the employer and to Acas.

6.4.3   Response (Rule 16)

The employer should file a response on prescribed form ET3. Rule 16 states that if a response is not presented on the prescribed form, or where the response does not include all the required information or it is received outside the required time-limit, the response shall be rejected (the respondent can apply for reconsideration of that decision under Rule 19 if he considers the rejection erroneous).

The form should be submitted within 28 days of the date on which the ET1 was sent by the tribunal to the respondent. Rule 4(3) states that:

> where any act must or may be done within a certain number of days of or from an event, the date of that event shall not be included in the calculation. For example, a response shall be presented within 28 days of the date on which the respondent was sent a copy of a claim: if the claim was sent on 1st October, the last day for presentation of the response is 29th October.

A copy of the response will be sent to all parties.

Rule 17 states that the following information must be provided:

(a)   respondent's full name;

(b)   respondent's full address;

(c)   whether or not the respondent wishes to resist the claim in whole or in part; and

(d)   if the respondent wishes to resist, on what grounds.

Rule 20 allows the respondent to apply for an extension of time within which to submit his ET3. The application for an extension must be made in accordance with Rule 20. Any application should set out reasons why an extension is sought.

Where a respondent fails to enter a response within the time-limits (or to apply for an extension under Rule 20) a tribunal judge shall decide whether a determination can be made and, if it can, issue a judgment. Otherwise a hearing will be listed. Even where a respondent is barred from contesting liability (for example because it fails to present a response in time), it should normally be able to participate in a remedy hearing (*Office Equipment Systems Ltd v Hughes* [2018] EWCA Civ 1842).

6.4.4 Initial consideration (Rule 26)

Once a claim form and response have been received, an Employment Judge will conduct an initial consideration of the case. The Employment Judge may make a case management order, or list the case for a preliminary or final hearing, or propose mediation or some other form of dispute resolution; or (Rule 27), if the Employment Judge considers that there is no jurisdiction to hear the claim, or that it or a part of it has no reasonable prospect of success, he may dismiss the claim or part of it (subject to giving the claimant the opportunity to make written representations explaining why it should not be dismissed). Rule 28 contains similar powers with regard to dismissing a response.

6.4.5 Applications to amend

There is nothing in the Rules dealing specifically with amendments. Such applications may give rise to subsidiary considerations about whether claims are made in time. One alternative to seeking to amend an existing claim is to issue a new claim and, if necessary, apply for permission to present it out of time (see **6.3.1** for time-limits and extensions). However, claimants need to remember that under the Early Conciliation rules (**6.2.2**), before a claim is brought an Early Conciliation certificate must be obtained. It is not clear how this will apply to an application to amend a pre-existing claim, where there is a new cause of action not covered by any existing certificate.

The principal authorities with regard to amendments are *Cocking v Sandhurst* [1974] ICR 650, *British Newspaper Printing Corporation (North) Ltd v Kelly* [1989] IRLR 222, *Selkent Bus Co v Moore* [1996] IRLR 661, *Housing Corporation v Bryant* [1999] ICR 123, *Harvey v Port of Tilbury (London) Ltd* [1999] ICR 1030 and *Ali v Office of National Statistics* [2005] IRLR 201. The EAT in *Selkent* stated a number of general principles which it said were applicable to the amendment of tribunal claims:

(4) Whenever the discretion to grant an amendment is invoked, the tribunal should take into account all the circumstances and should balance the injustice and hardship of allowing the amendment against the injustice and hardship of refusing it.

(5) What are the relevant circumstances? It is impossible and undesirable to attempt to list them exhaustively, but the following are certainly relevant:

(a) *The nature of the amendment*

Applications to amend are of many different kinds, ranging, on the one hand, from the correction of clerical and typing errors, the additions of factual details to existing allegations and the addition or substitution of other labels for facts already pleaded to, on the other hand, the making of entirely new factual allegations which change the basis of the existing claim. The tribunal have to decide whether the amendment sought is one of the minor matters or is a substantial alteration pleading a new cause of action.

(b) *The applicability of time limits*

If a new complaint or cause of action is proposed to be added by way of amendment, it is essential for the tribunal to consider whether that complaint is out of time and, if so, whether the time limit should be extended under the applicable statutory provisions ...

(c)   *The timing and manner of the application*

An application should not be refused solely because there has been a delay in making it. There are no time limits laid down in the Rules for the making of amendments. The amendments may be made at any time – before, at, even after the hearing of the case. Delay in making the application is, however, a discretionary factor. It is relevant to consider why the application was not made earlier and why it is now being made: for example, the discovery of new facts or new information appearing from documents disclosed on discovery. Whenever taking any factors into account, the paramount considerations are the relative injustice and hardship involved in refusing or granting an amendment. Questions of delay, as a result of adjournments, and additional costs, particularly if they are unlikely to be recovered by the successful party, are relevant in reaching a decision.

Even in the most extreme case, ie where there is a finding that, as 'a new' claim, that claim would be out of time (allowing for the relevant 'escape clause'), the authorities do not suggest that that would be fatal to an application to amend. Conversely, the fact that an amendment could be commenced as a new claim within the time-limit, while a significant feature, is not conclusive in favour of granting an application (see *Gillett v Bridge 86 Ltd* (UKEAT/0051/17) and *Patka v BBC* (UKEAT/0190/17)).

The Court of Appeal in *Office of National Statistics v Ali* [2005] IRLR 201 considered an appeal relating to an application to amend an ET1. The claim form alleged direct racial discrimination. Even though there was an argument about whether it included some aspects of indirect racial discrimination, it did not allege the indirect racial discrimination upon which the employee wished to rely. The details of complaint in the ET1 clearly referred to race as the reason for the treatment of which complaint was made. Mr Ali was originally unrepresented. After counsel was instructed, an application to amend the ET1 was made specifying the basis of a claim for indirect discrimination. The employment tribunal took the view that the ET1 raised the issue of whether there was something about the respondent's recruitment practice which had the effect of excluding black people and concluded that the ET1 included a claim of indirect race discrimination and no amendment was required. The Court of Appeal (Waller LJ) held, at para 39:

In my view the question whether an originating application contains a claim has to be judged by reference to the whole document. That means that although box 1 may contain a very general description of the complaint and a bare reference in the particulars to an event (as in *Dodd v* [*British Telecommunications* [1988] IRLR 16]), particularisation may make it clear that a particular claim, for example for indirect discrimination, is not being pursued. That may at first sight seem to favour the less particularised claim as in *Dodd*, but such a general claim cries out for particulars and those are particulars to which the employer is entitled so that he knows the claim he has to meet. An originating application which appears to contain full particulars would be deceptive if an employer cannot rely on what it states. I would for my part think that insofar as *Quarcoopome* [*v Sock Shop Holdings Ltd* [1995] IRLR 353] suggests to the contrary it should not be followed. Therefore I would hold that paragraph 25A seeks to bring into the proceedings a new claim.

For other decisions on amendment see, for example, *Baker v Commissioner of Police of the Metropolis* (UKEAT/0201/09/CEA), *Enterprise Liverpool Ltd v Jonas and Others* (UKEAT/0112/09), *Thompson v East Dumbartonshire Council* (UKEATS/0049/13), *Wade v CT Plus Community Interest Company* (UKEAT/0510/13) and *Makauskiene v Rentokil Initial Facilities Services (UK) Ltd* (UKEAT/0503/13). In *New Star v Evershed* [2010] EWCA Civ 870, the Court of Appeal held that adding a public interest disclosure claim to an unfair dismissal claim with similar facts did not require 'wholly different evidence' such that the application to amend should be refused. The claimant sought to add an 'automatic' unfair constructive dismissal claim by asserting that the reason, or principal reason, for his dismissal was that he had made a protected disclosure and that it was a 'whistle-blowing' claim. He had made allegations about being bullied in the context of his unfair dismissal claim, where he argued that it contributed to the intolerable atmosphere causing him to resign. Although the respondent said the allegations were irrelevant to the unfair dismissal claim, they had not been struck out and remained part of the case. The Court of Appeal accepted that this was not a mere 're-labelling' and specific findings would have to be made about the individual components of the public interest disclosure claim; but it upheld the reasoning of the EAT that there was a substantial overlap in the issues. The EAT held in *Amey Services Ltd v Aldridge* (UKEAT/0007/16) that the time issue must, where relevant, be decided before determining the amendment application.

6.4.6   Case management (Rule 29)

Under the Rules, the Employment Judge has wide case management powers. The Employment Judge may, for example, strike out a claim (Rule 37), make an unless order (Rule 38) or order a deposit (Rule 39). If there is a hearing, it will be a preliminary hearing (Rule 53) (see **6.4.7**). Preliminary hearings are normally in private (unless they involve the determination of a preliminary issue or consideration to strike out a claim or response). The Employment Judge may require:

(a)   a party to provide additional information;

(b)   a party to disclose documents;

(c)   a party to provide written answers to questions;

(d)   attendance of witnesses;

(e)   provision and exchange of witness statements.

An example of a pro forma template agenda for a case management discussion at a preliminary hearing is set out at the end of **Appendix 3**, along with the detailed (and helpful) Guidance issued by the President of the Employment Tribunals. One important process that is conducted at a preliminary case management hearing is to set out a list of issues, which should be agreed if possible between the parties. In *Land Rover v Short* (UKEAT/0496/10), the EAT noted that agreed lists of issues were usually of considerable assistance to tribunals and contributed to the natural justice requirements that a party should know the case it has to meet. The Court of Appeal in *Scicluna v Zippy Stitch Ltd* [2018] EWCA Civ 1320 held that an agreed list of issues is 'the road map by which the judge is to navigate his or her way to a just determination', and departure from it should only occur in exceptional circumstances. The EAT held that it is not open to the employment tribunals to limit the issues a claimant can pursue (subject to claims being struck out, which will be rare in discrimination claims (see **6.4.8.2**)) (*Tarn v Hughes and Others* (UKEAT/0064/18).

Employment Judges can suggest to the parties at the case management discussion that the case be referred to judicial mediation. This involves bringing the parties in a case together. The Employment Judge will try to assist the parties to resolve the dispute. The judicial mediation will be heard in private and will be entirely confidential. All jurisdictions (except equal pay) may be referred to the scheme.

The President of the Employment Tribunals has identified minimum criteria that will be applied in considering whether judicial mediation can be offered. The most significant of these is that the case would be listed in the normal course of events for a minimum of three days. Another important factor in assessing suitability is whether there is an on-going employment relationship (see **6.6** below). A fee applies (see **6.2.1**).

The President of the Employment Tribunals has also issued guidance on the basis on which the employment tribunals will offer to parties the facility of judicial assessment of their cases. Judicial assessment is an impartial and confidential assessment by an Employment Judge, at an early stage in the proceedings, of the strengths, weaknesses and risks of the parties' respective claims, allegations and contentions (<www.judiciary.gov.uk/wp-content/uploads/2013/08/presidential-guidance-rule-3-judicial-assessments.pdf>). If the parties consent, the Employment Judge may then give an assessment of the liability and/or remedy aspects of the case (see too **6.4.8.5**).

6.4.6.1   Additional information

A request for additional information should first be made directly to the other party before seeking an order from the tribunal. A tribunal may order a party to the proceedings to provide additional information about the grounds upon which he relies and of any facts or contentions relevant thereto, and it may impose a time-limit by which the order is to be complied with.

The purpose of additional information is to remedy any deficiency in the case stated in the claim or response form, in order that the parties will know in advance reasonable details of the nature of the complaints that each side is going to make at the hearing. For example, additional information may be ordered about a vague allegation such as 'the claimant failed to perform her duties satisfactorily'.

6.4.6.2   Disclosure of documents (Rule 31)

Again, a request should first be made to the other party before seeking an order. The tribunal has powers similar to those of the county court in ordering disclosure and inspection (CPR 1998, Part 31; see *Civil Litigation*, **Chapter 11**). The CPR 1998 provide for disclosure of:

(a)   the documents on which a party relies; and

(b)   the documents which:

    (i)   adversely affect a party's own case,

    (ii)   adversely affect another party's case, or

    (iii)   support another party's case.

The main purpose of the disclosure and inspection stage of the litigation process is to enable the parties better to evaluate the strength of their opponent's case in advance of the trial. The parties have to reveal to each other the documents which have a bearing on the disputed issues in the case. The process is intended to promote settlements and therefore a saving in costs. It ensures that the parties are not taken by surprise at the trial and that the court has all relevant information in order to do justice between the parties. The Court of Appeal held in *Canadian Imperial Bank of Commerce v Beck* [2009] IRLR 740 that 'the test is whether or not an order for [disclosure] is necessary for fairly disposing of the proceedings ... The fact that some documents may be confidential does not confer immunity on them.'

Privilege

There are some circumstances in which a party will not have to allow the other party to inspect a disclosed document. One of those is where a party relies on the document being protected by legal professional privilege. The rules on privilege are also the same as those that apply in the civil courts. In brief, there are two types of legal professional privilege:

(a)   *Advice privilege*

Communications passing between a party and his legal advisers, or between a party's legal advisers, are privileged from inspection, provided they are written by or to the solicitor in his professional capacity and for the sole or dominant purpose of obtaining legal advice or assistance for the client. 'Legal advice' is not confined to telling the client the law; it includes information passed by solicitor to client, or vice versa, so that advice may be sought and given, and it includes advice about what should prudently and sensibly be done in the relevant legal context.

Privilege, however, does not extend without limit to all solicitor/client communications. The range of assistance given by solicitors to their clients has greatly broadened in recent times; for example, many solicitors now provide investment advice to clients. The scope of legal professional privilege has to be kept within reasonable bounds. See further *Three Rivers District Council and Others v Governor and Company of the Bank of England* [2004] UKHL 48, [2004] 3 WLR 1274. Nor does it extend to communications with third parties (see the (criticised) case of *Three Rivers DC and Others v Bank of England (No 5)* [2003]

EWCA Civ 474 (between an employee and the company lawyer) and *Glaxo Wellcome UK Ltd v Sandoz* [2018] EWHC 2747 (Ch)).

The privilege extends to communications between a party and his solicitor's employee or agent, and also to communications between a party and a solicitor in his service, for example a solicitor to a government department or in a legal department of a commercial enterprise. The privilege also covers instructions and briefs to counsel, counsel's opinions, and counsel's drafts and notes.

There is an exception to legal advice privilege where 'sharp practice' or iniquity is involved. See *X v Y Ltd* (UKEAT/0261/17) where the EAT held that an email sent by a lawyer to a client containing legal advice on the dismissal of an employee crossed the threshold of iniquity because it was in fact advice on how to use redundancy to cloak an unfair and discriminatory dismissal. As such, the advice was not protected by legal advice privilege.

(b) *Litigation privilege*

(i) Communications passing between the solicitor and a third party are privileged from production and inspection only if:

(1) they come into existence after litigation is contemplated or commenced (see *Director of the Serious Fraud Office v ENRC Ltd* [2018] EWCA Civ 2006 where the Court of Appeal held that criminal proceedings were reasonably contemplated when ENRC initiated an investigation into allegations made by a whistleblower); and

(2) they are made with a view to the litigation, either for the sole or dominant purpose of obtaining or giving advice in regard to it, or for obtaining evidence to be used in it. In the ENRC case (above) the Court of Appeal held that the notes of employee interviews were made with the dominant purpose of avoiding and/or dealing with litigation and met the test.

Examples of documents which may come within this head of privilege are a report from an expert obtained by a solicitor with a view to advising his client about existing or contemplated litigation, or witness statements obtained by a solicitor for the purpose of existing or contemplated litigation.

(ii) Communications between the client and a third party are privileged if the sole or dominant purpose for which they were produced was to obtain legal advice in respect of existing or contemplated litigation, or to conduct, or aid in the conduct, of such litigation. It must be the case that litigation was reasonably in prospect at the time when the document was brought into existence, and that the sole or dominant reason for obtaining the document was to enable solicitors to advise as to whether a claim should be made or resisted, or to have it as evidence.

Where a client is not an individual, this form of privilege is also applied to communications between individuals within that organisation. Thus, a memorandum sent by one partner of a firm to another would be privileged if it was prepared for the dominant purpose of obtaining legal advice in respect of existing or contemplated litigation, or to aid the conduct of such litigation.

In *Scotthorne v Four Seasons Conservatories (UK) Ltd* (UKEAT/0178/10) the EAT decided that litigation privilege extended to protect advice given by a firm of employment law consultants to the employees and that the claimant did not have the right to inspect such communications. The EAT considered that legal advice given by non-legally qualified staff was not covered by legal advice privilege.

Waiver of privilege

The privilege is the client's and not the solicitor's, and therefore it may be waived by the client but not by the solicitor. Once a copy of a privileged document is served on the other side, the privilege is waived.

Confidentiality

If one party is seeking the disclosure of documents which the other side regards as being of a confidential nature (eg references, assessments, etc), the judge should inspect the documents in order to satisfy himself that disclosure is necessary. The judge will usually order disclosure where the content of the document is relevant and necessary to dispose of the case fairly (see, eg, *Nasse v SRC* [1979] IRLR 465; *Canadian Imperial Bank of Commerce v Beck* [2009] EWCA Civ 619). If appropriate, parts of the documents may be covered up (redacted), for example the name of an employee.

Voluntary disclosure

There is no general duty of disclosure in the absence of an order. However, if voluntary disclosure is made, there is a duty not to be selective by withholding documents and creating a false impression.

Without prejudice communications

In general, without prejudice communications are not disclosable. One exception to that rule is where there is unambiguous impropriety.

The EAT had an opportunity to consider the 'without prejudice' rule in *BNP Paribas v Mezzotero* [2004] IRLR 508. Where settlement discussions between parties are 'without prejudice', communications between the parties are not usually admissible in evidence in tribunal proceedings. In this case, however, the EAT held that for the rule to be effective there must be a genuine dispute between the parties and that, on the facts in the *BNP Paribas* case, there was not, despite the fact that the employee had raised a grievance as to how she was being treated upon her return from maternity leave. The employer called her into a meeting after she raised the grievance and told her it was a 'without prejudice' meeting. The EAT made it clear that the rule applies only where there is already a dispute between the parties, and the communications to which the rule is said to attach must be made for the purpose of a genuine attempt at compromise. More interestingly, the EAT also said that even if there had been a genuine dispute, it was 'unrealistic ... to refer to the parties as expressly agreeing to speak without prejudice, given the unequal relationship of the parties, the vulnerable position of the applicant in such a meeting as this, and the fact that the suggestion was made by the respondent only once the meeting had begun'. The EAT held in essence that the respondent's conduct was an abuse.

In *Brunel University v Vaseghi* [2007] IRLR 592, without prejudice discussions took place in an (unsuccessful) attempt to settle discrimination claims. The discussions were revealed during the course of internal grievance hearings. During the subsequent tribunal hearing, the employees tried to introduce evidence of the without prejudice discussions. The University objected, but the tribunal and EAT allowed the evidence in. The EAT said that failure to allow evidence of what was said during the without prejudice discussions would severely hamper the employees' ability to establish their victimisation claim. The EAT commented that 'in discrimination cases the necessity of getting to the truth of what occurred and if necessary eradicating the evil of discrimination may tip the scales as against the necessity of protecting the "without prejudice" privilege'. The Court of Appeal dismissed the appeal on the basis there had been bilateral waiver. It declined to comment on the suggestion by the EAT below and in *Mezzotero* that there was a particular exception to the without prejudice rule which applied only in discrimination and victimisation cases.

In *Woodward v Santander UK plc* (UKEAT/0250/09), the EAT, after considering the leading modern authorities concerning the without prejudice rule and the policy underlying the rule (namely that parties should not be discouraged from settling their disputes by fear that something said in the course of negotiations might be used against them) went on to hold:

58. Reading the judgment in *Mezzotero* as a whole, we do not think that it establishes any new exception to the without prejudice rule. In paragraph 38 Cox J expressly stated that she would regard the employer's alleged conduct as an exception to the without prejudice rule 'within the abuse principle'....

59. We doubt whether Cox J intended to say that it was unnecessary, in a discrimination case, to find unambiguous impropriety. We appreciate that paragraph 38 of her reasons, in which she refers to 'the unattractive task of attaching different levels of impropriety to fact sensitive allegations of discrimination', can be read in that way. But Cox J went on to say that she regarded the employer's alleged conduct as 'within the abuse principle'.

60. We would observe that the policy underlying the 'without prejudice' rule applies with as much force to cases where discrimination has been alleged as it applies to any other form of dispute. Indeed the policy may be said to apply with particular force in those cases where the parties are seeking to settle a discrimination claim.

61. Discrimination claims often place heavy emotional and financial burdens on claimants and respondents alike. It is important that parties should be able to settle their differences (whether by negotiation or mediation) in conditions where they can speak freely. A claimant must be free to concede a point for the purposes of settlement without the fear that if negotiations are unsuccessful he or she will be accused for that reason of pursuing the point dishonestly. A respondent must be free to adhere to and explain a position, or to refuse a particular settlement proposal, without the fear that in subsequent litigation this will be taken as evidence of committing or repeating an act of discrimination or victimisation. And it is idle to suppose that parties, when they participate in negotiation or mediation, will always be calm and dispassionate. They should be able, within limits, to argue their case and speak their mind.

62. What are the limits? To our mind they are best stated in terms of the existing exception for impropriety. This exception, as we have seen, applies only to a case where the Tribunal is satisfied that the impropriety alleged is unambiguous. It applies only in the very clearest of cases. A court or Tribunal is therefore required to make a judgment as to whether the evidence which it is sought to adduce meets this test. Words which are unambiguously discriminatory will of course fall within the exception: see the example given by Cox J at para 37 of *Mezzotero*.

63. It may at first sight seem unattractive, given the fact sensitive nature of discrimination cases, to exclude any evidence from which an inference of discrimination could be drawn. But it would have a substantial inhibiting effect on the ability of parties to speak freely in conducting negotiations if subsequently one or other could comb through the content of correspondence or discussions (which may have been lengthy or contentious) in order to point to equivocal words or actions in support of (or for that matter in order to defend) an inference of discrimination. Parties should be able to approach negotiations free from any concern that they will be used for evidence-gathering, or scrutinised afterwards for that purpose.

64. We therefore reject Mr Bacon's submission that there ought to be a wider exception to the without prejudice rule where discrimination is alleged. We do not think such an exception is consistent with the policy behind the rule. We cannot see any workable basis for applying such an exception while preserving the parties' freedom to speak freely in conducting negotiations.

In *Portnykh v Nomura International plc* (UKEAT/0448/13), the employment tribunal held that the without prejudice rule did not apply as there was no 'dispute' in existence when certain correspondence was entered into. The EAT disagreed. It held, looking at the factual matrix prior to the exchange of correspondence, that there was clearly a dispute in existence: if an employer announces an intention to dismiss an employee for misconduct, and there are then discussions about an alternative manner of dismissal, there is either a present dispute or the potential for a future dispute.

These cases highlighted the problems which can arise where termination discussions take place when there is no existing dispute. As a result, the Government inserted a new provision (s 111A) in the ERA 1996 to extend 'without prejudice' protections to make it easier for employers to make 'without prejudice' offers to employees. See **6.5.1** below.

6.4.6.3   'Written answers' to specific questions

The aim of written answers is to identify and narrow the issues; they need not be confined to amplification of the grounds upon which the party relies and are thus wider in scope than additional information. A similar approach is likely to be taken to such requests in the civil courts, so 'fishing' questions, for example, will not be allowed, neither will questions which relate solely to the evidence which a party intends to adduce. They are unlikely to be ordered where other procedural processes would be more appropriate, for example a request for additional information or a request for disclosure.

6.4.6.4   Disclosure of documents and attendance of witnesses (Rules 31 and 32)

The power to order disclosure and to issue witness orders is discretionary. The tribunal will normally need to be satisfied that the witness's evidence/document is sufficiently relevant.

6.4.6.5   Provision and exchange of witness statements

Tribunals almost invariably order that the parties' representatives prepare witness statements for the witnesses, and such statements stand as the witnesses' evidence-in-chief. The general rule (Rule 43) is that witness statements should not be read out but should be taken as read. In a case pre-dating the introduction of that rule, the President of the EAT gave guidance on the practice of reading out witness statements in tribunals. In *Mehta v Child Support Agency* (UKEAT/0127/10) he said that very often reading witness statements aloud 'achieves nothing of value' and 'wastes the time of tribunal and the parties', but that sometimes it might be helpful to read out a statement or part of a statement if matters might need clarifying or elucidation, or to help 'settle' an individual before he is cross-examined. He suggested that where both parties were represented, a procedure should be agreed. Where a party is not represented, a tribunal should ensure he understands the implications of what is proposed. Tribunals were cautioned against having a policy of not allowing a claimant to read out his statement – the appropriate procedure should be decided on a case by case basis at the tribunal's discretion. The tribunal will also usually order that statements are exchanged on an agreed date. Further detail may be found in **Civil Litigation, Chapter 12.**

6.4.6.6   The 'reasonable bounds' test

In *Hendricks v Commissioner of Police for the Metropolis* [2003] IRLR 96, Ms Hendricks' discrimination claim related to most of her 11 years at the force, involving nearly 100 specific allegations against 50 or so officers. The Court of Appeal stated that there must be close case management in lengthy discrimination cases, with agreed lists of issues and attempts to keep the proceedings within 'reasonable bounds' by concentrating on the most serious and most recent allegations. This approach was endorsed by the EAT in *HSBC Asia Holdings BV v Gillespie* (UKEAT/0417/10), which held that tribunals have wide discretionary case management powers and gave, obiter, guidance on the issue of pursuing 'sample' claims. It stated that there was no reason in principle why a tribunal could not hive off claims which it regarded as secondary or repetitive or otherwise unnecessary to a second hearing, allowing it to focus on claims considered to be more key.

However, there are limits to this. In *Tarn v Hughes* (UKEAT/0064/18), there were over 40 acts of discrimination alleged, requiring determination of 180 issues. The employment tribunal ordered Dr Tarn to select a sample of the 10 most recent and serious allegations to pursue. The EAT said that the order was perverse. While the tribunal has wide case management powers, limiting the claim in this way might undermine a just determination of the case. Claims should only be limited in exceptional cases. A tribunal has no power to prevent a claimant pursuing a properly arguable claim, even if it forms one of many similar claims (see *Ma v Merck, Sharp and Dohme Ltd* [2008] EWCA Civ 1426 and *Franco v Bowling and Co* (UKEAT/0280/09)).

6.4.7   Privacy and restrictions on disclosure (Rule 50)

Tribunals, like most courts, should hold most of their proceedings in open court (see ECHR, Article 6 and **6.4.14**). The principle that justice should be open is one of the foundations of the common law (see eg *Scott v Scott* [1913] AC 417 and *Global Torch Ltd v Apex Global Management Ltd* [2013] 1 WLR 2993) and applies as much to employment tribunals as to any other court. Rule 50, however, permits a tribunal at any stage of the proceedings to make an order to prevent or restrict the public disclosure of any aspect of the proceedings, if it considers it necessary in the interests of justice or in order to protect the Convention rights of any person. This gives a tribunal very wide powers to hold hearings or part of hearings in private, and to give anonymity to parties, witnesses and others.

The ETA 1996, ss 10–12 also give tribunals powers to make restricted reporting orders (RROs) in cases involving national security, confidential information, sexual offences or misconduct and disability.

An order can prevent publication of the name of the applicant (or respondent, or other persons affected by the allegation) or any other matter that is likely to lead to the identification of the individual in question. The RRO can last until the tribunal's written decision is sent to the parties. Where an allegation of a sexual offence is involved, the central register (see **6.4.12**) may be altered to delete any 'identifying material'.

In EF *v* AB (UKEAT/0525/13), the EAT overturned an employment tribunal's refusal to extend an RRO following the bringing of tribunal proceedings by a former employee for constructive dismissal and sexual harassment. The claims involved lurid revelations and allegations of sexual misconduct made against a senior manager and his wife. The tribunal made an RRO under Rule 50 and s 11(1)(b) of the ETA 1996, preventing a number of individuals, and various corporate respondents, from being identified until the determination of liability and remedy. The tribunal also made a register deletion order, because the proceedings involved allegations of sexual offences. Meanwhile, the Chief Executive Officer (CEO) obtained an interim injunction in the High Court restraining the claimant from making the allegations public. The High Court privacy proceedings were then stayed pending the outcome of the tribunal case. The claims were eventually dismissed in their entirety, the tribunal finding them wholly without merit. The tribunal ordered that the RRO remain in force in respect of four individuals. However, it refused to make the RRO permanent in respect of the CEO and others and the corporate respondents. It referred to the 'substantial public interest' in the issues raised by the case, and applying the balancing test found that the interests of open justice outweighed the right to respect for private life under Article 8 of the ECHR. The CEO appealed and the EAT allowed the appeal. The EAT found that the tribunal had erred in considering that there was a public interest in the claimants' identities being revealed, and in giving weight to the right of other employees to know what was going on. The EAT held that the tribunal erred in concluding that the 'public interest' outweighed the CEO's right to privacy.

In BBC *v* Roden (UKEAT/0385/14), the EAT overturned an RRO that had been made at the conclusion of employment tribunal proceedings. The claimant had been dismissed after his employer had been informed that serious allegations of a sexual nature had been made against him in relation to young men with whom he had been in contact in the course of his work. He brought a claim for unfair dismissal. The employment tribunal made an order granting anonymity to the claimant throughout the hearing, because the allegations of serious sexual assaults would be raised at the hearing but, as they were not in issue, the tribunal would not have an opportunity to make a specific finding that the allegations were not proved, which would affect the claimant's reputation. In finding against the claimant on his substantive claim, the tribunal found that he had misled his employer about an earlier incident and that this was a fundamental breach of his employment contract. The BBC applied to set aside the earlier RRO. The employment tribunal refused this application. The central plank of the Employment Judge's reasoning was that the public would conclude that the claimant was guilty of the allegations. The BBC appealed to the EAT. It submitted that the Employment Judge had failed to properly balance the claimant's Article 8 rights against the principles of open justice and freedom of expression, and that as a result the anonymity order constituted a disproportionate and unlawful interference with those competing rights. It further contended that the Judge had failed to take account of relevant considerations and took account of irrelevant ones. The EAT agreed, holding that the anonymity order constituted a disproportionate and unlawful interference with the principle of open justice and the strong public interest in full publication. The decision in *EF v AB* (above) is an example of the same principles being applied to produce the opposite result, as the Article 8 rights of the parties in that case, and the lack of any discernible public interest, were found to outweigh the rights of freedom of expression under Article 10 and open justice under Article 6. The judgment in *Roden* provides a helpful summary of the principles relevant to anonymity applications, and is a useful reference point for consideration of the issues involved in these sorts of cases. See too *Fallows v News Group Newspapers* (UKEAT/0075/16) (a case relating to Elton John's hairdresser) where the employment tribunal, upheld by the EAT, and applying the balancing exercise, declined to make an order.

There is a developing area of law to the effect that documents referred to in open court, including but not limited to witness statements and skeleton arguments, should be made available to the media on request (see *R (on the application of Guardian News and Media Ltd) v City of Westminster Magistrates' Court* [2012] EWCA Civ 420).

6.4.8   Hearings – general

In *Rackham v NHS Professionals Ltd* (UKEAT/0110/15), the EAT looked at the tribunal's obligation to make reasonable adjustments to ensure that a claimant (with Asperger's syndrome and anxiety) was able to access and fully participate in the proceedings. The EAT said that when considering whether proposed adjustments were fair and reasonable, this had to be judged by reference to both parties, proportionality and making sure the hearing proceeded. The autonomy of the disabled person (including parties, witnesses and lawyers) is of great importance, and those who have disabilities are entitled to have their voice listened to. This will probably mean in practice that any reasonable adjustments need to be worked out (and agreed if possible) in advance of the commencement of the substantive hearing.

There are two different types of hearing that may be held: preliminary and final. The text below deals with preliminary hearings. The final hearing is examined at **6.4.9**.

The Court of Appeal held in *Ezsias v North Glamorgan NHS Trust* [2007] EWCA Civ 330 that where there are facts in dispute, it would be exceptional for a case to be struck out without hearing the evidence at a full merits hearing. Only if the facts alleged by the claimant disclose no arguable case should it be struck out.

6.4.8.1   Preliminary hearings (Rules 53–56)

Preliminary hearings are interim hearings, which should be held in private (unless they are determining any preliminary issue or whether to strike out a claim). Rule 53 allows the Employment Judge, at a preliminary hearing, amongst other things, to:

(a)   conduct a preliminary consideration of the claim and make a case management order;

(b)   determine preliminary issues (eg an issue as to whether the claim was brought in time, or whether the claimant has sufficient continuity of service or whether the employee was dismissed). The Employment Judge can give judgment at the hearing on preliminary matters, which may result in the proceedings being struck out so that a final hearing is no longer required (see Rule 37 below);

(c)   consider whether to strike out a claim (see **6.4.8.2** below);

(d)   order payment of a deposit under Rule 39 (see **6.4.8.4** below);

(e)   explore the possibility of settlement;

(f)   conduct a judicial assessment of the case (if the parties agree) (from 3 October 2016).

6.4.8.2   Striking out

Rule 37 states that a claim or response may be struck out at any stage of the proceedings if:

(a)   the claim or response is scandalous, vexatious or has no reasonable prospects of success;

(b)   the manner in which proceedings have been conducted by the claimant or respondent is scandalous, unreasonable or vexatious;

(c)   the claimant or respondent has failed to comply with any tribunal orders;

(d)   the claim has not actively been pursued;

(e)   it is not possible to have a fair hearing of the claim.

In *Blockbuster Entertainment Ltd v James* [2006] IRLR 630, CA, it was held that a power to strike out was a 'draconic power not to be too readily exercised'. See too *Tayside Public Transport Co Ltd v Reilly* [2012] IRLR 755 (Court of Session), *Rodrigues v Co-Op Group Ltd* (UKEAT/0022/12) and *Harris v Academies Enterprise Trust* [2015] IRLR 208.

The power to strike out a claim on the ground that it has no reasonable prospect of success should only be exercised in rare circumstances (*Tayside Public Transport Co Ltd v Reilly*). It should not be struck out where the central facts are in dispute (see *North Glamorgan NHS Trust v Ezsias* [2007] EWCA Civ 330). Discrimination cases should, say the courts, rarely be struck out. In *Anyanwu v South Bank Students' Union* [2001] IRLR 305, HL, Lord Steyn stated:

> For my part such vagaries in discrimination jurisprudence underline the importance of not striking out such claims as an abuse of the process except in the most obvious and plainest cases. Discrimination cases are generally fact-sensitive, and their proper determination is always vital in our pluralistic society. In this field perhaps more than any other the bias in favour of a claim being examined on the merits or demerits of its particular facts is a matter of high public interest.

The EAT stated in *Bolch v Chipman* [2004] IRLR 140 that:

(1)   There must be a conclusion by the Tribunal not simply that a party has behaved unreasonably but that the proceedings have been conducted by or on his behalf unreasonably.

(2)   Assuming there be a finding that the proceedings have been conducted scandalously, unreasonably or vexatiously, that is not the final question so far as leading on to an order that the Notice of Appearance must be struck out.

(3)   Once there has been a conclusion, if there has been, that the proceedings have been conducted in breach of Rule 15(2)(d), and that a fair trial is not possible, there still remains the question as to what remedy the tribunal considers appropriate, which is proportionate to its conclusion. It is also possible, of course, that there can be a remedy, even in the absence of a conclusion that a fair trial is no longer possible, which amounts to some kind of punishment, but which, if it does not drive the defendant from the judgment seat (in the words of Millett J) may still be an appropriate penalty to impose, provided that it does not lead to a debarring from the case in its entirety, but some lesser penalty.

See *Chidzoy v BBC* (UKEAT/0097/17) for a recent case on striking out a claim on the unreasonable conduct ground.

In *Arriva London North Ltd v Maseya* (UKEAT/0096/16), Simler J stated there is nothing automatic about a decision to strike out. Rather, a tribunal is required to exercise a judicial discretion by reference to the appropriate principles.

6.4.8.3   Unless orders

Rule 38 gives a tribunal powers to make an unless order, whereby if an order is not complied with by a specified date, the claim or response will automatically be dismissed. Rule 38(2) allows such orders to be set aside if it is in the interests of justice to do so.

In *Enamejewa v British Gas Trading Ltd* (UKEAT/0347/14), the EAT looked at the approach to be taken to an application to revoke an unless order made under Rule 38(2). The claimant was dismissed for gross misconduct in January 2013. He claimed that he had been wrongfully and unfairly dismissed, and that he had also been the subject of discrimination on the ground of race. The employers disputed all of his claims. A case management discussion took place on 4 June 2013, and the case was listed for a hearing in December 2013. Following an argument between the parties about what was to be included in the agreed bundle, the employers' solicitor applied for an unless order requiring the claimant to provide his witness statement by 27 November. On 21 November, the claimant was told to disclose his witness statement 'forthwith'; if he did not, an 'unless order' would be made on 22 November. On 22 November, the employers' solicitors said that the claimant had not provided the witness statement. On 27 November, an unless order was made to the effect that both sides were to exchange witness statements by 12 noon on 29 November; and unless that happened, 'the claim or response as appropriate shall stand dismissed without further order'. On 29 November, at 11.33 am, the employers' solicitors emailed their witness statements to the claimant. The claimant emailed his witness statement to the employers' solicitors at 12.08, eight minutes after the deadline. At 12.19, the employers' solicitors emailed the tribunal, pointing out that the claimant had not complied with the unless order and inviting the tribunal to treat the claim as struck out without further order. On 3 December, the employment tribunal stated that the claimant's complaints had been dismissed and cancelled the hearing. The claimant's application for a review was rejected. The claimant appealed. The EAT said that while the reasons for making an unless order in the first place are 'highly relevant factors', they are not only factors to consider when reviewing an unless order under Rule 38(2). Those factors can include events that have occurred subsequent to the making of the order, such as, for example, a sudden incapacity or power failure. As Underhill J (the EAT President) observed in *Thind v Salvesen Logistics Ltd* (UKEAT/0487/09):

> The tribunal must decide whether it is right, in the interests of justice and the overriding objective, to grant relief to the party in default notwithstanding the breach of the unless order. That involves a broad assessment of what is in the interests of justice, and the factors which may be material to that assessment will vary considerably according to the circumstances of the case and cannot be neatly categorised. They will generally include, but may not be limited to, the reason for the default, and in particular whether it is deliberate; the seriousness of the default; the prejudice to the other party; and whether a fair trial remains possible. The fact that an unless order has been made, which of course puts the party in question squarely on notice of the importance of complying with the order and the consequences if he does not do so, will always be an important consideration. Unless orders are an important part of the tribunal's procedural armoury (albeit one not to be used lightly), and they must be taken very seriously; their effectiveness will be undermined if tribunals are too ready to set them aside. But that is nevertheless no more than one consideration. No one factor is necessarily determinative of the course which the tribunal should take. Each case will depend on its own facts.

The EAT remitted the case to the same Employment Judge, to reconsider in the light of the approach to the law set out by it.

6.4.8.4   Requirement to pay a deposit (Rule 39)

Rule 39 allows for a party to be ordered to pay a deposit of up to £1,000 in order to continue to take part in proceedings, where the Employment Judge considers any argument or allegation in a claim or response has 'little reasonable prospect of success'. Before so ordering, the Employment Judge must make reasonable enquiries as to the party's ability to pay (see, for example, *Hemdan v Ishmail* (UKEAT/0021/16)). The Employment Judge must set out his grounds for making such an order and give a copy of the document recording his reasons to the parties, and explain to the party against whom the order is made the potential consequences of the order. If the party does not pay the deposit by the date specified on the order, the claim or response will be struck out. A deposit order cannot be made merely because the claimant's case is unclear (*Tree v South East Coastal Services Ambulance NHS Trust* (UKEAT/0043/17)).

6.4.8.5   Judicial assessment

Judicial assessment will generally be offered at the first case management hearing after the issues have been clarified and case management orders made. Paragraph 21 of the Presidential Guidance states:

> If the parties consent, the Employment Judge may then give an assessment of the liability and/or remedy aspects of the case. It will be made clear that the assessment is provisional and that the Employment Tribunal hearing the case may come to a different view. In conducting the assessment the Employment Judge must make it clear that they are assessing the case on the state of the allegations and not evaluating the evidence, which has not been heard or seen, and assessing provisionally the risks as to liability and, typically, brackets of likely compensation on remedy. The Employment Judge will encourage parties to approach the process with an open mind and to be prepared to enter into the assessment pragmatically and to be receptive and listen to the Employment Judge's views.

6.4.8.6   Withdrawal (Rules 51 and 52)

Rule 51 permits a claimant to withdraw all or part of a claim at any time, subject to costs.

Rule 52 provides that where a claim has been withdrawn, a tribunal shall issue a judgment dismissing it (which means that the claimant cannot bring a further claim against the employer raising the same complaint) unless the claimant indicates a wish to reserve a right to bring a further claim, or the tribunal believes it is not in the interests of justice to issue a judgment. Claimants need to be careful about the impact of a dismissal, which will prevent them from bringing a claim in the civil courts. The EAT reiterated the obligation on the tribunal to ensure that the withdrawal is clear and unambiguous before dismissing a claim in *Campbell v OCS Group UK Ltd* (UKEAT/0188/16).

6.4.8.7   Role of Acas

A copy of the claim form and response will normally be sent to Acas by the tribunal, because Acas has a statutory duty to endeavour to promote settlement under most employment protection legislation (ETA 1996, s 18, as amended). Section 18C, which came into force on 6 April 2014, provides that Acas is under a duty to conciliate where a claim has been presented to an employment tribunal, provided it is requested to do so by the parties or it considers there is a reasonable prospect of achieving a settlement.

6.4.8.8   Preparation for the full hearing

The date, time and place of the hearing will be fixed, and a notice of hearing sent to the parties. Before the date has been fixed, the parties will be asked for dates to avoid. The parties should then ensure that their witnesses will be available.

Before the hearing the parties should prepare a bundle of documents for use at the hearing. The tribunal will often direct who is responsible for preparing the bundle. It should include all correspondence and other documents on which the parties intend to rely, arranged in correct sequence and numbered consecutively. It is desirable, wherever possible, that there should be an agreed bundle. At least six bundles should be available at the hearing, one for each member of the tribunal, one for each side and one for use by the witnesses. Some tribunals ask for the bundle to be lodged in advance of the hearing, others prefer it to be brought to the tribunal on the day of the hearing.

6.4.8.9   Postponement

A new Rule 30 provides that applications to postpone the hearing must be made as soon as possible after the need arises, and that applications made less than seven days before the hearing is due to begin can only be granted where the parties consent, and it is appropriate to allow the parties to settle their dispute by agreement or otherwise in accordance with the overriding objective, or the application was necessitated by fault of the other party or there are exceptional reasons. Costs may follow (see **6.4.11**).

6.4.9   The final hearing (Rules 57–59)

Subject to Rules 50 and 94, the final hearing shall be in public. It can determine liability and/or remedy and/or costs.

The Employment Tribunals Act 1996 (Tribunal Composition) Order 2012 (SI 2012/988) allows an Employment Judge to hear unfair dismissal cases sitting alone. Employment Judges were already able to sit alone in certain circumstances, for example in cases brought under Pt II of the ERA 1996 (protection of wages), reg 30 of the Working Time Regulations (holiday pay entitlement) or where the parties consented to this (ETA 1996, s 4(3)). Section 4(5) of the ETA 1996 still provides that, in certain circumstances, an Employment Judge may order a hearing by a full panel, including where there is a likelihood of a dispute arising on the facts. Section 4(5) also provides that the views of any of the parties should be taken into account.

The EAT expressed some reservations about judges sitting alone, in *McCafferty v Royal Mail Group* (UKEATS/0002/12). Mr McCafferty was a postman with 19 years' service, who had been dismissed for gross misconduct by reason of alleged dishonesty. The lay members of the tribunal found the dismissal fair. The Employment Judge, in the minority, considered that the dismissal was unfair. On appeal, the decision of the majority that the dismissal was fair was upheld. Lady Smith pointed out that the lay members of the employment tribunal reached their conclusion drawing on their 'valuable common sense'. Lady Smith remarked that this underlines the need to give careful consideration to any views expressed by parties as to whether proceedings should be heard by an Employment Judge and members. The EAT decided in *Sterling Developments v Pagano* (UKEAT/0511/06) that the Employment Judge need not consider s 4(5) before hearing a case alone where neither party made representations.

There is also provision in the ETA 1996 (as amended by s 4 of the Employment Rights (Dispute Resolution) Act 1998) for hearings to be heard by a tribunal judge and one member where the parties consent.

6.4.9.1   Representation

The parties may appear in person, or be represented by a friend, union representative or professional adviser. In England and Wales, public funding is not available for representation at the hearing, although a solicitor may advise prior to the hearing under the Legal Help scheme (subject to the usual restrictions). Note that under the Compensation Act 2006, non-lawyers are prohibited from representing litigants and charging them a fee, unless they are formally registered with and regulated by the Regulated Claims Management Service. Breach of the registration requirements is punishable by up to two years in prison. Free representation does not need to be regulated. A party is not obliged to attend a hearing and a tribunal may hear a case in a party's absence without further inquiry (see *Cooke v Glenrose Fish Co Ltd* [2004] IRLR 866).

6.4.9.2   Opening the case

The case will usually be opened by the side with the burden of proof for the first point in issue: for example, if it is alleged that the applicant has been constructively dismissed, the applicant will open. If there is no dispute as to dismissal, the respondent will open. Some tribunals will hear an opening speech, others prefer to hear witnesses immediately. There is generally no formal right to make an opening speech. An opening speech should briefly outline the facts (indicating areas of dispute), introduce the evidence and summarise the legal principles involved. In practice, opening speeches are very rare.

6.4.9.3 Presentation of evidence

Witnesses may give evidence under oath or by affirming. Pursuant to Rule 41, the rules of evidence are not strictly applicable. Rule 41 provides, inter alia:

> The tribunal shall seek to avoid undue formality and may itself question the parties or any witness so far as appropriate in order to clarify the issues or elicit the evidence. The tribunal is not bound by any rule of law relating to the admissibility of evidence in proceedings before the courts.

Therefore, for example, the tribunal can hear hearsay evidence. It is a matter for the tribunal to decide the weight to attach to such evidence. Often the witness will have signed a written statement, and this may be used as evidence-in-chief. The tribunal can, and very often will, order the exchange of statements before the hearing (see **6.4.6.5** above). Since April 2012, the general rule is that witnesses should not read out statements (see also **6.4.6.5** above). The tribunal may or may not allow supplementary questions by the witness's representative. This is then followed in the usual way by cross-examination and re-examination. The tribunal may intervene and ask questions of a witness at any time. This frequently happens.

Where a tribunal grants a witness order to a party, it should normally copy that to the other side (see *Jones v Secretary of State for Business, Innovation and Skills* (UKEAT/0238/16); Rules 32 and 60).

The overarching rule that governs the admissibility of evidence, including the making of witness attendance orders (see *Remploy Ltd v Lowen-Bulger* (UKEAT/0027/18)), is relevance. For further information, see **Civil Litigation**.

Increasingly, parties seek to rely on social media content as evidence in employment disputes: it may be used to undermine the evidence of a witness or a party (see, eg, *Gill v SAS Ground Services Ltd* (ET/2705021/09), *Young v Argos Ltd* (ET/1200382/11), *Teggert v TeleTech UK Ltd* (NIET/00704/11) and *Dixon v GB Eye Ltd* (ET/2203642/10)). Evidence of disparaging or offensive remarks about an employer, its products or a colleague may be produced (see, eg, *Whitham v Club 24 Ltd t/a Ventura* (ET/1810462/10), *Crisp v Apple Retail UK Ltd* (ET/1500258/11), *Taylor v Somerfield Stores Ltd* (ETS/107487/07) and *Smith v Trafford Housing Trust* [2012] EWHC 3221 (Ch)). Such content may not be in standard documentary form – it may be electronically stored, it may comprise screen shots, it may be available because a user has not paid much attention to his privacy settings, so that his personal information is accessible – but none the less it should still be included in any disclosure if it is material to the case.

Another evidential matter that is becoming increasingly common in tribunal hearings centres around the admissibility of covert recordings. Often employees record exchanges or conversations or even disciplinary hearings on mobile devices. Rule 41 gives tribunals very broad powers to 'regulate their own procedure', stating:

> The Tribunal may regulate its own procedure and shall conduct the hearing in the manner it considers fair, having regard to the principles contained in the overriding objective. The following rules do not restrict that general power. The Tribunal shall seek to avoid undue formality and may itself question the parties or any witnesses so far as appropriate in order to clarify the issues or elicit the evidence. The Tribunal is not bound by any rule of law relating to the admissibility of evidence in proceedings before the courts.

This Rule gives tribunals a very wide discretion in relation to the admissibility and exclusion of evidence. The EAT held in *HSBC Asia Holdings BV v Gillespie* [2011] IRLR 209 that, despite the absence of any express power, tribunals have the same powers as a civil court (see CPR 1998, r 32.1) with regard to the exclusion of evidence.

Tribunals will normally look first at whether any covert evidence that is sought to be admitted is relevant or material to any of the issues in the case. If it is, the tribunal will then move on to consider whether to exercise its discretion to admit or exclude that evidence. Even if evidence is relevant, tribunals have a discretion to exclude it.

One consideration that they will balance when deciding whether to exercise their discretion to admit such evidence is the public policy in preserving the integrity and confidentiality of employers' private deliberations. This has led, in some instances, to a distinction being drawn between recordings of hearings or discussions in 'public', ie when the employee is present, and deliberations that occur in 'private'. In *Chairman & Governors of Amwell View School v Dogherty* [2007] IRLR 198, the EAT held that 'no ground rule could be more essential to ensuring a full and frank exchange of views between members of the adjudicating body ... than the understanding that their deliberations would be conducted in private and remain private'.

Tribunals also have to bear in mind Rule 2 (see **6.4** above) which sets out that the 'overriding objective' is to 'enable Employment Tribunals to deal with cases fairly and justly'. The public interest in preserving private discussions will be balanced, for example, against the benefit of the tribunal having before it all the relevant evidence, particularly if there is a factual dispute between the parties that the evidence could help resolve. In *Amwell*, the EAT stated that:

> The balance between the conflicting public interests might well have fallen differently if the claim had been framed in terms of unlawful discrimination, where the decision was taken by a panel which gave no reasons for its decision, and where inadvertent recording of private deliberations (or the clear account of one of the panel members participating in those deliberations) had produced the only evidence – and incontrovertible evidence – of such discrimination.

On the other hand, Rule 2(b) provides that cases should be dealt with in ways that are proportionate to the complexity and importance of the issues. In *Vaughan v London Borough of Lewisham & Others* (UKEAT/0533/12), an employment tribunal refused to allow the claimant to produce 39 hours' worth of covert recordings of meetings between her, her colleagues and managers over the course of a year. The EAT, upholding the tribunal's decision, referred to the importance of proportionality and the need for a focused and selective application. The EAT said that it might have been different if the claimant 'produc[ed] the transcripts and the tapes of the material on which she wishe[d] to rely, and accompan[ied] them with a clear explanation of why they are said to be relevant'.

In *Punjab National Bank (International) Ltd & Others v Gosain* (UKEAT/0003/14), the claimant made allegations of sex discrimination, sexual harassment and constructive dismissal. She had made secret recordings of both the public and private parts of her grievance and disciplinary hearings. She alleged that the recordings contained evidence that inappropriate comments and considerations had occurred during the private parts of the employer's discussions. The evidence was admitted by the employment tribunal. On appeal, the EAT upheld that decision.

In *Wiggan v Wooler & Co Ltd* (UKEAT/0285/07), the EAT said that it will be rare for a case to be dismissed at half-time on the ground that it has no reasonable prospect of success (see the Court of Appeal decision in *Logan v Commissioner of Customs and Excise* [2004] IRLR 63).

6.4.9.4 Closing the case

Closing speeches may be made by the parties; whoever opened the case will make the final closing speech. The purpose of a closing speech is to review the evidence and to remind the tribunal of the relevant law.

6.4.9.5 The decision

The tribunal will then give its decision, with reasons (Rules 60–62). Rule 1 sets out the definitions of 'order', 'decision' and 'judgment'. A judgment is a decision which finally determines any part of a claim, including jurisdictional issues. The tribunal may give an oral decision immediately with oral reasons, or may follow an oral decision with written reasons. If the tribunal gives oral reasons for its decision, the parties may apply for written reasons. In complex cases, a decision may be reserved to a later date. The decision is formally recorded in a central register held at the Central Office of the Employment Tribunals in Bury St Edmunds (Rule 67). This register is open to the public. Sometimes a tribunal will adjourn at this stage to allow the parties to reach an agreement on quantum. Failing this, evidence will be heard relating to losses, etc (if not already dealt with in examination-in-chief during the hearing). Practice varies as to when the tribunal will hear evidence relating to quantum at the same time as liability.

Where there has been a hearing, an employment tribunal decision which is a judgment must (Rule 62(5)):

(a) identify the issues which the tribunal has determined;

(b) state the findings of fact relevant to the issues which have been determined;

(c) concisely identify the relevant law;

(e) state how that law has been applied to the findings of fact in order to decide the issues; and

(f) where the judgment includes a financial award, include a table or other means of showing how the amount or sum has been calculated.

A failure to do this will amount to an error of law (see *Balfour Beatty Power Networks Ltd v Wilcox* [2007] IRLR 63). In *Meek v City of Birmingham District Council* [1987] IRLR 250, Bingham LJ (see in particular paras 8 to 12) provided useful guidance on the minimum requirements as to what should be contained in an employment tribunal judgment (a case decided under the old rules). Paragraph 8 stated as follows:

> It has on a number of occasions been made plain that the decision of an Industrial Tribunal is not required to be an elaborate formalistic product of refined legal draftsmanship, but it must contain an outline of the story which has given rise to the complaint and a summary of the Tribunal's basic factual conclusions and a statement of the reasons which have led them to reach the conclusion which they do on those basic facts. The parties are entitled to be told why they have won or lost. There should be sufficient account of the facts and of the reasoning to enable the EAT or, on further appeal, this court to see whether any question of law arises; and it is highly desirable that the decision of an Industrial Tribunal should give guidance both to employers and trade unions as to practices which should or should not be adopted.

In other words, tribunals must provide a sufficient outline of the complaint along with a summary of its conclusions and its reasons for reaching those conclusions, so that the parties have enough detail to be able to work out why the decision was made. In *Greenwood v NWF Retail* (UKEAT/0409/09) the EAT re-examined whether a tribunal's written reasons were sufficient. The EAT made it clear that an employment tribunal is required, amongst other things, to decide relevant facts and how those facts should be applied to the law, and that a failure to do so will amount to an error of law. The EAT commented that the 'constituent parts [of a judgment] will need to be more than a formal statement paying lip service to the subparagraphs of the rule'. See also, eg, *Mak v Wayward Gallery Ltd* (UKEAT/0589/10) and *Cossington v C2C Rail Ltd* (UKEAT/0053/13).

6.4.10 Awards

The sum payable is due within 14 days of the judgment. Interest is payable (at 8%) from the day after the decision day, unless paid within 14 days. Unpaid awards must be enforced through the courts (see also **6.4.15**).

6.4.11 Costs

Although costs are not often awarded against the losing party in tribunal cases, there are limited powers to make costs orders (ETA 1996, s 13 and Rules 74–84 of the Tribunal Rules). Costs orders can be made where a party is legally represented or represented by a lay representative. A legal representative is defined as a person who has a general qualification within the meaning of s 71 of the Courts and Legal Services Act 1990 (Rule 74(2)). Tribunals also have a power to make preparation time orders where a party is not legally represented (see **6.4.11.3**).

The Tribunals Service Quarterly Report for 2016/2017 published by the Ministry of Justice shows that 297 awards were made in favour of claimants and 182 in favour of respondents. The median award was £925, the largest award £58,022 and the average award £3,747.

Three sorts of costs orders may be made:

(a)   costs orders (**6.4.11.1** and **6.4.11.2**);

(b)   preparation time orders (**6.4.11.3**); and

(c)   wasted costs orders (**6.4.11.4**).

6.4.11.1   Costs orders

Employment tribunals are established under, and derive their powers from, regulations made under statute (see **Chapter 1**). It has been a consistent feature of those regulations that the power to make an order containing an award of costs against a party to proceedings before an employment tribunal has been subject to a restriction relating to conduct. Formerly, the power could only be exercised if, in the opinion of the tribunal, the party had acted frivolously or vexatiously in bringing or conducting the proceedings. The threshold was subsequently lowered by the addition of the words 'or otherwise unreasonably', and it was later further reduced by the addition of conduct that was abusive or disruptive. The Employment Tribunals (Constitution and Rules of Procedure) Regulations 2001 (SI 2001/1171) continued the trend towards a reduction of the threshold by including:

(a)   cases where the bringing or conducting of the proceedings by a party had been misconceived; and

(b)   cases where it was the conduct of the proceedings by the party's *representative* that had been vexatious, abusive, disruptive or otherwise unreasonable.

The rules on costs were further developed by the 2004 Tribunal Rules (SI 2004/1861). Rule 41(2) stated that a 'tribunal or Employment Judge may have regard to the paying party's ability to pay when considering whether it or he shall make a costs order or how much that order should be'. Rule 2(1) also provided that the term 'misconceived' (see (a) above – which appeared in Rule 40(3)), 'includes having no reasonable prospect of success'. The 2013 Rules (SI 2013/1237) made yet further changes by removing the second part of Rule 40(3) ('or the bringing or conducting of the proceedings by the paying party has been misconceived') and replacing it with the second limb of Rule 76(1), namely, that costs might be awarded where a 'claim or response had no reasonable prospect of success'. Underhill J, in his Review of Employment Tribunal Rules in June 2012, said that he saw 'no case for changing the substantive criteria for the award of costs'. As such, it is unlikely that this latter change was intended to make a substantive difference to the threshold test.

The general powers to make costs orders are now set out in Rule 76. Costs orders (including fees) may be made where a party is legally represented or represented by a lay representative. The circumstances in which a tribunal *must* make a costs order are set out in Rule 76(3): a tribunal *must* make a costs order against a respondent in an unfair dismissal case where reinstatement or re-engagement is in issue and a hearing has to be postponed because of the respondent's failure to adduce evidence about the availability of the suitable employment. There is no definition of what constitutes 'costs' in Rule 76. The EAT in *Sunuva Ltd v Martin* (UKEAT/0174/17) said that costs orders can be awarded in respect of costs incurred before a claimant receives the ET3 Response.

Under Rule 76(1) a tribunal *may* make a costs order in a wide variety of circumstances, including, as mentioned above, where it considers that a party (or that party's representative) has acted vexatiously, abusively, disruptively or otherwise unreasonably in bringing or conducting the proceedings or any claim or response had no reasonable prospect of success, or a hearing was postponed on the application of a party less than seven days before the hearing was due to begin.

If a tribunal concludes that the commencement or pursuit of the claim was vexatious, abusive, disruptive or otherwise unreasonable, or had no reasonable prospect of success (see further below), then the tribunal must proceed to consider whether to make a costs order. However, it is not *obliged* to make a costs order – that process is discretionary. At this stage a tribunal may, but is not obliged to, take into account, both in terms of whether to make an order at all and, if so, the amount, the paying party's means.

In *AQ Ltd v Holden* (UKEAT/0021/12), the EAT said, at para 41:

> The threshold tests in Rule 40(3) are the same whether a litigant is or is not professionally represented. The application of those tests should, however, take into account whether a litigant is professionally represented. A tribunal cannot and should not judge a litigant in person by the standards of a professional representative. Lay people are entitled to represent themselves in tribunals; and, since legal aid is not available and they will not usually recover costs if they are successful, it is inevitable that many lay people will represent themselves. Justice requires that tribunals do not apply professional standards to lay people, who may be involved in legal proceedings for the only time in their life. As Mr Davies submitted, lay people are likely to lack the objectivity and knowledge of law and practice brought by a professional legal adviser. Tribunals must bear this in mind when assessing the threshold tests in Rule 40(3). Further, even if the threshold tests for an order for costs are met, the tribunal has discretion whether to make an order. This discretion will be exercised having regard to all the circumstances. It is not irrelevant that a lay person may have brought proceedings with little or no access to specialist help and advice.

But Judge Richardson continued:

> This is not to say that lay people are immune from orders for costs: far from it, as the cases make clear. Some litigants in person are found to have behaved vexatiously or unreasonably even when proper allowance is made for their inexperience and lack of objectivity.

Until 2004, there was no express provision about tribunals taking into account the paying party's means. Cases decided under the Tribunal Rules prior to 2004 need to be treated with some caution, as there was at that time no express requirement, nor provision of any machinery, for an inquiry into a party's means.

The current power is now set out in Rule 84 of the 2013 Rules, but it is still entirely a matter for the tribunal's discretion whether to take ability to pay into account (see *Vaughan v Lewisham LBC* [2013] IRLR 713). In *Jilley v Birmingham and Solihull Mental Health NHS Trust* (UKEAT/0584/06), the EAT considered the exercise by a tribunal of its discretion, under what was then Rule 40(3) of the 2004 Rules, whether to take into account the paying party's ability to pay. It held that if a tribunal decides not to do so, it should say why:

> If it decides to take into account ability to pay, it should set out its findings about ability to pay, say what impact this has had on its decision whether to award costs or on the amount of costs, and explain why. Lengthy reasons are not required. A succinct statement of how the Tribunal has dealt with the matter and why it has done so is generally essential. The Tribunal has no absolute duty to do so. ... In many cases it will be desirable to take means into account before making an order; ability to pay may affect the exercise of an overall discretion, and this course will encourage finality and may avoid lengthy enforcement proceedings. But there may be cases where for good reason ability to pay should not be taken into account: for example, if the paying party has not attended or has given unsatisfactory evidence about means. A question for the Tribunal in this case will be whether to take into account means given that in any event it has no power to do so in respect of the first proceedings. It may or may not be desirable to do so; it will depend on the submissions which are made to the Tribunal. If the Tribunal decides not to take means into account, it should express that conclusion, and say why. If the Tribunal decides to take means into account, it will then need to set out its findings about ability to pay, decide whether to make a costs order at all in the light of the paying party's means, and if it does what the order should be; and it give succinct reasons for its conclusions.

In the case of *Arrowsmith v Nottingham Trent University* [2011] EWCA Civ 797, it was held that a costs order need not be confined to sums the party could pay, as it might well be that the party's circumstances would improve in the future. In *Chadburn v Doncaster & Bassetlaw Hospital*

NHS Foundation Trust (UKEAT/0259/14), the EAT reviewed the legal framework and principles that should be considered when assessing the means of the paying party. It held that a costs award can still be made against a party who cannot afford to pay, if it is reasonable to believe that that party's financial situation might improve in the future: as the tribunal did not have to take the paying party's financial position into account at all when making a costs order, it must be able to take account of other matters.

The exercise of the tribunal's discretion is not dependent upon the existence of any causal nexus between the conduct relied upon and the costs incurred (Macpherson v BNP Paribas (London Branch) [2004] IRLR 558.). In Barnsley Metropolitan BC v Yerrakalva [2011] EWCA Civ 1255, the Court of Appeal had to look at the relationship between causation and the costs awarded, where a 100% costs order had been made in the respondent employer's favour. In Yerrakalva, the claimant's conduct in the proceedings was held to be unreasonable, which gave the employment tribunal jurisdiction to order costs. However, the Court of Appeal said, it did not follow that the claimant should pay all the Council's costs of the entire proceedings. The employment tribunal had rejected some of the Council's criticisms of the claimant. It had also criticised the Council for making more of a meal than was necessary to respond to the claimant's case. Those factors, the Court of Appeal said, are relevant to how the cost's discretion should be exercised, and operated against a 100% order in the Council's favour. Mummery LJ said:

> The vital point in exercising the discretion to order costs is to look at the whole picture of what happened in the case and to ask whether there has been unreasonable conduct by the claimant in bringing and conducting the case and, in doing so, to identify the conduct, what was unreasonable about it and what effects it had.

In Casqueiro v Barclays Bank plc (UKEAT/0085/12) (a case on wasted costs, looking at which costs or what part of the costs had been caused by the unreasonable conduct of the claimant), Slade J (at [22]–[23]) suggested that if a party wished to rely on limited evidence of his means, that evidence should be submitted with some level of formality: 'He should make a statement with supporting evidence for such an argument, such statement and documentation should be disclosed to the Respondent three weeks before any hearing and he should tender himself for cross-examination.' In Shields Automotive Ltd v Grieg (UKEATS/0024/10), the EAT said that where a tribunal has decided to have regard to a party's means, it is required to look at his whole means, and that included his capital resources.

In summary, when considering a costs application, a tribunal must ascertain whether a party has acted vexatiously, abusively, disruptively or otherwise unreasonably either in bringing the proceedings (or part), or in the way the proceedings (or part) have been conducted; or whether the claim had no reasonable prospect of success. If any one or more of these threshold triggers is met then the tribunal must go on to consider whether to make a costs order, but is not obliged to make one. When exercising its discretion as to whether to make a costs order, the tribunal may, but is not obliged to, have regard to the paying party's ability to pay. Where the tribunal has decided to make a costs order, again it may, but is not obliged to, have regard to the paying party's ability to pay in determining the amount of the award.

As far as what might amount to unreasonable conduct, in Topic v Hollyland Pitta Bakery (UKEAT/523/11), HHJ Burke QC said (at [27]) that lies do not automatically lead to a finding of unreasonableness, but no lies do not mean there cannot be unreasonableness; it is necessary to '[l]ook at the whole picture bearing in mind that costs are rarely awarded in the [employment tribunal]'. In Kapoor v Governing Body of Barnhill Community High School (UKEAT/0352/13), the EAT held that an employment tribunal was wrong to find that a claimant had conducted her case unreasonably, such as to warrant a costs award against her, on the simple basis that she had given false evidence: the case had to be considered as a whole, including, for example, the fact that the school's efforts to have the claim struck out had not always found favour. Beynon v Scadden [1999] IRLR 700 is authority for the proposition that a litigant should be expected to take stock of matters once all evidence is disclosed and the weaknesses of a complaint are identified. To carry on after a fundamental weakness is revealed, may amount to unreasonableness. Likewise, a refusal of an offer to settle might form the basis of unreasonableness.

In *Nicolson v Highlandwear Ltd* [2010] IRLR 859, the EAT allowed an appeal against a tribunal's refusal to award costs against an employee, where the tribunal found it was open to an employee to pursue an unfair dismissal claim purely in order to obtain a 'simple finding' of unfair dismissal 'without the objective of obtaining money'. The EAT pointed out that the ET1 form specified only three remedies and, unlike a discrimination claim, there was no provision for a declaration as a remedy. Commentators have pointed out that an employee may bring a claim to clear his name. It is also, arguably, inconsistent with *Telephone Information Services Ltd v Wilkinson* [1991] IRLR 148, where the EAT held that an employer's offer to pay the maximum unfair dismissal compensation did not render it frivolous or vexatious for the employee to continue the claim when unfairness was not admitted.

The Court of Appeal offered some advice to tribunals when deciding whether to make costs orders in late withdrawal cases, in *McPherson v BNP Paribas* [2004] IRLR 558 (decided under the 2004 Rules but still of assistance). Mr McPherson had withdrawn his tribunal claim about two weeks before the hearing, citing ill-health. There were doubts about the extent of his ill-health. He had also failed to comply with a number of tribunal orders. The tribunal and the EAT held that the late withdrawal, when taken against the background of his non-compliance with tribunal orders, amounted to unreasonable conduct. He was ordered to pay all of BNP Paribas's costs. The Court of Appeal agreed that Mr McPherson had acted unreasonably, but allowed his appeal to the extent that it varied the amount of costs he should have to pay. It held (Mummery LJ) that

> it would be legally erroneous if, acting on a misconceived analogy with the CPR, tribunals took the line that it was unreasonable conduct for employment tribunal claimants to withdraw claims and that they should accordingly be made liable to pay all the costs of the proceedings. It would be unfortunate if claimants were deterred from dropping claims by the prospect of an order for costs on withdrawal, which might well not be made against them if they fought on to a full hearing and failed. ... withdrawal could lead to a saving of costs. Also, ... notice of withdrawal might in some cases be the dawn of sanity and the tribunal should not adopt a practice on costs, which would deter applicants from making sensible litigation decisions. On the other side, ... tribunals should not follow a practice on costs, which might encourage speculative claims, by allowing applicants to start cases and to pursue them down to the last week or two before the hearing in the hope of receiving an offer to settle, and then, failing an offer, dropping the case without any risk of a costs sanction. The solution lies in the proper construction and sensible application of rule [76 (the relevant rule under the 2013 Rules)]. The crucial question is whether, in all the circumstances of the case, the claimant withdrawing the claim has conducted the proceedings unreasonably. It is not whether the withdrawal of the claim is in itself unreasonable.

The EAT decided in *Ibarz v University of Sheffield* (UKEAT/0018/15) that employment tribunal fees can be reimbursed to the claimant, even if they were paid by the claimant's trade union. (There is an EAT decision to the contrary, but the authors' view is that this decision is correct.)

6.4.11.2 Amount of costs (Rule 78)

Costs include fees, disbursements or expenses incurred by or on behalf of a party in relation to the proceedings (Rule 74(1)). They can include the costs of an in-house employed lawyer (see Rule 74(2)).

A costs order can be made against a respondent in respect of issue and hearing fees, even if they have been paid by a third party such as a trade union or insurance company (see *Ibarz v University of Sheffield* (UKEAT/0018/15)).

The costs ordered will either be a specified sum summarily assessed not exceeding £20,000, an agreed sum or a sum assessed by detailed assessment carried out by the county court or tribunal (which may exceed £20,000) (Rule 78). Rule 84 states that a tribunal may have regard to the paying party's ability to pay when considering (i) whether to make a costs order, or (ii) how much it should be, but there is no absolute duty to take this into account (see *Jilley v Birmingham and Solihull Mental Health NHS Trust* (UKEAT/0584/06)). Readers are referred to **Civil Litigation** for further details. The employment tribunal will have regard to the CPR 1998 and their accompanying practice directions and, for summary assessment, the 'Guideline Rates'.

6.4.11.3   Preparation time orders

Tribunals have the power to make 'preparation time orders' (Rules 76–79), where parties are not legally represented, in respect of carrying out preparatory work relating to but not including the hearing. The grounds for making such orders are the same as for a costs order (Rule 76). The Rules allow a rate of £37 per hour (from 6 April 2017; £38 per hour from April 2018) (up to a maximum of £20,000), in the same circumstances in which costs orders may be made. This may include time spent by the party (or its employees). Rule 79 deals with the assessment of preparation time orders.

Where a party is represented for only part of the proceedings, the tribunal can award costs and preparation time orders (see *Dunhoe v Support Services Group Ltd (in liquidation)* (UKEAT/0102/15)).

The ERRA 2013 enables tribunals to award both preparation time orders and witness expenses to litigants in person. This became effective from 25 June 2013.

6.4.11.4   Wasted costs orders (Rules 80–82)

Rule 80 permits tribunals to make a 'wasted costs' order against a party's representative (except not-for-profit representatives) as a result of 'any improper, unreasonable or negligent act or omission' by the representative. In *Mitchells Solicitors v Funkwerk Information Technologies* (UKEAT/0541/07), the EAT said that the threshold for a wasted costs order was high. The representative must not only have acted improperly, unreasonably or negligently, but must also have lent assistance to proceedings which amount to an abuse of process. Rule 80 is based on the wasted costs provision set out in s 51(7) of the Senior Courts Act 1981 for civil courts. The Court of Appeal's guidance on s 51(7), as set out in *Ridehalgh v Horsefield* [1994] 3 WLR 462, is therefore relevant and should be consulted.

In *Ratcliffe Duce & Grammer v Binns* (UKEAT/0100/08), the EAT confirmed that a wasted costs order cannot be made against a solicitor simply because the employment tribunal thinks that the client's pursuance of his claim is unreasonable and that the solicitor should have known that it was. The EAT repeated the three-stage test in *Ridehalgh* (above):

(1)   Has the legal representative of whom complaint is made acted improperly, unreasonably, or negligently?

(2)   If so, did such conduct cause the applicant to incur unnecessary costs?

(3)   If so, is it in the circumstances just to order the legal representative to compensate the applicant for the whole or any part of the relevant costs?

(See *Godfrey Morgan Solicitors Ltd v Cobalt Systems Ltd* [2012] ICR 305 for useful guidance.)

In *Hafiz and Haque Solicitors v Mullick* (UKEAT/0356/14), the EAT held that an employment tribunal erred in making a wasted costs order against a solicitor based on an inference that an unrealistic schedule of loss produced by the solicitor gave the claimant unreasonable expectations and prevented the claim's being settled earlier. The relevant principles were set out by the House of Lords in *Medcalf v Weatherill* [2002] UKHL 27, which emphasised the difficulties faced by a representative responding to an allegation of negligent conduct in circumstances where legal professional privilege prevented the representative from revealing details of the instructions given and the material provided by the client. The EAT said that tribunals should be 'very slow' to make wasted costs orders in cases where legal professional privilege prevented a representative from revealing details of the client's instructions.

In *Isteed v London Borough of Redbridge* (UKEAT/0442/14) the EAT again repeated the three-stage test set out in *Ridehalgh* (above) and held that the tribunal had focused only on question (1) and had not addressed the causation question. The tribunal must conduct a rigorous examination of the conduct in question and identify the improper, unreasonable or negligent acts relied upon. Mere allegations will not suffice (see *Wentworth-Wood v Maritime Transport Ltd* (UKEAT/0184/17)).

6.4.11.5   Financial penalties on employers that lose at tribunal

From April 2014, employment tribunals have the power to impose a penalty of up to £5,000 on a losing respondent employer, payable to the Secretary of State, where the employer's breach of the employee's rights 'has one or more aggravating features' (Enterprise and Regulatory Reform Act 2013, s 16, introducing s 12A into the Employment Tribunals Act 1996). 'Aggravating features' is not defined, although the explanatory notes to the 2013 Act provide non-exhaustive examples. If a financial award is made against the employer, the penalty must be 50% of that, subject to the £5,000 maximum penalty. The employer can pay only 50% of the penalty if he pays within 21 days. In January 2016, it was reported that only 12 such penalties had been imposed (written parliamentary questions, 26 January 2016).

In April 2016, a new Part 2A was inserted into the Employment Tribunals Act 1996 and came into force to introduce a new scheme for penalising employers who fail to pay tribunal or settlement sums under a COT3. The penalty will be 50% of the unpaid sum to a maximum of £5,000. Interest will accrue on the penalty. The penalty is payable to the Government (not the party awarded the sum due).

6.4.12   Reconsideration of tribunal decisions (Rules 70–73)

A party may, within 14 days, ask for decisions and judgments of the tribunal to be reconsidered where it is in the interests of justice. The tribunal can also reconsider of its own initiative. See *Sodexho v Gibbons* (UKEAT/0318/05) for a decision about tribunals' powers of reconsideration (decided under the 2004 Rules but still helpful) and *Outasight VB Ltd v Brown* (UKEAT/0253/14) (decided under the new Rules).

6.4.13   Appeals to the EAT

An appeal may be made from a decision of the employment tribunal, on a point of law only, to the EAT (ETA 1996, s 21). As with employment tribunals, the EAT must guard against substituting its own subjective response to an employer's conduct (see *Brent v Fuller* [2011] ICR 806). The EAT must pay proper regard to the decision of the employment tribunal, 'to whom Parliament has entrusted the responsibility of making what are, no doubt sometimes, difficult and borderline decisions' (see *Bowater v North West London Hospitals NHS Trust* [2010] IRLR 331).

Determining what is the difference between a question of law and findings of fact and inference is crucial but difficult: an error of law can be found if a tribunal fails to make a finding of fact where there is uncontroverted evidence, or has made a finding contrary to all the evidence. But there is no error of law where some evidence points one way and some evidence points another way (see *Yeboah v Crofton* [2002] IRLR 634 and *Brent v Fuller* [2011] ICR 806). Nor may an appellant try to reargue factual issues.

The procedures of the EAT are governed by rules in the Schedule to the Employment Appeal Tribunal Rules 1993 (SI 1993/2854), which have been amended on a number of occasions, most recently by the Employment Appeal Tribunal (Amendment) Rules 2013 (SI 2013/1693), to bring them into line with changes to the Employment Tribunal Rules. Any appeal must be made within 42 days after written reasons are sent out by the tribunal. The EAT's time-limit is enforced strictly (see, eg, the Court of Appeal's decision in *Greg O'Cathail v Transport for London* [2012] EWCA Civ 1004). In *Haydar v Pennine Acute Hospitals NHS Trust* [2018] EWCA Civ 1435, the Court of Appeal refused to extend time for a claimant to submit his appeal, after his original was lost in the post. When the employment tribunal sends out judgments to parties, it refers in its standard letter to a booklet entitled 'The judgment', which says that a party appealing should make a check with the EAT if no acknowledgement of the appeal is received within seven days. The claimant waited six weeks before checking with the EAT, and the Court of Appeal found that the claimant had failed to check with the EAT soon enough and his delay was serious and significant. However, in *Rana v London Borough of Ealing* [2018] EWCA Civ 2074, where the tribunal failed to send a judgment to the correct address, the Court of Appeal said that this was a situation where the discretion to allow an appeal 'out of time' should be exercised.

A new Practice Direction dealing with EAT procedure came into force on 29 July 2013. The Rules set out instructions as to the documents to be submitted when lodging an appeal, improve the procedures for weeding out unmeritorious appeals, and contain costs rules for the EAT, in line with the costs rules for employment tribunals.

Previously, most EAT cases were determined by a panel consisting of a judge and lay members. The ERRA 2013, which received Royal Assent on 25 April 2013, requires all EAT cases to be heard by a judge alone, unless a judge orders otherwise or any order specifies that certain proceedings are to be heard by a panel. The change applies to all EAT hearings that started on or after 27 June 2013.

6.4.14   The public tribunal register

Claims which are settled are not matters of public knowledge. Since late 2016, employment tribunal judgments go online (see <www.gov.uk/employment-tribunal-decisions>).

6.4.15   Enforcement

Employment tribunals are not responsible for enforcement of an award. This must be done in the civil courts as if it were a county court judgment.

Section 27(1)–(4) of the Tribunals, Courts and Enforcement Act 2007, which came into force on 1 April 2009, removed the previous requirement to register unpaid tribunal awards before they could be treated as enforceable. Claimants may go directly to the county court (or High Court) for enforcement. Form N322B, which is available on the court services website at <http://www.hmcourts-service.gov.uk>, needs to be completed to allow enforcement of a decision or an Acas settlement (Form COT3).

Employers or individuals who fail to pay employment tribunal or EAT awards in England and Wales, will now be added to the *Register of Judgments, Orders and Fines* once enforcement proceedings are brought against them (Register of Judgments, Orders and Fines (Amendment) Regulations 2009 (SI 2009/474)).

6.4.16   Funding

Apart from paying privately, there are a number of other options:

(a)   *Legal aid.* This is *only* available for complaints under the Equality Act 2010, and is subject to complex financial conditions and does not cover advocacy in the employment tribunal (but does so in the EAT). For further information, see the Legal Aid, Sentencing and Punishment of Offenders Act 2012.

(b)   *Damages-based agreements.* These are arrangements whereby the representative takes an agreed percentage of the damages the client receives, up to a maximum of 35% (excluding disbursements which can be charged on top). Readers should refer to the Damages-Based Agreements Regulations 2013 (SI 2013/609) and the Courts and Legal Services Act 1990 (amended 2013).

(c)   Conditional fee agreements. Readers should refer to the Courts and Legal Services Act 1990 (amended 2013). Success fees cannot be recovered from the opponent.

For a good overview of the above types of funding, see *Civil Litigation* at **2.4**.

6.4.17   Human Rights Act 1998

Under Article 6 of the ECHR, everyone is entitled, 'in the determination of his civil rights and obligations', to 'a fair and public hearing within a reasonable time by an independent and impartial tribunal established by law'. Any party to an employment-related dispute, whether it takes place in the courts or before a tribunal, is therefore entitled to a fair trial. Case law from Strasbourg has suggested, however, that employment disputes may not come within the definition of 'civil rights and obligations' because they are essentially concerned with private rights. Nonetheless, under the HRA 1998, courts and tribunals are obliged to act compatibly with the HRA 1998 (s 6), and therefore, when determining an employment dispute between private parties, will still have to apply Convention rights.

Inherent in the concept of a fair trial is equality of arms between the parties. This may render the lack of legal representation in employment tribunal proceedings open to challenge, although because such proceedings are set up to be conducted in a practical and straightforward manner, without undue formality, such a challenge may not succeed. The ECtHR has held that the unavailability of legal assistance in respect of complex issues is a breach of the principles of a fair trial. The Scottish Executive made a decision to make public funding available in some circumstances to individuals pursuing employment cases in Scotland amid fears that a failure to do so is in contravention of Article 6. Public funding is available where the claimant can show that his claim is arguable and too complex for him to litigate without assistance. The Lord Chancellor stated on 5 July 2001 that he was 'confident' that the public funding in England and Wales is fully compliant with the ECHR. (See too the judgment of the Supreme Court in *Coventry v Lawrence* [2015] UKSC 50.)

Readers should refer to **Chapter 15** for cases involving the HRA 1998.

6.5   SETTLEMENTS

Many complaints are settled without a hearing. In the first quarter of 2018–19, for example, 69% of all cases were withdrawn or settled before a full hearing. 25% were settled through Acas. Only 8% of cases were determined at a final hearing by the tribunal. The usual terms of settlement involve the employee agreeing not to start or proceed with a claim in consideration of the employer making a monetary payment and sometimes agreeing to provide a reference. Employers should be careful when providing a reference in these circumstances. A negligent reference that causes loss may be actionable by the recipient (*Hedley Byrne & Co Ltd v Heller & Partners Ltd* [1964] AC 465) or by the employee (*Spring v Guardian Assurance plc and Others* [1994] 3 All ER 129) (see **1.7.1.5**). Even in cases where the employer has a reasonable chance of success, it may be worth settling to avoid the cost of a tribunal hearing. This is a commercial decision to be taken by the employer. The effect of the recoupment regulations is also avoided (see **5.7.2.4**).

Broadly, by s 203 of the ERA 1996, any provision in an agreement is void in so far as it purports to exclude or limit the operation of any of the provisions of the Act, or to preclude a person from bringing any proceedings under the Act before an employment tribunal (this prevents an employee waiving their statutory rights – such as relating to unfair dismissal, redundancy payment, discrimination or holiday pay), unless:

(a)   a conciliation officer has taken action under s 18 of the ETA 1996. Conciliation officers are designated by Acas. Where a complaint is presented to a tribunal, it is the duty of the Secretary of the Tribunals to send copies of all documents to an appropriate conciliation officer. The officer's duties are to promote a settlement and ensure that both parties understand its effect. He does not have a duty to ensure that the settlement is fair (*Moore v Duport Furniture Products Ltd* [1980] IRLR 158, CA). He must be involved in promoting the settlement. He will not merely 'rubber-stamp' an agreement already reached between the parties. Any settlement achieved in this way is recorded on a COT3. A COT3 will be a legally binding and enforceable contract.

Note that personal injury claims cannot be settled through Acas, but if both parties agree, waivers in respect of existing claims can be included in the agreement.

It is common practice to exclude all possible claims by the employee in return for the settlement. However, care should be taken in drafting. In *Bank of Credit and Commerce International SA (in liquidation) v Ali and Others (No 1)* [2001] 2 WLR 735, the House of Lords held that a COT3 agreement containing a general release under which the employee accepted an additional payment on being dismissed for redundancy which was expressed as being 'in full and final settlement of all or any claims whether under statute, common law or in equity of whatsoever nature that exists or may exist' did not preclude a claim for 'stigma' damages which the parties could not have contemplated at the time the agreement was signed because the decision in *Malik* was not handed down until some eight years later. The House of Lords held that clear language leaving no scope for doubt is needed for an employee to be held to have intended to surrender rights and claims of which they were unaware and could not have been aware. Similarly, in *Royal National Othopaedic Hospital Trust v Howard* [2002] IRLR 849, the EAT held that an agreement settling a complaint of sex discrimination which was stated to be 'in full and final settlement ... of all claims which the applicant may have against the respondent' did not preclude her from bringing a victimisation claim later. The EAT held that, if such a result is intended, the language must be absolutely clear and leave no room for doubt that the agreement relates to future claims; or

(b) a written agreement (a 'settlement agreement') is entered into. Other than by involving Acas, a settlement agreement is therefore the only way in which an employee can effectively waive any statutory claims. Although it is not legally necessary to use this route to waive purely contractual disputes (such as breach of contract, notice, contractual holiday pay), it makes sense to include everything in one document. In order for a settlement agreement to be binding it must comply with the following conditions:

(i)   it must be in writing, identify the adviser, relate to the particular complaint and state that the relevant statutory conditions are satisfied,

(ii) the employee or worker must have received advice from a relevant independent adviser as to the terms and effect of the proposed agreement and, in particular, its effect on his ability to pursue his rights before an employment tribunal, and

(iii) there must be in force, when the adviser gives the advice, a contract of insurance, or an indemnity provided for members of a profession or professional body, covering the risk of a claim by the employee or worker in respect of loss arising in consequence of the advice.

A person is a relevant independent adviser:

(a) if he is a qualified lawyer;

(b) if he is an officer, official, employee or member of an independent trade union who has been certified in writing by the trade union as competent to give advice and as authorised to do so on behalf of the trade union;

(c) if he works at an advice centre (whether as an employee or a volunteer) and has been certified in writing by the centre as competent to give advice and as authorised to do so on behalf of the centre; or

(d) if he is a person of a description specified in an order made by the Secretary of State, eg a Fellow of the Institute of Legal Executives employed by a solicitors' practice.

However, a person is not a relevant independent adviser:

(a)   if he is employed by or is acting in the matter for the other party or a person who is connected with the other party;

(b)   in the case of a person within (b) or (c) above, if the trade union or advice centre is the other party or a person who is connected with the other party;

(c)   in the case of a person within (c) above, if the complainant makes a payment for the advice received from him; or

(d)   in the case of a person within (d) above, if any condition specified in the order in relation to the giving of advice by persons of that description is not satisfied.

A qualified lawyer is a barrister or solicitor who holds a practising certificate.

The conditions are applied strictly, such that if any one of the conditions is not satisfied the agreement is not binding.

Note: The settlement agreement must relate to a 'particular complaint'; a settlement agreement which seeks to exclude all possible claims will fall foul of ERA 1996, s 203, which contains restrictions on contracting out of statutory rights. In *Sutherland v Network Appliance Ltd* [2001] IRLR 12, the applicant's employment with the respondent was settled on agreed terms by way of a settlement agreement. The terms stated that the settlement was in 'full and final settlement of any claims you may have against the company'. The EAT confirmed that the agreement was void in respect of statutory claims but held that the agreement was enforceable to the extent that it contained a compromise of contractual claims. Thus a settlement agreement must only seek to settle those statutory claims which have already been raised (either by presentation to the tribunal or raised by the employer prior to the issue of proceedings). The Court of Appeal gave guidance on settlement agreements in *Hinton v University of East London* [2005] IRLR 522. Smith LJ stated that it is not adequate for settlement agreements to use 'a rolled up expression such as "all statutory rights"'. Instead the particular proceedings must be identified, 'either by a generic description such as "unfair dismissal" or by reference to the section of the statute giving rise to the claim'. She agreed with Mummery LJ's statement that 'it is good practice for the particulars of the nature of the allegations and of the statute under which they are made or the common law basis of the alleged claim to be inserted in the ... agreement in the form of a brief factual and legal description'. Readers should pay careful attention to this case when drafting settlement agreements.

Where an agreement is concluded either through a conciliation officer or as a settlement agreement, any proceedings will normally be adjourned generally. If the employer complies with the agreement, the employee is barred from continuing with his complaint. If the employer does not comply with the agreement, the employee can either return to the tribunal to continue with the complaint, or sue for breach of contract in the county court or High Court or the tribunal itself.

In *Collidge v Freeport plc* [2008] EWCA Civ 485, the Court of Appeal held that an employer was entitled to withhold payment under a settlement agreement where the employee was in breach of a warranty he had given in the agreement, whereby the employee stated that he knew of no circumstances which would amount to a repudiatory breach of contract.

Where a settlement does not bind an employee, any sums paid under it will be taken into account by the tribunal in making any award. However, as a result of s 124(5) of the ERA 1996, the maximum compensatory award (£78,335 as at April 2015) must be applied after all deductions have been made.

Whatever method of settlement is used, the employee's adviser should ensure that any personal injury claims or claims arising out of employment pension benefits are expressly excluded from the settlement. There is an ongoing, unresolved, debate as to whether future rights can be settled using a settlement agreement.

On 29 July 2013, Acas published a Statutory Code of Practice on Settlement Agreements. Failure to follow the Code will not automatically make an employer liable, but tribunals can take the guidance into account. The Code states that as a general rule, a minimum of 10 calendar days should be given for parties to consider terms and take independent advice. It also states that it would be best practice at such meetings to allow employees to be accompanied by a work colleague or trade union official. The Code includes a basic model form of settlement agreement. Typically, such an agreement will look to contain provisions relating to:

- any contractual payments due up to and on termination;
- any ex gratia payment as compensation for loss of employment and/or in consideration for the waiver/withdrawal of claims;
- an express waiver;
- provisions as to any ongoing confidentiality obligations. Note that there has been a lot of controversy about the use of confidentiality provisions or 'gagging clauses in NHS and #MeToo' sexual harassment and abuse claims. In March 2018, the Solicitors Regulation Authority (SRA) issued a warning notice about use of non-disclosure agreements that they must not be used to prevent disclosure of otherwise reportable conduct, or as a means of 'exerting' inappropriate influence over people not to make disclosures which are protected by statute or reportable to regulators or law enforcement agencies. The SRA warns that failure to comply with the notice may lead to disciplinary action (see www.sra.org.uk/solicitors/code-of-conduct/guidance/warning-notices/use-of-non-disclosure-agreements-(ndas)--warning-notice.page).

  Care should be taken to ensure that such clauses are drafted so as not to be seen as preventing individuals from raising legitimate public interest or safety concerns, such as those listed in the Public Interest Disclosure Act 1998 (see **Chapter 5**). The EHRC has suggested that such clauses should not be used in public sector settlements;

- provisions as to any ongoing restrictive covenants;
- practical provisions, such as payments into pensions;
- contributions to legal fees;
- indemnities regarding the tax treatment of any payments (it will usually be the obligation of the employee to declare payments to HMRC).

6.5.1 Pre-termination negotiations – protected conversations

The ERRA 2013 included a new provision in the ERA 1996 (s 111A) to make it easier for employers to make settlement offers to employees without this being admissible in subsequent unfair dismissal proceedings. The relevant provision (s 14) came into force on 29 July 2013 and inserted a new s 111A into the ERA 1996. Before this section was introduced, the common law 'without prejudice' rule prevented any statement made during a 'without prejudice' discussion from being used in a court or a tribunal (see **6.4.5.2** on without prejudice communications). Section 111A of the ERA 1996 allows greater flexibility, so that confidential discussions may be initiated as a means of negotiating the ending of an employment relationship without the need for an 'existing dispute', with such discussions being protected from disclosure unless there has been improper behaviour. Where a valid settlement agreement is concluded, an employee will be unable to bring an employment tribunal claim. Where a settlement agreement is not concluded, such that an employee can still bring a claim, s 111A will exclude evidence about termination discussions in unfair dismissal cases. An employer is therefore able to make an offer to 'pay off' an employee before any performance management or disciplinary proceedings have started, and before any dispute has arisen between them. Such offers are admissible in evidence in discrimination claims and any claims of automatically unfair dismissal, and also admissible if anything 'improper' is said or done. The Acas Statutory Code gives guidance on what might constitute improper behaviour, including:

- bullying and intimidation through the use of aggressive behaviour or offensive words
- putting undue pressure on a party, eg by not giving reasonable time for consideration
- saying that if a settlement proposal is rejected, the employee will be dismissed.

The first appellate judgment on s 111A was given by the EAT in *Faithorn Farrell Timms LLP v Bailey* (UKEAT/0025/16). The EAT noted that case law on 'without prejudice' discussions was not applicable to pre-termination negotiations, and s 111A had to be read on its own terms. Claims not covered by s 111A (eg discrimination) would still be governed by normal 'without prejudice' principles, so evidence may be admitted for a discrimination claim but remain excluded regarding unfair dismissal. The EAT held that the protection of s 111A is broader than it is for 'without prejudice' communications, in that it covers not just the content of a protected conversation but also the fact of them taking place. It would also cover an employer's internal discussions about a protected conversation. Section 111A did not allow for any waiver of the protection, although it noted that the 'improper behaviour' exception was broader than the 'unambiguous impropriety' test required to admit 'without prejudice' communications. See also *Greco v General Physics UK Ltd* (UKEAT/0114/16) and *Lenlyn UK Ltd v Kular* (UKEAT/0108/16) for two other cases looking at the impact of this provision. The EAT held in *Graham v Agilitas IT Solutions Ltd* (UKEAT/0212/17) that an employer cannot seek to use the s 111A shield in relation to part of a discussion but at the same time seek to rely on other parts of the same discussion to raise disciplinary allegations. In *Basra v BJSS Ltd* (UKEAT/0090/17), the EAT held that there is an exception to the general rule that pre-termination discussions cannot be referred to, namely where the date of the termination is in dispute:

> The chronological dividing line between what is, and what is not, admissible ... lies on the point at which the contract is terminated. ... where there is a dispute as to whether or not the contract was terminated on a particular date, the Tribunal would not be in a position to say what evidence should be excluded until that dispute is determined.

Acas has published a code of practice on settlement agreements which includes guidance on how to carry out settlement negotiations.

6.5.2 Recording the settlement

Once a claim has been presented, this needs to be withdrawn by the claimant in one of two ways:

(a) the terms of the settlement may be recorded and registered with the employment tribunal on Form COT3. This is the usual method used where a settlement is reached after a conciliation officer has taken action;

(b) alternatively, the claimant may merely decide to withdraw his claim to the tribunal, for example in compliance with a settlement agreement. Form COT4 can be used for this purpose, or a letter to the tribunal will suffice.

6.6 ALTERNATIVES TO TRIBUNAL PROCEEDINGS

Acas was given power to run a statutory arbitration scheme, as an alternative to the employment tribunal for unfair dismissal cases, by the Employment Rights (Dispute Resolution) Act 1998. The ACAS Arbitration Scheme (England and Wales) Order 2001 (SI 2001/1185) is intended to be 'confidential, informal, relatively fast and cost-efficient'. Procedures are 'non-legalistic' and flexible. Awards are final, with very limited opportunity to appeal. The scheme applies only to unfair dismissal complaints or claims under the flexible working law (see **14.19**). Full details of the scheme, including a guide to the scheme, may be found on the Acas website <http://www.acas.org.uk>. To use the scheme, both the employer and the employee must agree to enter into voluntary arbitration. An Acas officer will listen to the arguments of both sides and decide whether compensation should be awarded and, if so, how much.

The arbitrator cannot deal with 'jurisdictional matters' (eg whether the worker was an employee; whether the complaint was presented in time; or whether the employee has sufficient continuity of service). A dispute is referred to arbitration by the parties entering into an arbitration agreement. A waiver form under which the parties agree to arbitration and waive the right to return to the employment tribunal must accompany the agreement. If the employee withdraws from the scheme his claim is dismissed. The employer cannot unilaterally withdraw from the scheme.

Once the parties have agreed to arbitration the procedure in outline is as follows.

At least 14 days before the arbitration hearing each party must send to the Acas Arbitration Section:

(a)   a written statement of case;

(b)   supporting documents;

(c)   a list of witnesses.

In deciding whether the dismissal was fair or unfair, the arbitrator must have regard to general principles of fairness and good conduct rather than legal rules. He must still apply EU law and the HRA 1998. Witnesses cannot be cross-examined by the parties; it is for the arbitrator to establish facts.

The arbitrator's decision must identify the reason for dismissal, the main considerations taken into account in reaching the decision, state the decision, the remedy awarded and the date it was made. Awards are binding and there is generally no right of appeal.

As indicated above (see **6.4.6**), Employment Judges can suggest to the parties at the case management discussion that the case be referred to judicial mediation. Judicial mediation is voluntary and provides parties to an employment tribunal claim with a confidential, alternative settlement option that tries to avoid the need for a full merits hearing. It operates in addition to, and not as a substitute for, the role of Acas or privately negotiated settlements. The judicial mediation takes place in private. A trained Employment Judge acts as an impartial mediator to try to help the parties to resolve their dispute. This judge will not hear the case if the mediation fails.

The principal criteria which identify cases as being suitable for judicial mediation are:

(a)   a full hearing has been fixed for the substantive issues of at least three days in length;

(b)   the case will usually involve at least one element of discrimination although some other complex cases are included;

(c)   the claims are generally single claims, but occasionally judicial mediation can incorporate small multiples (ie two or three claimants);

(d)   there must be no proceedings in other jurisdictions; and

(e)   there must be no insolvency involved.

If a settlement is achieved, the terms are agreed in writing. The parties may finalise the settlement terms by entering into a compromise agreement or by using a COT3 Form if Acas is involved. The Law Society has now published a Practice Note to support judicial mediation. This is available at <http://www.lawsociety.org.uk/productsandservices/practicenotes/judicialmediation.page>.

Acas also offers a pre-claim conciliation scheme. The details are available on the Acas website (see above).

6.7   OVERLAPPING CLAIMS AND AWARDS

A dismissed employee may have more than one potential claim against his employer. For example, a dismissal that is both unfair and without proper notice or within a fixed term may give rise to both an unfair dismissal claim and a wrongful dismissal claim. If an employee is unfairly selected for redundancy, he will be entitled to a redundancy payment and be able to present an unfair dismissal claim. All three claims of wrongful dismissal, redundancy payment and unfair dismissal would be available to the employee unfairly dismissed without proper notice by reason of redundancy.

6.7.1 Wrongful and unfair dismissal

The wrongful dismissal claim is a breach of contract action which may be brought as a court action or pursued in an employment tribunal. The unfair dismissal claim is pursued only in an employment tribunal. Both may be pursued. In the case of a less well-paid employee who is entitled to only a short period of notice, the unfair dismissal claim is usually more advantageous, as compensation for future loss may extend beyond the employee's notice period.

If both claims are brought, and both succeed, the basic principle is that compensation will not be awarded for the same loss twice. The tribunal will deduct the breach of contract damages awarded from the compensatory award for unfair dismissal.

6.7.2 Redundancy payment and unfair dismissal

The redundancy payment will be set against the unfair dismissal award. Usually it will simply offset the basic award, but if it exceeds the basic award (eg because the basic award has been reduced by contributory fault) the remainder will reduce the compensatory award. The excess redundancy payment should be deducted *after* the other deductions (eg for contributory fault) have been made (see **5.6.2.2**).

6.7.3 Redundancy payment and wrongful dismissal

Since a redundancy payment is a reward for past services, and a wrongful dismissal payment is an award for future loss, a redundancy payment is not taken into account in awarding damages for wrongful dismissal.

6.7.4 A discriminatory dismissal

If a person is dismissed for reasons relating to a protected characteristic, such as sex or race, this is not automatically unfair but, in practice, will often be found to be unfair.

A claim for unfair dismissal may be pursued alongside a discrimination claim. Discrimination awards are not subject to any maximum figure and may include an award in respect of injured feelings. In addition, no eligibility conditions need be satisfied. As against this, the award for unfair dismissal includes a basic award in addition to compensation. Alternatively, re-engagement or reinstatement may be ordered. If both claims are pursued, s 126 of the ERA 1996 provides that compensation cannot be awarded again in respect of any loss or other matter which has already been taken into account in dealing with the other claim. (See **Chapters 8–13** for further details of discrimination claims.)

6.7.5 Compensation

The general rule of the compensation regime is that the employee cannot be compensated twice for the same *financial* loss.

---

1. Compensation in respect of time spent at work
- unfair dismissal basic award
- redundancy payment
- no other regimes

NB Employee will not be paid both

---

2. Compensation in respect of actual losses
- unfair dismissal compensatory loss to date of employment tribunal hearing
- wrongful dismissal damages (eg notice)
- discrimination pecuniary loss claims to date of employment tribunal hearing

NB Employee can recover these only once

---

3. Compensation in respect of future losses
- unfair dismissal compensatory loss from date of employment tribunal hearing
- discrimination future pecuniary loss claims from date of hearing

NB Employee can recover these only once

See further the diagram set out below.

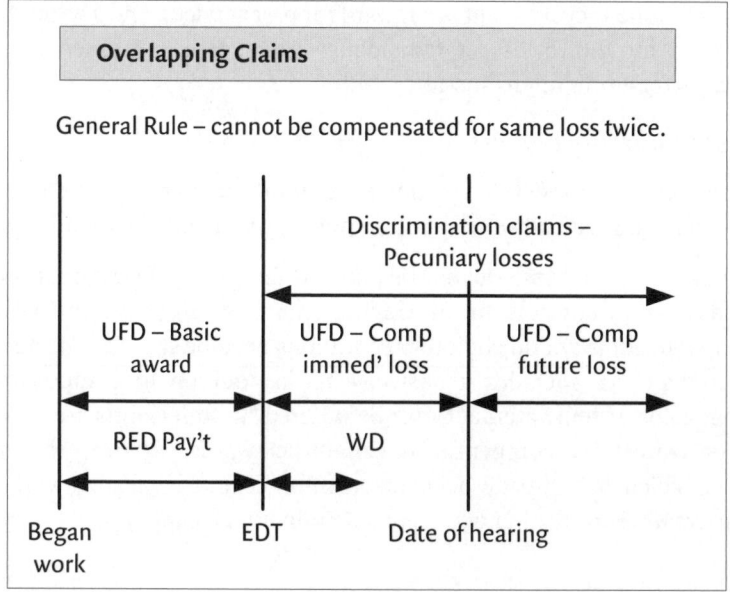

6.8 CASE STUDY: UNFAIR DISMISSAL

(1)   Chronology and facts

(2)   Particulars of response

(3)   Tribunal orders

(4)   Witness statement

(5)   Judgment

IN THE GUILDSHIRE EMPLOYMENT TRIBUNAL   CASE NUMBER: 1234/2018

BETWEEN

	MRS JANE MINNERY	Claimant
	- and -	
	GUILDSHIRE PRIMARY CARE TRUST ('PCT')	Respondent

CHRONOLOGY of
EVENTS

NUMBER	EVENT	DATE
1	Claimant commences employment with the Respondent	08/09/2011
2	Claimant's daughter made allegations of child abuse – Claimant's children taken into care	26/01/2018
3	Claimant's children voluntarily accommodated per Section 20 of the Children Act 1989	29/01
4	Claimant contacts acting senior nurse manager to notify Respondent of need to take emergency annual leave – no mention of superseding allegations	29/01
5	A one-week sick note is received by the Respondent from the Claimant	05/02
6	A further ten-day sick note received by the Respondent from the Claimant	09/02
7	Case Conference meeting – children placed on the Child Protection Register for emotional and physical abuse & Respondent notified	09/02 14/02
8	Claimant informed of her suspension by the Respondent	15/02
9	Children returned to the family home	22/02
10	Guildshire Police state that no criminal prosecution will be taken against the Claimant but that a notation will be made on the Criminal Records Bureau register.	01/03
11	Dr Francis meets with Claimant to assess the Claimant's fitness/competence to work	30/04
12	Dr Francis' investigations recommend Claimant is dismissed	21/05
13	Disciplinary panel meeting chaired by the PCT's Group Manager for Children's Services	02/07
14	Written confirmation of outcome of Disciplinary hearing	10/07
15	Claimant notifies the Respondent of her wish to appeal against the disciplinary panel's decision to dismiss her	17/07
16	Appeal panel hearing chaired by the PCT's Director of Children Services	07/09

NUMBER	EVENT	DATE
17	Written confirmation of outcome of Appeal hearing	10/09
18	Proceedings commenced in Tribunal. The Claimant alleges unfair dismissal on the grounds that: • Insufficient evidence presented to the hearing to justify dismissal • Decision based primarily on suspicion rather than evidence of wrongdoing • PCT's decision based on the CRB notation but those who presented the PCT's case could not say how long it would remain on file • The allegation of abuse was retracted • It was not true that the claimant did not have an insight on how personal life would impact on job – the claimant outlined that she would use reflection, support of colleagues and supervision, along with policies and procedures to deal with similar child protection issues. • No formal warnings given • Previous good service not taken into account	05/10
19	Tribunal Hearing: The Tribunal had an agreed bundle of documents The Tribunal had Witness Statements from the Claimant on her own behalf; and from Dr M Francis, Consultant Paediatrician for the PCT; the PCT's Group Manager of Children's Services who chaired the disciplinary hearing; and the PCT's Director of Children Services who chaired the appeal hearing.	17–19/2/2019

Tribunal's findings of fact

1.   The Claimant began her employment with the Respondent in September 2011, starting as a student health visitor. She qualified in August 2012. The Claimant's line manger told Dr Francis, the Trust's consultant paediatrician, that she had always found the Claimant to be hardworking, reliable and flexible. She assessed the Claimant as being a good colleague.

2.   The Claimant has two daughters who live with her.

3.   On 12 January 2018 the Claimant spoke to her line manager about allegations that had been made against her by her daughter which involved allegations of physical abuse, being hit with a belt by her mother.

4.   Social services wrote to the Respondent on 14 February, reporting that both the Claimant's daughters had been removed from the family home on 26 January due to allegations of physical harm made by one daughter. The children had been placed on the Child Protection Register under categories of 'physical harm and emotional abuse' on 9 February.

5.   The Respondent suspended the Claimant on 15 February. The decision to suspend was made because of the serious nature of the allegations. The Claimant remained on full pay and was told that the suspension was a neutral act, not disciplinary.

6.   Dr Francis was asked by the Respondent to investigate. By the time he met with the Claimant her children had returned home, and the Claimant had signed a written

agreement saying she would not cause emotional harm to her daughters and that she would work in partnership with the authorities.

7. Dr Francis interviewed the Claimant's line manager, the council's social worker and the Claimant.

8. The social worker told Dr Francis that she was concerned about the Claimant's perception of child abuse and physical chastisement. The Claimant was, she said, still attributing her actions to her upbringing and culture.

9. Dr Francis noted that no criminal charges were brought against the Claimant but that the investigation carried out by the police would appear as a notation on the Criminal Records Bureau record.

10. Dr Francis interviewed the Claimant on 30 April. He asked her about her practice as a health visitor. He then asked her about the recent events and for her assessment of how the incident would affect her work. The Claimant said that she did not think that it would affect her work, and that children were the priority in the service and that she would not impose her own values on her work. The Claimant told Dr Francis that her daughter had retracted her allegations, but there was no evidence of this. The Claimant appeared to think, Dr Francis notes, that if this was the case then there was no issue for the Respondent to take up with her.

11. Dr Francis recommended dismissal for the following reasons:

    (i)   The Claimant's refusal fully to accept responsibility for the offence that had occurred, instead attempting to justify her action because of her culture, knowing full well, through her child protection and health visitor training, that this was not acceptable. Instead the Claimant continued to focus on issues relating to her being misconstrued and misrepresented in the child protection investigation.

    (ii) The Claimant's unwillingness to acknowledge that the events which occurred in her private life would impact on her work and practice as a health visitor.

    (iii) His concern that the Claimant's experiences would affect her attitude and her ability to work jointly with agencies involved in child protection investigations, and in particular with social services.

    (iv) His concern that because of the issues raised in the investigation, the Claimant's duty to assess risks and make appropriate referrals to social services where there were child protection concerns might be affected, as this was dependent not just on her knowledge but also on her attitude. The concern was that it would be difficult for any manager to have confidence that the Claimant was making the correct decisions and taking appropriate actions, especially in child protection cases, given the independent way that health visitors work.

12. Dr Francis was also concerned about whether the Claimant could maintain her credibility among her colleagues and other professionals if they became aware of events that had occurred, and that the Respondent would be taking a risk if it continued to employ her as a health visitor. Should there be any other child protection issues in connection with the Trust's clients, where her judgment was called into question because of this background, the Respondent could be seen to be at fault.

13. Dr Francis also produced a document entitled: 'Management case relating to Jane Minnery'. The risks were listed as follows:

    1. 'The welfare, safety and health of children must always be paramount. This is an overriding responsibility of Guildshire PCT.

    2. As a health visitor [the Claimant] will present a risk to the children and families she will be working with because her current knowledge and attitude could impair her judgment and her ability to manage cases appropriately.

3. The organisation will be at risk if it continues to employ a health visitor who has been the executor of child abuse, and whose CRB check will contain a notification of this abuse.'

14. The Claimant was told in a letter dated 4 June that there would be a disciplinary hearing on 26 June to consider her dismissal due to the Claimant's conduct, and in light of the need to protect children and of the risk to the children and the PCT.

15. The Claimant was told that the hearing could result in the termination of her employment, and that she was entitled to be accompanied to the hearing by a trade union representative or friend or colleague. The disciplinary hearing took place on 2 July, not 26 June, at the Claimant's request as she wanted to go on holiday to recover from the trauma of recent events.

16. At the hearing Dr Francis presented the Respondent's case, summarising its concerns as that the Claimant had not seen the problem that he was trying to highlight to her when he had questioned her. He said that she was unable to make the connection between what she had experienced personally and how it could possibly affect her ability to do her job. He did not believe she was capable of being credible to other professionals, and he thought that it could be a problem employing someone carrying a CRB notation. For this reason she should be dismissed, he said. The Respondent made it clear to the Claimant that it was not concerned with the details surrounding her children's being taken into care. The Respondent was only concerned with its duty to protect clients from potential harm and with how what had happened had affected the Claimant's ability to carry out her job. The Respondent had to investigate that risk.

17. The Claimant's representative asked the Claimant a series of questions to enable her to give answers which would deal with the Respondent's apparent concerns. The Claimant confirmed that she would follow the Respondent's policies and procedures should she have to deal with a child at risk. She did not explain how that would work in practice. The Claimant confirmed that she did not feel compromised as a health visitor since the incident.

18. The Respondent wrote the Claimant a letter of dismissal dated 10 July. The reasons given for the decision to dismiss were:
   - It has been deemed not suitable for you to continue in your role as a health visitor due to 'some other substantial reason'. That is, given the PCT's overriding responsibility to protect its clients, the potential risk of employing a frontline health visitor with a CRB notation for physical and mental abuse of children outweighs the arguments to continue to employ you in that capacity.
   - For the same reason it has been deemed not suitable for the PCT to offer you alternative employment within adult services as a 'Registered General Nurse'. The Claimant was offered an administrative post.

19. The Claimant was told that her employment would be terminated with three months' notice, and she was told of her right to appeal within 21 days. Otherwise the dismissal would take effect from date of the hearing, 2 July.

20. The Claimant did appeal on 17 July. The appeal hearing was heard on 7 September. The central theme in the appeal was that as no evidence of wrongdoing had ever been presented against her, she should not have been dismissed. The Claimant relied heavily upon the absence of any formal finding of guilt against her as a result of the investigation carried out by the police and social services. She also stated that allegations by family members had subsequently been retracted, which should have made a difference to the outcome of the disciplinary hearing.

21 The CRB notation was discussed at the appeal hearing. The Respondent confirmed that it had relied on the police and social services investigation, which had concluded that there was insufficient evidence for a criminal prosecution but that there was enough for a CRB notation, which reflected the seriousness of the allegations.

22. The appeal panel decided as follows:
    - The panel had serious concerns about the impact of Jane Minnery working with vulnerable children and her lack of insight.
    - The appeal hearing considered whether she was suitable for a clinical alternative and decided (like the disciplinary panel) that the risks were too great.
    - The panel had confidence in the professional advice that personal behaviour impacts on professional behaviour, and confirmed that as a health visitor advising on child protection, there would be a risk.
    - The panel did not have confidence in the level of the Claimant's acceptable behaviour in parenting.

23. It had been noted during the hearing that the Claimant would not be supervised unless she reported a case to her team leader. As a band 7 employee she would be expected to assist with supervising junior staff and to have an in-depth knowledge of child protection matters, and to take a lead role in resolving those issues within families.

24. The appeal panel confirmed the disciplinary panel's decision on 10 September. The panel had reviewed the earlier decision to ensure it was fair and reasonable, taking into account the facts and circumstances.

25. It had been apparent to the appeal panel that the Claimant lacked insight into how her private behaviour could impact on her professional ability to make objective decisions about vulnerable children. The advice the panel had received was that the Claimant's conduct towards her children could not be separated from the risks presented by her continuing to work as a health visitor. The Respondent has to be responsible for children in the borough, and the children's needs remain paramount.

26. The appeal panel therefore agreed with the panel that the risks in continuing to employ the Claimant as a health visitor were too high.

IN THE GUILDSHIRE EMPLOYMENT TRIBUNAL   CASE NUMBER: 1234/2018

BETWEEN

MRS JANE MINNERY   Claimant

- and -

GUILDSHIRE PRIMARY CARE TRUST   Respondent

PARTICULARS OF RESPONSE

1. The Respondent is a Primary Care Trust commissioning and providing health services to members of the general public in the Guildshire area.

2. It is admitted that the Claimant was employed as a Health Visitor by the Respondent from September 2011 to July 2018. It is admitted that the Claimant was dismissed. It is not admitted that the dismissal was unfair.

3. Unless admitted in these Particulars of Response the Respondent denies all of the Claimant's allegations.

4. The Respondent has an overriding duty and responsibility to protect members of the public, especially children, who use the services it commissions or provides. That duty includes ensuring that any employee who comes into contact with children presents no risk of harm. Section 11 of the Children Act 2004 places a statutory duty on NHS bodies, amongst others, to make arrangements to safeguard and promote the welfare of children. Statutory guidance was first issued in 2005 and revised guidance was published in April 2007. The NHS bodies that are covered by this statutory duty include Strategic Health Authorities, NHS Trusts, NHS Foundation Trusts and Primary Care Trusts.

5. As part of its overriding duty to protect the welfare of children the Respondent has to ensure that staff coming into contact with children present no risk in themselves to the children who are referred to services operated or commissioned by the Respondent. It is averred that this overriding duty is such that the Respondent must also consider any potential risk to service users and act accordingly.

6. As stated above the Claimant was employed by the Respondent as a Health Visitor. In that role she regularly came into contact with vulnerable children. In February 2016 it was brought to the Respondent's attention that a Child Protection Section 47 investigation had been undertaken by Social Services together with a police investigation in respect of the Claimant's two children. Both children were put on the Child Protection Register and placed in foster care.

7. Although the police subsequently confirmed that no further action would be taken against the Claimant, they made a notation with the Criminal Records Bureau ('CRB'). The Claimant's two children were returned to her care in due course.

8. Because of the Respondent's overriding duty subject to the Children Act 2004 and also the Children Act 1989 ('The welfare, safety and health of children must always be paramount'), the Respondent considered it imperative to initiate an investigation into the Claimant's conduct and professional suitability to be in contact with children. The investigation was undertaken by Dr Francis, Consultant Paediatrician. The Claimant was invited by letter dated 4 June to a disciplinary hearing.

9. The disciplinary hearing took place on 2 July and the Claimant was notified of the outcome by letter dated 10 July. The panel concluded that the Claimant was unable to continue in her role as a Health Visitor due to its overriding duty to protect clients, and the potential risk of continuing to employ a health visitor with a CRB notation for physical and emotional abuse outweighed arguments to continue to employ her in that role. Equally the Respondent did not consider it suitable to continue to employ the Claimant as a Registered General Nurse within the Adult Service, and as such the

Claimant's contract as a health visitor with the Respondent would terminate three months from 2 July. The Respondent offered to re-deploy the Claimant into an administrative post.

10.   The Claimant appealed the decision of the disciplinary panel by letter dated 17 July. An appeal hearing took place on 7 September. The appeal panel upheld the decision of the disciplinary panel and the Claimant was notified of that decision by letter dated 10 September.

11.   The Human Resources Manager subsequently had a telephone conversation with the Claimant and discussed vacant posts within the Respondent. The posts included a clerical officer post and a post as a personal assistant. It was left for the Claimant to express an interest in either post but the Claimant failed to do so. The Claimant would certainly have been appointed to the clerical officer position if she had confirmed she wanted that post.

12.   In all the circumstances the Respondent maintains that the dismissal was fair. The Respondent denies that the Claimant was unfairly dismissed as alleged and denies that the Claimant is entitled to the relief sought or at all.

Advocate & Co
Solicitor for the Respondent
19 October 2018

IN THE GUILDSHIRE EMPLOYMENT TRIBUNAL   CASE NUMBER: 1234/2018

BETWEEN

MRS JANE MINNERY   Claimant

- and -

GUILDSHIRE PRIMARY CARE TRUST   Respondent

CASE MANAGEMENT ORDER

Employment Tribunal Rules of Procedure 2013 Rule 29

TO ALL PARTIES

Employment Judge Hazel has made the following Orders on his own initiative. Under Rule 29 any party affected by the Order may apply to have it varied or revoked. Such an application must be made in writing to this office before the date ordered for compliance and must include reasons for the application. All parties are required by Rule 30(2) to provide all other parties in writing with the information set out in that Rule.

ORDERS

1. **DISCLOSURE OF DOCUMENTS:**

   On or before **29th November 2018** each party shall send to the other a list of the documents in their possession or control relevant to the claims and to the grounds of resistance. Additionally, the Claimant shall send to the Respondent a 'schedule of loss', ie a written statement of what is claimed, including a breakdown of the sums concerned showing how they are calculated; and the Claimant's list of documents should include any documents relevant to the schedule of loss.

2. **INSPECTION OF DOCUMENTS:**

   If either party requests a copy of any document on the other party's list, that other party shall provide a clear photocopy within 14 days of the request. Alternatively, that other party shall allow the requesting party on reasonable notice and at a reasonable time to inspect the original documents on the list and to make photocopies of them. That inspection shall take place where the documents are normally situated, but the parties may agree that inspection shall take place at some other convenient location. The provision of copies in compliance with this order shall entitle the supplying party to reimbursement of reasonable copying expenses, but not to delay or withhold provision of the copies pending such reimbursement.

3. **BUNDLE OF DOCUMENTS:**

   For the Hearing, the parties shall agree a bundle of documents limited to those which are relevant to the determination by the Tribunal of the issues in the case. Because it appears likely that the Respondent has most of the original documents, the Respondent shall create the bundle unless the parties specifically agree otherwise. On or before **20th December 2018** the Claimant shall notify the Respondent of the relevant documents to be included on behalf of the Claimant. On or before **8th January 2019** the Respondent shall provide to the Claimant a clear, indexed, paginated copy of the bundle, assembled in chronological order (save in respect of formal policies or procedures, which may be placed together) and containing all the relevant documents which any party wishes to be included. The Respondent shall also bring 4 copies to the Hearing (3 for the Tribunal and one for any witness).

4.   **WITNESS STATEMENTS:**

Not later than **7 days** before the hearing the parties shall exchange written witness statements (including one from a party who intends to give evidence). The witness statement should set out all of the evidence of the relevant facts which that witness intends to put before the Tribunal. If it is intended to refer to any document, the witness statement should refer to page/s in the agreed bundle. A failure to comply with this order may result in a witness not being permitted to give evidence because it has not been disclosed in a witness statement; or in an adjournment of the hearing and an appropriate order for costs caused by such adjournment. Each party shall bring 4 copies of any such witness statement to the hearing. The Claimant's statement should contain evidence relevant to the schedule of loss.

5.   **HEARING TIME:**

The case will be listed for a **3 days** hearing on the Chairman's estimate of the time required for it. That estimate is intended to include the time needed for considering the oral and written evidence; each party's closing statements; the consideration and delivery of the judgment of the Tribunal; and consideration and judgment on remedy, if arising. The Tribunal will require the case to be completed within the time allocated to it and the parties must now consider the question, whether that time is adequate. If you consider that the hearing may require a time longer than that which has been set aside for it, you must write to the Tribunal as soon as possible, giving your own estimate of the time required, with reasons, and with an indication of the extent of the witnesses and documents which constitute the evidence in the case.

Notes:

(1)   Any person who without reasonable excuse fail to comply with an order to which s 7(4) of the Employment Tribunals Act 1996 applies shall be liable on summary conviction to a fine of £1,000.00.

(2)   Under Rule 6, if this order is not complied with, the Tribunal may take such action as it considers fair and just which may include (a) waiving or varying the requirement; (b) striking out the claim or response, in whole or part, in accordance with Rule 37; (c) barring or restricting a party's participation in the proceedings; and/or (d) awarding costs under Rules 74–84.

(3)   You may apply under Rule 29 for this order to be varied, suspended or set aside.

IN THE GUILDSHIRE EMPLOYMENT TRIBUNAL   CASE NUMBER: 1234/2018

BETWEEN

MRS JANE MINNERY   Claimant

- and -

GUILDSHIRE PRIMARY CARE TRUST   Respondent

WITNESS STATEMENT OF
DR MIKE FRANCIS

I, Dr Mike Francis MAKE OATH AND SAY as follows:

1. I am employed as a Consultant Paediatrician by Guildshire Primary Care Trust. The statements made within this witness statement are based upon facts within my own knowledge, save where I have indicated the source of my information or belief. Where matters are not directly within my knowledge, I believe them to be true.

2. I was appointed as the Designated Doctor for Child Protection for Guildshire in 1999 and continue to hold that post. I have worked in the speciality of paediatrics for 24 years, and I have had a significant experience managing cases where child abuse is suspected. In the last 13 years as Consultant Paediatrician and Designated Doctor for Child Protection, I have led the service strategically in the field of safeguarding children. I provide advice and supervision to clinicians, social workers and other professionals, and also to senior management within the health organisations locally.

3. I make this statement in support of the Respondent in respect of the claim that has been commenced by the Claimant in the Employment Tribunal alleging unfair dismissal.

4. I was asked by the Head of Children's Services for the Respondent to undertake an investigation surrounding allegations of physical abuse that had been made about the Claimant by her children. I wrote to the Claimant on 23 March 2016 informing her of my role and explaining that as part of my investigation I would be obtaining information about the allegations from Guildshire County Council Social Services and the section 47 investigation that had been completed. (A section 47 investigation requires the Local Authority to make enquiries when a child is suspected to be suffering, or likely to suffer, significant harm, in order to enable the Local Authority to decide whether it should take any action to safeguard and promote the welfare of the child.) I told the Claimant that as part of the investigation I would need to interview the relevant people concerned, which included herself, and I would write to her in due course to arrange a date for that interview. I told her she would be able to be accompanied by a trade union representative, work colleague or friend at the interview. I gave her my contact details so that she could contact me if she had any queries. (p52 Hearing Bundle)

5. I arranged to meet the Claimant on 19 April, but she cancelled that appointment two days beforehand (p55) and we eventually met on 30 April. The Claimant was accompanied at the meeting by her representative from the Royal College of Nursing, and notes were taken by my personal assistant.

6. At the start of the meeting I again confirmed that I had been asked to conduct an investigation by the Respondent and explained the reasons for the investigation, ie that it had been alleged that the Claimant had physically abused her children. I told her that I would prepare a report following our meeting which would be sent to her prior to being finalised, and at that point she would be asked to sign a copy of the final version.

7. The Claimant told me that after qualifying as a health visitor she was offered a substantive post as a health visitor with the Respondent. She said that her caseload was heavy, but she received support from the senior health visitors with whom she worked and also her manager and supervisor.

8. I explored with the Claimant the allegations and what had happened afterwards. She told me that she understood that the allegations had to be investigated but said that she felt what she had told the social worker had been misconstrued. One of the allegations that had been made was that she had hit her children with a belt. The Claimant told me that she had been asked by the social worker if she had ever hit her children with a belt but she said that the children were only ever smacked on their bottoms with the hand. She did concede that in the culture she came from, using a belt as a means of punishment was acceptable, but she said that through her health visitor training she had realised that was not the way forward. She was concerned that the report prepared by social services incorrectly conveyed what had been discussed and what she had said at the child protection conference when she and her partner had been interviewed by the Senior Practitioner, Child Protection Investigation Team, although she did accept that she had been given an opportunity to check the report and correct any inaccuracies. I took it that she had objected to the report, but she confirmed that the comments she had been concerned about were still in the report, so I presume that the social worker felt that the report was an accurate reflection of what had been discussed.

9. The Claimant also told me that she did not consider that the allegations about abuse, and the fact that her children had been taken into care, would affect her work as a health visitor. She told me that the children with whom she came into contact through her work were her priority, and she assessed each case on the evidence and merits, and not according to her personal beliefs or cultural background. The notes of my meeting with the Claimant are at page 68.

10. Also as part on my investigation I interviewed the Claimant's immediate line manager (p66); the social worker who conducted the investigation into the abuse allegations (p71); and I also reviewed the Child Protection Conference report (p80) prepared by the social worker; and liaised with Guildshire Police (p86).

11. When I interviewed the social worker on 19 April, she confirmed that she had not had any contact with the Claimant's family prior to the allegations, although one of her colleagues had been involved previously. She explained that the Claimant had acknowledged hitting her children with her hand and had in the past hit the elder daughter with a belt, but there had been no physical signs of abuse on either of the children, although the elder daughter had told her school that she was afraid to go home as she might be beaten. This had been mentioned to teachers at the school on a number of occasions but it was the first time that social services had been involved, and the referral by the school was prompted by the elder daughter alleging, on 26 January, that the Claimant had grabbed her around the neck and shaken her several times. Whilst the social worker confirmed that the elder daughter had subsequently stated that the smacking by hand and belt at home had stopped, she did not say that it had never happened; and the social worker felt that the daughter was intelligent and articulate, and had been reliable and consistent in the accounts that she had given.

12. The social worker told me that the Claimant had said that she (the Claimant) had been treated in the same manner at home when she was a child, ie hit with a belt, and that such chastisement was culturally acceptable. She said that the Claimant told her that following her health visitor training, she realised that type of behaviour was wrong, although the social worker suspected that it was possible that the abuse had continued after that point in time. Although the Claimant, when she was interviewed during the child protection conference on 8 February, confirmed that she had smacked both children in the past and had used a belt on the hands of the elder child, and appeared to have taken responsibility for her actions, that acknowledgement and acceptance for that type of punishment was subsequently retracted by the Claimant. However, when the Claimant's children were interviewed on 26 April, the social worker was told that the smacking by belt and hand had stopped, which would suggest to me that at some point in time in the past the Claimant had used a belt to punish her children.

13.   As a result of the initial Child Protection Conference, it was recommended that the Claimant and her partner should attend meetings and parenting courses, to which they agreed. The fact that the Claimant had two jobs also probably contributed to the stress that the Claimant was under, and would not have helped with the Claimant's attempts to cope with her children at home. I was told that the next review was due on 26 April (p87), but at the time of our meeting the children remained on the Child Protection Register, although there were no active concerns about their welfare at that time. I explained to the council's social worker that my concerns were around the Claimant's ability to care for her children without using physical violence or emotional pressure. I also had some concerns about the advice that she would give to clients, and whether she could properly decide when a referral was necessary if there were child protection concerns.

14.   I met the claimant's line manager on 2 May. She confirmed that she first met the Claimant when the Claimant was training to be a health visitor, and she became her line manager in August 2010. She told me that although she did not monitor the Claimant's work each day, when the Claimant was sick her cases were allocated to other health visitors who did not discover any issues with the management of her cases. She found the Claimant to be hard-working and reliable.

15.   Her line manager confirmed that health visitors worked independently and effectively managed themselves, but they could contact their line managers if there were problems, specifically with child protection issues. I asked her to explain how the Claimant could be monitored or supervised if she came back into practice. She was unable to explain how such monitoring would take place as it was not something that had happened before. I explained that I had concerns about the Claimant's attitude towards Social Services which could perhaps affect her willingness to report appropriate child protection issues.

16.   In addition to interviewing the above-named witnesses, I also carefully studied the initial Child Protection Conference report (p80), which was appendix 7 of my report. The report confirmed that following the allegations made on 26 January, the Claimant's two daughters were made subjects of a Police Protection Order and placed in local authority care. On 29 January the Claimant and her partner agreed to the children remaining in foster care, and then proposed that the children should be placed with family members rather than remaining in foster care, which happened on 6 February. The report noted that both the Claimant and her partner had admitted physically chastising their children, which included smacking the children's bottoms with their hands and hitting the elder child on the hand with a belt, but later commented that it was not illegal to chastise children reasonably.

17.   The report noted that both the Claimant and her partner agreed to sign a parental agreement, by which they agreed not to use any form of physical chastisement at any time against their children in the family home. In addition, the Claimant and her partner accepted that disciplining their children by the use of physical chastisement was not acceptable and could not continue.

18.   The report also noted that although the Claimant and her partner had admitted using a belt to chastise their elder daughter, that admission was retracted to some extent later by the Claimant, as it was reported that, according to her, there had been a misunderstanding in relation to the use of the belt and she had not used it for two years to punish her elder daughter.

19.   The report recommended that the children should be placed on the Child Protection Register under the category of Physical Abuse, and whilst it was proposed that the children should be returned to the family home on a gradual basis, they should be closely monitored by professionals to ensure their safety, and the Claimant and her partner were to attend a parenting course, amongst other requirements.

20.   I also contacted Guildshire Police to determine if any formal charges had been made against the Claimant and her partner, and I was informed that they had not been cautioned

and there was insufficient evidence to proceed with a criminal prosecution. I was told, however, that the incident would show up on a CRB check, but whether or not the information was released would depend upon the nature of the job for which the Claimant applied (p54). I was also subsequently informed by the social worker that the children had been removed from the Child Protection Register as they were no longer considered to be at risk of harm, and the Claimant and her partner had agreed to cooperate with the Child Protection Plan, and the children were classified as Children in Need (p87).

21.   In the light of the evidence that I had gathered, the witnesses I had interviewed, including the Claimant, and the report from the Initial Child Protection Conference, I had to decide whether or not I considered the Claimant presented a risk to clients, and children in particular, if she was allowed to resume her job as a health visitor. I felt that the Claimant was not able to accept responsibility for her actions in relation to her children, and continued to deny that she had done anything wrong when I interviewed her. The Claimant was of the view that as her children had been returned to her then that was evidence that there had not been any abuse and that nothing wrong had occurred. I could not see any degree of reflection about the events that had happened, which is what I would have expected, and especially from somebody working as a health visitor.

22.   Although the Claimant's children had been returned to her, this did not mean that there was no risk, or no continuing risk, or that there had not been any abuse. I must explain that child protection issues are based on the balance of probabilities. Initially the balance of probabilities in this case was that the children had either been significantly harmed, or were at risk of significant harm. Subsequently, when the children's names were removed from the register, it was felt that the risks were not as high as previously because of the work that had gone into the case.

23.   Upon concluding my investigation I had to consider whether or not I could recommend that the Claimant should be allowed to return to her job as a health visitor, albeit with supervision, or if I should recommend that she could not work with vulnerable clients, particularly children. I felt that the Claimant would need extensive supervision, and I came to the conclusion that as health visitors by the nature of the job work on their own a lot, it would have been difficult to be entirely confident that the Claimant did not pose a risk to children, either through failing to identify a risk or by condoning practices that she might have considered to be acceptable. I came to the conclusion that this was too high a risk to accept. The Children Act 2004 (p162) places a statutory obligation to promote and safeguard the welfare of children. Not only did I believe that to have allowed the Claimant to return to her position as a health visitor would have put that duty in jeopardy, but fundamentally I believe that my duty, and that of the Respondent, is to try to address the imbalances that exist when children are involved. The overriding duty of the Respondent, and its employees, is to protect and safeguard the welfare of children generally, and especially those considered to be at risk. It was my professional opinion that to return the Claimant to her role as a health visitor would have meant that the Respondent would not have been fulfilling its obligations and duty to protect the welfare of children, and as such I had to recommend that the Claimant should be dismissed from her position as a health visitor.

24.   I prepared a Management Statement of Case (p90) for the hearing, and on the basis of the risks I had assessed as to allowing the Claimant to continue to work as a health visitor, I recommended that she should be dismissed from that post. I presented the Management Case at the hearing on 2 July. I had no further involvement with the matter after that date save for my involvement as a witness for the Respondent in respect of the claim brought by the Claimant in the Employment Tribunal.

I confirm that the contents of this my witness statement are true.

Signed:

Date:

Judgment of the Employment Tribunal

The unanimous decision of the Tribunal is that the Claimant's dismissal was for some other substantial reason and was fair and reasonable in the circumstances.

REASONS

1. The Claimant brought a claim of unfair dismissal against the Respondent. The Respondent resisted her complaint.

EVIDENCE

2. The Tribunal had before it an agreed bundle of documents. The Tribunal had witness statements from the Claimant on her own behalf; and from Dr Francis, Consultant Paediatrician, Mr Y, Group Manager Children's Services and Z, Director of Adult and Children Services; all on behalf of the Respondent.

ISSUES

3. The tribunal had to determine the following issues:
   (a) the reason for the Claimant's dismissal
   (b) whether the reason fell within one of the permitted reasons under s 98(2) ERA 1996, and if so;
   (c) whether the Respondent had conducted a reasonable investigation on which to base its beliefs with regard to the Claimant;
   (d) whether it was reasonable in all the circumstances for the Respondent to treat it as a sufficient reason for dismissing the Claimant.

FINDINGS OF FACT [see the facts at pp 278–281 above]

LAW

4. The tribunal needs to consider the reason for the Claimant's dismissal and whether that reason is one that is proved by the employer; as the burden is on the employer to show the reason for the dismissal and that it is a reason falling under sub-section (2) of section 98 ERA 1996 or some other substantial reason of a kind such as to justify the dismissal of an employee holding the position which the employee did.

5. It is the Respondent's case that they dismissed for SOSR.

6. In order to prove that the dismissal has been for SOSR, the Respondent would need to prove that it is a substantial reason and thus not frivolous or trivial.

7. If the tribunal decides that the reason for dismissal is proven by the employer and that it is one of the reasons set out in section 98(2) ERA 1996, then the tribunal needs to decide if it was fair and reasonable in all the circumstances. The tribunal has to decide whether taking into account all the relevant circumstances, including the size and administrative resources of the employer's undertaking and the substantial merits of the case, the employer has acted reasonably treating that reason as a sufficient reason for dismissing the employee. In determining this, the tribunal has to be mindful not to substitute its views for that of the employer.

8. The tribunal is also aware of the Police Act and the Home Office Circular 5/2005 entitled 'Criminal Records Bureau: Local checks by police forces for the purpose of enhanced disclosure'.

APPLYING THE LAW TO THE FACTS:

Was the dismissal unfair?

9. In our judgment Dr Francis' investigation was thorough and fair. In conducting his investigation Dr Francis interviewed the Claimant after interviewing most of the

witnesses. The brief that he was given by the Respondent was properly focused in that he was not concerned with the details of what occurred between the Claimant's daughter and herself so much as with the Claimant's reaction to what had happened and her perspective on it, given the nature of her duties as a health visitor. After Dr Francis saw the Claimant he met her line manager who was supportive of the Claimant and stated that in her opinion the Claimant had been hard-working, reliable as a colleague and flexible whenever cover was required in managing their caseload.

10. The line manager confirmed that health visitors work independently, self-supervising on the whole, and that they would be monitored only if there were issues of concern.

11. When Dr Francis met the Claimant he asked her wide-ranging questions which allowed her the opportunity to give her version of the incident, and also to discuss broadly how the incident might affect her practice and influence her thinking or how she would work to ensure it did not do.

12. In our view Dr Francis was correct not to reinvestigate the child's allegations. As the Claimant's employer the Respondent's only interest in the situation would be how what has occurred in the Claimant's private life affects her ability to do her job. In order to do so, it was able to rely on the findings and judgment of the police and social services after their investigation into the child's allegations.

13. The social services and the police had decided that the children needed to be placed on the Register, even for a short period of time. Also, that although the children were returned to the family eventually, work needed to be done with both parents around parenting issues thrown up by the incident, and this occurred over a number of weeks from the date of the incident.

14. Lastly, the Respondent was aware from information provided by the police that there would be a notation on any Criminal Records Bureau disclosure that was obtained in respect of the Claimant in relation to working with children or vulnerable adults.

15. From those circumstances it was quite right for the Respondent to accept the fact that the Claimant had behaved in such a way toward her daughter that it warranted a CRB notation, even if there had been no conviction at the magistrates' court.

16. The disciplinary hearing was a hearing in which the Respondent balanced the risks involved in continuing to employ the Claimant (who it was aware, and which was noted in the minutes, had a good record prior to this incident and who would now have a CRB notation if a search were made); and the risks posed to the children in need within its catchment area, being the need to protect the safety of children, the risk to children and the risk to the PCT. The Respondent is entitled to weigh up those risks.

17. It was noted that if the Claimant was a new applicant for a job as a health visitor, with a CRB notation for physical and emotional abuse of her own children she would not have been employed. The difference is that the Claimant is an existing employee with a previous unblemished record. As she was a longstanding employee, it was the Respondent's duty to treat the Claimant fairly and reasonably, and to consider in the light of her previous employment with the Respondent whether or not that outweighed the risks.

18. In our judgment the Respondent was also entitled to take into consideration some of the inconsistencies in the evidence which was given by the Claimant to the Respondent in interviews and at the hearing. The Claimant stated that she used to condone chastisement with a belt, but that she stopped doing so when she undertook health visitor training and learnt this was not a suitable way to discipline her children. However, the Claimant became a qualified health visitor three years before the incident but she stated that she stopped using the belt against her children only two years prior to the incident. That would mean she continued to use the belt even after she completed her training, and therefore challenges her earlier statement.

19. The Claimant also stated during the course of the internal proceedings that she no longer believed that physical chastisement of children was appropriate. However, in her answer to Dr Francis at the investigatory interview, she stated that she would not impose her own values on her work and that each case was to be judged on its own merit and not on her beliefs. This would tend to suggest that she continues to believe that that method of discipline is still appropriate but that she is endeavouring to keep those beliefs to herself. There is a significant difference between the two positions.

20. In presenting her case to the Respondent at the disciplinary and appeal hearing and at the tribunal Hearing, the Claimant appeared to be suggesting that the fact that there was no evidence of abuse, that there had been no conviction at the magistrates' court, and that the children were returned to her and removed from the at risk register, meant that the Respondent should not have considered that anything significant had occurred but should instead consider that everything had, in effect, 'gone back to normal'. This would suggest to the Respondent that the Claimant did not appreciate that the fact that this had occurred at all would give the Respondent cause for concern.

21. The Respondent is therefore, in the tribunal's judgment, correct in its judgment that it could not have any confidence that the Claimant's personal opinions had in fact changed with regard to the correct methods for disciplining children. Instead it appears that the Claimant was going to keep her personal feelings to herself, which is different and less reliable.

22. The Respondent's real concern was that if the Claimant did not consider that whatever was happening with a particular child was wrong or was inappropriate, she was unlikely even to be aware that she had condoned it, and would not have flagged it up for advice from anyone.

23. When questioned about how she saw issues in her personal life affecting her work, the Claimant's answer was that there were policies and procedures that dealt with those issues. This answer demonstrated that she was not aware of a potential conflict between her apparent beliefs and the duties of the job.

24. The Respondent weighed up its duty towards the Claimant and the risks involved in continuing to employ her. The risks outweighed any duty towards her as a longstanding employee with no previous disciplinary record and a good work record, and this is why the decision was made to dismiss her.

25. It is therefore our judgment that the decision to dismiss was for some other substantial reason and that it was reasonable in all the circumstances that it should be considered as an appropriate reason for dismissing the Claimant.

26. The Respondent not only took into account the CRB notation but also took into consideration the Claimant's attitude to the existence of the notation, the investigation by social services and the police, and the effect of the whole incident on her practice. The claimant showed that she had failed to analyse the situation in a way which showed she appreciated the risks that faced the Respondent.

27. The Respondent was not weighing up the risk that the Claimant might abuse children; this was not the issue. The issue was that she might observe something in her work that should give her cause for concern and cause her to report the family to the authorities, but that she would not do so because she would not consider what she had observed as wrong or worrying. There were concerns that if she harboured personal views that physical chastisement of children with a belt or a hand was actually acceptable in her 'culture' or otherwise, she would not take up the issue with the family or her employers, as appropriate, and as required by the Respondent in satisfaction of its duties to protect children in its care.

28. The Claimant's job required her to work independently. The Respondent therefore had to be reassured that she would be able to perform her duties professionally and without any personal issues clouding matters. And even though the Claimant states that she

would not allow them to do so, the possibility that she might still hold those beliefs reasonably gave the Respondent cause for concern.

29. The Respondent is an independent organisation and is entitled to come to its own decision based on the facts. The Respondent's decision to dismiss that Claimant for some other substantial reason was fair and reasonable in the circumstances, and although it was unfortunate, considering the Claimant's unblemished work record up until that date, it was not unfair.

Signed

....

Employment Judge

Judgment sent to the Parties on

....

and entered on the Register

....

For Secretary of the Tribunals

6.9   FURTHER READING

Lewis, *Employment Law: an adviser's handbook*, 12th revised edn (LAG, 2017).

Cunningham and Reed, *Employment Tribunal Claims – Tactics and Precedents*, 4th edn revised (LAG, Dec 2013).

Harvey, *Industrial Relations and Employment Law* (Butterworths), Div PI.

Blackstone's Employment Law Practice, 10th edn (OUP, 2019).

Barnett, Cooper and Palka, *Costs in Employment Tribunals*, 2nd edn (Jordans, 2014)

SUMMARY

A wide range of different statutory claims may be brought by presenting a complaint to an employment tribunal (**6.2**). In most instances these claims must be brought by employees, but some claims by workers may also be dealt with (**1.3** and **6.2**). There are a number of different time-limits within which claims to tribunals must be submitted, depending upon the nature of the complaint. Care needs to be taken with these rules as the time-limits are relatively short (in most cases three months) and enforced strictly (**6.3**). For example, an unfair dismissal claim must normally be presented within three months starting with the effective date of termination (EDT – see **3.5.2**), or within such further period as the tribunal considers reasonable where it was not reasonably practicable for the complaint to be presented within three months (ERA 1996, s 111). The EDT for these purposes is the basic EDT defined by ERA 1996, s 97.

Since May 2014, claimants must make an early notification to Acas, to see whether the claim can be resolved through conciliation. If a settlement is not possible, a certificate will be issued, which is needed before a claim can be lodged at a tribunal. See **6.2.2**.

The practice and procedure of employment tribunals is governed by Rules set out in Sch 1 to the Employment Tribunals (Constitution and Rules of Procedure) Regulations 2013. These cover such matters as the form and substance of the claim form (ET1) and the response (ET3), case management, ancillary applications for information or documents, preliminary hearings and costs (**6.4**).

Many employment tribunal claims are settled without a hearing. Settlements, to be binding, may be negotiated either through an Acas conciliation officer or via a compromise agreement (**6.5**).

There are options other than bringing tribunal proceedings, including using ADR, the Acas statutory scheme and judicial mediation (**6.6**).

A dismissed employee may have more than one potential claim against an employer, eg unfair dismissal, wrongful dismissal and a redundancy payment claim. However, as a general rule an employee cannot be compensated twice for the same financial loss (**6.7**).

The following practical steps should be taken when bringing a claim:

- Consider whether to bring the claim in the tribunal or in a civil court (see **Chapter 1**).
- Check that the tribunal has jurisdiction. There is a list of all the tribunal jurisdictions at <http://www.employmenttribunals.gov.uk/FormsGuidance/jurisdictionList.htm>.

- Check time-limits. For example, for unfair dismissal, a claim must be received by the tribunal within three months starting with the EDT (or within such further period as the tribunal considers reasonable in all the circumstances: ERA 1996, s 111). In discrimination cases or complaints relating to non-payment of wages or holiday pay, the three-month period begins when the matter complained about happened. This may mean that time can start running in some cases before termination of employment. There are special rules for equal pay and redundancy payment claims.

- Notify Acas for Early Conciliation. Obtain a certificate.

- Submit the claim on the approved ET1 form and ensure all required information is provided.

- If the claim is posted (it is also possible to send it using a downloadable pdf via the employment tribunals website), the postcode for the place where the employee normally worked should be used to identify the correct tribunal office address to use. If the employee has never worked for the respondent, identify the correct tribunal office postal address by using the postcode for the place where the matter being complained about happened. There is a list on the employment tribunal website which indicates the correct tribunal office: <http://www. employmenttribunals.gov. uk/Documents/HearingCentres/Postcodelist_1st April2010.pdf>.

- Once the tribunal office has received and accepted the claim, it will give it a case number. If the claim is accepted, the tribunal office will send a letter to confirm this, together with a booklet about what the next steps are. At the same time, the tribunal office will send the respondent a copy of the claim form together with a form [ET3] for its response. In most cases, the tribunal office will also send a copy of the claim to Acas. The forms and guidance notes are available on the employment tribunal website.

- If the claim is not accepted, the tribunal office will return the form with a letter explaining the reason why the claim has not been accepted and what action needs to be taken. In these cases it will be very important to ensure that the form is resubmitted within the time limits.

- The response form and guidance notes are available on the employment tribunal website. If a response is not on the approved form, is not received within the specified time limit, or does not contain: (i) the employer's full name and address; (ii) whether the employer wants to defend all or part of the claim; and (iii) the grounds on which the claim is being defended, it will not be accepted.

- If the response is not accepted, it will be returned by the tribunal office. In these cases it will be very important to ensure that the form is resubmitted within the time-limits.

- If the response is accepted, a copy will be sent to the claimant.

- If no proper response is received within 28 days, the tribunal judge shall decide whether, on the material available (including further information requested), a determination can be made; and if so, judgment will be issued. Otherwise a hearing will be fixed. The respondent will be entitled to participate in a hearing only to the extent permitted by a judge, unless and until an extension of time is granted.

- A respondent should consider whether it wishes to make a counterclaim. Any such counterclaim must be made within six weeks of receiving the copy of the claim from the tribunal office. If a counterclaim is being made, the tribunal office can be asked to send the appropriate form.

- Once the claim and response have been received and accepted, the parties need to consider whether there are any issues they want to be dealt with or any orders which should be made before the claim should proceed further. The tribunal may give directions or orders on a variety of matters (see **6.4.6**), including further information, documents and witnesses. If a party decides that it needs more information or documents from the other party, it should first ask for these to be provided voluntarily by writing to the other party, giving a reasonable time limit for responding. If matters do not get resolved voluntarily, a party should write to the tribunal and ask the tribunal to issue an order.

- The final hearing will determine whether the claim succeeds or fails (ie on liability) and, if it succeeds, what remedy is appropriate. A full hearing will normally be conducted by an Employment Judge sitting alone, unless the case involves a claim of discrimination, in which case there will also be two non-legal members.

- A preliminary hearing (see **6.4.8.1**) can be held to determine jurisdictional issues, for example: (i) whether the claim or response should be struck out; (ii) questions of entitlement to bring or defend a claim; (iii) if either side's case appears weak, whether a deposit needs to be paid and, if so, how much, before that side can go ahead. This type of hearing is normally held in public before an Employment Judge sitting alone, but may also be held over the phone.

- In a straightforward case, the tribunal will issue, of its own motion, a short set of directions to help the parties prepare for the substantive hearing. In a more complex case, the tribunal may hold a preliminary hearing to deal with any outstanding matters. It may be held over the phone or in person. It is normally held in private. A preliminary hearing will normally seek to: (i) clarify the issues in the case; (ii) decide what orders should be made about matters such as documents and witnesses; and (iii) decide the time and length of the main hearing. The time and length of the main hearing will be given automatically in the standard directions.

- The length of time allocated to a case includes time for: (i) the substantive hearing on liability; (ii) any issues or evidence on remedy; and (iii) the tribunal to deliberate and deliver a judgment. Hearing dates are postponed only where there is a good reason and/or it is in the interests of justice to postpone a hearing.

- All or part of a claim (or responses) may be withdrawn at any time before or during the hearing, by telling the tribunal and the other parties in writing. Withdrawals should be done as soon as possible.

- If a case settles before the hearing, the parties should let the tribunal office know as soon as possible.

- Prior to the hearing it will be necessary for the parties to prepare and agree between them a bundle of documents for use at the hearing (see **6.4.8.7**). This is usually done by the respondent. It will also be necessary for the parties to have prepared witness statements for their witnesses and to have provided copies of these in advance in accordance with any case management directions to the other party. Signed copies must be brought to the tribunal.

- See **6.4.9** for the conduct of the main hearing, **6.4.11** for the rules on costs, and **6.4.12** and **6.4.13** for reconsiderations and appeals.

TRANSFER OF UNDERTAKINGS

LEARNING OUTCOMES

After reading this chapter you will be able to:

- explain when the Transfer of Undertakings (Protection of Employment) Regulations 2006 (as amended) apply
- identify what constitutes a 'relevant transfer'
- list and understand the *Spijkers* factors
- understand the effect of a 'relevant transfer' and who is covered by it
- describe the implications of dismissals connected to a transfer
- explain the impact of a transfer on an employer's ability to vary the terms of a contract of employment
- be aware of the requirements to inform and consult under the Regulations.

7.1 INTRODUCTION

In this chapter, we consider the protection afforded to employees by the Transfer of Undertakings (Protection of Employment) Regulations 2006 (SI 2006/246) ('the 2006 Regulations'), which replaced the 1981 Regulations (SI 1981/1794), and the new Collective Redundancies and Transfer of Undertakings (Protection of Employment) (Amendment) Regulations 2014 (SI 2014/16) ('the 2014 Amendment Regulations'), which came into force in January 2014.

The BIS Guide, *Employment Rights on the Transfer of an Undertaking* (July 2009), as amended to take account of the 2014 Amendment Regulations – available at <https://www.gov.uk/government/uploads/system/uploads/attachment_data/file/275252/bis-14-502-employment-rights-on-the-transfer-of-an-undertaking.pdf> – summarises the effect of the Regulations as follows:

> Broadly speaking, the effect of the Regulations is to preserve the continuity of employment and terms and conditions of any employees who are transferred to a new employer when a relevant transfer takes place. This means that employees employed by the previous employer (the 'transferor') when the transfer takes effect automatically become employees of the new employer (the 'transferee') on the same terms and conditions (except for certain occupational pensions rights). It is as if their contracts of employment had originally been made with the transferee employer. However, the Regulations provide some limited opportunity for the transferee or transferor to vary the terms and conditions of

employment contracts in a range of stipulated circumstances, even though the sole or principal reason for the variation is the transfer.

… The Regulations can apply regardless of the size of the transferred business: so the Regulations equally apply to the transfer of a large business with thousands of employees or of a very small one (such as a shop, pub or garage). The Regulations also apply equally to public or private sector undertakings and whether or not the business operates for gain, such as a charity.'

The 2006 Regulations were introduced to comply with various EC Directives concerning the transfers of undertakings. The main Directives are:

(a)   the Acquired Rights Directive (77/187/EC);

(b)   the Acquired Rights Directive (98/50/EC);

(c)   the Acquired Rights Amendment Directive (2001/23/EC).

As part of the Government's plans to deregulate business, in January 2013 it issued a consultation on reforming the 2006 Regulations. In November 2013, it published draft Regulations to implement a number of proposed amendments. These (the 2014 Amendment Regulations) became effective in January 2014. They include:

*   changes to the definition of 'entailing changes in the workforce' to include a change in location (see **7.5.3**)

*   amendments which are meant to make it easier for an employer to change employees' terms and conditions (see **7.6**).

Most of the changes introduced by the 2014 Amendment Regulations apply to transfers on or after 31 January 2014, although readers should be aware that there were some (albeit limited) transitional provisions that are beyond the scope of this work.

At common law in the UK, the transfer of an undertaking by one employer to another automatically terminates the employee's contract of employment, ie there is a dismissal. In this situation the reason for the dismissal will generally be redundancy (as the employer's requirement for employees to do work of a particular kind has ceased or diminished). Should the undertaking's new owner require the employee's services, he will offer a new contract of employment, and can do so on whatever terms he likes. Depending on the timing of the dismissal, the employee may still retain continuity in this situation (see ERA 1996, s 218(2) and *Clark & Tokely Ltd (t/a Spellbrook Ltd) v Oakes* [1998] 4 All ER 353). The 2006 Regulations altered the legal position by providing that where there is a 'relevant transfer', there will not be any automatic termination of the contract of employment. There will not be a dismissal simply because there is a transfer. In that situation, the employee will transfer with the undertaking and will be employed by the new owner under his original contract. If there are any dismissals, whether actual or constructive, and whether before or after the transfer, if those dismissals are connected with the transfer, they will be automatically unfair unless, effectively, there is a genuine redundancy situation (see **7.5** below).

7.2   WHEN DO THE 2006 REGULATIONS APPLY?

7.2.1   Applicability

The 2006 Regulations contain a number of exclusions and limitations. The most important ones are as follows:

(a)   There must be a transfer from one person to another; consequently, there must be a change in the employer, not merely in the ownership. The 2006 Regulations do not, therefore, apply to share sale transfers or where a purchaser buys a majority shareholding in a company, thereby gaining control. This is because there is no change in the identity of the employer. (See *Brookes and Others v Borough Care Services and CLS Care Services Ltd* [1998] IRLR 636, EAT, for confirmation of this principle.) A transfer which is caught by the Regulations can occur alongside or after a share sale (see, for example,

Millam v The Print Factory (London) 1991 Ltd [2007] IRLR 526 and *Jackson Lloyd Ltd and Mears Group plc v Smith and Others* (UKEAT/0127/13)).

The ECJ in *Allen and Others v Amalgamated Construction* (Case C-234/98) [2000] IRLR 119 ruled that the then applicable 1981 Regulations were capable of applying to transfers between two companies belonging to the same group, or where one subsidiary subcontracts work to another, provided the transfer involves the transfer of an 'economic entity' (see **7.2.2**). By way of guidance, the Regulations have been found to apply to mergers, sale of part of a going concern, changes of franchisee, sale of a sole trader's business or partnership. The Regulations do not apply to transfers of assets only. (See *Jackson Lloyd Ltd and Mears Group plc v Smith and Others* (UKEAT/0127/13).) For example, on insolvency the receiver may break up the business and sell off its assets to various buyers, the plant to one buyer and the premises to another.

Only a transfer of an undertaking or a service provision change (see **7.2.2**) will be covered by the 2006 Regulations.

(b)   The EAT, in *Holis Metal Industries v GMB* [2008] IRLR 187, confirmed that the Regulations can apply where the ownership of a company is transferred to a company operating outside the EU.

(c)   There are special provisions regarding insolvency (regs 8 and 9) which are beyond the scope of this book, but where there are bankruptcy or insolvency proceedings (but not administration proceedings – see *Key2Law (Surrey) LLP v De'Antiquis* [2011] EWCA Civ 1567), contracts of employment will not be transferred automatically.

(d)   Regulation 4 (automatic transfer of contract of employment together with all rights and liabilities (see **7.3.1** and **7.4**)) does not apply to rights under or in connection with an occupational pension scheme (reg 10). For this purpose, any provisions of an occupational scheme which do not relate to benefits for old age, invalidity or survivors are treated as not being part of the pension scheme, with the result that these benefits will be transferred. Some pension protection is now afforded to employees transferred by virtue of the Pensions Act 2004 (see **7.4.1.3**).

(e)   Regulation 4 (above) also does not transfer any liability of any person to be prosecuted for, convicted of and sentenced for any criminal offence. So, for example, if the transferor is liable to be prosecuted for breach of the HSWA 1974, that liability cannot pass to the transferee on the transfer of a business (reg 4(6)).

(f)   Regulation 7 (dismissals connected to the transfer are automatically unfair unless economic, etc reason (see **7.5**)) applies only to employees who satisfy the usual qualifying conditions for unfair dismissal protection (see **Chapter 3**), for example two years' continuous employment (see **7.5**).

(g)   The 2006 Regulations apply to England, Wales, Scotland and Northern Ireland; the 2014 Regulations do not apply to Northern Ireland.

(h)   Whether the 2006 Regulations apply to 'workers' (as opposed to employees) is not clear. The IWGB is supporting a claim alleging that a worker's contract transferred to CitySprint under the Regulations.

7.2.2 A relevant transfer – reg 3

The 2006 Regulations apply only to what are known as 'relevant transfers', which may occur in a wide range of situations. There are two broad categories of relevant transfers: business transfers (reg 3(1)(a)); and service provision changes (reg 3(1)(b)). Some transfers will comprise both a business transfer and a service provision change. The two definitions are not mutually exclusive – as long as one definition is satisfied, it does not matter if the other one is not.

We shall look at both types of relevant transfer in more detail below.

Regulation 3 also endeavours to clear up some areas where there had previously been uncertainty. It makes clear that the 2006 Regulations:

(a)   apply to public and private undertakings engaged in economic activities, whether or not they are operating for gain;

(b)   can apply to a transfer or service provision change howsoever effected, notwithstanding:

    (i)   that the transfer of an undertaking, business or part of an undertaking or business situated in the UK pre-transfer is governed or effected by the law of a country or territory outside the United Kingdom, or that the service provision change is governed or effected by the law of a country or territory outside Great Britain;

    (ii)   that the employment of persons employed in the undertaking, business or part transferred, or, in the case of a service provision change, persons employed in the organised grouping of employees, is governed by any such law.

As far as a business transfer is concerned (see **7.2.2.1** below), the 2006 Regulations apply so long as the undertaking itself (comprising, amongst other things, premises, assets, fixtures and fittings, and goodwill as well as employees) is situated in the UK; and so far as a service provision change is concerned, provided there is an organised grouping of employees situated in the UK immediately before the service provision change (therefore if an employee is part of team but works abroad, that should not prevent the Regulations from applying; but if the whole team worked abroad, that would fall outside the definition);

(c)   apply to a transfer of an undertaking, business or part of an undertaking or business (which may also be a service provision change) where persons employed in the undertaking, business or part transferred ordinarily work outside the UK, provided, of course, that the undertaking itself is situated in the UK immediately before the transfer;

(d)   do *not* apply to an administrative reorganisation of public administrative authorities or the transfer of administrative functions between public administrative authorities (reg 3(5)). For a recent case on what constitutes the exercise of public authority (as well as reviewing existing European and UK case law on whether there is an economic activity), see *Nicholls v London Borough of Croydon* (UKEAT/0003/18 and 0004/18). (Note: many such transfers are in fact covered by similar protection under other statutes, eg the Local Government Act 2003 applies in relation to the reorganisation of service provision within local government. See the Cabinet Office Statement of Practice, 'Staff Transfers in the Public Service' for more details.)

Regulation 3 also provides that:

(e)   a relevant transfer may be effected by a series of two or more transactions;

(f)   a relevant transfer may take place whether or not any property is transferred to the transferee by the transferor.

7.2.2.1   Business transfers

Under reg 3(1)(a), a business transfer is 'a transfer of an undertaking, business or part of an undertaking or business situated immediately before the transfer in the United Kingdom to another person where there is a transfer of an economic entity which retains its identity'. Regulation 3(2) defines 'economic entity' as 'an organised grouping of resources which has the objective of pursuing an economic activity, whether or not that activity is central or ancillary'. The expression 'organised grouping of resources' is derived from *Suzen v Zehnacker Gebaudereinigung GmbH Krankenhausservice* [1997] IRLR 255.

At the heart of this definition is the principle that to qualify as a business transfer, the identity of the employer must change. This is why the Regulations do not apply to transfers by share takeover because, when a company's shares are sold to new shareholders, there is no transfer of a business or undertaking – the same company continues to be the employer.

The key ECJ case outlining the general tests to be applied in determining whether there is a business transfer is *Spijkers v Gebroeders Benedik Abattoir CV* [1986] ECR 1119, ECJ. In *Spijkers*, the transferor owned and ran a slaughterhouse. The business came to an end, whereupon the premises, certain goods and all employees bar Mr Spijkers were transferred to the transferee. It was held that the fact that there was a break in time between the old business ceasing and the new one starting, and the lack of a transfer of goodwill, did not prevent the application of the Acquired Rights Directive. The Court said:

> It appears from the general structure of Directive 77/187 and the wording of Article 1(1) that the Directive aims to ensure the continuity of existing employment relationships in the framework of an economic entity irrespective of a change of owner. It follows that the decisive criterion for establishing the existence of a transfer within the meaning of the Directive is whether the entity in question retains its identity.

> Consequently, it cannot be said that there is a transfer of an enterprise business or part of a business on the sole ground that its assets have been sold. On the contrary, in a case like the present, it is necessary to determine whether what has been sold is an economic entity which is still in existence, and this will be apparent from the fact that its operation is actually being continued or has been taken over by the new employer, with the same economic or similar activities.

> To decide whether these conditions are fulfilled it is necessary to take account of all the factual circumstances of the transaction in question, including the type of undertaking or business in question, the transfer or otherwise of tangible assets such as buildings and stocks, the value of intangible assets at the date of transfer, whether the majority of the staff [in terms of numbers or skills] are being taken over by the new employer, the transfer or otherwise of the circle of customers and the degree of similarity between activities before and after the transfer and the duration of any interruption in those activities. It should be made clear, however, that each of these factors is only a part of the overall assessment which is required and therefore they cannot be examined independently of each other.

So, from *Spijkers* and later ECJ decisions, we may state that the decisive criterion for establishing the existence of a transfer within the meaning of the Directive is whether the entity in question retains its identity after the transfer. The key question is whether there is a transfer of an economic entity that retains its identity.

In *Holis Metal Industries Ltd v GMB* (see **7.2.1**), the EAT held that the 2006 Regulations might apply to a transfer from the UK to a non-UK country; the test is the same – is there an economic entity and has it transferred?

Is there an economic entity?

Regulation 3(2) defines 'economic entity' as 'an organised grouping of resources which has the objective of pursuing an economic activity, whether or not that activity is central or ancillary'. The reference to 'economic' appears to suggest that the 'undertaking' being transferred does need to have some sort of cost centre.

The BIS Guide says that 'the economic entity test ... means the Regulations apply where there is an identifiable set of resources (which includes employees) ... and that set of resources retains its identity after the transfer'.

The definition applies to the transfer not just of an undertaking but also of part of an undertaking. An illustration is *Fairhurst Ward Abbotts Limited v Botes Building Limited* [2004] IRLR 304, where an operation was split into two geographical units when it was re-tendered, and it was held that there were transfers to each of the two successful new contractors.

Even though it pre-dates the 2006 Regulations, the domestic authority that gives the best general guidance on whether there has been a business transfer is *Cheesman v R Brewer Contracts*

[2001] IRLR 144 (approved by the Court of Appeal in *Balfour Beatty Power Networks Ltd v Wilcox* [2007] IRLR 63).

In *Cheesman*, when looking at the question whether there was an undertaking, the EAT said that:

(a)   there needs to be found an economic entity, which is stable and discrete and whose activity is not limited to performing one specific works contract, an organised grouping of wage earners and assets enabling the exercise of an economic activity;

(b)   the entity must be sufficiently structured and autonomous but will not necessarily have significant assets;

(c)   in certain sectors the entity can essentially be based on manpower;

(d)   the identity of the entity emerges from factors such as its workforce, management staff, the way work is organised and operating methods.

In *Fairhurst Ward Abbotts Ltd* (above), the Court of Appeal confirmed that there is no requirement that the part of an undertaking transferred is itself a separate economic entity in the hands of the transferor; it is enough if part of a larger stable economic entity is identified for the first time as a separate economic entity on the occasion of the transfer separating a part from the whole.

This is therefore essentially a factual exercise. Once it has been determined that an entity exists, it is then necessary to ask 'Has that entity transferred?'

Has that entity transferred?

The *Spijkers* factors (see above) are particularly pertinent here. The decisive criterion established by *Spijkers* is whether 'the entity in question retains its identity'. This may be ascertained by looking at whether its operations are continued or resumed after the transfer. *Spijkers* laid down seven factors that tribunals should consider:

(a)   the type of undertaking or business;

(b)   the transfer or otherwise of tangible assets such as building, equipment and stocks;

(c)   the value of intangible assets at the date of transfer (eg goodwill);

(d)   whether the majority of the staff (in terms of numbers or skills) are being taken over by the new employer;

(e)   the transfer or otherwise of the circle of customers;

(f)   the degree of similarity between activities before and after the transfer;

(g)   the duration of any interruption in those activities.

The ECJ in *Spijkers* emphasised that all factors must be taken into account and that 'they cannot be examined independently of each other'.

The EAT confirmed in *Cheesman* (above) that where an economic entity can function without assets, the lack of assets transferred does not preclude a transfer; and where no staff are transferred, the reasons why may be relevant. (In *ECM (Vehicle Delivery Service) Ltd v Cox and Others* [1999] IRLR 559, the Court of Appeal held that the tribunal was entitled to have regard to the reasons why the employees were not taken on by the transferee – namely because it wished to avoid the (old) Regulations applying.)

The EAT overturned the decision of the tribunal that there was no transfer where the workforce of the transferor was not taken on. A tribunal should ask itself which, if any, of these factors are present. If the answer is all of (or in some cases several of) the above factors, it is generally going to be safe to assume that there has been a transfer of a stable economic entity.

The BIS Guidance suggests that 'resources' in reg 3(2) includes not only tangible and intangible assets but also employees. It is unclear how the reg 3(2) definition will work where only part of a large business is transferred, as it may be difficult to ascertain (particularly if resources are shared by different parts of the business) whether resources transferred were part of an 'organised grouping' capable of satisfying the reg 3 requirement. The Guidance states that in this situation the resources in question do not need to be used exclusively by the part of the business being transferred for the 2006 Regulations to apply.

For useful case law on the implications of the transferee not taking on former employees, see *RCO Support Services Ltd and Another v Unison and Others* [2002] ICR 751 and *Astle and Others v Cheshire County Council and Another* [2005] IRLR 12.

In *Camden Primary Care Trust and University College London v Skittrall and Others* (UKEAT/0078/05) (a contracting out case), UCL's degree level course in podiatry was taken over by the University of East London (UEL). The parties agreed that the Transfer Regulations applied. Six staff objected to the transfer and a tribunal was asked to make a preliminary determination as to whether there had been a relevant transfer. The tribunal said there had not, primarily because the economic entity had not retained its identity after the transfer as the course offered by UEL was a new, distinct course. The EAT said the tribunal had defined the economic entity too narrowly. If the economic entity was the UCL degree course in podiatry, there could never be a transfer unless UCL had successfully re-tendered for the contract tendered by Camden PCT. The differences that the tribunal found between the two courses were changes to the mode of delivery and location rather than changes to the actual *activity*. The EAT said that the course had retained its identity.

In *Jouini v Princess Personal Service GmbH* (PPS) [2007] IRLR 1005 a group of workers, comprising administrative staff and temporary staff who were transferred to a temporary work agency, was held to fall within the scope of the Directive. Dr John McMullen, Professor of Labour Law at Leeds University, has described the case as 'an excellent example of how the jurisprudence of the ECJ is built up in an incremental way from which the Court applies accrued principles to new situations'.

In *Klarenberg v Ferrotron Technologies GmbH* [2009] IRLR 301, the ECJ held that where a business was integrated into the transferee business to the extent that employees were integrated into different units, undertaking duties relating to the existing business, there was still a relevant transfer. There was no need for a transferee to retain the same organisational structure, as long as some functional link was maintained so that the transferee continued the same or a similar economic activity. A change in organisational structure did not prevent the Directive applying.

In *Wood v London Colney Parish Council* (UKEAT/0528/09), the EAT held that a temporary cessation in running a bar (caused by the loss of the premises licence) meant that the economic entity was suspended, but there was still a relevant transfer when the new owner later obtained his own licence. In *Colino Siguenza v Ayuntamiento de Valladolid* (Case C-472/16), the ECJ found that a five-month gap before the new contractor commenced its activities did not preclude there being a transfer. There was only a temporary suspension.

The High Court held in *Law Society v Secretary of State for Justice and Office for Legal Complaints* [2010] EWHC 352 (QB) that the cessation of the Law Society's complaints service and the start of a new complaints service was not a relevant transfer because none of the tangible or intangible assets transferred, nor did the existing caseload. In addition, the new provider was given wider powers.

See too *Ferreira da Silva e Brito and Ors v Estado Portugues* [2015] All ER (D) 47, where the ECJ held that there was a relevant transfer if a majority shareholder took over its subsidiary's activities after the subsidiary was wound up. The ECJ provides a useful summary of key principles in this case.

The EAT confirmed in *Hyde Housing Association and Ors v Layton* (UKEAT/0124/15) that there is not a relevant transfer in circumstances where an employee moves from an employment contract with one employer to one with several employers, including the original employer.

In *Ricardo v Portimão Urbis, EM, SA, in liquidation, Município de Portimão Emarp – Empresa Municipal de Águas e Resíduos de Portimão, EM, SA* (Case C-416/16), the CJEU examined whether a decision by a local Portuguese council to wind up its trading company and continue its activities by other means, was a transfer of an undertaking within the meaning of the Acquired Rights Directive (ARD).

The claimant, Mr Ricardo, was a director of the trading company, which had responsibility for all tourist matters, including street trading and cultural services. The Council decided to wind it up. At the time of the winding up, Mr Ricardo had been (at his request) on unpaid leave for three years. Some of the activities were taken over by the Council itself and the remainder of its activities were outsourced to another entity, Emarp (of which the Council was also the sole shareholder). There was an arrangement to transfer the staff to the Council and Emarp, but Mr Ricardo was not included in those plans. He was informed that his employment would end on the final closure of the trading company. He therefore brought a claim on the basis that there had been a transfer of an undertaking.

Where a transfer relates to public authorities, it is necessary to examine whether there is a transfer of an economic entity (ie of an undertaking engaged in economic activities) or an administrative reorganisation of public administrative authorities or the transfer of administrative functions between public administrative authorities. The first of these is a transfer of an undertaking. The latter two are not. In the *Portimão Urbis* case, the CJEU looked at these distinctions:

> The Court has made clear in that regard that the notion of economic activity encompasses any activity consisting in offering goods or services on a given market. Activities which fall within the exercise of public powers are excluded as a matter of principle from classification as economic activity. However, services which are carried out in the public interest and without a profit motive and are in competition with those offered by operators who seek to make a profit may be classified as economic activities for the purposes of [the ARD].

In this case, the Court considered that the various activities engaged in by the Council did not fall within the exercise of public powers, and were capable of being classified as economic activities for the purposes of the ARD:

> It is necessary in this regard to consider all the facts characterising the transaction at issue in the main proceedings, including, in particular, the type of undertaking or business in question, whether or not its tangible assets, such as buildings and movable property, are transferred, the value of its intangible assets at the time of the transfer, whether or not the majority of its employees are taken over by the new employer, whether or not its customers are transferred, the degree of similarity between the activities carried on before and after the transfer, and the period, if any, for which those activities were suspended. However, all those circumstances are merely single factors in the overall assessment which must be made and cannot therefore be considered in isolation.

Ultimately this will be a matter for national courts to decide.

7.2.2.2   Service provision changes

Background

As noted earlier, the most typical situation where the 2006 Regulations apply is the sale of a business as a going concern. Regulation 3(1)(b) was included in the 2006 Regulations in order to reduce the previous uncertainty which had existed in the 1981 Regulations about whether changes in service provision contracting would be captured by the Regulations or not.

Since the early 1980s, one of the developing trends within the public and private sector has been to externalise service functions, such as cleaning, catering, maintenance and IT systems, support and development. In this way, a particular organisation can concentrate its efforts on the core business, leaving ancillary services to those better equipped and qualified to provide them. Further, it allows businesses to deal more effectively with fluctuating demand for support services. Such externalisation has often involved contracting out, a process where the ancillary function which the organisation no longer wishes to manage is awarded, by contract, to another organisation. Contracting out is one of the most common 'atypical' transfer situations.

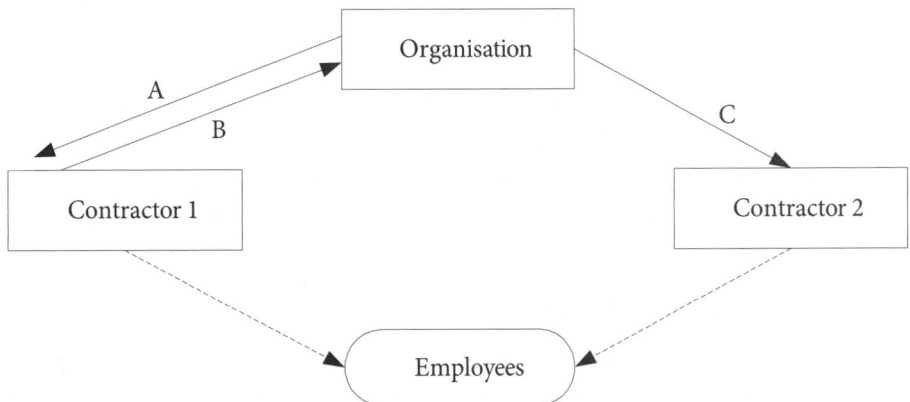

'First generation' contracting out occurs where the organisation awards a contract for some ancillary function to contractor 1 (arrow A). 'Second (third, fourth, etc) generation' contracting out occurs where an organisation ends a contract with one contractor (arrow B), and awards it to another (arrow C). Here, there is no contract between contractor 1 and contractor 2. The Regulations were, eventually, held to be capable of applying to all these scenarios.

When determining whether a business had retained its identity before and after the transfer, the courts focused on the nature of the activity rather than on the nature of the business. For example, on the contracting out of a canteen, the courts focused on whether *a* canteen existed after the transfer, rather than on whether *the* canteen (ie substantially the same business as before) existed after the transfer. In this way, it was not easy to see circumstances in which contracting out would fall outside the scope of the Acquired Rights Directive, and hence the Regulations, because where an organisation contracts out services, by definition, those activities will be continued or resumed by the (new) contractor.

In *Suzen v Zehnacker Gebaudereinigung GmbH Krankenhausservice* [1997] IRLR 255, the ECJ held that the Directive did not apply to the dismissal of a cleaner. Mrs Suzen was employed by Zehnacker as a cleaner at secondary church-run school, whose premises Zehnacker had contracted to clean. Mrs Suzen was dismissed along with seven other cleaners at the school when Zehnacker lost the contract. She claimed that the dismissal was automatically unfair, relying upon the Acquired Rights Directive.

The ECJ determined that the Directive did not apply to a change of contractor if there was no accompanying transfer from one undertaking to another of significant tangible or intangible assets, or taking over by the new employer of a major part of the workforce, in terms of their numbers and/or skills, assigned by the transferor to the performance of the contract:

> The decisive criterion for establishing the existence of a transfer within the meaning of the Directive is whether the entity in question retains its identity, as indicated inter alia by the fact that its operation is actually continued or resumed ...
>
> For the Directive to be applicable, however, the transfer must relate to a stable economic entity whose activity is not limited to performing one specific works contract. The term entity thus refers to an organised grouping of persons and assets facilitating the exercise of an economic activity which pursues a specified objective ... the fact that the service provided by the old and new awardees of a

contract is similar does not therefore support the conclusion that an economic entity has been transferred. An entity cannot be reduced to the activity entrusted to it ... the mere loss of a service contract to a competitor cannot therefore by itself indicate the existence of a transfer within the meaning of the Directive.

The ECJ felt able to come to this conclusion on the same authority as it had done in *Spijkers* (see **7.2.2.1**), namely, whether the entity in question retains its identity. This is because the factors to be taken into account in determining whether the entity in question retains its identity are varied and may be applied by the courts at their discretion. In *Suzen*, the decisive criterion applied was whether there was an accompanying transfer from one undertaking to another of significant tangible or intangible assets or taking over by the new employer of a major part of the workforce (in terms of numbers or skills), ie *Suzen* sets a minimum precondition in these situations.

The 2006 Regulations aim to clear up most, if not all, of the previous uncertainties by including an express provision that the 2006 Regulations will apply to a 'service provision change'.

Service provision changes

Regulation 3(1)(b) states that a service provision change may exist in any one of three possible situations, provided that certain specified conditions are satisfied. The three situations are:

(a) *activities cease to be carried out by a person ('a client') on his own behalf and are carried out instead by another person on the client's behalf ('a contractor')* – outsourcing or contracting out (ie client to contractor) (reg 3(1)(b)(i));

(b) *activities cease to be carried out by a contractor on a client's behalf (whether or not those activities had previously been carried out by the client on his own behalf) and are carried out instead by another person ('a subsequent contractor') on the client's behalf* – second generation contracting (ie contractor to contractor) (reg 3(1)(b)(ii)); or

(c) *activities cease to be carried out by a contractor [or sub-contractor] or a subsequent contractor on a client's behalf (whether or not those activities had previously been carried out by the client on his own behalf) and are carried out instead by the client on his own behalf* – insourcing or contracting back in-house (ie contractor to client) (reg 3(1)(b)(iii)).

Note: The 2014 Amendment Regulations inserted a new reg 3(2A) into the 2006 Regulations, which reads:

> References in paragraph (1)(b) to activities being carried out instead by another person are to activities which are fundamentally the same as the activities carried out previously.

While this is mainly cosmetic, in that it reflects existing case law (see, eg, *Metropolitan Resources Ltd v Churchill Dulwich Ltd* [2009] IRLR 700, below), it is intended to assist in the definition of 'activities' in reg 3(1)(b) by making it clear that the activities pre- and post-change must be fundamentally or essentially the same.

The EAT confirmed in *Arch Initiatives v Greater Manchester West Mental Health NHS Foundation* (EAT/ 0267/15) that a service provision change does not require the whole of the service carried out by the transferor to transfer (see analysis below).

The preconditions which must be satisfied (reg 3(3)) are that:

(a) immediately before the service provision change:
   (i) there is an organised grouping of employees situated in Great Britain which has as its principal purpose the carrying out of the activities concerned on behalf of the client,
   (ii) the client intends that the activities will, following the service provision change, be carried out by the transferee other than in connection with a single specific event or task of short-term duration; and

(b)   the activities concerned do not consist wholly or mainly of the supply of goods for the client's use. If there is a mixture, the service element will need to be predominant. (See *Pannu and Others v Geo W King (in liquidation) and Others* (UKEAT/0021/11) for a case in which the EAT upheld a decision that this exclusion applied.)

The wording of reg 3(3)(a) does not therefore cover transactions where there is no identifiable group of employees dedicated to meeting one client's needs.

Analysis

A service provision change will occur when a client who engages a contractor to do work on its behalf is either:

(a)   reassigning such a contract; or

(b)   bringing the work 'in-house'.

In *CT Plus (Yorkshire) CIC v Black and Others* (UKEAT/0035/16), the appellant ran a 'park-and-ride' service under a contract with the local council. The second respondent decided to run a commercial service on the same route, using its own staff and buses, without a subsidy from the Council. As a result, the Council (the first respondent) terminated its contract with the appellant. The appellant contended that the second respondent was a subsequent contractor carrying out the same activities 'on the client's behalf', the Council being the client. The Employment Judge found that the second respondent was not carrying out the activities on the 'client's' (the local council's) behalf, but as a commercial venture on its own behalf. The EAT agreed. 'Client' means an organisation that is in a position to carry out activities either itself or by commissioning them from others to carry out those activities on its behalf. The Council had not commissioned the second respondent's services.

Note that reg 2 provides that 'contractor' includes subcontractors. It has nonetheless been a matter of some contention as to whether the 2006 Regulations protect the interests of subcontractors in the event of a service provision change. In *Jinks v London Borough of Havering* (UKEAT/0157/14), the EAT had to consider the interpretation of the word 'client'. Havering Council had contracted with a third party (S) to operate an ice rink and car park. S subcontracted the running of the car park to another company (R). The subcontract ended when the Council transferred the car park to a local NHS Trust. The question arose whether there was a relevant transfer of the running of the car park operation to the Council, so that R's staff, including the claimant, who wanted to bring an unfair dismissal claim, transferred to the Council's employment. The employment tribunal found that the Council was the client of S, not R, and that there was no service provision change as the client must be the same both before and after the transfer. As there was no contractual relationship between the Council and R, the activities could not be 'carried on behalf of the client'. The EAT disagreed and adopted a wider interpretation of 'client'. It said that the question that should be asked was: On whose behalf was the car park being run? The identification of the 'client' is a question of fact, not law, and the EAT said that there can be more than one client in any given case. A strict legal or contractual relationship was not essential. Regulation 3(1)(b)(iii) must be read with reg 2: R was in reality carrying out activities 'on behalf' of the Council. The case was remitted to the employment tribunal to reconsider. In *Ottino Property Services Ltd v Duncan* (UKEAT/0321/14), the EAT also confirmed that the references to 'a client' and 'the client' in reg 3(1)(b) not only applied to a single client, but could also apply where there was a change in the provision of activities carried out on behalf of a group of clients. There are two provisos to this: (i) the identity of the clients must remain the same before and after the service provision change (see *McCarrick v Hunter* [2013] IRLR 26); and (ii) the clients must be able to demonstrate (reg 3(3)(a)(ii)) a common intention.

It will *not* be a service provision change if:

(a)   the contract is wholly or mainly for the supply of goods for the client's use (eg client engages a contractor to supply sandwiches and drinks to its canteen every day to sell on to staff) (see *Pannu* (above)); or

(b)   the activities are carried out in connection with a single specific event or a task of short-term duration. This suggests that where something is a 'one-off' job it will not be covered by the 2006 Regulations. There is a lack of clarity in the drafting of this exception. This wording may be read in one of two ways: either the exclusion applies to an activity (an 'event' or 'task') that is a one-off job *and* is of short duration, or it applies where the service activity in question is either a single specific event *or* a task of short-term duration.

The BIS Guidance supports the former interpretation, giving as an example two hypothetical contracts covering security for the Olympic Games. The first contract concerns the provision of security advice to the event organisers and covers a period of several years running up to the event. The second contract concerns hiring staff to protect athletes during the Games themselves. Both contracts are one-off in the sense that they relate to the holding of a specific event. The first contract runs for a significantly longer period than the second and would be covered by the Regulations, but the second would not.

This issue was considered by the EAT in *Liddell's Coaches v Cook* (UKEATS/0025/12), with the EAT disagreeing with the BIS Guidance: the phrase, it said, must be considered disjunctively. A single specific event did not need to be of short-term duration. The EAT looked at this again in *Swanbridge Hire & Sales Ltd v Butler & Others* (UKEAT/0056/13). The EAT held, disagreeing with *Lidell*, that the phrase 'short term' qualifies single events as well as tasks. Slade J's decision in *Swanbridge* is supported by the President of the EAT and should, for the moment, be preferred to that in *Lidell* (see *SNR Denton UK LLP v Kirwan & Others* (UKEAT/0158/12)).

Swanbridge was applied by the EAT in *Horizon Security Services Ltd v Ndeze and the PCS Group* (UKEAT/0071/14). In *Horizon*, PCS had been engaged to provide security services for Workplace Plc, which was looking after a business centre on a site owned by the London Borough of Waltham Forest. Waltham Forest's contract with Workplace plc was terminated and Waltham Forest engaged a new security company (Horizon) directly to look after the site for a limited period of eight to nine months, pending demolition of the buildings on the site for the purpose of building a new supermarket. Employees working for PCS, who were not kept on, brought claims of unfair dismissal, arguing there was a service provision change and that they should have been taken on by Horizon. The EAT held that as PCS worked for Workspace and Horizon for Waltham Forest, which was a different legal entity, there was no continuity of client and the employees were not entitled to transfer. The question of intention needed to be looked at immediately before the purported change. Further, tasks rather than activities should be the focus: in *Horizon*, to determine whether the period of eight to nine months was short-term, looking at the current and past task could be relevant. The case would have been remitted back to the employment tribunal to determine whether it was short-term, had the appeal on the first ground not succeeded. In *Robert Sage Ltd t/a Prestige Nursing Care Ltd v O'Connell and Others* (UKEAT/0336/13), the EAT upheld a tribunal decision that 'a hope and wish' that something would be short-term was not sufficient at the point of change to amount to 'an intention';

(c)   the client is not the same client. In *McCarrick v Hunter* [2013] IRLR 26, the Court of Appeal upheld the EAT's decision that there cannot be a service provision change in circumstances in which the client changes as well as the service provider: the client must be the same throughout. This was the first case in which the Court of Appeal considered the definition of a service provision change in reg 3(1)(b). (See also *SNR*

Denton UK LLP v Kirwan & Others [2012] IRLR 966 for a similar analysis and *Horizon* (above).)

Note: These are exceptions to reg 3(1)(b). Regulation 3(1)(a) may still apply in such situations, facts permitting.

Under reg 3(3)(a)(i), for there to be a service provision change, there does not have to be an 'economic entity' before the alleged transfer, so long as there is an organised grouping of employees and the other tests above are met. The term 'organised grouping of employees' is probably best summarised by the word 'team' (but note it is also stated that a single employee can satisfy the test – reg 2(1)). The EAT held in *Argyll Coastal Services Ltd v Mr I Stirling and Others* (UKEATS/0012/11) that the phrase 'organised grouping of employees' 'connotes a number of employees ... organised for the purpose of carrying out activities ... who work as a team'. Further, it does not matter whether the new contractor takes on any of the old contractor's employees; the transferee cannot now seek to argue that the 2006 Regulations do not apply because he did not take on any employees. So long as the same activities are carried out for the client before and after the transfer, there is a transfer.

The EAT gave helpful guidance on the concept of an 'organised grouping of employees' in *Eddie Stobart Ltd v Moreman* [2012] IRLR 356:

> The paradigm of an 'organised grouping' is indeed the case where employees are organised as 'the [Client A] team', though no doubt the definition could in principle be satisfied in cases where the identification is less specific .

Most recently, in *Amaryllis v McLeod* (EAT/0273/15) the EAT, referring to the *Moreman* case, said that what must be focused on was what the grouping of employees were doing immediately before the transfer, and not what happened historically. It is not enough that a department carries out significant work for a client – as the EAT said in Moreman, 'the regulation does not merely say that employees should in their day-to-day work in fact (principally) carry out the activities in question; it says that carrying out those activities should be the (principal) purpose of an "organised grouping to which they belong".'

Where the grouping comes about by virtue of 'coincidences of working patterns', that is unlikely to be enough – there needs to be an element of planning and deliberate organisation (see *Ceva Freight*, below).

The BIS Guidance offers the following analysis:

> This is intended to confine the Regulations' coverage to cases where the old service provider (ie the transferor) has in place a team of employees to carry out the service activities, and that team is essentially dedicated to carrying out the activities that are to transfer (though they do not need to work exclusively on those activities but carrying them out for the client does need to be their principal purpose). It would therefore exclude cases where there was no identifiable grouping of employees or where it just happens in practice that a group of employees works mostly for a particular client. This is because it would be unclear which employees should transfer in the event of a change of contractor, if there was no such grouping. For example, if a contractor was engaged by a client to provide, say, a courier service, but the collections and deliveries were carried out each day by various different couriers on an ad hoc basis, rather than by an identifiable team of employees, there would be no 'service provision change' and the Regulations would not apply. It should be noted that a 'grouping of employees' can constitute just one person as may happen when the cleaning of small business premises is undertaken by a single person employed by a contractor.

In one of the first cases to consider the new law, the tribunal held in *Hunt v Storm Communications Ltd and Others* (ET/2702546/06) that there was a service provision change when the client terminated its contract with Storm and awarded a new contract to a different agency. The claimant was employed by Storm as an account manager who spent about 70% of her time working on one client's account. The tribunal held that there was a 'service provision change'; the claimant was an 'organised grouping of employees' whose principal purpose was to provide services to the client, and the same activity was carried on when the new agency took over the account previously managed by Storm. See also *Rynda (UK) Ltd v Rhijnsburger* [2015] EWCA Civ 75, where the Court of Appeal held that a single employee was an 'organised grouping'. The Court identified a four-stage process for tribunals to follow in a service provision change case:

- Identify the service the transferor (the outgoing employer) was providing to the client.
- List the activities the staff of the transferor performed in order to provide that service.
- Identify the employee(s) of the transferor who ordinarily carried out those activities.
- Consider whether the transferor organised the employee(s) who were leaving into a 'grouping' for the principal purpose of carrying out the listed activities.

In *Kimberley Group Housing Ltd v Hambley* [2008] IRLR 682, the EAT gave some guidance on applying the provisions. First, the tribunal should identify the activities the current supplier has ceased to carry out. On the facts, the tribunal found that the activities were of providing suitable accommodation and related support services to asylum seekers in the towns concerned. The EAT did not interfere with this decision, but it did comment that 'care may need to be taken … in deciding what constitutes the relevant activities'. Secondly, it should ask whether an organised grouping of employees had as its *principal* purpose the carrying out of those particular activities for a client. The tribunal found that it did and the EAT agreed. The EAT stated that the word 'principal' qualifies the purpose and that '[a] distinction is to be drawn between a principal purpose and one which is merely ancillary'. Lastly, the tribunal should ascertain whether the new contractor(s) is/are engaged in the same activities as the old contractor. In this case they were, given the finding that the relevant activities were of providing suitable accommodation and related support services to asylum seekers in the towns concerned.

In *Clearsprings Management Ltd v Ankers and Others* (UKEAT/0054/08), the EAT confirmed that while under the 2006 Regulations one transferor could transfer the provision of a service to more than one transferee, there may be some circumstances in which, if the relevant activities are sufficiently split up and fragmented between a number of new contractors of the service, there is no service provision change. On the facts, the EAT agreed with the tribunal that because the allocation of asylum seekers showed no obvious pattern of re-allocation to the three incoming contractors, the activity carried on by Clearsprings, the outgoing contractor, was so fragmented that no relevant transfer took place within the meaning of reg 3 of the 2006 Regulations. More recently, in *London Care Ltd v Henry* (UKEAT/0219/17), the EAT held that it was important to identify what the pre-transfer activity was, when provision afterwards was allocated to multiple providers. If the work transferring to each of the new contractors was itself an 'activity', the activity would remain the same post-transfer. However, if the activity was the whole service then it would not be the same after the transfer. Where activities are randomly distributed among new contractors and are not easily identifiable as the activity carried out by the original contractor, it is unlikely that TUPE will apply.

In *Metropolitan Resources Ltd v Churchill Dulwich Ltd* [2009] IRLR 700, the EAT held that the question for tribunals is simply whether, on the facts, one of the three situations set out in reg 3(1)(b) exists and whether the conditions set out in reg 3(3) are satisfied, and that a commonsense and pragmatic approach is required. The tribunal should ask itself whether the activities carried on by the alleged transferee are fundamentally or essentially the same as those carried out by the alleged transferor. The answer to that question will be one of fact and degree, to be assessed by the tribunal on the evidence in the individual case before it. The pre-2006 case law is irrelevant for this purpose.

For an example of a case where it was held that a change of contractor did not fall within the 'service provision' definition because of a difference in activity before and after the change of contractor, see *OCS Group UK Ltd v Jones* (UKEAT/0038/09). The EAT refused to overturn the tribunal's decision that a canteen service that provided hot meals prepared by chefs was very different from a counter selling pre-prepared sandwiches, and that therefore the 2006 Regulations did not apply. That is a very narrow interpretation, in the authors' view.

In *Enterprise Management Services Ltd v Connect-Up Ltd and Others* (UKEAT/0462/10), the EAT set out a useful statement of the law:

(2)   The expression 'activities' is not defined in the Regulations. Thus the first task for the Employment Tribunal is to identify the relevant activities carried out by the original contractor: see *Kimberley*, para 28; *Metropolitan*, paras 29–30. That was the issue on appeal in *OCS*, where the Appellant's challenge to the activities identified by the Employment Tribunal failed.

(3)   The next (critical) question for present purposes will be whether the activities carried on by the subsequent contractor after the relevant date ... are fundamentally or essentially the same as those carried on by the original contractor. Minor differences may properly be disregarded. This is essentially a question of fact and degree for the Employment Tribunal (*Metropolitan*, para 30).

(4)   Cases may arise (eg [*Clearsprings*]) where the division of services after the relevant date, known as fragmentation, amongst a number of different contractors means that the case falls outside the service provision change regime, as explained in *Kimberley* (para 35).

(5)   Even where the activities remain essentially the same before and after the putative transfer date as performed by the original and subsequent contractors, [a service provision charge] will only take place if the following conditions are satisfied:

      (i)   there is an organised grouping of employees in Great Britain which has as its principal purpose the carrying out of the activities concerned on behalf of the client;

      (ii)   the client intends that the transferee post-service provision change will not carry out the activities in connection with a single event of short-term duration;

      (iii)   the activities are not wholly or mainly the supply of goods rather than services for the client's use. ...

(6)   Finally, by reg 4(1) the Employment Tribunal must decide whether each Claimant was assigned to the organised grouping of employees.

In *Nottinghamshire Healthcare NHS Trust v Hamshaw and Others* (UKEAT/0037/11), the EAT held that there was no relevant transfer in circumstances where a Healthcare NHS Trust which ran a care home shut the home and re-housed the residents into homes of their own. The residents' care was transferred to two new independent providers and the activities carried on by the new providers were 'materially different'. The clients were, in the judge's words, being moved from 'institution' to home; from 'management' to 'support'.

According to the EAT, there was neither a transfer of an economic entity retaining its identity under reg 3(1)(a) nor a service provision change under reg 3(1)(b). Under the new arrangements, former residents were to live in their own flats. The care provided was different. The economic entity had lost its identity. Nor was there a service provider change because the activity carried on by the new provider was not 'fundamentally or essentially' the same as the service provided before the change.

In *Anglo Beef Processors UK v Longland* (UKEATS/20025/15), the EAT stressed again the importance of taking a common sense and pragmatic approach to the meaning of the word 'activities'. The employment tribunal had examined the facts and concluded that 'there was really very little room for doubt that the activities carried out by [Anglo Beef] after the transfer were fundamentally the same as that carried out by [the predecessor company]'. The EAT saw no reason to overturn the tribunal's reasoning.

By analogy with *ECM v Cox* (above at **7.2.2.1**) it is possible that tribunals will be sceptical about deliberate fragmentation, which they may regard as an avoidance measure, but no such cases have emerged yet.

The statement of law set out in *Enterprise Management Services Ltd* (above) was endorsed in *Johnson Controls Ltd v Campbell and Another* (UKEAT/0042/12). The EAT added that the identification of 'activity' is critical in many cases and that tribunals must be careful to ensure that they do not take too narrow a view of that term. The EAT said that

> if for instance the activity performed by a given employee is after a service provision change to be performed by two or three employees in the transferee or, in a 3(1)(b)(iii) situation, by the client itself, then it may well be that the approach of the Tribunal should recognise that the same activity may well be carried on, though it is performed now by three people rather than by the one person who earlier performed it.

In *Ceva Freight (UK) Ltd v Seawell Ltd* [2013] CSIH 59, the Court of Session held that there was no service provision change when a client took back services previously carried out on its behalf by a contractor. Although one employee of the contractor spent all his time working for the client, it did not mean that he was an 'organised grouping of employees which has as its principal purpose the carrying out of the activities concerned on behalf of the client'. The employee was part of a team of employees who worked on 'outbound' services for the client and other clients, and did not have as its principal purpose the carrying out of activities to be done for Seawell.

In *Rynda (UK) Ltd v Rhijnsburger* [2015] EWCA Civ 75, the Court of Appeal upheld an employment tribunal decision that a single employee was an organised grouping that carried out the activity of management of a portfolio of commercial properties in The Netherlands. A deliberate decision had been taken by the transferor before the transfer, to organise the employee to work on these properties. See also *Robert Sage v O'Connell* (above), where the EAT overturned a tribunal's finding that an employee who was prohibited from working for a client, X (because he was suspended) was assigned to the group of employees working with X. The EAT held that as the employee was prohibited from working with the group of employees who were subject to the service provision change, that employee could not be said to be 'assigned' to that group.

In *Tees Esk & Wear Valleys NHS Foundation Trust v Harland* (UKEAT/0173/16) the EAT upheld the tribunal's conclusion that there was no service provision change for the purpose of reg 3(3). The claimants had been employed by the Trust as part of an organised grouping of employees put together to look after CE. Over time, CE had improved and his need for assistance had reduced from seven-to-one to one-to-one. The team put together by the Trust had nonetheless been retained, but the staff were required to look after other service users in the Trust's care, in the same location. That remained the position up to when the contract to provide care for CE was taken over by another provider. The tribunal found that the principal purpose of the grouping had been diluted such that it was no longer the provision of care to CE. There was, therefore, no service provision change for the purpose of reg 3(3).

In *London Care Ltd v Henry and Others* (EAT/0219/17 and 0220/17) the EAT confirms that fragmentation must be considered when deciding whether the activities taken on by the new contractors are essentially the same as those carried out by the previous contractor (see *Kimberley* above). Only then will it be possible to ascertain whether there is an organised grouping of employees with the principal purpose of carrying out the activities.

7.2.2.3 Cross-border transfers of undertakings

There has long been uncertainty about whether the Directive/Regulations apply in relation to the transfer of a UK-based business even if the purchaser is outside the European Union. This was looked at by the EC Commission, which reported on 18 June 2007. It did not reach a definitive conclusion! In *Holis Metal Industries Ltd v GMB & Newell Ltd* [2008] IRLR 187, the EAT said the UK Regulations could apply transnationally.

7.2.2.4 Time of transfer

Practically speaking, a transfer of an undertaking may extend over a period of time rather than being an event staged to take place for the purposes of the Acquired Rights Directive and the

2006 Regulations at any one particular moment in time. However, the legal requirement for certainty, so as to be able to identify, at the least, the date when a transfer took place, may conflict with practical realities. Sometimes the point of transfer is expressly pinpointed in sale documentation or otherwise agreed by the parties, but if it is not, tribunals have to identify as best they can when the actual transfer took place. The date of transfer may be important.

The ECJ considered the 'time' of transfer in *Celtec v Astley* (Case C-478/03) [2005] IRLR 647, where it had to decide whether a relevant transfer could be a gradual process occurring over a period of several years. The ECJ ruled that the use of the word 'date' (singular) in the Acquired Rights Directive, combined with the need for legal certainty, meant that the claimants in that case had to be able to point to a specific date on which they said the transfer occurred. A transfer *cannot* occur over a period of time (see paras 32–36). The ECJ went on to find:

> 29. … [T]he reference to 'date of a transfer' in [the Acquired Rights Directive] is designed to identify the workers who may rely on the protection established by that provision. That protection therefore covers workers assigned to the unit affected by the transfer whose contract of employment or employment relationship is in force on the 'date of a transfer' and not those who have ceased to be employed by the transferor on that date (see Case 19/83 *Wendelboe and Others* [1985] ECR 457, paragraphs 13 and 15) or those who were engaged by the transferee after that date (see *Ny Mølle Kro*, cited above, paragraphs 24 to 26).
>
> 30. Both the choice of the word 'date' and reasons of legal certainty indicate that, in the mind of the Community legislature, the workers entitled to benefit from the protection established by [the] Directive must be identified at a particular point in the transfer process and not in relation to the length of time over which that process extends.
>
> …
>
> 36. In those circumstances, the term 'date of a transfer' in [the Directive] must be understood as referring to the date on which responsibility as employer for carrying on the business of the unit in question moves from the transferor to the transferee.

In support of that interpretation, the Court observed, first, that the Acquired Rights Directive gives the Member States the option of providing that, after the date of transfer, the transferor is to be liable, alongside the transferee, for the obligations arising from a contract of employment or employment relationship. Such a rule implies that in any event those obligations are transferred to the transferee on the date of the transfer (*Rotsart de Hertaing v Benoidt SA and IGC Housing Service SA* (Case C-305/94) [1997] IRLR 127, para 23).

Lastly, the Court considered that to allow the transferor or transferee the possibility of choosing the date from which the contract of employment or employment relationship is transferred would amount to allowing employers to derogate, at least temporarily, from the provisions of the Directive, whereas those provisions are mandatory, and it is thus not possible to derogate from them in a manner unfavourable to employees (*Rotsart de Hertaing*, paras 17 and 25).

Having established that the Directive refers to a transfer taking place on a particular date, the ECJ went on to consider the issue of how that date was to be identified. The ECJ referred to Article 1(1) of the Acquired Rights Directive, which refers to the change in the legal or natural person responsible for carrying on the business and who continues or resumes the operation. The ECJ concluded that what was significant was to identify 'the date on which responsibility as employer for carrying on the business of the unit in question moves from the transferor to the transferee'.

Following the ECJ's ruling that a relevant transfer cannot take place over a period of time but only on a specific date, the House of Lords gave its opinion on the actual facts in *Celtec*. The House of Lords had to decide whether the date of the transfer was the date the employees were originally seconded. Their Lordships found that there was a deemed transfer of the claimants' contracts to the Training and Enterprise Council at the date of the original secondment, even though for three years the claimants thought they were civil service employees. This was when responsibility for carrying on the business had passed to the transferee.

The EAT followed *Celtec* in *Housing Maintenance Solutions Ltd v McAteer and others* (UKEAT/0440/ 13). That case concerned a contract for the repair and maintenance of housing association properties in Liverpool. The housing association terminated its contract with its existing contractor on 9 June 2011. Staff were made redundant and told that their contracts terminated on that date. The housing association began the process of setting up a subsidiary company, Housing Maintenance Solutions Ltd, to carry out the role. Housing Maintenance Solutions Ltd did not start operating until 1 July 2011. A number of employees brought claims for unfair dismissal, unpaid wages during the interval, and a failure to inform and consult. A key issue was the identity of the employer between 9 June and 1 July. The employment tribunal said the transfer took place on 9 June 2011 because that was the date that Housing Maintenance Solutions Ltd 'accepted responsibility for the claimants as employees'. The EAT disagreed and said that the date of transfer was the date when management responsibility for the employer's business transferred. The legal assumption of responsibility for the employees occurs on the date of transfer and not vice versa. The case was remitted to the employment tribunal to determine the date of the transfer.

In all cases, in determining when a relevant transfer takes place it will be essential to consider when responsibility for carrying on the business or service had transferred from one entity to another. In practice, if the transfer is a sale of a business and there is a gap between exchange of contracts and completion, it will be the date of completion which is the date of transfer for the purposes of reg 4.

7.3 EFFECT OF A RELEVANT TRANSFER

Once it has been established that a relevant transfer has occurred, it is necessary to consider what effect that has on the employment relationship.

7.3.1 Automatic transfer of contracts of employment

Regulation 4(1) of the 2006 Regulations provides:

> Except where objection is made under paragraph (7), a relevant transfer shall not operate so as to terminate the contract of employment of any person employed by the transferor and assigned to the organised grouping of resources or employees that is subject to the relevant transfer, which would otherwise be terminated by the transfer, but any such contract shall have effect after the transfer as if originally made between the person so employed and the transferee.

In other words, an employee's contract of employment does not end by reason of the transfer; instead the contract will be transferred from the old employer to the new on the existing terms and conditions, and with the employee's existing continuity of service (see *Jackson v Computershare Investment Services plc* [2008] IRLR 70). (Employees do, however, have the right to object to the transfer of their contracts (see **7.3.2.3**).) Note that the reference to employees is likely to include workers too (see reg 2(1)). Note too that where there is a pre-transfer dismissal, that dismissal is effective and contracts do not then transfer. Liability for the dismissal *may* transfer (see **7.3.2**).

In *G4S Justice Services (UK) Ltd v Anstey* [2006] IRLR 588, the EAT held that employees who had been dismissed for gross misconduct but who had an internal appeal pending at the date of a relevant transfer had their employment preserved only for the purpose of the appeal. If the appeal failed, the dismissal stood and the employees would not have been employed immediately before the transfer. If the appeal succeeded and the dismissal was set aside then it 'vanished', and the employees would be treated as if they were employed immediately before the transfer, so they continued in employment with the transferee.

Regulation 4(2) states that on the completion of a relevant transfer:

(a)   all the transferor's rights, powers, duties and liabilities under or in connection with any such contract shall be transferred by virtue of this regulation to the transferee; and

(b)   any act or omission before the transfer is completed, of or in relation to the transferor in respect of that contract or a person assigned to that organised grouping of resources or employees, shall be deemed to have been an act or omission of or in relation to the transferee.

The employees, in other words, have the same rights against the transferee as they had against the transferor and their continuity of employment is not affected by the transfer.

Regulation 8 sets out the position in respect of insolvent businesses. The detail is beyond the scope of this book.

7.3.2   Who is covered by reg 4(1)?

Regulation 4(3) states that any reference

to a person employed by the transferor and assigned to the organised grouping of ... employees that is subject to a relevant transfer, is a reference to a person so employed immediately before the transfer, or who would have been so employed if he had not been dismissed in the circumstances described in regulation 7(1) ...

Regulation 4(3) clearly applies to all employees employed by the transferor immediately before the transfer. In *Secretary of State for Employment v Spence* [1986] IRLR 248, CA, the Court of Appeal said that the phrase 'immediately before' means at the precise moment of transfer.

However, reg 4(3) of the 2006 Regulations also applies to employees who would have been so employed had they not been unfairly dismissed in the circumstances described in reg 7(1) (see **7.5**). This statutory provision encapsulates the House of Lords' judgment in *Secretary of State for Employment v Litster* [1989] IRLR 161. In that case the employees were dismissed one hour before the transfer. The House of Lords made it clear that a transferee may still be liable for any claims arising out of a pre-transfer dismissal, and reg 4(3) preserves that rule. This means that a transferee cannot circumvent the 2006 Regulations by insisting that the transferor dismiss some or all of the workforce prior to completion.

Thus a relevant transfer will:

(a)   transfer the contracts of anyone who is employed by the transferor immediately before the relevant transfer and who is assigned to the relevant group of employees that is the subject of the transfer. Their contracts of employment will transfer to the transferee and they will be employed by the transferee under the terms and conditions of those contracts;

(b)   pass liability for any pre-transfer dismissals falling within the circumstances described in reg 7(1) to the transferee. In other words, the transferee will be liable for any claims arising out of pre-transfer dismissals (actual or constructive (see reg 4(11)), or 'deemed' (see reg 4(9)) – see **7.3.2.1**) if those dismissals were by reason of the transfer, and those dismissals will be automatically unfair (see **7.5**) unless there is an economic, technical or organisational reason entailing changes in the workforce. Although the dismissal is effective (see **7.6**) and the employee is therefore not employed by the transferee, all rights, duties, and liabilities relating to his previous employment will transfer in addition to the claim of unfair dismissal, including, for example, any wrongful dismissal claim or any claim for discrimination.

7.3.2.1   Meaning of dismissal

Dismissal includes actual and constructive dismissal (see reg 4(11) at **7.3.2.3**). However, the term also includes, for the purpose of the 2006 Regulations, 'deemed' dismissal. This is because reg 4(9) provides that where a relevant transfer involves or would involve a substantial change in working conditions to the material detriment of a person whose contract of employment is or would be transferred under paragraph (1) [of reg 4], such an employee may treat the contract of employment as having been terminated, and the employee shall be treated for any purpose as having been dismissed by the employer.

The wording in reg 4(9) is wider than the meaning of constructive dismissal, where the employee must prove that he resigned as a result of a repudiatory breach of contract (see **Chapter 3**). The regulation will apply even when there is no fundamental breach of contract.

The BIS Guidance suggests that a substantial change in working conditions is likely to include a major relocation of the workplace which makes it difficult or much more expensive for an employee to travel, or the withdrawal of a right to a tenured post.

The EAT considered the meaning of reg 4(9) in *Tapere v South London and Maudsley NHS Trust* (UKEAT/0410/08). The EAT pointed out that there are two components to reg 4(9):

(a)   a 'substantial change in working conditions';

(b)   'to the material detriment of a person whose contract of employment is ... transferred'.

The EAT held that the term 'working conditions' should be interpreted widely following the decision of the ECJ in *Merckx and Neuhuys v Ford Motors Belgium SA* [1996] IRLR 467. In that case, salesmen were transferred to a new dealership at a different workplace without any guarantee as to client base or sales figures, so that there was potential for an adverse impact on commission. These components were regarded by the ECJ as 'working conditions'. The phrase therefore applies, according to the EAT, to contractual terms and conditions as well as physical conditions. On the facts, therefore, a change of workplace was a change to 'working conditions'. The question of whether it is a change of substance is, according to the EAT, a question of fact, and the employment tribunal will need to consider the nature, as well as the degree, of the change in order to decide whether it is substantial. The character of the change is likely to be the most important aspect of determining whether the change is substantial. In *Merckx*, the ECJ regarded the change as substantial because it was a change in remuneration. The EAT gave another example: a change in the method of salary payment. Moving from cash payment to bank, or from weekly to monthly payment would be a change of substance, even if the amount of remuneration was not altered. Therefore a change of workplace, on the facts, is also a change of substance.

On the phrase 'material detriment', the EAT held that 'material' simply means not trivial or fanciful, and that what has to be considered is the impact of the proposed change from the employee's point of view. On the facts of *Tapere* the change of location meant potential disruption to child-care arrangements and a longer journey, or an altered journey involving travelling on the M25, which the appellant did not find attractive. The tribunal should ask whether the employee regarded those factors as detrimental and, if so, whether that was a reasonable position for the employee to adopt. On the facts the claimant was therefore deemed to have been dismissed under reg 4(9).

In *Abellio London Ltd (Formerly Travel London Ltd) v Musse and Others* [2012] IRLR 360 (EAT), the EAT held that a move from north to south of the river in London (six miles) was substantial and that an increase in the working day of one to two hours was a material detriment, and that it was irrelevant that the contract contained a mobility clause. There was therefore a reg 4(9) dismissal, notwithstanding that there was no breach of contract. *Cetinsoy & Others v London United Busways Ltd* (UKEAT/0042/14) involved the transfer of a bus route from one company to another. As with the *Abellio* case, the transfer resulted in a move to a different depot. Although the contract specified that the employees should work at various locations, that did not include the new depot. The EAT upheld the employment tribunal decision that while the requirement to work at the new depot was a breach of contract, it was not a fundamental (repudiatory) breach. Furthermore, the move (which added between 30 minutes' and 60 minutes' travelling time a day) did not involve a substantial change in working conditions and was not to the material detriment of the employees.

Note that an employee who resigns in reliance on reg 4(9) cannot make a claim for notice pay. The employee should give notice and work it out (reg 4(10)).

7.3.2.2 Employees whose contracts would 'otherwise have been terminated by the transfer'

Those employees whose contracts would not be terminated by the transfer do not come within reg 4. This may, for example, apply to an employee who is retained by the transferor and redeployed in some other part of his operation within the terms of the employee's contract or with his consent. Such redeployment should take place before the transfer.

Where part of a business is transferred, employees will not be affected by reg 4 if they did not work in the part transferred. Even employees who perform duties in relation to the part transferred (eg administrative duties) will not be covered unless they are assigned to the part transferred, ie the organised grouping.

The question of whether an employee is assigned to the relevant grouping is a question of fact. The 2006 Regulations do not provide much by way of assistance as to what is meant by 'assigned'. Regulation 2(1) provides that it means 'assigned other than on a temporary basis'. For the time being, therefore, existing domestic and European case law will still be relevant. See, for example, *Securiplan v Bademosi* (UKEAT/1128/02) and *Gale v Northern General Hospital* [1994] IRLR 292. In general the case law confirms that where the employee was assigned is a matter of overall impression for the tribunal. This may often be decided as a mathematical question of how the employee spent most of his time, but sometimes a different approach may be called for.

The BIS Guidance suggests that in determining whether an assignment is temporary, factors such as 'the length of time the employee has been there and whether a date has been set by the transferor for his return or re-assignment to another part of the business or undertaking' should be taken into account.

Regard should also be had to the test laid down in *Botzen v Rotterdamsche Droogdok Maatschappij BV* (Case 186/83) [1986] 2 CMLR 50, ECJ. The ECJ said, in summary, that the test is whether there is a transfer of the part of the undertaking to which the employees 'were assigned and which formed the organisational framework within which their employment relationship took effect'.

Useful guidance on the *Botzen* test was given by the EAT in *Duncan Webb Offset (Maidstone) Ltd v Cooper and Others* [1995] IRLR 633. Factors which should be taken into account include how much time was spent on different parts of the business, how much value has been given to each part, what the contract said about the employee's duties, and how the cost of the employee was shared between the various parts of the business.

Further guidance may be found in the Court of Appeal decision in *CPL Distribution Ltd v Todd* [2003] IRLR 23. In *Argyll Coastal Services Ltd* (see **7.2.2.2** above), the EAT confirmed that involvement in carrying out the activity will not necessarily mean that the employee was assigned to the organised group, eg where the employee was covering for a colleague. In *BT Managed Services Ltd v Edwards & Another* (UKEAT/0241/14), the EAT held that an employee on long-term sick leave with no possibility of returning to work was not assigned to an organised grouping and so his employment did not transfer. Although it was a question of fact in each case, here he did not contribute to the 'economic activity' of the grouping (reg 3(2)), was unlikely to do so in the future, and a mere administrative connection was insufficient to constitute assignment.

In *Carsway Cleansing Consultants Ltd v Richards & Cooper Cleaning Services* (UKEAT/629/97), the EAT held that an employer could not 'off-load' an unwanted employee by deliberately moving him to a part of the undertaking that the employer knew was about to be transferred. The EAT held that such an act was fraudulent and, accordingly, void. The employee was not 'employed in the part of the undertaking' being transferred.

In *Jakowlew v Nestor Primecare (t/a Saga)* and others (UKEAT/0431/14), the EAT considered whether the client can determine who is assigned to the organised grouping. In a previous case (*Robert Sage Ltd t/a Prestige Nursing Care Ltd v O'Connell and Others* (UKEAT/0336/13), see **7.2.2.2** above) the EAT had held that this issue is to be determined by asking the question: Where would the employee be required to work immediately before the transfer? While the terms of any contract plays a part in answering that question, in some cases the contract can be superseded by the practical situation. In *Sage*, the EAT had held that as the employee had been prohibited from undertaking work with the organised group immediately before the transfer, and that prohibition was permanent, she could not be regarded as being assigned to it. *Jakowlew* asked the same question, but came to a different conclusion on the facts. N was a contractor who employed the claimant in providing care services. E was the client. The contract between N and E came to an end on 30 June 2013, and W took it over from 1 July 2013. The claimant was told that her employment would transfer from N to W. However, from February 2013, the claimant had, with others, been suspended for disciplinary reasons. The contract between N and E provided that E had the right to reject staff it considered unsuitable. E was concerned about the continued employment of the suspended employees, and on 19 June, E told N that it did not want the three suspended employees to continue working on its contract. N refused this request, saying that it was vexatious and not valid. On 27 June, three days before the transfer, the claimant was disciplined and given a final written warning. After the transfer, N reviewed the situation; it decided that E's request was valid and hence that the claimant should have been taken off the contract. As a result, it said that the claimant was not transferred. N had lost two contracts with E, and as a result had closed its office, so was in a position to make straightforward redundancies. The claimant was made redundant by N in September 2013. The claimant issued proceedings against both N and W, claiming that she was assigned to the organised grouping of employees that had transferred from N to W. The employment tribunal held that E's request was effective and that, as at the date of the transfer, this meant that the claimant was not assigned to the organised grouping. The EAT allowed the claimant's appeal and held that it was up to the employer, not the client, to decide who was assigned where. At the time of the transfer the claimant was no longer suspended and remained working for N: N had not accepted E's demand for the employee to be removed from the contract.

See also *Salmon v Castlebeck Care (Teesdale) Ltd (in administration) and others* (UKEAT/0304/14), which looked at the effect of a post-transfer internal appeal against dismissal following a relevant transfer, holding, in line with earlier authorities, that if an appeal against dismissal succeeds, an employee is reinstated with retrospective effect; if it fails, dismissal takes effect from the original date. Unlike the need to communicate a decision to dismiss, a successful appeal decision does not need to be communicated, as it has the effect of automatically reviving a contract at common law. Where there is a relevant transfer, a successful appeal will have the effect of bringing a contract back to life, such that an employee will be employed immediately prior to transfer, and so he and his rights will transfer to the transferee.

In *Kimberley Group Housing v Hambley* (above at **7.2.2.2**) the EAT held that there may be a transfer to more than one transferee under the Regulations. On the facts there were two overlapping contracts post-transfer, providing for activities done pre-transfer by one provider. By analogy with *Duncan Webb* above, the EAT found that the transferor's employees transferred to the transferee taking over the majority of the services, in this case Kimberley which took over 79% of the activities performed in one area and 97% in the other area of the country. See also *Costain v Armitage* (UKEAT/0048/14).

For a useful analysis of the tribunal's role in assessing whether an employee is 'assigned', see *London Borough of Hillingdon v Gormanley & Others* (UKEAT/0169/14). The EAT upheld a tribunal's decision that an employee on long-term sick leave who had been off sick for more than five years was not assigned to the group that transferred because there was, on the tribunal's findings, no prospect of the employee returning (*BT Managed Services Ltd v Edwards & Another* (UKEAT/0241/14)).

In *Ricardo v Portimão Urbis, EM, SA, in liquidation, Município de Portimão Emarp – Empresa Municipal de Águas e Resíduos de Portimão, EM, SA* (Case C-416/16), the CJEU had to consider whether the claimant, Mr Ricardo, who was a director of a local council's trading company, which was being wound up by the Council and its activities continued by other means, was covered by the concept of 'employee' within the meaning of the Acquired Rights Directive (ARD) such that his employment contract should transfer. Mr Ricardo had been (at his request) on unpaid leave for three years. There was an arrangement to transfer the staff to the Council and a new entity, but Mr Ricardo was not included in those plans. He was informed that his employment would end on the final closure of the trading company. The Court noted that any person who is considered to be an employee under the relevant national employment will be covered, so their employment contract will exist at the date of the transfer. Portuguese legislation provides that whilst an employment contract is suspended, the rights, obligations and safeguards of parties who are not required to be in active service are maintained. Therefore, said the Court, in such a case, the ARD will protect an employee who is not actually performing his duties because his employment contract is suspended.

7.3.2.3   The employee's right of objection

In the UK, employees can object to the transfer of their employment contract. If they do this, their employment is treated as terminated by operation of law and there is no dismissal.

Regulation 4(7) states:

> Paragraphs (1) and (2) shall not operate to transfer the contract of employment and the rights, powers, duties and liabilities under or in connection with it of an employee who informs the transferor or the transferee that he objects to becoming employed by the transferee.

Under reg 4(8):

> Subject to paragraphs (9) and (11), where an employee so objects, the relevant transfer shall operate so as to terminate his contract of employment with the transferor but he shall not be treated, for any purpose, as having been dismissed by the transferor.

And under reg 4(11):

> Paragraphs (1), (7), (8) and (9) are without prejudice to any right of an employee arising apart from these Regulations to terminate his contract of employment without notice in acceptance of a repudiatory breach of contract by his employer.

The transfer of the contract of employment and rights, powers, duties and liabilities under and in connection with it, will not occur if the employee informs the transferor or the transferee that he objects to becoming employed by the transferee. In that event, the transfer will terminate the employee's contract of employment with the transferor, but he will not be treated for any purpose as having been dismissed by the transferor, ie he will be regarded as having resigned (reg 4(7) and (8)) unless the reason for the objection is that the transfer will involve a significant and detrimental change in working conditions (reg 4(9)) (see **7.3.2.1** above), or the employee is alleging constructive dismissal (reg 4(11)). Therefore, if an employee exercises this right, he will lose all his rights against both the transferor and the transferee, unless he has been caused to resign by a change in working conditions or a breach of contract by his employer. Interestingly, the Court of Appeal has held that as the effect of the objection was that the contract of employment did not transfer to the transferee, neither did liability for any claims flowing from a constructive or reg 4(9) dismissal, which therefore remain with the transferor. In a case of this type, reg 4(3)/*Litster* does not apply to transfer liability (*University of Oxford v Humphreys* [2000] IRLR 183, CA).

There is nothing to prevent an employee in this situation being re-engaged by the transferee on new terms, although his continuity would be broken.

The right of employees to object to a transfer of their employment on a business transfer was also considered in *Senior Heat Treatment Ltd v Bell* [1997] IRLR 614. In this case, the employer decided to move its Heat Treatment Department to a vacant factory and new employer six miles away. The employees were given the following options:

(a)   transfer to the new factory and new employer;

(b)   opt out of the transfer and receive a payment equivalent to statutory redundancy pay, pay in lieu of notice and a further ex gratia sum.

The employees were given a form on which to state their preference. Having ticked the box objecting to the transfer, they received payments in accordance with the severance package. However, they had *already* signed employment contracts with the new employer and then turned up for work for the new employer the following Monday. When they were dismissed 10 months later, they claimed unfair dismissal and/or redundancy payments in the employment tribunal.

When the case reached the EAT, it was found that on the peculiar facts of this case the former employees were entitled to count their employment before the transfer towards their continuity of service, and as a result they had two years' service and could bring claims in the employment tribunal. The reasoning was that the employees had already signed contracts with the new employer before they completed the forms provided by their old employer. As a result, the EAT found they had not objected to the transfer even though they had said they wished to 'opt out' of it.

Opting out was also considered by the EAT in *Capita Health Solutions v BBC and McLean* (UKEAT/0034/07). The BBC transferred its occupational health unit to an outside contractor. Mrs McLean 'objected' and 'resigned' on the day before the transfer, stating that she would work 'a period of secondment' with the contractor while she served out her notice. The employment tribunal said that on the facts, Mrs McLean had not objected and her contract still transferred. The EAT agreed. Regulation 4 states that an objection will stop a transfer occurring and end the contract. There is no provision for working out notice. If Mrs McLean had objected successfully, she could not have continued as the BBC's employee.

It is now clear that neither the general application of the automatic transfer principle nor the existence of the employee's right to object is subject to a precondition that employees have knowledge of both the fact of a transfer and the identity of the transferee (*Secretary of State for Trade and Industry v Cook and Others* [1997] ICR 288, EAT).

Note that according to the High Court, employees may object after a transfer where they do not know the identity of the transferee pre-transfer, so long as they do so promptly (see *New ISG Ltd v Vernon* [2008] IRLR 115). In this case the High Court, interpreting the 2006 Regulations purposively, made it clear that where the identity of the buyer is not known until the sale is completed, the right to object would be meaningless if it could be exercised only pre-sale.

7.4 WHAT THE TRANSFEREE ACQUIRES

The transferee inherits those employees employed by the transferor on their existing terms and conditions, assuming that they do not object (reg 4(2)).

Equally, the transferred employee has no right to insist that he be given the benefit of any superior terms and conditions enjoyed by the transferee's existing staff. In addition, the transferee inherits the legal responsibilities for any employees dismissed by reason of the transfer or for a reason connected with the transfer, where no ETO reason exists (see **7.5.2** below).

7.4.1 Rights transferring – employees employed immediately before the transfer

The transferee inherits all the employees employed immediately before the transfer, together with all the contracts of employment of the transferred employees. The transferee cannot pick and choose which employees to take on. The only exceptions to this are where:

(a)   employees are 'temporarily' assigned to the 'organised grouping' (see **7.3.2.1**);

(b)   the employee has objected (see **7.3.2.2**).

The transferee also inherits all the accrued rights and liabilities connected with the contract of the transferred employee (except for criminal liabilities (reg 4(6)) and some benefits under an occupational pension scheme (see **7.4.1.3**)).

If, for example, the transferor was in arrears with wages at the time of the transfer, the employee can sue the transferee as if the original liability had been the transferee's. The transferor is relieved of his former obligations without any need for the employee's consent. All liability for tortious claims, for example personal injury claims, will also pass to the transferee whether the accident happens before the transfer or after the transfer but due to the pre-transfer negligence of the transferor (*Bernardone v Pall Mall Services Group and Others* [2000] IRLR 487, CA and *Baker v British Gas Services Ltd* [2017] EWHC 2302 (QB)). Note that where an entitlement is inextricably linked to the identity of the transferor (eg profit-sharing schemes), the employee's post-transfer entitlement, according to the EAT in *MITIE Managed Services Ltd v French* [2002] IRLR 512, is to participate 'in a scheme of substantial equivalence'.

Equally, the transferee may sue an employee for a breach of contract committed against the transferor prior to transfer.

The transferee will also inherit all the statutory rights and liabilities which are connected with the individual contract of employment, for example unfair dismissal, redundancy and discrimination.

Regulations 11 and 12 contain provisions requiring the transferor to notify the transferee in writing of 'liability' information about an employee who is 'assigned to the organised grouping of employees or resources that is the subject of a relevant transfer'. This includes providing details of the identity and age of the employee, the particulars of employment (ERA 1996, s 1), and information relating to disciplinary and grievance procedures involving the employee. If a transferor fails to provide this information in whole or part, the transferee may complain to an employment tribunal, which may award compensation of not less than £500 per employee (see **7.7**).

In *Born London Ltd v Spire Production Services Ltd* (UKEAT/0255/16), a transferor incorrectly stated that a Christmas bonus was non-contractual, when it turned out to be contractual. The question arose as to whether this was a breach of reg 11, such as to give rise to a compensation claim. The employment tribunal found that the claim had no reasonable prospect of success, and the EAT agreed. Even assuming that the bonus was contractual, all reg 11 requires is for particulars of employment to be provided as defined by s 1 of the ERA 1996. That did not impose a requirement to state whether a bonus was contractual or not. Saying that the bonus was non-contractual went further than the particulars required to be provided by reg 11. The way to avoid this sort of problem is a practical one: the transferee could have undertaken more due diligence on the question of whether remuneration was contractual or not. If the warranties and indemnities had covered this, then the transferee might have had a contractual claim against the transferor under the transfer contract.

The 2014 Amendment Regulations, which came into force on 31 January 2014, made changes to reg 11, so that the deadline for notification of employee information is increased from not less than 14 days before the transfer to not less than 28 days before the transfer. This will assist incoming contractors and transferees by giving them more information earlier about the employees they will be taking on.

The transferred employee's period of continuous employment will date from the beginning of his period of employment with the transferor, and the statutory particulars of terms and conditions of employment, which every employer is obliged to issue, must take account of any continuity enjoyed by virtue of the Regulations.

7.4.1.1 Restrictive covenants

In the case of restrictive covenants, these will normally be expressed in terms of protecting customers of the transferor. In essence, following the transfer of an undertaking a restrictive covenant should be read as being enforceable by the transferee, but only in respect of customers of the transferor who fall within the protection. (Great care needs to be taken if restrictive covenants are re-drafted post-transfer. See *Credit Suisse First Boston (Europe) Ltd v Padiachy and Others* [1998] IRLR 504 and *Credit Suisse First Boston (Europe) Ltd v Lister* [1998] IRLR 700.)

7.4.1.2 Collective agreements

Under the 2006 Regulations, any collective agreements made with a union by the transferor are deemed to have been made by the transferee (reg 5). Further, the transferee is deemed to recognise the trade union to the same extent as did the transferor (reg 6). In effect, the transferee steps into the shoes of the transferor. Neither the 2006 Regulations nor the general law prevent the employer from seeking to derecognise the union entirely, or from amending the basis of the recognition. This lack of an effective remedy undermines the protection given to trade unions on a relevant transfer. Note that the ERA 1999 contains detailed statutory procedures for the recognition and de-recognition of trade unions for collective bargaining. The procedures are beyond the scope of this book.

The ECJ held in *Alemo-Herron & Others v Parkwood Leisure Ltd* [2013] EUECJ C-426/11, [2013] WLR(D) 288 that where transferring employees' contracts provide for terms to be determined in accordance with a collective agreement, the transferee cannot be bound by post-transfer collectively agreed terms where it does not have the option of participating in the negotiation process of the collective agreement or does not consent to the arrangement (see *Asklepios Kliniken Langen-Seligenstadt GmbH v Felja* (Case C-680/15) [2017] IRLR 653, ECJ).

In *Unionen v Almega Tjänsteförbunden ISS Facility Services AB* (Case C-336/15), the ECJ confirmed that employees cannot be made subject to less favourable working conditions than those applicable prior to a transfer and that a transferee is required to take into account service with the transferor when calculating notice periods. Four employees with long service transferred to ISS. After some years of service with ISS they were all made redundant. At the date of redundancy all had total service with the transferor and ISS in excess of 10 years. However, they had all only been employed for periods between two and six years with ISS (the transferee) since the transfer. Both the transferor and transferee were parties to a collective agreement, which gave different periods of notice depending on the length of service of the particular employee. This provided for extended notice in cases where length of service exceeded 10 years and the employee was aged over 55 years. Under Swedish law, compliance with collective agreements entered into by the transferee was only required for one year after the transfer. The ECJ stated that although one year had passed, so ISS was entitled for economic reasons not related to the transfer to no longer continue to observe the original terms and conditions, no amendments had been made to the terms and conditions of the collective agreement and they continued to apply.

The 2014 Amendment Regulations inserted a new reg 4A into the 2006 Regulations, so that collectively agreed rights which come into force after the date of transfer will not transfer if the transferee is not a party to the collective bargaining for that right. See too **7.6** on varying collectively agreed terms post-transfer.

7.4.1.3 Pensions

Regulation 10 provides that regs 4 and 5 do not apply to occupational pension schemes (although a contractual provision that an employer would pay a certain percentage of salary into a personal pension fund would transfer). However, separate regulations have been issued under the Pensions Act 2004, which provide that when a relevant transfer occurs and employees had the benefit of an occupational pension scheme (with employer contributions) before transfer, the transferee *must* provide membership of an equivalent scheme. The detail is beyond the scope of the book; see Transfer of Employment (Pension Protection) Regulations 2005 (SI 2005/649) (as amended) and <http://www.dwp.gov.uk>.

7.4.1.4 'Liability for failure to consult'

Regulation 15(9) makes the transferor and the transferee jointly and severally liable in respect of compensation payable as a result of a failure to consult (see **7.7**).

7.4.2 Rights and liabilities which are not assigned under the 2006 Regulations

The 2006 Regulations do not have the effect of assigning:

(a)   criminal liabilities (reg 4(6)); or

(b)   liability (in a health and safety context) under a continuation order.

7.5 DISMISSAL OF AN EMPLOYEE BECAUSE OF A RELEVANT TRANSFER

If an employee is dismissed, before of after a relevant transfer, the dismissal is effective and the contracts ends. Depending on the facts, liability may fall on the transferor or the transferee.

The 2014 Amendment Regulations, which came into force on 31 January 2014, made changes to reg 7 of the 2006 Regulations. The wording of reg 7(1)–(3A) is now:

(1)   Where either before or after a relevant transfer, any employee of the transferor or transferee is dismissed, that employee is to be treated for the purposes of Part X of the 1996 Act (unfair dismissal) as unfairly dismissed if the reason for the dismissal is the transfer.

(2)   Paragraph (1) does not apply to dismissals that may take place for economic, technical or organisational reasons entailing changes in the workforce of either the transferor or transferee before or after a relevant transfer.

(3)   If a dismissal takes place for a reason referred to in paragraph (2), without prejudice to the application of section 98(4) of the 1996 Act (test of fair dismissal), for the purposes of sections 98(1) and 135 of that Act (reason for dismissal)—

    (a)   the dismissal is regarded as having been for redundancy where section 98(2)(c) of that Act applies; or

    (b)   in any other case, the dismissal is regarded as having been for a substantial reason of a kind such as to justify the dismissal of an employee holding the position which that employee held.

(3A)   In paragraph (2), the expression 'changes in the workforce' includes a change to the place (within the meaning of section 139 of the 1996 Act) where employees are employed by the employer to carry on the business of the employer or to carry out work of a particular kind for the employer.

This aims to clarify the definition of an 'economic, technical or organisational reason entailing changes in the workforce' ('ETO') and bring it more into line with the definition of redundancy. It also removed a phrase ('connected with the transfer') which had caused uncertainty as to its scope. This amended wording is intended to make it easier for employers to make post-transfer changes to contracts. This may give employers greater flexibility post-transfer, as a dismissal is now automatically unfair only if the reason or principal reason for the dismissal is the transfer itself, but the authors advise caution as the phrase 'the transfer' may yet be interpreted by courts to include 'transfer-connected reasons'.

If an employee is dismissed (whether actually (see **3.4.1**) or constructively (see **3.4.3**), or within the meaning of reg 4(9) (see **7.3.2.1**), and whether before or after the transfer), if the sole or principal reason for the dismissal is the transfer then, by reg 7 of the 2006 Regulations, the dismissal is automatically unfair (ie there is no need to consider whether the dismissal is reasonable in accordance with ERA 1996, s 98(4) (reg 7(1)). However, if the sole or principal reason for the dismissal is an ETO reason entailing changes in the workforce (of either the transferor or the transferee before or after a relevant transfer), there is no automatically unfair dismissal. The dismissal shall (without prejudice to the application of s 98(4) of the ERA 1996), for the purposes of ss 98(1) and 135 of the 1996 Act, be regarded as having been for redundancy where s 98(2)(c) of that Act applies (see **5.2.1**), or otherwise for a substantial reason of a kind such as to justify the dismissal of an employee holding the position which that employee held (reg 7(2)and (3)). The effect of this is that a presumption is created that ETO dismissals will be for the potentially fair reasons of either redundancy or some other substantial reason, and reasonableness will be determined in the usual way (see **Chapter 5**), liability lying with the employer who carried out the dismissals.

Regulation 7(4) states that reg 7 applies irrespective of whether the employee in question is assigned to the organised grouping of resources or employees that is, or will be, transferred. This means that the protection of reg 7 is available to *all* employees. It is important, therefore, that transferees are aware that their existing employees, as well as the transferring employees, are protected against transfer-related dismissal.

To bring a claim of unfair dismissal arising out of a transfer-related dismissal, an employee still needs to have a minimum of one or two years' continuous employment (dependent on when the employment commenced).

7.5.1 When is a dismissal by reason of the transfer itself?

It will be a question of fact for the tribunal to determine whether a dismissal is by reason of the transfer itself. The BIS Guidance gives the following example in connection with changing terms and conditions, but it is useful by way of analogy:

Q.   When is the sole or principal reason for a purported variation of contract the transfer?

A.   Where an employer changes terms and conditions simply because of the transfer and there are no extenuating circumstances linked to the reason for that decision, then the reason for the change is the transfer.

Where there are some extenuating circumstances, then whether or not the sole or principal reason for any purported variation is the transfer is likely to depend upon the circumstances.

If the new employer wishes merely to bring into line the terms and conditions of transferred staff with those of existing staff, then the transfer would be the reason for this change (due to the way in which the Courts have interpreted the Acquired Rights Directive).

In the authors' opinion, a dismissal following collusion between a transferor and a transferee with regard to dismissals (ie the transferee was involved in some way in the decision to dismiss) might be regarded as a dismissal by reason of the transfer itself, but as yet there is no authority supporting this proposition. In *Wheeler v Patel* [1987] IRLR 211 (a case decided under the old law), Mrs Wheeler was employed by the vendor of a shop in his business which he proposed to sell. Before the shop was transferred to a prospective purchaser, Mrs Wheeler was dismissed, in order to achieve agreement for sale. The EAT held (under the old law) that this dismissal was for a reason connected with the transfer, but it may be seen under the new law as a dismissal by reason of the transfer itself.

Although dismissals which occur shortly before or after the transfer are more likely to be by reason of it, an employee may have difficulty convincing the tribunal that a dismissal which took place weeks or even months before the transfer was by reason of the transfer, unless a court now determines that 'the transfer' includes 'transfer-connected reasons'.

One area of difficulty was whether it was sufficient for the employee to show that his dismissal was by reason of transfers generally as opposed to a specific transfer. There was a conflict of EAT decisions under the 1981 Regulations on this point. In *Ibex Trading Company Ltd v Walton and Others* [1994] IRLR 564, the EAT held that the actual transferee had to be identified. Dismissal in respect of transfers generally was not sufficient. The employees in this case were held to be dismissed by reason of 'a' transfer, rather than 'the' transfer.

However, in *Harrison Bowden Ltd v Bowden* [1994] ICR 186, and subsequently in *Morris v John Grose Group Ltd* [1998] IRLR 499 and *CAB Automotive Ltd v Blake and Others* (UKEAT/0298/07), the EAT held that the words 'the transfer' did not necessarily have to refer to the particular transfer that had actually occurred. That this is the correct approach was confirmed by the Court of Appeal in *Spaceright Europe Ltd v Baillavoine and Another* [2011] EWCA Civ 1565.

In the *Spaceright* case, the claimant was the managing director of a business which was up for sale. Although no buyer had been identified, a view had been taken that an incumbent managing director was too expensive for a purchaser. The claimant was dismissed, ostensibly on the grounds of redundancy, but the business was always going to need a managing director, and there was always going to be an ongoing business. The EAT agreed that the dismissal was connected with the transfer which was contemplated. The Court of Appeal agreed with this approach, holding that an ETO reason is not available where an employee is dismissed to make a business more attractive to prospective transferees.

This approach, said Mummery LJ, accords with the Acquired Rights Directive. The fact that no transferee can be identified at the moment of dismissal does not prevent employees' rights from being protected by the Directive.

In *Dynamex Friction Ltd and Another v Amicus and Others* [2008] IRLR 515, when the company got into difficulties, joint administrators were appointed. The administrators decided to dismiss the workforce on the basis that the company had no money to pay them. The Court of Appeal upheld the tribunal decision that the sole reason for the dismissals was economic, as there was no money to pay the workforce, and so was not transfer-related. It was the administrator's decision to dismiss, and just because there was collusion between the director of the insolvent company and the transferee did not make the dismissals transfer-related in circumstances where the administrator was not involved in the collusion.

For a recent decision, see *Hare Wines Ltd v Kaur* (UKEAT/0752/16) where a tribunal found that the dismissal of an employee immediately before a transfer was automatically unfair because the principal reason was the transfer.

7.5.2 Establishing an ETO reason which entails a change in the workforce

If there is a pre-transfer dismissal because of the transfer, the transferee (ie the new employer) will be liable for *all* claims by the dismissed employee (reg 4(3)) unless the dismissal was for an ETO reason which entailed a change in the workforce, in which case liability for a pre-transfer dismissal will lie with the transferor (ie the old employer). Liability for a post-transfer dismissal will always lie with the transferee.

If there is an ETO reason, the dismissal will be either for redundancy, or for 'a substantial reason' under s 98(1) and s 135 of the ERA 1996. Even where the employer can show such a reason, the employment tribunal must still be satisfied that the employer has acted reasonably within s 98(4) of the ERA 1996.

The employer must show an ETO reason entailing a change in the workforce, otherwise the dismissal will be automatically unfair.

Note that the wording of reg 7 mirrors the wording of reg 4(4) (see **7.6** below) There is no statutory definition of an ETO reason. According to the BIS Guidance, it is likely to include:

(a)   a reason relating to the profitability or market performance of the transferee's business (ie an economic reason);

(b)   a reason relating to the nature of the equipment or production processes which the transferee operates (ie a technical reason); or

(c)   a reason relating to the management or organisational structure of the transferee's business (ie an organisational reason). (See below.)

Likewise there is no statutory definition of the phrase 'entailing changes in the workforce'. Previous interpretations of the phrase by the courts under the 1981 Regulations (see, eg, *Berriman v Delabole Slate Ltd* [1985] ICR 546 and below) restricted it to changes in the numbers employed, or to changes in the functions performed by employees. The BIS Guidance suggests a functional change could involve a new requirement on an employee who held a managerial position to enter into a non-managerial role, or to move from a secretarial to a sales position. The amendments made by the 2014 Regulations have added a further situation to be covered by the phrase, namely a change to the place where employees are employed to carry on the business of the employer or particular work for the employer.

Two cases under the 2006 Regulations were regarded in particular as providing authoritative guidance on the concept of an ETO reason. An 'economic' reason must relate to the future conduct of the business as such, and does not include dismissing employees simply to obtain an enhanced price or to achieve an agreement for sale (*Wheeler v Patel*, **7.5.1** above; *Spaceright*, **7.5.2** above). It may, however, include an administrator's dismissing employees to keep a business running in the hope of a future sale. In *Crystal Palace FC & Another v Kavanagh & Others* [2013] EWCA Civ 1410, 29 staff were dismissed over the summer 'closed period', as they were not needed for the core operations. The tribunal held that reducing the wage bill to enable the club to continue as a going concern was an economic reason, separate from the longer-term objective of selling the business. The Court of Appeal upheld the tribunal's findings: the dismissals of the employees entailed changes in the workforce, and it was permissible on the facts for the tribunal to conclude there was an economic reason behind them).

The Court of Session confirmed in *Hynd v Armstrong* [2007] IRLR 338 that a transferor employer cannot rely on the transferee's reason for dismissal in order to establish an 'economic, technical or organisational reason' so as to provide a potential defence under the Regulations. In this case a pre-transfer dismissal of a solicitor by the transferor because the transferee did not require him was held to be automatically unfair. The Court of Session held that it is 'reasonably clear' that the Transfer Directive would not 'permit dismissal in such circumstances'. A transferor can only rely on a reason of its own.

Sarah Lamont of Bevan Brittan summarised at the time the practical effects of the case:

•   Where an employee is dismissed by the transferor prior to the transfer, the reason for the dismissal must relate to the transferor's future conduct of its business in order to be an ETO reason

•   That will never be the case where, as here, the transferor has no intention of continuing the business after the transfer

•   Often this situation arises where the transferor carries out dismissals at the request of the transferee, who does not want to take on the employees concerned, usually because it will leave him overstaffed and he does not want to carry out a redundancy exercise after the transfer

•   Where there are pre-transfer dismissals in connection with the transfer and there is no ETO reason, liability for unfair dismissal will pass to the transferee under TUPE

•   Although this is a case decided under TUPE 1981, it would apply equally to TUPE 2006, which replaced and amended the old version of the Regulations

- As a Court of Session case, this decision is not strictly binding on tribunals in England and Wales or the EAT sitting in England, but it is likely to be followed by them in practice.

According to the Court of Appeal in *Berriman* (see above), the ETO reason must entail a 'change in the workforce'. For a change in the workforce there has to be a change in the composition of the workforce, or possibly a substantial change in job descriptions. Changes in the identity of the individuals who make up the workforce do not constitute changes in the workforce itself so long as the overall numbers and functions remain the same.

In *London University v Sackur* (UKEAT/0286/06), an employer, following a transfer and wanting to harmonise terms and conditions after a period of consultation lasting two years, dismissed staff and offered to re-engage them on new terms. The EAT upheld a tribunal's finding of fact that a transfer of an undertaking was the sole reason for the dismissal of the employees, even though the dismissals occurred two years after the transfer. They then looked at whether harmonisation of terms was an ETO reason. Referring to *Berriman*, they said that that case established that for an ETO reason to entail changes in the workforce, it must involve changes in the 'strength' or 'establishment' of the workforce. That means changes in the overall numbers or functions of employees. Effectively, therefore, an ETO reason entailing a change in the workforce will have to be a genuine redundancy situation. A mere change in the terms and conditions enjoyed by the workforce will not suffice, neither will the mere substitution of one employee for another. Consequently, a transferee who provokes an actual or a constructive dismissal by attempting to change the terms and conditions of the transferred employees to harmonise with those of his existing workforce would be unable to rely on the defence. The EAT in *Meter U Ltd v Hardy and Others* [2012] IRLR 367 followed the guidance in *Berriman*, as did the Court of Appeal in *The Manchester College v Hazel and Another* (see below).

For a case in which the tribunal's finding that the change to the claimants' bonus scheme was done for an ETO reason entailing a change in the work force, see *Nationwide Building Society v Benn & Others* (UKEAT/0273/09). In that case the principal reason for the change in a bonus scheme was connected to the claimants' job functions since it was driven by the product range and funds available to the respondent at that time.

In *Spaceright* (**7.5.1** above), the Court of Appeal held that there was no ETO reason entailing a change in the workforce. The reason did not relate to the conduct of the business as a going concern; the business was always going to need a managing director. It did not involve a diminution in the number of employees in the transferred business: the claimant was replaced. The reason related to the sale of the business, not to the conduct of the business.

In *The Manchester College v Hazel and Another* [2014] EWCA Civ 72, the Court of Appeal upheld a tribunal's decision that harmonisation of terms and conditions six months after a transfer did not effect changes in the workforce, and that as dismissals were connected to the transfer they were automatically unfair. Shortly after a transfer of the provision of offender learning services from the Prison Service to the College, which resulted in the transfer of 1,500 employees, the College realised that large cost savings were needed. As part of a raft of proposals, it asked two employees to take pay reductions (of 18% and 13.2%). They refused and were dismissed. The Court of Appeal held that simple harmonisation of terms was not an ETO reason (although it did confirm that there can be an ETO reason even where there is not a change to numbers and functions). The appropriate remedy, on the facts, was reinstatement on the new terms and conditions but at the old salaries, which would be frozen until other employees caught up.

Because the *Berriman* decision left little scope for a change of workplace to amount to an ETO reason (unless it was accompanied by a change in numbers or functions), the 2014 Amendment Regulations inserted the new subs (3A) into reg 7 of the 2006 Regulations (see **7.5** above for the new wording), which expressly expanded the definition of 'changes in the workforce' to include a change to the place of work and to refer specifically to the definition of 'redundancy' in s 139 of the ERA 1996. The aim of this is to ensure that dismissal due to changes in the location of a business, or part of it, will not automatically be unfair; instead, the fairness of such dismissals will be considered in accordance with the familiar test under s 98(4) of the ERA 1996. So, the employer will need to make sure as with dismissal for redundancy, that selection for dismissal is fair and not based simply on the fact that the person is a transferred employee. Dismissed employees may also be entitled to a redundancy payment if they have been employed for two years or more. Employers must further ensure that the required period for consultation with employees' representatives is allowed (see **7.7** below).

For a recent decision of the EAT, see *Osborne v Capita Business Services Ltd* (UKEAT/0048/16). Capita's arguments in this case that there were 'economic, technical or organisational reasons' for its dismissal of a group of employees who had transferred to it under a TUPE transfer succeeded in regard to all but two employees. Seven employees were dismissed because their job functions were split and redistributed across several different sites: this entailed changes in the job functions of the workforce. Two employees were relocated with no significant change to their function. As the transfer occurred before the 2014 amendments, Capita could not rely on relocation to meet the 'changes in the workforce' condition. These two were therefore automatically unfairly dismissed.

As it will sometimes be unclear whether the 2006 Regulations apply, and therefore whether the previous or the new employer is responsible for making redundancy payments (because if the 2006 Regulations do not apply then liability for the dismissals will not pass to the transferee but will remain with the transferor), employees are best advised to make any claims against both employers at an employment tribunal.

In certain circumstances, reg 9 allows for variations to be agreed to where a transferor is subject to 'relevant insolvency proceedings' (as defined). The detail of this is beyond the scope of this book.

7.5.3 Summary

In summary, therefore:

(a)   Where the sole or principal reason for a dismissal is the transfer itself, the dismissal will be automatically unfair under reg 7(1). Irrespective of whether the dismissal occurred before or after the transfer, the claim will be against the transferee.

(b)   Where the sole or principal reason for a dismissal is not the transfer itself but is an ETO reason, under reg 7(2) and (3) the dismissal will be potentially fair on the basis of either redundancy (in which case a redundancy payment may also be appropriate) or some other substantial reason, subject to the normal unfair dismissal tests. In this situation, while the transferee will remain liable for any post-transfer dismissals, the transferor will be liable for pre-transfer dismissals.

(c)   Where the sole or principal reason for a dismissal is not the transfer, the usual unfair dismissal principles will apply.

(d)   An employee who has been dismissed, or who has resigned in circumstances in which he considers he was entitled to resign because of the consequences or anticipated consequences of the transfer, needs to have the requisite continuous employment, although the qualifying period does not apply where an employee claims that he was dismissed for asserting his statutory rights under the 2006 Regulations (reg 19) (see **5.5.3**).

(e)   Any complaints must be brought within three months of the date when employment ended.

(f)   Because it may be unclear whether claims should be made against the previous employer or the new employer, employees should consider whether to claim against both employers.

7.6 POST-TRANSFER VARIATIONS TO TERMS AND CONDITIONS

One of the aims of the 2006 Regulations was to clarify what the position was post-transfer, where variations were made to contracts. The Regulations ensure that employees retain the same terms and conditions post-transfer as they enjoyed pre-transfer, and that they are not penalised when they are transferred by being given inferior terms and conditions. This is achieved by two routes. First, the 2006 Regulations state (reg 4(1)) that the contract of employment of any transferred employee 'shall have effect after the transfer as if originally made between the person so employed and the transferee'. This ensures that the pre-existing terms and conditions are transferred across on the first day of the employee's employment with the transferee. Secondly, by way of reinforcement, the Regulations also impose limitations on the ability of the transferee and employee to agree variations to those terms and conditions.

The 2014 Amendment Regulations, which came into force on 31 January 2014, made changes to reg 4(4) and (5). The new wording is now as follows:

    (4)   Subject to regulation 9, any purported variation of a contract of employment that is, or will be, transferred by paragraph (1), is void if the reason for the variation is the transfer.

    (5)   Paragraph (4) does not prevent a variation to the contract of employment—

        (a)   if the reason for the variation is an economic, technical or organisational reason entailing changes in the workforce; or

        (b)   if the reason for the variation is the transfer, provided that the terms of that contract permit the employer to make such a variation.

    (5A)   In paragraph (5), the expression 'changes in the workforce' includes a change to the place (within the meaning of section 139 of the 1996 Act) where employees are employed by the employer to carry on the business of the employer or to carry out work of a particular kind for the employer.

    (5B)   Paragraph (4) does not apply in respect of a variation of contract in so far as it varies a term or condition incorporated from a collective agreement, provided that—

        (a)   the variation of the contract takes effect on a date more than one year after the date of the transfer; and

        (b)   following that variation, the rights and obligations in the employee's contract, when considered together, are no less favourable to the employee than those which applied immediately before the variation.

    (5C)   Paragraphs (5) and (5B) do not affect any rule of law as to when a contract of employment is effectively varied.

Any purported variation of a contract of employment that is transferred under reg 4(1) will thus be void if the reason for the variation is the transfer, but in certain situations (reg 4(5), (5B)) a variation may not be void, eg where there is an ETO or where a contract expressly permits changes. The definition of 'entailing changes in the workforce' will include changes to the place of work, as discussed in **7.5.2** above in connection with reg 7, so as to bring the definition more into line with the definition of 'redundancy' in s 139 of the ERA 199, and to take geographic or locational redundancies outside the scope of automatically unfair redundancies. Some caution is needed, as until the courts start interpreting the new wording, it is unclear how widely they will view 'the transfer'. The BIS Guidance suggests that where there are transfer-connected reasons for varying a contract, these might be caught by the phrase 'the transfer'. The advice currently therefore is that where there is a transfer-connected reason for varying contracts, it is sensible to ensure that there is also an ETO justification for it. Note that there are special provisions in reg 5B which relate to changes to terms incorporated from collective agreements.

Thus, reg 4(5) now permits a transferee or a transferor to agree to vary an employment contract with an employee where the sole or principal reason falls within the definition of an 'economic, technical or organisational reason entailing changes in the workforce' or the terms of the contract permit such a variation. Note that an employer cannot unilaterally change or impose new terms and conditions without the agreement of the employee (see *Regent Security Services v Power* [2008] IRLR 226). The BIS Guidance suggests that a reason unrelated to a transfer could include the sudden loss of an expected order by a manufacturing company, or a general upturn in demand for a particular service or a change in a key exchange rate.

Where a change occurs after the transfer, it will be a question of fact whether the change was related to the transfer. One relevant factor will be the length of time between the date of the transfer and the change, but the gap is only one factor. In *Taylor v Connex South Eastern Ltd* (UKEAT/1243/99), a case decided under the old law, the EAT held that there was still a connection between the transfer and an attempt to force changes in terms and conditions two years after the relevant transfer, because the subject matter of the insistence by the respondents on the contractual change was an important term which had been transferred across on the occasion of the transfer. However, in *Tabberer v Mears Ltd* (UKEAT/0064/17), the EAT upheld a tribunal's decision that the respondent's reason for ending an allowance was not connected with the transfer but, rather, because the allowance was 'outdated'.

It is unlikely that an attempt by a transferee to change the terms and conditions of a transferring employee in order to harmonise them with those of the existing workers would be covered by this wording. Any wish to harmonise terms and conditions is really a reason related to the transfer, and it is difficult to see how it could fall within the wording of reg 4(5). There is no hard-and-fast rule as to how long after a transfer it would 'safe' for the transferee to vary contracts because of the passage of time. The BIS Guidance points out that while there is likely to come a time when the link with the transfer can be treated as no longer effective, this must be assessed in the light of all the circumstances of the individual case, and will vary from case to case.

In summary, therefore, the Regulations draw a distinction between four situations:

(a)   cases where the sole or principal reason for a purported contractual variation is the transfer itself (void);

(b)   cases where the reason is entirely unconnected with the transfer (eg a misconduct dismissal) (valid);

(c)   cases where the reason is an ETO reason (valid);

(d)   cases where the terms of the contract permit the employer to make the variation (valid); and

(e)   cases where the changes are made to a collective agreement term more than one year post-transfer where the changes are entirely to the benefit of the employee (valid).

In the first situation any purported variation will be void, but this will not prevent a valid variation being agreed in the remaining situations.

Some commentators have raised questions about the compatibility of reg 4(5)(a) with the Acquired Rights Directive. The Directive does not deal with post-transfer contract variations, but in *Foreningen af Arbejdsledere I Danmark v Daddy's Dance Hall A/S* [1988] IRLR 315, the ECJ held that changes made 'by reason of the transfer' are on the whole invalid. There is no mention of an ETO exception. The UK Government has taken the view that because the Directive creates an exception for dismissals due to the transfer, the same should logically apply to contractual variations, which are a 'lesser interference' with an employee's rights.

In *Regent Security Services v Power* (above), the Court of Appeal held that favourable transfer-related variations (where no ETO existed) are valid, notwithstanding the statutory language. The Court held that the employee does not waive his transferred rights but rather obtains an extra right which co-exists with the original right. On the facts, Mr Power could therefore choose to retire at 60 (the transferred right) or 65 (the additional right).

Note that reg 9 allows for variations to be agreed in certain circumstances where a transferor is subject to 'relevant insolvency proceedings' (as defined). The detail of this is beyond the scope of this book.

7.6.1 Practical advice

Where acting for a transferee, it is imperative to carry out full due diligence of all transferring employees' terms and conditions, since the transferee will inherit on those terms and conditions, and may not be able to vary the terms and conditions even with the employees' consent (see also **7.7.1**).

Where acting for the transferee, an indemnity should be gained from the transferor in the event of there being any difference between the terms and conditions detailed in the due diligence process by the transferor, and the actual terms and conditions on which employees transfer across.

A transferee who wishes to be sure that old terms and conditions do not apply, and/or to harmonise terms and conditions with the existing workforce, may dismiss those employees post-transfer or get the transferor to dismiss pre-transfer, with a view to re-engaging them on new terms. Such dismissals will be effective, but will give rise to the risk of unfair dismissal claims. Such dismissals will be 'automatically' unfair, unless there is an ETO reason. In *Berriman* (**7.5.2** above), the Court of Appeal held that an ETO reason entailing changes in the workforce involves more than a mere change in terms and conditions. If transferees wish to have contractually binding and harmonious terms, they will have to bear in mind the potential costs of any consequential unfair dismissal claims. Alternatively, they will have to try to ensure that changes are not connected with the transfer.

One area where post-transfer contractual variations can cause problems is in the 'offshoring of services' – ie where work is transferred from the UK to abroad. This was the scenario considered by the EAT in *Xerox Business Services Philippines Inc Ltd v Zeb* (UKEAT/0121/16). From 2009, Mr Zeb worked for a financial accounting team, and in 2011 his employment transferred under TUPE to Xerox UK. He was based in Wakefield. In 2014, the financial accounting team function was offshored to Xerox Philippines. Xerox believed that the place of work of employees would remain in Wakefield, and because Xerox Philippines had no need for staff based in Wakefield, there would be a genuine redundancy. It gave staff various options, including being made redundant by Xerox UK with an enhanced package, transferring via TUPE and being made redundant by Xerox Philippines with a standard package, or relocating to the Philippines on local terms and conditions (which were considerably less generous than those in the UK). Mr Zeb argued that he should be able to relocate on his existing terms, so he did not object to the transfer and was then made redundant by Xerox Philippines.

The EAT, overturning the employment tribunal's finding of an automatically unfair dismissal, said that, under TUPE, Xerox Philippines had been obliged to employ Mr Zeb at Wakefield and pay his UK salary but had not been obliged to employ him in Manila at the same salary. TUPE permits variation of contracts but such variations must be agreed. Here, there was no meeting of minds on terms, so there was no variation. TUPE did not permit Mr Zeb unilaterally to vary his place of work. The statutory definition of redundancy was met and it appeared to be an ETO reason for dismissal.

7.7 THE PROVISION OF INFORMATION AND CONSULTATION UNDER THE 2006 REGULATIONS

Regulations 11–16 of the 2006 Regulations impose duties upon both the transferor and the transferee to provide information to each other, and to provide information to and consult the representatives of employees who may be affected by the transfer.

7.7.1   The provision of employee liability information

Article 3(2) of the Acquired Rights Directive (as amended in 2014) gives Member States the option to introduce provisions 'to ensure that the transferor notifies the transferee of all the rights and obligations which will be transferred to the transferee ... so far as those rights and obligations are or ought to have been known to the transferor at the time of the transfer'. As a result, from 6 April 2006, under reg 11 of the 2006 Regulations, transferors became obliged, for the first time, to give transferees written information about 'any person employed by [the transferor] who is assigned to the organised grouping of resources or employees that is the subject of a relevant transfer' and all the associated rights and obligations towards them, ie 'employee liability information'. This information includes, for example, the identity and age of the employees who will transfer, information contained in the employees' written particulars of employment under s 1 of the ERA 1996 (see *Born London Ltd v Spire Production Services Ltd* (UKEAT/0255/16)), any disciplinary and grievances procedures within the last two years, details of any claims that the transferor reasonably believes might be brought and information about any collective agreements. This is aimed at helping the transferee to prepare for the arrival of the transferred employees, and ensuring that it is fully aware of all its inherited obligations.

The obligation includes a duty to provide employee liability information relating to any person who would have been employed by the transferor and assigned to the organised grouping of resources or employees that is the subject of a relevant transfer immediately before the transfer if he had not been dismissed in the circumstances described in reg 7(1) (see **7.5**), including, where the transfer is effected by a series of two or more transactions, a person so employed and assigned, or who would have been so employed and assigned, immediately before any of those transactions (reg 11(4)).

The information, which need not be provided all in one go, should be given in writing or in any other form that is accessible to the transferee (eg as computer data files). The information may also be provided via a third party. For example, where a client is re-assigning a contract from an existing contractor to a new contractor, that client organisation may act as the third party in passing the information to the new contractor. The information must be provided not less than 28 days before the transfer or, if special circumstances make this not reasonably practicable, as soon as reasonably practicable thereafter (reg 11(6) and (7)). There is no provision entitling the transferor and the transferee to agree to contract out of the duty to supply the employee liability information.

If the transferor does not provide this information, within three months after the transfer the transferee may complain to an employment tribunal that the transferor has failed to comply with any provision of reg 11. The tribunal may make a declaration and award such compensation, as it considers just and equitable. Compensation starts at a minimum of £500 for each employee in respect of whom the information was not provided or was defective (reg 12).

7.7.2   The duty to inform and consult

Regulation 13 of the 2006 Regulations imposes duties upon both the transferor and the transferee to provide information to, and to consult, the representatives of employees who may be affected by the transfer.

An employer must inform and consult appropriate representatives, who may be:

(a)   elected employee representatives;

(b)   representatives of an independent trade union recognised by an employer. (Where there is a recognised trade union, the employer must consult with representatives of that trade union rather than with employee representatives.)

Regulation 14 lays down detailed requirements for the election of employee representatives. See the BIS Guidance for more information on how this works. Representatives and candidates for election have certain rights and protections to enable them to carry out their function properly. The dismissal of an elected representative will be automatically unfair if the reason, or the main reason, related to the employee's status or activities as a representative. An elected representative also has the right not to suffer any detriment short of dismissal on the grounds of his status or activities. Candidates for election enjoy the same protection.

The obligation to consult and provide information applies in relation to

> any employees of the transferor or the transferee (whether or not assigned to the organised grouping of resources or employees that is the subject of a relevant transfer) who may be affected by the transfer or may be affected by measures taken in connection with it; and references to the employer shall be construed accordingly.

Categories of 'affected employees' might include not only the individuals who are to be transferred, but also their colleagues in the transferor who will not transfer but whose jobs might still be affected by the transfer, and their new colleagues in employment with the transferee whose jobs might also be affected by the transfer.

In *I Lab Facilities Ltd v Metcalfe and Others* (UKEAT/0224/12), the EAT held that employees assigned to part of a business that was wound up, did not have to be consulted in respect of the transfer of the part of the business that was sold. The EAT held that those employees were not 'affected' by the transfer.

7.7.2.1   The duty to inform

The obligation to provide information arises whenever a relevant transfer is planned. The information must be provided 'long enough before a relevant transfer to enable the employer to consult with the employees' representatives' (reg 13(2)). There is no firm guidance on time limits. In particular, it is clear that they are not the same as redundancy time limits, ie 90 or 30 days. In practice, consultation under the Regulations often lasts for relatively short periods. The information to be given to the representatives is to be delivered to them personally or by post, or (in the case of union representatives) sent by post to the union's head office.

The employer of affected employees must inform all the appropriate representatives of the following:

(a)   the fact that a relevant transfer is to take place;

(b)   when it is to take place (approximately);

(c)   the reasons for it;

(d)   the legal, economic and social implications of the transfer for the affected employees;

(e)   the measures which he envisages taking (eg if a re-organisation will result) in relation to those employees (and if no measures are envisaged, that fact);

(f)   if the employer is the transferor, the measures, in connection with the transfer, which he envisages the transferee will take in relation to any affected employees who will become employees of the transferee after the transfer (and if no measures are envisaged, that fact). The transferee must give the transferor the necessary information so that the previous employer is able to meet this requirement.

7.7.2.2   The duty to consult

If action is envisaged which will affect the employees, the employer must consult the representatives of the employees affected about that action. The consultation must be undertaken with a view to seeking agreement of the employee representatives to the intended measures (reg 13(6)). In practice, this means that the management must consider representations made and reply to the same; and if they choose to reject them, they should state the reasons for this. There is clearly an obligation to negotiate in good faith. The employer must consider any representations made by the appropriate representatives and reply to those representations; and if he rejects any of those representations, he must state his reasons (reg 13(7)). The employer must permit the appropriate representatives access to any affected employees, and must provide them with such accommodation and other facilities as may be appropriate (reg 13(8)).

The 2014 Amendment Regulations inserted a new reg 13A into the 2006 Regulations, which allows an employer with fewer than 10 employees to fulfil its reg 13 obligation by consulting directly with the workforce, provided there are no appropriate representatives (as defined by reg 13(3)). This change applies to transfers taking place on or after 31 July 2014.

It is a defence for the employer to show that there were special circumstances which rendered it not reasonably practicable to perform the duty in question, provided that he took whatever steps to perform that duty as were reasonably practicable in the circumstances. The tenor of the case law is that this defence is to be construed extremely narrowly. The circumstances must be out of the ordinary and relate to the particular situation and not merely to general circumstances which may create pressure or problems for the employer.

Confidentiality will not in itself be enough to invoke the defence. A mere desire to preserve confidentiality, rather than it being a prerequisite for the purchase to go ahead, will not be adequate.

With regard to a financial crisis in a redundancy situation, the tribunal will look to the practicability of consultation in light of the suddenness of the situation and the extent of prior knowledge.

There is no case law on the point which often arises in the context of listed companies, ie whether the defence is available where the disclosure of information would amount to a disclosure of price-sensitive information. In the authors' view, this argument is unlikely to persuade most employment tribunals. The tribunal would no doubt counter-suggest that appropriate representatives could have been asked to agree to confidentiality obligations and that the Listing Rules allow a company to disclose information about impending developments/negotiations to employee or trade union representatives.

7.7.2.3 Failure to comply

The relative inadequacy of the remedy for a failure to inform and consult means that many companies will probably opt to put other business concerns, such as confidentiality, ahead of their obligations under the 2006 Regulations.

Any of the affected employees, or their appropriate representatives, may bring a complaint (no later than three months after the date of the transfer) to an employment tribunal (reg 15). They can choose against whom they bring their complaint. Where either the transferor or the transferee is the sole defendant, he may seek to join the other employer to the case. The 2006 Regulations resolve one previous area of uncertainty, as to whether the transferor or the transferee was liable for any award made by a tribunal for a failure to comply: both the transferee and the transferor are now jointly and severally liable in respect of any compensation payable (reg 15(9)).

If a complaint is upheld, the tribunal must make a declaration and has a discretion to order the employer to pay appropriate compensation to such descriptions of affected employees as may be specified in the award. 'Appropriate compensation' in reg 15 means such sum not exceeding 13 weeks' pay for the employee in question as the tribunal considers just and equitable having regard to:

(a)   the seriousness of the failure of the employer to comply with his duty;

(b)   any loss sustained by the transferee attributable to the matters complained of; and

(c)   the terms of any contract between transferor and transferee under which the transferor may be liable to pay a sum to the transferee in respect of failure to provide such information (reg 16(3)).

The last provision is to prevent any element of double recovery. It is for a tribunal to decide when it would be 'just and equitable' to award less than the maximum, although the Government has commented that if a failure was 'minimal or trivial', the minimum award need not apply. Note that whether a week's pay for this purpose is subject to the statutory maximum (currently £479) imposed by s 227 of the ERA 1996 was the subject of an appeal in *Zaman v Kozee Sleep Products Ltd* (EAT/0312/10). The EAT said that even though reg 16 did cross-refer to s 227 of the ERA 1996, there was no intention to apply the cap. If there had been such intention, it would have been necessary either to amend s 227 to include a specific reference or include an express provision in the 2006 Regulations. The Court of Appeal confirmed in *Sweetin v Coral Racing* [2006] IRLR 252 (following *Susie Radin Ltd v GMB* [2004] IRLR 400 – see **4.8.1.2**) that where there is a complete failure to engage in the consultation process, a tribunal should start at the 13-week maximum and work down as appropriate (see eg *Cable Realisations Ltd v GMB Northern* [2010] IRLR 42 and *Todd v Care Concern* (UKEAT/0057/2010)).

Compensation for a failure to inform and consult cannot be set off against other obligations, for example damages for breach of contract or for a 'protective award' under the collective redundancy obligations.

In *Royal Mail Group v CWU* [2009] EWCA Civ 1045, Royal Mail was planning to franchise a number of post office branches to WH Smith. It believed, however, that there was no relevant transfer as a result because Royal Mail was offering voluntary redundancy and/or redeploying staff using an express contractual right. Because Royal Mail believed that there was no transfer, it believed that there was no need to inform and consult the union about the transfer. The CWU complained to an employment tribunal, which found that Royal Mail had failed to comply with the obligation to inform and consult. The EAT and the Court of Appeal disagreed and overturned the tribunal's decision. They accepted that where an employer genuinely believes that no transfer will take place, it will not be in breach of its obligations to inform and consult.

7.7.3   Other duties to consult and inform

In addition to the obligations under regs 11–16 of the 2006 Regulations, the Information and Consultation of Employees Regulations 2004 (SI 2004/3426) (implementing the EC Directive on information and consultation) apply to undertakings employing 50 or more employees. The Regulations provide for a comprehensive scheme of consultation and the provision of information to employees (see **4.8.2**).

Again, where there is an overlap, the 2004 Regulations cease to apply once the employer has notified the representatives that he will be complying with his duties under the 2006 Regulations.

Note: The 2014 Amendment Regulations, which became effective in January 2014, amended the Trade Union and Labour Relations (Consolidation) Act 1992 by inserting a new provision (s 198A), which allows pre-transfer consultation by the transferee to take place (where the transferor agrees) and for such pre-transfer consultation to count for collective redundancy consultation purposes (see **4.8** above).

7.8   FURTHER READING

BIS Guide, *Employment Rights on the Transfer of an Undertaking*.

Selwyn's Law of Employment, 20th edn (OUP, 2018).

Blackstone's Employment Law Practice, 10th edn (OUP, 2019).

Derbyshire & Hardy, *TUPE: Law and Practice*, 4th edn (Spiramus, 2014).

Harvey, *Industrial Relations and Employment Law* (Butterworths), Div F.

Lewis, *Transfer of Undertakings* (Sweet and Maxwell, Last Release: November 2018).

McMullen, *Business Transfers and Employee Rights* (LNUK).

The blog <tupe.uk.net> endeavours to gather together information and case law on TUPE and contains a number of useful and updated resources. It is compiled by a practising barrister.

SUMMARY

At common law in the UK, the transfer of a business undertaking by one employer to another would automatically terminate the employee's contract of employment, ie there is a dismissal. The Transfer of Undertakings (Protection of Employment) Regulations 2006 alter the legal position by providing that where there is a 'relevant transfer', there will not be any automatic termination of the contract of employment simply by reason of the transfer. Where there is a 'relevant transfer', the employee will transfer to the new owner and will be employed by him on the same terms as under his original contract. If there are any dismissals, whether actual, constructive or deemed, and whether they are before or after the transfer of the business, if those dismissals are related to the transfer, they will be automatically unfair unless, effectively, there is a genuine redundancy situation (an economic, technical or organisational (ETO) reason for the dismissal; **7.1**).

For the 2006 Regulations to apply, there must be a transfer from one person to another; consequently, there must be a change in the employer, not merely in the ownership. The 2006 Regulations do not therefore apply to transfers by share takeover or to transfers of assets only, or to a situation where a purchaser buys a majority shareholding in a company, thereby gaining control. This is because there is no change in the identity of the employer – in all these situations it will remain the same company. The 2006 Regulations do apply to mergers, sales of part of a going concern, changes of franchisee, sale of a sole trader's business or partnership and to transfers between two companies belonging to the same group, or where one subsidiary subcontracts work to another, provided the transfer involves the transfer of an 'economic entity' (see *Allen and Others v Amalgamated Construction* (Case C-234/98) [2000] IRLR 119) (**7.2**).

Regulation 3 of the 2006 Regulations expressly covers 'service provision changes' such as contracting-out exercises (eg catering, cleaning, security) where services are outsourced, insourced or assigned to a new contractor. However, the Regulations will not apply to service provision changes that take place 'in connection with a single specific event or task of short term duration'.

Regulation 4(3) of the 2006 Regulations operates so as to transfer the contracts of any individuals who are:

(a)   employed by the transferor immediately prior to the transfer (or would have been had they not been dismissed for a reason related to the transfer – in this latter situation the dismissal will be effective but liability for any claims the dismissed employee may have may fall upon the transferee); and

(b)   assigned to the relevant grouping of employees that is transferred.

The Regulations state that there will be no transfer of employees who are only 'temporarily assigned' to a particular undertaking (**7.3** and **7.4**).

Regulations 4(5) and 7(1) clarify when the 'economic technical or organisational' (ETO) defence applies, and the ability to change terms and conditions on a transfer.

The 2006 Regulations permit variations of contract, which may be agreed between transferees and transferred employees, and which are done either for an ETO reason entailing changes in the workforce, or where the contract permits such variations. 'Entailing changes in the workforce' is not defined in the 2006 Regulations, but it has been interpreted by tribunals under predecessor Regulations as meaning changes in the 'numbers' employed. The 2014 Amendment Regulations have extended this meaning to include locational changes.

Regulation 4(7) and (8) allow an employee to object to a transfer, but specify that where this right is exercised, the employee shall be treated as having resigned (**7.5** and **7.6**).

Regulations 8 and 9 cover what happens where there is a rescue of failing businesses.

Regulations 11 and 12 create an obligation for the current employer to provide employee information to the transferee, so that the transferee is made fully aware of the employees' rights, obligations and liabilities upon transfer (**7.7**).

Flowcharts showing the steps to be taken to determine whether a dismissal before a relevant transfer or a dismissal on or after a relevant transfer is fair, are set out in **Figures 7.1** and **7.2** respectively below.

Figure 7.1 Dismissals before a relevant transfer

NB – ALSO check for redundancy payment claims and/or WD claims. Claim will be against the same party as the claim for UD.

Figure 7.2 Dismissals on or after a relevant transfer

Was there a relevant transfer?

Reg 3(1)(a): business transfer: two-limb test:
(a) Is there an economic entity? – question of fact;
(b) Has that entity transferred? – *Spijkers*
OR
Reg 3(1)(b) and reg 3(3) Service provision changes

→ NO → Usual employment rules apply

↓ YES

Effect of relevant transfer (reg 4) = Contract continues with transferee and statutory rights, etc preserved

↓ YES

Check eligibility re UD – usual rules include **one or two years' continuous employment + has there been a dismissal?**

→ NO → NO UD CLAIM

↓ YES

Was the transfer the sole or principal reason for the dismissal?

→ NO → Apply usual UD rules against **Transferee**

↓ YES

(Reg 7 provides that the dismissal = **AUTO UD** against the **Transferee** unless there is an ETO reason *entailing a change in the workforce*)

Was there an ETO reason entailing a change in the workforce?
- Look for redundancy as the typical example – if established the dismissal will be deemed to be for redundancy/substantial reason [for purpose of ERA 1996, s 98]

→ NO → Dismissal is automatically **unfair (reg 7)** Claim against Transferee **(reg 4(3))**

↓ YES

Claim against Transferee
Was dismissal handled fairly under s 98(4)?

→ NO → Dismissal unfair – claim against **Transferee**

↓ YES

Dismissal will be fair

NB – ALSO check for redundancy payment claims and/or WD claims. Claim will be against the Transferee.

DISCRIMINATION AND EQUAL PAY

LEARNING OUTCOMES

After reading this chapter you will be able to:

- understand the underlying principles of discrimination law and when and to whom it applies in an employment context
- list the grounds ('protected characteristics') in the Equality Act 2010 upon which discrimination is deemed unlawful
- describe and explain each of the protected characteristics
- list the four types of prohibited conduct
- understand the significance of occupational requirements and the reasonable steps defence
- describe the remedies available where a complaint of discrimination is made out.

8.1 INTRODUCTION

The first anti-discrimination legislation in the UK was passed in 1965. In 1975, Great Britain became a member of the European Community (which became the European Union in 1992 when the Maastricht Treaty was signed), but the then Government opted out of the Social Chapter provisions of the Treaty, which included anti-discrimination provisions. In 1997, the then Labour Government opted into the Social Chapter provisions of the Treaty. In 2000, the EU introduced a number of new directives protecting people on the basis of sexuality, religion, belief and age, as well as revising previous protections around disability, race and gender. Much of current UK anti-discrimination law mirrors these EU directives. Since the UK voted to leave the EU in June 2016, it remains uncertain what the position will be going forward as far as anti-discrimination law is concerned, as so much UK law in this area is EUgrounded. However, until Article 50 of the TEU is triggered, the UK will continue to be bound by its EU obligations.

A single Equality Bill, intended to harmonise and consolidate in one place most existing anti-discrimination and equality legislation (such as the SDA 1975, the RRA 1976 and the DDA 1995), was published on 27 April 2009. The Equality Act 2010 received Royal Assent on 8 April 2010. The Act replaced most of the previous discrimination legislation and, as well as codifying the different strands of the old statute-based law on discrimination (eg, direct discrimination still occurs when 'someone is treated less favourably than another person because of a protected characteristic'), also made a number of changes to the existing law (eg, employees may now complain about harassment even if it is not directed at them, if they can demonstrate that it creates an offensive environment for them). Additionally, it extended some aspects of the old law (eg, associative discrimination – direct discrimination against someone because he or she associates with another person who possesses a protected characteristic). Under the old law, discrimination by association applied only to race, religion and belief, and sexual orientation. It has now been extended to cover age, disability, gender reassignment and sex. Some entirely new concepts (eg, the concept of discrimination arising from disability, which occurs if a disabled person is treated unfavourably because of something arising in consequence of his or her disability) were introduced for the first time. Most of the employment provisions came into force on 1 October 2010.

In March 2011 the Government announced that it would not be implementing the 'dual' discrimination provisions (contained in s 14 of the Equality Act 2010), which were introduced to allow individuals who believed they had been discriminated against because of a combination of two protected characteristics to bring a combined claim.

The Equality and Human Rights Commission (EHRC) has created a series of non-statutory guidance documents to help explain the Act and provide practical examples. Its website <http://www.equalityhumanrights.com> has detailed guidance (running to hundreds of pages) for employers, workers, service providers, service users, education providers and public sector bodies. In line with its statutory powers (Equality Act 2006, s 14(1)), the EHRC has also published a code of practice on employment and one on equal pay. The purpose of these codes is to explain the statutory provisions of the Equality Act 2010. They draw on precedent and case law. The codes came into force on 6 April 2011. Courts and tribunals must take into account any part of the code that appears to them relevant to any questions arising in proceedings.

The Acas website <http://www.acas.org.uk> also contains a wealth of guidance on the Equality Act 2010.

This chapter and the following chapters on discrimination set out the current law. All the chapters on discrimination refer by way of illustration and example to the pre- and post-Equality Act 2010 case law. Although the Government believes, in many places, that there have been no changes, care is still needed where pre-Equality Act 2010 case law is relied upon as there are some nuanced differences.

8.1.1   Background

The general common law rule is that an employer is free to offer employment to whomsoever he chooses (*Allen v Flood and Taylor* [1898] AC 1). This common law freedom has been restricted by statute. The employer may be in breach of statutory requirements if he discriminates against a person on the grounds of:

(a)   sex or marital status;

(b)   gender reassignment;

(c)   race;

(d)   religion or belief;

(e) sexual orientation;

(f) trade union membership;

(g) part-time work;

(h) age;

(i) disability;

(j) fixed (limited)-term work;

(k) pregnancy and maternity.

In all areas of discrimination law it is important to appreciate the influence of EU law. In the area of sex discrimination, the Equal Treatment Directive (76/207) provided that there should be no discrimination on grounds of sex, either directly or indirectly, nor by reference to marital or family status, in access to employment, training, working conditions, promotion or dismissal. The UK first implemented the Directive by way of the SDA 1975, which made it unlawful to discriminate against women, men, married persons or persons who intend to undergo, or have undergone, a gender reassignment. The Equal Treatment (Amendment) Directive (2002/73) amended the Equal Treatment Directive, most importantly by adding definitions of 'sexual harassment' and 'harassment'. The UK initially implemented the changes required by the Directive in October 2005, by way of the Employment Equality (Sex Discrimination) Regulations 2005 (SI 2005/2467).

Influenced by international law and EU law (the Race Discrimination Directive (2000/43)), the RRA 1976 prohibited discrimination on the grounds of colour, race, nationality or ethnic or national origins.

Article 157 TFEU (ex 141 EC) established the principle that men and women should receive equal pay for equal work. This was implemented into UK law by way of the Equal Pay Act (EPA) 1970 (as amended).

The Framework Directive for Equal Treatment in Employment and Occupation (2000/78) required Member States to implement legislation prohibiting discrimination on grounds of sexual orientation and religion. The UK enacted law to comply with its EU obligations by way of the Employment Equality (Religion or Belief) Regulations 2003 (SI 2003/1660) ('the Religion or Belief Regulations'), the Employment Equality (Sexual Orientation) Regulations 2003 (SI 2003/1661) ('the Sexual Orientation Regulations') and the Disability Discrimination Act 1995 (Amendment) Regulations 2003 (SI 2003/1673), which amended the DDA 1995. The Sexual Orientation Regulations were amended in 2005 to take account of the Civil Partnership Act 2004. A revised Code of Practice on Racial Equality in Employment came into effect in April 2006. The Employment Equality (Age) Regulations 2006 (SI 2006/1031) ('the Age Regulations') were the last plank of the UK's implementation of the Equal Treatment Framework Directive.

The Equality Act 2006 received Royal Assent on 16 February 2006. It provided for the establishment of the EHRC, which came into being in October 2007. The EHRC took on the work of the former equality Commissions (the EOC, the DRC and the CRE), and additionally assumed responsibility for promoting equality and combating unlawful discrimination in three new strands, namely sexual orientation, religion or belief, and age. The EHRC also has responsibility for the promotion of human rights.

Much of the UK legislation referred to above has now been consolidated into the Equality Act 2010. All references in **Chapters 8** to **13** to 'the Act' are to the Equality Act 2010.

In May 2012, the Government announced various proposed changes to the Equality Act 2010 aimed at reducing 'red tape' in equality law. It further consulted on repealing provisions in the Act that made employers liable for harassment by third parties. On 1 October 2013, those provisions were repealed for post-1 October 2013 acts (see **11.4**). The Government abolished the statutory questionnaire procedure in April 2014 (see **8.8.1.2**).

Section 64 of the Enterprise and Regulatory Reform Act (ERRA) 2013 curbed the EHRC's duties and powers. Whilst the Commission retains its 'general duty', its 'good relations duty' and 'power of conciliation for non-workplace disputes' were repealed from 25 June 2013.

The Government removed employment tribunals' power to make wider recommendations on an employer's policies and procedures on discrimination from October 2015 (see **8.8.2.1**).

In 2016/17 there were issued in the employment tribunal 2,240 race, 4,000 disability, 7,500 age and some 20,000 sex (including equal pay and pregnancy) discrimination claims. Only 3% of issued race discrimination claims go all the way to a final hearing and succeed; 36% of claims are settled before a hearing. The statistics are broadly similar for sex and age discrimination claims. Disability (4% win; 42% settle) and pregnancy (6% win; 47% settle) claims have a slightly higher success rate. (See <www.gov.uk/government/collections/tribunals-statistics>.)

8.1.2   Who is protected?

The Act protects, amongst others, employees (s 39), job applicants (s 39), contract workers (s 41), office holders (s 50) and trade union members (s 57). It also protects employees after their employment has ended (s 108). Section 83(2) of the Act defines 'Employment' as '(a) employment under a contract of employment, a contract of apprenticeship or a contract personally to do work'. This definition is wider than the definition of 'employee' in s 230(1) of the ERA 1996 (see **1.3.2** and **1.3.4.2** above).

Sections 39 and 40 make it unlawful for an employer to discriminate against, or to harass or to victimise employees and people seeking work. It applies where the employer is making arrangements to fill a job, and in respect of anything done in the course of a person's employment (see **8.4** below). Section 41 makes it unlawful for a person (referred to as a 'principal') who makes work available to contract workers to discriminate against, harass or victimise them (see *Leeds City Council v Woodhouse* [2010] IRLR 625).

Section 108 makes it unlawful to discriminate against or harass someone after a relationship covered by the Act has ended (see **8.4** below).

The Supreme Court held, in *Hounga v Allen & Another* [2014] UKSC 47, that the defence of illegality does not always defeat a discrimination complaint (see **5.4.2.4**).

There is a general interpretation section in s 212, and an index to defined expressions in s 214 and Sch 28.

8.1.3   Territorial jurisdiction

Unlike previous discrimination legislation, the Act does not deal with territorial scope. Most of the old legislation applied to employment 'at an establishment in Great Britain', and provided protection to those who worked 'wholly or partly' in Great Britain as well as to those who worked wholly outside Great Britain but fulfilled specific criteria. It is therefore left to employment tribunals to determine whether the Act applies in any given situation.

According to the Explanatory Notes, the decision to remove territorial scope from the Act follows the precedent of the ERA 1996 (s 196, which determined whether it applied to employees who ordinarily work outside Great Britain, was repealed by the ERA 1999). The EHRC Code states that discrimination protection is required where there is a sufficiently close link between the employment relationship and Great Britain (see *Lawson* and *Ravat* at **3.7** above).

In *Clyde & Co LLP and Another v Bates van Winkelhof* [2012] EWCA Civ 1207, the Court of Appeal upheld an employment tribunal's decision with regard to jurisdiction and agreed that it was right to apply the *Serco v Lawson* test to discrimination and/or whistleblowing claims (see **3.7**). In this case, Mrs Bates van Winkelhof spent the majority of her time working abroad. The

Court confirmed that the test to be applied in that situation (ie where the person lives and/or works for at least part of the time in Great Britain) is whether an individual has a sufficiently strong connection with Great Britain. By contrast, in cases where the individual works wholly abroad, a comparative exercise will be appropriate (ie connections with Great Britain will need to outweigh connections with the other jurisdiction). Although the issue of whether the individual was a worker was appealed to the Supreme Court, the jurisdiction issue was not, and the Court of Appeal's analysis remains good law.

The High Court applied the *Lawson* test in R (*on the application of Hottak and Anor*) *v Secretary of State for Foreign and Commonwealth Affairs and Anor* [2015] IRLR 827, QBD. It held that two Afghan interpreters working for the armed forces in Afghanistan could not bring discrimination claims because they were not expat or peripatetic workers and did not have a closer connection to Great Britain than Afghanistan.

8.1.4 Interpretation

Section 137 provides that any final finding in a claim brought under the previous discrimination legislation is to be treated as conclusive in proceedings under the Act. A finding is considered final when an appeal against it is dismissed, withdrawn or abandoned, or where the time-limit for appealing against it has expired. This is intended to prevent matters that were determined under the previous legislation being relitigated under the Act.

8.1.5 Scope of this and following chapters on discrimination

This chapter deals with the matters that are common to all the protected characteristics. It, together with **Chapters 9, 10** and **11,** deals with discrimination on the grounds of sex, race, religion or belief, marriage and civil partnership, pregnancy and maternity, and sexual orientation. This chapter also looks briefly at equal pay, discrimination against part-time workers and discrimination on grounds of trade union membership or activities.

Chapter 12 deals with age discrimination and **Chapter 13** covers discrimination on the ground of disability, because these follow slightly different regimes from the other protected characteristics.

8.2 PROTECTED CHARACTERISTICS

Section 4 of the Equality Act 2010 sets out certain 'protected' characteristics. These are the grounds upon which discrimination is deemed unlawful.

The characteristics relevant to this chapter and **Chapters 9–11** are:

- gender reassignment (s 7)
- marriage and civil partnership (s 8)
- race (s 9)
- religion or belief (s 10)
- sex (s 11)
- sexual orientation (s 12)
- pregnancy and maternity (s 18).

The characteristic relevant to **Chapter 12** is age (s 5) and to **Chapter 13** is disability (s 6 and Sch 1). The definitions in relation to the protected characteristics of age and disability are dealt with separately in **Chapters 12** and **13**. Pregnancy and maternity, which are discussed separately in s 18, are covered under direct discrimination (see **9.4**).

The EHRC Code of Practice on Employment contains a wealth of information, and tribunals are obliged to take it into account when it appears relevant. Readers should refer to the Code for further guidance on protected characteristics.

8.2.1 Sex

Sex is defined in s 11 of the Act:

> In relation to the protected characteristic of sex—
>
> (a) a reference to a person who has a particular protected characteristic is a reference to a man or to a woman;
>
> (b) a reference to persons who share a protected characteristic is a reference to persons of the same sex.

8.2.2 Race

'Race' is defined non-exhaustively in s 9 of the Act:

> (1) Race includes—
>
>   (a) colour;
>
>   (b) nationality;
>
>   (c) ethnic or national origins.
>
> (2) In relation to the protected characteristic of race—
>
>   (a) a reference to a person who has a particular protected characteristic is a reference to a person of a particular racial group;
>
>   (b) a reference to persons who share a protected characteristic is a reference to persons of the same racial group.
>
> (3) A racial group is a group of persons defined by reference to race; and a reference to a person's racial group is a reference to a racial group into which the person falls.
>
> (4) The fact that a racial group comprises two or more distinct racial groups does not prevent it from constituting a particular racial group.
>
> (5) A Minister of the Crown may by order—
>
>   (a) amend this section so as to provide for caste to be an aspect of race;
>
>   (b) amend this Act so as to provide for an exception to a provision of this Act to apply, or not to apply, to caste or to apply, or not to apply, to caste in specified circumstances.
>
>   ...

The Explanatory Notes give the following examples:

- Colour includes being black or white.
- Nationality includes being a British, Australian or Swiss citizen.
- Ethnic or national origins include being from a Roma background or of Chinese heritage.
- A racial group could be 'black Britons' which would encompass those people who are both black and who are British citizens.

The Code of Practice also gives useful examples.

The courts have often had to consider the meaning of 'ethnic origins'. In *Mandla and Another v Dowell Lee and Another* [1983] 2 AC 548, HL, Lord Fraser identified two essential characteristics of an ethnic group:

(a) a long shared history; and

(b) a cultural tradition of its own.

On that basis, for example, Sikhs are a distinct ethnic group for these purposes.

In addition to these essential characteristics, his Lordship identified others which, although not essential, could be expected to be displayed, such as a common language, or a common geographical origin. The principles in *Mandla* have been applied in a number of cases, so, for example, gypsies have been held to constitute an ethnic group, but not Rastafarians.

In *BBC Scotland v Souster* [2001] IRLR 150, the Court of Session confirmed that the Scots and English are separate racial groups, defined by reference to their national origins (although not by reference to their ethnic origins).

In *Dizedziak v Future Electronics Ltd* (UKEAT/0270/11), the EAT upheld a decision that the claimant had been subjected to direct discrimination on grounds of her nationality when she was instructed by her line manager not to speak in 'her own language' at work (the claimant was a Polish national); but see too *Kelly v Covance* at **9.2.5.2**.

In *Moxam v Visible Changes Ltd and Another* (UKEAT/0267/11), the EAT confirmed that the phrase 'on racial grounds' protects a person against discrimination on grounds of race, not just on the ground of that person's race.

The Supreme Court held, in *Taiwo and Onu v Olaigbe and Akwiwu* [2016] UKSC 31, that mistreatment of a worker on the grounds of 'immigration status' was not race discrimination because immigration status could not be equated with nationality: while immigration status is a function of nationality, it is not so closely associated with it as to be indissociable from it. Discrimination on the grounds of their 'precarious' immigration status could not be said to be the same as discrimination on the ground of their race. It was not direct discrimination because the mistreatment was due to their vulnerable migrant status, not because of their nationality. It was not indirect discrimination because no 'provision, criterion or practice' has been applied. (Baroness Hale suggested that Parliament might have to consider whether to give employment tribunals jurisdiction to award compensation under s 8 of the Modern Slavery Act 2015 where vulnerable migrant workers suffer ill-treatment.) See too *Mruke v Khan* [2018] EWCA Civ 280, where the Court of Appeal held that the claimant's socio-economic circumstances were the reason for the less favourable treatment and not her nationality.

Section 97 of the ERRA 2013 (amending s 9 of the Equality Act 2010) came into effect on 25 June 2013, but the provision states only that a Minister must 'by order amend [the Equality Act] to provide for caste to be an aspect of race'. No draft Regulations have been produced yet. The EHRC published a report on the nature of caste prejudice and harassment in Spring 2014, and the Government consultated on prospective legislation from March–September 2017. The Government has recently announced that, for now, it will not legislate but will keep cases under review to 'ensure the principles established by the *Tirkey* judgment [see below] are upheld'. The EAT in *Chandok v Tirkey* (UKEAT/0190/14) found that as many elements implicit in caste identity may reflect an employee's ethnic origin, caste will be covered by the broad protected characteristic of race (note that *Tirkey* was a trafficking case).

8.2.3 Religion or belief

Religion or belief is defined in s 10 of the Act:

(1)   Religion means any religion and a reference to religion includes a reference to a lack of religion.

(2)   Belief means any religious or philosophical belief and a reference to belief includes a reference to a lack of belief.

(3)   In relation to the protected characteristic of religion or belief—

     (a)   a reference to a person who has a particular protected characteristic is a reference to a person of a particular religion or belief;

     (b)   a reference to persons who share a protected characteristic is a reference to persons who are of the same religion or belief.

The Explanatory Notes give the following examples:

- The Baha'i faith, Buddhism, Christianity, Hinduism, Islam, Jainism, Judaism, Rastafarianism, Sikhism and Zoroastrianism are all religions for the purposes of this provision.

- Beliefs such as humanism and atheism would be beliefs for the purposes of this provision but adherence to a particular football team would not be.

Note: Jews may also a constitute a racial group under the definition in s 9 (see **8.2.2**).

In *R v Secretary of State for Education and Employment & Others, ex parte Williamson & Others* [2005] 2 AC 246 (a case brought under Article 9 of the ECHR), the House of Lords considered the meaning of 'religious belief' and held that the court is concerned to ensure that the assertion of religious belief is made in good faith:

> 'neither fictitious, nor capricious, and that it is not artifice' ... but emphatically it is not for the court to embark on an inquiry into the asserted belief and judge its 'validity' by some objective standard ... Freedom of religion protects the subjective belief of an individual ... The belief must be consistent with basic standards of human dignity or integrity ... [and] possess an adequate degree of seriousness and importance ... [and] be coherent in the sense of being intelligible and capable of being understood. But again, too much should not be demanded in this regard ... Overall, these threshold requirements should not be set at a level which would deprive minority beliefs of the protection they are intended to have ...

The Explanatory Notes state that the criteria for determining what constitutes a 'philosophical belief' are that it must:

(a)   be genuinely held;

(b)   be a belief and not an opinion or a viewpoint based on the present state of information available;

(c)   be a belief as to a weighty and substantial aspect of human life and behaviour;

(d)   attain a certain level of cogency, seriousness, cohesion and importance; and

(e)   be worthy of respect in a democratic society, compatible with human dignity and not conflict with the fundamental rights of others.

These criteria are founded upon the ECtHR's decision in *Campbell and Cosans v UK* (1982) 4 EHRR 293.

In *McClintock v Department of Constitutional Affairs* [2008] IRLR 29, the EAT said that to constitute a belief, there must be a religious or philosophical viewpoint in which one actually believes; it is not enough to have an opinion based on some real or perceived logic, or based on information or lack of information.

The EAT had previously endorsed the above criteria in *Nicholson v Grainger plc* [2010] IRLR 4 (a case decided under the old law), and it is clear that the criteria will also apply to religious beliefs.

8.2.3.1   Some examples from case law

Religious belief

In *Hussain v Bhullar Bros* (ET/1806638/04), a tribunal held that attendance at home following the bereavement of a close family member was a religion-based practice or belief. The tribunal held that if a person genuinely believes that his faith requires a particular course of action then it is sufficient to make it part of his belief. It said that attempting to differentiate between cultural manifestation, traditions and religious observance would lead to 'unnecessary complications and endless debate'.

In *Trayhorn v Secretary of State for Employment* (UKEAT/0304/16) the EAT held that it was neither direct nor indirect discrimination to discipline an employee who was a Pentecostal Christian, who condemned homosexuality and spoke about repentance during a church service. The EAT said that it was not the manifestation of his belief that caused him to be disciplined but the way in which he had behaved.

The manifestation of religious beliefs can differ widely. The EHRC Employment Statutory Code of Practice states that 'a person does not have to prove that the manifestation of their religion or belief is a core component of the religion or philosophical belief they follow. It may instead be a means by which they choose to express their adherence to their religious belief.'

In *Gareddu v London Underground Ltd* (UKEAT/0086/16) the EAT emphasised that, to attract legal protection, the employee's expressed need to manifest their beliefs in a certain way must be genuine. On the facts (Mr Gareddu, who was a practising Roman Catholic from Sardinia, wished to take an extended five-week holiday to attend a number of religious festivals in Sardinia in August), while attendance at festivals in Sardinia was accepted as a manifestation of religious belief for Mr Gareddu, this was not the genuine reason for his extended holiday request. (Had it been genuine, the employer may have been able to justify refusing the request by showing that its practice of limiting holidays to a maximum of three weeks at a time was a proportionate means of achieving a legitimate end.)

Philosophical belief

In *Nicholson v Grainger plc* [2010] IRLR 4, the EAT adopted an expansive approach when it upheld a tribunal decision that an employee's belief that action was urgently needed to address climate change, could amount to a philosophical belief as it was cogent, serious, coherent and worthy of respect in a democratic society. The EAT rejected the argument that political or science-based beliefs could not fall with the meaning of 'philosophical belief', but any such belief must be 'worthy of respect in a democratic society'.

In November 2012, the ECtHR upheld a complaint by Arthur Redfearn, a bus driver in Bradford (serving a largely Asian population) who was dismissed when he stood as a BNP candidate, that he had been discriminated against on the grounds of political opinion or affiliation, which put the UK in breach of Article 11 of the ECHR (freedom of association) (*Redfearn v United Kingdom* [2012] ECHR 1878). This was a case heard in the UK courts before the Religion or Belief Regulations 2003 were implemented. The Court of Appeal (see *Redfearn v Serco Ltd t/a West Yorkshire Transport Service* [2006] IRLR 623) rejected Mr Redfearn's claim that he had been discriminated against on racial grounds. (He did not have sufficient service to bring an unfair dismissal claim.) Mummery LJ concluded that, 'properly analysed', Mr Redfearn's complaint was of discrimination on political grounds, which falls outside the anti-discrimination laws: Mr Redfearn was not dismissed simply because he was white – so he was not discriminated against, and Serco would have dismissed any driver of any race who stood for a similarly racially-segregated political party – so he did not suffer indirect discrimination either. The Religion or Belief Regulations 2003 (which have now been replaced by the Equality Act 2010) did contain protection for 'philosophical beliefs', but early decisions rejected arguments that this phrase included 'political beliefs'; and BNP members have not managed to persuade tribunals that theirs amounts to a philosophical belief (see, eg, *Wingfield v North Cumbria Mental Health and Learning Disabilities NHS Trust* (ET/2510953/05) and *L'Anson v Chief Constable of West Yorkshire Police* (ET/1804854/09)).

The ECtHR has previously distinguished between political opinions that are legal but extreme (eg the National Front) and those that are illegal (eg supporting terrorism). In this case, the ECtHR was split 4:3 in Mr Redfearn's favour. It did not find that Mr Redfearn was either unfairly dismissed or discriminated against; it held that there was not a proper opportunity for him to argue his case. While s 10 of the Equality Act 2010 (replacing the Religion or Belief Regulations 2003) does not expressly include political beliefs, the Equality Directive 2007/78/EC contains no such qualification; it is arguable that Serco, which was treated as a private employer, is an emanation of the State, such that the Equality Directive was directly enforceable against it. At the time the case was argued before the Court of Appeal, the BNP was characterised as a party that confined its membership to white people. Since then, following proceedings brought against the BNP by the EHRC, this is no longer strictly true, which may make it harder to dismiss BNP members from sensitive posts.

It is helpful to look at some employment tribunal decisions. In *Olivier v DWP* (ET/1701407/13), the tribunal held that a political belief (in this case a belief in democratic socialism (going beyond mere support for a political party) could amount to a philosophical belief, applying the *Nicholson* criteria (above).

In *Hashman v Milton Park (Dorset) Ltd* (ET/3105555/09), a gardener's belief in the sanctity of life, extending to a fervent anti-fox hunting stance, was held to be a protected philosophical belief; in *Lisk v Shield Guardian Ltd* (ET/3300873/11), a belief that individuals should wear poppies was held to be too narrow to constitute a protected belief; in *Maistry v BBC* (ET/1313142/10), a journalist's belief in the 'higher purpose' of public service broadcasting was a philosophical belief (that finding was not appealed, but the Court of Appeal held that the claimant was not dismissed because of his belief, in circumstances where those involved in the decision to dismiss were unaware that the claimant held such a belief); in *Arya v London Borough of Waltham Forest* (ET/3200/396/11), the claimant's belief that 'the Jewish religion's professed belief in Jews being "God's chosen people" was at odds with meritocratic and multicultural society', and was not therefore capable of being a philosophical belief; and in *Hawkins v Universal Utilities Ltd t/a Unicom* (ET/2501234/12), a tribunal held that a belief that 'it is wrong to lie under any circumstances' amounted to a philosophical belief. In *Gray v Mulberry Co (Design) Ltd* (UKEAT/0040/18), the EAT held that the tribunal had been right to find that a belief in 'the statutory human and moral right to own the copyright and moral rights of her own creative works and output' was not a 'belief' under s 10. The EAT held that the tribunal had correctly concluded that the belief did not attain a certain level of 'cogency, seriousness, cohesion and importance'.

There are two particularly tricky issues when looking at religion or belief discrimination. One concerns the extent to which law protects the manifestation of beliefs as opposed to the holding of them, particularly at work (see **10.2.3** below). There is a helpful ECHR Guidance Note on 'Religion or Belief and the Workplace', available at <http://www.equalityhumanrights.com/private-and-public-sector-guidance/employing-people/religion-or-belief-guidance-employers>. In May 2018, Acas issued new Guidance on Religion and Belief which, as well as providing an explanation of the law, contains practical guidance on talking about religion at work, food and fasting, and washing and changing rooms. Another difficult area is the apparent conflict with the protection of sexual orientation (see **9.2.5.2** below).

8.2.4   Sexual orientation

Sexual orientation is defined in s 12 of the Act:

(1)   Sexual orientation means a person's sexual orientation towards—

(a)   persons of the same sex,

(b)   persons of the opposite sex, or

(c)   persons of either sex.

(2)   In relation to the protected characteristic of sexual orientation—

(a)   a reference to a person who has a particular protected characteristic is a reference to a person who is of a particular sexual orientation;

(b)   a reference to persons who share a protected characteristic is a reference to persons who are of the same sexual orientation.

The Explanatory Notes give examples:

•   A man who experiences sexual attraction towards both men and women is 'bisexual' in terms of sexual orientation even if he has only had relationships with women.

•   A man and a woman who are both attracted only to people of the opposite sex from them share a sexual orientation.

•   A man who is attracted only to other men is a gay man. A woman who is attracted only to other women is a lesbian. So a gay man and a lesbian share a sexual orientation.

8.2.5   Gender reassignment

Gender reassignment is defined in s 7 of the Act:

(1)   A person has the protected characteristic of gender reassignment if the person is proposing to undergo, is undergoing or has undergone a process (or part of a process) for the purpose of reassigning the person's sex by changing physiological or other attributes of sex.

(2)   A reference to a transsexual person is a reference to a person who has the protected characteristic of gender reassignment.

(3)   In relation to the protected characteristic of gender reassignment—

 (a)   a reference to a person who has a particular protected characteristic is a reference to a transsexual person;

 (b)   a reference to persons who share a protected characteristic is a reference to transsexual persons.

The Explanatory Notes give examples:

- A person who was born physically male decides to spend the rest of his life living as a woman. He declares his intention to his manager at work, who makes appropriate arrangements, and she then starts life at work and home as a woman. After discussion with her doctor and a Gender Identity Clinic, she starts hormone treatment and after several years she goes through gender reassignment surgery. She would have the protected characteristic of gender reassignment for the purposes of the Act.

- A person who was born physically female decides to spend the rest of her life as a man. He starts and continues to live as a man. He decides not to seek medical advice as he successfully 'passes' as a man without the need for any medical intervention. He would have the protected characteristic of gender reassignment for the purposes of the Act.

Note that the requirement that previously existed under the SDA 1975 of being under medical supervision has been removed. This is because gender reassignment is recognised as a personal process rather than a medical one.

8.2.6   Marriage and civil partnership

Marriage and civil partnership is defined in s 8 of the Act:

(1)   A person has the protected characteristic of marriage and civil partnership if the person is married or is a civil partner.

(2)   In relation to the protected characteristic of marriage and civil partnership—

 (a)   a reference to a person who has a particular protected characteristic is a reference to a person who is married or is a civil partner;

 (b)   a reference to persons who share a protected characteristic is a reference to persons who are married or are civil partners.

The Explanatory Notes give examples:

- A person who is engaged to be married is not married and therefore does not have this protected characteristic.

- A divorcee or a person whose civil partnership has been dissolved is not married or in a civil partnership and therefore does not have this protected characteristic.

Marriage and civil partnership does not include those who are single and cohabiting.

Civil partnerships were introduced into the UK on 5 December 2005. Paragraph 18 of Sch 9 to the Equality Act 2010 provides that it is lawful to discriminate against an employee who is in a civil partnership or same-sex marriage by preventing or restricting them from having access to a benefit, facility or service, the right to which accrued before 5 December 2005 or which is payable in respect of periods of service before that date. In *Walker v Innospec Ltd* [2017] UKSC 47, the Supreme Court upheld a discrimination claim from Mr Walker that this provision was incompatible with the Framework Directive (2000/78/EC), as it amounted to direct discrimination in that it permitted an employer to treat a same-sex partner less favourably than an opposite-sex spouse. If Mr Walker had been married to a woman, she would have been entitled to a pension of about £45,700 pa. The impact of para 18 of Sch 9 meant that Mr Walker's husband would be entitled to a pension of about £1,000 pa. The Supreme Court referred to two decisions from the CJEU on survivors' pension rights for same-sex couples (*Maruko v Versorgungsanstalt der deutschen Bühnen* (Case C-267/06) and *Römer v Freie und Hansestadt*

Hamburg (Case C-147/08)) in declaring that para 18 of Sch 9 was incompatible with EU law and must be disapplied.

8.2.7 Pregnancy and maternity leave

See **9.4** below.

8.3 PROHIBITED CONDUCT

The Act outlaws:

(a)   direct discrimination (s 13) (see **Chapter 9**);

(b)   indirect discrimination (s 19) (see **Chapter 10**);

(c)   harassment (s 26) (see **Chapter 11**);

(d)   victimisation (s 27) (see **Chapter 11**);

(e)   instructing, causing, inducing and helping discrimination;

in relation to each of the protected characteristics. There are some differences with regard to age and disability. These characteristics are therefore dealt with separately in **Chapters 12** and **13**.

Direct and indirect discrimination are two different causes of action. They are different statutory torts (see R *(on the application of Elias) v Secretary of State for Defence* [2006] IRLR 934 and *National Statistics v Ali* [2005] ICR 201).

The Act also outlaws discrimination where a person is absent from work because of gender reassignment (s 16) (see **9.3**) and discrimination where a woman is absent from work as a result of pregnancy or illness caused by the pregnancy (s 18) (see **9.4**).

The prohibited conduct gives rise to a cause of action only if it falls within an area that the Act makes unlawful. The relevant part of the Act for employment purposes is Part 5 'Work'. Section 120 provides that an employment tribunal has jurisdiction to determine complaints relating to a breach of Part 5 provisions (see **8.4** for the relevant unlawful acts).

The EHRC non-statutory core guidance on 'Recruitment' gives the following examples of the various types of discrimination:

- You must not treat a person worse than another job applicant because of a protected characteristic (this is called **direct discrimination**).

> **Examples**
> - An employer does not interview a job applicant because of the applicant's ethnic background.
> - An employer says in a job advert 'this job is unsuitable for disabled people'.

- You must not do something which has (or would have) a worse impact on a job applicant and on other people who share a particular protected characteristic than on people who do not have that characteristic. Unless you can show that what you have done, or intend to do, is **objectively justified**, this will be **indirect discrimination**. 'Doing something' can include making a decision, or applying a rule or way of doing things.

> **Example**
> A job involves travelling to lots of different places to see clients. An employer says that, to get the job, the successful applicant has to be able to drive. This may stop some disabled people applying if they cannot drive. But there may be other perfectly good ways of getting from one appointment to another, which disabled people who cannot themselves drive could use. So the employer needs to show that a requirement to be able to drive is objectively justified, or they may be discriminating unlawfully against people who cannot drive because of their disability.

- You must not treat a disabled person **unfavourably** because of something connected to their disability where you cannot show that what you are doing is **objectively justified**. This only applies if you know or could reasonably have been expected to know that the person is a disabled person. The required knowledge is of facts of the applicant's disability. An employer does not need to realise that those particular facts are likely to meet the legal definition of disability. This is called **discrimination arising from disability.**

> **Example**
>
> An employer tells a visually impaired person who uses an assistance dog that they are unsuitable for a job because the employer is nervous of dogs and would not allow it in the office. Unless the employer can objectively justify what they have done, this is likely to be discrimination arising from disability. The refusal to consider the visually impaired person for the job is unfavourable treatment which is because of something connected to their disability (their use of an assistance dog). It may also be a failure to make a reasonable adjustment.

- You must not treat a person worse than someone else because they are **associated with** a person who has a protected characteristic.

> **Example**
>
> An employer does not give someone the job, even though they are the best-qualified person, just because the applicant tells the employer they have a disabled partner. This is probably direct discrimination because of disability by association. Direct discrimination cannot be justified, whatever the employer's motive.

- You must not treat a person worse than another job applicant because you incorrectly think they have a protected characteristic (**perception**).

> **Example**
>
> An employer does not give an applicant the job, even though they are the best-qualified person, because the employer incorrectly thinks the applicant is gay. This is still direct discrimination because of sexual orientation.

- You must not treat a job applicant badly or **victimise** them because they have complained about discrimination or helped someone else complain or have done anything to uphold their own or someone else's equality law rights.

> **Example**
>
> An employer does not shortlist a person for interview, even though they are well-qualified for the job, because last year the job applicant said they thought the employer had discriminated against them in not shortlisting them for another job.

- You must not **harass** a person.

> **Example**
>
> An employer makes someone feel humiliated by telling jokes about their religion or belief during the interview. This may amount to harassment.

In addition, to make sure that disabled people have the same access to everything that is involved in getting and doing a job as a non-disabled person you must make **reasonable adjustments**.

If an applicant asks for information about the job and the application form (if there is one), in an **alternative format** which they require because they are a disabled person then you must provide this, so long as it is a reasonable adjustment – and it is likely to be.

If an applicant needs reasonable adjustments to participate in any interview or assessment process, then you must make them.

When you assess a disabled job applicant's suitability for the job, you must take account of any reasonable adjustments which are needed to enable them to do the job.

If, after taking reasonable adjustments into account, the disabled applicant would not be the best person for the job, you do not have to offer it to them.

But if they would be the best person with the reasonable adjustments in place, you must offer them the job. In any event, it would make sense for you to do this, as you want the best person for the job.

...

- You must not **discriminate** against a person or harass or victimise them even after your employment relationship with them ends if what you are doing arises out of and is closely connected to the employment relationship that you had with them.

Example

A job applicant complains that you treated them worse than others in an interview because of their ethnic background. In response you tell another employer with whom you do business that it would not be a good idea to offer the applicant a job and when the applicant applies to that employer, he is refused an interview because of what you have said. This will be unlawful victimisation.

Distinguishing between direct and indirect discrimination

Direct and indirect discrimination are mutually exclusive, in that a single act, if it is discriminatory, cannot be both. It can sometimes be hard to determine whether a complaint is of direct or indirect discrimination. Generally, a provision, criterion or practice (PCP) (which is a requirement of an indirect discrimination claim) must be apparently neutral (see *James v Eastleigh Borough Council* [1990] ICR 554). If a PCP is very closely linked to a protected characteristic of an individual, it is more likely to be a direct discrimination claim.

The distinction between direct and indirect can be significant because whereas indirect discrimination can be justified, in most cases (but see direct age discrimination, **Chapter 12**) direct discrimination cannot. In practice, most claimants would be advised, where it is not clear, to claim under both heads.

Worked example (with thanks to the LSE-Featherstone Moot and Verity Bell)

Jessica is a transgender woman early in her transition and is employed as a receptionist at a city university. The university has a swimming pool which all employees are allowed to use. Jessica wanted to use the women only changing facilities but other pool users complained about a man using the changing rooms. When there was a complaint the lifeguard had to shut down the pool to investigate. The university then required Jessica to use the accessible staff changing facility and did not allow her to use the women's changing facility. Gender reassignment is a protected characteristic and is defined in section 7 of the Equality Act.

Should Jessica bring her claim of gender reassignment discrimination under section 13(1) or section 19(1) of the Equality Act?

Direct discrimination under section 13 occurs when, because of a protected characteristic, one party treats another less favourably. Direct gender discrimination cannot be justified. Here, Jessica would argue that being compelled to use the accessible changing facilities constituted less favourable treatment by reference to a comparator of someone who was not undergoing gender reassignment. The university would argue that their actions did not constitute less favourable treatment as all the facilities – male, female and accessible were equivalent in terms of the available facilities and ease of access to the pool.

An indirect discrimination claim under section 19 occurs where a provision, criterion or practice ('PCP') is applied, apparently neutrally to people, but which impacts on people with a relevant protected characteristic by putting them at a particular disadvantage when compared with persons who do not share that protected characteristic, and the individual claimant shares that protected characteristic. A discriminatory PCP can be justified if it is a proportionate means of achieving a legitimate aim. Here, Jessica would argue that the university was applying a PCP that the users of the gender-segregated changing facilities are 'somatically' consistent in appearance with the sex group of the facilities and that this puts those undergoing gender reassignment at a particular disadvantage. The university would most likely seek to justify any finding of indirect discrimination on the grounds that it had to consider the comfort and facility of all users and this included a convention that women were entitled to safe segregated spaces without physical male intrusion.

Although direct discrimination uses the term 'less favourable treatment' and indirect discrimination uses the term 'particular disadvantage', in practice the same factual matters are likely to be argued in support of both. So, for example, the requirement not to use the female only facilities / to use the accessible facilities. Direct discrimination requires a 'causal' link between the treatment and the protected characteristic, whereas indirect discrimination requires a 'causal' link between the PCP and the disadvantage. The PCP here is arguably so closely aligned to the protected characteristic of undergoing gender reassignment, that it in effect creates a closed category of potential users which only comprises those with the protected characteristic. If all of the people who suffer disadvantage share the same protected characteristic, the discrimination is going to be direct rather than indirect. If Jessica establishes that there is less favourable treatment which relates to the opportunity to use the changing rooms that match her gender identity, she should win. The university may argue, successfully, that it was not *because of* her gender identity but because of the physical manifestation (which might be related to the protected characteristic of sex), and / or that if the claimant was further down the line in her transition, it would allow her to use the women only changing rooms, and problems from public complaints and disruption. The case of *James v Eastleigh Borough Council* [1990] 2 AC 751 established that there will be direct discrimination if the PCP used exactly corresponds with a protected characteristic. If there was a finding that the PCP was not a closed category, and the case were to proceed as an indirect discrimination claim, justification would most likely be the main focus. That would involve considering whether the PCP was a proportionate means of achieving a legitimate aim. The university might seek to rely on the comfort of all the pool users, the claimant might counter that there are more proportionate options such as seeking to educate the public or installing private individual cubicles in the women's changing facilities.

Conclusion

Before looking in detail at each of these types of discrimination (in their individual chapters), we shall first consider what constitutes an unlawful act of discrimination. Discrimination is not in itself outlawed: it must be accompanied by an unlawful act.

8.4 UNLAWFUL ACTS OF DISCRIMINATION – IN THE EMPLOYMENT FIELD

Unlawful discrimination in the employment field against job applicants and employees/workers is prohibited by ss 39 and 40 of the Act. These sections make it unlawful for an employer directly or indirectly to discriminate against, victimise or harass employees and people seeking work. They apply where the employer is making arrangements to fill a job, and in respect of anything done in the course of a person's employment.

Other sections create causes of action for contract workers (s 41), police officers (ss 42–43), partnerships (ss 44–46), barristers and advocates (ss 47–48), office holders (ss 49–52, Sch 6) and trade union members (s 57). Section 108 prohibits discrimination and harassment against former employees and other groups referred to in this section. For a pre-Equality Act 2010 decision on the meaning of 'contract worker' in discrimination legislation, see *Leeds City Council v Woodhouse* [2010] IRLR 625, where the Court of Appeal rejected a submission that it is necessary for the alleged contract worker to show that the respondent had control or influence over the work that he did.

8.4.1 Recruitment

Under s 39(1) of the Act:

An employer (A) must not discriminate against a person (B)—

(a)   in the arrangements A makes for deciding to whom to offer employment;

(b)   as to the terms on which A offers B employment;

(c)   by not offering B employment.

Section 39(3) contains an identical provision with regard to victimisation, and s 40(1) protects job seekers from harassment.

Readers should note that under the Immigration, Asylum and Nationality Act 2006, an employer is expected to ensure that any migrant workers whom it employs are eligible to work in the UK (the Asylum and Immigration Act 1996 applies to those employed pre-February 2008). Section 15 of the 2006 Act provides that an employer who employs a person subject to immigration control who does not have the right to take employment, shall be guilty of a civil offence and liable to payment of a civil financial penalty (see **1.2.6**). The 2006 Act allows employers to avoid the penalty if they have carried out specific checks on documents. Checking the documents of prospective employees provides an employer with what is known as a 'statutory excuse'. For workers with a time-limit on how long they can stay in the UK, employers must repeat the document checks at least once a year to retain the 'statutory excuse'. The 2006 Act also (s 21) makes it a criminal offence knowingly to employ someone who has no permission to work in the UK. (For a case where the EAT considered the immigration rules, see *Kelly v University of Southampton* (UKEAT/0295/07).)

Tough penalties are in force for anyone caught employing illegal migrants. However, an employer also needs to take care that, when implementing or exercising measures to prevent illegal working, he also avoids unlawful discrimination. While taking proper steps to ascertain that an employee does have a right to work, careful consideration must be given to when to ask questions of applicants to avoid discriminating on the grounds of race (see, eg, *Osborne Clarke Services v Purohit* [2009] IRLR 341). Guidance ('An employer's guide to right to work checks') and a Code of Practice (on preventing illegal working/avoiding discrimination) are available on the Home Office website at <www.gov.uk>.

The best way for employers to ensure that they do not discriminate is to treat all job applicants the same way at each stage of the recruitment process. In other words, to carry out document checks on all prospective employees and not make assumptions about a person's right to work based on that person's background, appearance or accent.

In 2013, the UK Border Agency, which had, inter alia, responsibility for immigration enforcement, was abolished. A new executive agency, Immigration Enforcement, under the supervision of the Home Office, is now responsible for enforcing the UK's immigration laws and targeting illegal working. The Criminal and Financial Investigation Department is responsible for investigating criminality surrounding immigration, including trafficking and modern slavery.

The various EU equality directives permit positive action. Section 159 of the 2010 Act allows (but does not require) an employer to take a protected characteristic into account when deciding whom to recruit, where persons who share a protected characteristic suffer a disadvantage connected to the characteristic, or participation in an activity by persons who share a protected characteristic is disproportionately low. This can be done only where candidates are equally qualified. This does not allow employers automatically to prefer such candidates. Each case must be considered on its merits, and any action must be a proportionate means of addressing such disadvantage or under-representation.

8.4.2 Promotion and dismissal

Under s 39(2) of the Act:

> An employer (A) must not discriminate against an employee of A's (B)—
> (a)   as to B's terms of employment;
> (b)   in the way A affords B access, or by not affording B access, to opportunities for promotion, transfer or training or for receiving any other benefit, facility or service;
> (c)   by dismissing B;
> (d)   by subjecting B to any other detriment.

Dismissal, for the purposes of the Act, includes constructive dismissal (s 39(7)). Detriment does not include harassment (s 212). The EAT confirmed in *Cordant Security Ltd v Singh & Another* (EAT/0144/15) that it is a necessary part of any discrimination complaint that an unlawful act is made out. In that case, the employee could not have suffered a detriment because if the complaint had been investigated, it would have been found to be untrue because it was entirely fabricated. The employee could not be said to have suffered any injustice as a result of the less favourable treatment he suffered because the grievance was fabricated. Of course, a genuinely believed grievance might turn out to be unsubstantiated but that grievance is still a detriment.

Section 39(4) contains an identical provision with regard to victimisation.

Section 40(1) protects employees from harassment but does not refer to dismissal (see **11.3.1**).

8.4.3 Post-employment discrimination

Section 108 prohibits discrimination after the employment relationship has ended. Where an employment relationship has come to an end, it is unlawful for the employer to discriminate against the former employee or by harassing the former employee where the discrimination arises out of and is closely connected to that former relationship.

The Explanatory Notes give examples, one of which is:

> A[n] ... employer refuses to give a reference to an ... ex-employee because of his or her religion or belief. This would be direct discrimination.

Although s 108(7) of the 2010 Act states that post-employment victimisation is not covered, the Court of Appeal held in *Jessemey v Rowstock Ltd and anor* [2014] EWCA Civ 185 that this was a drafting error, and that post-employment victimisation is covered (see **11.7.2**).

8.4.4 Advertisements

Under the old discrimination legislation, there were specific provisions concerning discriminatory advertisements (for example in s 29 of the RRA 1976 and s 38 of the SDA 1975; there was never a specific prohibition in the now repealed Age Regulations). These were all repealed by the Act, along with the specific sections of the Equality Act 2006 which dealt with advertising. There is no specific provision in the Act regarding discriminatory advertisements, so publishers are no longer required to prove they relied reasonably on an assurance from the creator of an advertisement. Instead, s 13 of the Act, which prohibits direct discrimination, is intended to embrace discriminatory advertisements. The Explanatory Notes gives this as an example of direct discrimination:

> If an employer advertising a vacancy makes it clear in the advert that Roma need not apply, this would amount to direct race discrimination against a Roma who might reasonably have considered applying for the job but was deterred from doing so because of the advertisement.

In March and April 2016, the EHRC produced a series of four guides to advertising, which outline key aspects of equality law in relation to advertising job opportunities, as well as goods, services and accommodation.

The EHRC has enforcement powers that cover both direct and indirect discrimination, and may bring prosecutions against employers.

8.5 OCCUPATIONAL REQUIREMENTS

Schedule 9, Pt 1, para 1 to the Equality Act 2010 provides:

> (1) A person (A) does not contravene a provision [in relation to recruitment, training or dismissal] by applying a requirement to have a particular protected characteristic, if A shows that, having regard to the nature or context of the work—
>
> (a) it is an occupational requirement,
>
> (b) the application of the requirement is a proportionate means of achieving a legitimate aim, and
>
> (c) the person to whom A applies the requirement does not meet it (or A has reasonable grounds for not being satisfied that the person meets it).

The Act therefore provides a general exception to what would otherwise be unlawful direct discrimination in relation to work.

The exception in para 1 applies where being of a particular sex, race, religion or belief, sexual orientation or age – or not being a transsexual person, married or a civil partner – is a requirement for the work, and the person to whom it is applied does not meet it (or, except in the case of sex, does not meet it to the reasonable satisfaction of the person who applied it). The requirement must be crucial to the post and not merely one of several important factors. It also must not be a sham or pretext. In addition, applying the requirement must be a proportionate way of achieving a legitimate aim, ie it must be the least restrictive way of achieving the aim.

Examples of para 1 occupational requirements given in the Explanatory Notes to the Act include:

- The need for authenticity or realism might require someone of a particular race, or sex for acting roles (for example, a black man to play the part of Othello) or modelling jobs.
- Considerations of privacy or decency might require a public changing room or lavatory attendant to be of the same sex as those using the facilities
- Unemployed Muslim women might not take advantage of the services of an outreach worker to help them find employment if they were provided by a man.

In *Amnesty International v Ahmed* [2009] IRLR 884, the EAT suggested that Amnesty might have been able to rely on an 'occupational requirement' (under the predecessor law) when it refused to promote a North Sudanese woman to a post in Sudan because of fears for her and others' safety.

Schedule 9, Pt 1, para 2 to the Act provides for exceptions in relation to religious requirements relating to sex, transsexuals, married persons and civil partners, and sexual orientation:

(1)   A person (A) does not contravene a provision by applying [in relation to recruitment, training or dismissal] a requirement to which subparagraph (4) applies if A shows that—

    (a)   the employment is for the purposes of an organised religion,

    (b)   the application of the requirement engages the compliance or non-conflict principle, and

    (c)   the person to whom A applies the requirement does not meet it (or A has reasonable grounds for not being satisfied that the person meets it).

    ...

(5)   The application of a requirement engages the compliance principle if the application is a proportionate means of complying with the doctrines of the religion.

(6)   The application of a requirement engages the non-conflict principle if, because of the nature or context of the employment, the requirement is applied so as to avoid conflicting with the strongly held religious convictions of a significant number of the religion's followers.

The exception in para 2 allows the employer to apply a requirement to be of a particular sex or not to be a transsexual person, or to make a requirement related to the employee's marriage or civil partnership status or sexual orientation, but only if:

(a)   appointing a person who meets the requirement in question is a proportionate way of complying with the doctrines of the religion; or

(b)   because of the nature or context of the employment, employing a person who meets the requirement is a proportionate way of avoiding conflict with a significant number of the religion's followers' strongly held religious convictions.

Examples of para 2 occupational requirements given in the Explanatory Notes to the Act include:

- a requirement that a Catholic priest be a man and unmarried.
- unlikely to permit a requirement that a church youth worker who primarily organises sporting activities is celibate if he is gay, but it may apply if the youth worker mainly teaches Bible classes.
- would not apply to a requirement that a church accountant be celibate if he is gay.

In *Sheridan v Prospects for People with Learning Disabilities* (ET/2901366/06), a tribunal held that a Christian charity providing support services for people with learning disabilities could not rely on the (as it was then) 'genuine occupational requirement' exemption to operate a blanket 'Christians only' policy as the work was primarily secular in nature: it could not be said that being of a particular religion was essential for performing the functions of the post. See more recently *Pemberton v Former Acting Bishop of Southwell and Nottingham* (UKEAT/0072/16), where a refusal to grant an Extra Parochial Ministry Licence to a priest who had married his long-term, same-sex partner, because the view of marriage as between a man and a woman was part of the Church's doctrine, was held not to be unlawful direct discrimination, whether because of sexual orientation or marital status, relying on the religious occupation exception.

In the context of age, the ECJ held in *Vital Pérez v Ayuntamiento de Oviedo* (Case C-416/13) [2015] IRLR 158 that an age restriction of 30 to join the local police was not a genuine occupational requirement as the evidence was too weak. However, it upheld an age limit of 35 in *Salaberria Sorondo v Academia Vasca de Policia y Emergencias* (Case C-258/15) because the evidence was that the job was more physically demanding and dangerous.

8.6 VICARIOUS LIABILITY

Under s 109 of the Act, an employer is vicariously liable for acts of discrimination (including harassment) committed by his employees 'in the course of ... employment', as are principals for the acts of their agents. This is so whether or not the acts were done with the employer's knowledge or approval. The Court of Appeal held in *Kemeh v Ministry of Defence* [2014] EWCA Civ 91 that an employee of an independent contractor is not an agent of the third party employer simply because he carries out work for the third party. However, it is a defence for the employer to show that he took such steps as were reasonable to prevent an employee doing the act complained of.

8.6.1 Course of employment

In *Jones v Tower Boot Co Ltd* [1997] IRLR 168, CA, Mr Jones was subjected to acts of racial harassment by other employees, including having his arm burnt with a hot screwdriver; having metal bolts thrown at his head; having his legs whipped with a piece of welt; and being called 'chimp', 'monkey' and 'baboon'. The EAT held that the acts complained of could not by any stretch of the imagination be regarded as an improper mode of performing authorised tasks, and found for the employers. This decision initially caused much concern because no one is employed to harass another employee. However, the Court of Appeal reversed the decision because the EAT had erred in applying the old common law test of an employer's vicarious liability. The words 'in the course of employment' should be interpreted in the sense in which they are employed in everyday speech and not restrictively by reference to the old principles laid down for establishing an employer's vicarious liability for the torts committed by an employee. Otherwise, the more heinous the act of discrimination, the less likely it would be that the employer would be liable. Note, too, that the House of Lords reassessed the test used to establish the vicarious liability of employers at common law for the tortious acts of employees. The decision in *Lister and Others v Hesley Hall Ltd* [2001] IRLR 472 brings the statutory and common law approaches to vicarious liability more in line. (For an interesting, decision on the scope of vicarious liability – but not specifically in a discrimination context – see *Maga v Birmingham Roman Catholic Archdiocese Trustees* [2010] All ER (D) 141.) The EAT commented in *Livesey v Parker Merchanting Ltd* (UKEAT/0755/03) that the statutory test is to be regarded as at least as wide as, if not wider than, the *Lister* test.

In *Chief Constable of the Lincolnshire Police v Stubbs and Others* [1999] IRLR 81, a police officer was found to be acting 'in the course of employment' when he subjected the applicant to inappropriate sexual behaviour, even though the incidents occurred at social gatherings either immediately after work or at an organised leaving party. They were not chance meetings. The officer's employer was, on the facts, held to be vicariously liable for his actions under s 41 of the SDA 1975.

In *Sidhu v Aerospace Composite Technology Ltd* [2000] IRLR 602, the Court of Appeal upheld the tribunal's decision that a racial assault upon the applicant by a colleague during a family day out organised by the employer had not taken place 'in the course of employment', since the outing was in a public place, the employees had attended during their own time, and the majority of those attending were family and friends of the employees as opposed to employees.

The Court of Appeal considered the matter in two joined cases in 2012. In *Weddell v Barchester Healthcare Ltd* and *Wallbank v Wallbank Fox Designs Ltd* [2012] EWCA Civ 25, the Court decided that the employer was not vicariously liable for the actions of an employee who attacked his manager at the workplace but whilst he was off duty (*Weddell*), but that the employer was liable for an employee's attack on his manager carried out during work in response to a lawful instruction (*Wallbank*). In the former case, the act was not so closely connected with employment as to render the employer liable; the act was an 'independent venture ... distinct from [his] employment'. In the latter case, the sufficiently close connection was established because reacting to instructions was part of the job.

The Court of Session held, in *Vaickuviene and Others v J Sainsbury plc* [2013] CSIH 67, that the employer was not liable for verbal and physical abuse, which ultimately resulted in murder, because the act was not 'so closely connected with the employment'. The Supreme Court, in two cases, looked at the sort of relationship which has to exist between an individual and a defendant before the defendant can be made vicariously liable in tort. In *Cox v Ministry of Justice* [2016] UKSC 10, a sack of rice was accidentally dropped on the claimant's back, injuring her. The person who dropped the sack was a prisoner working in the prison kitchen. The question arose as to whether the Ministry of Justice was vicariously liable for the prisoner's negligence. The Court found that prisoners working in kitchens were integrated into the operation of the prison. They worked under the direction of prison staff. The prison service was therefore found liable to the claimant. (Contrast the facts with those in *Warren v Henlys Ltd* [1948] 2 All ER 935, where the relationship had changed from that of customer and representative of the company to complainant and subject of the complaint on the facts.) The Court referred to five factors (identified in *Various Claimants v Catholic Child Welfare Society* [2012] UKSC 56) which make it 'fair, just and reasonable' to impose tortious vicarious liability. This extended the scope for vicarious liability beyond the responsibility of an employer for acts and omissions of its employees 'in the course of their employment', but not so widely as to impose liability for acts of independent businesses or third parties. In *Mohamud v WM Morrison Supermarkets plc* [2016] UKSC 11, the Supreme Court held that a supermarket was vicariously responsible for an employee's unprovoked attack on a customer because the act was sufficiently connected to the employee's employment – his job was to deal with customers and the violence was carried out whilst dealing with a customer. The Supreme Court's judgment in *Mohamud* provides a useful review of the legal principles.

There are, according to *Mohamud*, two questions to be considered:

(a)   First, looking at matters broadly, what were the functions or what was the field of activities entrusted by the employer to the relevant employee, ie what was the nature of his or her job?

(b)   Secondly, was there sufficient connection between the position in which the person was employed and his or her wrongful conduct to make it right for the employer to be held liable under the principle of social justice?

In *Bellman v Northampton Recruitment Ltd* [2017] ICR 543, the High Court held that the employer was not liable for one employee's violent attack on another during an 'impromptu drink' after the firm's Christmas party: the drinks were after the party and at a different location; partners and other guests were present, and the conversation was, in the main, non-work-related. The

Court of Appeal overturned the decision ([2018] EWCA Civ 2214) and held that there was a sufficient nexus between the job and the act: the employee was senior, and the function was not purely social – it followed on from a work event where the company paid for taxis and drinks. In that case, the employee was the managing director and the other employee was left with severe brain damage. The Court noted the power and authority that the managing director had over his staff.

In *WM Morrison Supermarkets PLC v Various Claimants* [2018] EWCA Civ 2239, the Court of Appeal held that an employer was vicariously liable for the actions of an employee who disclosed the personal information of colleagues on the internet and was later convicted of fraud and offences under the Computer Misuse Act 1990 and s 55 of the Data Protection Act 1998. Employees issued proceedings against Morrisons seeking to hold it vicariously liable for the employee's misuse of their personal data. The Court of Appeal upheld the High Court's decision that Morrisons was liable. There was, said the High Court, 'a sufficient connection between the position in which [the employee] was employed and his wrongful conduct, put into the position of handling and disclosing the data as he was by Morrisons (albeit it was meant to be to KPMG alone), to make it right for Morrisons to be held liable "under the principle of social justice which can be traced back to Holt CJ"'.

In *Barclays Bank v Various Claimants PLC* [2018] EWCA Civ 1670, the Court of Appeal confirmed that organisations can be vicariously liable for the actions of third party contractors, in this case a doctor who carried out examinations of employees and prospective employees on behalf of the bank.

8.6.2   Reasonable steps' defence

Section 109(4) sets out the 'reasonably practicable' defence:

> In proceedings against A's employer (B) in respect of anything alleged to have been done by A in the course of A's employment it is a defence for B to show that B took all reasonable steps to prevent A—
>
> (a)   from doing that thing, or
>
> (b)   from doing anything of that description.

This defence is often unsuccessful. The employer must take preventative action. A written equal opportunities policy is unlikely to succeed unless it is implemented actively.

The European Recommendation and Code of Practice on the Dignity of Women and Men at Work (92/131/EEC) makes specific recommendations to employers on how to combat sexual harassment. Tribunals will look at whether employers have complied with these recommendations in deciding whether the employer is liable. The Code recommends that:

(a)   employers should issue a policy statement which expressly states that all employees have the right to be treated with dignity, that sexual harassment at work will not be permitted or condoned and that employees have the right to complain about it should it occur;

(b)   the policy should then be communicated to all employees so that they are aware that they have a right to complain and to whom they should complain. In this way, employees are made aware of the likely consequences of engaging in sexual harassment;

(c)   managers and supervisors have a particular duty to ensure that sexual harassment does not occur in the area for which they are responsible; they should explain the policy to their staff, and be responsive and supportive in confidentiality to anyone who complains;

(d)   managers and supervisors should be given training on their responsibilities in relation to sexual harassment and to ensure that they are aware of the factors which contribute to a working environment free from sexual harassment.

The Code also makes some recommendations as to the procedures which employers should follow when dealing with allegations of sexual harassment:

(a)   both formal and informal methods of resolving the problems created by harassment should be available;

(b)   employers should designate someone to provide advice and assistance to employees who are subjected to sexual harassment;

(c)   a formal procedure should specify to whom complaints should be brought, and also set out an alternative if complaining to that person would be inappropriate for the employee in question;

(d)   internal investigations of complaints should be seen to be independent, objective and handled with due respect for the rights of both the complainant and the alleged harasser. Those carrying out the investigation should not be connected with the allegations;

(e)   violations of the employer's policy on sexual harassment should be treated as a disciplinary offence.

The EHRC's Code of Practice suggests that reasonable steps will include training and implementation of an equality policy. An extract appears below:

18.5 It is essential that a written equality policy is backed by a clear programme of action for implementation and continual review. It is a process which consists of four key stages: planning, implementing, monitoring and reviewing the equality policy.

...

18.7 A written equality policy should set out the employer's general approach to equality and diversity issues in the workplace. The policy should make clear that the employer intends to develop and apply procedures which do not discriminate because of any of the protected characteristics, and which provide equality of opportunity for all job applicants and workers.

Planning the content of equality policies

18.8 Most policies will include the following:

- a statement of the employer's commitment to equal opportunity for all job applicants and workers;
- what is and is not acceptable behaviour at work (also referring to conduct near the workplace and at work-related social functions where relevant);
- the rights and responsibilities of everyone to whom the policy applies, and procedures for dealing with any concerns and complaints;
- how the policy may apply to the employer's other policies and procedures;
- how the employer will deal with any breaches of policy;
- who is responsible for the policy; and
- how the policy will be implemented and details of monitoring and review procedures.

18.9 It will help an employer avoid discrimination if the equality policy covers all aspects of employment including recruitment, terms and conditions of work, training and development, promotion, performance, grievance, discipline and treatment of workers when their contract ends. ...

Planning an equality policy – protected characteristics

18.10 It is recommended that adopting one equality policy covering all protected characteristics is the most practical approach. Where separate policies are developed, such as a separate race equality or sex equality policy, they should be consistent with each other and with an overall commitment to promoting equality of opportunity in employment.

Implementing an equality policy

18.11 An equality policy should be more than a statement of good intentions; there should also be plans for its implementation. The policy should be in writing and drawn up in consultation with workers and any recognised trade unions or other workplace representatives, including any equality representatives within the workforce.

...

Promotion and communication of an equality policy

18.13 Employers should promote and publicise their equality policy as widely as possible and there are a number of ways in which this can be done. Promoting the policy is part of the process of effective implementation and will help an employer demonstrate that they have taken all reasonable steps to prevent discrimination.

18.14 Employers may use a number of methods of communication to promote their policy, including:

- email bulletins
- intranet and/or website
- induction packs
- team meetings
- office notice boards
- circulars, newsletters
- cascade systems
- training
- handbooks
- annual reports.

18.15 These methods of communication may not be appropriate in all cases.... Employers must also consider whether reasonable adjustments need to be made for disabled people so that they are able to access the information.

18.16 Promoting and communicating an equality policy should not be a one-off event. It is recommended that employers provide periodic reminders and updates to workers and others such as contractors and suppliers. Employers should also periodically review their advertising, recruitment and application materials and processes ...

Implementing an equality policy – training

18.18 Employers should ensure that all workers and agents understand the equality policy, how it affects them and the plans for putting it into practice. The best way to achieve this is by providing regular training.

18.19 Some workers may need more specific training, depending on what they do within the organisation. For example, line managers and senior management should receive detailed training on how to manage equality and diversity issues in the workplace.

18.20 The training should be designed in consultation with workers, their workplace representatives and managers and by incorporating feedback from any previous training into future courses.

18.21 Employers should make sure in-house trainers are themselves trained before running courses for other workers. External trainers also need to be fully informed about the employer's policies, including their equality policy ...

Monitoring and reviewing an equality policy

18.23 Equality monitoring enables an employer to find out whether their equality policy is working ...

In *Caspersz v Ministry of Defence* (UKEAT/0599/05), the EAT held that the tribunal was correct to take the two-stage approach referred to in *Canniffe v East Riding of Yorkshire Council* [2000] IRLR 555, which is that a tribunal should:

(a)   identify whether a respondent took any steps at all to prevent the employee from doing the act or acts complained of; and

(b)   having identified what steps, if any, the employer took, consider whether there were any further steps that the employer could have taken that were reasonably practicable.

The EAT accepted in that case that the defence was satisfied: the employer had a 'Dignity at Work' policy that had been carefully implemented.

8.6.3   Personal liability of employees

By virtue of s 110 of the Act, the employee for whose act the employer is liable (or would be so but for establishment of a defence that he took all reasonable steps) is deemed to have aided that unlawful act. This means that the complainant may claim against both the employer and the employee who carried out the act of discrimination. It is not now necessary (as it was under the previous legislation) to show that the employee or agent knew that the act was unlawful. Section 111 covers instructing, causing or inducing contraventions of the Act, codifying the situation in *Weathersfield Ltd v Sargent* [1999] IRLR 94. It permits the intended victim to bring proceedings even if the instruction has not been carried out. Both the EHRC and B and/or C (if they are subjected to a detriment as a result of A's conduct, even where the instruction is not carried out) may bring enforcement proceedings in relation to any breach.

Note that if the employer is not vicariously liable for the acts of the employee because the acts did not take place during the course of employment, there can be no claim against the employee who carried out the discriminatory act. However, if the acts were committed during the course of employment then, even if the employer establishes the reasonably practicable defence, the employee may still be personally liable (*Yeboah v Crofton* [2002] IRLR 634). The Explanatory Notes give this example:

> A factory worker racially harasses her colleague. The factory owner would be liable for the worker's actions, but is able to show that he took all reasonable steps to stop the harassment. The colleague can still bring a claim against the factory worker in an employment tribunal.

The EAT held, in *Barlow v Stone* [2012] IRLR 898, that an employment tribunal had jurisdiction to consider a claim of victimisation brought by an employee against a fellow employee, even though no claim had been brought against their mutual employer, where the employer would have been liable under s 109 (see **8.6**).

8.7   RETIREMENT

The age at which the State retirement pension is payable is permitted to be discriminatory (EC Directive 79/7, Article 7). It is currently 65 for a man and between 60 and 65 for a woman. The State pension age for women has been increasing gradually since 2010, so that by 2018 it will be 65. By 2020 the State pension age for men and women will be 66, and by 2028 it will be 67. By the mid-2030s it is predicted to be 68, in the 2040s to be 69 and in the 2060s to be 70.

8.8   ENFORCEMENT AND REMEDIES

Enforcement proceedings may be brought either by an individual, or by the EHRC. The EHRC has power to investigate discriminatory practices and may serve a non-discrimination notice. Additionally, the EHRC can give assistance to an individual pursuing a claim.

The EHRC issued a Code of Practice which came into force on 6 April 2011. Whilst breach of the Code does not give rise to any legal liability, tribunals must take it into account if relevant.

The employment tribunal derives its jurisdiction from s 113 and ss 120–135 of the Act. An employment tribunal has jurisdiction, inter alia, to determine a complaint relating to a contravention of Pt 5 (work) (ss 39–83), s 108 (prohibited conduct where work relationships have ended). Note that members of the armed forces must have first utilised the armed forces procedure before they can complain to an employment tribunal under Pt 5 (s 121).

8.8.1   Enforcement by an individual

8.8.1.1   Time-limits

A complaint should be made to an employment tribunal within three months (less a day) of the act complained of or such other period as the tribunal thinks just and equitable (s 123). In considering whether to exercise its discretion, the employment tribunal should consider the prejudice that each party would suffer as a result of granting or refusing an extension of time, and should have regard to all the other relevant circumstances. In *British Coal Corporation v Keeble* [1997] IRLR 336, the court said that tribunals should adopt the factors mentioned in s 33 of the Limitation Act 1980 as a useful checklist. That is:

- the length of and reasons for the delay
- the extent to which the cogency of the evidence is likely to be affected by the delay
- the extent to which the party sued had co-operated with any requests for information
- the promptness with which the claimant acted once he knew of the possibility of taking action
- the steps taken by the claimant to obtain appropriate professional advice once he knew of the possibility of taking action.

In *London Borough of Southwark v Afolabi* [2003] IRLR 220, the Court of Appeal held that a tribunal is not required to go through the matters listed in s 33(3) of the Limitation Act 1980 as a checklist in considering whether it is just and equitable to extend time, provided no significant factor has been left out of account by the tribunal in exercising its discretion. The Court of Appeal confirmed in *Apelogun-Gabriels v London Borough of Lambeth* [2002] IRLR 116 that there is no general principle that it will be just and equitable to extend the three-month time-limit where the delay was caused by the applicant's seeking to deal with the matter internally. In *Robertson v Bexley Community Centre* [2003] IRLR 434, the Court of Appeal emphasised that there is no presumption that tribunals should extend time: the claimant must persuade the tribunal that it is just and equitable to do so. In *Pathan v South London Islamic Centre* (UKEAT/0312/13), the EAT held that the test is not, however, one of exceptional circumstances, it is whether it is 'just and equitable' to extend time. If the claim is brought against more than one respondent, the tribunal must decide whether it is just and equitable to extend time in each case separately (*Harden v Wootlif & Anor* (UKEAT/0448/14)).

In *British Transport Police v Norman* (UKEAT/0348/14), the EAT held that an employment tribunal had erred when it decided that it was just and equitable to extend the time-limit for a claim in circumstances where it had not first established the extent of and the reasons for the delay. The relevant questions were those proposed by Langstaff P in *ABM University Local Health Board v Morgan* (UKEAT/ 0305/13) (at para 52):

(a)   Why was it that the primary time-limit had been missed?

(b)   Why, after expiry of the primary time-limit, was the claim not brought sooner than it was?

However, in *Rathakrishnan v Pizza Express (Restaurants) Ltd* (EAT/0073/15), the EAT held that an employment tribunal erred because it had failed to take into account the balance of prejudice between the parties and the prospective merits of the claim. The tribunal was wrong not to weigh those factors in the balance. The EAT rejected the submission that a failure to provide a good excuse for the delay in bringing the relevant claim will inevitably result in an extension of time being refused. See, most recently, the Court of Appeal's approach in *Abertawe Bro Morgannwg University Local Health Board v Morgan* [2018] EWCA Civ 640, where the Court explored the principles behind extending time-limits. The Court confirmed that, in a complaint about an omission to act, such as a failure to make reasonable adjustments, the time-limit does not run from the date when the breach occurred, but rather begins to run at the end of the period in which the employer might reasonably have been expected to comply with the relevant duty.

Where there is a continuing act of discrimination, the three months do not start to run until the discrimination ceases (s 123(3)). The concept of 'continuing acts' of discrimination has generated much case law over the years and is a matter that requires very careful consideration. Continuing acts are distinguishable from one-off acts that have continuing consequences; time will run from the date of the one-off act complained of. Readers should refer to the Court of Appeal decision in *Hendricks v Commissioner of Police for the Metropolis* [2003] IRLR 96 on the question of continuing acts for further guidance. In that case the Court held that the test is whether the employer is responsible for 'an ongoing situation or a continuing state of affairs'. See also *Aziz v FDA* [2010] EWCA Civ 304 and *Okoro and anor v Taylor Woodrow*

Construction Ltd and Others [2012] EWCA Civ 1590 for more recent Court of Appeal decisions. In *Veolia Environmental Services Ltd v Gumbs* (UKEAT/0487/12), two allegations of discrimination over a long period were held to be linked by the employee's manager, who had made decisions adverse to the claimant on both occasions.

Where the discrimination consists of a failure to do something, the time-limit starts to run when the person decides not to do the thing in question. Note that the Act states (s 212(2) and (3)) that a reference (however expressed) to an act includes a reference to an omission; and a reference (however expressed) to an omission includes a reference to:

(a)   a deliberate omission to do something;

(b)   a refusal to do it;

(c)   a failure to do it.

Where an employer fails to make a reasonable adjustment for a disabled person, because it simply fails to consider doing so, time runs from a notional date – the date on which the employer might reasonably have been expected to make the adjustment. Given that a claimant will not know what that date is, one might expect tribunals to have 'sympathetic regard' to that difficulty in applying the just and equitable extension.

Readers should also remember that the Early Conciliation procedure must be complied with before a complaint is presented to the tribunal (see **6.3.7**).

8.8.1.2   Questionnaire procedure

Section 138 allowed a complainant to deliver a standard form of questionnaire to a respondent, to enable the complainant to decide whether to institute proceedings and, if so, how to present his case.

Although a respondent was not obliged to reply to the questionnaire, failure to reply, or the giving of evasive replies, allowed a tribunal to draw an inference that discrimination had occurred. In *D'Silva v NATFHE* (UKEAT/0384/07), the EAT held that an employer's failure fully to answer a questionnaire did not automatically raise a presumption of discrimination. The real significance was whether the failure could support an inference that the employer committed the discriminatory act: there might be situations in which a failure to deal with a questionnaire, however reprehensible, had no bearing at all on the employer's defence.

The Government abolished the questionnaire procedure in April 2014. It took the view that the questionnaire process did not assist in pre-hearing settlements or in reducing claims, but in fact created a significant burden for employers. While removing the formal procedure, claimants will still be able to seek such information through pre-action requests, by asking questions of the employer or by making applications to tribunals for orders for further information or disclosure. Employers who refuse to answer will still run the risk that adverse inferences may be drawn. See, for example, *Dattani v Chief Constable of West Mercia Police* [2005] IRLR 327. Employees can also make data subject access requests, to see what information the employer holds about them. The Acas Guide recommends a six-step process for pre-action questions, and a three-step process for respondents to follow (see <www.acas.org.uk/media/pdf/m/p/asking-and-responding-to-questions-of-discrimination-in-the-workplace.pdf>).

8.8.2   Remedies

Under the previous discrimination legislation, tribunals' powers to award the same remedies were to be exercised where the tribunal considered it just and equitable to do so. Section 124 does not contain the words 'just and equitable', but because the words referred to the choice of remedy and not the amount of compensation to be awarded, the authors do not consider that the change of wording is significant.

8.8.2.1   Declaration, orders and recommendations

Under s 124 of the Act, if the complaint is well founded:

> (2)   The tribunal may—
>
>> (a)   make a declaration as to the rights of the complainant and the respondent in relation to the matters to which the proceedings relate;
>>
>> (b)   order the respondent to pay compensation to the complainant;
>>
>> (c)   make an appropriate recommendation.
>
> (3)   An appropriate recommendation is a recommendation that within a specified period the respondent takes specified steps for the purpose of obviating or reducing the adverse effect on the complainant of any matter to which the proceedings relate.

Failure to comply with a recommendation in so far as it relates to the complainant, without reasonable excuse, can lead to an increase in the compensation ordered (s 124(7)).

The power to make a recommendation does not include a power to recommend that the employee should be promoted to the next suitable vacancy (*British Gas v Sharma* [1991] IRLR 101).

The Government removed the powers of tribunals to make 'wider' recommendations (ie that obviate or reduce the adverse effect on anyone other than the claimant) with effect from 1 October 2015. Since then, a tribunal can only make a recommendation relating to the claimant.

In *Lycée Français Charles de Gaulle v Delambre* (UKEAT/0563/10), the EAT upheld the tribunal's recommendations that the respondent circulate the judgment to the Governing Board and management team, that the respondent review existing equal opportunities policies, and that it undertake a programme of formal equality and diversity training.

A declaration is an important statement of the decision. Most tribunals' findings result in a compensation order. The tribunal has power to order the respondent to pay compensation of an amount corresponding to the damages that could be ordered in a county court. There is no upper limit to the amount that may be ordered. Unlike compensation for unfair dismissal, compensation for discrimination is awarded on tortious principles. This means that the tribunal must, as far as it can, put the claimant in the position he would have been in 'but for' the discriminatory act. An employee has a duty to mitigate his losses. Although the Act no longer specifically refers to an award being made if the tribunal considers it just and equitable to do so, there is no reason to believe this will change the way in which tribunals make such awards.

There is some uncertainty as to whether a compensatory award for discrimination may be reduced to take account of contributory fault. In *Way v Crouch* [2005] IRLR 603, the EAT concluded that compensation in discrimination cases may be subject to a deduction for contributory conduct on the part of the claimant (although the EAT found no grounds for any such deduction on the facts of the case). The EAT held that since an award of compensation in a discrimination case is of an amount corresponding to any damages that could have been ordered by a county court, it followed that any such award must be subject to the Law Reform (Contributory Negligence) Act 1945, which allows for reduction in compensation where the claimant's *conduct itself amounts to negligence or breach of a legal duty and contributed to the damage suffered*. This appears to be a much higher test than that applied in unfair dismissal cases (see **5.6.2.2**). The EAT did not elaborate, however, on the kind of situations that would be likely to give a tribunal grounds for holding that a victim of discrimination has contributed to the loss or injury he has suffered.

8.8.2.2 Assessment of compensation

Readers may find it useful to read *Michalak v Mid Yorkshire Hospitals NHS Trust* (ET/1810815/08) and *Lokhova v Sberbank CIB (UK) Ltd* (2015). The claimants were awarded £4.5 million and £3.2 million respectively in discrimination and harassment claims.

In deciding the appropriate level of compensation, the following matters will be taken into account:

(a) Pecuniary loss arising directly from an act of discrimination, including past loss to the date of the hearing and future losses (to put the claimant in the position he would have been if the discrimination had not occurred). As far as the duty to mitigate is concerned, see **5.6.2.2**

(b) Injury to feelings. Whilst an award for injury to feelings is not made automatically, in the majority of cases it will be almost inevitable. Awards for injury to feelings are compensatory: they should not be about punishment; they should be just to both parties. Awards need to be sufficient to command public respect for the policy underlying anti-discrimination legislation. The guidance in *HM Prison Service v Johnson* [1997] IRLR 162 gives a good summary of the approach to injury to feelings:

   a. Awards for injury to feelings are compensatory. They should be just to both parties. They should compensate fully without punishing the tortfeasor. Feelings of indignation ... should not be allowed to inflate the award.

   b. Awards should not be too low, as this would diminish respect for the policy of the anti-discrimination legislation. Society has condemned discrimination and awards must ensure that it is seen to be wrong. On the other hand, awards should be restrained, as excessive awards could ... be seen as the way to untaxed riches.

   c. Awards should bear some broad similarity to the range of awards in personal injury cases. We do not think this should be done by reference to any particular type of personal injury award; rather to the whole range of such awards.

   d. In exercising their discretion in assessing a sum, tribunals should remind themselves of the value in everyday life of the sum they have in mind. This may be done by reference to purchasing power or by reference to earnings.

   e. Finally, tribunals should bear in mind ... the need for public respect for the level of awards made.

In *Vento v Chief Constable of West Yorkshire Police* [2003] IRLR 102, the Court of Appeal handed down guidance on awards for injury to feelings. The Court said that the top band of awards should normally be between £15,000 and £25,000, and apply only to the most serious cases. The middle band of £5,000–£15,000 should be used for serious cases not meriting the top award, and awards of £500–£5,000 should be made for less serious cases (eg, an isolated incident). Awards of less than £500 should be avoided. The EAT set out new guideline figures in *Da'Bell v NSPCC* (UKEAT/0227/09) to take account of inflation. The ranges were:

(i)   The lower band – the upper limit for this band rose to £6,000.

(ii) The middle band – the upper limit rose to £18,000.

(iii) The upper band – the upper limit rose to £30,000.

Underhill P said in *Bullimore v Pothecary Witham Weld Solicitors (No 2)* [2011] IRLR 18 (EAT) that, '[a]s a matter of principle, employment tribunals ought to assess the quantum of compensation for non-pecuniary loss in "today's money"', although it would not be an error of law not to do so (see too *AA Solicitors Ltd (t/a AA Solicitors) & Another v Majid* (EAT/0217/15)).

The EAT decision in *St Andrews School v Blundell* (UKEAT/0330/09) reviews some post-*Vento* authorities.

The Court of Appeal held in *Simmons v Castle* [2012] EWCA Civ 1039 that general damages (which would include injury to feelings damages) should be increased by 10%

after 1 April 2013. This was revised slightly a year later (see *Simmons v Castle* [2012] EWCA Civ 1288), to make clear that the 10% did not apply to claimants covered by s 44(6) of the Legal Aid, Sentencing and Punishment of Offenders Act 2012 (which applied to certain types of 'no win, no fee' agreements). The EAT held, in *Cadogan Hotel Partners Ltd v Ozog* (UKEAT/0001/14), *Sash Window Workshop Ltd & Another v King* (EAT/0057/14), *Beckford v London Borough of Southwark* (EAT/0210/14) and *Olayemi v Athena Medical Centre & Another* (EAT/0140/15) and again in *AA Solicitors v Majid*, that the 10% uplift applied to injury to feelings awards. Given that the Court of Appeal held in *Summers v Bundy* [2016] EWCA Civ 126 (a non-employment case) that the uplift applies 'across the board' (save in s 44(6) cases), it seems likely that it applies to injury to feelings awards too. ET Presidential Guidance also supports an uplift of 10%. The Court of Appeal in *De Souza v Vinci Construction UK Ltd* [2017] EWCA Civ 879 held that the 10% increase should also apply to injury to feelings awards. In September 2017, the Presidents of the Employment Tribunals issued joint guidance on the bands for injury to feelings and psychiatric injury. The new bands for injury to feelings awards for claims presented from September 2017 were:

- lower: £800 to £8,400
- middle: £8,400 to £25,200
- higher: £25,200 to £42,000

In Joint Presidential Guidance dated 23 March 2018, the uprated amounts are:

- lower: £900 to £8,600
- middle: £8,600 to 25,700
- upper: £25,700 to £49,900

See www.judiciary.uk/wp-content/uploads/2015/03/vento-bands-presidential-guidance-20170905.pdf.

In *AA Solicitors* (above), the EAT stated that appeals against amounts of awards for injury to feelings would rarely succeed unless the award was placed in the wrong *Vento* band.

(c) Aggravated damages where the respondent has behaved in a high-handed, malicious, insulting or oppressive manner. Aggravated damages, which are an aspect of the injury to feelings award, are compensatory in nature, not punitive (see *Commissioner of Police for the Metropolis v Shaw* (UKEAT/0125/11). The power to award aggravated damages is not statutory; it derives from other, non-statutory torts.

In *Shaw*, the EAT considered the three categories of circumstances identified in the Law Commission Report on Aggravated, Exemplary and Restitutionary Damages (1997) (Law Comm No 247) that may attract an award of aggravated damages. The first concerned the *manner* in which the wrong was committed. The distress caused by an act of discrimination may be made worse by its being done in an 'high-handed, malicious, insulting or oppressive' way (May LJ used this expression in *Alexander v Home Office* [1988] ICR 685). The EAT warned that this should not be treated as an exhaustive definition of the kind of behaviour which may justify an award of aggravated damages, pointing out that, as the Law Commission Report made clear, an award may be made in the case of any exceptional or contumelious conduct which has the effect of seriously increasing the claimant's distress. The second circumstance identified in the Report was the respondent's motive. The EAT said that conduct which is spiteful or vindictive, or based on prejudice or animosity, is more likely to cause distress. The third circumstance was the respondent's conduct after the tort which related to it. This might include, depending on the circumstances, a failure to apologise, or not taking a complaint seriously.

The EAT commented on the difficulty of distinguishing between the injury caused by the discriminatory act itself and the injury attributable to the aggravating elements: tribunals had to be aware of the risks of compensating claimants under both heads for the same loss. The ultimate question is whether the overall award is proportionate to the totality of the suffering caused. The EAT cautioned on the dangers of focusing too much on the conduct – which could lead down the dangerous route of equating damages with punishment. While the EAT expressed doubt as to the desirability of awarding aggravated damages as a separate head of compensation, as there was no 'bright line' by which to distinguish what part of the injury to the claimant's feelings resulted from the core act and what resulted from an exceptional feature, it felt the practice had been approved too many times to suggest that it was wrong, but suggested a better way of dealing with it might be to include it as a subheading of injury to feelings, ie 'injury to feelings in the sum of £x, incorporating aggravated damages in the sum of £y'. This might reduce the risk of a tribunal unwittingly introducing a punitive element into the calculation.

In *Zaiwalla & Co and Another v Walia* [2002] IRLR 697, the EAT held that employment tribunals can, exceptionally, award aggravated damages by reference to the conduct of the respondent in defending a claim. The Court of Appeal upheld an award of aggravated damages in *BT v Reid* [2004] IRLR 327. The Court said that on the facts the tribunal was entitled to take into account the fact that the transgressor was not punished and was indeed promoted before the charges against him were determined. The Court emphasised it was not 'laying down any principle that an employer cannot promote [in the circumstances, but it may, depending on the facts,] demonstrate the high-handedness of an employer'. The employee must have some awareness of the improper conduct or motive (*Ministry of Defence v Meredith* [1995] IRLR 52). Conduct in the course of litigation may be taken into account (*City of Bradford Metropolitan Council v Arora* [1991] IRLR 165, CA). In *Tameside Hospital NHS Foundation Trust v Mylott* (UKEAT/0352/09 and UKEAT/0399/10), the EAT quashed a tribunal award of aggravated damages where the tribunal found that a manager had acted in a brusque and insensitive manner towards the employee, and that in giving evidence she was dismissive and evasive: none of these was sufficient to support the making of an award of aggravated damages.

In *Michalak* (above), the tribunal awarded £30,000 for injury to feelings and £56,000 for psychiatric damage but, despite being 'positively outraged' by the conduct of the employer, made no award for aggravated damages, in light of the guidance in *Shaw* (above). It did, however, award exemplary damages (see (d) below).

(d) Exemplary damages may be awarded in discrimination cases but are rare. Exemplary damages punish the wrongdoer and should be awarded only for 'arbitrary and outrageous use of executive power' (see, eg, *Kuddus v Chief Constable of Leicestershire Constabulary* [2001] UKHL 29).

In *Husain v Chief Constable of Kent* (ET, 6 April 2006), the employment tribunal awarded exemplary damages of £5,000 due to the seriousness of the discrimination. The police force had suggested that Mr Husain had falsified his qualifications and professional experience, and had circulated a report to this effect to other forces. Subsequently, Mr Husain was arrested and detained when he applied for a new job. The tribunal held that the suggestion that he was falsifying his qualifications was the result of racial stereotyping.

In *Ministry of Defence v Fletcher* (UKEAT/0044/09), the EAT looked at the relationship between aggravated and exemplary damages, and upheld the aggravated damages award but overturned the exemplary damages award, finding no 'conscious and contumelious' wrongdoing.

In *Michalak* (above), the employment tribunal awarded exemplary damages for 'oppressive, arbitrary or unconstitutional' behaviour. The NHS Trust had, the tribunal held, acted in such a manner when it failed to follow government procedures prescribed for NHS Trusts, in a deliberate attempt to deprive the claimant of her rights.

(e)   Compensation for personal injury (psychiatric or physical injury) caused by the discrimination can be awarded, for example, for depression or post-traumatic stress – see *Sheriff v Klyne Tugs (Lowestoft) Ltd* [1999] IRLR 481, CA. In *HM Prison Service v Salmon* [2001] IRLR 425, a female prison officer was awarded £21,000 for injury to feelings and £11,250 for personal injury in respect of psychiatric damage caused by sexual harassment. On appeal, the EAT recognised that there was a risk of double recovery, but that in principle injury to feelings and psychiatric injury are distinct, although in practice not always easy to separate.

In *Essa v Laing Ltd* [2004] IRLR 313, the Court of Appeal held that compensation for unlawful discrimination is not limited to cases of reasonably foreseeable harm. A claimant simply has to show that the discrimination caused the harm (it is sufficient to show that it was a substantial and effective cause, even if not the dominant cause). (See also *Taylor v XLN Telecom* (EAT/0383/09) for confirmation that a claimant is entitled to recover for injury (to feelings or personal injury) attributable to the act complained of (eg a racially motivated dismissal) and does not have to prove that the injury resulted from actual knowledge of the discrimination.)

In a case of psychiatric injury (and in some other cases where the claimant is 'only' seeking an injury to feelings award) medical evidence will normally be required (see **Chapter 6**), but see *Hampshire County Council v Wyatt* (UKEAT/0013/16) where the EAT held that an employment tribunal was entitled to make a personal injury award for depression in a disability discrimination case, despite no medical evidence being produced by the employee. The EAT did, however, confirm that it would be advisable for suitable medical evidence to be obtained by employees.

The Court of Appeal confirmed in *BAE Systems (Operations) Ltd v Konczak* [2017] EWCA Civ 1188 that where psychiatric injury is caused by an employer's wrongdoing, a tribunal needs to examine whether the harm suffered should be apportioned (where part was caused by the employer and part was not so caused).

(f)   In a case of indirect discrimination where the respondent proves that there was no intention to treat the claimant unfavourably, a tribunal cannot award damages to a claimant unless it has first considered making either a declaration or a recommendation (s 124(4) and (5)). The EAT held, in *JH Walker Ltd v Hussain and Others* [1996] IRLR 11, that a person will have intended an act if he intended the consequences of his act, ie he knew when he did the act that those consequences would follow and he wanted those consequences to follow. So, in this case, the company knew that the Islamic festival of Eid was important to Muslim employees, that only they were affected by prohibiting holidays from May to July, and that they were required to work on that day. Such discrimination was not, therefore, unintentional.

(g)   Pregnancy dismissals – loss of career prospects or congenial employment does not form a separate head of damage and should be catered for in the award for injury to feelings ((b) above). Estimated child-care costs should be set off against future loss of earnings.

(h)   Accelerated receipt – a discount should normally be applied (see **2.4.1.9**).

(i)   Section 207A of the TULR(C)A 1992 gives the tribunals discretion to increase or reduce awards by up to 25% where the employer or employee unreasonably fails to comply with the 2009 Acas Code.

(j)   Taxation – see **Table 5.1** at **5.6.2.5**. While the Court of Appeal in *Moorthy v Commissioners for HMRC* [2018] EWCA Civ 847 confirmed that awards for injury to feelings (under the Income Tax (Earnings and Pensions) Act 2003) are exempt from tax, it is of limited impact because, from 6 April 2018, s 406 of the 2003 Act has been amended to specify that a payment for injury to feelings in respect of discrimination connected with termination of employment now falls outside the tax free exemption for personal injury (unless it is a psychiatric injury). A payment for injury to feelings which is *not* related to termination can still be paid tax free.

(k)   Interest – tribunals must consider whether to award interest. Any award must be calculated in accordance with the Employment Tribunals (Interest on Awards in Discrimination Cases) Regulations 1996 (SI 1996/2803) and the Employment Tribunals (Interest on Awards in Discrimination Cases) (Amendment) Regulations 2013 (SI 2013/1669). Interest on past pecuniary losses will generally be awarded from the midpoint date between the act of discrimination and the date of the tribunal hearing. Interest on injury to feelings runs from the date on which the unlawful act took place to the date of leaving. The rate from 28 July 2013 is 8%.

Note that there is no upper limit on the amount of compensation which may be awarded.

8.8.2.3   Joint and several liability

Employees who are held to have knowingly aided the employer are treated as if they themselves did the unlawful act(s), and tribunals have power to make a separate award against each respondent (see *Gilbank v Miles* [2006] IRLR 538). In practice, tribunals often make substantial awards against an employer and a small award against any individual who has been found to have committed any actual acts of discrimination. Tribunals may also treat the parties as joint tortfeasors and make one award against all respondents jointly and severally.

In *Way and Another v Crouch* [2005] IRLR 603, the EAT held that it is proper to make both the employer and any individual who has been found to have committed any actual acts of discrimination liable on a joint and several basis. In practice this allows the employee to sue the individual harasser for the full amount of any compensation if the employer turns out to be insolvent. The EAT emphasised that when making joint and several awards, tribunals must apportion the respective shares, so that if a claimant chooses to enforce against only one respondent, that respondent can still seek a suitable contribution. Any apportionment should be on the basis of respective culpability (and not on the financial strengths of the parties).

In *Munchkins Restaurant Ltd and Another v Karmazyn and Others* (UKEAT/0359/09), the EAT said (casting doubt on *Way v Crouch*) that the appropriate principle where there is an award of joint and several liability is that any one of the respondents is liable for the full extent of the damages to the claimant. Although, as between respondents, a respondent may have a right to seek contribution from a co-respondent, depending upon the relative contribution and responsibility of each of the respondents to the wrong which has been done, that should not affect the position of a claimant, who is entitled, if the award is joint and several, to receive the full extent of his award from any of the respondents as he chooses. The EAT held:

> [A]s a matter of general approach, where there is more than one respondent to a claim ... a Tribunal will have to decide whether or not it is to make a joint and several award. In some cases the reason for it doing so will be obvious and need very little elaboration.

In *London Borough of Hackney v Sivanandan and Others* [2013] EWCA Civ 22 the employment tribunal found complaints of victimisation were valid, and determined that the respondents were jointly and severally liable to pay the claimant £421,415. The tribunal declined to apportion liability as between the respondents. The Court of Appeal held that the employment tribunal's decision not to apportion was correct, and that there is no power in law allowing employment tribunals to apportion damages. In *Brennan and Others v Sunderland District Council and Others* (UKEAT/0286/11), the EAT, following *Sivanandan*, said that the employment tribunal has no jurisdiction to determine claims for contribution under the Civil Liability (Contribution) Act 1978.

8.8.3   Removal of contractual term

Section 142 provides that a contractual term 'is unenforceable against a person in so far as it constitutes, promotes or provides for treatment of that or another person that is of a description prohibited by this Act'. The provisions also provide that a county court may, on the application of an interested party, make an order removing or modifying a term which is unenforceable against that party (s 143).

In *Mead-Hill v The British Council* [1995] IRLR 478, an employee sought to rely on these provisions in relation to a mobility clause. It was held that the insertion of the clause could amount to indirect discrimination against women, who form a higher proportion of secondary earners and, as such, are less likely to be able to relocate. However, it was open to the employers to show justification irrespective of sex.

8.9 EQUAL PAY AND THE EQUALITY CLAUSE

8.9.1 Introduction

What follows is merely a very brief introduction to this complex area of the law, the detail of which is beyond the scope of the book. The law was previously contained in the EPA 1970 as amended (principally by the SDA 1975); it is now contained in Pt 5 (work), Ch 3 (equality of terms) of the Equality Act 2010, which is designed to ensure that men and women within the same employment receive equal pay (and other contractual terms) for equal work. Equal pay for men and women for equal work is a requirement of EU law under Article 157 TFEU (ex 141 EC). The law works by implying an 'equality clause' into a contract. Lord Nicholls, in *Glasgow City Council and Others v Marshall and Others* [2000] 1 WLR 333, set out what was regarded as the proper approach (under the old law as set out in s 1 of the EPA 1970) to equal pay claims.

It is important to consider whether the claim is one that should be brought under the equal pay provisions, or one that should be brought under the discrimination provisions (above):

* If the less favourable treatment relates to the payment of money which is regulated by a contract of employment, only the equal pay provisions can apply.

* If the employee is treated less favourably than an employee of the other sex who is doing the same or broadly similar work, or whose work has been given an equal value under a job evaluation, and the less favourable treatment relates to some matter which is regulated by the contract of employment of either of them, only the equal pay provisions can apply. However, if the less favourable treatment relates to a matter not included in the contract, only the sex discrimination provisions can apply.

* If the less favourable treatment relates to a matter (other than the payment of money) in a contract, and the comparison is with workers who are not doing the same or broadly similar work, or work which has been given an equal value under a job evaluation, only the sex discrimination provisions can apply.

* Lastly, if the complaint relates to a matter which is regulated by an employee's contract of employment, but is based on an allegation that an employee of the other sex would be treated more favourably in similar circumstances (ie it does not relate to the actual treatment of an existing employee of the other sex but rather requires a hypothetical comparator), only the sex discrimination provisions can apply.

The distinctions are crucial in practice because there are different time-limits. In some cases, it may be advisable to bring a discrimination claim and an equal pay claim, in the alternative, to protect the client's position.

In *Birmingham City Council v Abdulla and Others* [2012] UKSC 47, the Supreme Court decided that equal pay claims, which would have been out of time in an employment tribunal, could be brought in the High Court.

8.9.1.1 The equality clause

Section 64(1) states that ss 66 to 70 apply where:

(a)   a person (A) is employed on work that is equal to the work that a comparator of the opposite sex (B) does;

...

By s 66:

(1)   If the terms of A's work do not (by whatever means) include a sex equality clause, they are to be treated as including one.

(2)   A sex equality clause is a provision that has the following effect—

(a)   if a term of A's is less favourable to A than a corresponding term of B's is to B, A's term is modified so as not to be less favourable;

(b)   if A does not have a term which corresponds to a term of B's that benefits B, A's terms are modified so as to include such a term.

This has the effect of implying an equality clause into the contract of employment of a woman (or man), so that she (or he) is entitled to be treated no less favourably than a man (or woman) in the same employment.

Section 65 deals with what is meant by equal work:

(1)   For the purposes of this Chapter, A's work is equal to that of B if it is—

(a)   like B's work,

(b)   rated as equivalent to B's work, or

(c)   of equal value to B's work.

(2)   A's work is like B's work if—

(a)   A's work and B's work are the same or broadly similar, and

(b)   such differences as there are between their work are not of practical importance in relation to the terms of their work.

It will be necessary for a claimant in an equal pay case to be able to point to an actual (not hypothetical) comparator in the 'same establishment' (Equality Act 2010, s 79), or at different establishments where common terms apply, or where there is a single source of pay and conditions of work between the claimant and the comparator (see *Lawrence v Regent Office Care Ltd* [2003] ICR 1092) (however, note that no comparator is needed if it can be shown that the reason for not paying a woman the same as a man is because she is pregnant – see *Alabaster v Woolwich plc and DWP* [2005] IRLR 576). In *Walton Centre for Neurology v Bewley* (UKEAT/0564/07), the EAT held that a woman's successor in the job cannot be used as a comparator for the purposes of an equal pay claim. The comparator must be employed contemporaneously or be a predecessor. If there is no actual comparator available, the woman must bring a claim of direct sex discrimination claim against the employer. The example given in the Explanatory Notes is as follows:

> An employer tells a female employee 'I would pay you more if you were a man' ... In the absence of any male comparator the woman cannot bring a claim for breach of an equality clause but she can bring a claim of direct sex discrimination ... against the employer.

For decisions on the meaning of 'same establishment', including common terms and conditions and a single source of pay and conditions, see *Dumfries and Galloway Council v North* [2013] ICR 993 and *Fox Cross Claimants v Glasgow CC* [2013] ICR 954. These cases were decided under the old Equal Pay Act. Whilst the Equality Act 2010 is similar, there are subtle changes that readers will need to take into account. The EAT held in *Asda Stores Ltd v Brierley* (UKEAT/0092/16) that the '*North* hypothetical test remains good law' (see *North* above). In other words, where there is not a comparator at the establishment where the claimant works, comparison is permitted where common terms apply *or would apply* at those establishments.

8.9.1.2   Defences

It is a defence to an equal pay claim to show that the difference in pay is due to a material factor which is relevant and significant, and which does not directly or indirectly discriminate against the worker because of her sex (s 69) . If there is evidence that the factor which explains the difference in terms is not directly discriminatory but would have an adverse impact on people of her sex (that is, without more, it would be indirectly discriminatory), the employer must show that it is a proportionate means of meeting a legitimate aim or the sex equality clause will apply. For these purposes, the long-term objective of reducing pay inequality will always count as a legitimate aim.

The EAT provided a useful step-by-step summary of the defence in *Bury Metropolitan Borough Council v Hamilton and Others; Council of the City of Sunderland v Brennan and Others* (UKEAT/0413–5/09):

(1) It is necessary first to identify the explanation for the differential complained of. (In the language of the statute, this is the 'factor' to which the differential is 'due'; but the terminology of 'explanation' used by Lord Nicholls in *Marshall* [*Glasgow City Council v Marshall* [2000] ICR 196] is generally less clumsy.) The burden of proof is on the employer.

(2) It is then necessary to consider whether that explanation is 'tainted with sex'. What that not altogether happy metaphor means is that the explanation relied on must not itself involve sex discrimination, whether direct or indirect (see per Lord Browne-Wilkinson in *Wallace* [*Strathclyde Regional Council v Wallace* [1998] ICR 205], at pp 211H–212A and per Lord Nicholls in *Marshall*, at pp 202H–203A).

(3) In considering whether the explanation involves direct or indirect discrimination, the ordinary principles of the law of discrimination apply. That means that:

   (a) if the differential is the result of direct discrimination (in the sense established in *Nagarajan v London Regional Transport* [1999] ICR 877) the defence under section 1(3) will fail;

   (b) if the differential involves indirect discrimination of either the 'PCP' or 'Enderby' type – as to this distinction, see para 16 below – the defence will fail unless the employer proves that the differential is objectively justified, applying the classic proportionality test;

   (c) if the employer's explanation involves neither direct nor indirect discrimination the defence will succeed, even if the factor relied on cannot be objectively justified – this is most vividly illustrated by the 'mistake' cases such as *Yorkshire Blood Transfusion Service v Plaskitt* [1994] ICR 74 and *Tyldesley v TML Plastics* [1996] ICR 356, approved in *Wallace*.

(4) In conducting the exercise under (3), the ordinary principles governing the burden of proof in discrimination claims will apply. Thus if the claimant shows a prima facie case of discrimination (in the sense explained in *Madarassy v Nomura International plc* [2007] ICR 867), the burden shifts to the employer to prove the absence of discrimination.

In *Allen and Another v GMB* [2008] IRLR 690, the Court of Appeal upheld a tribunal decision that the GMB Union indirectly discriminated against union members by recommending acceptance of a 'single status' pay deal which grossly underestimated the compensation to be paid to female equal pay claimants. Although the objective of securing a fair single status pay deal was legitimate, the means used by the union were not proportionate. Permission to appeal to the House of Lords was refused. The Court of Appeal found that a pay protection policy was prima facie indirectly discriminatory against women in *Haq & Others v Audit Commission* [2013] IRLR 206. However, the Court held by a majority that it was objectively justified because the policy was a proportionate way of achieving a legitimate aim.

In *Clark v Metropolitan Police Authority* (Mayor and City of London Court, Case No OMY00263, 26 May 2011), a part-time female inspector successfully challenged the Metropolitan Police's pay scheme. While, on its face, the terms were equal, and both full- and part-timers were paid for the hours they were due to work (for full-timers 40 hours and for part-timers according to their rotas), any hours worked over this were not paid. The effect was that if part-time and full-time inspectors worked the same number of hours but that number was greater than the part-timers' rota hours, the full-timers would be paid more. That pay differential was tainted by sex, as 96% of part-timers were women and 86% of full-timers were men. The Metropolitan Police Authority argued that the scheme had been agreed through collective bargaining, but the court said that was not sufficient to justify the inequality.

In *Calmac Ferries Ltd v Wallace & Another* (UKEATS/0014/13) (see also **Chapter 6**), the EAT held that since the burden lies on the employer to prove a material factor defence, strike out of such claims is wrong at the preliminary stage.

In *Glasgow City Council v UNITE Claimants* [2017] CSIH 34, when the Council implemented a job evaluation scheme, it implemented a three-year pay protection system to protect bonuses and other payments for so-called 'red-circled' employees (employees whose roles had been downgraded) who were typically men and who would otherwise have seen their pay fall because of the changes. Other employees, who were predominantly female, were not red-circled because their jobs had not been downgraded. This had the effect of keeping men's overall pay higher than women performing equivalent roles. The Court of Session held that treating differently red-circled employees and the other employees whose work has been rated as equivalent could not be justified on the facts because there was no evidence before the employment tribunal that the appellant had even considered the position of the other employees who had not been red-circled. As was observed in *Bury MBC v Hamilton* [2011] ICR 655, at para 78:

> [A] local authority cannot prove unaffordability by mere assertion. A case of justification on this basis can only be proved by adducing sufficiently detailed evidence, both of the costs themselves and of the financial context, to enable the Tribunal to reach an informed view ... That need not involve an exhaustive review of the Council's finances, but the Tribunal must be put in a position where it can assess the broad picture.

The equality clause does not apply to any provision affording women special treatment in connection with pregnancy or childbirth.

Readers should note that the EAT confirmed in *McNeil & Others v Commissioners for HM Revenue & Customs* (UKEAT/0183/17) that, as the judgment of the Supreme Court in *Essop/Naeem* (below at **10.2.3**) held, in a claim based on unlawful indirect discrimination:

69.   (i)   once it has been established ... that a PCP places people with relevant protected characteristics at a particular disadvantage compared with others, that is sufficient to require objective justification ...;

(ii)   it is irrelevant whether or not the reason why the PCP puts that group at a particular disadvantage is itself related to the protected characteristic;

(iii)   the only required causal link is between the PCP and the particular disadvantage.

70.   [T]hose principles apply equally to an equal pay claim based on indirect discrimination.

71.   Accordingly, to the extent that the line of authority based on *Armstrong v Newcastle upon Tyne NHS Hospital Trust* [2006] IRLR 124 has been understood as holding that it is open to a respondent to rebut a finding made of particular disadvantage by showing that the underlying reason for the particular disadvantage was not itself related to the protected characteristic in issue, it is inconsistent with the ratio of *Essop/Naeem* and can no longer be regarded as good law.

8.9.1.3 Enforcement

In the event of a breach of the equality clause, the remedy is to present a complaint to an employment tribunal within six months of the end of the employment contract, or in some circumstances to bring a breach of contract claim in the civil courts within six years (*Birmingham City Council v Abdulla and Others* [2012] UKSC 47). The tribunal, if the complaint is well founded, may award arrears of remuneration and damages going back for up to six years for breach of the equality clause.

Note that unlike in sex discrimination claims, damages for non-pecuniary loss (such as injury to feelings and aggravated damages) cannot be recovered in equal pay claims (because such claims are based on contract and are not based on a statutory tort as in a discrimination claim) – see *Council of the City of Newcastle upon Tyne v Allan and Others* [2005] IRLR 504 and *BMC Software Ltd v Shaikh* (UKEAT/0092/16). Nor can tribunals make recommendations in equal pay cases.

8.9.1.4 Equal pay audit

The ERRA 2013, which received Royal Assent on 25 April 2013, enabled the Secretary of State to require tribunals to order an equal pay audit where an employer is found to have breached the equal pay provisions in the Equality Act 2010, subject to exemptions and exceptions. The Government introduced the power on 1 October 2014 (see Equality Act 2010 (Equal Pay Audits) Regulations 2014 (SI 2014/2559). The Regulations require a tribunal to order an employer found to be in breach of equal pay law to undertake an equal pay audit in certain circumstances.

8.9.1.5 Gender pay gap reporting

The Equality Act 2010 (Gender Pay Gap Information) Regulations 2017 (SI 2017/172) came into force on 6 April 2017. The Regulations apply to public sector employers with 250 or more employees (and include 'workers') (see **Chapter 1**). Employers have until 4 April 2018 to publish details of their gender pay gap.

8.10 PART-TIME WORKERS

The Part-time Workers (Prevention of Less Favourable Treatment) Regulations 2000 (SI 2000/1551) implement the European Part-time Work Directive (97/81/EC). Clause 4(1) of the Directive provides:

> In respect of employment conditions, part-time workers shall not be treated in a less favourable manner than comparable full-time workers solely because they work part time unless different treatment is justified on objective grounds.

What follows is an overview.

The 2000 Regulations make it unlawful for employers to treat part-time workers less favourably than full-time workers (unless different treatment can be objectively justified – reg 5) in their terms and conditions, in areas such as:

(a)   hourly rates of pay;

(b)   overtime rates;

(c)   access to occupational pension schemes;

(d)   training;

(e)   (pro rata) holiday entitlement;

(f)   (pro rata) maternity/paternal leave;

(g)   (pro rata) sick pay.

Part-time workers should also be treated no less favourably when being selected for redundancy, unless the different treatment can be justified objectively.

The 2000 Regulations apply to 'workers', not just 'employees'. A part-time worker who is treated less favourably than a full-time worker is now able to bring a claim regardless of whether he or she is a man or a woman. Before the 2000 Regulations came into force, because part-time work is overwhelmingly done by women, claims of indirect sex discrimination were possible, but only by women part-time workers. Nevertheless, at present, if advising women, it would seem wise to run claims under both the Equality Act 2010 and the 2000 Regulations. Readers should consult the Regulations for detailed guidance.

Key to claims under the 2000 Regulations is whether the worker and his or her comparator are engaged in the same or broadly similar work (reg 2(4)(a)(ii)). This has generated a fair amount of case law.

In *Wippel v Peek and Cloppenburg GmbH* [2005] IRLR 211, the ECJ looked at the definition of worker, and said that national law needed to be looked at in Member States, who have wide discretionary powers. *Wippel* is often referred to in the UK cases on part-time workers.

The first UK case on what is required to make a part-time worker comparable with a full-time worker was decided by the House of Lords on 1 March 2006 (*Matthews v Kent and Medway Towns Fire Authority* [2006] IRLR 367). Retained firefighters (ie, part-time firefighters) claimed parity of employment terms with full-time, regular firefighters. They sought to belong to the pension scheme, and to be paid the same rate for additional duties and sick pay. The Court of Appeal ([2004] IRLR 697) held that retained firefighters are not engaged in the same or broadly similar work as regular firemen having regard to their level of qualification, skills and experience. The House of Lords said that the tribunal (which, along with the EAT, had found that the new workers were engaged on different contracts and that the Part-time Workers Regulations did not apply) had taken the wrong approach to the question of whether the workers did the same or broadly similar work. Their Lordships said that the question to ask is whether the main duties and responsibilities of the two jobs were the same or similar. This will involve looking at the work done by both groups, and taking into account similarities and differences. If the answer to the above question is 'Yes', the next stage is to look at the differences and decide whether they are so important as to prevent the work being regarded as the same or broadly similar. Their Lordships commented that just because the full-timers carried out some extra tasks, this would not prevent the jobs being the same or broadly similar. The case was sent back to the tribunal for reconsideration.

In *Moultrie and Ors v Ministry of Justice* (UKEAT/0239/14), the EAT upheld a tribunal's decision that fee-paid medical members of tribunals were not engaged in the same or broadly similar work as salaried medical members, because 15% of the work that the fee-paid members do is of such importance that it could not be said to be the same or broadly similar work.

Another more recent case looking at whether the (part-time) claimant and his (full-time) comparator were engaged in the same or broadly similar work is *Roddis v Sheffield Hallam University* (UKEAT/0299/17), which looked at whether an associate lecturer engaged on a zero hours contract was employed under the same type of contract as a full-time lecturer. The EAT said that the proper approach to reg 2(3) was to look at the 'comprehensive' list of categories of contract in reg 2(1), (2) and (4) and bear in mind that the purpose of the Regulations is to provide a threshold for comparison which is deliberately set not too high. Just because there are different terms and conditions or workers are treated differently does not automatically mean that they are not engaged in the same work.

In *Carl v University of Sheffield* (UKEAT/0261/08), a part-time teacher of shorthand complained that she had been treated less favourably than a full-time sociology lecturer, who was better qualified and taught at a higher level. She also argued that she could use a hypothetical comparator. The EAT said that a hypothetical comparator was not permissible in respect of a claim of less favourable treatment in a part-time work context. A claimant must be able to point to a real comparator. The claimant also failed in her claim based on an actual comparator, as the difference in skills and qualifications meant (unlike in *Matthews v Kent and Medway Towns Fire Authority*) that she had not identified an actual full-time comparator. (There is conflicting Scottish authority – see *Gibson v Scottish Ambulance Service* (EATS/0052/04).)

In *Sharma and Others v Manchester CC* [2008] IRLR 336, the EAT held, contrary to decisions in the Scottish courts, that once it is found that the part-timer is treated less favourably than a full-time comparator, and being part-time is *one* of the reasons, that will suffice to trigger the Regulations.

The Court of Appeal held in *BA plc v Pinaud* [2018] EWCA Civ 2427 that a part-time crew member who was required to be available for 53.5% of the full-time equivalent hours but was only paid 50% of the salary of the full-timer was treated less favourably.

Although the language used is the language of discrimination, there is no provision to make any award for injury to feelings. No adjustment to compensation for failure to comply with the

2009 Acas Code is possible, because a claim under the Regulations is not one of the listed Sch 2 jurisdictions.

The ECJ has ruled (see *Istituto nazionale della previdenza social (INPS) v Bruno* [2010] IRLR 890) on how the Part-time Work Directive applies to occupational pension rights. That case suggests that the protection goes beyond mere access to such schemes. In *O'Brien v Ministry of Justice* (Case C-393/10), the ECJ held that if fee-paid, part-time judges are workers, the national law that excludes fee-paid judges from the pension scheme is discriminatory, unless it can be objectively justified. The case was heard by the Supreme Court on 4 July 2012, and its reasons were given on 6 February 2013 ([2013] UKSC 6). The Supreme Court held that a part-time Crown Court recorder was a part-time worker for the purposes of the Part-time Workers Regulations, and that the differences in treatment between part-time, fee-paid recorders and full-time, salaried recorders regarding pensions was not objectively justified. Lady Hale gave the judgment of the Supreme Court on the justification issue. She referred (at [46]) to the opinion of Advocate-General Kokott, implicitly endorsed by the ECJ, that unequal treatment must be justified by

> the existence of precise, concrete factors, characterising the employment condition concerned in its specific context and on the basis of objective and transparent criteria for examining the question whether that unequal treatment responds to a genuine need and whether it is appropriate and necessary for achieving the objective pursued ...

Lady Hale emphasised that European case law clearly established that a discriminatory rule or practice could not be justified by reference to the simple saving of costs. The case was remitted back to the employment tribunal to determine the amount of pension to which the claimant was entitled. The EAT held that Mr O'Brien's pension should only be calculated with reference to his service after 7 April 2000 (the date the Part-time Workers Directive should have been implemented in the UK) (UKEAT/0466/13).

The issue of the amount of pension due to Mr O'Brien came before the Supreme Court at the same time as *Walker v Innospec* (see **8.2.6** above). A majority of the Supreme Court believed that the relevant date for the purposes of when discrimination occurred was not when the pension was earned but when it came to be paid. On this view, it would be the future effect of a past situation, in which case service before 7 April 2000 should be taken into account. The Court was unsure on this point and referred it to the CJEU, whose ruling was handed down on 7 November 2018. The CJEU (Case C-432/17) held that part-time work carried out before the deadline for implementing the Directive on 7 April 2000 must be taken into account.

8.11   FIXED-TERM EMPLOYEES

The Fixed-term Employees (Prevention of Less Favourable Treatment) Regulations 2002 (SI 2002/2034) work on a similar basis to the Part-time Workers Regulations 2000 (see **8.10**). However, there is one important distinction. The Fixed-term Employee Regulations apply only to employees, not to the wider category of workers.

Again, the detail of the legislation is beyond the scope of this book but, briefly, the 2002 Regulations cover the following:

(a)   A right for a fixed-term employee not to be treated less favourably than a comparable permanent employee (see *Carl v University of Sheffield* (**8.10** above)) on the grounds that he is a fixed-term employee, unless objectively justified. Objective justification is deemed to be made out where the fixed-term employee's contractual rights are, as a whole, at least as favourable as the permanent employee's. Otherwise, the employer will have to show that there is an objective reason for treating the fixed-term employee less favourably. Archived BIS Guidance gives an example an employee on a three-month fixed-term contract, who is not provided with a company car because the cost of doing so is so high, and the employee's travel needs can be met in another way.

(b)   An obligation on employers to advertise permanent vacancies in such a way as is reasonably likely to come to the fixed-term employee's attention.

(c)   A right to receive a written statement of reasons for treatment, if the employee believes less favourable treatment has occurred.

(d)   Provision that any dismissal for seeking to enforce these rights is automatically unfair.

(e)   Provision that a fixed-term contract will be converted to a permanent contract upon the next renewal/extension if the employee has been employed on a fixed-term contract for over four years (unless the employer can demonstrate an objective justification for continued fixed-term employment). The archived BIS Guidance gives as an example professional sports people, where it is traditional practice for employees to work on fixed-term contracts.

For some case law on the 2002 Regulations, see *Duncombe and Others v Secretary of State for Children, Schools and Children* [2011] UKSC 14, *The Manchester College v Mr M Cocliff* (UKEAT/0035/10), *Hall v Xerox UK Ltd* (UKEAT/0061/14) and *Ibarz v University of Sheffield* (UKEAT/0018/15) (time-limits).

8.12   TRADE UNION MEMBERSHIP OR ACTIVITIES

Section 137 of the Trade Union and Labour Relations (Consolidation) Act 1992 (TULR(C)A 1992) abolishes the pre-entry closed shop (ie the refusal to employ a person who is not a member of a trade union). It also prohibits an employer from refusing to employ someone because he is a member of a trade union or takes part in trade union activities.

8.12.1   Refusal of employment

It is unlawful to refuse to employ a person on the grounds that he is, or is not, a member of a trade union. It is also unlawful to refuse to employ a person if he does not agree to become, or remain or cease to be a member of a trade union (TULR(C)A 1992, s 137(1)).

8.12.2   Remedies

If a person has been refused employment on the grounds that he is, or is not, a member of a trade union, he may present a complaint to an employment tribunal within three months of the act complained of. The complainant may apply for interim relief (see **5.5.1**).

The tribunal may make an order for compensation, including injury to feelings, or a recommendation that the effect of the act be obviated or reduced. This could involve, for example, a recommendation that the complainant be offered employment. If a recommendation is not complied with, the compensation award can be increased. The maximum compensation currently awardable is £78,335 (at 6 April 2015).

8.13   DISCRIMINATION UNDER THE HUMAN RIGHTS ACT 1998

The ECHR ('the Convention') was incorporated into domestic law by the Human Rights Act (HRA) 1998. This means that individuals are able to enforce Convention rights in the UK's domestic courts and tribunals (see **Chapter 15**).

Article 14 of the Convention contains a wide prohibition against discrimination. It states that the enjoyment of rights and freedoms set forth in the Convention shall be secured

> without discrimination on any ground such as sex, race, colour, language, religion, political or other opinion, national or social origin, association with a national minority, property, birth or other status.

However, Article 14 does not create any 'freestanding' right to freedom from discrimination, and is thus limited to the right to enjoy the other Convention rights without discrimination. Protocol 12 prohibits discrimination in the enjoyment of any right granted by national law, but the UK has not ratified the Protocol.

There have been a number of cases before the ECtHR looking at violations of Article 14 (in conjunction with Article 2 (right to education)) by States in connection with education policies relating to the children of Roma parents (see, eg, *DH and Others v The Czech Republic* (App No 57325/00) and *Sampanis v Greece* (App No 32526/05), which contain useful statements on indirect discrimination and the shifting burden of proof).

Article 9 of the Convention contains the rights to freedom of thought and religion. It will cover, for example, religious groups who are not currently covered under the definition of 'race' under the Equality Act 2010 (eg Muslims; Rastafarians). If employers discriminate on grounds of belief or religion, that will be unlawful. However, the Court has been restrictive of these rights and has given only limited protection. See, for example, *Ahmad v UK* (1982) 4 EHRR 126, *Stedman v UK* (1997) 23 EHRR CD 168, ECtHR and *Kontinnen v Finland* (1996) 87 DR 68, ECtHR, where the ECtHR accepted that the right could be limited by contractual provisions. In these cases, the view taken was that if, for example, working hours conflict with religious convictions, the applicant is free to resign. However, the ECtHR held more recently in *Eweida & Others v UK* [2013] IRLR 231 that, given the importance in a democratic society of freedom of religion, rather than holding that the possibility of changing job would negate any interference with the right, the better approach is to weigh that possibility in the overall balance when considering whether or not the restriction is proportionate.

Even though discrimination on grounds of sexual orientation has, until very recently, not been covered by UK or EU law, sexual orientation has been recognised as part of an individual's private life under Article 8 of the Convention. If there is a dismissal on such grounds, Article 8 can be used to give strength to an argument that there is an unfair dismissal. If there is an act by a public authority, Article 8 will give rise to a direct cause of action. Article 8, in conjunction with Article 14, was significant in *EB v France* (App No 43546/02), where the ECtHR found breaches of the Convention when a lesbian's application to adopt a child was refused.

Particularly gross forms of harassment and discrimination may amount to inhuman or degrading treatment under Article 3 of the Convention.

8.14 FURTHER READING

Barnard, *The Substantive Law of the EU: The Four Freedoms*, 5th edn (OUP, 2016).

Barnard, *EU Employment Law*, 4th edn (OUP, 2012).

Wadham, Robinson, Ruebain and Uppal, *Blackstone's Guide to the Equality Act 2010*, 3rd edn (OUP, 2016).

Harvey, *Industrial Relations and Employment Law* (Butterworths), Divs K and L.

Discrimination Law (Bloomsbury Professional, 2016).

Tolley's Employment Handbook, 32nd edn (2018).

Jackson and Banerjee, *Disability Discrimination: Law and Case Management*, 2nd edn (Law Society Publishing, 2019).

The Government Equalities Office (GEO) website:
<http://www.equalities.gov.uk>.

The Advisory, Conciliation and Arbitration Service (Acas) Guidance at:
<http://www.acas.org.uk>.

See also the Acas advisory booklet, *Tackling discrimination and promoting equality – good practice guide for employers*, available from the Acas website at <http://www.acas.org.uk/publications>.

SUMMARY

The general common law rule is that an employer is free to offer employment to whomsoever he chooses (*Allen v Flood and Taylor* [1898] AC 1). This common law freedom has been restricted by statute. The EC Equal Treatment Directive (76/207) provides that there should be no discrimination on grounds of sex, either directly or indirectly, nor by reference to marital or family status, in access to employment, training, working conditions, promotion or dismissal. In the UK, under the provisions of the Equality Act 2010, an employer may be in breach of statutory requirements if he discriminates against a person on a large number of protected characteristics including:

(a)   sex, maternity, pregnancy or marital status;

(b)   gender reassignment;

(c)   colour, race, nationality or ethnic or national origins;

(d)   religion or belief;

(e)   sexual orientation;

(f)   age;

(g)   disability (**8.1**).

The Equality and Human Rights Commission (EHRC) has responsibility for promoting equality and combating unlawful discrimination on grounds of sex, race, disability, sexual orientation, religion or belief, and age. It also has responsibility for the promotion of human rights.

This chapter has looked at the matters which are common to all the protected characteristics. Provisions in the Equality Act 2010 relating to age and disability discrimination are in some ways different from the other protected characteristics, and so age discrimination (**Chapter 12**) and disability discrimination (**Chapter 13**) are dealt with separately.

Four main types of discrimination in the employment field are outlawed by UK legislation on these grounds. These are:

(a)   direct discrimination (ie being subject to less favourable treatment than others because of sex, race, religion or belief, sexual orientation, age, etc) (see **Chapter 9**);

(b)   indirect discrimination (ie the application of a provision, criterion or practice which disadvantages people of a particular sex, race, religion or belief, sexual orientation, age, etc) (see **Chapter 10**);

(c)   harassment (unwanted conduct that violates a person's dignity, or creates an intimidating, hostile, degrading, humiliating or offensive environment for him or her having regard to all the circumstances, including the perception of the victim) (see **Chapter 11**); and

(d)   victimisation (because the victim has been subject to a detriment because he has done a protected act) (see **Chapter 11**).

In most cases, indirect discrimination may be justified 'objectively' where the discrimination is a 'proportionate means of achieving a legitimate aim' (**Chapter 10**).

Discrimination is outlawed (Equality Act 2010, ss 39 and 40) in the employment field against job applicants (ie recruitment) and employees and former employees. It is unlawful for a person, to discriminate against a person employed by him (**8.4**):

(a)   in the way he affords him or her access to opportunities for promotion, transfer or training, or to any other benefits, facilities or services; or

(b)   by dismissing him or her, or subjecting him or her to any other detriment.

An employer may have a defence under the occupational requirements provisions of the Equality Act 2010 (**8.5**) and under the 'reasonable steps' defence (**8.6.2**), if he can show that he took such steps as were reasonably practicable to prevent an employee doing the act complained of. Employers may be vicariously liable for the acts of their employees during the course of employment (**8.6**).

Remedies and enforcement are dealt with at **8.8**. Tribunals may, on making a finding of discrimination, as they consider just and equitable, make:

(a)   an order declaring the rights of the complainant;

(b)   an order requiring the respondent to pay the complainant compensation; and/or

(c)   a recommendation that the respondent take, within a specified period, practicable action to obviate or reduce the adverse effect of any act of discrimination.

The general principle as far as compensation is concerned is that, as far as possible, complainants should be placed in the same position as they would have been but for the unlawful act (see *Ministry of Defence v Wheeler* [1998] IRLR 23). In addition to awarding compensation for foreseeable damage arising directly from the unlawful act, a tribunal has jurisdiction to award compensation for personal injury, including both physical and psychiatric injury, and for injury to feelings (**8.8.2.2**).

DIRECT DISCRIMINATION

LEARNING OUTCOMES

After reading this chapter you will be able to:

- understand the definition of direct discrimination
- explain what is meant by 'less favourable treatment'
- describe how direct discrimination protects women who are pregnant or on maternity leave
- explain what is meant by the shifting burden of proof
- list the potential remedies that are available where a complaint of discrimination is made out.

9.1 INTRODUCTION

This chapter considers direct discrimination in respect of the following protected characteristics listed in s 4 of the Equality Act 2010 ('the Act') (see **8.2.1**):

- gender reassignment (s 7)
- marriage and civil partnership (s 8)
- race (s 9)
- religion or belief (s 10)
- sex (s 11)
- sexual orientation (s 12)
- pregnancy and maternity (s 18).

This chapter refers, by way of illustration and example, to the pre- and post-Equality Act 2010 case law.

9.2 DIRECT DISCRIMINATION

9.2.1 Definition

Direct discrimination occurs where the reason for a person being treated less favourably than another is a protected characteristic listed in s 4 of the Act (see **9.1**). This definition is broad enough to cover cases where the less favourable treatment is because of the victim's association with someone who has that characteristic (eg is disabled – see **Chapter 13**), or because the victim is wrongly thought to have it (eg a particular religious belief) (see **9.2.2**).

Note that men cannot claim privileges for women connected with pregnancy or childbirth (s 13(6)(b)).

The definition of 'direct discrimination' is set out in s 13 of the Act:

(1)   A person (A) discriminates against another (B) if, because of a protected characteristic, A treats B less favourably than A treats or would treat others.

...

(4)   If the protected characteristic is marriage and civil partnership, this section applies to a contravention of Part 5 (work) only if the treatment is because it is B who is married or a civil partner.

(5)   If the protected characteristic is race, less favourable treatment includes segregating B from others.

(6)   If the protected characteristic is sex—

(a)   less favourable treatment of a woman includes less favourable treatment of her because she is breast-feeding;

(b)   in a case where B is a man, no account is to be taken of special treatment afforded to a woman in connection with pregnancy or childbirth.

(7)   Subsection (6)(a) does not apply for the purposes of Part 5 (work).

(8)   This section is subject to section ... 18(7) [see **9.4**].

The Explanatory Notes give examples:

- If an employer recruits a man rather than a woman because she assumes that women do not have the strength to do the job, this would be direct sex discrimination.

- If a Muslim shopkeeper refuses to serve a Muslim woman because she is married to a Christian, this would be direct religious or belief-related discrimination on the basis of her association with her husband.

- If an employer rejects a job application form from a white man who he wrongly thinks is black, because the applicant has an African-sounding name, this would constitute direct race discrimination based on the employer's mistaken perception.

- If an employer advertising a vacancy makes it clear in the advert that Roma need not apply, this would amount to direct race discrimination against a Roma who might reasonably have considered applying for the job but was deterred from doing so because of the advertisement.

In *Islington Borough Council v Ladele* [2009] ICR 387, the EAT explained direct discrimination as follows (para 32) (the case was appealed to the Court of Appeal but the explanation remains a valid one):

> The concept of direct discrimination is fundamentally a simple one. A claimant suffers some form of detriment (using that term very broadly) and the reason for that detrimental treatment is the prohibited ground. There is implicit in that analysis the fact that someone in a similar position to whom that ground did not apply (the comparator) would not have suffered the detriment. By establishing that the reason for the detrimental treatment is the prohibited reason, the claimant necessarily establishes at one and the same time that he or she is less favourably treated than the comparator who did not share the prohibited characteristic.

Only direct discrimination because of age may be justified (Article 6 of the Framework Directive and Equality Act 2010, s 13(2); see, for example, *Seldon v Clarkson Wright and Jakes* [2012] UKSC 16, **Chapter 12**.)

9.2.2 Association and perception

Associative discrimination occurs when someone who does not have a protected characteristic themselves is discriminated against because of someone else's protected characteristic. Perceptive discrimination is discrimination against an individual because others think (wrongly) that they possess a particular protected characteristic. In *EAD Solicitors LLP & Ors v Abrams* (UKEAT/0054/15), the EAT held that a limited company can bring a claim that it has been directly discriminated against where it suffers detrimental treatment because of the protected characteristics of someone it is associated with. Detrimental treatment can be applied to any person, natural or legal, and either or both can bring proceedings.

Associative and perceptive discrimination were covered under some but not all of the old discrimination legislation. For example, while the Employment Equality (Age) Regulations 2006 (SI 2006/1031) defined direct age discrimination as occurring where A treats B less favourably than others 'on grounds of B's age', the RRA 1976 referred to 'on racial grounds'. This wider wording meant that discrimination was not just with regard to the race of the person concerned – it could be with regard to the race of someone else.

In *Showboat Entertainment Centre v Owens* [1984] IRLR 7, a white employee was dismissed for failing to obey an order not to admit young black men into an amusement arcade; this was held to be a discriminatory dismissal. He was discriminated against on the grounds of someone else's race. In *Showboat*, Browne-Wilkinson P said (at para 11):

> Therefore the only question is whether Mr Owens was treated less favourably 'on racial grounds'. Certainly the main thrust of the legislation is to give protection to those discriminated against on the grounds of their own racial characteristics. But the words 'on racial grounds' are perfectly capable in their ordinary sense of covering any reason for an action based on race, whether it be the race of the person affected by the action or of others.

The decision in *Showboat* was subsequently approved by the Court of Appeal in *Weathersfield Ltd v Sargent* [1999] IRLR 94, which was another case in which an employee had resigned and was found to have been constructively dismissed, after having been given an unlawful instruction to discriminate on racial grounds against blacks and Asians. The crucial test under the old case law was whether the protected characteristic had a significant influence on the outcome which it was claimed was discriminatory.

For other pre-Equality Act cases, which are still illustrative of the likely approach in this area, see *Saini v All Saints Haque Centre* [2009] IRLR 74, *English v Thomas Sanderson Blinds Ltd* [2009] IRLR 206 and *Lisboa v Real Pubs Ltd* (EAT/0224/10).

The wording of the definition of 'direct discrimination' in the Act is wide enough to now cover both associative and perceptive discrimination: the reference in s 13 (see **9.2.1**) is to treatment 'because of [protected characteristic]' as opposed to 'on grounds of' A's protected characteristic. This broader wording removes the need to consider whether the complainant's protected characteristic was the reason for the treatment complained of. It means that so-called 'associative discrimination' is covered. If A treats B less favourably because B cares for an elderly relative, A may be held to have discriminated against B *because of age*, even though B's age is not the reason for the treatment.

The Explanatory Notes state that direct discrimination occurs where the reason for a person being treated less favourably than another is a protected characteristic listed in s 4, and that the definition (save in the case of marriage and civil partnership) is broad enough to cover cases where the less favourable treatment is because of the victim's association with someone who has that characteristic (eg, is black) (association), or because the victim is wrongly thought to have it (eg, a particular religious belief) (perception).

Note that a different approach applies where the reason for the treatment is marriage or civil partnership, in which case only less favourable treatment because of the victim's status amounts to discrimination. It must be the victim, rather than anybody else, who is married or a civil partner, and a perception that the victim is married or a civil partner is not sufficient.

Until recently, it was thought that associative discrimination was limited to direct discrimination and harassment. However, two recent cases, *CHEZ Razpredelenie Bulgaria* (Case C-83/14) and *Thompson v London Central Bus Company Ltd* (UKEAT/0108/15) suggest that it may also apply to cases of indirect discrimination and victimisation (see **10.2.4** and **11.7.1**).

See too the case of *Lee v McArthur and Ashers Baking Co Ltd* [2016] NICA 39, discussed at **9.2.5.3** below, which the Northern Ireland Court of Appeal held was a case of associative discrimination.

It is not clear how perception discrimination will work where the protected characteristic is disability (see **13.3.9**).

9.2.3   Reason for the less favourable treatment

Section 13 of the Act uses the words 'because of' where the previous legislation used the words 'on grounds of'. The Explanatory Notes state that this difference in wording does not change the legal meaning of the definition but rather is designed to make it more accessible to the ordinary user of the Act. In *Amnesty International v Ahmed* [2009] IRLR 884, Mr Justice Underhill stated that

> there can be no objection to the use of the phrase 'because of' if used as a synonym for the phrase 'on grounds of' as long as the phrase is not used to import a 'causation' (or a 'but for') test.

(For a case where the tribunal erroneously used the 'but for' test, see *Chief Constable of Greater Manchester Police v Bailey* [2017] EWCA Civ 425.)

9.2.4   What is less favourable treatment?

Less favourable treatment is a wide concept: it covers any 'disadvantage' (see, eg, *Jeremiah v Ministry of Defence* [1979] IRLR 436). It does not require any tangible loss (see *Chief Constable of West Yorkshire Police v Khan* [2001] IRLR 830). A mere deprivation of choice will be sufficient to found a claim of less favourable treatment (see, eg, *Gill v El Vino Co Ltd* [1983] QB 425 and *R v Birmingham City Council, ex p Equal Opportunities Commission* [1989] IRLR 173).

In *Dansie v The Commissioner of Police for the Metropolis* (UKEAT/0234/09), D, a police recruit, was forced to cut his shoulder length hair or face disciplinary action. It was common ground that a female police recruit would not have been required to cut her hair. D claimed he had been unlawfully discriminated against on the ground of his sex. The EAT, in upholding the tribunal's decision, said that requiring a conventional standard of appearance is not in itself discriminatory, provided that, looking at the code as a whole, neither sex is treated less favourably as a result of its enforcement.

Although there was some suggestion in recent but pre-Equality Act 2010 case law that the test may be a subjective one (see *Chief Constable of West Yorkshire v Khan*), the wording in s 13 appears to suggest that the test is objective: the question is whether the complainant would have been treated:

(a)   differently; and

(b)   more favourably,

had it not been because of sex, race, religion or belief, sexual orientation, gender reassignment or marital/civil partnership status. The reason for the less favourable treatment must be because of sex, race, etc. The tribunal must ask what the 'conscious or subconscious reason for treating the claimant less favourably was'. If a protected characteristic was one of the reasons for the treatment, that is enough to establish direct discrimination. It need not be the sole or main reason, as long as it had a significant influence on the outcome. (See *Nagarajan v London Regional Transport* [1999] IRLR 572, HL.)

What amounts to less favourable treatment is for the tribunal to decide, but the hurdle is generally not a difficult one to satisfy. In considering the meaning to be given to 'less favourable', the courts have generally adopted the same test as that applied to determine whether a 'detriment' has occurred. In *Chief Constable of West Yorkshire Police v Khan* (above), the employer refused to give the claimant a reference, and he claimed that this was racially discriminatory. The employer argued that the claimant was better off without a reference, because any such reference would have been unfavourable and that there was, therefore, no less favourable treatment. The House of Lords held it was enough that the claimant 'could reasonably say that he would have preferred not to have been treated differently in this way'. In *Metropolitan Police v Keohane* (UKEAT/0463/12), the claimant was a police dog handler: the removal of her work dog when she went on maternity leave was not a detriment on its own, but the potential resultant loss of overtime and career disadvantage upon the claimant's return from leave was.

A recent judgment of the CJEU on headscarf bans illustrates how difficult it can sometimes be to determine what is less favourable treatment in a direct discrimination context. The judgment is also illuminating on how the lines between direct and indirect discrimination can get blurred. In the cases of *Achbita v G4S Secure Solutions* (Case C-157/15) and *Bougnaoui v Micropole Univers* (Case C-188/15), the CJEU found that prohibitions on wearing an Islamic headscarf do not constitute direct religious discrimination but may amount to indirect discrimination unless they are objectively justified by a legitimate aim. In these cases, before they reached the CJEU, two different Advocates General had expressed different views. In *Achbita*, one Advocate General gave an opinion that banning the wearing of an Islamic headscarf at work could be justified when an employer has a policy of neutrality and when the ban is applied equally to all visible signs of religious beliefs, ie not just where they relate to one religion. However, in *Bougnaoui*, a different Advocate General gave an opinion that it was unlawful to ban a Muslim employee from wearing her headscarf when in contact with clients. Both cases raised the question as to whether a prohibition for employees against wearing visible characteristics of political, philosophical or religious belief violates Directive 2000/78/EC.

In *Achbita*, Ms Achbita, a Muslim female, was hired as a receptionist at G4S Secure in Belgium. G4S had an unwritten rule (which subsequently became officially incorporated) that employees were not allowed to wear *visible characteristics* of their religious, political or philosophical convictions while working. In 2006, Ms Achbita informed her management that she would start wearing a headscarf during working hours. She was told this violated the company policy. She was eventually dismissed by G4S due to her firm intention to wear an Islamic headscarf. She sued G4S relying on the Directive and Belgian courts found for G4S. A Belgian court then referred the case to the ECJ. The Advocate General in her opinion stated that the main issue was whether the prohibition represented direct or indirect discrimination. She stated that there was no direct discrimination based on religion when an employee with Islamic faith was prohibited from wearing a headscarf at the workplace, if this prohibition was based on a general internal company rule which prohibits visible political, philosophical and religious symbols at the workplace and not on stereotypes or prejudices against one or more specific religions or against religious persuasions in general. She went on to say, however, that it might be indirect discrimination as there is a risk that the prohibition would particularly affect Muslim females more severely. On that basis, she considered whether the treatment was justified, concluding that:

> a prohibition as the one determined by G4S may be regarded as a regular, decisive and legitimate professional requirement as dealt with under Article 4 (1) of Directive 2000/78 which as a rule may substantiate unfair treatment – regardless it is of direct or indirect nature – due to religion provided that the principle of proportionality is complied with.

As an employee cannot leave his gender, his skin colour, his ethnic background, his sexual orientation, his age or his disability 'outside the door' when he enters the employer's premises, there may, according to the Advocate General in connection with the person in question exercising her religion at the workplace, however, be required a certain amount of restraint whether or not it involves religious practice, religiously motivated behaviour or – as in the matter in hand – the relevant person's clothing.

In *Bougnaoui*, Ms Bougnaoui was also a Muslim female. She was employed in France as a design engineer by Micropole SA, an IT consultancy company. She wore an Islamic headscarf whilst at work including when she was visiting clients at their premises. The headscarf covered her head but not her face. When Ms Bougnaoui had been recruited, she had been told that the company had a religious neutrality principle and that it 'entirely respect[ed] the principle of freedom of opinion and the religious beliefs of everyone, but that, since [she] would be in contact internally or externally with the company's clients, [she] would not be able to wear the [headscarf] in all circumstances'. Subsequently, a client complained about Ms Bougnaoui's headscarf saying it 'embarrassed a number of its employees' and asked Micropole that she not wear it on future visits. Micropole asked her to remove her headscarf when visiting clients. She refused to do so and was dismissed. She brought a claim for discrimination based on her religious beliefs. Two French courts held that the dismissal was well founded on the basis of a 'genuine and serious reason'. The matter was then referred to the ECJ for a preliminary ruling. The Advocate General decided that Ms Bougnaoui was treated less favourably on the ground of her religion, since a comparator (a design engineer who had not chosen to manifest their religious belief) would not have been dismissed. As such, therefore, her dismissal did constitute unlawful direct discrimination on the grounds of religion or belief. There was no occupational requirement on the facts of this case. For example, it was considered that it would be proportionate to exclude a Sikh who wore a turban from working in a post that required the wearing of protective headgear, for health and safety reasons.

The CJEU's substantive conclusion and analysis is found in *Achbita*. The CJEU in *Achbita* agreed with the Advocate General that her case did not meet the criteria for direct discrimination but held that it was capable of constituting indirect discrimination. In terms of justification, the Court accepted that there was a legitimate aim (wanting a neutral image) but had more difficulty with whether the ban was proportionate. In *Bougnaoui* the CJEU was asked to consider a much narrower question than in *Achbita*. The Court said that the absence of religious clothing could not be a genuine occupational requirement, and nor could a desire to accommodate the cultural expectations and prejudices of customers.

In the UK, employers are generally free to set whatever dress codes for staff that they wish, as long as the requirements are not discriminating. In May 2018, the Government Equalities Office and the Department for International Development issued guidance, entitled 'Dress codes and sex discrimination: what you need to know'. It advises that while dress codes do not need to be identical, gender-specific rules, such as any requirement to wear make-up, have manicured nails, wear hair in certain styles or wear specific types of hosiery, should be avoided. Requiring female employees to wear high heels but not having footwear requirements for men, for example, is likely to constitute direct discrimination. (It could also amount to indirect discrimination against disabled employees.) Having requirements to dress smartly, however, which are not gender-specific, would be lawful. While problems with dress codes tend to be associated with sex discrimination claims, rather than religion, restrictions on the display of religious symbols (see eg *Eweida v British Airways* at **10.2.3** below) can also be problematic, more particularly in the context of indirect discrimination. At the end of April 2017, the Government published its response to the House of Commons Petitions Committee and Women and Equalities Committee joint report on dress codes on the workplace. Guidance on heels, make-up, manicures, skirt length, and the like, is due shortly.

In *Wasteney v East London NHS Foundation Trust* (EAT/0157/15), the EAT held that an evangelical 'born again' Christian worker accused of 'grooming' a female Muslim member of staff had not been discriminated against nor harassed on the grounds of her religion or belief when she was disciplined for seeking to impose her religious views on her colleague, who complained that the claimant had tried to pray with her, made repeated invitations to her to attend her church and gave her a book concerning the conversion of a female Muslim to the Christian faith. The Trust found that this was misconduct, namely the blurring of professional boundaries and subjecting a junior colleague to improper pressure and unwanted attention. She was issued with a final written warning, which was reduced to a first written warning on appeal. The claimant complained to an employment tribunal of direct discrimination and harassment because of/related to her religion and belief, and the manifestation of her belief. The employment tribunal did not uphold her complaints. She appealed to the EAT on grounds including that Article 9 of the European Convention on Human Rights (see **Chapter 15**) protected her right to manifest her belief and that the sanction imposed was 'oppressive'. The EAT dismissed her appeal, pointing out that the rights under Article 9 are qualified and limited, and finding that the sanction imposed was proportionate.

Note that in HM *Chief Inspector of Education, Children's Services and Skills v The Interim Executive Board of Al-Hijrah School* [2017] EWCA Civ 1426, the Court of Appeal held that segregation of girls and boys in a mixed school from age 9 was direct discrimination against both girls and boys. Where there is mirror discrimination (ie both genders suffer a detriment), there can still be a finding of less favourable treatment under s 13, as that section protects the individual, so a group comparison is not relevant.

9.2.5 The 'reason why question'

9.2.5.1 Comparison by reference to circumstances

The Explanatory Notes explain that s 23 provides that like must be compared with like in cases of direct discrimination. The treatment of the claimant must be compared with that of an actual or a hypothetical person – the comparator – who does not share the same protected characteristic as the claimant but who is (or is assumed to be) in not materially different circumstances from the claimant.

The use of the words 'would treat' in s 13(1) (see **9.2.1**) allows for a hypothetical rather than an actual comparator. The relevant circumstances of the complainant and the comparative group should be the same or not materially different. In *Chief Constable of West Yorkshire v Vento* [2001] IRLR 124, the EAT made an important point about comparing like with like and the use of hypothetical comparators where there is no actual comparator. In such cases, where the tribunal has to construct the probable treatment of a hypothetical comparator, it is legitimate to see how unidentical but not wholly dissimilar instances had been dealt with in the past. This would not infringe the principle of comparing like with like. For example, a woman might say that cases of alleged misconduct are investigated swiftly and in detail by the employer, whereas there was a slow and half-hearted investigation into her claim of sexual harassment. Thus, in the *Vento* case, the EAT held that the tribunal had not erred in constructing an inference from the hypothetical case of how the employers had treated four actual, unidentified but not wholly dissimilar comparators. The Court of Appeal approved *Vento* in *Balamoody v United Kingdom Central Council for Nursing, Midwifery and Health Visiting* [2002] IRLR 288, and ruled that the question of the correct comparator is a question of law.

The House of Lords emphasised the importance of the hypothetical comparator in *Shamoon v Chief Constable of the Royal Ulster Constabulary* [2003] IRLR 285. Their Lordships stated that 'in most cases a suitable actual comparator will not be available and a hypothetical comparator will have to constitute the statutory comparator'. As Michael Rubenstein notes in 'Highlights IRLR May 2003', 'the way others are treated whose circumstances are insufficiently similar to be actual comparators then becomes evidence of how a hypothetical comparator would be treated'. In *Shamoon*, the House of Lords also indicated that instead of relying on like with like comparators, a claimant may rely on the 'evidential significance' of non-exact comparators in support of an inference of direct discrimination, even though their evidential value will become weaker the greater the difference in circumstances. In that case, a Chief Inspector was removed from staff appraisal duties following complaints. The claimant sought to compare her treatment to that of two male officers who were in many respects directly comparable with her, save that no complaints had been made against them. That meant that they were inappropriate comparators. The comparator had to be a male officer against whom similar complaints had been made.

9.2.5.2   Reason for the treatment

Importantly, in *Shamoon* (**9.2.5.1** above) Lord Nicholls said (at para 11) that

> employment tribunals may sometimes be able to avoid arid and confusing disputes about the identification of the appropriate comparator by concentrating primarily on why the claimant was treated as she was. Was it on the proscribed ground which is the foundation of the application?

This approach has been adopted in a number of subsequent cases. In *London Borough of Islington v Ladele* (UKEAT/0453/08), Elias J (the then President) said that often, in practice, a tribunal will be unlikely to be able to identify who the correct comparator is, without first asking and answering the question why the claimant was treated as he was. Until that question is answered, he said, the appropriate attributes of the comparator will not be known. His conclusion was that whilst comparators may have evidential value, often they cast no light on the 'reason why question'. Elias J gave a useful example (at paras 36–37):

> A claimant alleges that he did not get a job because of his race. The employer says that it is because he was not academically clever enough and there is evidence to show that the person appointed had better academic qualifications. The claimant alleges this was irrelevant to the appointment; it was not therefore a material difference. The employer contends that it is a critical difference between the two situations. If the Tribunal is satisfied that the real reason is race, then academic qualifications are irrelevant. The relevant circumstances are not therefore materially different. It is plain that the comparator was treated differently. If the Tribunal is satisfied that the real reason is the difference in academic qualifications, then that provides a material difference between the claimant and the comparator.

> The determination of the comparator depends on the reason for the difference in treatment.

See also:

- *Amnesty International v Ahmed* [2009] IRLR 884 – consideration of what the characteristic of a hypothetical comparator should be is 'often a less useful way of addressing the questions raised by an issue of direct discrimination than focusing on the fundamental question of the reason for the act complained of' (para 25);
- *Aylott v Stockton-on-Tees Borough Council* [2010] IRLR 994 – 'there is no obligation … to construct a hypothetical comparator in every case' (para 37); and
- *Cordell v Foreign and Commonwealth Office* [2012] ICR 280:

> [D]irect discrimination [requires answers to] two questions – (a) whether the Claimant has been treated less favourably than an actual or hypothetical comparator with the same characteristics [other than the proscribed ground] ('the less favourable treatment question'), and (b) whether that treatment was [because of the proscribed ground] ('the reason why question'). … Where there is an actual comparator, asking the less favourable treatment question might be the most direct route to answer both questions; but where there is none it will usually be better to focus on the reason why question than to get bogged down in the often arid and confusing task of 'constructing a hypothetical comparator'.

See too *Martin v Devonshires Solicitors* [2011] ICR 352 for further discussion of some of these cases.

In *Azmi v Kirklees Metropolitan Borough Council* [2007] IRLR 484, the EAT upheld a tribunal's decision that the suspension of a teaching assistant for refusing an instruction not to wear a veil when assisting a male teacher in front of pupils, was not directly discriminatory on the grounds of religion or belief. Mrs Azmi had not been treated less favourably than a comparator (a person who wore a face covering) would have been in similar circumstances.

In *Glasgow City Council v Mr D McNab* [2007] IRLR 476, the EAT upheld a tribunal's decision that an atheist teacher employed by a local authority-maintained Catholic school had suffered direct discrimination when he was refused an interview for the post of Acting Principal Teacher of Pastoral Care. The post was not on the list of positions for which the Roman Catholic Church required a teacher to be Catholic, and therefore the Council should not have presumed that the Church would not have approved the appointment. There was no occupational requirement. A local authority has no religious ethos and cannot take advantage of the occupational requirements even in respect of employment in a religious school.

In *Ladele v The London Borough of Islington* [2010] IRLR 211, Ms Ladele was the registrar at Islington Council. She said that same-sex civil partnerships conflicted with her strict Christian beliefs, and refused to conduct same-sex civil partnership ceremonies. She was disciplined by the Council as a result. The EAT found that Ms Ladele was disciplined because she was refusing to carry out her duties, not because of her religious beliefs. Elias J said:

> The proper hypothetical or statutory comparator here is another registrar who refused to conduct civil partnership work because of antipathy to the concept of same sex relationships but which antipathy was not connected [to] or based upon his or her religious belief.

The Court of Appeal agreed with that view, and therefore held that there was no basis upon which the employment tribunal could have made a finding of direct discrimination ([2009] EWCA Civ 1357).

In *McFarlane v Relate Avon Ltd* [2010] ICR 50, EAT, the claimant entered into a contract of employment with the employer as a paid counsellor in August 2003. Upon doing so he expressly signed up to the employers' equal opportunities policy. The claimant is a Christian. In the course of his employment he experienced no difficulties of conscience in counselling same-sex couples where no sexual issues arose. At length, however, he sought to be exempted from any obligation to work with same-sex couples in cases where issues of psycho-sexual therapy ('PST') were involved. The EAT held that the tribunal was correct in its finding that there was no direct discrimination:

> [W]e concluded, firstly, that it was necessary for an actual or hypothetical comparator to be identified and, secondly, that an appropriate comparator would be another counsellor who, for reasons unrelated to Christianity, was believed by the respondent to be unwilling to provide PST counselling to same sex couples and therefore unwilling to abide by the respondent's Equal Opportunities and Ethical Practice Policies. The question, therefore, is whether the respondent would have treated [such] a comparator differently, and in our view it would not.

In other words, while religious belief was the claimant's motivation for his actions, the employer had dismissed him because he refused to comply with its equal opportunities policy.

The courts' analysis of direct discrimination in *Ladele* and *McFarlane* is not affected by the ECtHR's decisions (see **10.2.6**).

The clash between religious freedom and sexuality has manifest itself in a number of discrimination claims that are primarily based around religious objections to same-sex equality rights. There can seem to be irreconcilably conflicting rights. This has led to a distinction being drawn between the absolute right to hold a particular belief and the way in which that belief manifests itself. Manifestation is something that can and has been constrained by the law. Once religion enters the public domain, it effectively becomes a qualified right that is limited by other rights, which the law seeks to balance. (See *R v Secretary of State for Education and Employment, ex parte Williamson* [2005] UKHL 15, where the House of Lords held that freedom of religion was qualified when it came to manifestation by the need for a balance to be struck 'between the freedom to practise one's own religion and the interests of others affected by those practices'.) In addition to *Ladele* and *McFarlane*, see *McClintock v Department of Constitutional Affairs* [2008] IRLR 29 and *Lee v Ashers Baking Co Ltd and Others* [2018] UKSC 49 (**9.2.5.3** below).

In *Dziedziak v Future Electronics Ltd* (UKEAT/0270/11) the EAT upheld the tribunal's conclusion that the claimant, who is Polish, was subjected to direct discrimination on grounds of nationality when told by her line manager that she should not speak to colleagues 'in her own language', as those words demonstrated an 'intrinsic link' with her nationality. However, the EAT held in *Kelly v Covance Laboratories Ltd* (EAT/0186/15) that the 'intrinsic link' test in *Dziedziak* only went to shift the burden of proof to the respondent and that in *Kelly* the employer had a reasonable explanation for its actions unrelated to the claimant's race or national origins. The Court of Appeal held that the employment tribunal had been correct to focus on the decision maker's mental process in *CLFIS (UK) Ltd v Reynolds* [2015] EWCA Civ 549, because only he had taken the decision; none of the other players who influenced his reasoning were parties to the decision. Were it alleged that another player has provided tainted information, the correct approach is to treat that conduct as a separate act of discrimination from that of the person who acts upon it.

The EAT held, in *Grace v Places for Children* (UKEAT/0217/13), that the employment tribunal had been entitled to find that an employee was dismissed for the way in which she chose to manifest her religion, as opposed to her religious belief. There was therefore no direct discrimination. Paragraph 2.6.1 of the Employment Statutory Code of Practice issued by the EHRC states:

> Manifestations of a religion or belief could include treating certain days as days for worship or rest .... There is not always a clear line between holding a religion or belief and the manifestation of that religion or belief. Placing limitations on a person's right to manifest their religion or belief may amount to unlawful discrimination; this would usually amount to indirect discrimination.

The EAT agreed with that statement.

9.2.5.3 Motive

The motive or intentions behind the action are irrelevant and there is no defence once direct discrimination has been proved (see *Birmingham City Council v EOC* [1989] AC 1155). For example:

(a)   If the only woman remaining on a work experience scheme is withdrawn 'for her own good', this will be direct discrimination.

(b)   If the temporary appointment of a black person as a refuse collector is withdrawn due to fear of industrial action by the other workers, this will amount to direct discrimination even though the employer's intention was not to discriminate but to avoid disrupting the service.

In *Amnesty International v Ahmed* (UKEAT/0447/08), Amnesty declined to appoint a northern Sudanese woman to the position of researcher because it was concerned that her ethnic origin might compromise her impartiality and her safety. The tribunal upheld the claim of direct discrimination, as 'but for' her Sudanese origins she would have been appointed. The EAT upheld the tribunal's finding and approach. It made clear that the explanation for the discrimination was irrelevant and that this was a clear case where the employer's decision was overtly made on basis of the claimant's race (see *James v Eastleigh BC* [1990] 2 AC 751). Underhill J referred to the 'reason why question' as the discriminator's 'motivation' and to the explanation for the discrimination as his 'motive'. He explained (at paras 33–34):

> In some cases the ground, or the reason, for the treatment complained of is inherent in the act itself. If an owner of premises puts up a sign saying 'no blacks admitted' race is, necessarily, the ground on which (or the reason why) the black person is excluded. *James v Eastleigh* is a case of this kind ... In cases of this kind what was going on inside the head of the putative discriminator – whether described as his intention, motive, his reason or his purpose – will be irrelevant. The 'ground' of his action being inherent in the act itself, no further inquiry is needed. It follows that, as the majority in *James v Eastleigh* decided, a respondent who has treated a claimant les favourably on the ground of his or her sex or race cannot escape liability because he had a benign motive.

But that is not the only kind of case. In other cases – of which *Nagarajan* is an example – the act complained of is not itself discriminatory but is rendered so by a discriminatory motivation, ie by the 'mental processes' (whether conscious or unconscious) which led the putative discriminator to do the act ... Even in such a case, however, it is important to bear in mind that the subject of the inquiry is the ground of, or reason for, the putative discriminator's actions, not his motive; just as in the kind of case considered in *James v Eastleigh*, a benign motive is irrelevant.

What is important, therefore, is to discover what caused someone to act as he did, as opposed to a consideration of that person's motive, intention, reason or purposes; or to put it another way, in order to establish if direct discrimination has occurred, it is necessary to identify only 'the factual criteria that determined the decision made by the discriminator', as opposed to the motive for the discrimination. Motive may, however, be relevant to remedy.

In *Lee v Ashers Baking Co Ltd and Others* [2018] UKSC 49, the Supreme Court held that there was no unlawful discrimination, on grounds of sexual orientation, in a baker refusing to supply a cake iced with 'support gay marriage' because the objection was to the message, not to Mr Lee's sexual orientation (ie a distinction between the man and the message); the baker would have refused to supply the cake to anybody, whatever the characteristics. It was not therefore direct discrimination. Daphne Romney QC asks: 'Would it be different if the cake was to be iced with the words "Congratulations Bill and Ben or Congratulations Betty and Barbara"'? See 'The Consequences of the Ashers Cake Judgment', Oxford Human Rights Hub, 12 October 2018 (http://ohrh.law.ox.ac.uk/the-consequences-of-the-ashers-cake-judgment/).

See *Bull and Another v Hall and Another* [2013] UKSC 73, in which a bed and breakfast's refusal to allow a gay couple a room was found to be discriminatory on sexual orientation grounds.

9.2.6 Irrelevance of alleged discriminator's characteristics

Section 24 of the Act provides that it is no defence to a claim of direct discrimination that the alleged discriminator shares the protected characteristic with the victim. The discriminator will still be liable for any unlawful discrimination.

The Explanatory Notes provide an example:

An employer cannot argue that because he is a gay man he is not liable for unlawful discrimination for rejecting a job application from another gay man because of the applicant's sexual orientation.

9.2.7 Stereotypical assumptions

Stereotypical assumptions may amount to direct discrimination. For example:

(a) Assuming that a woman with young children will be an unreliable employee is direct discrimination.

(b) Assuming that the husband is the breadwinner and that his wife will resign and follow him, in the event of the husband being relocated, without asking the wife what her intentions are, also amounts to direct discrimination.

The courts have held, however, that it is not discriminatory to take into account natural differences between the sexes, for example to tell men that their hair must be worn above the collar, whereas, although women are allowed long hair, they are also subject to a rule prohibiting 'unconventional hair styles'.

9.2.8 Illegality

Note that the Supreme Court held, in *Hounga v Allen & Another* [2014] UKSC 47 (see **5.4.2.4**), that the illegality defence did not defeat a discrimination claim, as there was no 'sufficiently close connection between the illegality [the claimant had no right to work in the UK] and the tort to bar the claim'.

9.3   GENDER REASSIGNMENT AND ABSENCE FROM WORK

Section 16 of the Act provides that it is also discrimination against transsexual people if they are treated less favourably for being absent from work because they propose to undergo, are undergoing or have undergone gender reassignment than they would be if they were absent because they were ill or injured. Transsexual people are also discriminated against in relation to absences relating to their gender reassignment if they are treated less favourably than they would be for absence for reasons other than sickness or injury and it is unreasonable to treat them less favourably.

The Explanatory Notes give an example:

> A female to male transsexual person takes time off work to receive hormone treatment as part of his gender reassignment. His employer cannot discriminate against him because of his absence from work for this purpose.

9.4   PREGNANCY AND MATERNITY DISCRIMINATION

Section 18 of the Act defines what it means to discriminate because of a woman's pregnancy or maternity, as distinct from her sex, in specified situations within work. It protects a woman from discrimination because of her current or a previous pregnancy. It also protects her from maternity discrimination, which includes treating her unfavourably because she is breast-feeding, for 26 weeks after giving birth, and provides that pregnancy or maternity discrimination as defined cannot be treated as sex discrimination. Maternity is defined in s 213 of the Act. There is no definition of pregnancy.

Section 18 provides as follows:

(1)   This section has effect for the purposes of the application of Part 5 (work) to the protected characteristic of pregnancy and maternity.

(2)   A person (A) discriminates against a woman if, in the protected period in relation to a pregnancy of hers, A treats her unfavourably—

(a)   because of the pregnancy, or

(b)   because of illness suffered by her as a result of it.

(3)   A person (A) discriminates against a woman if A treats her unfavourably because she is on compulsory maternity leave.

(4)   A person (A) discriminates against a woman if A treats her unfavourably because she is exercising or seeking to exercise, or has exercised or sought to exercise, the right to ordinary or additional maternity leave.

(5)   For the purposes of subsection (2), if the treatment of a woman is in implementation of a decision taken in the protected period, the treatment is to be regarded as occurring in that period (even if the implementation is not until after the end of that period).

(6)   The protected period, in relation to a woman's pregnancy, begins when the pregnancy begins, and ends—

(a)   if she has the right to ordinary and additional maternity leave, at the end of the additional maternity leave period or (if earlier) when she returns to work after the pregnancy;

(b)   if she does not have that right, at the end of the period of 2 weeks beginning with the end of the pregnancy.

(7)   Section 13, so far as relating to sex discrimination, does not apply to treatment of a woman in so far as—

(a)   it is in the protected period in relation to her and is for a reason mentioned in paragraph (a) or (b) of subsection (2), or

(b)   it is for a reason mentioned in subsection (3) or (4).

In *Webb v EMO Air Cargo (UK) Ltd* [1993] IRLR 27, the House of Lords held that to dismiss a woman because she was pregnant, or to refuse to employ her because she was or might become pregnant, was unlawful direct discrimination. In *Brown v Rentokil Ltd* [1998] IRLR 445, the ECJ held that dismissal during pregnancy for absences due to incapacity for work 'must ...

be regarded as essentially based on the fact of pregnancy'. The ECJ decided that since pregnancy can affect only women, action taken on the grounds of a pregnancy-related illness constitutes direct discrimination on the grounds of sex.

Section 18 of the Act codifies the *Webb* decision above and sets out the meaning of discrimination because of a woman's pregnancy or pregnancy-related illness, or because she takes or tries to take maternity leave. Under s 18, a person discriminates against a woman in relation to her pregnancy or maternity leave if, during the protected period of her pregnancy and maternity leave, he treats her less favourably because of her pregnancy (or an illness resulting from it) or maternity leave. The period during which protection from these types of discrimination exists is the period of pregnancy and any statutory maternity leave to which the woman is entitled. Section 13 (see **9.2.1**) does not apply during these periods. There is no need for a comparator during the protected period. Where a woman is treated unfavourably because of pregnancy or a pregnancy-related illness, and the decision to treat her in that way was taken during the protected period but not implemented until after the end of that period, the treatment is regarded as occurring during the protected period (s 18(5)).

The Explanatory Notes give examples:

- An employer must not demote or dismiss an employee, or deny her training or promotion opportunities, because she is pregnant or on maternity leave.
- An employer must not take into account an employee's period of absence due to pregnancy-related illness when making a decision about her employment.

Section 18(7) means that a claim in respect of pregnancy and maternity discrimination during the protected period cannot be brought as direct sex discrimination under s 13. A claim for direct discrimination outside that protected period would fall under s 13. When a pregnancy-related illness arises during pregnancy or maternity leave (the protected period) and persists after the end of that leave, an employer is, however, permitted to take into account such absences after the maternity leave period in computing periods of absence justifying dismissal, in the same way that a man's absence for illness would be taken in to account (see *Larsson v Føtex Supermarked* (Case C-400/95) [1997] ECR I-2757 and *Lyons v DWP Jobcentre Plus* (UKEAT/0348/13)).

In *Sahota v The Home Office* (UKEAT/0342/09), the EAT considered the extent to which discrimination on the ground that an employee was receiving IVF treatment was to be regarded as discrimination on the ground of her pregnancy. It was common ground that after implantation, the claimant was to be regarded as being pregnant. The EAT, considering a decision of the ECJ in *Mayr v Backerei und Konditorei Gerhard Flockner OHG* [2008] IRLR 387, held that the pregnancy principle applied to adverse treatment during the interval between follicular puncture and an imminent or immediate implantation attempt, but said it did not go any wider.

In *Nixon v Ross Coates Solicitors* (UKEAT/0108/10) the EAT held that gossip about the paternity of a baby that a female employee was expecting (following her behaviour at an office party) amounted to sex discrimination, pregnancy discrimination and harassment.

In *Eversheds v De Belin* (UKEAT/0352/10), the EAT held that the obligation to protect employees who are pregnant or on maternity leave is limited to treatment that is 'reasonably necessary [meaning proportionate] to compensate them for the disadvantages occasioned by their condition'. In this case, the claimant had been scored lower in a redundancy exercise than a colleague who was on maternity leave solely because the colleague was given a maximum notional score for one of the criteria. The EAT upheld the tribunal's finding of sex discrimination and unfair dismissal: the maternity benefit applied was disproportionate because there were less discriminatory alternative measures that could be adopted, such as measuring performance at a time when both candidates were still at work. Thus, the claimant who had been disadvantaged by this was entitled to claim sex discrimination. However, applying the approach in *Polkey* (see **5.6.2.2**), as there was cogent evidence that the claimant would have been made redundant in any event some nine months later, the claim was remitted to a different tribunal to consider whether the claim for loss of earnings should be capped or discounted on that basis.

In *CD v ST* [2014] EUECJ C-167/12, the ECJ held that a commissioning mother in a surrogacy arrangement did not fall within the scope of the Pregnant Workers Directive.

In *Interserve FM Ltd v Tuleikyte* (UKEAT/0267/16), the EAT emphasised the 'because of' question – the unfavourable treatment must be 'because of' maternity leave, etc (the 'reason why' question applies just as much here as it does under s 13 (see **9.2.5.2**)).

In *Really Easy Car Credit Ltd v Thompson* (UKEAT/0197/17), the EAT held that an employer must believe or know that the employee is pregnant if a claim for pregnancy discrimination (or a claim for automatic unfair dismissal because of pregnancy) is to succeed. The decision to dismiss in this case was taken before the employer had belief or knowledge of the pregnancy. There is no provision against less favourable treatment because of something arising from pregnancy (as there is with disability discrimination). The case was remitted back to the tribunal to determine whether, on the facts, the real reason for the dismissal was pregnancy.

9.5 BURDEN OF PROOF

9.5.1 The shifting burden of proof

The legislation provides that where a complainant can establish facts from which the tribunal could decide that there has been a contravention of a provision of the Act, the tribunal *must* make a finding of unlawful discrimination *unless* the employer shows it did not contravene the provision (s 136). The Explanatory Notes explain that the burden of proving a case starts with the claimant. Once the claimant has established sufficient facts which, in the absence of any other explanation, point to a breach, then the burden shifts on to the respondent to show that it did not breach the Act. This has been held to mean that the complainant does have to establish some facts from which a tribunal could decide that there has been discrimination.

The EAT had the chance to consider the burden of proof in *Barton v Investec Henderson Crosthwaite Securities Ltd* [2003] IRLR 332 (a sex discrimination case decided under the old law). Ansell J gave guidance on the new burden of proof in practice in direct discrimination claims. That guidance was amended by the Court of Appeal in *Igen Ltd and Others v Wong* [2005] IRLR 258 and approved again in *Madarassy v Nomura International plc* [2007] EWCA Civ 33. Although these cases involved sex or race discrimination, the Court of Appeal in *Igen* made it clear that they apply to all the discrimination strands. The revised guidance is as follows:

1.   [It] was for the claimant who complained of sex discrimination to prove on the balance of probabilities facts from which the tribunal could conclude, in the absence of an adequate explanation, that the respondent had committed an act of discrimination against the claimant which was unlawful ...

2.   If the claimant did not prove such facts he or she would fail.

3.   It was important to bear in mind in deciding whether the claimant had proved such facts that it was unusual to find direct evidence of sex discrimination. Few employers would be prepared to admit such discrimination, even to themselves. In some cases the discrimination would not be an intention but merely based on the assumption that 'he or she would not have fitted in'.

4.   In deciding whether the claimant had proved such facts, it was important to remember that the outcome at this stage of the analysis by the tribunal would therefore usually depend on what inferences it was proper to draw from the primary facts found by the tribunal.

5.   It was important to note the word 'could' in s [136]. At this stage the tribunal did not have to reach a definitive determination that such facts would lead it to the conclusion that there was an act of unlawful discrimination. At this stage a tribunal was looking at the primary facts before it to see what inferences of secondary fact could be drawn from them.

6.   In considering what inferences or conclusions could be drawn from the primary facts, the tribunal must assume that there was no adequate explanation for those facts.

7.   Those inferences could include, in appropriate cases, any inferences that it was just and equitable to draw in accordance with s [138] ... from an evasive or equivocal reply to a questionnaire or any other questions that fell within s [138] ...

8.   Likewise, the tribunal must decide whether any provision of the relevant code of practice was relevant and if so take it into account in determining such facts ... This meant that inferences might also be drawn from any failure to comply with any relevant code of practice.

9.   Where the claimant had proved facts from which conclusions could be drawn that the respondent had treated the claimant less favourably on the ground of sex, then the burden of proof moved to the respondent.

10.   It was then for the respondent to prove that he had not committed, or as the case might be, was not to be treated as having committed, that act.

11.   To discharge that burden it was necessary for the respondent to prove, on the balance of probabilities, that the treatment was in no sense whatsoever on the grounds of sex, since 'no discrimination whatsoever' was compatible with the burden of proof Directive (Council Directive 97/80/EC).

12.   That required a tribunal to assess not merely whether the respondent had proved an explanation for the facts from which such inferences could be drawn, but further that it was adequate to discharge the burden of proof on the balance of probabilities that sex was not a ground for the treatment in question.

13.   Since the facts necessary to prove an explanation would normally be in the possession of the respondent, a tribunal would normally expect cogent evidence to discharge that burden of proof. In particular, the tribunal would need to examine carefully explanations for failure to deal with the questionnaire procedure and/or code of practice.

To summarise, following *Igen*, it has become accepted practice that, in a discrimination case, a claimant must prove, on the balance of probabilities, facts from which a (reasonable) tribunal could conclude, in the absence of an adequate explanation, that the respondent has discriminated against the claimant. The claimant must produce some evidence of discrimination before the burden will pass to the respondent. If the claimant does this then the respondent must prove that it did not commit the act. This is known as the shifting burden of proof – once the claimant has established a prima facie case (which will require the tribunal to hear evidence from the claimant and the respondent to see what proper inferences may be drawn (see *Madarassy v Nomura International* above and below)), the burden of proof shifts to the respondent to disprove the allegations, which will require consideration of the subjective reasons that caused the employer to act as he did. The respondent will have to show a non-discriminatory reason for the difference in treatment.

On the facts of *Barton v Investec*, the EAT found that Mrs Barton had produced sufficient evidence of sex discrimination to shift the burden of proof to the respondent, but that the tribunal had not considered what the employer's explanation was. The EAT found that, in hearing her claim for equal pay, the tribunal erred in that it failed to take into account Investec's reluctance to answer Mrs Barton's questionnaire and provide her with the information she requested concerning pay and bonuses.

The Court of Appeal in *Madarassy v Nomura* (above) took a further look at the burden of proof in discrimination cases. Essentially, it upheld the approach of the Court of Appeal in *Igen* and said that 'the correct legal position' was made plain in paras 28 and 29 of the judgment. The material parts of those paragraphs stated as follows:

28.   ... It is for the complainant to prove the facts from which ... the employment tribunal could conclude, in the absence of an adequate explanation, that the respondent committed an unlawful act of discrimination. It does not say that the facts to be proved are those from which the employment tribunal could conclude that the [respondent] 'could have committed' such act.

29.   The relevant act is, in a race discrimination case ... , that (a) in circumstances relevant for the purposes of any provision of the ... Act ...(b) the alleged discriminator treats another person less

> favourably and (c) does so on racial grounds. All those facts are facts which the complainant, in
> our judgment, needs to prove on the balance of probabilities …

The bare facts of a difference in status and a difference in treatment indicate only a possibility of discrimination: They are not, without more, sufficient material from which a tribunal 'could conclude' that, on the balance of probabilities, the respondent had committed an unlawful act of discrimination.

Evidence supporting a prima facie case might include breaches of the Codes of Practice (the tribunal must consider the reason for the failure – see *Tera (UK) Ltd v Mr A Goubatchev* (UKEAT/ 0490/08)), or an evasive reply to questions asked or a witness's lack of veracity (*Solicitors Regulation Authority v Mitchell* (UKEAT/0497/12) (see **8.8.1.2**), protected characteristic-related comments (*Cromwell Garage Ltd v Doran* (UKEAT/0369/10); *James v Gina Shoes Ltd and Ors* (UKEAT/ 0384/11)), or an employer's failure to provide information about recruitment criteria (*Meister v Speech Design Carrier Systems GmbH* (Case C-415/10) [2012] ICR 1066). Evidence against a prima facie case might be, for example, evidence of how the respondent treats (or mistreats) others (and not just the complainant). In *Laing v Manchester City Council* [2006] IRLR 748, the claimant's case failed at the first stage because the respondent gave evidence that the claimant was treated in the same way as all subordinate employees.

Usefully, the Court of Appeal in *Madarassy* made it clear (at paras 56 and 70) that although s 136 involves a two-stage test, the tribunal does not hear evidence in two stages; rather, it will hear all the evidence in a case before applying the two-stage analysis. Readers should study the case carefully before advising in discrimination cases. In *Gay v Sophos plc* (UKEAT/0452/10) the EAT confirmed that the tribunal is not obliged to follow the two-stage approach: if it finds that the employer was motivated by non-discriminatory considerations, the burden of proof has been discharged.

The burden of proof was considered by the Supreme Court in *Hewage v Grampian Health Board* [2012] UKSC 37. The Supreme Court declined to give any further guidance beyond *Igen* and *Madarassy*. Lord Hope, giving the unanimous judgment, reiterated that a complainant must prove facts from which the tribunal could conclude, in the absence of an adequate explanation, that the respondent had committed an act of unlawful discrimination, 'so the prima facie care must be proved, and it is for the claimant to discharge that burden'. Lord Hope repeated (at para 32) what Underhill J had pointed out in *Martin v Devonshires Solicitors* [2011] ICR 352 (at para 39), to the effect that

> it is important not to make too much of the role of the burden of proof provisions. They will require
> careful attention when there is room for doubt as to the facts necessary to establish discrimination. But
> they have nothing to offer where the tribunal is in a position to make positive findings on the evidence
> one way or the other.

The Supreme Court did say that inferences might be drawn by considering how others are treated, even if the situations compared are not exactly the same.

Some doubt was cast upon this previously accepted approach to s 136 by the EAT in *Efobi v Royal Mail Group* (UKEAT/0203/16) where the EAT said that there was no burden on claimants to prove facts from which a tribunal could decide that the employer has discriminated. The EAT said, rather, that:

> Section 136(2) … requires the ET, instead, to consider all the evidence, from all sources, at the end of
> the hearing, so as to decide whether or not 'there are facts etc' (cf paragraph 65 of Madarassy). Its
> effect is that if there are such facts, and no explanation from [the employer], the ET must find the
> contravention proved. If, on the other hand, there are such facts, but [the employer] shows he did not
> contravene the provision, the ET cannot find the contravention proved. … The word 'facts' in section
> 136(2) rather than 'evidence' shows, in my judgment, that Parliament requires the ET to apply section
> 136 at the end of the hearing, when making its findings of fact. It may therefore be misleading to refer
> to a shifting of the burden of proof, as this implies, contrary to the language of section 136(2), that
> Parliament has required a Claimant to prove something. It does not appear to me that it has done.

> I acknowledge that this is not the way in which section 136 is interpreted in the Explanatory Notes. ...

In reaching this conclusion, the EAT pointed out that cases such as *Igen* were based on predecessor legislation (eg the Sex Discrimination Act 1975) which was worded differently to s 136.

Those predecessor provisions had been introduced as a result of previous acknowledgment by UK courts that proving unlawful discrimination presented particular evidential problems, as it was extremely unusual to find explicit evidence of unlawful discrimination. As Lord Browne-Wilkinson put it, in *Glasgow City Council v Zafar* [1998] ICR 120, 'those who discriminate on the grounds of race or gender do not in general advertise their prejudices: indeed they may not even be aware of them'. It had been recognised by the courts, for example in *King v Great Britain China Centre* [1992] 1 ICR 529, that the outcome of a discrimination case would depend on what inferences it was proper to draw from the primary facts found by the court or tribunal. The problem was also acknowledged in Europe, in cases such as *Danfoss* (*Handels- og Kontorfunktionærernes Forbund i Danmark v Dansk Arbejdsgiverforening, acting on behalf of Danfoss* (Case C-109/88) [1989] ECR 3199) and *Enderby* (*Enderby v Frenchay Health Authority* (Case C-127/92) [1993] ECR I-5535). In 1997, the Council of the European Union adopted Directive 97/80 on the burden of proof in cases of discrimination based on sex. This Directive codified the case law of the ECJ on the reversal of the burden of proof. Provisions identical to Article 4(1) were included in the Racial Equality Directive, the Framework Directive and by Article 19(1) of Directive 2006/54 on the implementation of the principle of equal opportunities and equal treatment of men and women in matters of employment and occupation (also known as the recast Equal Treatment Directive).

Following these changes in Europe, the wording of the various relevant national UK discrimination statutes were amended to introduce a specific provision on the burden of proof. So, for example, s 63A was inserted into the Sex Discrimination Act 1975 (by the Sex Discrimination (Indirect Discrimination and Burden of Proof) Regulations 2001) and read as follows (emphasis added):

(1)   This section applies to any complaint presented under section 63 to an employment tribunal.

(2)   Where, on the hearing of the complaint, *the complainant proves* facts from which the tribunal could, apart from this section, conclude in the absence of an adequate explanation that the respondent—

   (a)   has committed an act of discrimination against the complainant which is unlawful by virtue of Part II, or

   (b)   is by virtue of section 41 or 42 to be treated as having committed such an act of discrimination against the complainant,

the tribunal *shall* uphold the complaint *unless the respondent proves that he did not commit, or, as the case may be, is not to be treated as having committed,* that act.

Section 54A of the Race Relations Act 1976 and s 17A(1C) of the Disability Discrimination Act 1995 were inserted in similar terms. These were the provisions that were examined and considered by the series of cases starting with *Barton v Investec*, *Igen* and *Madarassy*, following which the approach to the burden of proof in discrimination cases had been thought to have been settled. What had emerged from the authorities (and has recently been approved – see *Ayodele* below) was a consensus that the burden of proof did not shift simply on proof of a difference in race (to take one example) and a difference in treatment. So the mere fact that a person of a particular race was not appointed to a particular job, coupled with the fact that the job was given to a person of a different race, would not normally be enough to shift the burden of proof. In addition, the complainant in such a case would have to show, not only that they met the stated qualifications etc for the post, but also that they were at least as well qualified as the successful candidate (see for example *Dresdner Kleinwort Wasserstein Ltd v Adebayo* [2005] IRLR 514). The views on the burden of proof expressed in *Madarassy* were endorsed as recently as 2012 by Lord Hope in *Hewage v Grampian Health Board* [2012] UKSC 37. At para 31, he stated:

> The complainant must prove facts from which the tribunal could conclude, in the absence of an adequate explanation, that the respondent has committed an act of discrimination against the complainant which is unlawful. So the prima facie case must be proved, and it is for the claimant to discharge that burden.

Section 136(2) of the Equality Act 2010 is worded differently from this predecessor legislation. It states:

> If there are facts from which the Court could decide, in the absence of any other explanation, that a person (A) contravened the provision concerned, the Court must hold that the contravention occurred.

Section 136(3) provides, 'But subsection (2) does not apply if A shows that A did not contravene the provision.'

In other words, the reference to 'the complainant proving facts' had gone. Although the slightly different wording was acknowledged by commentators at the time, it had been assumed that, as the Equality Act 2010 was in effect a consolidating act and was not making new law or changing old law other than in very clearly identified circumstances, nothing followed from this. This is reflected in, for example, the Explanatory Notes to s 136, which state as follows (emphasis added):

> This section provides that, in any claim where a person alleges discrimination, harassment or victimisation under the Act, *the burden of proving his or her case starts with the claimant. Once the claimant has established sufficient facts*, which in the absence of any other explanation point to a breach having occurred, the burden shifts to the respondent to show that he or she did not breach the provisions of the Act. The exception to this rule is if the proceedings relate to a criminal offence under this Act.
>
> *Background*
>
> Under previous legislation, *in most cases the burden of proof was reversed once the claimant had established a case to an initial level*. However, the burden of proof was not previously reversed in race discrimination claims brought because of colour and nationality; claims of victimisation which related to race discrimination; non-work disability discrimination claims; and sex discrimination claims which related to the exercise of public functions. In these areas the burden of proof is now reversed once the claimant establishes his or her case to an initial level.
>
> *Example*
>
> A man of Chinese ethnic origin applies for a promotion at work but is not given an interview for the job. He finds that a number of white colleagues were given interviews despite having less experience and fewer qualifications. He brings a case for race discrimination before the employment tribunal and provides sufficient evidence to show that he had been treated less favourably because of his ethnic origin. It would then be up to his employer to prove that she had not discriminated against him in the promotion process.

The EAT in *Efobi* held that the employment tribunal had misdirected itself about the appropriate test for the burden of proof, and doubted whether, in the light of those misdirections, the tribunal had imposed a sufficiently rigorous standard of proof on the respondent. 'It is clear that, because of those misdirections, the ET decided that the claimant had not "got to first base".' Had the tribunal appreciated that the claimant did not have to get to first base, but that it had to consider all the evidence in the round, it might have concluded that s 136(2) was satisfied, and then have subjected the respondent's explanation to more rigorous scrutiny than it did. The EAT added that even if its interpretation of s 136 was wrong, 'and it is to be interpreted, despite the fact that its language is significantly different from the language of the predecessor sibling provisions, as imposing an initial burden of proof on a Claimant', that it nonetheless would have still allowed the claimant's appeal. This was because:

> The doubts I have expressed about the ET's approach apply with equal force if section 136 is to be interpreted in line with its predecessor provisions. Even if the ET directed themselves correctly about the effect of section 136, and it does impose an initial burden of proof on a Claimant, their approach to the evidence means that I am not confident that they did understand that there might have been, in this case, facts from which a Court could have concluded that (in the absence of an explanation) the

Respondent had discriminated against the Claimant, and that, because they failed to appreciate that, they did not scrutinise the Respondent's explanation rigorously enough.

It has of course always been the case, even under the old burden of proof provisions (see for example *Laing* and *Gay* above), that a tribunal needs to hear all the evidence, and it is not obliged to follow the two-stage approach. In *Laing* (approved by the Court of Appeal in *Madarassy*), Elias J held that an employment tribunal in drawing inferences (ie stage one) might have to and should legitimately consider all the evidence put before it prior to concluding whether the burden of proof had shifted to stage 2 for an explanation from the employer. *Laing* drew a distinction between facts – that is evidence – and explanation. Elias J noted that an employment tribunal did not necessarily fall into error merely because it failed to adopt a two-stage approach. The Court of Appeal in *Brown v Croydon London Borough Council* [2007] IRLR 259 agreed that whilst it is generally good practice to follow the two-stage test, there is no necessary error of law if it fails to do so.

However, the Court of Appeal restored the orthodoxy in *Ayodele v Citylink Ltd* [2017] EWCA Civ 1913 and held that the EAT's decision in *Efobi* should not be followed. Singh LJ held that the difference in wording between the old and the new was no more than a legislative 'tidying up' exercise. He approved the previous decisions in, for example, *Igen* and *Hewage*. In many cases, a tribunal will not need to have recourse to s 136 at all. As Lord Hope made clear in *Hewage*, s 136 and the shifting burden of proof rules have no relevance where a tribunal can make positive findings on the evidence one way or another as to whether a claimant was discriminated against. A respondent should not have to discharge the burden of proof unless and until a claimant has shown that there is a prima facie case of discrimination which needs to be answered. Section 136 has an important role to play in cases where there is room for doubt as to the facts necessary to establish discrimination.

9.5.2 Case law – drawing inferences

9.5.2.1 Cases decided prior to *Barton v Investec*

In *Strathclyde Regional Council v Zafar* [1998] IRLR 36, the House of Lords held that mere unreasonable treatment by the employer 'casts no light whatsoever' on the question whether he has treated the employee 'unfavourably' (see also *Martins v Marks and Spencer plc* [1998] IRLR 326). In *Law Society and Others v Bahl* [2003] IRLR 640, the EAT agreed that mere unreasonableness is not enough. Elias J commented that

> all unlawful discriminatory treatment is unreasonable, but not all unreasonable treatment is discriminatory, and it is not shown to be so merely because the victim is either a woman or of a minority race or colour ... Simply to say that the conduct was unreasonable tells nothing about the grounds for acting in that way ... The significance of the fact that the treatment is unreasonable is that a tribunal will more readily in practice reject the explanation given for it than it would if the treatment were reasonable.

A tribunal must also take into consideration all potentially relevant non-discriminatory factors that might realistically explain the conduct of the alleged discriminator.

These cases are still useful and relevant.

9.5.2.2 Cases decided after *Barton v Investec*

In *University of Huddersfield v Wolff* [2004] IRLR 534, the EAT overturned the tribunal's decision that, since there was less favourable treatment and a difference in sex, the burden shifted to the employer to provide an explanation. The EAT stated that 'the burden moves where the applicant has proved facts from which inferences could be drawn that the respondents have treated the applicant less favourably on the grounds of sex'. It is clear that more than simply being of a different sex/race is required to shift the burden of proof.

In *Igen Ltd and Others v Wong* (see **9.5.1** above), the Court of Appeal stated: 'The finding of unexplained unreasonable conduct enabled the Tribunal to draw the inferences satisfying the requirements of the first stage.' So it seems that unreasonable behaviour by an employer, combined with a relevant difference (sex, race, etc) may lead to a finding that the claimant has satisfied the initial evidential burden. However, Gibson LJ warned tribunals against

> too readily infer[ring] unlawful discrimination on a prohibited ground merely from unreasonable conduct where there is no evidence of other discriminatory behaviour on such ground, [although on the facts] the tribunal was not wrong in law to draw that inference.

In *Moonsar v Fiveways Express* [2005] IRLR 9, the EAT held, applying the *Barton* guidelines (**9.5.1** above), that downloading pornography in an office or other place where it could be seen by a woman gave rise to a prima facie case of less favourable treatment (by affecting the woman's dignity and creating an intimating atmosphere) which shifted the burden of proof onto the employer to establish a non-discriminatory reason, such as the woman was party to what was going on. The employment tribunal had found that the conduct of the male employees did not amount to sex discrimination by way of sexual harassment because the claimant had not complained of the behaviour at the time and the images had not been shown to her. The EAT said that the fact that the claimant did not complain at the time did not afford a defence where the behaviour was so obvious and there was evidence that she found the behaviour unacceptable. Having established that there was a case to answer, the burden then shifted to the employer to show that the conduct was not discriminatory.

In *DKW Ltd v Adebayo* [2005] IRLR 514, a race case, the EAT gave guidance on the level of evidence that is required to establish a prima facie case so that the burden of proof passes to the employer. The claim in *Adebayo* followed the summary dismissal of an employee of black African origin, employed as a senior trader, for breach of trading guidelines. The claim for race discrimination was based on the fact that other traders who had breached the guidelines in the same way had not been disciplined. The EAT confirmed that the tribunal was correct to accept that the applicant had established a prima facie case not only because other, white traders had not been disciplined for the same offence, but also because there had apparently been a number of procedural failings in the way the employers dealt with the case. The employers had failed to put forward an adequate explanation, and the fact that they had a genuine belief in the applicant's misconduct was not sufficient. The case establishes that all that an applicant needs to do is to show some primary facts from which inferences could be drawn. The EAT emphasised that it is not sufficient at the first stage for an applicant to show simply that a comparator of a different race was promoted to a post for which the applicant had also applied – he would need to show that a comparator of a different race was promoted to the post *and* that he was at least as well qualified.

In *Mohmed v West Coast Trains Ltd* (UKEAT/0682/05), the EAT upheld the tribunal's finding that the applicant had failed to prove facts from which a tribunal could conclude, in the absence of a non-discriminatory explanation from the employer, that the employer had discriminated against him. The EAT said that it was open to the tribunal to conclude that no inference of less favourable treatment could be drawn in circumstances where it was agreed that the employee could maintain his beard at one fist's length, in accordance with his religion, provided it was tidy. No prima facie case of unlawful discrimination had been made out.

The Scottish Court of Session in *Bvunzai v Glasgow City Council* [2005] CSIH 85 upheld a tribunal's decision that it would be legitimate to draw an adverse inference that an interview panel's assessment of the claimant at interview was influenced by racial factors. That inference was based on the manner in which the claimant and another applicant for the job were scored, and the fact that the respondent was unable credibly to explain how it had scored the job applicants. Moreover, the respondent had also departed from its Code of Conduct and could not credibly explain why.

In *Komeng v Sandwell Metropolitan Borough Council* (UKEAT/0592/10) the EAT said that tribunals should take care before accepting an employer's explanation that the treatment was meted out by reason of poor administration. In the circumstances, the tribunal must consider carefully why the claimant was treated the way he was (see also *Eagle Place Services Ltd v Rudd* (UKEAT/0497/08).

In *Hussain v Vision Security Ltd and Anor* (UKEAT/0439/10), the EAT held that, on the facts, an untruthful explanation of difference in treatment, together with the other facts, was sufficient to shift the burden of proof.

In *Veolia Environmental Services Ltd v Gumbs* (UKEAT/0487/12), the EAT held that whilst the substance of an employer's explanation for the treatment should be excluded from consideration when deciding whether the burden of proof shifted, the fact that explanations were inconsistent could be taken into account.

9.6 REMEDIES

See **8.8**. An employment tribunal can order a respondent to pay compensation including interest. Compensation can include damages for hurt feelings and the loss of the job. The tribunal can also make declarations or recommendations as to what action an employer could take to limit or restrict any damage done. Exemplary damages may be available.

9.7   CASE STUDY: DIRECT RACE DISCRIMINATION CLAIM – BURDEN OF PROOF

Facts

(1)   C was employed as a cleaning supervisor by Veryclean Bus Services Ltd (R) at its main London depot, from 25 April 2017 until her dismissal on 30 September 2018. R's business is that of providing bus-cleaning services. R has over 500 members of staff across 15 sites. R issued an equal opportunities policy in 2006. R's workforce consists of people from a variety of racial and national origins. C worked 40 hours per week, from 6pm until 2.30am on each weekday night. Her job involved management responsibilities, supervising in total 30 night and day workers at the depot. C's main job role was to ensure the proper and adequate cleaning of buses that were bought to the depot as part of a weekly maintenance and service check. At the end of the maintenance and service work, R needed to clean the buses, prior to their being sent back into service. It was C's responsibility to oversee that cleaning operation. With effect from 1 June 2018, C's line manager changed. There was no evidence that, prior to X becoming C's line manager, there had been any concerns about the way in which C carried out her job. X became dissatisfied (based partly on comments that he said he received from London Underground about the state of some of the buses, and based partly on his own observations) about the standard of the cleaning, and spoke about this to C informally on two occasions, on 20 July and 11 August. C maintained she had given X legitimate explanations for what he had observed. X noted on the second of these occasions that C's perception was that he was picking on her.

(2)   In addition to the two incidents on 20 July and 11 August, there were a number of other criticisms recorded by X about C on 19/08, 22/08, 28/08, 4/09 and 20/10. The final incident (20/10) related to an occasion on which X recorded that when he arrived at the site, he was told by a cleaner that C had gone home, that she had not told him, that he had tried to phone her and that she had said that she was sick. C did not deny that she was at home sick on this date.

(3)   Following that incident, X hand-delivered to C's home a letter of termination giving C one week's notice. The letter set out no reasons for the termination. Notwithstanding that R had a disciplinary procedure which was stated to apply to all staff after the completion of their probationary period, there had been no investigation, and no disciplinary process or procedure was followed. Subsequently, in response to a suggestion by C's representative that the dismissal was discriminatory, X wrote:

> As you are aware, C's employment with Veryclean Bus Services was less than 24 months, therefore we are under no legal obligation to supply you with the reasons for her dismissal. However, in the interest of fairness, openness and to dispel any suggestion that there may have been discrimination of any description, I am prepared to do so on this occasion. During her employment with us the following issues in regard to her performance conduct were raised but failed to be adequately addressed:
>
> •   Failure to perform the necessary quality control measures that were fundamental to her role. For example, the completion and standard of the rota cleaning.
>
> •   Failure to take reasonable action to ensure that the staff reported to her while performing their duties adequately and conducting themselves properly.
>
> •   Failure to advise her area manager of absence from site.
>
> •   Complaints from clients regarding the standard of cleaning.
>
> Should C wish to exercise her right of appeal we are willing to extend the deadline for this request to 10 October 2018 as per your request.

(4)   C's representative responded, stating that his client believed that she had been dismissed on the grounds of her race and that, in particular, she believed that there was an informal policy of replacing black workers with white Portuguese workers.

(5) On 11 October 2018, C submitted a race questionnaire to R; and on 26 October, she submitted an appeal against the termination of her employment. She made no mention of or nor complained about discrimination in that appeal. That appeal stated:

> I was not given any warning and carried out my duties to the best of my knowledge. We have to clean rota buses before they are inspected and before the engineers get to repair them and repair could last up to two days sometimes even longer and the buses are sent back during the day with oil/grease etc.

No appeal took place. R subsequently submitted additional information in response to the questionnaire.

(6) After C was dismissed, her job was offered to M, a black African, who was a supervisor at an another of R's bus depots, who turned it down. Subsequently, a Portuguese worker, N, took over C's position.

Claims

(7) C's complaint is that her dismissal amounted to direct discrimination under s 13 of the Equality Act 2010 on racial grounds. She is of black African origin. The alleged less favourable treatment is her dismissal and the manner of her dismissal. As C had less than two years' service with R, she was unable to bring an unfair dismissal claim arising out of her dismissal.

(8) R says it has not discriminated against C. It says the dismissal was not because of C's race.

Evidence

(9) Disclosure took place in the usual way and paginated bundles were prepared which included extracts from C's personal file, extracts from the staff handbook on *Disciplinary Procedures, Grievances and Appeals*, papers relating to the C's dismissal and a Schedule of Loss from C setting out her claim for compensation.

(10) Statistically, the evidence proved in response to the RRA questionnaire showed a total of 29 leavers between April 2017 and February 2018. There were 19 black leavers out of 29, which would be two-thirds of the total leavers. In terms of information relating to X, he supervised a total of nine sites. As regards the other site supervisors or managers, out of nine, one was Portuguese, two were South American, one was Asian and one was Eastern European. The remainder were black Africans.

(11) Witness statements were exchanged prior to the hearing. At the hearing all witnesses who gave oral evidence were cross-examined and the tribunal had the opportunity to ask questions of them.

(12) At the conclusion of the evidence, both sides made oral submissions on liability and remedy.

(13) All these matters were taken into consideration by the tribunal before reaching its decision.

The issues to be decided

(14) The tribunal will have to determine:
  (a) Has C been treated less favourably than a real or hypothetical comparator?
  (b) If so, is the comparator from a different racial group from C?
  (c) If so, has C proved facts from which the tribunal could conclude that the difference in treatment was because of race?
  (d) If so, has R proved that it did not treat C less favourably in any sense whatsoever because of race?

(15) Depending on the outcome of the matters, the tribunal will have to determine what amount of compensation, if any, should be awarded.

Submissions

(16) R submitted that the tribunal needed to take note that there was a very diverse ethnic pattern within R's workforce, which was also affected by influxes of different nationalities. It submitted that C was not doing her job. It accepted that if this was an unfair dismissal case, the dismissal would be unfair, but said that that was not relevant to this claim. R submitted that there was an informal practice with regard to employees with less than one year's service, but there was nothing in writing about that. R referred the tribunal to *Igen Ltd v Wong* [2005] IRLR 258, where the Court of Appeal set out a number of guidelines with regard to the burden of proof. R submitted that, in the first instance, the burden did not shift from C to R. In the alternative, it submitted that if the burden did shift, R had discharged its obligations in terms of showing that C's dismissal was not connected in any way whatsoever to her race. R said that the fact that it did not comply with its own disciplinary procedures could not shift the burden of proof on its own; even if there was unreasonableness, there needed to be something else to shift the burden. The evidence was that the post was initially offered to M, who was a black African like C. Alternatively, if the burden shifted then there was an adequate explanation, which was that provided by M.

(17) C submitted that the appropriate comparator was a white Portuguese person. In that context, it was submitted that N, who eventually took over the post, might well be a suitable actual comparator, but in any event, C said that a hypothetical white Portuguese comparator would suffice. She said that the tribunal needed to look at the imbalance between black non-Portuguese and white Portuguese/others. C's case was that X had a policy of dismissing black workers and replacing them with Portuguese workers, and that she had been a victim of this policy. C's evidence was that there had been mainly black Africans in the workplace before X started work. After X arrived, 22 out of 39 staff were white, of whom 16 were white European. C says she complained about race discrimination to X in August 2016. There was a suspicion that the notes of these meetings had not been recorded contemporaneously as X had claimed. R had not applied its own procedure. There was no reason for the dismissal. As far as *Igen v Wong* is concerned, C had been dismissed, no – and no fair – procedure had been followed, and C had been displaced by a Portuguese worker; these matters were, she said, sufficient to shift the burden of proof.

(18) As far as statistics were concerned, C relied upon the statistics which indicated that out of 10 white leavers, 6 had been dismissed and 4 had resigned (one of whom returned); and that there had been 17 black leavers, of whom only 2 had resigned. Proportionately, she said, it was significant that there had been a large number of black leavers over a relatively short period of time. C submitted that the burden of proof shifted to R, who needed to provide an explanation. She said that R had failed to show that in no way whatsoever was race the reason for C's dismissal.

Tribunal findings

(19) The unanimous judgment of the tribunal was that C's complaint of racial discrimination was not made out and it was dismissed.

(20) *Comparator.* C's chosen comparator was a white Portuguese person who would not have been dismissed in the way and in the circumstances that C was, and/or who was promoted when C was dismissed.

(21) *Has C proved facts from which the Tribunal could conclude that the treatment was because of her race?* The tribunal found as follows:

    21.1 C had been treated unreasonably, in that no proper process had been followed with regard to any investigation or disciplinary hearing in connection with allegations about her conduct or capability; R had failed in that regard to follow its own procedures; however, the tribunal accepted the evidence advanced by both

R's witnesses, which the tribunal regarded as being supported by the documents, that R had in practice disregarded a fair procedure when it dismissed *anyone* who had less than two years' service. The tribunal noted in particular that the dismissal letter sent to C was in virtually identical terms to (i) that sent by X's predecessor, Y, who was white British [against whom no complaint was or had been made] and (ii) that sent by X to B, described as white European; and (iii) was not dissimilar in terms to that sent by X to D, described as white European. As indicated by the EAT in *Laing* and approved by the Court of Appeal in *Madarassy*, having regard to all the evidence, the treatment or mistreatment (of others by the alleged discriminator) can be a highly material fact. On balance, the tribunal did not believe that the unreasonable treatment meted out to C was aimed only at her or at individuals of her race; it believed that all employees with less than two years' service were treated in this dismissive and unfair way by R. The tribunal was not convinced on the evidence before it that M and/or the hypothetical comparator would have been treated differently from C in similar circumstances relating to dissatisfaction with the way they carried out their jobs. On that basis, the tribunal did not find that this amounted to a proven fact from which it could conclude that C's less favourable treatment was because of race.

21.2 R was inconsistent in the reason it gave for C's dismissal – it had originally given no reason for the dismissal; subsequently it had said it was for 'operational' reasons; later, the letter of explanation set out reasons relating to C's capability. The tribunal accepted that R knew staff with less than two years' service did not have to be given a reason for dismissal. On balance, the tribunal did not believe that this alleged inconsistency amounted to a proven fact from which it could conclude that C's less favourable treatment was because of race.

21.3 A white Portuguese person eventually got C's job. Having heard the sworn testimony of M, who was a black African, the tribunal was satisfied that he had been offered the job by R. The tribunal did not find that the eventual appointment of a white Portuguese man amounted to a proven fact from which it could conclude that C's less favourable treatment was because of race. Neither did it give rise to any inference that C's treatment was because of race.

21.4 *Statistical evidence.* As far as statistics were concerned, there had been mainly black Africans in the workplace before X arrived. After he arrived, 22 out of 39 staff were white, of whom 16 were white European. Out of a total of 29 leavers between April 2017 and February 2018, there were 10 (British and European) white leavers (6 of whom were dismissed and 4 of whom had resigned (one of whom returned)); in contrast there had been 19 (African, British and European) black leavers, of whom only 2 had resigned. Proportionately, C relied on these figures to support her allegation that X was dismissing black Africans and replacing them with white Europeans. There was no specific information available as to who, in terms of race, had replaced those who had been dismissed over this period, although by extrapolation from the information to answers in the Questionnaire, it would appear that out of a total of 69 staff recruited, 23 were black Africans, of whom 11 left [just under 50%] and 22 were white Europeans, of whom 6 left [just under 25%]. There is clearly, on any analysis, a very high turnover of staff – of 69 recruited, 30 had left and 39 had remained. The statistics relating to black leavers did on their face appear to be significant – there was a higher proportion of black leavers over that period, and particularly black leavers who were dismissed (17/29 compared to 6/29). R relied upon the fact that, out of the sites managed by X and/ or over which he had responsibility for recruitment, almost half of the managers who were in a position directly comparable to that of C were black African. There was only one Portuguese manager. Further, if the leaving figures were narrowed down from the broad groupings replied upon by C [all blacks against all whites], so as to focus on the treatment of black Africans against white Europeans, the apparent disparity between dismissals decreased quite significantly – 11 black Africans compared to 6 white Europeans. The statistics indicated that 6 out of 10 white people were dismissed rather than resigned, and that 17 out of 19 black people were dismissed rather than resigned. There was a slight weighting in favour of black people over white people in the tribunal's judgment, when looked at in the round; while the statistical evidence provided some support for C's thesis, it was not particularly determinative and was not, in isolation, sufficient to amount to a fact from which it could conclude that this dismissal was because of race. It was not enough to shift the burden onto R to give an explanation.

(22) On balance, therefore, it was the tribunal's judgment that C had not succeeded in discharging the initial burden of proof to show facts from which the tribunal could conclude that her dismissal because of race, and she accordingly did not get to stage two, such as to require an explanation from R.

(23) The tribunal added that in case it was wrong with regard to its assessment of the evidence at stage one, it would in any event have found that R had proved that it did not treat C any less favourably in any sense whatsoever because of race. In particular, the tribunal found R had proved to its satisfaction two matters, which it regarded as compelling, namely, that:

23.1 prior to the appointment of N, the job had been offered to M, who had turned it down;

23.2 R treated everyone with less than two years' service in the same unreasonable way.

(24) On that basis, it was the unanimous decision of the tribunal that C's claim for race discrimination failed.

SUMMARY

This chapter has looked at direct discrimination in respect of the following protected characteristics listed in s 4 of the Equality Act 2010:

(a) sex;

(b) marriage and civil partnership;

(c) pregnancy and maternity;

(d) gender reassignment;

(e) race;

(f) religion or belief;

(g) sexual orientation (**9.1**).

(Age and disability are dealt with in separate chapters.)

One of the four main types of discrimination in the employment field outlawed by UK legislation is direct discrimination. Direct discrimination occurs when the reason for a person being treated less favourably than another is because of one of the protected characteristics (sex, race, religion or belief, sexual orientation, age, etc). The definition of direct discrimination is set out in s 13 of the Equality Act 2010 (**9.2**).

Less favourable treatment is a wide concept, which covers any 'disadvantage' – it does not require any tangible loss (**9.2.5**). Motive or intention is irrelevant and there is no defence once direct discrimination has been proved (save for age discrimination). There are special rules relating to pregnancy and maternity (**9.4**).

The burden of proving discrimination is a shifting one. The burden starts with the claimant. Once the claimant has established sufficient facts that, in the absence of any other explanation, point to a breach, the burden shifts to the employer. Section 136 provides that where a complainant can establish facts from which a tribunal could decide that there has been a contravention of a provision of the Equality Act 2010, the tribunal *must* find unlawful discrimination, *unless* the employer shows that it did not contravene the provision (**9.5**).

Remedies and enforcement are dealt with at **8.8**. Tribunals may, on making a finding of discrimination, as they consider just and equitable, make:

(a)   an order declaring the rights of the complainant;

(b)   an order requiring the respondent to pay the complainant compensation; and/or

(c)   a recommendation that the respondent take, within a specified period, practicable action to obviate or reduce the adverse effect of any act of discrimination.

The general principle as far as compensation is concerned is that, as far as possible, complainants should be placed in the same position as they would have been but for the unlawful act (see *Ministry of Defence v Wheeler* [1998] IRLR 23). In addition to awarding compensation for foreseeable damage arising directly from the unlawful act, a tribunal has jurisdiction to award compensation for personal injury, including both physical and psychiatric injury, and for injury to feelings (**8.8.2.2**).

A flowchart summarising direct discrimination is set out at **Figure 9.1**.

Figure 9.1 Flowchart – Direct Discrimination

ELIGIBILITY

time-limit – within 3 months of act of discrimination

↓

UNLAWFUL ACT

discrimination in recruitment, promotion, dismissal, harassment, post-employment matters or subjecting a person to detriment

↓

TYPE OF CLAIM

[NB some situations can give rise to more than one type of discrimination claim]

↓

DIRECT DISCRIMINATION

- Has C been treated differently and less favourably because of a protected characteristic?
- Need actual or hypothetical comparator (*Shamoon*)?
- 'Reason why question'
- *Barton v Investec/Igen v Wong*
  - initial evidential burden on C to prove facts from which ET could conclude that reason for less favourable treatment is because of sex, etc
  - legal burden passes to R to show cogent reason for less favourable treatment; it was in no way whatsoever to do with C's sex, etc
  - if R's explanation is inadequate, ET must find that R committed an act of unlawful discrimination
- Exception. Is there an occupational requirement (OR) exception?

↓

NO DEFENCE

↓

VICARIOUS LIABILITY

R will be vicariously liable for acts of employees committed in the course of employment (*Jones v Tower Boot Co/Chief Constable of Lincolnshire Police v Stubbs/Bellmann v Northampton* etc) unless R took all reasonably practicable steps to stop/avoid the discrimination (statutory defence – s 109(4))

↓

REMEDIES

- declaration of employee's rights
- recommendation that employer take action to alleviate or reduce the effect of the discrimination on C or the wider workforce
- order for compensation (no maximum)
  - pecuniary losses
  - aggravated damages if employer has behaved in a high-handed, malicious, insulting or aggressive manner
  - injury to feelings (*Vento/Da'Bell*)
  - psychiatric or physical injury
  - possibility of exemplary damages
  - increase/decrease for any unreasonable failure to comply with the Acas Code of Practice

INDIRECT DISCRIMINATION

LEARNING OUTCOMES

After reading this chapter you will be able to:

- understand the definition of indirect discrimination
- explain what is meant by the shifting burden of proof
- describe how the justification defence works
- list the potential remedies that are available where a complaint of indirect discrimination is made out.

10.1 INTRODUCTION

This chapter considers indirect discrimination in respect of the following protected characteristics listed in s 4 of the Equality Act 2010 (see **8.2.1**):

- gender reassignment (s 7)
- marriage and civil partnership (s 8)
- race (s 9)
- religion or belief (s 10)
- sex (s 11)
- sexual orientation (s 12)
- pregnancy and maternity (s 18).

This chapter refers, by way of illustration and example, to the pre- and post-Equality Act 2010 case law.

10.2 INDIRECT DISCRIMINATION

10.2.1 Definition

Indirect discrimination occurs when there is equal treatment of all groups but the effect of the provision, criterion or practice (PCP) imposed by an employer has a disproportionate adverse impact on one group, unless the requirement can be justified. The definition of indirect discrimination is set out in s 19 of the Act:

(1) A person (A) discriminates against another (B) if A applies to B a provision, criterion or practice which is discriminatory in relation to a relevant protected characteristic of B's.

(2) For the purposes of subsection (1), a provision, criterion or practice is discriminatory in relation to a relevant protected characteristic of B's if—

(a) A applies, or would apply, it to persons with whom B does not share the characteristic,

(b)   it puts, or would put, persons with whom B shares the characteristic at a particular disadvantage when compared with persons with whom B does not share it,

(c)   it puts, or would put, B at that disadvantage, and

(d)   A cannot show it to be a proportionate means of achieving a legitimate aim.

Baroness Hale said in *Secretary of State for Trade and Industry v Rutherford and Another* [2006] IRLR 551, HL, that some points stand out:

(a)   the concept is normally applied to a rule or requirement which *selects* people for a particular advantage or disadvantage;

(b)   the rule is applied to a group of people who *want* something. The disparate impact complained of is that they cannot have what they want because of the rule, whereas others can.

The Explanatory Notes provide examples:

- A woman is forced to leave her job because her employer operates a practice that staff must work in a shift pattern which she is unable to comply with because she needs to look after her children at particular times of day, and no allowances are made because of those needs. This would put women (who are shown to be more likely to be responsible for childcare) at a disadvantage, and the employer will have indirectly discriminated against the woman unless the practice can be justified.

- An observant Jewish engineer who is seeking an advanced diploma decides (even though he is sufficiently qualified to do so) not to apply to a specialist training company because it invariably undertakes the selection exercises for the relevant course on Saturdays. The company will have indirectly discriminated against the engineer unless the practice can be justified.

Other examples include the following:

(a)   A Sikh boy who was refused entrance to public school unless he cut his hair and stopped wearing a turban was indirectly discriminated against (*Mandla (Sewa Singh) and Another v Dowell Lee and Another* [1983] 2 AC 548; see now the approach in *R (on the application of Watkins-Singh) v Aberdare Girls' High School and Another* [2008] EWHC 1865 (Admin) and *G v Headteacher and Governors of St Gregory's Catholic Science College* [2011] EWHC 1452 (Admin), discussed at **10.2.3** below). Readers should note that on 1 October 2015, the right for Sikhs to wear turbans instead of safety helmets was extended to most workplaces.

(b)   To impose a requirement that a job applicant must weigh at least 12 stone would be discriminatory against women unless the minimum weight was a genuine requirement of the job.

(c)   The imposition of an age requirement of 17½ to 28 for promotion to executive officer was held to be indirect 'discriminatory', as more women than men would be out of the labour market between those ages having children. It could also discriminate against immigrant applicants, who may obtain qualifications at a later age than those educated in the UK.

(d)   The requirement that an employee should work full time as opposed to part time may indirectly discriminate against women (*Home Office v Holmes* [1984] 3 All ER 549).

(e)   In order to increase efficiency a company decided that no holidays could be taken during the May to July peak period. When Eid fell in June 1992, the company refused to make any exceptions to its policy, even though its Muslim employees offered to work extra hours to compensate. The rule was indirectly discriminatory (*JH Walker Ltd v Hussain and Others* [1996] IRLR 11).

(f)   A requirement to be available for duty 24 hours a day, seven days a week, taken together with a restriction on bringing relatives abroad to facilitate childcare, was indirectly discriminatory on grounds of sex and race (*Ministry of Defence v DeBique* (UKEAT/0048/09)).

(g)   A height requirement for police was not justified (*Ypourgos Esoterikon and Another v Kalliri* (Case C-409/16)).

Elements of an indirect discrimination claim

To bring a claim of indirect discrimination, a claimant must first show that he belongs to a particular protected group. He must also show that he is put to the disadvantage to which the protected group to which he belongs is put. A provision, criterion or practice (PCP) must then be identified which is applied to the claimant and has or would have an adverse impact on the claimant. The PCP must be apparently neutral; if it is premised on a rule that is itself discriminatory, the claim is likely to be one of direct discrimination (*James v Eastleigh Borough Council* [1990] ICR 554).

The only defence to an indirect discrimination claim is justification, ie that the application of the PCP constituted a proportionate means of achieving a legitimate aim.

10.2.2   Meaning of provision, criterion or practice

The phrase 'provision, criterion or practice' (PCP) is not defined but must be apparently neutral and will cover informal and formal working practices, and will therefore allow for examination of, for example, recruitment and promotion policies and working practices that do not operate as absolute requirements for the job in question (see, eg, *BA plc v Sturmer* [2005] IRLR 862). The EAT held in *Nottingham City Transport Ltd v Harvey* (UKEAT/0032/12) that a one-off flawed disciplinary procedure did not amount to a PCP. A practice, it held, must have an element of repetition. See too *H Fox (Father of G Fox, deceased) v BA plc* (UKEAT/0315/14). However, it can be sufficient for it to be applied to just the claimant.

It is necessary to determine a PCP in order to assess whether something an employer does to its employees gives rise to a difference in outcome, or has an adverse disparate impact, depending on the characteristics of its employees. In indirect discrimination claims, the adverse disparate impact must be shown to affect one group (to which the claimant belongs) more than it does to another group. Defining the PCP is key to finding whether there has been indirect discrimination. The leading decision is *Environment Agency v Rowan* [2008] IRLR 20, which was approved by the Court of Appeal in *Newham Sixth Form College v Sanders* [2014] EWCA Civ 734. See also *Unison v Lord Chancellor* [2017] UKSC 51 at [121]–[131].

10.2.3   Impact of provision – group disadvantage

PCPS cannot be considered in isolation. The adverse disparate impact must also be established. Once a PCP has been established, the complainant must show that the PCP is to the disadvantage of his or her group. Before any assessment of the impact of the PCP can be made, the appropriate pool for comparison must be identified. There has been some doubt as to whether the identification of the appropriate pool for comparison is a question of fact or law for the tribunal. If it is a question of fact, that means that a tribunal's decision cannot easily be appealed.

However, in *Allonby v Accrington and Rossendale College and Others* [2001] IRLR 364, Sedley LJ characterised the identification of the pool as a 'matter ... of logic', such that once the PCP has been identified, 'there is likely to be only one pool which serves to test its effect'. If the wrong pool is used, this will probably now be an error of law.

In *Jones v University of Manchester* [1993] IRLR 218 (a claim under the SDA 1975), the University had advertised a post requiring a graduate aged between 27 and 35. Mrs Jones argued that this indirectly discriminated against women. She was aged 46. The pool for comparison, Mrs Jones argued, should be graduates who had obtained their degrees as mature students. The tribunal agreed and upheld her complaint, as statistics showed that the proportion of women graduates obtaining their degrees as mature students (aged over 25) who could comply with the requirement was considerably smaller than the proportion of male graduates who had obtained their degrees as mature students. However, the EAT held that the wrong pool for comparison had been chosen, and the Court of Appeal upheld this view. The Court held that the appropriate pool for comparison was all men and women with the required qualifications for the job, not including the requirement complained of (ie, all graduates with relevant experience, ignoring age, and not just those who had graduated as mature students).

It will often be the case in recruitment situations that the appropriate pool for comparison is all those who are qualified for the post in question, including all those who would be so qualified were it not for the alleged discriminatory requirement. In other cases, where the complainant alleges that a practice of the employer is discriminatory, the pool might be the workforce to whom that requirement applies (see, eg, *London Underground Ltd v Edwards* [1998] IRLR 364, where the pool was all London Underground train drivers). The EAT held, in *Naeem v Secretary of State for Justice* (UKEAT/0215/14) that the tribunal had erred in selecting a pool comprised of all prison chaplains to whom the PCP applied. To include pre-2002 chaplains, when no Muslim chaplains were recruited pre-2002, only 'served to highlight a material difference between the [two groups]'. The PCP could only be tested in relation to persons employed since 2002.

Once a pool for comparison has been established, the tribunal must consider whether the PCP *would* put persons of the group in question at a *particular disadvantage* when compared to persons of the other group. Thus, for example, in a indirect sex discrimination claim, the tribunal must compare the proportion of women within the pool who suffer a disadvantage with the proportion of men. Under the old law it was necessary to show that the proportion of one sex or one race *who could comply* with the requirement was *considerably smaller* than that of the comparative group. The change suggested that statistical evidence would not always be required to prove this.

In *Homer v Chief Constable of West Yorkshire Police* [2012] IRLR 601, the Supreme Court confirmed that the new formulation was intended to do away with statistical comparisons where no statistics exist, and that now what is required is a particular disadvantage when compared with others who do not share the protected characteristic in question. On that basis, the employer's introduction of the need to have a degree to reach a higher grade worked to the comparative disadvantage of persons approaching compulsory retirement age, and was indirectly discriminatory on the ground of age.

In *London Underground Ltd v Edwards* (above) (a sex discrimination case), London Underground imposed a requirement to work flexible hours. All 2,023 men could comply (100%) and 20 out of the 21 women could comply (95.2%). The Court of Appeal held that the requirement was indirectly discriminatory. The Court accepted that a percentage difference of no more than 5% would often lead a tribunal to the conclusion that the then 'considerably smaller' requirement had *not* been made out. However, by taking into account wider national statistics (10 lone mothers for each father), the Court of Appeal was able to uphold the tribunal's findings of indirect discrimination. A similar approach was taken by the EAT in *Chief Constable of Avon Constabulary v Chew* (UKEAT/503/00), [2001] All ER (D) 101 (Sep).

In *Hacking and Paterson and Another v Wilson* (UKEAT/0054/09), the EAT commented that society has changed, and men now take on more childcare responsibilities. Whether the statistics bear that out is, in the authors' view, doubtful.

In *Cross and Others v BA plc* [2005] IRLR 423, the EAT upheld the tribunal's decision that the provision, providing for a compulsory retirement age of 55 for cabin crew and pilots, was to the detriment of a considerably larger proportion of women than men. The statistics presented to the tribunal showed that 90.28% of men were disadvantaged compared to 98.55% of women; and that 9.72% of men could comply with the provision, etc, compared to 1.45% of women. The employer argued on appeal that the tribunal should have ignored the smaller advantaged group and instead concentrated on the disadvantaged group statistics; it would, according to the employer, have been bound to find that there was no clear case of adverse impact. The EAT held that the tribunal was entitled to look at all the figures; and that in cases of less obvious adverse impact it should use more than one form of comparison.

In 1998, a challenge was launched to the UK's cut-off age of 65 for unfair dismissal claims and redundancy compensation (*Secretary of State for Trade and Industry v Rutherford and Another* [2006] IRLR 551, HL). In the absence of any age equality legislation at that time, the claim was brought based on indirect sex discrimination. Mr Rutherford had been made redundant in 1998 at the age of 67 by his employer, Harvest Town Circle Ltd. He claimed that the cut-off age of 65 indirectly discriminated against men, because more men than women continued to work past 65. Harvest subsequently went into liquidation and the defence of the claim was taken over by the Secretary of State. A tribunal held that the cut-off provisions did amount to indirect sex discrimination against men. It found, after a detailed statistical analysis, that in the pool of employees affected by the cut off, the proportion of men who were disadvantaged (ie all those over 65) was greater than the proportion of disadvantaged women. The EAT ([2001] IRLR 599 and [2003] IRLR 858) and the Court of Appeal ([2004] IRLR 892) disagreed with the way the tribunal had analysed the statistics. The case went to the House of Lords, which gave its decision on 3 May 2006. Unhelpfully, while there was a unanimous conclusion that there was no unlawful discrimination, each of their Lordships adopted a slightly different approach. However, the analysis in the House of Lords judgment of the principles of and the approach to the indirect discrimination claims is important, and should be considered fully by anyone wishing to bring or defend an indirect discrimination claim. The point to note here is that the House of Lords focused on relative proportions within the *advantaged* group in this case.

However, the Court of Appeal, in *Grundy v BA plc* [2007] EWCA Civ 1020, held that the employment tribunal did not err when it focused on the *disadvantaged* group, where the women disadvantaged outnumbered men 14:1, rather than on the make-up of the advantaged group, which contained 99% of all employees in the relevant pool, when deciding whether the practice disadvantaged considerably more women. The Court said that there is no rule that the focus should be on the advantaged or disadvantaged group. It depends on the facts. The pool, said the Court of Appeal,

> must be one which suitably tests the particular discrimination complained of; [there is no universal formula for locating the correct pool]. It needs to include, but not be limited to, those affected by the term of which complaint is made, which can be expected to include both people who can and people who cannot comply with it.

In *Somerset CC and Another v Pike* [2009] EWCA Civ 808, the Court of Appeal held that rules in the Teachers' Pension Scheme that prevented retired teachers who returned to part-time work from joining the scheme (those who returned full-time were allowed to rejoin) could be indirectly discriminatory. Mrs Pike took early retirement from teaching on grounds of ill-health in 1993. She returned to part-time work in 1994, but under the rules of the Scheme she was prevented from rejoining the Scheme. It was argued that this amounted to indirect sex discrimination because it disadvantaged a substantially higher proportion of women than men, as women are statistically more likely to work on a part-time basis. An employment tribunal decided that the correct pool of comparison was the whole of the teaching profession, which resulted in only a slightly adverse disparate impact of the rule on women of 0.3%. On that basis the tribunal found no detriment. The EAT held that the pool should consist only of teachers wishing to return to work, and excluding those who were not included in the post-retirement rules. On this basis, the disparity in relation to women assessed over a 13-year period was more significant – 15% more women than men were in non-pensionable employment and, comparing the proportion of advantaged women over the same period, 38% more men than women were advantaged. The Court of Appeal, applying the House of Lords decision in *Rutherford* (above), agreed. By adopting the entire teaching profession as the pool of comparison, the employment tribunal had brought into the equation people who had no interest in the advantage or disadvantage in question. The case was remitted to the employment tribunal to consider whether or not the rule could be justified.

In *Eweida v British Airways* [2009] IRLR 78, the EAT said that a dress code that prevented an employee from wearing a visible cross was not unlawful indirect discrimination. British Airways' policy did not permit personal items of jewellery to be visible over a uniform unless they were mandatory religious items which could not be concealed. When E insisted on wearing her cross visibly, having been warned not to do so, she was sent home. She was offered an alternative job for which a uniform was not required, but she refused it. She said that the policy was indirectly discriminatory. The EAT said that the policy did not put Christians as a group at a *particular disadvantage*, as there was no evidence that other Christians felt disadvantaged, and this decision was upheld by the Court of Appeal ([2010] EWCA Civ 80). However, the ECtHR held that she had been indirectly discriminated against and the policy was not justified (see **10.2.7** below) because her beliefs were not reasonably accommodated. In religious belief cases, it seems that the hurdle of showing 'group disadvantage' may no longer be necessary and that it will be enough to demonstrate individual disadvantage, because someone else is likely to share the religious belief. See *Mba v Mayor and Burgesses of the London Borough of Merton* [2013] EWCA Civ 1562 (below).

In *G v Headteacher and Governors of St Gregory's Catholic Science College* [2011] EWHC 1452 (Admin), the High Court had to consider whether a school's uniform and hair policy, which prohibited boys from wearing their hair in cornrows, was unlawful discrimination on sex and/or racial grounds. G, who was 11 and of African-Caribbean ethnicity, was due to start his secondary education at St Gregory's Catholic Science College, a strict but high-performing inner-London school. Since birth, G had not cut his hair and, in accordance with family tradition, kept his hair in cornrows. African-Caribbean girls were permitted to wear their hair in cornrows as the School recognised that this helped keep long hair neat and under control. The school's written uniform policy did not explicitly prohibit cornrows for boys, but the cornrow ban was outlined at an introductory meeting at the school in September 2009, which G missed. G was unwilling to comply with the school's policy and was therefore unable to take up his place at the school. He subsequently brought judicial review proceedings, alleging that the school's policy amounted to indirect race discrimination and sex discrimination. (He also launched a claim for damages in the county court alleging sex and race discrimination.)

The school had a strong Catholic ethos. One of its principal aims behind the ban on cornrows was to keep gang culture out of the school, to avoid ethnic tensions and violence. The school considered that distinctive haircuts could be 'badges of ethnic or gang identity in an aggressive or unwelcome sense and can help foster disunity rather than unity'. It therefore adopted a zero tolerance approach to all male hairstyles.

To prove indirect race discrimination, G had to show that the school's policy placed a racial group at a particular disadvantage and also that he, as an individual, suffered that disadvantage. The case is a good example of the difficulties of proving group discrimination where not all those who share a protected characteristic are equally affected by the policy. Compare *Mandla* (see **10.2.1**), where all Sikh men are required to wear their hair long and would be disadvantaged by a prohibition on wearing turbans, with *Eweida* (above), where the Court found that the employee's belief in the requirement to wear a visible cross was a personal one. The courts have been clear that 'the whole purpose of indirect discrimination is to deal with the problem of group discrimination' (per Elias J in *Eweida*), but there is no agreement as to how large or small a group must be to be protected. The Court of Appeal in *Eweida* expressed concern that a wide interpretation of 'group' risks placing 'an impossible burden on employers to anticipate and provide for what may be parochial or even factitious beliefs in society at large'.

In G's case, the judge concluded that the 'group disadvantage test' was satisfied as there was evidence that there were groups of African-Caribbean ethnicity who, for reasons based on their culture and ethnicity, regard the cutting of their hair to be wrong, so that it is necessary for them to keep their hair in cornrows. Collins J said:

> It may be that those who regard it as an obligation rather than a preference are in the minority, but on the material before me, I am satisfied that there is a group who could be particularly disadvantaged by a refusal to permit them to wear their hair in cornrows.

The judge also concluded that the school's refusal to allow G to attend school, and the trauma he suffered in being turned away on his first day, amounted to a sufficient individual disadvantage. The judge rejected the school's defence of justification, namely that its policy was a 'proportionate means of achieving a legitimate aim'. Collins J concluded that although the aim of the policy was legitimate, the school's argument that introducing exceptions would undermine the whole uniform policy was not a valid one. He concluded that a blanket policy without exceptions could not be justified.

The judge rejected G's sex discrimination claim. Applying *Smith v Safeway* [1996] ICR 868, he concluded a dress code will not be discriminatory where it enforces a common standard of conventionality for both men and women. On the facts, the school's rationale for permitting African-Caribbean girls to wear their hair in cornrows (keeping long hair neat and under control) was not evidence of sex discrimination.

In *Mba v Mayor and Burgesses of the London Borough of Merton* [2013] EWCA Civ 1562, when a practising Christian was rostered to work on Sundays, she brought an indirect discrimination claim. Two of the three judges in the Court of Appeal concluded, albeit obiter, that group disadvantage is not required in religious belief cases and that only individual disadvantage is necessary. The ECtHR has issued a guidance note on 'Religion or Belief and the Workplace', available at <http://www.equalityhumanrights.com>. There is also, separately, an Acas guidance note on dress codes, available at <http://www.acas.org.uk/dresscode>.

The Supreme Court in joined appeals in *Essop v Home Office (UK Border Agency); Naeem v Secretary of State for Justice* [2017] UKSC 27 considered issues arising from claims of indirect discrimination on grounds of race and/or age and/or religion. Mr Essop was the lead appellant in a group of 49 people, six of whom had been chosen as test cases. They are, or were, all employed by the Home Office. They were required to pass a Core Skills Assessment (CSA) as a prerequisite to promotion to certain civil service grades. A report in 2010 established that Black and Minority Ethnic (BME) candidates, and older candidates, had lower pass rates than white and younger candidates. No-one had been able to identify why this was. The claims alleged that the requirement to pass the CSA constituted indirect discrimination on the grounds of race or age. The Home Office argued that s 19(2)(b) of the Equality Act 2010 required the appellants to prove the reason for the lower pass rate. The Court of Appeal agreed, upholding the decision of the Employment Judge.

Mr Naeem is an imam who works as a chaplain in the Prison Service. Before 2002, Muslim chaplains were engaged on a sessional basis only, because it was believed that there were too few Muslim prisoners to justify employing them on a salaried basis, as some Christian chaplains were. Mr Naeem worked on a sessional basis from 2001 but in 2004 became a salaried employee. At this date the pay scheme for chaplains incorporated pay progression over time. The average length of service of Christian chaplains was longer, which led to a higher average basic pay. Mr Naeem argued that the incremental pay scheme was indirectly discriminatory against Muslim or Asian chaplains, resulting in lower pay in a post where length of service served no useful purpose as a reflection of ability or experience. Mr Naeem's claim was rejected by the employment tribunal which found that the indirect discrimination was justified. The EAT held that the scheme was not indirectly discriminatory at all because chaplains employed before 2002 should be excluded from the comparison between the two groups. The Court of Appeal held that it was not enough to show that the length of service criterion had a disparate impact upon Muslim chaplains: it was also necessary to show that the reason for that disparate impact was something peculiar to the protected characteristic of race or religion.

The Supreme Court unanimously allowed the *Essop* appeal. It unanimously dismissed Mr Naeem's appeal but confirmed the point that it is not necessary to answer the 'reason why' question. Mr Naeem lost because the employer had justified the PCP – the pay structure was a proportionate means of achieving a legitimate aim. The judgment makes clear that:

(a)   once it has been established (whether by statistical evidence or otherwise) that a PCP places people with relevant protected characteristics at a particular disadvantage compared with others, that is sufficient to require objective justification by a respondent of its use of the PCP;

(b)   it is irrelevant whether or not the reason why the PCP puts that group at a particular disadvantage is itself related to the protected characteristic;

(c)   the only required causal link is between the PCP and the particular disadvantage.

In the *Essop* case, it was irrelevant that some BME or older candidates could pass the CSA: the group was at a disadvantage because the proportion who could pass was smaller than the proportion of white or younger candidates. It is always open to a respondent to show that the PCP is justified. There may well be a good reason for it. A wise employer will, however, try to see if PCPs which do have a disparate impact can be modified to remove that impact while achieving the desired result. The disadvantage suffered by the individual must correspond with the disadvantage suffered by the group. The disadvantage in *Essop* was that members of the group failed the CSA disproportionately and the appellants suffered this disadvantage. However, a candidate who fails the CSA because he did not prepare or did not turn up for or finish the CSA has not suffered harm as a result of the PCP in question, and in such a case it is open to the respondent to show that the causal link between the PCP and the individual disadvantage is absent.

In Mr Naeem's case, the reason why the pay scale put Muslim chaplains at a disadvantage was known. It was because they have on average shorter lengths of service than Christian chaplains. The Court of Appeal was wrong to require the reason to relate to the protected characteristic. The pool of comparators comprises all workers affected by the PCP in question. In this case the incremental pay structure affected all chaplains in the Prison Service and this did put the Muslim chaplains at a disadvantage compared with the Christians. As regards justification, it was not in dispute that the pay scheme had a legitimate aim but the means adopted needed to be proportionate. The employment tribunal found as a fact that six years was the most required for newly appointed chaplains to have the skills and experience for reward at the top of the scale, but that in the circumstances the disadvantage suffered by Mr Naeem was no more than was necessary as the transition to a new shorter pay scale took its course. This Supreme Court said that was the correct test. It is not open to the courts on an appeal to disturb that finding, even if there were alternative means to reduce the disadvantage more quickly which could have been considered.

The decision in these two cases has been seen by commentators as helpful for both employers and employees. As far as employees are concerned, while a claimant will still need to show a causal link between the PCP and their own disadvantage, the Court stated that the purpose behind indirect discrimination legislation is to protect people with a protected characteristic from suffering disadvantage where an apparently neutral PCP is applied. It is about achieving a level playing field and removing hidden barriers. This makes it clear therefore that there is no obligation on an employee to explain why a PCP puts a group at a disadvantage when compared to others: it is enough simply to show that there is disadvantage. However, there is positive news for employers as well: the Court said that the requirement to justify a PCP should not be seen as placing an unreasonable burden on employers or as 'casting some sort of stigma upon them'. The Court also clarified that all workers affected by a PCP, whether positively or negatively, should be placed in the pool for comparison. There is a useful note about the cases on the 11KBW website by Sean Jones QC and Amy Rogers, entitled 'The Supreme Court makes indirect discrimination simple again'.

The EAT held in *Pendleton v Derbyshire CC & Another* (UKEAT/0238/15) that those who hold a religious belief in the sanctity of marriage face a particular disadvantage if forced to choose between their husband/wife and their career.

10.2.4 Complainant's disadvantage

The complainant must suffer a disadvantage and show why the PCP caused that disadvantage. Hypothetical cases cannot be brought. The House of Lords confirmed in *Shamoon v Chief Constable of the Royal Ulster Constabulary* [2003] IRLR 285 that, in order to qualify as a disadvantage, the disadvantage must arise in the employment field. But once this requirement is satisfied, as the House of Lords confirmed in *Shamoon*, the only other limitation that can be read into the words is:

> Is the treatment of such a kind that a reasonable worker would or might take the view that in all the circumstances it was to his detriment? An unjustified sense of grievance cannot amount to 'detriment' ... [b]ut ... it is not necessary to demonstrate some physical or economic consequence.

An obvious example of disadvantage in the employment context is not getting promoted or being dismissed.

In *Keane v Investigo and Others* (UKEAT/0389/09), the EAT dismissed the claimant's claims of age discrimination because she had applied for jobs only in order to claim compensation, and on that basis had not suffered a detriment (ie she had no interest in the job vacancies).

Readers should note the ECJ's decision in *CHEZ Razpredelenie Bulgaria* (Case C-83/14) (ECJ, 16 July 2015), which established that an individual may be able to claim indirect discrimination under the Race Discrimination Directive (2000/43) on the basis of associative discrimination. Section 19 of the Equality Act 2010 defines indirect discrimination: the complainant must share the same protected characteristic as the disadvantaged group. The ECJ decided in the *CHEZ* case that the Race Discrimination Directive does not require the complainant to share the protected characteristic (in this case, race) to bring a claim of indirect discrimination, as long as the complainant suffers the *same* disadvantage. The case illustrates the point: a utility company in Bulgaria had a practice of placing electricity meters at an unaccessible height in a district largely populated by people of Roma ethnic origin. The complainant was of non-Roma origin, but the ECJ held that she could allege indirect discrimination as she suffered the *same* disadvantage as those persons of Roma origin – namely, not being able to check electricity usage.

The judgment may mean that s 19 of the 2010 Act will need amending, but in the meantime employees could seek to rely directly or indirectly on relevant EU directives, to allege indirect discrimination (by association), where they do not share the protected characteristic.

10.2.5 Direct v indirect discrimination

Readers are referred to the ECJ cases of *Achbita* and *Bougnaoui* and the judgment, in particular, of Lady Hale in *Essop and Naeem* (above) at [17]–[25].

10.2.6 Dual discrimination

In *Ministry of Defence v DeBique* (UKEAT/0048/09), the EAT held that the claimant, a female soldier from St Vincent with childcare commitments, had been the victim of sex and race discrimination by reason of two 'provisions, criteria or practices' (PCPs): one requiring that she be available for deployment on a 24/7 basis ('the 24/7 PCP'), which disadvantaged her as a female single parent; the second prohibiting her from inviting a member of her extended family not of British origin to stay with her in Services Family Accommodation (and thereby assist with childcare) ('the immigration PCP'), which disadvantaged her as a foreign national. On this basis, the EAT upheld the employment tribunal's conclusion that indirect discrimination claims under the RRA 1976 and the SDA 1975 were made out when the combined effect of the two PCPs were considered. The EAT commented that 'discrimination is often a multi-faceted experience' and should not be artificially compartmentalised. When the two PCPs were considered together, their discriminatory effect could not be justified.

10.2.7   Employer's defence

The employer must show that the PCP is 'a proportionate means of achieving a legitimate aim' (s 19(2)(d) of the Act). The Directive uses slightly different language: 'objectively justified by a legitimate aim and the means of achieving that aim are appropriate and necessary'. The (old) CRE commented as follows:

> It is our belief that the 'proportionality test' is a more limited test than that provided for by the Directive ie that the means used are 'appropriate and necessary'.

In *Chief Constable of West Midlands Police v Harrod* [2015] IRLR 790, the EAT emphasised that justification is an objective evaluation. Further what has to be justified is the outcome, not the process followed. In *Allonby v Accrington and Rossendale College and Others* [2001] IRLR 364, the Court of Appeal made it clear that

> once an employment tribunal has concluded that [the PCP] has a disparate impact on a protected group it must carry out a critical evaluation of whether the reasons demonstrate a real need to take the action in question. This should include consideration of whether there was another way to achieve the aim in question.

The EAT emphasised in *Rajaratnam v Care UK Clinical Services Ltd* (UKEAT/0435/14) that it is the rule that needs to be justified and not its application to the individual concerned.

Courts and tribunals must carry out a balancing exercise between the degree of discrimination caused and the object or aim to be achieved, taking into account the surrounding circumstances (*Cobb v Employment Secretary* [1989] IRLR 464).

The Supreme Court held, in *Homer v Chief Constable of West Yorkshire Police* [2012] UKSC 15, that to be proportionate, a measure must be an appropriate and necessary means of meeting the legitimate aim. The ECHJ held in *Dansk Jurist- og Økonomforbund v Indenrigs- og Sundhadsministeriet* [2013] EUECJ C-546/11 that actions will not be proportionate if less discriminatory means to achieve the result were available.

So, for example, a rule prohibiting beards in a chocolate factory may be considered a proportionate response and justifiable in the interests of hygiene; but rather than not employing bearded persons, the employer should look at other means of achieving the objective, such as the covering up of beards. The 'appropriate and necessary' test requires consideration of whether there are less discriminatory alternative measures to achieve the aim; the proportionality test requires the same consideration.

In *Hardys & Hansons v Lax* [2005] EWCA Civ 846, (a case under the SDA 1975), the Court of Appeal held that the 'range of reasonable responses' test (see **5.3.1.1**) does not apply when tribunals have to decide whether an otherwise discriminatory practice is objectively justified. (See too *Board of Governors of St Matthias Church of England School v Crizzle* [1993] ICR 401, *Azmi v Kirklees Metropolitan Borough Council* [2007] IRLR 484 and *Allen and Another v GMB* [2008] IRLR 690.) The Court in *Hardys* said that the principle of proportionality required the tribunal to take into account the reasonable needs of the business. But it had to make its own judgment, upon a fair and detailed analysis of the working practices and business considerations involved, as to whether the proposal was reasonably necessary. The reasonableness qualification did not permit the margin of discretion or range of reasonable responses for which the respondent contended. The Court also added that, where an employer is relying on the economic needs of the business, it would be expected to adduce sufficient evidence of that business need to enable the tribunal to 'set out at least a basic economic analysis of the business and its needs'.

In *XC Trains Ltd v CD* (UKEAT/0331/15) the EAT upheld the employment tribunal's decision that the requirement to work anti-social hours put women at a particular disadvantage, but held that the employment tribunal had failed to weigh the legitimate aims of the employer against the discriminatory impact of the requirement.

Examples of objective justification under the old and new definitions of 'indirect discrimination' include the following:

(a)   In *Panesar v Nestlé Co* [1980] ICR 144, a factory rule prohibiting beards and long hair had a disproportionate impact on Sikhs, but it was held to be objectively justified on the grounds of hygiene.

(b)   In *London Underground Ltd v Edwards* (a sex discrimination case) (**10.2.3** above), the EAT held that the tribunal was entitled to find that the employers had not justified the requirement to work flexible hours. There was good evidence that the employer could have made arrangements which would not have been damaging to its business plans but which would have accommodated the reasonable needs of its employees.

(c)   There is some conflicting case law on whether cost alone may be relied upon to justify an otherwise discriminatory policy. In *Cross and Others v BA plc* (**10.2.3** above), a case decided under the equivalent of the new law, the EAT held that the employment tribunal had been entitled to take the cost to the employer of changing the offending provision into account when deciding whether the employer could justify the provision. The EAT added that costs could not be the sole justification, but they were nevertheless a relevant factor. (See also *BA plc v Starmer* [2005] IRLR 862, where the employer failed in its attempt to justify a refusal to halve the hours of a full-time female airline pilot with childcare responsibilities.) In *Bressol v Gouvernement de la Communauté Française* (Case C-73/08) the ECJ considered a costs plus justification advanced by a State. In *Woodcock v Cumbria Primary Care NHS Trust* [2012] EWCA Civ 330, the Court of Appeal held that a dismissal carried out in such a way as to avoid additional costs to the Trust of the employee attaining the age of 50 years before the end of his notice period, and thus being entitled to enhanced redundancy payments, was justified because the decision to terminate his employment by reason of redundancy was genuine and legitimate, and it was a part of that aim to ensure that the Trust also saved money through the timing of the notice given (the 'costs plus' approach). See too *Kapenova v Department of Health* (UKEAT/0142/13) where the Department of Health was able to rely on on a 'costs plus' justification on registration rules for trainee doctors (which operate to the disadvantage of medical students from some European countries).

(d)   In *Williams Drabble v Pathway Care Solutions Ltd and Another* (ET/2601718/04), the employment tribunal held that the employer had indirectly discriminated against a Christian employee when it imposed a requirement to work on Sundays. The employer had imposed a PCP on all staff, but it put practising Christians at a disadvantage and the employer was not able, on the facts, to show that the requirement to work on Sundays was a proportionate means of achieving a legitimate aim.

(e)   In *Azmi v Kirklees Metropolitan Borough Council* [2007] IRLR 484, the tribunal's finding was that refusing to permit a Muslim woman teacher to wear a full veil did not amount to indirect religious discrimination because the treatment was justified – the need to communicate effectively was a legitimate aim and was proportionate – the woman could wear a veil at all other times when not working directly with the children.

(f)   The ECtHR held in *Eweida & Others v UK* [2013] ECHR 37 that, while British Airways' wish to protect its image was legitimate, the policy interfered with Mrs Eweida's right to manifest her religion, and a fair balance was not struck by British Airways. Mrs Eweida's cross was discrete and did not encroach on others' interests. However, the ECtHR rejected complaints from three others (Mrs Chaplin – her cross interfered with health and safety and was therefore legitimately banned; Ms Ladele and Mr McFarlane's religious beliefs had to be balanced against competing Convention rights, and the Court allows a wide margin of appreciation when balancing competing rights).

(g)   In *Mayuuf v Governing Body of Bishop Challenor Catholic Collegiate School and Another* (ET/3202398/2004) (see <www.practicallaw.com/3-369-5996>), the claimant's beliefs required attendance at a mosque every Friday. The school required him to teach at that time (in 2003/04), and he brought a claim of indirect discrimination. The tribunal held that the school's actions were objectively justified, balancing the discriminatory effect on Mr Mayuuf against:

    (i)   declining standards in maths and the new arrangements in place;

    (ii)   the fact that all the Year 11 maths classes had to take place at the same time, so that pupils could be moved up or down between sets according to ability;

    (iii) the fact that it was impossible to rewrite the timetable to free the relevant period; and

    (iv)   the fact that providing a supply teacher would have affected the continuity of education and have been too costly.

(h)   In *Joseph Estorninho v Zoran Jokic t/a Zorans Delicatessen* (ET/2301487/06), the claimant was held to have been indirectly discriminated against when he was told that he would be required to work on Sundays. As a practising Catholic he attended church on a Sunday, and he was thereby placed at a 'particular disadvantage' compared with non-Catholics. Moreover, the employer had not considered other ways of arranging Sunday working, and thus had not adopted proportionate means.

(i)   In *Cherfi v G4S Security Services Ltd* (UKEAT/0379/10), the EAT upheld the tribunal's decision that a requirment that security guards be on site during the whole of their shift was a proportionate means of achieving a legitimate aim, in circumstances where the claimant had access to an on-site prayer facility and had been offered different shifts.

(j)   In *Mba v Mayor and Burgesses of the London Borough of Merton* (see **10.2.3** above), the Court of Appeal held that requiring all care workers at a children's home to work some Sundays in accordance with their contracts was objectively justified. Elias LJ pointed out in that case that the more widely shared the belief, the more difficult it will be for an employer to accommodate it.

(k)   In *Ypourgos Esoterikon and Another v Kalliri* (Case C-409/16), the ECJ held that the requirement for candidates for the Greek police academy to be at least 170cm tall amounted to indirect sex discrimination which could not be objectively justified. While ensuring operational capacity and proper functioning of the police force was a legitimate aim, maintaining a certain physical aptitude was not an appropriate way of achieving that aim.

10.3   BURDEN OF PROOF

The burden of proving objective justification is on the employer. The employer needs to produce cogent evidence that the justification defence is made out (see *British Airways v Starmer* [2005] IRLR 862 and *Osborne Clarke Services v Purohit* [2009] IRLR 341). However, the claimant has to show some evidence of disparate impact before the burden of proof is placed on the employer. The Court of Appeal held in *Bailey and Others v The Home Office* [2005] IRLR 369 that the tribunal had been entitled to conclude that there was a prima facie case of discrimination where the advantaged group was predominantly male but the disadvantaged group was mixed, containing both men and women. Waller LJ made clear the claimant's burden:

> [T]hus, where a difference in pay is established, and statistics seem to indicate a possibility of a disproportionate impact on women when looking at both the advantaged and disadvantaged groups as a whole, those statistics must provide sufficient evidence to get those carrying the burden over the hurdle of placing the onus on the employer ...

The Court of Appeal's judgment was given before a new definition of 'indirect discrimination' was brought into effect in October 2005 by the Employment Equality (Sex Discrimination) Regulations 2005. The definition in the Equality Act 2010 is identical. Commentators, at the time the new definition became law, queried *when* the burden of proof shifts in an indirect discrimination case. Taking the new definition into account, Claire Hockney of the EOC suggested that the burden of proof would transfer to the employer where the claimant could show:

(a)   the existence of a PCP; and

(b)   facts that 'indicate a possibility' that a particular group has been disadvantaged without the need to provide supporting statistics.

She said:

> [A]rguably, the intention of the legislation is that all the claimant is required to do is produce some evidence (even their own oral evidence) from which a tribunal could infer disparate impact. Once they do this the burden shifts to the respondent to show otherwise by cogent evidence.

A respondent could, at this stage, for example, put in evidence showing others are also at a disadvantage. This analysis still appears relevant today.

10.4 REMEDIES

See **8.8**. In a case of indirect discrimination, where the tribunal is satisfied there was no intent to discriminate, the tribunal must not award compensation without first considering whether to make a declaration or recommendation (s 124(4) and (5)).

SUMMARY

This chapter has looked at indirect discrimination in respect of the following protected characteristics listed in s 4 of the Equality Act 2010:

(a)   sex;

(b)   marriage and civil partnership;

(c)   pregnancy and maternity;

(d)   gender reassignment;

(e)   race;

(f)   religion or belief;

(g)   sexual orientation (**8.1**).

(Age and disability are dealt with in separate chapters.)

One of the four main types of discrimination in the employment field outlawed by UK legislation is indirect discrimination. Indirect discrimination occurs when there is equal treatment of all groups but the effect of a PCP imposed by an employer has a disproportionate adverse impact on one group, unless the requirement can be justified. The definition of indirect discrimination is set out in s 19 of the Equality Act 2010 (**10.2**).

Once a provision, etc has been established, the complaint must show that it is to the detriment of his group, ie it would put persons of the group at a particular disadvantage. The complainant must also suffer a disadvantage, so hypothetical cases cannot be brought (**10.2.3** and **10.2.4**). An employer has a defence to an indirect discrimination claim if he can show that the PCP is a 'proportionate means of achieving a legitimate aim' (**10.2.6**).

The burden of proving discrimination is a shifting one. The burden starts with the claimant. Once he has established sufficient facts that, in the absence of any other explanation, point to a breach, then the burden shifts to the employer. Section 136 provides that where a complainant can establish facts from which a tribunal could decide that there has been a contravention of a provision of the Equality Act 2010, the tribunal *must* find unlawful discrimination *unless* the employer shows it did not contravene the provision (**10.3** and **9.5**).

Remedies and enforcement are dealt with at **8.8**. Tribunals may, on making a finding of discrimination, as they consider just and equitable, make:

(a)   an order declaring the rights of the complainant;

(b)   an order requiring the respondent to pay to the complainant compensation; and/or

(c)   a recommendation that the respondent take, within a specified period, practicable action to obviate or reduce the adverse effect of any act of discrimination.

The general principle as far as compensation is concerned is that, as far as possible, complainants should be placed in the same position as they would have been but for the unlawful act (see *Ministry of Defence v Wheeler* [1998] IRLR 23). In addition to awarding compensation for foreseeable damage arising directly from the unlawful act, a tribunal has jurisdiction to award compensation for personal injury, including both physical and psychiatric injury, and for injury to feelings (**8.8.2.2**).

A flowchart summarising indirect discrimination is set out at **Figure 10.1**.

Figure 10.1 Flowchart – Indirect Discrimination

ELIGIBILITY
time limit – within 3 months of act of discrimination

UNLAWFUL ACT
discrimination in recruitment, promotion, dismissal, harassment, post-employment matters or subjecting a person to detriment

TYPE OF CLAIM
[NB some situations can give rise to more than one type of discrimination claim]

INDIRECT DISCRIMINATION
- Has R applied a PCP that applies equally to all?
- Does that PCP put persons of one group at a particular disadvantage compared to others? (group disadvantage required in religious belief cases?)
  – Particular disadvantage?
  – Pool of comparison required?
- Has C suffered a disadvantage?

POTENTIAL DEFENCE: JUSTIFICATION
Can R show that the PCP is a proportionate means of achieving a legitimate aim?

REMEDIES
- declaration of employee's rights
- recommendation that employer take action to alleviate or reduce the effect of the discrimination on the claimant
- order for compensation (no maximum)
  – pecuniary losses
  – aggravated damages if employer has behaved in a high-handed, malicious, insulting or aggressive manner
  – injury to feelings (*Vento/Da'Bell*)
  – psychiatric or physical injury
  – possibility of exemplary damages
  – increase/decrease for any unreasonable failure to comply with the Acas Code of Practice

HARASSMENT AND VICTIMISATION

> **LEARNING OUTCOMES**
>
> After reading this chapter you will be able to:
>
> - explain what is meant by harassment and what the different types of harassment are
> - explain when employers are liable for the acts of third parties
> - explain what is meant by victimisation
> - list the potential remedies that are available where a complaint of harassment or victimisation is made out.

11.1 INTRODUCTION

This chapter considers harassment and victimisation in respect of the following protected characteristics listed in s 4 of the Equality Act 2010 (see **8.2.1**):

- gender reassignment (s 7)
- race (s 9)
- religion or belief (s 10)
- sex (s 11)
- sexual orientation (s 12).

Section 26 (harassment) does not include marriage and civil partnership, or pregnancy and maternity: this is because pregnancy and maternity are covered by harassment related to sex, and as there is no evidence that people have been harassed due to marriage and civil partnership, it was not considered necessary to include these characteristics. These grounds are not covered by European law. One view is that harassment relating to those matters may be brought under s 13 as direct discrimination; another view is that as s 26 does not specifically disapply those protected characteristics, they are still included.

This chapter refers, by way of illustration and example, to the pre- and post-Equality Act 2010 case law.

11.2 BURDEN OF PROOF

The reversed burden of proof applies in both harassment and victimisation cases (s 136). Thus, where a prima facie case of harassment or victimisation is made out by a claimant, the tribunal will be required to find for the claimant unless the defendant can prove that his or her conduct was not unlawful (see **9.5** and **10.3**).

11.3 HARASSMENT

11.3.1 Definition

The definition of harassment is set out in s 26 of the Act.:

> (1)   A person (A) harasses another (B) if—
>
> > (a)   A engages in unwanted conduct related to a relevant protected characteristic, and
> >
> > (b)   the conduct has the purpose or effect of—
> >
> > > (i)   violating B's dignity, or
> > >
> > > (ii)   creating an intimidating, hostile, degrading, humiliating or offensive environment for B.
>
> (2)   A also harasses B if—
>
> > (a)   A engages in unwanted conduct of a sexual nature, and
> >
> > (b)   the conduct has the purpose or effect referred to in subsection (1)(b).
>
> (3)   A also harasses B if—
>
> > (a)   A or another person engages in unwanted conduct of a sexual nature or that is related to gender reassignment or sex,
> >
> > (b)   the conduct has the purpose or effect referred to in subsection (1)(b), and
> >
> > (c)   because of B's rejection of or submission to the conduct, A treats B less favourably than A would treat B if B had not rejected or submitted to the conduct.
>
> (4)   In deciding whether conduct has the effect referred to in subsection (1)(b), each of the following must be taken into account—
>
> > (a)   the perception of B;
> >
> > (b)   the other circumstances of the case;
> >
> > (c)   whether it is reasonable for the conduct to have that effect.
>
> ...

As with direct discrimination, s 26 prohibits harassment based on association and perception; to bring a claim, a victim of harassment does not have to possess the 'protected characteristic' himself: '... A engages in unwanted conduct *related to* a relevant protected characteristic' (s 26(1)(a)) (emphasis added).

Note that under the law, where the complaint is about harassment, the complainant cannot also claim direct discrimination, because 'detriment' does not include subjecting a person to harassment: see the definition of 'detriment' in s 212(1) of the Act: '"detriment" does not, subject to subsection (5), include conduct which amounts to harassment'.

There are three different types of harassment:

(a)   'Characteristic-related harassment' applies to all the protected characteristics listed in **11.1** above. It involves unwanted conduct which is related to a relevant characteristic and has the purpose or effect of creating an intimidating, hostile, degrading, humiliating or offensive environment for the complainant, or violating the complainant's dignity.

(b)   Sexual harassment is unwanted conduct of a sexual nature, where this has the purpose or effect of creating an intimidating, hostile, degrading, humiliating or offensive environment for the complainant, or violating the complainant's dignity.

(c)   The third type of harassment is treating someone less favourably because that person has either submitted to or rejected sexual harassment, or harassment related to sex or gender reassignment which had the purpose or effect of creating an intimidating, hostile, degrading, humiliating or offensive environment for the complainant, or violating the complainant's dignity.

Each will be dealt with in more detail below.

The EAT confirmed in *Timothy James Consulting Ltd v Wilton* (UKEAT/0082/14) that a resignation that amounts to a constructive dismissal does not of itself fall within the meaning of 'harassment', because s 26 of the Equality Act 2010 makes no reference to dismissal (cf s 39 of the Equality Act 2010 at **8.4.2**); it simply provides that employers must not harass employees and job applicants. However, prior acts which give rise to the constructive dismissal can be relied upon, and an actual dismissal can amount to something done 'in relation to employment' and therefore amount to harassment (see *Urso v Department for Work and Pensions* (UKEAT/0045/16)).

11.3.2 Characteristic-related harassment

European Union law defines harassment (Equal Treatment Directive (Recast) 2006/54) as:

> where unwanted conduct related to the [sex, etc] of a person occurs with the purpose or effect of violating the dignity of a person, and of creating an intimidating, hostile, degrading, humiliating or offensive environment.

To be unlawful under the old law, harassment had to be 'on the ground' of sex, etc. In *Equal Opportunities Commission v Secretary of State for Trade and Industry* [2007] IRLR 327, the EOC successfully challenged the UK legislation (in so far as it dealt with harassment in sex cases) in judicial review proceedings. The EOC submitted that the use of the words 'on the ground of' in SDA 1975, s 4A imported causation into the Act, requiring an investigation of the reason for the conduct complained of, whereas the Directive, by referring to conduct 'related to' the sex, etc of a person, defined harassment by association with sex, etc. The High Court held:

> [T]he use of the words 'on the ground of her sex' impermissibly imports causation – the reason why issue – into the concept of harassment. There can be conduct which is related to sex, but not of a sexual nature, which has the effect of creating an offensive working environment for a woman ... That would not fall within [the law] on a straightforward reading, as it would not be conduct on the ground of the woman's sex.

The law was amended in 2008 where the characteristic was sex, which meant that there were different definitions depending on the characteristic in question.

The Equality Act 2010 follows through that change in respect of all the protected characteristics in **11.1**: harassment no longer needs to be 'on the grounds' of but rather 'related to' a protected characteristic. The view is therefore that causation is no longer relevant, and that no comparator is needed. This means that an employer can no longer rely on the *Brumfitt* type defence by arguing that its conduct was not discriminatory because it treated everyone alike (in *Brumfitt v MOD* [2005] IRLR 4 (a case decided under the old test), the complainant lost her case because the obscene language used by the alleged harasser was directed at both men and women).

The courts have encouraged a three-stage approach (see *Richmond Pharmacology v Dhaliwal* [2009] ICR 724 and *Bakkali v Greater Manchester Buses (South) Ltd t/a Stage Coach Manchester* (UKEAT/0176/17):

(1)   Did the respondent engage in unwanted conduct?

(2)   Did the conduct in question either:

    (a)   have the *purpose* or

    (b)   have the *effect* of either (i) violating the claimant's dignity or (ii) creating an adverse environment for her ('the proscribed consequences')?

(3)   Was the unwanted conduct related to a relevant protected characteristic?

The Explanatory Memorandum to the 2008 amendments gave an example which is still useful: where male colleagues dislike a female colleague and decide to put the office equipment on a high shelf to make it hard for her to reach it, the old definition would not help as the men are acting out of dislike rather than because their colleague is a woman, ie not on the 'ground of her sex'; under the new definition such conduct might be actionable because it is 'related to sex', ie woman are on average shorter than men.

It is not necessary to have the protected characteristic in order to be covered by the protection. In *English v Thomas Sanderson Blinds Ltd* [2008] IRLR 342, Mr English complained about homosexual banter directed at him. He was not a homosexual and his colleagues knew this. He found the banter degrading and offensive. The Court of Appeal concluded that he had been harassed within the definition: although the banter was not based on a perception or assumption that he was homosexual, it was enough that Mr English was taunted as if he were gay. The banter created a degrading and hostile working environment, on the grounds of sexual orientation.

The law also covers a person who is a witness to harassment. The Explanatory Notes provide an example:

- A white worker who sees a black colleague being subjected to racially abusive language could have a case of harassment if the language also causes an offensive environment for her.

11.3.3   Sexual harassment

Sexual harassment encompasses any conduct of a sexual nature which has the purpose or effect of violating a person's dignity or of creating an intimidating, hostile, degrading, humiliating or offensive environment. Conduct of a sexual nature is not defined in the Act. The example given by the EHRC is unwelcome sexual advances – touching, standing too close, the displaying of offensive pictures.

The Explanatory Notes provide an example:

- An employer who displayed any material of a sexual nature, such as a topless calendar, may be harassing her employees where this makes the workplace an offensive place to work for any employee, female or male.

In August 2016, the Trades Union Congress (TUC) published a Report, 'Still just a bit of banter?'. See the Introduction for more details, but key findings included that more than half (52%) of all the women polled have experienced some form of sexual harassment, 28% of women have been subject to comments of a sexual nature about their body or clothes, and nearly one-quarter of women have experienced unwanted touching (such as a hand on the knee or lower back).

11.3.4   Less favourable treatment

An employer may also be liable where there is less favourable treatment of a person by reason of that person's submission to or rejection of sex- or gender reassignment-related harassment or sexual harassment which had the purpose or effect of violating that person's dignity or of creating an intimidating, hostile, degrading, humiliating or offensive environment.

The Explanatory Notes provide an example:

- A shopkeeper propositions one of his shop assistants. She rejects his advances and then is turned down for promotion which she believes she would have got if she had accepted her boss's advances. The shop assistant would have a claim of harassment.

11.3.5   'Purpose or effect ...'

All three types of harassment require that the conduct has the purpose or effect of (s 26(1) – see **11.3.1**):

    (i)   violating B's dignity, or

    (ii)   creating an intimidating, hostile, degrading, humiliating or offensive environment for B.

If the conduct was intended to have the effect of violating dignity or creating a hostile, etc environment, it amounts to harassment whatever the actual effect. If there is no such intent then the conduct may be treated as having the effect of violating dignity or creating a hostile, etc environment only if 'it should reasonably be considered as having that effect'; as part of that assessment, the victim's perspective is a relevant circumstance to take into account (s 26(4)). It is therefore for the tribunal to decide, based on the evidence, whether the effect of the conduct was to create a hostile, etc working environment.

In *Richmond Pharmacology v Dhaliwal* [2009] IRLR 336, the EAT noted that the fact that, at least in some cases, there will be substantial overlaps between the questions that arise in relation to each element (eg, the question whether the conduct complained of was 'unwanted' will overlap with the question of whether it creates an adverse environment for the employee) and between the two defined proscribed consequences (many or most acts which are found to create an adverse environment for an employee will also violate her dignity). The EAT went on to state that

> 14. ... an employer may be held liable on the basis that the effect of his conduct has been to produce the proscribed consequences even if that was not his purpose; and, conversely, that he may be liable if he acted for the purposes of producing the proscribed consequences but did not in fact do so (or in any event has not been shown to have done so). ... In most cases the primary focus will be on the effect of the unwanted conduct rather than on the employer's purpose ... .

> 15. ... A respondent should not be held liable merely because his conduct has had the effect of producing a proscribed consequence: it should be reasonable that that consequence has occurred. That ... creates an objective standard. The proscribed consequences are, of their nature, concerned with the feelings of the putative victim: that is, the victim must have felt, or perceived, her dignity to have been violated or an adverse environment to have been created. That can, if you like, be described as introducing a 'subjective' element; but overall the criterion is objective because what the tribunal is required to consider is whether, if the claimant has experienced those feelings or perceptions, it was reasonable for her to do so. Thus if, for example, the tribunal believes that the claimant was unreasonably prone to take offence, then, even if she did genuinely feel her dignity to have been violated, there will have been no harassment within the meaning of the section. Whether it was reasonable for a claimant to have felt her dignity to have been violated is quintessentially a matter for the factual assessment of the tribunal. It will be important for it to have regard to all the relevant circumstances, including the context of the conduct in question. One question that may be material is whether it should reasonably have been apparent whether the conduct was, or was not, intended to cause offence (or, more precisely, to produce the proscribed consequences): the same remark may have a very different weight if it was evidently innocently intended than if it was evidently intended to hurt.

In *Pemberton v Inwood* [2018] EWCA Civ 564, Underhill LJ revised his guidance in para 15 above. He noted that under the predecessor law, 'Conduct shall be regarded as having the effect [of violating that other person's dignity, or creating an intimidating, hostile, degrading, humiliating or offensive environment for him] only if, having regard to all the circumstances, including in particular the perception of that other person, it should reasonably be considered as having that effect', so that it was a requirement of liability that it was reasonable that the conduct should have the effect in question. However, under s 26 (above), perception, circumstances and reasonableness are now expressed as matters to be taken into account in deciding whether the effect has occurred. He did not believe that the difference in the structure of the successor provision was intended to make any substantive difference, but he amended the guidance as follows:

> In order to decide whether any conduct falling within sub-paragraph (1)(a) has either of the proscribed effects under sub-paragraph (1)(b), a tribunal must consider both (by reason of sub-section (4)(a)) whether the putative victim perceives themselves to have suffered the effect in question (the subjective question) and (by reason of sub-section (4)(c)) whether it was reasonable for the conduct to be regarded as having that effect (the objective question). It must also, of course, take into account all the other circumstances – sub-section (4)(b). The relevance of the subjective question is that if the claimant does not perceive their dignity to have been violated, or an adverse environment created, then

the conduct should not be found to have had that effect. The relevance of the objective question is that if it was not reasonable for the conduct to be regarded as violating the claimant's dignity or creating an adverse environment for him or her, then it should not be found to have done so.

In *Thomas Sanderson Blinds Ltd v English* (UKEAT/0316/10), the EAT held that a heterosexual employee who was subject to homophobic banter was not harassed because the banter did not have the effect of violating his dignity or creating a hostile etc environment – on the facts he had remained friends with his tormentors and had not complained.

In *Weeks v Newham College of Further Education* (UKEAT/0630/11), the EAT held that the word 'environment' is a 'state of affairs', which may be created by one incident if the effects are of longer duration.

In *Heathfield v Times Newspapers Ltd* (UKEAT/1305/12), the EAT upheld the tribunal's decision that offence caused by reference to 'the f***ing Pope' did not amount to harassment because, to the extent the claimant felt his dignity had been violated or a hostile environment created, that was not a reasonable reaction in the context of the case facts.

In *Betsi Cadwaladr University Health Board v Hughes and Others* (UKEAT/0179/13), a loss of status was held to amount to harassment related to the claimant's disability.

11.4 REMEDIES FOR HARASSMENT

See **8.8**. The main remedy is compensation, although tribunals can also make declarations and recommendations. In the recent case of *AA Solicitors v Majid* (EAT/0217/15), the EAT (noting the contrary decision in *De Souza* which was pending appeal) confirmed that the 10% uplift to general damages introduced in *Simmons v Castle* applied to injury to feelings. It also added that employment tribunals should be entitled to take the effect of inflation into account when assessing damages going forward. The claimant won her claim of sexual harassment and was awarded £14,000 for injury to feelings amongst other awards, based on the middle *Vento* band. The respondent, while accepting that the award was within the correct band, appealed, arguing that the award was excessive (the claimant had been dismissed after six weeks in her job; she cited about 40 acts of sexual harassment including asking her out, touching, and attempting to hug her; the respondent said that this was a case merely of persistent unwanted attentions but without serious physical contact, that was no worse than gauche and insinuating). The EAT dismissed the appeal. The claimant's dignity as a worker had been violated and she had been subject to humiliation. The award was not, in the EAT's judgment, 'manifestly excessive'.

There is no legal limit on the amount of compensation that can be awarded. While the *Vento* bands (see **8.8.2.2**) set limits for injury to feelings, there is no limit on other awards, such as for loss of earnings. In *Lokhova v Sberbank CIB (UK) Ltd* (2015), an employment tribunal awarded an employee nearly £3.2 million for sexual harassment, of which £44,000 was awarded for injury to feelings and £15,000 for aggravated damages; the remainder consisted of compensation for future loss of earnings for the claimant (who had earned £750,000 a year in salary and bonuses, but who the tribunal found 'will never work in financial services again, on the basis of the medical evidence').

11.5 EMPLOYERS' LIABILITY FOR THE ACTS OF EMPLOYEES

Readers are reminded of the principle of vicarious liability, and should refer to **8.6** above.

11.6 EMPLOYERS' LIABILITY FOR THE ACTS OF THIRD PARTIES

Employers could, until 2003, be liable for the acts of a person who was not an employee. In *Burton and Another v De Vere Hotels* [1996] IRLR 596, the applicants were employed as casual waitresses at one of the respondent's hotels, working at a dinner organised by the City of Derby Round Table. The stand-up comedian Bernard Manning had been booked as the guest speaker.

The two women were working in the banqueting hall where Mr Manning was speaking. He used words such as 'wog', 'nigger' and 'sambo', and said that 'darkies were good at giving blow jobs'. The applicants brought claims under the RRA 1976. The tribunal held that the respondent was not liable because it was not the respondent that had subjected the applicants to the racial harassment. The EAT held the respondent liable. The EAT said that an employer subjects an employee to racial harassment if he causes or permits racial harassment to occur in circumstances which he can control, whether it happens or not, and where an application of good employment practice would prevent or reduce the harassment. In the present case, it would have been good employment practice for the manager to warn his assistants to keep a look out for Mr Manning, and to withdraw the waitresses if things became unpleasant.

However, in *Macdonald v Advocate General for Scotland; Pearce v Governing Body of Mayfield Secondary School* [2003] IRLR 512, the House of Lords disapproved of the decision in *Burton*. Their Lordships stated that whilst an employer's failure to prevent third parties committing acts of sexual/racial harassment might amount to discrimination by the employer, it would do so only if the employer failed to take such steps *because* of the employee's sex/race.

In *EOC v Secretary of State for Trade and Industry* (**11.3.2** above), the High Court agreed with the EOC that the law needed to be re-cast so as to facilitate claims that an employer subjected an employee to harassment by knowingly failing to protect that employee from repetitive harassment by a third party, such as a supplier or customer. The High Court said that

> [s]o long as [the law] is framed in terms of unwanted conduct engaged in on the ground of a woman's sex by the employer, it is difficult to see how an employer could be held liable for the knowing failure to take steps to prevent harassment by others, since such knowing failure would have to amount to unwanted conduct by the employer on the ground of her sex.

Section 40 of the 2010 Act was aimed at dealing with this issue of protecting employees against persistent harassment by third parties (on at least two occasions). However, following a Government consultation in 2012, s 40 was repealed with effect from 1 October 2013 by s 65 of the ERRA 2013, because it was deemed unworkable. It is still open to employees to argue that an employer's failure to act in such circumstances amounts to unwanted conduct by the employer, relying on s 26 of the 2010 Act (see **11.3** above), as long as the tribunal is satisfied that the reason for the failure to act was 'related to' a protected characteristic. That should be easier to demonstrate than showing that the inaction is 'because of' the protected characteristic, but time will tell.

11.7 PROTECTION FROM HARASSMENT ACT 1997

Additionally, an employee may be able to bring a claim under the Protection from Harassment Act 1997. This allows for victims of harassment to claim damages and/or injunctive relief in the civil courts and to prosecute in the criminal courts. To bring a claim under the 1997 Act, it is not necessary to show that the harassment was done on any particular prohibited ground or basis. Harassment is not defined in the Act, but it includes 'alarming [a]person or causing a person distress'. The Act prohibits a course of conduct (defined as at least two occasions of harassment) that amounts to harassment, or which a person knows, or ought to know, amounts to harassment. There is no statutory defence available to an employer under the Act, which enables victims of harassment in the workplace to pursue claims against their employer through the civil courts (through the principle of vicarious liability) and/or through the employment tribunal (see *Majrowski v Guy's and St Thomas's NHS Trust* [2005] IRLR 340, CA (upheld by the House of Lords [2006] UKHL 34) and *Banks v Ablex Ltd* [2005] IRLR 357 for two decisions in this area).

Claims under the 1997 Act have a number of advantages over other more traditional 'employment' routes such as discrimination or unfair dismissal. The provisions will apply to workers as well as to employees. Unlike an unfair dismissal claim, compensation for injury to feelings can be recovered as well as loss of earnings. Claims under the 1997 Act can be brought in the courts, so there is no three-month limitation on bringing the claim. However, the realisation that the Act might give rise to claims for damages for what might be viewed as relatively trivial acts of harassment, led the Court of Appeal to re-examine what amounted to harassment under the Act. In *Conn v Sunderland City Council* [2007] EWCA Civ 1492, the trial judge found that two incidents involving verbal threats amounted to harassment under the Act and awarded a small sum by way of damages. The Court of Appeal made it clear that 'bad-mannered' behaviour should not give rise to criminal penalties or a civil claim for damages. It held that for the Protection from Harassment Act to be engaged, harassment had to amount to conduct that is, viewed objectively, likely to cause distress to the victim and is unacceptable and oppressive, and probably criminal. There must be two or more incidents which are each sufficiently serious.

However, see now *Veakins v Kier Islington Ltd* [2009] EWCA Civ 1288, where the Court of Appeal provided guidance on the sort of conduct that would be needed before an employee could successfully bring a claim under the Protection from Harassment Act 1997. In the leading judgment given by Maurice Kay LJ, the Court emphasised that

> since *Majrowski*, courts have been enjoined to consider whether the conduct complained of is 'oppressive and unacceptable' as opposed to merely unattractive, unreasonable or regrettable. The primary focus is on whether the conduct is 'oppressive and unacceptable' albeit that the court must keep in mind that it must be of an order which 'would sustain criminal liability'.

One of the perceived limitations on a claim under the Protection from Harassment Act was the requirement for harassment to arise out of a course of conduct, ie conduct occurring on at least two occasions. However, the provisions implemented by the Act now import a similar requirement into claims of third party harassment.

11.8 CASE STUDY: HARASSMENT

Facts

(1)   R1 is the operator of an adventure park. R2 is an employee of R1. He is the operations manager of R1, and was the line manager of C, who was a member of his operations team. C had been in post for nine months. On a previous occasion, another member of the operations team, 'F', complained informally to 'S' (the managing director of R1) about R2's conduct towards her, following which she then submitted a formal grievance in writing. C says she had a number of informal conversations with R2, making him aware that she was uncomfortable with his engaging her in conversations of an explicit sexual nature and/or making sexual innuendos. R2 says that staff accepted a level of ribald language and that swearing was common amongst all staff.

(2)   Following one particular incident when R2 made further remarks that C regarded as lewd, C sent R1 a letter giving one month's notice of her intention to resign. In this letter she said she had recently 'found working conditions intolerable due to your apparent disregard for the welfare of staff and your resultant failure to appropriately address or bring about a satisfactory conclusion regarding my concerns about R2 and the sexist and abusive behaviour others females and I have repeatedly endured'. She enclosed a copy of a diary she had been keeping, which she said contained examples of R2's behaviour. R1 did not take her complaint seriously and did nothing about it. C subsequently left.

(3)   C issued a claim form to the employment tribunal.

Claims

(4)   C complained of harassment under s 26(1) and (2) and of direct discrimination because of sex under s 13.

(5)   C claimed against R1 and R2.

(6) She indicated on the claim form that she only wanted compensation.

(7) R1 and R2 did not admit that the alleged incidents of discrimination relied upon by C took place, and denied that any incidents that did take place were acts of discrimination.

Evidence

(8) Disclosure took place in the usual way, and paginated bundles were prepared which included extracts from C's personal file, extracts from the staff handbook on *Grievances and Appeals*, papers relating to previous complaints and a Schedule of Loss from C setting out her claim for compensation.

(9) Witness statements were exchanged prior to the hearing.

(10) At the hearing all witnesses who gave oral evidence were cross-examined and the tribunal had the opportunity to ask questions of them. On C's behalf, oral evidence at the hearing was given by C and F. C also submitted witness statements from a number of former employees who did not appear to give evidence. As their evidence could not be tested by cross-examination, the tribunal gave their testimony less weight evidentially. For R1 and R2, oral evidence was given by R2, S, T, and W (a junior manager).

(11) At the conclusion of the evidence, both sides made oral submissions on liability and remedy.

(12) All these matters were taken into consideration by the tribunal before reaching its decision.

The issues to be decided

(13) C complained of both characteristic (sex)-related harassment and sexual harassment and direct sex discrimination. Where R1's conduct was directed at other female staff, it was characteristic-related harassment. R1 does not admit that the alleged incidents took place, and denies that any incidents that did take place were acts of harassment. The tribunal will need to determine:

  13.1 whether R2 subjected C to harassment either by way of conduct of a sexual nature directed at her, or by way of conduct directed at other female staff;

  13.2 whether R1 was responsible for any such harassment.

  13.3 The direct discrimination claims related to the way R1 responded to C's complaints about R2 and to the act of C's resignation.

(14) Depending on the outcome of the matters, the tribunal will have to determine what amount of compensation, if any, should be awarded.

Tribunal findings

(15) The unanimous decision of the tribunal is that:

  15.1 R1 and R2 unlawfully discriminated against C;

  15.2 R1 and R2 are to pay C £7,419.77 by way of compensation.

Reasons

Harassment claim

(16) The tribunal took account of s 136 of the Equality Act 2010 on the burden of proof. It noted that in *Igen v Wong* [2005] IRLR 258 (a race discrimination case determined under pre-Equality Act 2010 legislation), subject to one amendment, the Court of Appeal upheld the guidance given by the EAT in a sex discrimination case, *Barton v Investec Securities Ltd* [2003] ICR 1205, in particular, to summarise that guidance, that it is for the claimant who complains of sex discrimination to prove on the balance of probabilities facts from which the tribunal could conclude, in the absence of an adequate explanation, that the employer has committed an unlawful act of discrimination against

the claimant. Where the claimant proves facts from which inferences could be drawn that the employer has treated the applicant less favourably on the grounds of sex, then the burden of proof moves to the employer. It is then for the employer to prove that he did not commit, or, as the case may be, is not to be treated as having committed, that act. To discharge that burden it is necessary for the employer to prove, on the balance of probabilities, that the treatment was 'in no sense whatsoever on the grounds of sex', since 'no discrimination whatsoever' is compatible with the Burden of Proof Directive 97/80. That requires a tribunal to assess not merely whether the employer has proved an explanation for the facts from which such inferences can be drawn, but further that it is adequate to discharge the burden of proof on the balance of probabilities that sex was not a ground for the treatment in question. The tribunal also noted the decision of the Court of Appeal in *Madarassy v Nomura International plc* [2007] EWCA Civ 33, which emphasised that the court in *Igen* expressly rejected the argument that it was sufficient for the complainant simply to prove facts from which the tribunal could conclude that the respondent 'could have committed an unlawful act of discrimination'. It held that the bare facts of a difference in status and a difference in treatment only indicate a possibility of discrimination. 'They are not, without more, sufficient material from which a tribunal "could conclude" that, on the balance of probabilities, the respondent had committed an unlawful act of discrimination'.

(17)   The tribunal also considered the definition of harassment set out in s 26(1) and (2) of the Equality Act 2010. It noted that both types of harassment required that the conduct complained of had the purpose or effect of violating C's dignity or creating an intimidating, hostile, degrading or humiliating or offensive environment for C. It noted the case of *Reid and Bull Information Systems Ltd v Stedman* [1999] IRLR 299 (a pre-Equality Act 2010 case but one which it considered remained relevant on overall approach). It noted that in *Wileman v Minilec Engineering Ltd* [1988] IRLR 144, the EAT acknowledged that a person may be happy to accept the remarks of A or B in a sexual context and be wholly upset by similar remarks made by C; and that in *Driskel v Peninsula Business Services Ltd* [2000] IRLR 151, the EAT had held that a tribunal should not lose sight of the significance of the sex of both the complainant and the alleged discriminator. Sexual badinage with a heterosexual male by another man could not be completely equated with like badinage by him with a woman.

Tribunal's findings

Workplace culture

(18)   The tribunal found from the evidence of a number of witnesses that general ribald banter and mickey-taking was common in the workplace, and that there was a lot of sexual banter and swearing. It was not a 'cloistered' environment. There was also girly gossip about sex. R2 struggled with the 'overly emotional' reaction of some of the young women to his remarks, which left him bewildered. The tribunal noted that C was open in discussion about her relationship with her boyfriend. Overall it found C was uncomfortable with R2's conversations and behaviour, and R2 knew this but persisted with his conduct. This was backed up by the diary that C kept. The tribunal held that even in an environment where it was accepted that bad language was commonplace, the continued use of this sort of language when objection has been taken to it, particularly when it is used by a more senior manager to his junior staff, was not acceptable conduct. The tribunal found therefore that harassment was made out under s 26(2) but not under s 26(1). The tribunal did not believe that any of R2's language or behaviour was directed specifically at C because of her sex.

(19)   It held S did not do enough to set standards for his staff about this. Neither did he really take it seriously. It found there was a stark contrast between the way he treated C and the way he responded to a previous complaint about another member of staff. The tribunal

found that the different treatment was not, however, because of C's sex; it stemmed from the fact that S was not willing to tolerate any criticism of R2 because he considered him a valuable asset. The tribunal was not satisfied that this treatment fell within the definition of direct discrimination.

(20) On balance, the tribunal found that the comments made by R2 did amount to sexual harassment – his intention was irrelevant. It also found that given that C's resignation was caused principally by R2's remarks and S's failure to take her concerns seriously, those actions amounted to less favourable treatment because of her sex. An employer is vicariously liable for the acts of employees carried out within the course of their employment. R2 carried out these acts of harassment during the course of his employment. R1 had not sought to avail itself of the 'reasonably practicable steps' defence in s 109 of the Equality Act 2010. On that basis, the tribunal found R1 was liable for the acts of R2 and the omissions of S.

Remedies

(21) Section 124 of the Equality Act 2010 sets out the remedies available on a finding of discrimination. The general principle as far as compensation is concerned is that, as far as possible, complainants should be placed in the same position as they would have been but for the unlawful act (see *Ministry of Defence v Wheeler* [1998] IRLR 23). Another way of looking at it is to ask what loss has been caused by the discrimination in question. It is important to remember that the loss must be caused by the discrimination and, secondly, that the loss must not be too remote a consequence of the discrimination. In *Skyrail Oceanic Ltd v Coleman* [1981] ICR 864 (a pre-Equality Act 2010 sex discrimination claim), Lawton LJ explained this by saying that, 'Compensation is to be awarded for foreseeable damage arising directly from an unlawful act of discrimination'. Compensation for unlawful discrimination falls under two heads: financial loss, and non-financial loss. Financial loss covers matters such as loss of earnings, both past and future; while non-financial loss covers matters such as injury to feelings. In addition to awarding compensation for foreseeable damage arising directly from the unlawful act, an employment tribunal has jurisdiction to award compensation by way of damages for injury to feeling and personal injury, including both physical and psychiatric injury, caused by the unlawful discrimination. Where compensation is assessed under the discrimination regime, the Employment Protection (Recoupment of Jobseeker's Allowance and Income Support) Regulations 1996 do not apply.

(22) Principles relating to compensatory awards for injury to feelings for unlawful discrimination are set out in *Armitage and HM Prison Service v Johnson* [1997] IRLR 162, *Vento v Chief Constable of West Yorkshire Police* [2003] IRLR 102 and *Da'Bell v NSPCC* (UKEAT/ 0227/09). *Da'Bell* set out new guideline figures which the tribunal inserted into the *Vento* guidance. In *Vento* (original figures now adjusted for inflation and for the 10% uplift in general damages (which took effect from 1 April 2013) and which the EAT confirmed in *Cadogan Hotel Partners Ltd v Ozog* (UKEAT/0001/14) applies to injury to feelings awards in discrimination cases – see *Simmons v Castle* [2012] EWCA Civ 1039 – but see now **8.8.2.2**), the Court of Appeal observed that there were three broad bands of compensation for injury to feelings, as distinct from compensation for psychiatric or similar personal injury: (1) The top band should normally be between £19,800 and £33,000. Sums in this range should be awarded in the most serious cases, such as where there has been a lengthy campaign of discriminatory harassment on the ground of sex or race. Only in the most exceptional case should an award of compensation for injury to feelings exceed £33,000. (2) The middle band of between £6,600 and £19,800 should be used for serious cases which do not merit an award in the highest band. (3) Awards of between £660 and £6,600 are appropriate for less serious cases, such as where the act of discrimination is an isolated one or a one-off occurrence. Defining injury to feelings is

more a broadbrush exercise of estimation than of calculation, comparison with precedents or cold logic.

(23) Since the Court of Appeal's ruling in *Sheriff v Klyne Tugs (Lowestoft) Ltd* [1999] ICR 1170 (a race discrimination case), tribunals have jurisdiction to award compensation for personal injury arising out of unlawful sex, race or disability discrimination. This includes compensation for psychiatric illness. In *HM Prison Service v Salmon* [2001] IRLR 425, the EAT considered the possibility of overlap and double recovery where a tribunal awards separate sums for psychiatric damage and injury to feelings. The EAT accepted that injury to feelings can cover a wide range of injury, from minor upset to serious and prolonged feelings of humiliation and depression, and that in practice psychiatric damage may be compensated under this heading. It also accepted that there was a risk of double recovery where separate awards were made, and stated that tribunals should be aware of the risk.

(24) In *Snowball v Gardner Merchant Ltd* [1987] IRLR 397, the EAT said that evidence as to the complainant's attitude to matters of sexual behaviour was relevant and admissible for the purpose of determining the degree of injury to feelings that the complainant suffered as a result of sexual harassment. Compensation for sexual harassment must relate to the degree of detriment, and evidence as to whether she had talked freely to fellow employees about her attitude to sexual matters was relevant for determining whether the claimant was unlikely to be very upset by a degree of familiarity with a sexual connotation, so as to challenge the alleged detriment suffered and any hurt feelings

Tribunal's findings

(25) C had less than one year's continuous service. A sensible average weekly figure for her wages was £173.41. This was agreed by the parties. C did not have a job to go to when she resigned. She obtained some part-time work over the Christmas period. She later went full-time. That work is on-going. She set out in her Schedule of Loss the details of these earnings. In her current job she was getting paid more than she had earned with R1 (approx £202.00 per week). C said she was depressed as a result of her treatment. She referred to her GP's notes, indicating that she was struggling with money problems and had headaches, and continued to suffer anxiety and headaches. However, she was now working a 40-hour week without any sickness problems.

(26) The tribunal can make separate awards against R1 or R2. It is common in such cases to make a larger award against the employer and a smaller award against the individual harasser. The tribunal can also make one award and make both parties jointly and severally liable for that award. When making joint and several awards, tribunals must apportion the respective shares, so that if a claimant chooses to enforce only against one respondent, that respondent can still seek a suitable contribution from the other respondent. Any such apportionment should be on the basis of respectively culpability. The tribunal in this case made only one award. While R2 was the perpetrator, S's attitude was primarily responsible for what happened in allowing R2 to continue with his objectionable conduct. The tribunal concluded that S (and therefore R1) was substantially culpable for what happened. The tribunal apportioned blame on the basis of 20% to R2 and 80% to R1.

(27) *Compensatory element.* By the date of the hearing, taking account of C's actual earnings over the period against what she would have earned, her actual losses were £1,419.77. There were no future losses continuing to accrue.

(28) In terms of an award for *injury to feelings*, the tribunal felt that this case fell towards the top of the lower *Vento* band, in that it had not found there was any deliberate or ongoing campaign against C, but this was not just one isolated incident; a number of lewd remarks were made, which occurred as a result of a careless disregard for C's

sensitivities once they had been made known. Judging from the medical evidence, there were no lasting effects suffered by C. In the circumstances, the tribunal made an award, inclusive of interest, of £6,000 for injury to feelings.

(29) Accordingly, the tribunal found that the respondents were to pay C a total sum of £7,419.77. The Recoupment Regulations do not apply to this award.

11.9 VICTIMISATION

The victimisation provisions aim to give protection to workers who bring complaints of discrimination or other proceedings aimed at enforcing compliance with equal treatment principles.

11.9.1 Definition

The definition of victimisation is set out in s 27 of the Act:

(1) A person (A) victimises another person (B) if A subjects B to a detriment because—

    (a) B does a protected act, or

    (b) A believes that B has done, or may do, a protected act.

(2) Each of the following is a protected act—

    (a) bringing proceedings under this Act;

    (b) giving evidence or information in connection with proceedings under this Act;

    (c) doing any other thing for the purposes of or in connection with this Act;

    (d) making an allegation (whether or not express) that A or another person has contravened this Act.

(3) Giving false evidence or information, or making a false allegation, is not a protected act if the evidence or information is given, or the allegation is made, in bad faith.

...

The Explanatory Notes make it clear that the Act changes the old law, in that there is no longer a requirement for the tribunal to construct a comparator. However, a comparison of the claimant's treatment with that of an appropriate comparator will often be an effective way of establishing the reason for the treatment. Was the treatment *because* the claimant had done a protected act?

The Explanatory Notes give examples:

- A woman makes a complaint of sex discrimination against her employer. As a result, she is denied promotion. The denial of promotion would amount to victimisation.

- A gay man sues a publican for persistently treating him less well than heterosexual customers. Because of this, the publican bars him from the pub altogether. This would be victimisation.

- An employer threatens to dismiss a staff member because he thinks she intends to support a colleague's sexual harassment claim. This threat could amount to victimisation.

- A man with a grudge against his employer knowingly gives false evidence in a colleague's discrimination claim against the employer. He is subsequently dismissed for supporting the claim. His dismissal would not amount to victimisation because of his untrue and malicious evidence.

Some of the case law based on the pre-Equality Act 2010 law is still relevant. In *Chief Constable of West Yorkshire Police v Khan* [2001] 1 WLR 1947, the House of Lords confirmed that the less favourable treatment must be by reason of the protected act (ie motivated by it). In this case, the reason the employer refused to provide a reference was to preserve his position in pending litigation and not the fact that the worker had commenced proceedings.

According to the Court of Appeal in *Nagarajan v London Regional Transport* [1998] IRLR 73, there must be *conscious motivation* by the discriminator to treat the employee less favourably because of the protected act. The case was appealed to the House of Lords. Their Lordships (Lord Browne-Wilkinson dissenting) held that the Court of Appeal had erred in holding that the alleged victimiser must have been consciously motivated by the race relations legislation. The question that must be asked, according to their Lordships, is 'Did the defendant treat the employee less favourably because of his knowledge of a protected act?'. If the answer to that question is yes, the case will fall within the law, even if the victimiser did not consciously realise that he or she was prejudiced by the defendant's having done the protected act (*Nagarajan v London Regional Transport* [1999] IRLR 572).

In *St Helens Metropolitan Borough Council v Derbyshire* [2004] IRLR 851; [2005] EWCA Civ 977; [2007] IRLR 540, the EAT upheld a tribunal finding that female catering staff who had brought equal pay claims had also been victimised. The employer wrote to all catering employees (not just the women who brought the claims) and said that if the claims were successful, the cost of a school meal would rise so as to 'make provision of the service wholly unviable', which might lead to large numbers of redundancies. The employer also wrote to the women concerned and said, amongst other things, 'I am greatly concerned about the likely outcome of this matter ... [I would urge you to consider] the original offer of settlement'. The EAT held that this constituted victimisation and stated that a direct threat of dismissal or other sanction made to the individual claimant is not a necessary element for establishing less favourable treatment.

This decision was upheld on appeal by the House of Lords, which held that while an employer may seek to dissuade an employee from bringing a claim, it must seek to avoid putting unreasonable pressure on the employee. In this case, the House of Lords held that the letter was not reasonable and therefore amounted to victimisation.

In *McIntosh v Governing Body of St Mark's Primary School* (UKEAT/0226/13), the protected act was held not to be the cause of the unfavourable treatment. The tribunal's decision was that the claimant had been dismissed due to a breakdown in the relationship between the claimant and the headteacher 'which was irretrievable'.

In *Martin v Devonshires Solicitors* (UKEAT/0086/10), the EAT upheld a tribunal's decision that the claimant's dismissal was 'properly and genuinely separable' from the fact of her complaints. The EAT held that in principle a distinction can be made between subjecting a person to a detriment by reason of a complaint which amounted to a protected act, and by reason of the facts and features of the manner in which it was made. In *Martin*, the claimant suffered from a mental illness that led her to make claims of discrimination, which she believed to be true but were false, and she could not accept that they were false. *Martin* was an exceptional case (see too *Micheldever Tyre Service Ltd v Burrell* (UKEAT/0427/12) and *McIntosh v Governing Body of St Mark's Primary School* (UKEAT/0226/13)). In *Woodhouse v West North West Homes Leeds Ltd* (UKEAT/0007/12), the EAT held that the claimant's dismissal was victimisation and could not properly be separated from the claimant's complaints. In that case the employee's numerous grievances were dismissed by the employer, and the employee was then dismissed on the basis that their relationship had broken down as a result of the employee's 'uncurable disaffection'. The EAT overturned the tribunal's decision and held this was victimisation. The claimant was not mentally ill (cf *Martin*) and that grievance (past and future) caused the dismissal and therefore amounted to victimisation.

In *Chief Constable of Greater Manchester Police v Bailey* [2017] EWCA Civ 425, the Court of Appeal held that the tribunal had erred in law in applying a 'but for' test. The tribunal found for the claimant, stating that the treatment complained of was 'inextricably linked' to his previous protected act. The tribunal should, held the Court of Appeal, have asked whether the treatment complained of was by reason of the protected acts, which requires a consideration of the employer's motivation (conscious or unconscious). The tribunal's decision that the treatment 'flow[ed] from [the Claimant's] position under the Compromise Agreement, and hence also ... from his protected act' was:

> wrong in law – and, with all respect to the Tribunal, obviously so. It is self-evidently the case that there would have been no secondment to terminate if the Claimant had not brought his earlier claims, but

that kind of 'but for' causative link does not mean that the termination was 'because of' his earlier claims in the relevant sense.

The Court of Appeal confirmed, in *Deer v University of Oxford* [2015] EWCA Civ 52, that the manner in which a grievance is treated by the employer can amount to victimisation if the grievance process is less favourable than it would have been were it not for an earlier claim brought by the employees, *even if* the grievance was bound to fail. That latter fact will be relevant to compensation, but it does not defeat the victimisation claim. (See too *A v Chief Constable of West Midlands Police* (UKEAT/0313/14).)

In *Thompson v London Central Bus Company Ltd* (UKEAT/0108/15), the EAT considered that associative discrimination (see **9.2.2**) could apply to a victimisation claim. The issue is not whether there is a relationship between the victim and the third party with the protected characteristic, or how close that relationship is – while the more tenuous the relationship is, the harder it will be to prove causation, as a matter of law there is no minimum degree of association that needs to be established. This therefore appears to increase the scope of protection available to employees and workers under the Equality Act 2010, even if they have not carried out a protected act themselves.

The EAT held in *Saad v Southampton Hospitals NHS Trust* (UKEAT/0276/17) that the claimant's subjective belief that he had carried out a protected act was sufficient to counter a suggestion of bad faith under s 27(3) of the Equality Act 2010.

11.9.2 Remedies

See **8.8** above.

11.9.3 Protection of former employees

Section 108 protects against post-employment discrimination and harassment, but s 108(7) states expressly that 'conduct is not a contravention of this section in so far as it also amounts to victimisation of B by A' (see **8.4.3**). However, the Court of Appeal held, in *Jessemey v Rowstock Ltd and anor* [2014] EWCA Civ 185, that post-termination victimisation is proscribed by the 2010 Act, that s 108(7) was a 'plain case of drafting mistake', and that there was no reason why the Equality Act 2010 should not be construed to cover post-employment victimisation. At the time the Equality Act was drafted, post-termination victimisation was unlawful (see *Rhys-Harper v Relaxion Group* [2003] IRLR 484), and there was no indication that the Government intended to withdraw that protection in the Equality Act 2010.

SUMMARY

This chapter has looked at harassment and victimisation in respect of the following protected characteristics listed in s 4 of the Equality Act 2010:

(a)   sex;

(b)   gender reassignment;

(c)   colour, race, nationality or ethnic or national origins;

(d)   religion or belief;

(e)   sexual orientation (**8.1**).

(Age and disability are dealt with in separate chapters.) Harassment does not include marriage and civil partnership, or pregnancy and maternity (**11.1**).

Two of the four main types of discrimination in the employment field outlawed by UK legislation are harassment and victimisation.

Harassment is unwanted conduct that violates a person's dignity, or which creates an intimidating, hostile, degrading, humiliating or offensive environment for that person having regard to all the circumstances including the perception of the victim. The definition of 'harassment' is set out in s 26 of the Equality Act 2010 (**11.3**).

There are three different types of harassment (**11.3**):

(a)   'characteristic-related harassment', which involves unwanted conduct which is related to a relevant characteristic and has the purpose or effect of creating an intimidating, hostile, degrading, humiliating or offensive environment for the complainant, or violating the complainant's dignity;

(b)   sexual harassment, which is unwanted conduct of a sexual nature, where this has the purpose or effect of creating an intimidating, hostile, degrading, humiliating or offensive environment for the complainant, or violating the complainant's dignity;

(c)   treating someone less favourably because that person has either submitted to or rejected sexual harassment, or harassment related to sex or gender reassignment which had the purpose or effect of creating an intimidating, hostile, degrading, humiliating or offensive environment for the complainant, or violating the complainant's dignity.

Employers will be vicariously liable for the acts of their employees, unless they have taken such steps as were reasonable to prevent an employee doing the act complained of (see **8.6**). They will also be liable for the acts of third parties in some circumstances (see **11.4.2**).

The victimisation provisions aim to give protection to workers who bring complaints of discrimination or other proceedings aimed at enforcing compliance with equal treatment principles. Victimisation occurs when a person has been subject to a detriment because he has done a 'protected act'. This may include bringing a tribunal claim or giving evidence in connection with such a claim. The definition of 'victimisation' is set out in s 27 of the Equality Act 2010.

The same shifting burden of proof applies in both harassment and victimisation cases (**11.2** and **9.5**). Section 108 protects against post-employment discrimination and harassment, and victimisation (**11.7.2**).

Remedies and enforcement are dealt with at **8.8** above. A flowchart summarising harassment and victimisation is set out at **Figure 11.1**.

Figure 11.1 Flowchart – Harassment and Victimisation

ELIGIBILITY

time-limit – within 3 months of act of discrimination

↓

UNLAWFUL ACT

discrimination in recruitment, promotion, dismissal, harassment, post-employment matters or subjecting a person to detriment

↓

TYPE OF CLAIM

[NB some situations can give rise to more than one type of discrimination claim]

HARASSMENT	VICTIMISATION
<ul><li>character-related harassment – unwanted conduct related to a protected characteristic; or</li><li>sexual harassment – unwanted conduct of a sexual nature; or</li><li>less favourable treatment – where C has rejected unwanted conduct of a sexual nature or conduct related to sex of gender reassignment;</li><li>which has the purpose or effect of violating C's dignity or creating an intimidating, hostile, degrading, humiliating or offensive environment for C;</li><li>if unintended, having regard to all the circumstances, including C's perception, should conduct be reasonably considered as having that effect?</li></ul>	<ul><li>has C been subject to a detriment because C has done a protected act (eg brought/ intends to bring proceedings or has given/intends to give evidence or information in connection with such proceedings)?</li><li>No comparator needed</li><li>No bad faith</li></ul>

↓

NO DEFENCE

↓

VICARIOUS LIABILITY

R will be vicariously liable for acts of employees committed in the course of employment (*Jones v Tower Boot Co/Chief Constable of Lincolnshire Police v Stubbs*) unless R took such steps as were reasonable to stop/avoid the discrimination (statutory defence – s 109(4))

↓

REMEDIES

- declaration of employee's rights
- recommendation that employer take action to alleviate or reduce the effect of the discrimination
- order for compensation (no maximum)
  - pecuniary losses
  - aggravated damages if employer has behaved in a high-handed, malicious, insulting or aggressive manner
  - injury to feelings (*Vento/Da'Bell*)
  - psychiatric or physical injury
  - possibility of exemplary damages
  - increase/decrease for any unreasonable failure to comply with the Acas Code of Practice

AGE DISCRIMINATION

LEARNING OUTCOMES

After reading this chapter you will be able to:

- understand the underlying principles of age discrimination law, and when and to whom it applies in an employment context
- list the four types of prohibited conduct
- describe how the justification defence works in a direct age discrimination claim
- describe how the justification defence works in an indirect age discrimination claim
- explain how a compulsory retirement age may operate
- describe the remedies available where a complaint of age discrimination is made out.

12.1 INTRODUCTION

This chapter gives an overview of age discrimination. The Framework Directive for Equal Treatment in Employment and Occupation (2000/78) required Member States to implement legislation prohibiting discrimination on grounds of age by 2 December 2006. The UK enacted law to comply with its Community obligations by way of the Employment Equality (Age) Regulations 2006 (SI 2006/1031) ('the Age Regulations'), which were the last plank of the UK's implementation of the Equal Treatment Framework Directive. These have now been consolidated and harmonised in the Equality Act 2010. The EHRC has responsibility for the promotion of equality and combating discrimination on the grounds of age (see **8.1**).

The protection against discrimination because of age applies to all employers, private and public sector, and employment agencies, vocational training providers, trade unions, professional organisations, employer organisations, and trustees and managers of occupational pension schemes. It applies to employees, job applicants, ex-employees, contract workers, office holders and partners. The protection applies to a broad definition of workers and employees (see **1.3**). As with sex, race, disability, religious belief and sexual orientation discrimination, 'employment' is defined as 'employment under a contract of service or of apprenticeship or a contract personally to execute any work or labour' (s 83). This is a wider definition than that of 'employee' in the ERA 1996, and means that certain categories of individuals who are not covered by other statutory rights (eg job applicants, office holders, police officers and the self-employed) are covered by the Equality Act 2010.

Much of the terminology used is familiar discrimination terminology: under the Act direct age discrimination is prohibited (ie persons being subject to less favourable treatment than others because of their age) as well as indirect age discrimination (ie the application of a provision, criterion or practice which disadvantages people of a particular age), although (unlike other forms of discrimination) direct age discrimination can be justified 'objectively' where the discrimination is a 'proportionate means of achieving legitimate aim'. Both harassment (being unwanted conduct that violates a person's dignity, or creates an intimidating, hostile, degrading, humiliating or offensive environment for that person having regard to all the circumstances, including the perception of the victim) and victimisation (because the victim has brought proceedings under the Act, or has given evidence or information in connection with proceedings under the Act) are also prohibited.

12.2 THE PROTECTED CHARACTERISTIC

Section 4 of the Equality Act 2010 sets out certain 'protected' characteristics (see **8.2**). These are the grounds upon which discrimination is deemed unlawful. Age is listed as a protected characteristic in s 5:

(1)   In relation to the protected characteristic of age—

(a)   a reference to a person who has a particular protected characteristic is a reference to a person of a particular age group;

(b)   a reference to persons who share a protected characteristic is a reference to persons of the same age group.

(2)   A reference to an age group is a reference to a group of persons defined by reference to age, whether by reference to a particular age or to a range of ages.

This section establishes that where the Act refers to the protected characteristic of age, it means a person belonging to a particular age group. An age group includes people of the same age and people of a particular range of ages. Where people fall in the same age group, they share the protected characteristic of age.

The Explanatory Notes give the following examples:

- An age group would include 'over fifties' or twenty-one year olds.
- A person aged twenty-one does not share the same characteristic of age with 'people in their forties'. However, a person aged twenty-one and people in their forties can share the characteristic of being in the 'under fifty' age range.

Section 14 provides for the discrimination prohibited by the Act to include direct discrimination because of a combination of two protected characteristics ('dual discrimination'), eg age and gender, or disability and race (see **9.2.3**). The Government considers it too complicated and burdensome to allow claims on three or more different discrimination grounds.

12.3 PROHIBITED CONDUCT

As referred to at **12.1** above, there are four main types of age discrimination outlawed in the employment field by the Equality Act 2010 so far as the protected characteristic of age is concerned:

(a)   direct discrimination (s 13), eg refusing employment on the ground of a person's being too young or too old;

(b)   indirect discrimination (s 19), eg refusing employment on the ground of a person's having too few or too many years' service;

(c)   harassment (s 26);

(d)   victimisation (s 27).

These will be dealt with in more detail below.

12.4   UNLAWFUL ACTS OF DISCRIMINATION

As with sex and race, etc, discrimination in the employment field against job applicants, employees and former employees is prohibited by ss 39 and 40 of the Act. These sections make it unlawful for an employer to discriminate against, victimise or harass employees and people seeking work. The prohibition applies where the employer is making arrangements to fill a job, and in respect of anything done in the course of a person's employment. The provisions apply to recruitment, terms and conditions, promotions, transfers, dismissals and training. See **8.4** for more details.

In *Keane v Investigo and Others* (UKEAT/0389/09), K a 51-year-old accountant with a number of years' experience, applied for a large number of positions that were advertised as being for a recently-qualified accountant with limited experience. She was not interviewed for these posts and brought tribunal proceedings against 11 agencies, a number of whom settled. There were five left by the time of the tribunal hearing. At the hearing it was argued that K had no genuine interest in the jobs and had brought the claims to make a broader point about age discrimination. The tribunal found that there was no direct or indirect discrimination as K did not want the jobs. The EAT upheld that decision, finding that there was no 'less favourable treatment' or 'disadvantage' caused to K:

> [W]e do not see how an applicant who is not considered for a job in which he or she is not in any event interested can in any ordinary sense of the word be said to have suffered a detriment – or to be more precise, to have been (comparatively) unfavourably 'treated' or put at a 'disadvantage'.

The imposition of age limits has proved particularly problematic in European law – whether as a minimum or maximum at point of entry for a particular career, or when employment automatically terminates, or for the availability of certain benefits. On their face, all these limits amount to direct age discrimination. This treatment can be justified (see below) (under the Equal Treatment Framework Directive 2000/78) if it is 'objectively and reasonably justified by a legitimate aim ... and if the means of achieving that aim are appropriate and necessary'. This is why some time-limits are permitted (see for example *Rosenbladt* (Case C-45/09), *Hornfeldt* (Case C-141/11), *Goergiev* (Cases C-250/09 and C-268/09) and *Fries* (Case C-190/16)) and others are not (see for example *Prigge* (Case C-447/09), *Petersen* (Cases C-229/08 and C-341/09) and *Commission v Hungary* (Case C-286/12)).

12.5   OCCUPATIONAL REQUIREMENTS

See **8.5** for a more detailed discussion of occupational requirements.

12.6   DIRECT DISCRIMINATION

12.6.1   Definition

Direct discrimination occurs where the reason for a person being treated less favourably than another is a protected characteristic listed in s 4 of the Act (see **9.2.1**).

The definition of 'direct discrimination' in connection with a person's age is the same as for sex, race, etc, and is set out in s 13 of the Act:

> (1)   A person (A) discriminates against another (B) if, because of a protected characteristic, A treats B less favourably than A treats or would treat others.

(2)   If the protected characteristic is age, A does not discriminate against B if A can show A's treatment of B to be a proportionate means of achieving a legitimate aim.

The Explanatory Notes give the following by way of example:

If the manager of a nightclub is disciplined for refusing to carry out an instruction to exclude older customers from the club, this would be direct age discrimination against the manager unless the instruction could be justified.

Acas gives the following example of direct discrimination in its booklet *Age and the Workplace*:

Whilst being interviewed, a job applicant says that she took her professional qualification 30 years ago. Although she has all the skills and competences required of the job holder, the organisation decides not to offer her the job because of her age.

Note that, unlike the other types of protected characteristics, direct age discrimination can be justified (see **12.6.2**): for age, different treatment that is justified as a proportionate means of meeting a legitimate aim is not direct discrimination.

The definition is wide enough to cover discrimination by association, ie cases where the less favourable treatment is because of the victim's association with someone who has the protected characteristic. It is also (see **9.2.4**) wide enough to include discrimination on the ground of a person's apparent age; it will not be a defence for the employer to say that the person in question appeared to be older or younger than he or she in fact was. This would apply where, for example, someone is refused employment because he looks too old or too young.

It is therefore unlawful to decide not to employ someone on the ground of age, to dismiss him, to refuse to provide him with training, to deny him promotion, to give him adverse terms and conditions, or to retire him without an objective justification.

In *Swann v GHL Insurance Services UK Ltd* (ET/2306281/07), an employment tribunal decided (by a majority) that a flexible benefits package containing a medical insurance option, where the premium was calculated according to age, did not amount to unlawful age discrimination, because all the employees were given the same flexible benefits package and the calculation of the package was not age-related. (See also *Live Nation (Venues) UK Ltd v Hussain* (UKEAT/ 0234/ 08), where the EAT overturned the tribunal's funding of direct age discrimination.)

The Court of Appeal held in *Lockwood v DWP & Another* [2013] EWCA Civ 1195 that the protected characteristic cannot be used to argue that the circumstances of the claimant and the comparator are not materially similar. The discussion at **9.2.5.2** is relevant here.

12.6.2   Justification

One important distinction between direct age discrimination and most other forms of direct discrimination under UK law, is that direct age discrimination can be objectively justified if the treatment in question is shown to be a proportionate means of achieving a legitimate aim. The test is the same for both direct and indirect discrimination (see **12.6.1** above and **12.7** below) but the tests are slightly different in the Equal Treatment Framework Directive. In relation to direct discrimination, the question is whether the treatment is 'objectively and reasonably justified by a legitimate aim' (Article 6).

In *Seldon v Clarkson Wright & Jakes (A Partnership)* [2012] UKSC 16, the Supreme Court held that the test for justifying direct age discrimination is narrower than that for justifying indirect discrimination (see below). The case was brought by a partner in the respondent firm who was made to retire at 65. The Court held that direct age discrimination can only be justified if the employer's legitimate aim is a 'public interest' aim as specified in EU law, as opposed to purely individual aims being pursued by the business (eg redundancy costs). Lady Hale said, drawing from the ECJ's jurisprudence:

If it is sought to justify direct age discrimination under article 6(1), the aims of the measure must be social policy objectives, such as those related to employment policy, the labour market or vocational training. These are of a public interest nature, which is 'distinguishable from purely individual reasons particular to the employer's situation, such as cost reduction or improving competitiveness'.

Lady Hale summarised the legitimate aims recognised by the ECJ in the context of direct age discrimination claims:

(i)   promoting access to employment for younger people (*Palacios de la Villa, Hütter, Kücükdeveci*);

(ii)   the efficient planning of the departure and recruitment of staff (*Fuchs*);

(iii) sharing out employment opportunities fairly between the generations (*Petersen, Rosenbladt, Fuchs*);

(iv)   ensuring a mix of generations of staff so as to promote the exchange of experience and new ideas (*Georgiev, Fuchs*);

(v)   rewarding experience (*Hütter, Hennigs*);

(vi)   cushioning the blow for long serving employees who may find it hard to find new employment if dismissed (*Ingeniørforeningen i Danmark*);

(vii) facilitating the participation of older workers in the workforce (*Fuchs*, see also *Mangold v Helm*, Case C-144/04 [2006] 1 CMLR 1132);

(viii) avoiding the need to dismiss employees on the ground that they are no longer capable of doing the job which may be humiliating for the employee concerned (*Rosenbladt*); or

(ix)   avoiding disputes about the employee's fitness for work over a certain age (*Fuchs*).

The Supreme Court accepted that staff retention and workforce planning were directly related to the legitimate social policy aim of sharing out professional employment opportunities fairly between the generations, and that the need to expel partners by way of performance management was directly related to 'dignity' aims accepted as legitimate by the ECJ in *Rosenbladt* and *Fuchs*.

As far as proportionality is concerned, this will involve an employer showing that what it is doing is necessary to achieve the legitimate aim and is the least onerous way of doing so. It will be open to employers to demonstrate that any aim they are pursing is legitimate. Examples of treatment that a court or tribunal may find to be a proportionate way of achieving a legitimate aim could include setting age requirements in order to ensure the protection of, or to promote the vocational integration of, people in a particular age group, or the fixing of a minimum age to qualify for certain advantages linked to employment in order to recruit or retain older people. Acas gives the following advice in *Age and the Workplace*:

•   if your aim is to encourage loyalty then you ought to have evidence that the provision or criterion you introduce is actually doing so;

•   the discriminatory effect should be significantly outweighed by the importance and benefits of the legitimate aim;

•   you should have no reasonable alternative to the action you are taking. If the legitimate aim can be achieved by less or non discriminatory means then these must take precedence.

The case returned to the employment tribunal to make a decision on the facts. The dignity justification was not actively promoted before the tribunal. On the intergenerational fairness justification relied upon, the tribunal held that while the firm might have selected other ages within a narrow band (64 or 66) to achieve the aims, 65 was proportionate to the aims of retention and workforce planning, so that the mandatory retirement age of 65 was justified overall (ET 1100275/07). Mr Seldon appealed this decision. The EAT held that the tribunal had applied the correct test (UKEAT/0434/13). The proper analysis was to consider whether the chosen retirement age was reasonably necessary to achieve the aims, given the realities of setting a bright-line date. The decision does not provide an unqualified authority for companies to justify a mandatory retirement age of 65: this was a fact-sensitive decision since there was an agreed retirement age in the partnership deed; Mr Seldon was a partner, not an employee; and the case was decided using statistics relating to 2006, before the abolition of the default retirement age in 2011.

The EAT set out a useful summary of the legal position in *Magoulas v Queen Mary University of London* (UKEAT/0244/15):

> (1) an employee will only justify a PCP if it shows that the PCP is a proportionate means of achieving a legitimate aim; (2) the test is an objective test and not a band of reasonable responses test; (3) the Tribunal must not conflate legitimate aim and proportionality; (4) what amounts to a legitimate aim is not defined in the 2010 Act and is a question of fact for the Tribunal; (5) the measure must pursue the aim, but it is not necessary for this to have been specified at the time, and an *ex post facto* justification is possible (see *Seldon v Clarkson Wright & Jakes* [2012] IRLR 590); (6) an aim that is inherently discriminatory will not suffice and will not be a legitimate aim; (7) reducing cost can be a legitimate aim in some circumstances, for example in allocating resources between competing demands, but it cannot justify an otherwise discriminatory provision; (8) the principle of proportionality requires the Tribunal to strike an objective balance between the discriminatory effect of the PCP and the reasonable needs of the employer's business; (9) there is no guidance in the 2010 Act about this, and it is for the Tribunal to assess proportionality; (10) in general, the greater the disadvantage caused by the PCP, the more cogent the justification that is needed; (11) an employer can rely on a justification defence not thought of at the time of the discrimination (see *Cadman v Health & Safety Executive* [2004] IRLR 971); and (12) some evidence is required to establish the defence, but see the *Seldon* case per Elias P, as he then was, at para 73. There is an important citation from that decision at para 36 of the ET's Decision:
>
> > 'We do not accept the submissions ... that a tribunal must always have concrete evidence, neatly weighed, to support each assertion made by the employer. Tribunals have an important role in applying their common sense and their knowledge of human nature ... Tribunals must, no doubt, be astute to differentiate between the exercise of their knowledge of how humans behave and stereotyped assumptions about behaviour. But the fact that they may sometimes fall into that trap does not mean that the Tribunals must leave their understanding of human nature behind them when they sit in judgment.'

In *McCririck v Channel 4 & Another* (ET/2200478/2013), an employment tribunal held that Channel 4 had a legitimate aim – attracting a wider audience to horse racing (a public interest objective) – and that the means adopted to achieve the aim were proportionate – the dismissal. Mr McCririck was dismissed by Channel 4, for which he had worked as a television presenter. He alleged discrimination.

The Court of Appeal held, in *Woodcock v Cumbria PCT* [2012] EWCA Civ 330, that cost alone cannot justify discrimination, but that where there is another factor (here there was a redundancy situation too), the discrimination may be justified on a 'costs plus' basis. In *Sturmey v The Weymouth and Portland BC* (UKEAT/0114/14), the EAT held that *Woodcock* was not intended to lay down 'any general principle as to whether omitting or eliding stages in a redundancy process to save pension costs will always be a proportionate means of [achieving a legitimate aim]'. That will depend on the facts.

The Court of Appeal held in *Lockwood* (see **12.6.1**) that an enhanced supplement payable on voluntary redundancy to employees aged 35 and over, was objectively justified on the basis that younger employees remain unemployed for a shorter period and have fewer family and financial responsibilities.

In *Abercrombie & Fitch Italia Srl v Bordonaro* [2017] IRLR 1018, the ECJ held that the use of zero hours terms for people under 25 was justified because the rule sought to achieve a legitimate aim (help young people into jobs) and that it was a proportionate way of achieving the aim. Less rigid contracts of employment were an appropriate and necessary way to achieve labour market flexibility. See too *Air Products PLC v Cockram* [2018] EWCA Civ 346 for a recent decision of the Court of Appeal on objective justification. The aim of 'intergenerational fairness', achieved by limiting the advantage enjoyed by one age group over another, was a legitimate social policy. Balancing retention of employees and opportunities for younger employees with incentives for retirement after the age of 55 was a proportionate approach to the problem.

An area of particular difficulty is around the introduction by the Government of transitionary provisions seeking to make changes to public service pension schemes. These are often, by their very nature, age (and possibly sex and race) discriminatory, but the Government has argued that they are objectively justified. *Lord Chancellor and Secretary of State for Justice and another v McCloud and others* (UKEAT/0071/17) concerned judicial pension provisions introducing a less favourable pension scheme for judges but which included transitional protection for those within 10 years of pensionable age. It was argued that this directly discriminated against those who were not protected by the transitional arrangements. The EAT held that the tribunal had erred in law in concluding that the appellants had not established a legitimate aim but that it had been entitled to find that the chosen means were not appropriate or reasonably necessary to achieve the aim. The EAT was satisfied that the 'the conclusions of the EJ, at para 114, that the extremely severe impact of the transitional provisions on the Claimants far outweighed the public benefit of applying the policy consistently across the whole public service pension sector cannot be faulted and cannot be characterised as perverse'.

Sargeant v London Fire and Emergency Planning Authority (UKEAT/0116/17) also concerned transitional arrangements for pensions in respect of firefighters. In this case, the EAT held that the tribunal had been right to conclude that the Government was pursuing a legitimate aim but wrong to conclude that the measure was proportionate because, whilst Member States enjoy a broad discretion in their choice of the aims and of the means to pursue them, it had not applied the domestic case law requiring a balancing exercise. The means employed had to be both appropriate and necessary. The EAT said:

> ... whilst an Employment Tribunal is obliged, when considering both legitimate aim and proportionate means to recognise the margin of discretion which the CJEU line of authority accords Governments, when taking and implementing decisions about social policy, the Supreme Court in *Seldon* sought to reconcile the two lines of authority by enabling an Employment Tribunal, in an appropriate case, to consider for itself whether the aim is legitimate in the particular circumstances of the employment (*Seldon* paragraph 61) and to *scrutinise the means used to achieve the aim in the context of the particular business to see whether they meet the objective, and whether there are other less discriminatory measures which would do so* (*Seldon* paragraph 62). The reasoning in *Lockwood* involved the Court of Appeal following the guidance in *Seldon* by applying the approach described in *Hardy and Hansons* and *MacCulloch* (see *Lockwood v DWP* ...). (emphasis added)

12.7 INDIRECT DISCRIMINATION

Indirect discrimination occurs when there is equal treatment of all groups but the effect of the provision, criterion or practice imposed by an employer has a disproportionate adverse impact on one group, unless the requirement can be justified.

The definition of 'indirect discrimination' in connection with a person's age is the same as for sex, race, etc, and is set out in s 19 of the Act:

(1) A person (A) discriminates against another (B) if A applies to B a provision, criterion or practice which is discriminatory in relation to a relevant protected characteristic of B's.

(2) For the purposes of subsection (1), a provision, criterion or practice is discriminatory in relation to a relevant protected characteristic of B's if—

(a) A applies, or would apply, it to persons with whom B does not share the characteristic,

(b) it puts, or would put, persons with whom B shares the characteristic at a particular disadvantage when compared with persons with whom B does not share it,

(c) it puts, or would put, B at that disadvantage, and

(d) A cannot show it to be a proportionate means of achieving a legitimate aim.

For example, in *Kraft Foods v Hastie* (UKEAT/0024/10), Kraft had an 'exceptionally generous' contractual redundancy scheme. Because of the high levels of payment under the scheme, it capped redundancy payments at the sum that a redundant employee would have earned if he had remained in employment until normal retirement age. Mr Hastie, who was 62, had his redundancy payment capped at £76,560. This was what he would have earned if he had remained employed until 65. If no cap existed, he would have received about £90,000. He complained that the cap amounted to indirect discrimination on grounds of age, as it would only 'bite' against older workers. The EAT held that the cap was justified. The company's aim of preventing employees receiving a 'windfall' met a legitimate aim, namely giving appropriate payments to employees to compensate them for future loss of earnings. They said the cap was a proportionate means of achieving that aim.

In *Rolls Royce plc v Unite the Union* [2009] IRLR 576, an issue arose as to whether a collectively agreed redundancy selection matrix which included an award of points for length of service was indirect age discrimination. The Court of Appeal said that rewarding long service was a reasonable and legitimate policy. It held that, viewed objectively, including a length of service criterion amongst a substantial number of other criteria was proportionate. The legitimate aim was to reward loyalty, and to achieve a stable workforce in the context of a fair process of redundancy selection. (For cases looking at contractual redundancy schemes based on age, see *MacCulloch v ICI plc* [2008] IRLR 846 and *Loxley v BAE Systems (Munitions and Ordnance) Ltd* [2008] IRLR 853.)

In *HM Land Registry v Benson* (UKEAT/0197/11), the EAT said that an employer's decision not to select employees aged 50–54 for voluntary redundancy/early retirement because they were too expensive was justified indirect age discrimination. The selection of cheapness as a criteria, which allowed the release of as many employees as possible within budget, was a proportionate means of achieving this legitimate aim. The EAT, while considering that whether this was a 'costs plus' case was debatable, did not need to challenge the tribunal's finding of fact on that (see **10.2.6** above). See also *Harrod v Chief Constable of West Midlands Police* [2017] EWCA Civ 191, where the Court of Appeal held that the tribunal should not have rejected the 'justification case on the basis that the respondent should have pursued a different aim which would have had a less discriminatory impact'.

In *Chief Constable of West Yorkshire Police v Homer* [2009] IRLR 262, the EAT overturned a tribunal's finding of indirect age discrimination where an employer introduced a requirement that, to be graded at the top grade and to receive the higher salary linked to that grade, an employee had to have a law degree. The tribunal had concluded that there was discrimination directed against those without a law degree who were within the 60–65 age bracket. The tribunal considered the issue of justification but concluded that, although the employers were seeking to achieve a legitimate objective, namely the recruitment and retention of staff of an appropriate quality, nonetheless the imposition of this criterion was not a proportionate means of achieving it.

The EAT held that there was no age discrimination. It held that such a requirement did not put a 61-year-old employee at a particular disadvantage on the grounds of his age, even though he could not have obtained a degree (studying part-time) before he retired. He was treated in precisely the same way as everyone else. The requirement for a law degree was not something required only of those over a certain age. Neither was it in principle more difficult for an older person to obtain the qualification than it was for a younger person. Any disadvantage could properly be described as the consequence of age, but it was not the consequence of age discrimination (para 39). However, had the claimant been able to establish the requisite age group disadvantage, the EAT would have upheld the finding that any age discrimination was not justified, as the requirement was not a proportionate means of achieving the recruitment and retention of appropriately qualified staff. The Court of Appeal agreed with the EAT ([2010] All ER (D) 189) that the employee's problem was not his age per se, but rather that he would retire before he could get the necessary qualification.

The Supreme Court disagreed with the Court of Appeal and held that the employer did indirectly discriminate on grounds of age, subject to justification. Therefore, a requirement which works to the comparative disadvantage of a person approaching compulsory retirement age is discriminatory on grounds of age. The tribunal decided, when the question of justification was remitted back to it, that the respondent could not justify the policy of requiring a law degree to justify promotion to the highest grade – it was not a proportionate means of achieving a legitimate aim because the respondent could have treated new employees differently to existing employees ([2013] EQLR 295).

In *Braithwaite and Others v HCL Insurance BPO Services Ltd and Another* (EAT/152/14/DM; 0153/14), the respondent was facing financial difficulties and required employees to agree new terms and conditions or be dismissed. This put older employees at a disadvantage because they would lose contractual benefits built up through longer service. The tribunal found that the requirement to enter a new contract was objectively justified and dismissed the claim. The EAT held that the tribunal was entitled to find that the provision, criterion or practice (PCP) was justified as a proportionate means of achieving the legitimate. The respondent had a legitimate aim, namely reducing staff costs to ensure its future viability and to have in place a market-competitive, non-discriminatory set of terms and conditions.

See **Chapter 10** for more a more detailed analysis of the underlying principles of indirect discrimination.

12.7.1 Age groups

Bringing a claim for age discrimination will involve comparing the claimant's 'age group' with another group. Section 5(2) states that 'age group' means 'a group of persons defined by reference to age, whether by reference to a particular age or a range of ages'. There is no further definition of age groups in the Act. This was the same wording as used by the Age Regulations 2006. However, it is still unclear whether 'age group' will be interpreted widely or narrowly. Acas suggests that companies could undertake age monitoring using age bands 16–21, 22–30, 31–40, 41–50, 51–60, 60–65 and 65+. Whatever age group an employee chooses, it will still be open to an employer to challenge the group on the basis that it is not appropriate.

In *Lockwood* (**12.6.1** above), the Court of Appeal compared the circumstances of the claimant's age group (under 30) and that of the older age group (35 and over) to hold that the claimant had suffered less favourable treatment because of her age (a reduced redundancy award). However, the scheme rules were held to be objectively justified by social policy objectives (reflecting the extra difficulties faced by older workers on redundancy).

For a recent analysis, see *Donkor v Royal Bank of Scotland* (EAT/0162/15). The case is a useful reminder of the importance of the 'reason why' question (see **9.2.5**).

12.8 HARASSMENT AND VICTIMISATION

As with the other areas covered by discrimination legislation, harassment is a specific separate ground of complaint. The definitions used in connection with a person's age are identical to those used for sex, race, etc, ie harassment includes behaviour that is intimidating, hostile, degrading, humiliating or offensive.

The IDS Brief, *Focus on Age Discrimination* (805, May 2006), gave some useful practical examples of the protection against harassment provisions:

- an employee whose father works in the same office is subjected to jokes about the father's age. Even though the victim's own age is not the subject of the jokes, this behaviour may still qualify as harassment on the ground of age

- an older employee is not asked to after-work drinks and events as his younger colleagues believe he would not fit in with their social culture. As this is likely to make the older worker feel excluded, it could come within the definition of offensive conduct

- an older employee is subjected to jokes about baldness, wrinkles, etc. Any offensive behaviour based on physical traits that become apparent as one gets older could be argued to be on the ground of age.

In *Lambert v BAT (Investments) Ltd* (ET/3100897/08), the tribunal held that an e-mail entitled 'The perks of being over 50' amounted to 'unwanted conduct which had the effect of violating [the claimant's] dignity'.

The victimisation provisions aim to ensure that individuals are not discouraged from bringing complaints of age discrimination. The protected acts include bringing proceedings under the Act; giving evidence in connection with a case; and alleging that someone has done something which would be unlawful under the Act. Victimisation cannot be justified.

See **Chapter 11** for a more detailed analysis of the underlying principles of victimisation and harassment.

12.9   EXCEPTIONS

Many service-related benefits (see Sch 9, para 10) and the minimum pay rates applicable to younger workers under the minimum wage legislation (Sch 9, para 11) are exempt from the provisions of the Act. Schedule 9, Pt 2 also makes special provision for exemption of or modification to the normal rules in the case of retirement and enhanced redundancy payments (para 13). While certain age-related criteria have been removed (the upper and lower age limits for redundancy payments), the two-year qualifying service period, the length of service used to calculate the payment, and the age-based multipliers for unfair dismissal and redundancy payment awards all remain.

There are a number of other grounds set out in Sch 9, Pt 2 on which otherwise discriminatory acts are lawful: see, eg, para 14 (life assurance) and para 15 (childcare provision for children of a particular age group). The full details of these are beyond the scope of this book.

12.10   VICARIOUS LIABILITY

Section 109 provides that employers are vicariously liable for any acts of their workers, done in the course of their employment, that are unlawful under the Act. Likewise, it extends to the acts of agents. This is so whether or not the acts were done with the employer's knowledge or approval. However, it is a defence for the employer to show that he took such steps as were reasonably practicable to prevent an employee doing the act complained of. See **8.6** for a more detailed discussion of vicarious liability.

12.11   BURDEN OF PROOF

The burden of proof for age discrimination is the same as in all the other main areas of discrimination, as set out in s 136(2) of the Act, namely:

> If there are facts from which the court could decide, in the absence of any other explanation, that a person (A) contravened the provision concerned, the court must hold that the contravention occurred.

In other words, once a complainant has established facts from which a tribunal could conclude there has been discrimination, the tribunal will have to make a finding of discrimination, unless the employer proves he did not commit the act of discrimination (see **9.5**).

In *McCoy v McGregor & Sons Ltd, Dixon and Aitken* (IT/00237/07), the tribunal held that a job advert requiring 'youthful enthusiasm', taken in the context of other evidence, gave rise to a prima facie case of direct discrimination and therefore shifted the burden to the employer.

12.12   PRACTICAL CONSIDERATIONS

12.12.1   Advertising and recruitment

Care should be taken with the language used in job advertisements. Words such as 'mature', 'senior', 'energetic' and 'junior' could all be problematic. Advertisements should focus on the job requirement and the tasks, and not on the person. Consider why and, if so, what experience is needed. Care also needs to be taken about where job advertisements are placed. Recruitment criteria need to be looked at to see if they could have a discriminatory impact. Avoid focusing on a particular age group to satisfy customer prejudice or targets. Using an agency to recruit staff does not avoid the risk of age discrimination.

12.12.2 Application forms and interviews

The Acas booklet recommended banishing questions about age and date of birth from application forms, and suggests that this information could be collected through a separate diversity monitoring form. Application forms should also avoid requesting information from which a job applicant's age can be inferred, unless such information is necessary (eg the dates when an applicant attended school). Employers should consider why they need this information so that, if necessary, they can avail themselves of the justification defence. Interviewers should have had age diversity training. Make sure that each candidate is asked the same questions in the same order. Focus on the job requirement, the tasks involved and the competencies needed for the job.

12.12.3 Contracts

Employment contracts, policies and procedures, and terms and conditions all need to be checked to ensure that they comply with the Act. If any policies or practices are potentially discriminatory, consideration will need to be given as to whether they can be justified. The Act requires that if changes are to be made to the contracts of more than 20 employees, there must be collective consultation with either unions or employee representatives. Similar consultation obligations apply as are to be found in large-scale redundancy situations.

12.12.4 Pensions and insurance benefits

The provisions of the Act relating to pensions are set out in s 61. While the Act makes it unlawful for trustees and managers of occupational pension schemes to discriminate against members or prospective members on the ground of age, there are lots of exemptions (which are beyond the scope of this book) (see, eg, s 197 and Schs 7 and 9). BIS published 'Guidance on the Age Regulations and their impact on pension schemes' in December 2006, which is still a useful reference.

The Act, like the Age Regulations, outlaws age discrimination in respect of employment-related insured benefits (private medical, motor insurance, etc). The cost to employers of providing insured benefits in relation to older staff, particularly those over 65, can be very high. Insurance companies are free to impose age limits or higher premiums on insurance policies, as insurance providers are not covered by the age discrimination legislation. There is concern amongst both employer and employee organisations that the absence of any exemptions for insurance benefits may cause employers to level down or remove insured benefits for all staff.

The Government has not ruled out introducing an exemption for insured benefits, but to date no action has been taken.

12.12.5 Dismissal and retirement

If an employer wishes to retire an employee, the employer will have to ensure that a fair procedure is followed under the ordinary unfair dismissal rules. Retirement is no longer a potentially fair reason for dismissal, so employers will need to show that the dismissal was for one of the potentially fair reasons for dismissal set out in s 98 of the ERA 1996 (capability, conduct, illegality, redundancy or some other substantial reason). This will mean that if an employer feels that an employee is under-performing then the employer should deal with the employee in the same manner as any other under-performing employee, ie by following a fair capability process that focuses on the employee's performance and not on his age. There has been concern that older employees will be particularly sensitive to this, and employers will have to ensure that any such disciplinary/capability procedures are handled sensitively and fairly.

Employers may still be able to operate a compulsory retirement age, provided that they can objectively justify it. They must show that the discrimination is a proportionate means of achieving a legitimate aim (see **12.6.2**).

Commentators have advised that there are now broadly two options for employers – to have and operate a contractual retirement age and be willing and able to justify it (s 13(2) of the Act) if an employee complains of direct discrimination; or to treat retirement on a case-by-case basis using ordinary capability and disciplinary procedures; but otherwise to leave it up to employees to decide when they want to retire. Clauses in contacts specifying that the contract may come to an end automatically when the employee reaches his 65th birthday may need to reviewed.

With regard to the first option, as indicated above, there is a consistent body of decisions from the ECJ adopting a liberal stance towards justifying compulsory retirement ages. The EHRC's Code of Practice on Employment – which is admissible as evidence – should be referred to. In *Seldon* (**12.6.2** above) the tribunal accepted that the following aims were potentially legitimate aims:

- retention reasons – giving younger senior solicitors the opportunity of partnership so that they do not leave;
- facilitating partnership and workforce planning so as to provide promotion opportunities (and see the Acas booklet, *Working within the DRA*); and
- limiting the need to expel partners by way of performance management, including potential health and safety arguments.

In addition to being required to meet a legitimate aim, the retirement age will have to be a proportionate means of achieving that aim. The EHRC Code of Practice states (para 4.31) that:

> EU law views treatment as proportionate if it is an appropriate and necessary means of achieving a legitimate aim. ... [I]t is sufficient that less discriminatory measures could not achieve the same aim. A balance must be struck between the discriminatory effect of the practice and A's reasons for applying it, taking into account all the relevant facts.

Even where an employer can show that a compulsory retirement age is justified, it will still be necessary where an individual is to be dismissed to show that the dismissal was for a potentially fair reason. The most likely category of the five potentially fair reasons for dismissal that could be used here would appear to be some other substantial reason. Where there is no contractual date, an employer will have to rely on one of the other potentially fair reasons, from which capability seems to be the one most employers will probably rely on. For a detailed analysis of capability dismissals, see **5.2.2.1** and **5.4.2.1** above. It should be noted that in addition to capabilities and qualifications, the definition of capability includes skills, aptitude and health, as well as 'any other physical or mental quality'.

12.12.6 Redundancy

Note that enhanced redundancy schemes may be unlawful if they pay out based on differential age grounds (likely to be direct discrimination unless exempted under Sch 9 or objectively justified) or on length of service (indirect discrimination unless exempted under Sch 9 or objectively justified). Paragraph 13 of Sch 9 to the Equality Act 2010 allows for enhanced redundancy schemes that essentially mirror the statutory redundancy payment scheme, although employers can derogate from the statutory cap on a week's wage and/or the multiple used. See **12.6** and **12.7** above.

12.13 ENFORCEMENT AND REMEDIES

Chapter 3 of Pt 9 of the Act contains the enforcement and remedies regime. Readers are referred to **8.8** for a more detailed discussion of enforcement and remedies. In essence, the same regime applies as applies to the other grounds of discrimination. Section 124 permits the making of a declaration of rights, an order to pay compensation and a recommendation that the employer take, within a specified period, specific steps for the purpose of obviating or reducing the adverse effect on the complainant or any other person of any matter to which the complaint relates.

SUMMARY

Age is a protected characteristic under s 4 of the Equality Act 2010 (**12.2**). The provisions of the 2010 Act apply to employees, job applicants, ex-employees, contract workers, office holders and partners. They outlaw age discrimination in terms of recruitment, promotion and training, transfers and dismissals (**12.4**); ban all retirement ages below 65 (except where objectively justified); and remove the current upper age limits for unfair dismissal and redundancy (**12.12.5**).

Four main types of age discrimination in the employment field are outlawed by UK legislation. These are:

(a) direct discrimination (ie being subject to less favourable treatment than others because of age) (**12.6**);

(b) indirect discrimination (ie the application of a provision, criterion or practice which disadvantages people of a particular age) (**12.7**);

(c) harassment (unwanted conduct that violates a person's dignity, or creates an intimidating, hostile, degrading, humiliating or offensive environment for him having regard to all the circumstances including the perception of the victim) (**12.8**); and

(d) victimisation (because the victim has been subject to a detriment because he has done a protected act) (**12.8**).

Much of the terminology used is familiar 'discrimination' terminology. Unlike other forms of discrimination, both direct and indirect age discrimination may be justified 'objectively' where the discrimination is a 'proportionate means of achieving legitimate aim' (**12.6.2** and **12.7.2**). Harassment and victimisation cannot be justified.

The Equality Act 2010 also removes the age limits for statutory sick pay, statutory maternity pay, statutory adoption pay and statutory paternity pay. The Employment Equality (Age) Regulations 2006, Sch 6 further introduced a right for employees to request to be permitted to work beyond retirement age, and a duty on employers to consider that request, and a requirement for employers to give at least six months' notice to employees about their intended retirement date so that individuals might plan better for retirement and be confident that 'retirement' is not being used as a cover for unfair dismissal. The Regulations also made changes to the existing unfair dismissal regime. In particular, 'retirement' is now a potentially fair reason for dismissal. The Equality Act 2010 does not affect the age at which people may claim their State pensions.

Remedies and enforcement are dealt with at **8.8** above.

DISABILITY DISCRIMINATION

LEARNING OUTCOMES

After reading this chapter you will be able to:

- understand the underlying principles of disability discrimination and how it differs from other areas of discrimination
- explain the four cumulative elements that make up the meaning of 'disability'
- list the six types of prohibited conduct and explain how they differ from each other
- describe the remedies available where a complaint of disability discrimination is made out.

13.1 INTRODUCTION

This chapter considers disability discrimination. Traditionally, disability discrimination has been treated differently from discrimination because of sex, race, religion or belief, etc. The pre-Equality Act 2010 legislation, the Disability Discrimination Act 1995 (DDA 1995) (as amended by the Disability Discrimination Act 1995 (Amendment) Regulations 2003 and the Disability Discrimination Act 2005) was different from other discrimination legislation in a number of ways. In relation to sex, race, religion or belief, etc, the emphasis is on treating all people the same. In disability discrimination, the opposite is often the case – a person's individual circumstances have to be considered, and such consideration is crucial to avoid discrimination. Many of the differences that existed between the DDA 1995 and the rest of the UK anti-discrimination legislation have been maintained in the Equality Act 2010, eg the concept of 'reasonable adjustments' (see **13.5.2** below), whereby employers need to treat disabled people differently in order to achieve substantive equality.

The relevant parts of the 2010 Act in so far as they relate to disability discrimination were implemented in October 2010.

The EHRC has responsibility for the promotion of equality and for combating discrimination on the grounds of disability. The EHRC published a Code of Practice on Employment, which came into force on 6 April 2011.

The protection against discrimination because of disability applies to all employers, private and public sector, and employment agencies, vocational training providers, trade unions, professional organisations, employer organisations, and trustees and managers of occupational pension schemes. It applies to employees, job claimants, ex-employees, contract workers, office holders and partners. The protection applies to a broad definition of workers and employees (see **1.3**). As with sex, race, age, etc, 'employment' is defined as 'employment under a contract of employment, a contract of apprenticeship or a contract personally to do work' (s 83). This is a wider definition than that of 'employee' as contained in the ERA 1996, and means that certain categories of individuals who are not covered by other statutory rights (eg job claimants, office holders, police officers and the self-employed) are covered by the Equality Act 2010.

Much of the terminology used is familiar discrimination terminology; under the Act direct disability discrimination is prohibited (ie being subjected to less favourable treatment than others because of disability) as is indirect disability discrimination (ie the application of a provision, criterion or practice (PCP) which disadvantages the disabled person). Both harassment (being unwanted conduct that violates a person's dignity, or creates an intimidating, hostile, degrading, humiliating or offensive environment for him having regard to all the circumstances, including the perception of the victim) and victimisation (because the victim has brought proceedings under the Act, or has given evidence or information in connection with proceedings under the Act) are also unlawful. However, some of the terminology is new and relevant to disability discrimination only (eg the duty to make reasonable adjustments; discrimination arising from a disability).

13.2 THE PROTECTED CHARACTERISTIC

Section 4 of the Act sets out certain 'protected' characteristics (see **8.2**). These are the grounds upon which discrimination is deemed unlawful. Disability is listed as one of the protected characteristics in s 4.

13.3 THE MEANING OF 'DISABILITY' AND 'DISABLED PERSON'

13.3.1 Introduction

Crucial to the operation of the disability discrimination regime in the Act are the definitions of 'disability' and 'disabled person' in s 6. This section establishes who is to be considered as having the protected characteristic of disability and is a disabled person for the purposes of the Act.

Section 6 provides as follows:

> (1)   A person (P) has a disability if—
>
>   (a)   P has a physical or mental impairment, and
>
>   (b)   the impairment has a substantial and long-term adverse effect on P's ability to carry out normal day-to-day activities.
>
> (2)   A reference to a disabled person is a reference to a person who has a disability.
>
> (3)   In relation to the protected characteristic of disability—
>
>   (a)   a reference to a person who has a particular protected characteristic is a reference to a person who has a particular disability;
>
>   (b)   a reference to persons who share a protected characteristic is a reference to persons who have the same disability.
>
> (4)   This Act (except Part 12 and section 190) applies in relation to a person who has had a disability as it applies in relation to a person who has the disability;
>
>   accordingly (except in that Part and that section)—
>
>   (a)   a reference (however expressed) to a person who has a disability includes a reference to a person who has had the disability, and
>
>   (b)   a reference (however expressed) to a person who does not have a disability includes a reference to a person who has not had the disability.

A person has a disability, therefore, if he has:

- a physical or mental impairment, which has
- a substantial and
- long-term adverse effect on his ability to carry out
- normal day-to-day activities. (s 6(1))

A 'disabled person' means a person who has a disability (s 6(2)). In essence, s 6 requires a tribunal to look at four different (cumulative) conditions.

Section 6 replaces similar provisions in the DDA 1995. The stated intention was that the 2010 Act would make it easier for a person to show that he is disabled. It introduces one major change from the DDA 1995, by removing a previous requirement to consider a specific list of eight capacities (such as mobility or speech, hearing or eyesight) which were said to constitute 'normal day-to-day activities', when considering whether or not a person was disabled (see **13.3.3** below). This change is intended to make it easier for some people to demonstrate that they meet the definition of a 'disabled person'.

A number of other sources also provide assistance, including Sch 1 to the Act; the Equality Act 2010 (Disability) Regulations 2010 (SI 2010/2128); and the 'Guidance on matters to be taken into account in determining questions relating to the definition of disability' ('the Guidance') which came into force on 1 May 2011. The Guidance is published by the Office for Disability Issues (ODI) which is a cross-government organisation that works with government departments, disabled people and a wide range of external groups: see <http:// www.officefordisability.gov.uk>. The Guidance does not impose any legal obligations in itself, nor is it an authoritative statement of the law. However, para 12 of Sch 1 to the Act requires that an adjudicating body which is determining for any purpose of the Act whether a person is a disabled person must take into account any aspect of the Guidance which appears to it to be relevant.

In *HK Danmark (acting on behalf of Ring) v Dansk almennyttigt Boligselskab* (Case C-335/11) [2013] IRLR 571, the ECJ held that the concept of 'disability' in the Equal Treatment Directive 2000/ 78 must be interpreted in a manner consistent with the United Nations Convention on the Rights of Persons with Disabilities approved by the EU in Decision 2010/48, and that accordingly 'disability' referred to a long-term limitation which results in particular from physical, mental or psychological impairments which in interaction with barriers may hinder the full and effective participation of the person concerned in professional life on an equal basis with others. See too *Chacón Navas v Eurest Colectivadades SA* [2006] IRLR 706, where the ECJ focused on whether the disability hinders a person's full and effective participation in society on an equal basis. The domestic definition of disability in the Equality Act 2010 will have to be interpreted in a manner consistent with this approach.

We look at each of the various elements of the definition of 'disability' in s 6 of the Act in more detail below.

13.3.2 The impairment condition

The claimant must have a physical or mental impairment. There is no definition in the Act of either physical or mental impairment. The Guidance states that the term should be given its ordinary meaning. Examples given include sensory impairments, organ specific diseases such as asthma, progressive diseases such as MS, and mental health conditions such as depression, OCD and eating disorders. The Guidance states that if the condition amounts to an impairment, it is *not* necessary to consider how the impairment was caused, and confirms the case law reported at **13.3.2.1** below in this respect.

The Equality Act 2010 (Disability) Regulations 2010 provide that an addiction to alcohol, nicotine or any other substance will not be an impairment for the purposes of the Equality Act

2010. In addition, a tendency to set fires, a tendency to steal, a tendency to physical or sexual abuse of other persons, exhibitionism (a compulsive desire to expose one's genital organs publicly), voyeurism (obtaining sexual pleasure from the observation of people undressing and having intercourse) and seasonal allergic rhinitis (hay fever) (although it may be taken into account for the purposes of the Act where it aggravates the effect of any other condition) are not recognised as impairments.

The 2010 Regulations also confirm that people who are certified blind, severely sight impaired, sight impaired or partially sighted by a consultant ophthalmologist are deemed disabled, and will automatically qualify for protection under the Act.

13.3.2.1   Case law

In *Dunham v Ashford Windows* [2005] IRLR 608, the EAT held that general learning disabilities could amount to a mental impairment; and in *Paterson v The Commissioner of Police of the Metropolis* (UKEAT/0635/06), that the claimant's dyslexia had an adverse effect on his normal day-to-day activities (being written assessments of work).

The Guidance emphasises that it is not how an impairment is caused that is important, but rather the effect it has. In *Power v Panasonic UK Ltd* [2003] IRLR 151, the EAT said that where depression was caused by alcohol addiction, the fact that the *cause* of the impairment was an addiction did not mean it was not covered.

In *J v DLA Piper UK LLP* (UKEAT/0263/09) the claimant's job offer was withdrawn soon after she revealed a history of depression. She tried (unsuccessfully) to convince the tribunal that she was in fact disabled and so entitled to protection under the pre-Equality Act 2010 legislation (DDA 1995). She maintained that her disability consisted of clinical depression, being a 'mental impairment which has a substantial and long-term adverse effect on [her] ability to carry out normal day-to-day activities'. She asserted that the condition had an adverse effect on her ability to concentrate. The tribunal decided that J did not suffer from a sufficiently well-defined impairment. J appealed and submitted that the existence of an impairment will, in most cases, be evident from the existence of an adverse effect on a claimant's ability to carry out day-to-day activities, and so the tribunal should examine that issue first. The EAT accepted that there will be cases where identifying the nature of the impairment in question involves difficult medical questions and that, in most such cases, it will be easier and legitimate for the tribunal to 'park' that issue and first consider adverse effect: it will not always be essential to identify a specific 'impairment' (within the words of s 1 of the DDA 1995) if the existence of one can be established from evidence of an adverse effect on the claimant's abilities.

Thus it may be easier to address the second and third conditions at **13.3.3** and **13.3.4** below first, ie whether there is a substantial effect on ability to carry out day-to-day activities. In the event that the tribunal decides that those conditions are made out, an impairment may be inferred. So if, for example, the claimant's symptoms have a substantial effect on normal day-to-day activities caused by symptoms characteristic of depression, the tribunal is likely to conclude that the impairment condition is also made out: that the claimant is suffering from clinical depression. In this case the medical evidence was ambiguous. The EAT stated that it remains good practice for the tribunal to state its conclusions on the issues of impairment and effect separately, as recommended in *Goodwin v Patent Office* (see **13.3.3.1**), but, in reaching those conclusions, the tribunal need not proceed by rigid consecutive stages. Specifically, where there may be a dispute about the existence of an impairment, it will make sense to make findings on the question of substantial adverse effect and then consider impairment in the light of those findings.

In *Walker v Sita Information Networking Computing Ltd* (UKEAT/0097/12), the EAT confirmed that the focus is on the effect of the impairment and *not* how the impairment was caused. The ECJ confirmed in *FOA, acting on behalf of Karsten Kaltoft v Kommunernes Lansforening (KL)* (Case C-354/

13) [2015] ICR 322, that obesity does not, in itself, constitute a disability; but said that obesity can constitute a disability if it entails a limitation resulting from long-term physical or mental impairments that hinder the full and effective participation of that person in professional life. That accords with the UK case law. When the case was then remitted back to the Danish court, it held that:

(1)   the employee's weight fulfilled the criteria for obesity, but obesity alone did not constitute a disability;

(2)   the employee had not established on the evidence that he suffered from impairments that prevented him from fully and effectively performing his work on an equal basis with other employees;

(3)   the discomfort described by the employee (which included restricted mobility) did not prevent him from carrying out his work (as a child minder). Accordingly, the court found that he was not disabled at the time of the dismissal.

13.3.3   The adverse effect on normal day-to-day activities condition

The tribunal must ascertain whether the identified impairment adversely affects the claimant's ability to carry out normal day-to-day activities. These are not defined in the Act. The Guidance states that the term 'normal day-to-day activities' are things that people do on a regular or daily basis, such as shopping, reading, getting dressed, etc. The Guidance confirms that the term is not intended to include activities which are normal only for a particular person or group of people. In any individual case, the activities carried out may be highly specialised, for example the playing of a particular game, taking part in a particular hobby, playing a musical instrument, playing sport or performing a highly-skilled task. Impairments which affect only such an activity and have no effect on 'normal day-to-day activities' are not covered. Nevertheless, the EAT held in *Cruickshank v VAW Motorcast Ltd* [2002] IRLR 24 that if, while at work, a claimant's symptoms have a significant and long-term effect on his ability to perform day-to-day tasks, such symptoms should not be ignored simply because the work itself is specialised, so long as the effect of the disability can be measured in terms of the claimant's ability to carry out day-to-day tasks. The EAT confirmed in *Paterson v Commissioner of Police of the Metropolis* [2007] IRLR 763, that 'normal day-to-day activities', includes 'the activities which are relevant to participation in professional life'. The Guidance confirms this.

The Guidance says as follows:

> It is not possible to provide an exhaustive list of day-to-day activities, although guidance on this matter is given here and illustrative examples of when it would, and would not, be reasonable to regard an impairment as having a substantial adverse effect on the ability to carry out normal day-to-day activities are shown in the Appendix. In general, day-to-day activities are things people do on a regular or daily basis, and examples include shopping, reading and writing, having a conversation or using the telephone, watching television, getting washed and dressed, preparing and eating food, carrying out household tasks, walking and travelling by various forms of transport, and taking part in social activities.
>
> The term 'normal day-to-day activities' is not intended to include activities which are normal only for a particular person, or a small group of people. In deciding whether an activity is a normal day-to- day activity, account should be taken of how far it is normal for a large number of people, and carried out by people on a daily or frequent and fairly regular basis. In this context, 'normal' should be given its ordinary, everyday meaning.
>
> A normal day-to-day activity is not necessarily one that is carried out by a majority of people. For example, it is possible that some activities might be carried out only, or more predominantly, by people of a particular gender, such as applying make-up or using hair curling equipment, and cannot therefore be said to be normal for most people. They would nevertheless be considered to be normal day-to-day activities.

The Guidance gives these examples:

A woman plays the piano to a high standard, and often takes part in public performances. She has developed carpal tunnel syndrome in her wrists, an impairment that adversely affects manual dexterity. She can continue to play the piano, but not to such a high standard, and she has to take frequent breaks to rest her arms. This would not of itself be an adverse effect on a normal day-to-day activity. However, as a result of her impairment she also finds it difficult to operate a computer keyboard and cannot use her PC to send emails or write letters. This is an adverse effect on a normal day-to-day activity.

A man works in a warehouse, loading and unloading heavy stock. He develops heart problems and no longer has the ability to lift or move heavy items of stock at work. Lifting and moving such unusually heavy types of item is not a normal day-to-day activity. However, he is also unable to lift, carry or move moderately heavy everyday objects such as chairs, either at work or around the home. This is an adverse effect on a normal day-to-day activity.

A man has had chronic fatigue syndrome for several years and although he has the physical capability to walk and to stand, he finds these very difficult to sustain for any length of time because of the overwhelming fatigue he experiences. As a consequence, he is restricted in his ability to take part in normal day-to-day activities such as travelling, so he avoids going out socially, and works from home several days a week. Therefore there is a substantial adverse effect on normal day-to-day activities.

13.3.3.1 Case law

In *Paterson v Commissioner of Police of the Metropolis* (**13.3.3** above), the EAT held, following an ECJ decision, that career exams and assessments could constitute normal day-to-day activities. In *Chief Constable of Lothian and Borders Police v Cumming* (UKEATS/0077/08), the EAT held that the claimant's minor eyesight impairment did not have a substantial adverse effect on normal day-to-day activities, albeit that she could not progress in her job because of the stringent medical criteria. In *Chief Constable of Dumfries and Galloway Constabulary v Mr C Adams* (UKEATS/0046/08), the EAT held that normal day-to-day activities, albeit carried out during the nightshift, fell within the definition of 'normal day-to-day activities'.

The EAT emphasised in *Goodwin v Patent Office* [1999] IRLR 4 that the DDA 1995 was not concerned with what a person *can* do. Neither was the 1995 Act concerned with whether the claimant had so modified his lifestyle that he might, in fact, manage reasonably well. It required tribunals to look, instead, at the person's ability to carry out daily activities. If the person managed reasonably well because he had adapted his lifestyle, he was still regarded as disabled if his ability to carry out one or more daily activities would clearly be regarded as adversely affected (*Vicary v BT plc* [1999] IRLR 680). On the facts of *Goodwin*, the EAT stated that the tribunal's error was that it had looked at the claimant's abilities to cope at home and come to a conclusion that he was not, therefore, disabled within the meaning of the Act. Instead, said the EAT, the tribunal should have looked at what the claimant could not do, eg carry on a normal conversation with work colleagues. The EAT concluded that the claimant was disabled.

In *Leonard v Southern Derbyshire Chamber of Commerce* [2001] IRLR 19, the issue for the EAT was whether the claimant's clinical depression had a substantial adverse effect on her ability to carry out normal day-to-day activities. The tribunal said she could catch a ball, and eat and drink, and weighed these against what she could not do, such as negotiate pavement edges safely. This, the EAT said, was inappropriate, since her ability to catch a ball did not diminish her inability to negotiate pavement edges safely. A tribunal should, the EAT repeated, concentrate on what claimants cannot do or only do with difficulty, rather than on things they can do (see *Paterson v Commissioner of Police of the Metropolis* (above) and *Aderemi v London and South Eastern Railway Ltd* (UKEAT/0316/12)). In *Banaszczyk v Booker Ltd* (UKEAT/0132/15), the EAT provided some useful guidance as to the meaning of normal day-to-day activities in the context of work activities.

13.3.4 The substantial condition

Section 212(1) of the Act defines 'substantial' to mean 'more than minor or trivial'. The Guidance states that this requirement 'reflects the general understanding of "disability" as a limitation going beyond the normal differences in ability which may exist among people'.

The Guidance suggests a number of factors to consider, including the time taken to carry out an activity, the way in which an activity is carried out, the cumulative effects of an impairment, the effects of behaviour and the effects of the environment. In one case the EAT said, albeit *obiter*, that someone whose hearing impairment merely requires him to view the television with the volume up, and which results in occasional difficulty in hearing speech, may have difficulty in showing 'substantial adverse effect' (*London Underground Ltd v Bragg* (UKEAT/847/98)).

The Guidance states that the time taken by a person with an impairment to carry out a normal day-to-day activity should be considered when assessing whether the effect of that impairment is substantial. It should be compared with the time it might take a person who did not have the impairment to complete an activity. It gives the following example:

> A ten-year-old child has cerebral palsy. The effects include muscle stiffness, poor balance and uncoordinated movements. The child is still able to do most things for himself, but he gets tired very easily and it is harder for him to accomplish tasks like eating and drinking, washing, and getting dressed. Although he has the ability to carry out everyday activities such as these, everything takes longer compared to a child of a similar age who does not have cerebral palsy. This amounts to a substantial adverse effect.

The Guidance states that another factor to be considered when assessing whether the effect of an impairment is substantial is the way in which a person with that impairment carries out a normal day-to-day activity. The comparison should be with the way that the person might be expected to carry out the activity if he did not have the impairment. It gives the following example:

> A person who has obsessive compulsive disorder follows a complicated ritual of hand washing. When preparing a simple meal, he washes his hands carefully after handling each ingredient and each utensil. A person without the disorder might wash his or her hands at appropriate points in preparing the meal, for example after handling raw meat, but would not normally do this after every stage in the process of preparation.

In relation to the cumulative effects of a condition the Guidance gives the following example:

> A man with depression experiences a range of symptoms that include a loss of energy and motivation that makes even the simplest of tasks or decisions seem quite difficult. For example, he finds it difficult to get up in the morning, get washed and dressed, and prepare breakfast. He is forgetful and cannot plan ahead. As a result he has often run out of food before he thinks of going shopping again. Household tasks are frequently left undone, or take much longer to complete than normal. Together, the effects amount to a substantial adverse effect.

In the Appendix to the Guidance, further illustrative and non-exhaustive examples are given of circumstances in which it would be reasonable to regard as substantial the adverse effect of the ability to carry out a normal day-to-day activity. In addition, illustrative and non-exhaustive examples are given of circumstances where it would not be reasonable to regard the effect as substantial. The EAT upheld the tribunal's decision in *Anwar v Tower Hamlets College* (UKEAT/0091/10) that the effect, although 'more than trivial', was still minor and therefore not substantial. With respect, it is hard to see how that interpretation can be correct – the test is whether the effect is more than minor *or* trivial. The EAT, in *Aderemi v London and South Eastern Railway Ltd* (UKEAT/0316/12), held that any matter that cannot be classified as 'trivial' or 'insubstantial' must be treated as substantial.

If an impairment ceases to have a substantial adverse effect on a person's ability to carry out normal day-to-day activities, it is to be treated as continuing to have that effect if that effect is likely to recur (Sch 1, para 1).

Progressive conditions (eg rheumatoid arthritis) do not have to have a *substantial* adverse effect if the condition is *likely to* result in such an impairment (Sch 1, para 8). However, they need to have *some* effect. Therefore, once a person with a progressive condition experiences symptoms which have *any* effect on his normal day-to-day activities, he will fall within the definition of 'disability', so long as the effect of the impairment is likely to become substantial in the future (see *Mowat-Brown v University of Surrey* [2002] IRLR 235 and *Kirton v Tetrosyl Ltd* [2002] IRLR 840). As to whether type 2 diabetes falls under progressive conditions, see *Taylor v Ladbrokes Betting and Gaming Ltd* [2017] IRLR 312. (Note that the Act covers from the date of diagnosis people who have cancer, HIV/AIDS and multiple sclerosis – see **13.3.11**.)

An impairment which consists of a severe disfigurement is deemed to have a substantial effect on the ability of the person to carry out normal day-to-day activities (Sch 1, para 3). The Guidance indicates that assessing severity will be mainly a matter of the degree of the disfigurement. Examples of disfigurements include scars, birthmarks, limb or postural deformation, or diseases of the skin. The Equality Act 2010 (Disability) Regulations 2010 make clear (reg 5) that a severe disfigurement is not to be treated as having a substantial adverse effect on the ability of the person concerned to carry out normal day-to-day activities if it consists of either a tattoo (which has not been removed) or a piercing of the body for decorative or other non-medical purposes, including any object attached through the piercing for such purposes.

13.3.5   Medical evidence

Medical evidence has traditionally played an important role in disability discrimination cases. In *Kapadia v London Borough of Lambeth* [2000] IRLR 699, the tribunal discounted uncontested medical evidence and held that the claimant's medical condition did not have a substantial adverse effect on his ability to carry out day-to-day-activities. The Court of Appeal, agreeing with the EAT, held that the tribunal had erred in rejecting the medical evidence, and reversed the decision. Pill LJ said that uncontested medical evidence need not be accepted by the tribunal where the evidence, on the basis of which the doctor has formed an opinion, is rejected, or where the doctor has misunderstood the evidence he was invited to consider. Nevertheless, the Court of Appeal said the issue of whether an individual has a disability within the meaning of the DDA 1995 is a legal issue, and is one to be determined by the tribunal itself, in light of the medical evidence. In *Abadeh v British Telecommunications plc* [2001] IRLR 23, the EAT held that the tribunal had erred in deciding that an employee was not disabled within the meaning of the DDA 1995 by, in effect, adopting the doctor's assessment as to whether the adverse effects of the impairment were substantial, instead of making its own assessment based on the medical evidence. In *McKechnie Plastic Components v Grant* (UKEAT/0284/08), the EAT held that the tribunal had been free to reach a finding of discrimination when an agreed expert's medical report did not support such a finding, except that it had failed to apply the correct test with respect to whether the impairment was long-term.

In *J v DLA Piper UK LLP* (see **13.3.2.1** above) the EAT remitted the case to the employment tribunal because the tribunal had wrongly declined to give effect to the evidence provided by the claimant's GP on the issues of impairment and 'deduced effect' (see **13.3.7**), having concluded that the GP was not a specialist.

Reference should be made to the EAT's judgments in *De Keyser v Wilson* [2001] IRLR 324 and *City Facilities Management (UK) Ltd v Ling* (UKEAT/0396/13) for guidance as to how expert evidence should be collected and whether it is required in employment tribunal cases.

The EAT held in *East of England Ambulance Service NHS Trust v Sanders* (UKEAT/0217/14) that the employment tribunal acted improperly when it searched for evidence which it found supported the claimant's case that she was disabled.

The EAT confirmed in *Mutombo-Mpania v Angard Staffing Solutions Ltd* (UKEAT/0002/18) that the burden of proof is on the claimant to prove disability.

13.3.6 The long-term condition

Under Sch 1, para 2, the effect of an impairment is long-term if it has lasted for at least 12 months, it is likely to last for at least 12 months, or it is likely to last for the rest of the life of the person affected.

The long-term question should be answered as at the date of the alleged discriminatory acts, not with the benefit of hindsight at the date of the hearing (*Richmond Adult Community College v McDougall* [2008] ICR 431).

In *SCA Packaging Ltd v Boyle* [2009] UKHL 37, the House of Lords held that the word 'likely' should be interpreted as meaning 'could well happen' rather than 'more likely than not'. Their Lordships rejected previous authority that 'likely' in the DDA 1995 was taken to mean a 51% chance, and applied a lower standard. The EAT held that to be the correct test more recently in *Martin v University of Exeter* (UKEAT/0092/18).

The Act states that if an impairment has had a substantial adverse effect on a person's ability to carry out normal day-to-day activities but that effect ceases, the substantial effect is treated as continuing if it is likely to recur. Conditions with effects which recur only sporadically or for short periods can still qualify as impairments for the purposes of the Act in respect of the meaning of 'long-term' (Sch 1, para 2(2)).

The Guidance gives as an example a person with rheumatoid arthritis, who may experience substantial adverse effects for a few weeks after the first occurrence and then have a period of remission. If the substantial adverse effects are likely to recur, the Guidance says they are to be treated as if they were continuing. If the effects are likely to recur beyond 12 months after the first occurrence, they are to be treated as long-term. It should be noted that some impairments with recurring or fluctuating effects may be less obvious in their impact on the individual concerned than is the case with other impairments where the effects are more constant. Likelihood of recurrence should be considered taking all the circumstances of the case into account. This should include what the person could reasonably be expected to do to prevent the recurrence. See *Williams v Leukaemia and Lymphoma Research* (UKEAT/0493/13) and *Thyagarajan v Cap Gemini UK plc* (UKEAT/0264/14) for a recent cases on recurring conditions.

The Act provides that a person who has had a disability within the definition is protected from some forms of discrimination even if he has since recovered or the effects have become less than substantial. In deciding whether a past condition was a disability, its effects count as long-term if they lasted 12 months or more after the first occurrence, or if a recurrence happened or continued until more than 12 months after the first occurrence (s 6(4) and Sch 2, para 2).

13.3.7 Examples of disabilities under the Act

The Explanatory Notes to the Act give the following examples:

- A man works in a warehouse, loading and unloading heavy stock. He develops a long-term heart condition and no longer has the ability to lift or move heavy items of stock at work. Lifting and moving such heavy items is not a normal day-to-day activity. However, he is also unable to lift, carry or move moderately heavy everyday objects such as chairs, at work or around the home. This is an adverse effect on a normal day-to-day activity. He is likely to be considered a disabled person for the purposes of the Act.
- A young woman has developed colitis, an inflammatory bowel disease. The condition is a chronic one which is subject to periods of remissions and flare-ups. During a flare-up she experiences severe abdominal pain and bouts of diarrhoea. This makes it very difficult for her to travel or go to work. This has a substantial adverse effect on her ability to carry out normal day-to-day activities. She is likely to be considered a disabled person for the purposes of the Act.
- A man with depression finds even the simplest of tasks or decisions difficult, for example getting up in the morning and getting washed and dressed. He is also forgetful and can't plan ahead. Together, these amount to a 'substantial adverse effect' on his ability to carry out normal

day-to-day activities. The man has experienced a number of separate periods of this depression over a period of two years, which have been diagnosed as part of an underlying mental health condition. The impairment is therefore considered to be 'long-term' and he is a disabled person for the purposes of the Act.

In the recent case of *Herry v Dudley Metropolitan Council* (UKEAT/0100/16) the EAT drew a distinction between a mental impairment, such as clinical depression or anxiety (which could be a disability), and stress caused by adverse life events (including difficulties at work), which will not be a disability without 'something more'.

In *Walker v Sita Information Networking Computing Ltd* (UKEAT/0091/10), the EAT held that while obesity is not a disability, the conditions caused by it are likely to render someone disabled. The claimant weighed over 21 stone and suffered from a number of conditions, including asthma, diabetes, high blood pressure, anxiety and depression. This resulted in various physical and mental symptoms which could not be attributed to any pathological or mental cause. The EAT emphasised that what was important was not the cause but the effect of the impairments on the claimant's day-to-day activities. However, the EAT said that obesity was not a clinically recognised condition which would itself justify a finding of disability. The EAT did recognise the possibility that an obese person who was determined to lose weight and return to normal weight levels within 12 months might not have a long-term impairment. What is important is that tribunals examine the impact of the obesity on the individual and his ability to carry out normal day-to-day activities, not the cause of any symptoms arising from it.

The ECJ reached the same conclusion in *Kaltoft* (Case C-354/13), see **13.3.2.1**. It held that obesity is not in itself a disability, but that if

> the obesity of the worker concerned entails a limitation which results in particular from physical, mental or psychological impairments that in interaction with various barriers may hinder the full and effective participation of that person in professional life on an equal basis with other workers, and that limitation is a long-term one, obesity can be [a disability].

13.3.8   The effect of medical treatment

Where measures are being taken to treat or correct an impairment that would be *likely* to have a substantial adverse effect on the ability of the person to carry out normal day-to-day activities but for the fact that measures are being taken to treat or correct the condition, the effects of treatment are disregarded and that impairment is still treated as amounting to a disability (save that spectacles and contact lenses are taken into account) (Sch 1, para 5). The Court of Appeal held in *Woodrup v London Borough of Southwark* [2003] IRLR 111 that clear medical evidence will be required in 'deduced effect' cases. However, the EAT observed in *Fathers v Pets at Home Ltd and anor* (UKEAT/0424/13), that relatively little evidence may be required in some cases, eg that to stop taking anti-depressants would lead to a serious effect on ability to carry out day-to-day activities.

Further analysis of the statutory provisions relating to the effects of medical treatment under the old law may be found in *Abadeh v British Telecommunications plc* [2001] IRLR 23.

The EAT held, in *Metroline Travel Ltd v Stoute* (UKEAT/0302/14), that the avoidance of sugary drinks was not sufficient to amount to a particular diet such that it would be ignored when considering the adverse effects of a disability.

13.3.9   Perceived disabilities

The new definition in the Act is wide enough to include people who are discriminated against because they are perceived to be disabled, ie where the discriminator thinks that a person has a disability which he does not have, and discriminates against him for that reason. This is achieved by the use of the terms 'because of' (direct discrimination, s 13) and 'related to' (harassment, s 26) – see **13.5** below.

Two pre-Equality Act 2010 cases looked at the issue of perception discrimination – see J v DLA Piper UK LLP (UKEAT/0263/09) and Aitken v Commissioner of Police of the Metropolis (UKEAT/0226/ 09). Although in neither case was the issue properly before the EAT, it made clear its rejection of the claimants' arguments. One of the reasons given by the EAT in J v DLA Piper for rejecting perception discrimination was the conceptual difficulty in fitting it into the framework of the DDA 1995. In particular, how would a tribunal establish that what the employer 'perceives' actually amounts to a disability? The Foreword to IDS Brief 905 (July 2010) suggests that similar difficulties may apply under the 2010 Act, which retains the same definition of 'disability' as the DDA 1995:

> For example, suppose an employer suspected a job applicant to be emotionally unstable and refused a job on that basis. Could the applicant bring a claim on the basis that the employer had discriminated on the basis of a perceived disability, such as depression? Or would the employer easily defeat the claim on the basis that, while he perceived that the claimant was irrationally and unpredictably moody and so would be difficult to work with, he was perceiving something less than an actual disability? Adopting a broad and purposive approach, tribunals might consider it sufficient that an employer declines to employ because he perceives some adverse effect on the employee's ability to do the job in question. This could be evidence that he perceived the employee's 'condition' to be serious enough to qualify as a disability. However, such an interpretation would deprive the word 'disability' of its specific, technical meaning. It would also potentially mean that any job applicant rejected because of the employer's perception that they would be difficult to work with would have an arguable claim.

It is not clear whether the employee must be perceived as having an impairment (that has a substantial and long-term adverse effect, etc) or whether having a noticeable impairment is sufficient.

13.3.10   Past disabilities

Past disabilities, for example a mental illness which is now cured, are protected under Sch 1, para 9 to the Act. It provides that:

(1)   A question as to whether a person had a disability at a particular time ('the relevant time') is to be determined, for the purposes of section 6, as if the provisions of, or made under, this Act were in force when the act complained of was done had been in force at the relevant time.

(2)   The relevant time may be a time before the coming into force of the provision of this Act to which the question relates.

13.3.11   Certain medical conditions

The Act covers from the time of diagnosis people who have cancer (see Lofty v Harris t/a First Café (UKEAT/0177/17) where the EAT held that Sch 1, para 6 does not distinguish between invasive and other types of cancer), HIV/AIDS and multiple sclerosis (Sch 1, para 6). This means that such people do not have to rely on the condition having 'some' effect as a progressive condition (see **13.3.4**). Otherwise, conditions which will develop into a disability in the future are not protected until the person develops some symptoms, but those symptoms do not have to have a substantial adverse effect if the condition is a progressive one (Sch 1, para 8).

13.3.12   Relationship between the disability and the allegedly discriminatory act

The EAT, in Cruickshank v VAW Motorcast Ltd [2002] IRLR 24, held that the tribunal must assess, on the basis of the evidence available at that time, whether the claimant had a disability *at the time of the alleged discriminatory act*, rather than at the time of the hearing. That approach was confirmed by the Court of Appeal in Richmond Adult Community College v McDougall [2008] ICR 431 in the context of when to determine whether the effect of an impairment is likely to last for at least 12 months (see **13.3.6**). At the time the decision (not to employ) was taken, there was no evidence that the illness was likely to recur, and the tribunal held that it did not therefore have a long-term effect.

13.3.13 The definition of disability under the EC Equal Treatment Framework Directive

The EC Equal Treatment Framework Directive (2000/78) sets out a framework for eliminating employment and occupational discrimination in a number of areas, including disability. The concept of disability is not defined in the Directive. In *Chacón Navas v Eurest Colectividades SA* (Case C-13/05) [2006] IRLR 706, the ECJ had to decide if a sickness that might cause what might constitute a disability in the future, could be equated with disability. The ECJ said not. The ECJ's approach to what amounted to a disability was broadly the same as that contained in the DDA 1995, although interestingly the Court focused on the effect of any impairment on the employee's *professional* life, in contrast to the Act's focus on the impact on 'normal day-to-day activities'. (See also *HK Danmark (acting on behalf of Ring) v Dansk almennyttigt Boligselskab* (Case C-335/11) (**13.3.1** above) and *FOA, acting on behalf of Karsten Kaltoft v Kommunernes Lansforening (KL)* (Case C-354/13) (**13.3.2.1** above).)

13.4 UNLAWFUL DISCRIMINATION IN EMPLOYMENT

13.4.1 Recruitment

Under s 39(1) of the Act, it is unlawful for an employer to discriminate against a disabled person:

(a) in the arrangements which he makes for the purpose of determining to whom he should offer employment;

(b) in the terms on which he offers that person employment; or

(c) by refusing to offer or deliberately not offering him employment.

There is a new provision in the Act (s 60) which prevents a prospective employer asking an applicant for work about his health before work is offered or he has been included in a pool of successful candidates to be offered a job when a vacancy arises. This is not, however, a blanket ban on pre-employment health enquiries. There is a limited set of circumstances in which health-related inquiries can be made. For instance, s 60 does not apply to questions that are necessary to establish whether the applicant will be able to carry out a function intrinsic to the work concerned. Only the EHRC can enforce a breach of this provision, but where the employer asks such questions and rejects the applicant, if the applicant brings a claim of direct discrimination, it will be for the employer to show that he has not discriminated against the applicant.

Section 159 allows an employer to take disability into account when deciding whom to recruit, where disabled people are at a disadvantage or under-represented. This can be done only where candidates are equally qualified. This does not allow employers automatically to prefer disabled candidates. Each case must be considered on its merits, and any action must be a proportionate means of addressing such disadvantage or under-representation.

13.4.2 Promotion and dismissal

Under s 39(2) of the Act, it is unlawful for an employer to discriminate against a disabled person whom he employs:

(a) in the terms of employment which he affords him;

(b) in the opportunities which he affords him for promotion, a transfer, training or receiving any other benefit;

(c) by refusing to afford him, or deliberately not affording him, any such opportunity; or

(d) by dismissing him, or subjecting him to any other detriment (dismissal, for the purposes of the Act, includes constructive dismissal (s 39(7)). Detriment does not include harassment (s 212).

Section 159 allows an employer to take disability into account when deciding whom to promote, where disabled people are at a disadvantage or under-represented. This can be done only where candidates are equally qualified. This does not allow employers automatically to prefer disabled employees. Each case must be considered on its merits, and any action must be a proportionate means of addressing such disadvantage or under-representation.

13.4.3 Post-employment discrimination

Section 108 prohibits discrimination after relationships have ended. Where an employment relationship has come to an end, it is unlawful for the employer to discriminate against the former employee or harass the former employee where the discrimination arises out of and is closely connected to that former relationship. This means, for example, that former employees are protected from being discriminated against on grounds of disability so far as references are concerned, or in a post-dismissal appeal (see also **8.4.3**).

Article 5 of the Equality Act 2010 (Consequential Amendments, Saving and Supplementary Provisions) Order 2010 made changes to s 108(4). The amendment was intended to ensure that the new provision replicated the 'old' law (ie, that even if a person becomes disabled after the relationship has ended, the duty to make a reasonable adjustment (see **13.5.2**) still applies). The original provision could have been interpreted as meaning that the duty arose only if the person already had a disability at the time the relationship ended.

13.5 TYPES OF DISCRIMINATION

There are six ways in which an employer may discriminate against a disabled claimant, employee or former employee. Each will be considered in more detail below. As a matter of ease of approach, the various heads have been considered in this order: direct discrimination, failure to make reasonable adjustments, discrimination arising from disability, indirect discrimination, harassment and victimisation. This approach has been adopted because discrimination arising from disability and indirect discrimination may be justified.

13.5.1 Direct discrimination

Section 13 provides:

> (1) A person (A) discriminates against another (B) if, because of a protected characteristic, A treats B less favourably than A treats or would treat others.
>
> ...
>
> (3) If the protected characteristic is disability, and B is not a disabled person, A does not discriminate against B only because A treats or would treat disabled persons more favourably than A treats B.

Direct discrimination occurs where the reason for a person being treated less favourably than another is a protected characteristic listed in s 4. The language of s 13 explicitly involves a comparison between how the claimant and another person without that protected characteristic is treated – the less favourable treatment. Direct discrimination occurs where someone is discriminated against *because* he is disabled.

Therefore an employer's treatment of a disabled person will amount to direct discrimination if:

(a) the treatment is because of his disability;

(b) the treatment is less favourable in comparison to the treatment of a person not having that protected characteristic is (or would be); and

(c) the relevant circumstances, including the abilities, of the person with whom the comparison is made are the same as, or not materially different from, those of the disabled person (but without the disability).

The Code gives an example of treatment that might amount to direct discrimination:

> During an interview, a job applicant informs the employer that he has multiple sclerosis. The applicant is unsuccessful and the employer offers the job to someone who does not have a disability. In this case,

it will be necessary to look at why the employer did not offer the job to the unsuccessful applicant with multiple sclerosis to determine whether the less favourable treatment was because of his disability.

Note that the tribunal case of *Attridge Law v Coleman* [2007] ICR 654 was referred to the ECJ for clarification as to whether the UK's then current discrimination legislation properly implemented the EC Equal Treatment Framework Directive. Mrs Coleman was not disabled, but her son was. She resigned after allegedly being refused flexible working. She claimed constructive unfair dismissal, direct discrimination and harassment related to disability under the DDA 1995. The ECJ ruled ([2008] IRLR 722) that the EC Framework Directive covers discrimination by association, and sent the case back to the tribunal to see if it could 'fit it into' the current UK law, ie whether the DDA 1995 could be construed to give effect to this interpretation (Case C-303/06). In *Coleman v EBR Attridge Law LLP and Another* (ET/2303745/2005) the tribunal held that the DDA 1995 was capable of an interpretation consistent with the Directive so as to include discrimination by association. The respondent appealed on the basis, inter alia, that the tribunal had 'distorted and rewritten' the DDA 1995. The EAT upheld the tribunal's decision (UKEAT/0071/09) and read words into the DDA 1995 to achieve 'the purpose and effect of the directive'.

The definition of direct discrimination in the Act now states that direct discrimination occurs where the reason for a person being treated less favourably than another is a protected characteristic listed in s 4, and the definition is broad enough to cover cases where the less favourable treatment is because of the victim's association with someone who is disabled, or because the victim is wrongly thought to have a disability. (See too *Chief Constable of Norfolk v Coffey* (UKEAT/0260/16) where the EAT held that an employee whom the employer thinks might become disabled in the future falls within the ambit of disability law.) The definition in the Act also states that, in relation to disability, it is not discrimination to treat a disabled person more favourably than a person who is not disabled.

There is a new exception to what would otherwise be direct disability discrimination in Sch 9, para 1 ('work occupational requirements'). Where being disabled is an occupational requirement for work and a person does not meet that requirement, it will not be discriminatory to reject that person. The requirement must be a 'proportionate means of pursing a legitimate aim', and the burden of showing that rests on those seeking to rely on it. An example might be where an organisation advertises for a deaf person who uses British Sign Language (BSL) to work as a counsellor for other deaf people who use BSL.

The wording used for direct discrimination because of disability is now identical to the wording used in connection with other protected characteristics, and readers are referred to **Chapter 9** for more details about direct disability discrimination, including:

(a)   association and perception (see **9.2.3**);

(b)   the interpretation of the phrase 'because of' (see **9.2.4**);

(c)   what amounts to 'less favourable treatment' (see **9.2.5**);

(d)   the use of comparators (the treatment of the claimant must be compared with that of an actual or a hypothetical person – the comparator – who does not share the same protected characteristic as the claimant (or, in the case of dual discrimination, either of the protected characteristics in the combination) but who is (or is assumed to be) in not materially different circumstances from the claimant. The Code gives an example in a disability case:

> A disabled man with arthritis who can type at 30 words per minute applies for an administrative job which includes typing, but is rejected on the grounds that his typing is too slow. The correct comparator in a claim for direct discrimination would be a person without arthritis who has the same typing speed with the same accuracy rate. In this case, the disabled man is unable to lift heavy weights, but this is not a requirement of the job he applied for. As it is not relevant to the circumstances, there is no need for him to identify a comparator who cannot lift heavy weights.

The Court of Appeal's judgment in *Aitken v Commissioner of Police of the Metropolis* [2012] ICR 78 provides useful guidance on how to construct the correct hypothetical comparator in a direct disability discrimination claim (see **9.2.5**). In *Cordell v Foreign and Commonwealth Office* (UKEAT/0016/11), the EAT re-emphasised that it will often be better 'to focus on the reason-why question than to get bogged down in the often arid and confusing task of "constructing a hypothetical comparator"' (see **9.2.5**). In *Aitken*, the Court of Appeal upheld the tribunal's decision that the proper hypothetical comparator was someone who did not have the claimant's disability but used aggressive words and behaviour frightening to a reasonable person; and

(e)   motive (see **9.2.7**).

13.5.2 Failure to comply with the duty to make reasonable adjustments

An employer also discriminates against a disabled person if he fails (without justification) to make reasonable adjustments, in circumstances where it is under a duty to do so.

Sections 20 and 21 of the Act provide as follows:

20   Duty to make adjustments

(1)   Where this Act imposes a duty to make reasonable adjustments on a person, this section, sections 21 and 22 and the applicable Schedule apply; and for those purposes, a person on whom the duty is imposed is referred to as A.

(2)   The duty comprises the following three requirements.

(3)   The first requirement is a requirement, where a provision, criterion or practice of A's puts a disabled person at a substantial disadvantage in relation to a relevant matter in comparison with persons who are not disabled, to take such steps as it is reasonable to have to take to avoid the disadvantage.

(4)   The second requirement is a requirement, where a physical feature puts a disabled person at a substantial disadvantage in relation to a relevant matter in comparison with persons who are not disabled, to take such steps as it is reasonable to have to take to avoid the disadvantage.

(5)   The third requirement is a requirement, where a disabled person would, but for the provision of an auxiliary aid, be put at a substantial disadvantage in relation to a relevant matter in comparison with persons who are not disabled, to take such steps as it is reasonable to have to take to provide the auxiliary aid.

(6)   Where the first or third requirement relates to the provision of information, the steps which it is reasonable for A to have to take include steps for ensuring that in the circumstances concerned the information is provided in an accessible format.

(7)   A person (A) who is subject to a duty to make reasonable adjustments is not (subject to express provision to the contrary) entitled to require a disabled person, in relation to whom A is required to comply with the duty, to pay to any extent A's costs of complying with the duty.

(8)   A reference in section 21 or 22 or an applicable Schedule to the first, second or third requirement is to be construed in accordance with this section.

(9)   In relation to the second requirement, a reference in this section or an applicable Schedule to avoiding a substantial disadvantage includes a reference to—

(a)   removing the physical feature in question,

(b)   altering it, or

(c)   providing a reasonable means of avoiding it.

(10)   A reference in this section, section 21 or 22 or an applicable Schedule (apart from paragraphs 2 to 4 of Schedule 4) to a physical feature is a reference to—

(a)   a feature arising from the design or construction of a building,

(b)   a feature of an approach to, exit from or access to a building,

(c)   a fixture or fitting, or furniture, furnishings, materials, equipment or other chattels, in or on premises, or

(d)   any other physical element or quality.

(11)   A reference in this section, section 21 or 22 or an applicable Schedule to an auxiliary aid includes a reference to an auxiliary service.

21   Failure to comply with duty

(1)   A failure to comply with the first, second or third requirement is a failure to comply with a duty to make reasonable adjustments.

(2)   A discriminates against a disabled person if A fails to comply with that duty in relation to that person.

13.5.2.1   Duty to adjust

Under ss 20 and 21 an employer can be liable for failing to take positive steps to help overcome the disadvantages resulting from disability. An employer is under a duty to make reasonable adjustments where a disabled person is placed at a substantial disadvantage in comparison with non-disabled people.

The first requirement (s 20(3)) covers changing the way things are done (such as changing a practice), the second (s 20(4)) covers making changes to the built environment (such as providing access to a building) and the third (s 20(5)) covers providing auxiliary aids and services (such as providing special computer software or providing a different service).

Where the first or third requirement involves the way in which information is provided, a reasonable step includes providing that information in an accessible format (s 20(6)). Under the second requirement, taking steps to avoid the disadvantage will include removing, altering or providing a reasonable means of avoiding the physical feature, where it would be reasonable to do so (s 20(9)). It also makes clear that, except where the Act states otherwise, it would never be reasonable for a person bound by the duty to pass on the costs of complying with it to an individual disabled person (s 20(7)).

The Court of Appeal in *Cave v Goodwin and Another* [2001] EWCA Civ 391 stressed that the duty does not arise where the disabled person is not placed at a substantial disadvantage. The Act defines substantial as more than minor or trivial (s 212).

The duty applies in recruitment and during all stages of employment, including dismissal (see *Aylott v Stockton-on-Tees Borough Council* [2010] EWCA Civ 910).

Section 21 makes clear that a failure to comply with any one of the reasonable adjustment requirements amounts to discrimination against a disabled person to whom the duty is owed. It also provides that, apart from under this Act, no other action can be taken for failure to comply with the duty.

The EAT held in *Environment Agency v Rowan* (UKEAT/0060/07) that a tribunal *must* identify:

(a)   the provision, criterion or practice applied, or the physical feature, or the auxiliary aid not supplied;

(b)   the identity of non-disabled comparators (where appropriate); and

(c)   the nature and extent of the substantial disadvantage suffered by the claimant.

The Court of Appeal endorsed this approach in *Newham Sixth Form College v Sanders* [2014] EWCA Civ 734.

Note that the duty applies to the disabled worker, and the principle of associative discrimination does not extend to the duty to make reasonable adjustments (*Hainsworth v Ministry of Defence* [2014] EWCA Civ 763).

Advisers are therefore required to consider these matters with their clients.

13.5.2.2   'Provision, criterion or practice'

The Code states that 'provisions, criteria and practices' (PCPs) should be construed widely and include formal and informal policies, rules, one-off decisions and actions etc. The duty to make reasonable adjustments will apply, for example, to selection and interview procedures as well as to job offers, contractual arrangements and working conditions.

Physical features, according to the Code, include, for example, steps, kerbs, parking areas, lighting, furniture etc. Auxiliary aids include, for example, specialist equipment, sign language interpreters and support workers.

Nonetheless, there are examples of things found not to amount to a 'provision, criterion or practice':

(a)   inefficiency by an employer's human resources department (*Newcastle Upon Tyne Hospitals NHS Foundation Trust v Bagley* (UKEAT/0417/11));

(b)   a one-off flawed disciplinary procedure (*Nottingham City Transport Ltd v Harvey* (UKEAT/0032/12));

(c)   incompetently-run disciplinary proceedings (*Carphone Warehouse plc v Martin* (UKEAT/0371/12)).

In *Secretary of State for Justice v Prospere* (UKEAT/0412/14), the EAT re-emphasised the importance of the tribunal properly identifying the PCP at the outset of a case, since the steps which a respondent is under a duty to take must depend on the particular PCP applied.

In *Griffiths v Secretary of State for Work and Pensions* [2015] EWCA Civ 1265, the claimant was dismissed for sickness absence. She argued that the employer's sickness absence policy should be modified to allow her, as a disabled person, to have longer periods of illness absence before she faced the risk of sanctions than would be permitted for employees not subject to disability-related illnesses.

Elias LJ held that the PCP was that 'the employee must maintain a certain level of attendance at work in order not to be subject to the risk of disciplinary sanctions. That is the provision breach of which may end in warnings and ultimately dismissal.'

In *Carreras v United First Partners Research* (UKEAT/0266/15), the EAT confirmed that an expectation that an employee would work long hours could be a PCP that puts a disabled employee at a substantial disadvantage compared to non-disabled employees. Mr Carreras was an analyst working for an independent brokerage and research firm. Initially, he worked long hours (often at least 12 hours a day). However, in 2012, he had a serious cycling accident. On his return to work he experienced dizziness, fatigue and headaches, had difficulty concentrating and found it difficult to work in the evenings. For the first six months after his return to work, he worked no more than eight hours a day. However, he then began to increase those hours, working from 8am until 6.30pm to 7pm until the end of 2013. From October 2013, he initially made some requests to work late but it became assumed that he would work late. In February 2014, Mr Carreras objected to being asked to work late and, following a heated dispute over this, resigned from his employment. He subsequently brought claims for constructive unfair dismissal and a failure to make reasonable adjustments. An employment tribunal dismissed both his claims. In relation to the reasonable adjustments claim, the PCP he was relying on was a 'requirement' that he work late hours. The respondent argued he had been asked, but not made, to work late. The tribunal agreed with the respondent. Because the PCP Mr Carreras was relying on as a 'requirement' was not made out, his reasonable adjustments claim failed.

Mr Carreras appealed. The EAT overturned the tribunal's decision and said that it had adopted 'an overly technical approach' to the PCP. The EAT referred to the EHRC Code of Practice, which made it clear that a PCP had to be construed broadly: 'Adopting a real world approach, whilst "requirement" might be taken to imply some element of compulsion, an expectation or assumption placed upon an employee ... might well suffice.' The EAT's judgment was approved by the Court of Appeal, which stated that a 'pattern of repeated requests' can be sufficient ([2018] EWCA Civ 323). The case was remitted back to the tribunal.

13.5.2.3   Identifying the comparator and the substantial disadvantage

The s 20 duty arises when the PCP, or physical feature or failure to provide an auxiliary aid places the disabled person at a substantial disadvantage when compared with the non-disabled. 'Substantial' again means 'more than minor or trivial'. It is important that the disadvantage allegedly suffered is *identified* by the claimant or claimant's representative for the tribunal.

The House of Lords, in *Archibald v Fife Council* [2004] IRLR 651, identified how the non-disabled comparator should be identified. In that case, the employee had been a road sweeper with the Council. She had minor surgery which gave rise to complications, leaving her virtually unable to walk and therefore unable to do her job. The Council took various positive steps to seek to redeploy her, such as by retraining her and short-listing her for various posts for which she might be eligible. However, she was not appointed to an alternative post and was dismissed for failing to be able to carry out her job. She claimed that her employers had failed to make reasonable adjustments because she had still had to go through a competitive interview process. In the course of his speech, Lord Rodger identified the comparator as being those employees who were not disabled, could carry out the functions of their job and were therefore not at risk of dismissal.

In *Smith v Churchills Stairlifts plc* [2006] IRLR 41, the Court of Appeal considered the judgment in *Archibald* and concluded that 'the comparator is readily identified by the disadvantage caused by the relevant arrangements'. In that case the claimant was prevented from attending a training course because he could not carry a radiator cabinet, because of his disability. The Court of Appeal held that the correct comparators were the other candidates who attended the training course. On that basis, the claimant was placed at a substantial disadvantage compared to the comparators who could attend the course. As he could not attend, he could not be appointed to the position. The EAT made it clear in *Fareham College v Walters* (UKEAT/ 0396/08) that in many cases the facts will speak for themselves, and the identity of the non-disabled comparator will be clear from the PCP found to be in play. In that case, the PCP was conceded as the refusal to allow the claimant a phased return to work. The EAT held that the correct comparator group was non-disabled employees who could attend work forthwith. That placed the claimant at a substantial disadvantage compared to the comparators. The employees in the comparator group would not be dismissed because they could attend work without a phased return. That approach accords with the Court of Appeal's decision in *Smith v Churchills Stairlifts* (above).

A less generous approach to comparators was initially taken by the EAT in sickness absence cases. *Rider v Leeds CC* (UKEAT/0243/11) and *London Borough of Hillingdon v Bailey* (UKEAT/0421/ 12) concerned the enforcement of the respondents' respective sickness absence policies. In the *Rider* case, the EAT said that the correct comparator was someone who was not disabled but was subject to the policy because of illness. As such, the claimant was not at a disadvantage at all. In the *Bailey* case, the EAT held again that the correct comparators were employees who were ill and subject to the sickness policy but non-disabled. However, the Court of Appeal in *Griffiths* (above) held that the claimant was placed at a substantial disadvantage compared to non-disabled persons. The requirement to maintain a certain level of attendance at work in order not to be subject to the risk of disciplinary sanctions placed the claimant, whose disability led to disability-related absences which would not be the case with the able-bodied, at a substantial disadvantage. *Bailey* and *Rider* are therefore no longer good law.

As the EAT noted, in *General Dynamics Information Technology Ltd v Carranza* (UKEAT/0107/14), employees would also be well advised to bring a claim of discrimination arising from a disability in the alternative in circumstances where they are dismissed for poor attendance. Elias LJ noted in *Griffiths* that '[i]t would be open to a tribunal to find that the dismissal for disability-related absences constituted discrimination arising out of disability contrary to section 15, if, for example, the absences were the result of the disability and it was not proportionate in all the circumstances to effect the dismissal' (see **13.5.4**).

13.5.2.4   Has the employer made reasonable adjustments?

Once a comparison has identified a substantial disadvantage, the question will be whether the employer has made reasonable adjustments – the onus is on the employer to show this. This will depend on the circumstances of each case. That question has to be determined objectively. In the *Smith v Churchills Stairlifts* case (at **13.5.2.2** above), the position was summarised as follows (section numbers adjusted to reflect the amended legislation):

> There is no doubt that the test required by [s 20] is an objective test. The employer must take 'such steps as it is reasonable, in all the circumstances of the case ...' The objective nature of the test is further illuminated by [the draft Code]. Thus, in determining whether it is reasonable for an employer to have to take a particular step, regard is to be had, amongst other things, to ... the financial and other costs which could be incurred by the employer in taking the step and the extent to which taking it would disrupt any of his activities.
>
> It is significant that the concern is with the extent to which the step would disrupt any of his activities, not the extent to which the employer reasonably believes that such disruption would occur. The objective nature of this test is well established in the authorities: see *Collins v Royal National Theatre Board Ltd* [2004] EWCA Civ 144, [2004] IRLR 395 in which Sedley LJ said (at paragraph 20):
>
>> 'The test of reasonableness under [s 20] ... must be objective. One notes in particular that [s 21] speaks of 'such steps as it is reasonable ... for him to have to take.'

A duty is imposed on the employer only to take such steps as are reasonable in all the circumstances of the case. The employer can therefore undertake a cost–benefit analysis when considering reasonable adjustments.

The Code provides that, in determining whether it is reasonable for an employer to have taken a particular step in order to comply with the duty, the following factors *might be taken into account*:

(a)   whether taking any particular steps would be effective in preventing the substantial disadvantage;

(b)   the practicability of the step;

(c)   the financial and other costs of making the adjustment and the extent of any disruption caused;

(d)   the extent of the employer's financial or other resources;

(e)   the availability to the employer of financial or other assistance to help make an adjustment (such as advice through Access to Work); and

(f)   the type and size of the employer.

The following are examples of steps which an employer might take in relation to a disabled person in order to comply with the duty to adjust. The examples are from the Code:

- making adjustments to premises;
- providing information in accessible formats;
- allocating some of the disabled person's duties to another worker;
- transferring him to fill an existing vacancy;
- altering his hours of working or training;
- assigning him to a different place of work or training or arranging home working;
- allowing him to be absent during working hours for rehabilitation, assessment or treatment;
- giving or arranging for training or mentoring (whether for the disabled person or any other person);
- acquiring or modifying equipment;

- modifying procedures for testing or assessment;
- providing a reader or interpreter;
- providing supervision or other support;
- allowing the person to take disability leave;
- employing a support worker;
- modifying disciplinary or grievance procedures;
- adjusting redundancy selection criteria;
- modifying performance-related pay arrangements.

The EAT held, in *Kenny v Hampshire Constabulary* [1999] IRLR 76, that the duty to adjust under the DDA 1995 was limited to job-related matters. So, in this case, the provision of a carer to assist a disabled person when using the toilet was not something the employer had to provide under the duty to adjust. However, the EAT thought that if the worker had his own personal carer then the employer would be expected to make physical arrangements to accommodate the carer at the workplace.

In *British Gas Services Ltd v McCaull* [2001] IRLR 60, the EAT ruled that there was nothing in the Act which prevented an employer arguing at a tribunal that a particular step was not a reasonable one, even if it did not put its mind to the question of accommodation at the time. The obligation to make adjustments is an ongoing one (*Wilding v British Telecommunications plc* [2002] IRLR 524). For another decision on reasonable adjustments, see *Home Office v Collins* [2005] EWCA Civ 598.

The House of Lords in *Archibald v Fife Council* (see **13.5.2.3**) considered whether the duty to make reasonable adjustments applied to the position of a disabled employee who became totally incapable of doing the job for which she was originally employed but who could do another job in the same organisation. Mrs Archibald was interviewed for a sedentary post, but a more qualified person was appointed and Mrs Archibald was dismissed. The House of Lords held that there was a positive duty to make reasonable adjustments. Unlike sex and race discrimination, an employer was obliged to discriminate positively in favour of disabled people. The House of Lords gave a very wide meaning to the concept of 'arrangements'. In this case, there was, it said, an 'arrangement' which placed Mrs Archibald at a substantial disadvantage, namely that if she was physically unable to work as a road sweeper, she was liable to be dismissed. The positive obligation to make reasonable adjustments potentially includes allowing disabled persons to 'trump' candidates for other jobs, even if the disabled employee is not the best candidate, if the disabled employee is suitable to do that work.

As Baroness Hale said:

> [In the cases of sex and race discrimination] men and women or black and white, as the case may be, are opposite sides of the same coin. Each is to be treated in the same way ... Pregnancy apart, the differences between the genders are generally regarded as irrelevant. The 1995 Act, however, does not regard the differences between disabled people and others as irrelevant. It does not expect each to be treated in the same way. It expects reasonable adjustments to be made to cater for the special needs of disabled people. It necessarily entails an element of more favourable treatment.

This decision made clear that employers needed to take proper medical advice and consult with the employee before making decisions about reasonable adjustments (see, eg, *Southampton City College v Randall* [2006] IRLR 24). It is also clear that the need to make reasonable adjustments continues throughout the employment on an ongoing basis. In *Rothwell v Pelikan Hardcopy Scotland* [2006] IRLR 24, the EAT held that the employer's failure to consult with the employee (after having accommodated his disability for many years) before dismissing him on grounds of ill-health was a failure to make reasonable adjustments. In *Greenhof v Barnsley Metropolitan Borough Council* [2006] IRLR 98, the EAT suggested that a serious failure to make a reasonable adjustment would almost inevitably amount to a breach of the implied term of trust and confidence, so entitling an employee to resign and claim constructive dismissal. The EAT confirmed in *Nottingham City Homes Ltd v Brittain* (UKEAT/ 0038/18) that:

> [a]n employer cannot benefit from their own failure to obtain evidence as to whether an employee with a disability can return to work with reasonable adjustments. As explained in *Doran*, whether the employer has complied with their duty to make reasonable adjustments will be judged not only on what they knew but on what should have been known to them had they made reasonable enquiries.

In *Environment Agency v Rowan* [2008] IRLR 20, the EAT held that a trial period (of home working on the facts) could not normally be a reasonable adjustment. The EAT said that a trial period would be a means of assessing whether a future adjustment was a reasonable adjustment, rather than the adjustment in itself.

In *Secretary of State for Work and Pensions (Job Centre Plus) and Others v Wilson* (UKEAT/0289/09), an agoraphobic employee requested to work from home. The EAT held that the tribunal had been wrong to focus on the employer's failure to accede to this request without first considering whether the adjustment would have been futile. The evidence showed that the work, which involved face-to-face interviews with the public and handling confidential files that others in the office needed to access, could not be done effectively from home. In addition, the employer had considered alternative work, at a more senior grade, which might not involve such responsibilities, but no such work was available.

In *Chief Constable of South Yorkshire Police v Jelic* [2010] EWCA Civ 744 the EAT held that reasonable adjustments may extend to swapping roles of employees within an organisation.

There have been conflicting decisions on whether an employer's failure to make an assessment of a disabled employee is of itself a failure to make a reasonable adjustment (see, eg, *Mid-Staffordshire General Hospitals NHS Trust v Cambridge* [2003] IRLR 566). However, in *Tarbuck v Sainsbury's Supermarkets Ltd* [2006] IRLR 664, the EAT said it was not. That approach was confirmed again by the EAT in *Spence v Intype Libra Ltd* (UKEAT/0617/06), where the claimant sought to argue on appeal that *Tarbuck* had been wrongly decided or could be distinguished on its facts. The EAT upheld the tribunal's decision. In *Scottish and Southern Energy plc v Mackay* (UKEAT/0075/06), the EAT said 'we follow the *Tarbuck* line'.

The EAT in *Tameside Hospital NHS Foundation Trust v Mr Mylott* (UKEAT/0352/09) (a case decided under s 4A of the DDA 1995) held that the duty to make reasonable adjustments involves taking steps to enable the employee to stay in employment, not to compensate him for having to leave it – so in Mr Mylott's case, there was no duty to offer him ill-health retirement.

The EAT held in *Salford NHS PCT v Smith* (UKEAT/0507/10) that a career break could not amount to a reasonable adjustment, because it would not have prevented the provisions, criteria and practices placing the claimant at a substantial disadvantage in comparison with persons who were not disabled. Reasonable adjustments are, the EAT held, concerned with enabling the disabled person to remain at or return to work (see also *Conway v Community Options* (UKEAT/0034/12)).

The EAT clarified in *Noor v Foreign and Commonwealth Office* (UKEAT/0470/10) that, 'although the purpose of reasonable adjustments is to prevent a disabled person from being at a substantial disadvantage, it is certainly not the law that an adjustment will only be reasonable if it is completely effective'.

The EAT gave guidance on the costs issue in *Cordell v Foreign and Commonwealth Office* (UKEAT/ 0016/11) and said that it must be weighed with the other factors, but that cost 'is one of the central considerations in the assessment of reasonableness'. It stated that tribunals 'must make a judgment, ultimately, on the basis of what they consider right in their capacity as an industrial jury'.

In *G4S Cash Solutions (UK) Ltd v Powell* (UKEAT/0243/15), the EAT said that where an employee is unable to continue in their original role, it may be a reasonable adjustment both to move them to a new role and to maintain their former rate of pay, if that was higher than the usual rate for the new role.

The EAT held in *Croft Vets Ltd v Butcher* (UKEAT/0430/12) that the respondent failed to make reasonable adjustments by refusing to pay for private counselling. The EAT held that the issue was not 'the payment of private medical treatment in general, but, rather, payment for a specific form of support to enable the claimant to return'.

The EAT confirmed in *Wade v Sheffield Hallam University* (UKEAT/0194/12) that the duty to adjust does not require an employer to redeploy a disabled employee to a role for which he does not meet most of the essential criteria. In *HK Danmark (acting on behalf of Ring) v Dansk almennyttigt Boligselskab* (Case C-335/11) (see **13.3.1** above), the ECJ held that reducing an employee's working hours could be a reasonable adjustment, though it would depend on the facts.

Elias LJ held in *Griffiths* (above) that whilst the sickness absence policy placed the claimant at a substantial disadvantage:

> the steps required to avoid or alleviate such disadvantages are not likely to be steps which a reasonable employer can be expected to take. The *O'Hanlon* case ... provides an example. The sick pay rules in that case were found to constitute a substantial disadvantage for reasons already discussed, but the Court of Appeal agreed with the EAT in holding that increasing the period during which the disabled claimant could claim full pay whilst sick would not be a reasonable step to expect the employer to take. ... Hooper LJ also approved an observation by the EAT that:
>
> > 'The Act is designed to recognise the dignity of the disabled and to require modifications which enable them to play a full part in the world of work, important and laudable aims. It is not to treat them as objects of charity which, as the tribunal pointed out, may in fact sometimes and for some people tend to act as a positive disincentive to return to work.'

Elias LJ upheld the employment tribunal's conclusion on the facts that modifying the policy to allow the claimant to have longer periods of illness absence before she faced the risk of sanctions than would be permitted for employees not subject to disability-related illnesses, was not a reasonable adjustment. He noted, however, that where periods of absence were limited and occasional, it might be possible to modify the policy in a principled and rational way, and it might be unreasonable not to do so. It will, of course, depend on the facts.

In *G4S Cash Solutions (UK) Ltd v Powell* (UKEAT/0243/15) the EAT held that an employer cannot impose as a reasonable adjustment something that is incompatible with the terms of the employment contract (the employee offered a job at a reduced rate of pay) unless the employee consents. There is no reason in principle why pay protection, in conjunction with other measures, cannot be a reasonable adjustment. The question would be whether it was reasonable for the employer to take that step.

13.5.2.5 Knowledge of disability

Note that the duty in s 20 is not to make adjustments to facilitate the employment of disabled people generally. The duty arises only in relation to particular identifiable individuals. Schedule 8, Pt 3, para 20 states that an employer is not subject to a duty to make reasonable adjustments if the employer does not know, and could not reasonably be expected to know, that a person has (or has had) a disability and is likely to be placed at a substantial disadvantage. That language reflects wording that was used previously, where an employer was exempted from the duty to make reasonable adjustments if 'he did not know, and could not reasonably be expected to know, that someone was likely to be placed at a substantial disadvantage'. In *DWP v Alan* (UKEAT/0242/09) the EAT held that, to ascertain whether that exemption applies, two questions arise:

1.   'Did the employer know both that the employee was disabled and that his disability was liable to affect him in the manner set out in [s 20]'. If the answer is no, then the second question is:

2. 'Ought the employer to have known both that the employee was disabled and that his disability was liable to affect him in the manner set out in [s 20]'. If the answer to this question is also no, there is no duty to make reasonable adjustments.

(See too *Wilcox v Birmingham CAB Services Ltd* (UKEAT/0293/10).)

In *Department of Work and Pensions v Hall* (UKEAT/0012/05), the employer was held to have constructive knowledge of an employee's disability because, inter alia, the employee's manager had seen her application for disabled person's tax credit.

In *Wilcox* (above), the EAT held that the employer did not and could not have reasonably known about the claimant's disability until it had received a consultant's report that had been commissioned (on the order of the tribunal).

In *Gallop v Newport CC* [2013] EWCA Civ 1583, the Court of Appeal overturned a tribunal's finding that the employer did not have knowledge because it was entitled to rely on advice from an occupational health adviser that the employee was not disabled. The Court of Appeal held that the question was not what the occupational health department had reported, but rather whether the employer had actual or constructive knowledge of the facts constituting the claimant's disability. The employer does not also need to know that the consequence of those facts is that the employee is, as a matter of law, disabled. The case was remitted for a re-hearing. On remission, the employment tribunal held that the decision maker did not, nevertheless, have actual knowledge of the claimant's disability and that his decision was not because of an intention or motivation stemming from the claimant's disability, so there was no direct disability discrimination. That decision was upheld on appeal (UKEAT/0118/15). Note, however, the important clarification provided by the Court of Appeal in *Donelien v Liberata UK Ltd* [2018] EWCA Civ 129 that the basis of *Gallop* was that an employer cannot simply rely on its own unquestioning adoption of occupational health's unreasoned opinion, which the Court said is a long way from saying that an employer may not attach great weight to the informed and reasoned opinion of an occupational health consultant:

> It seems that there was some concern following the decision in Gallop that it raised a serious question about whether employers in a case of this kind were entitled to attach weight to advice from occupational health consultants about whether an employee was suffering from a disability within the meaning of the 1995 Act. It was explicitly for that reason that Judge Richardson, when permitting the appeal in the EAT to proceed, directed that it be heard by a tribunal that included lay members. In my view it is plain that Rimer LJ did not intend generally to discount the value of such advice. The basis on which the employee's appeal was allowed was that the ET had found that the employer was entitled to rely, and rely exclusively, on the opinion of the occupational health advisers in circumstances where that opinion was worthless because it was unreasoned. That is perhaps most clear from para 42 of Rimer LJ's judgment ('relying *simply* on its *unquestioning* adoption of OH's *unreasoned* opinion') but equally from paras 40 and 43 ('he cannot simply rubber-stamp the adviser's opinion'). That is very far from saying that an employer may not attach great weight to the informed and reasoned opinion of an occupational health consultant. That was the view of the EAT, and in particular of the lay members, in the present case. Having expressed at para 30 of his judgment essentially the same view as me about the ratio of *Gallop*, Langstaff J went on to say, at para 31, that while an ET will 'look for evidence that the employer has taken its own decision ... the lay members sitting with me in this case would wish to emphasise that in general great respect must be shown to the views of an Occupational Health doctor', though such views should not be followed uncritically.

The Code states that 'an employer must do all [it] can reasonably be expected to do to find out if a worker has a disability ... [and this is] an objective assessment'.

In *Abertawe Bro Morgannwg University Local Health Board v Morgan* [2018] EWCA Civ 640, the Court of Appeal held that the time by which an employer should comply with its duty to make reasonable adjustments is not the same as when a failure to comply with that duty begins. The duty to make reasonable adjustments begins as soon as an employer is able to take steps to avoid any relevant disadvantage to its employee, and that depends on its knowledge of an employee's disability. However, in assessing time, the Court said that the correct approach is to 'establish a default rule that time begins to run at the end of the period in which the respondent might reasonably have been expected to comply with the relevant duty' and that date must be assessed in light of the facts as they would reasonably have appeared to the claimant, including what the claimant was told by the respondent.

13.5.2.6   Concluding remarks

Schedule 8 to the Act sets out further guidance in respect of reasonable adjustments. If two or more people have a duty to make reasonable adjustments for the same person, each of them must comply with the duty in so far as it is reasonable for each of them to do so.

The Explanatory Notes to the Act give the following examples of reasonable adjustments:

- A utility company knows that significant numbers of its customers have a sight impairment and will have difficulty reading invoices and other customer communications in standard print, so must consider how to make its communications more accessible. As a result, it might provide communications in large print to customers who require this.

- A bank is obliged to consider reasonable adjustments for a newly recruited financial adviser who is a wheelchair user and who would have difficulty negotiating her way around the customer area. In consultation with the new adviser, the bank rearranges the layout of furniture in the customer area and installs a new desk. These changes result in the new adviser being able to work alongside her colleagues.

- The organiser of a large public conference knows that hearing-impaired delegates are likely to attend. She must therefore consider how to make the conference accessible to them. Having asked delegates what adjustments they need, she decides to engage BSL/English interpreters, have a palantypist and an induction loop to make sure that the hearing-impaired delegates are not substantially disadvantaged.

- An employee develops carpal tunnel syndrome which makes it difficult for him to use a standard keyboard. The employer refuses to provide a modified keyboard or voice-activated software which would overcome the disadvantage. This could be an unlawful failure to make a reasonable adjustment which would constitute discrimination.

- A private club has a policy of refusing entry to male members not wearing a collar and tie for evening events. A member with psoriasis (a severe skin condition which can make the wearing of a collar and tie extremely painful) could bring a discrimination claim if the club refused to consider waiving this policy for him.

- A visually-impaired prospective tenant asks a letting agent to provide a copy of a tenancy agreement in large print. The agent refuses even though the document is held on computer and could easily be printed in a larger font. This is likely to be an unlawful failure to make a reasonable adjustment which would constitute discrimination.

Note: In *Hainsworth v Ministry of Defence* [2014] EWCA Civ 763, the Court of Appeal held that employers are not obliged to consider making reasonable adjustments to accommodate employees who have an association with a disabled person (see *Coleman v EBR Attridge Law* at **13.5.1**, and **9.2.3**, where the claimant complained of direct discrimination by association). The claimant was employed by the Ministry of Defence in Germany. Her daughter had Down's Syndrome, and the educational establishment provided by the Ministry of Defence in Germany did not cater for her educational requirements. The claimant requested a transfer to the UK to help her meet her daughter's needs. This was refused and she brought a claim under s 20 of the Equality Act 2010.

While the definition of harassment and direct discrimination in the Equality Act 2010 were changed so as to cover associative discrimination, the Act states only that reasonable adjustments must be made to assist the *disabled person* in question. This reflects the wording in Article 5 of the Equal Treatment Framework Directive. The tribunal rejected the claim, holding that the Equality Act only required an employer to make reasonable adjustments for an employee or job applicant who is disabled; it does not oblige an employer to make adjustments for a non-disabled employee who is associated with a disabled person. The EAT and the Court of Appeal upheld the tribunal's decision: the Equality Act 2010 did not entitle the claimant to any reasonable adjustments, and the EU Directive focused on disabled employees and not on others.

13.5.3 Background to discrimination arising from disability and indirect discrimination – disability-related discrimination and the House of Lords decision in Malcolm

Under the DDA 1995, an employer discriminated against a disabled person if, for a reason relating to the person's disability, he treated him less favourably than a person to whom that reason did not apply and he could not show that the treatment was justified. The reason for the less favourable treatment only needed to be related to the person's disability, not necessarily on the grounds of it.

In *Clark v Novacold Ltd* [1999] IRLR 318, the employee was dismissed after a period of long-term absence by reason of ill health following a work accident. The Court of Appeal held that he had been dismissed for a reason relating to his disability, and gave the following further example:

> If no dogs are admitted to a café, the reason for denying access to refreshment in it by a blind person with his guide dog would be the fact that no dogs are admitted. That reason 'relates to' his disability. ...

The House of Lords, in *London Borough of Lewisham v Malcolm* [2008] IRLR 700, overruled that analysis. Their Lordships held that 'a reason which relates to a person's disability' has to be construed narrowly. *Malcolm* was not an employment case. Mr Malcolm was a tenant of the London Borough of Lewisham. He suffered from a form of chronic schizophrenia which had led to a number of hospital admissions, some of them involuntary. His illness was not disabling when controlled by appropriate medication; but when such medication was not taken, his ability to carry out normal day-to-day activities was substantially impaired. Contrary to Lewisham's rules, Mr Malcolm sublet his flat. Lewisham sought to obtain possession, and an issue arose as to whether in doing so it was discriminating against him (under what was then s 22(3)(c) of the DDA 1995, which stated that 'It is unlawful for a person managing any premises to discriminate against a disabled person occupying those premises ... by evicting the disabled person, or subjecting him to any other detriment'). Section 24(1) provided that, for the purposes of s 22, a person discriminated against a disabled person if:

(a)   for a reason which relates to the disabled person's disability, he treats him less favourably than he treats or would treat others to whom that reason does not or would not apply; and

(b)   he cannot show that the treatment in question is justified.

This wording was identical to the equivalent employment provision in s 3A(1) of the DDA 1995. So, although the case was a housing case, it had direct relevance to the employment context.

The House of Lords decided that Mr Malcolm was a disabled person but that the reason for Lewisham's treatment of him did *not* relate to Mr Malcolm's disability. The House of Lords said the real reason for the treatment was that Lewisham, as a social landlord with a limited stock of housing and a heavy demand from those on its waiting list, acted as it did because it was not prepared to allow tenancies to continue where the tenant was not living in the premises demised. Their Lordships went on to hold (with some reservations, as they felt that 'but for' his mental illness, Mr Malcolm would probably not have behaved so irresponsibly as to sublet his flat and move elsewhere) that Lewisham's reason for seeking possession – that Mr Malcolm had sublet the flat and gone to live elsewhere – was a pure housing management decision which had nothing whatever to do with his mental disability. Lord Bingham held that that the expression 'a reason which relates to the disabled person's disability' denoted 'some connection, not necessarily close, between the reason and the disability'. On the facts, there was no evidence that the Council was aware that Mr Malcolm suffered from a disability.

Lord Scott stated:

> If the physical or mental condition that constitutes the disability has played no motivating part in the decision of the alleged discriminator to inflict on the disabled person the treatment complained of, the alleged discriminator's reason for that treatment cannot ... relate to the disability.

His Lordship (using the 'no dogs' policy example given above) said that if a restaurant refuses to allow a blind person to bring his dog onto the premises, there is no discrimination in such a case because 'the problem is the dog', not the disability.

Importantly, however, Lord Scott did accept that in the *Clark* case the employer's reason for the dismissal was that the employee's injury was going to keep him off work for a year or so. This was plainly a reason that had been caused by, and, in that sense, *related* to the employee's disability.

Until the House of Lords decision in *Malcolm*, the correct comparator in these cases was said to be someone to whom that reason (for the treatment) did not or would not apply (*Clark v Novacold Ltd*). In *Clark*, the reason for the treatment was C's inability to do his job. Therefore, the correct comparator was someone who was able to perform the main functions of his job. Such a person would not have been dismissed, and therefore Mr Clark had been treated less favourably than someone to whom the reason for the treatment did not apply. In *Malcolm*, their Lordships, assuming (contrary to their actual conclusion) that the reason for the treatment related to Mr Malcolm's disability, went on to consider who the appropriate comparator should be in such a case. Referring to the 'care and detail' of Mummery LJ in *Clark v Novacold*, the House of Lords said the issue in Mr Malcolm's case was whether 'the others' with whose treatment the treatment of Mr Malcolm was to be compared were:

(a)   persons without a mental disability who have sublet a Lewisham flat and gone to live elsewhere, or

(b)   tenants of Lewisham flats who have not sublet or gone to live elsewhere, or

(c)   some other comparator group, and if so what?

Lord Bingham, with whom Lords Scott, Brown and Neuberger agreed, commented that, based on his understanding of the judgment in *Clark v Novacold*, the correct comparison would be with group (b). But, he went on to say, he found that decision 'difficult to accept' for the reason succinctly given by Toulson LJ in the Court of Appeal (at para 155):

> [T]he complainant is logically bound to be able to satisfy the requirement of showing that his treatment is less favourable than would be accorded to others to whom the reason for his treatment did not apply. For without the reason there would not be the treatment.

Lord Bingham, finding that this would defeat Mr Malcolm's complaint of discrimination, went on to say that 'a more natural comparison, as it seems to me, is with group (a)'. On this analysis, the comparison would fall to be made on the bases rejected in *Clark v Novacold*, ie with a person who had a dog but no disability, or a diner who was a very untidy eater but had no disability-related reason for eating in that way. Looking at group (c) as a possibility, he said it would make it attractive, if possible, to identify an intermediate comparator group (c), as this 'would avoid absurdity and give fair effect to the statute. But I do not think that any such intermediate comparator group has been suggested, and none is identified by the statutory language'. On that basis, he said, 'I find it hard to accept that *Novacold* was rightly decided. I am in any event satisfied that a different principle must be applied in the present context.'

Lord Scott said:

> The Lord Justice's [Mummery's] conclusion in *Clark* emasculates the statutory comparison. What is the point of asking whether a person has been treated 'less favourably than others' if the 'others' are those to whom the reason why the disabled person was subjected to the complained of treatment cannot apply?

He went on:

> Confusion regarding the blind man and his guide dog example has, I think, crept in because of the over-concentration on the refusal to admit entry to the dog. The dog is not a potential beneficiary of

the 1995 Act. It is the blind man who is. If he is refused entry it is not because he is blind but because he is accompanied by a dog and is not prepared to leave his dog outside. Anyone, whether sighted or blind, who was accompanied by a dog would have been treated in the same way. The reason for the treatment would not have related to the blindness; it would have related to the dog.

Baroness Hale in her dissenting speech pointed out that Parliament introduced the new definition of direct discrimination on the assumption that *Clark* was properly decided.

The view of most commentators was that the effect of imposing a much stricter comparator test in these claims would be that claimants would rarely be able to clear the hurdle of showing less favourable treatment. The decision appeared to render the disability-related provisions of the DDA 1995 meaningless, and to make it extremely hard (if not impossible) for a claimant to succeed in a claim of disability-related discrimination which existed under the DDA 1995.

In late November 2008, the Government announced that it would be issuing a consultation document setting out its proposals for dealing with the problems posed by *Malcolm*. The Government published its response to the consultation in April 2009. In brief, it proposed removing disability-related discrimination as a concept, and replacing it with 'indirect' discrimination. The intention was that there would also be a provision requiring a duty-holder to fulfil the duty to make reasonable adjustments before he could seek objectively to justify indirect discrimination (see **13.5.5** below).

It is against this background that the measures in the 2010 Act relating to discrimination arising from disability and indirect discrimination were introduced.

13.5.4   Discrimination arising from disability

Section 15 of the Act was enacted with the intention of rebalancing the situation, post-*Malcolm*, which it was felt had restricted the wider purpose of the DDA. Section 15 provides:

> (1)   A person (A) discriminates against a disabled person (B) if—
>
>> (a)   A treats B unfavourably because of something arising in consequence of B's disability, and
>>
>> (b)   A cannot show that the treatment is a proportionate means of achieving a legitimate aim.
>
> (2)   Subsection (1) does not apply if A shows that A did not know, and could not reasonably have been expected to know, that B had the disability.

The explanatory notes state that s 15 is aimed at 're-establishing an appropriate balance between enabling a disabled person to make out a case of experiencing a detriment which arises [from] his or her disability, and providing an opportunity for an employer or other person to defend the treatment'. It provides that it is discriminatory to treat a disabled person unfavourably not because of the person's disability itself, but because of something arising from, or in consequence of, his or her disability, such as the need to take a period of disability-related absence. While the language of s 13 on direct discrimination explicitly involves a comparison with persons without the protected characteristic, s 15 only refers to 'unfavourable treatment' and does not therefore necessitate a comparator. It is, however, possible to justify such treatment if it can be shown to be a proportionate means of achieving a legitimate aim.

The EAT gave guidance on the meaning of 'unfavourable' in *Swansea University Pension Scheme Trustees v Williams* [2015] IRLR 885 and said that 'unfavourable' should be measured against an objective sense of that which is adverse as compared with that which is beneficial. On appeal (*Williams v Trustees of Swansea University Pension and Assurance Scheme* [2017] EWCA Civ 1008), the Court of Appeal held that an employee was not unfavourably treated because of something arising in consequence of his disability. The appellant suffers from a number of conditions, including Tourette's syndrome, obsessive compulsive disorder and depression. After having worked full time for a number of years, he asked to wok part time because of his disabilities:

his hours (and pay) were reduced. He then applied for ill health retirement (at the age of 38). Under the Scheme's rules, he was provided with an enhanced benefit up to what would have been his normal retirement age. No actuarial reduction was made for early receipt; however, his enhanced benefits were calculated using his part-time salary at the date of his retirement, and the claimant complained under s 15 that this was unfavourable treatment because a person working full time would have had their pension calculated using their full-time pay. The Court rejected his claim: Mr Williams had actually been treated advantageously in consequence of his disability (although not as advantageously as a person with a different disability or medical history would have been treated).

Discrimination arising from disability is different from direct discrimination in that the question is whether the person has been treated unfavourably *because of something arising in consequence* of his disability (cf direct discrimination which is *less favourable* treatment *because of the disability* and requires a comparator). So, for example, this section may be relied on by persons who are dismissed while on long-term sick leave; if the absence is due to a disability, the dismissal would appear to be potentially unlawful discrimination arising from the person's disability. In *Buchanan v Commissioner of Police of the Metropolis* (UKEAT/0112/16) the EAT emphasised that a key facet of s 15 (unlike s 19) claims is that it is individualised: it is not sufficient to show that there is a policy that has been considered and applied to everyone; it is the treatment arising from the policy in the individual case that needs to be justified. The EAT held in *Hall v Chief Constable of West Yorkshire Police* (UKEAT/0057/15) that a s 15 claim could succeed where the disability had a significant influence on, or was an effective cause of, the treatment.

In *Hall v Chief Constable of West Yorkshire Police* (above) the EAT emphasised that it was not necessary for the disability to be the cause of the unfavourable treatment. The burden on a claimant to establish causation in a claim for discrimination arising from disability is low. It will be sufficient to show that there is a 'loose' causal link and that the unfavourable treatment has been caused by an outcome or consequence of the disability, and the employer's motivation is irrelevant. The EAT in *Charlesworth v Dransfields Engineering Services Ltd* (UKEAT/0197/16) said that s 15 requires unfavourable treatment to be 'because of something' arising in consequence of the disabled person's disability. If the 'something' is an effective cause – an influence or cause that operated on the mind of the alleged discriminator to a significant extent (whether consciously or unconsciously) – the causal test is satisfied. However, even if a claimant succeeds in establishing discrimination arising from disability, the employer can defend such a claim by showing either that the treatment was objectively justified or that it did not know or could not reasonably have known that the employee was disabled.

A similar approach was taken in *Risby v London Borough of Waltham Forest* (EAT/0318/15) where it was held that an employee's loss of temper, for which he was dismissed, arose from his disability because, although his loss of temper was unrelated to his disability per se, it arose from the employer's decision to hold a course in a venue the employee could not access because of his disability. The EAT provided a clear analysis of s 15 of the Equality Act 2010 in *T-Systems Ltd v Lewis* (EAT/0042/15) and made reference to some of the examples set out in the EHRC Code of Practice on Employment (see above).

In *City of York Council v Grosset* [2018] EWCA Civ 1105, the claimant was a teacher suffering from a disability (cystic fibrosis). He was employed by the respondent with full knowledge of this. The claimant's case was that he was subjected to an increased workload; he was unable to absorb the increased pressure of work by working in his own time, by reason of the time-consuming exercise regime he has to pursue to keep his disease under control. He became very stressed. Whilst subject to this high level of stress, the claimant showed a class of 15-year-olds an 18-rated horror film, *Halloween*. When the school learned about this, disciplinary charges were brought against the claimant. These resulted in his summary dismissal for gross misconduct.

The claimant accepted at the disciplinary hearing that showing the film was inappropriate and maintained that it had happened as a result of an error of judgment on his part arising from the high level of stress he was under at the time in consequence of his disability.

The employment tribunal was satisfied that the error of judgment for which the claimant was dismissed arose in consequence of his disability. The respondent appealed to the EAT in relation to the finding of the tribunal that there had been a breach of s 15 in relation to the dismissal of the claimant. The EAT dismissed the appeal.

The respondent argued in the Court of Appeal that the claimant had to show that the respondent itself appreciated that the claimant's behaviour in showing the film arose in consequence of his disability for the s 15 claim to succeed, and that he could not do so. The tribunal had accepted that the decision-makers for the respondent did not believe the claimant's claim that his behaviour was the result of a misjudgment caused by levels of stress arising in consequence of his disability.

The Court of Appeal pointed out that s 15(1)(a) requires an investigation of two distinct causative issues: (i) did A treat B unfavourably because of an (identified) 'something'? and (ii) did that 'something' arise in consequence of B's disability? The CA held:

> 37. The first issue involves an examination of A's state of mind, to establish whether the unfavourable treatment which is in issue occurred by reason of A's attitude to the relevant 'something'. In this case, it is clear that the respondent dismissed the claimant because he showed the film. That is the relevant 'something' for the purposes of analysis. This is to be contrasted with a case like *Charlesworth v Dransfields Engineering Services Ltd*, EAT (Simler J), UKEAT/ 0197/16/JOJ, unrep, judgment of 12 January 2017, in which the reason the claimant was dismissed was redundancy, so that no liability arose under section 15 EqA, even though the redundancy of the claimant's job happened to be brought into focus by the ability of the defendant employer to carry on its business in periods when he was absent from work due to a disability. In that case, therefore, the relevant 'something' relied upon by the claimant was the claimant's absence from work due to sickness, but he was not dismissed because of that but because his post was redundant.

> 38. The second issue is an objective matter, whether there is a causal link between B's disability and the relevant 'something'. In this case, on the findings of the ET there was such a causal link. The claimant showed the film as a result of the exceptionally high stress he was subject to, which arose from the effect of his disability when new and increased demands were made of him at work in the autumn term of 2013.

> 39. In my view, contrary to Mr Bowers' argument, it is not possible to spell out of section 15(1)(a) a further requirement, that A must be shown to have been aware when choosing to subject B to the unfavourable treatment in question that the relevant 'something' arose in consequence of B's disability (ie that A should himself be aware of the objective causation referred to in issue (ii) above).

The EAT referred to the Grosset case in *Sheikholeslami v University of Edinburgh* (UKEAT/0014/17) in deciding that the employment tribunal erred when it failed to consider the possibility that the causal connection between the something that causes unfair treatment and the disability may involve several links. See too *South Warwickshire NHS Foundation Trust v Lee and Others* (UKEAT/0287/17) and *Dunn v Secretary of State for Justice* [2018] EWCA Civ 1998.

The Code gives an example of how this works:

> An employer dismisses a worker because she has had three months' sick leave. The employer is aware that the worker has multiple sclerosis and most of her sick leave is disability-related. The employer's decision to dismiss is not because of the worker's disability itself. However, the worker has been treated unfavourably because of something arising in consequence of her disability (namely, the need to take a period of disability-related sick leave) …

> It is irrelevant whether or not other workers would have been dismissed for having the same or similar length of absence. It is not necessary to compare the treatment of the disabled worker with that of her colleagues or any hypothetical comparator. The decision to dismiss her will be discrimination arising from disability if the employer cannot objectively justify it.

The Explanatory Notes give the following examples:

- An employee with a visual impairment is dismissed because he cannot do as much work as a non-disabled colleague. If the employer sought to justify the dismissal, he would need to show that it was a proportionate means of achieving a legitimate aim.

- The licensee of a pub refuses to serve a person who has cerebral palsy because she believes that he is drunk as he has slurred speech. However, the slurred speech is a consequence of his impairment. If the licensee is able to show that she did not know, and could not reasonably have been expected to know, that the customer was disabled, she has not subjected him to discrimination arising from his disability.

- However, in the example above, if a reasonable person would have known that the behaviour was due to a disability, the licensee would have subjected the customer to discrimination arising from his disability, unless she could show that ejecting him was a proportionate means of achieving a legitimate aim.

13.5.4.1   Objective justification

The s 15 defence applies if an employer can show that the (unfavourable) treatment is a proportionate means of achieving a legitimate aim. See *Swansea University Pension Scheme Trustees v Williams* (above), *Griffiths v Secretary of State for Work and Pensions* [2015] EWCA Civ 1265 and *DL Insurance Services Ltd v O'Connor* (UKEAT/0230/17) for recent cases on how the justification defence is applied in a s 15 case. A different approach is adopted in these cases from justification in an indirect discrimination case under s 19 (see **13.5.5** below).

The EAT held in *Dominique v Toll Global Forwarding Ltd* (UKEAT/0308/13) that there is no legal obligation to consider any failure to adjust before considering objective justification. However, the EAT held that any relevant failure to adjust will be pertinent to the necessary balancing exercise required. The EHRC's Code states:

> If an employer has failed to make a reasonable adjustment which would have prevented or minimised the unfavourable treatment, it will be very difficult for them to show that the treatment was objectively justified.

In *Hensman v Ministry of Defence* (UKEAT/0067/14), the EAT overturned a tribunal's decision that the dismissal was disproportionate, holding that it had failed to carry out the necessary balancing exercise. The employment tribunal had focused on what the Crown Court had said about the actions of Mr Hensman in filming a colleague in the shower not being his fault because of his medical condition, rather than balancing that against the employer's concerns relating to trust and confidence.

The EAT held, in *Burdett v Aviva Employment Services Ltd* (UKEAT/0439/13), that the employment tribunal failed to balance the discriminatory impact of the measure (dismissal for sexual assault of two female employees when the claimant stopped his medication) against other options open to the employer (eg allowing the claimant to work from home). The employment tribunal had held that the discrimination was justified.

13.5.4.2   Knowledge of disability

For discrimination arising from a disability to occur, the employer or other person must know, or reasonably be expected to know, that the disabled person has a disability.

Section 15(2) states that 'subsection (1) does not apply if A shows that A did not know, and could not reasonably have been expected to know, that B had the disability'. That is the same wording used with regard to s 21, so readers should have regard to the interpretation given to the phrase in *DWP v Alan* (UKEAT/0242/09) (see **13.5.2.5**).

Where employers are dealing with misconduct issues with a disabled employee, they are well advised to get informed medical advice on whether a link exists or is likely to exist between the conduct and the disability.

13.5.5   Indirect discrimination

Section 19 provides:

(1)   A person (A) discriminates against another (B) if A applies to B a provision, criterion or practice which is discriminatory in relation to a relevant protected characteristic of B's.

(2)   For the purposes of subsection (1), a provision, criterion or practice is discriminatory in relation to a relevant protected characteristic of B's if—

(a)   A applies, or would apply, it to persons with whom B does not share the characteristic,

(b)   it puts, or would put, persons with whom B shares the characteristic at a particular disadvantage when compared with persons with whom B does not share it,

(c)   it puts, or would put, B at that disadvantage, and

(d)   A cannot show it to be a proportionate means of achieving a legitimate aim.

The other provision, which was introduced as a consequence of *Malcolm* (above), is one familiar to employment lawyers in relation to discrimination on other grounds (see **Chapter 10**). Indirect discrimination occurs when a policy that applies in the same way to everybody has an effect which particularly disadvantages people with a protected characteristic. Where a particular group is disadvantaged in this way, a person in that group is indirectly discriminated against if he is put at that disadvantage, unless the person applying the policy can justify it. The 2011 Guidance on Disability states, by way of example, that a disabled person with a mobility impairment will have 'the particular characteristic of being mobility impaired' and 'would share the protected characteristic with other people who have mobility impairments'. Thus the focus should be on symptoms. Unlike discrimination arising from disability, there is no requirement in s 19 that an employer need know about an employee's disability.

Indirect discrimination may also occur when a policy would put a person at a disadvantage if it were applied. This means, for example, that where a person is deterred from doing something, such as applying for a job or taking up an offer of service, because a policy which would be applied would result in his disadvantage, this may also be indirect discrimination.

In order objectively to justify indirect discrimination, the employer will need to show that there is a legitimate aim and that the PCP is a proportionate way of achieving that aim.

The definition and interpretation of indirect discrimination in this context are identical to those set out in the Equality Act 2010 for the other protected characteristics (see **Chapter 10**). However, the reference in s 19 to persons who share a protected characteristic is defined as a reference to persons who have the *same disability* (s 6(3)) (the guidance suggests that this is assessed in terms of symptoms – eg mobility impaired). Indirect discrimination may cause difficulties for a disabled person who has to show a group disadvantage under this section. In *Russell v College of North West London* (UKEAT/0314/13), the EAT pointed out that to establish a claim it was necessary to show that a PCP caused a particular disadvantage to employees who shared the protected characteristic of the claimant. This is because s 6(3)(b) of the Equality Act 2010 makes it clear that the disadvantage has to apply to people who share the same disability rather than to disabled people as a whole. On that basis, the claimant failed because she had not put forward any evidence as to the impact the PCP had on people with Meniere's Disease. For a case on applying multiple choice tests in a recruitment exercise, see *GLS v Brookes* (UKEAT/0302/16).

Readers should refer to **Chapter 10** for more details.

13.5.6   Harassment

The definition of 'harassment' (s 26) for disability discrimination is identical to that set out in the Act for the other protected characteristics. See **11.2** for more details.

The Code provides an example:

> A worker has a son with a severe disfigurement. His work colleagues make offensive remarks to him about his son's disability. The worker could have a claim for harassment related to disability.

Note that the Act prohibits harassment based on association and perception: the prohibition on harassment 'related to' disability can cover treatment of the employee based on the disability of a third party (see *Coleman v Attridge Law* at **13.5.1** above). The definition of 'harassment' may well also cover combined discrimination because the harassment 'relates' to each of the grounds (see the House of Lords debates on the Equality Bill, *Hansard HL*, cols 546–47, 13 January 2010). Harassment by an employer also covers harassment by a third party where the employer has failed to take such steps as are reasonably practicable to prevent the party from so acting. This will not apply unless the employer knows the employee has been harassed in his employment on at least two other occasions by a third party, although this does not have to be the same party on each occasion.

See *Peninsula Business Service Ltd v Baker* (UKEAT/0241/16), where a harassment claim based on a 'perception' of disability failed. The definition of actual disability in s 6 appears problematic in this type of case. In order to bring a successful disability discrimination claim, a disability need to be established, unless either (a) an individual is subjected to conduct related to a protected characteristic they are wrongly perceived to have, (b) an individual closely associated with someone with a protected characteristic suffers harassment related to that characteristic (even if they do not share it), or (c) a protected characteristic is attributed to someone and they are harassed because of it.

13.5.7 Victimisation

The definition and interpretation of victimisation (s 27) are identical to those set out in the Act for the other protected characteristics. If a worker or employee is treated less favourably as a result of complaining about discrimination, or raising the issue or doing any other 'protected act', the claimant will be able to complain to the tribunal of unlawful victimisation. See **11.3** for more details.

13.6 BURDEN OF PROOF

The burden of proof is on the employer (s 136). The legislation provides that where a complainant can establish facts from which the tribunal could decide there has been direct discrimination, the tribunal *must* make a finding of unlawful discrimination *unless* the employer proves that there is a non-discriminatory explanation. This means that the complainant does have to establish some facts from which a tribunal could decide that there has been discrimination before looking to the employer for a non-discriminatory explanation. See **9.5.10.3** and **11.2** for more details.

13.7 VICARIOUS LIABILITY

An employer is vicariously liable for acts of discrimination by its employees during the course of their employment by virtue of s 109 of the Act (see **8.6** for more details).

13.8 ENFORCEMENT AND REMEDIES

The employment tribunal has exclusive jurisdiction to consider claims of disability discrimination in the field of employment. The complaint must be presented within three months beginning with the date of the act complained of, unless the tribunal considers that it is just and equitable in the circumstances to hear the claim outside that period. In cases of failure to make reasonable adjustments, the Court of Appeal held in *Matuszowicz v Kingston upon Hull City Council* [2009] EWCA Civ 22 that the three-month period runs from the point at which the employer makes it clear that no adjustment or further adjustment can be made. In cases where the employer simply does nothing, time, said the Court, will run from when, if the employer had been acting reasonably, it would have made the adjustment. That will be an artificial date, and difficult to second-guess what the tribunal will conclude. It is unfortunate, in the authors' view, to impose a start date that the parties may not realise has begun. Of course, the employment tribunal retains a discretion to extend time if it considers it just and equitable to do so – where, for example, the employee did not realise time had begun to run.

Enforcement proceedings may be brought by an individual or by the EHRC. The EHRC has power to conduct formal investigations and serve non-discrimination notices, and to give assistance to an individual pursuing a claim. The same principles apply to those in relation to sex, race, etc discrimination. Compensation may be awarded for injury to feelings. The EAT held in *Instant Muscle Ltd v Khawaja* (UKEAT/216/03) that the guidance in *Vento* should be applied to awards for injury to feelings in a case under the DDA 1995. See **8.8** for more details.

SUMMARY

Provisions relating to disability in the Equality Act 2010 are in some ways very different from other discrimination legislation, such as that relating to sex, race, religion or belief, sexual orientation or age, where the emphasis is on treating all people the same. In disability discrimination, the opposite may be true – a person's individual circumstances must be considered, and such consideration is crucial to avoid discrimination (**13.1**).

A person has a disability if he has a physical or mental impairment which has a substantial and long-term adverse effect on his ability to carry out normal day-to-day activities (s 6(1)). A 'disabled person' means a person who has a disability (s 6(2)). It also covers, from the time of diagnosis, people who have cancer, HIV/AIDS and multiple sclerosis (**13.3**).

Under s 39(1) of the Equality Act 2010, discrimination is outlawed in the employment field against job applicants, employees and former employees. It is unlawful (s 39(2)) for an employer to discriminate against a disabled person whom he employs in terms of access to opportunities for promotion, transfer or training, or other benefits, facilities or services; or by dismissing him or subjecting him to any other detriment (**13.4**).

There are six ways in which an employer may discriminate against a disabled applicant, employee or former employee.

(a) Direct discrimination (s 13). This is where someone is discriminated against because he is disabled. Such discrimination cannot be justified (**13.5.1**).

(b) Failure to make reasonable adjustments (ss 20–22). An employer may be liable for failing to take positive steps to help overcome the disadvantages resulting from disability. The defence of justification is not relevant here (**13.5.2**).

(c) Disability arising from disability (s 15). An employer may discriminate against an individual if he treats that individual unfavourably because of circumstances arising out of his disability (**13.5.4**). An employer may justify such treatment if he can show that it was a proportionate way of achieving a legitimate aim.

(d) Indirect discrimination (s 19). This covers the application of a PCP that disadvantages a disabled person (**13.5.5**). An employer may justify such treatment if he can show that it was a proportionate way of achieving a legitimate aim.

(e) Harassment (s 26). The definition is the same as for sex, race, religion or belief, etc (**13.5.6**).

(f) Victimisation (s 55). The definition is the same as for sex, race, religion or belief, etc (**13.5.7**).

Remedies and enforcement are dealt with at **8.8**. A flowchart summarising disability discrimination is set out at **Figure 13.1**.

Figure 13.1 Flowchart: Disability Discrimination

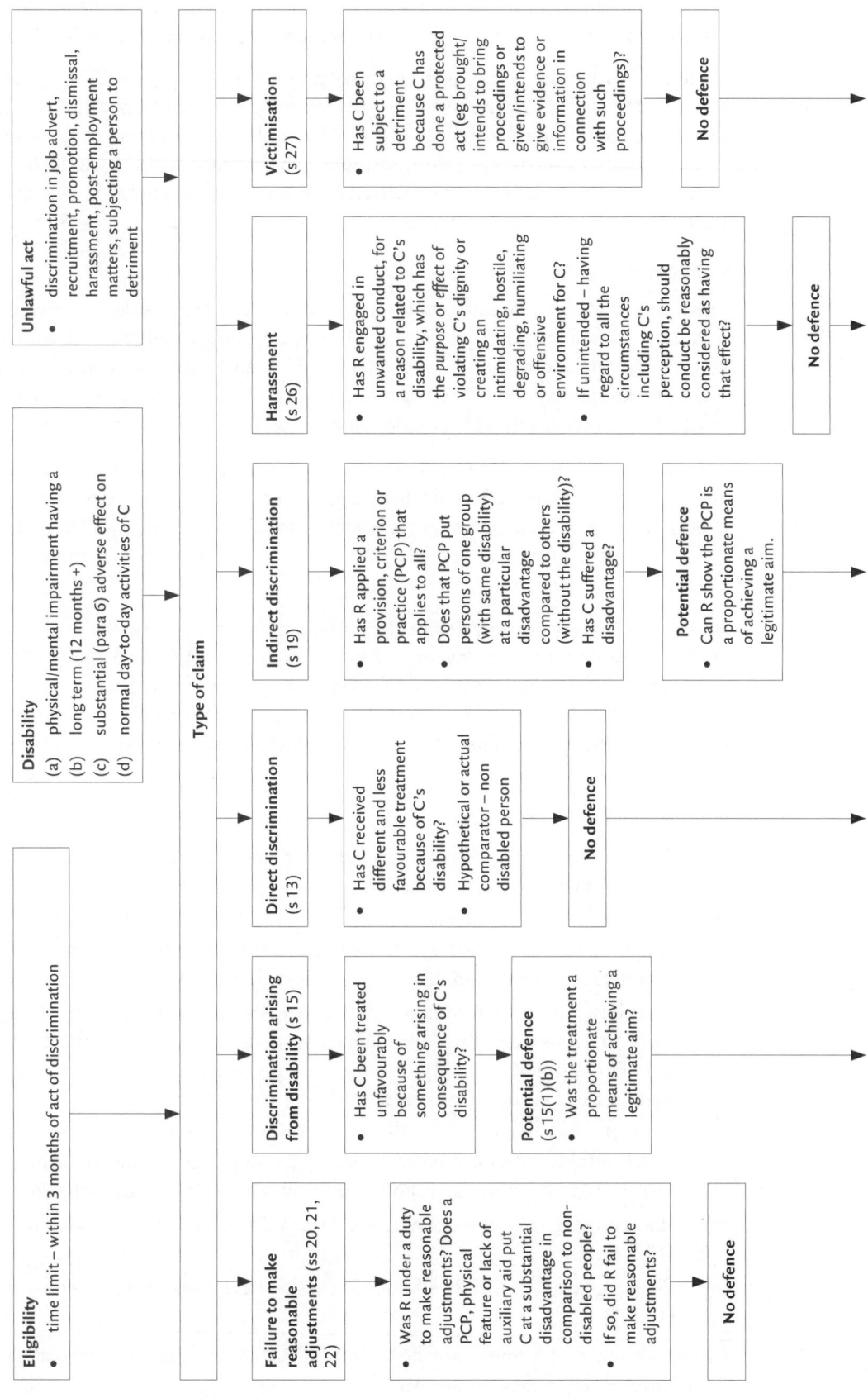

Vicarious liability

R will be vicariously liable for acts of employees committed in the course of employment (*Jones v Tower Boot Co/Chief Constable of Lincolnshire Police v Stubbs*) unless R took all reasonably practicable steps to stop/avoid the discrimination (s 109(4))

Remedies

- Declaration of employee's rights
- Recommendation that employer take action to alleviate or reduce the effect of the discrimination on the claimant or wider workforce
- Order for compensation (no maximum)
  - pecuniary losses
  - aggravated damages if employer has behaved in a high-handed, malicious, insulting or aggressive manner
  - injury to feelings (*Vento/Da'Bell*)
  - psychiatric or physical injury
  - possibility of exemplary damages
  - increase or decrease if employer or employee unreasonably fails to comply with Acas 2009 Code

CHAPTER 14

FAMILY-FRIENDLY RIGHTS AND THE RIGHT TO REQUEST FLEXIBLE WORKING

> **LEARNING OUTCOMES**
>
> After reading this chapter you will be able to:
>
> - describe the special rights afforded to pregnant women and women on maternity leave
> - explain the differences between the ordinary and additional maternity leave regimes
> - understand the significance of automatically unfair dismissal under s 99 of the ERA 1996
> - list the other family-friendly rights.

14.1 INTRODUCTION

In this chapter we look briefly at family-friendly rights, including some of the special rights afforded to pregnant women. The chapter also briefly considers the laws which create other family-friendly rights such as adoption, paternity and parental leave, as well as the right to request flexible working arrangements and to unpaid time off work to deal with emergencies at home. Only employees working under contracts of employment (see **1.3**) are entitled to these rights (but note that workers do have protection from discrimination (see **1.3.4.2**)).

The law concerning maternity, paternity, and parental and adoption leave rights is contained in the ERA 1996, as amended. However, much of the detail in respect of maternity rights and parental leave, etc is contained in secondary legislation, the Maternity and Parental Leave etc Regulations 1999 (SI 1999/3312) (MPLR 1999), as amended by the Paternity and Adoption Leave Regulations 2002 (SI 2002/2788) and the Shared Parental Leave Regulations 2014 (SI 2014/3050). The European Commission published a 'Roadmap' for the formulation of proposals to improve women's participation in the labour market and enable parents and carers to better balance their caring and work responsibilities. More detail is expected in 2016.

Legislation relating to pay is contained principally in the Social Security Contributions and Benefits Act 1992, the Statutory Maternity Pay Regulations 1986 (SI 1986/1960) and the Statutory Paternity Pay and Statutory Adoption Pay Regulations 2002 (SIs 2002/2818, 2820 and 2822).

The detail about flexible working is contained in the ERA 1996 and the Flexible Working Regulations 2014 (SI 2014/1398).

14.2 MATERNITY LEAVE

Only employees who work under contracts of employment are entitled to maternity leave. Workers who do not fit the definition of 'employee' set out in s 230(1) of the ERA 1996 (see **1.3**) do not qualify for the right to time off, but they do have protection from discrimination (see **1.3.4.2**, **Chapters 8** and **9** and **14.11**).

All pregnant women are entitled to up to 52 weeks' maternity leave. The first 26 weeks are known as 'ordinary maternity leave' (OML). The remaining period of up to 26 weeks is known as 'additional maternity leave' (AML), which commences on the day after the last day of a woman's OML. There are few differences between the two regimes which are dealt with below. Statutory maternity pay (SMP) is currently payable for 39 weeks to women with 26 weeks' service by the beginning of the 14th week before the expected week of childbirth (EWC).

Parents are able to share up to 50 weeks of this leave and 37 weeks' maximum pay (see **14.16**). (Mothers are still obliged to take two weeks' leave immediately after the birth – see **14.4**.)

14.3 ORDINARY AND ADDITIONAL MATERNITY LEAVE

Section 71 of the ERA 1996 (as amended) provides for ordinary maternity leave.

14.3.1 Notice provisions (MPLR 1999, reg 4(1))

No later than the end of the fifteenth week before the EWC, or, where that is not practicable, as soon as reasonably practicable, a woman should notify her employer of:

(a)   her pregnancy;

(b)   the EWC;

(c)   the date on which she intends to start her maternity leave. This part of the notice must be in writing if the employer so requests;

and in addition, if the employer requests,

(d)   provide him with a certificate from a registered medical practitioner or registered midwife stating the EWC.

A woman who has given notice under reg 4 can revise the date by giving further notice. If she wants to postpone the start date, she must give at least 28 days' notice before the date previously notified. If she wants to start leave earlier, she must give at least 28 days' notice before the new start date, unless it is not reasonably practicable to do so (eg, if the baby is born early).

If the woman fails to serve the correct notices, she may not be able to start her leave on the intended date.

14.3.2 When can a woman start her maternity leave? (MPLR 1999, reg 4(2))

A woman cannot start her maternity leave period earlier than the eleventh week before the EWC, unless the baby is born before the eleventh week; and the maternity leave cannot start later than the birth of the baby.

Subject to the above, a woman can start her leave when she chooses. So, for example, she could take 11 weeks before the birth of the baby and the remainder after, or she could take six weeks before and the rest after, or work up to the birth and take all her maternity leave after.

However, if a woman is absent from work wholly or partly because of pregnancy in the four-week period before the EWC, she may have to start her leave on that date (reg 6(1)). The woman must notify her employer as soon as reasonably practicable that she is absent for a reason related to pregnancy (reg 4(3)). The employer might agree to waive the pregnancy related absence. Additionally, maternity leave will be automatically triggered where childbirth occurs before the date she has notified, or, before she has notified a date. In that event, she must notify her employer as soon as reasonably practicable of the date of the birth (reg 4(4)).

14.3.2.1 Employer's notice

An employer who is notified of the date on which an employee's maternity leave will start or has started shall, within 28 days of notification, notify the employee of the date her AML will end (reg 7(6)).

14.3.3 Additional maternity leave (ERA 1996, s 73 as amended)

Additional maternity leave will commence on the day after the last day of a woman's OML period (MPLR 1999, reg 6(3)) and continue for *up to* 26 weeks from the day it begins.

The woman does not have to tell her employer that it is her intention to take AML when she gives her initial maternity leave notice.

14.3.4 Sickness at the end of maternity leave

Where a woman is unable to return to work at the end of her maternity leave, according to BIS guidance, the normal contractual arrangements for sickness will apply. She should be treated like any other sick employee. Generally, if an employee has a pregnancy-related sickness after the end of her maternity leave, she does not have *automatic* protection from sex discrimination (see **14.13**).

14.3.5 Rights and obligations during maternity leave (ERA 1996, s 71)

14.3.5.1 Rights

During the maternity leave period, the woman's contract of employment continues. A woman is entitled to the benefit of all the terms and conditions of employment which would have applied to her had she not been absent, including non-contractual benefits, except remuneration. The ECJ ruled, in *Gillespie v Northern Health* [1996] IRLR 214, that nothing in EU equal pay law requires that a woman on maternity leave should receive her normal full pay while on leave. The law only requires that the amount paid complies with the Pregnant Workers Directive and is adequate, and not so low as to jeopardise the general purpose of maternity leave. Remuneration is defined as 'sums payable to the employee by way of wages or salary' (MPLR 1999, reg 9). Thus, a woman on maternity leave is entitled to continue to receive benefits in kind, such as private medical insurance, the company car (if for company and personal use), club membership, subsidised loans, etc, and she will continue to accrue statutory and contractual holiday entitlement. The EAT held in *Peninsula Business Services Ltd v Donaldson* (EAT/0249/15) that childcare vouchers provided under a salary sacrifice scheme were part of an employee's remuneration under reg 9 and did not have to continue during maternity leave. The key distinction was that the vouchers were paid under a salary sacrifice scheme and not in addition to salary.

If the employer denies the woman such benefits, he will be acting in breach of contract, and such action will also be discriminatory if the denial is because of maternity leave or pregnancy (Equality Act 2010, s 18 – see **14.11** below). Section 47C of the ERA 1996 also protects the woman from being subjected to any detriment short of dismissal because she took maternity leave (see **14.6**).

The woman who takes maternity leave continues to be bound by express and implied contractual terms and conditions, for example the implied duty of good faith. The obligation does not extend to terms that are inconsistent with the right to maternity leave, for example the obligation to turn up and work.

14.3.5.2   Working during maternity leave

Regulation 12A of the MPLR 1999 enables an employee on maternity leave to agree with her employer to work for up to 10 days during the statutory maternity leave period without bringing that period to an end as a result of carrying out the work. For the purposes of that provision, 'work' may include training or any other activity undertaken to assist the employee in keeping in touch with the workplace. The provision also sets out that reasonable contact, which employers and employees are entitled to have with each other during the maternity leave period, does not bring that period to an end. Any such work must be by agreement between the parties, and there is no right for an employer to demand that an employee undertake any such work, nor for an employee to do such work. The regulation also provides that any such days' work shall not have the effect of extending the maternity leave period.

14.3.6   Right to return to what?

14.3.6.1   After OML

A woman who takes only OML is entitled to return to the job in which she was employed before her absence with her seniority, pension rights and similar rights as they would have been had she not been absent, and terms and conditions no less favourable than they would have been had she not been absent. The OML period counts towards the woman's period of continuous employment for both statutory and contractual rights. 'Job' is defined in MPLR 1999, reg 2(1) and has the same meaning as that described below in relation to AML (see **14.3.6.2**).

14.3.6.2   After AML

A woman does not have to give any notice if she simply intends to return at the end of the AML period. However, if she intends to return earlier than the end of the AML period, she must give her employer eight weeks' notice of the date on which she intends to return (reg 11(1)). If she fails to do so, the employer is entitled to postpone her return to work to a date that will ensure he receives eight weeks' notice, unless the employer has failed to comply with his duty under reg 7(6), in which case the employer cannot prevent her from returning early (see **14.3.2.1**).

The statutory right is to return to the job in which she was employed before her absence, or, if not reasonably practicable for the employer to allow her to return to that job, for a reason other than redundancy, to a suitable and appropriate job:

(a)   on no less favourable terms and conditions as to remuneration than those which would have been applicable had she not been absent;

(b)   with seniority, pension and similar rights preserved as they would have been if the period of employment prior to AML were continuous with her employment following her return to work.

So, for example, if all employees of her grade received a pay rise during her leave, the woman will be entitled to this higher rate of pay on her return. The AML period will not count towards service related contractual benefits, but will be counted for the purpose of statutory rights that depend on length of service.

'Job', for the purposes of AML, is defined as the nature of the work which she is employed to do in accordance with her contract and the capacity and place in which she is employed (MPLR 1999, reg 2(1)). So, if for example her contract provides that she can be required to work in one of three departments (A, B and C), although she actually worked in Department A, she could be taken back in Department B or C.

In *Blundell v Governing Body of St Andrew's Catholic Primary School* [2007] IRLR 652, the EAT gave guidance on what the 'same job' is, saying that a returner should come back to a work situation as near as possible to that which she left, but held that a teacher could not insist on returning to teach the same class after her leave.

If it is not reasonably practicable *for a reason other than redundancy* for the employer to let the woman return to the job in which she was employed before her AML (eg due to a business reorganisation or some other substantial reason), the employer must allow her to return to another job which is both suitable for her and appropriate for her to do in the circumstances (MPLR 1999, reg 18(2)) (see *Kelly v Secretary of State for Justice* (UKEAT/0227/13)). The terms and conditions of the job offered must not be less favourable than those that applied (or would have applied) to the old job. The BIS guidance states that if the offer is suitable and the woman refuses the job, she will have 'effectively resigned'. This view has not been tested, and in the authors' view she is more likely to have been dismissed. Such dismissal will not be automatically unfair but may be 'ordinarily' unfair, depending on the facts. If the offer is not suitable, the woman can bring a complaint of unfair dismissal (and perhaps pregnancy/maternity discrimination/wrongful dismissal (see below)).

Returning on different terms and conditions

An employee may wish to return to work on different terms and conditions, for example part time or working different hours to fit in with her family responsibilities. She has no such right under the existing statutory provisions. She may, however, be able to allege indirect sex discrimination if the employer refuses, for example, to allow her to return on a part-time basis (see generally **Chapter 8** and *Sibley v The Girls Day School Trust, Norwich High School for Girls* (UKEAT/1368/01)). In addition, employees have a right to request flexible working patterns (see **14.16**).

Failure to return at the end of AML

A failure to return at the end of AML will not of itself terminate the contract of employment. The court will look at the intention of the employee: if the employee intended her failure to return to end the contract then the court will interpret her act as terminating the contract. Failing any express intention, employers will need to take steps to discover the reason for any late return before deciding what action to take (eg whether to treat it as a disciplinary matter) (see *Rashid v Asian Community Care Services Ltd* (UKEAT/480/99). A failure to treat an AML late returner in the same way as any other late returner could also give rise to a potential discrimination claim under the general provisions of the SDA 1975 (see **14.11** and **Chapters 8 and 9** generally) or unfair dismissal (see **14.7**). Furthermore, if the employer has failed to specify the return date (see **14.3.2.1**) and the woman reasonably believed that her maternity leave had not ended, then any dismissal will be automatically unfair (see **14.7**).

14.4   COMPULSORY MATERNITY LEAVE

Section 72 of the ERA 1996 prescribes a mandatory period of maternity leave. An employer must prohibit a woman from returning to work during a two-week period from the date of childbirth. To allow her to return in that period is a criminal offence and the employer will be liable, on conviction, to a fine not exceeding level 2 on the standard scale (currently £500). This applies to employees and workers.

This period counts as time worked for the purposes of a discretionary bonus.

14.5 REDUNDANCY DURING MATERNITY LEAVE

Section 74 of the ERA 1996 provides that Regulations may be made to make provision about redundancy. Regulation 10 of the MPLR 1999 provides that if it is not practicable for the employer, by reason of redundancy, to continue to employ the woman under her existing contract of employment, she is entitled to be offered a suitable available vacancy before the contract ends, where there is a suitable vacancy (in priority to other employees). The new contract must be such that:

(a)   the kind of work to be done under it is both suitable in relation to the employee and appropriate for her to do in the circumstances; and

(b)   its provisions as to capacity and place in which she is employed, and as to other terms and conditions of her employment, are not substantially less favourable than her previous contractual terms and conditions (MPLR 1999, reg 10).

If the woman is dismissed by reason of redundancy and this provision is not complied with, the dismissal will be automatically unfair (MPLR 1999, reg 20, see **14.7**).

In *Simpson v Endsleigh Insurance Services Ltd* (UKEAT/0544/09) the EAT gave guidance on the right of employees facing redundancy while on maternity leave to be offered a 'suitable available vacancy'. The EAT held that the suitability of the vacancy is to be assessed by the employer, having regard to the employee's personal circumstances and work experience. In *Sefton BC v Wainwright* (UKEAT/0168/14), the EAT held that if there is a suitable vacancy, it should be offered to the woman, even if her (non-pregnant) colleague was the better candidate, unless the employer could offer the woman another suitable vacancy.

14.6 PROTECTION FROM DETRIMENT SHORT OF DISMISSAL

The ERA 1996, s 47C contains special protection from acts short of dismissal for pregnant/maternity leave employees. The situations when that protection arises are set out in MPLR 1999, reg 19. They are similar to those set out in s 99 (see **14.7** below) relating to dismissal.

The woman can complain to the tribunal that she has been subjected to a detriment in contravention of s 47C under ERA 1996, s 48. Her remedies will be a declaration and/or compensation.

Note that no period of continuous employment is required to claim under the above provisions.

14.7 AUTOMATICALLY UNFAIR DISMISSAL

Under s 99 of the ERA 1996, a woman who is dismissed is entitled to be regarded as unfairly dismissed if the reason or the principal reason is connected, inter alia, with:

(a)   the pregnancy of the employee (MPLR 1999, reg 20(3)(a));

(b)   the fact that she has given birth to a child (reg 20(3)(b));

(c)   the fact that she is on maternity suspension under ERA 1996, s 66 (reg 20(3)(c));

(d)   the fact that she took OML, or sought to take OML or availed herself of the benefits of any of the terms and conditions of her employment preserved by ERA 1996, s 71 (reg 20(3)(d));

(e)   the fact that she took AML or sought to do so (reg 20(3)(e));

(f) a failure to return after AML in a case where the employer did not give her notice of the date on which the AML would end and she reasonably believed that that period had not ended; or the employer gave less than 28 days' notice of the end of AML and it was not reasonably practicable for her to return on that date (reg 20(3)(ee));

(g) the fact that she undertook, considered undertaking or refused to undertake work in accordance with reg 12A (reg 20(3)(eee)).

If the dismissal is shown to be for any of the above reasons, then the tribunal does not have to go on and consider whether the dismissal was reasonable in accordance with ERA 1996, s 98(4).

The MPLR 1999, reg 20(3)(b) applies only where the dismissal ends the employee's OML or AML period (reg 20(4)). This means that a woman will not be protected under this provision from a childbirth-related dismissal that occurs after the end of her maternity leave.

A dismissal is also automatically unfair under s 99 if the reason or principal reason for the dismissal is that the employee was redundant and that MPLR 1999, reg 10 has not been complied with (see above at **14.5**). In other words, she has not been offered suitable alternative employment before the end of her existing contract (where a vacancy exists) and the dismissal ends the woman's OML or AML period. The duty to offer a suitable alternative vacancy appears to be an absolute one; if a suitable vacancy exists, it must be offered to the woman on OML or AML in preference to any other affected employee.

If reg 10 has been complied with, the dismissal may still be automatically unfair, if the reason or principal reason for her dismissal is that the employee was redundant, and it is shown that the circumstances constituting redundancy applied to other employees who held similar positions and the reason for which the woman was selected for redundancy was for a reason in reg 20(3) (see (a)–(g) above).

The employee is not required to prove that her dismissal was for one of the above reasons. She only has to adduce some evidence to create a presumption and, if the employer is arguing that the dismissal was for a reason other than pregnancy, the burden is on him to prove this. If it is found that the reason for dismissal fell within the above provisions, there is no scope for the employer to argue that it was nonetheless reasonable in all the circumstances. The dismissal is automatically unfair.

Note again that no period of continuous employment is required to claim automatically unfair dismissal under the above provision.

If the woman's dismissal is not automatically unfair under the above provisions, it may still be unfair under the ordinary principles in ERA 1996, s 98(4) (see **Chapter 5**).

14.7.1 Exception to protection from automatically unfair dismissal

The automatic unfair dismissal protection contained in s 99 of the ERA 1996 does not apply where it is not reasonably practicable for a reason other than redundancy for the employer to allow the woman to return from OML or AML to a job which is suitable for the employee and appropriate for her to do in the circumstances, but an associated employer offers her a job of that kind and the employee accepts the job or unreasonably refuses that offer (MPLR 1999, reg 20(7)).

Of course, even where these exceptions apply, a woman could still claim that her dismissal was unfair under ERA 1996, s 98(4) (see **Chapter 5**).

14.7.2 Written reasons for dismissal (ERA 1996, s 92(4))

If a woman is dismissed while pregnant or during the OML/AML periods, she is entitled, without prior request, to a written statement giving the reason for her dismissal.

14.8   REMEDIES FOR UNFAIR DISMISSAL

A complaint must be brought within three months of the date of dismissal. If the complaint is upheld, the usual remedies are available. If reinstatement is ordered, it will be in the job to which the woman was allowed to return. If the dismissal occurred before the commencement of leave, the tribunal may include in the reinstatement order a declaration that all rights in connection with maternity leave are to be restored (see **Chapters 5** and **6**).

14.9   REDUNDANCY PAYMENTS

If no suitable alternative vacancy exists and the woman is genuinely redundant within the meaning of ERA 1996, s 139 (see **Chapter 4**) then, provided she is eligible, she will be entitled to a redundancy payment.

If a suitable alternative job is offered and she unreasonably refuses it, the right to a payment will be lost.

14.10   WRONGFUL DISMISSAL

If the woman is dismissed during pregnancy, OML or AML, or after she has returned from leave, she is entitled to receive proper notice, unless she has acted in repudiatory breach of contract. If the woman does not receive proper notice she will be able to claim wrongful dismissal. Even if she is on maternity leave, she is entitled to full pay if her notice period is the statutory period under s 86 (see s 87(4)).

14.11   PREGNANCY/MATERNITY DISCRIMINATION

In addition to the statutory right to leave described above and the right to pay described below, there is also protection from discrimination.

Section 18 of the Equality Act 2010 reads:

> (1)   This section has effect for the purposes of the application of Part 5 (work) to the protected characteristic of pregnancy and maternity.
>
> (2)   A person (A) discriminates against a woman if, in the protected period in relation to a pregnancy of hers, A treats her unfavourably—
>
> > (a)   because of the pregnancy, or
> >
> > (b)   because of illness suffered by her as a result of it.
>
> (3)   A person (A) discriminates against a woman if A treats her unfavourably because she is on compulsory maternity leave.
>
> (4)   A person (A) discriminates against a woman if A treats her unfavourably because she is exercising or seeking to exercise, or has exercised or sought to exercise, the right to ordinary or additional maternity leave.
>
> (5)   For the purposes of subsection (2), if the treatment of a woman is in implementation of a decision taken in the protected period, the treatment is to be regarded as occurring in that period (even if the implementation is not until after the end of that period).
>
> (6)   The protected period, in relation to a woman's pregnancy, begins when the pregnancy begins, and ends—
>
> > (a)   if she has the right to ordinary and additional maternity leave, at the end of the additional maternity leave period or (if earlier) when she returns to work after the pregnancy;
> >
> > (b)   if she does not have that right, at the end of the period of 2 weeks beginning with the end of the pregnancy.
>
> (7)   Section 13, so far as relating to sex discrimination, does not apply to treatment of a woman in so far as—
>
> > (a)   it is in the protected period in relation to her and is for a reason mentioned in paragraph (a) or (b) of subsection (2), or
> >
> > (b)   it is for a reason mentioned in subsection (3) or (4).

Section 18 makes it unlawful during the protected period to treat a woman unfavourably on the ground of her pregnancy, or on the ground that she is exercising or seeking to exercise a statutory right to maternity leave. No comparator is needed and no justification defence is available. Pregnancy or maternity leave must be a substantial reason for the treatment (see *O'Neill v Governors of St Thomas More* [1996] IRLR 372). Once the protected period has ended, a comparator will be needed. Note that as the right to maternity leave is generally statutory (unless an employer has a contractual scheme), only employees have the right to maternity leave, and therefore workers are not protected under s 18 (other than during their pregnancy or for their two weeks' compulsory leave after giving birth (see **14.4**)). Section 18 also covers less favourable treatment as a result of pregnancy-related illness. However, where a woman falls ill with a pregnancy-related illness, such as post-natal depression, after she returns from maternity leave, that illness is not subject to any special protection.

The protected period referred to in s 18 above is defined (following *Brown v Rentokil* [1998] IRLR 445, ECJ) as beginning with pregnancy and ending at the end of the maternity leave period or, if the woman returns to work before then, when she returns to work. It goes without saying that the employer must know that the woman is pregnant (actual knowledge) (*Ramdoolar v Bycity Ltd* [2005] ICR 368 and see too *Really Easy Car Credit Ltd v Thompson* (UKEAT/ 0197/17)).

14.12 OTHER MATERNITY-RELATED RIGHTS

14.12.1 Suspension from work on maternity grounds

It may happen that a pregnant woman cannot safely continue with her existing job. Her employer cannot simply dismiss her without falling foul of ERA 1996, s 99. He could, however, suspend her under s 66. This will amount to a suspension on maternity grounds if it is due to:

(a)   any statutory requirement (eg Ionising Radiation Regulations 1985); or

(b)   any recommendation contained in a Code of Practice issued under the HSWA 1974.

If an employer has available suitable alternative employment (on terms and conditions not 'substantially less favourable'), he must offer the pregnant woman such work on full pay before suspending her on maternity grounds (see *BA Ltd v Moore and Botterill* [2000] IRLR 296). A failure to make such an offer may result in the woman bringing a complaint to the employment tribunal.

A woman who is suspended on maternity grounds is entitled to be paid in full (see *Mahlburg v Land Mecklenburg-Vorpommern* [2000] IRLR 276, ECJ).

As both men and women are entitled to parental, paternity and adoption leave, it is unlikely that either sex will have a claim for direct sex discrimination if dismissed, or if subjected to any other detriment in relation to taking time off. If, however, it is less acceptable in a particular workplace for a man rather than a woman to take parental, paternity or adoption leave, and as a result he is treated less favourably, this would be direct discrimination.

14.12.2 Health and safety risk assessments

Regulation 3(1) of the Management of Health and Safety at Work Regulations 1999 (SI 1999/ 3242) imposes a general duty on an employer to safeguard the health and safety of its employees by making a suitable and sufficient assessment of the risks to which they are exposed at work. A failure to carry out a risk assessment may amount to a detriment under s 26 of the Equality Act 2010, as well as unlawful discrimination under s 18 of that Act (see **14.11**) (see *Day v T Pickles Farms Ltd* [1999] IRLR 217 and *Hardman v Mallon* [2002] IRLR 516).

The ECJ held in *Otero Ramos v Servicio Galego de Saúde* (Case C-531/15) [2018] IRLR 159 that the reverse burden of proof applies to the Pregnant Workers Directive where a worker is denied a risk assessment or a satisfactory risk assessment because any less favourable treatment of a female worker due to pregnancy or maternity leave, here due to her being a breastfeeding woman, constitutes direct sex discrimination. That meant that the woman had to present facts or evidence capable of showing that the risk assessment was not done properly and, if so, the burden was on the employer to prove no discrimination.

If there is a causally linked dismissal, it will be automatically unfair under ERA 1996, s 99 or reg 20 of the MPLR 1999 (see **14.7**).

14.12.3 Maternity pay

The ECJ ruled in *Gillespie v Northern Health and Social Services Board* [1996] IRLR 214, that nothing in EU equal pay law requires that a woman on maternity leave should receive her normal full pay while she is on leave. It requires only that she receives an amount that is adequate and not so low as to jeopardise the general purpose of maternity leave (see the Pregnant Worker Directive).

A woman on maternity leave may be entitled to receive statutory maternity pay (SMP). This is paid by the employer who recoups it from the State. It is paid for a maximum period of 39 weeks, which may begin at the start of the eleventh week before the expected week of confinement.

Statutory maternity pay is presently set at 90% of the woman's normal weekly earnings for the first six weeks, and for 33 weeks thereafter at £145.18 per week or 90% of the normal weekly earnings if this is less than £145.18 (for babies due on or after 1 April 2018).

14.12.4 Time off for ante-natal care (ERA 1996, s 55)

A pregnant woman has the right not to be unreasonably refused time off during her working hours to attend ante-natal appointments. She is entitled to be paid for such absence (ERA 1996, s 56). From 1 October 2014, partners are also entitled to time off to attend ante-natal appointments (and adoption appointments – see **14.13** below).

The right is available only to employees. Case law suggests that tribunals are reluctant to find refusals reasonable where appointments have been made on proper medical advice. The employer may ask for evidence of the appointment, except in the case of the first appointment (ERA 1996, s 55(2) and (3)).

An employee who is the husband, civil partner or partner of a pregnant women, the father or parent of a pregnant women's expected child or an intended parent in a surrogacy arrangement who meets specified conditions, has the right to take (unpaid) time off (up to a maximum of six and a half hours) during working hours to accompany the woman to up to two ante-natal appointments. Such employees are protected against detrimental treatment or dismissal in connection with the exercise of these rights (ERA 1996, s 572ZE, as inserted by the Children and Families Act 2014, s 127(1)).

14.12.5 Surrogacy and infertility

Most of the legal protections accorded to pregnancy and maternity do not currently apply to the commissioning parents in a surrogacy arrangement. While the surrogate mother will be entitled to the protections accorded to any pregnant woman, in *CD v ST* (Case C-167/12) the ECJ held that a mother who becomes the parent through a surrogacy arrangement (the 'commissioning' mother), even if she is the biological mother and even if she is treated in law (under s 54 of the Human Fertilisation and Embryology Act 2008) as the legal parent, is not entitled to the paid leave that other new parents are, although she may take unpaid parental leave (see **14.16** below) and, with an employer's consent, other periods of leave. In the instant case, the employee was heavily involved in the baby's life from the outset, and breastfed the baby within an hour of the birth and continued to so for three months, but the ECJ said the decision by the employer (an NHS Trust) not to pay either maternity or adoption pay was correct as neither applied to the employee. The ECJ also held that the refusal of the employer to provide maternity leave to a commissioning mother does not constitute discrimination on the grounds of sex contrary to the Equal Treatment Directive.

The Children and Families Act 2014, which received Royal Assent on 13 March 2014 and came into force in December 2014 where the EWC was on or after 5 April 2015, includes provisions that enable the commissioning parents in a surrogacy arrangement to utilise adoption leave and pay (see **14.13** below).

The ECJ in *CD v ST* (above) also considered whether the employee's gynaecological condition amounted to a disability, but found it did not. Some care may be needed in this area, as infertility may be the result of or lead to a medical condition which may fall within the definition of disability.

Employees under going fertility treatment such as IVF also have limited legal protection. In particular, currently, a woman is not entitled to take paid or unpaid time off to undergo fertility treatments. A woman undergoing IVF does enjoy statutory protection from sex discrimination during a limited period of time when the ova are collected, fertilised and 'immediately' thereafter implanted. The position may be different where there is a gap between fertilisation and implantation. A woman also benefits from the protection of UK maternity laws, as being in a 'protected period', once a fertilised ovum is implanted (ie once the woman is regarded as being pregnant). If the implantation fails and the pregnancy ends, the protected period ends after a further two-week period. There is a Code of Practice issued by the EHRC which provides guidance in this area. The EHRC Code recommends that employers treat requests for time off for IVF treatment 'sympathetically'.

14.13 ADOPTION LEAVE

Since April 2003, employees have had the right to take time off work after adopting a child. The statutory right is set out in the ERA 1996, ss 75A–75D, and the detail is contained in the Paternity and Adoption Leave Regulations (PALR 2002) (SI 2002/2788) (as amended). Until 5 April 2015, there was a requirement for 26 weeks' continuous service, but on 5 April 2015 the entitlement became a 'day one' employment right. The law is very similar to the law which applies to women taking OML and AML. The summary below sets out in outline only the legal framework.

As a basic proposition all employees are entitled to take up to 52 weeks' adoption leave if they:

- are matched for adoption;
- foster a child with a view to adoption;
- are intended parents in a surrogacy arrangement who have or intend to apply for a parental order.

An employee who is entitled to ordinary adoption leave (OAL) will also be entitled to 26 weeks' additional adoption leave (AAL), which will start on the day after the last day of the OAL period (reg 20). This is the same period as AML (**14.3.3**).

The employer must notify the employee of the date AAL will end, in the same way that an employer must tell a woman of the date her OML or AML will end (see **14.3.2.1**).

The terms and conditions of employment that apply during ordinary adoption leave (OAL) are exactly the same as those which apply to a woman during OML (see **14.3.5.1**).

The terms and conditions of employment which apply during AAL are exactly the same as those which apply during AML (see **14.3.5.1**)

Exactly the same rules that apply to women returning from OML or AML apply to employees returning from OAL or AAL (see **14.3.6.2**). In essence, eight weeks' notice must be given of any return to work if the employee intends to return earlier than the end of the AAL period (MPLPAL(A)R 2006, reg 15).

Returning employees are entitled to almost the same rights as those which apply to women returning from OML or AML (see **14.3.6**).

The rules which apply when a redundancy situation arises during an employee's OAL or AAL are the same as those which apply to redundancy situations which arise while a woman is on OML or AML (see **14.5**).

Employees who take or seek to take adoption leave are protected in the same way as women who take or seek to take maternity leave (see **14.6**; **14.7**) against detrimental treatment, and will be regarded as automatically unfairly dismissed if the reason for their dismissal was connected to the fact that they took or sought to take adoption leave.

Where a couple is notified of being matched with a child for adoption on or after 3 April 2011, additional paternity leave can be taken (Additional Paternity Leave Regulations 2010, reg 3(2)) – see **14.14** for more details.

As both men and women are entitled to parental, paternity and adoption leave, it is unlikely that either sex will have a claim for direct sex discrimination if dismissed, or if subjected to any other detriment in relation to taking time off. If, however, it is less acceptable in a particular workplace for a man rather than a woman to take parental, paternity or adoption leave, and as a result he is treated less favourably, this would be direct discrimination.

Adopters are entitled, since 5 April 2015, to paid time off work to attend appointments to have contact with the child prior to the adoption's taking place.

An employee who adopts a child and takes adoption leave may be entitled to statutory adoption pay (SAP). The qualifying conditions are set out in the Social Security Contributions and Benefits Act 1992 (as amended) and the Statutory Paternity Pay and Statutory Adoption Pay (General) Regulations 2002 (SI 2002/2822). Detail of the provisions are outside the scope of this book, but essentially an employee who is eligible for adoption leave and who takes that leave will normally be entitled to SAP.

Statutory adoption pay is paid for 39 weeks by the employer at a weekly rate of £145.18 (from 1 April 2018) or 90% of the employee's normal weekly earnings, whichever is the lower.

The administrative requirements which pertain to SAP are extremely complex; the rules are contained in the Statutory Paternity Pay and Statutory Adoption Pay (Administration) Regulations 2002 (SI 2002/2820).

Adoption leave can also be converted to shared parental leave (see **14.2** and **14.16** below).

14.14 PATERNITY LEAVE

The Employment Act 2002 (EA 2002) introduced a new right for fathers and other eligible employees to take up to two weeks' paid paternity leave (ordinary paternity leave: OPL). The right is also available to foster parents and parents in a surrogacy arrangement. The EA 2002 introduced ss 80A–80D into the ERA 1996, which allows the Secretary of State to make Regulations governing the new right. Such Regulations have been made in the form of the PALR 2002, where the detail of how the right works is set out.

Statutory paternity pay is currently £145.18 (from 1 April 2018) a week or 90% of normal weekly earnings if less, and is payable for a maximum of 28 weeks.

Additional paternity leave has been abolished. Its place is taken by shared parental leave (see **14.16**).

The provisions and requirements that apply to employees taking paternity leave are exactly the same as those that apply to women taking OML (see **14.3**).

14.15 PARENTAL LEAVE

Parental leave is available to birth and adoptive parents, and to anyone with parental responsibility for a child. Eligible employees can take up to 18 weeks' leave (unpaid) for each child at any time before the child's fifth birthday. Parents of disabled children can take 18 weeks' unpaid leave until their child's 18th birthday. No more than four weeks' leave may be taken in any one year, and leave must be taken in one-week blocks.

During parental leave, the contract continues in a limited form, and the employee continues to accrue holiday. Readers should consult the legislation for the details of parental leave.

The Government has passed the Parental Bereavement (Leave and Pay) Act 2018, which will provide a right to two weeks' leave and pay (how much is unknown at this stage) to parents who lose a child under 18. It is not expected to come into force until 2020.

14.16 SHARED PARENTAL LEAVE

The Shared Parental Leave Regulations 2014 (SI 2014/3050) came into force on 1 December 2014, for babies expected on or after 5 April 2015 or matched/placed for adoption on or after 5 April 2015. They also apply to foster parents and intended parents in a surrogacy arrangement. They are aimed at allowing partners to be more involved in the first year, and at allowing mothers to return to work while ensuring that there is still parental care. Employees must have 26 weeks' continuous employment to be entitled to share the leave. Mothers must take a two-week compulsory maternity leave period. Save for that restriction, the Regulations allow parents to share the leave as they wish, but there are procedural requirements that must be complied with. Similarly, parents can share statutory pay.

The new shared parental leave rights allow eligible employees to share up to 50 weeks' leave and 39 weeks' pay in the year following a child's birth or adoption. The 50-week period starts two weeks after the birth and applies to children born/placed for adoption/placed with foster parents who are approved prospective adopters/placed with parents in a surrogacy arrangement who have or expect to acquire a parental order (under the Human Fertilisation and Embryology Act 2008) on or after 5 April. Parents can take the leave alternatively or simultaneously, the intention being to allow parents more flexibility in sharing the care of a child during the first year after its birth. Shared parental leave does not need to be taken as one consecutive period but can be taken in one block or several discontinuous blocks (up to a maximum of three blocks of leave per person, although an employer could voluntarily agree more), and employees can return to work between blocks. If a child's parents choose not to take shared parental leave then a mother's right to 52 weeks' maternity leave is unaffected.

Shared parental leave is available to the mother of the child and either the father or the person who at the date of the child's birth is the mother's spouse, civil partner or partner. 'Partner' is defined as the person who lives with the mother in an 'enduring family relationship' but is not a relative. Both parents must have shared responsibility for the care of the child.

The procedure to be followed, and the information that has to be provided, is complex, and a detailed analysis is beyond the scope of this work. However, it is the employee's responsibility to check eligibility. In broad terms, a mother must first curtail her maternity leave. To do this, a mother must give at least eight weeks' notice to her employer that she wishes to do so. Secondly, either the mother and/or the partner (depending on who is making the request) must serve a written (non-binding) Notice of Entitlement at least eight weeks before the first period of shared parental leave. The Notice of Entitlement must contain certain information, including the names of both parents, the start and end dates of maternity leave, and how much shared parental leave each intends to take and an indication of when they intend to take it. Both parents must also provide signed declarations to the relevant employer confirming that the information in the Notice of Entitlement is correct. Thirdly, and subsequently, a Period of Leave notice must be served on the employer, setting out the start and end dates of each period of shared parental leave. The Period of Leave notice must be served at least eight weeks before the start of the first period of leave. A maximum of three Period of Leave notices can be served. Provided these procedural requirements are complied with, and the request is for one or more periods of continuous leave, an employer must allow the request. However, an employer retains discretion to refuse or negotiate requests for discontinuous shared parental leave. Requests must be granted or refused within 14 days of the date of the Period of Leave notice.

Parents can also share statutory parental leave pay (£145.18 as of 1 April 2018) for up to 37 weeks. There are some employment and earnings tests where a partner is not employed.

An employee's rights during and on return from shared parental leave are similar to those enjoyed by mothers on maternity leave (see **14.3.5** and **14.3.6**).

Two useful Acas guides are available – 'Shared Parental Leave: a good practice guide for employers and employees' and 'Shared parental leave summary process' – as well as a BIS guidance note, 'Shared parental leave and pay: employer guide'. An online calculator is available at <http://www.gov.uk/government/news/calculate-your-leave-and-pay-when-you-have-a-child>. IDS Employment Law Briefs 1010 and 1011 also contain a detailed two-part analysis of the right and BIS has published an 'Employers' Technical Guide to Shared Parental Leave and Pay'.

Note: Concern has been expressed that where employees offer enhanced maternity pay, failing to offer enhanced shared parental leave pay may be discriminatory. The Government believes this is discretionary and not discriminatory. Two employment tribunals have looked at this and come to different conclusions. In *Hextall v Chief Constable of Leicestershire Police* (ET/2601223/2015), the tribunal found it was not a discriminatory practice (see too *NJ Shuter v Ford Motor Company* (ET/3203504/2013) where a similar outcome resulted). But in *Ali v Capita Customer Management Ltd* (ET/1800990/2016), the tribunal found that it was direct discrimination (which meant the employer had no opportunity to justify it) not to pay full salary to a father taking shared parental leave in circumstances where a mother on maternity leave during the same period would have received full pay.

The EAT disagreed with the tribunal's decision in *Ali* (see *Capita Customer Management Ltd v (1) Ali (2) Working Families (Intervenor)* (UKEAT/0161/17)). The EAT held that the employment tribunal had adopted the wrong comparator and therefore had erred in holding that the circumstances of the claimant father were comparable to those of a woman who had recently given birth, as both had leave to care for their child. It said that the tribunal's finding failed to have regard to the purpose of maternity leave and pay, being the health and wellbeing of a woman in pregnancy, confinement and after recent childbirth. The correct comparator, the EAT said, should have been a woman on shared parental leave, who would have been given leave on the same terms as Mr Ali. Furthermore, even if the tribunal's proposed comparator had been correct, the more favourable treatment accorded to the mother would have been disregarded under s 13(6)(b) as special treatment afforded to women in connection with pregnancy or childbirth. It may be that from 14 weeks (the period protected by the Pregnant Workers Directive) or 26 weeks (the period suggested by Working Families, which intervened in the case) after childbirth, it might be possible to draw a valid comparison between a father on shared parental leave and a mother on maternity leave.

In *Hextall v (1) Chief Constable of Leicestershire Police (2) Working Families (Intervenor)* (UKEAT/0139/17), the EAT remitted the case back to the tribunal, deciding that the tribunal had erred when adopting the same reason for rejecting women on maternity leave as comparators for a direct discrimination claim, for the purposes of the indirect discrimination claim. 'The identification of a pool' for testing the impact on men and women was different from direct discrimination claims, as fathers had no choice but to take shared parental leave. The EAT appeared, therefore, to accept that enhancing maternity leave pay, but not pay for shared parental leave, may give rise to *indirect* sex discrimination claims by fathers, because mothers have a choice as to whether to take maternity leave or shared parental leave.

The situation as to whether a failure to offer enhanced shared parental pay, where enhanced maternity pay is available, is discriminatory therefore remains unclear. Indirect discrimination appears to be the more logical route to go down, but as, unlike direct discrimination, employers can justify indirect discrimination, it remains to be seen how and when this may apply and when there is a shift from provisions about the health and recovery of the mother to those about the care of the child. In *Shuter*, the employment tribunal accepted that paying women on maternity leave for a full year in order to recruit and retain them in a male-dominated workforce was a valid justification.

14.17 RIGHT TO REQUEST FLEXIBLE WORKING

Amended legislation concerning the right to request flexible working was brought into force on 30 June 2014. The scheme is set out in ss 80F–80I of the ERA 1996 and the Flexible Working Regulations 2014 (SI 2014/1398). In summary, all employees with at least 26 weeks' continuous employment can request to work flexibly if the change relates to hours, times or place of work. The employer must deal with an application 'reasonably', and can only refuse a request for one of eight statutory reasons. An employee can complain to a tribunal if, for example, the employer does not deal with her application reasonably or rejects it on a non-statutory ground. Acas has published a Code of Practice and guidance (see <http://www.acas.org.uk>). Employment tribunals must take the Acas guidance into account when considering relevant claims.

14.17.1 The application

A flexible working application must be in writing, state whether the employee has made a previous application (only one application per 12 months is permitted) and be dated.

14.17.2 Grounds for refusal

Employers are under a duty to consider requests reasonably and to notify the decision, including any appeal, within three months (or such longer period as agreed) (s 80G).

An employer can refuse an employee's request for flexible working only where one or more of the grounds in s 80G of the ERA 1006 applies, ie:

- additional costs
- detrimental effect on ability to meet customer demand
- inability to reorganise work among existing staff
- inability to recruit additional staff
- detrimental impact on quality
- detrimental impact on performance
- insufficiency of work during the periods the employee proposes to work
- planned structural changes.

The Acas Guide provides examples, and readers are recommended to read it before advising.

In *Whiteman v CPS Interiors Ltd* (ET/2601103/2015), a claim for breach of the flexible working legislation was rejected. The tribunal emphasised that there is no 'right' to work flexibly, only a right to request it and to have the request dealt with in a reasonable manner. Provided an employer follows the Acas Code and its approach is not discriminatory (see **14.17.6**), an employer is free to reject requests on one of the specified grounds. See also *Smith v Gleacher Shacklock LLP* (ET/2202747/2015), where a claim was also rejected, along with an indirect sex discrimination claim.

14.17.3 Complaining to the tribunal

If an employer refuses a request to work flexibly, an employee can complain to an employment tribunal on grounds that the employer:

- failed to deal with the application in a reasonable manner;
- failed to decide within the decision period (three months);
- rejected the application for a reason other than one of the statutory grounds;
- based its decision on incorrect facts.

Tribunals do not have the power to question the commercial validity of the employer's decision to refuse an application. The tribunal's role is essentially to ensure that the employer has taken the request seriously and that its refusal was based on the correct facts. Complaints must be brought within three months from the date on which the employee was notified of the decision. The tribunal may extend the deadline if it was not reasonably practicable for the employee to present the complaint within the three-month period.

14.17.4 Remedies

Remedies are dealt with under s 80I of the ERA 1996 and reg 6 of the Flexible Working Regulations 2014. The maximum compensation that a tribunal may award is eight weeks' pay (subject to the statutory maximum – currently £475 at 1 February 2015). The amount awarded will depend on what the tribunal considers just and equitable.

14.17.5 Detriment and automatic unfair dismissal (ERA 1996, ss 47E and ERA 1996, s 104C)

Employees who make an application to work flexibly, or who exercise their rights under the above provisions to work flexibly, are protected against detrimental treatment in the same way as women who take or seek to take maternity leave, and will be regarded as automatically unfairly dismissed if the reason for their dismissal was connected to the fact that they sought to work flexibly or exercised their rights under the above provisions. An employee who is dismissed because she tried to exercise the right to work flexibly may also bring a claim to have been dismissed for asserting a statutory right under s 104(1)(a) or (b) (see *Horn v Quinn Walker Securities* (ET/2505740/03) for an example).

So long as the employee has two years' service (or one year if employed before 6 April 2012), she could also bring a normal unfair dismissal claim (see, for an example, *Superdrug Stores plc v Fannon* (UKEAT/1190/96)).

If an employer acts perversely or unreasonably in dealing with or refusing a request, an employee may be entitled to resign and claim constructive dismissal (see *Clarke v Telewest Communications plc* (ET/1301034/04)).

14.17.6 Overlap with sex discrimination law

Where a woman returning from maternity leave asks to work part time, she may, if the employer refuses her request, have a claim of unlawful indirect sex discrimination. To bring a claim of indirect sex discrimination, an individual will need to establish a PCP that appears to be gender neutral, which puts a person of that sex at a particular disadvantage which cannot be justified. If she made the request under the above statutory provisions, she may also, depending on the facts, have a complaint under s 80H of the ERA 1996, for unjustified refusal of a request for flexible working (see, for an example, *Girvin v Next Retail Ltd* (ET/1900767/05)). A man may also be able to bring a direct sex discrimination claim if he can show that a woman's request would have been treated more favourably.

14.18 TIME OFF TO CARE FOR DEPENDANTS

As a basic proposition, all employees are entitled to reasonable unpaid time off work to look after a dependant (dependant care leave) (ERA 1996, s 57A).

14.18.1   Entitlement to dependant care leave

Section 57A(1) of the ERA 1996 states that an employee is entitled to be permitted to take a reasonable amount of unpaid time off work in order to take action necessary:

(a)   to assist a dependant who is ill, has given birth, is injured or assaulted;

(b)   to arrange care for an ill or injured dependant;

(c)   as a result of the death of a dependant;

(d)   due to care arrangements being disrupted or ending;

(e)   to deal with an incident at the child's school.

The amount of time the employee can take off work to care for a dependant is a reasonable amount of time to take *necessary* action. In *Royal Bank of Scotland plc v Harrison* (UKEAT/0093/08) the EAT gave guidance on what was meant by 'necessary'. It said that there was no justification for inserting words such as 'sudden' or 'emergency' into s 57A(1)(d).

In order to be entitled to take time off to care for a dependant, the employee must tell his employer:

(a)   the reason for his absence as soon as reasonably practicable; and

(b)   How long he expects to be absent (s 57A(2)).

'Dependant' is defined in s 57A(3), (4) and (5) as follows:

(a)   The employee's spouse, civil partner, child, parent or person who lives in the same household (but not a tenant, lodger or boarder). The definition clearly extends to non-married partners.

(b)   'Dependant' also includes anybody who *reasonably relies upon* the employee for help when a person is ill or injured or assaulted or to make arrangements for care. The BIS guidance states that this may be where the employee is the primary carer for another person, or is the only person who can help in an emergency: for example, an elderly neighbour living alone who falls and breaks a leg, where the employee is closest at hand at the time of the fall.

14.18.2   Meaning of reasonable amount of time off

The decision in *Qua v John Ford Morrison Solicitors* [2003] IRLR 184 was the first reported appellate decision on the right to time off to care for dependants. Ms Qua was absent from work for 17 days (over a period of eight separate occasions) as a result of her young son's medical problems.

The EAT considered the meaning of 'reasonable amount of time off work' and stated that when determining what is a reasonable amount of time off work, a tribunal should always take into account the circumstances of that individual and should ignore any disruption to the employers' business. The EAT pointed out that an employee is entitled to be permitted to take a reasonable amount of time off work to take the action needed to deal with a sick child. But, as the EAT indicated, the section is dealing with the unforeseen. Once a parent knows that a child is suffering from an underlying medical condition which is likely to cause further relapses, such a situation no longer falls within the section. The employee would, in such a situation, be entitled to a reasonable period off work to make arrangements for longer-term care. Thus the advice to the employer in respect of an employee who wishes to take three weeks off work to care for her sick child is that the employee cannot do this. She is entitled to take time off to make arrangements for his care, but not to take the three weeks and care for him herself.

In *Royal Bank of Scotland plc v Harrison* (UKEAT/0093/08) an employee learnt on 8 December that her childminder would be unavailable on 22 December and argued that the time she took off to look after her child was time off to care for a dependant under s 57A. The Bank argued that absence of anyone to care for her child was not unexpected and s 57A only applied to situations that arose suddenly or in an emergency. The EAT disagreed. It held that an event is 'unexpected' at the moment the employee learns of it. Once aware of it, he or she must try to make alternative arrangements, but if it is not possible to do so, it will become necessary for the employee to take time off under s 57A.

14.18.3   Detriment and automatic unfair dismissal (ERA 1996, s 99 and MPLR 1999, regs 19 and 20)

Employees who take or seek to take dependant care leave are protected in the same way as women who take or seek to take maternity leave against detrimental treatment, and will be regarded as automatically unfairly dismissed if the reason for their dismissal was connected to the fact that they took or sought to take dependency leave (MPLR 1999, regs 19 and 20(3)(e)(iii)). (See **14.6** and **14.7**.)

Similarly, an employee will be regarded as automatically unfairly dismissed if there was a redundancy situation and those circumstances (ie the redundancy situation) applied to other employees, and the reason the employee was selected for redundancy, was because he took or sought to take dependency leave (reg 20(2)).

In *Ellis v Ratcliffe Palfinger Ltd* (UKEAT/0438/13), the EAT upheld an employment tribunal decision that an employee had not been automatically unfairly dismissed for exercising his right to take time off for dependants because he had not told his employer the reason for his absence 'as soon as reasonably practicable'. Under the terms of his contract, Mr Ellis was obliged, if absent due to illness, to notify his line manager no later than 30 minutes after he should have started work and was required to stay in regular contact. As a result of attendance issues, Mr Ellis received a final written warning on 25 November 2011, which was to remain on his file for 12 months. On 6 February 2012, Mr Ellis took his heavily pregnant partner to hospital several times. However, he did not telephone his line manager. His father telephoned in later in the day. Mr Ellis did not attend work for the rest of the week and did not keep in touch with his employer. He was called to a disciplinary meeting on 12 February. He said his mobile phone battery had run out and he could not remember his employer's telephone number. He was dismissed and brought proceedings for automatically unfair dismissal under s 57A of the ERA 1996. The tribunal judge found that Mr Ellis could have made contact with his employer on a number of occasions and that he had not, therefore, told his employer the reason for his absence 'as soon as reasonably practicable', which is a mandatory requirement of s 57A. On that basis he was not covered by the automatically unfair dismissal protection.

14.18.4   Remedies

The remedies available to employees in relation to their right to take time off to care for a dependant are set out in s 57B of the ERA 1996. The time-limit for making a complaint is three months from the date of the refusal. If the tribunal decides that the complaint was well-founded, it may make a declaration and/or award compensation, of such amount as the tribunal considers to be just and equitable having regard to the employer's behaviour and any loss sustained by the employee.

14.19   PARENTAL BEREAVEMENT LEAVE

The Parental Bereavement (Pay and Leave) Act 2018 has received royal assent. It entitles employed parents who have lost a child under 18 to take two weeks' statutory paid leave to allow them time to grieve. Previously, employees had to rely either on contractual rights or employer goodwill in such situations. Although s 57A of the ERA 1996 allows an employee to take a reasonable amount of time off work to deal with an emergency, this is unpaid and there is no definition of reasonable. Mothers who lose a child after 24 weeks of pregnancy or during maternity leave will not lose their entitlement to maternity pay and leave.

All the details will appear in supporting regulations, which have not yet been published. The Government has said that it anticipates introducing regulations by April 2020. Acas has produced guidance on managing bereavement in the workplace. This highlights some of the potential difficulties in this area:

- Details of death are covered by data protection rights.
- Religious observance rights need to be taken into account, or there is a risk that religious or racial discrimination may arise.
- The impact of grief can have an effect on performance and behaviour.

14.20 FURTHER READING

Blackstone's Employment Law Practice, 10th edn (OUP, 2019).

Harvey, *Industrial Relations and Employment Law* (Butterworths), Vol 2, Div J.

SUMMARY

The provisions relating to maternity rights have been implemented as a result of the Equal Treatment Directive 1976 and the Pregnant Workers Directive 1992. The law is contained in the ERA 1996, as amended. However, much of the detail in respect of maternity rights and parental leave is contained in the Maternity and Parental Leave etc Regulations 1999 (as amended) (**14.1**). The following checklist summarises points of importance when considering maternity rights:

- Length of service.
- Detrimental treatment.
- Dismissal.
- Reason for dismissal – ERA 1996, s 99/other.
- If not s 99, eligibility/fairness of employer's actions under s 98(4).
- Whether entitled to a redundancy payment and/or to claim sex discrimination and/or wrongful dismissal.

The main rights afforded to pregnant woman relate to the right to take maternity leave and to return to work after that leave expires. In most instances, some of that leave will be paid for. All pregnant women are entitled up to 52 weeks' maternity leave. The first 26 weeks are known as 'ordinary maternity leave' (OML) (**14.3**). The remaining period of up to 26 weeks is known as 'additional maternity leave' (AML) (**14.3.3**).

A woman who wants to take maternity leave must notify her employer of the fact of her pregnancy, the expected week of childbirth and the date she intends to start her maternity leave. There are rules about the time by which this must be done (**14.3.1**).

During maternity leave, the woman's contract of employment continues. A woman is entitled to the benefit of all the terms and conditions of employment which would have applied to her had she not been absent during the maternity leave period, including non-contractual benefits, except remuneration. A woman who takes OML is entitled to return to the job in which she was employed before her absence, with her seniority, pension rights and similar rights as they would have been had she not been absent, and on terms and conditions no less favourable than they would have been had she not been absent. The statutory right to return to a job after AML is more restricted than after OML. A woman on maternity leave may be entitled to receive statutory maternity pay (SMP), which is paid for a maximum period of 39 weeks (**14.12.3**). The maternity leave period counts towards the woman's period of continuous employment for both statutory and contractual rights (**14.3.6.1**).

An employee on maternity leave may agree with her employer to work for up to 10 days during her maternity leave without bringing that period to an end. 'Work' may include training or any other activity undertaken to assist the employee to keep in touch with the workplace (**14.3.5.2**).

Under ss 47C and 99 of the ERA 1996, pregnant/maternity leave employees have special protection from acts short of dismissal and/or dismissal (**14.6** and **14.7**). Section 18 of the Equality Act 2010 states that it will be sex discrimination where a woman is treated less favourably because she is pregnant or exercising or seeking to exercise, or has exercised her right to maternity leave (**14.11**).

Since April 2003, employees have the right to take time off work after adopting a child. The law is very similar to the law which applies to women taking maternity leave. An employee who adopts a child and takes adoption leave may be entitled to statutory adoption pay (SAP) (**14.13**).

The Employment Act 2002 (EA 2002) introduced a right for fathers and other partners to take up to two weeks' paid paternity leave. The Paternity and Adoption Leave Regulations 2002 set out the relevant details. Employees who take or seek to take paternity leave are protected against detrimental treatment in the same way as women who take or seek to take maternity leave, and will be regarded as automatically unfairly dismissed if the reason for their dismissal was connected to the fact that they took or sought to take paternity leave. An employee who takes paternity leave is entitled to statutory paternity pay (SPP) (**14.14**).

New provisions, which became effective from 5 April 2015, allow parents to take shared parental leave (**14.16**).

Under the Maternity and Parental Leave etc Regulations 1999 (as amended), an employee is entitled to take up to 18 weeks' unpaid parental leave (18 weeks for a disabled child). Employees who take or seek to take parental leave are protected against detrimental treatment in the same way as women who take or seek to take maternity leave, and will be regarded as automatically unfairly dismissed if the reason for their dismissal was connected to the fact that they took or sought to take parental leave (**14.16**).

The detail about flexible working is contained in the Flexible Working (Eligibility, Complaints and Remedies) and (Procedural Requirements) Regulations 2002. The right to request flexible working applies to carers of children and carers of adults (**14.17**).

Under the ERA 1996, s 57A, all employees are entitled to unpaid time off work to look after a dependant who is ill, has given birth, is injured or assaulted, or who has died, and to deal with an incident at a child's school. The amount of time the employee may take off work to care for a dependant is a reasonable amount of time to take necessary action (**14.18**).

Table 14.1 summarises the main rights and remedies available with regard to maternity leave, parental leave, time off for dependants, paternity leave, adoption leave and requests for flexible working.

Table 14.1 Summary of main rights and remedies

The right (primary jurisdiction in brackets)	Main features	Who qualifies?
Rights and remedies covering maternity leave, parental leave, time off for dependants, paternity leave, adoption leave, requests for flexible working (the detail is contained in the MPL, PAL and SPL Regs)		
Pregnancy/maternity discrimination (Equality Act 2010, ss 18 and 39)	Unfavourable treatment because of pregnancy/maternity leave	All female workers who are pregnant, employees on maternity leave & workers for 2 weeks after the birth
Sex discrimination (direct and indirect) (Equality Act 2010, ss 13, 19 and 26) and harassment	Where there is less favourable treatment on grounds of sex/marital status or unjustified PCP which disadvantages one sex	All workers, male and female
Automatic unfair dismissal (ERA ss 99 and 104C, MPL Regs 10 & 20, PAL Regs 28 & 29, APL Reg 34)	Automatic unfair dismissal if the only or principal reason is connected with a right to leave for family reasons, or requesting flexible work	All employees regardless of length of service
Protection from detriment (ERA s 47C & 47E)	Covers leave for family and domestic reasons and in relation to flexible working	All employees regardless of length of service
'Ordinary' unfair dismissal (ERA s 98)	Where the dismissal is not fair. Note also the possibility of automatic unfair dismissal under ss 100 (H&S) and 104 ERA (asserting a statutory right)	Employees with two years' service (for those who start work on or after 6 April 2012)
Written reasons for dismissal (ERA 1996 s 92(4) & (4A))	Applies if s/he is dismissed when pregnant or on maternity or adoption leave	All employees whether or not they have requested the reasons in writing
Specific rights and remedies		
Time off for antenatal care (ERA ss 55–56)	Reasonable paid time off	All employees
Refusal of time off for antenatal care (ERA s 57)	Specific remedy in addition to protection from dismissal, detriment and discrimination	
H&S protection (Management of Health and Safety at Work Regulations 1999 and ERA ss 66–69)	Protection from risks is the employer's responsibility culminating in suspension on full pay	All employees, must notify pregnancy in writing to benefit from alternative work & paid suspension
Breach of H&S provisions	Compensation (ERA s 70), automatic unfair dismissal in relation to suspension (MPL Regs 20(3)(c)), sex discrimination	Note: a dismissed employee may have a claim under ERA s 100 and the employer is also liable to prosecution
Ordinary maternity leave (OML) (ERA s 71, MPL Regs 4–11)	26 weeks	All employees regardless of length of service
Additional maternity leave (AML) (ERA s 73, MPL Regs 5–12)	Starts when OML ends and runs for 26 weeks	All employees regardless of length of service
Refusal of maternity leave (ERA s 99 and 47C)	Automatic unfair dismissal or detriment	
Contractual rights during OML and AML (ERA s 71, MPL Reg 9)	All rights set out in contract continue to accrue apart from remuneration	

The right (primary jurisdiction in brackets)	Main features	Who qualifies?
Parental leave (ERA s 76, MPL Regs 13–18)	Thirteen weeks for each parent for each child under 5 years old (18 weeks if the child is disabled)	Employees with responsibility for a child who have been employed for one year
Shared parental leave (SPL Regs)	Parents can share up to 50 weeks' leave	Employees with 26 weeks' continuous employment
Parental leave: unreasonable postponement or refusal (ERA s 80)	Declaration and compensation under ERA s 80	
Time off for dependants (ERA s 57A)	Time off to care for dependant in an emergency	All employees
Refusal of time off for dependants (ERA s 57B)	Declaration and compensation under ERA s 57B	
Paternity leave (ERA s 80A, PAL Regs)	2 weeks' leave to be taken together	Employees with 26 weeks' service by the 15th week before the EWC or the date of matching for adoption
Additional paternity leave	2–26 weeks paid leave	If partner returns to work before the end of their maternity (or adoption leave) period
Refusal of paternity leave (ERA s 99 & 47C)	Automatic unfair dismissal or detriment	
Adoption leave (ERA s 75A, PAL Regs)	52 weeks' leave	All employees
Refusal of adoption leave (ERA s 99 and 47C)	Automatic unfair dismissal or detriment	
Redundancy during maternity or adoption or shared parental leave (ERA ss 74 and 75C, MPL Reg 10, PAL Reg 23, SPL Reg 39)	Right to be given first refusal of any suitable alternative job available	All employees on OML and AML and adoption leave
Return to work after OML (ERA s 71); up to 26 weeks' – SPL (SPL Reg 40); OAL (PAL Reg 26)	Right to return to the same job	
Return to work after AML (ERA s 73, MPL Reg 18); up to 26 weeks' – SPL (SPL Reg 40); AAL (PAL Reg 26)	Right to return to the same job. Only if that is not reasonably practicable may the employer offer a suitable alternative	All employees
Statutory Maternity Pay/Adoption Pay/SPL Pay)	90% of salary for 6 weeks, 33 weeks at £145.18 pw	All employees and other workers who have NI deducted at source and who have been employed for 26 weeks by the 15th week before the EWC & earn at least £116 a week in an 8 week 'relevant period'
Failure to pay SMP	Unlawful deduction from wages (see ERA s 27(1)(c))	Note: the employer is also liable to prosecution
Maternity allowance	£145.18 (or 90%, whichever is the lower) payable by the DSS for 39 weeks	Employed and self-employed workers who work during their pregnancy but do not qualify for SMP
Means tested benefits	Support from the welfare benefits safety net via DWP for women who cannot claim SMP or MA	

The right (primary jurisdiction in brackets)	Main features	Who qualifies?
Statutory paternity pay	Fixed rate for 2 weeks of £145.18 or 90% gross earnings	Average earnings must be £116 pw (or more)
Refusal of paternity pay	Unlawful deduction from wages (ERA s 27(1)(ca))	
Additional statutory paternity pay	£145.18 pw or 90% gross earnings	26 weeks' continuous employment/£116 pw
Refusal of adoption pay	Unlawful deduction from wages (ERA s 27(1)(cb))	
Flexible working (ERA s 80F, FW Regs 2014)	The right to ask for flexible working for all employees	Employees with 26 weeks' service.
Refusal of FW	ERA s 80H and possibly indirect sex discrimination	

© Palmer Wade (adapted)

CHAPTER 15

HUMAN RIGHTS, MONITORING AND DATA PROTECTION

LEARNING OUTCOMES

After reading this chapter you will be able to:

- understand how the Human Rights Act 1998 may influence UK law

- explain when Article 6 may impact upon internal disciplinary proceedings

- explain how Article 6 impacts upon employment tribunal hearings

- describe how Article 8 is relevant to employment tribunal claims

- describe the relevance of the Regulation of Investigatory Powers Act 2000 and of the Data Protection Act 1998.

15.1 HUMAN RIGHTS ACT 1998 – INTRODUCTION

The HRA 1998 came into force on 2 October 2000. It incorporates into domestic law the European Convention for the Protection of Human Rights and Fundamental Freedoms 1950 ('the Convention' or 'ECHR'). The ECHR is an instrument of the Council of Europe, which has 47 Member States, including the UK and Russia. It is enforced by the European Court of Human Rights (ECtHR) based in Strasbourg. It is completely separate from the EU. The EU has its own Charter of Fundamental Rights, which is overseen by the Court of Justice of the EU (ECJ), based in Luxembourg. Although the UK was already a signatory to the Convention and was therefore bound by it as a matter of international law, until the HRA 1998 came into force the Convention was not directly part of UK domestic law and individuals could not enforce Convention rights in the domestic courts.

In his speech to the Conservative Party conference on 10 October 2014, the then Prime Minister, David Cameron, said that his party would replace the HRA 1998 with a 'British Bill of Rights and Responsibilities' if it won the General Election in May 2015. An official document, released on 2 October 2014, set out the party's proposals at that time and suggested a draft Bill would be published. The intent then was to put the text of the Convention into primary legislation so as to break the formal link between British courts and the European Court of Human Rights (ECtHR). In September 2015, the Government said that its proposals to replace the HRA 1998 would be launched in autumn 2015, and that there would be a 'full and thorough consultation'. In October 2015 the Government announced that it intended to fast-track the Bill of Rights, but a further delay was announced in December 2015 and a draft Bill is still awaited.

15.2   THE SCHEME OF THE HUMAN RIGHTS ACT 1998

Schedule 1 to the HRA 1998 sets out the relevant Convention rights which are protected under the Act.

Section 3 of the Act states that 'so far as it is possible to do so' primary and secondary legislation must be read and given effect in a way which is compatible with the Convention rights; this includes (s 2) taking account of any judgments and decisions of the European Court of Human Rights. In order to give effect to the spirit of the Convention, UK courts and tribunals adopt a 'purposive' approach to the interpretation of such legislation. This is an area with which the UK courts are reasonably familiar, albeit in a different context, as they have been applying a purposive approach to EU Regulations and Directives for some time. For example, the House of Lords in *Litster v Forth Dry Dock and Engineering Co Ltd* [1989] IRLR 161 (see **7.3.2**) had to put a very strained interpretation on the Transfer of Undertakings (Protection of Employment) Regulations 1981 in order to make them comply with the (old) Acquired Rights Directive which they were intended to implement.

If any primary or subordinate legislation is found to be incompatible with a Convention right, the HRA 1998 provides that such legislation remains effective. In such a situation, certain courts (the Supreme Court and some named appellate courts, but not including employment tribunals or the EAT) can make (s 4) a 'declaration of incompatibility' in relation to that legislation, upon which Parliament may act if it wishes. (This allows for the sovereignty of Parliament to remain unchallenged.) The declaration does not affect the validity of the law and is not binding on the parties to the proceedings.

The HRA 1998 creates a new free-standing cause of action for the victims of unlawful acts by public authorities. Victims are entitled to rely on their Convention rights in proceedings brought against public authorities, or in conjunction with other existing causes of action – for example breach of contract or unfair dismissal claims. Public authorities are defined as 'including' the courts and tribunals, and 'any person certain of whose functions are functions of a public nature' (s 6). Section 6 provides that it is unlawful for a public authority to act in a way which is incompatible with Convention rights. It allows 'victims' who claim that a public authority has acted (or proposes to act) unlawfully to bring proceedings in the 'appropriate court or tribunal' (s 7). Section 8 deals with remedies.

The important Convention rights, from an employment perspective, are identified at **15.4**. Most of those rights are not absolute rights but are limited by counter-balances which permit legitimate interferences with those rights in certain situations. Most human rights cases are not about whether the right exists but whether there has been an interference with the right, and whether that interference is legitimate and necessary. That will involve questions of proportionality and relevance being considered (see **15.4** below).

15.3   KEY DEFINITIONS

The mainstay of the HRA 1998 is that it permits victims to sue public authorities.

15.3.1   Public authorities

Case law has considered the meaning of 'public authority' and recognised three categories of legal persons for the purposes of the Act:

(a)   clear public authorities (eg central and local government, the police, HM Revenue and Customs, courts and tribunals);

(b)   mixed authorities (eg privatised utilities like Railtrack, which retain some public functions, or private companies which carry out some public duties, like G4S);

(c)   private persons.

The scope of the Act differs according to each category. Clear public authorities fall within the scope of s 6 (ie they have to act in a way which is compatible with the Convention rights) in relation to all their activities. Mixed authorities fall within the scope of s 6 in relation only to those acts they carry out which are of a public nature. Private persons are entirely outside the direct scope of s 6.

Defining within which category a particular body falls is a difficult area. As far as mixed authorities are concerned, determining whether acts are private acts or public acts is a distinction with which the UK courts are familiar, not least in determining whether bodies are susceptible to judicial review. The boundaries between public and private law continue to be hotly contested by parties in judicial review proceedings and are beyond the scope of this book, but we set out some of the HRA case law on this issue below.

In a case involving a housing association in Poplar (*Poplar Housing and Regeneration Community Association Ltd v Donoghue* [2002] QB 48), the Court of Appeal held that housing associations were not to be regarded as public authorities for all purposes. The fact that the association was a charity motivated by the public interest did not point towards it being a public authority. However, the Court said that an act which would otherwise be private, could become public if it had features that imposed a 'public stamp', and concluded, on the facts, that the role of the housing association was so 'closely assimilated' to that of the local authority that it should be regarded as a 'hybrid' public authority for the purposes of s 6. In (R *(Heather and Others) v Leonard Cheshire Foundation and Others* [2002] 2 All ER 936) the Court of Appeal decided that the Leonard Cheshire Foundation, which was a charitable voluntary organisation, was not performing a public function within the meaning of s 6(3) because the provision of care was not a 'public function', although the fees for the care were paid by the local authority.

Similarly, in *YL v Birmingham City Council* [2007] UKHL 27, the House of Lords held (3:2) that a private care home for the elderly under contract with a local authority was not exercising 'functions of a public nature'. Baroness Hale, dissenting, concluded that the fact the care was paid for by the local authority was supportive of the home's performing public functions.

In R *(on the application of Susan Weaver) v London and Quadrant Housing Trust* [2008] EWHC 1377 (Admin), a registered social landlord's management and allocation of housing functions were held to be functions of a public nature. The Court of Appeal upheld the High Court's decision ([2009] EWCA Civ 587) and the Supreme Court refused leave to appeal.

15.3.2   Victims

A 'victim' can bring proceedings against a public authority, relying on a Convention right.

A victim is defined (s 7(7)) to include a person, non-governmental organisation or group of individuals. Thus, in addition to individuals, victims may include companies, political parties, professional bodies and trade unions. Victims must be 'directly affected' by the act complained of (or at risk of being so affected). But note that in some situations the ECtHR has allowed those 'indirectly affected' (eg relatives of a dead victim) to bring a complaint. The ECtHR has not allowed pressure group claims, and the scope for representative actions is limited.

15.3.3   Reliance

Section 6 creates a free-standing cause of action for victims of unlawful acts done by public authorities (see **15.3.1** above). They do not need to 'hang' such a claim on any other existing cause of action. Such persons are therefore entitled to bring a claim under s 7 in the 'appropriate court or tribunal'. Employment tribunals and the EAT fall within that definition. They can adjudicate on free-standing claims under the HRA 1998, have to interpret any legislation in accordance with Convention rights (s 3) and, as they are themselves public authorities, are obliged to act in compliance with Convention rights in accordance with s 6.

Those persons who do not fall within the category of persons who may bring direct free-standing claims (eg private sector employees) will still be able to avail themselves of Convention rights but not as a free-standing claim. Because tribunals are themselves public authorities, and are obliged to act in compliance with Convention rights under s 6, and because they will have to interpret UK legislation in accordance with Convention rights under s 3, such other persons can rely on Convention rights to help in the interpretation and application of any existing causes of action (eg unfair dismissal or breach of contract claims).

15.4   RELEVANT CONVENTION RIGHTS

Identified briefly below are those Convention rights which may be of relevance to UK employment law. Reference is also made in other chapters, where appropriate, to specific employment law areas where the HRA 1998 may have application.

15.4.1   Article 6

This creates a right to a 'fair and public hearing within a reasonable time by an independent and impartial tribunal established by law'. Article 6 may be used to challenge areas such as the following:

(a)   A right to legal representation at disciplinary hearings.

There has been much discussion about whether Article 6 applies to employers' internal disciplinary procedures (see **15.3.1**).

In R (G) v The Governors of X School [2011] UKSC 30, the Supreme Court held (by a 4:1 majority) that a teaching assistant's rights under Article 6 of the European Convention on Human Rights had not been breached by the school's decision to prohibit legal representation at his internal disciplinary hearing. The claimant was employed as a teaching assistant at a primary school. He was accused of kissing and having sexual contact with a 15-year old boy, who was undergoing a period of work experience at the school. As a result of the accusations the claimant was suspended and disciplinary proceedings were commenced. Criminal proceedings were not brought against the claimant. The claimant asked for legal representation at the disciplinary hearing, which was to take place before the school's governors. This request was refused as the school's disciplinary policy provided for accompaniment only by a work colleague or union representative. The disciplinary hearing resulted in a finding that the allegations were substantiated, and the claimant was summarily dismissed.

Statutory provisions obliged the school, when it made a serious finding of misconduct, to make a reference to what became the Independent Safeguarding Authority (ISA) (originally the Secretary of State) to consider whether the claimant should be should be placed on the 'children's barred list' and prevented from working with children in the future. Under this statutory framework, the claimant would have a right to legal representation before the ISA; and if dissatisfied with its decision, there was a right of appeal.

The claimant appealed the decision of the school's disciplinary committee to the appeal committee of the school's governors. He requested permission to be legally represented at this hearing, but this was refused. He brought judicial review proceedings, alleging that the disciplinary proceedings were unfair and constituted a breach of his rights to a fair hearing under Article 6 of the Convention. His appeal to the appeal committee of the school's governors was stayed, pending the outcome of the civil proceedings.

The Court of Appeal held that where the consequences of an internal disciplinary proceeding were sufficiently linked to the determination of an individual's civil right to practise his chosen profession (in the sense of having a 'substantial influence or effect' on the outcome of a subsequent process which is determinative of civil rights (in this case the outcome of the ISA's process, which could have meant that the claimant's name was added to the register)), the school had to have regard to Article 6. Laws LJ said (para 47):

> It seems to me that there is every likelihood that the outcome of the disciplinary process in a case like this, where there has been a finding of abuse of trust by virtue of sexual misconduct, will have a profound influence on the decision-making procedures relating to the barred list …

Having concluded that Article 6 was 'engaged', the Court of Appeal decided that Article 6 required that the claimant should be allowed legal representation in the disciplinary proceedings.

The Supreme Court agreed with the Court of Appeal on the appropriate test to be applied in determining whether Article 6 is engaged in the course of an internal disciplinary procedure. The Supreme Court, by a majority, applying the 'substantial influence or effect' test, overruled the Court of Appeal's finding that Article 6 required that the claimant should be allowed legal representation in the disciplinary proceedings

In its view, the fact that the ISA was required by statutory provisions and published guidance to 'exercise its own independent judgment both in relation to finding facts and making an assessment of their gravity and significance', before forming a view as to whether G should be placed on the barred list, was significant. The Supreme Court considered that the governors' determination that G had been guilty of gross misconduct would *not* have a 'substantial influence or effect' on the ISA's decision-making process. It followed that G's Article 6 rights were not engaged at the internal disciplinary stage, but only at the subsequent ISA hearing.

In his dissenting judgment, Lord Kerr considered that the ISA's decision in the barring procedure would inevitably be affected by the governors' report on the allegations. Accordingly, in Lord Kerr's view, Article 6(1) required that G should have been permitted legal representation by the school governors at the internal disciplinary hearing.

In *Mattu v The University Hospitals of Coventry and Warwickshire NHS Trust* [2012] IRLR 619, the Court of Appeal rejected the proposition that the fair trial guarantees contained in Article 6(1) were engaged at the stage of disciplinary proceedings brought by an employer that could lead to dismissal and career damage. This was a different situation from *R (G) v The Governors of X School* (above), as it was the effect of dismissal that could render the employee unemployable in the NHS thereafter. All three members of the Court of Appeal agreed that Article 6 would not be engaged by the decision to dismiss. It also said that dismissal was a contractual matter, not the determination of a civil right.

Provided there is no contractual obligation to permit legal representation, it appears that, while employers should always consider in any particular case the gravity of the allegations and the possible implications of an adverse finding, the vast majority of employers will not need to be concerned by requests for legal representation at disciplinary hearings.

(b)   *Access to the courts.* In *Devlin v UK* [2002] IRLR 155, the ECtHR held that a total block on the applicant bringing proceedings for religious discrimination on grounds of national security, amounted to a disproportionate restriction on the applicant's right of access to a court and was therefore in breach of Article 6. By contrast, in *Fogarty v UK* [2002] IRLR 148, the same court held that excluding an employee of the US embassy from bringing discrimination proceedings did not breach Article 6 because there was a legitimate aim being pursued and the exclusion was proportionate, namely, the promotion of good relations between States through respect for State sovereignty.

In *Benkharbouche and Anor v Embassy of the Republic of Sudan* [2015] IRLR 301, the Court of Appeal held that immunity from proceedings conferred on two embassies by the State Immunity Act 1978 in respect of two members of staff (non-diplomatic) was contrary to Article 6 because there were no special features present in the case. The Supreme Court upheld that decision in *Benkharbouche v Secretary of State for Foreign and Commonwealth Affairs* [2017] UKSC 62.

(c)   *Limitation periods.*

(d)   *Qualifying periods.*

(e)   *Court fees.*

(f)   *Funding.* In *Airey v Ireland* (1979) 2 EHRR 305, the ECtHR found that while there is no general right to legal aid in civil cases, legal aid is required when legal representation is compulsory, because of the complexity or nature of the case or the ability of a person to self-represent. In *Steel and Morris v The UK* [2005] ECHR 103 (the 'McLibel' case), the ECtHR held that the lack of civil legal aid in this case was in violation of Article 6. The case was factually and legally complex, and 'equality of arms' was central to a fair hearing.

(g)   *Refusal to grant adjournments* (see *Teinaz v London Borough of Wandsworth* [2002] IRLR 721 and *Andreou v Lord Chancellor's Department* [2002] IRLR 728). In *Iqbal v Metropolitan Police Service & Another* (UKEAT/0186/12), the EAT held that a tribunal had been wrong to refuse an adjournment on medical grounds, referring to the guidance in *Teinaz*.

(h)   *Delays in hearings.* For example, Article 6 may allow a challenge to the lengthy delays in equal pay cases. In *Somjee v UK* [2002] IRLR 886, the ECtHR held that the delays caused by the conduct of the employment tribunal and EAT amounted to a breach of Article 6. It took eight and seven years respectively for the claimant's claims to be disposed of, and despite the fact that some of the delays were caused by the claimant herself and that the proceedings were complex, because the employment tribunal and EAT had contributed to the delays, there was a breach of Article 6. In *Kwamin and Others v Abbey National plc and other cases* [2004] ICR 841, the EAT held that excessive delay between hearing and decision renders the decision unfair. The EAT said that Article 6 requires a fair hearing to be conducted within a reasonable period. In *Elliot v Whitworth Centre Ltd* (UKEAT/0030/13), the EAT upheld an Employment Judge's decision to strike out the claimant's claim on the ground that a fair trial was no longer possible two years after the claim was issued. The tribunal had not communicated with either the claimant or the respondent, and the claimant did not chase the tribunal until nearly two years later.

(i)   *Independence and impartiality.* The House of Lords held in *Lawal v Northern Spirit Ltd* [2003] IRLR 538 that there is a real possibility of bias where counsel appears as representative in front of a division of the EAT where he has previously sat as part-time judge with one or both wing members. The House of Lords stated that '[they] consider that the present practice in the EAT tends to undermine public confidence in the system. It should be discontinued.' Part-time judges have now been phased out.

In *Breeze Benton Solicitors v Miss A Weddell* (UKEAT/0873/03), the appeal by the solicitors' firm was based on the refusal of the employment tribunal chairman to recuse himself following previous proceedings involving the same firm and the firm's complaint concerning the chairman's conduct. The EAT said with regard to the test of bias:

(i)   that the test properly applied requires the tribunal to recuse itself if there is a real possibility of bias. If such a risk is found, the tribunal is not entitled to balance against that risk considerations of prejudice to the other party resulting from delay,

(ii)   that if in any case there is a real ground for doubt, that doubt should be resolved in favour of recusal,

(iii)   that it is no answer to a recusal application to say that the chairman was only one of three members with an equal vote, given the important position of the legally qualified and presiding member of a tribunal of three members, and

(iv) unless he admits to the possibility of bias, the claim of the person asked to recuse himself that he will not be or is not partial is of no weight because of 'the insidious nature' of bias.

Applying these principles to the facts, the EAT concluded that the fair-minded and informed observer, having considered all the facts, would decide that there was a real possibility of bias and that the chairman should thus have recused himself.

(j) *Fairness in terms of 'equality at arms'* (eg the right of both parties to present their cases without being placed at a substantial disadvantage when compared to the means of and resources available to the other party).

(k) *Use of a closed material procedure.*

In *Home Office v Tariq* [2011] UKSC 35, the Supreme Court held that the use of a closed material procedure in employment tribunal proceedings is compatible with Article 6 of the European Convention and EU law. Mr Tariq was suspended from his job as an immigration officer with the Home Office after the arrest of his brother and cousin as part of a major counter-terrorism investigation. There was no suggestion that Mr Tariq had been involved in any terrorism. He brought direct and indirect discrimination claims on the grounds of race and religion. The Home Office made an application for the use of a closed material procedure, on grounds of national security. The use of the procedure would mean that Mr Tariq and his representative would be excluded from certain aspects of the proceedings. His interests would be represented by the appointment of a special advocate, who is allowed to see the material but not to tell his client about it. The Court of Appeal dismissed Mr Tariq's appeal but held that Article 6 required Mr Tariq to be provided with the gist of the allegations made against him. The Home Office appealed against that decision and Mr Tariq cross-appealed against the conclusion that a closed material procedure could be used. The Supreme Court unanimously dismissed Mr Tariq's cross-appeal and by a majority of 8:1 allowed the Home Office's appeal. It held that ECtHR case law has established that national security may require the imposition of special systems whereby a party may not be permitted to know about secret material which is protected by national security. There were sufficient safeguards in the availability of special advocates. As far as the right to know the gist of the case was concerned, the Supreme Court said that ECtHR case law provides that where the liberty of the subject is involved, Article 6 requires the gist be provided, but this case did not involve the liberty of the subject.

15.4.2 Article 8

This provision gives a right to respect for private and family life, home and correspondence. Article 8(2) permits 'interference' by a public authority which is in accordance with the law and is necessary in a democratic society in the interests of national security, public safety or the economic well-being of the country, for the prevention of disorder or crime, for the protection of health or morals, or for the protection of the rights and freedoms of others. In *Botta v Italy* (1998) 26 EHRR 241, at para 32, the ECtHR said:

> Private life, in the court's view, includes a person's physical and psychological integrity; the guarantee afforded by [Article 8] is primarily intended to ensure the development, without outside interference, of the personality of each individual in his relations with other human beings.

See also *Niemietz v Germany* (1992) 16 EHRR 97, *Bensaid v UK* (2001) EHRR 205 and *Pretty v UK* (2002) 35 EHRR 1.

Common law in the UK has been moving towards protecting privacy through the law of confidence (see, eg, *Douglas v Hello!* [2005] EWCA Civ 595; *McKennitt v Ash* [2005] EWHC 3003 (QB); and *Browne v Associated Newspapers Ltd* [2007] EWCA Civ 295). In *Campbell v Mirror Group Newspapers plc* [2004] UKHL 22, the House of Lords held tht where a person has a reasonable expectation of privacy, that engages the right to an action for breach of confidence, enshrined in Article 8.

In the employment context, Article 8 may be used to protect employees' privacy. It may allow employees to challenge over-intrusive policies by employers. For example, if the employer opens 'private and confidential' mail addressed to an employee, the employee may be able to bring a claim under Article 8. If the employee is a public sector employee, he may (see **15.3.1**) have a free-standing claim under Article 8. If the employee is a private sector employee, he may be able to rely indirectly on Article 8 in an unfair dismissal or breach of contract context.

Note that Article 8 has been specifically relied upon by the courts in cases involving disabled persons (see, eg, *Price v UK* (2001) 34 EHRR 1285; *JAB and Y v East Sussex CC* [2003] EWHC 167 (Admin)) to recognise that the concept embraced in 'physical and psychological integrity', protected by Article 8, is the right of the disabled to participate in the life of the community.

In *Halford v UK* [1997] IRLR 471, Alison Halford, an Assistant Chief Constable with the Merseyside Police, brought an allegation that private conversations from a phone she had been given expressly for her private use had been intercepted. It was an extreme case and the ECtHR had no difficulty in finding that her rights under Article 8 had been violated. In *Copland v UK* [2007] ECHR 253, the ECtHR held that an employer risked breaching Article 8 if it monitored an employee's phone, email or Internet usage without having an 'acceptable use' policy in place or informing the employee of the monitoring. In *Atkinson v Community Gateway Association* (UKEAT/0457/12), the EAT held that accessing an employee's emails in the course of a disciplinary investigation into his conduct was not a breach of Article 8. There was no reasonable expectation of privacy where the employee sent emails from his work account in breach of the email policy. Further, such emails were not marked 'personal/private'.

In *McGowan v Scottish Water* [2005] IRLR 167, the employee alleged a breach of Article 8. The claimant was dismissed following covert surveillance of his house which confirmed he was falsifying time sheets. The EAT said that covert surveillance of a home 'raises at least a strong presumption that the right to have one's private life respected is being invaded'. Nevertheless, on the facts the employer was justified in its actions because it was seeking to preserve its assets and investigating a crime. Similarly, in *City & Council of Swansea v Gayle* (UKEAT/0501/12), the EAT considered that an employee has no expectation of privacy in a public place. If it was engaged, the limited interference with the claimant's right to privacy would be justified where, as here, the employee was playing squash during working time.

In *Copland v UK* [2007] ECHR 253, the ECtHR held that the collection and storage by an employer of information regarding an employee's telephone, e-mail and Internet use was, in the absence of any legal provision, unjustified (but see now the Telecommunications (Lawful Business Practice) (Interception of Communications) Regulations 2000 (SI 2000/2699), made under Regulation of Investigatory Powers Act 2000 (see **15.5.1**), which allow monitoring subject to certain conditions).

In *Garamukanwa v Solent NHS Trust* (EAT/0245/15) the EAT confirmed the employment tribunal's decision that Article 8 was not engaged where an employer used, as part of its disciplinary procedures, material seized and provided by the police following the claimant's arrest after a complaint was made over 'malicious emails' sent to another employee. The EAT said that there was no reasonable expectation of privacy in this case, because the claimant had brought relevant matters into the workplace himself.

See too *Barbulescu v Romania* [2016] ECHR 61 for confirmation that surveillance may or may not be justified and it will always depend on the facts. Certainly, there is no absolute right for employers to monitor their employees' emails without needing both adequate contractual cover (eg an appropriate policy) and proper justification.

Article 8 was used to protect the interests of homosexuals serving in the armed forces. See *Lustig Prean v UK* [1999] IRLR 734, where the ECtHR held that the applicants' discharge from the armed forces as part of a blanket ban on homosexuals infringed their right to respect for their private life. The internal investigation which was carried out prior to their discharge was also found to be a breach of Article 8. The UK Government was unable to show that either breach was necessary in a democratic society.

In *Jones v University of Warwick* [2003] 1 WLR 954, the Court of Appeal held that evidence gathered in breach of Article 8 (secret footage of the claimant filmed in her home) was admissible as it was relevant, and so it was in the interests of justice for it to be considered.

In *Hanlon v Kirklees Council* (UKEAT/0119/04) the EAT upheld the decision of a tribunal to strike out the claimant's case because he refused to consent to the disclosure of his medical records under the Access to Medical Reports Act 1988. The claimant argued that it was a breach of his right to respect for private life to have to consent. The EAT pointed out that the right to respect for private life had to be balanced against a protection for the rights of others, and in litigation the right of the other party to a fair trial was important. Striking out the claimant's case did not offend against the claimant's right to respect for private life.

If an employer insists on pre-employment screening or testing without proper justification (eg there will be some groups of workers where there is a genuine risk that they could infect others – such as surgeons), or, for example, asks questions about whether an applicant/employee is HIV-positive, that may itself give rise to an Article 8 complaint. Article 8 may also be relevant to the question of whether employers can search their employees or test them for drugs (see *O'Flynn v Airlinks Airport Coach Company Ltd* (UKEAT/0269/01).

In *X v Y* [2004] IRLR 625, the Court of Appeal dealt with the question of whether tribunals must take account of Convention rights (in this case Article 8) when deciding unfair dismissal claims brought against private sector employers. Mr X was a charity worker and worked with young offenders. He was arrested after a 'passing' policeman discovered him and a man he did not know 'engaging in sexual activity' in the toilets of a transport café. Mr X accepted a caution, and his name was placed on the Sex Offenders Register. Subsequently, his employers, who worked closely with the Probation Service, discovered this and dismissed him on the grounds of gross misconduct. The tribunal found the dismissal was fair. The Court of Appeal had to decide whether a tribunal, when deciding whether a dismissal is fair or unfair, was bound to have regard to the right to respect for privacy in private life. The employer here, however, was a private sector employer. The EAT did not answer the question. It got round the point by holding that Article 8 was not engaged. The EAT considered that an act of 'gross indecency', committed in a public place, which attracted a caution, was a public matter not a private one. ('We are not persuaded that transitory sexual encounters between consenting male adults in public lavatories fall within the right to respect for private life enshrined in Article 8.')

The majority of the Court of Appeal (Mummery and Dyson LJJ) agreed with the EAT that Article 8 was not engaged. Brooke LJ doubted this (on the basis that acts in a secluded room in private could be private in nature), but thought that the acceptance of the caution by Mr X subsequently removed the private aspect of it. Mummery LJ went on to state that there should be no difference in approach whether the employer is private or public sector. He described the effect of the Convention as 'oblique', rather than horizontal. He said the HRA 1998 did not give an applicant any cause of action against a respondent that was not a public authority. In this sense, he said the HRA 1998 did not have full horizontal effect. However, he said the effect of s 6 in a case involving a claim against a private employer was to reinforce the strong interpretative obligation imposed on a tribunal by s 3. By a process of interpretation, the right to privacy was 'blended' with the law on unfair dismissal, but without creating new private law causes of action against private employers.

In *Pay v Lancashire Probation Service* [2004] IRLR 129, the EAT agreed that s 98(4) of the ERA 1996 must be read in a way which is compatible with human rights. However, on the facts, the EAT decided that because the activities the applicant was involved in (performing in fetish clubs and merchandising of products connected with bondage, domination and sado masochism; photographs were also available on the Internet of him involved in these activities) were not private, and that the interference with freedom of expression was justified, there was no infringement of the applicant's rights under Article 8 or 10 (freedom of expression) of the Convention. Mr Pay was a probation officer who worked with sex offenders. The EAT said that the interference with Article 10 was justified on the facts because of the competing interests of the employer to protect their reputation and maintain public confidence. Dismissal was a proportionate response on the facts. The ECtHR agreed ([2009] IRLR 139).

In *Whitfield v General Medical Council* [2003] IRLR 39, the Privy Council rejected a claim for breach of Article 8 where a doctor relied on the provision in an appeal against the GMC condition that he abstain from all alcohol and submit to random testing. The doctor argued this was a breach of his right to respect for private and family life as it deprived him of the enjoyment of social drinking on family occasions. The Privy Council said that there was nothing to stop him going out and drinking soft drinks, and, moreover, that the interference was justified on public safety grounds.

In *Turner v East Midlands Trains Ltd* [2013] IRLR 107, the Court of Appeal held that the range of reasonable responses test for unfair dismissal is sufficiently robust and objective to ensure compliance with Article 8. The Court proceeded on the basis that the damage to a claimant's reputation flowing from a serious charge of dishonesty did engage Article 8.

In *Williams v Architects Registration Board* (Administrative Court, 20 May 2016), Mr Williams, a registered architect, received a criminal conviction for a benefit fraud. He failed to attend any professional conduct hearings, was found guilty of misconduct as a result of his conviction and was struck off, with an order that the finding subsist for five years. He appealed to the Administrative Court, arguing that his Article 8 rights were breached because, under the Rehabilitation of Offenders Act 1974, his conviction would become spent after two years. The court accepted his Article 8 rights were engaged but held that any interference was necessary and proportionate. The 1974 Act did not bind disciplinary proceedings. Publishing a sanction was an important part of disciplinary proceedings and involved an element of public deterrence and maintaining standards.

The Supreme Court held, in *R (on the application of T and anor) v Secretary of State for the Home Department and Others* [2014] UKSC 35, that automatic disclosure of all spent convictions on an enhanced CRB check is incompatible with Article 8. The Government has introduced a 'filter', which results in certain old and minor offences not being disclosed, but only where a person has a single conviction, ie not for persons with more than one conviction.

In *R (on the applications of P and Another) v Secretary of State for Justice and Another* [2016] EWHC 89 (Admin), the High Court held that the single conviction 'filter' is arbitrary and lacks any means for assessing proportionality, and that there had therefore been an unjustified interference with the claimants' Article 8 rights.

The ECtHR considered the lawfulness of covert camera surveillance of employees at work in *López Ribalda v Spain* (Application Nos 1874/13 and 8567/13). The surveillance was carried out to monitor suspected thefts by employees, and on the facts it was held to breach Article 8. See too *Köpke v Germany* (Application No 420/17) where the surveillance of *one* employee suspected of theft was held not to breach Article 8. The difference between the two cases is that in *Köpke*, the surveillance was targeted at a particular employee; in *López Ribalda* it was not. See too *Antovic v Montenegro* (Application No 70838/13) where the Court held (by a majority of 4:3) that cameras in lecture theatres (installed to protect property and people and to monitor teaching) breached Article 8.

The issues raised by Article 8 are also reflected in two other pieces of legislation – the Regulation of Investigatory Powers Act 2000 (RIPA 2000) and the Data Protection Act 1998 (DPA 1998) (see **15.5**).

15.4.3 Articles 9 and 10

Article 9 protects freedom of thought, conscience, and religion. Article 10 gives the right to freedom of expression. Both these provisions are subject to restrictions similar to those contained in Article 8. These Articles are most likely to be relevant to, for example, employees' attendance at religious ceremonies and employers' imposition of dress codes. In terms of the latter, there would be no need for a comparison between the sexes as, under the Equality Act 2010, the issue would be simply whether the interference with the freedom could be justified by the employer (eg on health and safety grounds – but what about enhancing the employer's business reputation?). To a large extent the protection offered by Article 10 is mirrored in the Public Interest Disclosure Act 1998. Article 10 may also impact on confidentiality clauses in contracts (see also **1.8.6**).

In *Copsey v WWB Devon Clays Ltd* [2005] IRLR 811 (a case decided before the Religion and Belief Regulations 2003 came into force), the Court of Appeal considered the issue of whether and when a refusal to work on a Sunday is unfair. The case looks at the impact of Article 9 on UK unfair dismissal law. For different reasons (there are three separate judgments) the Court of Appeal held that such a dismissal was not unfair. However, the decision makes clear that employers must try to minimise the impact of changes to working hours (for example by offering alternative jobs) where employees hold strong religious beliefs.

In *Eweida & Others v UK* [2013] ECHR 37, the ECtHR held that the UK failed to comply with its legal obligation under Article 9 in respect of one of the four claimants – Ms Eweida – because although her right to manifest her religion by wearing a cross whilst at work on the check desk at British Airways (BA) was sufficiently protected, a fair balance was not struck between her rights and those of others, in circumstances where there was no evidence of any real encroachment on the interests of others – the cross was discreet and did not detract from her professional appearance. Moreover, BA had subsequently amended its uniform policy to allow for the visible wearing of religious symbolic jewellery. However, the other three claimant's all lost on the facts:

(a)   Ms Chaplin worked as a nurse on a geriatric ward, and the ban on jewellery was therefore proportionate, given clinical safety concerns.

(b)   Ms Ladele had objected to conducting same-sex civil ceremonies. The Court held that the UK was allowed a wide margin of appreciation in striking a balance between Convention rights, and that in this case the aim of providing access to services, irrespective of sexual orientation, was a legitimate aim and that the means used to pursue this aim (Ms Ladele was dismissed and the tribunal rejected her discrimination complaint) were proportionate, given the competing rights of freedom of religion and non-discrimination on grounds of sexual orientation.

(c)   Mr McFarlane refused to counsel safe-sex couples, and his complaint that his Article 9 rights had been breached was dismissed. The UK courts enjoyed a wide margin of appreciation in deciding where to strike the balance between the claimant's rights to manifest his religious beliefs and his employer's interest in securing the rights of others. It was not, on the facts, exceeded.

In *Mba v Mayor and Burgesses of the London Borough of Merton* [2014] IRLR 145, a case brought under what was reg 3(1)(b) of the Employment Equality (Religion or Belief) Regulations 2003 (now s 19 of the Equality Act 2010), the claimant, who was a Christian, was employed at a children's home. All full-time staff had to work on two of three weekends over a three-week period. After two years of accommodating the claimant's wish not to work on Sundays, the respondent required her to start working on Sundays. She refused, resigned and brought a discrimination claim. The employment tribunal found that she was put at a particular disadvantage, but that this was a proportionate means of achieving a legitimate aim. While the claimant's belief that Sunday should be a day of rest was deeply held, the tribunal said it was 'not a core component of the Christian faith', such that any group impact was limited. The Court of Appeal noted that where the right to religious freedom under Article 9 was engaged, it does not require a group disadvantage to be shown (see *Eweida* above). While the Regulations do require the group position to be considered, it is still possible to apply the concept of justification in a way that is compatible with Article 9. In that context, the fact that the claimant's beliefs were not more widely shared, or did not constitute a 'core' belief, could not weaken her case on justification.

In *Hill v Governing Body of Great Tey Primary School* (UKEAT/0237/12), the EAT looked at the correct approach to be adopted when assessing compensation where a dismissal engaged Article 10. The claimant, a school dinner assistant, had told a child's parents that during a break, the child had been tied to a railing and whipped across the legs by other pupils. She was suspended for allegedly breaching the school's policy on confidentiality. She then complained to the media about her treatment, repeating what she had told the child's parents. She was subsequently dismissed for breaches of confidentiality, but also for bringing the school into disrepute. The tribunal found the dismissal was procedurally unfair. At the remedy hearing, the tribunal awarded compensation of two months' wages on the basis that the claimant would still have been dismissed after that period of time if a proper procedure had been adopted (following *Polkey*, see **5.6.2.2**), reduced by 80% for contributory fault. The claimant argued that the tribunal had not taken proper account of her Article 10 right to freedom of expression, and that this had impacted both on its assessment of *Polkey* and contributory fault. The EAT accepted these criticisms and said that the tribunal should have adopted a structured approach to Article 10, assessing in particular whether dismissal was a proportionate response to the claimant's actions.

In *Matuz v Hungary* [2014] ECHR 1112, the EctHR held that the dismissal of a Hungarian State television journalist related to and interfered with the journalist's Article 10 rights. The journalist was dismissed after publishing a book, which breached his contractual duty of confidentiality, containing allegations of censorship against his employer.

In *Rubins v Latvia* [2015] ECHR 2, a majority of the ECtHR held that a Latvian university had infringed a professor's right to freedom of expression by dismissing him after his allegations of mismanagement were published in the national press. The case is controversial, as some commentators regard it not as a whistleblowing case but rather as a blackmail case, because the professor had offered to withdraw all his complaints if the university revoked a number of decisions concerning the merger of his Department or paid him compensation. When the university refused, the national news agency published his criticisms of the university's management.

One area where Article 10 is becoming increasingly prominent relates to the rights of employers to take action against employees who express their views and opinions on social media platforms such as Facebook and Twitter. According to an Acas Research Paper in 2010 ('Workplaces and Social Networking: The Implications for Employment Relations'), dismissals concerning employees' use of social media are increasing (see, eg, *Preece v JD Wetherspoons plc* (ET/2104806/2010), *Crisp v Apple Retail UK Ltd* (ET/1500258/11), *North West London Hospitals NHS Trust v Bowater* [2011] EWCA Civ 63, *Smith v Trafford Housing Trust* [2012] EWHC 3221 (Ch), *Redfearn v United Kingdom* [2012] ECHR 1878 and *Teggart v TeleTech UK Ltd* [2014] IRLR 625).

Tribunals have been slow to recognise that employees may have Article 10 rights in such situations, of which proper account will need to be taken when considering whether a dismissal is fair. There is a tendency, where the speech at issue is considered 'unimportant' or of low social value or public contribution, to belittle the Article 10 right, which may be relevant to the reasonableness of a dismissal but should not intrude into an assessment of the proportionality of the interference (interference with Article 10, as a qualified right is justified only when prescribed by law, where there is a legitimate aim (see Article 10(2)) and when it is proportionate to that aim), which is a separate issue. For example, in *Gosden v Lifeline Project Ltd* (ET/2802731/2009), the claimant's contract of employment stated that gross misconduct included 'any act which is or is calculated to or may damage the company's reputation or integrity'. The claimant had forwarded, while at home, an offensive e-mail from his private e-mail account to the private e-mail account of an acquaintance, who worked for his employer's biggest client. The employment tribunal found that dismissal was justified, as this was something that 'might' damage the employer's reputation, even though there was no clear evidence of actual harm and it had been the client's employee who had subsequently distributed the e-mail.

In *Game Retail Ltd v Laws* (UKEAT/0188/14), the claimant was dismissed after he was found to have tweeted offensive posts. He had been employed since 1997 and was required to investigate losses, fraud and theft, and to conduct audits in those stores for which he had responsibility. The stores used Twitter and other social media as tools for marketing and communications. Each store had its own Twitter profile and feed, to which the manager and/ or deputy manager had access for posts. Some time prior to July 2012, the claimant opened his own Twitter account and began to follow the respondent's stores for which he had responsibility in order to be able to monitor their tweets. He said the purpose was for his own private communications conducted outside of work; however, a number of the respondent's stores followed his posts. In July 2013, an unidentified store manager notified one of the respondent's managers about tweets posted by the claimant on his Twitter feed. There was an investigation by a senior manager, who identified a number of tweets as being offensive, threatening and obscene. None of the tweets was directed at or against the respondent. The claimant was dismissed. A tribunal found that the dismissal was unfair. The claimant argued in part that the respondent was seeking to restrict his freedom of speech. The EAT, in allowing the employer's appeal, acknowledged that, generally speaking, employees must have the right to express themselves, 'providing it does not infringe on their employment and/or is outside the work context. That said, we recognise that those questions might themselves depend on the particular employment or work in question'. The EAT remitted the case to a different tribunal to reconsider the range of reasonable responses test, and the application of that test in respect of the sanction.

In *British Waterways Board v Smith* (UKEAT/0004/15) the EAT had to decide whether it was unfair to dismiss an employee who, it transpired, as a result of a separate and unrelated investigation, had two years previously made derogatory comments on his Facebook page about his colleagues and made comments about drinking while on standby. The employment tribunal held the dismissal was unfair. The EAT allowed the employer's appeal and substituted a finding that dismissal was not unfair. The EAT accept the submission for the respondent that there was no need for special rules in respect of cases relating to the use of Facebook. It relied on the EAT's decision in *Game Retail*. The EAT held that there had been a reasonable investigation, that the employer had lost confidence in the employee and that a fair procedure was followed, and said that in the circumstances the only decision an employment tribunal properly directing itself could make was that dismissal was not unfair.

It is clear from these decisions that it is important that employers have clear, effective and well-communicated policies around the use of social media, both within and outside the workplace. This will make it easier for employers to take disciplinary action if employees post negative or derogatory comments.

15.4.4   Article 11

Article 11 protects the right to freedom of association, including the right to form and join a trade union, and is outside the scope of this book.

15.4.5   Article 14

This prohibits discrimination, but only in the context of other Convention rights (see **8.13** for more detail). For cases, see *Webster v The Attorney General of Trinidad and Tobago* [2015] UKPC 10, *R (JS) v Secretary of State for Work and Pensions* [2015] UKSC 16, *Mathieson v Secretary of State for Work and Pensions* [2015] UKSC 47 and *Boyraz v Turkey* [2015] IRLR 164.

15.5   DATA PROTECTION

Employers need to ensure that they comply with the law when they process their employees' data. All employers have data protection obligations and risk substantial penalties for non-compliance with their obligations.

What follows is a very brief overview. Readers are advised to consult the legislation and the Information Commissioner's Office for further information and guidance (https://ico.org.uk/). The Information Commissioner has responsibility for upholding information rights in the public interest, promoting openness by public bodies and data privacy for individuals.

15.5.1   The General Data Protection Regulation and the Data Protection Act 2018

The EU has passed a new General Data Protection Regulation (GDPR) (Regulation (EU) 2016/679) (replacing the Data Protection Directive 95/46 on which previous UK law was based in the Data Protection Act 1998), which applies to personal data processing (Article 2). The GDPR applies to all Member States from 25 May 2018. The GDPR has direct effect in each EU Member State without the need for further implementing legislation. However, Article 88 of the GDPR permits Member States to provide for more specific rules (by way of legislation or collective agreements) to ensure the protection of the rights and freedoms in respect of processing employees' personal data.

The European Data Protection Board will seek to ensure that the GDPR is applied consistently across the EU (see www.i-scoop.eu/gdpr/european-data-protection-board-edpb/#The_European_Data_Protection_Board_and_binding_decision_making). The European Commission has published guidance on its website (https://ec.europa.eu/commission/priorities/justice-and-fundamental-rights/data-protection/2018-reform-eu-data-protection-rules_en).

The UK Government passed the Data Protection Act (DPA) 2018 in order to implement the GDPR into UK domestic law. This received Royal Assent on 23 May 2018. The Data Protection Act 2018 (Commencement No 1 and Transitional and Saving Provisions) Regulations 2018 (SI 2018/625) brought the majority of the provisions of the DPA 2018 into force on 25 May 2018 (on which date the DPA 1998 was repealed).

The Information Commissioner's Office (ICO) is the UK's independent body, set up to uphold information rights. It will investigate complaints of GDPR breaches. The ICO has published guidance on the GDPR on its website (https://ico.org.uk/for-organisations/guide-to-the-general-data-protection-regulation-gdpr/). Employers will need to show that they have complied with the legislation when carrying out data processing and monitoring in the workplace and can demonstrate compliance. The ICO's Guide on the GDPR should help organisations comply with the GDPR/DPA 2018 requirements.

From 25 May 2018, the Data Protection (Charges and Information) Regulations 2018 (SI 2018/480) require every employer who processes personal information to pay a data protection fee to the ICO unless they are exempt (see the self-assessment tool: https://ico.org.uk/for-organisations/data-protection-fee/).

> **What is personal data**
>
> Personal data is information that relates to an individual (GDPR, Article 4). The individual must be identified or identifiable either directly or indirectly from one or more identifiers or from factors specific to the individual. The ICO has issued guidance on what constitutes personal data. It includes many useful examples (see https://ico.org.uk/for-organisations/guide-to-the-general-data-protection-regulation-gdpr/what-is-personal-data/).

Article 4 defines 'processing' as:

> any operation or set of operations which is performed on personal data or on sets of personal data, whether or not by automated means, such as collection, recording, organisation, structuring, storage, adaptation or alteration, retrieval, consultation, use, disclosure by transmission, dissemination or otherwise making available, alignment or combination, restriction, erasure or destruction.

Employers need to identify the types of processing that they carry out.

Article 5 of the GDPR sets out the principles of data protection with which data controllers (employers) must comply (see Article 4 definition clause):

- lawfulness, fairness and transparency;
- purpose limitation ('collected for specified, explicit and legitimate purposes ...');
- data minimisation ('... limited to what is necessary ...');
- accuracy;
- storage limitation;
- integrity and confidentiality;
- accountability.

Article 6 sets out the (alternative) bases for processing data under the GDPR:

(a) *Consent* – the individual has given consent for their personal data to be processed for a specific purpose. The ICO states that '... employers and other organisations in a position of power over individuals should avoid relying on consent unless they are confident they can demonstrate it is freely given'.

(b) *Contract* – the processing is necessary for performance of the contract or to take steps prior to agreeing the contract.

(c) *Legal obligation* – the processing is necessary to comply with the law.

(d) *Vital interests* – the processing is necessary to protect the vital interests of the individual.

(e) *Performance of a task carried out in the public interest* – processing is necessary to perform a task in the public interest or in the exercise of official authority, and has a clear basis in law.

(f) *Legitimate interests* – the processing is necessary for the purposes of the legitimate interests of the controller or a third party except where such interests are overridden by the fundamental rights of the individual.

It will be noted that all bar one of the above depend upon the processing being 'necessary'. The ICO suggests that this does not mean that processing always has to be essential but that it must be a targeted and proportionate way of achieving the purpose. A lawful basis will not apply if you can reasonably achieve the purpose by some other less intrusive means.

The ICO advises that employers may need to consider a variety of factors, including:

- What is your purpose – what are you trying to achieve?
- Can you reasonably achieve it in a different way?
- Do you have a choice over whether or not to process the data?
- Are you a public authority?

The ICO gives the following guidance:

- You must have a valid lawful basis in order to process personal data.
- There are six available lawful bases for processing. No single basis is 'better' or more important than the others – which basis is most appropriate to use will depend on your purpose and relationship with the individual.
- Most lawful bases require that processing is 'necessary'. If you can reasonably achieve the same purpose without the processing, you won't have a lawful basis.
- You must determine your lawful basis before you begin processing, and you should document it. Take care to get it right first time – you should not swap to a different lawful basis at a later date without good reason.
- Your privacy notice should include your lawful basis for processing as well as the purposes of the processing.
- If your purposes change, you may be able to continue processing under the original lawful basis if your new purpose is compatible with your initial purpose (unless your original lawful basis was consent).
- If you are processing special category data [see GDPR, Article 9] you need to identify both a lawful basis for general processing and an additional condition for processing this type of data.
- If you are processing criminal conviction data or data about offences you need to identify both a lawful basis for general processing and an additional condition for processing this type of data.

To lawfully process some 'special' categories of personal data (defined in Article 9 to include racial or ethnic origin, political opinions, religious beliefs, trade union membership, health data or data concerning sexual orientation), one of the Article 9 bases must be established (eg explicit consent, employment and social security law necessity, etc).

The GDPR provides the following rights for individuals:

(a)   the right to be informed (Article 13);

(b)   the right of access (Article 15);

(c)   the right to rectification (Article 16);

(d)   the right to erasure (Article 17);

(e)   the right to restrict processing (Article 18);

(f)   the right to data portability (Article 20);

(g)   the right to object (Article 21);

(h)   rights in relation to automated individual decision making, including profiling (Article 22).

The ICO suggests that there a number of steps that employers need to take to comply with the GDPR's accountability obligations, including:

- adopting and implementing data protection policies;
- taking a 'data protection by design and default' approach;
- putting written contracts in place with organisations that process personal data on your behalf;
- maintaining documentation of your processing activities;
- implementing appropriate security measures;
- recording and, where necessary, reporting personal data breaches;
- carrying out data protection impact assessments for uses of personal data that are likely to result in high risk to individuals' interests;
- appointing a data protection officer; and
- adhering to relevant codes of conduct and signing up to certification schemes.

Article 33 of the GDPR requires the data processor to notify the data controller on becoming aware of a data breach. The ICO states:

- The GDPR introduces a duty on all organisations to report certain types of personal data breach to the relevant supervisory authority. You must do this within 72 hours of becoming aware of the breach, where feasible.

- If the breach is likely to result in a high risk of adversely affecting individuals' rights and freedoms, you must also inform those individuals without undue delay.

- You should ensure you have robust breach detection, investigation and internal reporting procedures in place. This will facilitate decision-making about whether or not you need to notify the relevant supervisory authority and the affected individuals.

- You must also keep a record of any personal data breaches, regardless of whether you are required to notify.

The ICO goes on to say:

> When a personal data breach has occurred, you need to establish the likelihood and severity of the resulting risk to people's rights and freedoms. If it's likely that there will be a risk then you must notify the ICO; if it's unlikely then you don't have to report it. However, if you decide you don't need to report the breach, you need to be able to justify this decision, so you should document it.

Failing to notify a breach when required to do so can result in a fine of up to €10 million or up to 2% of global turnover, whichever is higher. The fine can also be combined with the ICO's corrective powers under Article 58.

Article 35 of the GDPR introduces the concept of a Data Protection Impact Assessment (DPIA) as a tool which can help employers. A DPIA will be required when data processing is 'likely to result in a high risk to the rights and freedoms of natural persons'.

The GDPR sets out the minimum features that must be included in a DPIA:

- a description of the processing operations and the purposes, including, where applicable, the legitimate interests pursued by the data controller;

- an assessment of the necessity and proportionality of the processing in relation to the purpose;

- an assessment of the risks to individuals;

- the measures in place to address risk, including security, and to demonstrate that the data controller is complying with the GDPR.

Before doing a DPIA, a data protection officer, if one has been appointed, should be consulted along with the views (where appropriate) of data subjects or their representatives. The views of the ICO may also need to be sought. Data controllers will be obliged to retain a record of the DPIA. Failure to carry out a DPIA when one is required can result in an administrative fine of up to €10 million or, in the case of an undertaking, up to 2% of the total worldwide annual turnover of the preceding financial year, whichever is higher.

15.5.2 Specific issues

15.5.2.1 Employee consent to data processing

The Information Commissioner has warned employers that consent may not be adequate in the employment context due to the imbalance of power inherent in an employment relationship. The ICO states:

> **What's new?**
>
> The GDPR sets a high standard for consent, but the biggest change is what this means in practice for your consent mechanisms.
>
> The GDPR is clearer that an indication of consent must be unambiguous and involve a clear affirmative action (an opt-in). It specifically bans pre-ticked opt-in boxes. It also requires distinct ('granular') consent options for distinct processing operations. Consent should be separate from other terms and conditions and should not generally be a precondition of signing up to a service.
>
> You must keep clear records to demonstrate consent.

The GDPR gives a specific right to withdraw consent. You need to tell people about their right to withdraw, and offer them easy ways to withdraw consent at any time.

Public authorities, employers and other organisations in a position of power may find it more difficult to show valid freely given consent.

You need to review existing consents and your consent mechanisms to check they meet the GDPR standard. If they do, there is no need to obtain fresh consent.

Why is consent important?

Consent is one lawful basis for processing, and explicit consent can also legitimise use of special category data. Consent may also be relevant where the individual has exercised their right to restriction, and explicit consent can legitimise automated decision-making and overseas transfers of data.

Genuine consent should put individuals in control, build trust and engagement, and enhance your reputation.

Relying on inappropriate or invalid consent could destroy trust and harm your reputation – and may leave you open to large fines.

When is consent appropriate?

Consent is one lawful basis for processing, but there are alternatives. Consent is not inherently better or more important than these alternatives. If consent is difficult, you should consider using an alternative.

Consent is appropriate if you can offer people real choice and control over how you use their data, and want to build their trust and engagement. But if you cannot offer a genuine choice, consent is not appropriate. If you would still process the personal data without consent, asking for consent is misleading and inherently unfair.

If you make consent a precondition of a service, it is unlikely to be the most appropriate lawful basis.

Public authorities, employers and other organisations in a position of power over individuals should avoid relying on consent unless they are confident they can demonstrate it is freely given.

What is valid consent?

Consent must be freely given; this means giving people genuine ongoing choice and control over how you use their data.

Consent should be obvious and require a positive action to opt in. Consent requests must be prominent, unbundled from other terms and conditions, concise and easy to understand, and user-friendly.

Consent must specifically cover the controller's name, the purposes of the processing and the types of processing activity.

Explicit consent must be expressly confirmed in words, rather than by any other positive action.

There is no set time limit for consent. How long it lasts will depend on the context. You should review and refresh consent as appropriate.

How should we obtain, record and manage consent?

Make your consent request prominent, concise, separate from other terms and conditions, and easy to understand. Include:

- the name of your organisation;
- the name of any third party controllers who will rely on the consent;
- why you want the data;
- what you will do with it; and
- that individuals can withdraw consent at any time.

You must ask people to actively opt in. Don't use pre-ticked boxes, opt-out boxes or other default settings. Wherever possible, give separate ('granular') options to consent to different purposes and different types of processing.

Keep records to evidence consent – who consented, when, how, and what they were told.

Make it easy for people to withdraw consent at any time they choose. Consider using preference-management tools.

Keep consents under review and refresh them if anything changes. Build regular consent reviews into your business processes.

Further guidance produced by the European Data Protection Board (EDPB) can be found here: http://ec.europa.eu/newsroom/article29/item-detail.cfm?item_id=623051.

15.5.2.2   Providing information to employees

Article 12(1) of the GDPR says that information collected must be provided to employees in 'a concise, transparent, intelligible and easily accessible form, using clear and plain language ...'. Articles 13 and 14 list the information that must be provided, depending on whether the data is collected from the employee or not.

The ICO states:

> You can provide this information through a variety of media:
> *   Orally – face to face or when you speak to someone on the telephone (it's a good idea to document this).
> *   In writing – printed media; printed adverts; forms, such as financial applications or job application forms.
> *   Through signage – for example an information poster in a public area.
> *   Electronically – in text messages; on websites; in emails; in mobile apps.

It is good practice to use the same medium you use to collect personal data to deliver privacy information. So, if you are collecting information through an online form you could provide a just-in-time notice as an individual fills in the form. You can combine this with more detailed information on your website, accessible through a clear and prominent link on the online form.

15.5.2.3   Subject access requests

Employees have the right (under the GDPR, Article 15 and the DPA 2018) to be told, upon request (requests must be dealt with without 'undue delay' and at the very latest within one month of receiving the request), whether personal data about them are being processed and, if so, to be told what the specific data are, why they are being processed and to whom they are going. This is known as a 'subject access request' (SAR). The DPA 2018 provides for some exemptions, eg confidential references given by the data controller but not received by the data controller; legally privileged information. If personal data on one employee contain personal data on another, the employer will, according to a majority decision of the Court of Appeal in *B v GMC* [2018] EWCA Civ 1497, have to consider if disclosure is reasonable having regard to all the relevant circumstances by considering the statutory balancing of interests test, including taking any objection into consideration. If an employee withholds consent, that might, in some situations, tip the balance against disclosure, according to the Court of Appeal, if other interests were balanced. Personal data may include copies of appraisals, disciplinary records, sickness/holiday forms, as well as informal notes/emails passing between managers about the employee. Generally, no fee is payable.

The right to make a SAR existed under the DPA 1998, but there are some changes, for example to the timeframe for responding (see above), and a fee can no longer be charged (unless the requests are 'manifestly unfounded or excessive' or for further copies, in which case a reasonable fee can be charged (GDPR, Articles 12 and 15)).

Employees sometimes use their right to make a SAR in the context of a dispute with their employer. A failure to respond by the employer could make a dismissal unfair (see the unreported employment tribunal decision in *McWilliams v Citibank NA*, 19 April 2016). If an employer refuses to comply with such a request, the employee can complain to the Information Commissioner. Alternatively, an employee could apply to the High Court for an order that the employer comply. In *Gurieva v Community Safety Development (UK) Ltd* [2016] EWHC 643 (QB), the High Court said that employees are not obliged to give reasons for making a SAR, and there is nothing inherently wrong with an employee using such a request for the purposes of obtaining early access to information that they might get later via disclosure in litigation.

In 2017, the ICO published a Code of Practice on SARs. It has not yet been updated to take into account the DPA 2018. The Code reflected case law in the courts. Readers are referred, inter alia, to the Court of Appeal case of *Dawson-Damer v Taylor Wessing LLP* [2017] EWCA Civ 74 (impact of legal professional privilege on a SAR; disproportionate effect exemption) and the employment tribunal case of *McWilliams v Citibank NA* (above) (where a refusal to comply with a SAR contributed to the unfairness of a dismissal). See too, *B v GMC* (above).

15.6   MONITORING IN THE WORKPLACE

There are many reasons why businesses might wish to monitor or record telephone or email use. Some financial or insurance firms may be legally obliged to record calls when executing transactions over the telephone; others may wish to monitor calls for quality or compliance purposes. Monitoring may also be useful to ensure that employees are not misusing the communications facilities provided to them. The law looks to balance these objectives, which will generally be considered legitimate, against the need to protect the privacy of employees and external callers. Employers should always be up-front about what and when they are monitoring, and should have social media, internet and email policies in place. Employers should also seek to avoid breaching the implied duty of trust and confidence in some monitoring circumstances. See too cases decided under Article 8 ECHR above.

From 27 June 2018, monitoring and recording of electronic communications is regulated by the Investigatory Powers Act (IPA) 2016 and the Investigatory Powers (Interception by Businesses etc for Monitoring and Record-keeping Purposes) Regulations 2018 (SI 2018/356) (which replace the Regulation of Investigatory Powers Act (RIPA) 2000 and the Telecommunications (Lawful Business Practice) (Interception of Communications) Regulations 2000 (SI 2000/2699)), in addition to the GDPR and DPA 2018 (above). What follows is a very brief introduction to the provisions that currently apply in the workplace. Readers will need to keep up to date with the changing legal position, and this section will be fully updated in the next edition.

The IPA 2016 regulates when a person may make an 'interception of a communication in the course of transmission'. Interception includes 'monitoring or interference with a private telecommunication system which makes the communication available to someone other than the sender or the recipient'. While most of the Act is aimed at the security services and the State, the provisions on the interception of communications sent and received on public and private telecommunication systems, where they impact on aspects of the employment relationship, and the provisions on surveillance and covert sources (set out in Part II) are of much more general application. As far as the interception of communications is concerned, unless there is (expressly or by implication) consent (by both parties to the communication) to the interception, a criminal offence may be committed. An employer can lawfully intercept communications without consent (from both parties to the communication) only if it complies with the provisions of the 2018 Regulations. The Regulations create in effect a number of 'lawful purposes' whereby employers can monitor and record communications between parties without their consent, provided that the employer has made 'all reasonable efforts to inform' every person who uses the telecommunication system that their communications may be monitored and recorded. Lawful purposes are (reg 3):

(a)   to establish the existence of facts;

(b)   ensuring compliance with regulatory or statutory rules;

(c)   ascertaining or demonstrating employee standards;

(d)   national security;

(e)   prevention or detection of crime;

(f)   investigating the unauthorised use of the telecommunications system;

(g)   to secure the effective operation of the telecommunication system.

Note that the Investigatory Powers Tribunal ruled in *C v Police and Secretary of State for the Home Department* (November 2014, IPT/03/32) that not all covert surveillance of employees was covered by RIPA 2000, and that will continue to be the case under the revised legislation.

In practice, the RIPA 2000 caused few problems for employers, and that is likely to continue to be the case under the IPA 2016 – it permits most types of surveillance, provided they are for business-related reasons.

Readers should refer to the 2016 Act and 2018 Regulations for the detail.

15.6.1 Guidance

Part 3 of the ICO's Employment Practices Code contains guidance on monitoring at work. It provides that it will normally be intrusive to monitor workers; employers should normally carry out an impact assessment before monitoring and should be sure that the monitoring is justified by real benefits; workers should normally be told if and why they are being monitored; employers should be careful when monitoring personal communications such as emails that are clearly personal; employers should not undertake covert monitoring except in the rarest circumstances where there are grounds for suspecting criminal activity, it has been authorised at the highest level of the business, and where there is a risk that notifying workers of the monitoring would prejudice the prevention or detection of that criminal activity. At the heart of the Code is proportionality.

The Article 29 Working Party (now European Data Protection Board (made up of a representative from each EU Member State's data protection authority, together with the European Data Protection Supervisor and the European Commission)) has published both an Opinion on data processing at work and a set of Data Protection Impact Assessment (DPIA) guidelines which set out criteria for assessing when data processing is high risk.

The criteria for assessing when data processing will be considered to be high risk include:

(1)   any evaluation or scoring, especially based on a data subject's performance at work, economic situation, health, personal preferences or interests, reliability or behaviour, location or movements;

(2)   automated decision-making with legal or similar significant effects;

(3)   systematic monitoring of individuals;

(4)   sensitive data;

(5)   personal data on a large scale;

(6)   datasets that have been matched or combined;

(7)   data concerning vulnerable data subjects;

(8)   data transfers across borders outside the EU;

(9)   data that prevents data subjects from exercising a right or using a service or a contract.

Any sort of employee monitoring is very likely to be considered as high-risk processing (see criteria 3, 7 and 9).

Article 4(11) of the GDPR states:

'Consent' of the data subject means any freely given, specific, informed and unambiguous indication of the data subject's wishes by which he or she, by a statement or by a clear affirmative action, signifies agreement to the processing of personal data relating to him or her.

According to the ICO draft guidance on the GDPR:

> Consent will not be freely given if there is imbalance in the relationship between the individual and the controller – this will make consent particularly difficult for public authorities and for employers, who should look for an alternative lawful basis.

It is unlikely therefore that employers will be able to rely on consent where surveillance is concerned. Given that surveillance is usually undertaken to prevent or detect crime or to detect or stop misuse of the employer's resources, an employer may be able to rely on Article 6(1)(f) – processing for 'the purposes of the legitimate interests pursued by the data controller or by a third party, except where such interests are overridden by the interests or fundamental rights and freedoms of the data subject which require protection of personal data, in particular where the data subject is a child'. However, there is a potential problem for local authority and government employers, as Article 6 states that the legitimate interests condition shall not apply to processing carried out by public authorities in the performance of their tasks. Such organisations may have to fall back on Article 6(1)(c) and 6(1)(e).

Employers, as data controllers, also have an obligation to ensure that they are transparent in terms of the how they use employees' information. Consideration will also have to be given as to what extent general information will have to be supplied to employees in respect of the employer's surveillance activities (see Articles 13 and 14 of the GDPR on privacy notices).

The Article 29 Working Party Opinion on data processing at work (Opinion 2/2017: http://ec.europa.eu/newsroom/article29/item-detail.cfm?item_id=610169) complements Opinion 8/2001 on the processing of data protection in the employment context and its 2002 Working Document on the surveillance of electronic communications in the workplace (http://ec.europa.eu/newsroom/article29/item-detail.cfm?item_id=611236). 'The Opinion makes a new assessment of the balance between legitimate interests of employers and the reasonable privacy expectations of employees by outlining the risks posed by new technologies and undertaking a proportionality assessment of a number of scenarios in which they could be deployed.' One matter the 2017 Opinion stresses is the need for transparency, so that employees are properly informed about any processing taking place in a clear and accessible manner. Another area that the Opinion identifies as potentially problematic is the tracking of employees across devices, and the potential for reducing anonymity that may impact on whistleblowing. It suggests that data collected during recruitment, for example, should be deleted as soon as it is clear that a candidate is not going to be employed. Key to all this going forward will be the understanding by employers that they can only collect data for legitimate purposes, with any processing taking place needing to be proportionate, necessary, for a real and present interest, and in a lawful, articulated and transparent manner. The fact that an employer may 'own' the electronic means does not mean that employees are not entitled to have their communications kept secret. If an employer has a policy of allowing employees to 'bring your own devices' into work, for example, employees should try to ensure that their devices have the ability to shield private communications from work-related monitoring.

15.6.2   Use of personal devices at work

Employers need to have in place proper measures to make sure that they secure and protect data that they process or retain, whether those data relate to employees or to third party customers/clients. Many employees use their own mobile devices to access their employers' corporate networks and systems. This can create potential problems, both in distinguishing between work information and personal information (eg, who 'owns' a contact list (see **1.8.6.2**)) and with regards to the access to, storage of, and processing and security of personal data (eg, customer or client profiles).

In March 2013, a YouGov survey found that while 47% of all UK adults were using personal devices at work, relatively few were given any guidance on their use. The ICO was concerned about the implications of employees using their own personal devices for the security of personal data. This includes employees' use of personal iPads, smartphones and other personal devices for work purposes. Often, personal devices are not very secure – even if they have passwords, they will not be using technologically secure methods to send and receive information – yet if used for work purposes, they will start to store data that it will be hard for employers to monitor properly. The use of own devices can also blur the line between work and private life. This may create problems not only regarding who 'owns' what information, but also about what rights the employer has to access information on the device. Travelling abroad with devices can constitute a transfer of data, which may cause problems with individual countries' data protection obligations. As all data controllers in the UK are responsible for ensuring that personal data are processed in accordance with the DPA 2018, this means that employers are responsible for ensuring that they take appropriate technical and organisational measures against accidental loss, destruction or damage. Employers should conduct an audit of what personal data are being processed, where such data are stored, which devices are being used and by whom, how data are accessed and transferred, and the potential for leakage, and how losses, theft, etc will be dealt with. Employers should then maintain an 'acceptable use' policy for BYOD. The ICO has issued guidance on 'Bringing Your Own Devices' (BYOD) to work.

Employers will need to consider, inter alia, whether to prohibit or limit personal activity on the use of company-owned devices and how to ensure company data on such devices is held securely. Practically, if employers are to include this in a policy, they will need to consider how they will monitor such use and enforce the policy. Where employees use their own devices and are allowed access to company systems and information, policies should clearly state how data and information are expected to be treated and protected. Clear information should be given as to what an employee should do if a device is lost or stolen. It will be necessary to delineate how the company will treat and have access to personal information (which should be private) and how it will treat and have access to work-related information. The policy should state what will happen on the termination of the employment, both with regard to the physical device *and* with regard to information stored on it.

15.6.3   Transfers of personal data outside the EU

On of the most vexing issues arising out of the General Data Protection Regulation (see **15.5.1**) relates to the transfer of personal data outside the EU. This can impact on UK and other European companies who have US subsidiaries or parents with regard to both customers'/clients' personal data as well as employees' personal data.

In October 2015, in a case decided under the Data Protection Directive, the ECJ, in the case of *Schrems v Irish Data Protection Commissioner* (Case C-362/14), invalidated the Safe Harbor arrangements that had governed transfers of personal data between the EU and the United States. The Data Protection Directive prohibited transfers of personal data outside the EU to a third country unless the country in question ensured an adequate level of data protection. In July 2000, the European Commission approved (executive decision 2000/520/EC) what were known as the Safe Harbor Principles, whereby the US provided safeguards for data protection. The Safe Harbor arrangements consisted essentially of American undertakings voluntarily self-assessing and self-certifying against an agreed set of principles.

Some or all of the data provided by subscribers to Facebook is transferred from Facebook's Irish subsidiary to servers located in the United States, where it is kept. Max Schrems, an Austrian citizen and privacy campaigner, had been a Facebook user since 2008. He lodged a complaint with the Irish data protection authority (the Data Protection Commissioner) against Facebook Ireland Ltd, contending that, in the light of the revelations made by Edward Snowden in 2013 concerning the activities of the United States intelligence services (including the National Security Agency (NSA)), the law and practices of the United States offered no real protection against surveillance by the United States of any data transferred to it. The Data Protection Commissioner rejected the complaint on the ground, in particular, that the European Commission had approved the Safe Harbor scheme. Mr Schrems appealed the decision to the Irish High Court, which referred various questions to the ECJ for a preliminary ruling. The ECJ held that the Safe Harbor arrangements failed to protect privacy, were inadequate and therefore invalid.

After the ruling, a number of American-based companies, such as Facebook and Microsoft, invoked template standard model agreements from the European Commission on the basis that these allowed them to continue to transfer data to the US. Schrems brought a further complaint to the Irish Data Protection Commission in respect of this usage. In May 2016, the Data Protection Commission referred the case to the ECJ.

The European Commission has produced a communication on the international transfer of personal data which is based on guidance from the Article 29 Working Party (made up of all the European data protection authorities).

On 2 February 2016, the European Commission and the US Government reached a political agreement on a new framework for transatlantic exchanges of personal data for commercial purposes to replace Safe Harbor: the EU–US Privacy Shield (IP/16/216). This was put before the Article 29 Working Party, the European Data Protection Supervisor and the European Parliament, and a number of clarifications and improvements were made. In July 2016, this was formally adopted by the European Commission and notified to Member States. US companies were able to certify with the US Commerce Department starting from 1 August 2016.

The European Commission believes that the EU–US Privacy Shield is a robust new system that brings stronger data protection standards than under the Safe Harbor Principles, and which are better enforced, as well as providing safeguards on government access to personal data and easier redress for individuals in case of complaints. The General Data Protection Regulation (GDPR), like its predecessor, does not allow the transfer of data on EU citizens outside the EU unless that country has adequate data privacy laws. It is likely that being certified under the EU–US Privacy Shield will comply with most GDPR requirements, but it is not a substitute for GDPR compliance. It is likely that there will be challenges to its adequacy under the GDPR regime.

Readers should note that the above is only a very brief overview of this complex area, and reference should be made to the legislation and the ICO website for further details.

15.7 FURTHER READING

Allen, Crasnow, Beale, McCann and Barnett, *Employment Law and Human Rights*, 3rd edn (OUP, 2018).

Carey, *Data Protection – A Practical Guide to UK and EU Law*, 5th edn (OUP, 2018).

SUMMARY

The Human Rights Act 1998 incorporates the European Convention for the Protection of Human Rights and Fundamental Freedoms 1950 ('the Convention') into domestic law. Although the UK was already a signatory to the Convention and was therefore bound by it as a matter of international law, until the HRA 1998 came into force the Convention was not directly part of UK domestic law and individuals could not enforce Convention rights in the domestic courts (**15.1**).

Schedule 1 to the HRA 1998 sets out the relevant Convention rights that are to be protected under the Act:

- Article 6 creates a right to 'a fair and public hearing within a reasonable time by an independent and impartial tribunal established by law'.
- Article 8 gives a right to respect for private and family life and correspondence.
- Article 9 protects freedom of thought, conscience and religion.

- Article 10 gives the right to freedom of expression.
- Article 11 protects the right to freedom of association, including the right to form and join a trade union.
- Article 14 prohibits discrimination, but only in the context of other Convention rights (**15.2**).

The important Convention rights, from an employment perspective (eg Articles 6, 8, 9 and 10), are not absolute rights but are limited by counter-balances which permit legitimate interferences with those rights in certain situations. Most human rights cases are not about whether the right exists but whether there has been an interference with the right, and whether that interference is legitimate and necessary. That will involve questions of proportionality and relevance (**15.4**).

United Kingdom courts and tribunals must (HRA 1998, s 3) adopt a 'purposive' approach to the interpretation of UK legislation. If primary legislation is found to be incompatible with a Convention right, the HRA 1998 provides that such primary legislation remains effective but permits certain courts (the High Court and named appellate courts, but not employment tribunals or the EAT) to make (s 4) a 'declaration of incompatibility' in relation to that primary legislation, upon which Parliament may act if it wishes (**15.2**). (This allows for the sovereignty of Parliament to remain unchallenged.) Secondary legislation may, however, be struck down.

The GDPR and the DPA 2018 apply to the 'processing of the data'. This covers most of the routine personnel tasks, from the creation of personnel information to its filing, retention and storage. Personal data must be obtained only for specific and lawful purposes, must be processed fairly and lawfully, and must be kept accurate and up to date. There are special restrictions on the processing of 'sensitive' personal data – these include data about an employee's racial or ethnic origins, political beliefs, physical or mental health or sex life, and the commission of offences.

The Investigatory Powers Act 2016 and the Investigatory Powers (Interception by Businesses etc for Monitoring and Record-keeping Purposes) Regulations 2018 provide, as far as the interception of internal communications is concerned, that unless there is (expressly or by implication) consent (by both parties to the communication) to the interception, a criminal offence may be committed. The Regulations create in effect a number of 'lawful purposes' whereby employers can monitor and record communications between parties without their consent, provided that the employer has made 'all reasonable efforts to inform' every person who uses the telecommunication system that their communication may be monitored. These lawful purposes include:

(a)   ensuring compliance with regulatory or statutory rules;

(b)   ascertaining or demonstrating employee standards;

(d)   prevention or detection of crime.

The Information Commissioner has responsibility for the working and policing of the law. The Information Commissioner has published an Employment Practices Code, relating to recruitment and selection, employee records, monitoring at work and workers' health. Although the Code contains guidance and is not legally binding, it provides the benchmarks the Commissioner will use. It has not been updated post-GDPR/DPA 2018.

Appendix 1

Statement of Terms and Service Contract Examples

Example of Statement of Terms under the Employment Rights Act 1996, s 1

[Section 1 of the ERA 1996 requires an employer to give an employee a written statement of terms and conditions within two months of employment commencing and must set out certain matters relating to the employment relationship. If there is a separate written contractual agreement then it is not necessary also to provide a separate set of terms: see **1.4.2**. A written statement or contract – see below – can also contain additional matters that have specifically been offered to/accepted by the employee.]

[In this example the employer is a limited company. The employee is a clerk.]

| From | [| Employer |] |
| To | [| Employee |] |

This statement sets out certain particulars, as at the date of the statement of the terms and conditions of your employment which are required to be given to you under s 1 of the Employment Rights Act 1996.

1. Your employment commenced on [ ]. No employment with a previous employer counts as part of your period of continuous employment.

[Length of service can be important in terms of determining unfair dismissal rights as well as in the calculation of notice and unfair dismissal awards. In this context, continuity can also be important, especially if, for example, someone has transferred as a result of a TUPE transfer: see **3.5**.]

2. The title of your job is [ ]. [The duties which this job entails are set out in the attached job description [ ] and in addition to those duties you may be required to undertake additional or other duties as necessary to meet the needs of the business.

[It is important to be precise when defining the job description and duties. Job descriptions can be important, for example, when determining whether a redundancy situation has arisen: see **1.8.2** and **4.2.3**.]

3. Your place of work is [ ].

[Place of work can be important, for example, when determining whether a redundancy situation has arisen: see **1.8.2.3** and **4.2.2**.]

4. Your remuneration is [ ] per year, payable at [ ] intervals on [ ] directly into your bank account.

[The remuneration clause should specify how an employee's remuneration is calculated. Where appropriate, it should set out an hourly rate, when payment is due, whether it is paid in advance or in arrears, along with any fringe benefits. Consideration also needs to be given to the national minimum wage requirements and, where appropriate, the 'living wage' rate for over-25s: see **1.8.3.1**.]

5. Your normal hours of work are from [ ] to [ ] Monday to Friday inclusive. A [ ] hour break may be taken for lunch.

[It may be useful to specify whether the lunch hour is included as part of the weekly hours worked and to make clear if it is unpaid.]

6. You are entitled to [ ] days paid holiday in each calendar year to be taken at times convenient to us, in addition to public holidays. During holidays you will be entitled to your normal basic remuneration. On termination of your employment your entitlement to accrued holiday pay will be in direct proportion to the length of your service during the calendar year in which termination takes place. No holidays may be taken during a period of notice.

[Paid holidays can often be a source of confusion and dispute between employer and employee. Bearing in mind the statutory minimum (see **1.8.3.4**, **1.12**), it is important to set out clearly how much paid holiday an employee is entitled to, when it accrues from, and when the holiday year runs from/to: see **1.8.3.3**. Although certain minimum information must be set out in the written terms, it is acceptable to refer employees to a more detailed separate document that is reasonably accessible to the employee, such as a staff handbook. Such a document may allow an employer to give a much clearer account of how the holiday policy works in practice. It also allows, where an employee is part time, to set out how a pro rata entitlement is calculated and what the appropriate procedure is when time off is requested. Where additional documents are referred to setting out more fuller policy details, employers often include a sentence that says that the policy does not form part of the contract of employment, so as to give them flexibility to amend the policy. See **1.9** on variation of contractual terms.]

7.   You will be paid your normal remuneration during absence through sickness or injury up to a maximum [   ] weeks in any period of 12 months, provided that you supply a medical certificate in the event of any such absence for seven or more consecutive days. Such remuneration will discharge our liability to pay you Statutory Sick Pay and you will be required to give credit for any other national insurance sickness benefits payable to you as a result of such absence.

[The contract terms should state whether the employer pays more than statutory sick pay (SSP). There is no legal right for an employee to be paid anything more than SSP. SSP is paid at a prescribed rate and is payable for up to 28 weeks. If additional ('enhanced') contractual sick pay is paid, the contract should set out whether a medical certificate is required, the period for which it is paid, the amount and whether SSP is deducted when calculating it. Although certain minimum information must be set out in the written terms, it is acceptable to refer employees to a more detailed separate document which sets out these matters: see **1.8.3.3**. In practice, employers will need to provide information about the entitlement to sick pay as well as sickness absence reporting procedures.]

8.   [You are eligible to join the [   ] pension scheme. Full details can be found in the booklet entitled [   ], a copy of which can be obtained from [   ]. [No pension scheme is applicable to your employment, but we shall provide you with access to a designated stakeholder pension scheme. We do [not] make contributions.]

[All employers will be obliged to offer eligible employees access to a workplace pension by 2018. Employees who qualify for a workplace pension will be those who are aged between 22 and the State Pension age, earn at least £10,000 a year and work in the UK. Employers must pay at least 1% of their employee's 'qualifying earnings' into their workplace pension. This will rise to 3% in 2019 if approved by Parliament. Employees can choose to opt out. If the employee has opted out, this should be reflected in the agreement. Employers are obliged to re-enroll eligible employees every 3 years. The contract terms should state the relevant details. Although certain minimum information must be set out in the written terms, it is acceptable to refer employees to a more detailed separate document which sets out these matters: see **1.8.4**.]

9.1   The disciplinary rules which will apply to you are set out in the booklet entitled [   ] [a copy of which can be obtained from   ]. The rules do not form part of your contract of employment.

9.2   If you are dissatisfied with any disciplinary decision relating to you, you may appeal to [   ] for the matter to be reconsidered.

9.3   If you have any grievance relating to your employment you may seek redress by applying to [   ]. The steps consequent upon an application of this kind are set out in the booklet entitled [   ] a copy of which can be obtained from [   ]. The rules do not form part of your contract of employment.

[Although certain minimum information must be set out about disciplinary procedures in the written terms, it is acceptable to refer employees to a more detailed separate document which sets out these matters: see **1.8.8**.]

10.1   The length of notice which you are obliged to give to us to terminate your employment is [   ].

10.2   The length of notice you are entitled to receive from us to terminate your employment is (subject to 10.3):

10.2.1   One week's notice if your period of continuous employment is less than two years.

10.2.2   One week's notice for each year of continuous employment, if your period of continuous employment is two years or more, subject to a maximum of 12 weeks' notice after 12 years' continuous employment.

10.3   You may be dismissed without notice in the event of your committing an act of gross misconduct.

[Although there are set statutory minimum notice periods, these must be set out in the contract. Employers can impose longer notice periods by contract if required. Following the decision of the Supreme Court in Haywood (2.3.3) that a term will be implied into all contracts of employment that notice will only start to run from the date an employee receives written notice and has had a reasonable opportunity to consider it, employers now need to make sure that their contracts of employment set out expressly how notice can be served and when it will be considered to have been received.]

11.   There is no collective agreement in force which affects your terms and conditions of employment.

[Collective bargaining consists of negotiations between an employer and a group of employees so as to determine the conditions of employment. The result of collective bargaining procedures is usually reflected in a collective agreement. Employees are often represented in bargaining by a union or other labour organisation. Where there are collective agreements in place that regulate the terms and conditions of employees in their workplace, these must be stated.]

Dated [   ]

Signed Employee [   ]

For and on behalf of Employer [   ].

Example of Service Contract

[In this example the employer is a partnership. The employee is a member of the firm's middle management. In order to avoid the necessity of a separate statement of terms, the requirements of ERA 1996, s 1 have also been included. It has been shortened by incorporating a number of standard written policies around grievances and disciplinary hearings. Contracts should always be reviewed when employees are promoted. Commentary on the standard minimum terms as required by the ERA 1996, s 1 is included in the sample statement above; additional commentary has been added here only around additional clauses.]

THIS AGREEMENT dated [   ] [*year*] is made BETWEEN:

(1)   [   ] ('the Employer')

(2)   [   ] ('the Employee')

1. Definitions

'Business' the business carried on from time to time by the Employer

'Confidential Information' includes any trade secrets, secret manufacturing processes, technical data, know-how and all information relating to the affairs and finances of the Employer (including business contacts)

[One of the major advantages of tailored and agreed contractual terms is that express confidentiality clauses can be agreed. While all contracts will imply a duty of mutual obligation, fidelity and trust, that is of a narrow nature and limited, and it is always advisable, where employees have access to confidential information, to include carefully drafted and tailored terms: see **1.7.2.8**, **1.8.6.1** and clauses 5, 12, 13, 14 below. Including an express term allows an employer to make clear what sort of matters and information it considers to be 'confidential'.]

'Employment' the Employee's employment under this agreement

'Incapacity' any illness accident or similar reason preventing the Employee from properly carrying out the Employment

'Partner' any partner in the firm [   ]

'Partners' the partners for the time being of the firm [   ]

2. Job title and length of employment

2.1   Subject to clause 18, the Employer agrees to employ the Employee as [   ] from (and including) [   ].

2.2   No employment with a previous employer counts as part of the Employee's period of continuous employment with the Employer.

3. Duties

3.1   The duties which this job entails are set out in [   ] and in addition to those duties the Employee may be required to undertake additional or other duties as necessary to meet the needs of the Business.

3.2   The Employee must:

3.2.1   perform to the best of his/her ability all the duties of the job,

3.2.2   do all in his/her power to promote, develop and extend the Business,

3.2.3   comply with the reasonable directions of the Partners.

4. Place of work

4.1   The Employee's usual place of work is [   ] but the Employee may be required to work in any place which the Partners may reasonably require.

4.2   The Employee may also be required to travel on the business of the Employer anywhere within the European Union.

[Express mobility clauses are sometimes included in contracts to allow employers to have the flexibility to move an employee to a different place of work. If there is no express mobility clause, an employer may be able to rely on an implied clause if relocation is still within reasonable travelling distance of an employee's home. Even if there is an express mobility clause, it must still be enforced reasonably (see *Courtaulds v Sibson* and *Kellogg Brown & Root (UK) Ltd v Fitton*). If an employee is senior, it can be important for the place of work ('mobility') clause to be widely drawn to allow flexibility. If an employee is expected to work outside the UK, this should be stated. For more junior employees, a narrower mobility clause may be preferable. Employment tribunals generally interpret mobility clauses restrictively – ie with ambiguities resolved in the employee's favour.]

5. To devote full time

5.1   The Employee's normal hours are [   ] to [   ], but he/she will be expected to work whatever other hours are necessary to meet the needs of the Business.

5.2   The Employee must (unless prevented by Incapacity) devote his/her whole time and attention to the Business.

5.3   The Employee must not without the prior written consent of the Partners:

    (a)   take part in any other business or employment (of whatever nature), or

    (b)   except where permitted by clause 5.4, have an interest in any other business which is similar to or competes with the Business.

5.4   The Employee may have an interest in shares or other securities which are quoted on a recognised stock exchange, so long as the interest does not extend to more than 2% of the total amount of the shares or securities of the company in question.

5.5   [Working time opt out if appropriate: see **1.11.3.4**.]

[This can enable an employer to be more specific about what constitutes fidelity and good faith. It may be helpful to identify where potential competition might be perceived and where financial or other conflicts of interest can arise.]

6. Remuneration

6.1   The Employer agrees to pay to the Employee a salary (accruing from day to day) at the rate of [£   ] per year payable in arrear by equal monthly instalments on the 5th day of each month directly into the Employee's bank account.

6.2   The Partners must review this salary annually and may increase the salary with effect from the review date.

[6.3   Include any other benefits that may arise]

7. Expenses

7.1   Subject to 7.2, the Employer agrees to repay the Employee for all reasonable hotel and other expenses wholly and exclusively incurred by him/her in the performance of the Employment.

7.2   The Employee must give the Employer receipts or other evidence of these expenses.

8. Company car

8.1   The Employer agrees to provide a car for the Employee in accordance with the Firm's car policy as published and varied by the Employer from time to time.

8.2   The Employee must:

    8.2.1   take good care of the car,

    8.2.2   comply with the provisions of any insurance policy relating to it, and

    8.2.3   return the car and its keys to the Employer at its principal place of business (or any other place the Employer may reasonably specify) immediately upon the ending of the Employment.

9. Holidays

9.1   The Employer's holiday year runs from 1st January to 31st December.

9.2   The Employee is entitled to [   ] working days' paid holiday in each holiday year (in addition to the usual public holidays) to be taken when convenient to the Employer.

9.3   The Employee may not without the consent of the Partners carry forward any unused part of his/her holiday to a subsequent holiday year.

9.4   On termination of this employment, the Employee's entitlement to accrued holiday pay will be in direct proportion to the length of service during the calendar year in which termination takes place.

9.5   The Employee will be required to repay to the Employer pay received for holiday taken in excess of basic holiday entitlement accrued at termination.

10. Private health and permanent sickness insurance

The Employer agrees to cover the cost of the Employee's membership of an appropriate permanent sickness insurance and private patients' medical plan with such reputable insurance schemes as the Employer may decide from time to time.

11. Pension

On completion of [   ] months' employment the Employee may join the [   ] pension scheme. Details are set out in the booklet [   ]. A copy can be obtained from any Partner.

[Many employment contracts contain a reference to contracting out. However, this is no longer relevant as it ended in April 2016. In addition to the basic State Pension, the State previously provided a second-tier top-up pension, based on how much an employee earned. This was introduced in 1978 and was originally called the State Earnings Related Pension Scheme (Serps). It became State Second Pension (S2P) in 2002. Before rules were changed in 2012, employees were allowed to 'contract out' of this additional pension. In exchange for lower National Insurance contributions, they gave up part or all of it and received extra pension from their occupational scheme or personal/stakeholder pension instead. In April 2016, the Government introduced a raft of pension reforms, and contracting out was abolished. If employees still have these provisions in their contract, the statutory reform provisions automatically repealed them.]

12. Confidentiality during the Employment

12.1   The Employee is aware that in the course of the Employment he/she may be given or come across Confidential Information.

12.2   The Employee must not disclose or use any Confidential Information (except in the proper course of his/her duties).

12.3   The Employee must use his/her best endeavours to prevent the disclosure of any Confidential Information.

12.4   All notes of any Confidential Information which the Employee acquires or makes during the Employment belong to the Employer. When the Employment ends (or at any time during the Employment should any Partner so request) the Employee must hand over these notes to someone duly authorised by the Partners to receive them.

[One of the major advantages of tailored and agreed contractual terms is that express confidentiality clauses can be agreed: see **1.7.2.8**, **1.8.6.1** and see also clauses 5, 12, 13, 14 which may together make up a package of restrictions. During employment, there is always an implied term of 'fidelity' or good faith which can be replied upon to ensure an employee does not reveal confidential information. However, including an express term allows an employer, for example, to make clear exactly what sorts of information it considers to be 'confidential'.]

13. Confidentiality after the Employment ends

After the Employment ends, the Employee must not disclose or use any of the Firm's trade secrets or any other information which is of a sufficiently high degree of confidentiality as to amount to a trade secret.

[After employment, only very highly sensitive confidential information is protected by any implied term. An express term allows this cover to be widened. See **1.8.6.2**.]

14. Unfair competition after the Employment ends

14.1   The Employer is entitled to protect its Confidential Information, its goodwill and its trade connections from any unfair competition by the Employee.

14.2   Therefore

14.2.1   For [   ] months after the Employment ends, the Employee agrees not to seek business from any person, firm or company who at any time during the [   ] months immediately preceding the ending of the Employment has been a customer of the Employer, or done business with it and with whom the Employee has had personal contact.

14.2.2   For [   ] months after the ending of the Employment, the Employee agrees not to be associated with the business of [   ]

(a)   within [   ] miles of the Employer's premises at [   ] or

(b)   within [   ] miles of any other premises of the Employer where the Employee was employed for at least [   ] months in the last [   ] months of the Employment.

[In order to prevent unfair competition after employment ends, employers should consider inserting a restrictive covenant into an employee's contract. This can restrain an ex-employee from working in a competing business, soliciting customers or poaching other staff. Such clauses, to be enforceable and not to amount to an unlawful restraint of trade, must be clear, must be aimed at protecting a legitimate business interest and must not be over-restrictive or unduly onerous. See **1.8.7**. Not all employees will need such clauses. Most arguments about restrictive covenants arise at the end of the employment relationship. However, when a court is asked to determine the enforceability of a restrictive covenant, it will have to consider the job role of the employee at the point when the covenant was entered. Restrictive covenants should therefore be appropriate for the role in question or they risk being unenforceable (see *PAT Systems v Neilly*, *Bartholomews Agri Foods Ltd v Thornton* and *Egon Zehnder Ltd v Tillman*). What are known as 'garden leave' clauses may also be considered. These allow an employer to require an employee who has been given and paid notice to stay at home during the notice period rather than coming into work. This can prevent an employee immediately joining a competitor. See **1.8.7.3**.]

15. Incapacity

15.1   If the Employee cannot work because of Incapacity, he/she must immediately tell a Partner. The Employee must provide a medical certificate, specifying the nature of the Incapacity and its likely duration, within eight days of the start of his/her absence and then at weekly intervals.

15.2   The Employee will be paid during absence due to Incapacity (payment to be inclusive of statutory sick pay) for a total of up to [   ] weeks in any one calendar year of the Employment.

15.3   After that, the Employee will continue to be paid salary only at the discretion of the Employer.

15.4   The Employee must inform the Employer of the amount of any social security benefit he/she receives and the Employer may deduct this from the salary paid to him/her under this clause.

16. Grievance Procedure

A copy of the current edition of the Grievance Procedure is attached. The procedure is revised by the Firm from time to time and the Employee may apply to a Partner at any time to inspect the most recent copy.

17. Disciplinary Procedure

A copy of the current edition of the disciplinary procedure affecting the Employee is attached to this agreement, although it does not form part of this contract and will not have contractual effect. The procedure is revised by the Firm from time to time and the Employee may apply to a Partner at any time to inspect the most recent edition.

18. Collective Agreement

There is no collective agreement in force which affects your terms and conditions of employment.

19. Ending the Employment

The Employer may end the Employment without notice or pay in lieu of notice in the following circumstances:

19.1   If the Employee has committed a serious or repeated breach of any of his/her obligations under this agreement or the Employer has reasonable grounds for believing he/she has done so.

20. Notice of termination

20.1   The Employee is obliged to give the Employer [   ] weeks' notice in order to terminate this contract.

20.2   The Employee is entitled to receive [   ] weeks' notice from the Employer in order to terminate his/her contract (subject to clause 19.1).

[20.3   Consider including an option to make a payment in lieu of notice ('PILON' clause). See **2.3.3**.]

[20.4   Consider a fixed term as an alternative.]

[Although there are set statutory minimum notice periods, employers can impose longer notice periods by contract if required. 'Garden leave' clauses may also be considered. These allow an employer to require an employee who has been given and paid notice to stay at home during the notice period rather than coming into work. This can prevent an employee immediately joining a competitor. See **1.8.7.3**. A PILON clause allows an employer to protect against a wrongful dismissal claim (see **Chapter 3**) if it makes a payment instead of requiring an employee to work out his notice period.]

21. Notices

21.1   Notices by the Employee must be by letter addressed to the Employer at its principal place of business. Notices by the Employer must be by letter addressed to the Employee at his/her last known address in Great Britain.

21.2   Any notice given by letter will be treated as being given at the time at which the letter would be delivered in the ordinary course of second class post. Any notice delivered by hand will be treated as being given upon delivery. In proving service by post it will be enough to prove that the notice was properly addressed and posted.

[Following the decision of the Supreme Court in *Haywood* (**2.3.3**) that a term will be implied into all contracts of employment that notice will only start to run from the date an employee receives written notice and has had a reasonable opportunity to consider it, employers now need to make sure that their contracts of employment set out expressly how notice can be served and when it will be considered to have been received.]

SIGNED by ....

In signing this, the Employee acknowledges and confirms that s/he agrees that these terms constitute his/her contract of employment with the Employer.

[It is always useful to get the employee to sign a contract as then there is express evidence that he received and so was aware of the contractual terms and staff policies.]

[Note: This is not an exhaustive list. Increasingly contracts may include clauses relating to social media (including cyber-bullying), e-mail and Internet use (in order to comply with the notice requirements under the Telecommunications (Lawful Business Practice) (Interception and Communications) Regulations 2000), records and monitoring (see **Chapter 15**), bonuses, whistleblowing (see **5.6.5**), equal opportunities (see **Chapter 8**), health and safety, maternity, paternity and flexible working, etc (see **Chapter 14**). Consideration must be given as to whether such terms are to be contractual or not (see **1.8** and **1.9**).]

Appendix 2
Case Study

Claim form

You must complete all questions marked with an '*'

Official Use Only			
Tribunal office			
Case number		Date received	

More than a single claimant	Additional Claimants supplied as CSV file	Additional information supplied as RTF file

1 Your details

1.1	Title	✔ Mr ☐ Mrs ☐ Miss ☐ Ms

1.2* First name (or names): James

1.3* Surname or family name: Gold

1.4 Date of birth: 3 0 / 0 6 / 1 9 5 6   Are you? ✔ Male ☐ Female

1.5* Address

Number or name: 12

Street: Douglas Crescent

Town/City:

County: Guildshire

Postcode: G U 1 2 8 Q Y

1.6 Phone number
Where we can contact you during the day: 01111 123456

1.7 Mobile number (if different):

1.8 How would you prefer us to contact you?
(Please tick only one box): ✔ Email ☐ Post ☐ Fax   Whatever your preference please note that some documents cannot be sent electronically

1.9 Email address: james.gould@hotmail123.com

1.10 Fax number:

2 Respondent's details (that is the employer, person or organisation against whom you are making a claim)

2.1* Give the name of your employer or the person or organisation you are claiming against (If you need to you can add more respondents at 2.4): Car Parking PLC

2.2* Address

Number or name:

Street:

Town/City:

County: Guildshire

Postcode:

Phone number: 01234 567 789

2.3   If you worked at a different address from the one you have given at 2.2 please give the full address

Address

Number or name

Street

Town/City

County

Postcode |___|___|___|___| **|** |___|___|___|

Phone number

2.4   If there are other respondents please tick this box and put their names and addresses here. ☐

(If there is not enough room here for the names of all the additional respondents then you can add any others at Section 13.)

Respondent 2

Name

Address

Number or name

Street

Town/City

County

Postcode |___|___|___|___| **|** |___|___|___|

Phone number

Respondent 3

Name

Address

Number or name

Street

Town/City

County

Postcode |___|___|___|___| **|** |___|___|___|

Phone number

3 Multiple cases

3.1 Are you aware that your claim is one of a number of claims against the same employer arising from the same, or similar, circumstances?

☐ Yes ☑ No

If Yes, and you know the names of any other claimants, add them here. This will allow us to link your claim to other related claims.

4 Cases where the respondent was not your employer

4.1 If you were not employed by any of the respondents you have named but are making a claim for some reason connected to employment (for example, relating to a job application which you made or against a trade union, qualifying body or the like) please state the type of claim you are making here. (You will get the chance to provide details later):

Now go to Section 8

5 Employment details

If you are or were employed please give the following information, if possible.

5.1 When did your employment start?

9/11/15

Is your employment continuing?

☐ Yes ☑ No

If your employment has ended, when did it end?

30/04/18

If your employment has not ended, are you in a period of notice and, if so, when will that end?

5.2 Please say what job you do or did.

Team Leader

6 Earnings and benefits

6.1 How many hours on average do, or did you work each week in the job this claim is about? `40`   hours each week

6.2 How much are, or were you paid?

Pay before tax £ `1916.00`   ☐ Weekly ☑ Monthly

Normal take-home pay
(Incl. overtime, commission, bonuses etc.) £ `1482.00`   ☐ Weekly ☑ Monthly

6.3 If your employment has ended, did you work (or were you paid for) a period of notice? ☑ Yes ☐ No

If Yes, how many weeks, or months' notice did you work, or were you paid for? `2` weeks ☐ months

6.4 Were you in your employer's pension scheme? ☐ Yes ☑ No

6.5 If you received any other benefits, e.g. company car, medical insurance, etc, from your employer, please give details.

7 If your employment with the respondent has ended, what has happened since?

7.1 Have you got another job? ☐ Yes ☑ No

If No, please **go to section 8**

7.2 Please say when you started (or will start) work.

7.3 Please say how much you are now earning (or will earn). £

8 Type and details of claim

8.1* Please indicate the type of claim you are making by ticking one or more of the boxes below.

- [✔] I was unfairly dismissed (including constructive dismissal)
- [ ] I was discriminated against on the grounds of:

  - [ ] age
  - [ ] gender reassignment
  - [ ] pregnancy or maternity
  - [ ] sexual orientation
  - [ ] religion or belief

  - [ ] race
  - [ ] disability
  - [ ] marriage or civil partnership
  - [ ] sex (including equal pay)

- [ ] I am claiming a redundancy payment
- [ ] I am owed
  - [ ] notice pay
  - [ ] holiday pay
  - [ ] arrears of pay
  - [ ] other payments

- [ ] I am making another type of claim which the Employment Tribunal can deal with.
  (Please state the nature of the claim. Examples are provided in the Guidance.)

8.2*   Please set out the background and details of your claim in the space below.

The details of your claim should include **the date(s) when the event(s) you are complaining about happened.** Please use the blank sheet at the end of the form if needed.

9 What do you want if your claim is successful?

9.1   Please tick the relevant box(es) to say what you
      want if your claim is successful:

      ☐ If claiming unfair dismissal, to get your old job back and compensation (reinstatement)

      ☐ If claiming unfair dismissal, to get another job with the same employer or associated
         employer and compensation (re-engagement)

      ☑ Compensation only

      ☐ If claiming discrimination, a recommendation (see Guidance).

9.2   What compensation or remedy are you seeking?

      If you are claiming financial compensation please give as much detail as you can about how much you are claiming and how you have calculated this sum.
      (Please note any figure stated below will be viewed as helpful information but it will not restrict what you can claim and you will be permitted to revise the sum claimed
      later. See the Guidance for further information about how you can calculate compensation). **If you are seeking any other remedy from the Tribunal which you have
      not already identified please also state this below.**

      The claimant seeks loss of earnings from 30 April 2018 to the date of the hearing and future loss of earnings.
      The claimant seeks an uplift of any award because the respondent unreasonably failed to comply with Acas.

10   Information to regulators in protected disclosure cases

10.1   If your claim consists of, or includes, a claim that you are making a protected disclosure under the Employment Rights Act 1996 (otherwise known as a 'whistleblowing' claim), please tick the box if you want a copy of this form, or information from it, to be forwarded on your behalf to a relevant regulator (known as a 'prescribed person' under the relevant legislation) by tribunal staff. (See Guidance). ☐

11   Your representative

If someone has agreed to represent you, please fill in the following. We will in future only contact your representative and not you.

11.1   Name of representative

Fred McLean

11.2   Name of organisation

Collaws Solicitors LLP

11.3   Address

Number or name | 20

Street | The Street

Town/City |

County | Guildshire

Postcode | G U 1 2 1 G G

11.4   DX number (If known)

11.5   Phone number

07777 123456

11.6   Mobile number (If different)

11.7   Their reference for correspondence

FM/JG

11.8   Email address

fm@collaws.co.uk

11.9   How would you prefer us to communicate with them? (Please tick only one box)   ☑ Email   ☐ Post   ☐ Fax

11.10   Fax number

12   Disability

12.1   Do you have a disability?   ☐ Yes   ☑ No

If Yes, it would help us if you could say what this disability is and tell us what assistance, if any, you will need as your claim progresses through the system, including for any hearings that maybe held at tribunal premises.

13   Details of additional respondents

Section 2.4 allows you to list up to three respondents. If there are any more respondents please provide their details here

Respondent 4

Name

Address

    Number or name

    Street

    Town/City

    County

    Postcode

Phone number

Respondent 5

Name

Address

    Number or name

    Street

    Town/City

    County

    Postcode

Phone number

14   Fee

**Please re-read the form and check you have entered all the relevant information.
Once you are satisfied, please tick this box.** ☐

For those submitting their claim by post

☑ I enclose the appropriate fee

OR

☐ I enclose an application for remission of the fee

If you fail to do so your claim form will be returned to you and you will be told it has been rejected. This means that any time limit which applies to your claim will still be running and the claim form will have to be re-submitted within that time limit.

Data Protection Act 1998.
We will send a copy of this form to the respondent and Acas. We will put the information you give us on this form onto a computer. This helps us to monitor progress and produce statistics. Information provided on this form is passed to the Department for Business, Innovation and Skills to assist research into the use and effectiveness of employment tribunals. (URN 05/874)

15 Additional information

Please use this space to provide any important additional information about your claim which you have not been able to include so far.

Please see separate sheet.

Employment Tribunals – Multiple Claim form

Please use this form if you wish to present two or more claims which arise from the same set of facts. Use additional sheets if necessary.

The following claimants are represented by [   ]

and the information required for all the additional claimants is the same as stated in the main claim of

[   ]

| Title | ☐ Mr   ☐ Mrs   ☐ Miss   ☐ Ms |

First name (or names) [   ]

Surname or family name [   ]

Date of birth [ ] [ ] / [ ] [ ] / [ ] [ ] [ ] [ ]

Address

Number or name [   ]

Street [   ]

Town/City [   ]

County [   ]

Postcode [| | | | | |]

| Title | ☐ Mr   ☐ Mrs   ☐ Miss   ☐ Ms |

First name (or names) [   ]

Surname or family name [   ]

Date of birth [ ] [ ] / [ ] [ ] / [ ] [ ] [ ] [ ]

Address

Number or name [   ]

Street [   ]

Town/City [   ]

County [   ]

Postcode [| | | | | |]

Title
☐ Mr   ☐ Mrs   ☐ Miss   ☐ Ms

First name (or names)
[   ]

Surname or family name
[   ]

Date of birth
[ ][ ] / [ ][ ] / [ ][ ][ ]

Address

Number or name
[   ]

Street
[   ]

Town/City
[   ]

County
[   ]

Postcode [| | | | | |]

Title
☐ Mr   ☐ Mrs   ☐ Miss   ☐ Ms

First name (or names)
[   ]

Surname or family name
[   ]

Date of birth
[ ][ ] / [ ][ ] / [ ][ ][ ]

Address

Number or name
[   ]

Street
[   ]

Town/City
[   ]

County
[   ]

Postcode [| | | | | |]

Title   ☐ Mr   ☐ Mrs   ☐ Miss   ☐ Ms

First name (or names)   _____

Surname or family name   _____

Date of birth   [|] / [|] / [| |]

Address   Number or name   _____

                    Street   _____

                 Town/City   _____

                   County   _____

                 Postcode   [| | | | | |]

Title   ☐ Mr   ☐ Mrs   ☐ Miss   ☐ Ms

First name (or names)   _____

Surname or family name   _____

Date of birth   [|] / [|] / [| |]

Address   Number or name   _____

                    Street   _____

                 Town/City   _____

                   County   _____

                 Postcode   [| | | | | |]

HM Courts & Tribunals Service

Diversity Monitoring Questionnaire

It is important to us that everyone who has contact with HM Courts & Tribunals Service, receives equal treatment. We need to find out whether our policies are effective and to take steps to ensure the impact of future policies can be fully assessed to try to avoid any adverse impacts on any particular groups of people. That is why we are asking you to complete the following questionnaire, which will be used to provide us with the relevant statistical information. **Your answers will be treated in strict confidence.**

Thank you in advance for your co-operation.

Claim type

Please confirm the type of claim that you are bringing to the employment tribunal. This will help us in analysing the other information provided in this form.

- (a) ☑ Unfair dismissal or constructive dismissal
- (b) ☐ Discrimination
- (c) ☐ Redundancy payment
- (d) ☐ Other payments you are owed
- (e) ☐ Other complaints

Sex

What is your sex?

- (a) ☐ Female
- (b) ☑ Male
- (c) ☐ Prefer not to say

Age group

Which age group are you in?

- (a) ☐ Under 25
- (b) ☐ 25-34
- (c) ☐ 35-44
- (d) ☐ 45-54
- (e) ☑ 55-64
- (f) ☐ 65 and over
- (g) ☐ Prefer not to say

Ethnicity

What is your ethnic group?

White

- (a) ☑ English / Welsh / Scottish / Northern Irish / British
- (b) ☐ Irish
- (c) ☐ Gypsy or Irish Traveller
- (d) ☐ Any other White background

Mixed / multiple ethnic groups

- (e) ☐ White and Black Caribbean
- (f) ☐ White and Black African
- (g) ☐ White and Asian
- (h) ☐ Any other Mixed / multiple ethnic background

Asian / Asian British

- (i) ☐ Indian
- (j) ☐ Pakistani
- (k) ☐ Bangladeshi
- (l) ☐ Chinese
- (m) ☐ Any other Asian background

Black / African / Caribbean / Black British

- (n) ☐ African
- (o) ☐ Caribbean
- (p) ☐ Any other Black / African / Caribbean background

Other ethnic group

- (q) ☐ Arab
- (r) ☐ Any other ethnic group

- (s) ☐ Prefer not to say

Disability

The Equality Act 2010 defines a disabled person as 'Someone who has a physical or mental impairment and the impairment has a substantial and long-term adverse effect on his or her ability to carry out normal day-to-day activities'.

Conditions covered may include, for example, severe depression, dyslexia, epilepsy and arthritis.

Do you have any physical or mental health conditions or illnesses lasting or expected to last for 12 months or more?

(a) ☐ Yes

(b) ☑ No

(c) ☐ Prefer not to say

Marriage and Civil Partnership

Are you?

(a) ☐ Single, that is, never married and never registered in a same-sex civil partnership

(b) ☐ Married

(c) ☐ Separated, but still legally married

(d) ☑ Divorced

(e) ☐ Widowed

(f) ☐ In a registered same-sex civil partnership

(g) ☐ Separated, but still legally in a same-sex civil partnership

(h) ☐ Formerly in a same-sex civil partnership which is now legally dissolved

(I) ☐ Surviving partner from a same-sex civil partnership

(J) ☐ Prefer not to say

Religion and belief

What is your religion?

(a) ☑ No religion

(b) ☐ Christian (including Church of England, Catholic, Protestant and all other Christian denominations)

(c) ☐ Buddhist

(d) ☐ Hindu

(e) ☐ Jewish

(f) ☐ Muslim

(g) ☐ Sikh

(h) ☐ Any other religion (please describe)

[   ]

(I) ☐ Prefer not to say

Caring responsibilites

Do you have any caring responsibilities, (for example; children, elderly relatives, partners etc.)?

(a) ☐ Yes

(b) ☑ No

(c) ☐ Prefer not to say

Sexual identity

Which of the options below best describes how you think of yourself?

(a) ☑ Heterosexual/Straight

(b) ☐ Gay /Lesbian

(c) ☐ Bisexual

(d) ☐ Other

(e) ☐ Prefer not to say

Gender identity

Please describe your gender identity?

(a) ☑ Male (including female-to-male trans men)

(b) ☐ Female (including male-to-female trans women)

(c) ☐ Prefer not to say

Is your gender identity different to the sex you were assumed to be at birth?

(f) ☐ Yes

(g) ☑ No

(h) ☐ Prefer not to say

Pregnancy and maternity

Were you pregant when the issue you are making a claim about took place?

(a) ☐ Yes

(b) ☑ No

(c) ☐ Prefer not to say

Thank you for taking the time to complete this questionnaire.

Employment Tribunals check list and cover sheet

Please check the following:

1. Read the form to make sure the information given is correct and truthful, and that you have not left out any information which you feel may be relevant to you or your client.
2. Do not attach a covering letter to your form. If you have any further relevant information please enter it in the 'Additional Information' space provided in the form.
3. Send the completed form to the relevant office address.
4. Keep a copy of your form posted to us.

If your claim has been submitted on-line or posted in with the appropriate fee you should receive confirmation of receipt from the office dealing with your claim within five working days. If you have not heard from them within five days, please contact that office directly. If the deadline for submitting the claim is closer than five days you should check that it has been received before the time limit expires. Claims which include an application for a full or partial remission of the fee may take a little longer to deal with.

You have opted to print and post your form. We would like to remind you that forms submitted on-line are processed much faster than ones posted to us. If you want to submit on-line please go back to the form and click the submit button, otherwise follow the check list before you post the completed form to the relevant office address.

A list of our office's contact details can be found at the hearing centre page of our website at – www.justice.gov.uk/tribunals/employment/venues ; if you are still unsure about which office to contact please call our national enquiry line on 0845 7959775 (Mon – Fri, 9am – 5pm) or Minicom 0845 757 3772; they can also provide general procedural information about the employment tribunals.

IN THE Guildshire Employment Tribunal

Case Number 123456/2018

Mr J Gold (Claimant)
v
Car Parking PLC (Respondent)

Statement of Case

1. The Claimant was employed by the respondent as a Team Leader based at the Guildshire car park.

2. He started working in this role in November 2015. He was dismissed on the grounds of redundancy on the 30th April 2018 and was paid a redundancy payment.

3. The Claimant does not accept that there was a genuine redundancy situation and understands that a new employee is currently employed in his role at the car park.

4. The Claimant further argues that the selection criteria were unfair in that his level of experience and expertise was underscored.

5. He appealed his dismissal but was unsuccessful in the appeal which was heard on the 20th April 2018. The Claimant only saw the scoring for the first time after the appeal so he didn't have an opportunity to contest the score before the appeal, or at the appeal. The scoring was only forwarded to him after the appeal hearing was adjourned. The Claimant expected to return to the appeal to raise his complaints but this didn't happen and he received a letter confirming his dismissal. The Claimant has worked previously for the respondent for a number of years and was Tupe'd out to a different employer. He has worked in this industry for approximately 4 years. He argues the procedure adopted was unfair and predetermined.

6. On viewing the score he was horrified to see he had been scored 1 for his skills for the current position and job. He had no performance issues and had a good appraisal. There was simply no justification to score him one meaning 'not acceptable'.

7. In conclusion the respondent did not allow the claimant the opportunity to contest his scores. They concluded the appeal then sent him his score, and when he saw his score he found that the score was unfair and didn't reflect his skills and ability. The Claimant had no performance issues and was never advised that his performance was below par. He would have expected to score 4 'good' and not 1.

8. His comparators in the pool were 3. The Claimant asked for an alternative role locally. He was aware that two members of staff in a more junior role were leaving. His request was ignored by the contractor manager. These jobs were given to two more junior staff with no rail experience at all; they were only used to off street car parks. The machinery and procedures are very different in the rail track contract sites. The Claimant could easily have done either role. The respondents offered a junior role miles from his home and on less pay.

EMPLOYMENT TRIBUNALS

To: Car Parking PLC

e-mail: GuildshireET@tribunals.gsi.gov.uk

Case Number: 123456/2018

Mr J Gold	**Claimant**
v	
Car Parking PLC	**Respondent**

NOTICE OF A CLAIM

The Claim

The Employment Tribunal has accepted a claim for unfair dismissal against the above respondent. It has been given the above Case Number, which should be quoted in any communication relating to this case.

A copy of the claim is enclosed for the respondent.

The Response

To submit a response, a prescribed form must be used. Alternatively you may respond on-line at www.employmenttribunals.gov.uk. It must be received at this office by 26/07/2018. If a response is not received by then, and no extension of time has been applied for and given, the claim will proceed undefended, or a default judgment may be made.

Acas

Acas (whose services are free) may be able to help the parties resolve the matter at any time.

Representative

If you appoint a representative to act for you, please pass these documents to your representative as soon as possible. You remain responsible for ensuring that the representative deals with all matters promptly.

Enclosures

A copy of the claim

A prescribed response form

A copy of the booklet 'Responding to a claim' can be found on our website at www.employmenttribunals.gov.uk/Publications/publications.htm

If you do not have access to the internet, paper copies can be obtained by telephoning the tribunal office dealing with the claim

Signed *D Smith*

D SMITH

For the Tribunal Office

Guildshire ET

Dated: 28 June 2018

cc   Acas

RESPONSE TO AN EMPLOYMENT TRIBUNAL CLAIM

In the claim of:

Mr J Gold

-v-

Car Parking PLC

Case Number: 123456/2018
(please quote this in all correspondence)

This requires your immediate attention. If you want to resist the claim made against you, you must use the prescribed response form. Your completed form must reach the tribunal office within 28 days of the date of the attached Notice. If the form does not reach us by 26/07/2018 you will not be able to take part in the proceedings and a default judgment may be entered against you.

Please read the guidance notes and the notes on this page carefully **before** filling in this form.

By law, you **must** provide the information marked with ⋆ and, if it is relevant, the information marked with • (see guidance on Pre-acceptance procedure).

Please make sure that all the information you give is as accurate as possible.

Where there are tick boxes, please tick the one that applies.

If you fax the form, do not send a copy in the post.

You must return the full form, including this page, to the tribunal office.

ET3

Employment Tribunal

Response form

| Case number | 123456/2016 |

You must complete all questions marked with an '*'

1   Claimant's name

| 1.1 | Claimant's name | James Gold |

2   Respondent's details

| 2.1* | Name of individual, company or organisation | Car Parking PLC |
| 2.2 | Name of contact | Mrs J Price |

2.3*	Address		
		Number or name	The Business Centre
		Street	
		Town/City	
		County	Guildshire
		Postcode	G U 1 2 8 Q Y

| | DX number (If known) | |

| 2.4 | Phone number
Where we can contact you during the day | 01234 567789 |
| | Mobile number (If different) | |

2.5   How would you prefer us to contact you?
(Please tick only one box)   ☑ Email   ☐ Post   ☐ Fax   Whatever your preference please note that some documents cannot be sent electronically

| 2.6 | Email address | j.price@carparkingplc.co.uk |
| | Fax number | |

| 2.7 | How many people does this organisation employ in Great Britain? | 1500 |

2.8   Does this organisation have more than one site in Great Britain?   ☑ Yes   ☐ No

| 2.9 | If Yes, how many people are employed at the place where the claimant worked? | 8 |

3 Employment details

3.1 Are the dates of employment given by the claimant correct?   ☑ Yes   ☐ No

If Yes, please **go to question 3.2**

If No, please give the dates and say why you disagree with the dates given by the claimant

When their employment started | 09-11-2015

When their employment ended or will end | 30-04-2018

I disagree with the dates for the following reasons

3.2 Is their employment continuing?   ☐ Yes   ☑ No

3.3 Is the claimant's description of their job or job title correct?   ☑ Yes   ☐ No

If Yes, please **go to Section 4**

If No, please give the details you believe to be correct

4 Earnings and benefits

4.1 Are the claimant's hours of work correct?   ☑ Yes   ☐ No

If No, please enter the details you believe to be correct.   _____ hours each week

4.2 Are the earnings details given by the claimant correct?   ☑ Yes   ☐ No

If Yes, please **go to question 4.3**

If No, please give the details you believe to be correct below

Pay before tax (Incl. overtime, commission, bonuses etc.)   £ _____   ☐ Weekly   ☐ Monthly

Normal take-home pay (Incl. overtime, commission, bonuses etc.)   £ _____   ☐ Weekly   ☐ Monthly

4.3   Is the information given by the claimant
      correct about being paid for, or working a   ☑ Yes   ☐ No
      period of notice?

      If Yes, please **go to question 4.4**

      If No, please give the details you believe to
      be correct below. If you gave them no
      notice or didn't pay them instead of letting
      them work their notice, please explain what
      happened and why.

4.4   Are the details about pension and other
      benefits e.g. company car, medical   ☑ Yes   ☐ No
      insurance, etc. given by the claimant correct?

      If Yes, please **go to Section 5**

      If No, please give the details you believe to
      be correct.

5   Response

5.1* Do you defend the claim?   ☑ Yes   ☐ No

      If No, please **go to Section 6**

      If Yes, please set out the facts which you rely on to defend the claim.
      (See Guidance - If needed, please use the blank sheet at the end of this form.)

> The respondent is the UK's leading provider of 'off-street' parking services. It has approximately 1,500 employees. The claimant worked as a Team Leader at its car parks in Guildshire, where about 8 people work. The Claimant was employed from 9th November 2015 until 30th April 2018, when he was dismissed by reason of redundancy. The Claimant's claims are denied in their entirety.
>
> On 16th February, the Claimant and his colleagues were invited to a meeting on 21st February about proposed changes to the workplace. The Respondent operated what was known as the 'First Contract' at 3 railway stations. There were three Team Leaders, including the Claimant. In order to increase focus and accountability and to reduce the overhead cost, the business proposed to reduce the Team Leaders to two, who would be expected to cover the three stations. The three Team Leaders were told of the proposal and were informed that they were at risk of redundancy and would be consulted severally.
>
> Martin Smith, the Contract Manager, and Jack Tawse, from the Human Resources department, conducted the first consultation with the Claimant on 23rd February. The restructuring proposed was discussed, along with the process of consultation and selection. The Claimant was told that a process of selection would determine which one of the three Team Leaders would be at risk of redundancy. The Claimant had no question or comment.
>
> A second consultative meeting took place with the Claimant on 7th March. The Claimant was asked whether he had any questions or comments. He did not. He was given estimates of the payments that he would receive if he were made redundant. He was told about the internal vacancies. The Claimant had no questions outstanding.
>
> A third meeting took place on 22nd March. The Claimant again had no comments or questions.
>
> So, on 22nd March, Martin Smith undertook to score the Claimant and his two colleagues against the following criteria:
>
> See continuation sheet

6 Employer's Contract Claim

6.1 Only available in limited circumstances where the claimant has made a contract claim. (See Guidance)

6.2 If you wish to make an Employer's Contract Claim in response to
the claimant's claim, please tick this box and complete question 6.3 ☐

6.3 Please set out the background and details of your claim below, which should include all important dates
(see Guidance for more information on what details should be included)

7 Your representative

If someone has agreed to represent you, please fill in the following. We will in future only contact your representative and not you.

7.1	Name of representative	V Alavy
7.2	Name of organisation	Swallows & Co LLP

7.3 Address

Number or name	12
Street	High Street
Town/City	
County	Guildshire
Postcode	G U 1 2 1 A B

7.4	DX number (If known)	
7.5	Phone number	01999 234567
7.6	Mobile phone	
7.7	Their reference for correspondence	
7.8	How would you prefer us to communicate with them? (Please tick only one box)	☑ Email ☐ Post ☐ Fax
7.9	Email address	v.alavy@swallows.co.uk
7.10	Fax number	

8 Disability

8.1 Do you have a disability?   ☐ Yes   ☑ No

If Yes, it would help us if you could say what this disability is and tell us what assistance, if any, you will need as your claim progresses through the system, including for any hearings that maybe held at tribunal premises.

Please re-read the form and check you have entered all the relevant information. Once you are satisfied, please tick this box. ☑

Data Protection Act 1998.

We will send a copy of this form to the claimant and Acas. We will put the information you give us on this form onto a computer. This helps us to monitor progress and produce statistics. Information provided on this form is passed to the Department for Business, Innovation and Skills to assist research into the use and effectiveness of employment tribunals. (URN 05/874)

Employment Tribunals check list and cover sheet

Please check the following:

1. Read the form to make sure the information given is correct and truthful, and that you have not left out any information which you feel may be relevant to you or your client.
2. Do not attach a covering letter to your form. If you have any further relevant information please enter it in the 'Additional Information' space provided in the form.
3. Send the completed form to the relevant office address.
4. Keep a copy of your form posted to us.

Once your response has been received, you should receive confirmation from the office dealing with your claim within five working days. If you have not heard from them within five days, please contact that office directly. If the deadline for submitting the response is closer than five days you should check that it has been received before the time limit expires.

You have opted to print and post your form. We would like to remind you that forms submitted on-line are processed much faster than ones posted to us. If you want to submit on-line please go back to the form and click the submit button, otherwise follow the check list before you post the completed form to the relevant office address.

A list of our office's contact details can be found at the hearing centre page of our website at – www.justice.gov.uk/tribunals/employment/venues ; if you are still unsure about which office to contact please call our national enquiry line on 0845 7959775 (Mon – Fri, 9am – 5pm) or Minicom 0845 757 3772; they can also provide general procedural information about the employment tribunals.

Continuation sheet

Skills for the current position/job:
Performance; Skills for other positions/jobs with Car Parks PLC; Length of service; Disciplinary record.
They were rated as follows:
Not acceptable/incomplete 1; Acceptable 2; Good 4; Exceptional 5.
The Claimant's colleagues scored 18 and 24.
Unfortunately the Claimant's experience was at one of the three sites only. The other two Team Leaders had experience at the other sites.

At the next consultative meeting on 25th March the Claimant was told that, because he had recorded the lowest score, he was at risk of redundancy. He was served with the notice that his employment would be terminated on 30th April, unless alternative employment could be found. The Claimant was sent the company's weekly bulletin of internal vacancies and asked to indicate any that were of interest. This was confirmed to the Claimant in writing, including the Claimant's right of appeal, on 25th March.

The Claimant was off sick from 1st April.

The Claimant appealed by letters dated 5th April and 11th April. He said that:

1 he had shown unquestionable loyalty
2 he carried out all instructions, often going beyond what was asked of him
3 he had built a strong team in the site where he worked
4 he had had to query why a number of his staff were not receiving their expenses, some of which were outstanding
5 he had supported the staff team at night and at weekends when proper cover could not be found
6 he had been working 'on-call' without receiving any payment
7 he had not been shown the scoring process
8 he thought that there would be more work not less, so could not understand the reduction in the staff.

Alan Savage, the Head of Operations, conducted the appeal hearing on 20th April. Jack Tawse was present. The Claimant confirmed that he was satisfied with the process, but his main concern was not having received details of what he scored. These were given to him.

On appeal, the dismissal was upheld. Unfortunately, no alternative employment acceptable to the Claimant could be found. Before the employment tribunal the Respondent will argue:

– that was a genuine reason for the redundancy
– that the selection process was fair
– that the dismissal of the Claimant by reason of redundancy was fair and reasonable in all the circumstances
– that, contrary to his assertion, the Claimant has not been 'replaced'.

EMPLOYMENT TRIBUNALS

Case No. 123456/2018

Mr J Gold	**Claimant**
v	
Car Parking PLC	**Respondent**

ORDER FOR DIRECTIONS

An Employment Judge has directed that:

1   This case will be given a one day hearing.

1.1   The parties are required to prepare and present their cases to enable the Tribunal to deal with all the issues, and remedy if applicable, in that time.

1.2   You **must** inform the Tribunal **immediately** if you believe the hearing date, time or length is not appropriate and, if so, give detailed reasons why.

2   No later than **10 September 2018** the Claimant **must** send a **Schedule of Loss** to the Respondent and the Tribunal.

3   No later than **24 September 2018** each party **must** send to each other party a **copy of any document** it has relevant to the claims in the proceedings.

4   The parties **must** agree **a bundle** of **documents** for the tribunal hearing. The [First] Respondent **must** ensure that **six copies of the bundle** are available at the tribunal hearing.

5   **No documents or copy correspondence should be sent to the Tribunal before the hearing date unless a party is required to do so.**

6   Each party must prepare **six copies of a written witness statement** for each person who is to give evidence at the hearing. This includes the Claimant and any personal Respondent. The statements will normally be read aloud at the hearing and the person will then be questioned about the contents.

7   The statement shall contain **all** of that person's evidence. No person can give evidence without a statement unless the Tribunal agrees.

8   **Not later than 14 days before the hearing** there shall be simultaneous exchange of witness statements by each party providing to each other party one copy of each witness statement.

GUIDANCE ON THE ABOVE ORDERS IS GIVEN BELOW

GUIDANCE

Schedule of Loss

1   A Schedule of Loss **must** set out the money you want as compensation for each part of your claim and the way it has been calculated. You may find it helpful to use a spreadsheet program.

Documents

2   'Documents' includes letters, notes, emails, memos, diary entries, audio or visual recordings, text messages and any other legible records.

3   If extensive hand-written document/s are being relied on a typescript **must** be provided by the party relying on the document/s.

4   If a recording is being relied on a transcript **must** be prepared by the party relying on it. That typescript **must** be included in the bundle and sent to any other party, together with a copy of the recording.

Bundles of Documents

5   The bundle **must** contain a copy of any relevant document any party intends to use at the Tribunal hearing. Two-sided copying is encouraged.

6   The parties **must** agree on the inclusion of only relevant extracts of lengthy documents. A full copy of such a document should be brought to the Hearing.

7   All the documents **must** be in date order, with the oldest at the front.

8   Each page **must** be numbered.

9   The bundle **must** have an index showing the date, description and page number of each document.

10   The bundle **must** be held together so it opens flat.

11   Witness statements **must not** be included in a bundle.

Witness Statements

12   Each witness statement (including the claimant's) **must**:

12.1   have page numbers, be typed single-sided with double line spacing with at least 2.5cm page margins;

12.2   use a 'standard' (e.g. Arial, Times New Roman or similar) size 12 font;

12.3   contain **all** the evidence of the witness;

12.4   be laid out in short consecutively **numbered** paragraphs;

12.5   set out **in chronological order,** with dates, the facts which the witness can state;

12.6   not contain matters irrelevant to the issues;

12.7   refer **by page number in the bundle of documents** to any document mentioned in the statement;

12.8   be signed and dated;

12.9   not be contained in a bundle.

NOTES

1   Failure to comply with an Order for DISCLOSURE/INSPECTION may result on summary conviction in a fine of up to £1,000 being imposed upon a person in default under section 7(4) of the Employment Tribunals Act 1996.

2   If a person does not comply with Orders made under the Employment Tribunals Rules of Procedure 2013, rule 8 of the Employment Tribunals (Levy Appeals) Rules of Procedure or rule 7 of the Employment Tribunals (Health and Safety – Appeals against Improvement and Prohibition Notices) Rules of Procedure an Employment Judge or Tribunal may:

2.1   make an order in respect of costs or preparation time (if applicable) under rules 74 to 84; or

2.2   at a Preliminary Hearing or a Final Hearing make an order to strike out the whole or part of the claim or, as the case may be, the response and, where appropriate, order that a respondent be debarred from responding to the claim altogether.

3   The Tribunal may also make a further Order (an 'Unless Order') providing that unless it is complied with, the claim or, as the case may be, the response shall be struck out on the date of non-compliance without further consideration of the proceedings under rule 38.

4   An Order may be varied or revoked upon application by a person affected by the Order or by an Employment Judge on his own initiative.

Dated: 18 August 2018

Employment Judge

ORDER SENT TO THE PARTIES ON

.......19 August 2018........

....
FOR THE TRIBUNAL OFFICE

[Guildshire Employment Tribunal]

To: Mr Fred Mclean
       Collaws Solicitors LLP
       20 The Street, Guildshire, GU12

       V Alavy
       Swallows & Co LLP
       12 High Street, Guildshire GU12

Cc: Acas

EMPLOYMENT TRIBUNALS

To: Mr Fred Mclean
Collaws Solicitors LLP
20 The Street, Guildshire, GU12

V Alavy
Swallows & Co LLP
12 High Street, Guildshire GU12

Case Number: 123456/2018

Mr J Gold	Claimant
v	
Car Parking PLC	Respondent

NOTICE OF HEARING
Employment Tribunals Rules of Procedure 2013

The claim will be heard by an Employment Tribunal at **Guildshire House, Guildshire,** on **29 October 2018** at **10:00 am** or as soon thereafter on that day as the Tribunal can hear it. The Tribunal may transfer your case at short notice to be heard at another hearing centre within the region.

The Hearing has been allocated **1 day** including remedy, if appropriate. If you think that is not long enough, you must give your reasons, in writing, and your time estimate within 14 days of this Notice.

Unless there are exceptional circumstances, no application for a postponement will be granted. Any such application must be in writing. The application should include any dates agreed for re-listing the case or should advise the Tribunal of your unavailable dates within two months of the original Hearing.

You may submit written representations for consideration at the hearing. If so, they must be sent to the tribunal and to all other parties not less than 7 days before the hearing. You will have the chance to put forward oral arguments in any case.

It is your responsibility to make sure that your witnesses come to the Hearing.

You must comply with any Case Management Order issued in relation to this case and refer to the guidance in the booklet 'The hearing'.

A copy of the booklet 'The hearing' and expenses leaflet can be found on our website at www.employmenttribunals.gov.uk/Publications/publications.htm

A location map for the office can be found at www.employmenttribunals.gov.uk/HearingCentres/hearingCentres.htm

If you do not have access to the Internet, paper copies can be obtained by telephoning the tribunal office dealing with the claim.

To   Mr Fred Mclean
       Collaws Solicitors LLP
       20 The Street, Guildshire, GU12

and

       V Alavy
       Swallows & Co LLP
       12 High Street, Guildshire GU12   Signed R *Drummond*
                                                 For the Secretary of Employment Tribunals

       Dated: 20 August 2018

cc   Acas

Mr J Gold v Car Parking PLC

Case number: 123456/2018

SCHEDULE OF DOCUMENTS

Page	Description	Number of sheets
	Tribunal Papers	
1–11	Claim	11
12–18	Response	7
19–21	Order for Directions	3
22–23	Notice of Hearing	2
	Documents	
24–26	Offer letter dated 6th November 2015	3
27	Letter to the Claimant dated 16th February 2018	1
28	Announcement	1
29	Letter to the Claimant dated 21st February	1
30–33	Notes of first meeting dated 23rd February	4
34	Letter to the Claimant dated 25th February	1
35	Notes of second meeting dated 7th March	1
36	Letter to the Claimant dated 17th March	1
37	Notes of third meeting dated 22nd March	1
38–39	Blank criteria for selection	2
40–42	Criteria for selection – the Claimant	3
43–46	Criteria for selection – others	4
47	Letter to the Claimant dated 23rd March	1
48	Letter to the Claimant dated 25th March	1
49	Letter to the Claimant dated 25th March	1
50–51	Fit note dated 1st April	2
52	Letter from the Claimant dated 5th April	1
53	Letter to the Claimant dated 6th April	1
54	Letter from the Claimant dated 11th April	1
55	Letter to the Claimant dated 15th April	1
56–57	Fit note dated 18th April	2
58 – 61	Letter to the Claimant dated 20th April	4
62–64	Document headed 'Monday to Friday 17.00–08,00 (if no team leader)'	3
	Remedy	
65	Schedule of loss	1
66–94	Evidence of job searching	29
95–112	Payslips	18

Guildshire Employment Tribunal

Case Number 123456/2018

Mr John Gold (Claimant)

v

Car Parking PLC (Respondent)

CLAIMANT'S WITNESS STATEMENT

1. Prior to commencing employment with the respondent, I was in the army for 10 years. I was employed for 8 years of this in the transport section. I joined Car Parking PLC in March 2014 on the network rail contract; that contract covered 4 mainline stations and I was employed as a team leader managing 17 staff. I was transferred under the TUPE rules to a different employer in 2013. I remained in this role until I was made redundant in July 2015. This information is relevant because it shows I had previous service with the company with more responsibility and it also shows a degree of management experience and flexibility. I had 4 years experience managing staff in car parks.

2. I started working for the respondents as a team leader at the Guildshire Car Park. Guildshire is an International Station and as such the role and nature of the duties differed to that of the normal shopping type car park. There are security issues because of customs and immigration, there are terrorist issues and there is liaison with lots of other agencies. I commenced my employment in November 2015. I refer to my contractual offer letter (p 24–26). This is not accurate. I received this document having already started work.

3. The machinery and equipment differed, it was antiquated and prone to breakdowns, the staff were expected to provide more information to customers utilising the service, the staff had to be on the concourse near the car park machines to assist passengers to pay for their parking, car-parking could also be for longer periods than normal. There are two external car parks with 300 plus spaces. Then there is a six floors multi-storey car park with about 1200 spaces. The car parks are linked to the station. The car park is manned 24 hours a day all year round. There are two staff on days and two on nights. Other staff are on rest days and holidays. I covered a forty plus hours shift covering as and when required. I was on call when I was not working.

4. I was in charge of 8 staff based at this large car park. The car park is very busy and I certainly considered that I was busy and that the role I performed did not cease or diminish.

5. The normal car parks in Guildshire operate not on a 24 hour basis and they are closed in the evenings, they are primarily for shopping centre users and 9 to 5 staff working in the city centre.

6. On 16th February I received a letter (p 27). The letter invited me to attend a briefing. At this briefing I would then refer to the announcement document and point out that in this document it states 'we will comply fully with all our obligations for consultation'. The document also says that they will answer **'any questions or challenges which you may have'**. On 21st February the 30 day consultation started. I now refer to the various notes regarding the meetings. You will note that I am not provided any great detail on why the business has decided to remove my post. I am aware that I am entering an assessment process. I now refer to the selection criteria for the surviving positions. I do not recall seeing the criteria at all during the process. Looking at the criteria now under skills for my current position I had been doing the same job since 2014 and in fact my previous role was more complex and I had more staff to manage. I also had extensive management experience and that can be seen throughout my level of experience. I would challenge anyone who suggests that I am not qualified to do the role I was employed to do.

7. In relation to performance I prided myself on running an efficient service, we had very few customer complaints, the staff worked well with me and I worked well with them. My attendance was excellent, my service although broken was linked and I think that my previous service should have been taken into account as it was not my fault I was transferred under the TUPE process. I had no disciplinary history.

8. I can only describe the consultation process as a tick box exercise. I had nothing to say because I did not know how I was being scored and who was in my pool for redundancy. I now refer you to the document that I only received after my appeal hearing had concluded and when I was advised that I had no further right of appeal. I refer the appeal outcome letter that clearly shows this was the case. It scores me under the skills section not acceptable. The criteria is training courses or from experience with CP PLC or elsewhere. I had a great deal of experience with CP PLC previously and elsewhere doing the identical job at a much higher level. I would say my score should have been exceptional. I would also point out that it lists my job as a customer service advisor; that really worries me I am a team leader not a customer service advisor. It is dated 22nd March yet it takes them until 20th April to send it to me. My last consultation meeting took place on the 22nd March. That is the date when apparently I was scored. The question is did the scoring take place before or after this meeting. Mr Smith provides no information to me at this meeting about my scores, he asks me no questions about my experience.

9. How can this process I say amount to meaningful consultation?

10. I was in a position where I was fighting in the dark. I had no idea what reason I was scored down on to cause me to be made redundant. I only obtained this information after my appeal. It was in my view that they were deliberately concealing my scores because they could not fairly justify them until I had had my appeal.

11. Since I now have had sight of the criteria and my scores and the apparent reasons for the scores I would make the following comments under each criteria head;

12. **Skills and Knowledge for the current Position/Job**

    I had several years experience in the role. So I clearly had the relevant skills to do the job I was employed to do at Guildshire. The criteria refer to experience with CP PLC or elsewhere. The criteria does not ask about performance in my role; it clearly excluded that the score should be based on the actual skills and experience in the role. I have skills and other positions that would cover knowledge of other systems in other sites (p 40). I refer to the reasons (p 41–42). I am scored down because of a perceived lack of knowledge on the different parking system at used at the other two stations. Firstly that was not the site I was employed at. If the other team leaders attended my site they couldn't operate the machines on my site easily either. The criteria are irrelevant to the job I was employed at. Secondly on the occasions I attended at these sites I gained a working knowledge of this system and familiarised myself with it. I just hadn't been formally trained on it because it was not my normal site. To score me at one was frankly an insult with my level of experience and cannot be justified according to the criteria. A fairer score would have been 4.

13. **Performance**

    The site ran efficiently. Problems were always solved at the site without the need for outside help. No examples are given of how I do not solve problems. This is simply rubbish and is not supported by proof. I am scored 2 and yet if you now look at my Comparators you will note that basically this is an assessment based purely on the perception of the person scoring. It is not based on any evidence. I was well respected, problems solved and I always met what was asked of me yet I only score 2? (p 43–46).

14. **Skills for other positions and jobs**

    I had done the job previously. I had helped set up the systems at one of the other stations and I was familiar with all necessary skills apart from being formally trained on the different parking system. Again a score of 4 would have been appropriate.

15.   In my view the scorer didn't apply the criteria correctly or provide evidence to support his conclusions. The scores were in effect one person's preferences.

16.   In relation to length of service they could for example have considered my previous service which was only broken because of Tupe. You will note that I am scored below Good on all aspects and only scored exceptional when all those comparators are scored the same.

17.   In conclusion the consultation process was in my view a tick box process, I expected to be given at some point my scores and the criteria and an explanation with evidence of how my scores had been arrived at. This didn't happen. I had been through a similar process in the past and it had happened on that occasion. My second one to one dealt with internal vacancies, how to apply etc. At this point though I was at risk I didn't know I was selected so I had no real comments. My third one to one dealt with the criteria that was to be used but the scoring was not yet done. It was on 25th March I was told I was selected for redundancy and that I was dismissed. At no time during the consultation could I know of or discuss my actual scores. I was shocked that I had been selected and became ill with stress at work. I appealed verbally and confirmed it in writing. I also applied for the more junior role at Ashford. I was unsuccessful despite having managed staff which really was humiliating. I submitted details of my appeal. You will note that I specifically refer in my appeal to not being shown the scoring. At the time of preparing this statement the respondents have not produced the minutes of the appeal. In the appeal I clearly said that I had no opportunity to put my case and that I should have the scores. Despite making this clear in my appeal letter they still had not bothered to show me my scores. The whole process was unfair and predetermined. At the appeal I recall being told that the appeal would be adjourned so I could get my scores and then once I had them it would be reconvened so that I could put my points.

18.   That's not what happened I get instead a decision with my scores and the letter makes it clear the process is over (p 58).

19.   I consider that the process was completely unfair and that if a fair process had taken place I would not have been selected for redundancy. I consider that when I received my scores after the process concluded it showed me that this was simply Mr Smith taking a personal view on me and it had little or nothing to do with the evidence.

20.   In relation to steps of mitigation I would say as follows. I was sick with work related stress for approximately 3 weeks after my dismissal. I then signed on for Job Seekers Allowance. I looked at various job agencies but I could find little to apply for so I decided to seek work via the Job Centre via newspapers and through online web sites.

21.   As you will see I looked at a wage spectrum of jobs in the junior management level. I have also obtained job details via an ex forces agency. I have had five interviews to date. The first was in mid-April with a security firm. I was then interviewed on 14th July for the position of Department Manager at Parkhome Leisure.

22.   The third was an interview for a company called Petrol Services as an account manager. The fourth was for the position of Facilities Manager at Dupont College Guildshire on the 3rd of August. I have also recently been interviewed on 20th September for the position of assistant Project Manager. I have been unsuccessful in all my interviews.

23.   I have tried for jobs with salaries as low as £14,000.

24.   I refer to the various positions I have applied for and the documents in support of the same.

25.   In conclusion this Statement is true to the best of my knowledge and belief.

Signed *J Gold*

25 October 2018

Mr J Gold v Car Parking PLC

Case number: 123456/2018

STATEMENT OF EVIDENCE OF MARTIN SMITH

My name is Martin Smith

1. I am employed by the Respondent as Contract Manager. I have worked in that capacity since November 2013. For 6 months prior to this I was acting as Duty Manager to become familiar with the role. At the time of the Claimant's dismissal I was responsible for the car parks attached to the 'First Contract' three rail stations. I have experience of the CP PLC dismissal procedures and have received a one day training course on the company dismissal procedures.

2. The claimant worked as a Team Leader at the CP PLC car parks in Guildshire International. The Claimant was employed from 9th November 2015 until 30th April 2018, when he was dismissed by reason of redundancy. His contract appears at page 24 to 26 of the bundle. The Claimant was always located at Guildshire International apart from when he was required to cover a Team Leader at one of the other sites. I am aware that the Claimant had previously worked for the Respondent but this was before my time.

3. On 16th February, I invited the Claimant and his two colleagues to a meeting on 21st February about proposed changes to the workplace. My letter appears at page 27 of the bundle.

4. There were three Team Leaders, including the Claimant. In order to increase focus and accountability and to reduce the overhead cost, the business proposed to reduce the Team Leaders to two. The two would be expected to cover the three stations. The three Team Leaders were told of the proposal and were informed that they were at risk of redundancy and would be consulted individually. The announcement appears at page 28 of the bundle. I read this out to them when they were all together.

5. I, along with Jack Tawse, from the Human Resources department, conducted the first consultation with the Claimant on 23rd February. My letter inviting the Claimant to that meeting appears at page 29 of the bundle.

6. The restructuring proposed was discussed, along with the process of consultation and selection. The Claimant was told that a process of selection would determine which one of the three Team Leaders would be at risk of redundancy. He was told the selection would be by way of a desk top exercise. In front of me during the meeting was the template criteria for selection for redundancy which appears at page 38-39 of the bundle. I explained the criteria that were to be used. The Claimant had no question or comment and in fact said he had been through the process four times before. To me that meant he was familiar with the process which is why he did not ask any questions. The notes of the meeting appear at page 30-33 of the bundle. I followed the same format for the other two Team Leaders who were at risk.

7. A second consultative meeting took place with the Claimant on 7th March. My invitation to him appears at page 34 of the bundle. At this point I had not conducted the desk top selection exercise. But I went through with him other opportunities that were available in CP PLC. It followed the same process with all three of the Team leaders who were at risk. The Claimant was asked whether he had any questions or comments. He did not. He was given estimates of the payments that he would receive if he were made redundant. He was told about the internal vacancies. The Claimant had no questions outstanding. The notes of the meeting appear at page 35 of the bundle. At that meeting we did not discuss the selection process any further.

8. A third meeting took place on 22nd March. The invitation appears at page 36 of the bundle. The Claimant again had no comments or questions. The notes of the meeting are at page 37 of the bundle. I confirmed to him and the other two Team Leaders that I would now conduct the desk top selection exercise.

9.   So, on 22nd March, I undertook to score the Claimant and his two colleagues against the following criteria:

Skills for the current position/job

Performance

Skills for other positions/jobs with NCP

Length of service

Disciplinary record

They were rated as follows:

Not acceptable/incomplete	1
Acceptable	2
Good	4
Exceptional	5

The Claimant scored 16.

The Claimant's colleagues scored 18 and 24.

Whilst I was scoring the candidates I was looking at suitability for the job going forward. There was to be two team leaders covering the three sites. One of the requirements would be to produce compliance and audit documentation which unfortunately the Claimant did not do to the extent of the other Team Leaders. Unfortunately the Claimant's primary experience was at Ashford International only. The other two Team Leaders had experience at the other sites. In addition the Claimant had only been in post since November 2015.

The scoring charts appear at pages 40–46 of the bundle.

10.   Before I met with the three Team leaders again I sent the scoring assessment that I had done on each to Dave Hirst, Head of Operations to review what I had done. He confirmed to me that it was in order and I arranged to see the three Team Leaders to confirm the outcome.

11.   At the next consultative meeting on 25th March I informed the Claimant that, because he had recorded the lowest score, he was at risk of redundancy. He was served with the notice that his employment would be terminated on 30th April, unless alternative employment could be found. The letter inviting the Claimant to the meeting appears at page 47 of the bundle and the letters confirming that he was at risk of redundancy and giving notice of redundancy appears at page 48–49 of the bundle. I would have sent him both letters dated 25th March. One confirms that the position of Team Leader that he held was redundant and the other was a personal letter to the Claimant giving him notice of redundancy including details of his right of appeal.

12.   At the meeting I told the Claimant he had been selected for redundancy. I had the scoring sheet in front of me. But unfortunately the Claimant said a few words and stood up and walked out of the office. I was unable to provide him with any more details of the scoring as he had left. Jack Tawse from Human Resources was also present during the meeting.

13.   That was the last I heard until Dave Hirst asked me for the details of the scoring process and the consultation process. I gave Dave the relevant paperwork.

14.   I understand that the Claimant has said that he was unable to challenge the scores that I gave him in the desk top selection exercise. Firstly I would say that the Claimant did not contribute to any of the meetings that I had with him. Secondly I would say that the scores would not have changed. His length of service is a fact. And it was a fact that he did not have certain skills required for the job going forward. So, even if he had raised an objection his scores would have remained the same.

15.   This statement is true to the best of my knowledge and belief.

Signed   M Smith

Dated 27.10.18

Mr J Gold v Car Parking PLC

Case number: 123456/2018

STATEMENT OF EVIDENCE OF JACK TAWSE

My name is Jack Tawse

1.   I am employed by the Respondent as Human Resources Business Partner. I have worked in that capacity for just over 4 years. I started with respondent around 2012 when I joined as Human Resources Policy Manager. As Human Resources Business Partner I provide HR support and advice to the managers in the area.

2.   The Respondent does not have a Redundancy Policy. The approach adopted will depend upon the particular circumstances. We have been involved in situations which have required collective consultation as well as individual consultation in the past.

3.   I provided Human Resources advice and assistance throughout the process of consultation, selection, dismissal and appeal in relation to the Claimant.

4.   I am providing this evidence as the Employment Tribunal refused to postpone the hearing when it learnt that Dave Hirst, the manager hearing the appeal, was unavailable. I was present during the appeal hearing to provide HR advice to Dave Hirst.

5.   I was involved in the first consultation meeting with the Claimant. I do recall Martin Smith going through the agenda items outlined at page 30 of the bundle. I also recall Martin Smith specifically explaining the desk top selection exercise to the Claimant and the other two Team Leaders. At that stage we were seeking comments from the Team Leaders about the proposal itself and selection methodology proposed. The Claimant had no comment to make.

6.   I was also involved in the meeting on 25th March with the Claimant. Martin Smith confirmed that the Claimant had been selected for redundancy. The purpose of the meeting was to explain the selection process. But when the Claimant was informed that he had been selected, he said something along the lines of that he felt it had been a foregone conclusion and he left without Martin being able to explain his rationale and his scoring.

7.   On 1st April, after the Claimant received notification of his redundancy, he was off sick. The sick notes appear at pages 50–51 of the bundle.

8.   The Claimant appealed to Dave Hirst by letter dated 5th April. It appears at page 52 of the bundle. In preparing for the Employment Tribunal proceedings I have discussed matters with Dave Hirst. After the Claimant appealed on 5th April, he had been in touch with Dave Hirst and arranged to meet him informally. The Claimant was asking whether there were any openings in CP PLC in the south area. At that time all that Dave was aware of was a Mobile Support Officer. The Claimant said he would think about it and in the meantime confirmed that his letter of appeal dated 5th April should be ripped up. Dave Hirst became aware that the Claimant was not interested in the vacancy and wanted to pursue his appeal.

9.   We then received the letter dated 11th April. He said that:

(a)   he had shown unquestionable loyalty

(b)   he carried out all instructions, often going beyond what was asked of him

(c)   he had built a strong team in Ashford with limited support from Ebbsfleet

(d)   he had had to query why a number of his staff were not receiving their expenses, some of which were outstanding

(e)   he had supported the staff team at night and at weekends when proper cover could not be found

(f)   he had been working 'on-call' without receiving any payment

(g)   he had not been shown the scoring process

(h)   he thought that there would be more work not less, so could not understand the reduction in the staff.

The Claimant's letter appears at page 54 of the bundle.

10.   Dave Hirst, the Head of Operations, conducted the appeal hearing on 20th April. The invitation appears at page 55 of the bundle. I was present.

11.   I accept that there are no notes of the appeal hearing. It was a quick meeting. During the appeal the Claimant confirmed that he was satisfied with the process, but his main concern was not having received details of what he scored. These were shown to him at the appeal hearing. But he said nothing. He said he did not have a copy so it was agreed a copy would be sent to him by post, which is what was done.

12.   I recall however that Dave did take the opportunity to review the scores not least because he was surprised that it had been the Claimant who had had the lowest score. But when looking at the scores and the rationale that Martin Smith had given, Dave was satisfied that they had been correct.

13.   So, on appeal, the dismissal was upheld. Unfortunately, no alternative employment acceptable to the Claimant could be found.

14.   The outcome letter appears at page 58 of the bundle.

15.   Overall, I would say that the Claimant was a good employee and had the business not been in a position where it needed to reduce numbers he would have still been employed. It had not been a foregone conclusion. It had been a fair process and each Team Leader was assessed objectively and fairly. It was unfortunate that the Claimant's score was the lowest.

16.   This statement is true to the best of my knowledge and belief.

Signed J *Tawse*

Dated 27.10.18

EMPLOYMENT TRIBUNALS

Case No. 123456/2018

BETWEEN

Mr J Gold   Claimant

and

Car Parking PLC   Respondent

Held at Guildshire on   29 October 2018

Representation   **Claimant:**   Mr T Robinson, Non practising Barrister
                                  Respondent: Ms R Bates, Counsel

Employment Judge   Smith-Jones (sitting alone)

JUDGMENT

It was the unanimous decision of the Tribunal that the Claimant was unfairly dismissed by the Respondent.

REASONS

Introduction

1. The Tribunal convened on 29 October 2018 to hear the Claimant's claim, as set out in his ET1/Claim Form submitted on 22 June 2018 of unfair dismissal, namely that the Respondent had followed a flawed procedure when selecting him for redundancy, particularly with regard to the consultation and selection process adopted. The Respondent in its ET3 denied this claim. It submitted that the Claimant was dismissed for a fair reason, namely redundancy, following a reorganisation in response to a need to reduce operational costs. Further, it said that it acted reasonably within the meaning of section 98(4) ERA 1996. In particular, the Respondent said it carried out a fair consultation and selection procedure and explored options for alternative employment. There was no dispute that the Claimant had been dismissed. It was indicated at the commencement of the hearing by Mr Robinson that it was accepted that the dismissal was by reason of redundancy.

Issues

2. The matter was listed for a full merits hearing. The principal issues for us to determine were whether, in accordance with the principles set out in *Polkey v AE Dayton Ltd* [1988] ICR 142, the Respondent had:

    (a) Warned and consulted with the Claimant

    (b) Adopted a fair basis for selection, fairly applied

    (c) Taken such steps as may be reasonable to avoid or minimise redundancy

3. If we found that there was an unfair dismissal, then it would be necessary to consider what remedy was appropriate.

Witnesses/evidence

4. The Claimant provided a witness statement, which was taken as read. The Respondent's representative had the opportunity to cross-examine him and the Tribunal was able to ask questions of its own. On behalf of the Respondent, witness statements were

provided on behalf of Mr Martin Smith (Contract Manager) and Mr Jack Tawse (Human Resources Business Partner (South) who provided Human Resources advice and assistance to the Respondent with regard to the consultation, selection, dismissal and appeal of the Claimant). Both witness statements were taken as read by the Tribunal. The Claimant's representative had the opportunity to cross-examine them and the Tribunal was able to ask questions of its own.

5.   The Tribunal also had an agreed paginated bundle of documents. Where a number appears in brackets in this Judgment [ ] that is a reference to a page in this bundle. There was also a separate bundle of additional documents provided relating to the Claimant's job search and the issue of mitigation.

6.   Both representatives made short oral submissions at the close of the evidence. Both parties' submissions are summarised below. A brief oral judgment on liability and some matters of principle on remedy was given at the end of the hearing. This document formally records that judgment and gives the reasons for it. The parties subsequently agreed the remedy between themselves.

Brief Summary of Facts

7.   Mr Gold was employed as a Team Leader at the Respondent's car park at Guildshire, with effect from 9th November 2015. The Claimant was primarily based at Guildshire but was one of three Team Leaders covering three stations. He was required to cover at the other sites from time to time. A different (and older) technology system was employed by CP PLC to manage the car parking at Guildshire than was used at the other two sites.

8.   In early 2018, in order to increase focus and accountability and to reduce over head costs, a decision was taken by the Respondent to reduce the Team Leaders from three to two. On 16th February 2018, Mr Smith invited the Claimant and his two colleagues to a meeting on 21st February to discuss proposed changes to the workplace [27]. At that meeting, they were told of this proposal, informed that they were at risk and would be consulted individually [28]. The same procedure was followed with regard to each of the three Team Leaders.

9.   On 23rd February, a first consultation meeting took place with the Claimant, conducted by Mr Smith, accompanied by Mr Tawse [29, 30–33]. At this meeting, the restructuring was discussed, along with the proposed process for consultation and selection. The Claimant was told what the selection criteria were [38–39]. These included skills for the current job, performance skills for other jobs within CP PLC, length of service and disciplinary record. The Claimant made no comment. A second consultation meeting with the Claimant took place on 7th March [34, 35]. Possible vacancies were discussed and the Claimant was given estimates of any payments he might receive were he to be made redundant.

10.   A third consultation meeting took place on 22nd March [36, 37]. Following this meeting, Mr Smith conducted a selection procedure using the selection criteria referred to above. He carried out this exercise on his own using his personal knowledge and expertise of the three Team Leaders along with information from their personnel files. The Claimant was scored with the lowest mark of the three Team Leaders. Mr Smith's evidence was that while he was conducting the scoring he was looking at suitability going forward. There was not a revised job description for the new posts. Under the reorganised structure, it would however be necessary for a Team Leader to have responsibility for all three sites, and knowledge of and ability to use the system in place at the other two sites was deemed by Mr Smith to be essential. On any analysis. the Claimant had less experience of this system than the other two team leaders and would require training to operate it. Mr Smith thought such training might take a week and approximately a month on the job to assimilate it. He did not discuss this with the Claimant. The Claimant was given lower marks than his colleagues on the skills for the current job, performance, and skills for other jobs criteria. He also had less continuous service than the other Team Leaders [40–46].

11. A further meeting was held with the Claimant on 25th March [27]. He was informed that he had received the lowest score and was therefore at risk of redundancy. He was subsequently sent letters confirming he was at risk of redundancy [48] and was given notice including his right of appeal [49]. The Claimant stood up and left the meeting shortly after being told he had received the lowest score. Mr Smith said he was ready to give the Claimant his score but was unable to because the Claimant left the meeting.

12. The Claimant was signed off sick shortly afterwards [80–81]. He appealed the decision to dismiss him by letter dated 5th April [52] and subsequently by letter dated 11 April [54]. In his letter of appeal, the Claimant said, amongst a number of points, that he had not been shown the scoring process.

13. An appeal hearing was conducted by Mr Hirst on 20th April [55]. There are no notes of this meeting. It was not disputed that the meeting did not last long. The Claimant was told his scores, and these were later sent to him by post. No alternative employment was available. The Claimant rejected a lower grade job and there were no other suitable internal vacancies.

Claimant's Submissions

14. Mr Robinson submitted that the Respondent had not followed a fair and objective selection procedure. He submitted there was an unfair assessment of the Claimant's capabilities, and also that the consultation exercise was inadequate because no opportunity was given to the Claimant to discuss or challenge his scores. On this basis, he said the Claimant's dismissal was unfair. He had no issue with the pool of the three team leaders but said that the criteria were not fairly applied to the Claimant. The three consultation meetings all predated the scoring exercise. The meeting after it had been completed was a fait accompli – the Claimant was told he was dismissed. There was no meaningful consultation after the decision to dismiss had been taken. The Claimant was not shown the notes of the selection at the appeal and there was no opportunity given to him to embark on any meaningful review at that stage. Further, the scoring adopted was very subjective and appeared to be based on penalising the Claimant for lacking future skills, although the first criteria was only about his current skills. Although the Claimant was offered an alternative job this was a demotion and he was not obliged to accept it in order to mitigate his position.

15. Mr Hughes referred the Tribunal to *E-ZEC Medical Transport Services Ltd v Gregory* (UKEAT/ 0192/08) (a case where the EAT upheld a finding by an employment tribunal that a subjective marking system without prior consultation had led to a finding of unfair dismissal; and where a tribunal had found on the facts that a meeting which had been described as a consultation meeting was in essence a meeting to impart the scores and not to review the process); and *Budenberg Gauge Co Ltd v Griffiths* (UKEAT/43/93 and 162/ 93) (an appeal against a tribunal finding of unfairness centering around the use of selection criteria used in a redundancy exercise, where the Claimant was not shown her scores and was therefore unable to comment on them).

Respondent's Submissions

16. Ms Bates on behalf of the Respondent submitted that the Claimant was dismissed for a fair reason relating to redundancy. There was an economic/operational need to reduce the number of Team leaders from 3 to 2. The job had not changed but the individuals doing it needed to be more diverse. It was about capability going forwards. There was a group notification, followed by three separate consultation meetings. The selection criteria were put to Mr Gold and he raised no objection to them. They were objective. Mr Smith was the best placed manager to carry out the selection process. Unfortunately because the Claimant lacked experience of the newer parking system and he had less service, he was scored lower. Lack of experience on that system was a fair criteria for him to use. He had given Mr Gold proper credit for his previous experience. Because Mr Gold walked out of the meeting telling him about this, there was no opportunity to give him his scores. The issue was revisited on appeal but the decision was upheld by Mr Hirst. She submitted that there was a fair and reasonable procedure and proper

consultation and full discussion about all relevant matters. There were no other suitable equivalent vacancies but the Claimant had been offered employment, albeit of a lower status, but he had not wanted to take it. Ms Bates referred the Tribunal to the cases of *Buchanon v Tilcon* [1983] IRLR 417 and *British Airways v Greene*.

The law

Unfair dismissal – reason

17. Where there is a dismissal, an employer has to prove, in the sense that the burden of proof is on it, that the reason for the dismissal falls within one of the potentially fair categories listed in section 98 ERA 1996. These include redundancy. Where there is a potentially fair reason for dismissal, a tribunal must decide whether the employer acted reasonably or unreasonably in treating that as a sufficient reason for dismissal.

18. So far as material, section 98 ERA 1996 provides:

> '98   (1)   In determining for the purposes of this Part whether the dismissal of an employee is fair or unfair, it is for the employer to show–
>
>> (a)   the reason (or, if more than one, the principal reason) for the dismissal, and
>>
>> (b)   that it is either a reason failing within subsection (2) ...
>
> (2)   A reason falls within this subsection if it ...
>
>> (c)   is that the employee is redundant, ...'

19. It was said by Cairns LJ in *Abernethy v Mott Hay & Anderson* [1974] IRLR 213, at 215 that,

> 'A reason for the dismissal of an employee is a set of facts known to the employer, or it may be a set of beliefs held by him, which cause him to dismiss the employee.'

It is not for the employment tribunal to consider the substance of the employer's reasons at the section 98(1)(b) stage (provided they are more than *'whimsical or capricious'* [*Harper v National Coal Board* [1998] IRLR 260 at para 8, referred to in *Scott v Richardson* at paragraph 17]). As Griffiths LJ observed in *Kent County Council v Gilham* [1985] ICR 233, if on the face of it the employer's reason could justify the dismissal, then it passes as a reason and the enquiry moves on to section 98(4) and the question of reasonableness.

20. The definition of redundancy is set out at section 139 ERA. This provides, as far as relevant:

> '(1)   For the purposes of this Act an employee who is dismissed shall be taken to be dismissed by reason of redundancy if the dismissal is wholly or mainly attributable to–
>
>> (a)   the fact that his employer has ceased or intends to cease–
>>
>>> (i)   to carry on the business for the purposes of which the employee was employed by him, or
>>>
>>> (ii)   to carry on that business in the place where the employee was so employed, or
>>
>> (b)   the fact that the requirements of that business–
>>
>>> (i)   for employees to carry out work of a particular kind, or
>>>
>>> (ii)   for employees to carry out work of a particular kind in the place where the employee was employed by the employer,
>>
>> have ceased or diminished or are expected to cease or diminish'.

Unfair dismissal – reasonableness

21. Where there is a potentially fair reason for dismissal, a tribunal must then go on to decide whether the employer acted reasonably or unreasonably in treating that potentially fair reason as a sufficient reason for dismissal of the employee. The material statutory provisions are set out in section 98(4) Employment Rights Act 1996, which, so far as relevant, are as follows:

> '(4)   Where the employer has fulfilled the requirements of subsection (1), the determination of the question whether the dismissal is fair or unfair (having regard to the reason shown by the employer)–

(a) depends on whether in the circumstances (including the size and administrative resources of the employer's undertaking) the employer acted reasonably or unreasonably in treating it as a sufficient reason for dismissing the employee, and

(b) shall be determined in accordance with equity and the substantial merits of the case.'

22. *Iceland Frozen Foods v Jones* [1982] IRLR 439 (as confirmed by the Court of Appeal in the joined cases of *HSBC (formerly Midland Bank) v Madden and Post Office v Foley* [2000] IRLR 827), sets out that 'a decision to dismiss must be within the band of reasonable responses which a reasonable employer might have adopted'. Tribunals should not, when considering these matters, look at what they would have done but should judge, on the basis of the range of reasonable responses test, what the employers actually did. The appropriate test is whether the dismissal of the Claimant lay within the range of conduct that a reasonable employer could have adopted. The EAT, in *Sheffield Health and Social Care NHS Foundation Trust v Crabtree* (UKEAT/0331/09), reminded Employment Tribunals that the burden of proof under s 98 (4) is neutral.

Unfair dismissal – procedural fairness in a redundancy situation

23. In a redundancy case, the procedural circumstances identified in numerous cases including *Williams v Compair Maxam* [1982] IRLR 83, *Polkey v A E Dayton Services Ltd* [1987] IRLR 503 and as emphasised by the EAT in *Mugford v Midland Bank plc* [1997] IRLR 208, need to be considered. The principles which were put forward in *Williams* as generally accepted principles (where employees are represented by an independent union but have since been recognised as having more general application – see for example *Freud v Bentalls* [1982] IRLR 443 where it was held that the same principles would apply to a workplace where there was no trade union) were –

'1. The employer will seek to give as much warning as possible of impending redundancies so as to enable the union and employees who may be affected to take early steps to inform themselves of the relevant facts, consider possible alternative solutions and, if necessary, find alternative employment in the undertaking or elsewhere.

2. The employer will consult the union as to the best means by which the desired management result can be achieved fairly and with as little hardship to the employees as possible. In particular, the employer will seek to agree with the union the criteria to be applied in selecting the employees to be made redundant. When a selection has been made, the employer will consider with the union whether the selection has been made in accordance with those criteria.

3. Whether or not an agreement as to the criteria to be adopted has been agreed with the union, the employer will seek to establish criteria for selection which so far as possible do not depend solely upon the opinion of the person making the selection but can be objectively checked against such things as attendance record, efficiency at the job, experience, or length of service.

4. The employer will seek to ensure that the selection is made fairly in accordance with these criteria and will consider any representations the union may make as to such selection.

5. The employer will seek to see whether instead of dismissing an employee he could offer him alternative employment.'

24. In particular, the appropriate test of fairness under s 98(4) ERA 1996 in a redundancy situation was that an employer would be expected to (i) sufficiently warn and consult affected employees (unless the tribunal finds that the employer acted reasonably in taking the view that, in the exceptional circumstances of the case, consultation or warning would be 'utterly useless'); (ii) adopted a fair (objective) basis on which to select for redundancy; and (iii) take such steps as may be reasonable to avoid or minimise redundancy by redeployment within its own organisation. A failure to act in accordance with one of these does not necessarily mean a dismissal is unfair: the tribunal must consider this in the light of the circumstances known to the employer at the time he dismissed the employee. Issues of fairness and reasonableness need to be

judged by reference to the 'range of reasonable responses' test (see *Beddell v West Ferry Printers* [2000] ICR 1263).

25. <u>Warning and consultation</u>. <u>Consultation</u> should be 'genuine and meaningful'. Case law has established that, for redundancy dismissals to be fair, the employer must usually warn employees of the possibility of redundancy and then consult individually with them before reaching any conclusion regarding their dismissal. This rule is not absolute, and the courts have repeatedly stressed that a procedural failure does not inevitably lead to a finding of unfair dismissal. Rather, tribunals must focus on the overall picture when determining whether, in the particular case, the employer has acted reasonably in dismissing.

26. It is unclear on the authorities as to whether there are separate obligations of warning and consultation. In *Rowell v Hubbard Group Services Ltd* [1995] IRLR 195, the EAT said there were separate obligations to warn and consult. However, in *Coney Island Ltd v Eikouil* [2002] IRLR 174, the EAT, which was referred to *Rowell* as well as to *Compair Maxam* and *Polkey*, held that there is no separate duty to warn and that warning and consultation are part and parcel of one single process of consultation which begins with the employee being given notice that he is at risk. On either analysis, whether these are separate duties or combined, it is clear that a tribunal should look at whether, in all the circumstances, adequate and reasonable warning of impending redundancy has been given and should consider whether there has been fair and adequate consultation.

27. Consultation involves giving the person consulted a fair and proper opportunity to understand fully the matters about which he is being consulted, and to express their views on those subjects, with the consultor thereafter considering those views properly and genuinely. It would appear that employees themselves may sometimes have a responsibility to ensure the effectiveness of such consultation as does take place.

28. <u>Criteria for selection</u>. In *Drake International Systems Ltd v O'Hare* (UKEAT/0384103), the EAT emphasised that tribunals should not impose their own views as to the reasonableness of the selection criteria or the implementation of the criteria: the correct question was whether the selection was one that a reasonable employer acting reasonably could have made.

29. One distinction which case law has determined since *Williams* is that there is a distinction between an exercise which is selecting for redundancy from within an existing group – ie is looking solely at reducing numbers and an exercise which is seeking to achieve that by selecting for a new role. Where an employer has to decide which employees from a pool of existing employees are to be made redundant, the criteria will reflect a known job, performed by known employees over a period. Where, however, an employer has to appoint to new roles after a re-organisation, the employer's decision must of necessity be forward-looking. It is likely to centre upon an assessment of the ability of the individual to perform in the new role. In *Akzo Coatings v Thompson* (EAT/117/94) His Honour Judge Peter Clark said:

> 'There is, in our judgment, a world of difference between the way in which an employer approaches selection for dismissal in a redundancy pool where some will be retained and others dismissed. It is to that exercise which points 2-4 in the *Williams* guidelines are directed. These observations have no application when considering whether the employer has taken reasonable steps to look for alternative employment.'

30. In *Ball v Balfour Kilpatrick Ltd* (EAT/823/95) His Honour Judge Smith said that there is no rule of law that selection criteria must be exclusively objective. He went on to say:

> 'It is clear on the authority of *Akzo Coatings Plc v Thompson and Others* [1996] EAT (unreported) that the touchstone in such a situation is reasonableness rather than the application of either agreed selection criteria for redundancy or the application of objective criteria.'

31. In *Darlington Memorial Hospital NHS Trust v Edwards and Vincent* (EAT/678/95) His Honour Judge Hull said:

> 'If these are new posts with a different job description from anything which the various Applicants brought to them, then it seems to us that the employer is most certainly not under a

duty to carry out something very like the exercise which he has to carry out in deciding who to select for redundancy. On the contrary, if he is to be allowed to manage his business, he must select as he thinks right. If he tells the employees that they will be allowed to apply for new jobs, as was manifestly the case here, then of course he will be required to carry out the exercise in good faith. If they are to be allowed to apply their applications must be considered properly. If the criteria are different from the old jobs so be it, that was part of the original occasion of redundancy, it was as much reorganisation as redundancy, although redundancy was the result. But to say that they are the same process and that it must be based on similar principles is quite simply, in our view, wrong. It may be, we are not going to decide this, that the duty goes beyond faith, and it may be said that there is some sort of duty of care, but there it is, it is something which the employer has said he will do and he must do it. He must consider the applicants.'

32. Another difficult question for tribunals is to decide the extent to which they should examine the marking that has been applied in a selection exercise. The EAT and the courts have considered on a number of occasions the principles that pertain to the investigation of marking and scores in a redundancy exercise and have made clear that close scrutiny is inappropriate. What is in issue is the question of fairness of the selection procedure and marking should only be investigated where there are exceptional circumstances such as bias or obvious mistake: see *Eaton v King* [1995] IRLR 75 (subsequently upheld by the Court of Session). Lord Coulsfield observed at paragraph 11 that:

> 'every redundancy situation is one of distress for employees who are affected: and every redundancy situation is one in which hard decisions have to be made. It is, however, essential to remember that what is required of the employer is that he should act reasonably'

33. Further guidance is to be found in *British Aerospace plc v Green* [1995] IRLR 433:

> '13.   The whole tenor of the authorities to which I have already referred is to show, in both England and Scotland, the courts and tribunals (with substantial contribution from the lay membership of the latter) moving towards a clear recognition that if a graded assessment system is to achieve its purpose it must not be subjected to an over-minute analysis. That applies both at the stage when the system is being actually applied, and also at any later stage when its operation is being called into question before an industrial tribunal. To allow otherwise would involve a serious risk that the system itself would lose the respect with which it is at present regarded on both sides of industry, and that tribunal hearings would become hopelessly protracted.'

34. The judgment of Lord Johnston in relation to the issue of fair consultation (again in the context of a trade union consultation) in *John Brown Engineering v Brown Ltd* [1997] IRLR 90 is frequently cited. He started by referring to the judgment of Glidewell LJ in *R v British Coal Corporation, ex Parte Price and Others* [1994] IRLR 72:

> 'Fair consultation means:
> (a)   consultation when the proposals are still at a formative stage;
> (b)   adequate information on which to respond;
> (c)   adequate time in which to respond;
> (d)   conscientious consideration by an authority of a response to consultation.
>
> Another way of putting the point more shortly is that fair consultation involves giving the body consulted a fair and proper opportunity to understand fully the matters about which it is being consulted, and to express its views on those subjects, with the consultor thereafter considering those views properly and genuinely.'

35. Case law suggests that one of the requirements for fair consultation in a redundancy exercise involves giving an employee sufficient information about and explanation for his scoring so he understands it and has a meaningful chance to comment on and challenge it. See, for example, the two cases referred to by Mr Hughes (*E-ZEC Medical Transport Services Ltd v Gregory* (UKEAT/0192/08) and *Budenberg Gauge Co Ltd v Griffiths* (UKEAT/43/93 and 162/93). This was emphasised recently by the Court of Appeal in *Pinewood Repro Limited t/a County Print (County Print) v Page* (EAT/0028/10). In that case, the employer agreed the selection criteria (attendance, quality, productivity, abilities, skills, experience, disciplinary record and flexibility) with the trade union, ensured that the

scoring was carried out by two senior managers and gave the employee a right to appeal his selection for redundancy, but did not explain to Mr Page why he had received lower scores than the two other people in the selection pool. Mr Page was provided with a copy of his scores; he queried why he had been marked down for 'abilities, skills and experience' given his level of qualifications and 27 years experience. He also queried why he had been marked down for flexibility as he was 'as flexible as the next man.' He was given no explanation as to how the scores had been arrived at, being told only that 'we believe that the scores given by the assessors are responsible and appropriate'. On appeal, he was told that the employers were 'satisfied that the scoring was factual and correct'. A tribunal found that Mr Page had been unfairly dismissed. The EAT upheld their decision and took the opportunity to review the relevant authorities and, whilst cautioning against an impermissible 'microscopic analysis' of scoring by tribunals, indicated that, particularly with subjective criteria, employees should have sufficient information to understand their scores and an opportunity to challenge them. In *Dabson v David Cover & Sons*, (EAT/0374/2011), the EAT emphasised that when assessing the fairness of selection for redundancy, the marks awarded in the selection exercise should only be investigated in exceptional circumstances such as bias or obvious mistake.

36. Alternative employment. Following the principle in *Polkey*, dismissal will not normally be regarded as a reasonable step on the employer's part unless he takes such steps as would be reasonable to avoid or minimise redundancy by way of redeployment within his organisation. In *Thomas & Betts Manufacturing Ltd v Harding* [1980] IRLR 255, the Court of Appeal ruled that an employer should do what he can so far as is reasonable to seek alternative work. This does not mean, as the EAT pointed out in *MDFI Ltd v Sussex* [1986] IRLR 126, that an employer is obliged by law to enquire about job opportunities elsewhere, and a failure will not necessarily render a dismissal unfair. It is all a question of what is reasonable in the context. It was established in *Williams* that as a matter of good industrial practice, managers should make reasonable efforts to look for alternative employment for employees before making them redundant. The NIRC in *Vokes Ltd v Bear* [1973] IRLR 353, said that an employer who had failed to investigate whether there were job vacancies within the group which might have been offered to an employee as an alternative to making him redundant, had behaved unfairly:

   'The employer had not yet done that which in all fairness and reason he should do, namely to make the obvious attempt to see if Mr Bear could be placed somewhere else in this large group'.

37. None of the cases go so far as to amount to a proposition that there was a duty to find alternative employment (see *Brush Electrical Machines Ltd v Guest* (1976) EAT 382/76). The duty under s 98(4) is to take reasonable steps to try and find alternative employment.

Conclusions

38. The Claimant's claim was that he had been unfairly dismissed contrary to ss 94 and 98 of the Employment Rights Act 1996. There was no issue about the dismissal or about the requisite length of service to bring this claim. The Tribunal is satisfied that the exercise was genuinely implemented in an honest belief that it was the sensible way forward in order to achieve efficiencies and cost savings and was based on genuine commercial and operational reasons. I am satisfied that the definition of redundancy as per the three stage test identified particularly by the House of Lords in *Murray and Another v Foyle Meats Limited* [1999] IRLR 562 was met. The Claimant did not, before the Tribunal, dispute the existence of a potential redundancy situation.

39. I then moved on to look at fairness in three main areas, consultation, selection and the adequacy of searches with regard to alternatives to redundancy. I looked at the overall picture up to the date of termination to ascertain whether the employer has or has not acted reasonably in dismissing the employee on the grounds of redundancy.

40. With regard to the consultation, and subject to what I have to say below on the selection scoring, my view was that what the Respondent did here was reasonable. Overall, I was satisfied that the efforts the Respondent made did fall within the range of reasonable responses. There was, I felt, adequate warning, consultation about the impending

redundancy situation, why it had arisen and how the Respondent was intending to deal with it and the opportunity was given to the Claimant to discuss these issues. There were several meetings about the redundancy situation with the Claimant. What was done, which is what I have to look at as far as the law is concerned, was not so inadequate in my judgment as to fall outside the range of reasonable responses test. So I did not feel that the consultation process per se was such as to give rise to unfair dismissal.

41. I then moved on to consider the selection process. It is not for me, when I apply the range of reasonable responses test, to say what I would have done. I must look at what the Respondent actually did. In my view, the failure by the Respondent to give the Claimant his scores and to allow him an adequate opportunity to discuss them before indicating the finality of the decision that he was the one to be dismissed was unreasonable and fell outside the range of reasonable responses test. I bore in mind the Claimant's reaction to the meeting after the selection process had been concluded but I nonetheless felt that this meeting was not designed to be a meeting to discuss the scores as opposed to a meeting to tell the Claimant he had been selected and would be dismissed. This was borne out by the letters of 25th March [48, 49] – for example 'This desktop exercise has now been completed and unfortunately you have been selected for redundancy'. The Respondent could for example, have written to the Claimant after this meeting enclosing his scores and giving him an opportunity to discuss them before sending the letter of dismissal. I felt the lack of opportunity allowed to the Claimant to have a meaningful opportunity to contest his selection was not remedied by the appeal process, which still failed to allow the Claimant to engage in the process. Lack of consultation implies a loss of opportunity, not that the opportunity, if given, would have made necessarily any difference. I have not engaged in a remarking process but it was also in my judgment unfair that, in the circumstances in this case, Mr Smith applied criteria relating to what he regarded as future skills needed, when these were not on the face of it one of the criteria he was selecting under, so no-one was aware this was a relevant criteria and therefore did not have the opportunity to engage or challenge or discuss it; and further (as indicated from the analysis of the cases above), while there is nothing wrong in using future skills as a criteria where a new job is being proposed in this case, here there was no new job just the same job going forward. This could put another way be said to be a failure of the consultation process, in that consultation involves giving the person consulted a fair and proper opportunity to understand fully the matters about which he is being consulted, and to express their views on those subjects, with the consultor thereafter considering those views properly and genuinely. This did not happen in this case.

42. In my assessment, what was done here was I felt sufficiently inadequate as to fall outside the range of reasonable responses test.

43. On the third and final area, ie whether consideration was given to seeing if there was an alternative to making the Claimant redundant, on the facts, I was satisfied that the Claimant was provided with a list of vacancies and that neither he nor the Respondent identified any that might amount to suitable alternative employment opportunities within the Respondent. The opportunity offered was a clear demotion and could not be said to be a suitable alternative; I was satisfied that the vacancies mentioned by the Claimant were not available as at the date of his dismissal. I was satisfied that what was done was reasonable in the circumstances and fell within the range of reasonable responses test.

44. Having looked at all these matters in the round, as well individually, on balance I was satisfied that the Respondent's failings in the areas identified above were such as to give rise to an unfair dismissal. On that basis, my overall finding was that this was an unfair dismissal on the grounds of redundancy.

45. I went on to consider whether there should be any sort of *Polkey* deduction, on the basis of considering whether there was a chance that even had a fair procedure been followed, the Claimant would still have been dismissed. This is always to some extent going to be

a hypothetical exercise. However, I bore in mind that any unfairness that I have identified above with regard to the approach to and application of the selection criteria and discussion thereon may have resulted in different marks being applied to the others in the pool. Further, there were only three in the pool and one had to go. In addition, Mr Smith sent his scoring assessment to a third party, who was standing in for Dave Hirst, to review. He raised no concerns. Further, Mr Hirst had reviewed it and had identified no concerns such as to overturn it. On balance, I felt taking these matters into account there was still a chance that the Claimant might have been dismissed. I assessed that risk at 25%.

46. In the light of the findings indicated above, the parties subsequently reached an agreement between themselves as to the appropriate remedy. It was agreed that the proceedings would be stayed for a period of 14 days with liberty to restore if necessary. The Recoupment Regulations do not therefore arise for consideration.

Employment Judge Smith-Jones

Judgment and Reasons sent to the parties on 23 November 2018 and entered in the Register.

.... for the Tribunal Office

EMPLOYMENT TRIBUNALS

To: Mr Fred Mclean
       Collaws Solicitors LLP
       20 The Street, Guildshire, GU12

       V Alavy
       Swallows & Co LLP
       12 High Street, Guildshire GU12

Date: 23 November 2018

Case Number: 123456/2018

Mr J Gold	**Claimant**
v	
Car Parking PLC	**Respondent**

EMPLOYMENT TRIBUNAL JUDGMENT

A copy of the Employment Tribunal's judgment is enclosed. There is important information in the booklet 'The Judgment' which you should read. The booklet can be found on our website at www.employmenttribunals,gov.uk/Publications/publications.htm. If you do not have access to the internet, paper copies can be obtained by telephoning the tribunal office dealing with the claim.

The Judgment booklet explains that you may request the employment tribunal to <u>review</u> a judgment or a decision. It also explains the <u>appeal</u> process to the Employment Appeal Tribunal including the strict 42 day time limit. These processes are quite different, and you will need to decide whether to follow either or both. Both are **subject to strict time** limits. <u>An application to *review* must be made within 14 days of the date the decision was sent to you. An application to *appeal* must generally be made within 42 days of the date the decision was sent to you; but there are exceptions: see the booklet.</u>

The booklet also explains about asking for written reasons for the judgment (if they are not included with the judgment). These will almost always be necessary if you wish to appeal. You must apply for reasons (if not included with the judgment) within 14 days of the date on which the judgment was sent. If you do so, the 42 day time limit for appeal runs from when these reasons were sent to you. Otherwise time runs from the date the judgment was sent to you or your representative.

For further information, it is important that you read the Judgment booklet. You may find further information about the EAT at www.employmentappeals.gov.uk. An appeal form can be obtained from the Employment Appeal Tribunal at: Fleetbank House, 2–6 Salisbury Square, London EC4Y 8AE or in Scotland at 52 Melville Street, Edinburgh EH3 7HF.

Yours faithfully,

....

MISS R SMITH

For the Tribunal Office

INTEREST ON TRIBUNAL AWARDS

GUIDANCE NOTE

1.   This guidance note should be read in conjunction with the booklet, which you received with your copy of the Tribunal's judgment.

2.   The Employment Tribunals (Interest) Order 1990, 2013 Amendment provides for interest to be paid on employment tribunal awards (excluding discrimination or equal pay awards* or sums representing costs or expenses) if they remain wholly unpaid from the day after the relevant decision day.

3.   Time runs from the date on which the Tribunal's judgment is recorded as having been sent to the parties and is known as 'the relevant decision day'. The date from which interest starts to accrue is the day immediately following the relevant decision day and is recorded on the Notice attached to the judgment. If you have received a judgment and subsequently request a reasons (see 'The Judgment' booklet) the date of the relevant judgment day will remain unchanged.

4.   If the full amount is paid within 14 days of the relevant decision day, no interest is payable.

5.   'Interest' means simple interest accruing from day to day on such part of the sum of money awarded by the tribunal for the time being remaining unpaid. Interest does not accrue on deductions such as Tax and/or National Insurance Contributions that are to be paid to the appropriate authorities. Neither does interest accrue on any sums which the Secretary of State has claimed in a recoupment notice (see 'The Judgment' booklet).

6.   Where the sum awarded is varied upon a review of the judgment by the Employment Tribunal or upon appeal to the Employment Appeal Tribunal or a higher appellate court, then interest will accrue in the same way (from 'the calculation day'), but on the award as varied by the higher court and not on the sum originally awarded by the Tribunal.

7.   The Judgment booklet explains how employment tribunal awards are enforced. The interest element of an award is enforced in the same way.

---

* The Employment Tribunals (Interest on Awards in Discrimination Cases) Regulations 1996 prescribe the provisions for interest on awards made in discrimination and equal pay cases.

NOTICE

THE EMPLOYMENT TRIBUNALS (INTEREST) ORDER 1990

Tribunal case number(s): 123456/2018

Name of case(s): Mr J Gold v Car Parking PLC

The Employment Tribunals (Interest) Order 1990 (as amended) provides that sums of money payable as a result of a judgment of an Employment Tribunal (excluding discrimination or equal pay awards or sums representing costs or expenses), shall carry interest where the sum remains unpaid on the day after the day ('*the relevant decision day*') that the document containing the tribunal's judgment is recorded as having been sent to the parties, but that no interest shall be payable if the full amount of the award is paid within 14 days after the relevant decision day.

The rate of interest payable is that specified in section 17 of the Judgments Act 1838 on the relevant judgment day. This is known as 'the stipulated rate of interest' and the rate applicable in your case is set out below.

The following information in respect of this case is provided by the Secretary of the Tribunals in accordance with the requirements of Article 12 of the Order-

'the relevant decision day' is: 24 November 2018

'the stipulated rate of interest' is: 8%

....

MISS R SMITH

For the Tribunal Office

Appendix 3

Presidential Guidance – General Case Management

1. This Presidential Guidance was first issued in England & Wales on 13 March 2014 under the provisions of Rule 7 of the First Schedule to the Employment Tribunals (Constitution and Rules of Procedure) Regulation 2013 ("the Rules"). It is now amended and reissued on 22 January 2018 to take account of the decision of the UK Supreme Court in R *(on the application of UNISON) v Lord Chancellor* [2017] UKSC 51 so as to remove all relevant and related references to Employment Tribunal fees. The opportunity has also been taken to make other editorial amendments.

Note

2. Whilst the Employment Tribunals in England & Wales must have regard to such Presidential Guidance, they will not be bound by it and they have the discretion available to them as set out in the Rules as to how to apply the various case management provisions.

3. This Presidential Guidance in relation to General Case Management matters does not supersede or alter any other Presidential Guidance.

Background

4. The overriding objective set out in Rule 2 applies.

5. Rule 29 of the Rules permits a Tribunal to make Case Management Orders. The particular powers subsequently identified in the Rules do not restrict the general power contained in Rule 29.

6. Any Case Management Order may vary, suspend or set aside any earlier Case Management Order where that is necessary in the interests of justice. In particular, this may be necessary where a party affected by the earlier Order did not have a reasonable opportunity to make representations before it was made.

7. Rule 30 specifies details of how an application for a Case Management Order is made generally. Rules 31, 32, 34, 35, 36 and 37 deal with specific instances where Case Management Orders may be made.

8. Rule 38 deals specifically with the situation where Unless Orders can be made.

9. Rule 39 deals with the provision relating to Deposit Orders.

10. The Rules generally contain other Case Management provisions: for example, Rule 45 in relation to timetabling.

11. In applying the provisions of the Rules this Presidential Guidance attempts to set out the procedure, processes and considerations that will normally apply in the circumstances specified below.

Action by Parties

12. While any application for a Case Management Order can be made at the hearing or in advance of the hearing, it should ordinarily be made in writing to the Employment Tribunal office dealing with the case or at a Preliminary Hearing which is dealing with Case Management issues.

13. Any such application should be made as early as possible.

14. Where the hearing concerned has been fixed – especially with the agreement of the parties – that will be taken into account by the Employment Judge considering the application.

15. The application should state the reason why it is made. It should state why it is considered to be in accordance with the overriding objective to make the Case Management Order applied for. Where a party applies in writing, they should notify the other parties (or other representatives, if they have them) that any objections should be sent to the Tribunal as soon as possible.

16. All relevant documents should be provided with the application.

17. If the parties are in agreement, that should also be indicated in the application to the Tribunal.

Examples of case management

18. These are examples of case management situations:
    - amendment of claim and response
    - adding or removing parties
    - disclosure of documents
    - preparation of hearing bundles

- witnesses and witness orders
- preparation and exchange of witness statements
- disability issues
- timetabling
- remedies
- costs
- concluding a case without a hearing

Further Guidance Notes on these matters are appended to this Presidential Guidance.

19. Where the parties' circumstances or contact details have changed, such changes should be notified to the Employment Tribunal office and to the other parties immediately.

Action by the Employment Judge

20. Where the appropriate information has been supplied, an Employment Judge will deal with the matter as soon as practicable. If any information has not been supplied, an Employment Judge may request further relevant information, which will have the effect of delaying consideration of the application.

21. The decision of the Employment Judge will be notified to all parties as soon as practicable after the decision has been made

22. Orders are important. Non-compliance with them may lead to sanctions. Therefore, if a party is having difficulty in complying with such an Order, they should discuss it with the other parties and then apply to the Tribunal to vary the Order.

Agenda for Preliminary Hearing

23. In preparation for a Preliminary Hearing concerned with Case Management matters, the Tribunal will often send out an agenda to the parties in advance of such a Preliminary Hearing. The agenda should be completed in advance of that Preliminary Hearing and returned to the Tribunal. If possible it should be agreed by the parties. A copy of the current form of agenda can be found at: https://www.judiciary.gov.uk/publications/employment-rules-and-legislation-practice- directions/.

Alternative dispute resolution

24. There is separate Presidential Guidance in respect of alternative dispute resolution (ADR) and, in particular, judicial assessments and judicial mediation at: https://www.judiciary.gov.uk/publications/employment-rules-and-legislation-practice- directions/.

Brian Doyle

Judge Brian Doyle
President
22 January 2018

GUIDANCE NOTE 1:

AMENDMENT OF THE CLAIM AND RESPONSE INCLUDING ADDING AND REMOVING PARTIES

Amendment

1. Amendment means changing the terms of the claim or response. This note concentrates on amendments to the claim. The Employment Tribunal can allow amendments, but it will generally only do so after careful consideration and taking into account the views of the other parties. In some cases a hearing may be necessary to decide whether to allow an amendment.

2. Generally speaking, minor amendments cause no difficulties. Sometimes the amendment is to give more detail. There may have been a typographical error or a date may be incorrect. The Tribunal will normally grant leave to amend without further investigation in these circumstances.

3. More substantial amendments can cause problems. Regard must be had to all the circumstances, in particular any injustice or hardship which would result from the amendment or a refusal to make it.

If necessary, leave to amend can be made conditional on the payment of costs by the claimant if the other party has been put to expense as a result of a defect in the claim form.

4. In deciding whether to grant an application to amend, the Tribunal must carry out a careful balancing exercise of all of the relevant factors, having regard to the interests of justice and the relative hardship that will be caused to the parties by granting or refusing the amendment.

5. Relevant factors would include:

   5.1 *The amendment to be made.* Applications can vary from the correction of clerical and typing errors to the addition of facts, the addition or substitution of labels for facts already described, and the making of entirely new factual allegations which change the basis of the existing claim. The Tribunal must decide whether the amendment applied for is a minor matter or a substantial alteration, describing a new complaint.

   5.2 *Time limits.* If a new complaint or cause of action is intended by way of amendment, the Tribunal must consider whether that complaint is out of time and, if so, whether the time limit should be extended. Once the amendment has been allowed, and time taken into account, then that matter has been decided and can only be challenged on appeal. An application for leave to amend when there is a time issue should be dealt with at a preliminary hearing to address a preliminary issue. This allows all parties to attend, to make representations and possibly even to give evidence.

   5.3 *The timing and manner of the application.* An application can be made at any time, as can an amendment even after Judgment has been promulgated. Allowing an application is an exercise of a judicial discretion. A party will need to show why the application was not made earlier and why it is being made at that time. An example which may justify a late application is the discovery of new facts or information from disclosure of documents.

6. The Tribunal draws a distinction between amendments as follows:

   6.1 those that seek to add or to substitute a new claim arising out of the same facts as the original claim; and

   6.2 those that add a new claim entirely unconnected with the original claim.

7. In deciding whether the proposed amendment is within the scope of an existing claim or whether it constitutes an entirely new claim, the entirety of the claim form must be considered.

Re-labelling

8. Labelling is the term used for the type of claim in relation to a set of facts (for example, "unfair dismissal"). Usually, mislabelling does not prevent the re-labelled claim being introduced by amendment. Seeking to change the nature of the claim may seem significant, but very often all that is happening is a change of label. For instance, a claimant may describe his or her claim as for a redundancy payment when, in reality, he or she may be claiming that they were unfairly dismissed.

9. If the claim form includes facts from which such a claim can be identified, the Tribunal as a rule adopts a flexible approach and grants amendments that only change the nature of the remedy claimed. There is a fine distinction between raising a claim which is linked to an existing claim and raising a new claim for the first time. In the leading case, the claimant tried to introduce an automatically unfair dismissal claim on the specific ground of his trade union activity in addition to the ordinary unfair dismissal claim in his claim form. The appeal court refused the amendment because the facts originally described could not support the new claim. Furthermore, there would be a risk of hardship to the employer by increased costs if the claimant was allowed to proceed with this new claim.

10. While there may be a flexibility of approach to applications to re-label facts already set out, there are limits. Claimants must set out the specific acts complained of, as Tribunals are only able to adjudicate on specific complaints. A general complaint in the claim form will not suffice. Further, an employer is entitled to know the claim it has to meet.

Time Limits

11. The Tribunal will give careful consideration in the following contexts:

   11.1 The fact that the relevant time limit for presenting the new claim has expired will not exclude the discretion to allow the amendment. In one case, a Tribunal allowed the amendment of a claim form complaining of race discrimination to include a complaint of unfair dismissal. The appeal court upheld the Tribunal's decision, although the time limit for unfair dismissal had expired. The facts in the claim form were sufficient to found both complaints. The amendment would neither prejudice the respondent nor cause it any injustice.

11.2 It will not always be just to allow an amendment even where no new facts are pleaded. The Tribunal must balance the injustice and hardship of allowing the amendment against the injustice and hardship of refusing it. Where for instance a claimant fails to provide a clear statement of a proposed amendment when given the opportunity through case management orders to do so, an application at the hearing may be refused because of the hardship that would accrue to the respondent.

Seeking to add new ground of complaint

12. The Tribunal looks for a link between the facts described in the claim form and the proposed amendment. If there is no such link, the claimant will be bringing an entirely new cause of action.

13. In this case, the Tribunal **must consider** whether the new claim is in time.

14. The Tribunal will take into account the tests for extending time limits:

14.1 the "just and equitable" formula in discrimination claims;

14.2   the "not reasonably practicable" formula in most other claims;

14.3 the specific time limits in redundancy claims;

14.4 the special time limits in equal pay claims.

Adding a new party

15. The Tribunal may of its own initiative, or on the application of a party, or a person wishing to become a party, add any other person as a party by adding them or substituting them for another party. This can be done if it appears that there are issues between that person and any of the existing parties falling within the jurisdiction of the Tribunal and which it is in the interests of justice to have determined in the proceedings.

Adding or removing parties

16. These are some of the circumstances which give rise to addition of parties:

16.1 Where the claimant does not know, possibly by reason of a business transfer situation, who is the correct employer to be made respondent to the claim.

16.2 Where individual respondents, other than the employer, are named in discrimination cases on the grounds that they have discriminated against the claimant and an award is sought against them.

16.3 Where the respondent is a club or an unincorporated association and it is necessary to join members of the governing body.

16.4 Where it is necessary in order to decide a claim which involves a challenge to a decision of the relevant Secretary of State. The Secretary of State is responsible by statute for certain sums of money in different insolvency situations. The Tribunal decides if a refusal to pay is correct, provided conditions are met in relation to timing.

17. Asking to add a party is an application to amend the claim. The Tribunal will have to consider the type of amendment sought. The amendment may deal with a clerical error, add factual details to existing allegations, or add new labels to facts already set out in the claim. The amendment may, if allowed, make new factual allegations which change or add to an existing claim. The considerations set out above in relation to amendments generally apply to these applications.

18. When you apply to add a party you should do so promptly. You should set out clearly in your application the name and address of the party you wish to add and why you say they are liable for something you have claimed. You should further explain when you knew of the need to add the party and what action you have taken since that date.

19. The Tribunal may also remove any party apparently wrongly included. A party who has been added to the proceedings should apply promptly after the proceedings are served on them if they wish to be removed.

20. A party can also be removed from the proceedings if the Claimant has settled with them or no longer wishes to proceed against them.

21. The Tribunal may permit any person to participate in proceedings on such terms as may be specified in respect of any matter in which that person has a legitimate interest. This could involve where they will be liable for any remedy awarded, as well as other situations where the findings made may directly affect them.

GUIDANCE NOTE 2:
DISCLOSURE OF DOCUMENTS AND PREPARING HEARING BUNDLES

1. The Employment Tribunal often requires the parties to co-operate to prepare a set of documents for the hearing. Even if no formal order is made, the Tribunal prefers that documentary evidence is presented in one easily accessible set of documents (often known as "the hearing bundle") with everyone involved in the hearing having an identical copy.

Why have an agreed set of documents?

2. Early disclosure of documents helps the parties to see clearly what the issues are. It helps them to prepare their witness statements and their arguments. There is no point in withholding evidence until the hearing. This only causes delay and adds to the costs. It may put you at risk of having your case struck out.

3. Agreeing a set of documents means that all parties agree which documents are relevant and the Tribunal will need to see. It does not mean they agree with what the documents contain or mean.

4. It avoids problems at a hearing when a party produces a document which the other party has not seen before. This is unfair and may lead to the hearing being delayed or adjourned. This is costly to all concerned and may result in the offending party paying the costs of the adjournment.

5. An agreed set of documents – rather than each party bringing their own set of documents to the hearing – prevents uncertainty and delay at the hearing.

What is the disclosure of documents?

6. Disclosure is the process of showing the other party (or parties) all the documents you have which are *relevant* to the issues the Tribunal has to decide. Although it is a formal process, it is not a hostile process. It requires co-operation in order to ensure that the case is ready for hearing.

7. Relevant documents may include documents which record events in the employment history: for example, a letter of appointment, statement of particulars or contract of employment; notes of a significant meeting, such as a disciplinary interview; a resignation or dismissal letter; or material such as emails, text messages and social media content (Facebook, Twitter, Instagram, etc). The claimant may have documents to disclose which relate to looking for and finding alternative work.

8. Any relevant document in your possession (or which you have the power to obtain) which is or may be relevant to the issues must be disclosed. This includes documents which may harm your case as well as those which may help it. To conceal or withhold a relevant document is a serious matter.

9. A party is usually not required to disclose a copy of a "privileged" document: for example, something created in connection with the preparation of a party's Tribunal case (such as notes of interviews with witnesses); correspondence between a party and their lawyers; correspondence between parties marked "without prejudice"; or part of discussions initiated on a "without prejudice" basis with a view to settlement of the matters in issue; or records of exchanges with ACAS.

How and when does disclosure take place?

10. The process should start and be completed as soon as possible. A formal order for disclosure of documents usually states the latest date by which the process must be completed.

11. In most cases, the respondent (usually the employer) has most or all of the relevant documents. This often makes it sensible for the respondent to take the lead in disclosure. Each party prepares a list of all relevant documents they hold and sends it as soon as possible to the other party.

12. Sometimes the parties meet and inspect each other's documents. More commonly, they agree to exchange photocopies of their documents in the case, which should be "clean" copies (that is, unmarked by later notes or comments, unless those notes or comments are themselves evidence).

How is the hearing bundle produced?

13. The parties then co-operate to agree the documents to go in the hearing bundle. The hearing bundle should contain only the documents that are to be mentioned in witness statements or to be the subject of cross-examination at the hearing, and which are relevant to the issues in the proceedings. If there is a dispute about what documents to include, the disputed documents should be put in a separate section or folder, and this should be referred to the Tribunal at the start of the hearing.

14. One party then prepares the hearing bundles. This is often the respondent because it is more likely to have the necessary resources. Whoever is responsible for preparing the hearing bundles prepares the documents in a proper order (usually chronological), numbers each page (this is called

"pagination") and makes sufficient sets of photocopies, which are stapled together, tagged or put into a ring binder.

15.   Each party should have at least 1 copy. The Tribunal will need 5 copies for a full Tribunal panel or 3 copies if the Employment Judge is to sit alone. That is 1 copy for the witness table, 1 for each member of the Tribunal and 1 to be shown to the public or media, where appropriate. The copies for the Tribunal must be brought to the hearing. They should not be sent to the Tribunal in advance, unless requested.

Are the documents confidential?

16.   All documents and witness statements exchanged in the case are to be used only for the hearing. Unless the Tribunal orders otherwise, they must only be shown to a party and that party's adviser/ representative or a witness (insofar as is necessary). The documents must not be used for any purpose other than the conduct of the case.

17.   Because it is a public hearing, the Tribunal will enable persons (including the press and media) present at the hearing to view documents referred to in evidence before it (unless it orders otherwise).

GUIDANCE NOTE 3:
WITNESSES AND WITNESS STATEMENTS

Witnesses

1.   The parties should consider who they need to give evidence in support of their case at the Employment Tribunal hearing.

2.   As part of the Case Management of the proceedings, the Tribunal will need to know how many witnesses are to be called, so that the required length of the hearing can be properly allocated and, if necessary, timetabled. The identity of the witnesses and the relevance of their evidence to the issues will also often be important.

3.   Rule 43 provides that where a witness is called to give oral evidence, any witness statement of that person shall stand as that witness's evidence in chief unless the Tribunal orders otherwise. Witnesses are required to give their oral evidence on oath or affirmation.

4.   The Tribunal may exclude from the hearing any person who is to appear as a witness in the proceedings, until such time as that person gives evidence, if it considers it in the interests of justice to do so. This is not the usual practice of the Employment Tribunal in England & Wales.

Witness orders

5.   The Tribunal may order any person in Great Britain to attend a hearing to give evidence, produce documents or produce information (Rule 32).

6.   If a party believes that a person has relevant information or evidence to give, but that they might not attend the hearing voluntarily, that party can apply to the Tribunal for a witness order. A witness order requires the witness to attend the hearing. It can also be useful where the witness is willing to attend, but their employer will not release them to attend.

7.   An application for a witness order may be made at a hearing or by an application in writing to the Tribunal. In order that the Tribunal can send the witness order to the witness in good time before the hearing, it is important to make any application as early as possible. A witness order might be refused if the attendance of the witness cannot be ensured in time.

8.   The application will need to give the name and address of the witness; a summary of the evidence it is believed they will give (or a copy of their witness statement, if there is one); and an explanation as to why a witness order is necessary to secure their attendance.

9.   Exceptionally, an application for a witness order does not have to be copied to the other parties, unless the Tribunal considers that it is in the interests of justice to do otherwise. If the Tribunal grants a witness order, the other parties will then be informed that a witness order has been made and who the witness is, unless there is a good reason not to do so.

Witness statements

10.   The Tribunal often orders witness statements to be prepared and exchanged. Even if no formal order is made, the Tribunal generally prefers evidence to be presented by means of written statements. These are normally read in advance by the Tribunal so that they stand as the evidence in chief (that is,

the main evidence of the witness before questions are put in cross-examination) without being read out loud by the witness.

Why prepare witness statements?

11. It helps to write down what you have to say in evidence. You often remember much more and feel more comfortable when giving evidence having done so.

12. Early exchange of witness statements enables the parties to know the case they have to meet and what the issues are going to be. All the relevant evidence will come out at the hearing. There is nothing to gain (and much to lose) by withholding it until then.

13. Preparation of witness statements helps the Tribunal to identify the issues and to ensure that the case is completed in the time allowed.

14. A witness statement should be prepared for each witness who is to give evidence. This includes the claimant (and the respondent where he or she is an individual).

How should a witness statement be set out and what should it contain?

15. It is easier for everyone if the statement is typewritten or word-processed (although a clear and legible handwritten statement is acceptable) with each page numbered.

16. The witness statement should be in a logical order (ideally, chronological) and contain numbered paragraphs. It should cover all the issues in the case. It should set out fully what the witness has to tell the Tribunal about their involvement in the matter, usually in date order.

17. The statement should be as full as possible because the Tribunal might not allow the witness to add to it, unless there are exceptional circumstances and the additional evidence is obviously relevant.

18. When completed, it is good practice for the statement to be signed, particularly if the witness is unavailable to attend the hearing. The Employment Tribunal Rules of Procedure do not *require* a witness statement to contain a "statement of truth" (such as "This statement is true to the best of my knowledge and belief" or "I believe the facts in this statement to be true") at the end. There is no objection to a witness statement that does or does not contain such a statement of truth.

19. A copy of any witness statements should be provided to the other party. You should bring 5 copies with you to the hearing if there is a full Tribunal panel and 3 copies if the Employment Judge is to sit alone. That is 1 copy for the witness table, 1 for each member of the Tribunal and 1 to be shown to the public and media, where appropriate.

20. If you realise that your statement has left out something relevant when you receive the other party's statements, you should make a supplementary statement and send it immediately to the other party. You do not need to comment on or respond to every point in the other side's statements or repeat what you said originally.

How should a witness statement be exchanged?

21. When the witness statements are ready, a copy should usually be sent to the other side, whether or not their statements have been received or are ready to be exchanged.

22. Exchange of witness statements at the same time is the norm, but it is not always appropriate. In some cases, it makes sense for the claimant's witness statement to be sent first. The respondent will then know exactly what case has to be answered. This avoids irrelevant statements being taken from witnesses who are not needed. In other cases, however, it may make sense for the respondent's statements to be sent first. Any particular directions made by the Tribunal must be followed.

23. Unless there is a different date fixed, the exchange of witness statements should be completed by no later than 2 weeks before the hearing.

Inspection of witness statements

24. Rule 44 provides that any witness statement, which stands as evidence in chief, shall be available for inspection during the course of the hearing by members of the public (that includes the media) attending the hearing. That is, unless the Tribunal decides that all or any part of the statement is not to be admitted as evidence. In that case, the statement or that part of it shall not be available for inspection.

25. There are exceptions to this rule where the Tribunal has made an order protecting the privacy of a witness or restricting the disclosure of documents (rule 50) or in national security proceedings (rule 94).

GUIDANCE NOTE 4:
DISABILITY

1. The terms "disabled", "disabled person" and "disability" are words in common use. In disability discrimination cases in Employment Tribunals these terms have a particular meaning set out in section 6 of the Equality Act 2010 (and Schedule 1 to that Act) and regulations made under those provisions.

2. Reference should be made to those statutory provisions and to those regulations, as well as to the statutory *Guidance on matters to be taken into account in determining questions relating to the definition of disability* (2011) issued by the Secretary of State. That *Guidance* is available at: https://www.equalityhumanrights.com/en/publication-download/equality-act-2010-guidance-matters-be-taken-account-determining-questions.

Evidence of disability

2. A claimant who relies upon the protected characteristic of disability may be able to provide much of the information required without medical reports. A claimant may be able to describe their impairment and its effects on their ability to carry out normal day to day activities.

3. Sometimes medical evidence may be required. For instance, where there is a dispute about whether the claimant has a particular disability or whether an impairment is under effective control by medication or treatment.

4. The question then to be answered is what effects the impairment would have if the medication was withdrawn. Once more, a claimant may be able to describe the effects themselves, but respondents frequently ask for some medical evidence in support.

5. Claimants must expect to have to agree to the disclosure of relevant medical records or occupational health records.

6. Few people would be happy to disclose all of their medical records or for disclosure to be given to too many people. Employment Judges are used to such difficulties. They will often limit the documents to be disclosed and the people to whom disclosure should be made. Disclosure is generally for use only in the proceedings and not for sharing with third parties.

7. Even after a claimant's description of their impairment and disclosure of relevant documents in support, respondents may dispute that the claimant is disabled. If that happens the intervention of an Employment Judge may be necessary.

8. The following possibilities might arise, although there might be others:

9. That the claimant has to agree to undergo medical examination by a doctor or specialist chosen and paid for by the respondent.

    9.1 That the claimant agrees to provide further medical evidence at their own expense.

    9.2 That the claimant and the respondent may agree to get a report jointly. That would involve sharing the decision as to who to appoint, the instructions to be given and the cost of any report. This may be the most effective course, but neither party

    9.3 may in the end be bound by the findings of the report, even if they agree to this course of action.

10. It can be expensive to obtain medical evidence. Limited financial assistance may be available. Whether it is granted is a matter which only a member of the administrative staff of Her Majesty's Courts & Tribunals Service can decide. Any application for such assistance should be made to the manager of the relevant Employment Tribunal office.

11. Care should be taken to decide whether a medical report is necessary at all. For instance, if a claimant has epilepsy which is well-controlled by medication, then medical evidence may be unnecessary for a Tribunal to consider what effect would follow if the medication was not taken.

12. Claimants must remember that they have the burden of proving that they are disabled. They may be satisfied that they can do this, perhaps with the assistance of the records of their General Practitioner, their medical consultant and their own evidence.

Reasonable adjustments to the Tribunal hearing or procedure

13. If the disability of a party, representative, witness or other person might affect their participation in the Tribunal hearing or procedure, an application should be made to the Tribunal as soon as possible so that the Tribunal can consider what reasonable adjustments might be made.

GUIDANCE NOTE 5:
TIMETABLING

1. The overriding objective in Rule 2 of the Employment Tribunals Rules of Procedure means that each case should have its fair share of available time, but no more. Otherwise other cases would be unjustly delayed. Each party must also have a fair share of the time allowed for the hearing of their case.

What is timetabling?

2. Each party has a duty to conduct the case so that wherever possible the Tribunal can complete the case within the time allowed. Failing to do that may mean a delay of many weeks before the case can return for further hearing. It also means that other cases waiting to be heard might be delayed.

3. To avoid the risk of this happening the Tribunal sometimes divides up the total time allowed for a hearing into smaller blocks of time to be allowed for each part of the hearing. This is called "timetabling". It is necessary in particularly long or complicated hearings or sometimes where a party has no experience of conducting hearings.

4. Timetabling is permitted by Rule 45. It provides that a Tribunal may impose limits on the time that a party may take in presenting evidence, questioning witnesses or making submissions. The Tribunal may then prevent the party from proceeding beyond any time so allotted.

How and when is timetabling done?

5. Employment Judges estimate the amount of time to be allowed for a hearing based on all the information they have when the hearing is listed. In straightforward cases that might be when the claim first comes in or when the response arrives. In complex cases it is often done at a preliminary hearing as part of case management.

6. For very short cases it is rare for a formal timetable to be issued. Nevertheless, even for a hearing of one day it might be helpful for the judge and the parties to agree at the beginning of the hearing roughly how long they expect each of the various stages to take. For longer or more complex hearings a timetable is often decided in consultation with the parties at a preliminary hearing or at the start of the hearing itself.

7. Fairness does not always mean that the hearing time must be divided equally between the parties or each witness.

8. For example, the party giving evidence first – in unfair dismissal cases this is usually the employer, but in discrimination cases this is often the employee – will often have to explain the relevance of the documents referred to in the witness statements, which requires time. Also some witnesses might have to give evidence about many separate incidents, whereas others perhaps just one short conversation. If an interpreter is required extra time has to be allowed. The Tribunal will take these things into account when estimating how long the evidence and examination of each witness should take.

9. The Tribunal will set the timetable using its own experience, but the Employment Judge will often ask for the parties' views on how long each stage of the hearing might take.

10. The stages involved in a typical hearing are as follows:

    10.1 At the start of the hearing, if this has not already been done, the Tribunal should make sure that everybody understands the questions the Tribunal has to answer. This is about identifying the issues that are to be decided. The Tribunal will also check that everyone has copies of all of the documents, etc.

    10.2 Often the Tribunal will then read the witness statements and any pages in the agreed bundle of documents to which they refer.

    10.3 Each witness is then questioned on their own statement. This is called "cross–examination". The Tribunal may also ask questions of the witnesses. A specific time may be allocated for questions in respect of each witness and for the witness to clarify any points that have arisen from those questions (this is called "re- examination").

    10.4 When the evidence is finished, each party is entitled to make "submissions". This means that they may summarise the important evidence in their case and may highlight any weak parts of the other side's case. They may also refer the Tribunal to any legal authorities (statutory provisions or previous case law) which might be relevant. Although each party has the right to make submissions, they are not obliged to do so. Again, the Tribunal might timetable the amount of time for submissions.

    10.5 After submissions, the Tribunal will reach its decision. Sometimes it needs to "retire" or "adjourn" (which simply means to leave the hearing room) in order to consider everything that has been said. The length of time it needs to do this might just be a few minutes or an hour in a simple, straightforward case. It may be days or weeks in a very long or complex case, in which instance the parties will usually be sent away with an indication of when a decision might be expected.

10.6 The Tribunal will then tell the parties what has been decided and why. This is referred to as "delivering judgment". This might be done orally – that is, by telling the parties the decision in their presence in the hearing room. If the decision has been made later (a "reserved decision"), then it may be sent to the parties in writing.

10.7 After delivering judgment, the Tribunal will, if the claim succeeds, hear evidence about the claimant's loss. The parties may then make submissions on what award is necessary. The Tribunal may then have to retire or to adjourn again to decide on remedy. It will then deliver its judgment on remedy either orally or reserve it and send it later in writing.

10.8 Lastly, the Tribunal might have to consider orders in respect of any costs matters. Orders for costs are not the norm. The Tribunal will then give judgment with reasons on those matters, again either orally or in writing.

11. If a party believes that the time estimate for the whole or any part of the hearing is wrong, the Tribunal will expect them to say so as soon as possible. Waiting till the day before the hearing or the start of it to ask for extra time is not helpful. It can save time to try to agree a more accurate estimate and then to ask the Tribunal to change the timetable.

What can a party do to assist the Tribunal to keep to the timetable?

12. It is helpful for each party to make a list, for their own use, of the questions to be asked of the witnesses about each of the issues in the case. It is also useful to decide which of the questions are the most important, so that if time is running out the really important questions can be asked, even if others have to be abandoned.

13. Being able to find and quote the page number of the relevant documents in the bundle can save a lot of time. Asking questions using words the witness will understand, so that less time is wasted having to explain what is being asked, also saves time. A series of short, precise questions is generally better than one long, complicated one. They take less time to ask and to answer, and are easier for the witness and the Tribunal to understand and for everyone to take a note of.

14. There is nothing to be gained by asking the same question several times or to argue with the witness. That will just waste the time allowed. The purpose of asking questions is not to try to make the witness agree with the questioner, but to show the Tribunal which side's evidence is more likely to be accurate. If necessary, the Tribunal can be reminded in submissions at the end of the case that, for example, the witness would not answer a question or gave an answer which was not believable or which was not consistent with a document in the bundle, etc. An explanation of why your evidence is more reliable can be given at that stage.

What if the time allowed is exceeded?

15. The parties must try to conclude their questioning of each witness, and their submissions, within the time limit allocated. Usually the Employment Judge will remind a party of how long they have left when time is nearly up. If a party does not finish in time, they run the risk that the Tribunal may stop their questioning of that witness (which is sometimes called "guillotining" the evidence). This is not a step the Tribunal likes to take. Sometimes it is necessary, especially if one side takes so long that they might prevent the other side from having a fair opportunity to ask their own questions.

16. If later witnesses take less time than expected, it might be possible to "re-call" the witness who did not have enough time, if the Tribunal agrees.

GUIDANCE NOTE 6:
REMEDY

What is remedy?

1. After an Employment Tribunal has decided whether the claimant's claim succeeds it will consider how the successful party should be compensated. This part of the judgment is called "Remedy". Sometimes it is done immediately after the merits or liability judgment, but in long or complex cases it may be adjourned to another day.

2. The Tribunal has different powers for each different type of claim. It must calculate loss and order an appropriate remedy for each part of a successful claim. Accurate and often detailed information

from both parties is needed to make correct calculations and to issue a judgment which is fair to all. Sometimes the Tribunal can only estimate the loss: for example, for how long a party may be out of work.

Different types of remedy

3.   For some claims the only remedy is to order the employer/respondent to pay a sum of money: for example, wages due, holiday pay and notice pay.

4.   For unfair dismissal the Tribunal may:

    4.1   Order the employer to "reinstate" the dismissed employee. This is to put them back in their old job, as if they had not been dismissed; or to "re-engage" them, which is to employ them in a suitable but different job. In each case the Tribunal may order payment of lost earnings, etc.

    4.2   If those orders are not sought by the claimant or are not practicable, the Tribunal may order the employer to pay compensation. This is calculated in two parts:

        •   a "Basic Award", which is calculated in a similar way to a statutory redundancy payment; and

        •   a "Compensatory Award", which is intended to compensate the employee for the financial loss suffered.

5.   In claims of unlawful discrimination, the Tribunal may:

    5.1   make a declaration setting out the parties' rights; and/or

    5.2   order compensation to be paid by the employer and/or fellow workers who have committed discriminatory acts. If the employer can show that it has taken all reasonable steps to prevent employees from committing such acts (called the "statutory defence"), the only award which can be made is against the fellow worker, not the employer; and/or

    5.3   make a recommendation, such as for the claimant's colleagues or managers to be given training to ensure that discrimination does not happen again.

Mitigation

6.   All persons who have been subjected to wrongdoing are expected to do their best, within reasonable bounds, to limit the effects on them. If the Tribunal concludes that a claimant has not done so, it must reduce the compensation so that a fair sum is payable.

7.   The Tribunal will expect evidence to be provided by claimants about their attempts to obtain suitable alternative work and about any earnings from alternative employment.

8.   The Tribunal will expect respondents, who consider that the claimant has not tried hard enough, to provide evidence about other jobs which the claimant could have applied for.

Statement of remedy

10.   The Tribunal will usually order the claimant to make a calculation showing how each amount claimed has been worked out. For example: x weeks' pay at £y per week. Sometimes this is called a "Schedule of loss" or a "Statement of remedy".

11.   Tribunals are expected to calculate remedy for each different type of loss – sometimes called "Heads of loss" or "Heads of damage". Therefore the statement should show how much is claimed under each head.

12.   If the claimant has received State benefits, he or she should also specify the type of benefit, the dates of receipt, the amount received and the claimant's national insurance number. (See also "Recoupment" below).

13.   Typical heads of loss include;

    •   wages due

    •   pay in lieu of notice (where no notice or inadequate notice was given)

    •   outstanding holiday pay

    •   a basic award or redundancy payment

    •   past loss of earnings

    •   future loss of earnings

    •   loss of pension entitlements.

14.   In discrimination cases, the heads of loss will also typically include:

    •   injury to feelings

    •   aggravated or exemplary damages (which are rare)

    •   damages for personal injury (but only when the act of discrimination is the cause of the claimant becoming ill).

15. The Tribunal will usually order the statement to be produced early in the proceedings, as it can help in settlement negotiations, when considering mediation and when assessing the length of the hearing. It should be updated near to the hearing date.

Submissions on *Polkey* and contributory fault

16. In an unfair dismissal claim, if an employee has been dismissed, but the employer has not followed a proper procedure (such as the ACAS Code), the Tribunal will follow the guidance in the case of *Polkey v AE Dayton Services Limited* and subsequent cases. The Tribunal will consider whether, if a fair procedure had been followed, the claimant might still have been fairly dismissed, either at all, or at some later time. This question is often referred to as the "Polkey" question or deduction.

17. There are also cases where the dismissal may be procedurally unfair, but the employee's own conduct has contributed to the position they now find themselves in. This is called "contributory conduct".

18. Where either or both of these are relevant, the Tribunal will reduce the compensation awarded by an appropriate percentage in each case. This means that there may be two reductions, which, where there has been really serious misconduct, could be as high as 100%, so that nothing would be payable.

19. Generally the Tribunal will decide these issues at the same time as it reaches its decision on the merits of the claim. Sometimes this will be done at a separate remedy hearing. The Tribunal will usually explain at the start of the hearing which of those options it will follow. If it does not, then the parties should ask for clarification of when they are expected to give evidence and to make submissions on these matters.

Injury to Feelings

20. In discrimination cases and some other detriment claims, Tribunals may award a sum of money to compensate for injury to feelings. When they do so, they must fix fair, reasonable and just compensation in the particular circumstances of the case. The Tribunal will bear in mind that compensation is designed to compensate the injured party rather than to punish the guilty one. It will also remind itself that awards should bear some relationship to those made by the courts for personal injury.

21. The Tribunal will follow guidelines first given in the case of *Vento v Chief Constable of West Yorkshire Police* and in subsequent cases. These guidelines are referred to as the "Vento guidelines" or the "Vento bands". The President of Employment Tribunals will issue from time to time separate guidance on the present value of the Vento bands or guidelines.

22. The Tribunal will expect claimants to explain in their statement of remedy which Vento band they consider their case falls in. They will also expect both parties to make submissions on this during the remedy part of the hearing.

Information needed to calculate remedy

23. This varies in each case dependent on what is being claimed. Each party should look for any relevant information which could help the Tribunal with any necessary calculations in their case. They should provide copies of this information to each other and include those copies in the hearing bundle.

24. The types of information that could be relevant include:
    - the contract of employment or statement of terms & conditions with the old employer
    - the date the claimant started work with that employer
    - details of any pension scheme and pension contributions
    - pay slips for the last 13 weeks in the old employment
    - any other document showing the claimant's gross pay and net pay
    - proof of any payments actually made by the old employer, such as a redundancy payment or payment in lieu of notice
    - any document recording the day the claimant last actually worked
    - any document explaining how many days and hours per week the claimant worked
    - any document explaining how overtime was paid
    - any document recording when the holiday year started
    - any document recording when holiday has been taken in that year and what has been paid for those days
    - any documents setting out the terms of the old employer's pension scheme
    - any documents showing the claimant's attempts to find new or other work
    - contract of employment and payslips for any new job with a new employer

- documents such as bank statements, if losses for bank charges are claimed
- medical reports or "Fit notes" if unable to work since dismissal
- any documents showing that jobs were or are available in the locality for which the claimant could have applied.

25. The witness statements should tell the Tribunal which parts of these documents are important and why. Providing enough information to the Tribunal at an early stage could help to promote a settlement and so avoid a hearing.

Is all loss awarded?

26. For claims such as unpaid wages, holiday pay and notice pay the Tribunal will order the difference between what should have been paid and what has actually been paid. Wages and holiday pay are usually calculated gross, but pay in lieu of notice is usually calculated net of tax and national insurance. The judgment should specify whether each payment ordered has been calculated gross or net.

27. In the case of unfair dismissal there are several limits (called statutory caps) on what can be awarded.

Grossing up

28. The rules on when tax is payable on awards made by Tribunals are too complex for inclusion here. When it is clear that the claimant will have to pay tax on the sum awarded, the Tribunal will award a higher figure, calculated so that tax can be paid and the claimant will receive the net sum which properly represents the loss. This calculation is called "grossing up".

Interest

29. There are two separate situations where interest is relevant.

30. First, when a Tribunal calculates compensation for discrimination, it is obliged to consider awarding interest. If it decides to do so, it calculates interest from the date of the act of discrimination up to the date of the calculation. The exception is for interest on lost wages, where the calculation is made from the middle of that period (as that is simpler than calculating interest separately on each missing wage, but leads to a roughly similar result). The Tribunal will then include that interest in the award made.

31. In addition, interest is payable on awards for all claims if they are not paid when due. A note accompanying the Tribunal's judgment will explain how interest has been calculated. In respect of all claims presented on or after 29 July 2013 interest is calculated from the day after the day upon which the written judgment was sent to the parties, unless payment is actually made within the first 14 days, in which case no interest is payable.

32. The Employment Tribunal plays no part in enforcing payment of the award it makes. That is done by the civil courts, who issue separate guidance on how to enforce payments.

Recoupment

33. For some claims, such as unfair dismissal, if the claimant has received certain State benefits the Tribunal is obliged to ensure that the employer responsible for causing the loss of earnings reimburses the State for the benefits paid. In those cases the Tribunal will order only part of the award to be paid to the claimant straightaway, with the rest set aside until the respondent is told by the State how much the benefits were. The respondent then pays that money to the State and anything left over to the claimant.

34. This is called "recoupment". The Tribunal should set out in the judgment whether or not recoupment applies, and if it does, how much of the award is set aside for recoupment purposes. If either party is in any doubt about recoupment, they should ask the Tribunal to explain how it affects them.

Costs

35. See the separate guidance on "Costs".

Pensions loss

36. The President of Employment Tribunals has issued separated guidance and principles on the calculation of pensions loss. See:

https://www.judiciary.gov.uk/wp-content/uploads/2013/08/presidential-guidance-pension-loss-20170810.pdf

https://www.judiciary.gov.uk/wp-content/uploads/2015/03/principles-for-compensating-pension-loss-20170810.pdf.

GUIDANCE NOTE 7:

COSTS

1.   The basic principle is that Employment Tribunals do not order one party to pay the costs which the other party has incurred in bringing or defending a claim. However, there are a number of important exceptions to the basic principle, as explained below.

What are costs?

2.   "Costs" means some or all of the legal and professional fees, charges, payments or expenses incurred by a party in connection with the Tribunal case. It includes the expenses incurred by a party or witness in attending a hearing.

What orders for payment of costs can be made?

3.   There are three different types of payment orders: costs orders; preparation time orders (sometimes referred to as PTOs); and wasted costs orders. These specific terms have the following meanings.

4.   A costs order generally means that a party is ordered to pay some or all of the costs paid by the other party to its legal representatives (barristers and solicitors) or to its lay representative. No more than the hourly rate of a preparation time order can be claimed for a lay representative. Separately, costs orders can be made for the expenses reasonably and proportionately incurred by a party or witness in attending a hearing.

5.   Preparation time orders are for payment in respect of the amount of time spent working on the case by a non-represented party, including its employees or advisers, but not the time spent at any final hearing.

6.   Wasted costs orders are for payment of costs incurred by a party as a result of any improper, unreasonable or negligent act or failure to act by a representative or for costs incurred after such act where it would be unreasonable to expect the party to bear them. They require payment by a representative to any party, including the party represented by the payer.

When may orders for costs and preparation time be made?

7.   Apart from costs orders for the attendance of witnesses or parties at hearings, a party cannot have both a costs order and a preparation time order made in its favour in the same proceedings. So it is often sensible for a Tribunal in the course of the proceedings (for example, at a preliminary hearing) to decide only that an order for payment will be made, but to leave to the end of the case the decision about which type of order and for how much.

8.   Orders for payment of costs or for preparation time may be made on application by a party, a witness (in respect of their expenses) or on the Tribunal's initiative up to 28 days after the end of the case. If judgment on the claims is given at a hearing, it will usually be sensible to make any application for costs or PTOs then, in order to avoid delay and the additional cost of getting everyone back for another hearing.

9.   The circumstances when payment orders may be made are as follows.

10.   If an employer in unfair dismissal proceedings requires an adjournment to obtain evidence about the possibility of re-employment, the Tribunal must order the employer to pay the costs of the adjournment provided:

•   the claimant notified the desire to be re-employed at least 7 days before the hearing;

•   the employer cannot prove a special reason why it should not pay.

11.   A party may be ordered to pay costs or preparation time to the other party, without any particular fault or blame being shown, where:

•   the paying party has breached an order or practice direction; or

•   an adjournment or postponement is granted at the request of or due to the conduct of the paying party.

12.   A party may be ordered to pay costs in the form of the expenses incurred or to be incurred by a witness attending a hearing, without any particular fault or blame being shown. The order may be in favour of or against the party who called the witness. It may be made on the application of a party, the witness or at the Tribunal's own initiative. It may be payable to a party or to the witness.

13.   A party may be ordered to pay costs or preparation time to the other party where the Tribunal considers that:

•   a party has acted vexatiously, abusively, disruptively or otherwise unreasonably in bringing or defending the proceedings or in its conduct of the proceedings; or

- the claim or response had no reasonable prospect of success.

14. The circumstances described at paragraph 13 require a Tribunal to consider first whether the criteria for an order are met. Each case will turn on its own facts. Examples from decided cases include that it could be unreasonable where a party has based the claim or defence on something which is untrue. That is not the same as something which they have simply failed to prove. Nor does it mean something they reasonably misunderstood. Abusive or disruptive conduct would include insulting the other party or its representative or sending numerous unnecessary e- mails.

15. If the criteria are met, the Tribunal is at the threshold for making an order. It will decide whether it is appropriate to order payment. It will consider any information it has about the means of the party from whom payment is sought, the extent of any abusive or unreasonable conduct, and any factors which seem to indicate that the party which is out-of-pocket should be reimbursed. For example, sometimes it becomes clear that a party never intended to defend on the merits (that is, for example, whether the claimant was unfairly dismissed), but pretended that it was doing so until the last minute, causing the claimant to use his or her lawyer more, before conceding what was really always obvious.

When may a wasted costs order be made?

16. A Tribunal may consider making a wasted costs order of its own initiative or on the application of any party, provided the circumstances described at paragraph 6 above are established. This is a very rare event. When it happens, usually a party will seek costs from the other party and, in the alternative, wasted costs from that party's representative. The representative from whom payment is sought is entitled to notice and so is the party – because they may need separate representation at this costs hearing.

Amount of costs, preparation time and wasted costs orders

17. Broadly speaking, costs orders are for the amount of legal or professional fees and related expenses reasonably incurred, based on factors like the significance of the case, the complexity of the facts and the experience of the lawyers who conducted the litigation for the receiving party.

18. In addition to costs for witness expenses, the Tribunal may order any party to pay costs as follows:

    18.1 up to £20,000, by forming a broad-brush assessment of the amounts involved; or working from a schedule of legal costs; or, more frequently and in respect of lower amounts, just the fee for the barrister at the hearing (for example);

    18.2 calculated by a detailed assessment in the County Court or by the Tribunal up to an unlimited amount;

    18.3 in any amount agreed between the parties.

19. Preparation time orders are calculated at the rate of £33 per hour (until April 2014, when the rate increases by £1 as at every April) for every hour which the receiving party reasonably and proportionately spent preparing for litigation. This requires the Tribunal to bear in mind matters such as the complexity of the proceedings, the number of witnesses and the extent of documents.

20. Wasted costs orders are calculated like costs orders: the amount wasted by the blameworthy (as described at paragraph 6 above) conduct of the representative.

21. When considering the amount of an order, information about a person's ability to pay may be considered. The Tribunal may make a substantial order even where a person has no means of payment. Examples of relevant information are: the person's earnings, savings, other sources of income, debts, bills and necessary monthly outgoings.

GUIDANCE NOTE 8:
CONCLUDING CASES WITHOUT A HEARING

1. A claim or response which has been accepted may be disposed of by the Employment Tribunal at any point in any number of stages before the final hearing. This note sets out most of the situations generally encountered and refers you to the relevant rules.

Rejection at presentation stage

2. A claim may be rejected by an Employment Judge at the time of presentation under Rule 12 where there are certain substantive defects. A claimant may have a right to make representations and attend a hearing before this occurs.2

3.   The claimant may apply for reconsideration of that rejection by an Employment Judge within 14 days on the grounds that it is wrong or that the defect can be rectified. Unless the claimant asks for a hearing, the issue is decided on paper by the Employment Judge. If there is a hearing, only the claimant attends.

Failure to respond and Rule 21 judgment

4.   If no response to the claim is received from the respondent within the prescribed time, the Tribunal considers whether a judgment can be issued under Rule 21 on the available material. An Employment Judge may seek further information from the claimant or order a hearing. The respondent will receive notice of the hearing, but will only be allowed to participate in the hearing to the extent permitted by the judge.

Notice under Rule 26 after response received

5.   If a response to the claim from the respondent is accepted, the Tribunal conducts an initial consideration of the claim form and response form under Rule 26. If the Employment Judge considers that the Tribunal has no jurisdiction to hear the claim, or that the claim or the response has no reasonable prospect of success, notice will be sent to the parties setting out the judge's view and the reasons for it. The judge will order that the claim or response (or any part of it) shall be dismissed on a date specified unless the claimant or respondent (as the case might be) has before that date written to explain why that should not happen.

6.   If no representations are received then the claim or response or the relevant part will be dismissed. If representations are received, they will be considered by an Employment Judge, who will either permit the claim or response to proceed or fix a hearing for the purposes of deciding whether it should be permitted to do so. Such a hearing may consider other matters in relation to preparing the case for hearing.

Preparation for the final hearing

7.   If the Employment Judge directs the case is to proceed to final hearing, orders will normally be made under Rule 29 to prepare for the hearing which is listed. These may include disclosure of documents and exchange of witness statements. Failure to comply with these orders may lead to sanctions as set out below.

Striking out under Rule 37

8.   Under rule 37 the Tribunal may strike out all or part of a claim or response on a number of grounds at any stage of the proceedings, either on its own initiative, or on the application of a party. These include that it is scandalous or vexatious or has no reasonable prospect of success, or the manner in which the proceedings have been conducted has been scandalous, unreasonable or vexatious.

9.   Non-compliance with the rules or orders of the Tribunal is also a ground for striking out, as is the fact that the claim or response is not being actively pursued.

10.   The fact that it is no longer possible to have a fair hearing is also ground for striking out. In some cases the progress of the claim to hearing is delayed over a lengthy period. Ill health may be a reason why this happens. This means that the evidence becomes more distant from the events in the case. Eventually a point may be reached where a fair hearing is no longer possible.

11.   Before a strike out on any of these grounds a party will be given a reasonable opportunity to make representations in writing or request a hearing. The Tribunal does not use these powers lightly. It will often hold a preliminary hearing before taking this action.

12.   In exercising these powers the Tribunal follows the overriding objective in seeking to deal with cases justly and expeditiously and in proportion to the matters in dispute. In some cases parties apply for strike out of their opponent at every perceived breach of the rules. This is not a satisfactory method of managing a case. Such applications are rarely successful. The outcome is often further orders by the Tribunal to ensure the case is ready for the hearing.

13.   It follows that before a claim or response is struck out you will receive a notice explaining what is being considered and what you should do. If you oppose the proposed action you should write explaining why and seeking a hearing if you require one.

Unless orders under Rule 38

14.   The Tribunal may, in order to secure compliance with an order for preparation of the case, make an "unless order" under rule 38. This is an order that will specify that, if it is not complied with, the claim or response or part of it shall be dismissed without further order. The party may apply, within 14 days of the date that the "unless order" was sent, to have the order set aside or for time for

compliance to be extended. If the party does not comply with the order then the case is struck out without further order. A party may also apply after the strike out for the claim or response to be reinstated.

Deposit orders under Rule 39

15.   The Tribunal has power under Rule 39 to order that a deposit be paid on the ground that a specific allegation or argument has little reasonable prospect of success. If such an order is made the deposit must be paid in the time specified as a condition of continuing to advance the allegation or argument. If the party fails to pay the deposit by the date specified, the allegation to which the deposit relates is struck out.

Withdrawal under Rule 51

16.   When a claimant withdraws the claim it comes to an end. The Tribunal must issue a dismissal judgment under Rule 52, unless for some reason this is inappropriate. Often the settlement of a claim includes an agreement that the claimant withdraws the claim and that a dismissal judgment is made.

Compromise agreements and ACAS

17.   Section 203 of the Employment Rights Act 1996 and section 144 of the Equality Act 2010 restrict any contracting out of the provisions of these two Acts. Claims can be settled using an ACAS conciliator to produce a COT3 agreement or, where legal advice is available to the claimant, a compromise or settlement agreement.

Conclusion

18.   In the absence of one of the outcomes outlined above the case will be determined at a final hearing following consideration of the evidence and law by a Tribunal.

Index